MW00849062

Competitive Negotiation

The Source Selection Process

Third Edition

Wolters Kluwer
Law & Business

Competitive Negotiation

The Source Selection Process

Third Edition

John Cibinic, Jr.
Ralph C. Nash, Jr.
Karen R. O'Brien-DeBakey

National   Law   Center

Government Contracts Program

PREFACE

Since that passage of the Competition in Contracting Act in 1994, competitive negotiation has become the major procurement technique used by the government for purchases above the simplified acquisition threshold. It is described in many ways, such as "competitive proposals," "source selection," and "best value," but essentially it is a technique that permits the government to conduct negotiations with two or more competitors after the receipt of proposals. In 1993 we published the first edition of Competitive Negotiation: The Source Selection Process, which went into full detail on these rules. The passage of the Federal Acquisition Streamlining Act in 1994 and the Clinger-Cohen Act in 1996 along with the "Rewrite" of FAR Part 15 of the Federal Acquisition Regulation (FAR) made such significant changes in the competitive negotiation process that we published a second edition in 1999. This edition details the abundant case law as well as the statutory and regulatory changes that have occurred in the past decade since the re-write.

This book discusses all phases of the competitive negotiation process from the inception of the requirement for goods or services to the award of the contract and notification and debriefing of unsuccessful offerors. We organized the chapters to follow the discrete steps of the process, with the result that many topics are included in two or more chapters. For example, choosing evaluation factors is dealt with in Chapter 2, using the factors is dealt with in Chapter 6, and their impact on the source selection decision is dealt with in Chapter 10. We have generally included cross-references when this occurs but readers should also check topics in the index to ensure that they have all the material on each topic.

In the text, we have included citations to and quotations from the FAR as well as from agency regulations supplementing the FAR. To assist our readers, we have also included the full text of selected regulations and guidance documents as attachments in the back of the book. The text also includes citations to and quotations from numerous internal documents that amplify the FAR.

Once a reader becomes fully familiar with the book, it will be possible to quickly find the relevant guidance on any topic by referring to the detailed table of contents.

Since our co-author, John Cibinic, Jr. died in 2005, he did not participate in writing this third edition. However, we have retained his valuable insights from the first two editions in this edition and are grateful for his contributions in analyzing the source selection process.

ABOUT THE AUTHORS

Ralph C. Nash, Jr., is Professor Emeritus of Law of The George Washington University, Washington, D.C., from which he retired in 1993. He founded the Government Contracts Program of the university's National Law Center in 1960, was Director of the Program from 1960 to 1966 and from 1979 to 1984, and continues to be actively involved in the Program. He was Associate Dean for Graduate Studies, Research and Projects, of the Law Center from 1966 to 1972. Professor Nash has specialized in the area of Government Procurement Law. He worked for the Navy Department as a contract negotiator from 1953 to 1959, and for the American Machine and Foundry Company as Assistant Manager of Contracts and Counsel during 1959 and 1960. He graduated *magna cum laude* with an A.B. degree from Princeton University in 1953, and earned his Juris Doctor degree from The George Washington University Law School in 1957. He is a member of Phi Beta Kappa, Phi Alpha Delta, and the Order of the Coif.

Professor Nash is active as a consultant for government agencies, private corporations, and law firms on government contract matters. In recent years, he has served widely as neutral advisor or mediator/arbitrator in alternate dispute resolution proceedings. He is active in the Public Contracts Section of the American Bar Association, is a member of the Procurement Round Table, and is a Fellow and serves on the Board of Advisors of the National Contract Management Association.

During the 1990s, Professor Nash was active in the field of acquisition reform. He served on the "Section 800 Panel" that recommended revisions to all laws affecting Department of Defense procurement, the Defense Science Board Task Force on Defense Acquisition Reform, and the Blue Ribbon Panel of the Federal Aviation Administration.

In 2010 Professor Nash joined with other notable government contracts professionals to create the Public Contracting Institute, which provides industry leading acquisition related training to the public and private sectors. The Institute also sponsors the Ralph C. Nash, Jr. Foundation, which is dedicated to improving the acquisition profession through scholarships and participation in training and mentoring programs.

He is the coauthor with John Cibinic, Jr. of a casebook, *Federal Procurement Law* (3d ed., Volume I, 1977, and Volume II, 1980). He and Professor Cibinic also coauthored five textbooks: *Formation of Government Contracts* (3d ed. 1998), *Administration of Government Contracts* (4th ed. 2006), *Cost Reimbursement Contracting* (3d ed. 2004), *Government Contract Claims* (1981) and *Competitive Negotiation: The Source Selection Process* (2d ed. 1999). He is coauthor with Leonard Rawicz of the textbook *Intellectual Property in Government Contracts* (6th ed. 2008), coauthor with seven other authors of the textbook *Construction Contracting*

(1991), coauthor with Vernon Edwards, Steven L. Schooner and Karen O'Brien-DeBakey of *The Government Contracts Reference Book* (3d ed. 2007) and coauthor with Steven Feldman of *Government Contract Changes* (3d ed. 2007). He has written several monographs for The George Washington University Government Contracts Program monograph series, and has published articles in various law reviews and journals. Since 1987 he has been coauthor of a monthly analytical report on government contract issues, *The Nash & Cibinic Report.*

Karen R. O'Brien-DeBakey is a Director at Jefferson Consulting Group where she advises government and corporate clients on a wide range of acquisition issues. She provides expert assistance to government agencies in a wide range of acquisition services to include developing acquisition plans and strategies, analyzing acquisition operations, developing performance-based statements of work, and developing evaluation criteria and source selection plans that meet agencies' goals and objectives. Ms. O'Brien-DeBakey assists commercial clients in the acquisition process to understand federal regulations and implications for business operations.

Prior to joining Jefferson, she was Of Counsel to the firm of McCarthy, Sweeney and Harkaway, P.C., where she practiced government contract law. Prior to that, Ms. O'Brien-DeBakey was at ESI International managing the Government Contracts publications program of the George Washington University Law School. She began her career as a procurement law attorney in the Army Judge Advocate General's Corps. While in the Army, she served as legal advisor to the Principal Assistant Responsible for Contracting and the Head of Contracting Activity in Southwest Asia. She also served as a staff attorney for the DOD Advisory Panel on Streamlining and Codifying the Acquisition Process (Section 800 Panel). She is coauthor of *The Government Contracts Reference Book* with Ralph C. Nash, Jr., Vernon J. Edwards, and Steven L. Schooner; *Elements of Government Contracting* (3d ed. 2004), with Richard D. Lieberman, and *ILI/JCG Guide to Millennium Challenge Indicators and Source Data* with Allan V. Burman. She received a B.A. in accounting, magna cum laude, from Niagara University and a J.D., cum laude, from Vermont Law School.

SUMMARY TABLE OF CONTENTS

CONTENTS

Chapter 2
DEVELOPMENT OF THE SOURCE SELECTION PLAN **191**

Chapter 5
COMMUNICATIONS TO FACILITATE EVALUATION. 497

Chapter 6
EVALUATION AND RANKING OF PROPOSALS 533

Chapter 9
SOURCE SELECTION

Chapter 11
CONTRACT AWARD CONTROVERSIES 837

INTRODUCTION

In recent years procurement through competitive negotiation has become the major process used to acquire goods and services by the federal government. This process affords the government a greater degree of flexibility than is found in the other major process — sealed bidding. There are several aspects of this flexibility. The negotiation process permits discussion between the parties and modifications of proposals by offerors while sealed bidding does not. In negotiation the government's source selection officials have much greater discretion in selecting the successful offeror for award. They can exercise this discretion by selecting a procurement strategy designed to obtain the best value — either the tradeoff process, the lowest-price technically acceptable process, some combination of the two, or any other process that meets the statutory requirements. Further, negotiation permits considerable discretion in selecting the source when tradeoffs are made between cost or price and other factors. In contrast, in sealed bidding any factors used in source selection other than bid price must be converted to dollars. Proposals submitted in negotiated procurement are not available for public inspection prior to award, while under sealed bidding public opening of bids is a major part of the process and bids may be examined by any person at that time. In sealed bidding a contracting officer is prohibited by statute from considering a bid that contains material deviations from the invitation for bids and changes to bids are not permitted. Finally, in negotiated procurement the contracting officer is not required to reject proposals that vary from the RFP requirements, but may include them in discussions and permit offerors to change their proposals. Thus, negotiation does not involve the concept of responsiveness developed in sealed bidding even though the term is sometimes used in negotiations, *Pacificon Prods., Inc.*, Comp. Gen. Dec. B-196371, 80-2 CPD ¶ 58.

The standard method for competitive negotiation was originally inserted into the Armed Services Procurement Act in 1962 and was adopted by the Competition in Contracting Act of 1984 as the "competitive proposal" technique. These procedures are now embodied in similar language in 10 U.S.C. § 2305(b) and 41 U.S.C. § 253b, and are implemented in FAR Part 15.

This "competitive proposal" procedure is not a detailed procedure in either its statutory or regulatory form. Rather, it is a set of limitations on the freedom of the contracting officer in conducting competitive negotiations. However, as the statutory language was implemented by regulation and interpreted by numerous decisions, a detailed procedure was adopted by almost all agencies. This procedure involved the solicitation of complete proposals including technical, management, and cost or price elements from each competitor. If statutory standards were met, award was made on the basis of initial proposals. If award on initial proposals was not feasible or desirable, the contracting officer proceeded to conduct negotiations by evaluating and narrowing proposals to those within the competitive range, conducting meaningful written or oral discussions, calling for the submission of final proposal revisions, and awarding a contract without further discussions. In this book we have called this the "standard" process for competitive negotiations. This process is presented graphically in Figure 1.

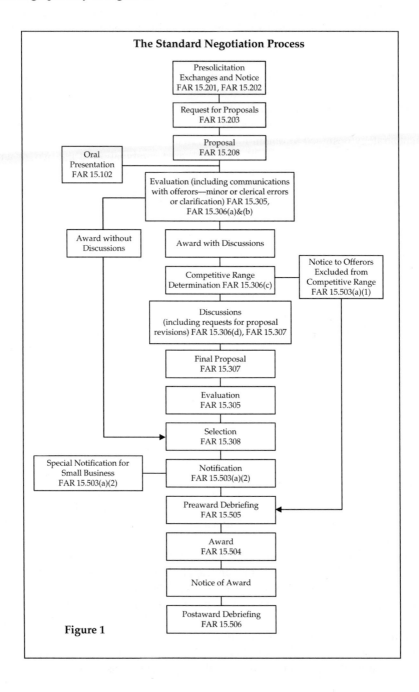

The Standard Negotiation Process

Presolicitation Exchanges and Notice FAR 15.201, FAR 15.202

Request for Proposals FAR 15.203

Proposal FAR 15.208

Oral Presentation FAR 15.102

Evaluation (including communications with offerors—minor or clerical errors or clarification) FAR 15.305, FAR 15.306(a)&(b)

Award without Discussions

Award with Discussions

Competitive Range Determination FAR 15.306(c)

Notice to Offerors Excluded from Competitive Range FAR 15.503(a)(1)

Discussions (including requests for proposal revisions) FAR 15.306(d), FAR 15.307

Final Proposal FAR 15.307

Evaluation FAR 15.305

Selection FAR 15.308

Special Notification for Small Business FAR 15.503(a)(2)

Notification FAR 15.503(a)(2)

Preaward Debriefing FAR 15.505

Award FAR 15.504

Notice of Award

Postaward Debriefing FAR 15.506

Figure 1

While this standard process for competitive negotiations is the norm, it can be followed using elaborate procedures or relatively simple procedures. During the 1980s many agencies adopted procedures requiring the expenditure of considerable time and money by both the competitors and the government agency conducting the procurement. Thus, elaborate technical and management proposals were solicited, large teams were charged with reviewing and scoring these proposals, extensive written or oral discussions were conducted with multiple offerors, major rewrites were permitted in best and final offers, and multi-tiered reviews were conducted in the final source selection process. It was not unusual for procurements to take over a year in these circumstances and one Government Accountability Office report, "Information Technology: A Statistical Study of Acquisition Time" (GAO/AIMO-95-65, Mar. 13, 1995), indicated that the average time for the award of information technology procurements over $25 million in value was 777 days. By the end of the 1980s some agencies had begun to realize that the process had become highly inefficient and took steps to adopt "acquisition streamlining" policies in order to make the competitive negotiation process more efficient. See Air Force Systems Command Regulation 550-23, *Streamlined Source Selection*, July 28, 1987, and National Aeronautics & Space Administration's *Streamlined Acquisition Handbook*, Feb. 16, 1990. The first edition of this book, published in 1993, documents the elaborate procedures that had developed and the initial efforts that had been taken to streamline the process.

After the adoption of the Federal Acquisition Streamlining Act of 1994, Pub. L. No. 103-355, and the Clinger-Cohen Act of 1996, Pub. L. No. 104-106, the streamlining initiatives gained momentum. *The Gore Report on Reinventing Government: Creating a Government that Works Better and Costs Less* (National Performance Review, 1993) recommended that the procurement process be simplified and stated:

> This administration will rewrite the 1,600-page FAR, the 2,900 pages of agency supplements that accompany it, and Executive Order 12352, which governs federal procurement. The new regulations will:
>
> - shift from rigid rules to guiding principles;
> - promote decision making at the lowest possible level;
> - end unnecessary regulatory requirements;
> - foster competitiveness and commercial practices;
> - shift to a new emphasis on choosing "best value" products;
> - facilitate innovative contracting approaches;
> - recommend acquisition methods that reflect information technology's short life cycle; and
> - develop a more effective process to listen to its customers: line managers, government procurement officers, and vendors who do business with the government.

In 1996 the FAR Councils undertook an effort to accelerate this effort to streamline the process by rewriting Part 15 of the Federal Acquisition Regulation to make the competitive negotiation process more efficient. The first draft of this rewrite issued in September 1996, 61 Fed. Reg. 48380, made substantial changes to the regulations giving greater flexibility to contracting agencies and removing a number of fixed requirements from the competitive negotiation process. After extensive public comment, a final rewrite was published in September 1997, 62 Fed. Reg. 51224, making less radical changes to the regulation but, nonetheless, permitting more streamlined procurements. The following comments of the FAR Council in issuing the regulation indicate its interest in promoting greater efficiency in the process:

> The goals of this rewrite are to infuse innovative techniques into the source selection process, simplify the process, and facilitate the acquisition of best value. The rewrite emphasizes the need for contracting officers to use effective and efficient acquisition methods, and eliminates regulations that impose unnecessary burdens on industry and on Government contracting officers.

This emphasis on minimizing the complexity of the negotiation process is reflected in FAR 15.002(b) as follows:

> (b) Competitive acquisitions. When contracting in a competitive environment, the procedures of this part are intended to minimize the complexity of the solicitation, the evaluation, and the source selection decision, while maintaining a process designed to foster an impartial and comprehensive evaluation of offerors' proposals, leading to selection of the proposal representing the best value to the Government (see 2.101).

The rewritten FAR did not mandate streamlined techniques nor did it contain streamlined procedures. It merely adopted procedures that its authors believed *permitted* streamlined procedures. Thus, the efficiency of the process is totally dependent on the processes that are used by contracting agencies on individual procurements. While a few agencies have adopted streamlined procedures in the 14 years since the FAR was rewritten, far more agencies have continued to conduct procurements in the old manner – soliciting technical and management proposals for the most simple products and services. In this regard, the major goal of the 1990s of making the competitive negotiation process more efficient has not been accomplished. The need for streamlined procedures is still apparent – as both government and contractor resources to conduct procurements have become more constrained – but it has proven exceedingly difficult to induce contracting agencies to seek more effective ways of conducting their procurements.

The major factor in the lack of streamlining is the use of too many evaluation factors. Many agencies continue to use a standard set of evaluation factors even when analysis of past procurements would show that many of the factors being used do not discriminate among the competitors. We have included extensive coverage of evaluation factors in Chapter 2 in an effort to aid agencies in reducing the number of evaluation factors.

Another major effort of the FAR Rewrite in 1997 was to allow more robust exchanges during the source selection process. The encouragement of more exchanges before receipt of proposals in FAR 15.201 appears to have given agencies more freedom in this area. However, the encouragement of more exchanges during evaluation of proposals in FAR 15.306 appears to have been a failure. We added Chapter 5, Communications to Facilitate Evaluation, to the second edition to allow full exploration of this part of the source selection process. In the ensuing years, we have realized, in reading the many protest decisions in this area, that these rules are seriously flawed. The fundamental problem is that the adoption of one rule in FAR 15.306(a) for permissible exchanges before award on the basis of initial proposals and another rule in FAR 15.306(b) for permissible exchanges before establishing a competitive range assumes that an agency has made the decision of which course of action to follow before it has read the proposals. This, of course, is a false assumption with the result that agencies have been reluctant to engage in robust exchanges during proposal evaluation. We have continued to use the title of Chapter 5 in this new edition but the fact is that the rule, as currently written, does not facilitate evaluation. Rather, it has had the opposite effect of inducing agencies to decide whether to award without discussions or undertake discussions without a full understanding of what each offeror is proposing.

Similarly the rewritten rule in FAR 15.306(d) was intended to encourage more robust exchanges after a competitive range was established. The FAR Rewrite adopted the term "negotiations" to describe this part of the process and we adopted that term in writing the second edition. We have continued to use that term in this edition but it is apparent that most contracting officers are not in favor of negotiations to assist each offeror in the competitive range to make its best offer in its final proposal revision. Contracting officers seem to be intrinsically opposed to such "technical leveling" even though the prohibition of that practice was removed from FAR 15.306(e). In sum, we have concluded that the rewritten FAR 15.306, in its entirety, is a failed rule that has not led to more robust exchanges and has introduced considerable confusion into the source selection process. We discuss these problems in detail in Chapters 5 and 8.

The other element of the rewrite that has caused confusion is the use of the word "proposal' without defining its meaning. The definition of the word "offer" in FAR 2.101 states that proposals are offers but the word "proposal" in FAR Part 15 appears to mean, in most instances, not only the offer but also the information submitted by each offeror. See, for example, FAR 15.208 containing the rules on submission and modification of "proposals" which appear to cover all information submitted by an offeror. Compare FAR 15.207 discussing "handling proposals and information" – apparently separating a proposal from information submitted by each offeror. Further confusion is created in the definition of "proposal revision" in FAR 15.001 as a "change to a proposal . . .as a result of negotiation" (do the parties negotiate about information?). In each chapter we have attempted to discern the meaning of "proposal" as used in the paragraph of the FAR being addressed, but we confess that the lack of clarity in the FAR makes this a difficult task. Perhaps the most trying aspect of this discernment is attempting in Chapter 5 to determine the extent of the Government Accountability Office's clarification rule which appears to depend on whether information sought by an agency is for the purpose of determining whether a proposal is "acceptable." We have done our best but it seems to us that offers are either acceptable or unacceptable but that acceptability of information is a strange concept.

In the face of these poorly drafted parts of the FAR, in this revised edition we have done our best to identify the way the regulations have been interpreted by the GAO and the Court of Federal Claims. We have also included, as in past editions, the history of the regulations and the legal rulings on those regulations. In some instances this older material is important because GAO has established a number of rules governing competitive negotiation that are independent of the specific regulations in effect at the time of a protester procurement. It is certainly clear that a practitioner cannot understand these rules without fully understanding the protest decisions. This fact that government contracting practices and procedures are an amalgamation of regulations and legal decisions is one of the unique aspects of government procurement.

This book assimilates the statutory and regulatory requirements with the numerous protest decisions into a single discussion of the procedures that can be followed. We have also made numerous references to the most helpful guidance from less formal publications such as internal directives and manuals to illustrate various policies and procedures. This does not necessarily mean that these policies and procedures would be applicable to all procurements or that other policies and procedures specified in the manuals are useful or helpful.

There are several basic principles that must be kept in mind dealing with statutes, regulations, decisions, and manuals:

1. The statutes and some regulations are *legally binding*. When promulgated pursuant to statutory authority, published regulations take on the status of law. Thus, statutes and published regulations using the terms "shall" or "may not" are mandatory and must be followed by a contracting agency unless a deviation from the regulation is obtained pursuant to FAR Subpart 1.4. Failure to follow mandatory rules will generally result in the granting of a protest and may even result in a declaration that the contract is void. See, for example, *CACI, Inc. v. Michael P.W. Stone*, 990 F.2d 1233 (Fed. Cir. 1993), holding that the failure to obtain a Delegation of Procurement Authority, as required by the statute governing the procurement of automatic data processing equipment, resulted in a void contract.

2. The manuals and handbooks of the agencies are *not legally binding, Motorola, Inc.,* Comp. Gen. Dec. B-247937.2, 92-2 CPD ¶ 334, but contain an agency's statement of what it considers to be *good business practice*. Since the second edi-

tion was written, most of the major agencies have moved a considerable amount of text from their FAR supplements to agency manuals and guidance documents. Both government employees and contractors dealing with an agency should be fully conversant with these subsidiary documents and should recognize that the agency is free to alter these documents without going through the onerous regulatory process.

3. While the decisions of the Government Accountability Office and the Court of Federal Claims may resolve protests, they are not necessarily guidance on good business practice. If a protest is granted, the procedure followed by the agency has been determined to be improper or incorrect. Obviously, this is a clear signal that the agency should not follow that practice in the future. Denial of a protest, however, does not necessarily mean that the agency has followed good business practice in the procurement. While in some cases the agency that wins a protest has engaged in a well conducted procurement, in many other winning protests the agency has met only the bare legal requirements. Thus, critical judgment must be exercised when using award decisions as a guide to future actions. Structuring a procurement to win protests is generally questionable policy. The key is to structure a procurement to obtain what the agency needs at a reasonable price in a way that is fair to the competitors.

This book discusses the use of the negotiation process from the inception of the requirement for goods or services to the award of the contract and the debriefing of the losing offerors. The eleven chapters are organized to follow the discrete steps in the competitive negotiation process — attempting to address each issue that arises in that step. While this makes each chapter somewhat self-sufficient, it causes some redundancy of coverage and requires some cross-referencing to obtain full comprehension of the topic. For example, proposal scoring systems are covered in Chapter 2 under the discussion of developing the source selection plan (information relevant to the selection of a system is covered). Scoring systems are discussed in Chapter 5, where their proper use (or their misuse) is covered. Similar treatment is given to many other topics. Readers should review both the index and the detailed table of contents to ensure that they find all of the coverage of any specific topic.

CHAPTER 1

ACQUISITION PLANNING

"Acquisition planning" is an expansive term that includes actions aimed at stating the government's needs, identifying potential sources, and determining the acquisition strategy that will be used to most effectively fulfill the agency need in a timely manner and at a reasonable cost, FAR 2.101. It is a process by which the efforts of all personnel responsible for an acquisition are coordinated and integrated through a comprehensive plan. The acquisition plan contains the documented results of acquisition planning. The goal of acquisition planning is to ensure that the government meets its needs in the most effective, economical and timely manner, consist with public policy, FAR 7.102(b).

This chapter reviews all elements of acquisition planning conducted by an agency. The first section explains the planning process as mandated by law and implemented by regulation. It focuses on who is responsible for planning, when acquisition planning should begin, the level of detail and formality of planning, and the consequences of inadequate planning. The integral role market research plays in acquisition planning is then discussed followed by a discussion of the policy favoring the purchase of commercial products or services. The first section concludes with a discussion of the types and scope of early exchanges of information among industry and the program, contracting and other participants in the acquisition process. The second section provides an in-depth discussion on each element of the acquisition plan.

I. PLANNING PROCESS

While planning is arguably one of most critical steps in the entire acquisition process, it is often performed as an afterthought. Sound acquisition planning ensures that the contracting process is conducted in a timely manner, in accordance with statutory, regulatory, and policy requirements, and reflects the mission needs of the agency.

A. Requirement for Planning

1. Policy

As a result of deficiencies in the planning process, a number of agencies began to focus on the need for more formalized acquisition planning in the 1970s. Congress also identified this need during discussions on the Competition in Contracting Act of 1984 (CICA). As a result, the Armed Services Procurement Act and the Fed-

1

eral Property and Administrative Services Act now require that an executive agency "use advance procurement planning and market research" in preparing for the procurement of property or services, 10 U.S.C. § 2305(a)(1)(A)(ii); 41 U.S.C. § 253a(a) (1)(B). FAR Part 7 implements this requirement, and FAR 7.102(a) requires agencies to perform acquisition planning and conduct market research for all acquisitions in order to promote and provide for (1) the acquisition of commercial items to the maximum extent practicable; and (2) full and open competition or, when full and open competition is not required or possible, maximum competition practicable.

2. Agency-head Responsibilities

The FAR does not provide detailed guidance on the acquisition planning process but rather places this responsibility on the agency head. FAR 7.103 provides that the agency-head or designee is responsible for —

- Promoting and providing for full and open competition
- Encouraging offerors to supply commercial items
- Establishing criteria and thresholds at which increasingly greater detail and formality in the planning process is required
- Writing plans either on a systems basis, on an individual contract basis, or on an individual basis, depending upon the acquisition
- Specifying when a written plan is required
- Designating planners for acquisitions
- Reviewing and approving acquisition plans
- Establishing standard acquisition plan formats
- Waiving requirements of detail and formality, as necessary, in planning for acquisitions

Because the breadth of responsibility is placed on the agency head, specific guidance on acquisition planning is contained in agency-specific regulations, manuals, and guides.

3. Contracting and Programmatic Responsibility for Planning

The agency-head designates the person or office responsible for acquisition planning, FAR 7.103. Often this is the program manager or other official responsible for the program. For example, DOD provides that the program manager or other official responsible for the program has overall responsibility for acquisition planning, DFARS 207.103(g). The Navy states that the program manager has overall responsibility for acquisition planning, while the contracting officer advises on contracting strategy, appropriate contract type election, and other contractual matters, Department of the Navy Acquisition Planning Guide (Mar. 2007). The Air Force requires that an acquisition strategy panel be created for all acquisitions requiring a written acquisition plan, AFFARS 5307.104-90. For NASA acquisitions requiring head-quarters approval, the responsible program operations division analyst serves as the coordinator in developing the procurement strategy, NFS 1807.170; NASA Guide for Successful Headquarters Procurement Strategy Meetings (rev. Sept. 2006). In both the Department of Health and Human Services and the Department of Justice responsibility is jointly shared between the program and contracting office, HHSAR 307.104(e) (contracting officer and project officer develop an acquisition planning schedule, which cannot be revised except by mutual agreement of these same individuals); JAR 2807.102(b) (acquisition planning is the joint responsibility of both the contracting and program offices).

The central role of the individual responsible for acquisition planning is to co-ordinate the plan and convene planning meetings with all those who have a responsibility for the development, management, or administration of the acquisition, DFARS 207.105. As depicted in the following chart, FAR 7.104(a) contemplates that acquisition planning be performed by a team consisting of all those who will be responsible for significant aspects of the acquisition, such as contracting, fiscal, legal, and technical personnel.

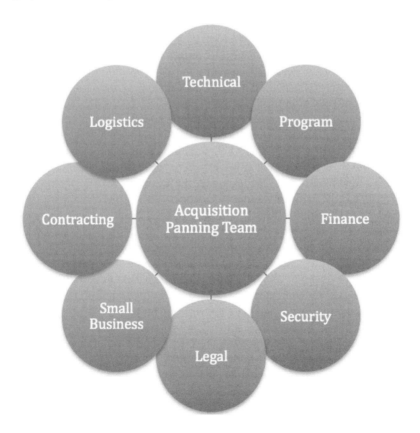

The most effective planning comes about through working in a collaborative relationship with those having a vested interest in the outcome of the procurement. DOE's Acquisition Guide (January 2009) emphasizes the importance of stakeholder involvement in planning, providing in Chapter 4:

> The process of planning involves lots of dialog with the user, the supporter, and the various functional experts assigned to the program management office and field staff organizations. In addition to using the team of specialists within the program office, you should use representatives from the functional staff offices to discuss and refine all planning issues. . . .
>
> Remember, an acquisition plan serves to generate commitment by all stakeholders to support execution of the plan. The best way to achieve this commitment by all stakeholders is to have them participate actively and early in the planning process. In order for the government to successfully meet its overall program objectives, everyone involved in planning and executing the program must feel some ownership.

When this collaborative process is formalized it is called an Integrated Product (or Project) Team (IPT). An IPT is a management technique that simultaneously integrates all essential acquisition activities through the use of multidisciplinary teams. The purpose of IPTs is to make team decisions based on timely input from the entire team (e.g. program management, engineering, manufacturing, test, logistics, financial management, procurement, and contract administration) including customers and suppliers. IPTs are generally formed at the program manager level. IPTs began to emerge in the Department of Defense in the 1980s to support concurrent engineering approaches and culminated in 1995 with the Secretary of Defense directing the Department to apply the Integrated Product and Process Development concept of using IPTs throughout the acquisition process. See DOD Directive 5000.01. Starting in the 1990s civilian agencies began using IPTs — or similar cross-functional teams. For example, the Department of Veterans Affairs requires the use of IPTs for all acquisitions valued at $5 million. See VA Office of Acquisitions and Logistics Information Letter, October 2009. The guidance further provides that IPTs are recommended for complex acquisitions valued at less than $5 million where there are considerable technical, program, or business risk to the government. IPTs should be assembled at the earliest possible stage of the acquisition cycle. IPTs are mandated by Department of Energy (DOE) Order 413.3 and DOE Manual 413.3-1. The Order directs that "all acquisition programs and projects shall use an integrated project team approach to managing projects.

Although the FAR does not discuss the role of competition advocates in the planning process, they have become actively involved in acquisition planning in most procuring agencies. Appointed pursuant to 41 U.S.C. § 418, competition advocates are responsible for challenging barriers to competition and promoting full and open competition. The agency-level advocate is given the additional duty of providing an annual report to the senior procurement executive on the agency's use of competition in contracting. They generally work at a high level in the procuring agency with commensurate influence in determining the strategy that will be used by the agency in the prospective procurement. They also approve or review virtually all justifications for the use of other than competitive procedures. In DHS, all written acquisition plans for acquisitions over $5 million require sign off by the competition advocate, HSAM, Chapter 3007 — Appendix H.

4. The Timing of Planning

It is essential that acquisition planning be done early in the process to ensure that all actions necessary to carry out an effective procurement can be performed within the procurement cycle. FAR 7.104(a) provides that "[a]cquisition planning should begin as soon as the agency need is identified, preferably well in advance of the fiscal year in which contract award is necessary." There are two levels of acquisition planning. An annual acquisition plan is prepared prior to the beginning of each fiscal year. The annual acquisition plan contains all anticipated acquisitions — to include new acquisitions as well as contract/order modifications over the simplified acquisition threshold expected to be awarded during the next fiscal year. The purpose of the annual acquisition plan is to provide for workload scheduling, monitoring and reporting purposes. See, for example, HHSAR 307.104(a). The Office of Small and Disadvantaged Business Utilization (OSDBU) will review the annual acquisition plan to ensure that small business goals will be met. The second level is a formal or informal acquisition plan, as appropriate, for an individual acquisition. The timing of the individual acquisition plan should follow right after the annual acquisition plan. See HUD Handbook 2210.3, Procurement Policies and Procedures, which provides:

> As soon as practicable after receipt of the strategic procurement plan within OCPO, the cognizant Contracting Officer, in conjunction with the Program Office, shall develop the acquisition plan for each new contract action over $100,000." There are three formats for the plans:
>
> Basic: $100,000-$1 million;
>
> Limited: $1,000,001-$5 million; and
>
> Comprehensive: Greater than $5 million

To maximize their value, individual acquisition plans should be developed and approved in advance of preparation of the procurement request package. This assures that the primary personnel (program and procurement officials) are in agreement concerning the acquisition strategy before time and effort are invested in preparing the work statement and request package.

5. The Acquisition Plan

The acquisition plan formally "documents" the overall strategy for accomplishing and managing an acquisition. The acquisition plan communicates to senior management information on the technical and business aspects of the acquisition upon which to base their decisions.

The FAR does not specify whether written or formal acquisition plans should be prepared but, rather, places this responsibility on agency heads, FAR 7.103(d). Specifically, the FAR allows the agency head to "establish criteria and thresholds at which increasingly greater detail and formality in the planning process is required as the acquisition becomes more complex and costly, specifying those cases in which a written plan shall be prepared," FAR 7.103(d). The thresholds at which greater detail and formality are required vary by agency.

Some agencies, such as DOD, require written plans only for large-dollar acquisitions (acquisitions for development when costs are $10 million or more and for production or services when costs are $50 million or more for all years or $25 million or more for any fiscal year) but permit the use of written plans for smaller procurements, DFARS 207.103(d)(i). The Army requires written acquisition plans in accordance with the dollar thresholds identified in DFARS 207.103(d)(i), AFARS 5107.103. The Air Force requires written acquisition plans for all acquisitions of $5 million or more, as well as for other high-risk acquisitions, AFFARS 5307.103(c) (i)(C). The Navy requires written acquisition plans for all acquisitions involving the development, production, or support of weapon systems, subsystems, or equipment that meet or exceed the thresholds of DFARS 207.103(c)(i) unless an exemption is applicable, NAPS 5207.103(c)(i).

Civilian agencies tend to require written acquisition plans at lower-dollar thresholds. For example, the General Services Administration requires written plans for acquisitions over the simplified acquisition threshold ($100,000), GSA Order, Acquisition Planning (OGP 2800.1) (Appendix 507A). This regulation also provides that the heads of contracting activities may authorize oral plans for acquisitions not exceeding $150,000, as long as the file contains the name of the individual who approved the plan. Generally more detailed written plans are required as the dollar amount of the acquisition increases. For instance, while GSA requires a limited acquisition plan at the simplified purchase threshold, a comprehensive plan is required for IT acquisitions over $20 million or for any acquisition over $50 million. In addition, the GSA Order provides that, regardless of the dollar threshold, a comprehensive plan is required when the acquisition is complex, critical to agency strategic objectives and mission, highly visible or politically sensitive, or for acquisitions with which GSA has little or no experience that may result in a need for greater oversight or risk management. Similarly, HUD has three levels of plans: basic acquisition plans for acquisitions over the simplified acquisition threshold up to $1 million, limited acquisition plans for acquisitions in the range of $1 million up to $5 million, and comprehensive acquisition plans for acquisitions over $5 million. The Department of Health and Human Services (HHS) requires a written acquisition plan for proposed acquisitions expected to exceed $500,000 (inclusive of options), HHSAR 307.7101(a).

The specific content of acquisition plans will vary, depending on the nature, circumstances, and stage of the acquisition. Acquisition plans for service contracts must describe the strategies for implementing performance-based contracting methods or must provide rationale for not using those methods. A synopsis of the elements of an acquisition plan is depicted in the chart below. A comprehensive discussion of each element is contained in Section II of this chapter.

Acquisition Plan Outline		
Element	**FAR Provision**	**Synopsis**
Background and Objectives		
Statement of Need	7.105(a)(1)	Introduce the plan by a brief statement of need. Summarize the technical and contractual history of the acquisition. Discuss feasible acquisition alternatives, the impact of prior acquisitions on those alternatives, and any related in-house effort.
Applicable Conditions	7.105(a)(2)	Identify and discuss all significant conditions affecting the acquisition, such as requirements for compatibility with current and/or future systems/programs.
Cost (life cycle, design-to-cost, should cost)	7.105(a)(3)	Set forth the cost goals for the acquisition and the rationale supporting them. This should include a discussion on how estimated costs were arrived.
Capability or performance	7.105(a)(4)	Provide a description of the required capabilities or performance characteristics of the supplies or performance standards for the services being acquired. Discuss how they are related to the need.
Delivery or performance-period requirements	7.105(a)(5)	Describe the basis for establishing the delivery or performance period requirements. Identify the number of years (base and option periods). Discuss briefly industry practices, market conditions, transportation time, and production time.
Tradeoffs	7.105(a)(6)	Provide a brief description of and expected consequences of trade-offs among the various cost, capability or performance, and schedule goals. Discuss which is most important and how it will impact the procurement in comparison of the other goals.
Risks	7.105(a)(7)	Discuss cost, technical and schedule risks. Describe the efforts to be taken to reduce risk and consequences of failure to achieve goals. Discuss effects on cost and schedule risks.

Acquisition Plan Outline		
Element	**FAR Provision**	**Synopsis**
Acquisition streamlining	7.105(a)(8)	Discuss plans and procedures to encourage industry participation by using draft solicitations, pre-solicitation conferences and any other means of stimulating industry involvement and select and tailor only necessary and cost effective requirements.
Plan of Action		
Sources	7.105(b)(1)	Indicate the prospective sources of supplies or services that can meet the need. Consider required sources of supplies or services — e.g., small businesses, service-disabled veteran owned businesses, HUB Zone businesses, etc. Address the extent and results of the market research and indicate their impact on the various elements of the plan.
Competition	7.105(b)(2)	Describe how competition will be sought, promoted and sustained throughout the acquisition. If not using full and open competition, cite the authority in FAR 6.302. Discuss the application of the authority.
Source selection procedures	7.105(b)(3)	Discuss the source selection procedures for the acquisition including timing for submission and evaluation of proposals and the relationship of evaluation factors to the attainment of acquisition objectives. Document the relative importance of non-cost factors in evaluation.
Contracting considerations	7.105(b)(4)	Identify and discuss the type of contract. If appropriate, discuss multi-year contracts and/or the inclusion of options. Discuss any other contracting methods and any special contract provisions or clauses. Discuss any incentive arrangement or document cross reference to the incentive plan.
Budgeting and funding	7.105(b)(5)	Develop and include budget estimates. Include the total value of the independent government cost estimate, including any options. Discuss the funding strategy.
Product or service description	7.105(b)(6)	Explain the use of a statement of work, performance work statement, statement of objectives, technical specifications, or other description of the requirement.
Priorities, allocations, and allotments	7.105(b)(7)	Discuss any priorities or urgent requirements. Specify the method and reason for obtaining and using priorities, allocations, and allotments.
Contractor versus Government performance	7.105(b)(8)	Address the requirement given to OMB Circular A-76.
Inherently governmental functions	7.105(b)(9)	See FAR 7.5. Document that the services do not constitute inherently governmental functions.

Acquisition Plan Outline		
Element	**FAR Provision**	**Synopsis**
Management information requirements	7.105(b)(10)	Discuss the management systems to be used to monitor the contractor's efforts.
Make or buy	7.105(b)(11)	Discuss any consideration given to make or buy programs (FAR 15.407-2).
Test and evaluation	7.105(b)(12)	If applicable, describe the test program of the contractor and the government. Describe the test program for each major phase of a system acquisition.
Logistics considerations	7.105(b)(13)	Describe, as applicable, logistic considerations such as timing, transition planning, etc.
Government-furnished property	7.105(b)(14)	Indicate whether property will be furnished to contractors, including material and facilities, and discuss any associated considerations, such as its availability or the schedule for its acquisition.
Government-furnished information	7.105(b)(15)	Indicate whether government information, such as manuals, drawings and test data, will be provided to prospective offerors and contractors.
Environmental and energy conservation objectives	7.105(b)(16)	Discuss the applicable environmental and energy conservation objectives associated with this acquisition, if applicable.
Security considerations	7.105(b)(17)	Discuss any security considerations — e.g., information security requirements for information technology acquisitions.
Contract administration	7.105(b)(18)	Describe how the contract will be administered — e.g., identify how inspections and acceptance corresponding to the work statement's performance criteria will be enforced.
Other considerations	7.105(b)(19)	Discuss other matters that are germane to the plan but not covered elsewhere.
Milestones for the acquisition cycle	7.105(b)(20)	Address milestones and any other steps appropriate.
Identification of participants in acquisition plan preparation	7.105(b(21)	E.g., contracting officer, contracting specialist, program manager, legal, government technical manager

a. Program and Phased Acquisition Plans

DOD provides that written acquisition plans for large-dollar acquisitions should be prepared on a program basis, while other acquisition plans may be written on either a program or individual-contract basis, DFARS 207.103(d). The Army policy is that, when feasible, acquisition plans will be written on a program/project basis for all procurement actions generally above $30 million, AFARS 7.103(c).

The Navy provides that for programs with multiple contracts, it may be beneficial to prepare one principal acquisition plan for the major procurement and prepare individual acquisition plans for the acquisition of equipment, software or services, Department of the Navy Acquisition Planning Guide (Mar. 2007) The Navy's guidance provides that when using multiple acquisition plans, the principal acquisition plan should:

a. Reference its subsidiary APs [acquisition plans] and vice versa.

b. Identify segments of the program to be assigned to field activities for contractual action.

c. Provide integrated planning for the total system, including an acquisition milestone chart.

NASA provides that acquisition plans should be prepared on a program or system basis when practical, NFS 1807.103(e). In such cases, the plan should fully address all component acquisitions of the program or system.

b. Revisions or Updates to the Acquisition Plan

The acquisition plan is required to be reviewed at least annually and changed whenever necessary. FAR 7.104(a) provides:

At key dates specified in the plan or whenever significant changes occur, and no less often than annually, the planner shall review the plan and, if appropriate, revise it.

The Department of the Navy Acquisition Planning Guide (Mar. 2007) provides examples of when an acquisition plan should be revised, which include:

a. The PM [program manager] is unable to meet a condition attached to a conditionally approved AP [acquisition plan].

b. The PM is unable to execute the competition plan set forth in the approved AP.

c. A major windfall or shortfall in program funding or a major stretch-out or compression in the program schedule is anticipated.

d. There is a substantial quantity increase and the program was previously approved on the basis of a sole source acquisition.

e. The source selection authority (SSA) proposes to change the source selection plan in a manner that would reduce the number of potential competitors adversely affect small business participation.

The Department of Health and Human Services requires the acquisition plan to be reviewed at least quarterly and modified as appropriate, HHSAR 307.104.

6. Adequacy of Planning

The lack of adequate acquisition planning can place an agency in a position where it will attempt to acquire supplies and services without obtaining full and open competition. In this regard lack of advance planning does not justify noncompetitive procurement, as stated in 10 U.S.C. § 2304 and 41 U.S.C. § 253:

(f) In no case may the head of an agency —

* * *

(5) enter into a contract for property or services using procedures other than competitive procedures on the basis of the lack of advance planning.

Nevertheless, the Government Accountability Office (GAO) has sanctioned continuation of a contract when it is impracticable to recommend corrective action. When this occurs, protesters excluded from the competition may be awarded protest costs, *RBC Bearings, Inc.*, Comp. Gen. Dec. B-401661, 2009 CPD ¶ 207 (failure to plan precluded agency from second source and resulted in sole source award); *Freund Precision, Inc.*, 66 Comp. Gen. 90 (B-223613), 86-2 CPD ¶ 543, *recons. denied*, 87-1 CPD ¶ 464 (failure to plan ahead precluded agency from evaluating protester's alternate product and resulted in sole source procurement); *Laidlaw Envtl. Servs. (GS) Inc.*, Comp. Gen. Dec. B-249452, 92-2 CPD ¶ 366 (failure to plan led to sole source extension of contract); and *Techno-Sciences, Inc.*, Comp. Gen. Dec. B-257686, 94-2 CPD ¶ 164 (failure to draft specification in a timely manner led to sole source award).

Where award has not been made, the GAO may recommend cancellation of the procurement, *TeQcom, Inc.*, Comp. Gen. Dec. B-224664, 86-2 CPD ¶ 700. There, failure to plan ahead effectively deprived offerors of any opportunity to qualify their products so that they could compete with the brand-name manufacturer. However, the GAO indicated that the agency could proceed on a sole source basis only for those quantities for which it had an urgent and compelling need.

Cases finding a lack of advance planning include *eFedBudget Corp.*, Comp. Gen. Dec. B-298627, 2006 CPD ¶ 159 (agency took no steps to end its reliance on the contractor's existing software systems); *VSA Corp.*, Comp. Gen. Dec. B-290452.3, 2005 CPD ¶ 103 (agency's predicament caused by its failure to consider meeting its requirement from any firm other than the incumbent and exacerbated by the fact that incumbent contract expired in May 2001 and had been extended on a sole source basis for four years); *HEROS, Inc.*, Comp. Gen. Dec. B-292043, 2003 CPD ¶ 111 (agency abandoned the updating of a manual considered critical to the agency's ability to conduct full and open competition for engine overhauls more than ten years prior to the earliest retirement date); *Signal & Sys., Inc.*, Comp. Gen. Dec. B-288107, 2001 CPD ¶ 168 (despite knowing of safety concerns with a vehicle control system that would have to be replaced, the agency took nearly two years to draft performance specifications that it intended to use to conduct a competitive procurement); *TLC Servs., Inc.*, Comp. Gen. Dec. B-252614, 93-1 CPD ¶ 481 (agency failed to draft necessary statement of work because of personnel vacancies, inexperienced staff, and high backlog of work); *K-Whit Tools, Inc.*, Comp. Gen. Dec. B-247081, 92-1 CPD ¶ 382 (agency took 10 months to determine requirements when it knew that the items were required by a fixed deadline); *Service Contractors*, Comp. Gen. Dec. B-243236, 91-2 CPD ¶ 49 (procurement process for ongoing services commenced six months after expiration of prior contract); and *Pacific Sky Supply, Inc.*, 66 Comp. Gen. 370 (B-225513), 87-1 CPD ¶ 358 (nine-week delay in processing paperwork on qualification requirement deprived protester of a reasonable opportunity to compete). In *WorldWide Language Resources, Inc.*, Comp. Gen. Dec. B-296984, 2005 CPD ¶ 206, the GAO sustained a protest finding the agency made an obvious error that constituted a lack of advance planning by attempting to place the requirement under an environmental services contract, which, on its face, did not include within its scope the bilingual-bicultural advisor requirement. In *New Breed Leasing Corp.*, Comp. Gen. Dec. B-274201, 96-2 CPD ¶ 202, the GAO sustained a protest, finding that had the agency engaged in reasonable advance planning, it would not have taken more than a year after the solicitations were issued to realize that the solicitations were fundamentally flawed in failing to contain basic information. Similarly, in *Commercial Drapery Contractors, Inc.*, Comp. Gen. Dec. B-271222, 96-1 CPD ¶ 290, an agency sought to justify its issuance of purchase orders to a Multiple Award Federal Supply Schedule contractor at higher prices than those offered by other Federal Supply Schedule contractors by arguing that it urgently needed the supplies and only the selected contractor could meet the delivery time. The GAO sustained the protest, finding that the urgency resulted from delays caused by the agency's prior improper issuance of purchase orders to the same contractor for the same requirement and the subsequent cancellation of those orders in response to clearly meritorious protests.

In deciding protests, both the GAO and Court of Federal Claims have applied a reasonable efforts test when reviewing advance planning efforts. Thus, advance planning need not be entirely error-free or actually successful for an agency to successfully defend a protest, *L-3 Communications Eotech, Inc. v. United States*, 87 Fed. Cl. 656 (2009); *Infrastructure Def. Techs., LLC v. United States*, 81 Fed. Cl. 375 (2008); *Cubic Def. Sys., Inc. v. United States*, 45 Fed. Cl. 239 (1999); *Sprint Communications Co., L.P.*, Comp. Gen. Dec. B-262003.2, 96-1 CPD ¶ 24. See *Honeycomb Co. of Am.*, Comp. Gen. Dec. B-225685, 87-1 CPD ¶ 579, where the agency made a reasonable but unsuccessful effort to obtain competition. The GAO distinguished such a case from those where there was an absence of advance planning. In *Rex Sys., Inc.*, Comp. Gen. Dec. B-239524, 90-2 CPD ¶ 185, the agency's continued negotiations with a failing contractor placed it in a position of urgency requiring a sole source award. Although the GAO, in hindsight, indicated that it might disagree with how long the negotiations were allowed to continue, it was unable to conclude that such actions were unreasonable. The GAO found that the efforts sought to establish the failing contractor as an alternate source and were therefore related to procurement planning and fostering competition. The fact that the efforts were unsuccessful did not constitute a lack of planning. The same reasoning was used to deny a protest in *Polar Power, Inc.*, Comp. Gen. Dec. B-270536, 96-1 CPD ¶ 157. See also *Datacom, Inc.*, Comp. Gen. Dec. B-274175, 96-2 CPD ¶ 199, rejecting the protester's claim that the urgency necessitating a noncompetitive sole-source award and contract modification resulted from the lack of advance planning. In that case the decision on how to conduct the procurement was the subject of significant congressional action. The GAO would not fault the Air Force for failure to compete its procurement in the face of a congressional report directing the agency to go no further in its effort to hold a competition of any kind.

B. Market Research

Market research is an integral element of the acquisition planning process. Acquisitions begin with a description of the government's needs stated in terms sufficient to allow conduct of market research, FAR 10.002. It is defined in FAR 2.101:

> "Market Research" means collecting and analyzing information about capabilities within the market to satisfy agency needs.

Increased emphasis on market research began in the early 1980s. In hearings before the Senate Armed Services Committee, the GAO stated that the failure to perform market research was a "major processing deficiency." Many witnesses testified that the failure to perform market research was one of the key factors responsible for the absence of competition in government procurement, Competition in Contracting Act of 1983: Hearings on S. 338 Before the Committee on Armed Services, United States Senate, 98th Cong., 1st Sess. (1983). The Senate Report on the CICA stated: "Competition in contracting depends on the procuring agency's understanding of the marketplace . . . . [M]arket research is essential to developing this understanding," S. Rep. No. 50, 98th Cong., 2d Sess. (1984).

1. Requirement for Market Research

As a result of the Congressional concern about the inadequacy of market research, CICA included a general requirement for market research in 10 U.S.C. § 2305(a)(1)(A) and 41 U.S.C. § 253a(a)(1). The Federal Acquisition Streamlining Act of 1994 (FASA) added new, more specific provisions at 10 U.S.C. § 2377(c) and 41 U.S.C. § 264b(c). These statutory provisions are prescribed in FAR Part 10. FAR 10.001 states the policy that agencies must:

(1) Ensure that legitimate needs are identified and trade-offs evaluated to acquire items that meet those needs;

(2) Conduct market research appropriate to the circumstances —

> (i) Before developing new requirements documents for an acquisition by that agency;

> (ii) Before soliciting offers for acquisitions with an estimated value in excess of the simplified acquisition threshold;

> (iii) Before soliciting offers for acquisitions with an estimated value less than the simplified acquisition threshold when adequate information is not available and the circumstances justify its cost;

> (iv) Before soliciting offers for acquisitions that could lead to a bundled contract (15 U.S.C. 644(e)(2)(A)).

> (v) Agencies shall conduct market research on an ongoing basis, and take advantage to the maximum extent practicable of commercially available market research methods, to identify effectively the capabilities, including the capabilities of small businesses and new entrants into Federal contracting, that are available in the marketplace for meeting the requirements of the agency in furtherance of a contingency operation or defense against or recovery from nuclear, biological, chemical, or radiological attack; and

(3) Use the results of market research to —

> (i) Determine if sources capable of satisfying the agency's requirements exist;

> (ii) Determine if commercial items or, to the extent commercial items suitable to meet the agency's needs are not available, nondevelopmental items are available that —

>> (A) Meet the agency's requirements;

>> (B) Could be modified to meet the agency's requirements; or

>> (C) Could meet the agency's requirements if those requirements were modified to a reasonable extent;

> (iii) Determine the extent to which commercial items or nondevelopmental items could be incorporated at the component level;

> (iv) Determine the practices of firms engaged in producing, distributing, and supporting commercial items, such as type of contract, terms for warranties, buyer financing, maintenance and packaging, and marking;

(v) Ensure maximum practicable use of recovered materials (see Subpart 23.4) and promote energy conservation and efficiency; and

(vi) Determine whether bundling is necessary and justified (see 7.107) (15 U.S.C. 644(e)(2)(A)).

(vii) Assess the availability of electronic and information technology that meets all or part of the applicable accessibility standards issued by the Architectural and Transportation Barriers Compliance Board at 36 CFR Part 1194 (see Subpart 39.2).

FAR 10.002(a) provides that the government's need should be stated in "terms sufficient to allow conduct of market research." Once the need is sufficiently stated, market research is conducted to determine if commercial items or nondevelopmental items are available to meet the government's needs or could be modified to meet the government's needs, FAR 10.002(b). Market research is also used to ensure that full and open competition will be obtained by determining if additional or more competent sources are available to perform the work.

One of the basic goals of market research is to obtain competition. See *Coulter Corp.; Nova Biomedical; Ciba Corning Diagnostics Corp.*, Comp. Gen. Dec. B-258713, 95-1 CPD ¶ 70. When other than full and open competition procedures are used, FAR 6.303-2(a)(8) requires that justifications describe the market research conducted or the reasons why it was not conducted. The GAO has held that an agency's reason for not conducting a market survey was adequate where it had supported the fact that a directed source was designated pursuant to an international agreement, *PacOrd*, Comp. Gen. Dec. B-238366, 90-1 CPD ¶ 466. The GAO also upheld an agency's decision not to conduct a market survey where the agency stated that it had recently determined that there was only one domestic source for a product, *Lister Bolt & Chain, Ltd.*, Comp. Gen. Dec. B-224473, 86-2 CPD ¶ 305.

2. Extent and Nature of Market Research

The extent and nature of market research conducted varies depending on such factors as urgency, estimated dollar value, complexity, and past performance, FAR 10.002(b)(1). FAR 10.002(b)(2) describes the various techniques that may be used to conduct market research:

(i) Contacting knowledgeable individuals in Government and industry regarding market capabilities to meet requirements.

(ii) Reviewing the results of recent market research undertaken to meet similar or identical requirements.

(iii) Publishing formal requests for information in appropriate technical or scientific journals or business publications.

(iv) Querying the Governmentwide database of contracts and other procurement instruments intended for use by multiple agencies available at www.contractdirectory.gov and other Government and commercial databases that provide information relevant to agency acquisitions.

(v) Participating in interactive, on-line communication among industry, acquisition personnel, and customers.

(vi) Obtaining source lists of similar items from other contracting activities or agencies, trade associations or other sources.

(vii) Reviewing catalogs and other generally available product literature published by manufacturers, distributors, and dealers or available on-line.

(viii) Conducting interchange meetings or holding presolicitation conferences to involve potential offerors early in the acquisition process.

See *McKesson Automation Systems, Inc.*, Comp. Gen. Dec. B-290969.2, 2003 CPD ¶ 24, where the GAO found market research to be adequate where the agency had reviewed an extensive independent report comparing various firm's systems approaches, held numerous meetings with the firms to obtain additional information, had site visits to inspect various systems, and made comparisons of the various features of each firms' systems.

3. Effect of Inadequate Market Research

Inadequate market research can be a fatal defect in the procurement process if there are sources available to meet the agency's needs that were not discovered. In *Rochester Optical Mfg, Co.*, Comp. Gen. Dec. B-292247, 2003 CPD ¶ 138, the GAO sustained a protest on the basis that the market research was materially deficient. The contracting officer's market research was geographically limited for no legitimate reason and she used inaccurate information for the basis of her research. The GAO found that the market research could not be relied upon in determining not to conduct the procurement as a small business set-aside. Similarly, in *SWR, Inc.*, Comp. Gen. Dec. B-294266, 2004 CPD ¶ 219, the GAO sustained a protest challenging an agency decision not to set aside a procurement for HUBZone small businesses for aircraft washing machines for three Marine Corps Air Stations. The contracting officer's basis for not setting aside the procurement for HUBZone concerns was because Pro-Net research did not identify any HUBZone concerns. However, more than a month prior to the issuance of the RFP the agency learned that the Charleston Air Force Base RFP for similar aircraft washing services was a HUBZone set-aside, not a 100% small business set-aside as the contracting specialist had mistakenly believed. The agency also learned of the existence of more than two HUBZone firms that were interested in the procurement. The GAO found that the agency's continued reliance on the contracting officer's Pro-Net research even after obtaining information that cast serous doubt on the validity of the research was unreasonable.

Market research may be found to be inadequate if available sources of information are not utilized. In *Information Ventures, Inc.*, Comp. Gen. Dec. B-294267, 2004 CPD ¶ 205, the GAO sustained a protest on the basis that the market research was unreasonably limited. Although the contracting officer searched the GSA Advantage database, she did not search the Central Contractor Registration database or SBA's PRO-Net, nor did she obtain input from the small business representative.

4. Relationship of Specifications to Market Research

The CICA statutory provisions requiring market research could be read to imply that specifications should not be drafted until the agency had conducted market research to identify the market conditions that would permit full and open competition. However, such a procedure was not in accord with the traditional practice of having the technical offices of the procuring agency draft the specifications prior to the commencement of the procurement based on their conception of the needs of the agency. It is doubtful that this somewhat vague statutory language altered this traditional practice in many agencies. Congress provided a far clearer statement of the policy in the commercial item provisions of the FASA requiring that market research be conducted "before developing new specifications," 10 U.S.C. § 2377(c) and 41 U.S.C. § 264(c). This statutory requirement is stated in FAR 10.001(a)(2)(i) requiring that market research be conducted before "developing new requirements documents." However, there is no clear statement of this policy in FAR Part 11, which enunciates the policy on preparing specifications to be used in the acquisition process. FAR 11.002(a)(1) merely states that agencies are required to specify their needs "using market research." In spite of this lack of clarity in the FAR, there should be no doubt that agencies should follow policies that require a thorough review of market conditions before new specifications are drafted. In some instances agencies may be able to prepare a new specification after a single exploration of market conditions to determine what products or services are available in the marketplace. However, the relationship between market research and specification drafting is more often an iterative process.

In some cases the agency's clear understanding of its needs and knowledge of the market may be such as to enable the preparation of a draft specification prior to discussions with potential offerors, and the market survey would consist of circulating the draft specification for comment. In other cases the market survey may be necessary to enable the agency to state its needs. This is particularly so when an agency is procuring a product or service not previously purchased — when it is imperative to determine whether there is market availability to meet, wholly or partially, the agency's needs. Whatever procedure is found to be most productive, it appears to be clear that the policy is that agencies should not finalize contract specifications until there has been thorough consultation with as many potential contractors as possible.

C. Policy Favoring Commercial Items and Nondevelopmental Products or Services

The initial consideration in the acquisition planning process is the determination of whether there are commercial items that will meet the government need. This determination is required by the statutory provisions added by FASA that clearly stated a preference for the acquisition of commercial products and services. See 10 U.S.C. § 2377 and 41 U.S.C. § 264b. This policy is implemented in FAR 12.101, which states:

> Agencies shall —
>
> (a) Conduct market research to determine whether commercial items or nondevelopmental items are available that could meet the agency's requirements;
>
> (b) Acquire commercial items or nondevelopmental items when they are available to meet the needs of the agency; and
>
> (c) Require prime contractors and subcontractors at all tiers to incorporate, to the maximum extent practicable, commercial items or nondevelopmental items as components of items supplied to the agency.

FAR 7.102(a) carries this requirement into the planning process by stating that acquisition planning must "promote and provide for" the acquisition of commercial items or, if commercial items are not available, nondevelopmental items "to the maximum extent practicable."

1. Definitions

The definitions of "commercial item" and "nondevelopmental item" are so broad that they can be interpreted to include almost all of the products and services procured by the government. "Commercial item," as defined in 41 U.S.C. § 403(12) and FAR 2.101, includes both commercial supplies and commercial services. However, supplies and services are given different treatment, with the definition of commercial supplies being broader than the definition of commercial services. The terminology is further complicated by the fact that when used alone, "item" most often refers to supplies only.

In addition, nondevelopmental items and commercially available off-the-shelf items are distinct subcategories of supplies. For guidance on strategies for acquiring commercial items, see Office of Defense Acquisition, Technology, and Logistics, Commercial Item Handbook (Draft Version 2.0, 2009).

a. Commercial Supplies

The following general definition of commercial supplies is contained in 41 U.S.C. § 403(12) and repeated verbatim in FAR 2.101:

(a) Any item, other than real property, that is of a type customarily used for non-governmental purposes and that —

(1) Has been sold, leased, or licensed to the general public; or,

(2) Has been offered for sale, lease, or license to the general public;

(b) Any item that evolved from an item described in paragraph (a) of this definition through advances in technology or performance and that is not yet available in the commercial marketplace, but will be available in the commercial marketplace in time to satisfy the delivery requirements under a Government solicitation;

(c) Any item that would satisfy a criterion expressed in paragraphs (a) or (b) of this definition, but for —

(1) Modifications of a type customarily available in the commercial market place; or

(2) Minor modifications of a type not customarily available in the commercial marketplace made to meet Federal Government requirements. "Minor" modifications means modifications that do not significantly alter the nongovernmental function or essential physical characteristics of an item or component, or change the purpose of a process. Factors to be considered in determining whether a modification is minor include the value and size of the modification and the comparative value and size of the final product. Dollar values and percentages may be used as guideposts, but are not conclusive evidence that a modification is minor;

(d) Any combination of items meeting the requirements of paragraphs (a), (b), (c), or (e) of this definition that are of a type customarily combined and sold in combination to the general public;

This exceedingly broad definition of commercial supplies includes a wide variety of products, as long as they meet the key test of being "of a type customarily used for nongovernmental purposes." Thus, the government can be the first purchaser of such an item even though it is not being sold commercially at the time of the procurement. Furthermore, the item being acquired need not be the same as items sold commercially — as long as it is the same class or "type" as items sold commercially. The definition also includes modified products as long as they are of the type customarily available in the marketplace or the modifications are minor. See *Electronic Vision Access Solutions*, Comp. Gen. Dec. B-401473, 2009 CPD ¶ 169 (Braille display system is commercially available even though it is not in current production or currently being sold to the general public); and *Precision Lift, Inc.*, Comp. Gen. Dec. B-310540.4, 2008 CPD ¶ 166 (Helicopter platforms were commercial, non-developmental items where item was previously offered for sale to the general public, although none had been sold). In a post-award protest filed at the Court of Federal Claims, *Precision Lift, Inc. v. United States*, 83 Fed. Cl. 661 (2008), Precision Lift sought to enjoin performance, arguing that the term "offer" in the FAR definition of "commercial item" should be considered synonymous with the contractual term "offer." The court disagreed, finding this to be a very narrow reading of the FAR. The court found the platforms had been offered for sale to the general public through various advertising and marketing efforts.

Determining whether a product is a commercial item is largely within the discretion of the contracting agency, and will not be disturbed by the GAO unless it is shown to be unreasonable. See *Aalco Forwarding, Inc.*, Comp. Gen. Dec. B-277241, 97-2 CPD ¶ 110 (agency properly determined that services could be acquired as commercial item under FAR part 12 procedures notwithstanding inclusion of government-unique requirements in solicitation); *Premier Eng'g & Mfg., Inc.*, Comp. Gen. Dec. B-283028, 99-2 CPD ¶ 65 (determination as to whether modifications to a commercial item are minor are within the agency's technical judgment that will be disturbed only where unreasonable). In *Nabco, Inc.*, Comp. Gen. Dec. B-293027, 2004 CPD ¶ 14, the GAO held that a door modification to an explosive ordnance disposal total containment vehicle was a minor modification that did not significantly alter the nongovernmental function or essential purpose of the vehicle. The vehicle had been sold commercially and the change in the door configuration, modifying it from a "slide out" to a "swing out" style to meet the Air Force requirements, was already available to commercial customers on other containment vessels. Similarly, in *GIBBCO LLC*, Comp. Gen. Dec. B-401890, 2009 CPD ¶ 255, modifications to commercial housing units to satisfy air quality standards were minor and did not alter the commercial nature, nongovernmental functions, or essential physical characteristics of the units. See also *Canberra Indus., Inc.*, Comp. Gen. Dec. B-271016, 96-1 CPD ¶ 269 (solicited item within FAR definition of commercial item where regularly sold to public and modification does not alter item's function or physical characteristics).

b. *Nondevelopmental Items*

Nondevelopmental items are covered by the statutes and regulations in two different ways. First, they are considered to be commercial items if they meet the following requirements contained in 41 U.S.C. § 403(12)(h) and FAR 2.101:

> (8) A nondevelopmental item, if the procuring agency determines the item was developed exclusively at private expense and sold in substantial quantities, on a competitive basis, to multiple State and local governments.

A broader definition of the term "nondevelopmental item" is contained in 41 U.S.C. § 403(13), which does not necessarily include commercial items. This definition, with minor modifications, is set forth in FAR 2.101 as follows:

(1) Any previously developed item of supply used exclusively for governmental purposes by a Federal agency, a State or local government, or a foreign government with which the United States has a mutual defense cooperation agreement;

(2) Any item of supply described in paragraph (1) of this definition that requires only minor modification or modifications of a type customarily available in the commercial marketplace in order to meet the requirements of the procuring department or agency; or

(3) Any item of supply being produced that does not meet the requirements of paragraph (1) or (2) solely because the item is not yet in use.

Care must be exercised in using these two definitions because some of the policies discussed in this section apply only to commercial items, while other policies apply as well to nondevelopmental items (as defined in the broader sense). If a solicitation permits proposals for either commercial items or nondevelopmental items, the second definition will be used and minor modifications will be acceptable, *Tremble Navigation, Ltd.*, Comp. Gen. Dec. B-271882, 96-2 CPD ¶ 102 (award on the basis of a proposed nondevelopmental item improper because modifications were major).

c. Commercially Available Off-the-Shelf (COTS) Items

This following definition is contained in 41 U.S.C. § 431(c) and incorporated into FAR 2.101:

(1) Means any item of supply (including construction material) that is —

(i) A commercial item (as defined in paragraph (1) of the definition in this section);

(ii) Sold in substantial quantities in the commercial marketplace; and

(iii) Offered to the Government, under a contract or subcontract at any tier, without modification, in the same form in which it is sold in the commercial marketplace; and

(2) Does not include bulk cargo, as defined in section 3 of the Shipping Act of 1984 (46 U.S.C. App. 1702), such as agricultural products and petroleum products.

To meet the COTS definition, the item must be offered to the government without modification, in the same form in which it is sold in the commercial marketplace. See *Cerner Corp.*, Comp. Gen. Dec. B-293093, 2004 CPD ¶ 34 (met COTS requirement where enterprise-wide scheduling and registration system currently used in healthcare environments). But see *Chant Eng'g Co.*, Comp. Gen. Dec. B-281521,

99-1 CPD ¶ 45 (new equipment like Chant's proposed test station, which may become commercially available as a result of the instant procurement, does not satisfy the RFP COTS requirement).

d. Commercial Services

The statute and the FAR include two types of services within the definition of commercial items.

(1) SERVICES IN SUPPORT OF A COMMERCIAL ITEM

The first type is described in 41 U.S.C. § 403(12) and repeated verbatim in FAR 2.101:

(5) Installation services, maintenance services, repair services, training services, and other services if —

(i) Such services are procured for support of an item referred to in paragraph (1), (2), (3), or (4) of this definition, regardless of whether such services are provided by the same source or at the same time as the item; and

(ii) The source of such services provides similar services contemporaneously to the general public under terms and conditions similar to those offered to the Federal Government.

These services are ancillary to commercial supplies but need not be procured at the same time or from the same supplier that provided the commercial supplies. The key requirement is that they be offered to the general public using the same workforce as will be used in providing the services to the government.

(2) STAND-ALONE SERVICES

The second type of commercial services are stand-alone services, defined in FAR 2.101 as follows:

(6) Services of a type offered and sold competitively in substantial quantities in the commercial marketplace based on established catalog or market prices for specific tasks performed or specific outcomes to be achieved and under standard commercial terms and conditions. For purposes of these services —

(i) Catalog price means a price included in a catalog, price list, schedule, or other form that is regularly maintained by the manufacturer or vendor, is either published or otherwise available for inspection by customers, and states prices at which sales are currently, or were last, made to a significant number of buyers constituting the general public; and

(ii) Market prices means current prices that are established in the course of ordinary trade between buyers and sellers free to bargain and that can be substantiated independent of the offerors.

The most difficult aspect of this definition is determining whether services have been sold "based on established . . . market prices." In many instances, services such as janitorial services or construction services are sold commercially by obtaining competitive prices against a specification calling for such services related to a specific building or project. Prices obtained in this way can be readily construed as "established market prices" because they were obtained in a highly competitive market. The following guidance in Appendix C of the DOD *Commercial Item Handbook* can be read to adopt this concept:

The . . . stand-alone definition does not preclude the inclusion of Government-unique requirements or terms and conditions, as long as there are sufficient "common characteristics" between the commercially available service and the service being acquired. Warehousing, garbage collection, and transportation of household goods are examples of services that are commercial. Other more sophisticated services (e.g., repair and overhaul work, research-related services, software design, testing, and engineering consultation) can also be commercial.

In order to meet the commercial item definition, the price for the stand-alone services must be "based on established catalog or market prices." The established market price for stand-alone services does not have to be published or written. Market research enables the Government to collect data from independent sources in order to substantiate the market price.

In contrast, the OFPP memorandum "Applicability of FAR Part 12 to Construction Acquisition" (July 3, 2003), states that construction should not be procured using the commercial item rule. The reason give for this policy is not that construction does not meet the commercial services definition but that contract clauses have not been drafted to permit the use of the rule for construction contracts. See also *Voith Hydro, Inc.*, Comp. Gen. Dec. B-401244.2, 2009 CPD ¶ 239, agreeing with an agency decision not to procure construction-type services as a commercial item procurement.

Agencies have considerable discretion to determine that work meets the definition of stand-alone commercial services. See *SHABA Contracting*, Comp. Gen. Dec. B-287430, 2001 CPD ¶ 105, rejecting a protest of an agency determination that tree thinning was a commercial service, stating:

Determining whether a particular service is a commercial item is a determination largely within the agency's discretion, which will not be disturbed by our office, unless it is shown to be unreasonable, *Crescent Helicopters*, B-284706 *et. al.*, May 30, 2000, 2000 CPD ¶ 90 at 2. Agencies are required to conduct market research pursuant to FAR part 10 to determine whether commercial items are available that could meet the agency's requirements. FAR 12.101(a). If through market research the agency determines that the government's needs can be met by an item customarily available in the commercial marketplace that meets the FAR 2.101 definition of a commercial item, the agency is required to use the procedures in FAR part 12 to solicit and award any resultant contract. FAR 10.002(d)(1), 12.102(a).

Here, the record shows that the Forest Service concluded, based upon an informal market survey, that these tree thinning services qualify as a commercial item because the services are not unique, are not used exclusively by the government, and are offered and sold competitively by forestry and nursery firms. For example, the Forest Service reports that there were more than 150 potential offerors on the mailing list for the services, that the local telephone book contained numerous sources for tree thinning services, and that the agency has personal knowledge of several commercial companies engaged in various types of tree services.

e. Combinations and Interorganizational Transfers

The statute and FAR 2.101 permit combinations of supplies and ancillary services in support of commercial supplies:

> (4) Any combination of items meeting the requirements of paragraphs (1), (2), (3), or (5) of this definition that are of a type customarily combined and sold in combination to the general public.

The statute and FAR 2.101 permit transfers between organizations with a contractor to be treated as commercial items:

> (7) Any item, combination of items, or service referred to in paragraphs (1) through (6) of this definition, notwithstanding the fact that the item, combination of items, or service is transferred between or among separate divisions, subsidiaries, or affiliates of a contractor.

f. Key Terms

The statutory and regulatory definitions of commercial items use a number of key terms that are not defined. The following definitions of these terms and related terms had been incorporated into FAR 15.804-3 but were removed from the FAR by Federal Acquisition Circular (FAC) 90-32, September 18, 1995.

"General public" is used in many parts of the statutory definition. The previous FAR definition stated:

> The "general public" is a significant number of buyers other than the Government or affiliates of the offeror; the item involved must not be for Government end use. For the purpose of this subsection 15.804-3, items acquired for "Government end use" include items acquired for foreign military sales.

The phrase "sold in substantial quantities" is applicable only to stand-alone services, nondevelopmental items, and commercially off-the-shelf supplies. The previous FAR definition stated:

> An item is "sold in substantial quantities" only when the quantities regularly sold are sufficient to constitute a real commercial market. Nominal quantities, such as models, samples, prototypes, or experimental units, do not meet this requirement. For services to be sold in substantial quantities, they must be customarily provided by the offeror, using personnel regularly employed and equipment (if any is necessary) regularly maintained solely or principally to provide the services.

2. Maximizing the Procurement of Commercial Items

The statutory goal is to use procurement procedures that "reduce any impediments . . . to the acquisition of commercial items," 10 U.S.C. § 2377(b)(5) and 41 U.S.C. § 264(b)(5). Such impediments should be identified by the contracting officer in the course of performing the required market research to determine the availability of commercial items as discussed earlier. See FAR 12.202. In general, it can be expected that the major impediments will be excessive requirements for proposal information and the use of terms and conditions in the contract that impose noncommercial requirements. Based on an understanding of the impact of such requirements on the government's ability to attract offers from commercial sellers, the procurement should be structured to minimize the affect of such impediments by streamlining the source selection process and minimizing the terms and conditions used in the contract. The procedural guidance discussed in this section contains sufficient flexibility to permit contracting with commercial sources in most situations.

a. Streamlining the Procurement

When it is determined that the work being procured falls within the definition of commercial item and does not exceed $6.5 million ($12 million for certain commercial items described in FAR 13.500(e)), the agency should plan to use streamlined procurement procedures. FAR 12.203 states:

> Contracting officers shall use the policies unique to the acquisition of commercial items prescribed in this part in conjunction with the policies and procedures for solicitation, evaluation and award prescribed in Part 13, Simplified Acquisition Procedures; Part 14, Sealed Bidding; or Part 15, Contracting by Negotiation, as appropriate for the particular acquisition. The contracting officer may use the streamlined procedure for soliciting offers for commercial items prescribed in 12.603. For acquisitions of commercial items exceeding the simplified acquisition threshold but not exceeding $6.5 million ($12 million for acquisitions as described in 13.500(e)), including options, contracting activities shall employ the simplified procedures authorized by Subpart 13.5 to the maximum extent practicable.

This gives the contracting officer complete freedom in selecting any existing procurement procedure. However, because the goal is to attract commercial sellers, it would be expected that the use of procedures described in Parts 14 and 15 would be minimized.

Unless the streamlined procedure of FAR 12.603 is used, the contracting officer must use Standard Form 1449, Solicitation/Contract/ Order for Commercial Items, when issuing written solicitations and awarding contracts and placing orders for commercial items. This form may also be used for documenting receipt, inspection, and acceptance of commercial items, FAR 12.204.

FAR 12.202(b) requires that the government's needs be described in "sufficient detail for potential offerors of commercial items to know which commercial products or services to offer." In *National Aeronautics & Space Admin.*, Comp. Gen. Dec. B-274748.3, 97-1 CPD ¶ 159, the GAO held that, although the use of functional or performance specifications is appropriate, the agency must advise offerors of its specific ideas of what features would satisfy its needs. Generally, it is desirable to permit suppliers to submit commercial product literature instead of specially written technical proposals. FAR 12.205 provides the following guidance:

> (a) Where technical information is necessary for evaluation of offers, agencies should, as part of market research, review existing product literature generally available in the industry to determine its adequacy for purposes of evaluation. If adequate, contracting officers shall request existing product literature from offerors of commercial items in lieu of unique technical proposals.

FAR 12.205 also suggests that commercial sellers be permitted to propose on more than one product:

> (b) Contracting officers should allow offerors to propose more than one product that will meet a Government need in response to solicitations for commercial items. The contracting officer shall evaluate each product as a separate offer.

FAR 12.205(c) permits the contracting officer to tailor the response time for the submission of the offer to meet the needs of the commercial marketplace. Thus, it permits response times of less than 30 days when appropriate.

FAR 12.301(b) provides two standard solicitation provisions, described as follows:

> (1) The provision at 52.212-1, Instructions to Offerors — Commercial Items. This provision provides a single, streamlined set of instructions to be used when soliciting offers for commercial items and is incorporated in the solicitation by reference (see Block 27a, SF 1449). The contracting officer may tailor these instructions or provide additional instructions tailored to the specific acquisition in accordance with 12.302.

(2) The provision at 52.212-3, Offeror Representations and Certifications — Commercial Items. This provision provides a single, consolidated list of representations and certifications for the acquisition of commercial items and is attached to the solicitation for offerors to complete. This provision may not be tailored except in accordance with Subpart 1.4. Use the provision with its Alternate I in solicitations issued by DoD, NASA, or the Coast Guard. Use the provision with its Alternate II in solicitations for acquisitions for which small disadvantaged business procurement mechanisms are authorized on a regional basis.

The FAR also permits the use of a "streamlined" procedure combining the synopsis and solicitation into a single document with a response time no longer than is necessary to give potential offerors a reasonable opportunity to respond to the solicitation. This allows greatly shortening the statutory requirements for standard procurement that require a 15-day synopsis period and a 30-day offer period. See *American Artisan Prod.*, Comp. Gen. Dec. B281409, 98-2 CPD ¶ 155 (contracting officer's decision to allow 15-day response time for commercial item acquisition reasonable based on prior experience with previous procurement) and *Gibbco LLC*, Comp. Gen. Dec. B-401890, 2009 CPD ¶ 255 (protester provided no information showing that the requirement for the submission of proposals within 22 days for this commercial item acquisition was unreasonable). The guidance on the use of this fast procedure is set forth in FAR 12.603.

b. Terms and Conditions

In order to attract commercial sellers, commercial item procurements should be planned to use the least intrusive terms and conditions possible. The FAR guidance is aimed at minimizing the contract language and simplifying the contract. FAR 12.301(a) provides that contracts include only those clauses —

(1) Required to implement provisions of law or executive orders applicable to the acquisition of commercial items; or

(2) Determined to be consistent with customary commercial practice.

Traditionally, FAR Part 12 required that contracts for commercial items be either firm-fixed price or fixed-price with economic price adjustment. As of 2007, FAR 12.207(b) provides that time-and-materials contract or labor-hour contract may be used for the acquisition of commercial services when —

(i) The service is acquired under a contract awarded using —

(A) Competitive procedures (e.g., the procedures in 6.102, the set-aside procedures in Subpart 19.5, or competition conducted in accordance with Part 13);

(B) The procedures for other than full and open competition in 6.3 provided the agency receives offers that satisfy the Government's expressed requirement from two or more responsible offerors; or

(C) The fair opportunity procedures in 16.505, if placing an order under a multiple award delivery-order contract; and

(ii) The contracting officer —

(A) Executes a determination and findings (D&F) for the contract, in accordance with paragraph (b)(2) of this section (but see paragraph (c) of this section for indefinite-delivery contracts), that no other contract type authorized by this subpart is suitable;

(B) Includes a ceiling price in the contract or order that the contractor exceeds at its own risk; and

(C) Authorizes any subsequent change in the ceiling price only upon a determination, documented in the contract file, that it is in the best interest of the procuring agency to change the ceiling price.

FAR 12.207(b)(2) provides that before entering into a T&M or LH contract for commercial services, the contracting officer must execute a Determination and Finding (D&F), which contains sufficient facts and rationale to justify that no other contract type authorized by this subpart is suitable. At a minimum it should consist of —

(i) Include a description of the market research conducted (see 10.002(e));

(ii) Establish that it is not possible at the time of placing the contract or order to accurately estimate the extent or duration of the work or to anticipate costs with any reasonable degree of certainty;

(iii) Establish that the requirement has been structured to maximize the use of firm-fixed-price or fixed-price with economic price adjustment contracts (e.g., by limiting the value or length of the time-and-material/labor-hour contract or order; establishing fixed prices for portions of the requirement) on future acquisitions for the same or similar requirements; and

(iv) Describe actions planned to maximize the use of firm-fixed-price or fixed-price with economic price adjustment contracts on future acquisitions for the same requirements.

If the T&M/LH contract, with options, exceeds three years, the D&F must be approved by the head of the contracting activity. See FAR 12.207(b)(3) and FAR 16.601(d)(1)(ii).

One of the major elements of the policy favoring the procurement of commercial items was the elimination of as many contract clauses as was practicable. The FASA amended a number of laws to state that they did not apply to the procurement of commercial items and added 41 U.S.C. § 430 requiring the FAR to include a list of laws that were not applicable to contracts and subcontracts for commercial items. Subsequently, § 4203 of the Clinger-Cohen Act of 1996 enacted 41 U.S.C. § 431 requiring that the FAR list laws that are not applicable to the procurement of COTS items.

FAR 52.212-4 provides a standard contract clause, Contract Terms and Conditions — Commercial Items, which contains 20 specific provisions to be used in contracts for commercial items. These provisions are greatly shortened versions of the standard clauses used in government procurement, such as the termination clauses, the inspection clauses, the changes clause, and the disputes clause. The contracting officer is authorized to "tailor" certain of these provisions but only to reflect commercial practices, FAR 12.302. However, the following clauses, which implement statutory requirements, may not be tailored:

(1) Assignments;
(2) Disputes;
(3) Payment (except as provided in subpart 32.11);
(4) Invoice;
(5) Other compliances; and
(6) Compliance with laws unique to Government contracts.

Tailoring may be needed to attract some sellers of commercial products. FAR 12.213 contains the following guidance to contracting officers on the subject of tailoring:

> It is a common practice in the commercial marketplace for both the buyer and seller to propose terms and conditions written from their particular perspectives. The terms and conditions prescribed in this part seek to balance the interests of both the buyer and seller. These terms and conditions are generally appropriate for use in a wide range of acquisitions. However, market research may indicate other commercial practices that are appropriate for the acquisition of the particular item. These practices should be considered for incorporation into the solicitation and contract if the contracting officer determines them appropriate in concluding a business arrangement satisfactory to both parties and not otherwise precluded by law or Executive order.

FAR 52.212-5 provides a standard clause, Contract Terms and Conditions Required to Implement Statutes or Executive Orders — Commercial Items, that sets forth the mandatory clauses that must be included in these procurements. This clause may not be tailored. The contracting officer must check the appropriate provisions in this clause in accordance with the instructions in FAR 12.503. Paragraph (e) (1) of the clause specifies the extent to which flow down is required in subcontracts for commercial items. See the guidance in FAR 12.504, which lists some statutes that remain applicable even though they are not specified in the clause. Contractors should be aware that other statutes of general applicability in the United States are also not listed in this clause.

Being a subset of commercial items, any laws listed in FAR 12.503 and FAR 12.504 are also inapplicable to contracts or subcontracts for the acquisition of COTS items, FAR 12.505. In addition, FAR 12.505 implements § 4203 of the Clinger-Cohen Act of 1996 (41 U.S.C. § 431) with respect to the inapplicability of certain laws to contracts and subcontracts for the acquisition of COTS items. This provision is intended to reduce the burden on contractors that provide COTS EPA-designated products that contain recovered materials and contractors that provide construction material or end products that are COTS items manufactured in the United States.

D. Early Exchanges with Potential Offerors

Successful acquisition planning requires exchanges of information between the procuring agency and potential offerors to ensure that the agency fully understands the products and services that are available and that the potential offerors fully understand the need that the agency is attempting to fulfill with the proposed procurement. Such exchanges permit the procurement to be structured in the way that will promote the most effective competition among informed offerors. However, the adoption of the procurement integrity provisions in the Office of Procurement Policy Act of 1989, 41 U.S.C. § 423, applied significant restraints to such exchanges, with the result that many agencies did not permit meaningful exchanges in the acquisition planning process. Two steps have been taken to correct this situation. First, the statutory procurement integrity provisions were substantially modified by the Clinger-Cohen Act of 1996, Pub. L. No. 104-106. Second, the rewrite of FAR Part 15 specifically addressed this problem and added a new provision encouraging exchanges for the purpose of improving procurements. FAR 15.201 now provides the following:

Exchanges with industry before receipt of proposals.

(a) Exchanges of information among all interested parties, from the earliest identification of a requirement through receipt of proposals, are encouraged. Any exchange of information must be consistent with procurement integrity requirements (see 3.104). Interested parties include potential offerors, end users, Government acquisition and supporting personnel, and others involved in the conduct or outcome of the acquisition.

(b) The purpose of exchanging information is to improve the understanding of Government requirements and industry capabilities, thereby allowing potential offerors to judge whether or how they can satisfy the Government's requirements, and enhancing the Government's ability to obtain quality supplies and services, including construction, at reasonable prices, and increase efficiency in proposal preparation, proposal evaluation, negotiation, and contract award.

(c) Agencies are encouraged to promote early exchanges of information about future acquisitions. An early exchange of information among industry and the program manager, contracting officer, and other participants in the acquisition process can identify and resolve concerns regarding the acquisition strategy, including proposed contract type, terms and conditions, and acquisition planning schedules; the feasibility of the requirement, including performance requirements, statements of work, and data requirements; the suitability of the proposal instructions and evaluation criteria, including the approach for assessing past performance information; the availability of reference documents; and any other industry concerns or questions. Some techniques to promote early exchanges of information are —

(1) Industry or small business conferences;

(2) Public hearings;

(3) Market research, as described in part 10;

(4) One-on-one meetings with potential offerors (any that are substantially involved with potential contract terms and conditions should include the contracting officer; also see paragraph (f) of this section regarding restrictions on disclosure of information);

(5) Presolicitation notices;

(6) Draft RFPs;

(7) RFIs;

(8) Presolicitation or preproposal conferences; and

(9) Site visits.

(d) The special notices of procurement matters at 5.205(c), or electronic notices, may be used to publicize the Government's requirement or solicit information from industry.

(e) RFIs may be used when the Government does not presently intend to award a contract, but wants to obtain price, delivery, other market information, or capabilities for planning purposes. Responses to these notices are not offers and cannot be accepted by the Government to form a binding contract. There is no required format for RFIs.

(f) General information about agency mission needs and future requirements may be disclosed at any time. After release of the solicitation, the contracting officer shall be the focal point of any exchange with potential offerors. When specific information about a proposed acquisition that would be necessary for the preparation of proposals is disclosed to one or more potential offerors, that information shall be made available to the public as soon as practicable, but no later than the next general release of information, in order to avoid creating an unfair competitive advantage. Information provided to a particular offeror in response to that offeror's request shall not be disclosed if doing so would reveal the potential offeror's confidential business strategy, and is protected under 3.104 or subpart 24.2. When conducting a presolicitation or prepproposal conference, materials distributed at the conference should be made available to all potential offerors, upon request.

This guidance permits exchanges with industry by program and technical personnel as well as contracting officers. It also describes a broader range of communication techniques than was provided for in the prior regulation. Thus, it greatly enhances the ability of agencies to perform fully effective acquisition planning. See NIH Policy Manual, 6315-1 Initiation, Review, Evaluation, and Award of Research & Development (R&D) Contracts (2004):

NIH encourages exchanges of information among all interested parties, from the earliest identification of a requirement through receipt of proposals. Any exchange of information must be consistent with procurement integrity requirements (see FAR 3.104). An early exchange of information among industry and the program manager, contracting officer, and other participants in the acquisition process can identify and resolve concerns regarding the acquisition strategy, including:

-proposed contract type, terms and conditions, and acquisition planning schedules;

-the feasibility of the proposal instructions and evaluation criteria; including the approach for assessing past performance information;

-the availability of reference documents; and

-any other industry concerns or questions.

There are also statutory requirements for notification of potential offerors of proposed procurements before a solicitation is issued, 15 U.S.C. § 637(e) and 41 U.S.C. § 416(a). The primary vehicle used is a synopsis of the proposed procurement in the governmentwide point of entry (GPE) located at http://www.fedbizopps. gov. While these notice requirements provide only minimal times for potential offerors to provide information as to their capabilities to the agency, they are the only mandatory part of this exchange of information process.

This section discusses all the techniques that are available to agencies to obtain full information for acquisition planning. Prior to the analysis of each technique, the current limitations imposed by the procurement integrity statute and its implementing regulations will be considered and the statutory synopsis requirement will be discussed.

1. Types of Exchanges

a. Solicitations for Planning Purposes

One technique for conducting market research is the use of solicitations for information or planning purposes. FAR 15.201(e) permits requests for information (RFIs) to be used in this manner as follows:

> RFIs may be used when the Government does not presently intend to award a contract, but wants to obtain price, delivery, other market information, or capabilities for planning purposes. Responses to these notices are not offers and cannot be accepted by the Government to form a binding contract. There is no required format for RFIs.

Some agencies require that solicitations for information or planning purposes may be used only when approved at a level above the contracting officer. See, for example, DEAR 915-201(e) (the head of contracting activity).

b. One-on-One Meetings

One-on-one meetings commonly known as "due diligence sessions" is a technique that promotes a fuller exchange of information with potential contractors during the acquisition planning process. FAR 15.201(c) provides:

> (4) One-on-one meetings with potential offerors (any that are substantially involved with potential contract terms and conditions should include the contracting officer; also see paragraph (f) of this section regarding restrictions on disclosure of information);

During due diligence, potential contractors have access to members of the acquisition team and program staff so that contractors may learn as much as possible about the agency's requirement.

The guidance on these meetings is contained in FAR 15.201(f) as follows:

> General information about agency mission needs and future requirements may be disclosed at any time. After release of the solicitation, the contracting officer must be the focal point of any exchange with potential offerors. When specific information about a proposed acquisition that would be necessary for the preparation of proposals is disclosed to one or more potential offerors, that information must be made available to the public as soon as practicable, but no later than the next general release of information, in order to avoid creating an unfair competitive advantage. Information provided to a particular offeror in response to its request must not be disclosed if doing so would reveal the potential offeror's confidential business strategy, and is protected under 3.104 or subpart 24.2.

Although this guidance is somewhat confusing, a clear distinction should be made between meetings that take place before the issuance of an RFP and those that occur after its issuance. Before the issuance of the RFP, agency technical and program personnel are permitted to meet with potential offerors to exchange information regarding "mission needs and future requirements" as long as they do not provide information on the specifics of elements of a procurement. If specific information is to be provided, the contracting officer should be made part of the exchange and care must be exercised to ensure that other potential contractors are given the same information. Although not covered by this guidance, it appears clear that agency technical and program personnel can obtain information from potential contractors in the course of performing market research.

After the issuance of an RFP, far greater care must be exercised to avoid unfair treatment of offerors. In general, the best course of action is to limit exchanges to the receipt of inquiries from potential offerors. Answers to such inquiries can be given if the inquiry will not have an impact on any other potential offeror. If the answer will impact other offerors, it should be given to all offerors at the same time whenever possible. Agency personnel should not assume that the guidance in ¶ (f) above permits such answers to be given to other offerors at the time of the "next general release of information" unless it is clearly established that this will not give one offeror a competitive advantage.

c. Draft Solicitations and Specifications

Several agencies use draft solicitations or draft specifications as a means of improving their clarity when the procurement is complex or of a high dollar amount, AFARS 5115.201(c)(6)(i) (Draft RFPs may be used when there are concerns with the statement of work or specifications or when there are significant technical risks and cost drivers); NFS 1815.201 (draft RFPs mandatory for all competitive negotiated procurements over $10 million).

To be useful, a draft solicitation must be as complete as possible, and sufficient time should be allowed to permit prospective offerors to respond meaningfully, NAVSEA Source Selection Guide, Part 2 (January 24, 2001).

A draft solicitation should invite comment on all aspects of the solicitation. NASA's guidance is set forth in NFS 1815.201, which provides:

> DRFPs shall invite comments from potential offerors on all aspects of the draft solicitation, including the requirements, schedules, proposal instructions, and evaluation approaches. Potential offerors should be specifically requested to identify unnecessary or inefficient requirements. If the DRFP contains Government-unique standards, potential offerors should be invited to identify voluntary consensus standards that meet the Government's requirements as alternatives to Government-unique standards cited as requirements, in accordance with FAR

11.101 and OMB Circular A-119. Comments should also be requested on any perceived safety, occupational health, security (including information technology security), environmental, export control, and/or other programmatic risk issues associated with performance of the work. When considered appropriate, the statement of work or the specifications may be issued in advance of other solicitation sections.

When issuing draft solicitations or specifications, potential offerors should be advised that the draft solicitation or specification is not a solicitation and the agency is not requesting proposals.

When draft solicitations or specifications are circulated for comment, they should be sent to all prospective offerors, and an announcement of their availability should be published through fedbizopps, FAR 5.205(c). Sufficient time should be given to potential offerors to submit meaningful comments, and the agency should take steps to assure all submitters that their comments have been given full consideration.

d. Sources-Sought Synopsis

Another technique for identifying potential sources is the issuance of a sources sought synopsis in fedbizopps. FAR 5.205 states that contracting officers may transmit to the GPE advance notices of their interest in potential R&D programs whenever market research does not produce a sufficient number of concerns to obtain adequate competition. This provision further states that advance notices will enable potential sources to learn of R&D programs and provide these sources with an opportunity to submit information that will permit evaluation of their capabilities. Under the FAR, such advance notices are called "Research and Development Sources Sought." Although the FAR appears to limit this technique for identifying potential sources to research and development contracts, it has been used for all types of procurement.

If an agency uses a sources-sought synopsis, it must make its essential requirements clear to potential offerors and allow them an opportunity to demonstrate their ability to comply before rejecting them as potential sources. In *M.D. Thompson Consulting, LLC*, Comp. Gen. Dec. B-297616, 2006 CPD ¶ 41, the GAO sustained a protest finding that the agency notice of intent to modify the contract to extend performance on a sole-source basis did not comply with the requirement for an accurate description of the services to be furnished. The agency had provided a bare-bones description of the requirement which was not sufficient to allow a prospective contractor to make an informed business judgment as to whether to request a copy of the solicitation. The GAO stated:

> By providing an inadequate description of its sole-source procurement in the synopsis, DOE restricted competition in violation of statute and regulation. Moreover, DOE compounded the shortcomings of this particular notice by providing

no information on the availability of a statement of work and by stating in the synopsis that the notice "is for informational purposes only and is not a request for proposals or other information." Cf. 41 U.S.C. sect. 416(b)(4); 15 U.S.C. sect. 637(f); FAR sect. 5.207(c)(15). The protesters and the Small Business Administration (SBA) argue, and we agree, that the language of the synopsis discouraged, and may have been intended to discourage, responses.

Similarly, in *Information Ventures, Inc.*, Comp. Gen. Dec. B-293518, 2004 CPD ¶ 76, the GAO found that the synopsis did not accurately describe the agency's requirement, stating:

> [T]he notice, while not entirely clear, indicates a need for a contractor to "plan and convene a conference" (described later in the notice as involving over 4,000 participants), and to provide training for conference participants on the Get Connected Toolkit. However, the requisition, including the scope of work, dated November 20, 2003, which presumably served as the basis for the notice, provides a markedly different description of the work here. Specifically, the requisition shows that the agency actually wanted a contractor to provide a geriatrics specialist and a conference coordinator to prepare a one-day training course in using the Get Connected Toolkit. This training course was to be offered during the course of the American Society of Aging (ASA)/NCOA conference on April 14, 2004, and the agency anticipated providing training to up to 60 individuals. See AR, Tab D, Statement of Work at 2-10. In our view, the agency's actual requirements are significantly different than "planning and convening a conference" for 4,000 people, as the notice advised. In light of the misleading notice used here, Information Ventures, as well as other potential contractors, was denied any realistic opportunity to compete for the agency's requirements.

For other cases sustaining a protest on the grounds that the description of the requirement in the synopsis was inaccurate, see *Sabreliner Corp.*, Comp. Gen. Dec. B-288030, 2001 CPD ¶ 170 (synopsis was inaccurate in that the actual requirement was to upgrade the engines to a military configuration not a commercial configuration); *Pacific Sky Supply Co.*, Comp. Gen. Dec. B225420, 87-1 CPD ¶ 206 (sole-source synopsis identified only 2 of 15 items included in the solicitation); and *Masstor Sys. Corp.*, 64 Comp. Gen. 118 (B-215046), 84-2 CPD ¶ 598 (agency rejected a potential source for failing to demonstrate compliance with a requirement that was neither set forth in the sources-sought synopsis nor otherwise made known to the vendor). The government should not, however, include proprietary information in the sources-sought synopsis. In *Research, Analysis & Dev., Inc. v. United States*, 8 Cl. Ct. 54 (1985), the plaintiff submitted an unsolicited proposal pertaining to a novel concept in state-of-the-art aircraft sensor technology. The proposal included the proper restrictive proprietary legend. After having agreed to maintain the confidentiality of the information, the agency issued a sources-sought synopsis requesting responses regarding the feasibility of a sensor system concept identical to that proposed by the plaintiff. The court held that the disclosure in the Commerce Business Daily (now fedbizopps) of the proprietary information associated with the unsolicited proposal violated the government's implied-in-fact contractual obligation to protect the data and entitled the company to damages. See also *Totolo/King (J.V.) v. United States*, 87 Fed. Cl. 680 (2009) (disclosure of a bond estimate in the sources-sought synopsis would conflict with the government's right and legal obligation to keep a project estimate confidential).

The results of a sources-sought synopsis may bear on the GAO's review of an agency's reasonableness in choosing specifications. In *Motorola, Inc.*, Comp. Gen. Dec. B-247913.2, 92-2 CPD ¶ 240, the protester challenged the agency's choice of procuring on a nondevelopmental item (NDI) basis. In concluding that the agency had a reasonable basis for its selection of NDI-only specifications, the GAO stated that through a sources-sought synopsis, the agency learned that there were offerors who would have an NDI available either by making minor modifications to existing items or by developing an item that would meet the agency's specifications and that such items would be available by the time the agency would award the contract. Thus, the GAO found that the agency had a sufficient basis to conclude that an NDI procurement was feasible.

Similarly, the results of a sources-sought synopsis may support the GAO's finding that an agency reasonably awarded on a sole-source basis. In *Polaris, Inc.*, Comp. Gen. Dec. B-218008, 85-1 CPD ¶ 401, the GAO held that an agency had properly awarded a sole-source contract because it had made a significant effort to determine whether other firms could meet the agency's needs. The agency had issued a sources-sought synopsis and received responses from six potential offerors which indicated that none could meet all its requirements. The GAO stated that the agency had properly concluded that the protester could not meet it needs because it had merely restated the agency's requirements in its response. Similarly, the results of a sources-sought synopsis may support an agency's determination not to set aside a procurement. In *E.L. Enters.*, Comp. Gen. Dec. B-271251.2, 96-2 CPD ¶ 29, the GAO upheld the agency's determination not to set aside a procurement, finding that the agency had made reasonable efforts to identify potential Indian concern offerors through a sources-sought synopsis. One firm responded to the synopsis, but the capability statement showed that the firm had limited corporate history and had never performed the services. The GAO will not consider a protest against a procuring agency issuing a potential sources-sought announcement. The GAO considers only protests against solicitations already issued by agencies and awards made or proposed to be made under those solicitations, *Pancor Corp.*, Comp. Gen. Dec. B-234168, 89-1 CPD ¶ 328.

2. Disclosure Prohibitions

There are several sanctions on disclosing or obtaining information related to the procurement process. 18 U.S.C. § 1905 imposes criminal sanctions on any government employee that discloses trade secrets and other proprietary data obtained from any person or organization. The procurement integrity provisions of the Office of

Procurement Policy Act of 1989, 41 U.S.C. § 423, as amended in 1996, prohibit any person from disclosing "contractor bid or proposal information" or "source selection information" before contract award, 41 U.S.C. § 423(a). There may also be improper conduct involved in obtaining information about a competitor.

a. Disclosure of Confidential Information

18 U.S.C. § 1905 provides:

> Whoever, being an officer or employee of the United States or of any department or agency thereof, any person acting on behalf of the Office of Federal Housing Enterprise Oversight, or agent of the Department of Justice as defined in the Antitrust Civil Process Act (15 U.S.C. 1311B1314), publishes, divulges, discloses, or makes known in any manner or to any extent not authorized by law any information coming to him in the course of his employment or official duties or by reason of any examination or investigation made by, or return, report or record made to or filed with, such department or agency or officer or employee thereof, which information concerns or relates to the trade secrets, processes, operations, style of work, or apparatus, or to the identity, confidential statistical data, amount or source of any income, profits, losses, or expenditures of any person, firm, partnership, corporation, or association; or permits any income return or copy thereof or any book containing any abstract or particulars thereof to be seen or examined by any person except as provided by law; shall be fined not more than $1,000, or imprisoned not more than one year, or both; and shall be removed from office or employment.

The conviction of a government employee under 18 U.S.C. § 1905 for improper disclosure of information was affirmed in *United States v. Wallington*, 889 F.2d 573 (5th Cir. 1989) (Act not overly broad to constitute a valid criminal statute).

b. Disclosure of Bid or Proposal Information or Source Selection Information

The Procurement Integrity Act, 41 U.S.C. § 423(a) as amended by the Clinger-Cohen Act of 1996, prohibits a "person" from knowingly disclosing "contractor bid or proposal information" or "source selection information" before award of a contract. The "persons" covered are defined in the Act, 41 U.S.C. § 423(a)(2), as any person who

> (A) is a present or former official of the United States, or a person who is acting or has acted for or on behalf of, or who is advising or has advised the United States with respect to, a Federal agency procurement; and

> (B) by virtue of that office, employment, or relationship has or had access to contractor bid or proposal information or source selection information.

The term "official" is defined in 41 U.S.C. § 423(f)(7) as (1) an officer as defined in 5 U.S.C. § 2104, (2) an employee as defined in 5 U.S.C. § 2105, and (3) a member of the uniformed forces as defined in 5 U.S.C. § 2101(3). FAR 3.104-1 adds to this the category of "special Government employees" as defined in 18 U.S.C. § 202.

The persons covered by the Act are those who have either "acted" or "advised" regarding a federal agency procurement and have obtained information through that contact with the procurement. Neither the statute nor the implementation of this part of the Act in FAR 3.104-3(a) contains any guidance on the meaning of "acted" or "advised," with the apparent effect that this rule applies to persons who have acted or advised no matter how small their contact with the procurement.

The Act applies only to a "federal agency procurement," which is defined in 41 U.S.C. § 423(f)(4) to mean only acquisitions using competitive procedures. This provision is implemented in FAR 3.104-3(a). However, FAR 3.104-4(a) contains a broader statement: "Except as specifically provided for in this subsection, no person or other entity may disclose contractor bid or proposal information or source selection information to any person other than a person authorized, in accordance with applicable agency regulations or procedures, by the agency head or the contracting officer to receive such information." This paragraph substantially broadens the scope of the Act by making it improper to disclose contractor bid or proposal information or source selection information on sole source procurements or contract modifications. It correctly reflects the fact that 18 U.S.C. § 1905 prohibits disclosure of proprietary information.

The term "contractor bid or proposal information," defined in 41 U.S.C. § 423(f)(1) and repeated verbatim in FAR 3.104-1:

(1) Cost or pricing data (as defined by 10 U.S.C. 2306a(h)) with respect to procurements subject to that section, and section 304A(h) of the Federal Property and Administrative Services Act of 1949 (41 U.S.C. 254b(h)), with respect to procurements subject to that section.

(2) Indirect costs and direct labor rates.

(3) Proprietary information about manufacturing processes, operations, or techniques marked by the contractor in accordance with applicable law or regulation.

(4) Information marked by the contractor as "contractor bid or proposal information" in accordance with applicable law or regulation.

(5) Information marked in accordance with 52.215-1(e).

The term "source selection information" is defined in 41 U.S.C. § 423(f)(2), and repeated verbatim in FAR 2.101:

any of the following information that is prepared for use by an agency for the purpose of evaluating a bid or proposal to enter into an agency procurement contract, if that information has not been previously made available to the public or disclosed publicly:

(1) Bid prices submitted in response to an agency invitation for bids, or lists of those bid prices before bid opening.

(2) Proposed costs or prices submitted in response to an agency solicitation, or lists of those proposed costs or prices.

(3) Source selection plans.

(4) Technical evaluation plans.

(5) Technical evaluations of proposals.

(6) Cost or price evaluations of proposals.

(7) Competitive range determinations that identify proposals that have a reasonable chance of being selected for award of a contract.

(8) Rankings of bids, proposals, or competitors.

(9) Reports and evaluations of source selection panels, boards, or advisory councils.

(10) Other information marked as "Source Selection Information — See FAR 2.101 and 3.104" based on a case-by-case determination by the head of the agency or the contracting officer, that its disclosure would jeopardize the integrity or successful completion of the Federal agency procurement to which the information relates.

Section 4304(h) of the Act contains a number of "savings provisions," as follows:

Savings Provisions. — This section does not —

(1) restrict the disclosure of information to, or its receipt by, any person or class of persons authorized, in accordance with applicable agency regulations or procedures, to receive that information;

(2) restrict a contractor from disclosing its own bid or proposal information or the recipient from receiving that information;

(3) restrict the disclosure or receipt of information relating to a Federal agency procurement after it has been canceled by the Federal agency before contract award unless the Federal agency plans to resume the procurement;

(4) prohibit individual meetings between a Federal agency official and an offeror or potential offeror for, or a recipient of, a contract or subcontract under a Federal agency procurement, provided that unauthorized disclosure or receipt of contractor bid or proposal information or source selection information does not occur;

(5) authorize the withholding of information from, nor restrict its receipt by, Congress, a committee or subcommittee of Congress, the Comptroller General, a Federal agency, or an inspector general of a Federal agency;

(6) authorize the withholding of information from, nor restrict its receipt by, the Comptroller General of the United States in the course of a protest against the award or proposed award of a Federal agency procurement contract; or

(7) limit the applicability of any requirements, sanctions, contract penalties, and remedies established under any other law or regulation.

These provisions are implemented at FAR 3.104-4(e) and (f). It seems clear that these rules should not prevent open communication between contracting agencies and potential offerors regarding the work to be procured and the procurement strategy before solicitations are issued as long as specific finalized source selection plans and technical evaluation plans are not revealed.

II. ELEMENTS OF THE ACQUISITION PLAN

The acquisition plan must identify all actions essential to the conduct of a successful procurement and establish milestones for their performance. The acquisition plan answers the "who-what-when-where-why-how" of the acquisition strategy planning process. FAR 7.105 provides the following general guidance regarding the elements of the acquisition plan:

In order to facilitate attainment of the acquisition objectives, the plan must identify those milestones at which decisions should be made (see paragraph (b)(18) below). The plan must address all the technical, business, management, and other significant considerations that will control the acquisition. The specific content of plans will vary, depending on the nature, circumstances, and stage of the acquisition. In preparing the plan, the planner must follow the applicable instructions in paragraphs (a) and (b) below, together with the agency's implementing procedures. Acquisition plans for service contracts or orders must describe the strategies for implementing performance-based acquisition methods or must provide rationale for not using these methods (see subpart 37.6).

FAR 7.105(a) contains a brief description of the elements of the acquisition plan under the category "Acquisition background and objectives," while FAR 7.105(b) describes additional elements under the category "Plan of action." The Acquisition background and objectives section considers what the government is buying, how it will evaluate price and other cost factors, where the work is to be performed, and the risks involved. The Plan of action section describes the steps necessary to procure the identified articles or services. Although the elements are discussed separately, they are interrelated. In this section, the topics are covered in the sequence they are listed in the FAR.

A. Background and Objectives

Eight specific factors are identified in FAR 7.105(a) for consideration in developing the procurement goals. This part of the regulation need not be regarded as an outline that the acquisition plan must follow but, rather, as issues that must be addressed.

1. Statement of Need

FAR 7.105(a)(1) states:

> Statement of need. Introduce the plan by a brief statement of need. Summarize the technical and contractual history of the acquisition. Discuss feasible acquisition alternatives, the impact of prior acquisitions on those alternatives, and any related in-house effort.

The need for the acquisition is identified and documented by the program or technical personnel in the agency who prepare the budget justification. Generally, the need will have been fully justified during the budget process and can merely be restated in the acquisition plan. If the acquisition planning is being done prior to preparing the budget, the agency will have to analyze its needs in a thorough manner as part of the acquisition plan.

This part of the plan should include the technical and contractual history of the procurement. The technical history of the product or service being procured should identify what specifications have been used in the past and any difficulties that have been encountered in performance against those specifications. The summary of the contractual history is normally done by the contracting officer and should identify each previous procurement that impacts the current planning. This is a key element in the planning process because it identifies how the current procurement fits in the overall conduct of the agency's business. The contractual history also identifies those cases where the procurement is part of an ongoing program, such as the development of a new product. In such cases, the agency normally will have adopted an acquisition plan for the entire program, and the planning for each step in the program will merely verify that the overall plan is still valid. On the other hand, the contractual history may identify previous procurements that have been unsuccessful — indicating that a new approach is needed. Thus, the contractual history is a key starting point for the preparation of the plan.

This section of the plan should include a discussion of feasible acquisition alternatives. For instance, the agency should consider and discuss performance in-house by government employees, performance under an agreement with another government agency, or performance by a contractor under an existing contract. The agency should also discuss the impact of prior acquisitions on the alternatives (i.e., whether an alternative is related to a prior or similar effort, whether multiple contracts were awarded previously and proved ineffective, etc.) as well as whether there is any related in-house effort. This element of the plan calls for innovative thinking, especially if the acquisition techniques used in the past have not been fully successful. Some aspects of the determination of the strategy are covered in the specific issues addressed below.

2. Applicable Conditions

This part of the plan identifies the constraints that must be imposed on the end product of the procurement, as set forth in FAR 7.105(a)(2):

> *Applicable conditions.* State all significant conditions affecting the acquisition, such as —
>
> > (i) Requirements for compatibility with existing or future systems or programs and
> >
> > (ii) Any known cost, schedule, and capability or performance constraints.

Precise identification of significant conditions early in the procurement process enables the agency to explore steps that can be taken to reduce or eliminate constraints that could have a detrimental impact on the procurement being planned. For example, if a product to be procured must be fully compatible with items in the agency's inventory, the agency may have to provide detailed drawings in the procurement package or induce the original manufacturer to license other sources in order to obtain sufficient competition to ensure a reasonable price. In such a case identification of this constraint would lead to the adoption of a strategy that would make detailed drawings available to a number of competitors through purchase of the rights or reverse engineering or establish an agreement with the original manufacturer to license additional sources.

Of course, identification of a constraint does not guarantee that there is a strategy that will completely overcome it. Many constraints must be accepted as an inherent element of the procurement. However, early identification of such constraints is beneficial because it assists all members of the planning team in recognizing the limitations that must be accepted in the conduct of the procurement being planned.

3. Cost

One of the major considerations in acquisition planning is the overall cost to the government. Acquisition techniques should be chosen to induce contractors to provide products and services at the lowest possible cost commensurate with high quality and timely performance. The costs considered should be both the initial acquisition cost of the product or service and the operating or use costs because the amount to be paid to a contractor may not be the only, or even the major, expenditure by the government in using the work obtained. Thus, it is important for the government to consider more than the contract price in determining what award is most advantageous to the government. FAR 7.105(a)(3) states:

> *Cost.* Set forth the established cost goals for the acquisition and the rationale supporting them, and discuss related cost concepts to be employed, including, as appropriate, the following items:
>
> > (i) *Life-cycle cost.* Discuss how life-cycle cost will be considered. If it is not used, explain why. If appropriate, discuss the cost model used to develop life-cycle cost estimates.
> >
> > (ii) *Design-to-cost.* Describe the design-to-cost objective(s) and underlying assumptions, including the rationale for quantity, learning-curve, and economic adjustment factors. Describe how objectives are to be applied, tracked, and enforced. Indicate specific related solicitation and contractual requirements to be imposed.
> >
> > (iii) *Application of should-cost.* Describe the application of should-cost analysis to the acquisition (see 15.407-4).

This part of the plan contains the agency's best analysis of the expected cost of the procurement and some of the techniques that will be used to ensure that this cost is reasonable and attainable.

a. Acquisition Cost

The plan must contain the agency's estimate of the amount of funds that will be needed to support the contract effort. This is usually done through the development of an independent government cost estimate (IGCE). An IGCE is the government's own estimated cost/price of the proposed acquisition. The IGCE serves as the basis for reserving funds for the contract as part of acquisition planning. The traditional use of the IGCE is to determine the reasonableness of a contractor's cost and technical proposals. Although § 3004 of FASA requires an IGCE before the development or production of a new military program, there is no similar statutory or regulatory requirement for supplies or services. However, the IGCE has become common practice and is often a required element of a proper contract file for supplies or services over the simplified acquisition threshold. The IGCE is prepared by either the program office or contracting officer. The estimate (including work sheets) is to remain confidential, and the government may not provide this information to contractors. See, e.g., Department of Commerce NOAA Independent Government Cost Estimate Guide (2007); EPA Guide for Preparing Independent Government Cost Estimates;

Department of State's Foreign Service Handbook 6 FAH-2 H-350; and Department of Army Procurement Advisory Notice 07-01 (Feb. 7, 2007). For standard materials readily available on the commercial market, catalog or market survey prices may suffice for the estimate. The below template may assist in the development of the IGCE when catalog or market prices are not available.

INDEPENDENT GOVERNMENT COST ESTIMATE (IGCE)

1. PROJECT TITLE				
2. PROJECT MANAGER	Period of Performance			
	FROM		TO	
DESCRIPTION OF COST ELEMENTS				
1. DIRECT LABOR (List Labor Categories)	ESTIMATED HOURS	RATED PER HOUR ($)	ESTIMATED COST ($)	TOTAL ESTIMATED COST ($)
			$0.00	
			$0.00	
			$0.00	
			$0.00	
			$0.00	
			$0.00	
	TOTAL DIRECT LABOR			$0.00
2. OVERHEAD	RATE (%)	TOTAL LABOR ($)	ESTIMATED COST ($)	TOTAL ESTIMATED COST ($)
				$0.00
3. MATERIALS/SERVICES (Excluding Information Technology (IT)			ESTIMATED COST ($)	TOTAL ESTIMATED COST ($)
				$0.00
4. INFORMATION TECHNOLOGY SUPPORT			ESTIMATED COST ($)	TOTAL ESTIMATED COST ($)
TOTAL IT SUPPORT				$0.00

5. TRAVEL		ESTIMATED COST ($)	TOTAL ESTIMATED COST ($)
			$0.00
6. SUBCONTRACTOR (S) CONSULTANT (S)		ESTIMATED COST ($)	TOTAL ESTIMATED COST ($)
TOTAL SUBCONTRACTOR (S) CONSULTANT(S)			$0.00
7. OTHER DIRECT COSTS		ESTIMATED COST (S)	TOTAL ESTIMATED COST ($)
			$0.00
8. TOTAL ESTIMATED COST			$0.00
TYPED NAME AND TITLE		SIGNATURE	
OFFICE/DIVISION/BRANCH		DATE	

Each period of performance requires an IGCE – (e.g., base award and all option periods).

The higher the degree of accuracy of the IGCE, the more smoothly the procurement will proceed because funds will be available as necessary to execute it. Thus, good acquisition planning demands that the agency devote sufficient effort to arriving at an accurate cost estimate.

b. Life-Cycle Cost

The plan must contain a discussion of how life-cycle cost logic will be used in the procurement. FAR 7.101 defines life-cycle cost to mean "the total cost to the government of acquiring, operating, supporting, and (if applicable) disposing of the items being acquired," but the FAR contains no guidance on the application of this technique. The cost of ownership of an asset or service is incurred throughout its whole life and does not all occur at the point of acquisition.

DOD Directive 5000.01, The Defense Acquisition System, May 12, 2003, and DOD Instruction 5000.02, Operation of the Defense Acquisition System, Dec. 8, 2008, provide guidance on life-cycle cost. For a defense acquisition program, life-cycle cost consists of research and development costs, investment costs, operating and support costs, and disposal costs over the entire life-cycle. The Instruction requires each program to have a life-cycle sustainment plan from the inception of the program through deployment of the system. The plan must be continually updated as the program progresses and must consider "supply; maintenance; transportation; sustaining engineering; data management; configuration management; HSI; environment, safety (including explosives safety), and occupational health; protection of critical program information and anti-tamper provisions; supportability; and interoperability."

In instances where the cost of operating and maintaining the acquired product will be much greater than the initial acquisition cost, conducting a procurement without factoring in life-cycle costs can greatly increase the ultimate costs to the government. For example, it may be more expensive to purchase equipment with a low initial price that requires significantly more personnel or energy to operate than does higher-priced equipment. Similarly, low-priced equipment that will be expensive to maintain may not be the best buy for the agency. Generally, these life-cycle costs are included in a procurement in one of two ways: by including specific contract provisions establishing design goals or stating mandatory contract requirements for such factors as operating costs, maintainability, and reliability; or by making life-cycle costs a part of the evaluation process in competitive source selections when the agency has a methodology to evaluate such costs during source selection.

Factoring life-cycle costs into a procurement by using clauses containing mandatory contract requirements forces the contractor to consider the cost in computing the contract price. Thus, a warranty clause calling for the equipment to function over a specified period of time would induce the contractor to include in its price either the cost of repair of equipment that did not meet the warranty or the cost of designing and manufacturing equipment that had the required life. Similarly, a clause requiring the contractor to reimburse the government for all energy costs over a certain required amount would motivate the contractor to include such costs in the price if its equipment did not meet the requirement. Such clauses are the most direct way of factoring life-cycle costs into the procurement process because they ensure that the offered prices include each offeror's evaluation of the cost impact of the requirement. It is difficult, however, for agencies to formulate a complete set of contract clauses covering all life-cycle costs anticipated in the use of a product.

Another way to deal with life-cycle costs is to include contract clauses establishing goals, such as maintenance labor hours per aircraft flight hour or fuel consumption of vehicles. In order to ensure that such goals are effective, agencies frequently specify contractual penalties for missing the goal or incentives for making the goal. Alternatively, these goals can be taken into account in subjective award-fee determinations. Such clauses generally have a less direct impact on the contractor than a clause requiring full reimbursement of the government for failure to meet the life-cycle cost requirement.

The use of evaluation factors in the source selection process is the other way of addressing life-cycle costs. If sufficient information is available, the agency can make a reasonable estimate of the life-cycle cost of each competitor and add that to the offered prices to determine whose price is lowest, *Columbia Inv. Group*, Comp. Gen. Dec. B-214324, 84-2 CPD ¶ 632, or the estimate can be used to assist the source selection official in making a best value determination, *Storage Tech. Corp.*, Comp. Gen. Dec. B-215336, 84-2 CPD ¶ 190. In *Ingalls Shipbuilding, Inc.*, Comp. Gen. Dec. B-275830, 97-1 CPD ¶ 180, the GAO found that the agency reasonably evaluated offerors' approaches to life-cycle cost reduction and concluded that awardee's proposal offered the highest likelihood of reducing life-cycle ownership costs. But see *Sikorsky Aircraft Co.*, Comp. Gen. Dec. B-299145, 2007 CPD ¶ 45, finding that the Air Force failed to reasonably perform the required Most Probable Life-Cycle Cost evaluation required by its own solicitation. The solicitation provided that for purposes of the source selection, cost/price would be calculated on the basis of the Most Probable Life Cycle Cost, including both contract and operations and support (O&S) costs. Thus, the solicitation provided for O&S costs to directly impact the overall evaluated cost. In addition, the solicitation requested detailed information quantifying the required maintenance for the proposed aircraft. The Air Force nevertheless normalized the cost of maintenance when calculating O&S costs, thereby ignoring the potentially lower cost of the protesters' asserted low maintenance helicopters. Similarly, see *The Boeing Co.*, Comp. Gen. Dec. B-311344, 2008 CPD ¶ 114, where the RFP made clear that the Most Probable Life-Cycle Cost was a key cost/price metric for source selection. In finding the agency's evaluation of military construction costs in calculating the offerors' most probable life-cycle costs for their proposed aircraft to be unreasonable, the GAO stated:

> An agency's life-cycle cost evaluation, like other cost analyses, requires the exercise of informed judgment concerning the extent to which proposed costs or prices represent a reasonable estimation of future costs. Our review of the agency's cost analysis is limited to the determination of whether the evaluation was reasonable and consistent with the terms of the RFP. See *Cessna Aircraft Co.*, B-261953.5, Feb. 5, 1996, 96-1 CPD ¶ 132 at 21. The agency's analysis need not achieve scientific certainty; rather, the methodology employed must be reasonably adequate to provide some measure of confidence that the agency's conclusions about the most probable costs under an offeror's proposal are realistic in view of other cost information reasonably available to the agency at the time of its evaluation. See *Information Ventures, Inc.*, B-297276.2 et al., Mar. 1, 2006, 2006 CPD ¶ 45 at 7.

Another possible technique is to make a subjective evaluation of life-cycle costs in the evaluation of the technical competence of the offeror. Such evaluation techniques will be far more accurate if the agency has valid information on the prospective life-cycle costs of the offered equipment — such as its energy usage or maintenance costs. See *Lockheed Aeronautical Sys. Co.*, Comp. Gen. Dec. B-252235.2, 93-2 CPD ¶ 80, sustaining a protest because the agency had based its award decision on a life-cycle cost analysis prepared by the winning contractor but that analysis used equipment reliability factors that were not being offered by the contractor.

Care must be used in specifying a particular product or performance technique on the basis of a life-cycle cost analysis. See *Moore Heating & Plumbing, Inc.*, Comp. Gen. Dec. B-247417, 92-1 CPD ¶ 483, granting a protest when the agency used a specification that prohibited buried cable in the installation of a heat distribution system on the basis that it would raise the life-cycle cost because of potential repair costs. When the protester was able to demonstrate that the agency's analysis was flawed, the GAO ruled that the specification was restrictive.

c. Design-to-Cost

When the acquisition is for the designated development of a new product, the plan must also contain a discussion of the use of design-to-cost techniques. FAR 7.101 defines "design-to-cost" as:

> a concept that establishes cost elements as management goals to achieve the best balance between life-cycle cost, acceptable performance, and schedule. Under this concept, cost is a design constraint during the design and development phases and a management discipline throughout the acquisition and operation of the system or equipment.

The purpose of this technique is to focus the contractor on the need to design an item that can be procured and used in the future at an affordable cost. The FAR contains no further guidance on how to use design-to-cost techniques in the procurement process.

d. Should-Cost Analysis

Should-cost analysis is a selective form of cost analysis used primarily on major procurements. This process is described in FAR 15.407-4(a), as follows:

> (1) Should-cost reviews are a specialized form of cost analysis. Should-cost reviews differ from traditional evaluation methods because they do not assume that a contractor's historical costs reflect efficient and economical operation. Instead, these reviews evaluate the economy and efficiency of the contractor's existing work force, methods, materials, equipment, real property, operating systems, and management. These reviews are accomplished by a multifunctional team of Government contracting, contract administration, pricing, audit, and engineering representatives. The objective of should-cost reviews is to promote both short and long-range improvements in the contractor's economy and efficiency in order to reduce the cost of performance of Government contracts. In addition, by providing rationale for any recommendations and quantifying their impact on cost, the Government will be better able to develop realistic objectives for negotiation.

DOD PGI 215.407-4 provides that DOD contracting activities should consider performing a program should-cost review before award of a definitive contract for a major system as defined by DoDI 5000.2. Should-cost analysis has been used most often on major contracts for the manufacture of high-priced equipment. It requires a detailed industrial engineering analysis of the specific methods used by the contractor to manufacture the product and a determination of more cost-effective methods that will reduce the costs. In this regard it is significantly different than conventional cost analysis because it challenges not the offeror's projections of current costs but, rather, the necessity for incurring those costs.

4. Capability or Performance

FAR 7.105(a)(4) provides the following guidance on capability or performance:

Capability or performance. Specify the required capabilities or performance characteristics of the supplies or the performance standards of the services being acquired and state how they are related to the need.

The requirement for a specific statement of the key performance characteristics of the supplies or services being acquired should assist the agency in identifying restrictive provisions in the statement of work that may preclude potential contractors from participating in the procurement. When such provisions are identified, an agency can address possible steps that can be taken to eliminate them. The guidance on restrictive specifications is reviewed below in the discussion of specifications.

This requirement should also assist the agency in determining whether the proposed contract specification contains too many detailed requirements that will preclude offerors from proposing innovative ways to meet the agency's needs with fewer resources. See FAR Subpart 37.6 requiring that service contracts be performance based to the maximum extent practicable. Thus, FAR 37.602 calls for service contract work statements to "[d]escribe the work in terms of the required results rather than either 'how' the work is to be accomplished or the number of hours to be provided."

5. Delivery or Performance-Period Requirements

FAR 7.105(a)(5) states:

Delivery or performance-period requirements. Describe the basis for establishing delivery or performance-period requirements (see Subpart 11.4). Explain and provide reasons for any urgency if it results in concurrency of development and production or constitutes justification for not providing for full and open competition.

The guidance in FAR Subpart 11.4 gives contracting officers a number of factors to consider in establishing the delivery schedule or performance period. FAR 11.401(a) also contains the following cautionary language as to establishing schedules that are too tight:

The time of delivery or performance is an essential contract element and shall be clearly stated in solicitations. Contracting officers shall ensure that delivery or performance schedules are realistic and meet the requirements of the acquisition. Schedules that are unnecessarily short or difficult to attain —

(1) Tend to restrict competition,

(2) Are inconsistent with small business policies, and

(3) May result in higher contract prices.

The agency should also consider whether any contractual provisions will be used to provide enhancement or enforcement of the performance or delivery schedule. The two most commonly used techniques are liquidated damages and delivery incentives. Liquidated damages are used quite frequently on construction contracts and occasionally on other types of contracts. By establishing a fixed amount of damages for each day of delay, they provide the government with a preestablished remedy for delay and limit the contractor's liability for such delay. FAR 11.502 provides the following guidance on liquidated damages:

(a) The contracting officer must consider the potential impact on pricing, competition, and contract administration before using a liquidated damages clause. Use liquidated damages clauses only when —

(1) The time of delivery or timely performance is so important that the Government may reasonably expect to suffer damage if the delivery or performance is delinquent; and

(2) The extent or amount of such damage would be difficult or impossible to estimate accurately or prove.

(b) Liquidated damages are not punitive and are not negative performance incentives (see 16.402-2). Liquidated damages are used to compensate the Government for probable damages. Therefore, the liquidated damages rate must be a reasonable forecast of just compensation for the harm that is caused by late delivery or untimely performance of the particular contract. Use a maximum amount or a maximum period for assessing liquidated damages if these limits reflect the maximum probable damage to the Government. Also, the contracting officer may use more than one liquidated damages rate when the contracting officer expects the probable damage to the Government to change over the contract period of performance.

There are two standard clauses for liquidated damages in fixed-price contracts — Liquidated Damages — Supplies, Services, or Research and Development, FAR 52.211-11, and Liquidated Damages — Construction, FAR 52.211-12. These clauses provide that the damages do not apply to excusable delays. See Chapter 10 of *Cibinic, Nagle & Nash, Administration of Government Contracts (4th ed. 2006)* for an in-depth discussion of liquidated damages.

Delivery incentives are used when the government wants to induce the contractor to perform earlier than required. FAR 16.402-3 provides:

(a) Delivery incentives should be considered when improvement from a required delivery schedule is a significant Government objective. It is important to determine the Government's primary objectives in a given contract (e.g., earliest possible delivery or earliest quantity production).

(b) Incentive arrangements on delivery should specify the application of the reward-penalty structure in the event of Government-caused delays or other delays beyond the control, and without the fault or negligence, of the contractor or subcontractor.

6. Tradeoffs

FAR 7.105(a)(6) provides the following guidance on tradeoffs:

Trade-offs. Discuss the expected consequences of trade-offs among the various cost, capability or performance, and schedule goals.

In arriving at an acquisition strategy, the agency must make explicit decisions to determine the best balance among cost, performance, and schedule. The agency should discuss which of these goals is most important and how they will impact the procurement in comparison with the other goals. The tradeoffs required to be addressed here are different than the cost/technical tradeoff performed as part of a best value basis for award. This section should address tradeoffs between competing government interests such as schedule adjustments and affect on performance, budget versus technical capabilities, and quicker delivery of equipment resulting in higher cost.

The January 2006 report of the Defense Acquisition Performance Assessment Project (DAPA) concluded that "the budget, acquisition and requirements processes [of the Department of Defense] are not connected organizationally at any level below the Deputy Secretary of Defense." As a result, DOD officials often fail to consider the impact of requirements decisions on the acquisition and budget processes, or to make needed tradeoffs between cost, schedule and requirements on major defense acquisition programs. To address this concern, § 201 of the Weapon Reform Act of 2009, Pub .L. No. 111-23 requires consultation between the budget, requirements and acquisition stovepipes — including consultation in the joint requirements process — to ensure the consideration of trade-offs between cost, schedule, and performance early in the process of developing major weapon systems.

7. Risks

FAR 7.105(a)(7) states:

Risks. Discuss technical, cost, and schedule risks and describe what efforts are planned or underway to reduce risk and the consequences of failure to achieve goals. If concurrency of development and production is planned, discuss its effects on cost and schedule risks.

GSA's Acquisition Planning Wizard provides the following guidance for identifying and mitigating risk:

Identify and describe any risks (and also rate as High, Moderate, or Low) associated with the project, e.g., —

1. Schedule
2. Cost
3. Funding/budget availability
4. Technical obsolescence
5. Technical feasibility
6. Risk implicit in a particular contract type
7. Dependencies between a new project and other projects or systems
8. The number of simultaneous high risk projects to be monitored
9. Project management risk
10 Operational

Describe actions to manage and mitigate risk for each risk identified during the acquisition. Techniques may include, but are not limited to —

1. Prudent project management, monitoring progress, costs, schedules, etc.
2. Use of modular contracting
3. Thorough acquisition planning tied to budget planning by the program, finance and contracting offices
4. Continuous collection and evaluation of risk-based assessment data
5. Prototyping prior to implementation
6. Post implementation reviews to determine actual project cost, benefits and returns
7. Focusing on risks and returns using quantifiable measures
8. Earned Value Management
9. Milestone Deliverables

There has been significant criticism of DOD major weapon systems programs for adopting requirements that impose undue risks that can not be achieved – resulting in substantial delays and cost increases. See, for example, *Defense Acquisitions: Assessment of Selected Weapon Programs*, GAO-1-388SP, March 2010, reviewing 42 ongoing programs and commenting on the extent to which they have conformed to the initiatives of the department to ensure that they were "knowledge-based." This "knowledge-based" requirement has been recommended by GAO for many years. It is based on the premise that a major program should not be permitted to proceed into development of a new system until all of the technology necessary to meet the requirement has been proven. DOD Instruction 5000.02, Operation of the Defense Acquisition System, implements this concept by inserting a Technology Development Phase in the acquisition process where all unproven technology that is specified for a system must "provide for two or more competing teams producing prototypes of the system and/or key system elements," with these prototypes "demonstrated in a relevant environment, or, preferably in an operational environment."

8. Acquisition Streamlining

Acquisition streamlining is an effort to reduce the costs of doing the acquisition by eliminating unnecessary procedures and practices. FAR 7.101 contains the following definition:

> "*Acquisition streamlining*," means any effort that results in more efficient and effective use of resources to design and develop, or produce quality systems. This includes ensuring that only necessary and cost-effective requirements are included, at the most appropriate time in the acquisition cycle, in solicitations and resulting contracts for the design, development, and production of new systems, or for modifications to existing systems that involve redesign of systems or subsystems.

FAR 7.105(a)(8) states:

> *Acquisition streamlining.* If specifically designated by the requiring agency as a program subject to acquisition streamlining, discuss plans and procedures to
>
> > (i) Encourage industry participation by using draft solicitations, presolicitation conferences, and other means of stimulating industry involvement during design and development in recommending the most appropriate application and tailoring of contract requirements;
> >
> > (ii) Select and tailor only the necessary and cost-effective requirements; and
> >
> > (iii) State the timeframe for identifying which of those specifications and standards, originally provided for guidance only, shall become mandatory.

The FAR guidance focuses on the first element of streamlining — the adoption of contract specifications and other solicitation provisions that are clearly understood by the potential competitors and that permit open competition. Open exchanges with industry during the planning process are also encouraged by FAR 15.201. This FAR guidance does not address the need to reduce the complexity and cost of many procurements that require the preparation of extensive technical and management plans, the evaluation of those plans by numerous government evaluators, the coordination of such evaluations, and the ultimate extensive decision process. However, this type of acquisition streamlining is highly necessary if an agency is to adopt a truly streamlined acquisition process. This issue is extensively discussed in Chapter 2.

In contrast to the numerous over-complex government processes, commercial contracting practices utilize a highly streamlined solicitation, which is generally only one quarter the size of a standard government services solicitation. The standard times can be compressed, proposals and evaluations are highly streamlined, and commercial pricing is obtained. See FAR Part 12.

B. Plan of Action

This section covers 21 specific factors that are identified in FAR 7.105(b) as being elements of most acquisition plans. This part of the regulation need not be regarded as an outline that the acquisition plan must follow but, rather, as issues that must be addressed.

1. Sources

FAR 7.105(b)(1) states:

(1) *Sources*. Indicate the prospective sources of supplies or services that can meet the need. Consider required sources of supplies or services (see Part 8) and sources identifiable through databases including the Governmentwide database of contracts and other procurement instruments intended for use by multiple agencies available at http://www.contractdirectory.gov. Include consideration of small business, veteran-owned small business, HUBZone small business, and small disadvantaged business, and women-owned small business concerns (see Part 19), and the impact of any bundling that might affect their participation in the acquisition (see 7.107) (15 U.S.C. 644(e)). When the proposed acquisition strategy involves bundling, identify the incumbent contractors affected by the bundling. Address the extent and results of the market research and indicate their impact on the various elements of the plan (see Part 10).

One of the most critical tasks in the acquisition planning process is the determination of the sources that are available to meet the government's needs. As discussed earlier, this is an essential element of the market research effort that agencies must undertake — with major emphasis on finding commercial sources that can meet the government's needs efficiently. However, as indicated above, there are other aspects to the determination of sources. For some products and services there are mandatory sources. In addition, there are statutory policies requiring procurement from small business concerns and small disadvantaged business concerns.

a. Mandatory Sources

Various statutes and regulations require agencies to attempt to satisfy their needs for goods and services from specific sources prior to contracting with commercial sources. FAR Part 8 contains detailed guidance on mandatory sources. See also DFARS Part 208 for guidance on mandatory sources for defense procurement.

FAR 8.002 ranks mandatory sources in order of priority. Existing agency inventory is the first source considered for supplies. If the needed supply is not available from existing inventory, FAR 8.002(a)(1) directs the agency to consider other sources in the following order: other agencies (excess supplies), Federal Prison Industries, the Committee for Purchase from People Who Are Blind or Severely Disabled, government wholesale supply sources, mandatory federal supply schedules, optional federal supply schedules, and commercial sources. If the agency's requirement is for services, sources are considered in the following sequence: the Committee for Purchase from People Who Are Blind or Severely Disabled, mandatory federal supply schedules, optional federal supply schedules, Federal Prison Industries, and commercial sources, FAR 8.002(a)(2). The following discussion examines these mandatory sources of supply.

(1) EXCESS PERSONAL PROPERTY

The administrator of the GSA is authorized to prescribe policies and methods to promote utilization of excess personal property by the federal agencies pursuant to 40 U.S.C. § 483. This statute requires agencies to utilize excess personal property of other agencies to the fullest extent possible. The statute also charges agencies with the duty of monitoring excess property and either transferring or disposing of it as promptly as possible. The GSA maintains catalogs of available excess property, issues bulletins, and provides other assistance to facilitate acquisition of excess personal property. FAR 8.102 requires procurement personnel to make positive efforts to satisfy agency requirements by obtaining and using excess personal property before initiating a contract action.

(2) GOVERNMENT PRINTING OFFICE

Virtually all printing, binding, and blankbook work for Congress, the Executive Office of the President, the judiciary (except the Supreme Court), and every executive department, independent office, and establishment of the government must be done by or through the Government Printing Office (GPO), absent a waiver from the Joint Committee on Printing, 44 U.S.C. § 501. Section 207 of the Legislative Branch Appropriations Act of 1993, Pub. L. No. 102-392, prohibits, with limited exceptions, the use of appropriated funds by the executive branch agencies for the procurement of printing other than by or through the GPO. Section 207 was amended by the Legislative Branch Appropriations Act of 1995, Pub. L. No. 103-283, and added "duplicating" to the definition of "printing." In response to OMB Memorandum M-02-7 (May 2001) announcing that executive departments and agencies should not be required to procure printing through GPO and advising agencies to select printing and duplicating services based on best quality, cost, and time of delivery, Congress enacted § 117 of Pub. L. No. 107-229, as amended by § 4 of Pub. L. No. 107-240. This legislation prohibits agencies from using appropriated funds to implement or comply with OBM Memorandum M-0207 and prohibits the use of any appropriated funds to pay for the printing of the President's Budget. See *Letter to Chairman, Committee on Appropriations*, Comp. Gen. Dec. B-300192, Nov. 13, 2002, where the GAO upheld the general rule that all printing and binding for the government "shall be done" through the GPO and found that failure to abide by § 117 would constitute a violation of the Anti-Deficiency Act. In *Bureau of Land*

Management, Payment of Pocatello Field Office Photocopying Costs, Comp. Gen. Dec. B-290901, 2003 CPD ¶ 2, the GAO held that photocopying services procured by another BLM field office from a commercial source in violation of 44 U.S.C. § 501 were not authorized and could not be paid for with federal funds.

FAR 8.802 mandates compliance with the regulations of the Congressional Joint Committee on Printing and vests responsibility for obtaining waivers and dealing with the Joint Committee in certain officials.

Individual printing orders costing not more than $1,000 are, under certain conditions, not required to be printed by the GPO, Pub. L. No. 102-392, Title II § 207(a), codified at 44 U.S.C. § 501 note.

(3) GOVERNMENT WHOLESALE SUPPLY SOURCES

The administrator of the GSA is authorized to operate supply centers and procure and supply personal property for executive agencies, 40 U.S.C. § 481. Pursuant to this authority, the GSA operates supply distribution facilities and maintains an inventory of stock items that constitute a mandatory source for executive agencies located within the United States. See 41 C.F.R. § 101-26.301. The GSA publishes a supply catalog that lists all items available from GSA stock. The GSA also has an electronic catalog, "GSA Advantage!," which is an on-line ordering system that allows agencies to search through all GSA sources of supply and select the item that best meets their requirements.

Other wholesale supply sources include the defense supply centers of the Defense Logistics Agency, 41 C.F.R. § 101-26.6, and the inventory control points of the military departments, 41 C.F.R. § 101-26.606. For example, under DLA, gasoline, fuel oil, and kerosene may be purchased from the Defense Energy Support Center, 41 C.F.R. § 101-26.602-3. The Department of Veterans Affairs is a wholesale source for nonperishable items, 41 C.F.R. § 101-26.704.

(4) GENERAL SERVICES ADMINISTRATION MOTORPOOLS

The Federal Property and Administrative Services Act of 1949 authorizes the General Services administrator to "consolidate, take over, acquire, or arrange for the operation by any executive agency of" motor vehicles, 40 U.S.C. § 491. The Act authorizes the GSA to enter into rental or other arrangements and to utilize government-owned vehicles. The Act provides that requisitioning agencies should be charged for services rendered at prices calculated to recover all elements of cost.

The procedures for the leasing, from commercial concerns, of motor vehicles that comply with the Federal Motor Vehicle Safety Standards and applicable state motor vehicle safety regulations are covered in FAR Subpart 8.11. Under these procedures, FAR 8.1102 provides that contracting officers must obtain a written certification before preparing solicitations for leasing of motor vehicles that —

(1) The vehicles requested are of maximum fuel efficiency and minimum body size, engine size, and equipment (if any) necessary to fulfill operational needs and meet prescribed fuel economy standards;

(2) The head of the requiring agency, or a designee, has certified that the requested passenger automobiles (sedans and station wagons) larger than Type IA, IB, or II (small, subcompact, or compact) are essential to the agency's mission;

(3) Internal approvals have been received;

(4) The General Services Administration has advised that it cannot furnish the vehicles.

(5) FEDERAL PRISON INDUSTRIES

Federal Prison Industries (FPI), also referred to as UNICOR, is a wholly owned government corporation created by Congress in 1934 to administer industrial operations in federal penal and correctional institutions. FPI is authorized to produce commodities for consumption in penal institutions or for sale to the government but is prohibited from selling to the public, 18 U.S.C. §§ 4121-4129. Until 2001 the legislation that created UNICOR remained unchanged. It required federal agencies to purchase FPI products to meet their requirements as long as FPI's prices were competitive. UNICOR's mandatory source status ended in 2002. As amended, 10 U.S.C. § 2410n states that if the product is not comparable in price, quality, or time of delivery to products available from the private sector that best meet the Department's needs, competitive procedures shall be used for the procurement. This is implemented in the FAR. The purchase of FPI supplies are mandatory where, after market research, the agency determines that the FPI items are comparable to private sector items in terms of price, quality, and time of delivery, FAR 8.602(a)(3). If the item is not found to be comparable, agencies are to acquire items meeting their needs through competitive procedures and to include FPI in the solicitation process, FAR 8.602(a)(4)(i), (ii). See *Gentex Corp.*, Comp. Gen. Dec. B-400328, 2008 CPD ¶ 186 (protest that agency should have provided for cost analysis under OMB Circular A-76 based on award to FBI denied as no statute or regulation requires an agency to conduct an A-76 study and competition, or otherwise adjust its evaluation to account for any FPI competitive advantages simply because FPI is a potential or actual competitor).

Section 827 of the National Defense Authorization Act for Fiscal Year 2008, Pub. L. No. 110-181, further amended 10 U.S.C. § 2410n. Effective March 31, 2008, § 827 requires DoD contracting activities to use competitive procedures when procuring products for which FPI has significant market share (defined as being greater than 5% in any Federal Supply Code (FSC)). In using these procedures, FPI must be included in the solicitation process. See DFARS 208.602-70. The objective of the rule is to provide for competition in the acquisition of items for which FPI has a significant market share. The rule is expected to benefit small business concerns that offer items for which FPI has a significant market share, by permitting those concerns to compete for additional DoD contract awards.

Federal Prison Industries maintains a list of supplies manufactured and services performed by FPI (http://www.unicon.gov).

(6) Surplus Strategic and Critical Materials

The General Services administrator has the authority to purchase strategic and critical materials for government stockpiles and for use or resale to stimulate exploration, development, and mining of these materials under Exec. Order No. 10480, 18 Fed. Reg. 4939 (1953), which delegates presidential authority as contained in 50 U.S.C. App. § 2093.

FAR 8.003 requires government agencies to satisfy their requirements for strategic and critical materials from or through surplus holdings that are maintained by the Defense National Stockpile Center. Under Part 8, the Defense National Stockpile Center transfers material to federal agencies, which in turn provide it to their contractors as government furnished material.

(7) Committee for Purchase From People Who Are Blind or Severely Disabled

The Javits-Wagner-O'Day Act, now known as the AbilityOne Program, mandates that commodities or services on the Procurement List required by government entities be procured from a nonprofit agency employing persons who are blind or have other severe disabilities, if that commodity or service is available within the normal period required by that government entity, 41 U.S.C. §§ 46-48. The Committee for Purchase From People Who Are Blind or Severely Disabled (Committee) is the federal agency authorized to administer the program. It has designated two Central Nonprofit Agencies, National Industries for the Blind and NISH, to assist with program implementation. This Act is implemented in FAR Subpart 8.7.

The Procurement List may be accessed at: http://www.abilityone.gov/. Many items on the Procurement List are identified in the General Services Administration Supply Catalog and GSA's Customer Service Center Catalogs with a black square and the words "NIB/NISH Mandatory Source," and in similar catalogs issued by the Defense Logistics Agency and the Department of Veterans Affairs. GSA, DLA, and

VA are central supply agencies from which other federal agencies are required to purchase certain supply items on the Procurement List.

The Committee determines the suitability of adding a commodity or service to the Procurement List based on the employment potential for persons who are blind or have other severe disabilities, the qualifications and capability of the nonprofit agency, and whether or not a proposed addition to the Procurement List is likely to have a severe adverse impact on the current contractor for the specific commodity or service, 41 C.F.R. §§ 51-2.4. The Committee is also responsible for determining fair market prices for commodities and services on the Procurement List, 41 C.F.R. §§ 51-2.7. The fair market price is derived at by negotiations between the contracting activity and the nonprofit agency that will produce or provide the commodity or service to the government, assisted by the appropriate central nonprofit agency.

Ordering offices may acquire supplies or services on the Procurement List from commercial sources only if the acquisition is specifically authorized in a purchase exception granted by the designated central nonprofit agency, FAR 8.706. The central nonprofit agency will grant an exception when the AbilityOne participating nonprofit agencies cannot provide the supplies or services within the time required, and commercial sources can provide them significantly sooner in the quantities required. The central nonprofit agency will also grant an exception when the quantity required cannot be produced or provided economically by the AbilityOne participating nonprofit agencies, FAR 8.706 and 41 C.F.R. §§ 51-5.4.

(8) FEDERAL SUPPLY SCHEDULES

Administered by the GSA, the Federal Supply Schedule (FSS) program has been designed to provide agencies with a simple process for acquiring commonly used supplies and services in varying quantities at volume discounts. Orders placed pursuant to a multiple-award schedule (MAS) are considered to be issued pursuant to full and open competition, 10 U.S.C. § 2302(2)(C); 41 U.S.C. § 259(b)(3). Although included under FAR Part 8, Required Sources of Supplies and Services, these schedules are non-mandatory, *Murray-Benjamin Elec. Co., LP*, Comp. Gen. Dec. B-298481, 2006 CPD ¶ 129.

When using a schedule, ordering activities are to place orders with the schedule contractor who can provide the supply or service that represents the best value. Before placing an order, an ordering activity must consider reasonably available information about the supply or service offered under MAS contracts by surveying at least three schedule contractors through the GSA Advantage! on-line shopping service, or by reviewing the catalogs or pricelists of at least three schedule contractors, FAR 8.405-1.

FSS orders may not cover supplies or services not covered by a schedule contract, *OMNIPLEXWorld Servs. Corp.*, Comp. Gen. Dec. B-291105, 2002 CPD ¶ 199. The rule requires that all labor categories to perform required services be included in the schedule contract. See, for example, *CDM Group, Inc.*, Comp. Gen. Dec. B-291304.2, 2002 CPD ¶ 221, finding that the agency properly rejected the protester's quotation that was based on labor categories not included in its FSS contract. However, agencies have reasonable discretion in interpreting the scope of schedules. See, for example, *Information Ventures, Inc.*, Comp. Gen. Dec. B-291952, 2003 CPD ¶ 101, denying a protest that the services required by the agency were not available under the FSS.

The General Services Administration has eased this scope problem by including blanket schedule item numbers (SINs) on some of the schedules to be used when an agency needs services that are listed under several different SINs. This permits award to a contractor with a contract listing only the blanket SIN. See *Avalon Integrated Servs. Corp.*, Comp. Gen. Dec. B290185, 2002 CPD ¶ 118, finding that it was "irrelevant" that a contractor who held an FSS contract for the blanket SIN used by the agency did not also hold a schedule contract for other SINs under which services were sought. There are also "corporate schedule contracts" covering broad scopes of work. See *Planned Systems Int'l, Inc.*, Comp. Gen. Dec. B-292319.3, 2003 CPD ¶ 198, permitting use of this schedule. It appears that these techniques will not permit award for work by categories of labor that are not included in these broad schedules. See *Symplicity Corp.*, Comp. Gen. Dec. B-291902, 2003 CPD ¶ 89, granting a protest where the agency failed to consider whether the services offered by the task order awardee were covered by its FSS contract.

(9) HELIUM

FAR 8.5 implements the requirements of the Helium Act, 50 U.S.C. § 167a et seq., concerning the acquisition of liquid or gaseous helium by federal agencies or by government contractors or subcontractors for use in the performance of a government contract. It requires that to the extent that supplies are readily available, all major helium requirements purchased by a government agency or used in the performance of a government contract must be purchased from federal helium suppliers, FAR 8.502. See also 43 C.F.R. Part 3195. The Bureau of Land Management maintains a list of Federal Helium Suppliers at http://www.nm.blm.gov.

b. Small and Disadvantaged Businesses

It is the policy of the government to place a "fair proportion" of contracts with small businesses, 15 U.S.C. § 631(a). The FAR implements this policy stating that the government should provide maximum practicable opportunities in its acquisitions to small business, veteran-owned small business, service-disabled veteran-owned small business, HUBZone small business, small disadvantaged business, and women-owned small business concerns, FAR 19.201(a). FAR Part 19 contains detailed guidance on requirements to procure from small businesses and small disadvantaged businesses.

(1) STRUCTURING PROCUREMENTS

During the acquisition planning process, agencies must structure their procurements to carry out these policies. FAR 19.202-1 contains the following guidance:

Small business concerns shall be afforded an equitable opportunity to compete for all contracts that they can perform to the extent consistent with the Government's interest. When applicable, the contracting officer shall take the following actions:

(a) Divide proposed acquisitions of supplies and services (except construction) into reasonably small lots (not less than economic production runs) to permit offers on quantities less than the total requirement.

(b) Plan acquisitions such that, if practicable, more than one small business concern may perform the work, if the work exceeds the amount for which a surety may be guaranteed by SBA against loss under 15 U.S.C. 694b.

(c) Ensure that delivery schedules are established on a realistic basis that will encourage small business participation to the extent consistent with the actual requirements of the Government.

(d) Encourage prime contractors to subcontract with small business concerns (see Subpart 19.7).

(e)(1) Provide a copy of the proposed acquisition package to the SBA procurement center representative (or, if a procurement center representative is not assigned, see 19.402(a)) at least 30 days prior to the issuance of the solicitation if —

(i) The proposed acquisition is for supplies or services currently being provided by a small business and the proposed acquisition is of a quantity or estimated dollar value, the magnitude of which makes it unlikely that small businesses can compete for the prime contract;

(ii) The proposed acquisition is for construction and seeks to package or consolidate discrete construction projects and the magnitude of this consolidation makes it unlikely that small businesses can compete for the prime contract; or

(iii) The proposed acquisition is for a bundled requirement. (See 10.001(c)(2)(i) for mandatory 30-day notice requirement to incumbent small business concerns.) The contracting officer shall provide all information relative to the justification of contract bundling, including the acquisition plan or strategy, and if the acquisition involves substantial bundling, the information identified in 7.107(e). When the acquisition involves substantial bundling, the contracting officer shall also provide the same information to the agency Office of Small and Disadvantaged Business Utilization.

(2) The contracting officer also must provide a statement explaining why the —

(i) Proposed acquisition cannot be divided into reasonably small lots (not less than economic production runs) to permit offers on quantities less than the total requirement;

(ii) Delivery schedules cannot be established on a realistic basis that will encourage small business participation to the extent consistent with the actual requirements of the Government;

(iii) Proposed acquisition cannot be structured so as to make it likely that small businesses can compete for the prime contract;

(iv) Consolidated construction project cannot be acquired as separate discrete projects; or

(v) Bundling is necessary and justified.

(3) The 30-day notification process shall occur concurrently with other processing steps required prior to the issuance of the solicitation.

(4) If the contracting officer rejects the SBA representative's recommendation made in accordance with 19.402(c)(2), the contracting officer shall document the basis for the rejection and notify the SBA representative in accordance with 19.505.

FAR 19.202-2 requires contracting officers to make every effort to locate small business sources. This goal is accomplished by (1) making every reasonable effort to find additional small business concerns prior to issuing solicitations, unless lists are already excessively long and only some of the concerns on the list will be solicited (this effort should include contacting the SBA procurement center representative); and (2) publicizing solicitations and contract awards through the governmentwide point of entry (see subparts 5.2 and 5.3).

Agencies have been criticized for not coordinating with the Small Business Administration when they remove work from the small-business program. See, for example, *Letter to the Air Force and Army concerning Valenzuela Eng'g, Inc.*, Comp. Gen. Dec. B-277979, 98-1 CPD ¶ 51. In that case, the Air Force had ordered services using the Economy Act from an Army task order contract instead of renewing or recompeting for the work on the small business set-aside basis that had been used in the past. The GAO ruled that this violated FAR 19.202-1(e) because Economy Act purchases were acquisitions requiring coordination. See also *TRS Research*, Comp. Gen. Dec. B-290644, 2002 CPD ¶ 159 (agency's failure to coordinate the current consolidation of requirements with the SBA procurement center representative was inconsistent with the requirements of the Act and implementing regulations).

There has also been substantial criticism of contracting agencies for not following these policies when they "bundled" their contract requirements in order to achieve efficiencies. As a result, the Small Business Reauthorization Act of 1997, Pub. L. No. 105-135, contains provisions requiring federal agencies to "avoid unnecessary and unjustified bundling of contract requirements that precludes small business participation in procurements as prime contractors," 15 U.S.C. § 631. 15 U.S.C. § 632(o)(2), defines bundling as:

> consolidating 2 or more procurement requirements for goods or services previously provided or performed under separate smaller contracts into a solicitation of offers for a single contract that is likely to be unsuitable for award to a small-business concern due to —
>
> (A) the diversity, size, or specialized nature of the elements of the performance specified;
>
> (B) the aggregate dollar value of the anticipated award;
>
> (C) the geographical dispersion of the contract performance sites; or
>
> (D) any combination of the factors described in subparagraphs (A), (B), and (C).

See also FAR 2.101 and 13 C.F.R. § 125.2(d)(1)(i). The term "separate smaller contract" is defined as "a contract that has been performed by 1 or more small business concerns or was suitable for award to 1 or more small business concerns." 15 U.S.C. § 632(o)(3); 13 C.F.R. § 125.2(d)(1)(ii). See *Vox Optma, LLC*, Comp. Gen. Dec. B-400451, 2008 CPD ¶ 212 (no consolidation found where two of the contract actions identified — a task order under which protester was a subcontractor and work performed by a second subcontractor under the same task order — were under a contract executed by an entirely different activity); *USA Info. Sys., Inc.*, Comp. Gen. Dec. B-291417, 2002 CPD ¶ 224 (solicitation does not represent a "consolidation" of two or more requirements, inasmuch as the record establishes that all of the requirements here were previously provided under the one predecessor contract); and *Outdoor Venture Corp.*, Comp. Gen. Dec. B-299675, 2007 CPD ¶ 138 (not considered consolidation of two or more requirements where requirement is currently being procured as a packaged system under one contract).

A procurement that is exclusively set aside for small business concerns cannot constitute improper bundling under the Small Business Act, *Phoenix Scientific Corp.*, Comp. Gen. Dec. B-286817, 2001 CPD ¶ 24; *Health & Human Services Group*, Comp. Gen. Dec. B-294703, 2005 CPD ¶ 6.

When a proposed acquisition involves bundled requirements, the agency must first conduct market research to determine whether the bundling is necessary and justified, given the potential impact on small business participation, by ascertaining whether the government will derive measurably substantial benefits from the bundling and quantifying these benefits, 15 U.S.C. § 644(e)(2); FAR 7.107(a). In addition, the agency must, at least 30 days before issuing a solicitation, provide its acquisition package to the SBA procurement representative for review and also provide a statement why the (1) proposed acquisition cannot be divided into reasonably smaller lots for small businesses, (2) delivery schedules cannot be established that will encourage small business participation, (3) proposed acquisition cannot be structured so to make it likely that small businesses can compete for the prime contract, (4) consolidated construction project cannot be acquired as separate discrete projects, or (5) bundling is necessary and justified, FAR 19.202-1(e). Furthermore, within the same 30 days, an agency must notify any affected incumbent small business concerns of the government's intention to bundle the requirement, FAR 10.001(c)(2). See *Sigmatech, Inc.*, Comp. Gen. Dec. B-296401, 2005 CPD ¶ 156, sustaining a protest on the basis that the Army failed to perform a bundling analysis as required FAR 7.107(a), (b), or comply with the requirements of FAR 19.202-1 in providing notice of bundling to the SBA. The record further showed that the agency failed to provide notice to Sigmatech (the incumbent small business concern) of its intent to bundle the requirements and thus failed to comply with FAR 10.001(c)(2). The requirements that agencies perform a bundling analysis and notify the SBA when requirements are bundled is applicable to Blanket purchase agreements (BPAs) and orders placed against FSS contracts, FAR 8.404(a).

The key requirement is that the agency must find measurably substantial benefits to justify bundling, with the limitation that reduction of administrative or personnel costs are not a sufficient justification unless the cost savings are expected to be at least 10% of the estimated contract value (including options) of the bundled requirements, FAR 7.107.

Measurably substantial benefits may include individually or in any combination or aggregate: cost savings or price reduction, quality improvements that will save time or enhance performance or efficiency, reduction in acquisition cycle times, better terms and conditions, and any other benefits, FAR 7.107(b). The agency must quantify the identified benefits and explain how their impact would be measurably substantial. The benefits must be equivalent to 10% of the estimated contract or order value (including options) if the value is $86 million or less; or 5% for estimated contracts (including options) over $86 million, FAR 7.107(b). See *Nautical Eng'g, Inc.*, Comp. Gen. Dec. B-309955, 2007 CPD ¶ 204 (justification reasonably relied on two different benefits to the government: decreased maintenance and repair costs quantified as a savings of 5.29% and an 18% increase in time that the cutters will be performing their duties); and *B.H. Aircraft Co.*, Comp. Gen. Dec. B-295399.2, 2005 CPD ¶ 138 (substantial benefit of $28.3 million over five years, which was an amount well above the amount necessary to justify bundling).

For acquisition planning purposes, when the proposed acquisition strategy involves "substantial bundling," defined as bundling resulting in a contract or order that meets the following dollar amounts: $7.5 million or more for the Department of Defense; $5.5 million or more for NASA, GSA, and DOE; and $2 million or more for all other agencies (FAR 7.104(d)(2)), FAR 7.107(e) provides that the acquisition strategy must additionally —

(1) Identify the specific benefits anticipated to be derived from bundling;

(2) Include an assessment of the specific impediments to participation by small business concerns as contractors that result from bundling;

(3) Specify actions designed to maximize small business participation as contractors, including provisions that encourage small business teaming;

(4) Specify actions designed to maximize small business participation as subcontractors (including suppliers) at any tier under the contract, or order, that may be awarded to meet the requirements;

(5) Include a specific determination that the anticipated benefits of the proposed bundled contract or order justify its use; and

(6) Identify alternative strategies that would reduce or minimize the scope of the bundling, and the rationale for not choosing those alternatives.

Challenges to bundling may also be made under the Competition in Contracting Act (CICA), 10 U.S.C. § 2304 and 41 U.S.C. § 253. Under CICA, requirements may be determined to be bundled whenever aggregated requirements are found to be unduly restrictive of competition. The reach of the restrictions against total package or bundled procurements in CICA is broader than the reach of restrictions against bundling under the Small Business Act, *Phoenix Scientific Corp.*, Comp. Gen. Dec. B-286817, 2001 CPD ¶ 24. CICA generally requires that solicitations include specifications which permit full and open competition and contain restrictive provisions and conditions only to the extent necessary to satisfy the needs of the agency, 10 U.S.C. § 2305(a)(1)(A), (B); 41 U.S.C. § 253a(a)(2)(B). Because procurements conducted on a bundled or total package basis can restrict competition, the GAO will sustain a challenge to the use of such an approach where it is not necessary to satisfy the agency's needs, *Better Serv.*, Comp. Gen. Dec. B-265751.2, 96-1 CPD ¶ 90. The determination of a contracting agency's needs and the best method for accommodating them are matters primarily within the agency's discretion, *Specialty Diving, Inc.*, Comp. Gen. Dec. B-285939, 2000 CPD ¶ 169. Because of the restrictive impact of bundling, protests challenging a bundled solicitation will be sustained, unless an agency has a reasonable basis for its contention that bundling is necessary, *National Customer Eng'g*, Comp. Gen. Dec. B-251135, 93-1 CPD ¶ 225.

Administrative convenience is not a legal basis to justify bundling of requirements, if the bundling of requirements restricts competition, *EDP Enters., Inc.,* Comp. Gen. Dec. B-284533.6, 2003 CPD ¶ 93 (protest of bundling of food services in the same RFP with base, vehicle, and aircraft maintenance services for administrative convenience sustained); *Vantex Serv. Corp.,* Comp. Gen. Dec. B-290415, 2002 CPD ¶ 131 (protest of bundling of portable latrine rental services with waste removal services, each of which is classified under a different North American Industrial Classification System code and is generally performed by a different set of contractors sustained); and *National Customer Eng'g,* Comp. Gen. Dec. B-251135, 93-1 CPD ¶ 225 (bundling computer hardware and software maintenance restricted competition because it clearly excluded companies that performed only one of these types of maintenance). But see *AirTrak Travel,* Comp. Gen. Dec. B-292101, 2003 CPD ¶ 117, finding that the grouping of travel locations by geographic region and issuing a single consolidated procurement were not based solely on administrative convenience. There, the GAO stated that the underlying purposes behind the agency's single procurement included the legitimate requirement to reengineer the antiquated and costly DOD travel process, in part by consolidating the process and structuring geographical groupings to allow for more small business participation.

Bundling is proper in order to have a single contractor be responsible for work that is integrated by its nature. The need for integration of the work is generally viewed as a technical determination that the GAO will not challenge. See for example, *Outdoor Venture Corp.,* Comp. Gen. Dec. B-299675, 2007 CPD ¶ 138 (need for proven integration and compatibility of systems); *USA Information Sys., Inc.,* Comp. Gen. Dec. B291417, 2002 CPD ¶ 224 (single web-based information retrieval system for on-line documentation as opposed to obtaining information from multiple vendors found reasonable); *Phoenix Tech. Servs. Corp.,* Comp. Gen. Dec. B-274694.2, 97-2 CPD ¶ 142 (engineering support services for all aspects of two different aircraft); *Magnavox Elec. Sys. Co.,* Comp. Gen. Dec. B-258037, 94-2 CPD ¶ 227 (missiles containing a new mid-course guidance system as a single system); *Titan Dynamics Simulations, Inc.,* Comp. Gen. Dec. B-257559, 94-2 CPD ¶ 139 (pyrotechnic simulators along with the new system for which the simulators are to be used); *Resource Consultants, Inc.,* Comp. Gen. Dec. B-255053, 94-1 CPD ¶ 59 (modifications of interrelated simulators in a single contract); and *Space Vector Corp.,* 73 Comp. Gen. 24 (B-253295.2), 93-2 CPD ¶ 273 (three launch vehicles in a single procurement).

Bundling will be found to be reasonable if a consolidation will result in significant cost savings or efficiencies, *Teximara, Inc.,* Comp. Gen. Dec. B-293221.2, 2004 CPD ¶ 151 (aligning areas that are integrally linked maximizes cross-utilization and cross-training opportunities between service areas). See also *Nautical Eng'g, Inc.,* Comp. Gen. Dec. B-309955, 2007 CPD ¶ 204 (consolidation of dockside and shipside maintenance and repair work found reasonable to achieve maintenance and repair cost savings and increased operational time); *2B Brokers,* Comp. Gen. Dec. B-298651, 2006 CPD ¶ 178 (consolidation of transportation coordination and freight transportation services would increase optional effectiveness and improve shipment efficiency); *B.H. Aircraft Co.*, Comp. Gen. Dec. B-295399.2, 2005 CPD ¶ 138 (bundled performance-based logistics supply chain management contract found reasonable to alleviate shortages of parts, increase availability of needed parts and maintain the military readiness of the aircraft); *Reedsport Mach. & Fabrication*, Comp. Gen. Dec. B-293110.2, 2004 CPD ¶ 91 (combination of two motor life boats reasonable in order to generate sufficient repair work to meet the $10,000 minimum amount under the contemplated IDIQ contract and to achieve economies of scale); *S&K Elecs.*, Comp. Gen. Dec. B-282167, 99-1 CPD ¶ 111 (single procurement for all desktop IT requirements — rather than continuing to rely on the current frag- mented approach of using different sources for hardware/software and services— will result in significant quality improvements as a result of (1) having a single con- tractor responsible for infrastructure interoperability and product compatibility, (2) eliminating the confusion, delays and denials of responsibility for service interrup- tions or installation problems, and (3) facilitating consistent, timely upgrades and refreshment of technology); *National Airmotive Corp.*, Comp. Gen. Dec. B-280194, 98-2 CPD ¶ 60 (maintenance of several jet engines); *Building Sys. Contractors, Inc.*, Comp. Gen. Dec. B-266180, 96-1 CPD ¶ 18 (new energy management control sys- tem with the replacement of the heating, ventilating and air-conditioning system); *Tucson Mobilephone, Inc.*, Comp. Gen. Dec. B-256802, 94-2 CPD ¶ 45 (procure- ment and installation of new telecommunications equipment); *Iowa-Illinois Clean- ing Co.*, Comp. Gen. Dec. B-260463, 95-1 CPD ¶ 272 (custodial and mechanical maintenance services for single building); *Resource Consultants, Inc.*, Comp. Gen. Dec. B-255053, 94-1 CPD ¶ 59 (combining several tasks to support a modifica- tion to a weapon training system); *Ryder Aviall, Inc.*, Comp. Gen. Dec. B-249920, 92-2 CPD ¶ 438 (both parts and labor for engine overhaul); *Delta Oaktree Prods.*, Comp. Gen. Dec. B-248903, 92-2 CPD ¶ 230 (various types of graphic arts servic- es); *LaQue Center for Corrosion Tech.*, Inc., Comp. Gen. Dec. B-245296, 91-2 CPD ¶ 577 (corrosion control services for life of product); *Institutional Electro-Methods, Inc.*, 70 Comp. Gen. 53 (B-239141.2), 90-2 CPD ¶ 363 (modification kits and engi- neering services for many modifications to an aircraft engine); *Massa Prods. Corp.*, Comp. Gen. Dec. B-236892, 90-1 CPD ¶ 38 (manufacturing of a number of similar transducers); *Great Lakes Towing Co.*, Comp. Gen. Dec. B-235023, 89-1 CPD ¶ 570 (maintenance and repair of vessel); *Eastman Kodak Co.*, 68 Comp. Gen. 57 (B-231952), 88-2 CPD ¶ 455 (photocopiers and related services); *Korean Maint. Co.*, 66 Comp. Gen. 12 (B-223780), 86-2 CPD ¶ 379 (custodial services for several buildings); and *Southwest Marine, Inc.*, Comp. Gen. Dec. B-204136, 82-2 CPD ¶ 60 (overhaul of two ships).

Bundling is most frequently rejected when there is no strong relationship among the items that are included in the package. For example, in *TRS Research*, Comp. Gen. Dec. B-290644, 2002 CPD ¶ 159, the GAO sustained a protest on the basis of improper bundling where the agency had consolidated nine IDIQ contracts into a single requirement for intermodal container equipment requirements worldwide. The nine previous IDIQ contracts varied in scope; although some vendors were awarded some of the same items, no two of the nine vendors were awarded contracts requiring exactly the same equipment. The agency contended that awarding a single contract to one contractor would cure performance problems experienced under the previous fragmented and inefficient approach, which required the administration of nine different IDIQ contracts. The agency argued that since the master license agreement sought to include all of the agency's intermodal container equipment requirements, the master license agreement and the nine resulting IDIQ contracts should be viewed as constituting one single broad procurement requirement for intermodal container equipment. The GAO disagreed, stating that the master license agreement was not a statement of a single procurement requirement, but instead functioned more as a list of a range of multiple procurement requirements and to read it so broadly could shield "from meaningful review the very sort of arbitrary consolidation of requirements that the Act's restrictions on bundling are intended to prevent." See also *Pemco Aeroplex, Inc.*, Comp. Gen. Dec. B-280397, 98-2 CPD ¶ 79, finding improper bundling where the Air Force combined the overhaul and repair of five different systems or subsystems into a single contract. Similarly, in *Richard M. Milburn High School*, Comp. Gen. Dec. B-244933, 91-2 CPD ¶ 496, the GAO rejected the packaging of five different types of training programs where only one required college accreditation.

(2) Set-Asides

The major method of ensuring that the government's small-business policies are implemented is the set-aside. FAR 19.501 contains the following guidance:

(a) The purpose of small business set-asides is to award certain acquisitions exclusively to small business concerns. A "set-aside for small business" is the reserving of an acquisition exclusively for participation by small business concerns. A small business set-aside may be open to all small businesses. A small business set-aside of a single acquisition or a class of acquisitions may be total or partial.

(b) The determination to make a small business set-aside may be unilateral or joint. A unilateral determination is one that is made by the contracting officer. A joint determination is one that is recommended by the Small Business Administration (SBA) procurement center representative (or, if a procurement center representative is not assigned, see 19.402(a)) and concurred in by the contracting officer.

(c) For acquisitions exceeding the simplified acquisition threshold, the requirement to set aside an acquisition for HUBZone small business concerns (see 19.1305 takes priority over the requirement to set aside the acquisition for small business concerns.

(d) The small business reservation and set-asides requirements at 19.502-2 do not preclude award of a contract to a service-disabled veteran-owned small business concern under Subpart 19.14.

(e) The contracting officer shall review acquisitions to determine if they can be set aside for small business, giving consideration to the recommendations of agency personnel having cognizance of the agency's small business programs. The contracting officer shall document why a small business set-aside is inappropriate when an acquisition is not set aside for small business, unless a HUBZone or service-disabled veteran-owned small business set-aside or HUBZone or service-disabled veteran-owned small business sole source award is anticipated. If the acquisition is set aside for small business based on this review, it is a unilateral set-aside by the contracting officer. Agencies may establish threshold levels for this review depending upon their needs.

(f) At the request of an SBA procurement center representative, (or, if a procurement center representative is not assigned, see 19.402(a)) the contracting officer shall make available for review at the contracting office (to the extent of the SBA representative's security clearance) all proposed acquisitions in excess of the micro-purchase threshold that have not been unilaterally set aside for small business.

(g) To the extent practicable, unilateral determinations initiated by a contracting officer shall be used as the basis for small business set-asides rather than joint determinations by an SBA procurement center representative and a contracting officer.

(h) All solicitations involving set-asides must specify the applicable small business size standard and NAICS code (see 19.303).

(i) Except as authorized by law, a contract may not be awarded as a result of a small business set-aside if the cost to the awarding agency exceeds the fair market price.

In accordance with these regulations, contracts should be designated for set-aside in the acquisition planning process in three circumstances: (1) the procurement is for $150,000 or less but over $3,000, (2) the procurement is for a product or service that has been acquired previously through a set-aside, and (3) the procurement is for a product or service where competition can be obtained from two or more small businesses. This "rule of two" is implemented with the following guidance in FAR 19.502-2:

(a) Each acquisition of supplies or services that has an anticipated dollar value exceeding $3,000 ($15,000 for acquisitions as described in 13.201(g)(1)), but not over $150,000 ($300,000 for acquisitions described in paragraph (1) of the Simplified Acquisition Threshold definition at 2.101), is automatically reserved exclusively for small business concerns and shall be set aside for small business unless the contracting officer determines there is not a reasonable expectation of obtaining offers from two or more responsible small business concerns that are competitive in terms of market prices, quality, and delivery. If the contracting officer does not proceed with the small business set-aside and purchases on an unrestricted basis, the contracting officer shall include in the contract file the reason for this unrestricted purchase. If the contracting officer receives only one acceptable offer from a responsible small business concern in response to a set-aside, the contracting officer should make an award to that firm. If the contracting officer receives no acceptable offers from responsible small business concerns, the set-aside shall be withdrawn and the requirement, if still valid, shall be resolicited on an unrestricted basis. The small business reservation does not preclude the award of a contract with a value not greater than $150,000 under Subpart 19.8, Contracting with the Small Business Administration, under 19.1007(c), Solicitations equal to or less than the ESB reserve amount, or under 19.1305, HUBZone set-aside procedures.

(b) The contracting officer shall set aside any acquisition over $150,000 for small business participation when there is a reasonable expectation that (1) offers will be obtained from at least two responsible small business concerns offering the products of different small business concerns (but see paragraph (c) of this subsection); and (2) award will be made at fair market prices. Total small business set-asides shall not be made unless such a reasonable expectation exists (but see 19.502-3 as to partial set-asides). Although past acquisition history of an item or similar items is always important, it is not the only factor to be considered in determining whether a reasonable expectation exists. In making R&D small business set-asides, there must also be a reasonable expectation of obtaining from small businesses the best scientific and technological sources consistent with the demands of the proposed acquisition for the best mix of cost, performances, and schedules.

The-set aside provisions of FAR 19.502-2(b) apply to competitions of task and delivery orders issued under multiple award, IDIQ contracts, *Delex*, Comp. Gen. Dec. B-400403, 2008 CPD ¶ 181 (Navy required to set aside the delivery order for the small business IDIQ contract holders); but not to orders issued under federal supply schedule contracts, GSA Acquisition Alert 2008-07 (Oct. 28, 2008).

A contracting officer's determination under FAR 19.502-2 concerns a matter of business judgment within the contracting officer's discretion that will not be disturbed absent a showing that it was unreasonable, *Quality Hotel Westshore*, Comp. Gen. Dec. B-290046, 2002 CPD ¶ 91; *Neal R. Gross & Co.*, Comp. Gen. Dec. B-240924.2, 91-1 CPD ¶ 53. The Court of Federal Claims similarly holds such determinations to be a matter of business judgment and within the contracting officer's discretion, *Rhinocorps Ltd. Co. v. United States*, 87 Fed. Cl. 261 (2009).

FAR 19.502-2 does not require the use of any particular method for assessing the availability of small business, *MCS Mgmt., Inc. v. United States*, 48 Fed. Cl. 506 (2000); *American Artisan Prods., Inc.*, Comp. Gen. Dec. B-292380, 2003 CPD ¶ 132. The decision whether to set aside a procurement may be based on an analysis of factors such as the prior procurement history, the recommendations of appropriate small business specialists, and market surveys that include responses to sources sought announcements, *SAB Co.*, Comp. Gen. Dec. B-283883, 2000 CPD ¶ 58; *PR Newswire*, Comp. Gen. Dec. B-279216, 98-1 CPD ¶ 118. See, for example,

FlowSense, LLC, Comp. Gen. Dec. B-310904, 2008 CPD ¶ 56 (agency reasonably determined there were no SDVOSB firms with the capabilities and capital to procure the necessary bonding and to perform the work associated with the project based on information contained in a database, which showed that the firm's total annual revenue was substantially below the estimated value of the contract which brought into question the firm's capacity to perform); and *MCS Mgmt., Inc.*, Comp. Gen. Dec. B-285813, 2000 CPD ¶ 187 (agency reasonably considered annual revenues and size of past contracts when examining whether small businesses were capable of performing contract for a set-aside solicitation). Because a decision whether to set aside a procurement is a matter of business judgment within the contracting officer's discretion, the GAO review generally is limited to ascertaining whether that official abused his or her discretion, *Admiral Towing & Barge Co.*, Comp. Gen. Dec. B-291849, 2003 CPD ¶ 164. The GAO will not question a small business set-aside determination where the record shows that the evidence before the contracting officer was adequate to support the reasonableness of the conclusion that small business competition reasonably could be expected, *National Linen Serv.*, Comp. Gen. Dec. B-285458, 2000 CPD ¶ 138; *Commonwealth Home Health Care, Inc.*, Comp. Gen. Dec. B-400163, 2008 CPD ¶ 140. In making set-aside decisions, agencies need not make either actual determinations of responsibility or decisions tantamount to determinations of responsibility; rather, they need only make an informed business judgment that there is a reasonable expectation of receiving acceptably priced offers from small business concerns that are capable of performing the contract, *ViroMed Labs.*, Comp. Gen. Dec. B298931, 2006 CPD ¶ 4.

There have been a number of cases where the GAO found the agency's decision not to set aside reasonable. See, for example, *Information Ventures, Inc.*, Comp. Gen. Dec. B-400604, 2008 CPD ¶ 232, where the GAO found reasonable an agency determination not to set aside based on the contracting officer's review of the information provided by small business concerns in their responses to the sources sought notice and review of the procurement history. The GAO further stated that the record confirms that the agency's small business specialist and the SBA's PCR were integrated in the contracting officer's decision-making process and they both concurred with his business judgment that the requirement should be competed on an unrestricted basis. See also *EMMES Corp.*, Comp. Gen. Dec. B-402245, 2010 CPD ¶ 53 (market research and publication of sources sought notice indicated agency was not likely to receive proposals from at least two small businesses); *The Protective Group, Inc.*, Comp. Gen. Dec. B-310018, 2007 CPD ¶ 208 (record showed agency was familiar with body armor marketplace, and responses from firms participating in industry day conference with agency demonstrated that it was not likely to receive proposals from at least two responsible small businesses); *International Filter Mfg., Inc.*, Comp. Gen. Dec. B-299368, 2007 CPD ¶ 70 (market research, a review of the drawings, and consultation with small business representative was sufficient to demonstrate that far less than 50% of the total cost of the kit could be manufactured by small businesses); *Shirlington Limousine & Transport, Inc.*, Comp. Gen. Dec. B-299241, 2007 CPD ¶ 52 (agency reasonably considered the responses it had received from two similar, although substantially smaller in scope, solicitations noting that in neither case did it receive two acceptable proposals); *American Artisan Productions, Inc.*, Comp. Gen. Dec. B-292380, 2003 CPD ¶ 132 (agency reasonably concluded—based on market surveys and concurrence of the SBA—that it could not expect to receive proposals from at least two responsible small business offerors at fair market prices); *Quality Hotel Westshore*, Comp. Gen. Dec. B290046, 2002 CPD ¶ 91(determination not to set aside procurement reasonable where based on a market survey, request for interest targeted at small businesses, and concurrence of the SBA and the agency's small business specialist); *Belleville Shoe Mfg. Co.*, Comp. Gen. Dec. B-287237, 2001 CPD ¶ 87 (set-aside not required where record supports finding that firm had never produced boots of the type and quantity required under the solicitation); *MCS Mgmt., Inc.*, Comp. Gen. Dec. B-285813, 2000 CPD ¶ 187 (set-aside not required where there was no indication that small business concerns could perform food service contracts of the scope and complexity required under the solicitation); *CardioMetrix*, Comp. Gen. Dec. B-276912, 97-2 CPD ¶ 45 (procurement history for the same services showed that it was unlikely that at least two small businesses would submit offers at a fair market price); *Ruchman & Assocs., Inc.*, Comp. Gen. Dec. B-275974, 97-1 CPD ¶ 155 (research and visit to other federal and private-sector entities showed that none were utilizing a small business to perform such work); and *CardioMetrix*, Comp. Gen. Dec. B-261327, 95-2 CPD ¶ 96 (agency's determination not to set aside reasonable where it had twice attempted to procure the follow-on services under a small-business set-aside but had to cancel the procurements because the agency did not receive a reasonably priced offer from a small business).

Cases where the GAO found the agency's decision to set aside reasonable include, *Med-South, Inc.*, Comp. Gen. Dec. B-401214, 2009 CPD ¶ 112 (in addition to surveying the market and contacting the OSDBU, the contracting officer reviewed GAO decisions challenging similar solicitation for home oxygen including one where the GAO upheld the decision to set aside the procurement for small business); *Logistics Health, Inc.*, Comp. Gen. Dec. B-400157, 2008 CPD ¶ 160 (determination made based on market research which indicated that there were a large number of small and large business vendors providing these services and pricing for the services would be competitively based); *Encompass Group, LLC*, Comp. Gen. Dec. B-296602; 2005 CPD ¶ 159 (protester's argument that there are no small business manufacturers of the bulk fabric does not show that the agency was unreasonable in concluding that it would obtain two or more offers from small business manufacturers of the sheets, pillow cases and blankets); *Moog Inc.*, Comp. Gen. Dec. B-294600, 2004 CPD ¶ 230 (agency reasonably determined that it could expect to receive offers from at least two responsible small business concerns at a fair market price where work was previously performed by a small business and the RFP did not require source approval to perform services); *Stewart Title Co. of Illinois*, Comp. Gen. Dec. B-283291, 99-2 CPD ¶ 71 (acquisition was of the same size and type as the successful set-asides in the southeast, and there was no apparent reason to expect a different outcome merely due to geography); *PR Newswire*, Comp. Gen.

Dec. B-279216, 98-1 CPD ¶ 118 (development of technological advances in industry strongly suggested that small business may now have capability to perform the contract); and *American Medical Response of Conn.*, Comp. Gen. Dec. B-278457, 98-1 CPD ¶ 44 (determination based on knowledge of previous participation in a procurement for the same services by at least two business concerns that had submitted at fair market prices).

The GAO will sustain a protest if it determines that an agency's decision not to set aside is unreasonable. See *Rochester Optical Mfg. Co.*, Comp. Gen. Dec. B-292247, 2003 CPD ¶ 138, where the agency made insufficient efforts to ascertain small business interest and capability to perform the requirement. See also *Delex*, Comp. Gen. Dec. B-400403, 2008 CPD ¶ 181, sustaining a protest finding unreasonable the agency's analysis of the procurement history in its determination not to set aside the task order for small businesses. The agency explained that the procurement history showed that the protester did not submit a proposal for the predecessor task order requirement; that while the protester had expressed interest in the last five delivery order acquisitions under the IDIQ contract, it submitted proposals for only three of the five acquisitions; and that in a previous delivery-order competition under this IDIQ contract where only the protester and one other contract holder submitted proposals, the protester's proposal was evaluated as unsatisfactory, leaving the agency with only the option of making award to the other contract holder. The GAO reasoned:

> [w]ith respect to the predecessor delivery order for this requirement, we agree with Delex that a small business could reasonably decide not to compete with the large business contract-holders for this work, and that an agency should not rely on the results of an unrestricted competition to determine the likelihood that a small business will participate in a set-aside competition. With respect to the five previous acquisitions, we again agree with Delex. We know of no requirement that a small business participate in every acquisition for which it is eligible to compete, especially when several of these acquisitions are occurring over a short period of time. Finally, we are concerned about the Navy's reliance on Delex's submission of an unsatisfactory proposal 2 years ago, as opposed to other more recent, and perhaps more relevant events.

Similarly, in *Thermal Solutions, Inc.*, Comp. Gen. Dec. B-259501, 95-1 CPD ¶ 178, the GAO found that an agency's decision not to set aside a procurement for small disadvantaged businesses (SDBs) was unreasonable. The decision not to set aside the procurement was based on prior SDB set-aside procurements for dissimilar work and prior procurements for similar work that were not set aside for SDBs. The GAO found that the agency received expressions of interest from five undisputed SDBs, and reasoned that SDBs often cannot effectively compete with non-SDB firms and, thus, may not submit offers on contracts that they are otherwise capable of performing. See also *Bollinger & ACCU-Lab Med. Testing*, Comp. Gen. Dec. B-270259, 96-1 CPD ¶ 106 (agency improperly withdrew set-aside by relying on the procurement history instead of investigating the numerous small-business responses to the CBD announcement and performing a current market study). In *LBM, Inc.*, Comp. Gen. Dec. B-290682, 2002 CPD ¶ 157, the contract for transportation motor pool services at Fort Polk, LA, had been a small business set-aside for ten years. When it came up for renewal the Army decided to include it under the Logistical Joint Administrative Management Support Services (LOGJAMSS) IDIQ contracts. The GAO sustained the protest, rejecting the Army's argument that it was a protest of the proposed award of a task order under a LOGJAMSS contract—thereby divesting the GAO of jurisdiction pursuant to the FASA—by explaining that it was a protest of whether work that had been previously set aside exclusively for small businesses could be transferred to LOGJAMSS. The GAO stated that this was a challenge to the terms of the underlying LOGJAMSS solicitation and was within its bid protest jurisdiction. It added that the FASA "was not intended to, and does not, preclude protests that timely challenge the transfer and inclusion of work in ID/IQ contracts without complying with applicable laws or regulations" and explained that Small Business Act requirements "were applicable to acquisitions prior to the enactment of [the] FASA, and nothing in that statute authorizes the transfer of acquisitions to ID/IQ contracts in violation of those laws and regulations." In *Dep't of the Army—Modification of Recommendation*, Comp. Gen. Dec. B-290682.2, 2003 CPD ¶ 123, the agency requested that the GAO modify its recommendation in LBM to recognize that the agency, having decided to acquire the services exclusively from small businesses, could limit the competition to those small businesses who hold IDIQ contracts for the services at issue. The GAO denied the request on the ground that CICA provides for full and open competition among eligible small businesses for acquisitions required to be set-aside for small businesses.

The agency must also consider making a partial set-aside in cases where a total set-aside is not possible. A partial set-aside would reserve a portion of a procurement for small businesses if they matched the highest price on the non-set-aside portion of the procurement. FAR 19.502-3 contains the following guidance:

> (a) The contracting officer shall set aside a portion of an acquisition, except for construction, for exclusive small business participation when —
>
> (1) A total set-aside is not appropriate (see 19.502-2);
>
> (2) The requirement is severable into two or more economic production runs or reasonable lots;
>
> (3) One or more small business concerns are expected to have the technical competence and productive capacity to satisfy the set-aside portion of the requirement at a fair market price;
>
> (4) The acquisition is not subject to simplified acquisition procedures; and

(5) A partial set-aside shall not be made if there is a reasonable expectation that only two concerns (one large and one small) with capability will respond with offers unless authorized by the head of a contracting activity on a case-by-case basis. Similarly, a class of acquisitions, not including construction, may be partially set aside. Under certain specified conditions, partial set-asides may be used in conjunction with multiyear contracting procedures.

The determination as to whether a particular acquisition should be partially set aside for small business is left to the discretion of the contracting officer. As with a total set-aside, that determination must be reasonably supported. See *Digital Sys. Group, Inc.*, Comp. Gen. Dec. B-258262.2, 95-1 CPD ¶ 30, finding that, although the agency's original rationale concerning the rejection of a partial set-aside was incomplete, its responses to the protest provided sufficient basis to support its decision. Specifically, the contracting officer considered a partial set-aside on the basis of agency size but rejected it because an agency's size was unrelated to its functional needs. The agency determined that functional needs determined the appropriate software, and because GSA could not ascertain those needs, a set-aside was not viewed as feasible. See also *Vox Optima, LLC*, Comp. Gen. Dec. B-400451, 2008 CPD ¶ 212, denying the protester's argument that since the solicitation contemplates the award of multiple IDIQ contracts, the requirement is necessarily severable into two or more lots, and thus is suitable for a partial set-aside. The GAO stated that the determination as to whether a particular acquisition should be partially set aside is left to the discretion of the contracting officer, provided the determination is reasonable. The GAO found that the agency reasonably determined not to set aside a portion of the work because there were no firms capable of performing the full-spectrum of services required by the agency. See, however, *Belleville Shoe Mfg. Co.*, Comp. Gen. Dec. B-287237, 2001 CPD ¶ 87, finding that the agency improperly failed to consider whether a partial set-aside was required.

Under the Small Business Competitiveness Demonstration Program, established by Pub. L. No. 100-656 and extended indefinitely by the Small Business Reauthorization Act of 1998, Pub. L. No. 105-135, agencies are directed not to use set-asides for four types of procurement as long as they meet certain percentage goals through open competition: (1) construction, (2) refuse systems and related procurements, (3) architectural and engineering services, and (4) nuclear ship repair. FAR Subpart 19.10 contains guidance on the implementation of this program. The program is based on the premise that small businesses in these industries can obtain a fair proportion of the work in a competitive environment. As long as selected agencies maintain awards in these industries at a level of at least 40% small business those agencies will use full and open competition rather than set-asides on all contracts expected to exceed $30,000. Contracts for amounts of $30,000 or less will continue to be set aside for emerging small businesses (ESBs) provided that the contracting officer determines that there is a reasonable expectation of obtaining offers from two or more responsible ESBs that will be competitive in terms of price, quality, and delivery, FAR 19.1007(c)(1). ESBs are defined as small businesses whose size is no greater than 50% of the small-business size standard applicable to the North American Industry Classification System code for the industry, FAR 19.1002. If the contracting officer proceeds with the ESB set-aside and receives a quotation from only one ESB at a reasonable price, the contracting officer must make the award, FAR 1007(c)(2). See *Cromartie Constr. Co.*, Comp. Gen. Dec. B-271788, 96-2 CPD ¶ 48. The determination of price reasonableness is within the discretion of the agency, and the GAO will not disturb such a determination unless it is unreasonable or there is fraud or bad faith on the part of contracting officers. See *Olsen Envtl. Servs., Inc.*, Comp. Gen. Dec. B-241475, 91-1 CPD ¶ 126, finding that the contracting officer had a rational basis for determining that the price submitted by the ESB was unreasonably high.

The program also requires participating agencies to target for expansion 10 industry categories with which they have had low small business involvement for special efforts to increase that involvement, FAR 19.1004. The participating agencies include: Departments of Agriculture, Defense, Energy, Health and Human Services, the Interior, Transportation, and Veterans Affairs; the Environmental Protection Agency; the General Services Administration; and the National Aeronautics and Space Administration. Each participating agency, in consultation with the SBA, must designate its own targeted industry categories for enhanced small business participation, FAR 19.1005(b). For a list of each participating agency's targeted industry categories, refer to the participating agency's regulations see DFARS 219.1005(b) and NFS 1819.1005(b).

(3) SMALL BUSINESS PROGRAMS AND PREFERENCES

There is one overarching small business program and five subsidiary programs. Four of the subsidiary programs have minimum goals set forth in 15 U.S.C. § 644:

Program	Goal
All small business concerns	23%
Small business concerns owned and controlled by service-disabled veterans	3%
Qualified HUBZone small business concerns	3%
Small business concerns owned and controlled by socially and economically disadvantaged individuals	5%
Small business concerns owned and controlled by women	5%
Veteran-owned small business concerns	No stated goal

These goals are government-wide goals with some flexibility in the statute for agencies to have different goals. See 15 U.S.C. § 644(g)(1), stating:

Notwithstanding the Government-wide goal, each agency shall have an annual goal that presents, for that agency, the maximum practicable opportunity for small business concerns, small business concerns owned and controlled by service-disabled veterans, qualified HUBZone small business concerns, small business concerns owned and controlled by socially and economically disadvantaged individuals, and small business concerns owned and controlled by women to participate in the performance of contracts let by such agency. The Administration and the Administrator of the Office of Federal Procurement Policy shall, when exercising their authority pursuant to paragraph (2), insure that the cumulative annual prime contract goals for all agencies meet or exceed the annual Government-wide prime contract goal established by the President pursuant to this paragraph.

The traditional technique for ensuring that small businesses obtain their fair share of government procurements is the set-aside, as discussed in the previous section. In addition, FAR Part 19 sets forth supplemental procedures for three of the subsidiary categories—service-disabled veterans, HUBZone small business concerns, and small business concerns owned and controlled by socially and economically disadvantaged individuals. There are no supplemental procedures for either veteran-owned small businesses or women-owned small businesses.

There is parity among each of the small business subcategories. The 2010 Small Business Jobs Act, P.L. 111-240, § 1347, re-established equality among each of the small business subcategories that competes for government contracts. The Act makes a technical revision to the 1953 Small Business Act by replacing the word "shall" in the Historically Underutilized Business Zone statute with the word "may." The old language in the Small Business Act stated that a procurement officer shall award contracts based on limited competition to HUBZone small businesses. But, the statutes creating the service-disabled veteran-owned small business program and the Small Business Administration's 8(a) Business Development Program used the word "may" when referring to set-aside contracts. The GAO and the U.S. Court of Federal Claims had determined the difference in "shall" and "may" unambiguously established a preference for HUBZone firms (see *Mission Critical Solutions v. United States*, 91 Fed. Cl. 386 (2010) and Comp. Gen. Dec. B-401057, 2009 CPD ¶ 93, *recons. denied*, 2009 CPD ¶ 148).

(A) Service-Disabled Veteran-Owned Smallbusiness Procurement Program

The Veterans Benefits Act, Pub. L. No. 108-183, § 308 (2003) amended the Small Business Act, 15 U.S.C. § 657(f) to establish the Service-Disabled Veteran-Owned Small Business Concern (SDVOSBC) Program. The program is implemented in FAR Subpart 19.14. The language of the Act is discretionary and permits, but does not require, a contracting officer to restrict competition to SDVOSBCs if certain conditions are satisfied, *DAV Prime, Inc.*, Comp. Gen. Dec. B-311420, 2008 CPD ¶ 90.

An agency is required to make reasonable efforts to ascertain whether an acquisition is suitable for a set-aside to an SDVOSBC before it can proceed with a small business set-aside, *MCS Portable Serv.*, Comp. Gen. Dec. B-299291, 2007 CPD ¶ 55 (Air Force failed to make reasonable efforts to ascertain whether the acquisition was suitable for an SDVOSBC set-aside when it disregarded an SDVOSBC's expression of interest). In *IBV, Ltd.*, Comp. Gen. Dec. B-311244, 2008 CPD ¶ 47, the GAO stated that while the record showed that at least two SDVOSBC firms were available and interested in competing on this requirement, this is only the first of two considerations that go into a set-aside decision. In addition, the contracting officer must have a reasonable expectation that award will be made at a fair market price. The GAO found the contracting officer's concern that the SDVOSBCs would not propose fair market pricing was confirmed by the pricing of those proposals. The SDVOSBC proposals received were priced at more than double the independent government estimate, and all exceeded the RFP's estimated price range.

FAR 19.1405 permits competitions restricted to service-disabled veteran-owned small business, as follows:

(a) The contracting officer may set-aside acquisitions exceeding the micro-purchase threshold for competition restricted to service-disabled veteran-owned small business concerns when the requirements of paragraph (b) of this section can be satisfied. The contracting officer shall consider service-disabled veteran-owned small business set-asides before considering service-disabled veteran-owned small business sole source awards (see 19.1406).

(b) To set aside an acquisition for competition restricted to service-disabled veteran-owned small business concerns, the contracting officer must have a reasonable expectation that —

(1) Offers will be received from two or more service-disabled veteran-owned small business concerns; and

(2) Award will be made at a fair market price.

(c) If the contracting officer receives only one acceptable offer from a service-disabled veteran-owned small business concern in response to a set-aside, the contracting officer should make an award to that concern. If the contracting officer receives no acceptable offers from service-disabled veteran-owned small business concerns, the service-disabled veteran-owned set-aside shall be withdrawn and the requirement, if still valid, set aside for small business concerns, as appropriate (see Subpart 19.5).

FAR 19.1406 permits sole source awards to service-disabled veteran-owned small business concerns as follows:

(a) A contracting officer may award contracts to service-disabled veteran-owned small business concerns on a sole source basis (see 19.501(d) and 6.302-5), provided —

(1) Only one service-disabled veteran-owned small business concern can satisfy the requirement;

(2) The anticipated award price of the contract (including options) will not exceed —

(i) $6 million for a requirement within the NAICS codes for manufacturing; or

(ii) $3.5 million for a requirement within any other NAICS code;

(3) The service-disabled veteran-owned small business concern has been determined to be a responsible contractor with respect to performance; and

(4) Award can be made at a fair and reasonable price.

To be considered a service-disabled veteran, the veteran must have an adjudication letter from the Veterans Administration, a Department of Defense Form 214, Certificate of Release or Discharge from Active Duty, or a Statement of Service from the National Archives and Records Administration, stating that the veteran has a service-connected disability. There is no minimum disability rating. A veteran with a 0 to 100% disability rating is eligible to self-represent as a service-disabled veteran for federal contracting purposes. A contractor officer has no obligation to investigate or question a contractor's claim of SDVOSBC status prior to making an award, *Major Contracting Services, Inc.*, Comp. Gen. Dec. B-400616, 2008 CPD ¶ 214.

The SBA is the designated authority for determining whether a firm is an eligible SDVOSBC, and it has established procedures for interested parties to challenge a firm's status as a qualified SDVOSBC, see 15 U.S.C. § 632(q), § 657b; 13 C.F.R. § 125.25, § 125.27 (2008); FAR 19.307; FAR 19.1403. If the SBA sustains the protest, and the contract has not yet been awarded, then the protested concern is ineligible for an SDVOSBC contract award, 13 C.F.R. § 125.27(g). See *Singleton Enters.—GMT Mech. (J.V.)*, Comp. Gen. Dec. B-310552, 2008 CPD ¶ 16 (agency properly rejected bid of joint venture under a solicitation set side for a SDVOSBC where the SBA had determined in another solicitation that the joint venture did not qualify as a SDVOSBC). However, there is no requirement that a contract be terminated if an awardee is found to be other than an SDVOSBC after award was made, *Major Contracting Servs., Inc.*, Comp. Gen. Dec. B-400616, 2008 CPD ¶ 214; *Veteran Enter. Tech. Servs., LLC*, Comp. Gen. Dec. B-298201.2, 2006 CPD ¶ 108. If a contract has already been awarded, and the SBA sustains the protest, the contracting officer cannot count the award as an award to an SDVOSBC and the concern cannot submit another offer as an SDVOSBC on a future SDVOSBC procurement unless it overcomes the reasons for the protest, 13 C.F.R. § 125.27(g).

The Veterans First Contracting Program, created by the Veterans Benefits, Health Care, and Information Technology Act of 2006, 38 U.S.C. § 8127, and administered by the VA, provides the VA with independent authority to make sole-source contract awards to SDVOSBCs and veteran-owned small business firms, *In & Out Valet Co.*, Comp. Gen. Dec. B-311141, 2008 CPD ¶ 71; *Apex Limited, Inc.*, Comp. Gen. Dec. B-402163, 2010 CPD ¶ 35. Specifically, 38 U.S.C. § 8127(c) states:

> (c) Sole Source Contracts for Contracts Above Simplified Acquisition Threshold. — For purposes of meeting the goals under subsection (a), and in accordance with this section, a contracting officer of the Department [of Veterans Affairs] may award a contract to a small business concern owned and controlled by veterans using procedures other than competitive procedures if —

>> (1) such concern is determined to be a responsible source with respect to performance of such contract opportunity;

>> (2) the anticipated award price of the contract (including options) will exceed the simplified acquisition threshold (as defined in section 4 of the Office of Federal Procurement Policy Act (41 U.S.C. 403)) but will not exceed $5,000,000; and

>> (3) in the estimation of the contracting officer, the contract award can be made at a fair and reasonable price that offers best value to the United States.

The Veterans First Contracting Program also includes a statement of priority for VA contract awards, which grants first priority to sole-source or set-aside contracts for SDVOSB firms, second priority to sole-source or set-aside contracts for veteran-owned small business firms, and lower priority for all other categories of small business firms, 38 U.S.C. § 8127(i).

(B) HUBZONE EMPOWERMENT PROGRAM

The HUBZone Empowerment Contracting Program was enacted into law as part of the Small Business Reauthorization Act of 1997, Pub. L. No. 105-135. See 15 U.S.C. § 631 note. This program is designed to provide federal contracting opportunities for certain qualified small business concerns located in distressed communities. The purpose is to promote private-sector investment and employment opportunities in these communities. A concern may be determined to be a "qualified HUBZone small-business concern" if it is located in an "historically underutilized business zone," is owned and controlled by one or more U.S. citizens, and at least

35% of its employees reside in a HUB Zone. FAR Subpart 19.13 implements this policy.

With regard to the HUBZone program, 15 U.S.C. § 657a(b)(2)(B) states that, "[n]otwithstanding any other provision of law,"

> a contract opportunity shall be awarded pursuant to this section on the basis of competition restricted to HUBZone small business concerns if the contracting officer has a reasonable expectation that not less than 2 qualified HUBZone small business concerns will submit offers and that the award can be made at a fair market price.

Mirroring the statutory language, the applicable FAR provision states that a contracting officer "shall set aside acquisitions exceeding the simplified acquisition threshold for competition restricted to HUBZone small business concerns," FAR 19.305(a), when the contracting officer has a reasonable expectation that offers will be received from two or more HUBZone small business concerns and award will be made at a fair market price, FAR 19.1305(b). See *SWR, Inc.*, Comp. Gen. Dec. B-294266, 2004 CPD ¶ 219. An agency must make reasonable efforts to ascertain whether it will receive offers from at least two HUBZone small business concerns, *USA Fabrics, Inc.*, Comp. Gen. Dec. B-295737, 2005 CPD ¶ 82; *Global Solutions Network, Inc.*, Comp. Gen. Dec. B-292568, 2003 CPD ¶ 174.

Contracting officers may also award sole-source contracts to HUBZone small businesses under essentially the same circumstances that are prescribed for service-disabled veteran-owned small businesses, FAR 19.1306. The contracting officer must determine that the HUBZone small business firm is the only such firm capable of doing the work, FAR 19.1306(a).

Another procedure that can be used to steer work to a HUBZone small business firm is a 10% evaluation preference, FAR 19.1307. This preference can be used by conducting a full competition among all types of firms and adding 10% to the prices of all competitors. The contracting officer must insert the clause at FAR 52.219-4, Notices of Price Evaluation Preference for HUBZone Small Business Concerns, in solicitations and contracts for acquisitions conducted using full and open competition. The clause is not to be used in acquisitions that do not exceed the simplified acquisition threshold. The preference is not to be used (1) in acquisitions expected to be less than or equal to the simplified acquisition threshold; (2) where price is not a selection factor so that a price evaluation preference would not be considered (e.g., Architect/Engineer acquisitions); and (3) where all fair and reasonable offers are accepted (e.g., the award of multiple award schedule contracts), FAR 19.1307(a).

FAR 19.1304 makes the HUBZ.3one procedures inapplicable to —

> (a) Requirements that can be satisfied through award to —

(1) Federal Prison Industries, Inc. (see Subpart 8.6); or

(2) Javits-Wagner-O'Day Act participating non-profit agencies for the blind or severely disabled (see Subpart 8.7);

(b) Orders under indefinite delivery contracts (see Subpart 16.5);

(c) Orders against Federal Supply Schedules (see Subpart 8.4);

(d) Requirements currently being performed by an 8(a) participant or requirements SBA has accepted for performance under the authority of the 8(a) Program, unless SBA has consented to release the requirements from the 8(a) Program;

(e) Requirements that do not exceed the micro-purchase threshold; or

(f) Requirements for commissary or exchange resale items.

(C) 8(A) PROGRAM

The 8(a) Program is established under 15 U.S.C. § 637(a), which authorizes the Small Business Administration to contract with procuring agencies and award the work under those contracts to small disadvantaged businesses. The small disadvantaged businesses eligible for this work are designated by the SBA pursuant to their regulations in 13 CFR § 124.101– 113. FAR 19.803 contains the following guidance on the designation of specific contracts for award under this program:

Through their cooperative efforts, the SBA and an agency match the agency's requirements with the capabilities of 8(a) concerns to establish a basis for the agency to contract with the SBA under the program. Selection is initiated in one of three ways —

(a) The SBA advises an agency contracting activity through a search letter of an 8(a) firm's capabilities and asks the agency to identify acquisitions to support the firm's business plans. In these instances, the SBA will provide at least the following information in order to enable the agency to match an acquisition to the firm's capabilities:

(1) Identification of the concern and its owners.

(2) Background information on the concern, including any and all information pertaining to the concern's technical ability and capacity to perform.

(3) The firm's present production capacity and related facilities.

(4) The extent to which contracting assistance is needed in the present and the future, described in terms that will enable the agency to relate the concern's plans to present and future agency requirements.

(5) If construction is involved, the request shall also include the following:

(i) The concern's capabilities in and qualifications for accomplishing various categories of maintenance, repair, alteration, and construction work in specific categories such as mechanical, electrical, heating and air conditioning, demolition, building, painting, paving, earth work, waterfront work, and general construction work.

(ii) The concern's capacity in each construction category in terms of estimated dollar value (e.g., electrical, up to $100,000).

(b) The SBA identifies a specific requirement for a particular 8(a) firm or firms and asks the agency contracting activity to offer the acquisition to the 8(a) Program for the firm(s). In these instances, in addition to the information in paragraph (a) of this section, the SBA will provide —

(1) A clear identification of the acquisition sought; e.g., project name or number;

(2) A statement as to how any additional needed equipment and real property will be provided in order to ensure that the firm will be fully capable of satisfying the agency's requirements;

(3) If construction, information as to the bonding capability of the firm(s); and

(4) Either —

(i) If sole source request —

(A) The reasons why the firm is considered suitable for this particular acquisition; e.g., previous contracts for the same or similar supply or service; and

(B) A statement that the firm is eligible in terms of NAICS code, business support levels, and business activity targets; or

(ii) If competitive, a statement that at least two 8(a) firms are considered capable of satisfying the agency's requirements and a statement that the firms are also eligible in terms of the NAICS code, business support levels, and business activity targets. If requested by the contracting activity, SBA will identify at least two such firms and provide information concerning the firms' capabilities.

(c) Agencies may also review other proposed acquisitions for the purpose of identifying requirements which may be offered to the SBA. Where agencies independently, or through the self marketing efforts of an 8(a) firm, identify a requirement for the 8(a) Program, they may offer on behalf of a specific 8(a) firm, for the 8(a) Program in general, or for 8(a) competition (but see 19.800(e)).

Procurements under the 8(a) Program must be competitive if there are at least two eligible firms and it is anticipated that the contract price will exceed $6.5 million in the case of manufacturing contracts and $4 million in the case of all other acquisitions, FAR 19.805-1(a). These competitive procurements may use either sealed bidding or competitive negotiation procedures, FAR 19.805-2(a).

2. Competition

Competition is the most fundamental goal of acquisition planning because it is believed that obtaining competition is the best method of ensuring that the government will receive the supplies and services it needs at fair and reasonable prices. Competition also furthers the congressional goal of providing all qualified sources an opportunity to participate in the procurement process. Thus, there are strong statutory provisions requiring competition in new procurements. The FAR guidance goes further than these requirements, addressing the need to plan the procurement to ensure that competition is possible, to the greatest extent practicable, in subcontracts and subsequent procurements of components and spare parts.

FAR 7.105(b)(2) states:

Competition. (i) Describe how competition will be sought, promoted, and sustained throughout the course of the acquisition. If full and open competition is not contemplated, cite the authority in 6.302, discuss the basis for the application of that authority, identify the source(s), and discuss why full and open competition cannot be obtained.

(ii) Identify the major components or subsystems. Discuss component breakout plans relative to these major components or subsystems. Describe how competition will be sought, promoted, and sustained for these components or subsystems.

(iii) Describe how competition will be sought, promoted, and sustained for spares and repair parts. Identify the key logistic milestones, such as technical data delivery schedules and acquisition method coding conferences, that affect competition.

(iv) When effective subcontract competition is both feasible and desirable, describe how such subcontract competition will be sought, promoted, and sustained throughout the course of the acquisition. Identify any known barriers to increasing subcontract competition and address how to overcome them.

The extent of competition required by the procurement statutes has been the subject of extensive debate and a number of statutory changes. Prior to passage of the CICA, the statutes provided that specifications and invitations for bids (IFBs) for formal advertising (now sealed bidding) "permit such free and full competition as is consistent with the procurement of property and services needed by the agency concerned," 10 U.S.C. § 2305(a) (pre-CICA version). See also the prior version of 41 U.S.C. § 253. For negotiated procurement, the Armed Services Procurement Act required that proposals be solicited from "the maximum number of qualified sources consistent with the nature and requirements of the supplies or services to be procured," 10 U.S.C. § 2304(g) (pre-CICA version). In 1984 the CICA amended the procurement statutes to require that full and open competition be used in sealed bid and competitive proposal procurements except when specifically exempted, 10 U.S.C. § 2304(a)(1)(A) and 41 U.S.C. § 253(a)(1)(A). The CICA defined "full and open competition" to mean that "all responsible sources are permitted to submit sealed bids or competitive proposals on the procurement," 41 U.S.C. § 403(6).

Based on claims that receipt in some cases of inordinately large numbers of proposals placed an undue and unnecessary burden on procurements, attempts were made to narrow the statutory definition. One draft of the Clinger-Cohen Act of 1996 provided for "efficient competition." However, the requirement for full and open competition was not changed. Instead, § 4101 of the Act added a new provision to 10 U.S.C. § 2304(j) and 41 U.S.C. § 253(h), as follows:

> The Federal Acquisition Regulation shall ensure that the requirement to obtain full and open competition is implemented in a manner that is consistent with the need to efficiently fulfill the Government's requirements.

Efficiency in competition was addressed in § 4103 of the Act, which provides that the contracting officer can limit the number of proposals in the competitive range "to the greatest number that will permit an efficient competition among the offerors rated most highly," 10 U.S.C. § 2305(b)(4)(B) and 41 U.S.C. § 253b(d)(2).

The current statutes address competition in a confusing manner. They require that full and open competition be obtained through the use of "competitive procedures," and provide that the agency "shall use the competitive procedure that is best suited under the circumstances of the procurement," 10 U.S.C. § 2304(a); 41 U.S.C. § 253(a)(1). Thus, in the planning process, agencies must first review the statutory competitive procedures to determine if any of them are appropriate. If no competitive procedure is usable, the statutes provide that agencies may use "procedures other than competitive procedures" if they are justified under any of seven stated exceptions, 10 U.S.C. § 2304(c); 41 U.S.C. § 253(c).

a. Competitive Procedures

The competition statutes define competitive procedures in an elliptical fashion. Competitive procedures are defined as "procedures under which an executive agency enters into a contract pursuant to full and open competition," 41 U.S.C. § 259(b). The Office of Federal Procurement Policy Act then provides that full and open competition "means that all responsible sources are permitted to submit sealed bids or competitive proposals," 41 U.S.C. § 403(6). The two standard competitive procedures where the agencies must obtain full and open competition are:

1. Sealed bids (previously formal advertising), 41 U.S.C. § 253(a)(2)(A) and 10 U.S.C. § 2304(a)(2)(A); and

2. Competitive proposals (formerly negotiation), 41 U.S.C. § 253(a)(2)(B) and 10 U.S.C. § 2304(a)(2)(B).

In addition, 41 U.S.C. § 259(b) and 10 U.S.C. § 2302(2) define "competitive procedures" to include five alternative procurement procedures, as follows:

1. Procurement of architectural or engineering services conducted in accordance with title IX of this Act (40 U.S.C. § 541 et seq.);

2. The competitive selection of basic research proposals resulting from a general solicitation and the peer review or scientific review (as appropriate) of such proposals;

3. The procedures established by the Administrator for the multiple awards schedule program of the General Services Administration if —

(A) Participation in the program has been open to all responsible sources; and

(B) Orders and contracts under such procedures result in the lowest overall cost alternative to meet the needs of the Government;

4. Procurements conducted in furtherance of section 15 of the Small Business Act (15 U.S.C. § 644) as long as all responsible business concerns that are entitled to submit offers for such procurement are permitted to compete; and

(5) A competitive selection of research proposals resulting from a general solicitation and peer review or scientific review (as appropriate) solicited pursuant to section 9 of the Small Business Act (15 U.S.C. § 638).

When a procurement falls within one of these five categories, the amount of competition obtained will be determined by the special procedure for that category. These procurement procedures are generally used in preference to using one of the two standard competitive procedures. For example, if the procurement involves architect and engineer services, the procedures of 40 U.S.C. § 541 must be used. Similarly, most agencies now use general solicitations of opportunities and peer review selection procedures for both standard research procurements and research procurements that are set aside for small business. The General Services Administration multiple award schedule program is also used as a standard practice for specified categories of commercial products.

When one of these five alternative procedures is not applicable, the agency must select the most effective standard competitive procedure — sealed bidding or competitive negotiation. This will be discussed in detail below in the section on contracting considerations.

Although the statutes specifically require full and open competition to be attained in the procurement process, the five alternative procedures each contain their own rules as to the extent of competition required (including limitations in most instances). Thus, the explicit requirement for full and open competition applies mostly to procurements using sealed bids or competitive proposals. Because sealed bidding is inherently full and open, as those procurements are publicly announced, the degree of competition is a significant issue primarily in the competitive negotiation procedure. The key requirement is the definition of full and open competition, which provides that all responsible sources are permitted to submit sealed bids or competitive proposals on the procurement, 41 U.S.C. § 403(6). Only a few exceptions to this rule are permitted when competitive negotiation procedures are used.

(1) INADVERTENTLY OMITTING SOURCES

Under the previous statutory provisions, the GAO upheld awards if the government obtained "adequate competition" and stated that the adequacy of competition did not depend on whether every prospective bidder was afforded an opportunity to bid. See *Culligan, Inc.*, 56 Comp. Gen. 1011 (B-189307), 77-2 CPD ¶ 242, which involved advertised procurement, and *John Bransby Productions, Ltd.*, Comp. Gen. Dec. B-198360, 80-2 CPD ¶ 419, dealing with negotiated procurement. These decisions permitted an agency to omit a source from the procurement if it made reasonable efforts to inform offerors generally of the proposed procurement and there was no probative evidence that the agency had a conscious or deliberate intent to impede the participation of the prospective bidders.

The GAO has continued this line of cases and will not require cancellation of a solicitation or an award merely because a prospective offeror was not furnished a copy of the solicitation, absent probative evidence of a conscious or deliberate effort to exclude the offeror. See *International Ass'n of Firefighters*, Comp. Gen. Dec. B-220757, 86-1 CPD ¶ 31, stating:

Generally, the risk of nonreceipt of a solicitation amendment rests with the offeror. *Maryland Computer Services, Inc.*, B-216990, Feb. 12, 1985, 85-1 CPD ¶ 187. The propriety of a particular procurement is determined on the basis of whether full and open competition was achieved and reasonable prices were obtained, *Metro Medical Downtown*, B-220399, Dec. 5, 1985, 85-2 CPD ¶ 631, and whether the agency made a conscious and deliberate effort to exclude an offeror from competing for the contract. *Reliable Service Technology*, B-217152, Feb. 25, 1985, 85-1 CPD ¶ 234.

See also *Kendall Healthcare Prods. Co.*, Comp. Gen. Dec. B-289381, 2002 CPD ¶ 42 (firm did not take reasonable measures to obtain a copy of the solicitation when it choose not to review an amendment because it was listed under a classification code not reviewed by the firm); *Cutter Lumber Prods.*, Comp. Gen. Dec. B-262223.2, 96-1 CPD ¶ 57 (inadvertent failure to solicit incumbent did not result in lack of full and open competition where 12 offers were received and awardee's price was lower than the other competitive prices as well as incumbent's prior contract price); *Transwestern Helicopters, Inc.*, Comp. Gen. Dec. 235187, 89-2 CPD ¶ 95 (inadvertent failure to solicit incumbent did not result in a lack of full and open competition where agency made reasonable efforts to publicize and distribute the solicitation and received 25 bids); *Shemya Constructors*, Comp. Gen. Dec. B-232928.2, 89-1 CPD ¶ 108 (24 firms were solicited and there was no attempt by the agency to exclude the offeror from the competition); *Metro Med. Downtown*, Comp. Gen. Dec. B-220399, 85-2 CPD ¶ 631 (full and open competition was present despite failure to solicit firm through apparent oversight because Commerce Business Daily notice resulted in solicitation of 24 firms, of which four submitted offers); *Denver X-Ray Instruments, Inc.*, Comp. Gen. Dec. B-220963, 85-2 CPD ¶ 562 (no evidence that prospective offeror was deliberately excluded from competition). However, in *Trans World Maint., Inc.*, 65 Comp. Gen. 401 (B-220947), 86-1 CPD ¶ 239, the GAO found that the agency failed to obtain full and open competition when it failed to solicit bids from the incumbent contractor, which had requested a copy of the solicitation at least four times before its issuance. In addition, the CBD notice did not indicate the date of the IFB or of the bid opening. See also *Abel Converting, Inc. v. United States*, 679 F. Supp. 1133 (D.D.C. 1988), where the court held that an agency's failure to solicit an incumbent contractor on a 33-item procurement would not be adequately remedied by the GAO's recommendation that the agency resolicit the 14 items on which it had received only one bid, because the agency had not received full and open competition. The court reasoned at 1141:

> While the GAO concluded that two bids constituted adequate competition on nineteen of the line items, the Court disagrees. When so few bidders participate in a solicitation, the absence of even one responsible bidder significantly diminishes the level of competition. This is particularly so when the absent bidder is the incumbent contractor since that contractor previously submitted the lowest bids. Because GSA's actions "prevented a responsible source from competing[,] . . . the CICA mandate for full and open competition was not met."

In *Republic Floors, Inc.*, Comp. Gen. Dec. B-242962, 91-1 CPD ¶ 579, the GAO required resolicitation of the procurement because only two responsive bids were received and the agency had failed to send the protester two material solicitation amendments. The GAO reasoned that when so few firms participated in the competition, the absence of even one responsive firm due to the agency's regulatory violation so diminished the level of competition and undermined the CICA mandate for full and open competition that it constituted a compelling reason for resolicitation. See also *Qualimetrics, Inc.*, Comp. Gen. Dec. B-262057, 95-2 CPD ¶ 228 (competition found inadequate even though numerous proposals were received because no other offeror proposed to supply the identical equipment that incumbent manufactured and solicitation was for multiple-award federal supply schedule contract); *Davis Enters.*, Comp. Gen. Dec. B-249514, 92-2 CPD ¶ 389 (competition found inadequate where six bids were received and incumbent was not provided a copy of the solicitation); *Professional Ambulance Inc.*, Comp. Gen. Dec. B-248474, 92-2 CPD ¶ 145 (competition found inadequate where incumbent was not provided a copy of the solicitation and only minimum competition (three offers) were received); and *Custom Envtl. Serv., Inc.*, 70 Comp. Gen. 563 (B-242900), 91-1 CPD ¶ 578 (competition found inadequate where only one responsive bid was received and at least three other prospective bidders were eliminated from the bidding as a result of using an obsolete mailing list).

(2) COMPETITION EXCLUDING PARTICULAR SOURCES

41 U.S.C. § 253(b)(1) and 10 U.S.C. § 2304(b)(1) provide that executive agencies are permitted to exclude particular sources in order to establish or maintain alternate sources if the agency head determines that to do so:

(A) would increase or maintain competition and would likely result in reduced overall costs for such procurement, or for any anticipated procurement, of property or services;

(B) would be in the interest of national defense in having a facility (or a producer, manufacturer, or other supplier) available for furnishing the property or service in a case of a national emergency or industrial mobilization;

(C) would be in the interest of national defense in establishing or maintaining an essential engineering, research, or development capability to be provided by an educational or other nonprofit institution or a federally funded research and development center.

The second and third of these reasons are similar to the former 10 U.S.C. § 2304(a)(16), which permitted the use of negotiated procurement to maintain multiple producers that were part of the mobilization base. The first reason gives statutory authority for developing a competitive second source by precluding an existing sole source contractor from participating in the second source competition or maintaining an alternate source by precluding the primary source from being awarded all of an agency's requirements. FAR 6.202(a) states the following justifications that may be used for excluding one or more sources:

> Agencies may exclude a particular source from a contract action in order to establish or maintain an alternative source or sources for the supplies or services being acquired if the agency head determines that to do so would —
>
>> (1) Increase or maintain competition and likely result in reduced overall costs for the acquisition, or for any anticipated acquisition;
>>
>> (2) Be in the interest of national defense in having a facility (or a producer, manufacturer, or other supplier) available for furnishing the supplies or services in case of a national emergency or industrial mobilization;
>>
>> (3) Be in the interest of national defense in establishing or maintaining an essential engineering, research, or development capability to be provided by an educational or other nonprofit institution or a federally funded research and development center;
>>
>> (4) Ensure the continuous availability of a reliable source of supplies or services;
>>
>> (5) Satisfy projected needs based on a history of high demand; or
>>
>> (6) Satisfy a critical need for medical, safety, or emergency supplies.

These provisions appear to allow agencies to create or maintain multiple sources for a product or service by excluding an existing source. If there are two or more sources performing at the time of the procurement, they could be used to allocate the new work between the sources. They are not applicable to single source situations, which are discussed below.

FAR 6.202(b) provides that a determination and findings (D&F) by an agency head or designee must support the decision to exclude particular sources. Class D&Fs are not permitted; thus, a D&F must be made for each individual procurement action. After exclusion of particular sources, an agency is required to establish full and open competition using one of the competitive procedures, FAR 6.201.

(3) SMALL-BUSINESS AND LABOR-SURPLUS SETASIDES

Set-asides limiting competition to small competition to small business firms conducted under competitive procedures are authorized by 41 U.S.C. § 253(b)(2) and 10 U.S.C. § 2304(b)(2), which state that an agency may provide for the procurement of property or services covered by this section using competitive procedures, but excluding other than small business concerns in furtherance of sections 9 and 15 of the Small Business Act (15 U.S.C. §§ 639, 644).

The decision as to when to use these set-asides was discussed earlier in the discussion of required sources.

(4) Reprocurement After Default Termination

FAR 49.402-6 provides that after a default termination, reprocurements of no more than the amount of work remaining to be performed are not subject to the statutory competition requirements, but reprocurements over the remaining quantity of work are to be treated as new acquisitions. The FAR requires in the former case that the agency obtain competition to the maximum extent practicable. The GAO has held that in the case of a reprocurement after default, the statutes and regulations governing regular federal procurements are not strictly applicable, *Aerosonic Corp.*, 68 Comp. Gen. 179 (B-232730), 89-1 CPD ¶ 45. See *Montage, Inc.*, Comp. Gen. Dec. B-277923.2, 97-2 CPD ¶ 176, stating that an agency may properly exclude a defaulted contractor from a reprocurement for the resulting work, explaining that

> contracting officers are invested with wide latitude to determine how needed supplies or services are to be reprocured after the default of a contract. In the absence of a countervailing law or regulation, such a broad grant of discretion necessarily includes determining, in view of the circumstances of the default, whether or not to solicit or allow the defaulted contractor to compete in the reprocurement. The agency, with its particularized knowledge of the contractor's past performance (or failure to perform) on the requirement being reprocured, is clearly in the best position to make that determination. Although "competition to the maximum extent practicable" must be obtained in the reprocurement, that standard does not, in our view, mean that an agency must consider an offer from a defaulted contractor for the reprocurement of the very work for which it was defaulted. Accordingly, and in light of the broad authority accorded contracting officers by FAR 49.402-6, we will not review an agency's decision not to solicit a defaulted contractor.

See also *Derm-Buro. Inc.*, Comp. Gen. Dec. B-400558, 2008 CPD ¶ 226 (reasonable to limit reprocurement competition to the only two firms on the qualified products list, and not subject to first article testing); *Essan Metallix Corp.*, Comp. Gen. Dec. B-310357, 2007 CPD ¶ 5 (reasonable to exclude protester from a reprocurement necessitated by the termination of its own contract); *Marvin Land Sys., Inc.*, Comp. Gen. Dec. B-276434, 97-2 CPD ¶ 4 (reasonable to award sole-source reprocurement contract including an option to a firm that was in production at the time of the termination, when this was the only contractor that could meet the delivery schedule for the original contract quantities); *International Tech. Corp.*, Comp. Gen. Dec. B-250377.5, 93-2 CPD ¶ 102 (reasonable to award sole-source reprocurement contract for services with two option years because the reprocurement was conducted only 60 days after the original contract was awarded where prices would not have changed significantly in such a short period). Compare *Master Sec., Inc.,* Comp. Gen. Dec. B-235711, 89-2 CPD ¶ 303, ruling that the inclusion of two one-year options in a sole-source reprocurement of a defaulted service contract violated the FAR requirement to obtain competition to the maximum extent practicable. In reaching this conclusion, the GAO used the same reasoning applied under the statutory requirements — because there was adequate time to obtain competition for this optional work, not obtaining such competition was improper.

There is no requirement that a reprocurement be conducted using precisely the same terms as in the original procurement. See, for example, *Vereinigte Gebudereinigungsgesellschaft,* Comp. Gen. Dec. B-280805, 98-2 CPD ¶ 117 (reprocurement may require proof of language capability prior to award although original procurement contained no such requirement); Bud *Mahas Constr., Inc.,* 68 Comp. Gen. 622 (B-235261), 89-2 CPD ¶ 160 (reprocurement of small business set-aside contract need not be restricted to small businesses).

b. Other Than Competitive Procedures

"Other than competitive procedures" are not statutorily defined; 41 U.S.C. § 253(c) and 10 U.S.C. § 2304(c) merely list seven specific procurement situations where full and open competition is not required. Depending upon the circumstances, such procurements may be made on either a sole source basis or with limited competition.

(1) ONLY ONE SOURCE AVAILABLE

The first exception in 41 U.S.C. § 253(c) and 10 U.S.C. § 2304(c) states:

> (1) the property or services needed by the executive agency are available from only one responsible source or only from a limited number of responsible sources and no other type of property or services will satisfy the needs of the executive agency;

This is the broadest and possibly most utilized exception to the requirement for full and open competition. It is intended to permit a sole-source procurement "only when truly warranted," Competition in Contracting Act: Report of Government Affairs Committee to Accompany S. 338, S. Rep. No. 8-50, 98th Cong., 1st Sess. 21 (1983). This section discusses the decisions contesting sole-source procurements under both the prior statutes and the current statute to determine the meaning of this exception.

(A) AGENCY DISCRETION

An agency determination that a proposed contractor is the only source capable of meeting the technical needs of the agency is subject to close scrutiny but will not be overturned if the agency has properly justified its needs and there is a reasonable basis for its determination, *Mine Safety Appliances Co.*, Comp. Gen. Dec. B-233052, 89-1 CPD ¶ 127; *WSI Corp.*, Comp. Gen. Dec. B-220025, 85-2 CPD ¶ 626. However, when a responsible source has expressed interest in the procurement, the agency must make reasonable efforts to permit the source to compete, *Neil R. Gross & Co.*, 69 Comp. Gen. 292 (B-237434), 90-1 CPD ¶ 212. If such efforts fail, however, the GAO is reluctant to question agency decisions. See, for example, *Automated Prod. Equip. Corp.*, Comp. Gen. Dec. B-210476, 84-1 CPD ¶ 269, where, despite observing that the agency's technical personnel were impressed with the protester's equipment demonstration, the GAO did not disturb the agency's determination that the protester did not supply sufficient data from which the agency could evaluate the functional equivalence of the protester's equipment. Similarly, in *Technology for Communications Int'l*, Comp. Gen. Dec. B-236922, 89-2 CPD ¶ 603, the GAO did not question an agency's determination that the protester, in response to a CBD notice seeking sources, did not submit sufficient technical data to justify permitting the protester to compete on the basis of developing a new product if it won the competition.

Nonetheless, the GAO has held that the availability of only one source has to be demonstrated convincingly, *Daniel H. Wagner Assocs.*, 65 Comp. Gen. 305 (B-220633), 86-1 CPD ¶ 166. In most protests of sole-source awards, agencies have been able to meet this test. For example, in *Amray, Inc.*, Comp. Gen. Dec. B-209186, 83-2 CPD ¶ 45, the protester complained of a sole-source procurement for a scanning microscope on the grounds that it, too, could meet the agency's needs. In rejecting the protest, the GAO noted that the agency's technical personnel reviewed the literature published by various manufacturers, spoke to their representatives, including Amray's, and reasonably determined the microscope to be unique. See also *Smith & Wesson, Inc.*, Comp. Gen. Dec. B-400479, 2008 CPD ¶ 215 (reasonable to sole-source pistol which was currently in use therein avoiding the need for retraining on a different model or the need to stockpile spare parts for a different model); *Kearfott Guidance & Navigation Corp.*, Comp. Gen. Dec. B-292895.2, 2004 CPD ¶ 123 (reasonable to determine that only one source had the unique, comprehensive overall knowledge of the critical elements of the guidance weapon system that could satisfy the agency's needs); *McKesson Automation Sys., Inc.*, Comp. Gen. Dec. B-290969.2, 2003 CPD ¶ 24 (reasonable to determine that only one responsible source could meet requirement for installation of a pharmacy robotic system); *Metric Sys. Corp.*, Comp. Gen. Dec. B-279622, 98-2 CPD ¶ 4 (reasonable to determine that only one source could complete the modification of an electronic warfare system to simulate advanced threats within the urgent time constraints of the procurement); *Datacom, Inc.*, Comp. Gen. Dec. B-274175, 96-2 CPD ¶ 199 (reasonable to determine that only one source would be able to produce a first article for approval and then production articles within the time in which the Air Force needed them); *Mnemonics, Inc.*, Comp. Gen. Dec. B-261476.3, 96-1 CPD ¶ 7 (reasonable to determine that only one source could supply critically required items under an expedited delivery schedule); *Navistar Marine Instrument Corp.*, Comp. Gen. Dec. B-262221,

95-2 CPD ¶ 232 (sole-source procurement proper where no other barometer had the ability to fit into a preexisting opening on the instrument control panel of the engine); *Nomura Enter., Inc.*, Comp. Gen. Dec. B-260977.2, 95-2 CPD ¶ 206 (sole-source contract for engineering support services related to howitzer proper because agency reasonably concluded that unacceptable delays would occur if award was made to another source); *Midwest Dynamometer & Eng'g Co.*, Comp. Gen. Dec. B-257323, 94-2 CPD ¶ 91 (reasonable to determine that only one source could furnish a dynamometer system meeting requirement for a system capable of running on existing software); *Litton Computer Servs.*, Comp. Gen. Dec. B-256225, 94-2 CPD ¶ 36 (reasonable to determine that only the developer of the original system had the necessary extensive system knowledge and experience to accomplish task); *Essex Electro Eng'rs, Inc.*, Comp. Gen. Dec. B-250437, 93-1 CPD ¶ 74 (procurement from only immediately available source justified to obtain backup electric power plants, which were in short supply because of Operation Desert Storm — even though units would be placed on standby status); *AGEMA Infrared Sys.*, Comp. Gen. Dec. B-240961, 91-1 CPD ¶ 4 (reasonable to determine that only one source was available where protester's equipment did not contain essential technical features needed by agency); *EG&G Astrophysics Research Corp.*, Comp. Gen. Dec. B-241171, 90-2 CPD ¶ 525 (agency had thoroughly reviewed protester's equipment and had reasonably determined it did not meet agency's needs); *Elbit Computers*, Ltd., Comp. Gen. Dec. B-239038, 90-2 CPD ¶ 26 (determination that no other contractor could supply the equipment reasonable); *Abbott Labs.*, Comp. Gen. Dec. B-230220, 88-1 CPD ¶ 468 (reasonable determination of agency requirement and no other source); and *C&S Antennas, Inc.*, Comp. Gen. Dec. B-224549, 87-1 CPD ¶ 161 (agency determination that only one product was compatible with its needs reasonable even though protester was meeting similar needs of another agency).

An agency's legitimate need to standardize equipment may provide a reasonable basis for imposing restrictions of competition. See *Chicago Dyer Co.*, Comp. Gen. Dec. B-401888 2009 CPD ¶ 253 (agency's sole-source award of flatwork ironer based on interoperability need of already installed VA equipment); *Brinkmann Instruments, Inc.*, Comp. Gen. Dec. B-309946, 2007 CPD ¶ 188 (agency's sole-source award based on need to acquire the same autotitrator previously fielded on the other nuclear submarines for purposes of standardization); *Advanced Med. Sys., Inc.*, Comp. Gen. Dec. B-259010, Jan. 17, 1995, *Unpub.* (agency's need to standardize fetal monitors in order to maximize patient care); and *Sperry Marine, Inc.*, Comp. Gen. Dec. B-245654, 92-1 CPD ¶ 111 (sole-source acquisition of particular radar system where agency needed to utilize the same radar system it had already deployed at training school).

Protest of sole source determinations have, however, been sustained if the facts indicate that other sources could satisfactorily meet the government's needs. In *Lockheed Martin Sys. Integration—Owego*, Comp. Gen. Dec. B-287190.2, 2001 CPD ¶ 110, the GAO sustained a protest to a sole-source award where the record showed that another potential vendor was given an incorrect understanding of the agency's requirements. In *Barnes Aerospace Group*, Comp. Gen. Dec. B-298864, 2006 CPD ¶ 204, the GAO sustained a challenge to a sole-source procurement because the presolicitation notice generated an expression of interest from a second source yet the J&A was prepared in advance of the notice and did not consider the viability of the second source. Similarly in *Precision Logistics, Inc.*, Comp. Gen. Dec. B-271429, 96-2 CPD ¶ 24, the GAO sustained a protest to a sole-source award for aircraft parts because, when offerors submitted alternate products, the government inordinately delayed evaluation of the products to determine their technical acceptability. See also *Support Servs. Int'l, Inc.*, Comp. Gen. Dec. B-271559, 96-2 CPD ¶ 20 (protest sustained because the incumbent contractor was not solicited due to the agency's unreasonable determination that it could not be expected to perform satisfactorily); *Data Based Decisions, Inc.*, Comp. Gen. Dec. B-232663, 89-1 CPD ¶ 87 (protest sustained because incumbent contractor was not solicited although able to compete for the work); *Design Pak, Inc.*, Comp. Gen. Dec. B-212579, 83-2 CPD ¶ 336 (protest to a noncompetitive award sustained because the agency confused its requirements with the characteristics of the sole-source contractor's product); and *Sidereal Corp.*, Comp. Gen. Dec. B-210969, 83-2 CPD ¶ 92 (protest sustained because the protester had recently won contracts for equipment similar to that procured, thus demonstrating that meaningful competition was possible). In making a determination that only one contractor is capable of meeting an agency's needs, it is improper for an agency to rely on the putative sole-source contractor for technical advice and expertise. The agency should independently evaluate technical data and draw its own conclusions, *Aero Corp. v. Navy*, 558 F. Supp. 404 (D.D.C. 1983).

(B) Privately Developed Items

The determination to procure on a sole source basis may be justified under certain circumstances if the items being procured were developed at private expense. The following material discusses the circumstances that preclude or permit sole source procurement of privately developed items.

(1) PATENTED ITEMS

The mere fact that an item is patented will not justify a sole source procurement. The statutory basis for this rule is 28 U.S.C. § 1498(a), which gives patent owners the right to reasonable compensation if an invention is used "by or for the United States without license" but does not permit patent owners to enjoin the use of patents in such cases. In 38 Comp. Gen. 276 (B-136916) (1958), the GAO ruled that this statute requires the use of competitive procurement techniques when purchasing patented items, reasoning at 278:

> It is our view, however, that section 1498 appears clearly to constitute a modification of the patent law by limiting the rights of patentees insofar as procurement of supplies by the Government may be concerned, and by vesting in the Government

a right to the use of any patents granted by it upon payment of reasonable compensation for such use. We believe that the statute is not consistent with any duty on the part of a contracting agency of the Government to protect the interests of patentees or licensees with respect to articles which it proposes to purchase, since the statute itself defines and provides an exclusive remedy for enforcement of the patentee's rights as to the Government. Any other interpretation would appear to us to impose an impossible burden upon Government procurement officials to determine the applicability and validity of any patents affecting any articles desired.

FAR 27.102(b) provides that generally the government will not refuse to award a contract on the grounds that the prospective contractor may infringe a patent. See also 53 Comp. Gen. 270 (B-177835) (1973), indicating that competitive negotiation could be used to obtain patented items if the circumstances for negotiation are present. The traditional practice to overcome the competitive advantage accorded to an infringing competitor by this policy has been to include a Patent Indemnity clause (transferring the risk of patent infringement to the contractor) in the contract. This practice was approved by the GAO in *Barrier-Wear*, Comp. Gen. Dec. B-240563, 90-2 CPD ¶ 421, and was permitted by FAR 27.203-1(b)(2)(ii) prior to December 2007. At that time, a revised Part 27 of the FAR became effective, omitting any coverage of this issue, 72 Fed. Reg. 63045, Nov. 11, 2007. There is no indication in the current FAR that a Patent Indemnity clause cannot be used for this purpose.

(II) COPYRIGHTED ITEMS

Although 28 U.S.C. § 1498(b) contains substantially the same language relating to copyrights as in 28 U.S.C. § 1498(a), the presence of a copyright has been held to be a valid reason for sole-source procurement. FAR 27.102(e) provides that generally the government requires that contractors obtain permission from copyright owners before including copyrighted works, owned by others, in data to be delivered to the government. See *ALK Assocs.*, Comp. Gen. Dec. B-237019, 90-1 CPD ¶ 113, upholding a sole-source procurement of copyrighted software because the agency needed the identical software to meet its needs. The GAO apparently reasoned that competitors could not recreate such software nor could the agency or its contractors take the software through eminent domain procedures (as can occur with patents). See also *Vorum Research Corp.*, Comp. Gen. Dec. B-255393, 94-1 CPD ¶ 155 (protest against a sole-source procurement denied based, in part, on the grounds that some of the software needed to perform the contract was copyrighted); *Federal Computer Int'l Corp.*, Comp. Gen. Dec. B-251132, 93-1 CPD ¶ 175 (protest against a sole-source procurement to maintain Xerox equipment denied because diagnostics, manuals, maintenance routines, software revisions, updates, modules, enhancements and source code were either copyrighted or maintained as trade secrets). The same logic probably explains the copyright provisions in ¶ (c)(2) of the Rights in Data — General clause in FAR 52.227-14 and ¶ (d) of the Rights in Technical Data — Noncommercial Items clause in DFARS 252.227-7013, stating that a contractor may not use copyrighted material in the performance of the contract without the consent of the contracting officer.

(III) ITEMS DESCRIBED BY PROPRIETARY DATA

Because there is no statute comparable to 28 U.S.C. § 1498 covering proprietary data, it is the policy of the government to honor proprietary rights in technical data, FAR 27.102. This policy, now incorporated into 41 U.S.C. § 418a(a) and 10 U.S.C. § 2320(a)(1), states that procurement regulations may not impair "any other right in technical data otherwise established by law." However, 10 U.S.C. § 2320(c)(1) does permit the use of contract clauses calling for expiration of a contractor's proprietary rights to the technical data after no more than seven years. This policy is not discussed in the current guidance on technical data in DFARS Subpart 227.71, which was issued in 1995. It was implemented in the prior DFARS 227.473-1(c)(3), which was effective from 1988 through 1995 and called for negotiation of time limitations between one and five years. The government's policy of honoring proprietary rights in technical data does not prevent the government from meeting its needs with an independent development project.

In some cases the GAO has held that agencies should prepare data packages or use performance specifications to facilitate competitive procurement. The fact that the agency would incur substantial cost in drafting a specification that could be used for competitive procurement was not adequate justification for sole-source procurement in *Techniarts*, Comp. Gen. Dec. B-193263, 79-1 CPD ¶ 246. But see *Compressor Eng'g Corp.*, Comp. Gen. Dec. B-213032, 84-1 CPD ¶ 180, stating that it would be unreasonable for the agency to bear the cost of testing parts that would facilitate a competitive procurement. In *Command, Control & Communications Corp.*, Comp. Gen. Dec. B-210100, 83-2 CPD ¶ 448, the GAO rejected the agency's arguments that the urgency of its needs and the lack of proprietary data precluded a competitive award. Although the GAO recognized that the agency might have to satisfy its immediate needs on a sole-source basis, urgency could not justify acquisition of computer systems over a five-year period where the systems were not complex technologically and the agency acknowledged that other vendors could duplicate the system "if given enough time."

The GAO has sustained sole-source procurements where the product being procured could be described only by proprietary data, *Aerospace Eng'g & Support, Inc.*, Comp. Gen. Dec. B-258546, 95-1 CPD ¶ 18 (agency had previously failed in attempting to qualify a second source without access to the proprietary data); *Litton Computer Servs.*, Comp. Gen. Dec. B-256225, 94-2 CPD ¶ 36 (agency reasonably determined that only the developer of the original system had the necessary extensive system knowledge and experience to accomplish task); *TSI Microelectronics Corp.*, Comp. Gen. Dec. B-243889, 91-2 CPD ¶ 172 (agency had found that it did not have sufficient data to generate a competitive procurement package); *Hydra Rig*

Cryogenics, Inc., Comp. Gen. Dec. B-234029, 89-1 CPD ¶ 442; *Turbo Mech., Inc.*, Comp. Gen. Dec. B-231807, 88-2 CPD ¶ 299; *Quality Diesel Engines, Inc.*, Comp. Gen. Dec. B-210215, 83-2 CPD ¶ 1. In such cases the GAO generally will not question an agency's legal determination that the sole-source contractor has proprietary rights, *Fil-Coil Co.*, Comp. Gen. Dec. B-198105, 80-2 CPD ¶ 304 (protester did not submit sufficient data to demonstrate that it had ability to manufacture acceptable part). Similarly, the Court of Federal Claim will uphold a sole-source contract where proprietary data rights preclude a competitive procurement, *FN Mfg., Inc. v. United States*, 44 Fed. Cl. 449 (1999). See also *Metric Sys. Corp. v. United States*, 42 Fed. Cl. 306 (1998) (declining to set aside sole-source contract for Mini-MUTES radar simulator for Air Force training under the one responsible source provision of CICA, noting that the awardee had the proprietary rights to the product).

The existence of proprietary software can also justify a sole-source procurement. See, for example, *MFVega & Assocs., LLC*, Comp. Gen. Dec. B-291605.3, 2003 CPD ¶ 65, holding that a contract to create a second-generation program management information system using the existing system was properly sole-sourced to the only contractor having access to the source codes of the software in the existing system. Similarly, in *Midwest Dynamometer & Eng'g Co.*, Comp. Gen. Dec. B-257323, 94-2 CPD ¶ 91, it was held that the agency reasonably determined that only one source could furnish a dynamometer system meeting its requirement for a system capable of running on existing software. See also *Metric Sys. Corp.*, Comp. Gen. Dec. B-279622, 98-2 CPD ¶ 4, where a sole-source procurement to upgrade a system was justified because only one company had experience with that system. Similarly, in *Bartlett Techs. Corp.*, Comp. Gen. Dec. B-218786, 85-2 CPD ¶ 198, a sole source was justified because the protester's software was not compatible with the product currently being used by the agency. The necessity for compatibility also justified a sole-source procurement in *Card Tech. Corp.*, Comp. Gen. Dec. B-275385, 97-1 CPD ¶ 76. However, a software specification is unduly restrictive if it prevents an offeror from proposing software that will perform as well as that specified, *Honeywell Information Sys., Inc.*, Comp. Gen. Dec. B-215224, 84-2 CPD ¶ 389. Compare *Lanier GmbH*, Comp. Gen. Dec. B-216038, 85-1 CPD ¶ 523, finding no undue restriction in the specifications for a computer system that merely required that it meet certain minimum requirements.

If an agency can overcome proprietary rights to software, it is expected to take steps to establish the basis for competitive procurement in the future. See, for example, *eFedBudget Corp.*, Comp. Gen. Dec. B-298627, 2006 CPD ¶ 159, where the agency had entered into a license with the developer of a software system providing that the agency could only use the system for internal purposes and that the company would make all improvements to the program available to the agency. While the GAO agreed that this limitation on the agency's rights was a valid reason for an immediate sole source procurement, it recommended that the agency explore methods of obtaining competition in the future, stating:

[W]e recommend that the agency conduct a documented cost/benefit analysis reflecting the costs associated with obtaining competition, either through purchasing additional rights to the proprietary software or some other means, and the anticipated benefits. If the cost/benefit analysis reveals a practicable means to obtain competition, we recommend that the agency proceed with a competitive procurement.

Sole source procurements have been justified where as a practical matter, it was not feasible to create a nonproprietary data package. See *Kessler Int'l Corp.*, Comp. Gen. Dec. B-230662, 88-2 CPD ¶ 27, where it was held that the agency reasonably determined that only one source could timely supply the needed part because it was a critical application part necessary for performing safety, mission, and readiness requirements. The government had no technical data package because the item had been developed at private expense under a nondevelopmental item contract. Similarly, in *Raytheon Co.-Integrated Defense Sys.*, Comp. Gen. Dec. B-400610, 2008 CPD ¶ 8, the GAO found unobjectionable an agency's awards of follow-on contracts for the continued development of a sophisticated weapon system. To justify the decision to proceed sole source the agency noted that the ongoing, concurrent hardware and software upgrades meant that the technical data package and government-purpose software licenses needed to support a competitive procurement were not available. Without the benefit of the technical data package and those licenses, the agency considered it likely that acquiring the services from some other source would result in unacceptable delays in meeting the government's requirements, because to integrate the new elements of the Aegis Modernization program, another contractor would need time to gain a working knowledge of the Aegis Weapon System software or to obtain direct assistance from the incumbent. In *Rack Eng'g Co.*, Comp. Gen. Dec. B-194470, 79-2 CPD ¶ 385, the GAO upheld the Navy's sole-source procurement for interchangeable spare-parts cabinets because the supplier had already supplied 87% of the Atlantic Fleet Carrier Force's needs, reasoning that the cost of redesigning and retooling to meet the interchangeability requirement would necessarily preclude any other offerors from competing. Thus, the most economically sound alternative to ensure interchangeability was to procure sole source from the existing supplier. In *Worldwide Marine, Inc.*, Comp. Gen. Dec. B-212640, 84-1 CPD ¶ 152, the GAO acknowledged there may have been some degree of agency negligence in failing to draft specifications but, nevertheless, held that faced with an urgent need for the purchase in question, the agency was justified in making a sole-source award to the only company that possessed adequate data to produce the item. See also *Piezo Crystal Co.*, 69 Comp. Gen. 97 (B-236160), 89-2 CPD ¶ 477, and *Rotek, Inc.*, Comp. Gen. Dec. B-240252, 90-2 CPD ¶ 341, upholding sole-source procurements justified by the agency's lack of a data package and an urgent need for initial deliveries of the product. In *Masbe Corp.*, Comp. Gen. Dec. B-260253.2, 95-1 CPD ¶ 253, the GAO upheld a sole-source procurement for a critical military aircraft engine part because the Air Force did not have adequate data to establish qualification requirements for the part (because this data was possessed by the original designer of the engine) and thus could not tell what variation in the configuration and manufacturing process led to acceptable performance. Similarly, in *KSD, Inc. v. United States*, 72 Fed. Cl. 236 (2006), a sole source procurement was upheld because the agency had induced the contractor to develop a new product using IR&D funds with the result that it had no access to the proprietary technical data resulting from the development work. The court found that the agency's action in negotiating away its data rights was not arbitrary and capricious. See also *Kearfott Guidance & Navigation Corp.*, Comp. Gen. Dec. B-292895.2, 2004 CPD ¶ 123 (product was too complicated to permit reverse engineering as a means of obtaining competition and contractor that designed equipment had unique knowledge of its details); *Cubic Defense Sys., Inc. v. United States*, 45 Fed. Cl. 239 (1999) (agency did not have access to proprietary data and there was insufficient time to permit reverse engineering).

Sole-source procurements will not be sustained when a protester shows that competition can be obtained without the use of proprietary technical data. See, for example, *Marconi Dynamics, Inc.*, Comp. Gen. Dec. B252318, 93-1 CPD ¶ 475, granting a protest against a sole-source procurement after reviewing the protester's detailed analysis of its ability to perform engineering services using its own resources plus those of the procuring agency without any requirement to use proprietary technical data of the original equipment manufacturer. See also *Test Sys. Assocs., Inc.*, 71 Comp. Gen. 33 (B-244007.2), 91-2 CPD ¶ 367, holding that a sole-source procurement to an incumbent contractor was not justified because there was no proprietary "unique data base" and no reason that a new contractor could not perform the work at a lower price than the incumbent. Similarly, in *Sabreliner Corp.*, Comp. Gen. Dec. B-288030, 2001 CPD ¶ 170, a protest of a sole-source procurement was granted when the agency was unable to demonstrate that the selected contractor actually had proprietary data necessary to perform the engineering and overhaul work. In a subsequent protest of the next attempt to procure this overhaul work, *HEROS, Inc.*, Comp. Gen. Dec. B-292043, 2003 CPD ¶ 111, the GAO granted the protest because the agency had not performed sufficient planning to determine if contractors could perform the work using information that was commercially available.

10 U.S.C. § 2305(d) and 41 U.S.C. § 253b(j) contain a requirement intended to foster subsequent competition when major systems are being procured. These statutes address both development and manufacturing contracts for major systems and require that procedures be used by the contracting officer to ensure that the contracting parties address the issue of obtaining competition when buying replenishment parts, components or systems in the future. The latter statute states:

(j) Planning for future competition. (1) (A) In preparing a solicitation for the award of a development contract for a major system, the head of an agency shall consider requiring in the solicitation that an offeror include in its offer proposals described in subparagraph (B). In determining whether to require such proposals, the head of the agency shall give due consideration to the purposes for which the system is being procured and the technology necessary to meet the system's required capabilities. If such proposals are required, the head of the agency shall consider them in evaluating the offeror's price. (B) The proposals that the head of an agency is to consider requiring in a solicitation for the award of a development contract are the following:

(i) Proposals to incorporate in the design of the major system items which are currently available within the supply system of the Federal agency responsible for the major system, available elsewhere in the national supply system, or commercially available from more than one source.

(ii) With respect to items that are likely to be required in substantial quantities during the system's service life, proposals to incorporate in the design of the major system items which the United States will be able to acquire competitively in the future.

(2) (A) In preparing a solicitation for the award of a production contract for a major system, the head of an agency shall consider requiring in the solicitation that an offeror include in its offer proposals described in subparagraph (B). In determining whether to require such proposals, the head of the agency shall give due consideration to the purposes for which the system is being procured and the technology necessary to meet the system's required capabilities. If such proposals are required, the head of the agency shall consider them in evaluating the offeror's price.

(B) The proposals that the head of an agency is to consider requiring in a solicitation for the award of a production contract are proposals identifying opportunities to ensure that the United States will be able to obtain on a competitive basis items procured in connection with the system that are likely to be reprocured in substantial quantities during the service life of the system. Proposals submitted in response to such requirement may include the following:

(i) Proposals to provide to the United States the right to use technical data to be provided under the contract for competitive reprocurement of the item, together with the cost to the United States, if any, of acquiring such technical data and the right to use such data.

(ii) Proposals for the qualification or development of multiple sources of supply for the item.

(3) If the head of an agency is making a noncompetitive award of a development contract or a production contract for a major system, the factors specified in paragraphs (1) and (2) to be considered in evaluating an offer for a contract may be considered as objectives in negotiating the contract to be awarded.

See also 10 U.S.C. § 2320(e) stating:

(e) The Secretary of Defense shall require program managers for major weapon systems and subsystems of major weapon systems to assess the long-term technical data needs of such systems and subsystems and establish corresponding acquisition strategies that provide for technical data rights needed to sustain such systems and subsystems over their life cycle. Such strategies may include the development of maintenance capabilities within the Department of Defense or competition for contracts for sustainment of such systems or subsystems. Assessments and corresponding acquisition strategies developed under this section with respect to a weapon system or subsystem shall —

(1) be developed before issuance of a contract solicitation for the weapon system or subsystem;

(2) address the merits of including a priced contract option for the future delivery of technical data that were not acquired upon initial contract award;

(3) address the potential for changes in the sustainment plan over the life cycle of the weapon system or subsystem; and

(4) apply to weapon systems and subsystems that are to be supported by performance-based logistics arrangements as well as to weapons systems and subsystems that are to be supported by other sustainment approaches.

The 2001 DOD Guide, *Intellectual Property: Navigating Through Commercial Waters* (www.acq.osd.mil/dpap/Docs/intelprop.pdf), recognizes the difficulty of factoring this competition principle into the acquisition of products and services embodying proprietary technology at 3-4:

The need for competition has stimulated much of the desire to acquire technical data and assert patent rights. In the past, to ensure that the prices for spare parts for maintenance were fair, programs would acquire technical data packages (e.g., detailed design drawings, manufacturing data, and source code). The technical data packages would be used for follow-on competitive reprocurement of spares, year after year, to support fielded systems maintained by the military services and stockpiled by the Defense Logistics Agency and military depots. However, in recent years, this type of competition strategy has become obsolete; DOD has moved instead from form, fit and function specifications to contractor logistics support strategies and just-in-time inventory spares/parts supply. With this in mind, contracting officers and program managers should look to satisfy competition requirements through alternative strategies such as

* long-term initial competitive contracts,

* cycling technical insertion in shorter increments by using form, fit, and function specifications that enable new entrants, and

* dissimilar competition (see DOD Directives 5000.1 and 5000.2).

For complete coverage of the various methods to work around proprietary rights and obtain competition see Chapter 8 of Nash & Rawicz, *Intellectual Property in Government Contracts* (6th ed. 2008).

(C) Unsolicited Proposals

Unsolicited proposals can provide the basis for a determination that the property or services are available from only one source. See 41 U.S.C. § 253(d)(1)(A), stating:

> [I]n the case of a contract for property or services to be awarded on the basis of acceptance of an unsolicited research proposal, the property or services shall be considered to be available from only one source if the source has submitted an unsolicited research proposal that demonstrates a unique and innovative concept the substance of which is not otherwise available to the United States and does not resemble the substance of a pending competitive procurement.

10 U.S.C. § 2304(d)(1)(A) is substantively the same.

FAR Subpart 15.6 goes beyond these statutes and provides guidance on the handling of all unsolicited proposals for research work and other types of work. However, this regulation establishes unsolicited proposals as the least desirable manner of submitting new and innovative ideas to an agency for evaluation. See FAR 15.602, which states:

> It is the policy of the Government to encourage the submission of new and innovative ideas in response to Broad Agency Announcements, Small Business Innovation Research topics, Small Business Technology Transfer Research topics, Program Research and Development Announcements, or any other Government-initiated solicitation or program. When the new and innovative ideas do not fall under topic areas publicized under those programs or techniques, the ideas may be submitted as unsolicited proposals.

FAR 15.606-2(a) requires that each proposal be comprehensively evaluated, considering, at a minimum, the following factors:

> (1) Unique, innovative, and meritorious methods, approaches, or concepts demonstrated by the proposal;
>
> (2) Overall scientific, technical, or socioeconomic merits of the proposal;
>
> (3) Potential contribution of the effort to the agency's specific mission;
>
> (4) The offeror's capabilities, related experience, facilities, techniques, or unique combinations of these that are integral factors for achieving the proposal objectives;

(5) The qualifications, capabilities, and experience of the proposed principal investigator, team leader, or key personnel critical to achieving the proposal objectives; and

(6) The realism of the proposed cost.

FAR 15.607 contains limitations on award of contracts based on unsolicited proposals:

(a) A favorable comprehensive evaluation of an unsolicited proposal does not, in itself, justify awarding a contract without providing for full and open competition. The agency point of contact shall return an unsolicited proposal to the offeror, citing reasons, when its substance —

(1) Is available to the Government without restriction from another source;

(2) Closely resembles a pending competitive acquisition requirement;

(3) Does not relate to the activity's mission; or

(4) Does not demonstrate an innovative and unique method, approach, or concept, or is otherwise not deemed a meritorious proposal.

FAR 15.607(b) goes on to state that if the unsolicited proposal has received a favorable comprehensive evaluation and is not subject to the above impediments, the agency can procure the work covered by the proposal. If it is for research work, such procurement can be on a sole source basis in accordance with FAR 6.302-1(a)(2)(i):

Supplies or services may be considered to be available from only one source if the source has submitted an unsolicited research proposal that —

(A) Demonstrates a unique and innovative concept (see definition at 2.101), or, demonstrates a unique capability of the source to provide the particular research services proposed;

(B) Offers a concept or services not otherwise available to the Government; and

(C) Does not resemble the substance of a pending competitive acquisition.

If the proposal is for other than research work, FAR 15.607(b) requires full and open competition unless one of the statutory exceptions is justified.

The GAO has held that these provisions do not require award of a contract to a submitter of an unsolicited proposal — they merely permit award if the proposal is unique and innovative. Even when the proposal is unique and innovative, agencies have the discretion not to award a sole-source contract, *S. T. Research Corp.*, Comp. Gen. Dec. B-231752, 88-2 CPD ¶ 152; *University of Dayton Research Inst.*, Comp. Gen. Dec. B-220589, 86-1 CPD ¶ 108. Further, the GAO "does not consider it appropriate to review a protest that an agency should procure from a particular firm on a sole-source basis," *Arctic Energies Ltd.*, Comp. Gen. Dec. B-224672, 86-2 CPD ¶ 571. Thus, it is very difficult to challenge an agency decision to reject an unsolicited proposal.

It is appropriate not to issue a sole-source contract based on an unsolicited proposal where the data necessary for a competitive procurement are otherwise available to the government, *Saratoga Indus.*, Comp. Gen. Dec. B-219341, 85-2 CPD ¶ 247 (information in the unsolicited proposal was available from previous specifications or from publicly available information); *Georgetown Air & Hydro Sys.*, Comp. Gen. Dec. B-210806, 84-1 CPD ¶ 186 (unsolicited proposal incorporated information related to a forthcoming solicitation). In *LW Planning Group*, Comp. Gen. Dec. B-215539, 84-2 CPD ¶ 531, the government was found to have properly decided that the work in the unsolicited proposal required the work of an architect-engineer contractor and the work could therefore not be awarded to the submitter without following the A/E procedures.

It appears that a proposal could be unique and innovative even though it does not include proprietary information. FAR 15.609 permits unsolicited proposals to contain a legend on each page prohibiting the disclosure, outside the government, of such information or the use of such information for any purpose other than evaluation of the proposal. This regulation also establishes a procedure for government protection of the information even if the legends are not placed on the proposal. See, however, *Xerxe Group, Inc. v. United States*, 278 F.3d 1357 (Fed. Cir. 2002), not recognizing this element of the regulation and holding that the submitter of an unsolicited proposal lost all rights to each page of the proposal which did not contain a proprietary legend. It has also been held that the government does not violate a protectable trade secret by competitively soliciting for the item using data that were independently developed by the government, *Zodiac of North Am., Inc.*, Comp. Gen. Dec. B-220012, 85-2 CPD ¶ 595; *Sellers, Connor & Cuneo*, 53 Comp. Gen. 161 (B-177436), *recons. denied*, 74-1 CPD ¶ 126.

The submission of advertising materials does not constitute an unsolicited proposal, *Metric Sys. Corp.*, Comp. Gen. Dec. B-271578, 96-2 CPD ¶ 8. In *Metric Systems*, the protester asserted that the brochure and pricing sheet it submitted to the Air Force constituted an unsolicited proposal and that the Air Force's use of that information to develop IFB specifications violated FAR 15.608(a) prohibitions. The GAO denied the protest, stating that an unsolicited proposal must be in the nature of a proposal for a contract, and that the brochure and pricing sheet did not meet this test because they did not include a signature of a person authorized to represent and contractually obligate the company, did not state the period of time for which the alleged proposal was to be valid or the type of contract preferred, and did not identify any proprietary data to be used only for evaluation purposes.

Many agencies now screen unsolicited research proposals to determine if they can be reviewed and considered under the broad agency announcement in effect at the time of receipt of the proposal. In most cases the proposal will fall within one of the categories of research covered by this announcement and can be treated as a research proposal.

(D) FOLLOW-ON CONTRACTS

Follow-on contracts are awards made to the contractor that has previously been awarded a design or manufacturing contract for the same item or that has previously performed the services being procured. The CICA enacted two special provisions on this issue. Sole-source contracting for follow-on contracts for major systems or equipment is permitted by 41 U.S.C. § 253(d)(1)(B) in the following circumstances:

[I]n the case of a follow-on contract for the continued development or production of a major system or highly specialized equipment when it is likely that award to a source other than the original source would result in

(i) substantial duplication of cost to the Government which is not expected to be recovered through competition, or

(ii) unacceptable delays in fulfilling the executive agency's needs, such property may be deemed to be available only from the original source and may be procured through procedures other than competitive procedures.

The same provision is contained in 10 U.S.C. § 2304(d)(1)(B) with additional language making it applicable to follow-on contracts for "highly specialized services." The Acts require the agency to determine and document that the cost of the initial capital investment made by the developer of new items cannot be offset by savings that would result from openly competing the item.

The GAO has considered the issue of follow-on contracts in a variety of cases. In *Sprint Communications Co.*, Comp. Gen. Dec. B-262003.2, 96-1 CPD ¶ 24, the agency justified a 15-month "bridge" contract on a sole-source basis to the original contractor to permit the award of several contracts designated to achieve significant economies of scale. In *International Harvester Co.*, 61 Comp. Gen. 388 (B-205073), 82-1 CPD ¶ 459, involving a sole-source award to the company that developed and hand-built four prototypes, the GAO urged the Army to limit its first production run to the minimum number needed to validate a data package and to consider whether competing the remainder of its requirements would result in savings despite the initial tooling cost incurred by the incumbent contractor. See also *Univox Cal., Inc.*, Comp. Gen. Dec. B-225449.2, 87-2 CPD ¶ 569, where the GAO permitted the limitation of competition to the two contractors that had developed competitive prototypes, but recommended that the agency quickly obtain technical data packages so that quantities in future years could be fully competed. Compare *Berkey Mktg. Cos.*, Comp. Gen. Dec. B-224481, 86-2 CPD ¶ 596, where the agency was permitted to continue buying "the only commercially available item within an acceptable price range that would meet the [agency's] minimum requirements"; and *SEAVAC Int'l, Inc.*, Comp. Gen. Dec. B-231016, 88-2 CPD ¶ 134, where urgency justified the agency's continuing to buy services from the incumbent contractor. See also *Magnavox Elec. Sys. Co.*, Comp. Gen. Dec. B-258076.2, 94-2 CPD ¶ 266, finding that a sole-source award on a follow-on contract was permissible because award to any other source would cause unacceptable delays. The GAO noted that another basis for awarding sole source to a follow-on contractor would be if the award to any other source would result in substantial duplication of cost that would not be expected to be recovered through competition. Because the decision was based on unreasonable delay, the GAO did not address the question of duplication of costs. In *Nomura Enter., Inc.*, Comp. Gen. Dec. B-260977.2, 95-2 CPD ¶ 206, the GAO found a sole-source award on a follow-on contract reasonable on the basis that unacceptable delays would occur if award was made to another source prior to the completion of current production due to massive amount of materials and equipment that would have to be transferred to the new contractor.

Mere prior experience of a contractor has been found to be insufficient grounds to support a sole-source procurement. In *Electronic Sys., U.S.A.*, Inc., Comp. Gen. Dec. B-200947, 81-1 CPD ¶ 309, the GAO stated:

> A company's prior experience with the procuring agency which may facilitate the company's performance of the required services and enable it to better anticipate problems in the implementation of the system is not a legally adequate justification to support a sole-source procurement. Furthermore, the fact that a particular contractor may be able to perform the services with greater ease than any other contractor does not justify a noncompetitive procurement to the exclusion of others.

In another decision a sole-source procurement of repairs to an oil distribution system was improper when justified on the basis that the selected contractor had installed the original system and had previously made repairs to it, *Titan Atl. Constr. Corp.*, Comp. Gen. Dec. B-200986, 81-2 CPD ¶ 12. See also *Metropolitan Radiology Assocs.*, Comp. Gen. Dec. B-195559, 80-1 CPD ¶ 265, ruling that a sole-source procurement was not justified on the basis of a long-standing relationship with a single contractor.

Justifications for award of sole-source procurements to the prior contractor have been most successfully challenged by the submission of proof that the competitor is equally capable of performing the work. For example, in *CK Techs., Inc.*, Comp. Gen. Dec. B-254271.2, 93-2 CPD ¶ 20, the GAO determined that the protester was capable of supplying the desired product, and the sole-source procurement was therefore improper. Similarly, sole source procurement was found improper in *Federal Data Corp.*, Comp. Gen. Dec. B-196221, 80-1 CPD ¶ 167, where, after the agency's publication of intent to procure on a sole-source basis, the agency received alternative responses indicating the likelihood that other concerns could meet the government's needs. In *Aerospace Research Assocs.*, Comp. Gen. Dec. B-201953, 81-2 CPD ¶ 36, a sole-source procurement for armored helicopter seats was improper because the agency was aware of two other contractors that could possibly "satisfy the Government's minimum needs without undue technical risk . . . within the required time" yet failed to contact them about the solicitation. See also *Consolidated Elevator Co.*, 56 Comp. Gen. 434 (B-187624), 77-1 CPD ¶ 210, where sole-source awards for elevator maintenance to the manufacturers of the respective elevators were found to be improper because evidence showed that companies other than the manufacturers could meet the government's maintenance needs. Similarly, in *Berkshire Computer Prods.*, Comp. Gen. Dec. B-240327, 91-1 CPD ¶ 464, sole-source awards to the original computer system contractor were found improper because the protester sold compatible equipment and software.

(2) Unusual and Compelling Circumstances

The second exception in 41 U.S.C. § 253(c) and 10 U.S.C. § 2304(c) states:

> (2) the agency's need for the property or services is of such an unusual and compelling urgency that the United States would be seriously injured unless the agency is permitted to limit the number of sources from which it solicits bids or proposals; This exception permits a procurement without full and open competition based on unusual and compelling urgency. This exception is narrowly construed because the acquisition planning process is intended to overcome all but the most compelling urgency situations. 10 U.S.C. § 2304(f)(5) and 41 U.S.C. § 253(f)(5) state that agencies may not enter into a contract for property or services using procedures other than competitive procedures on the basis of the lack of advance planning or concerns related to the amount of funds available to the agency for procurement functions.

Urgency has generally been found in circumstances where the agency has made reasonable efforts to obtain competition but has been unable to accomplish this goal because of insufficient time to fulfill critical agency requirements. For example, the need to continue weapon tests vital to the national security has met the urgency requirement, *Support Sys. Assocs.*, Comp. Gen. Dec. B-232473, 89-1 CPD ¶ 11. Urgency was also found to exist in *Greenbrier Indus., Inc.*, Comp. Gen. Dec. B-241304, 91-1 CPD ¶ 92, where the Marine Corps reasonably determined that only one company was capable of immediately supplying chemical protective suits for use in Operation Desert Shield; and *E. Huttenbauer & Son, Inc.*, Comp. Gen. Dec. B-252320.2, 93-1 CPD ¶ 499, where the agency reasonably determined that only one known firm was capable of meeting urgent supply requirement caused by Operation Restore Hope in Somalia. In *Alektronics, Inc.*, Comp. Gen. Dec. B-261431, 95-2 CPD ¶ 146, the GAO found reasonable a sole-source award of a critical military item where there was an inventory shortage and the awardee was the only approved source. Similarly, in *Gentex Corp.*, Comp. Gen. Dec. B-233119, 89-1 CPD ¶ 144, the GAO agreed that the agency was justified in refusing to consider an untested competitive product in a weapons program; and in *Forster Enters., Inc.*, Comp. Gen. Dec. B-237910, 90-1 CPD ¶ 363, the GAO permitted a sole-source contract to the only company with a qualified product for an unforeseen quantity of essential military items needed during the period the protester was qualifying its product under a new contract. See also the following decisions finding that urgency justified other than full and open competition: *T-L-C Sys.*, Comp. Gen. Dec. B-400369, 2008 CPD ¶ 195 (sole-source award on urgency reasonable where immediate replacement of failed fire alarms was necessary to prevent potential loss of life or property due to fire); *Eclypse Int'l Corp.*, Comp. Gen. Dec. B-274507, 96-2 CPD ¶ 179 (sole-source award to only approved source reasonable for urgently required deployable circuit analyzers); *BlueStar Battery Sys. Corp.*, Comp. Gen. Dec. B-270111.2, 96-1 CPD ¶ 67 (procurement restricted to two manufacturers that had supplied batteries to the Army under previous contracts); *All Points Int'l, Inc.*, Comp. Gen. Dec. B-260134, 95-1 CPD ¶ 252 (only one contractor was capable of meeting requirement relating to the growing Cuban and Haitian refugee population at the U.S. Naval Facility); *Purdy Corp.*, Comp. Gen. Dec. B-257432, 94-2 CPD ¶ 127 (no other source possessed or could reasonably access test stand that was needed quickly for examining discovered gearbox problem); *Logics, Inc.*, Comp. Gen. Dec. B-256171, 94-1 CPD ¶ 314 (agency solicited only known sources that had successfully manufactured filter assemblies because the agency encountered a critical supply shortage); *Sargent & Greenleaf, Inc.*, Comp. Gen. Dec. B-255604.3, 94-1 CPD ¶ 208 (sole-source award to only qualified firm for limited quantities of security containers because existing mechanical locks placed classified information at risk); *Braswell Servs. Group, Inc.*, Comp. Gen. Dec. B-245507, 92-1 CPD ¶ 72 (ship repair was urgent and critical to ship operations, and the ship's limited availability did not permit resolicitation on either a competitive basis or the basis of a limited competition); *Rotair Indus.*, Comp. Gen. Dec. B-239503, 90-2 CPD ¶ 154 (competition limited to two sources with qualified products when the protester had not completed the qualification of its product and the agency could wait no longer); *Astron*, Comp. Gen. Dec. B-236922.2, 90-1 CPD ¶ 441 (sole source justified because there was insufficient time to test another nondevelopmental item); and *Racal Corp.*, Comp. Gen. Dec. B-235441, 89-2 CPD ¶ 213 (contract awarded to the only contractor that could proceed without first-article testing because the agency had concluded that the risk of failure by another contractor was too great).

A finding of urgency has also been justified where the contractor currently performing the work provided an additional quantity while competition was being conducted for future requirements. In *Sun Dial & Panel Corp.*, Comp. Gen. Dec. B-277660, 97-2 CPD ¶ 146, the GAO stated that it was reasonable for the agency to make a sole-source award for a relatively small quantity of items on the basis of urgency until the agency could make an award for a larger quantity pursuant to a competitive procurement. See also *Datacom, Inc.*, Comp. Gen. Dec. B-274175, 96-2 CPD ¶ 199 (agency purchased limited number of items to meet its needs until it could complete its competitive buy); *Polar Power, Inc.*, Comp. Gen. Dec. B-270536, 96-1 CPD ¶ 157 (purchased limited quantity on sole-source basis with balance of requirement to be purchased under competitive procedures); *Elbit Computers, Ltd.*, Comp. Gen. Dec. B-239038, 90-2 CPD ¶ 26 (agency planned to purchase initial quantity on sole-source basis and then purchase additional quantities on a competitive basis using reprocurement data); and *Abbott Prods., Inc.*, Comp. Gen. Dec. B-231131, 88-2 CPD ¶ 119 (no option or variation in quantity was included in sole-source award, and future requirements would be selected competitively). However, urgency will not be justified on this basis if the urgency was brought about by poor planning. See *New Breed Leasing Corp.*, Comp. Gen. Dec. B-274201, 96-2 CPD ¶ 202 (sole-source extension of incumbent's contract was created by agency's failure to engage in advance planning); *TLC Servs., Inc.*, Comp. Gen. Dec. B-252614, 93-1 CPD ¶ 481 (urgency on which noncompetitive contract award was based was the result of lack of advance planning). An agency justification under this exception does not support the procurement of more than a minimum quantity needed to satisfy the urgent requirement and should not continue for more than a minimum time. See the next section on limitations on the use of other than competitive procedures where the GAO sustained protests on the basis that the agency should have procured only a limited amount of its needs on an urgency or sole-source basis, pending the development of competition.

A finding of urgency may be justified while an award protest is being decided. See *J&J Columbia Servs. MV LTDA*, Comp. Gen. Dec. B-299595.2, 2007 CPD ¶ 126, and *Unified Indus., Inc.*, 70 Comp. Gen. 142 (B-241010), 91-1 CPD ¶ 11, where, in both cases, the GAO found reasonable an agency's sole-source award of interim contracts. See also *Computers Universal, Inc.*, Comp. Gen. Dec. B-296536, 2005 CPD ¶ 160 (extension of sole-source task order reasonable pending protest).

Although the statute does not indicate what type of serious injury must result to justify limiting competition, the GAO has included possible financial injury within the scope of the term, *Arthur Young & Co.*, Comp. Gen. Dec. B-221879, 86-1 CPD ¶ 536. In that case the Navy was permitted to make a sole-source award because it claimed that the incumbent was the only firm that could perform a management study in time and that the study was necessary to achieve an estimated $1.5 billion savings. Serious injury was also found in a potential failure of the agency's telephone system, *AT&T Info. Servs., Inc.*, 66 Comp. Gen. 58 (B-223914), 86-2 CPD ¶ 447, and potential poor operation of the agency's computer facility, *Data Transformation Corp.*, Comp. Gen. Dec. B-220581, 86-1 CPD ¶ 55.

(3) INDUSTRIAL MOBILIZATION, ESSENTIAL CAPABILITY AND EXPERTS AND NEUTRALS

The third exception in 41 U.S.C. § 253(c) and 10 U.S.C. § 2304(c) states:

(3) it is necessary to award the contract to a particular source or sources in order (A) to maintain a facility, producer, manufacturer, or other supplier available for furnishing property or services in case of a national emergency or to achieve industrial mobilization, (B) to establish or maintain an essential engineering, research, or development capability to be provided by an educational or other nonprofit institution or a federally funded research and development center, or (C) to procure the services of an expert for use, in any litigation or dispute (including any reasonably foreseeable litigation or dispute) involving the Federal Government, in any trial, hearing, or proceeding before any court, administrative tribunal, or agency, or to procure the services of an expert or neutral for use in any part of an alternative dispute resolution process, whether or not the expert is expected to testify;

This exception deals with three dissimilar situations — maintaining a facility for industrial mobilization, establishing or maintaining critical engineering, research, or development capability provided by an educational or other nonprofit organization or federally funded research and development center, or procuring the services of an expert or neutral in a dispute.

With regard to the industrial mobilization element of this exception, an agency's decision will not be questioned as long as it can demonstrate that its determinations are related to its mobilization needs, *Outdoor Venture Corp.*, Comp. Gen. Dec. B-279777, 98-2 CPD ¶ 27; *Minowitz Mfg. Co.*, Comp. Gen. Dec. B-228502, 88-1 CPD ¶ 1. See *Honorable Dan Burton*, Comp. Gen. Dec. B-265884, Nov. 7, 1995, *Unpub.*, for a full explanation of this policy. See also *Ridgeline Indus., Inc.*, Comp. Gen. Dec. B-402105, 2010 CPD ¶ 22 (minimum sustaining rate sole source contract was necessary for the firm to continue operating its military specification tent production line); *Right Away Foods/Shelf Stable Foods*, Comp. Gen. Dec. B-259859.3, 95-2 CPD ¶ 34 (award to third mobilization base producer proper where agency reasonably determined that the failure of either of the current producers would be catastrophic in the event of a military emergency); *Kilgore Corp.*, Comp. Gen. Dec. B-253672, 93-2 CPD ¶ 220 (sole-source award to operate and maintain an ammunition plant based on mobilization need); *Lance Ordnance Co.*, Comp. Gen. Dec. B-246849, 92-2 CPD ¶ 29 (sole-source award made to one of two mobilization base producers for smoke and illumination signals); *Greenbrier Indus., Inc.*, Comp. Gen. Dec. B-248177, 92-2 CPD ¶ 74 (agency divided its requirements for chemical suits among four active mobilization base producers to provide a continuation of each firm's minimum sustaining rate of production); and *Propper Int'l, Inc.*, Comp. Gen. Dec. B-229888, 88-1 CPD ¶ 296 (Navy hat considered an essential part of the enlisted person's uniform and designated industrial mobilization item).

The second part of this exception is used primarily to award contracts to Federally Funded Research and Development Centers (FFRDCs), which were established under the authority of OFPP Policy Letter 84-1, 49 Fed. Reg. 14,462 (1984) (now rescinded), to "perform analyze, support and manage research and development activities of an agency." The provisions of Policy Letter 84-1 were implemented in FAR 35.017. See *SRI Int'l*, 69 Comp. Gen. 334 (B-237779), 90-1 CPD ¶ 318; 71 Comp. Gen. 155 (B-244564) (1992). These nonprofit organizations work in designated areas under "sponsoring agreements" in accordance with procedures set forth in FAR 35.017. Contracts must be awarded to FFRDCs within the scope of their designated areas on a sole-source basis because they are prohibited from competing with non-FFRDCs, FAR 35.017-1(c)(4). For cases holding that this non-competition requirement bars FFRDCs from acting as subcontractors, see *Logicon RDA*, Comp. Gen. Dec. B-276240, 97-1 CPD ¶ 219, and *Energy Compression Research Corp.*, Comp. Gen. Dec. B-243650.2, 91-2 CPD ¶ 466.

The third part of this exception was added by the FASA in 1994, with no statutory definition of the term "expert." However, in *SEMCOR, Inc.*, Comp. Gen. Dec. B-279794, 98-2 CPD ¶ 43, the GAO held that the term did not encompass the providing of litigation services which were performed, in major part, by paralegals, secretaries, editors and clerical personnel. This holding was based on the fact that, while these personnel had gained considerable experience from working on the major litigation for which the services were required, they did not have the "special skill or knowledge of a particular subject, combined with experience" which was required to establish that a person was an expert.

(4) Terms of International Agreement or Treaty

This exception in 41 U.S.C. § 253(c) and 10 U.S.C. § 2304(c) states:

> the terms of an international agreement or a treaty between the United States and a foreign government or international organization, or the written directions of a foreign government reimbursing the agency for the cost of the procurement of the property or services for such government, have the effect of requiring the use of procedures other than competitive procedures;

Terms of an international agreement or treaty may have the effect of requiring the use of other than competitive procedures. There is no requirement that the foreign government initiate a sole source designation. In the absence of bad faith or an intention to circumvent competition, it is immaterial whether a United States agency recommends specific items or advises a foreign government as to what items might satisfy its needs. See *Goddard Indus., Inc.*, Comp. Gen. Dec. B-275643, 97-1 CPD ¶ 104, finding proper a sole-source procurement that involved a foreign military sale and the foreign government on whose behalf the procurement was conducted requested purchase from a specified source. Similarly, in *Pilkington Aerospace, Inc.*, Comp. Gen. Dec. B-259173, 95-1 CPD ¶ 180, the GAO found proper a sole-source award of advanced design windshields for the F-15 aircraft because the procurement involved a foreign military sale and the foreign government on whose behalf the procurement was conducted requested that the item be manufactured by a specified source. See also *Optic-Electronic Corp.*, Comp. Gen. Dec. B-235885, 89-2 CPD ¶ 326 (sole-source award issued by the United States Army on behalf of the Egyptian government for laser range finders and ballistic computer systems proper); and *Kahn Indus., Inc.*, Comp. Gen. Dec. B-225491, 87-1 CPD ¶ 343 (sole-source awards for dynameters on behalf of the Republic of the Philippines and the Arab Republic of Egypt proper).

(5) AUTHORIZED BY ANOTHER STATUTE

This exception in 41 U.S.C. § 253(c) and 10 U.S.C. § 2304(c) states:

> (5) subject to subsection (j), a statute expressly authorizes or requires that the procurement be made through another executive agency or from a specified source, or the agency's need is for a brand-name commercial item for authorized resale;

The use of other than competitive procedures is permitted when a statute expressly authorizes or requires that a procurement be made through another agency or from a specified source. Sole source awards under the 8(a) set-aside procedure are usually justified under this exception. See *Bosco Contracting Inc.*, Comp. Gen. Dec. B-236969, 89-2 CPD ¶ 346, holding that the CICA's mandate for full and open competition does not apply to a procurement being conducted as an 8(a) set-aside under 15 U.S.C. § 637(a).

This exception also authorizes the use of other than competitive procedures when "the agency's need is for a brand-name commercial item for authorized resale." See *Defense Commissary — Request for Advance Decision*, Comp. Gen. Dec. B-262047, 96-1 CPD ¶ 115, holding that the Defense Commissary Agency could noncompetitively procure items bearing the USO Always Home brand name for resale in military stores.

Economy Act orders do not fall under this exception. The Economy Act generally permits agencies to procure services under another agency's contract without full and open competition only where that contract was awarded in compliance with CICA. See 10 U.S.C. § 2304(f)(5). In *Valenzuela Eng'g, Inc.*, Comp. Gen. Dec. B-277979, 98-1 CPD ¶ 51, although the protest was dismissed as untimely, the GAO stated by letter to the Secretary of Air Force that its review indicated that the contract violated CICA. Here, the Air Force attempted to satisfy its requirements for operation and maintenance services pursuant to the Economy Act by placing an order under an existing indefinite-delivery, indefinite-quantity contract (IDIQ) that had been awarded by the Army. However, the GAO found that this contract did not comply with the CICA requirement for full and open competition because the work statement did not reasonably describe the scope of the services needed and therefore did not provide potential offerors notice of work that would be within the scope of the resulting contract. The GAO stated that because an agency may not procure property or services from another agency unless that other agency has complied fully with the requirements of CICA, the Air Force acted improperly in using the Army contract.

(6) NATIONAL SECURITY

This exception in 41 U.S.C. § 253(c) and 10 U.S.C. § 2304(c) states:

(6) the disclosure of the agency's needs would compromise the national security unless the agency is permitted to limit the number of sources from which it solicits bids or proposals;

An agency may limit the number of sources from which it solicits offers if the disclosure of the agency's needs would compromise the national security. There are no protests on the use of this exception.

(7) PUBLIC INTEREST

This exception in 41 U.S.C. § 253(c) and 10 U.S.C. § 2304(c) states:

(7) the head of the agency —

(A) determines that it is necessary in the public interest to use procedures other than competitive procedures in the particular procurement concerned, and

(B) notifies the Congress in writing of such determination not less than 30 days before the award of the contract.

This exception enables the head of the agency to make a determination that it is necessary to the public interest to use other than competitive procedures in a particular procurement. See *Zublin Del., Inc.*, Comp. Gen. Dec. B-227003.2, 87-2 CPD ¶ 149, denying a protest that the Navy, after submission of initial offers, unreasonably restricted competition to United States firms for construction of Navy housing in the Philippines. The GAO held that the Secretary of the Navy, under 10 U.S.C. § 2304(c)(7), made the required determination that such a restriction was in the public interest because hiring foreign firms could jeopardize United States bases in the Philippines. See also *Spherix, Inc. v. United States*, 58 Fed. Cl. 514 (2004), holding the agency head properly exercised her statutory authority to award a sole source modification under 41 U.S.C. § 253(c)(7). The court found reasonable the D&F, which stated it is in the public interest to integrate agency recreation reservation requirements to provide a more comprehensive system with one-stop service. This decision followed an earlier case, *Spherix, Inc. v. United States*, 58 Fed. Cl. 351 (2003), addressing the court's jurisdiction under the public interest exception.

c. Limitations on Use of Other Than Competitive Procedures

Although a procurement may be conducted under other than competitive procedures, there are limitations on its use.

(1) COMPETITION REQUIRED WHERE PRACTICABLE

Justification for the use of other than competitive procedures on the basis of any exception other than (c)(1) does not necessarily permit the use of sole source contracting. Competition is required from as many potential sources as is practicable. See 41 U.S.C. § 253(e) and 10 U.S.C. § 2304(e), which state this rule for two of the exceptions:

> An executive agency using procedures other than competitive procedures to procure property or services by reason of the application of subsection (c)(2) or (c)(6) shall request offers from as many potential sources as is practicable under the circumstances.

The FAR is broader by not limiting the requirement to solicit from as many sources as is practicable to only (c)(2) and (c)(6). FAR 6.301(d) is applicable to (c)(3), (c)(4), (c)(5), and (c)(7) as well. It provides:

> When not providing for full and open competition, the contracting officer shall solicit offers from as many potential sources as is practicable under the circumstances.

Thus, procurements under all subsections except (c)(1) should be conducted with some degree of competition when circumstances permit.

Protests in this area have primarily been under subsection (c)(2). For instance, the GAO has held that even though urgency permitted a procurement without full and open competition, the agency violated the statute by awarding a sole-source contract, *TMS Bldg. Maint.*, 65 Comp. Gen. 222 (B-220588), 86-1 CPD ¶ 68; *Data Based Decisions, Inc.*, Comp. Gen. Dec. B-232663, 89-1 CPD ¶ 87. In *Major Contracting Servs., Inc.*, Comp. Gen. Dec. B-401472, 2009 CPD ¶ 170, while the GAO agreed with the agency that the circumstances met the requirement for an exception to full and open competition based on urgency, it held that the agency should have conducted a limited competition rather than extending the contract on a sole-source basis. Here the results of the market survey identified potential qualified sources and the requirement for portable chemical restrooms had been procured by contract for at least ten years, providing the agency full familiarity with the potential sources. The GAO has also held that an agency violated the statute where it had conducted the procurement so inefficiently that a competitor did not have time to compete for the entire quantity, *Arrow Gear Co.*, 68 Comp. Gen. 612 (B-235081), 89-2 CPD ¶ 135. See also *Bausch & Lomb, Inc.*, Comp. Gen. Dec. B-298444, 2006 CPD ¶ 135 (protest sustained because agency never considered the capabilities of the equipment of other interested firms); *AT&T Info. Servs., Inc.*, 66 Comp. Gen. 58 (B-223914), 86-2 CPD ¶ 447 (protest sustained when the agency could have conducted fast negotiations with another known source of the work); *Charles Snyder*, 68 Comp. Gen. 659 (B-235409), 89-2 CPD ¶ 208 (protest sustained where agency could have solicited nonlocal company that had previously expressed interest in procurement); *Ferranti Int'l Defense Sys., Inc.*, Comp. Gen. Dec. B-237760, 90-1 CPD ¶ 317 (protest sustained where agency could have negotiated with a third source that had expressed interest and had prior experience, without significantly delaying the ongoing procurement). In *Earth Property Servs., Inc.*, Comp. Gen. Dec. B-237742, 90-1 CPD ¶ 273, the agency was prohibited from soliciting only one source in an urgent procurement where a second offeror, that had previously done similar work for the agency, was available to perform on short notice. See also *Bay Cities Servs., Inc.*, Comp. Gen. Dec. B-239880, 90-2 CPD ¶ 271, holding that the incumbent contractor's refusal to provide cost data did not justify failing to solicit a proposal for an urgent procurement of additional effort for four months (two other proposals had been solicited).

Although an agency is required to seek competition from as many potential sources as is practicable, competition may be limited to one firm when it is justified, *Braswell Servs. Group, Inc.*, 92-1 CPD ¶ 72; *L-3 Communications Eotech, Inc. v. United States*, 85 Fed. Cl. 667 (2009) (government's decision to require type-classified close combat optics, which only the incumbent awardee could provide, was not meritless, but needed to help assure the weaponry was acceptable, safe, suitable, and supportable, pursuant to Army Regulation 700-142). In *Reliance Mach. Works, Inc.*, Comp. Gen. Dec. B-220640, 85-2 CPD ¶ 685, the GAO stated that where an agency conducts a limited competition in an emergency, the fact that an offeror was not one of two firms solicited will not be grounds for a protest. An agency conducting a procurement under the urgency exception may limit competition to the only firm it reasonably believes can perform the work promptly and properly, *Total Industry & Packaging Corp.*, Comp. Gen. Dec. B-295434, 2005 CPD ¶ 38; *McGregor Mfg. Corp.*, Comp. Gen. Dec. B-285341, 2000 CPD ¶ 151; *IMR Sys. Corp.*, Comp. Gen. Dec. B-222465, 86-2 CPD ¶ 36; *Arthur Young & Co.*, Comp. Gen. Dec. B-221879, 86-1 CPD ¶ 537; *Gentex Corp.*, Comp. Gen. Dec. B-221340, 86-1 CPD ¶ 195. In *Research Analysis & Maint., Inc.*, Comp. Gen. Dec. B-296206, 2005 CPD ¶ 182, the GAO denied a protest by the incumbent contractor that the agency improperly failed to consider it as a potential source for a bridge contract, finding that the agency had reasonably determined that the incumbent's performance under the contract was unacceptable and that its plan to correct the unacceptable performance had been inadequate.

(2) Procurement Pending Development of Competition

If the agency finds in the acquisition planning process that it has missed the opportunity for full and open competition because of faulty actions, it may be permitted to limit competition for a period of time while it establishes the conditions for full and open competition in the future. In several instances the agency's justification of single source or urgency has been provisionally accepted, but the GAO has limited the scope of the procurement to that period of work necessary to establish the conditions for full and open competition. For example, agencies have been required to sever procurements in order to minimize the amount of work that is not subject to full and open competition, *ABA Indus., Inc.*, Comp. Gen. Dec. B-250186, 93-1 CPD ¶ 38 (procurement limited to quantity urgently required; contract modified to delete the non-urgent units, and this quantity was to be resolicited); *Tri-Ex Tower Corp.*, Comp. Gen. Dec. B-239628, 90-2 CPD ¶ 221 (urgent sole-source procurement limited to portion of work); *Ricoh Corp.*, 68 Comp. Gen. 531 (B-234655), 89-2 CPD ¶ 3 (agency should procure only immediate needs on sole-source basis when other companies are developing capability to meet agency needs); *Freedom Marine*, Comp. Gen. Dec. B-229809, 88-1 CPD ¶ 289 (agency should have obtained competition for at least half of its quantity where there was adequate time to do so if the procurement had commenced at the time the sole source J&A was prepared). In *Arrow Gear Co.*, 68 Comp. Gen. 612 (B-235081), 89-2 CPD ¶ 135, the GAO recommended that the agency use the existing source for the minimum quantity needed to fulfill its needs while recompeting the requirement as to the quantity not urgently needed. The GAO held this was necessary because of the agency's dilatory conduct of the procurement. In *Signals & Sys., Inc.*, Comp. Gen. Dec. B-288107, 2001 CPD ¶ 168, while the J&A supported a tangible urgency requirement, the GAO sustained the protest because that the Army had not made a reasonable effort to ascertain the minimum quantity necessary to satisfy its immediate urgent requirement. The GAO recommended that the agency promptly undertake a review to determine the number of units needed to satisfy its immediate urgent requirement, as documented in its justification, and not acquire more than that number. In *Filtration Dev. Co., LLC v. United States*, 60 Fed. Cl. 371 (2004), the court held that the Army was justified in using the unusual and compelling urgency exception, but only for the exact number of kits required for helicopters deploying to Iraq in the immediate future. The court was "unwilling to condone an indefinite extension of the unusual and compelling urgency exception." The Army used the same reasoning, after the first protest had been decided, to sole source an additional two hundred inlet kits. See *Filtration Dev. Co., LLC v. United States*, 63 Fed. Cl. 418 (2004). While the court had previously limited the scope of the previous J&A document to the specific number of kits needed, the court did not prevent the use of another J&A that detailed the urgent and compelling rationale for more kits based upon a separate and independent justification. The J&A addressed the increased need and the depletion of the kits previously bought under the last exception.

The length of time of contracts awarded under the unusual and compelling urgency exception to full and open competition is now limited pursuant to § 862 of the Duncan Hunter National Defense Authorization Act for Fiscal Year 2009, Pub. L. No. 110-417, and an Office of Federal Procurement Policy Administrator's Memorandum (May 31, 2007), which sought to enhance competition in federal acquisitions. The rule at FAR 6.302-2(d) applies to contracts that exceed the simplified acquisition threshold and provides that the total period of performance for such contracts awarded pursuant to the exception cannot exceed the time necessary —

(A) To meet the unusual and compelling requirements of the work to be performed under the contract; and

(B) For the agency to enter into another contract for the required goods and services through the use of competitive procedures.

The total period of performance cannot exceed one year unless the head of the agency determines that "exceptional circumstances" apply, FAR 6.3022(d)(2). The determination of "exceptional circumstances" is in addition to the "justification and approval" required to invoke the unusual and compelling urgency exception, FAR 6.302-2(d)(4).

(3) Ordering Work Under Existing Contracts

Agencies often attempt to order work under existing contracts. Some contract clauses (changes and options) and contract types (indefinite delivery contracts calling for task and delivery orders) specifically provide the mechanism for such actions. In some cases the agency is authorized but not required to order additional work without competing the work or justifying a noncompetitive award. In other cases the work is considered a new procurement and competition or justification must precede the ordering. For changes, the work must be within the general scope, and for task and delivery orders the work must not increase the scope, period or maximum dollar value.

(A) Change Orders

Change orders issued under the various Changes clauses may be made on a sole-source basis if they are within the general scope of the contract. Although the GAO does not review contract administration matters, it will review an allegation that the government action should have been the subject of a new procurement, *Engineering & Professional Servs., Inc.*, Comp. Gen. Dec. B-289331, 2002 CPD ¶ 24; *Atlantic Coast Contracting, Inc.*, Comp. Gen. Dec. B-288969.2, 2002 CPD ¶ 104.

The test in determining whether a modification triggers the competition requirements is whether there is a material difference between the modified contract and the contract that was originally awarded, indicating that the "field of competition" is different than contemplated by the original competitors. See *Engineering & Professional Servs., Inc.*, Comp. Gen. Dec. B-289331, 2002 CPD ¶ 24, stating:

> In determining whether a modification triggers the competition requirements in the Competition in Contracting Act of 1984, 10 U.S.C. § 2304(a)(1)(A) (Supp. IV 1998), we look to whether there is a material difference between the modified contract and the contract that was originally awarded. *Neil R. Gross & Co., Inc.*, [B-237434, Feb. 23, 1990, 90-1 CPD ¶ 212] at 2-3; see *AT&T Communications, Inc. v. Wiltel, Inc.*, 1 F.3d 1201, 1205 (Fed. Cir. 1993).
>
> Evidence of a material difference between the modification and the original contract is found by examining any changes in the type of work, performance period, and costs between the contract as awarded and as modified. *Access Research Corp.*, B-281807, Apr. 5, 1999, 99-1 CPD ¶ 64 at 3-4; *MCI Telecomms. Corp.*, B-276659.2, Sept. 29, 1997, 97-2 CPD ¶ 90 at 7-8. The question for our review is whether the original nature or purpose of the contract is so substantially changed by the modification that the original and modified contract would be essentially different, and the field of competition materially changed. *Everpure, Inc.*, B-226395.4, Oct. 10, 1990, 90-2 CPD ¶ 275 at 4.

The Court of Federal Claims uses essentially the same test. In *Chapman Law Firm Co. v. United States*, 81 Fed. Cl. 323 (2008), the court articulated the test as follows at 326-27:

> In determining whether a modification is outside the scope of the original government contract, the Court applies the "cardinal change doctrine." [*AT & T Communications, Inc. v.*]*Wiltel*, 1 F.3d [1201 (Fed. Cir. 1883)] at 1205 (noting that CICA sets forth no standard for determining when a modification is within the scope of the original contract). "[A] cardinal change . . . occurs when the government effects an alteration in the work so drastic that it effectively requires the contractor to perform duties materially different from those originally bargained for." Id. If the contract as modified materially departs from the scope of the original procurement, then CICA's competition requirements will apply. *See, e.g., CWT/Alexandar Travel, Ltd. v. United States*, 78 Fed. Cl. 486, 494 (2007); *HDM Corp. v. United States*, 69 Fed. Cl. 243, 254 (2005). In its analysis, the Court should look to whether the original offerors were adequately advised of the potential for the types of changes that in fact occurred, and "whether the modification is of a nature which potential offerors would reasonably have anticipated." *Wiltel*, 1 F.3d at 1207 (quoting *Neil R. Gross & Co.*, B-237434, 90-1 CPD ¶ 212 at 3 (February 23, 1990).

The court found that the only changes were the geographic expansion of service and the possibility of new pricing, and that these changes were clearly contemplated in the contracts.

The critical issue in these cases is the determination of whether the original competitors would have foreseen the changes that the agency has ordered. Apparently, the logic is that the original prices would have reflected such changes and therefore that new competition is not needed to ensure that the prices have been established through competition. See, for example, *CWT/Alexander Travel, Ltd. v. United States*, 78 Fed. Cl. 486 (2007), where a issue was whether a delay in the contract start date of more than two years (from an anticipated April 2005 until October 2007) made moot the price data on which the offerors relied. The court found no change outside of the scope because the solicitation did not specify a definite start date for commencement of performance – it only contemplated that the work would begin with a modification some time after award, which is precisely what happened – and the nature of the travel services required under the contract made price changes inevitable. Further, the proposed price modifications were not enough alone or in combination with the start date modifications to establish a change outside of the scope. Similarly in *CESC Plaza Limited Partnership v. United States*, 52 Fed. Cl. 91 (2002), where the protesters argued that the sum of the changes materially altered the contract (rather than the specific changes themselves), the court held that they were foreseeable to the offerors because they did not materially alter the contract's cash flow features or shift the risk of performance. See also *HDM Corp. v. United States*, 69 Fed. Cl. 243 (2005) (modification to a contract for management of medical insurance records not outside the scope because consolidating responsibility for the crossover function was consistent with the broad objectives of the original contract); and *VMC Behavioral Healthcare Servs., Div. of Vasquez Group, Inc. v. United States*, 50 Fed. Cl. 328 (2001) (solicitation was for level of effort contract for employee assistance services, subject to modification as additional agencies were added to the contract's coverage). In contrast in *Cardinal Maint. Serv., Inc. v. United States*, 63 Fed. Cl. 98 (2004), the court found that the addition to, and deletion of, work from the contract materially changed the original competed contract. The changes were not of the type that were specifically authorized or even foreseen in the original contract. Rather, the modifications authorized substantial changes, which the contracting officer identified as "considerable" with costs that were potentially "extremely excessive." The contract had only contemplated "minimal additions and deletions of service" which would be accomplished through application of the Add/Delete of Service Cost Sheet, set forth in Section 1.6 of the solicitation. The modifications to the contract were not, however, made through this provision. Instead, the contracting officer eliminated the limitations by removing the Add/Delete of Service Cost Sheet. See also *CW Gov't Travel v. United States*, 61 Fed. Cl. 559 (2004), *reh'g denied*, 63 Fed. Cl. 459 (2005), *aff'd*, 163 Fed. Appx. 853 (Fed. Cir. 2005), where the court found that the addition, by contract modification, of traditional travel services to a contract to provide military travel services using a paperless automated travel management system was a material change. The original solicitation sought services for the construction of a web-based, wholly electronic travel services platform. When the platform ran into technical difficulties, the government modified the contract to provide traditional travel services. The court held that the new services were so far removed from the original requirements that they should have been independently solicited through full and open competition. See also *CCL, Inc. v. United States*, 39 Fed. Cl. 780 (1997) (modification increasing the number of locations where computer maintenance services were to be performed).

The Court of Federal Claims and GAO will look at the entire solicitation for the original contract to determine whether it adequately advised offerors of the potential for the type of changes found in the modification when making a scope determination. For instance, in *DOR Biodefense, Inc.*, Comp. Gen. Dec. B-296358.3, 2006 CPD ¶ 35, the protesters argued that the contract was improperly modified to require delivery of a bivalent serotype A/B vaccine, a product that was not listed among the optional RFP CLINs. The GAO determined that the type of work under the contract as modified remained substantially unchanged because the RFP advised offerors that the government reserved the right to change the list of vaccine sertoypes to add or delete products as need may arise. Similarly, in *Sallie Mae, Inc.*, Comp. Gen. Dec. B-400486, 2008 CPD ¶ 221, the protester argued that the modification of the contract to encompass the servicing of the non-defaulted FFELP loans was beyond the original scope of the contract. In support of its argument the protester stated that the statement of objectives (SOO) did not describe the servicing of non-defaulted FFELP loans. Moreover, the protester argued that offerors could not possibly have contemplated that the contract would include the servicing of the non-defaulted FFELP loans given that the legislation authorizing the loan purchase program was not enacted until May 2008. The GAO disagreed, determining that the SOO clearly placed offerors on notice that the agency intended to award a contract for the management of all types of student loans. The SOO also specifically instructed that the solution was to be flexible enough to handle new requirements generated by Congress and to respond to legislative mandates and policy changes. See also *Overseas Lease Group, Inc.*, Comp. Gen. Dec. B-402111, 2010 CPD ¶ 34 (contract modification within scope where solicitation's differentiation between "nontactical" and "up-armored" vehicles was sufficient to put protester on notice that term "non-tactical" was intended to refer to unarmored vehicles); *Lasmer Indus., Inc.*, Comp. Gen. Dec. B-400866.2, 2009 CPD ¶ 77 (delivery order for parts was within scope where part was specifically included in the contract, and the contract allowed the agency to order the part under a negotiated delivery schedule); *Armed Forces Hospitality*, Comp. Gen. Dec. B-298978.2, 2009 CPD ¶ 192 (lack of definitiveness in the original SOW provided the Army with additional contractual flexibility and latitude to reduce the number of rooms to be renovated and extend performance); and *HG Properties A, LP*, Comp. Gen. Dec. B-290416, 2002 CPD ¶ 128 (lease modification changing location of site for construction of offered building space remains within the scope of the underlying lease where the property location requirements were only general in nature and scope with wide location boundaries). But see *W.H. Mullins*, Comp. Gen. Dec. B-207200, 83-1 CPD ¶ 158, where a modification of an existing requirements contract was found to be beyond the scope of competition for the original contract because the parties could not have reasonably anticipated such a major change. Similarly, in *Sprint Communications Co.*, Comp. Gen. Dec. B-278407.2, 98-1 CPD ¶ 60, a modification adding transmission services was found to be outside the scope because the initial procurement had stated that such services were not required.

A contract may not be modified by changing or relaxing requirements where the resulting work is fundamentally different from the work anticipated by the original solicitation, *Avtron Mfg., Inc.*, 67 Comp. Gen. 404 (B-229972), 88-1 CPD ¶ 458 (modification to the performance specifications in the purchase description for aircraft generator test stands); and *Lamson Div. of Diebold, Inc.*, Comp. Gen. Dec. B-196029.2, 80-1 CPD ¶ 447 (change order issued almost immediately after contract award substituting a mail delivery system of electric cars on fixed tracks in lieu of the specialized system of stationary trays on moving belts). In *Poly-Pacific Techs., Inc.*, Comp. Gen. Dec. B-296029, 2005 CPD ¶ 105, the original solicitation sought proposals that required offerors to both lease plastic media and recycle in compliance with regulations, and offerors were required to propose technical solutions and pricing for both the lease and recycling components of the work. The GAO stated that an agency may not modify a contract by changing or relaxing requirements where the resulting work is fundamentally different from the work anticipated by the original solicitation. Here, the RFP did not anticipate that the contractor could be relieved of the recycling requirement or that a disposal effort could be ordered in lieu of recycling.

(B) Extensions and Options

Contract extensions, exercise of contract options, and lease renewals can also constitute de facto sole-source procurements. Extensions adding only time to permit the contractor to complete performance of the original work are almost always within the scope of the procurement. However, if the original contract is seen as a procurement of services for a specified period of time, extensions calling for additional time will frequently be held to be de facto sole-source procurements. The GAO has stated that "competition should be sought whenever it appears likely that the Government's position can be improved whether in terms of cost or performance," 51 Comp. Gen. 57 (B-165218) (1971). In *Saltwater Inc. — Recons & Costs*, Comp. Gen. Dec. B-294121.3, 2005 CPD ¶ 33, the GAO sustained a protest regarding a Department of Commerce contract for fisheries observer services because the contract was awarded for a period longer than that upon which the competition was based. Specifically, the award was for a 6-month contract period from July 1, 2004 to December 31, 2004, with an option to extend the contract 1 year, i.e., to December 31, 2005, which Commerce exercised. The extension of the contract beyond June 30, 2005 constituted an improper sole-source action, since it was not supported by a J&A. In *Washington Nat'l Arena Ltd. Partnership*, 65 Comp. Gen. 25 (B-219136), 85-2 CPD ¶ 435, the government issued an amendment retroactively extending a contract that had expired four months earlier. The GAO held that this action constituted an improper de facto sole-source award. In *Memorex Corp.*, 61 Comp. Gen. 42 (B-200722), 81-2 CPD ¶ 334, changing an "option to purchase" or a "lease-to-ownership" plan envisioning a five-year lease period was held to be outside the scope of the procurement. See also *Intermem Corp.*, Comp. Gen. Dec. B-187607, 77-1 CPD ¶ 263, where a mandatory requirements contract was modified twice to extend its expiration date. The agency issued a D&F (a written approval by an authorized official clearly justifying the specific determination made), concluding that the extensions were in the best interests of the government because a lapse would disrupt a government-wide mandatory source of equipment and services and user agencies would lose accumulated purchase credits. The GAO found that the extensions not justified became they necessary only because the agency failed to timely solicit a follow-on contract. In *Federal Data Corp.*, Comp. Gen. Dec. B-196221, 80-1 CPD ¶ 167, a short renewal of an ADPE lease pending replacement with government-owned equipment constituted an unjustified sole-source procurement where responses to a CBD notice evinced competitive interests in a solicitation. See also *Techno-Sciences, Inc.*, Comp. Gen. Dec. B-257686, 94-2 CPD ¶ 164, finding that the agency had improperly extended a contract on a sole-source basis, stating that other responsible sources could have competed for the requirement had the agency engaged in adequate advance procurement planning to allow a phase-in period for a new contractor.

Before an agency can exercise an option without competition or justification, "the option must have been evaluated as part of the initial competition," FAR 17.207(f). See also FAR 6.001, which contains the following statement of applicability of the competition requirements:

> This part applies to all acquisitions except —
>
> * * *
>
> (c) Contract modifications, including the exercise of priced options that were evaluated as part of the initial competition (see 17.207(f)), that are within the scope and under the terms of an existing contract.

Thus, the competition requirement does not apply to evaluated options because they are part of the original competition. However, FAR 17.207(d) requires some analysis of the reasonableness of the price before exercising options, *Banknote Corp. of Am.*, Comp. Gen. Dec. B-250151, 92-2 CPD ¶ 413 (improper to rely on original bid prices, especially when quantities were increasing); *AAA Eng'g & Drafting, Inc.*, Comp. Gen. Dec. B-236034.2, 92-1 CPD ¶ 307 (current market price must be checked to ensure that option price is reasonable). The GAO has been quite lenient in enforcing this requirement. See *Sippican, Inc.*, Comp. Gen. Dec. B-257047.2, 95-2 CPD ¶ 220, where the protester, a firm that had lost the competition, had informed the agency that it could offer the option quantities at lower prices because it had reduced its costs. The GAO held that the contracting officer had properly exercised his discretion in failing to conduct a competition for the option quantity, stating:

> As a general rule, option provisions in a contract are exercisable at the discretion of the government. See Far 17.201. An informal analysis of prices or an examination

of the market which indicates "that the option price is better than prices available in the market or that the option is the more advantageous offer" is one of three methods specifically set forth in FAR 17.207(d) as a basis for determining whether to exercise an option. *Person-System Integration, Ltd.*, B-246142; B-246142.2, Feb. 19, 1992, 92-1 CPD ¶ 204. The form of such examination is largely within the discretion of the contracting officer, so long as it is reasonable. See *Kollsman Instrument Co.*, 68 Comp. Gen. 303 (1989), 89-1 CPD ¶ 243; *Action Mfg. Co.*, 66 Comp. Gen. 463 (1987), 87-1 CPD ¶ 518. The FAR also permits a determination that the option price is the most advantageous based upon a finding that the time between contract award and option exercise is short enough and the market stable enough that the option price remains most advantageous. FAR 17.207(d).

Our Office will not question an agency's exercise of an option under an existing contract unless the protester shows that the agency failed to follow applicable regulations or that the determination to exercise the option, rather than conduct a new procurement, was unreasonable. *Tycho Technology, Inc.*, B-222413.2, May 25, 1990, 90-1 CPD ¶ 500. The intent of the regulations is not to afford a firm that offered high prices under an original solicitation an opportunity to remedy this business judgment by undercutting the option price of the successful offeror. *Person-System Integration, Ltd., supra.* We find no basis to question the agency's determination to exercise the option.

Similarly in *Antmarin, Inc.*, Comp. Gen. Dec. B-296317, 2005 CPD ¶ 149, the protester challenged the Navy's price analysis arguing that it was unreasonable to compare prices with those of the original competition because these prices were no longer valid due to the passage of time and changes in the market conditions. In finding that the Navy reasonably determined that exercising the option was reasonable the GAO stated:

The Navy did compare MLS's prices with those of the original competition and reasonably focused on the fact that MLS's price was approximately 43 percent lower than the other offerors' (a significant difference), and that MLS's escalation for its option year pricing was in line with the increases of the other offerors (demonstrating that MLS's did not offer overly inflated option year pricing in the original competition). Contrary to the protesters' suggestions, the Navy did not rely exclusively on a comparison of the prices from the original competition.

See also *Alice Roofing & Sheet Metal Works, Inc.*, Comp. Gen. Dec. B-283153, 99-2 CPD ¶ 70, holding that the agency's use of consumer price index to analyze the rate of increase of option pricing for roofing services was not unreasonable. The GAO determined that there was no reason to suspect that roofing prices had either declined or increased at lower rate than prices generally, and the protester did not furnish any evidence demonstrating that roofing prices were substantially different from those of the option prices. The same result was reached in *Bulova Techs., Inc.*, Comp. Gen. Dec. B-252660, 93-2 CPD ¶ 23, and *Valentec Wells, Inc.*, Comp. Gen. Dec. B-239499, 90-2 CPD ¶ 177.

In contrast, if an option was not evaluated under the initial competition, FAR 17.207(f) prevents its exercise absent competition or an appropriate justification and authorization that full and open competition is not required, *Major Contracting Servs.*, Comp. Gen. Dec. B-401472, 2009 CPD ¶ 170, *recons. denied*, 2009 CPD ¶ 250; *Stoehner Sec. Servs., Inc.*, Comp. Gen. Dec. B-248077.3, 92-2 CPD ¶ 285; *Kollsman Instrument Co.*, Comp. Gen. Dec. B-233759, 89-1 CPD ¶ 243.

(C) TASK AND DELIVERY ORDERS

Task (services) and delivery (supplies) order contracts are contracts that do not specify a firm quantity, 10 U.S.C. § 2304d(1) and (2) and 41 U.S.C. § 253k(1) and (2). FAR Subpart 16.5 provides that task or delivery order contracts may take the form of requirements contracts or indefinite-quantity contracts and that there is a preference for multiple-award contracts.

Procurement notices and the other requirements of CICA are not required for the issuance of task or delivery orders under either single award or multiple-award contracts, 10 U.S.C. § 2304c(a) and 41 U.S.C. § 253j(a). However, 10 U.S.C. § 2304c(b) and 41 U.S.C. § 253j(b) require that each contractor receiving an award of an original task or delivery order contract be "provided a fair opportunity to be considered" for each order unless

(1) the [executive] agency's need for the services or property ordered is of such unusual urgency that providing such opportunity to all such contractors would result in unacceptable delays in fulfilling that need;

(2) only one such contractor is capable of providing the services or property required at the level of quality required because the services or property ordered are unique or highly specialized;

(3) the task or delivery order should be issued on a sole-source basis in the interest of economy and efficiency because it is a logical follow-on to a task or delivery order already issued on a competitive basis; or

(4) it is necessary to place the order with a particular contractor in order to satisfy a minimum guarantee.

The statutory exemption of task and delivery orders from competition is implemented in FAR 6.001(d) and (f).

A task or delivery order may not "increase the scope, period or maximum value" of the contract. Such increases may be accomplished only "by modification of the basic contract," 10 U.S.C. § 2304a(e) and 41 U.S.C. § 253h(e). Although not specifically stated in these sections, procurement notices and competition would be required for such actions unless a noncompetitive award could be justified because the exemption from competition is only applicable to task orders. By contrast, the

FASA's coverage of task orders for advisory and assistance services specifically provides that contract modifications are subject to competition requirements, 10 U.S.C. § 2304b(f)(2) and 41 U.S.C. § 253i(f)(2). Under limited circumstances, a one-time extension not exceeding six months may be made on a sole-source basis, 10 U.S.C. § 2304b(g) and 41 U.S.C. § 253i(g).

The GAO has followed the same reasoning with task and delivery orders as with change orders. The test is whether the order is within the scope of the original competition. See *Lockheed Martin Fairchild Sys.*, Comp. Gen. Dec. B-275034, 97-1 CPD ¶ 28, finding modernization of computer-based training within the scope of a contract for automatic data processing systems integration and support services, stating:

> In determining whether a delivery order issued under an existing contract is beyond the contract's scope of work, we look to whether there is a material difference between the contract, as modified by the delivery order, and the original contract. *Indian and Native Am. Employment and Training Coalition*, 64 Comp. Gen. 460 (1985), 85-1 CPD ¶ 432; *Dynamac Corp.*, B-252800, July 19, 1993, 93-2 CPD ¶ 37. As to the materiality of a modification, we consider factors such as the extent of any changes in the type of work, performance period and costs between the contract as awarded and as modified by the delivery order, as well as whether the original contract solicitation adequately advised offerors of the potential for the type of delivery order issued. *Data Transformation Corp.*, B-274629, Dec. 19, 1996, 97-1 CPD ¶ 10.

Task orders were also found to be within the scope of the contract in *Outdoor Venture Corp.*, Comp. Gen. Dec. B-401628, 2009 CPD ¶ 260 (delivery order requirement for full concealment covers within scope since the SOW listed variations of Ultra Lightweight Camouflage Net Systems to be procured and noted that other versions not specifically identified could also be procured); *Morris Corp.*, Comp. Gen. Dec. B-400336, 2008 CPD ¶ 204 (logical connection between the broad scope of food service operations delineated in the IDIQ contract—the feeding of individuals housed within a specified Iraqi training camp and/or coalition base—and the food service operations required to feed detainees located within the camp); *Colliers Int'l*, Comp. Gen. Dec. B-400173, 2008 CPD ¶ 147 (task order to conduct feasibility study was within scope of IDIQ which was broad and specifically provided for unidentified "special studies"); *Relm Wireless Corp.*, Comp. Gen. Dec. B-298715, 2006 CPD ¶ 190 (tactical radio within scope of IDIQ because RFP's definition of Land Mobile Radio covered similar assets designated for contingency, tactical or war ready material purposes); *Specialty Marine, Inc.*, Comp. Gen. Dec. B-293871, 2004 CPD ¶ 130 (statement of work language encompasses a broad category of ships without limitation to size); *Symetrics Indus., Inc.*, Comp. Gen. Dec. B-289606, 2002 CPD ¶ 65 (retrofitting reasonably falls within definition of depot level maintenance); *Ervin & Assocs., Inc.*, Comp. Gen. Dec. B-279083, 98-1 CPD ¶ 126 (relevant language in the solicitation's statement of work sets forth the anticipated services in broad, general, and flexible terms); *Techno-Sciences, Inc.*, Comp. Gen. Dec. B-277260.3, 98-1 CPD ¶ 138 (tasks within general scope where the contract specifically contemplated that operations, maintenance, and technical support would include whatever was necessary to support mission); *Exide Corp.*, Comp. Gen. Dec. B-276988, 97-2 CPD ¶ 51 (delivery orders in excess of maximum order limitation and to be delivered after contract expiration within contract scope when its terms provided for such flexibility); *Master Security, Inc.*, Comp. Gen. Dec. B-274990.2, 97-1 CPD ¶ 21 (addition of number of hours and contract sites not considered material change); and *LDDS WorldCom*, Comp. Gen. Dec. B-266257, 96-1 CPD ¶ 50 (the added services could have been anticipated from the face of the contract and were not materially different than the services currently rendered under the contract); *Liebert Corp.*, Comp. Gen. Dec. B-232234.5, 91-1 CPD ¶ 413 (work within general scope but quantity beyond maximum stated in contract outside scope); and *Information Ventures, Inc.*, Comp. Gen. Dec. B-240458, 90-2 CPD ¶ 414 (tasks "logically related to the overall purpose" of the agreement).

When the original competitors would not have anticipated the order, it will be found to be outside the scope of the contract. For example, in *Anteon Corp.*, Comp. Gen. Dec. B-293523, 2004 CPD ¶ 51, the GAO stated that although an electronic passport cover is essentially an identification document that is not materially different in function from a smart identification card, the physical deliverables under the task order request were not reasonably within the scope of GSA's smart card contract. See also *Floro & Assocs.*, Comp. Gen. Dec. B-285451.3, 2000 CPD ¶ 172 (task order beyond the scope of a contract for noncomplex integration services of commercially available off-the-shelf hardware and software where it required the contractor to provide management services to assist in support of distance learning product lines); *Ervin v. Assocs., Inc.*, Comp. Gen. Dec. B-278850, 98-1 CPD ¶ 89 (task order beyond the scope when the work was not mentioned in the original solicitation); *Dynamac Corp.*, Comp. Gen. Dec. B-252800, 93-2 CPD ¶ 37 (order for support of a computerized information system outside the scope of a contract that was intended to provide engineering support for an agency's information resources management systems because the original solicitation for the contract did not adequately advise offerors of the potential for this type of order); *Data Transformation Corp.*, Comp. Gen. Dec. B-274629, 97-1 CPD ¶ 10 (operation of a nationwide debt collection system was held to be outside the scope of a litigation support contract – one factor supporting the decision was that the agency had historically procured the work under a separate contract); *Comdisco, Inc.*, Comp. Gen. Dec. B-277340, 97-2 CPD ¶ 105 (agency exceeded the scope of its task orders for computer equipment and related services by permitting computer hardware/software to constitute more than its allotted share of a contract); *Marvin J. Perry & Assocs.*, Comp. Gen. Dec. B-277684, 97-2 CPD ¶ 128 (modification of Federal Supply Schedule delivery orders to permit substitution of lower-grade, less expensive furniture materially altered the nature of the orders from those originally issued and thereby prejudiced the protester).

d. Post-Protest Justifications

Even if it has been determined that government action in modifying a contract has gone beyond the scope of the procurement and therefore constitutes a de facto sole-source procurement, the GAO will deny the protest if a new sole-source procurement could have been justified. In *Tilden-Coil Constructors, Inc.*, Comp. Gen. Dec. B-211189.3, 83-2 CPD ¶ 236, the Army modified an ongoing contract for the construction of eight buildings and a central energy plant to authorize the incumbent to construct two additional buildings. The GAO accepted the Army's explanation that additional costs and delayed completion dates would result from the overcrowding of the congested work site occasioned by the presence of another contractor. See also *Mediax Assocs.*, Comp. Gen. Dec. B-211350, 84-1 CPD ¶ 71, declining to determine whether a modification exceeded the scope of a procurement after first concluding that a sole-source award was justified. Similarly in *Lyntronics Inc.*, Comp. Gen. Dec. B-292204, 2003 CPD ¶ 140, neither the protester nor GAO raised the issue of whether the modification exceeded the scope of the procurement; rather the focus was on whether the sole-source modification was justified. According to the J&A, no other source could meet the agency's needs because any other source's product would have to undergo required safety and first article testing which would take a number of months and delay delivery. The protester stated it could have a first article testing completed in a matter of weeks, but did not describe how this would be achieved. The GAO found reasonable the agency's conclusion that there was only one responsible source. In *Hercules Aerospace Co.*, Comp. Gen. Dec. B-254677, 94-1 CPD ¶ 7, the protester asserted that a contract modification for additional rocket motors and engineering services amounted to a de facto sole-source procurement. Without deciding this issue, the GAO held that the agency's decision to modify the contract of the only qualified contractor due to unusual and compelling circumstances was reasonable. See also *Pegasus Global Strategic Solutions, LLC*, Comp. Gen. Dec. B-400422.3, 2009 CPD ¶ 73, where the GAO took as a "given" that the agency improperly modified the contract, but nonetheless found that the sole source modification was not unreasonable based on the agency's urgent requirement. Compare *Kent Watkins & Assocs.*, Comp. Gen. Dec. B-191078, 78-1 CPD ¶ 377, where the government apparently added another year's work by modification and later wrote a sole-source justification for a new procurement after the protest had been lodged. The supporting reasons cited included that the incumbent contractor submitted the only response to the solicitation, the incumbent had gained special experience, and additional costs would be incurred in changing contractors. However, because the agency was aware of other companies interested in the solicitation, the GAO found the sole-source award improper.

e. Justifications and Approvals

When the acquisition plan proposes a strategy that entails using a procurement that is other than competitive, 41 U.S.C. § 253(f) and 10 U.S.C. § 2304(f) require the contracting officer to provide written justification for the use of such procedures.

These statutes require that the justification contain the following six elements:

(A) a description of the agency's needs;

(B) an identification of the statutory exception from the requirement to use competitive procedures and a demonstration, based on the proposed contractor's qualifications or the nature of the procurement, of the reasons for using that exception;

(C) a determination that the anticipated cost will be fair and reasonable;

(D) a description of the market survey conducted or a statement of the reasons a market survey was not conducted;

(E) a listing of the sources, if any, that expressed in writing an interest in the procurement; and

(F) a statement of the actions, if any, the agency may take to remove or overcome any barrier to competition before a subsequent procurement for such needs.

See FAR 6.303-2 for additional guidance on the contents of this justification. These requirements generally apply without regard to which exemption from full and open competition resulted in the need to prepare a J&A.

This justification must be certified as accurate and complete by the contracting officer responsible for awarding the contract, 41 U.S.C. § 253(f)(1)(A), 10 U.S.C. § 2304(f)(1)(A). It must then be reviewed and approved pursuant to FAR 6.304, as follows:

Contract Amount		Approval Authority
Over	**Not in excess of**	
$500,000	$10,000,000	Competition advocate without delegation
$10,000,000	$50,000,000 ($75,000 for DOD, NASA & the Coast Guard)	Head of Procuring Activity or delegate (Flag Officer or GS-16 rank or above)
$50,000,000 ($75,000 for DOD, NASA & the Coast Guard)	———	Senior Procurement Executive of Agency without delegation

Justification and Approvals (J&As) should be prepared and approved during the acquisition planning process. However, they may be made subsequently and even after award if circumstances warrant, FAR 6.303-1(e). Although late preparation of a J&A may not represent good planning, the lateness will not affect the validity of an otherwise proper J&A, *AUTOFLEX, Inc.*, Comp. Gen. Dec. B-240012, 90-2 CPD ¶ 294 (J&A executed after the closing date for receipt of proposals but prior to award); and *Magnavox Elec. Sys. Co.*, Comp. Gen. Dec. B-258076.2, 94-2 CPD ¶ 266 (J&A not invalidated even though modified and signed by the approving authority after the lower-level officials had signed it and after a protest was filed). Similarly, if additional facts are learned after a J&A has been prepared, an amended J&A will satisfy the detailed requirements for information that must be included, *Minowitz Mfg. Co.*, Comp. Gen. Dec. B-228502, 88-1 CPD ¶ 1. Clerical errors in a J&A will not invalidate a procurement, *Mnemonics, Inc.*, Comp. Gen. Dec. B-261476.3, 96-1 CPD ¶ 7.

Procurements will be overturned if the J&A does not contain a reasonable explanation for the avoidance of full and open competition. See *Worldwide Languages Resources, Inc.*, Comp. Gen. Dec. B-296984, 2005 CPD ¶ 206 (agency's J&A in support of the sole-source award flawed because it was premised on the unsupported conclusion that only one contractor was capable of meeting the requirement in a timely and cost-effective manner); *VSE Corp.*, Comp. Gen. Dec. B-290452.3, 2005 CPD ¶ 103 (sole-source award improper because it is not supported by a written J&A); *Sabreliner Corp.*, Comp. Gen. Dec. B-288030, 2001 CPD ¶ 170 (J&A replete with errors and inconsistencies that could not reasonably justify sole-source award); *Sturm, Ruger & Co.*, Comp. Gen. Dec. B-235938, 89-2 CPD ¶ 375 (documentation not meeting the specific requirements applicable to J&As insufficient to justify the avoidance of full and open competition); and *NI Indus., Inc.*, Comp. Gen. Dec. B-223941, 86-2 CPD ¶ 674 (elimination of one of two mobilization base contractors not adequately justified where the J&A contained no statement of the particular facts and circumstances that would justify a sole-source award).

Class J&As are permitted if approved in writing in accordance with agency procedures, FAR 6.304(c). When class J&As are used, the approval level should probably be determined by the estimated total value of the class. Class J&As will not be sufficient if they do not relate to the particular facts and circumstances of the specific procurement being questioned, *NI Indus., Inc.*, Comp. Gen. Dec. B-223941, 86-2 CPD ¶ 674.

The National Defense Authorization Act for FY 2008 amended 10 U.S.C. § 2304(f)(1)(C) and 41 U.S.C. § 253(f)(1)(C) by requiring that agencies post the justification and approval documents for all contracts awarded in reliance on a CICA exception on fedbizopps within 14 days of contract award.

f. Continuous Competition

Section 202 of the Weapon Systems Acquisition Reform Act of 2009, Pub. L. No. 111-23, requires DOD to adopt acquisition strategies for major weapon systems that provide for continuous competition throughout the life of the program. The Act contains a list of strategies which have been inserted in DFARS 207.106 verbatim with no additional guidance:

(S-72)(1) In accordance with section 202 of the Weapon Systems Acquisition Reform Act of 2009 (Pub. L. 111-23), acquisition plans for major defense acquisition programs as defined in 10 U.S.C. 2430, shall include measures that —

(i) Ensure competition, or the option of competition, at both the prime contract level and subcontract level (at such tier or tiers as are appropriate) throughout the program life cycle as a means to improve contractor performance; and

(ii) Document the rationale for the selection of the appropriate subcontract tier or tiers under paragraph (S-72)(1)(i) of this section, and the measures which will be employed to ensure competition, or the option of competition.

(2) Measures to ensure competition, or the option of competition, may include, but are not limited to, cost-effective measures intended to achieve the following:

(i) Competitive prototyping.

(ii) Dual-sourcing.

(iii) Unbundling of contracts.

(iv) Funding of next-generation prototype systems or subsystems.

(v) Use of modular, open architectures to enable competition for upgrades.

(vi) Use of build-to-print approaches to enable production through multiple sources.

(vii) Acquisition of complete technical data packages.

(viii) Periodic competitions for subsystem upgrades.

(ix) Licensing of additional suppliers.

(x) Periodic system or program reviews to address long-term competitive effects of program decisions.

(3) In order to ensure fair and objective "make-or-buy" decisions by prime contractors, acquisition strategies and resultant solicitations and contracts shall—

(i) Require prime contractors to give full and fair consideration to qualified sources other than the prime contractor for the development or construction of major subsystems and components of major weapon systems;

(ii) Provide for Government surveillance of the process by which prime contractors consider such sources and determine whether to conduct such development or construction in-house or through a subcontract; and

(iii) Provide for the assessment of the extent to which the prime contractor has given full and fair consideration to qualified sources in sourcing decisions as a part of past performance evaluations.

(4) Whenever a source-of-repair decision results in a plan to award a contract for the performance of maintenance and sustainment services on a major weapon system, to the maximum extent practicable and consistent with statutory requirements, the acquisition plan shall prescribe that award will be made on a competitive basis after giving full consideration to all sources (including sources that partner or subcontract with public or private sector repair activities).

There is very little guidance on the implementation of these strategies. However, some have been discussed in other parts of this chapter. The guidance in DOD PGI 217.7504, discussed below, is also useful since it was originally written to provide guidance to agencies that were establishing second sources for weapons systems. See Chapter 8 of Nash & Rawicz, *Intellectual Property in Government Contracts* (6th ed. 2008), for more in-depth discussion of the techniques that involve working around proprietary data.

g. Obtaining Competition for Spare Parts

The FAR requirement for considering competition in the planning process calls for identification of the steps that will be taken to obtain competition for components and subsystems as well as spare parts. As discussed earlier, when life-cycle cost techniques are used, this can be accomplished by placing provisions in the original contract making the contractor responsible for the costs of subsystems, components and spare parts.

When the original contractor is not responsible for the life-cycle support of a product, the agency will have to plan the techniques that will be used in the future to obtain any necessary replacement subsystems, components, and parts. One way to accomplish this is to obtain a full data package with unlimited rights. However, there are limitations on this technique. See DFARS 227.7103-1 stating DOD's policy to permit the inclusion of proprietary items in designs and to avoid the acquisition of proprietary rights when procuring equipment:

(c) Offerors shall not be required, either as a condition of being responsive to a solicitation or as a condition for award, to sell or otherwise relinquish to the Government any rights in technical data related to items, components or processes developed at private expense except for the data identified at 227.7103-5(a)(2) and (a)(4) through (9).

(d) Offerors and contractors shall not be prohibited or discouraged from furnishing or offering to furnish items, components, or processes developed at private expense solely because the Government's rights to use, modify, release, reproduce, perform, display, or disclose technical data pertaining to those items may be restricted.

When these policies result in proprietary technical data packages, the agency must plan to obtain competition in the future acquisition of subsystems, components, and parts by working around the proprietary rights of the contractor that designed the equipment. The most useful guidance on the techniques that are available is set forth in DOD Procedures, Guidance and Information (PGI) 217.7504, stating the policy on the acquisition of parts when data is not available:

When acquiring a part for which the Government does not have necessary data with rights to use in a specification or drawing for competitive acquisition, use one of the following procedures in order of preference—

(1) When items of identical design are not required, the acquisition may still be conducted through full and open competition by using a performance specification or other similar technical requirement or purchase description that does not contain data with restricted rights. Two methods are —

(i) Two-step sealed bidding; and

(ii) Brand name or equal purchase descriptions.

(2) When other than full and open competition is authorized under FAR Part 6, acquire the part from the firm which developed or designed the item or process, or its licensees, provided productive capacity and quality are adequate and the price is fair and reasonable.

(3) When additional sources are needed and the procedures in paragraph (1) of this section are not practicable, consider the following alternatives —

(i) Encourage the developer to license others to manufacture the parts;

(ii) Acquire the necessary rights in data;

(iii) Use a leader company acquisition technique (FAR subpart 17.4) when complex technical equipment is involved and establishing satisfactory additional sources will require technical assistance as well as data; or

(iv) Incorporate a priced option in the contract which allows the Government to require the contractor to establish a second source.

(4) As a last alternative, the contracting activity may develop a design specification for competitive acquisition through reverse engineering. Contracting activities shall not do reverse engineering unless —

(i) Significant cost savings can be demonstrated; and

(ii) The action is authorized by the head of the contracting activity.

The most prevalent technique to obtain competition for spare parts is for the government to suggest that companies reverse engineer a product in order to compete for a quantity of items to be procured. The major way that an agency initiates this type of reverse engineering is by providing proprietary items to competitors. With regard to spare parts, this procedure is encouraged by 10 U.S.C. § 2320(d), which states:

The Secretary of Defense shall by regulation establish programs which provide domestic business concerns an opportunity to purchase or borrow replenishment parts from the United States for the purpose of design replication or modification, to be used by such concerns in the submission of subsequent offers to sell the same or like parts to the United States.

This technique is sometimes called "competitive copying." The key issue when using this technique is the method by which the procuring agency determines that the product to be supplied will meet the government's requirements. There are three methods being used: analysis of the technical data prepared by the new source, preaward testing of the product to be supplied, and postaward testing of the product.

Agencies may insist on the submission of the technical data that will be used to perform a contract for a proprietary item before the award of such a contract, *EG&G Sealol*, Comp. Gen. Dec. B-232265, 88-2 CPD ¶ 558; *Electro-Magnetic Processes, Inc.*, Comp. Gen. Dec. B-227912, 87-2 CPD ¶ 269. The Defense Logistics Agency uses the following Conditions for Evaluation and Acceptance of Offers for Part Numbered Items clause in DLAD 52.217-9002 for this purpose:

[T]he offeror must furnish with its offer legible copies of all drawings, specifications, or other data necessary to clearly describe the characteristics and features of the alternate product being offered. Data submitted must cover design, materials, performance, function, interchangeability, inspection and/or testing criteria, and other characteristics of the offered product. In addition, the offeror must furnish drawings and other data covering the design, materials, etc. of the exact product cited in the PID [procurement identification description] sufficient to enable the Government to determine that the offeror's product is equal to the product cited in the PID.

This clause is based on the premise that the government must review the technical data of an offeror that intends to provide the replenishment parts before it will award a contract for such parts. This is the most frequently used technique to ensure that these parts will meet the government's needs.

Alternatively, an agency may require preaward testing of an offered product to determine that it will perform as well as the sole source proprietary item, *Interstate Diesel Servs., Inc.*, Comp. Gen. Dec. B-230107, 88-1 CPD ¶ 480; *B.H. Aircraft Co.*, Comp. Gen. Dec. B-222565, 86-2 CPD ¶ 143. However, this may restrict competition because it requires the offeror to incur the costs of manufacturing the product and performing tests. Moreover, agencies must comply with the procedural requirements in 10 U.S.C. § 2319 or 41 U.S.C. § 253c when they use this technique. See FAR Subpart 9.2.

The least restrictive technique for determining product acceptability is to provide for post-award testing. Guidance on such first-article testing is contained in FAR Subpart 9.3. FAR 9.302 contains the following caution as to the possibility that this may impose the risk on the government if awarding to a contractor that cannot deliver a conforming product:

> First article testing and approval (hereafter referred to as testing and approval) ensures that the contractor can furnish a product that conforms to all contract requirements for acceptance. Before requiring testing and approval, the contracting officer shall consider the —
>
> (a) Impact on cost or time of delivery;
>
> (b) Risk to the Government of forgoing such test; and
>
> (c) Availability of other, less costly, methods of ensuring the desired quality.

Agencies sometimes create nonproprietary technical data packages by reverse engineering proprietary products. Reverse engineering is the process of developing design specifications by inspection and analysis of a product. Although DFARS PGI 217.7504 provides that reverse engineering by the government is the least desirable means of obtaining competition in the face of proprietary data, this practice has been found to be legal, *Westech Gear Corp. v. Dep't of the Navy*, 907 F.2d 1225 (D.C. Cir. 1990); *American Hoist & Derrick, Inc. v. United States*, 3 Cl. Ct. 198 (1983). Sometimes nonproprietary technical data packages are created by awarding a contract to perform the reverse engineering, *EG&G Sealol*, Comp. Gen. Dec. B-232265, 88-2

CPD ¶ 558. When reverse engineering is too expensive to justify the effort to obtain competition, an agency can reasonably decide to continue the sole-source procurement, *Gel Sys., Inc.*, Comp. Gen. Dec. B-231680, 88-2 CPD ¶ 316. See also *AAI ACL Techs., Inc.*, Comp. Gen. Dec. 258679.4, 95-2 CPD ¶ 243, finding a sole-source award proper given the risk and cost associated with reverse engineering.

Agencies also attempt to obtain competition in the face of proprietary data by having the contractor with the proprietary data license other contractors. This is permitted by 10 U.S.C. § 2320(a)(2)(G)(iii). One form of licensing occurs in leader/follower procurement described in FAR Subpart 17.4. In that situation the developer of a product or system is required to create a follower company that is fully capable of producing the product or system. DOD PGI 217.7504 encourages the development of sources for spare parts by using the leader/follower technique or by encouraging the contractor to license other sources. In *Leigh Instruments, Ltd.*, Comp. Gen. Dec. B-233642, 89-1 CPD ¶ 149, the licensee complained that the contractor had failed to honor the license with the result that the licensee could not successfully compete on a procurement. The GAO did not entertain the protest, characterizing such situations as disputes between two private parties.

3. *Source Selection Procedures*

FAR 7.105(b)(3) states:

Source-selection procedures. Discuss the source-selection procedures for the acquisition, including the timing for submission and evaluation of proposals, and the relationship of evaluation factors to the attainment of the acquisition objectives (see Subpart 15.3). When an EVMS is required (see FAR 34.202(a)) and a pre-award IBR is contemplated, the acquisition plan must discuss —

(i) How the pre-award IBR will be considered in the source selection decision;

(ii) How it will be conducted in the source selection process (see FAR 15.306); and

(iii) Whether offerors will be directly compensated for the costs of participating in a pre-award IBR.

This element of the planning process requires the formulation of a source selection plan—a major task that is discussed in detail in Chapter 2. It also requires the agency to determine the timing of submission and evaluation of proposals. The need for acquisition streamlining to reduce the time taken in the preparation and evaluation of proposals was previously discussed. The sequence of the entire competitive negotiation process will be discussed in the later treatment of the milestones for the acquisition cycle.

4. Acquisition Considerations

FAR 7.105(b)(4) states:

> *Acquisition considerations.* For each contract contemplated, discuss contract type selection (see Part 16); use of multi-year contracting, options, or other special contracting methods (see Part 17); any special clauses, special solicitation provisions, or FAR deviations required (see Subpart 1.4); whether sealed bidding or negotiation will be used and why; whether equipment will be acquired by lease or purchase (see Subpart 7.4) and why; and any other contracting considerations. Provide rationale if a performance-based acquisition will not be used or if a performance-based acquisition for services is contemplated on other than a firm-fixed-price basis (see 37.102(a), 16.103(d), and 16.505(a)(3)).

This part of the plan covers the structure of the contract that will be used to carry out the acquisition strategy. Depending on the nature of the program, these decisions can be relatively simple or extremely complex. The major issues are type of contract, special procurement techniques, and the use of sealed bidding.

a. Type of Contract

Although agency policies have changed from time to time, the basic statutory and regulatory policy has remained constant — calling for a balanced approach to the selection of the proper contract type. The statutory guidance is simple and direct. 41 U.S.C. § 254(b) and 10 U.S.C. § 2301(a)(2) give broad discretion to use the appropriate type of contract on negotiated procurements but prohibit any use of a cost-plus-a-percentage-of cost system of contracts. FAR 16.103 carries out this policy by emphasizing two basic principles: the need to tailor the type of contract to the facts of each procurement, and the advantage of using fixed-price contracts when possible. This section of the FAR provides very balanced guidance in this area:

> (a) Selecting the contract type is generally a matter for negotiation and requires the exercise of sound judgment. Negotiating the contract type and negotiating prices are closely related and should be considered together. The objective is to negotiate a contract type and price (or estimated cost and fee) that will result in reasonable contractor risk and provide the contractor with the greatest incentive for efficient and economical performance.

> (b) A firm-fixed-price contract, which best utilizes the basic profit motive of business enterprise, shall be used when the risk involved is minimal or can be predicted with an acceptable degree of certainty. However, when a reasonable basis for firm pricing does not exist, other contract types should be considered, and negotiations should be directed toward selecting a contract type (or combination of types) that will appropriately tie profit to contractor performance.

> (c) In the course of an acquisition program, a series of contracts, or a single long-term contract, changing circumstances may make a different contract type ap-

propriate in later periods than that used at the outset. In particular, contracting officers should avoid protracted use of a cost-reimbursement or time-and-materials contract after experience provides a basis for firmer pricing.

(d) Each contract file shall include documentation to show why the particular contract type was selected. Exceptions to this requirement are —

(1) Fixed-price acquisitions made under simplified acquisition procedures;

(2) Contracts on a firm fixed-price basis other than those for major systems or research and development; and

(3) Awards on the set-aside portion of sealed bid partial set-asides for small business.

FAR 16.104 provides a list of factors to be considered in selecting the contract type with guidance as to the application of each factor. This section of the FAR requires the contracting officer to impose financial risks on the contractor that are commensurate with the ability of the parties to define and price the work with some degree of accuracy. This guidance describes the factors as follows:

(a) Price competition. Normally, effective price competition results in realistic pricing, and a fixed-price contract is ordinarily in the Government's interest.

(b) Price analysis. Price analysis, with or without competition, may provide a basis for selecting the contract type. The degree to which price analysis can provide a realistic pricing standard should be carefully considered. (See 15-404-1(b).)

(c) Cost analysis. In the absence of effective price competition and if price analysis is not sufficient, the cost estimates of the offeror and the Government provide the bases for negotiating contract pricing arrangements. It is essential that the uncertainties involved in performance and their possible impact upon costs be identified and evaluated, so that a contract type that places a reasonable degree of cost responsibility upon the contractor can be negotiated.

(d) Type and complexity of the requirement. Complex requirements, particularly those unique to the Government, usually result in greater risk assumption by the Government. This is especially true for complex research and development contracts, when performance uncertainties or the likelihood of changes makes it difficult to estimate performance costs in advance. As a requirement recurs or as quantity production begins, the cost risk should shift to the contractor, and a fixed-price contract should be considered.

(e) Urgency of the requirement. If urgency is a primary factor, the Government may choose to assume a greater proportion of risk or it may offer incentives to ensure timely contract performance.

(f) Period of performance or length of production run. In times of economic uncertainty, contracts extending over a relatively long period may require economic price adjustment terms.

(g) Contractor's technical capability and financial responsibility.

(h) Adequacy of the contractor's accounting system. Before agreeing on contract type other than firm-fixed-price, the contracting officer shall ensure that the contractor's accounting system will permit timely development of all necessary cost data in the form required by the proposed contract type. This factor may be critical when the contract type requires price revision while performance is in progress, or when a cost-reimbursement contract is being considered and all current or past experience with the contractor has been on a fixed-price basis.

(i) Concurrent contracts. If performance under the proposed contract involves concurrent operations under other contracts, the impact of those contracts, including their pricing arrangements, should be considered.

(j) Extent and nature of proposed subcontracting. If the contractor proposes extensive subcontracting, a contract type reflecting the actual risks to the prime contractor should be selected.

(k) Acquisition history. Contractor risk usually decreases as the requirement is repetitively acquired. Also, product descriptions or descriptions of services to be performed can be defined more clearly.

This guidance sets forth the government's basic policy to use the type of contract that imposes sufficient risk on the contractor to motivate good performance yet relieves the contractor of risks over which it has no control and that are unpredictable. This goal requires the contracting parties to strike a delicate balance in the selection and negotiation of the contract type.

Because of the difficulties of selecting the proper type of contract for research and development contracts, FAR 35.006 contains the following special provisions dealing with the selection of the correct type of contract in this area:

(b) Selecting the appropriate contract type is the responsibility of the contracting officer. However, because of the importance of technical considerations in R&D, the choice of contract type should be made after obtaining the recommendations of technical personnel. Although the Government ordinarily prefers fixed-price arrangements in contracting, this preference applies in R&D contracting only to the extent that goals, objectives, specifications, and cost estimates are sufficient to permit such a preference. The precision with which the goals, performance objectives, and specifications for the work can be defined will largely determine the type of contract employed. The contract type must be selected to fit the work required.

(c) Because the absence of precise specifications and difficulties in estimating costs with accuracy (resulting in a lack of confidence in cost estimates) normally precludes using fixed-price contracting for R&D, the use of cost-reimbursement contracts is usually appropriate (see Subpart 16.3). The nature of development work often requires a cost-reimbursement completion arrangement (see 16.306(d)). When the use of cost and performance incentives is desirable and practicable, fixed-price incentive and cost-plus-incentive-fee contracts should be considered in that order of preference.

* * *

(e) Projects having production requirements as a follow-on to R&D efforts normally should progress from cost-reimbursement contracts to fixed-price contracts as designs become more firmly established, risks are reduced, and production tooling, equipment, and processes are developed and proven. When possible, a final commitment to undertake specific product development and testing should be avoided until —

> (1) Preliminary exploration and studies have indicated a high degree of probability that development is feasible and

> (2) The Government has determined both its minimum requirements and desired objectives for product performance and schedule completion.

For a detailed discussion of the selection and application of the various types of contracts, see Chapter 8 of Cibinic & Nash, *Formation of Government Contracts* (3d ed. 1998).

Congress has enacted special provisions covering the selection of the proper type of contract for DOD weapon systems procurements. In the Defense Appropriations Act of 1987, 101 Stat. 1329, § 8118 prohibited the use of firm fixed-price contracts for the development of such systems without Secretarial approval. This prohibition stayed in place until the enactment of the National Defense Authorization Act for Fiscal Year 2007, Pub. L. No. 109-364, which contained § 818 reversing the rule and favoring the use of fixed-price type contracts for weapon systems development. This provision is implemented in DFARS 234.004 as follows:

> (2) In accordance with Section 818 of the National Defense Authorization Act for Fiscal Year 2007 (Pub. L. 109-364), for major defense acquisition programs as defined in 10 U.S.C. 2430—

>> (i) The Milestone Decision Authority shall select, with the advice of the contracting officer, the contract type for a development program at the time of Milestone B approval or, in the case of a space program, Key Decision Point B approval;

>> (ii) The basis for the contract type selection shall be documented in the acquisition strategy. The documentation—

(A) Shall include an explanation of the level of program risk; and

(B) If program risk is determined to be high, shall outline the steps taken to reduce program risk and the reasons for proceeding with Milestone B approval despite the high level of program risk; and

(iii) If a cost-type contract is selected, the contract file shall include the Milestone Decision Authority's written determination that—

(A) The program is so complex and technically challenging that it would not be practicable to reduce program risk to a level that would permit the use of a fixed-price type contract; and

(B) The complexity and technical challenge of the program is not the result of a failure to meet the requirements of 10 U.S.C. 2366a.

b. Special Procurement Techniques

When the government has a firm determination of the quantity of articles or services needed and has available appropriations it will normally enter into a contract for the total quantity and obligate the funds. However, there are a number of situations where the quantity is uncertain or funds are not available for the full program. Thus, in this part of the acquisition plan, the agency should consider whether it will benefit by contracting for more work than is immediately required in the current fiscal year or over additional years. The major benefit that can be derived from such contracts is lower prices resulting from reduced contractor costs because of capital investments and other efficiencies that would not be achieved if the contract were for only the work that is immediately required. Contracting agencies also achieve benefits from longer contracts by stabilizing their contract administration processes and not incurring the costs of repetitive procurements. While there is no single clearly enunciated government policy with regard to the use of these forms of contracting, it is apparent that a fundamental goal of the government should be to buy articles or services in sufficient quantities over a sufficient period of time to permit efficient performance of the contract. This policy with regard to supplies is contained in 10 U.S.C. § 2384(a) and 41 U.S.C. § 253f(a) and implemented in FAR Subpart 7.2. The latter statute states:

Each executive agency shall procure supplies in such quantities as (A) will result in the total cost and unit cost most advantageous to the United States, where practicable, and (B) does not exceed the quantity reasonably expected to be required by the agency.

Contracts for more work than is immediately required must be written to comply with the Anti-Deficiency Act, 31 U.S.C. § 1341. This Act precludes the award of firm contracts for work until money has been appropriated to pay for it. The agency must use special contracting techniques to include such work in a contract. Four such techniques are widely used: multi-year contracts, options, task or delivery order contracts and requirements contracts.

(1) MULTI-YEAR CONTRACTS

Multi-year contracting was devised by DOD in the 1960s to enable the military services to procure weapon systems over a five-year period. The contracting technique has been expanded over the years to cover the procurement of both supplies and services, and statutes have been enacted placing some limitations on its use. See 10 U.S.C. § 2306b (procurement of supplies by DOD, NASA, and the Coast Guard); 10 U.S.C. § 2306(g) (procurement of services by DOD, NASA, and the Coast Guard); 41 U.S.C. § 254c (procurement of supplies and services by other agencies).

Under a multi-year contract the procuring agency may stop ordering the supplies or services if the requirement no longer exists, but the contractor is protected by the payment of a cancellation charge (up to a cancellation ceiling) covering costs that have not been recovered in the prices paid to the date of cancellation. FAR 17.103 describes this contracting technique:

> "Multi-year" contract means a contract for the purchase of supplies or services for more than 1, but not more than 5, program years. A multi-year contract may provide that performance under the contract during the second and subsequent years of the contract is contingent upon the appropriation of funds, and (if it does so provide) may provide for a cancellation payment to be made to the contractor if appropriations are not made. The key distinguishing difference between multi-year contracts and multiple year contracts is that multi-year contracts, defined in the statutes cited at 17.101, buy more than 1 year's requirement (of a product or service) without establishing and having to exercise an option for each program year after the first.

Multi-year contracts legally bind the government to order the stated requirements over the life of the contract as long as the requirement continues to exist and funding is available, *Applied Devices Corp. v. United States*, 219 Ct. Cl. 109, 591 F.2d 635 (1979). They are used to induce contractors to reduce their costs because they have some assurance of a long-term contract. FAR 17.105-2 lists the objectives of multi-year contracting:

> Use of multi-year contracting is encouraged to take advantage of one or more of the following:
>
> (a) Lower costs.
>
> (b) Enhancement of standardization.

(c) Reduction of administrative burden in the placement and administration of contracts.

(d) Substantial continuity of production or performance, thus avoiding annual startup costs, pre-production testing costs, make-ready expenses, and phaseout costs.

(e) Stabilization of contractor work forces.

(f) Avoidance of the need for establishing quality control techniques and procedures for a new contractor each year.

(g) Broadening the competitive base with opportunity for participation by firms not otherwise willing or able to compete for lesser quantities, particularly in cases involving high startup costs.

(h) Provide incentives to contractors to improve productivity through investment in capital facilities, equipment, and advanced technology.

FAR 17.105-1 recognizes the different statutory requirements for use of multi-year contracts:

(a) Except for DoD, NASA, and the Coast Guard, the contracting officer may enter into a multi-year contract if the head of the contracting activity determines that —

(1) The need for the supplies or services is reasonably firm and continuing over the period of the contract; and

(2) A multi-year contract will serve the best interests of the United States by encouraging full and open competition or promoting economy in administration, performance, and operation of the agency's programs.

(b) For DoD, NASA, and the Coast Guard, the head of the agency may enter into a multi-year contract for supplies if —

(1) The use of such a contract will result in substantial savings of the total estimated costs of carrying out the program through annual contracts;

(2) The minimum need to be purchased is expected to remain substantially unchanged during the contemplated contract period in terms of production rate, procurement rate, and total quantities;

(3) There is a stable design for the supplies to be acquired, and the technical risks associated with such supplies are not excessive;

(4) There is a reasonable expectation that, throughout the contemplated contract period, the head of the agency will request funding for the contract at a level to avoid contract cancellation; and

(5) The multi-year contracting method may be used for the acquisition of supplies or services.

Note that this guidance does not cover multi-year service contracts issued by DOD, NASA, or the Coast Guard pursuant to 10 U.S.C. § 2306(g). See DFARS 217.171 for guidance on this type of multi-year contracting.

(2) Options

An option is a unilateral right in a contract by which the government may, for a specified time, elect to purchase additional supplies or services called for by the contract, or elect to extend the term of the contract, FAR 2.101. Options have become the major means that agencies have avoided the need to obtain their requirements through annual purchases – hence avoiding the administrative cost and time of processing a procurement each year. Many agencies also use options for additional years' quantities of items as a means of inducing offerors to propose lower prices. This policy appears to be effective even though the options are not legally binding on the government. FAR 17.202(a) gives contracting officers broad authority to use options with the following limitations:

(b) Inclusion of an option is normally not in the Government's interest when, in the judgment of the contracting officer —

(1) The foreseeable requirements involve —

(i) Minimum economic quantities (i.e., quantities large enough to permit the recovery of startup costs and the production of the required supplies at a reasonable price); and

(ii) Delivery requirements far enough into the future to permit competitive acquisition, production, and delivery.

(2) An indefinite quantity or requirements contract would be more appropriate than a contract with options. However, this does not preclude the use of an indefinite quantity contract or requirements contract with options.

(c) The contracting officer shall not employ options if —

(1) The contractor will incur undue risks; e.g., the price or availability of necessary materials or labor is not reasonably foreseeable;

(2) Market prices for the supplies or services involved are likely to change substantially; or

(3) The option represents known firm requirements for which funds are available unless —

(i) The basic quantity is a learning or testing quantity; and

(ii) Competition for the option is impracticable once the initial contract is awarded.

Options have been widely used for additional years of work on services contracts. A major reason for this use of option is to maintain continuity of service when the agency is aware that it will have a continuing need for the services. See FAR 17.202 stating:

(d) In recognition of (1) the Government's need in certain service contracts for continuity of operations and (2) the potential cost of disrupted support, options may be included in service contracts if there is an anticipated need for a similar service beyond the first contract period.

In addition, FAR 17.204(e) requires that the total length of time of the basic contract and option periods shall not exceed five years for service contracts, and the total of the basic contract and option quantities shall not exceed the five-year requirements of the government for supply contracts. These limitations do not apply to information technology contracts.

When options are included in the contract, the agency must decide whether they will be evaluated in making the original source selection decision. If they are evaluated, they may be subsequently exercised without obtaining full and open competition pursuant to FAR 17.207. However, if they are not evaluated, the full and open competition requirement must be met, FAR 17.207(f). For this reason, most agencies evaluate options in the original procurement. FAR 17.206 provides the following guidance on evaluation of options:

(a) In awarding the basic contract, the contracting officer shall, except as provided in paragraph (b) of this section, evaluate offers for any option quantities or periods contained in a solicitation when it has been determined prior to soliciting offers that the Government is likely to exercise the options. (See 17.208.)

(b) The contracting officer need not evaluate offers for any option quantities when it is determined that evaluation would not be in the best interests of the Government and this determination is approved at a level above the contracting officer. An example of a circumstance that may support a determination not to evaluate offers for option quantities is when there is a reasonable certainty that funds will be unavailable to permit exercise of the option.

Protests will be sustained if an agency exercises an unevaluated option without justifying a non-competitive procurement in accordance with the CICA procedures. See *Major Contracting Servs., Inc.*, Comp. Gen. Dec. B-401472, 2009 CPD ¶ 170, *recons. denied*, 2009 CPD ¶ 250, explaining that this is the only rational interpretation of FAR 17.207(f). See also *Stoehner Security Servs., Inc.*, Comp. Gen. Dec. B-248077.3, 92-2 CPD ¶ 285, applying this regulation to the exercise of an unpriced option. In *Freightliner Corp. v. Caldera*, 225 F.3d 1361 (Fed. Cir. 2000), the court held that FAR 17.207(f) gives the contractor no rights with regard to the improper exercise of an unevaluated option.

(3) REQUIREMENTS CONTRACTS

Another method of contracting for supplies or services that are not currently funded or may not be needed is the requirements contract. This type of indefinite-delivery contract may be used when the exact times or quantities of future delivers are not known at the time of contract award, FAR 16.501-2(a). The requirements contract "provides for the filling of all actual purchase requirements of designated Government activities for supplies or services during a specified contract period, with deliveries or performance to be scheduled by placing orders with the contractor," FAR 16.503(a). Thus, the government is legally required to order the supplies or services specified in the contract as long as it has a requirement for such supplies or services, *Torncello v. United States*, 231 Ct. Cl. 436, 681 F.2d 756 (1982); *Mason v. United States*, 222 Ct. Cl. 436, 615 F.2d 1343 (1980).

A requirements contract is appropriate when the government anticipates re-curring requirements but cannot predetermine the precise quantities of supplies or services that the designated government activities will need during a definite period, FAR 16.503(b). The contract must contain a realistic estimated total quantity, FAR 16.503(a)(1). This estimate is not intended to be a representation to an offeror or contractor that the estimated quantity will be required or ordered or that conditions affecting requirements will be stable or normal. Rather, the estimate is solely for the benefit of the offerors, so that they have an idea of what will be expected of them under the contract. However, the agency must exercise care in computing the estimated requirement because the government will be liable if the estimate is inac-curate because of negligence, *Chemical Tech., Inc. v. United States*, 227 Ct. Cl. 120, 645 F.2d 934 (1981); *Hi-Shear Tech. v. United States*, 53 Fed. Cl. 420 (2002) (in estimating the number of components it needed, the government failed to allow for units returned from the field that would be repaired and returned to stock and a new program implemented to increase the number of units returned).

Requirements contracts may be for a single year or for multiple years. In most cases requirements contracts for more than one year include options for a specified number of additional years where appropriations are not available at the time of con-tracting. See, for example, *Free State Reporting, Inc.*, Comp. Gen. Dec. B-259650, 95-1 CPD ¶ 199 (requirements for support services for base year and two option years); *Tulane Univ.*, Comp. Gen. Dec. B-259912, 95-1 CPD ¶ 210 (requirements for services for two base years and three option years). Multiple year requirements contracts could also be issued as a single document, including later years not covered by current appropriations, if there is no possibility that the contractor could obligate the government by performing work prior to the issuance of a requirement. See

42 Comp. Gen. 272 (B-144641) (1962), where the GAO ruled that a requirements contract was in violation of appropriations law because the government would be obligated to pay for work in a later year not covered under the contract. See also 67 Comp. Gen. 190 (B-224081) (1988), and 48 Comp. Gen. 494 (B-164908) (1969). In cases where a requirement contract is used in this way, an agency will normally include an "availability of funds" clause stating that the government will not be liable to pay the contractor until funds for future years have been made contractually available. See *Funding of Maintenance Contract Extending Beyond Fiscal Year*, Comp. Gen. Dec. B-259274, 96-1 CPD ¶ 247, where the GAO approved a requirements contract when the requirement covered two fiscal years with the second year restricted by an Availability of Funds clause. The GAO stated that "a naked contractual obligation that carries with it no financial exposure to the government does not violate the Anti-Deficiency Act."

Agencies have also used multi-year requirements contracts when multiyear or no-year funds are being used for the procurement. This practice was explicitly permitted by FAR 17.104-4 until 1996, when the provision was deleted from the regulation. It is still legally permissible even though the FAR is silent on the subject. For examples of multi-year requirements contracts, see *Liebert Corp.*, 70 Comp. Gen. 448 (B-232234.5), 91-1 CPD ¶ 413 (agency issued firm-fixed-price requirements contract for services and materials over a five-year period); *CDI Marine Co.*, Comp. Gen. Dec. B-219934.2, 86-1 CPD ¶ 242 (agency issued a CPFF requirements contract for services performed over a three-year period).

(4) TASK AND DELIVERY ORDER CONTRACTS

Another form of contract providing for the ordering of supplies or services as the need is identified is the task or delivery order contract. These contracts are subject to the provisions of the Federal Acquisition Streamlining Act of 1994 (FASA), Pub. L. No. 103-355, dealing with "task order contracts" and "delivery order contracts," 10 U.S.C. § 2304a–2304d and 41 U.S.C. § 235h–235k. The following definitions are contained in 10 U.S.C. § 2304d and 41 U.S.C. § 253k:

> (1) The term "task order contract" means a contract for services that does not procure or specify a firm quantity of services (other than a minimum or maximum quantity) and that provides for the issuance of orders for the performance of tasks during the period of the contract.

> (2) The term "delivery order contract" means a contract for property that does not procure or specify a firm quantity of property (other than a minimum or maximum quantity) and that provides for the issuance of orders for the delivery of property during the period of the contract.

These statutory provisions are implemented in FAR Subpart 16.5, covering requirements contracts and indefinite-quantity contracts. Other types of contracts, such as level-of-effort contracts, may also provide for the ordering of work by tasks without calling for a "firm quantity" of work. If so, they would be subject to these statutes even though the FAR does not specify that they are covered.

One major purpose of these statutes is to ensure that these types of contracts will be sufficiently precise to enable offerors to ascertain the scope of the work to be ordered so that they can submit meaningful offers, as set forth at 10 U.S.C. § 2304a and 41 U.S.C. § 253h:

> (b) Solicitation. The solicitation for a task or delivery order contract shall include the following:
>
>> (1) The period of the contract, including the number of options to extend the contract and the period for which the contract may be extended under each option, if any.
>>
>> (2) The maximum quantity or dollar value of the services or property to be procured under the contract.
>>
>> (3) A statement of work, specifications, or other description that reasonably describes the general scope, nature, complexity, and purposes of the services or property to be procured under the contract.

In order to ensure that competition is maximized, these statutes favor the award of multiple contracts over single contracts for a designated series of task orders or delivery orders. See 10 U.S.C. § 2304a(d) and 41 U.S.C. § 253h(d), which grant authority to make single awards but state the following:

> (d) Single and Multiple Contract Awards. —
>
>> (1) The head of an agency may exercise the authority provided in this section —
>>
>>> (A) to award a single task or delivery order contract; or
>>>
>>> (B) if the solicitation states that the head of the agency has the option to do so, to award separate task or delivery order contracts for the same or similar services or property to two or more sources.
>>
>> (2) No determination under section 2304(b) of this title is required for award of multiple task or delivery order contracts under paragraph (1)(B).
>>
>> (3) (A) No task or delivery order contract in an amount estimated to exceed $100,000,000 (including all options) may be awarded to a single source unless the head of the agency determines in writing that —

(i) the task or delivery orders expected under the contract are so integrally related that only a single source can reasonably perform the work;

(ii) the contract provides only for firm, fixed price task orders or delivery orders for —

(I) products for which unit prices are established in the contract; or

(II) services for which prices are established in the contract for the specific tasks to be performed;

(iii) only one source is qualified and capable of performing the work at a reasonable price to the government; or

(iv) because of exceptional circumstances, it is necessary in the public interest to award the contract to a single source.

(B) The head of the agency shall notify Congress within 30 days after any determination under subparagraph (A)(iv).

(4) The regulations implementing this subsection shall —

(A) establish a preference for awarding, to the maximum extent practicable, multiple task or delivery order contracts for the same or similar services or property under the authority of paragraph (1)(B); and

(B) establish criteria for determining when award of multiple task or delivery order contracts would not be in the best interest of the Federal Government.

10 U.S.C. § 2304b(e) and 41 U.S.C. § 253i(e) contain special limitations on task order contracts for "advisory and assistance services" if the contract period exceeds three years and the estimated contract amount is over $10 million. In such cases a single contract can be awarded only if the head of the executive agency determines that because the services required under the contract are unique or highly specialized, it is not practicable to award more than one contract. "Advisory and assistance services" are defined in 31 U.S.C. § 1105(g):

[T]he term "advisory and assistance services" means the following services when provided by nongovernmental sources:

(i) Management and professional support services.

(ii) Studies, analyses, and evaluations.

(iii) Engineering and technical services.

Most task and delivery order contracts are structured as indefinite-delivery, indefinite-quantity contracts. FAR 16.504 contains the following guidance on these contracts:

(a) Description. An indefinite-quantity contract provides for an indefinite quantity, within stated limits, of supplies or services during a fixed period. The Government places orders for individual requirements. Quantity limits may be stated as number of units or as dollar values.

(1) The contract must require the Government to order and the contractor to furnish at least a stated minimum quantity of supplies or services. In addition, if ordered, the contractor must furnish any additional quantities, not to exceed the stated maximum. The contracting officer should establish a reasonable maximum quantity based on market research, trends on recent contracts for similar supplies or services, survey of potential users, or any other rational basis.

(2) To ensure that the contract is binding, the minimum quantity must be more than a nominal quantity, but it should not exceed the amount that the Government is fairly certain to order.

(3) The contract may also specify maximum or minimum quantities that the Government may order under each task or delivery order and the maximum that it may order during a specific period of time.

(4) A solicitation and contract for an indefinite quantity must —

(i) Specify the period of the contract, including the number of options and the period for which the Government may extend the contract under each option;

(ii) Specify the total minimum and maximum quantity of supplies or services the Government will acquire under the contract;

(iii) Include a statement of work, specifications, or other description, that reasonably describes the general scope, nature, complexity, and purpose of the supplies or services the Government will acquire under the contract in a manner that will enable a prospective offeror to decide whether to submit an offer;

(iv) State the procedures that the Government will use in issuing orders, including the ordering media, and, if multiple awards may be made, state the procedures and selection criteria that the Government will use to provide awardees a fair opportunity to be considered for each order (see 16.505(b)(1));

(v) Include the name, address, telephone number, facsimile number, and e-mail address of the agency task and delivery order ombudsman (see 16.505(b)(6)) if multiple awards may be made;

(vi) Include a description of the activities authorized to issue orders; and

(vii) Include authorization for placing oral orders, if appropriate, provided that the Government has established procedures for obligating funds and that oral orders are confirmed in writing.

An IDIQ contract differs from a requirements contract in that the IDIQ contract does not obligate the government to purchase more than a stated minimum quantity, whereas a requirements contract obligates the government to purchase all of its requirements from the contractor during a fixed period of time, *Travel Centre v. Barram*, 236 F.3d 1316 (Fed. Cir. 2001). See also *Varilease Tech. Group, Inc. v. United States*, 289 F.3d 795 (Fed. Cir. 2002); *IMS Engineers-Architects, P.C. v. United States*, 86 Fed. Cl. 541 (2009); and *J. Cooper & Assocs. v. United States*, 53 Fed. Cl. 8 (2002).

c. Sealed Bidding

A final contracting consideration that must be addressed in the planning process is whether sealed bidding is the most appropriate technique. One of the major changes to procurement policy in the CICA was the elimination of the absolute preference for formal advertising (renamed "sealed bidding") over negotiation. Instead, the CICA substituted the following rule in 10 U.S.C. § 2304(a)(2) and 41 U.S.C. § 253(a)(2):

In determining the competitive procedures appropriate under the circumstance, an executive agency —

(A) shall solicit sealed bids if —

(i) time permits the solicitation, submission, and evaluation of sealed bids;

(ii) the award will be made on the basis of price and other price-related factors;

(iii) it is not necessary to conduct discussions with the responding sources about their bids; and

(iv) there is a reasonable expectation of receiving more than one sealed bid;

However, 10 U.S.C. § 2304(a)(1)(B) and 41 U.S.C. § 253(a)(1)(B) also provide that in conducting a procurement, an agency shall use the competitive procedure or combination of competitive procedures that is best suited under the circumstances of the procurement.

The statutes thus give agencies considerable discretion in deciding whether to use sealed bidding. These provisions are implemented by FAR 6.401, which states:

> Sealed bidding and competitive proposals, as described in Parts 14 and 15, are both acceptable procedures for use under Subparts 6.1, 6.2; and, when appropriate, under Subpart 6.3.
>
>> (a) *Sealed bids.* (See Part 14 for procedures.) Contracting officers shall solicit sealed bids if —
>>
>>> (1) Time permits the solicitation, submission, and evaluation of sealed bids;
>>>
>>> (2) The award will be made on the basis of price and other price-related factors;
>>>
>>> (3) It is not necessary to conduct discussions with the responding offerors about their bids; and
>>>
>>> (4) There is a reasonable expectation of receiving more than one sealed bid.
>>
>> (b) *Competitive proposals.* (See Part 15 for procedures.)
>>
>>> (1) Contracting officers may request competitive proposals if sealed bids are not appropriate under paragraph (a) of this section.
>>>
>>> (2) Because of differences in areas such as law, regulations, and business practices, it is generally necessary to conduct discussions with offerors relative to proposed contracts to be made and performed outside the United States and its outlying areas.

Competitive proposals will therefore be used for these contracts unless discussions are not required and the use of sealed bids is otherwise appropriate. Contracting officers must use sealed bidding if none of the four exceptions set forth in 10 U.S.C. § 2304(a)(2) and 41 U.S.C. § 253(a)(2) can be demonstrated. The GAO explained this rule in *Defense Logistics Agency*, 67 Comp. Gen. 16 (B-227055.2), 87-2 CPD ¶ 365 at 17:

> It is true . . . that CICA eliminates the specific preference for formally advertised procurements ("sealed bids") and directs an agency to use the competitive proce-

dures, or combination of procedures, that is best suited under the circumstances of the procurement. However, CICA . . . does provide, in determining which competitive procedure is appropriate under the circumstances, that an agency "shall solicit sealed bids if": (1) time permits, (2) award will be based on price, (3) discussions are not necessary, and (4) more than one bid is expected to be submitted. As is evident, the plain language of the CICA provision is mandatory in nature. When the enumerated statutory conditions are present, the solicitation of sealed bids is, therefore, required, leaving no room for the exercise of discretion by the contracting officer in determining which competitive procedure to use.

In reaching this conclusion, the GAO relied on the legislative history of the CICA, stating:

> The legislative history of CICA also indicates the mandatory nature of the requirement to use sealed bidding when the statutory conditions are present. Senate Report No. 98-50, 98th Cong., 2nd Sess., reprinted in 1984 U.S. Code Cong. & Admin. News 2191, states, in pertinent part:
>
>> While competitive negotiation is recognized in S.338 as a bona fide competitive procedure, the Committee emphasizes that traditional formal advertising procedures are by no means cast aside. In fact, agencies are required . . . to solicit sealed bids [when the enumerated conditions are present.]
>
> House Conference Report No. 98-861, 98th Cong., 2nd Sess., reprinted in 1984 U.S. Code Cong. & Admin. News 2110, states:
>
>> In effect, the substitute, like the Senate amendment, removes the restriction from — and written justification required for — competitive proposal procedures and places them on a par with sealed bid procedures. The substitute maintains minimum criteria for sealed bid procedures to ensure their use when appropriate.

See also *Knoll N. Am., Inc.*, Comp. Gen. Dec. B-250234, 93-1 CPD ¶ 26. In *Racal Corp.*, 70 Comp. Gen. 127 (B-240579), 90-2 CPD ¶ 453, the GAO ruled that negotiation could not be used in a price-only procurement to ensure that offerors had a complete understanding of the specifications and to permit changes to the agency's requirements after submission of offerors. See also *Northeast Constr. Co.*, 68 Comp. Gen. 406 (B-234323), 89-1 CPD ¶ 402, holding that negotiation was not appropriate because the procurement was based on price alone and the RFP did not call for technical proposals. But see *TLT Constr. Corp.*, Comp. Gen. Dec. B-286226, 2000 CPD ¶ 179, denying a protest of the use of negotiation procedures, finding that the agency reasonably determined that discussions might be necessary to ensure that offerors fully understood the importance of timely, quality performance.

Agencies have great discretion to determine that a best value tradeoff analysis is necessary. See *Ceres Envt'l Servs., Inc.*, Comp. Gen. Dec. B-310902, 2008 CPD ¶

48, holding the use of negotiation procedures rather than sealed bidding to be appropriate because the accelerated schedule and complexity of the project necessitated consideration of non-price factors. In a unique case, *Weeks Marine, Inc. v. United States*, 79 Fed. Cl. 22 (2007), the court enjoined an agency from using negotiation procedures because it had not adequately justified their use. The Federal Circuit reversed this ruling in *Weeks Marine, Inc. v. United States*, 575 F.3d 1352 (Fed. Cir. 2009), stating at 1370-71:

> The Corps has put forth seven specific reasons for its procurement action, each of which represents a legitimate procurement objective. And as seen, in the case of each reason, the Acquisition Plan states the underlying rationale. Perhaps the Plan's fullest statement of an underlying rationale relates to emergency procurements.
>
> * * *
>
> [W]e hold that the Corps's decision to [use negotiation procedures] "evince[s] rational reasoning and consideration of relevant factors." Were we to conclude otherwise, we would be second-guessing the Corps's action. That is something we are not permitted to do. "If the court finds a reasonable basis for the agency's action, the court should stay its hand even though it might, as an original proposition, have reached a different conclusion as to the proper administration and application of the procurement regulations." *Honeywell, Inc. v. United States*, 870 F.2d 644, 648 (Fed. Cir. 1989) (quoting *M. Steinthal & Co. v. Seamans*, 455 F.2d 1289, 1301, 147 U.S. App. D.C. 221 (D.C. Cir. 1971)) (holding that the General Accounting Office's determination that a bid for a procurement contract was responsive and properly disclosed the bidder's identity had a rational basis).

Similarly, an agency's decision to use sealed bidding procedures instead of competitive negotiation will be upheld unless it is clearly unreasonable. In *Eagle Fire Inc.*, Comp. Gen. Dec. B-257951, 94-2 CPD ¶ 214, the protester argued that technical proposals were needed and discussions required; thus, the procurement should have been conducted using competitive procedures rather than sealed bidding procedures. The GAO found no basis to object to the Navy's choice of using sealed bidding because there was no ambiguity in the specification requirements and the Navy could conduct a preaward survey to determine whether the low bidder was qualified and capable of performing the contract. See also *Tennessee Apparel Corp.*, Comp. Gen. Dec. B-253178.3, 94-1 CPD ¶ 104, where the protester contended that negotiation procedures were required. The GAO found that the specifications identified in the IFB made price and price-related factors the only relevant evaluation criteria and made discussions unnecessary. Further, the GAO stated that the matters identified by the protester as necessary for discussions concerned a bidder's capacity to perform, which could be resolved through the conduct of a preaward survey. See also *Machinewerks, Inc.*, Comp. Gen. Dec. B-258123, 94-2 CPD ¶ 238 (sealed bidding with bid samples an appropriate technique to ensure that the proposed product met the agency's needs); *Virginia Blood Servs.*, Comp. Gen. Dec. B-259717, 95-1 CPD ¶ 185 (sealing bidding appropriate when agency reasonably concluded that there was no reason to conduct discussions or to consider factors other than price in selecting the contractor).

5. *Budgeting and Funding*

FAR 7.105(b)(5) states:

> Budgeting and funding. Include budget estimates, explain how they were derived, and discuss the schedule for obtaining adequate funds at the time they are required (see Subpart 32.7).

The government's full funding policy provides that budget authority sufficient to complete a useful segment of a capital project must be appropriated before any obligations for the useful segment may be incurred, otherwise a contract would violate the Anti-Deficiency Act. See OMB Circular A-11 (August 2009).

There are two situations, other than the special procurement techniques discussed above, where contracts can be awarded without full funding — incrementally funded contracts and contracts conditioned on the availability of funds.

a. *Incrementally Funded Contracts*

Incrementally funded contracts are contracts where the contract describes the work to be done in firm language but the scope of work is greater than the funds available to the agency at the time of contract award. The FAR contains no guidance on when an agency may use an incrementally funded contract. However, FAR 32.705-2(c) calls for the use of the Limitation of Funds clause in FAR 52.232-22 when an incrementally funded cost-reimbursement contract is used.

NASA gives the following guidance for using incrementally funded contracts at NFS 18-32.702-70:

> (a) Cost-reimbursement contracts may be incrementally funded only if all the following conditions are met:
>
> > (1) The total value of the contract (including options as defined in FAR Subpart 17.2) is — (i) $500,000 or more for R&D contracts under which no supplies are deliverable; or (ii) $1,000,000 or more for all other contracts.
> >
> > (2) The period of performance exceeds one year.
> >
> > (3) The funds are not available to fund the total contract value fully at award.
> >
> > (4) Initial funding of the contract is $100,000 or more.

(b) Fixed-price contracts, other than those for research and development, shall not be incrementally funded.

(c)(1) Fixed-price contracts for research and development may be incrementally funded if the conditions of 1832.702-70(a)(1) through (4) are met and the initial funding of the contract is at least 50 percent of the total fixed price.

(2) Incrementally funded fixed-price contracts shall be fully funded as soon as adequate funding becomes available.

(d) Except for a modification issued to fully fund a contract, incremental funding modifications shall not be issued for amounts totaling less than $25,000.

(e) Except for a modification issued to close out a contract, modifications deobligating funds shall not be issued for amounts totaling less than $25,000.

(f) The procurement officer, with the concurrence of the installation Chief Financial Officer, may waive any of the conditions set forth in paragraphs 1832.702-70(a) through (e). The procurement officer shall maintain a record of all such approvals during the fiscal year.

(g) A class deviation from the conditions set forth in paragraphs 1832.70270(a) through (e) exists to permit incremental funding of contracts under Phase II of the Small Business Innovation Research (SBIR) and Small Business Technology Transfer (STTR) programs. This deviation exists with the understanding that the contracts will be fully funded when funds become available.

b. Contracts Conditioned on Availability of Funds

FAR 32.703-2 provides for the limited use of contracts issued subject to the availability of funds (with an appropriate contract clause):

(a) Fiscal year contracts. The contracting officer may initiate a contract action properly chargeable to funds of the new fiscal year before these funds are available, provided that the contract includes the clause at 52.232-18, Availability of Funds (see 32.705-1(a)). This authority may be used only for operation and maintenance and continuing services (e.g., rentals, utilities, and supply items not financed by stock funds) —

(1) Necessary for normal operations; and

(2) For which Congress previously had consistently appropriated funds, unless specific statutory authority exists permitting applicability to other requirements.

(b) Indefinite-quantity or requirements contracts. A one-year indefinite-quantity or requirements contract for services that is funded by annual appropriations may extend beyond the fiscal year in which it begins; provided, that —

(1) Any specified minimum quantities are certain to be ordered in the initial fiscal year (see 37.106) and

(2) The contract includes the clause at 52.232-19, Availability of Funds for the Next Fiscal Year (see 32.705-1(b)).

(c) Acceptance of supplies or services. The Government shall not accept supplies or services under a contract conditioned upon the availability of funds until the contracting officer has given the contractor notice, to be confirmed in writing, that funds are available.

6. Product Descriptions

FAR 7.105(b)(6) states:

Product or service descriptions. Explain the choice of product or service description types (including performance-based acquisition descriptions) to be used in the acquisition.

The product description is included in Section C of the contract in the form of a specification or work statement. The type of product description used is a key element of the acquisition planning process because it is inherently related to the extent of competition and the procurement technique.

With respect to specifications and work statements to be used in the procurement process, 41 U.S.C. § 253a(a) provides:

(1) In preparing for the procurement of property or services, an executive agency shall —

(A) specify its needs and solicit bids or proposals in a manner designated to achieve full and open competition for the procurement;

* * *

(C) develop specifications in such manner as is necessary to obtain full and open competition with due regard to the nature of the property or services to be acquired.

(2) Each solicitation under this title shall include specifications which

(A) consistent with the provisions of this title, permit full and open competition;

(B) include restrictive provisions or conditions only to the extent necessary to satisfy the needs of the executive agency or as authorized by law.

The same requirements are set forth in 10 U.S.C. § 2305(a)(1). These statutory provisions contain a number of policy objectives to be served in selecting the product description for a contract — promoting the acquisition of commercial items, favoring the use of functional or performance specifications, and avoiding the use of restrictive provisions. It is also vital that the product description be clearly stated to obtain the most effective competition and avoid later disputes.

a. Government vs. Commercial Specifications

For many years the government followed a policy favoring the use of government-drafted specifications — based, apparently, on the belief that such specifications were more precisely drafted and more likely to ensure that the procuring agencies obtained products and services that met their needs. However, there were increasing indications that these specifications (Federal specifications and military specifications) were not keeping up with market conditions and not allowing government agencies to obtain the best products and services available at the most economical prices. The policy changed in the 1990s. On June 29, 1994, the Secretary of Defense issued a memorandum calling for the use of performance specifications or non-government standards for all new military systems and permitting the use of military specifications only when a waiver has been obtained. This memorandum stated:

> Military Specifications and Standards: Performance specifications shall be used when purchasing new systems, major modifications, upgrades to current systems, and nondevelopmental and commercial items, for programs in any acquisition category. If it is not practicable to use a performance specification, a non-government standard shall be used. Since there will be cases when military specifications are needed to define an exact design solution because there is no acceptable non-government standard or because the use of a performance specification or nongovernment standard is not cost effective, the use of military specifications and standards is authorized as a last resort, with an appropriate waiver.

The intent of the policy was not to eliminate military specifications altogether, but to curtail the automatic development and imposition of unique military specifications as the cultural norm within the Department of Defense.

At the same time, the FASA included 10 U.S.C. § 2377 and 41 U.S.C. § 264b, stating a preference for the acquisition of commercial and nondevelopmental items and requiring agencies to modify requirements in appropriate cases to ensure that the requirements can be met by commercial items or, to the extent that commercial items suitable to meet the agency's needs are not available, nondevelopmental items other than commercial items, state specifications in terms that enable and encourage bidders and offerors to supply commercial items or, to the extent that commercial items suitable to meet the agency's needs are not available, nondevelopmental items other than commercial items in response to the agency solicitations. This statutory coverage does not mandate the use of commercial standards but permits agencies to adopt any policy that will maximize the procurement of commercial items. FAR Part 11 preserves this agency discretion. FAR 11.002(a)(2)(ii) merely restates the first statutory requirement set forth above. FAR 11.101(a) revised the priority list for selection of specifications to remove military specifications and federal specifications from the list:

> Agencies may select from existing requirements documents, modify or combine existing requirements documents, or create new requirements documents to meet agency needs, consistent with the following order of precedence:
>
> > (1) Documents mandated for use by law.
> >
> > (2) Performance-oriented documents (e.g., a PWS or SOO). (See 2.101.)
> >
> > (3) Detailed design-oriented documents.
> >
> > (4) Standards, specifications and related publications issued by the Government outside the Defense or Federal series for the non-repetitive acquisition of items.

This guidance is silent as to the policies of the Department of Defense but apparently permits the use of federal specifications if none of the documents on the list will suffice. See FAR 11.201, which states:

> (a) Solicitations citing requirements documents listed in the General Services Administration (GSA) Index of Federal Specifications, Standards and Commercial Item Descriptions, the DoD Acquisition Streamlining and Standardization Information System (ASSIST), or other agency index shall identify each document's approval date and the dates of any applicable amendments and revisions. Do not use general identification references, such as "the issue in effect on the date of the solicitation." Contracting offices will not normally furnish these cited documents with the solicitation, except when —
>
> > (1) The requirements document must be furnished with the solicitation to enable prospective contractors to make a competent evaluation of the solicitation;
> >
> > (2) In the judgment of the contracting officer, it would be impracticable for prospective contractors to obtain the documents in reasonable time to respond to the solicitation; or
> >
> > (3) A prospective contractor requests a copy of a Government promulgated requirements document.
>
> (b) Contracting offices shall clearly identify in the solicitation any pertinent documents not listed in the GSA Index of Federal Specifications, Standards and Commercial Item Descriptions or ASSIST. Such documents shall be furnished with the solicitation or specific instructions shall be furnished for obtaining or examining such documents.

(c) When documents refer to other documents, such references shall —

(1) Be restricted to documents, or appropriate portions of documents, that apply in the acquisition;

(2) Cite the extent of their applicability;

(3) Not conflict with other documents and provisions of the solicitation; and

(4) Identify all applicable first tier references.

b. Functional and Performance Specifications

Specifications are usually referred to as design, performance, or functional specifications. These different types of specifications have different legal ramifications. See *Blake Constr. Co. v. United States*, 987 F.2d 743 (Fed. Cir. 1993), where the court described design specifications at 744:

Design specifications . . . describe in precise detail the materials to be employed and the manner in which the work is to be performed. The contractor has no discretion to deviate from the specifications, but is "required to follow them as one would a road map." "Detailed design specifications contain an implied warranty that if they are followed, an acceptable result will be produced." *Stuyvesant Dredging Co. v. United States*, 834 F.2d 1576, 1582 (Fed. Cir. 1987) (citing *United States v. Spearin*, 248 U.S. 132 (1918)).

In *Caddell Constr. Co. v. United States*, 78 Fed. Cl. 406 (2007), the contractor contended that the requirement to modernize a medical facility was a design specification while the government argued it was a performance specification. The court gave their contentions at 411-12:

Plaintiff argues that because the contract in this case "prescribe[s] in minute detail 'the character, dimension, and location of the construction work'" it is a design specification. In particular, plaintiff points to the fact that the contract specified "the type steel, bolts, tubing, washers, studs, nuts, zinc coating and fasteners to be used." In addition, plaintiff avers that the contract dictated how fabrication and erection were to be performed, inspected, and tested. Finally, plaintiff claims that the structural and architectural drawings "specify the exact dimensions, locations, sizes and connections for each piece of steel required to be fabricated and assembled to form the structural frame for this Project" indicating that this contract was a design specification and not a performance specification.

Defendant maintains that the contract in question was a performance specification because it "specified the end product (the building to be constructed) and left the discretion of how to construct the building almost entirely up to Caddell/ SSC." Although defendant admits that the contract documents were detailed, defendant argues that because these details are not instructions on how to construct the building, the contract was not a design specification. Finally, defendant avers that because the contract did not provide the "means and methods" for the construction, the contract was a performance specification.

The court agreed with the contractor that, at the very least, the structural steel portion of the contract was a design specification, stating at 412:

> Although the government did not dictate every aspect of the construction of the building and left certain key aspects of the construction, such as sequencing and scheduling, up to Caddell, the details and specifications for the structural steel were design specifications. Nine pages of the contract are devoted to specifications for the structural steel with specific instructions on what type of bolts, washers, nuts, welds, finishes, and connections, among other things could be used for the construction. This was clearly a "road map" for the structural steel fabricator to follow.

* * *

> Although defendant urges this court to follow the court's decision in *PCL Construction Services, Inc. v. United States*, the two cases are factually dissimilar. In *PCL Construction*, plaintiff "promised that its construction efforts would include. . . its own 'engineering efforts' to address design problems as they occurred." *PCL Construction Services, Inc. v. United States*, 47 Fed. Cl. 745, 798 (2000). Plaintiff made no such assurances with regard to the steel structure in this case. In fact, plaintiff was obligated to fabricate the steel exactly according to the plans and to clear any questions of discrepancies or missing information with the government. Plaintiff could not "fill in the blanks," if necessary.

When the government uses a design specification, it impliedly warrants that the specifications are suitable for their intended purposes. See Chapter 3 of *Cibinic, Nagle & Nash, Administration of Government Contracts (4th ed. 2006)*.

In *Blake Constr. Co. v. United States*, 987 F.2d 743 (Fed. Cir. 1993), the court also discussed performance specifications at 744:

> Performance specifications "set forth an objective or standard to be achieved, and the successful bidder is expected to exercise his ingenuity in achieving that objective or standard of performance, selecting the means and assuming a corresponding responsibility for that selection." *J.L. Simmons Co. v. United States*, 188 Cl. Ct. 684, 412 F.2d 1360, 1362 (Ct. Cl. 1969).

In general, performance-type specifications describe the government's requirements in terms of the agency's needs rather than in terms of a precise description of the work to be done. In many cases they promote more competition by giving contractors more flexibility and place the risk of nonperformance on the contractor. See, for example, *Daewoo Eng'g & Constr. Co. v. United States*, 73 Fed. Cl. 547

(2006), *aff'd*, 557 F.3d 1332 (Fed. Cir. 2009), rejecting an allegation that a specification was defective. The court held that the disputed requirement was a performance specification that placed responsibility for compliance on the contractor, adding that with performance specifications "[t]he Government does not care how the job is completed, so long as it obtains what it paid for." The GAO denied a protest that the use of such specifications placed too much risk on the contractor by requiring substantial design effort, *McDermott Shipyards*, Comp. Gen. Dec. B-237049, 90-1 CPD ¶ 121, citing *Pitney Bowes*, 68 Comp. Gen. 249 (B-233100), 89-1 CPD ¶ 157, for the view that such specifications are favored under the CICA.

A functional specification describes the work to be performed in terms of end purpose or the government's ultimate objective, rather than how the work is to be performed. Functional specifications may be regarded as a particular type of performance specification—one that describes the government's ultimate need or objective without specifying any particular approach or type of product that should be used to achieve the objectives.

This should be contrasted with a so-called "product-oriented" performance-type specification, which indicates the ultimate performance objectives of the government but also specifies a particular type of product or approach that must be used and the performance standards that must be met. Functional specifications have the advantage of permitting the widest possible competition. However, before functional specifications are introduced, the commercial market should be examined to guarantee that the needs of the government can and will be met through use of such specifications. Functional specifications must be carefully prepared to ensure that competitors are not misled by overly general statements of the agency's requirements. In *CompuServe*, Comp. Gen. Dec. B-188990, 77-2 CPD ¶ 182, the GAO discussed the benefits and disadvantages of functional specifications:

> To use the approach advocated by the protester — functional specifications — in a procurement such as the present one can increase competition, which is desirable. However, using functional specifications is not free from complex, and potentially costly, difficulties. Initially, the Government must expend considerable effort in drafting the specifications.

> Offerors must then translate the specifications into their own individual equipment and software approaches. This can involve a considerable amount of detail, may result in a variety of solutions to the Government's requirements and may be quite costly. A substantial effort on the part of the Government is then required to evaluate the proposals. Whether an agency conducting a procurement like the present one should be required to take a functional approach, as opposed to specifying a DBMS package, is a question which cannot be answered in the abstract.

See *Wincor Mgmt. Group, Inc.*, Comp. Gen. Dec. B-278925, 98-1 CPD ¶ 106, holding that a specification describing the agency requirement for commercial washers and dryers in "broad functional terms" was sufficiently detailed to provide offerors with a "common understanding" of the agency's needs so they could "compete intelligently on a relatively equal basis."

Agencies can choose among a number of types of specifications or combine types of specifications to identify its needs. 41 U.S.C. § 253a(a)(3) and 10 U.S.C. § 2305(a)(1)(C), as modified by the FASA, provide:

> [T]he type of specification included in a solicitation shall depend on the nature of the needs of the executive agency and the market available to satisfy such needs. Subject to such needs, specifications may be stated in terms of —
>
> (A) function, so that a variety of products or services may qualify;
>
> (B) performance, including specifications of the range of acceptable characteristics or of the minimum acceptable standards; or
>
> (C) design requirements.

FAR 11.002(a)(2)(i) describes the types of specifications omitting the reference to design specifications:

> State requirements with respect to an acquisition of supplies or services in terms of —
>
> (A) Functions to be performed;
>
> (B) Performance required; or
>
> (C) Essential physical characteristics;

These provisions contain no explicit statement of which type of specification is preferred, but they list functional and performance specifications ahead of design specifications. Thus, they imply a preference for these broader product descriptions. FAR 11.101(a) is more explicit, stating a preference for performance-oriented specifications over design-oriented specifications. However, the ultimate objective is to obtain the most effective competition to meet the agency's needs.

Few specifications are composed solely of one type. The government must often combine specification types in order to describe its needs adequately and ensure full and open competition. See *Blake Constr. Co. v. United States*, 987 F.2d 743 (Fed. Cir. 1993), stating at 746:

> [T]he distinction between design and performance specifications is not absolute, and does not dictate the resolution of this case. Contracts may have both design and performance characteristics. *See, e.g., Utility Contractors, Inc. v. United*

States, 8 Cl. Ct. 42, 50 n.7 (1985) ("Certainly one can find numerous government contracts exhibiting both performance and design specifications."), *aff'd mem.*, 790 F.2d 90 (Fed. Cir. 1986); *Aleutain Constructors v. United States*, 24 Cl. Ct. 372, 379 (1991) ("Government contracts not uncommonly contain both design and performance specifications." It is not only possible, but likely that a contractor will be granted at least limited discretion to find the best way to achieve goals within the design parameters set by a contract. *See, e.g., Penguin Indus., Inc. v. United States*, 209 Ct. Cl. 121, 530 F.2d 934, 937 (Ct. Cl. 1976). "On occasion the labels 'design specification' and 'performance specification' have been used to connote the degree to which the government has prescribed certain details of performance on which the contractor could rely. However, those labels do not independently create, limit, or remove a contractor's obligations." *Zinger Constr. Co. v. United States*, 807 F.2d 979, 981 (Fed. Cir. 1986) (citations omitted). These labels merely help the court discuss the discretionary elements of a contract. It is the obligations imposed by the specification which determine the extent to which it is "performance" or "design," not the other way around.

FAR Subpart 37.6 provides for the use of performance specifications in contracting for services. This gives the contractor the maximum opportunity to find the most efficient way to perform. FAR 37.602 states:

(a) A Performance work statement (PWS) may be prepared by the Government or result from a Statement of objectives (SOO) prepared by the Government where the offeror proposes the PWS.

(b) Agencies shall, to the maximum extent practicable —

(1) Describe the work in terms of the required results rather than either "how" the work is to be accomplished or the number of hours to be provided (see 11.002(a)(2) and 11.101);

(2) Enable assessment of work performance against measurable performance standards;

(3) Rely on the use of measurable performance standards and financial incentives in a competitive environment to encourage competitors to develop and institute innovative and cost-effective methods of performing the work.

(c) Offerors use the SOO to develop the PWS; however, the SOO does not become part of the contract. The SOO shall, at a minimum, include —

(1) Purpose;

(2) Scope or mission;

(3) Period and place of performance;

(4) Background;

(5) Performance objectives, i.e., required results; and

(6) Any operating constraints.

c. Specifications for Development Contracts

Specifications for development contracts have always been performance specifications. Traditionally, development specifications called for a considerable amount of innovative effort in order to meet the government's needs. DOD has now prohibited this flexibility by requiring a new phase in the development cycle. As discussed earlier, this constitutes an adoption of the policy of knowledge-based acquisition, which is a management approach requiring adequate knowledge at critical junctures (i.e., knowledge points) throughout the acquisition process to make informed decisions. The policy provides a framework for developers to ask themselves at key decision points whether they have the knowledge they need to move to the next phase of acquisition. DOD Directive 5000.1 calls for sufficient knowledge to reduce the risk associated with program initiation, system demonstration, and full-rate production, stating:

> E1.1.14. Knowledge-Based Acquisition. PMs shall provide knowledge about key aspects of a system at key points in the acquisition process. PMs shall reduce technology risk, demonstrate technologies in a relevant environment, and identify technology alternatives, prior to program initiation. They shall reduce integration risk and demonstrate product design prior to the design readiness review. They shall reduce manufacturing risk and demonstrate producibility prior to full-rate production.

Other methods of ensuring that development specifications do not require the use of innovative technologies in the development process have been called "evolutionary development" and "spiral development." DOD Instruction 5000.02 reemphasizes that "evolutionary acquisition is the preferred DOD strategy for rapid acquisition of mature technology for the user." "Spiral development" is no longer used as an evolutionary acquisition strategy term but it can still be used as an engineering term to describe a software development method. With regard to evolutionary development, the instruction states:

> An evolutionary approach delivers capability in increments, recognizing, up front, the need for future capability improvements. The objective is to balance needs and available capability with resources, and to put capability into the hands of the user quickly.

These techniques are endorsed by the Weapon Systems Acquisition Reform Act of 2009, Pub. L. No. 111-23. It requires that Department of Defense officials responsible for cost estimates, budgeting, and acquisition all weigh in on system capability documents before they are validated by the Joint Requirements Oversight Council. Thus, the DOD director of cost assessment and program evaluation; the Under Secretary of Defense (Comptroller); and the Under Secretary of Defense for Acquisition, Technology and Logistics are to comment on tradeoffs between cost, schedule, and performance objectives as part of the requirements development process. This is the first major paradigm shift in how requirements for major defense acquisition programs are validated.

d. Unduly Restrictive Specifications

The use of unduly restrictive specifications is prohibited by 41 U.S.C. § 253a(a) (2) and 10 U.S.C. § 2305(a)(1)(B). An unduly restrictive specification is one that limits competition by including a requirement that exceeds the needs of the government, *Kohler Co.*, Comp. Gen. Dec. B-257162, 94-2 CPD ¶ 88. The procuring agency has considerable discretion in determining its needs, and the GAO will not disturb the agency's determination unless a protester shows that the restrictive provision is unreasonable. See *AT&T Corp.*, Comp. Gen. Dec. B-270841, 96-1 CPD ¶ 237, stating:

> The governing statutes and regulations allow contracting agencies broad discretion in determining their minimum needs and the appropriate method for accommodating them. See 10 U.S.C. § 2305(a)(1)(A) (1994); Federal Acquisition Regulation § 6.101(b) and 7.103(c). Government procurement officials who are familiar with the conditions under which supplies, equipment, or services have been used in the past, and how they are to be used in the future, are generally in the best position to know the government's actual needs, and therefore, are best able to draft appropriate specifications. *Gel Sys., Inc.*, B-234283, May 8, 1989, 89-1 CPD ¶ 433. Although an agency is required to specify its needs in a manner designed to achieve full and open competition, and is required to include restrictive provisions or conditions only to the extent necessary to satisfy its needs, without a showing that competition is restricted, agencies are permitted to determine how best to accommodate their needs, *Mine Safety Appliances Co.*, B-242379.2; B-242379.3, Nov. 27, 1991, 91-2 CPD ¶ 506, and we will not substitute our judgment for that of the agency. *Simula, Inc.*, B-251749, Feb. 1, 1993, 93-1 CPD ¶ 86; *Purification Envtl.*, B-259280, Mar. 14, 1995, 95-1 CPD ¶ 142.

The GAO has also stated that an agency's basis for using a restrictive specification will be held to be reasonable if it can "withstand logical scrutiny," *Glock, Inc.*, Comp. Gen. Dec. B-236614, 89-2 CPD ¶ 593; *Chadwick-Helmuth Co., Inc.*, Comp. Gen. Dec. B-279621.2, 98-2 CPD ¶ 44. However, a stricter rule is applicable when the provision limits the competition to a single source, *Daniel H. Wagner, Assocs.*, 65 Comp. Gen. 305 (B-220633), 86-1 CPD ¶ 166.

The GAO will not rule on protests that the specification was less restrictive than proper to meet the needs of an agency, *Purification Envtl.*, Comp. Gen. Dec. B-259280, 95-1 CPD ¶ 142; *Technology Scientific Servs., Inc.*, Comp. Gen. Dec. B-245039, 91-2 CPD ¶ 233; *Terex Corp.*, 64 Comp. Gen. 691 (B-217053), 85-2 CPD ¶ 76. Of the various kinds of specifications, design specifications are the most likely to be unduly restrictive. They are likely to contain specific requirements that are not necessary to meet the agency's needs but that preclude some contractors from competing. See, for example, *Mossberg Corp.*, Comp. Gen. Dec. B-274059, 96-2 CPD ¶ 189 (requirement that shotguns be constructed with nonreflective steel receiver rather than aluminum and requirement for crossbolt-type safety versus top-of-the-receiver); *Kohler Co.*, Comp. Gen. Dec. B-257162, 94-2 CPD ¶ 88 (requirement that diesel engines in power generators be four-cycle); *Bardex Corp.*, Comp. Gen. Dec. B-252208, 93-1 CPD ¶ 461 (requirement for electromechanical shiplift rather than hydraulic lifting devices); *Data-Team, Inc.*, 68 Comp. Gen. 368 (B-233676), 89-1 CPD ¶ 355 (requirement that copying machines use dry toner); *North Am. Reporting, Inc.*, 60 Comp. Gen. 64 (B-198448), 80-2 CPD ¶ 364 (exclusion of electronic stenographic equipment); *Lanier Bus. Prods., Inc.*, Comp. Gen. Dec. B-193693, 79-1 CPD ¶ 232 (overly intricate features on text editing equipment); and *Constantine N. Polites & Co.*, Comp. Gen. Dec. B-189214, 78-2 CPD ¶ 437 (exclusion of metric threaded parts).

Specifications written around a certain product are particularly susceptible to being found unduly restrictive. See, for example, *Racal Corp.*, Comp. Gen. Dec. B-233240, 89-1 CPD ¶ 169 (make and model specification); *Southern Techs., Inc.*, 66 Comp. Gen. 208 (B-224328), 87-1 CPD ¶ 42 (specific product required); *Jarrell-Ash Div. of the Fisher Scientific Co.*, Comp. Gen. Dec. B-185582, 77-1 CPD ¶ 19 (specified feature found in only one product); and 48 Comp. Gen. 345 (B-164993) (1968) (commercial specification describing, in great part, the desk of one manufacturer). See, however, *Stavely Instruments, Inc.*, Comp. Gen. Dec. B-259548.3, 95-1 CPD ¶ 256, holding that the specifications for X-ray units were not unduly restrictive even though only one company manufactured the product and the specifications were written around that product; Stavely did not challenge the technical specifications or otherwise assert that the specifications overstated or otherwise exceeded the Air Force's actual needs. See also *Kenwood USA Corp.*, Comp. Gen. Dec. B-294638, 2004 CPD ¶ 239, where the protester alleged that the specifications were unduly restrictive because they mimic specifications listed in Motorola technical manuals, and that Motorola was the only entity that would be able to compete successful. The GAO found that there was no evidence that Kenwood was competitively harmed by the allegedly restrictive specifications, stating that Kenwood did not furnished it with an explanation as to how any of the challenged specifications prevent firms other than Motorola from competing effectively.

A specification will not be held to be unduly restrictive if the agency can show that it has a legitimate need for the specified restrictive feature. See, for example, *Messier-Bugatti, Safran Group*, Comp. Gen. Dec. B-401064, 2009 CPD ¶ 109 (designs indicates that lock-ring wheels have lower life-cycle costs, are logistically simpler to support, and offer improved maintainability over tie-bolt designs); *Shirlington Limousine & Transport, Inc.*, Comp. Gen. Dec. B-299241, 2007 CPD ¶ 68 (requirement that the secured storage facility be accessed by an electronic access control system results in higher levels of safety and efficiency); *General Electrodynamics Corp.*, Comp. Gen. Dec. B-298698, 2006 CPD ¶ 180 (electronic load cells outweighs the inherent reliability and maintainability risks of hydraulic load cells);

USA Fabrics, Inc., Comp. Gen. Dec. B-295737, 2005 CPD ¶ 82 (consignment inventory requirement intended to reduce the amount of time that it takes FPI to supply DSCP with T-shirts for the military); *Vertol Sys. Co.*, Comp. Gen. Dec. B-295936, 2005 CPD ¶ 80 (requirement of an appropriate certification by competent aviation authorities not unreasonable to ensure the safety of government personnel); *Ocean Servs., LLC*, Comp. Gen. Dec. B-292511.2, 2003 CPD ¶ 206 (RFP's provision that all vessels meet the SOLAS requirements set forth in Subchapter U in order to meet certain enhanced safety-related requirements); *NVT Techs., Inc.*, Comp. Gen. Dec. B292302.3, 2003 CPD ¶ 174 (bond requirement in nonconstruction contract necessary to protect the government's interests); *Caswell Int'l Corp.*, Comp. Gen. Dec. B-278103, 98-1 CPD ¶ 6 (interoperability requirement based on agency's need to ensure operational safety and military readiness); *CairnsAir, Inc.*, Comp. Gen. Dec. B-278141, 98-1 CPD ¶ 1 (specification for brand-name self-contained breathing apparatus which had to be compatible with components and with existing inventory); *Innovative Refrigeration Concepts*, Comp. Gen. Dec. B-272370, 96-2 CPD ¶ 127 (requiring particular type of heat exchanger and digital controller requiring less maintenance and was more efficient); *Laidlaw Envtl. Servs.*, Comp. Gen. Dec. B-272139, 96-2 CPD ¶ 109 (specification prohibiting use of open-burn/open-detonation technologies reflecting legitimate environmental concerns); *Purification Envtl.*, Comp. Gen. Dec. B-270762, 96-1 CPD ¶ 203 (requirement to use one particular design approach (oxidation process rather than new accelerated chemical treatment process) which was the only way to remove the contaminant without creating a hazardous waste); *Building Sys. Contractors, Inc.*, Comp. Gen. Dec. B-266180, 96-1 CPD ¶ 18 (specifications for a brand-name computerized energy management control system when the system had to be compatible with the other 23 facilities at the base); *T&S Prods., Inc.*, Comp. Gen. Dec. B-261852, 95-2 CPD ¶ 161 (requirement for pressure-sensitive adhesive shipping tape with a specified length where that tape quality was necessary to secure fiberboard shipping boxes); *Fisons Instruments, Inc.*, Comp. Gen. Dec. B-261371, 95-2 CPD ¶ 31 (specifications for a mass spectrometry system); *Electronic Office Env'ts*, Comp. Gen. Dec. B-254571, 93-2 CPD ¶ 342 (detailed design specifications for file cabinets when necessary to maintain aesthetic appearance); *Lenderking Metal Prods.*, Comp. Gen. Dec. B-252035, 93-1 CPD ¶ 393 (suspension system incorporating features of brand-name product when agency experience indicated that features necessary to meet agency's needs); *Absecon Mills, Inc.*, Comp. Gen. Dec. B-251685, 93-1 CPD ¶ 332 (upholstery fabrics to be used by Federal Prison Industries when necessary for aesthetics); *Trilectron Indus., Inc.*, Comp. Gen. Dec. B-248475, 92-2 CPD ¶ 130 (requiring air conditioners to use new coolant that reduces ozone release even though EPA regulations do not require its use); *Electro-Methods, Inc.*, 70 Comp. Gen. 53 (B-239141.2), 90-2 CPD ¶ 363 (buying entire modification kits rather than individual parts); *Pulse Elecs., Inc.*, Comp. Gen. Dec. B-240105, 90-2 CPD ¶ 309 (MIL-Q-9858A quality assurance requirement for complex item); *Allen Organ Co.*, Comp. Gen. Dec. B-231473.2, 88-2 CPD ¶ 196 (requirement for wind-blown pipe organ to harmonize with historic building even though it excluded electronic organs); *Milcare, Inc.*, Comp. Gen. Dec. B-230876, 88-2 CPD ¶ 29 (inward-opening doors on storage cabinetswhen agency had space shortage); and *Honeywell Inc.*, Comp. Gen. Dec. B-230224, 88-1 CPD ¶ 568 (detailed salient characteristics describing features of brand-name product when agency demonstrated its need for specified features).

Performance specifications are much less likely than design specifications to be found to be unduly restrictive unless they contain a restrictive design feature. See, for example, *Harris Enters., Inc.*, Comp. Gen. Dec. B-311143, 2008 CPD ¶ 60 (requirement that awardee be ISO compliant); *MCI WorldCom Deutschland GmbH*, Comp. Gen. Dec. B-291418, 2003 CPD ¶ 1 (requirement that telecommunication circuits be accredited); Mark Dunning Indus., Inc., Comp. Gen. Dec. B-289378, 2002 CPD ¶ 46 (in a solicitation for trash collection services, requirements that offerors employ an individual household weighing system in order to provide the agency with data on the trash and recycling habits of family housing residents not unduly restrictive); *CHE Consulting, Inc.*, Comp. Gen. Dec. B-284110, 2000 CPD ¶ 51 (requirement to obtain support agreements from 65% of the original equipment manufacturers); and *Sun Refining & Mktg. Co.*, Comp. Gen. Dec. B-239973, 90-2 CPD ¶ 305 (requirement for delivery of oil products by pipeline rather than by truck).

Performance requirements, however, can be unduly restrictive in some instances, *MadahCom, Inc.*, Comp. Gen. Dec. B-298277, 2006 CPD ¶ 119 (requirements requiring compliance with specific radio frequency standard and minimum transmission range for equipment); *Instrument Control Serv., Inc.*, Comp. Gen. Dec. B-289660, 2002 CPD ¶ 66 (unnecessary requirement that items be calibrated within 5 workdays); *Chadwick-Helmuth Co.*, Comp. Gen. Dec. B-279621.2, 98-2 CPD ¶ 44 (unnecessary requirement that commercial computer power supply operate all existing software when software is readily modified); *Prime-Mover Co.*, Comp. Gen. Dec. B-201970, 81-2 CPD ¶ 325 (unnecessary speed and mechanical requirements for forklift vehicles); *Globe Air, Inc.*, Comp. Gen. Dec. B-180969.2, 75-1 CPD ¶ 57 (requirement that rotor blades on helicopter be no more than 37 feet in diameter). Compare *Glock, Inc.*, Comp. Gen. Dec. B-236614, 89-2 CPD ¶ 593 (requirement that handguns be double-action first shot, single-action subsequent shots reasonable for safety purposes); *Fluid Eng'g Assocs.*, 68 Comp. Gen. 447 (B-234540), 89-1 CPD ¶ 520 (requirement for independent roughing/backing pump system reasonable based on analysis of agency needs); and *Hallmark Packaging Prods., Inc.*, Comp. Gen. Dec. B-232218, 88-2 CPD ¶ 390 (requirement that trash bags pass tear-resistance test reasonable because it is a standard commercial test).

e. Unclear or Ambiguous Specifications

If specifications are vague or ambiguous, they will not communicate the exact needs of the agency to the offerors. This will generally result in proposals that do not fully meet the agency's needs or do not give rise to the most satisfactory product or service that the offeror can provide. It may even result in some potential offerors deciding not to submit proposals because they assume the agency is not seeking their product or service. The outcome of such specifications is, thus, either reduced competition or the need for considerably greater clarification or discussion after the proposals have been submitted. Most protests of ambiguous or vague specifications have occurred in sealed bid procurements, where specification problems cannot be cleared up easily after bid opening. Although there is more flexibility in negotiated procurements, agencies are still required to provide clear and unambiguous specifications. The GAO stated the following rule in *Alpha Q, Inc.*, Comp. Gen. Dec. B-248706, 92-2 CPD ¶ 189:

> The government has a general obligation when seeking bids or proposals to draft solicitations in a way that identifies the agency's needs with sufficient detail and clarity so that all vendors have a common understanding of what is required under the contract in order that they can compete on an equal basis. *Dynalectron Corp.*, B-198679, Aug. 11, 1981, 81-2 CPD ¶ 115; *Worldwide Marine, Inc.*, B-212640, Feb. 7, 1984, 84-1 CPD ¶ 152. This means that a contracting agency normally must provide or at least reference the applicable specifications and drawings which are to govern the contractor's performance. Federal Acquisition Regulation (FAR) 10.008(d). Solicitations are not required to be so detailed as to eliminate all uncertainties, *AAA Eng'g & Drafting, Inc.*, B-236034, Oct. 31, 1989, 89-2 CPD ¶ 404, and in some cases the government cannot provide drawings or other data because they are either not available or not releasable. *See Oktel*, B-244956, B-244956.2, Dec. 4, 1991, 91-2 CPD ¶ 512; *American Diesel Engineering Co., Inc.*, B-245534, Jan. 16, 1992, 92-1 CPD ¶ 79. However, where relevant information is available for inclusion in a solicitation and would give offerors seeking to meet government requirements a clearer understanding of those requirements than they would otherwise have, the information should be provided.

The following discussion includes decisions on both sealed bid and competitively negotiated procurements where guidance is provided to ensure fair competition and obtain the best product or service to meet the agency's needs.

(1) REQUIREMENT FOR CLARITY

Specifications and solicitations that are susceptible to more than one reasonable interpretation of what kind of performance is contemplated are ambiguous. Such requirements are objectionable because they impede full and open competition by failing to ensure that offerors are competing on a common or equal basis. This rule is strictly enforced in sealed bid procurements and would appear to be equally applicable to competitively negotiated procurements using design specifications. See *North Am. Reporting, Inc.*, 60 Comp. Gen. 64 (B-198448), 80-2 CPD ¶ 364, stating at 69:

> We agree with the protester that the term "other service" as used in the amended IFB is ambiguous. . . . [T]he term "other service" may be any other delivery service each bidder cares to offer as long as the FERC is so advised. Thus, the bidders are, in effect, defining the term and, as they do so differently, their bids are not comparable because they are not bidding on the same delivery bases. *See* 39 Comp. Gen. 570, 572 (1960). Therefore, we believe that this portion of the IFB accelerated delivery specification is not sufficiently definite to permit the preparation and evaluation of bids on a common basis.

In *M.J. Rudolph Corp.*, Comp. Gen. Dec. B-196159, 80-1 CPD ¶ 84, the GAO recommended resolicitation of a contract to lease cranes for loading ships where the specifications were susceptible to more than one reasonable interpretation as to the necessary performance characteristics of the cranes. See also *Allied Signal, Inc.*, Comp. Gen. Dec. B-275032, 97-1 CPD ¶ 136 (RFP ambiguous where protester and awardee both have reasonable interpretations of a requirement that the proposed modules must be backward compatible with two existing intelligence terminals); *MLC Fed., Inc.*, Comp. Gen. Dec. B-254696, 94-1 CPD ¶ 8 (RFP's system architecture requirement that equipment proposed be of the latest line could have referred only to the conceptual structure and functional behavior of the machine as distinct from the physical design); *Consolidated Devices, Inc. — Recons.*, Comp. Gen. Dec. B-225602.2, 87-1 CPD ¶ 437 (RFP did not adequately define the torque/force tension ranges within which the calibrators were to operate); *University Research Corp.*, 64 Comp. Gen. 273 (B-216461), 85-1 CPD ¶ 210 (RFP contained vague description of training courses with result that incumbent contractor had unfair advantage); *Maron Constr. Co.*, Comp. Gen. Dec. B-193106, 79-1 CPD ¶ 169 (specifications were ambiguous as to the quantity of doors and frames required); *Kemp Indus., Inc.*, Comp. Gen. Dec. B-192301, 78-2 CPD ¶ 248 (specifications were ambiguous regarding a requirement that a specific motor assembly be used in the power pack supplying howitzers); *Orthopedic Equip. Co.*, Comp. Gen. Dec. B-189971, 78-1 CPD ¶ 391 (specifications were unclear as to whether or not leaded steel could be used in the production of mountain pilon snap links); *Flo Tek*, Inc., 56 Comp. Gen. 378 (B-187571), 77-1 CPD ¶ 129 (specifications were ambiguous as to the type of stainless steel required under the contract); *Learning Resources Mfg. Co.*, Comp. Gen. Dec. B-180642, 74-1 CPD ¶ 308 (specifications did not indicate whether modular counter units were to be constructed of particle board or plywood and particle board); 51 Comp. Gen. 635 (B-174813) (1972) (specifications did not indicate whether photo composition, Linotron 1010 system, or master typography program was to be furnished); 51 Comp. Gen. 518 (B-173244) (1972); Comp. Gen. Dec. B-173452, Sept. 27, 1971, *Unpub.* (inconsistent provisions in solicitation); 49 Comp. Gen. 713 (B-169368) (1970) (solicitation failed to specify delivery time); 52 Comp. Gen. 87 (B-175254) (1972) (unclear whether solicitation referred to gear box components formerly or currently used by manufacturer); 52 Comp. Gen. 842 (B-177879) (1973) (solicitation incorporated two inconsistent bid acceptance provisions causing 10 of 13 bidders to submit nonresponsive bids); *Air Plastics, Inc.*, 53 Comp. Gen. 622 (B-179836), 74-1 CPD ¶ 100 (specifications did not detail descriptive data required); *Jacobs Transfer, Inc.*, 53 Comp. Gen. 797 (B-180195), 74-1 CPD ¶ 213 (specifications failed to estimate the number of work units required); *Allied Contractors, Inc.*, Comp. Gen. Dec. B-186114, 76-2 CPD ¶ 55 (specification ambiguous as to whether prefabricated metal building was needed in sewage treatment plant).

Specifications are not ambiguous when they contain clear performance requirements. An agency can properly elect to state its needs in terms of performance or functional requirements in order to encourage greater competition. See *Memorex Corp.*, Comp. Gen. Dec. B-212660, 84-1 CPD ¶ 153, finding that it was proper to define the requirement in terms of the "required capability and characteristics of the requested equipment" in order to invite innovative and independent approaches to meeting the agency's needs. The GAO relied to some extent on the fact that five proposals had been submitted in response to the RFP. See also *Jackson Jordan, Inc.*, Comp. Gen. Dec. B-198072, 80-2 CPD ¶ 104, where, on a sealed bid procurement, the GAO held that a specification requiring "tamping 100% of the switch" was not ambiguous, although performance was impossible, because it provided the best method presently available to describe the performance characteristic. It is also proper to define the work in terms of sample tasks, *International Sec. Tech., Inc.,* Comp. Gen. Dec. B-215029, 85-1 CPD ¶ 6.

An agency can also impose risks on competitors when it does not have necessary information. See *ANV Enters., Inc.*, Comp. Gen. Dec. B-270013, 96-1 CPD ¶ 40 (specification to test soil for the proper fertilizer requirements and to furnish and apply fertilizer did not impose undue risk where agency provided information on the types and quantities of fertilizer used historically); *Cobra Techs., Inc.*, Comp. Gen. Dec. B-254890, 94-1 CPD ¶ 35 (failure to include an estimate of the hours required to assist tenant moves not undue risk because there was no historical data to use and the IFB described what was to be required); *Newport News Shipbuilding & Dry Dock Co.*, Comp. Gen. Dec. B-221888, 86-2 CPD ¶ 23 (statement that offerors should assume the work was similar to prior overhauls and that if not, price would be adjusted provided sufficient clarity); *Korean Maint. Co.*, 66 Comp. Gen. 12 (B-223780), 86-2 CPD ¶ 379 (requirement that offeror bear risk of utility costs for three-year performance period not undue risk where past usage data were included in RFP); *Dynalectron Corp.*, 65 Comp. Gen. 290 (B-220518), 86-1 CPD ¶ 151 (requirement that offeror bear risk of amount of materials needed to perform work not undue risk where neither agency nor offerors could make a good estimate because the past usage data were not segregated); *Analytics Inc.*, Comp. Gen. Dec. B-215092, 85-1 CPD ¶ 3 (requirement that equipment function with other unspecified equipment to be procured in the future not overly vague); and *Klein-Sieb Advertising & Pub. Relations, Inc.*, Comp. Gen. Dec. B-200399, 81-2 CPD ¶ 251, *recons. denied*, 82-1 CPD ¶ 101 (statement that agency could not compute amount of services required not overly vague where seven proposals received).

The apparent confusion of bidders evidenced by their varied responses to the solicitation can be indicative of ambiguity in the specification. One solicitation was canceled because six of nine bidders took exception to the specifications, Comp. Gen. Dec. B-177660, Apr. 24, 1973, *Unpub*. See also *Ferguson-Williams, Inc.*, Comp. Gen. Dec. B-258460, 95-1 CPD ¶ 39 (agency canceled solicitation where refuse collection and disposal requirements did not identify the agency's actual requirements and the three low bidders were misled). However, in *Bentley, Inc.*, Comp. Gen. Dec. B-200561, 81-1 CPD ¶ 156, the GAO overturned the agency's decision to cancel a solicitation for alleged ambiguity, relying in part upon the fact that none of the several bidders had complained that the solicitation was ambiguous.

The mere fact that there is a great variation in bid prices is not sufficient evidence of inadequate specifications to require cancellation, *Broken Lance Enters., Inc.*, Comp. Gen. Dec. B-193066, 78-2 CPD ¶ 328 (submission of low bids does not indicate ambiguity and is not a basis to challenge an award); *Arvol D. Hays Constr.*

Co., Comp. Gen. Dec. B-187526, 76-2 CPD ¶ 378 (wide disparity in bid prices does not automatically indicate defective IFB); *J.C.L. Servs., Inc.*, Comp. Gen. Dec. B-181009, 74-1 CPD ¶ 198 (that a wide range of bids was received does not necessarily indicate defect in the specifications).

(2) ERRORS OR OMISSIONS IN SPECIFICATIONS

Specifications may be improper due to errors or omissions even though they are definite and unambiguous, *Day & Zimmerman, Inc.*, Comp. Gen. Dec. B-212017, 84-1 CPD ¶ 377 (current operating data needed for competition for services); 50 Comp. Gen. 50 (B-169977) (1970) (erroneous provision expressed fixed level of labor hours required as opposed to estimated level); 51 Comp. Gen. 426 (B-174010) (1972) (solicitation omitted data requirements); Comp. Gen. Dec. B-173740.1, Nov. 17, 1971, *Unpub.* (specifications omitted test capability and one specific item); Comp. Gen. Dec. B-178482, July 10, 1973, Unpub. (explosive was erroneously classified in specifications as class "C" rather than class "B"); *Kleen-Rite Janitorial Servs., Inc.*, Comp. Gen. Dec. B-180345, 74-1 CPD ¶ 210 (bid sheet omitted blank space for an itemized price). See also *Hoechst Marion Roussel, Inc.*, Comp. Gen. Dec. B-279073, 98-1 CPD ¶ 127, granting a protest because the solicitation for drugs did not obtain competition on some of the dosages actually used by the agency when these dosages were available commercially at lower prices than the smaller dosages in the solicitation.

Government construction contracts often attempt to overcome this problem by including an Omissions and Misdescriptions clause that requires a contractor to perform omitted or misdescribed details of the work that are necessary to carry out the intent of the drawings or specifications. However, this clause applies only to details, not to new sections of unspecified work. For example, in *Strauss Constr. Co.*, ASBCA 22791, 79-1 BCA ¶ 13,578, a contractor was not required to provide a particular fire extinguishing system whose description was omitted from the specifications because the particular system was not a "detail" under the clause. Furthermore, the government may include contract clauses that require the contractor to assume the risk of specification or drawing errors or omissions. In 48 Comp. Gen. 750 (B-165953) (1968), the GAO approved the use of such a clause, stating at 754:

> [W]e are not aware of any situations where [the] doctrine of implied warranty or representation as to the adequacy of Government specifications has been extended to cases where the Government discloses the inadequacies of such specifications and permits or requires the contractor to make necessary corrections.

See also *Varo, Inc.*, Comp. Gen. Dec. B-193789, 80-2 CPD ¶ 44.

(3) OPEN OR INDEFINITE SPECIFICATIONS

Provisions permitting offerors to select the applicable specification, like ambiguous specifications, may preclude competition on a common basis. In *Alpha Q,*

Inc., Comp. Gen. Dec. B-248706, 92-2 CPD ¶ 189, the GAO ruled that a specification was improper because it required offerors to deliver parts for General Electric engines meeting "the latest revision of the General Electric drawing." The GAO reasoned that FAR 10.008(b) required that the government furnish such information. That provision, now in FAR 11.201, states:

> Do not use general identification references, such as "the issue in effect on the date of the solicitation."

See also *Pulse Elecs., Inc.*, Comp. Gen. Dec. B-244764, 91-2 CPD ¶ 468, finding a specification improper because it required offerors to comply with military specifications and standards "in effect as of the date set for receipt of proposals."

7. *Priorities, Allocations and Allotments*

FAR 7.105(b)(7) states:

> *Priorities, allocations, and allotments.* When urgency of the requirement dictates a particularly short delivery or performance schedule, certain priorities may apply. If so, specify the method for obtaining and using priorities, allocations, and allotments, and the reasons for them (see Subpart 11.6).

FAR Subpart 11.6 describes the application of the Defense Priorities and Allocation System under the Defense Production Act of 1950, 50 U.S.C. App. § 2061 et seq. This Act permits an agency awarding contracts in support of the national defense to designate such contracts with a DO or DX rating, which gives them priority over other orders received by suppliers of certain materials. FAR 11.603(f) provides that guidance on the use of these priorities is contained in agency instructions. See, for example, DOD Manual 4400.1-M (May 1995), which prescribes uniform procedures to assure priority treatment on contracts and orders for materials, components, and equipment on authorized programs to meet required delivery dates.

8. *Contractor versus Government Performance*

FAR 7.105(b)(8) states:

> *Contractor versus Government performance.* Address the considerations given to OMB Circular A-76 (see Subpart 7.3).

OMB Circular A-76, Policies for Acquiring Commercial or Industrial Services Needed by the Government, states a preference for contracting with private sources when an agency is obtaining commercial products or services. In most acquisition planning efforts this policy will not be an issue because the agency does not have the capability of performing the work with its own employees. This policy is operative primarily when the agency had decided to contract out work that has previously been performed by agency employees. In such cases the agency must conduct the procurement in accordance with the OMB Circular and the guidance in FAR Subpart 7.3. This entails the conducting of a competition between the agency activity and potential contractors. There may also be some situations when an agency activity will be permitted to compete for work that is designated for procurement from private sources. Contracting officers should review their agency regulations for guidance on contracting procedures to be used in this situation. See Chapter 3 of *Cibinic & Nash, Formation of Government Contracts (3d ed. 1998)* for a detailed discussion of the A-76 policy.

9. Inherently Governmental Functions

FAR 7.105(b)(9) states:

Inherently governmental functions. Address the consideration given to Subpart 7.5.

Certain governmental functions may not be contracted out to private firms. OFPP issued a proposed policy letter on March 31, 2010, adopting the FAIR Act definition as the single, government-wide definition. This definition reflects longstanding OFPP guidance that had been set out in OFPP Policy Letter 92-1, Sept. 30, 1992. The definition, which the draft guidance stated should be inserted in all existing regulations and policies, provides that an activity is "inherently governmental when it is so intimately related to the public interest as to mandate performance by federal employees." The draft also lists 20 examples of inherently governmental functions.

The proposed policy letter provides guidance to help agencies determine whether a given function meets the definition of an "inherently governmental function." The proposed policy letter retains a list of examples of inherently governmental functions, currently found in FAR Subpart 7.5. OFPP would also create tests for agencies to use in determining whether functions not appearing on the list otherwise fall within the definition of inherently governmental. The "nature of the function" test would ask agencies to consider whether the direct exercise of sovereign power is involved. Such functions are uniquely governmental and, therefore, inherently governmental. The "discretion" test would ask agencies to evaluate whether the discretion associated with the function, when exercised by a contractor, would have the effect of committing the government to a course of action. This test was included in OFPP Policy Letter 92-1, Inherently Governmental Functions, and currently may be found in OMB Circular A-76 (Attachment A, para. B(1)(b)), which rescinded Policy Letter 92-1.

The guidance seeks to clarify and reinforce that agencies have both pre-award and post-award responsibilities for evaluating whether a function is inherently governmental and taking steps to avoid transferring inherently governmental authority to a contractor, such as through inadequate attention to contract administration. For proposed work, a determination that the work is not inherently governmental should be made prior to issuance of the solicitation, preferably during acquisition planning. For ongoing contracts, agencies should review how work is performed; focusing, in particular, on functions that are closely associated with inherently governmental activities and professional and technical services, to ensure the scope of the work or the circumstances have not changed to the point that inherently governmental authority has been transferred to the contractor.

10. Management Information Requirements

FAR 7.105(b)(10) states:

Management information requirements. Discuss, as appropriate, what management system will be used by the Government to monitor the contractor's effort. If an Earned Value Management System is to be used, discuss the methodology the Government will employ to analyze and use the earned value data to assess and monitor contract performance. In addition, discuss how the offeror's/contractor's EVMS will be verified for compliance with the American National Standards Institute/Electronics Industries Alliance (ANSI/EIA) Standard-748, Earned Value Management Systems, and the timing and conduct of integrated baseline reviews (whether prior to or post award) (See 34.202).

Some agencies impose management information systems on major contractors to ensure that they receive timely information on the progress of the work during performance. See, for example, chapter 7 of DOD Regulation 5000.2-R, *Mandatory Procedures for Major Defense Acquisition Programs (MDAPs) and Major Automated Information System (MAIS) Acquisition Programs* (Apr. 5, 2002), which required reports from contractors on cost and schedule performance in order to assess whether programs are meeting their objectives. Generally, such reporting is not required on contracts for commercial items or for non-commercial items that were competitively procured on firm-fixed-price contracts. DFARS 234.201 requires that cost or incentive contracts and subcontracts valued at $20 million or more [in then year dollars] comply with the American National Standards Institute/Electronic Industries Alliance (ANSI/EIA) Standard 748—Earned Value Management Systems (ANSI/EIA-748). Cost or incentive contracts and subcontracts valued at $50 million or more are required to have an ANSI/EIA-748 compliant EVMS that has been determined acceptable by the Cognizant Federal Agency. The Defense Contract Management Agency is the executive agency for determining EVMS compliance when DoD is the Cognizant Federal Agency.

NASA Policy Directive 9501.1H, Oct. 7, 2005, establishes guidelines for a NASA contractor Financial Management Reporting System. Reporting is done by the contractor through the use of the NASA Form 533 series of Contractor Financial Management Reports. These reports supply the following: "(1) . . . correlated information needed by NASA project management for the evaluation of contractor cost as it relates to schedule and technical performance; (2) . . . actual and projected data necessary for assuring that contractor performance is realistically planned and supported by dollar and labor resources; and (3) . . . contractor cost information to the NASA accounting system as set forth in the Financial Management Manual

9060, 9100, and 9240." This system of reporting is applicable to all NASA cost-type contracts, price-redetermination contracts, and fixed-price incentive contracts. NASA Procedures and Guidelines (NPG 9501.2D), May 23, 2001, implements this directive. The report formats include NASA Form 553M, which provides monthly data on actual and planned costs and labor hours, short-term cost projections, estimates to complete, and contract values, and NASA Form 553Q, which provides quarterly time-phased cost and labor-hour estimates. The NASA Form 533M report is required when the contract value is $500,000 or greater and the period of performance is one year or more, or the contract value is $1 million or greater, regardless of the period of performance. The NASA Form 533Q is required only when the contract value is $1 million or greater and the period of performance is for one year or more.

The contractor's internal management system should be relied upon to the maximum extent possible, without requiring costly modifications, to furnish the data necessary for any management reporting system required by a government agency.

11. Make-or-Buy Programs

FAR 7.105(b)(11) states:

Make or buy. Discuss any consideration given to make-or-buy programs (see Subpart 15.407-2).

FAR 2.101 defines "make-or-buy program" as that part of a contractor's written plan for a contract identifying those major items to be produced or work efforts to be performed in the prime contractor's facilities and those to be subcontracted.

Make-or-buy programs are imposed on offerors or contractors to permit the contracting officer to make a detailed analysis of whether the contractor will perform the work in the most efficient manner. FAR 15.407-2(c) contains the following guidance on the use of such programs:

(1) Contracting officers may require prospective contractors to submit make-or-buy program plans for negotiated acquisitions requiring cost or pricing data whose estimated value is $11.5 million or more, except when the proposed contract is for research or development and, if prototypes or hardware are involved, no significant follow-on production is anticipated.

(2) Contracting officers may require prospective contractors to submit make-or-buy programs for negotiated acquisitions whose estimated value is under $11.5 million only if the contracting officer —

(i) Determines that the information is necessary; and

(ii) Documents the reasons in the contract file.

12. Test and Evaluation

FAR 7.105(b)(12) states:

Test and evaluation. To the extent applicable, describe the test program of the contractor and the Government. Describe the test program for each major phase of a major system acquisition. If concurrency is planned, discuss the extent of testing to be accomplished before production release.

FAR Part 46 contains detailed guidance on quality assurance and provides standard inspection clauses for use in different types of contracts. These standard clauses generally provide that the contractor is responsible for performing sufficient inspection and testing to ensure that supplies or services meet the contract requirements. However, FAR 46.201 gives agencies great latitude in imposing any inspection or testing requirement necessary to meet their needs. FAR 46.201(c) contains the following guidance:

Although contracts generally make contractors responsible for performing inspection before tendering supplies to the Government, there are situations in which contracts will provide for specialized inspections to be performed solely by the Government. Among situations of this kind are —

(1) Tests that require use of specialized test equipment or facilities not ordinarily available in suppliers' plants or commercial laboratories (e.g., ballistic testing of ammunition, unusual environmental tests, and simulated service tests); and

(2) Contracts that require Government testing for first article approval (see Subpart 9.3).

In the procurement of major systems, the Department of Defense is prohibited from proceeding "beyond low-rate initial production" until the completion of an initial operational test and evaluation (OT&E) program, 10 U.S.C. § 2399. DOD Regulation 5000.02, *Operation of the Defense Acquisition System*, Enclosure 6, Dec. 8, 2008, requires that each system acquisition have an integrated test program, including OT&E that ensures that each phase has been successfully competed:

1.b. The PM, in concert with the user and the T&E community, shall coordinate DT&E, OT&E, LFT&E, family-of-systems interoperability testing, information assurance testing, and modeling and simulation (M&S) activities, into an efficient continuum, closely integrated with requirements definition and systems design and development. The T&E strategy shall provide information about risk and risk mitigation, provide empirical data to validate models and simulations, evaluate technical performance and system maturity, and determine whether systems are operationally effective, suitable, and survivable against the threat detailed in the STAR or STA. The T&E strategy shall also address development and assessment of the weapons support equipment during the EMD Phase, and into production, to ensure satisfactory test system measurement performance, calibration traceability and support, required diagnostics, and safety. Adequate time and resources shall be planned to support pre-test predictions and post-test reconciliation of models and test results, for all major test events. The PM, in concert with the user and the T&E community, shall provide safety releases (to include formal Environment, Safety, and Occupational Health (ESOH) risk acceptance in accordance with Section 6 of Enclosure 12) to the developmental and operational testers prior to any test using personnel.

The regulation contains no guidance as to how much of this test activity is to be included in the acquisition plan, but it is clear that any work that must be performed or supported by contractors must be taken into account during the planning process.

13. Logistics Considerations

FAR 7.105(b)(13) states:

Logistics considerations. Describe —

(i) The assumptions determining contractor or agency support, both initially and over the life of the acquisition, including consideration of contractor or agency maintenance and servicing (see Subpart 7.3) support for contracts to be performed in a designated operational area or supporting a diplomatic or consular mission (see 25.301-3); and distribution of commercial items;

(ii) The reliability, maintainability, and quality assurance requirements, including any planned use of warranties (see Part 46);

(iii) The requirements for contractor data (including repurchase data) and data rights, their estimated cost, and the use to be made of the data (see Part 27); and

(iv) Standardization concepts, including the necessity to designate, in accordance with agency procedures, technical equipment as "standard" so that future purchases of the equipment can be made from the same manufacturing source.

This part of the plan is very important when the agency is purchasing equipment that it will use over a period of years. In such cases the maintenance of that equipment may cost considerably more than the cost of the original equipment. The agency must plan the procurement to ensure that these maintenance costs are minimized. This generally entails planning to contract for maintenance work or replacement parts or components at reasonable prices and/or including warranty clauses in the original contract..

a. Warranties

FAR Subpart 46.7 contains guidance on the use of warranties and provides, in general, that they should not be used unless they are cost-effective. Nonetheless,

FAR 46.710 specifies a number of standard warranty clauses for use when the contracting officer has decided that they are beneficial. FAR 46.703 contains the following guidance on the decision to use warranties:

> The use of warranties is not mandatory. In determining whether a warranty is appropriate for a specific acquisition, the contracting officer shall consider the following factors:
>
> > (a) *Nature and use of the supplies or services.* This includes such factors as —
> >
> > > (1) Complexity and function;
> > >
> > > (2) Degree of development;
> > >
> > > (3) State of the art;
> > >
> > > (4) End use;
> > >
> > > (5) Difficulty in detecting defects before acceptance; and
> > >
> > > (6) Potential harm to the Government if the item is defective.
> >
> > (b) *Cost.* Warranty costs arise from —
> >
> > > (1) The contractor's charge for accepting the deferred liability created by the warranty; and
> > >
> > > (2) Government administration and enforcement of the warranty (see paragraph (c) of this section).
> >
> > (c) *Administration and enforcement.* The Government's ability to enforce the warranty is essential to the effectiveness of any warranty. There must be some assurance that an adequate administrative system for reporting defects exists or can be established. The adequacy of a reporting system may depend upon such factors as the —
> >
> > > (1) Nature and complexity of the item;
> > >
> > > (2) Location and proposed use of the item;
> > >
> > > (3) Storage time for the item;
> > >
> > > (4) Distance of the using activity from the source of the item;
> > >
> > > (5) Difficulty in establishing existence of defects; and

(6) Difficulty in tracing responsibility for defects.

(d) *Trade practice.* In many instances an item is customarily warranted in the trade, and, as a result of that practice, the cost of an item to the Government will be the same whether or not a warranty is included. In those instances, it would be in the Government's interest to include such a warranty.

(e) *Reduced requirements.* The contractor's charge for assumption of added liability may be partially or completely offset by reducing the Government's contract quality assurance requirements where the warranty provides adequate assurance of a satisfactory product.

Prior to 1997, 10 U.S.C. § 2403 required DOD to obtain "guarantees" on major weapon systems contracts. This statute was repealed by § 847 of the FY 1998 Defense Authorization Act, Pub. L. No. 105-85.

b. Contracting for Parts or Components

The FAR contains no guidance on the steps necessary to ensure that replacement parts and components can be procured at reasonable prices. However, DOD PGI 217.75 provides that an agency may either acquire replenishment parts concurrently with production of the end item or acquire them competitively in a subsequent procurement when the agency has the right to use the technical data describing the parts. If neither of these can be accomplished, DOD PGI 217.7504 provides guidance on techniques that can be used to acquire the parts effectively. These techniques were discussed earlier in the material on obtaining competition. DOD PGI 217.7506 providing guidance on the need to "break out" spare parts from the contractor that designed a system so that they can be procured separately from the manufacturer of the parts or on a competitive basis. See ¶ 1-102 stating:

(b) The objective of the DoD Spare Parts Breakout Program is to reduce costs through the use of competitive procurement methods, or the purchase of parts directly from the actual manufacturer rather than the prime contractor, while maintaining the integrity of the systems and equipment in which the parts are to be used. The program is based on the application of sound management and engineering judgment in —

(1) Determining the feasibility of acquiring parts by competitive procedures or direct purchase from actual manufacturers; and

(2) Overcoming or removing constraints to breakout identified through the screening process (technical review) described in 3-302.

14. Government-Furnished Property

FAR 7.105(b)(14) states:

Government-furnished property. Indicate any Government property to be furnished to contractors, and discuss any associated considerations, such as its availability or the schedule for its acquisition (see Part 45.102).

FAR Part 45.102, Government Property, stipulates the following policy:

(a) Contractors are ordinarily required to furnish all property necessary to perform Government contracts.

(b) Contracting officers shall provide property to contractors only when it is clearly demonstrated —

(1) To be in the Government's best interest;

(2) That the overall benefit to the procurement significantly outweighs the increased cost of administration, including ultimate property disposal;

(3) That providing the property does not substantially increase the Government's assumption of risk; and

(4) That Government requirements cannot otherwise be met.

(c) The contractor's inability or unwillingness to supply its own resources is not sufficient reason for the furnishing or acquisition of property.

15. Government-Furnished Information

FAR 7.105(b)(15) states:

Government-furnished information. Discuss any Government information, such as manuals, drawings, and test data, to be provided to prospective offerors and contractors. Indicate which information that requires additional controls to monitor access and distribution (e.g., technical specifications, maps, building designs, schedules, etc.), as determined by the agency, is to be posted via the Federal Technical Data Solution (FedTeDS) (see 5.102(a)).

This is an important element of the acquisition planning process because the government is generally liable if it provides defective drawings or specifications to a contractor. See Chapter 3 of Cibinic, Nagle & Nash, *Administration of Government Contracts* (4th ed. 2006). The agency must determine whether any such information is accurate and must plan steps to avoid furnishing it, if possible, if its accuracy is questionable.

16. Environmental and Energy Conservation

FAR 7.105(b)(16) states:

Environmental and energy conservation objectives. Discuss all applicable environmental and energy conservation objectives associated with the acquisition (see Part 23), the applicability of an environmental assessment or environmental impact statement (see 40 CFR part 1502), the proposed resolution of environmental issues, and any environmentally-related requirements to be included in solicitations and contracts.

Some agencies have assigned one individual as an environmental advocate who is tasked with ensuring that environmental considerations are included in all procurement decisions.

FAR Part 23 is designed to improve the government's energy efficiency through proactive procurement decisions. These regulations were promulgated in 2001 in response to Executive Order No. 13123, "Greening the Government Through Efficient Energy Management," and substantially revised in 2007 in response to § 104 of the Energy Policy Act of 2005, Pub. L. No. 109-58 (codified at 22 U.S.C. §§ 16511–16514), and Executive Order No. 13423, "Strengthening Federal Environmental Energy, and Transportation Management," January 26, 2007.

FAR Subpart 23.2 addresses the acquisition of energy-efficient products and the use of energy-savings performance contracts. Agencies are required to purchase Energy Star and Federal Energy Management Program (FEMP)-designated energy efficient products unless the head of the agency determines that the products are not life cycle cost effective or are not reasonably available, FAR 23.203.

FAR 23.705 is specific to the government's acquisition of energy-efficient electronic products. Agencies are required to meet at least 95% of their annual acquisition requirements for electronic products with Electronic Product Environmental Assessment Tool (EPEAT)-registered products, unless an EPEAT standard for such products is unavailable.

The procurement preference for biobased products was added to the FAR in 2007 in Subpart 23.4, to implement the requirement in the Farm Security and Rural Investment Act of 2002, 7 U.S.C. § 8102, for federal agencies to give a preference to biobased products, as designated by the USDA, when procuring certain types of items. FAR Subpart 23.4 requires agencies to establish an affirmative procurement program for USDA-and EPA-designated items if the agency's purchase of a designated item exceeds $10,000 or the aggregate amount paid for designated items in the preceding fiscal year was $10,000 or more, FAR 23.400.

The second preference program in FAR Subpart 23.4 is for use of products containing recovered materials. "Recovered material" is defined as "waste materials and by-products recovered or diverted from solid waste, but the term does not include those materials and by-products generated from, and commonly reused within, an original manufacturing process," FAR 2.101. The EPA is required by the Resource Conservation and Recovery Act, Pub. L. No. 94-580 (codified at 42 U.S.C. § 6901 et. seq.), to designate products that are or can be made with recovered materials. FAR 23.404(b) provides that agency affirmative procurement programs must require that 100% of purchases of EPA designated products contain recovered material, unless the item cannot be acquired competitively within a reasonable time, meeting appropriate performance standards, or at a reasonable price.

FAR 23.202 implements the government's policy to acquire supplies and services that promote energy and water efficiency, advance the use of renewable energy products, and help foster markets for emerging technologies, FAR 23.202. This policy extends to all acquisitions, including those below the simplified acquisition threshold.

17. Security Considerations

FAR 7.105(b)(17) states:

Security considerations. For acquisitions dealing with classified matters, discuss how adequate security will be established, maintained, and monitored (see Subpart 4.4). For information technology acquisitions, discuss how agency information security requirements will be met. For acquisitions requiring routine contractor physical access to a Federally-controlled facility and/or routine access to a Federally-controlled information system, discuss how agency requirements for personal identity verification of contractors will be met (see Subpart 4.13).

FAR 4.403 requires contracting officers to ensure that any contractor has the appropriate security clearances when classified information is required for contract performance. This provision provides:

(a) *Presolicitation phase.* Contracting officers shall review all proposed solicitations to determine whether access to classified information may be required by offerors, or by a contractor during contract performance.

   (1) If access to classified information of another agency may be required, the contracting officer shall —

      (i) Determine if the agency is covered by the NISP; and

      (ii) Follow that agency's procedures for determining the security clearances of firms to be solicited.

   (2) If the classified information required is from the contracting officer's agency, the contracting officer shall follow agency procedures.

(b) *Solicitation phase.* Contracting officers shall —

> (1) Ensure that the classified acquisition is conducted as required by the NISP or agency procedures, as appropriate; and

> (2) Include —

>> (i) An appropriate Security Requirements clause in the solicitation (see 4.404); and

>> (ii) As appropriate, in solicitations and contracts when the contract may require access to classified information, a requirement for security safeguards in addition to those provided in the clause (52.204-2, Security Requirements).

(c) *Award phase.* Contracting officers shall inform contractors and subcontractors of the security classifications and requirements assigned to the various documents, materials, tasks, subcontracts, and components of the classified contract as follows:

> (1) Agencies covered by the NISP shall use the Contract Security Classification Specification, DD Form 254. The contracting officer, or authorized representative, is the approving official for the form and shall ensure that it is prepared and distributed in accordance with the Industrial Security Regulation.

> (2) Contracting officers in agencies not covered by the NISP shall follow agency procedures.

Contracting officers must insert FAR 52.204-2, Security Requirements, in solicitations and contracts when the contract may require access to classified information.

If any prospective contractors have not obtained clearances under the Defense Industrial Security Program, they will be unable to participate in any competition. This issue must be addressed in the acquisition planning process in order to provide time for such contractors to become part of the program and obtain security clearances for all their employees who would have to handle classified material during contract performance.

18. Contract Administration

FAR 7.105(b)(18) states:

> *Contract administration.* Describe how the contract will be administered. In contracts for services, include how inspection and acceptance corresponding to the work statement's performance criteria will be enforced.

FAR Part 42 provides guidance on the performance of contract administration and related audit services. The agency should decide, in the planning process, whether the contract will be administered by the procuring agency or by a field organization. FAR 42.201(b) notes that the Defense Contract Management Command is a major organization charged with the responsibility for contract administration. Other agencies have similar, but smaller, organizations. These organizations are listed in the Federal Directory of Contract Administration Services Components, FAR 42.203.

In order to ensure that contract administration is performed efficiently and effectively and that contractors are treated consistently on different contracts, FAR 42.002 requires that agencies use field offices that provide contract administration and audit services, as follows:

(a) Agencies shall avoid duplicate audits, reviews, inspections, and examinations of contractors or subcontractors, by more than one agency, through the use of interagency agreements.

(b) Subject to the fiscal regulations of the agencies and applicable interagency agreements, the requesting agency shall reimburse the servicing agency for rendered services in accordance with the Economy Act (31 U.S.C. 1535).

(c) When an interagency agreement is established, the agencies are encouraged to consider establishing procedures for the resolution of issues that may arise under the agreement.

FAR 42.202 provides guidance on the delegation of contract administration function to contract administration offices. The contract administration functions are listed in FAR 42.302, but the agency has the choice of which functions to delegate and which to retain.

If audit services will be required during the performance of a contract, the audit agency to provide such services should be determined in the planning process. The major agency providing such services is the Defense Contract Audit Agency, FAR 42.101(b). However, other agencies also provide such services with selected contractors — primarily educational institutions. DCAA maintains a Directory of Federal Contract Audit Offices, FAR 42.103. The procedure for requesting audit services is set forth in FAR 42.102.

19. Other Considerations

FAR 7.105(b)(19) states:

Other considerations. Discuss, as applicable:

    (i) Standardization concepts;

    (ii) The industrial readiness program;

    (iii) The Defense Production Act;

(iv) The Occupational Safety and Health Act;

(v) Support Anti-terrorism by Fostering Effective Technologies Act of 2002 (SAFETY Act) (see Subpart 50.2);

(vi) Foreign sales implications;

(vii) Special requirements for contracts to be performed in a designated operational area or supporting a diplomatic or consular mission; and

(viii) Any other matters germane to the plan not covered elsewhere.

This part of the plan can cover any matter not covered in other parts. The list in the FAR is clearly a partial list, and the agency should consider carefully any other issues that are relevant to a successful procurement.

One matter that should be considered in this part when supplies are being procured is whether the quantity needed is an "economic purchase quantity." FAR 7.202(a) and (b) provide the following guidance:

(a) Agencies are required by 10 U.S.C. 2384(a) and 41 U.S.C. 253(f) to procure supplies in such quantity as (1) will result in the total cost and unit cost most advantageous to the Government, where practicable, and (2) does not exceed the quantity reasonably expected to be required by the agency.

(b) Each solicitation for a contract for supplies is required, if practicable, to include a provision inviting each offeror responding to the solicitation (1) to state an opinion on whether the quantity of the supplies proposed to be acquired is economically advantageous to the Government, and (2) if applicable, to recommend a quantity or quantities which would be more economically advantageous to the Government. Each such recommendation is required to include a quotation of the total price and the unit price for supplies procured in each recommended quantity.

20. Milestones for the Acquisition

FAR 7.105(b)(20) states:

Milestones for the acquisition cycle. Address the following steps and any others appropriate:

Acquisition plan approval.

Statement of work.

Specifications.

Data requirements.

Completion of acquisition-package preparation.

Purchase request.

Justification and approval for other than full and open competition where applicable and/or any required D&F approval.

Issuance of synopsis.

Issuance of solicitation.

Evaluation of proposals, audits, and field reports.

Beginning and completion of negotiations.

Contract preparation, review, and clearance.

Contract award.

The milestone chart should contain a specific date for the completion of each step in the acquisition process and should identify the person or organization responsible for the action. When the procurement is being conducted by an acquisition team in accordance with FAR 1.102(d), the member of the team that will play the lead role in completing each action should be identified in the milestone chart. Any additional steps that are required to implement the acquisition plan should also be included in the milestone chart.

21. Participants

FAR 7.105(b)(21) states:

Identification of participants in acquisition plan preparation. List the individuals who participated in preparing the acquisition plan, giving contact information for each.

This list of participants in the acquisition planning process provides contacts if there are later questions about any element of the plan.

CHAPTER 2

DEVELOPMENT OF THE SOURCE SELECTION PLAN

As noted in Chapter 1, a key element of the acquisition plan is the source selection procedures that will be followed in the procurement. Most agencies prepare a source selection plan detailing these procedures based on the procurement strategy that will be used. The plan should include the evaluation factors and their relative importance as well as the internal procedures that will be used to make the ultimate source selection decision. While a complete source selection plan is not a legal requirement, its preparation has been adopted by agencies as good business practice.

The GAO has continuously held that failure to adhere to the source selection plan is not protestable because it is an internal agency document vesting no rights in offerors, *Sayres & Assocs. Corp.*, Comp. Gen. Dec. B-295946, 2005 CPD ¶ 90; *Islandwide Landscaping, Inc.*, Comp. Gen. Dec. B-293018, 2004 CPD ¶ 9; *Johnson Controls World Servs., Inc.*, Comp. Gen. Dec. B-289942, 2002 CPD ¶ 88; *Mid Pacific Envtl.*, Comp. Gen. Dec. B-283309.2, 2000 CPD ¶ 40. Some decisions of the Court of Federal Claims have agreed with this reasoning, *Manson Constr. Co. v. United States*, 79 Fed. Cl. 16 (2007); *ManTech Telecommunications & Information Sys. Corp. v. United States*, 49 Fed. Cl. 57 (2001); *C&L Constr. Co. v. United States*, 6 Cl. Ct. 792 (1984). In contrast, other decisions of the Court of Federal Claims have held that failure to adhere to the plan is grounds for granting a protest, *Fort Carson Support Servs. v. United States*, 71 Fed. Cl. 571 (2006) (agencies may change plans at will but "subordinate officials" may not deviate from approved plan); *Beta Analytics Int'l, Inc. v. United States*, 67 Fed. Cl. 384 (2005) (departure from plan indicated unequal treatment of offerors).

The statutes and FAR give agencies broad discretion in devising source selection procedures. For example, there is no requirement in the FAR for a written source selection plan, but many agencies require the preparation of such plans as the initial step in the competitive negotiation process. See DFARS 215.303(b)(2) requiring a source selection plan for "high-dollar value and other acquisitions." See also *Contracting for Best Value: A Best Practice Guide to Source Selection*, AMC-P 715-3 (Jan. 1, 1998); *NAVSEA Source Selection Guide*, Section 4 (Jan. 24, 2001; *Transportation Acquisition Manual* (TAM) 1215.303(b); and AFFARS *Informational Guidance* 5315.303 (Dec. 2008).

The goal of a source selection plan is to structure and implement each procurement to assure that the contract is awarded to the competitor with the most favorable offer. The source selection plan should enable the government: (1) to conduct a fair and unbiased competition and (2) to arrive at a contract that ensures that the contractor will fully meet the government's needs. The source selection plan should include source selection procedures that ensure these objectives are met. Moreover, in order to accomplish these two goals the agency must first organize a source selection team.

I. SOURCE SELECTION TEAM

In order to achieve the benefit of the various disciplines involved in selecting the procurement strategy and evaluation factors, it is essential that the source selection team be established at the outset. This requires a determination as to the number of people that will be involved in the process and the selection of people who are competent to evaluate proposals and make the source selection decision and are free from bias or conflict of interest.

A. Composition and Functions of Team

FAR 1.102(c) states the following expansive composition of the "Acquisition Team:"

> The Acquisition Team consists of all participants in Government acquisition including not only representatives of the technical, supply, and procurement communities but also the customers they serve, and the contractors who provide the products and services.

The statement of guiding principles in FAR 1.102 emphasizes that the "Acquisition Team" is responsible for successful procurement. FAR 1.102-3 states:

> The purpose of defining the Federal Acquisition Team (Team) in the Guiding Principles is to ensure that participants in the System are identified — beginning with the customer and ending with the contractor of the product or service. By identifying the team members in this manner, teamwork, unity of purpose, and open communication among the members of the Team in sharing the vision and achieving the goal of the System are encouraged. Individual team members will participate in the acquisition process at the appropriate time.

The functions of the "Acquisition Team" are set forth in FAR 1.102-4

> (a) Government members of the Team must be empowered to make acquisition decisions within their areas of responsibility, including selection, negotiation, and administration of contracts consistent with the Guiding Principles. In particular, the contracting officer must have the authority to the maximum extent practicable and consistent with law, to determine the application of rules, regulations, and policies, on the specific contract.

> (b) The authority to make decisions and the accountability for the decision made will be delegated to the lowest level within the System, consistent with law.

(c) The Team must be prepared to perform the functions and duties assigned. The Government is committed to provide training, professional development, and other resources necessary for maintaining and improving the knowledge, skills, and abilities for all Government participants on the Team, both with regard to their particular area of responsibility within the System, and their respective role as a team member. The contractor community is encouraged to do likewise.

(d) The System will foster cooperative relationships between the Government and its contractors consistent with its overriding responsibility to the taxpayers.

Many agencies adopted this team concept in the 1990s, referred to as Integrated Product Teams (IPTs), as the best way to perform the competitive negotiation process. An IPT was defined in *DOD Guide to Integrated Product and Process Development* (version 1.0) Feb. 5, 1996, as follows:

Integrated Product Teams are cross-functional teams that are formed for the specific purpose of delivering a product for an external or internal customer. IPT members should have complimentary skills and be committed to a common purpose, performance objectives, and approach for which they hold themselves mutually accountable. IPTs are the means through which IPPD is implemented. Members of an integrated product team represent technical, manufacturing, business, and support functions and organizations which are critical to developing, procuring and supporting the product. Having these functions represented concurrently permits teams to consider more and broader alternatives quickly, and in a broader context, enables faster and better decisions. Once on a team, the role of an IPT member changes from that of a member of a particular functional organization, who focuses on a given discipline, to that of a team member, who focuses on a product and its associated processes. Each individual should offer his/her expertise to the team as well as understand and respect the expertise available from other members of the team. Team members work together to achieve the team's objectives.

The Federal Aviation Administration, which operates outside the FAR and the standard procurement statutes, also structured its entire competitive negotiation process based on the use of IPTs. Paragraph 1.11 of the FAA Acquisition Management System stated:

Integrated Product Teams will be used for all acquisitions, whether at headquarters or for field activities, including those pre-existing to April 1, 1996. The size and composition of individual Integrated Product Teams will vary widely. A complex development of a NAS system may require an IPT of many people with varied capabilities. On the other hand, the procurement of low-cost products or services may involve an IPT of as few as two people, representing the provider and the user or customer.

For guidance on organizing and leading effective IPTs, see *Rules of the Road: A Guide for Leading Successful Integrated Product Teams* (Office of the Under Secretary of Defense, Nov. 1995). Additional guidance was contained in Part 5.4 of

DOD Regulation 5000.2-R, *Mandatory Procedures for Major Defense Acquisition Programs (MDAPs) and Major Automated Information System (MAIS) Acquisition Programs*, Mar. 15, 1996.

Although this was good guidance, it has been deleted from the current regulations. Thus, the FAA AMS no longer contains this requirement and DOD Regulation 5000.2-R has been superseded by DOD Instruction 5000.02, Dec. 8, 2008 (not discussing IPTs). Nonetheless, many agencies continue to use IPTs in their major procurements.

In spite of the fact that agency regulations do not call for a formal team structure, the source selection process in intrinsically a team endeavor. Thus, source selection teams should be established and "tailored" for each particular acquisition. In some cases this will mean that the team will consist of the contracting officer and a technical evaluator, while in other, larger or more complex procurements, the team will consist of many members from various disciplines. The Army Materiel Command guidance in *Contracting for Best Value: A Best Practice Guide to Source Selection*, AMC-P 715-3, Jan. 1, 1998, discussed the concept of "tailoring" the evaluation team:

> Source selection should be a multidisciplined team effort from the earliest planning stages. The size and composition of the team should be tailored specifically to the acquisition. In complex source selections you may have a larger team (e.g., 8 to 10 people) from various functional disciplines. In streamlined source selections, however, the team may consist of one or more technical evaluators and the contracting officer, who is also the source selection authority. Whether the team is large or small, it should be established to ensure continuity and active ongoing involvement of appropriate contracting, technical, logistics, legal, user, contract administrators, and other experts to ensure a comprehensive evaluation of each proposal.

Within the Acquisition Team, FAR 15.303(a) specifies the source selection and contracting process responsibilities. The contracting officer is the source selection authority (SSA) unless the agency head appoints another individual. FAR 15.303(b) and (c) provides guidance on the roles of the SSA and the contracting officer as follows:

> (b) The source selection authority shall —
>
> > (1) Establish an evaluation team, tailored for the particular acquisition, that includes appropriate contracting, legal, logistics, technical, and other expertise to assure a comprehensive evaluation of offers;
> >
> > (2) Approve the source selection strategy or acquisition plan, if applicable, before solicitation release;

(3) Ensure consistency among the solicitation requirements, notices to offerors, proposal preparation instructions, evaluation factors and subfactors, solicitation provisions or contract clauses, and data requirements;

(4) Ensure that proposals are evaluated based solely on the factors and subfactors contained in the solicitation (10 U.S.C. 2305(b)(1) and 41 U.S.C. 253b(d)(3));

(5) Consider the recommendations of advisory boards or panels (if any); and

(6) Select the source or sources whose proposal is the best value to the Government (10 U.S.C. 2305(b)(4)(B) and 41 U.S.C. 253b(d)(3)).

(c) The contracting officer shall —

(1) After release of a solicitation, serve as the focal point for inquires from actual or prospective offerors;

(2) After receipt of proposals, control exchanges with offerors in accordance with 15.306; and

(3) Award the contract(s).

1. Major Acquisitions

In procurements of special significance to an agency, because of dollar size or importance, more formal source selection procedures are followed. The distinguishing feature in these procedures is that the source selection authority (SSA) usually is not a member of the immediate source selection team but is a higher-ranking official of the agency. In such cases the source selection team usually contains one or more levels of personnel to advise and brief the SSA during the decisional process. Such personnel are necessary because the SSA is not expected to be a full participant in all the steps of the source selection process but is expected to make the competitive range and source selection decisions. DOD has imposed additional review processes and has mandated that officials not perform multiple functions in the source selection process. See DFARS 203.170 stating:

To ensure the separation of functions for oversight, source selection, contract negotiation, and contract award, departments and agencies shall adhere to the following best practice policies:

(a) Senior leaders shall not perform multiple roles in source selection for a major weapon system or major service acquisition. Departments and agencies shall certify every 2 years that no senior leader has performed multiple roles in the acquisition of a major weapon system or major service. Completed certifications shall be forwarded to the Director, Defense Procurement, in accordance with the procedures at PGI 203.170.

*   *   *

(c) Acquisition process reviews of the military departments shall be conducted to assess and improve acquisition and management processes, roles, and structures. The scope of the reviews should include –

    (1) Distribution of acquisition roles and responsibilities among personnel;

    (2) Processes for reporting concerns about unusual or inappropriate actions;

*   *   *

(d) Source selection processes shall be –

    (1) Reviewed and approved by cognizant organizations responsible for oversight;

    (2) Documented by the head of the contracting activity or at the agency level; and

    (3) Periodically reviewed by outside officials independent of that office or agency.

(e) Legal review of documentation of major acquisition system source selection shall be conducted prior to contract award, including the supporting documentation of the source selection evaluation board, source selection advisory council, and source selection authority.

Agencies often require the use of formal procedures for negotiated acquisitions over a specified dollar threshold, but the thresholds vary among the agencies. For example, the Air Force designates program personnel as the SSA for most acquisitions over $10 million with higher ranking officials as the SSA for many acquisitions over $100 million, AFFARS 5315.303(c). Other agencies have different thresholds. See NASA (NFS 1815.300-70(a) – acquisitions over $50 million) and DOT (TAM 1215.303 – "major systems" defined as systems with life-cycle costs of over $150 million or meeting other characteristics).

When formal procedures are used, it has been common for the source selection organization to include a source selection evaluation board (SSEB or SEB) and/ or a source selection advisory council (SSAC), but these names vary from agency to agency. The contracting officer usually serves only as an advisor to the SSA but continues to play a major role. Under FAR 15.303(c) the contracting officer must, at a minimum, serve as a focal point for inquiries from prospective offerors after release of the solicitation, control exchanges with offerors after receipt of proposals, and sign the contract.

The precise role of the SSEB and the SSAC is a matter of agency discretion. See AFFARS Mandatory Procedure 5315.3 containing the following descriptions of the functions of the source selection evaluation team (formerly the SSEB) and the SSAC:

> Source Selection Evaluation Team (SSET) is a group of government and, if needed, nongovernment personnel representing the various functional disciplines relevant to the acquisition. The Source Selection Evaluation Team evaluates proposals and reports its findings to the SSAC (if used) and the SSA.

> Source Selection Advisory Council (SSAC) is a group of senior government personnel who provide counsel during the source selection process and may prepare the comparative analysis of the Source Selection Evaluation Team's evaluation results, when directed by the SSA.

SSEBs are generally responsible for creating the evaluation plan and evaluating the proposals. They are composed of agency officials with expertise in the area of the procurement and frequently contain voting and nonvoting members. In most cases they establish evaluation panels containing additional people with expertise in specialized areas. See the NASA Source Selection Guide (http://ec.msfc.nasa.gov/hq/library/sourceselection/guide.pdf), which contains a description of all participants in the agency's SEB procedure as follows:

> 2.5.4 . . . The SEB Chairperson is the principal operating executive of the SEB. . . . The Chairperson is expected to manage the team efficiently without compromising the validity of the findings provided to the SSA as the basis for a sound selection decision. . . .

> 2.5.5 . . . The SEB Recorder functions as the principal administrative assistant to the SEB Chairperson. . . .

> 2.5.6 . . . If a committee is utilized, it functions as a fact-finding arm of the SEB, usually in a broad grouping of related disciplines (e.g., technical or management). . . . The committee examines in detail each proposal, or portion thereof, assigned by the SEB. It evaluates such proposals or excerpts in accordance with the approved evaluation factors and sub-factors before submitting a written report to the SEB summarizing its evaluation. . . .

Although these boards are generally composed of government employees, the FAR does not require this, and the GAO has approved the use of outside review committees in conjunction with in-house personnel, *Raytheon Co.*, Comp. Gen. Dec. B-261959.3, 96-1 CPD ¶ 37; *Tulane Univ.*, Comp. Gen. Dec. B-193012, 80-1 CPD ¶ 309. See NFS 1815.370(c)(2):

> While SEB participants are normally drawn from the cognizant installation, personnel from other NASA installations or other Government agencies may participate. When it is necessary to disclose the proposal (in whole or in part) outside the Government, approval shall be obtained in accordance with 18-15.207-70.

For guidance of other agencies on the use of outside evaluators, see DEAR 915.305(d), AFFARS 5315.305(c), and GSAM 515.305-70.

SSACs are composed of high-level agency employees who oversee the SSEB. They provide additional assistance and advice to the SSA. SSACs are not used in all cases. For example, they are not included in the standard organizations described in the NASA and GSA regulations.

Agencies have almost complete discretion as to the method used to convey evaluation results to the SSA and the role of the SSA in the source selection decision. However, the SSA must devote sufficient time to making the decision to be able to demonstrate that it was his or her independent judgment. See *Environmental Chem. Corp.*, Comp. Gen. Dec. B-275819, 97-1 CPD ¶ 154, stating:

> [S]election officials are not bound by recommendations made or price/cost evaluation methodologies used by an agency evaluation panel or other subordinate officials. *See Bell Aerospace Co.*, 55 Comp. Gen. 244 (1975), 75-2 CPD ¶ 168. Rather, source selection officials in negotiated procurements have broad discretion in determining the manner and extent to which they will make use of the technical and cost evaluation results. *Grey Advertising, Inc.*, 55 Comp. Gen. 1111 (1976), 76-1 CPD ¶ 325. In exercising that discretion, they are subject only to the tests of rationality and consistency with the established evaluation factors. *Id.*

This permits the SSA to accept the judgments of the lower-level officials or to make a totally independent assessment. For cases permitting adoption of the lower-level assessments, see *Planet/Space, Inc.*, Comp. Gen. Dec. B-401016, 2009 CPD ¶ 103 (protest that SSA had not considered a factor denied because he had been briefed on the issue and adopted risk assessment of SEB); *U.S. Facilities, Inc.*, Comp. Gen. Dec. B-293029, 2004 CPD ¶ 17 (protest of lack of independent decision denied because SSA participated in all major steps of procurement); *PRC, Inc.*, Comp. Gen. Dec. B-274698.2, 97-1 CPD ¶ 115 (protest that the SSA's analysis was superficial denied because the decision was reasonable based on the record). For a case where the SSA did a thorough assessment in making the decision, see *Microdyne Outsourcing, Inc. v. United States*, 72 Fed. Cl. 694 (2006).

A protest will be sustained if it is found that the SSA has not exercised independent judgment in arriving at the source selection decision. See *Information Sciences Corp. v. United States*, 73 Fed. Cl. 70 (2006), finding no independent decision where the SSA adopted, almost verbatim, a report of minority members of the technical evaluation team without any explanation of why that view was superior to the majority members' view. See also *AT&T Corp.*, Comp. Gen. Dec. B-299542.3, 2008 CPD ¶ 65 (SSA was apparently unaware of evaluation findings); and *IDEA Int'l, Inc. v. United States*, 74 Fed. Cl. 129 (2006) (SSA did not explain why he did not follow the recommendation of the technical evaluators). Protests have also been granted when it is clear that the SSA did not devote sufficient effort to understand the decision, *ProTech Corp.*, Comp. Gen. Dec. B-294818, 2005 CPD ¶ 73 (SSA did not follow evaluation factors); *Keeton Corrections, Inc.*, Comp. Gen. Dec. B-293348, 2005 CPD ¶ 44 (SSA did not notice mistake in evaluations); *Ashland Sales & Serv. Co.*, Comp. Gen. Dec. B-291206, 2003 CPD ¶ 33 (SSA relied on contracting officer document containing factual errors); *Shumaker Trucking & Excavating Contractors, Inc.*, Comp. Gen. Dec. B-290732, 2002 CPD ¶ 169 (SSA endorsed contracting officer document that contained no rationale for the decision).

There are numerous cases sustaining the SSA's independent assessment of the proposals. See *University Research Co.*, Comp. Gen. Dec. B-294358.6, 2005 CPD ¶ 83 (SSA thoroughly explained why he did not follows the views of the technical evaluators); *MW-All Star Joint Venture*, Comp. Gen. Dec. B-291170.4, 2004 CPD ¶ 98 (SSA reasonably assigned different ratings than evaluators); *Resource Mgmt. Int'l, Inc.*, Comp. Gen. Dec. B-278108, 98-1 CPD ¶ 29 (SSA's evaluation that protester's slightly higher technical rating did not merit the expenditure of additional funds reasonable notwithstanding the technical evaluation committee's recommendation to award to protester); *LTR Training Sys., Inc.*, Comp. Gen. Dec. B-274996, 97-1 CPD ¶ 71 (SSA reasonably evaluated technical proposals as equal in spite of SSET's evaluation that protester's proposal was superior); *EBA Eng'g, Inc.*, Comp. Gen. Dec. B-275818, 97-1 CPD ¶ 127 (SSA's decision to raise technical standing of awardee reasonable); *Juarez & Assocs., Inc.*, Comp. Gen. Dec. B-265950.2, 96-1 CPD ¶ 152 (SSA reasonably evaluated technical proposals as equal in spite of source evaluation group's evaluation that protester's proposal was superior). If the SSA adopts flawed assessments of the lower-level officials, the source selection decision will be overturned. See, for example, *New Breed Leasing Corp.*, Comp. Gen. Dec. B-259328, 96-2 CPD ¶ 84 (protest granted because decision was based on technical evaluation board report that misstated findings of evaluators).

2. Smaller Acquisitions

When acquisitions are not considered "major," far less formal procedures are generally followed. In such cases, the contracting officer is almost always the SSA and the source selection team is reduced to a few individuals. For example, in the Air Force, AFFARS 5315.303 states that for acquisitions of no more than $10 million:

> (a)(1) The contracting officer is the Source Selection authority (SSA) for acquisitions of $10M or less. Except as provided in paragraph (4) below, contracting officer is the SSA for acquisitions of any dollar value using Performance Price Tradeoff (PPT) or Lowest Price Technically Acceptable (LPTA) procedures, unless the acquisition plan approving authority designates otherwise.

The Army has more complete guidance in *Contracting for Best Value: A Best Practice Guide to Source Selection*, AMC-P 715-3 (Jan. 1, 1998), stating that in streamlined source selections "the team may consist of one or more technical evaluators and the contracting officer, who is the source selection authority." NASA is less explicit on the size and composition of the team in smaller procurements, merely providing discretion on the structure of the team when procurements are under $50 million, NFS 1815.300-70(a)(1)(ii).

It can be seen that in these smaller procurements, agencies generally have a great deal of discretion in structuring the source selection team. At a minimum, the contracting officer is expected to use agency employees with expertise in the technical aspects of the procurement to evaluate those elements of the proposals. In addition, many contracting officers use agency employees with technical expertise to assist them in making the best value decision in order to select the source. This permits the agency to arrive at a knowledgeable judgment as to the dollar value of the various aspects of the technical proposals submitted.

These less formal procedures have been recognized by the GAO. There is no legal requirement for source selection evaluation boards, and the evaluation can be conducted by one person if properly qualified, *Carol L. Bender, M.D.*, Comp. Gen. Dec. B-196912, 80-1 CPD ¶ 243. The GAO has offered little guidance with respect to the composition of evaluation teams because this is primarily a matter of agency discretion, *Washington School of Psychiatry*, Comp. Gen. Dec. B-189702, 78-1 CPD ¶ 176.

B. Qualifications of Team Members

Whatever organization is used in the source selection process, the members of the team must possess two traits. First, they must have the skill and ability to carry out their tasks in a professional manner. Second, they must be free from bias or conflict of interest.

1. Competence

Procuring agencies are highly dependent on the quality of the personnel performing the basic evaluation of the proposals. They must have the technical or business skills to evaluate all or part of the proposals. They should also be able to exercise good business judgment in determining which proposal is most advantageous to the government. See NFS 1815.370(c):

> *Designation.* (1) The SEB shall be comprised of competent individuals fully qualified to identify the strengths, weaknesses, and risks associated with proposals submitted in response to the solicitation. The SEB shall be appointed as early as possible in the acquisition process, but not later than acquisition plan or acquisition strategy meeting approval.

Neither the Court of Federal Claims nor the GAO has been willing to review the technical qualifications of members of the source selection team, *Software Eng'g Servs. Corp. v. United States*, 85 Fed. Cl. 247 (2009); *IMLCORP, LLC*, Comp. Gen. Dec. B-310582, 2008 CPD ¶ 15; *Eggs & Bacon, Inc.*, Comp. Gen. Dec. B-310066,

2007 CPD ¶ 209; *Glatz Aeronautical Corp.*, Comp. Gen. Dec. B-293968.2, 2004 CPD ¶ 160; *EBA Eng'g, Inc.*, Comp. Gen. Dec. B-275818, 97-1 CPD ¶ 127. See *Stat-a-Matrix, Inc.*, Comp. Gen. Dec. B-234141, 89-1 CPD ¶ 472, stating:

> The composition of technical evaluation panels is within the discretion of the contracting agency and, as such, will not be reviewed by our Office absent a showing of possible bad faith, fraud, conflict of interest, or actual bias on the part of evaluators. *New Mexico State University*, B-230669.2, June 2, 1988, 88-1 CPD ¶ 523. None of these factors is shown or even alleged here. Moreover, it is our view that the important and responsible positions held by the agency evaluators here constituted prima facie evidence that they were qualified to evaluate proposals. *Communications and Data Systems Assocs.*, B-223988, Oct. 29, 1986, 86-2 CPD ¶ 491.

Nonetheless, the Court of Federal Claims has ordered an agency to appoint a new SSA and a reconstructed SEB when it has found that the procurement was conducted improperly, *Wackenhut Servs., Inc. v. United States*, 85 Fed. Cl. 273 (2008). See also *Information Sciences Corp. v. United States*, 73 Fed. Cl. 70 (2006), ordering the agency to appoint a new SSA when the prior SSA did not exercise independent judgment in making the best value decision. The GAO has also recommended that new officials be appointed when improper conduct has occurred in the protest process. See *University Research Co., LLC*, Comp. Gen. Dec. B-294358, 2004 CPD ¶ 217 (appointment of new SSA recommended because prior SSA misstated technical finding in GAO protest); and *Beneco Enters., Inc.*, Comp. Gen. Dec. B-283512.3, 2000 CPD ¶ 176 (appointment of new SSA and SSEB recommended because prior officials had misrepresented facts).

2. Freedom from Bias or Conflict of Interest

Evaluators must be not only technically qualified, but also free from bias or conflict of interest. The Guiding Principles in FAR 1.102 emphasize this requirement. See FAR 1.102-2(c), which sets forth a "performance standard:"

> Conduct business with integrity, fairness, and openness. (1) An essential consideration in every aspect of the System is maintaining the public's trust. Not only must the System have integrity, but the actions of each member of the Team must reflect integrity, fairness, and openness. The foundation of integrity within the System is a competent, experienced, and well-trained, professional workforce. Accordingly each member of the Team is responsible and accountable for the wise use of public resources as well as acting in a manner which maintains the public's trust. Fairness and openness require open communication among team members, internal and external customers, and the public.

Evaluators are also subject to agency standards of conduct and the federal Standards of Ethical Conduct in 5 C.F.R. § 2635. See FAR 3.101-1, which states:

Government business shall be conducted in a manner above reproach and, except as authorized by statute or regulation, with complete impartiality and with preferential treatment for none. Transactions relating to the expenditure of public funds require the highest degree of public trust and an impeccable standard of conduct. The general rule is to avoid strictly any conflict of interest or even the appearance of a conflict of interest in Government-contractor relationships. While many Federal laws and regulations place restrictions on the actions of Government personnel, their official conduct must, in addition, be such that they would have no reluctance to make a full public disclosure of their actions.

The major conflicts of interest that must be avoided are financial interests in offerors and employment discussions with offerors. Government employees are prohibited from participating in a procurement with a company in which they hold a financial interest, 18 U.S.C. § 208. The definition of "financial interest" is included in 5 C.F.R. § 2635.403(c):

> (1) Except as provided in paragraph (c)(2) of this section, the term financial interest is limited to financial interests that are owned by the employee or by the employee's spouse or minor children. However, the term is not limited to only those financial interests that would be disqualifying under 18 U.S.C. § 208(a) and § 2635.402. The term includes any current or contingent ownership, equity, or security interest in real or personal property or a business and may include an indebtedness or compensated employment relationship. It thus includes, for example, interests in the nature of stocks, bonds, partnership interests, fee and leasehold interests, mineral and other property rights, deeds of trust, and liens, and extends to any right to purchase or acquire any such interest, such as a stock option or commodity future. It does not include a future interest created by someone other than the employee, his spouse, or dependent child or any right as a beneficiary of an estate that has not been settled.
>
> (2) The term financial interest includes service, with or without compensation, as an officer, director, trustee, general partner or employee of any person, including a nonprofit entity, whose financial interests are imputed to the employee under § 2635.402(b)(2)(iii) or (iv).

Employment negotiations are also a conflict of interest under 18 U.S.C. § 208. Guidance on this prohibition is contained in 5 C.F.R. § 2635.603. Employment negotiations are also covered in the Procurement Integrity Act, 41 U.S.C. § 423. See FAR 3.104-3, which contains the following guidance on the requirements of this Act:

> (c) *Actions required when an agency official contacts or is contacted by an offeror regarding non-Federal employment (subsection 27(c) of the Act).* (1) If an agency official, participating personally and substantially in a Federal agency procurement for a contract in excess of the simplified acquisition threshold, contacts or is contacted by a person who is an offeror in that Federal agency procurement regarding possible non-Federal employment for that official, the official must —

(i) Promptly report the contact in writing to the official's supervisor and to the agency ethics official; and

(ii) Either reject the possibility of non-Federal employment or disqualify himself or herself from further personal and substantial participation in that Federal agency procurement (see 3.104-5) until such time as the agency authorizes the official to resume participation in that procurement, in accordance with the requirements of 18 U.S.C. 208 and applicable agency regulations, because —

(A) The person is no longer an offeror in that Federal agency procurement; or

(B) All discussions with the offeror regarding possible non-Federal employment have terminated without an agreement or arrangement for employment.

For a full discussion of the standards of conduct see Chapter 1 of Cibinic & Nash, *Formation of Government Contracts* (3d ed. 1998).

The FAR 3.101-1 requirement "to avoid strictly any conflict of interest or even the appearance of a conflict of interest" is designed to ensure that offerors are cofindent of integrity in the procurement process. However, where the appearance of a conflict is not brought to light until after completion of evaluation there has been a reluctance on the part of the courts and the GAO to overturn a procurement unless there are hard facts showing bias or an actual conflict of interest. While such decisions may be justified on practical grounds, they should not be considered as endorsing the knowing use of personnel with the appearance of a conflict of interest.

If the contracting officer finds, during the conduct of the procurement, that any member of the team has an actual or apparent conflict of interest or bias, that person should be removed from the source selection team. A number of cases have upheld such removal. See, for example, *EBA Eng'g, Inc.*, Comp. Gen. Dec. B-275818, 97-1 CPD ¶ 127 (some members of evaluation panel replaced after they received letters from employees of incumbent contractor arguing that it should not be replaced); *Pemco Aeroplex, Inc.*, Comp. Gen. Dec. B-239672.5, 91-1 CPD ¶ 367 (some members of evaluation team replaced after flawed evaluation); *Louisiana Physicians for Quality Med. Care, Inc.*, 69 Comp. Gen. 6 (B-235894), 89-2 CPD ¶ 316 (new evaluation panel established after agency learned that chairman of original panel had close relationship with officer of competitor); *Applied Science Assocs., Inc.*, Comp. Gen. Dec. B-234467, 89-1 CPD ¶ 577 (evaluation panel member removed because his academic advisor was executive of offeror); *National Council of Teachers of English*, Comp. Gen. Dec. B-230669, 88-2 CPD ¶ 6 (outside evaluator dropped when competitor's proposal included evaluator's enthusiastic letter of endorsement); *Brown & Root Servs., Corp.*, Comp. Gen. Dec. B-227079.3, 88-1 CPD ¶ 324 (evaluator removed because he held stock in parent corporation of offeror); and

Pharmaceutical Sys., Inc., Comp. Gen. Dec. B-221847, 86-1 CPD ¶ 469 (initial evaluation panel disbanded when contracting officer was led to believe that it could not render an impartial recommendation).

In spite of the firm requirements that agency employees must be free from conflict of interest, it has been very difficult to successfully protest either bias or conflict of interest. The GAO has stated that any successful protest must be based on hard facts, not mere suspicion or innuendo, *Environmental Affairs Mgmt., Inc.*, Comp. Gen. Dec. B-277270, 97-2 CPD ¶ 93; *Dayton T. Brown, Inc.*, 68 Comp. Gen. 6 (B-231579), 88-2 CPD ¶ 314. The major situation where hard facts have been demonstrated is where an agency employee acknowledged bias in connection with a guilty plea on a charge that she engaged in employment discussions while serving as a major participant in source selections. See *Lockheed Martin Aeronautics Co.*, Comp. Gen. Dec. B-295401, 2005 CPD ¶ 41; and *Lockheed Martin Corp.*, Comp. Gen. Dec. B-295402, 2005 CPD ¶ 24.

The GAO has also held that it will not rule on a contention of bias if there is an ongoing investigation of the facts that are claimed to demonstrate bias, *Pemco Aeroplex, Inc.*, Comp. Gen. Dec. B-310372, 2008 CPD ¶ 2. Where an appearance of impropriety is alleged, the GAO frequently states that it will not overturn the agency's decision unless the protester can present evidence that the evaluator actually influenced the award of the contract, *ITECH, Inc.*, Comp. Gen. Dec. B-231693, 88-2 CPD ¶ 268; *Mariah Assocs., Inc.*, Comp. Gen. Dec. B-231710, 88-2 CPD ¶ 357. This same test was used by the court in *Dynalectron Corp. v. United States*, 4 Cl. Ct. 424 (1984), *aff'd*, 758 F.2d 665 (Fed. Cir. 1985) (statements of manager of evaluation team showing bias against protester but no proof of biased scoring of proposals). Compare *United States v. Mississippi Valley Generating Co.*, 364 U.S. 520 (1961), where the Court held that a contract was unenforceable due to the appearance of a conflict of interest on the part of an employee who played a minor role in the contract award process.

There are numerous cases upholding an agency determination that employees participating in the procurement had no actual bias or conflict of interest. For instance, in *CACI, Inc.-Fed. v. United States*, 719 F.2d 1567 (Fed. Cir. 1983), the court upheld an award where most of the technical evaluators had discussed employment with one of the offerors a year before the procurement and the offeror had been the government official in charge of the preceding contract. The court reasoned that there was no technical violation of 18 U.S.C. § 207 or § 208 and no hard facts proving an appearance of a conflict of interest. See also *Raydar & Assocs., Inc.*, Comp. Gen. Dec. B-401447, 2009 CPD ¶ 180 (allowing offeror access to government offices and property not proof of bias when offeror was incumbent contractor); *Integrated Mgmt. Resources Group, Inc.*, Comp. Gen. Dec. B-400550, 2008 CPD ¶ 227 (email requiring all planned awards to protester to be brought to attention of top agency officials does not prove bias); *Palmetto GBA, LLC*, Comp. Gen. Dec. B-298962, 2007 CPD ¶ 25 (evaluator's statement alluding to pressure to change a score not sufficient evidence of bias); *Hard Bodies, Inc.*, Comp. Gen. Dec. B-279543, 98-1 CPD ¶ 172 (contracting officer's ire at offeror's frequent phone calls insufficient to prove bias); *Cygnus Corp.*, Comp. Gen. Dec. B-275957, 97-1 CPD ¶ 202 (presence of vested marital property rights in assets or income of an offeror controlled by employee's spouse did not give government employee sufficient ownership or control over offeror so as to constitute a conflict of interest); *SF & Wellness*, Comp. Gen. Dec. B-272313, 96-2 CPD ¶ 122 (although awardee's spouse was a full-time government employee, he had no connection with Navy's physical fitness program or the awardee's operations); *DRI/McGraw-Hill*, Comp. Gen. Dec. B-261181, 95-2 CPD ¶ 76 (mere fact that member of technical evaluation panel had co-authored various publications with awardee insufficient to prove conflict of interest where there was no current economic relationship between technical evaluation panel member and awardee and no evidence that member had exerted improper influence on behalf of awardee); *Trataros/Basil, Inc.*, Comp. Gen. Dec. B-260321, 95-1 CPD ¶ 265 (allegation that evaluator was biased against offeror was not supported by any evidence — evaluator's scores were in line with other evaluators); *Docusort, Inc.*, Comp. Gen. Dec. B-254852.2, 95-1 CPD ¶ 107, *recons. denied*, 95-2 CPD ¶ 25 (mere fact that contracting officer proposed adding fee to awardee's contract price for phase-in costs insufficient to show bias where such fees were not added nor were phase-in costs evaluated); *Sprint Communications Co.*, Comp. Gen. Dec. B-256586, 94-1 CPD ¶ 300 (no conflict where member of evaluation committee, as president of a university, was entitled to a seat on the board of directors of an offeror's principal subcontractor; president himself was not a member of the subcontractor's board of directors and, in any event, did not participate in the award selection); *Jaycor*, Comp. Gen. Dec. B-240029.2, 90-2 CPD ¶ 354 (no clear proof that evaluator was biased against offeror or had employment discussions with winner); *Quality Sys., Inc.*, Comp. Gen. Dec. B-235344, 89-2 CPD ¶ 197 (no action taken when evaluator was personal friend of employee of offeror — no proof of bias or receipt of gratuities); *Laser Power Tech, Inc.*, Comp. Gen. Dec. B-233369, 89-1 CPD ¶ 267 (no action taken when chairman of technical evaluation panel discussed procurement with subcontractor shortly before issuance of RFP — no evidence of bias or disclosure of sensitive information); *Presearch, Inc.*, Comp. Gen. Dec. B-227097, 87-2 CPD ¶ 28 (heavy burden to show bias not met by protester); *Aqua-Chem, Inc.*, Comp. Gen. Dec. B-221319, 86-1 CPD ¶ 319 (no action taken where chairman of evaluation panel had tried to issue sole source contract to competitor, due to the lack of hard evidence); and *Ensign-Bickford Co.*, Comp. Gen. Dec. B-211790, 84-1 CPD ¶ 439 (protester failed to demonstrate any bias against its technical design on the part of the evaluator).

II. PROCUREMENT STRATEGIES

Once established, the source selection team must decide on the methodology that will be used to ultimately select the source. The procurement statutes give the agencies a great degree of discretion in devising competitive negotiation strategies designed to fulfill the government's needs. Three issues must be addressed in devising the best strategy: the selection of the appropriate competitive negotiation technique, the designation of mandatory requirements, and the possible use of a multistep process.

A. Selecting the Competitive Negotiation Technique

Prior to the FAR Part 15 rewrite, contained in FAC 97-02, Sept. 30, 1997, FAR 15.602 described two types of competitive negotiation: (1) "cost or price competition between proposals that meet the Government's requirements," and (2) "competition involving an evaluation and comparison of cost or price and other factors." The latter technique became know as the "best value" technique. In addition, FAR 15.613 permitted agencies to use "alternative source selection procedures."

The FAR rewrite uses the term "best value" more broadly. It encompasses all the strategies, whether or not based on tradeoffs between cost or price and other factors. FAR 15.402 states: "The objective of source selection is to select the proposal that represents the best value." The term is now defined in FAR 2.101:

> Best value means the outcome of an acquisition that, in the Government's estimation, provides the greatest overall benefit in response to the requirement.

FAR 15.100 makes it clear that the regulatory guidance under the rewritten FAR is only partial by stating:

> This subpart describes some of the acquisition processes and techniques that may be used to design competitive acquisition strategies suitable for the specific circumstances of the acquisition.

Thus, agencies are permitted to devise the appropriate strategy for each procurement. FAR 15.101, entitled "Best value continuum," elaborates on this concept:

> An agency can obtain best value in negotiated acquisitions by using any one or a combination of source selection approaches. In different types of acquisitions, the relative importance of cost or price may vary. For example, in acquisitions where the requirement is clearly definable and the risk of unsuccessful contract performance is minimal, cost or price may play a dominant role in source selection. The less definitive the requirement, the more development work required, or the greater the performance risk, the more technical or past performance considerations may play a dominant role in source selection.

The FAR then describes two specific techniques — the "tradeoff process" and the "lowest-price, technically acceptable source selection process." The following material discusses both processes. It also considers other strategies that have been used in the past.

1. Tradeoff Process

This strategy was previously known as the best value technique. The hallmark of the system is that it permits the determination of best value to be made *after the receipt and evaluation of proposals*. It is described in FAR 15.101-1:

(a) A tradeoff process is appropriate when it may be in the best interest of the Government to consider award to other than the lowest priced offeror or other than the highest technically rated offeror.

(b) When using the tradeoff process, the following apply:

(1) All evaluation factors and significant subfactors that will affect contract award and their relative importance shall be clearly stated in the solicitation; and

(2) The solicitation shall state whether all evaluation factors other than cost or price when combined are significantly more important than, approximately equal to, or significantly less important than cost or price.

(c) This process permits tradeoffs among cost or price and non-cost factors and allows the Government to accept other than the lowest priced proposal. The perceived benefits of the higher-priced proposal shall merit the additional cost, and the rationale for tradeoffs must be documented in the file in accordance with 15.406.

This process is the most widely used because it permits the source selection decision to be made after the proposals have been fully analyzed. However, it gives the source selection official very broad discretion because the ultimate decision is made on a *subjective* basis. The essence of the process is that, when the offeror with the lowest price is not evaluated best on the non-price factors, the selection decision is based on a business judgment as to whether the added value of non-price factors is worth a higher price. See *TRW, Inc. v. Widnall*, 98 F.3d 1325 (Fed. Cir. 1996); *Environmental Chemical Corp.*, Comp. Gen. Dec. B-275819, 97-1 CPD ¶ 154. It is clear that this judgment as to the value of the non-cost factors need not be quantified, FAR 15.308. See *Widnall v. B3H Corp.*, 75 F.3d 1577 (Fed. Cir. 1996), stating that these tradeoff decisions must be based on a "reasoned explanation" of the decision but need not be based on quantification of the non-cost factors. The same result was reached by the GAO in *Systems Mgmt., Inc.*, Comp. Gen. Dec. B-287032.5, 2002 CPD ¶ 29; *Suddath Van Lines, Inc.*, Comp. Gen. Dec. B-274285.2, 97-1 CPD ¶ 204; *Kay & Assoc., Inc.*, Comp. Gen. Dec. B-258243.7, 96-1 CPD ¶ 266; and *EG&G Team*, Comp. Gen. Dec. B-259917.3, 95-2 CPD ¶ 175. If the agency does quantify some of the non-cost evaluation factors, the GAO will not scrutinize the quantification for accuracy but will focus on the overall rationality of the best value decision, *DDD Co.*, Comp. Gen. Dec. B-276708, 97-2 CPD ¶ 44.

In the past, some agencies have attempted to devise numerical formulas to make this tradeoff appear to be *objective.* Some of these formulas have used a total point system by assigning points to the price, others have assigned dollar values to the non-price factors or have divided the price by the points assigned to non-price factors to come up with a dollars per point figure. Such techniques have been accepted as tools to be used in evaluating the relative merits of proposals. However, the GAO has indicated that these are only evaluation techniques and that the source selection official should still exercise judgment in determining whether the merits of the highest scored proposal are worth paying a higher price. See *C&B Constr., Inc., Comp. Gen. Dec.* B-401988.2, 2010 CPD ¶ 1, stating:

> [A] selection decision may not be made on point scores alone where the agency selection official has inadequate documentation on which to base a reasoned decision. *J.A. Jones Mgmt. Servs., Inc.,* B-276864, July 24, 1997, 97-2 CPD ¶ 47 at 4. . . . Since the record provides no contemporaneous tradeoff comparing Aquatic to C&B, other than on the basis of their point scores, we sustain the protest. *See, Shumaker Trucking & Excavating Contractors, Inc.,* B-290732, Sept. 25, 2002, 2002 CPD ¶ 169 at 8 (protest sustained where Forest Service relied solely on point scores and failed to document any comparison of protester's lower-priced and lower-rated proposal to awardee's higher-priced, higher-rated proposal, in source selection decision).

See also *Harrison Sys., Ltd.,* 63 Comp. Gen. 244 (B-212675), 84-1 CPD ¶ 572 (recommending that a total point system not be used in combination with a statement that award will be made to the offeror receiving the highest number of points); *Storage Tech. Corp.,* Comp. Gen. Dec. B-215336, 84-2 CPD ¶ 190 (dollar values assigned to non-price factors only to be used as a *guide* to the selection official); and *Moran Assocs.,* Comp. Gen. Dec. B-240564.2, 91-2 CPD ¶ 495 (cost/technical ratio formula only one tool to assure that the government was getting the best buy). In addition, a number of agencies have prohibited or strongly discouraged the use of such formulas.

When the tradeoff process is selected, the agency must decide whether negotiations will be necessary after the proposals have been evaluated or whether the award should be made without negotiations. The statutes give agencies broad discretion in making this decision. 10 U.S.C. § 2305(b)(4)(A) states:

> The head of an agency shall evaluate competitive proposals in accordance with paragraph (1) and may award a contract —
>
> > (i) after discussions with the offerors, provided that written or oral discussions have been conducted with all responsible offerors who submit proposals within the competitive range; or
>
> > (ii) based on the proposals received, without discussions with the offerors (other than discussions conducted for the purpose of minor clarification) provided that the solicitation included a statement that proposals are intended to be evaluated, and award made, without discussions, unless discussions are determined to be necessary.

Substantially the same language is contained in 41 U.S.C. § 253b(d)(1).

Under the original Competition in Contracting Act of 1984 (CICA), award without negotiations could be made only when it could be clearly demonstrated that such award would result in the lowest overall cost to the government. However, statutory changes in the 1990s deleted this requirement and gave agencies full discretion to use this process whenever they found it desirable. Furthermore, House Report 101-665, 101st Cong., 2d Sess. (accompanying Pub. L. No. 101-510, which initially changed the statutory requirement) stated that "the committee proposing the change did not recommend a preference" for one technique over the other but noted the following benefits of making award without negotiations:

Significant reduction of acquisition lead time

Permitting award on technical superiority when discussions are not needed

Lessening the chances of wrongful disclosure of source selection information

Reduction of the Government's overall acquisition costs by reducing the amount a contractor is spending on bid and proposal costs

An additional benefit is the avoidance of final proposal revisions that include arbitrary price reductions. Such reductions have resulted in excessively low prices, which can create serious difficulties during contract performance.

Considering these benefits, agencies have decided to award competitively negotiated procurements without negotiations as a way to streamline their process. The use of this technique should be considered when it appears that the offerors will have a sufficient understanding of the contract requirements to negate any requirement for negotiations.

2. Lowest-Price, Technically Acceptable Process

This strategy has been used for many years. The FAR now describes it as a best value procedure, but the best value determination is made by the agency *at the time the strategy is chosen*, before receipt or analysis of proposals. Thus, when an agency has decided to use this strategy, it has decided that the best value will be obtained by paying the lowest price offered by any offeror that submits an acceptable "technical proposal." FAR 15.101-2 describes this process:

(a) The lowest price technically acceptable source selection process is appropriate when best value is expected to result from selection of the technically acceptable proposal with the lowest evaluated price.

(b) When using the lowest price technically acceptable process, the following apply:

(1) The evaluation factors and significant subfactors that establish the requirements of acceptability shall be set forth in the solicitation. Solicita-

tions shall specify that award will be made on the basis of the lowest evaluated price of proposals meeting or exceeding the acceptability standards for non-cost factors. If the contracting officer documents the file pursuant to 15.304(c)(3)(iii), past performance need not be an evaluation factor in lowest price technically acceptable source selections. If the contracting officer elects to consider past performance as an evaluation factor, it shall be evaluated in accordance with 15.305. However, the comparative assessment in 15.305(a)(2)(i) does not apply. If the contracting officer determines that a small business' past performance is not acceptable, the matter shall be referred to the Small Business Administration for a Certificate of Competency determination, in accordance with the procedures contained in subpart 19.6 and 15 U.S.C. § 637(b)(7).

(2) Tradeoffs are not permitted.

(3) Proposals are evaluated for acceptability but not ranked using the non-cost/price factors.

(4) Exchanges may occur (see 15.306).

A key element of this technique is that the non-cost evaluation factors are all of equal importance. The failure of a proposal to meet any of the factors will preclude award to the offeror submitting the proposal. See, for example, *Synoptic Sys. Corp.*, Comp. Gen. Dec. B-290789.4, 2003 CPD ¶ 42, where two offerors were properly dropped from the competition after being scored unacceptable on two of a large number of factors. See also *Dubinsky v. United States*, 44 Fed. Cl. 509 (1999), holding that an agency may not award to an offer that has material failures to meet mandatory requirements. However, the offeror may be given an opportunity to cure the noncompliance through oral or written discussions if award on initial proposals will not be made and the proposal would otherwise be in the competitive range. Of course, this would require the agency to hold discussions with all other offerors in the competitive range and to permit them to submit final proposal revisions – with the potential result that one of them would become the low price offeror.

One major benefit of this strategy is that the agency can greatly shorten the evaluation process because, once the low price proposal has been found to be technically acceptable, there is no need to evaluate the acceptability of any of the other proposals. This streamlined process can be used as long as the agency has used the Instruction to Offerors – Competitive Acquisition solicitation provision in FAR 52.215-1 which states in ¶ (f)(4) that the agency intends to award without discussions.

The term "technically acceptable proposals" as used in the FAR refers to all non-cost factors. It includes factors dealing with the capability of the offerors, as well as the technical details of the performance that is offered in the proposal. Although FAR 15.101-2(b)(1) refers only to determinations of unacceptable past performance as requiring reference to the Small Business Administration (SBA), the same rule would apply to lack of acceptability based on any other capability factor. See, e.g., *Vantex Serv. Corp.*, Comp. Gen. Dec. B-266199, 96-1 CPD ¶ 29, holding that when traditional responsibility factors such as "experience" are evaluated on a go/no-go basis, the matter must be referred to the SBA if the proposal is determined unacceptable because of such factors. See also *R. L. Campbell Roofing Co.*, Comp. Gen. Dec. B-289868, 2003 CPD ¶ 37; *Dynamic Aviation — Helicopters*, Comp. Gen. Dec. B-274122, 96-2 CPD ¶ 166; and *Environsol, Inc.*, Comp. Gen. Dec. B-254223, 93-2 CPD ¶ 295.

The lowest-price, technically acceptable proposal technique has been used extensively in the past. See, for example, *Weinschel Eng'g Co.*, 64 Comp. Gen. 524 (B-217202), 85-1 CPD ¶ 574, where the GAO agreed with a source selection when the Navy awarded a fixed-price contract to the lowest-priced offeror meeting the RFP's technical specifications. In *Saxon Corp.*, Comp. Gen. Dec. B-216148, 85-1 CPD ¶ 87, the RFP provided for award to the offeror with the lowest overall price among those offers found acceptable in the technical and management areas. Technical and management factors were thus scored on a go/ no-go basis. In *Computer Sciences Corp.*, Comp. Gen. Dec. B-213287, 84-2 CPD ¶ 151, the RFP for a data base management system called for award to the vendor with the lowest evaluated price offering a system judged to have a "user-friendly, English-like syntax." Award may also be made to the technically acceptable proposal with the lowest total discounted life-cycle cost, *Hawaiian Tel. Co.*, Comp. Gen. Dec. B-187871, 77-1 CPD ¶ 298; *University Sys.*, GSBCA 10600-P, 90-3 BCA ¶ 23,085.

It has been held that "no narrative justifications" are required to support the assessment that an element of a technical proposal is unacceptable, *Al Ghanim Combined Group Co. Gen. Trad. & Cont. W.L.L. v. United States*, 56 Fed. Cl. 502 (2003) (evaluators merely circled "pass" or "fail" on an evaluation sheet). The court derived this rule from FAR 15.305(a)(3) stating that an "assessment of each offeror's ability to accomplish the technical requirements" was required only in tradeoff procurements. The court did not consider FAR 15.305(a) calling for documentation of "relative strengths, significant weaknesses, and risks."

The use of this method has on several occasions led to protests that sealed bidding was required for the procurement. In *Saxon Corp.*, Comp. Gen. Dec. B-216148, 85-1 CPD ¶ 87, the GAO upheld the use of negotiation, finding that it was impossible to draft sufficiently precise specifications for a sealed bid procurement where a high level of technical and management competence was needed. Similarly, in *Essex Electro Eng'rs, Inc.*, 65 Comp. Gen. 242 (B-221114), 86-1 CPD ¶ 92, the use of negotiation was upheld because of the agency's need to conduct discussions with offerors. The protester's argument that the agency could have obtained the necessary information through a preaward survey was rejected, as the discussion process can be used to negotiate contractual terms, as well as to obtain responsibility-related information. See also *Vantex Serv. Corp.*, Comp. Gen. Dec. B-266199, 96-1 CPD ¶ 29, where the RFP listed three technical evaluation factors that the agency stated would be evaluated on a go/no-go basis to determine the acceptability of an offeror's proposal. Once technical acceptability was established based on the evaluation factors, price would become the determinative factor for award. The GAO found proper the use of competitive negotiation because the agency reasonably determined that discussions were necessary.

3. Other Approaches

As discussed earlier, the FAR now permits the use of any other competitive negotiation approach that complies with the procurement statutes. One such approach is a combination of the tradeoff process and the lowest-price, technically acceptable proposal process suggested by FAR 15.101. Another possibility is a process calling for negotiations with only the winning contractor. A third possibility is a competitive negotiation process based solely on low price.

a. Combination of Tradeoff and Lowest-Price, Technically Acceptable Processes

Although FAR Part 15 does not directly address the combination of these two processes, FAR 15.101 indicates that a "combination of source selection approaches" may be used. Thus, an agency could subject some of the evaluation factors to a go/no-go test, while providing that others can be evaluated on a tradeoff logic. This technique would enable tradeoffs to be made for those factors subject to evaluation on their relative merits while requiring rejection of the proposals not meeting the minimum requirements for those subject to the go/no-go test. Another strategy might be to subject all factors to a go/no-go test for the proposal to receive further consideration and then to evaluate the relative merits of those determined to be acceptable. These types of strategies were discussed in Chapter 2 of the GSA Handbook, *Source Selection Procedures*, APD P 2800.2, July 21, 1987, which provided the following guidance:

> [A] go, no-go approach can be applied to some or all of the major evaluation factors or subfactors identified in the solicitation. When all factors are go, no-go the process is equivalent to the lowest-priced acceptable proposal approach discussed above. When the "greatest value concept" is used, some evaluation factors may be used as discriminators and be evaluated on a go, no-go basis. An evaluation factor such as "management" may be used as a discriminator for evaluation on a go, no-go basis. If the "management" factor is scored adequate, it may, or may not, have further relevance in the evaluation process. . . . The evaluation process may be structured so that the factor has no further relevance . . . if it is scored adequate. On the other hand, the evaluation process may be structured so that the factor is scored and the merits of the proposal considered in the ultimate award decision. An adequate score in such an area is therefore a minimum requirement for selection. . . . This approach is frequently used in situations in which the product is subject to testing to establish whether it meets certain requirements outlined in the solicitation.

This method has been used in a number of situations and has been approved by the GAO. See *Integrated Concepts & Research Corp.*, Comp. Gen. Dec. B-309803, 2008 CPD ¶ 117 (proper tradeoff of proposal risk, past performance and price among the acceptable technical proposals); *Utility Tool & Trailer, Inc.*, Comp. Gen. Dec. B-310535, 2008 CPD ¶ 1 (proper tradeoff of delivery, small business participation and price among the acceptable technical proposals); *Brewbaker White Sands JV*, Comp. Gen. Dec. B-295582.4, 2005 CPD ¶ 176 (proper tradeoff between past performance and price among the offerors that had submitted acceptable technical proposals); *Sterling Servs., Inc.*, Comp. Gen. Dec. B-286326, 2000 CPD ¶ 208 (proper evaluation of past performance in a "Technically Acceptable – Performance/Price Tradeoff" procurement); and *ECI Telecom, Inc.*, 64 Comp. Gen. 688 (B-218533), 85-2 CPD ¶ 73 (upholding a selection based on a go/no-go evaluation of all technical subfactors). See also *FMB Laundry, Inc.*, Comp. Gen. Dec. B-261837.2, 95-2 CPD ¶ 274, where the protester argued that the RFP was deficient because it failed to specify what weight would be accorded to the technical factors in relation to price. The GAO stated that the fact that relative weight of acceptability versus price was not spelled out was irrelevant because the solicitation did not contemplate gradations in acceptability rankings as it was essentially a go/no-go determination. This procedure has been upheld in a procurement containing a "5000 round service life" requirement, *Smith & Wesson Div., Bangor Punta Corp. v. United States*, 782 F.2d 1074 (1st Cir. 1986), *reh'g and reh'g en banc denied, Unpub.* (1986), where a product was excluded from further consideration based on tests of samples that cracked before firing 5,000 rounds. The GAO has approved similar procedures where offerors had an opportunity to correct deficiencies found in initial testing, *Centennial Computer Prods., Inc.*, Comp. Gen. Dec. B-212979, 84-2 CPD ¶ 295.

b. *Negotiations After Source Selection*

The "alternative source selection procedures" that were identified in the earlier FAR 15.613 were the NASA "source evaluation board" and the DOD "four-step" procedures for use in contracting for research and development. The essential distinguishing element of these procedures was the selection of the winning offeror before the conduct of negotiations. They are no longer alluded to in the FAR, but they appear to be acceptable procedures in contracting for technically complex work. This is explained in a comment by DOD in its promulgation of proposed revisions to the DFARS to implement the FAR Part 15 rewrite. This comment states at 62 Fed. Reg. 63050, Nov. 26, 1997:

> DFARS guidance on the four-step source selection process and the alternate source selection process have been removed, as the new guidance at FAR 15.101, best value continuum, clearly allows such source selection processes.

For an example of the current use of this procedure, see *Veterans Tech., LLC*, Comp. Gen. Dec. B-310303.2, 2008 CPD ¶ 31.

Under the Four-Step procedure, technical and cost proposals were submitted sequentially. Preselection discussions were conducted only to permit clarification of proposals, restricted best and final offers were solicited and followed by full negotiation with the winner. The major differences in this technique from the conventional competitive negotiation technique was the amount of discussion permitted prior to source selection and the extent of negotiation that occurred after source selection. The major purpose of the Four-Step technique was to select the source based on its original proposal rather than on its proposal as enhanced by discussions. Its fundamental premise was that the most competent contractor was the one submitting the best original proposal. In order to ensure that the government ultimately got the best possible contract, the Four-Step technique permitted full negotiation after source selection where the government agency had the opportunity to press for changes in the winner's proposal as long as they did not alter the basis for the source selection.

The original guidance on the procedure was contained in the 1970 NASA Procurement Directive 70-15, which stated in part:

> In cost-reimbursement type contracts and all research and development contracts, ambiguities and uncertainties in the proposals of such firms shall be pointed out during discussions by the contracting officer, but not deficiencies.

Although the GAO refused to rule that this original NASA procedure was in violation of the statutory requirement for discussions, it did find that it needed clarification, stating in 51 Comp. Gen. 621 (B-173677) (1972) at 622-23:

> We think the propriety of the prohibition in NASA Procurement Directive 70-15 against discussing "deficiencies" must be considered in the light of these problems. We think certain weaknesses, inadequacies, or deficiencies in proposals can be discussed without being unfair to other proposers. There well may be instances where it becomes apparent during the course of negotiations that one or more proposers have reasonably placed emphasis on some aspect of the procurement different from that intended by the solicitation. Unless this difference in the meaning given the solicitation is removed, the proposers are not competing on the same basis. Similarly, if a proposal is deemed weak because it fails to include substantiation for a proposed approach or solution, in the circumstance where the inadequacy appears to have arisen because of a reasonable misunderstanding of the amount of data called for, we believe the proposer should be given the opportunity, time permitting, to furnish such substantiation. Thus, it seems to us that the prohibition in NASA Procurement Directive 70-15 against discussing "deficiencies" needs clarification.

Subsequently, NASA made minor modifications to the policy. The complete regulatory statement was contained in NFS 18-15.613-71(b)(5):

> (ii) Cost-reimbursement contracts and all contracts for research and development.
>
> > (A) The contracting officer, in concert with or on behalf of the SEB, will conduct written and/or oral discussions of the effort to be accomplished

and the cost of the effort with all offerors determined to be within the competitive range. The discussions are intended to assist the SEB or other evaluators (1) in understanding fully each offeror's proposal and its strengths and weaknesses based upon the individual efforts of each offeror; (2) in assuring that the meanings and the points of emphasis of RFP provisions have been adequately conveyed to the offerors so that all are competing equally on the basis intended by the Government; (3) in evaluating the personnel proposed by each firm; and (4) in presenting a report to the Source Selection Official that makes the discriminations among proposals clear and visible. In this process, prior to contractor selection, the Government's interests are not served by its assuming the role of an information exchange or clearinghouse.

(B) In cost-reimbursement type contracts and all research and development contracts, the contracting officer shall point out instances in which the meaning of some aspect of a proposal is not clear and instances in which some aspects of the proposal failed to include substantiation for a proposed approach, solution, or cost estimate.

(C) However, where the meaning of a proposal is clear and the Board has sufficient information to assess its validity and the proposal contains a weakness which is inherent in an offeror's management, engineering, or scientific judgment, or which is the result of its own lack of competence or inventiveness in preparing its proposal, the contracting officer shall not point out the weaknesses. Discussions are useful in ascertaining the presence or absence of strengths and weaknesses. The possibility that such discussions may lead an offeror to discover that it has a weakness is not a reason for failing to inquire into a matter where the meaning is not clear or where insufficient information is available, since understanding of the meaning and validity of the proposed approaches, solutions, and cost estimates is essential to a sound selection. Offerors should not be informed of the relative strengths or weaknesses of their proposals in relation to those of other offerors.

This guidance was deleted from the regulation in 63 Fed. Reg. 44,408, Aug. 19, 1998.

The GAO commented on the revised procedure in *Sperry Rand Corp.*, 54 Comp. Gen. 408 (B-181460), 74-2 CPD ¶ 276:

The NASA procedure represents one approach to meeting the statutory requirement for written and oral discussions, 10 U.S.C. § 2304(g) [now 10 U.S.C. § 2304(a)]. In part, at least, the underlying rationale is that to point out deficiencies during the discussions would compromise the competition, because weaker proposals would be improved, and a leveling effect would occur. To avoid this, discussions are limited to clarification of proposals; after selection, the agency then negotiates the best possible contract on terms most advantageous to the Government. Considered in the abstract, potential conflicts between the procedure and the statutory requirement can be envisioned; for instance, as appears to be contemplated by [the protester], a situation where the discussions are so limited in scope and content that they amount to little more than a ceremonial exercise, with the meaningful discussions transposed almost entirely into the final negotiations stage.

NASA decisions to limit discussions based on this policy were affirmed in *Program Resources, Inc.*, Comp. Gen. Dec. B-192964, 79-1 CPD ¶ 281; *Pioneer Contract Servs., Inc.*, Comp. Gen. Dec. B-197245, 81-1 CPD ¶ 107; and *Taft Broadcasting Corp.*, Comp. Gen. Dec. B-222818, 86-2 CPD ¶ 125. However, discussions were not meaningful where NASA waived a regulation concerning interest rates for one offeror yet failed to inform the other offeror of the waiver during discussions. The GAO held that discussions were required because this was not a question of technical transfusion, *Union Carbide Corp.*, 55 Comp. Gen. 802 (B-184495), 76-1 CPD ¶ 134.

DOD adopted a similar procedure for R&D procurements when it developed its Four-Step negotiation process, DFARS 215.613 (pre-rewrite). Step one called for very limited discussions. DFARS 215.613-70(f) provided:

> (2) In conducting step one — (i) Limit discussions to only what is necessary to ensure that both parties understand each other; (ii) Do not tell offerors about deficiencies in their proposals; and (iii) Provide written clarifications to all offerors when it appears the Government's requirements have been misinterpreted.

The regulations concerning Four-Step negotiation did not cite technical transfusion as the reason for limiting discussions. Rather, this limitation on discussions was based on the premise that the competition was fairer if source selection was made on the basis of the initial position of the competitors rather than on their final position, which included modifications suggested or induced by the procuring agency through the process of discussions. The reason for not invoking technical transfusion as the reason for limiting discussions in step one may have been that the regulations anticipated that technical transfusion would take place with the selected offeror in step four. The DOD Four-Step procedure was challenged in *GTE Sylvania, Inc.*, 57 Comp. Gen. 715 (B-188272), 77-2 CPD ¶ 422, where the GAO made an extensive analysis of the procedure and concluded that the limited discussions actually conducted met the statutory requirement. For a full evaluation of the Four Step procedure, questioning whether it meets the statutory requirement for discussions, see Smith, *The New "Four Step" Source Selection Procedure: Is the Solution Worse Than the Problem?*, 11 Pub. Ct. L. Rev. 322 (1980).

EPA's version of the Four-Step procedure, PIN 77-15, was challenged in *Roy F. Weston, Inc.*, Comp. Gen. Dec. B-197949, 80-1 CPD ¶ 340. Although the protester contended that the items not brought up in discussion were deficiencies, the GAO stated:

> [W]e think a more accurate description would be that they were the differences in the relative merits of the proposals, as viewed by the [technical evaluation panel]. If they were truly weaknesses or deficiencies, then there would have been an ob-

ligation on the part of EPA to discuss the areas with Weston, assuming no danger of technical transfusion, notwithstanding PIN 77-15.

This would appear to indicate that the limitation on discussions in Four-Step procurement will not be permitted in some circumstances.

c. Price-Only Competitive Negotiation

A few agencies have used a competitive negotiation procedure with award to be made to the low-price proposal with no other evaluation factors. The justification for the use of negotiation in such cases has been the need to conduct discussions to ensure that the winning offeror understands the specifications. In *JT Constr. Co.*, Comp. Gen. Dec. B-244404.2, 92-1 CPD ¶ 1, the GAO held that the use of competitive procedures was appropriate because the contracting officer reasonably determined that discussions were necessary in order to gauge offeror understanding of specifications on a renovation project. See also *Claude E. Atkins Enters., Inc.*, Comp. Gen. Dec. B-241047, 91-1 CPD ¶ 42, where the GAO held that negotiation in such circumstances was proper on a contract for renovation of two buildings because of the complexity of the specifications, holding:

> The agency was faced with a complex procurement in which it anticipated possible problems with its specifications. It is clear from the record that one problem was whether the specifications reflected the agency's actual needs. Another was whether offerors could be expected to fully understand what the specifications required. Under these circumstances, we think the contracting officer had a reasonable basis for believing that discussions would be necessary prior to award so that offeror understanding could be gauged (we see no reason why price breakdowns alone, without technical proposals, could not be used for that purpose) and offeror input could be obtained for improving the specifications.

> In fact, the record shows that helpful changes to the project requirements, such as modifications to the phasing of the construction, were developed as the result of the discussions. When this is considered against the backdrop of the contracting officer's expected difficulty in receiving accurate pricing from offerors, the past performance problems which arose from misunderstandings about the technical requirements in a sealed bid procurement for a similar project and the problems with A/E firm's specification development efforts, we cannot conclude that the agency's judgment in choosing to use competitive negotiation here was unreasonable.

The use of negotiation procedures without technical/management proposals was also permitted in *Carter Chevrolet Agency, Inc.*, Comp. Gen. Dec. B-228151, 87-2 CPD ¶ 584. In this procurement of 19,349 vehicles of different types, the agency used competitive negotiation because it had experienced many problems on past sealed bid procurements — with regard to frequent exceptions to the specification, misunderstandings on statutory price limitations, and problems with model year changes. The GAO seemed to agree that these were valid reasons for using negotiation but based the decision primarily on the fact that competitive bids had not been received on many of the line items on past sealed bid procurements. The decision contains this interesting statement:

> [T]he purpose of the negotiation process is to develop through discussions, if necessary, the contractual terms themselves and thereby to define and frame the terms of a firm's offer. . . . Here since the specifications were varied, rather than just complicated, and it reasonably could be expected that offerors would propose numerous variations from the specifications for many of the vehicles, we cannot object to GSA's position that discussions were necessary.

See also *Military Base Mgmt., Inc.*, 66 Comp. Gen. 179 (B-224115), 86-2 CPD ¶ 720, where the GAO permitted the use of negotiation procedures without technical/management proposals because the agency had experienced difficulties in the past on sealed bid procurements, stating that it was proper to use negotiation procedures "to insure that a vendor understands just what the agency believes is required by the specifications."

This technique should be used with care because the GAO will carefully analyze its use to ensure that it does not violate the statutory requirement to use sealed bidding when the four statutory factors are present. See 10 U.S.C. § 2304(a)(2) and 41 U.S.C. § 253(a)(2), which states:

> In determining the competitive procedures appropriate under the circumstance, an executive agency —
>
> (A) shall solicit sealed bids if —
>
>> (i) time permits the solicitation, submission, and evaluation of sealed bids;
>>
>> (ii) the award will be made on the basis of price and other price-related factors;
>>
>> (iii) it is not necessary to conduct discussions with the responding sources about their bids; and
>>
>> (iv) there is a reasonable expectation of receiving more than one sealed bid; and
>
> (B) shall request competitive proposals if sealed bids are not appropriate under clause (A).

These factors were held to be present in *Racal Corp.*, 70 Comp. Gen. 127 (B-240579), 90-2 CPD ¶ 453, rejecting the use of price-only competitive negotiation in order to conduct discussions, stating at 129:

The Army asserts that discussions are necessary to ensure that all firms have a complete understanding of the specifications. The agency has failed to demonstrate, however, how it intended to utilize discussions to evaluate the understanding of responding offerors. In this regard, an offeror's understanding is typically reflected in its technical proposal, which the agency did not require in this case. . . . The agency has not explained how it would otherwise evaluate an offeror's understanding in this procurement.

Instead, the record reflects that the Army is in reality concerned that offerors may not have the capability to produce the canisters. . . . In this regard, the agency notes that one prior producer went bankrupt and unproven producers have submitted low priced proposals on previous RFPs. On the other hand, except for the bankrupt contractor, only experienced producers, that is, Racal and Mine Safety Appliance Co., have received awards for this item. While the agency's concern that prospective contractors have the capability to perform is legitimate, we think that where no technical proposal is required, an investigation of the offeror's responsibility, using such tools as a preaward survey, is generally the proper mechanism to ameliorate the agency's concerns. . . . Moreover, sealed bid procedures have a specific mechanism, pre-bid conferences, for the explicit purpose of briefing prospective bidders and explaining complicated specifications. FAR 14.207 (FAC 84-58). Under the circumstances, we find the agency's concerns here, that offerors be capable and understand the requirements, do not support a conclusion that discussions are therefore required.

Nor do we think the agency's other basic reason that negotiated procedures would better allow for possible changes in quantity, delivery schedules, opening dates, etc., serves as a rationale for discussions. Such changes are properly accomplished by an amendment, regardless of the procurement type.

The use of price-only competitive negotiation was also rejected in *Northeast Constr. Co.*, 68 Comp. Gen. 406 (B-234323), 89-1 CPD ¶ 402 (repair and improvement project is routine construction project where there is no need to have discussions to ensure understanding of specifications); and *ARO Corp.*, Comp. Gen. Dec. B-227055, 87-2 CPD ¶ 165 (no need for price discussion to ensure that price is fair and reasonable when item being procured is commercial pump). See also *Knoll North America, Inc.*, Comp. Gen. Dec. B-240234, 93-1 CPD ¶ 26, where the GAO rejected a protester's argument that competitive negotiation should have been used because the specifications were unclear and discussion was needed to work out specification problems.

B. Specifying Mandatory Requirements

In structuring the procurement strategy, the agency must determine which mandatory requirements will be specified. Agencies have frequently included numerous mandatory requirements in their specifications in order to ensure that the contractor would meet their needs. However, there are two significant disadvantages to this procedure. First, the specification of detailed requirements may keep the agency from obtaining the most current product or the most effective service. This was discussed in detail in the consideration of the specification in Chapter 1.

The second disadvantage of specifying numerous mandatory requirements is the inflexibility that it introduces into the procurement process. Because a contract may not be awarded to an offeror that does not agree to meet all of the mandatory requirements, the solicitation must be either amended or canceled if an advantageous offer proposes to deviate from such a requirement. See FAR 15.206, which states:

> (a) When, either before or after receipt of proposals, the Government changes its requirements or terms and conditions, the contracting officer shall amend the solicitation.

> *   *   *

> (d) If a proposal of interest to the Government involves a departure from the stated requirements, the contracting officer shall amend the solicitation, provided this can be done without revealing to the other offerors the alternate solution proposed or any other information that is entitled to protection (see 15.207(b) and 15.306(e)).

> (e) If, in the judgment of the contracting officer, based on market research or otherwise, an amendment proposed for issuance after offers have been received is so substantial as to exceed what prospective offerors reasonably could have anticipated, so that additional sources likely would have submitted offers had the substance of the amendment been known to them, the contracting officer shall cancel the original solicitation and issue a new one, regardless of the stage of the acquisition.

In view of these disadvantages, agencies should specify only their most essential requirements as mandatory. Other specific requirements can be specified as targets, FAR 11.002(e), or for guidance only, FAR 11.002(c). Alternatively, the agency can include a clause in the solicitation providing that failure to meet a mandatory requirement will not preclude award. Flexibility can also be achieved by avoiding the specification of detailed requirements and using performance requirements, FAR 11.002(a) (general guidance), FAR 37.602(b) (performance-based service contracts).

When agencies provide for flexibility in meeting their requirements, award can be made to an offeror that does not meet the requirement without amending the solicitation and informing other offerors of the deviation. See, for example, *Litton Sys., Inc. v. Dep't of Transportation*, GSBCA 12911-P, 94-3 BCA ¶ 27,263, holding that it was proper to award a contract without amending the solicitation to an offeror that had not agreed to meet the contract requirements. The board reached this conclusion because the solicitation stated that exceptions and deviations would not make the proposal automatically unacceptable. Similarly, in *Mantech Telecommunications & Information Sys. Corp. v. United States*, 49 Fed. Cl. 57 (2001), the court found that an experience requirement was not a mandatory minimum requirement because the

RFP stated that proposals would be excluded from the competition if *"significant deficiencies"* were identified. See also *Morse-Diesel Int'l, Inc.*, Comp. Gen. Dec. B-274499.2, Dec. 16, 1996, *Unpub.*, reaching the same conclusion when the solicitation contained the following language:

> Individual deficiencies do not necessarily render the whole proposal unacceptable to the Government. A proposal is considered unacceptable to the Government, as a whole, when it is deficient to the extent that, to allow an offeror to correct those deficiencies would constitute a complete rewrite of the proposal. The determination as to whether a proposal is deficient to that extent is made at the discretion of the Evaluation Board. In making such a determination, the Board will consider such things as the number and severity of the deficiencies.

In deciding whether to provide for such flexibility in the acquisition process, an agency must consider the ramifications for contract performance. Clearly, the flexible specification gives the contractor the power to select the precise manner of performance and an agency order to perform in a different manner will be a contract change for which the agency must provide an equitable adjustment. See, for example, *A.S. McGaughan Co. v. Barram*, 113 F.3d 1256 (Fed. Cir. 1997), where the court reversed GSBCA 13367, 96-1 BCA ¶ 28,261, and held that a constructive change had occurred when the contracting officer ordered the contractor to comply with a requirement that was noted on the drawings as "suggested" and "for design intent only." On the other hand, the government will less likely be subject to claims for defective specifications when it uses flexible specifications. See, for example, *Intercontinental Mfg. Co. v. United States*, 4 Cl. Ct. 591 (1984), where the court rejected a defective specification claim because the contractor had chosen the manufacturing processes used to meet the specifications. The court stated the general rule pertaining to performance specifications as follows at 595:

> [T]he planned methods of manufacture were of the contractor's own choosing and no representations as to their suitability had been made by the Government. In such a situation then, a case for defective specifications could exist only if performance had proven impossible, either actually or from a standpoint of commercial impracticability (i.e., commercial senselessness). Short of these extremes, however, the risk of unanticipated performance costs remains upon the contractor's shoulders alone.

For a complete discussion of the ramifications of using flexible specifications in the context of contract performance see Chapters 3 and 4 of Cibinic, Nagle & Nash, *Administration of Government Contracts* (4th ed. 2006).

C. Techniques for Limiting the Number of Competitors

Another issue that should be addressed in formulating the procurement strategy is whether a procedure that limits the number or type of competitors should be used. When an agency believes that it will receive a large number of proposals, such a procedure can be an effective way of initially screening the offerors to ensure that only those that are fully qualified participate in the competition. This saves the less qualified companies from incurring the proposal preparation costs and reduces the administrative burden on the agency from having to evaluate large numbers of proposals.

The legal authority to prevent offerors from competing on later stages of competitively negotiated procurement has been the subject of considerable contention. The early drafts of the FAR rewrite that were published for comment contained a proposed rule on a mandatory multistep procurement process, but the rule was criticized because it required almost full proposals in the first step. As a result, the final rule issued in FAC 97-02, Sept. 30, 1997, contained no provision on mandatory multistep procurement — only a provision on voluntary multistep procurement. Nonetheless, there are a number of procedures permitting a mandatory multistep process, and there are indications that some agencies have used mandatory multistep procedures in the course of conducting competitive negotiations. This section will consider the new advisory (voluntary) multistep procedure and the mandatory multistep procedures that are identified in statutes or regulations.

1. Advisory Multistep Procedure

The FAR rewrite added the following procedure in FAR 15.202:

Advisory multi-step process.

(a) The agency may publish a presolicitation notice (see 5.204) that provides a general description of the scope or purpose of the acquisition and invites potential offerors to submit information that allows the Government to advise the offerors about their potential to be viable competitors. The presolicitation notice should identify the information that must be submitted and the criteria that will be used in making the initial evaluation. Information sought may be limited to a statement of qualifications and other appropriate information (e.g., proposed technical concept, past performance, and limited pricing information). At a minimum, the notice shall contain sufficient information to permit a potential offeror to make an informed decision about whether to participate in the acquisition. This process should not be used for multi-step acquisitions where it would result in offerors being required to submit identical information in response to the notice and in response to the initial step of the acquisition.

(b) The agency shall evaluate all responses in accordance with the criteria stated in the notice, and shall advise each respondent in writing either that it will be invited to participate in the resultant acquisition or, based on the information submitted, that it is unlikely to be a viable competitor. The agency shall advise respondents considered not to be viable competitors of the general basis for that opinion. The agency shall inform all respondents that, notwithstanding the advice provided by the Government in response to their submissions, they may participate in the resultant acquisition.

This procedure can be an effective way to eliminate potential competitors that do not have the qualifications to perform the work. However, to be used successfully, the agency must make a reasoned assessment of the minimum qualifications required for the contract and of the qualifications of each potential offeror. Although the regulation calls for written advice of the agency assessment, agencies should consider meeting with companies that are found to be unqualified in order to explain the decision fully.

An agency cannot turn this into an involuntary downselect procedure, *Kathpal Techs., Inc.*, Comp. Gen. Dec. B-283137.3, 2000 CPD ¶ 6 (agency improperly excluded qualified offeror from making an oral presentation as called for by the RFP without considering price). An example of use of this procedure is found in *Spherix, Inc.*, Comp. Gen. Dec. B-294572, 2005 CPD ¶ 3 (three of ten companies found qualified but protest of one granted for defects in conducting competition).

2. Prequalification

Prequalification of offerors has been a controversial subject because it has the appearance of avoiding the full and open competition requirement. However, it was formally recognized by Congress in 1984, shortly after the passage of the CICA, with the enactment of 41 U.S.C. § 253c and 10 U.S.C. § 2319. These statutes provide that before enforcing any prequalification requirement with regard to a firm or a product, the head of the contracting agency must (1) demonstrate in writing a need for establishing the requirement; (2) specify all requirements that must be satisfied to become qualified in the least restrictive manner possible in the circumstances; (3) specify an estimate of the costs of testing and evaluation likely to be incurred by a potential offeror in order to become qualified; (4) ensure that prospective contractors are given a prompt opportunity to demonstrate their ability to meet the requirement; and (5) ensure that a potential offeror seeking qualification is promptly informed as to whether qualification is attained and, if not attained, is promptly furnished specific information explaining the outcome. These requirements are implemented in FAR Subpart 9.2. Neither the regulation nor the statutes contain any guidance as to the situations that can justify the necessity for qualification requirements.

These statutes authorize greater use of prequalification procedures than had been authorized prior to 1984. See *Vac-Hyd Corp.*, 64 Comp. Gen. 658 (B-216840), 85-2 CPD ¶ 2, commenting that although the applicable prequalification statute was not yet applicable to the procurement being protested, it "establishes a framework for future procurements." In *Vac-Hyd*, the GAO stated that the protested prequalification process for jet engine repair contracts was proper because it

> serves a bona fide need of the government — that is, it ensures a high level of maintenance on a critical aircraft part — yet it also allows nonapproved sources to submit proposals and become qualified.

However, the GAO criticized the way the agency had implemented the prequalification procedure because it had not given the protester sufficient opportunity to become qualified. Compare *Advanced Seal Tech., Inc.*, Comp. Gen. Dec. B-400088, 2008 CPD ¶ 137 (five days reasonable time to qualify product); *CM Mfg., Inc.*, Comp. Gen. Dec. B-293370, 2004 CPD ¶ 69 (reasonable opportunity given by placing requirements in procurement notice); and *Newguard Indus., Inc.*, Comp. Gen. Dec. B-257052, 94-2 CPD ¶ 70 (reasonable opportunity given by notification that item did not meet agency requirements).

Award of a long-term contract to the only prequalified source is improper when another source is in the process of qualifying, *Barnes Aerospace Group*, B-298864, 2006 CPD ¶ 217 (two year contract with three one-year options).

Prequalification procedures have been approved for repair and alteration of nuclear ships, *Southwest Marine, Inc.*, Comp. Gen. Dec. B-225559, 87-1 CPD ¶ 431; production of films and videos, *Video Educ. Television*, Comp. Gen. Dec. B-248596, May 19, 1992, *Unpub.*; and ship dismantling under master ship repair contracts, *Stevens Tech. Servs., Inc.*, Comp. Gen. Dec. B-250515.2, 93-1 CPD ¶ 385.

FAR 9.202 sets forth a number of procedures that an agency must follow to prequalify sources:

(a)(1) The head of the agency or designee shall, before establishing a qualification requirement, prepare a written justification —

(i) Stating the necessity for establishing the qualification requirement and specifying why the qualification requirement must be demonstrated before contract award;

(ii) Estimating the likely costs for testing and evaluation which will be incurred by the potential offeror to become qualified; and

(iii) Specifying all requirements that a potential offeror (or its product) must satisfy in order to become qualified. Only those requirements which are the least restrictive to meet the purposes necessitating the establishment of the qualification requirements shall be specified.

(2) Upon request to the contracting activity, potential offerors shall be provided —

(i) All requirements that they or their products must satisfy to become qualified;

(ii) At their expense (but see 9.204(a)(2) with regard to small businesses), a prompt opportunity to demonstrate their abilities to meet the standards specified for qualification using qualified personnel and facilities of the agency concerned, or of another agency obtained through interagency agreements, or under contract, or other methods approved by the agency (including use of approved testing and evaluation services not provided under contract to the agency).

(3) If the services in (a)(2)(ii) above are provided by contract, the contractors selected to provide testing and evaluation services shall be —

(i) Those that are not expected to benefit from an absence of additional qualified sources; and

(ii) Required by their contracts to adhere to any restriction on technical data asserted by the potential offeror seeking qualification.

(4) A potential offeror seeking qualification shall be promptly informed as to whether qualification is attained and, in the event it is not, promptly furnished specific reasons why qualification was not attained.

These prequalification procedures must be carefully followed. See *Stevens Tech. Servs., Inc.*, Comp. Gen. Dec. B-250515.2, 93-1 CPD ¶ 385, ruling that the protester was entitled to have the agency's determination that it was not a qualified contractor referred to the SBA in order to obtain a Certificate of Competency. The GAO reached this conclusion because the factors evaluated by the agency were the normal responsibility factors and did not include any of the exceptions in FAR 9.202(d) such as special testing requirements or quality assurance demonstrations. In *Digicomp Research Corp.*, Comp. Gen. Dec. B-262139, 95-2 CPD ¶ 246, the GAO held that the prequalification statutes, including all their procedural requirements, are applicable to procurements where the agency has justified limited competition rather than full and open competition.

FAR 9.206-2 requires that agencies include the Qualification Requirements clause in FAR 52.209-1 in all procurements subject to a qualification requirement. If this clause is not expressly incorporated in the solicitation, an agency may not enforce any qualification provisions, *Warren Pumps, Inc.*, Comp. Gen. Dec. B-258710, 95-1 CPD ¶ 79, *recons. denied*, 95-2 CPD ¶ 20 (inclusion of qualification requirement in specification not controlling when FAR clause omitted from solicitation); *Comspace Corp.*, Comp. Gen. Dec. B-237794, 90-1 CPD ¶ 217 (offer of product not meeting qualification requirement improperly rejected when only such requirement was in specifications). Furthermore, the absence of this clause is a clear indication that no such requirement pertains to the procurement, *Gentex Corp.*, Comp. Gen. Dec. B-271381, 96-1 CPD ¶ 281, *recons. denied*, 96-2 CPD ¶ 88.

Prior to 1984, prequalification of offerors — the limiting of competitors to those firms that had been determined to be responsible prior to the solicitation — had been held by the GAO to be a restriction on competition. See 53 Comp. Gen. 209 (B-178624) (1973), stating at 211:

It is the cornerstone of the competitive system that bids and/or proposals be solicited in such a manner as to permit the maximum amount of competition consistent with the nature and extent of the services or items being procured. Any establishment of presolicitation procedures for determining a prospective bidder's/offeror's responsibility whether relating to the manner of manufacture or capability to manufacture, is a restriction of full and free competition [the pre-CICA standard]. The question to be answered concerning the validity of the procedure is not whether it restricts competition per se, but whether it unduly restricts competition.

* * *

While determinations concerning a contractor's responsibility must be made before contract award, we have not ordinarily sanctioned such determinations prior to bid opening since to do so might foreclose the receipt of proposals from responsible contractors of whom the procurement agency is not aware. Thus, in the usual case, such prebid opening determinations have been considered as unduly restricting competition within the meaning of the statutes governing competition.

Following this reasoning, the GAO ruled that prequalification procedures were improper in contracts for restoration of historic buildings, 52 Comp. Gen. 569 (B-176940) (1973); supply of aircraft parts, *D. Moody & Co.*, 55 Comp. Gen. 1 (B-180732), 75-2 CPD ¶ 1; and operation of a sonobuoy test program, *VAST, Inc.*, Comp. Gen. Dec. B-182844, 75-1 CPD ¶ 71. None of these cases directly addressed the issue of whether there was a compelling agency need for prequalification. In *Dep't of Agriculture's Use of Master Agreement*, 54 Comp. Gen. 606 (B-182337), 75-1 CPD ¶ 50, the GAO ruled that mere administrative convenience was not a valid reason for the use of prequalification procedures. In that case the agency had used a system of prequalifying the 10 most qualified companies for each type of consulting services being procured. The GAO noted that this was considerably more restrictive than a system that prequalified all qualified firms. In *Dep't of Agriculture's Use of Master Agreements*, 56 Comp. Gen. 78 (B-182337), 76-2 CPD ¶ 390, the GAO approved modified prequalification procedures, awarding a master agreement to all qualified firms, on the grounds that this would enhance competition by permitting more firms to compete than the alternative of awarding a single requirements contract for the consulting services.

In spite of the general view that prequalification was restrictive, a number of prequalification systems were approved before 1984 as not being unduly restrictive. For example, prequalification of film and videotape producers was approved to permit more meaningful evaluation of offerors, *John Bransby Productions, Ltd.*, Comp. Gen. Dec. B-198360, 80-2 CPD ¶ 419, and prequalification of production lines for microcircuitry by NASA was also approved on the basis that such prequalification was necessary to assure a continuous supply of these items under stringent quality requirements, 50 Comp. Gen. 542 (B-171597) (1971). The GAO also permitted the Navy to require contractors to have or be eligible for a master ship repair contract (MSRC), which is a certification of responsibility, in order to receive an award, *Carolina Drydocks, Inc.*, Comp. Gen. Dec. B-218186.2, 85-1 CPD ¶ 629; *Fairburn Marine Aviation*, Comp. Gen. Dec. B-187062, 76-2 CPD ¶ 523. The GAO in *Carolina Drydocks* upheld a determination that the protester would not qualify for an MSRC. The determination was based on a survey revealing inadequate facilities and organization. Prequalification was also approved for use in the cut-make-and-trim industry where the agency demonstrated that reputable firms would not submit bids under normal sealed bidding conditions, Comp. Gen. Dec. B-135504, May 2, 1958, *Unpub.* See Lieblich, *Bidder Prequalifications: Theory in Search of Practice*, 5 Pub. Cont. L.J. 32 (1972).

The lack of fair prequalification procedures was the basis for sustaining a protest in *Algonquin Parts, Inc.*, 60 Comp. Gen. 361 (B-198464), 81-1 CPD ¶ 270. In that case the GAO stated that the Navy failed to institute formal qualification procedures for a known supplier or to act in conjunction with the Air Force in its qualification process of the same supplier for similar parts.

Prequalification has also been permitted by other statutes. See, for example, 10 U.S.C. § 2865, permitting prequalification of contractors to enter into shared energy savings contracts at military bases. In *Strategic Resource Solutions Corp.*, Comp. Gen. Dec. B-278732, 98-1 CPD ¶ 74, the GAO ruled that it was proper to restrict the competition to the 1997 list of prequalified companies even though the award was not going to be made until 1998. See also 10 U.S.C. § 2687, permitting prequalification of contractors to enter into contracts for certain environmental restoration activities.

The DOD suggests procurement of replenishment parts only from qualified contractors. DFARS 217.7502(b)(2) provides as follows:

> Replenishment parts must be acquired so as to ensure the safe, dependable, and effective operation of the equipment. Where this assurance is not possible with new sources, competition may be limited to the original manufacturer of the equipment or other sources that have previously manufactured or furnished the parts as long as the action is justified.

An agency may use a basic ordering agreement when procuring replenishment parts. However, when a basic ordering agreement is used in such cases, an agency must have procedures in place for qualifying additional suppliers. See *Rotair Indus.*, 58 Comp. Gen. 149 (B-190392), 78-2 CPD ¶ 410, where the agency used a basic ordering agreement for the procurement of helicopter parts. The protester contended that the procedures used by the Navy in procuring helicopter parts was unduly restrictive of competition. Specifically, the protester asserted that the lack of procedures for qualifying additional suppliers, continued use of restrictive procurement method coding on orders, and failure to publicize orders promptly in the *Commerce Business Daily* resulted in virtually automatic procurement of orders under Sikorsky's basic ordering agreement on a noncompetitive basis. The GAO agreed and sustained the protest.

3. Multiple Award Task and Delivery Order Contracts

The most common multistep procedure in use at the present time is the issuance of multiple-award task and delivery order contracts. Under a single solicitation, an agency awards separate task or delivery order contracts for the same or similar services or supplies to two or more contractors. Task or delivery orders can then be issued under these contracts through competitive or sole source procedures. However, FAR 16.505(b) states a preference for competition, as follows:

(1) *Fair opportunity.* (i) The contracting officer must provide each awardee a fair opportunity to be considered for each order exceeding $3,000 issued under multiple delivery-order contracts or multiple task-order contracts, except as provided for in paragraph (b)(2) of this section.

(ii) The contracting officer may exercise broad discretion in developing appropriate order placement procedures. The contracting officer should keep submission requirements to a minimum. Contracting officers may use streamlined procedures, including oral presentations. In addition, the contracting officer need not contact each of the multiple awardees under the contract before selecting an order awardee if the contracting officer has information available to ensure that each awardee is provided a fair opportunity to be considered for each order and the order does not exceed $5 million. The competition requirements in part 6 and the policies in subpart 15.3 do not apply to the ordering process. However, the contracting officer must —

(A) Develop placement procedures that will provide each awardee a fair opportunity to be considered for each order and that reflect the requirement and other aspects of the contracting environment;

(B) Not use any method (such as allocation or designation of any preferred awardee) that would not result in fair consideration being given to all awardees prior to placing each order;

(C) Tailor the procedures to each acquisition;

(D) Include the procedures in the solicitation and the contract; and

(E) Consider price or cost under each order as one of the factors in the selection decision.

(iii) Orders exceeding $5 million. For task or delivery orders in excess of $5 million, the requirement to provide all awardees a fair opportunity to be considered for each order shall include, at a minimum —

(A) A notice of the task or delivery order that includes a clear statement of the agency's requirements;

(B) A reasonable response period;

(C) Disclosure of the significant factors and subfactors, including cost or price, that the agency expects to consider in evaluating proposals, and their relative importance;

(D) Where award is made on a best value basis, a written statement documenting the basis for award and the relative importance of quality and price or cost factors; and

(E) An opportunity for a postaward debriefing in accordance with paragraph (b)(4) of this section.

(iv) The contracting officer should consider the following when developing the procedures:

(A)(1) Past performance on earlier orders under the contract, including quality, timeliness and cost control.

(2) Potential impact on other orders placed with the contractor.

(3) Minimum order requirements.

(4) The amount of time contractors need to make informed business decisions on whether to respond to potential orders.

(5) Whether contractors could be encouraged to respond to potential orders by outreach efforts to promote exchanges of information, such as —

(i) Seeking comments from two or more contractors on draft statements of work;

(ii) Using a multiphased approach when effort required to respond to a potential order may be resource intensive (e.g., requirements are complex or need continued development), where all contractors are initially considered on price considerations (e.g., rough estimates), and other considerations as appropriate (e.g., proposed conceptual approach, past performance). The contractors most likely to submit the highest value solutions are then selected for one-on-one sessions with the Government to increase their understanding of the requirements, provide suggestions for refining requirements, and discuss risk reduction measures.

(B) Formal evaluation plans or scoring of quotes or offers are not required.

(2) *Exceptions to the fair opportunity process.* The contracting officer shall give every awardee a fair opportunity to be considered for a delivery-order or task-order exceeding $3,000 unless one of the following statutory exceptions applies:

(i) The agency need for the supplies or services is so urgent that providing a fair opportunity would result in unacceptable delays.

(ii) Only one awardee is capable of providing the supplies or services required at the level of quality required because the supplies or services ordered are unique or highly specialized.

(iii) The order must be issued on a sole-source basis in the interest of economy and efficiency because it is a logical follow-on to an order already issued under the contract, provided that all awardees were given a fair opportunity to be considered for the original order.(iv) It is necessary to place an order to satisfy a minimum guarantee.

This is a multistep procedure because the government can effectively limit the number of competitors by issuing orders only to competitors with those awarded contracts. In addition, 10 U.S.C. § 2304c(e) and 41 U.S.C. § 253j(e) preclude protesting of the issuance of task or delivery orders of $10 million or less except "on the ground that the order increases the scope, period, or maximum value of the contract under which the order is issued." The issuance of task or delivery orders over $10 million can be protested to the GAO only.

The GAO has granted protests when a task or delivery order was, in effect, a "downselect" for the balance of the agency's needs. See *OTI America, Inc.*, Comp. Gen. Dec. B-295455.3, 2005 CPD ¶ 157, stating:

Where . . . an agency uses parallel contracts for the development and production of products to conduct a competition among the contractors resulting in the elimination of one or more contractors as sources for the agency's requirements for the duration of the contracts in question, we will consider protests concerning that competition and the decisions to eliminate contractors. *Electro-Voice, Inc.*, B-278319, B-278319.2, Jan. 15, 1998, 98-1 CPD ¶ 23 at 5; *Fermont Div., Dynamics Corp. of Am.*, B-257373.3, et al., Dec. 22, 1995, 96-1 CPD ¶ 78 at 1-2 n.1; *Mine Safety Appliances Co.*, B-238597.2, July 5, 1990, 90-2 CPD ¶ 11 at 4; see *Westinghouse Elec. Corp.*, B-189730, Mar. 8, 1978, 78-1 CPD ¶ 181 at 6. In the above cited cases, there was a "downselection" of a contractor based on a limited competition among the contract holders, as contemplated by the terms of the parallel contracts, and this downselection was implemented by issuing or not issuing delivery orders under the contracts, or exercising or not exercising contract options.

The Court of Federal Claims has followed this reasoning in taking jurisdiction of downselect protests of the issuance of task or delivery orders, *OTI America, Inc. v. United States*, 68 Fed. Cl. 108 (2005). Compare the court's narrow view of its jurisdiction in *A&D Fire Protection, Inc. v. United States*, 72 Fed. Cl. 126 (2006). See also *Global Communications Solutions, Inc.*, Comp. Gen. Dec. B-291113, 2002 CPD ¶ 194 (changing basis for selecting low price on contract line items to be procured from single contractor an improper downselect); *Teledyne-Commodore, LLC*, Comp. Gen. Dec. B-278408.4, 98-2 CPD ¶ 121 (task order being competed was for all work contemplated by base contract). Most protests of this nature have been denied because the GAO found that the order did not constitute a downselect, *L-3 Communications Co.*, Comp. Gen. Dec. B-295166, 2004 CPD ¶ 245 (order calling for design of product and stating that agency "may" order additional items left room for future competition); *Professional Performance Dev. Group, Inc.*, Comp. Gen. Dec. B-294054.3, 2004 CPD ¶ 191 (setting aside some work for small contractors not a downselect when large companies would be allowed to compete for other work); *Intrados Group*, Comp. Gen. Dec. B-280130, 98-1 CPD ¶ 168 (protester had successfully competed on prior task orders and would be able to compete for other task orders under the contract).

The statutes provide that agencies must provide an alternate procedure to ensure that orders are issued fairly by establishing "ombudsmen" to hear complaints regarding task or delivery orders. See FAR 16.505(b)(6) stating:

> The head of the agency shall designate a task-order and delivery-order ombudsman. The ombudsman must review complaints from contractors and ensure they are afforded a fair opportunity to be considered, consistent with the procedures in the contract. The ombudsman must be a senior agency official who is independent of the contracting officer and may be the agency's competition advocate.

The use of task and delivery order contracts as multistep procedures has been significantly enlarged in recent years by statutory provisions permitting multiple agencies to order from contracts issued by a single agency. See Chapter 8. However, these "government-wide agency contracts" and "multiple agency contracts" generally are awarded to a large number of contractors with the result that do not restrict the competition to the extent that occurs with some multiple award contracts issued for use by a single agency.

4. Award of Program Definition Contract

For many years the military services have awarded multiple contracts to define programs and have limited future competition to those companies or teams that have performed a program definition contract. Paragraph 1.4.3 of DOD Regulation 5000.2-R, *Mandatory Procedures for Major Defense Acquisition Programs (MDAPs) and Major Automated Information System (MAIS) Acquisition Programs*

(Mar. 15, 1996), contained the following description of the work to be done on such a contract:

> During this phase, the program shall become defined as one or more concepts, design approaches, and/or parallel technologies are pursued as warranted. Assessments of the advantages and disadvantages of alternative concepts shall be refined. Prototyping, demonstrations, and early operational assessments shall be considered and included as necessary to reduce risk so that technology, manufacturing, and support risks are well in hand before the next decision point. Cost drivers, life-cycle cost estimates, cost-performance trades, interoperability, and acquisition strategy alternatives shall be considered to include evolutionary and incremental software development.

This regulation was replaced by DOD Instruction 5000.02, *Operation of the Defense Acquisition System* (Dec. 8, 2008), which replaces this phase with a "technology development phase" where contracts are to be awarded to "two or more competing teams producing prototypes of the system and/or key system elements." The instruction contains no guidance on whether other contractors will be permitted to compete for the following "engineering and manufacturing development" phase but prior practice would indicate that competition for that contract is likely to be limited to the contractors in the technology phase.

In *Hughes Missile Sys. Co.*, Comp. Gen. Dec. B-272418, 96-2 CPD ¶ 221, Hughes protested the award of a contract for the definition and development of the joint air-to-surface standoff missile to Lockheed Martin and McDonnell Douglas. The solicitation contemplated the award of two cost-plus-fixed-fee contracts for a 24-month program definition and risk reduction (PDRR) phase, which would include priced options for a follow-on cost-plus-incentive-fee engineering, management and development phase, to be exercised on the basis of a downselect competition between the two PDRR contractors. Hughes contended that the agency did not adequately consider the complexity of the products being developed or procured when evaluating past cost/schedule performance and arriving at an overall rating. The GAO denied the protest, finding that the offerors were advised that the agency viewed program similarity as more important than product similarity. See also *Gentex Corp. – Western Operations*, Comp. Gen. Dec. B-291793, 2003 CPD ¶ 66, and *Gentex Corp. v. United States*, 58 Fed. Cl. 634 (2003), holding it was proper to allow a subcontractor on one of the two teams that had the PDRR contract to assume the role of lead contractor on the competition for the follow-on contract.

5. Two-Phase Design-Build Procedure

Traditionally, the federal government has obtained new buildings and other civil works by contracting with an architect/engineering firm (A/E) for design of the project, soliciting competitive bids or proposals for the construction of the project, and awarding a contract to the successful offeror. This is known as the design-bid-build delivery system. Although this system has worked well, it is relatively slow, and it separates design responsibility from construction responsibility. The system has been criticized for not bringing sufficient consideration of constructibility into the design process and for subjecting the government to claims of the construction contractor for design defects. In using detailed construction drawings, the government is liable to the contractor on a standard that approaches strict liability, yet its claim against the A/E for defective design is generally judged by a standard of negligence.

In order to overcome these problems, federal agencies such as the Postal Service, the General Services Administration, and the Army Corps of Engineers began to use a design-build delivery system where the tasks of both design and construction were combined into a single contract. This was done using the standard competitive negotiation process with extensive technical proposals. See the General Services Administration publication "Design-Build Request for Proposals Guide" (Nov. 1991) and the Corps of Engineers publication "Design-Build Instructions for Military Construction" (Sept. 26, 1994). This procedure placed a heavy burden on offerors because the agency frequently required extensive design work as a part of the competitive proposal.

Section 4105 of the Clinger-Cohen Act of 1996 amended 10 U.S.C. § 2305a and 41 U.S.C. § 253m to include new design-build selection procedures. This section of the Act establishes a series of new acquisition rules — known as two-phase selection procedures — that must be followed when an agency decides to use the design-build delivery system and concludes that extensive design proposals will be required. The regulatory implementation adds a new FAR Subpart 36.3.

The following statement on when the new procedure should be used is set forth in 10 U.S.C. § 2305a:

> Authorization — Unless the traditional acquisition approach of design-bid-build established under the Brooks Architect-Engineers Act (41 U.S.C. § 541 et seq.) is used or another acquisition procedure authorized by law is used, the head of an agency shall use the two-phase selection procedures for entering into a contract for the design and construction of a public building, facility, or work when a determination is made that the procedures are appropriate for use.

Almost identical language is used in 41 U.S.C. § 253m. FAR 36.104 uses virtually the same language but includes the following sentence:

> Other acquisition procedures authorized by law include the procedures established in this part and other parts of this chapter and, for DOD, the design-build process described in 10 U.S.C. § 2862.

Thus, there are essentially two delivery systems for construction projects — design-bid-build and design-build. If design-bid-build is chosen, the design effort must be done using the Brooks Act procedures. Thereafter, the construction can be procured using sealed bidding, negotiation, or construction management. If design-build is chosen, either a one-step or two-step procedure may be used. The one-step procedure would follow normal competitive negotiation procedures. The two-step procedure would follow this new statutory two-phase procedure.

Contracting officers must consider the following criteria set forth in 10 U.S.C. § 2305a and 41 U.S.C. § 253m to determine whether the two-phase procedure is appropriate:

> Criteria for use — A contracting officer shall make a determination whether two-phase selection procedures are appropriate for use for entering into a contract for the design and construction of a public building, facility, or work when the contracting officer anticipates that three or more offers will be received for such contract, design work must be performed before an offeror can develop a price or cost proposal for such contract, the offeror will incur a substantial amount of expense in preparing the offer, and the contracting officer has considered information such as the following:
>
> (1) The extent to which the project requirements have been adequately defined.
>
> (2) The time constraints for delivery of the project.
>
> (3) The capability and experience of potential contractors.
>
> (4) The suitability of the project for use of the two-phase selection procedures.
>
> (5) The capability of the agency to manage the two-phase selection process.
>
> (6) Other criteria established by the agency.

These criteria are repeated in FAR 36.301(b). The key criteria are the requirement for design work and the resulting incurrence of cost by offerors. If extensive design work will be required with commensurate high proposal costs, the two-phase design-build procedure should be used. If little design work or proposal costs will be required, the normal competitive negotiation procedure will likely be the most efficient procedure.

Even though capability criteria are used to select the Phase 1 contractors, they may also be used again in making the final source selection of the Phase

2 contractor, *Hines/Mortenson*, Comp. Gen. Dec. B-256543.4, 94-2 CPD ¶ 67. Challenges to the criteria used to select the competing contractors have been rejected, *King Constr. Co.*, Comp. Gen. Dec. B-298276, 2006 CPD ¶ 110 (experience in constructing buildings of the same type); *Parcel 47C LLC*, Comp. Gen. Dec. B-286324, 2001 CPD ¶ 44 (control of site to construct leased building). However, the GAO has agreed that it is proper to exclude a contractor from the competition because it has an organizational conflict of interest from drafting the specification and preparing the budget estimate, *SSR Eng'rs, Inc.*, Comp. Gen. Dec. B-282244, 99-2 CPD ¶ 27 (rejecting the argument that FAR 36.302 precludes the application of the OCI rules because it allows the use of contractors to perform these tasks).

Some agencies have awarded multiple award IDIQ contracts for smaller design-build projects. See, for example, holding that it is improper to select such contractors using fixed labor rates, *S. J. Thomas Co.*, Comp. Gen. Dec. B-283192, 99-2 CPD ¶ 73, holding that it is improper to use fixed labor rates, without an estimated quantity of labor, as the evaluation criteria.

6. *Federal Aviation Administration Screening Procedure*

The Federal Aviation Administration has adopted a multistep procedure as its basic procurement procedure for complex and noncommercial acquisitions. This was done under Pub. L. No. 104-50, which exempted the Federal Aviation Agency (FAA) from the Federal Property and Administrative Services Act, as well as a number of other designated statutes. As a result, on April 1, 1996, the FAA issued the *Federal Aviation Administration Acquisition Management System* (*AMS*), a separate procurement regulation. The AMS was issued in June 1997 and has been revised several times – the last revision being in October 2008. It is not published in the Federal Register but is available at http://fast.faa.gov/.

The AMS has a "Complex and Noncommercial Source Selection" process that is used for complex, large-dollar, developmental, and noncommercial items and services. Under AMS 3.2.2.3, there are five phases in the process:

Planning

Screening

Selection

Debriefing (as requested); and

Lessons learned

The screening process is the multistep procedure used by the FAA. A screening information request (SIR) is a request by the FAA for documentation, information, presentations, proposals, or binding offers. Once the public announcement has been released, the SIR may be released to start the competitive process, AMS 3.2.2.3.1.2.1. The number of distinct screening steps for a particular procurement will vary depending on the complexity of the procurement. Three categories of SIRs may be used according to the procurement strategy adopted by the procurement team: (1) qualification information, (2) screening information, and (3) requests for offers, AMS 3.2.2.3.1.2.1.

Qualification information is be used to qualify vendors and establish qualified vendor lists (QVLs). It should be used only if it is intended that the resultant QVL will be used for multiple FAA procurements. Requested qualification information should be tailored to solicit information that will allow the FAA to make a determination as to which vendors meet the FAA's minimum qualification requirements for the required products or services. The qualification information is evaluated in accordance with the evaluation plan. A QVL will then be established for the given product or service. Once the list is established, only qualified vendors may compete for the products or services. This list can be updated at the FAA's discretion.

The second category of SIR calls for screening information, AMS 3.2.2.3.1.2.1. This category allows the FAA to determine which offerors will provide the FAA with the best value. This SIR focuses on information that directly relates to the key discriminators for the procurement. Types of information that may form the basis of a screening request include equipment/products for FAA testing, capability statements, draft/model contracts, technical proposals (including oral presentations, if appropriate), commercial pricing information, financial information, cost or price information, and cost or price proposals, AMS 3.2.2.3.1.2.1. Each SIR requesting screening information must include some cost or pricing information appropriate to the specific SIR level of detail, AMS 3.2.2.3.1.2.1.

The last category of SIR is the request for offer, which is a request for an offeror to commit formally to provide the products or services required by the acquisition, AMS 3.2.2.3.1.2.1. The response to the request for offer is a binding offer and will become a binding contract if signed by the contracting officer, AMS 3.2.2.3.1.2.1. The request for offer may take the form of a formal solicitation, a proposed contract, or a purchase order.

III. EVALUATION FACTORS AND SUBFACTORS

The selection of the evaluation factors and subfactors that will be used for the procurement is a critical part of source selection planning. Evaluation factors and subfactors describe the matters that are to be considered in determining which proposal will be most advantageous to the government. In selecting the factors and subfactors, the agency should include those elements of the procurement that are critical to the selection of the source offering the best value but, at the same time, should limit the number of factors to permit the evaluation process to be completed in a short period of time — in most cases in one or two weeks and rarely longer than a month. Limiting the number of factors also permits the agency to focus on the key issues in making the source selection, whereas the use of a large number of factors and subfactors tends to obscure the importance of key issues. Striking this balance is difficult, but it must be accomplished to conduct an effective competitively negotiated procurement.

FAR 15.304 provides only minimal general guidance on the selection of evaluation factors:

(a) The award decision is based on evaluation factors and significant subfactors that are tailored to the acquisition.

(b) Evaluation factors and significant subfactors must —

(1) Represent the key areas of importance and emphasis to be considered in the source selection decision; and

(2) Support meaningful comparison and discrimination between and among competing proposals.

While this general guidance is imprecise, it does provide a degree of assistance in selecting an appropriate number of evaluation factors. First, it indicates that the decision on the evaluation factors to be used should be made on each source selection. Thus, ¶ (a) calls for "tailoring" the factors to the acquisition. This precludes merely using the same factors that have been used in the past on similar acquisitions and suggests a new analysis for each new source selection. Second, ¶ (b)(1) calls for factors that focus on "key areas of importance" – with the implication that only major areas of importance should be evaluated. In following this guidance, contracting officers must point out to the other members of the acquisition team that, as a general proposition, *all* key areas of importance will be included in the specifications as mandatory requirements. Thus, when the contract is awarded, the contractor will be obligated to meet these requirements. Since this is the case, there is no necessity to evaluate all of the key areas of importance – only the major areas need be evaluated. This proposition is reinforced by ¶ (b)(2) requiring evaluation factors to "support meaningful comparison and discrimination." This required the acquisition team to review past acquisitions of the same or similar products or services to ascertain which evaluation factors have actually discriminated among the competitors. When it is found that a factor has not served this purpose – with the competitors being given similar scores or ratings – that factor should not be used in the new procurement. Following this analytical process, the acquisition team should be able to select a small number of evaluation factors that permit award to the offeror that will provide the best value to the government.

Neither the statutes nor the FAR deal coherently with the classification of evaluation factors. However, they both describe evaluation factors in two categories: price or cost to the government, and non-price factors. From this perspective, non-price factors identify those elements of a tradeoff process procurement for which the agency is willing to pay a higher price. All such non-price factors are lumped together under the broad category "quality of the product or services." See 10 U.S.C. § 2305(a)(3)(A)(i) and 41 U.S.C. § 253a(c)(1)(A) specifying evaluation of the "quality of the product or services to be provided (including technical capability, management capability, prior experience, and past performance of the offeror)." FAR 15.304(c) contains this same classification, expanding on the quality factor and adding past performance and other factors:

> The evaluation factors and significant subfactors that apply to an acquisition and their relative importance are within the broad discretion of agency acquisition officials, subject to the following requirements:
>
> > (1) Price or cost to the Government shall be evaluated in every source selection (10 U.S.C. 2305(a)(3)(A)(ii) and 41 U.S.C. 253a(c)(1)(B)) (also see part 36 for architect-engineer contracts);
> >
> > (2) The quality of the product or service shall be addressed in every source selection through consideration of one or more non-cost evaluation factors such as past performance, compliance with solicitation requirements, technical excellence, management capability, personnel qualifications, and prior experience (10 U.S.C. 2305(a)(3) (A)(i) and 41 U.S.C. 253a(c) (1)(A)); and
> >
> > (3)(i) Except as set forth in paragraph (c)(3)(iii) of this section, past performance shall be evaluated in all source selections for negotiated competitive acquisitions expected to exceed the simplified acquisition threshold.
> >
> > > (ii) For solicitations involving bundling that offer a significant opportunity for subcontracting, the contracting officer must include a factor to evaluate past performance indicating the extent to which the offeror attained applicable goals for small business participation under contracts that required subcontracting plans (15 U.S.C. 637(d)(4)(G)(ii)).
> > >
> > > (iii) Past performance need not be evaluated if the contracting officer documents the reason past performance is not an appropriate evaluation factor for the acquisition.

(4) The extent of participation of small disadvantaged business concerns in performance of the contract shall be evaluated in unrestricted acquisitions expected to exceed $550,000 ($1,000,000 for construction) subject to certain limitations (see 19.201 and 19.1202).

(5) For solicitations involving bundling that offer a significant opportunity for subcontracting, the contracting officer must include proposed small business subcontracting participation in the subcontracting plan as an evaluation factor (15 U.S.C. 637(d)(4)(G)(I)).

(6) If telecommuting is not prohibited, agencies shall not unfavorably evaluate an offer that includes telecommuting unless the contracting officer executes a written determination in accordance with FAR 7.108(b).

This regulation emphasizes the long-standing rule of the GAO that agencies have broad discretion in selecting the factors and in determining their relative importance. See *Augmentation, Inc.*, Comp. Gen. Dec. B-186614, 76-2 CPD ¶ 235, stating:

[I]t is well settled that a determination of an agency's minimum needs and the selection and weights of evaluation criteria to be used to measure how well offerors will meet those needs are within the broad discretion entrusted to agency procurement officials.

A more coherent way to classify evaluation factors can be derived from a recognition that they are used to evaluate two different considerations in the source selection process — the *offer* made by each offeror and the *capability* of each offeror. The offer is comprised of those *promises* made by the offeror that will be included in the contract and will thus be contractually binding. This will be price or estimated cost and fee, at a minimum, plus other features that constitute contractual promises or undertaking. These other features might be the precise product or service to be furnished, an offered delivery schedule, a specific warranty, or any other promise solicited from the offeror that the agency concludes should be contractually binding. In contrast, the evaluation of capability of the offerors does not result in contractual promises. Rather, it is an evaluation of the offeror's ability to perform the promised work in order to assess the risk that the offeror will fail to carry out the contractual promises. Thus, there are two distinct types of evaluation factors — "offer factors" and "capability factors." In selecting the evaluation factors and subfactors for a procurement, it is helpful to distinguish between the two.

The distinction between "capability factors" and "offer factors" is blurred when the agency incorporates capability issues into the contract as contractually binding promises. For example, an agency might evaluate proposed key personnel to determine an offeror's capability and incorporate the names of key personnel into a Key Personnel clause. Similarly, an agency might evaluate the technique that the offeror intends to use to perform the work to determine its capability and also decide to make the technique contractually binding. In such cases the classification of the evaluation factors in these terms is not important, but it will guide the agency in specifying how the information to be used for evaluation should be submitted. In this regard it is good practice for the solicitation to inform the offerors which factors will be made contractual promises and which will be used solely for evaluation purposes. This matter will be discussed in Chapter 6.

This section deals with the types of evaluation factors and subfactors that might be used by an agency — organized in terms of offer factors and capability factors.

A. Offer Factors

Offer factors, as discussed in this book, are those factors that will result in contractual promises beyond the promises embodied in the request for proposals (RFPs). In the normal competitive procurement, the government spells out the greater portion of the offer it is soliciting in the RFP — including the contract specifications and the terms and conditions. If an offeror signs the proposal without taking exception to any mandatory element of the RFP, it has agreed to make the offer solicited by the government and those promises play no further role in the evaluation process. If an offeror takes exception to a mandatory element of the RFP, award to that offeror is precluded until the matter has been cleared up by amending the RFP or having the offeror withdraw the exception. See Chapter 6 for a full discussion of this process.

Every procurement has one offer evaluation factor — cost to the government; and in many procurements, this is the only offer factor. However, the agency may choose to solicit non-cost offers, of various types, when it desires to evaluate promises that are not contained in the RFP. Both cost and non-cost offer factors are considered in the following material.

1. Cost to the Government

The one offer evaluation factor that is present in every negotiated procurement is cost to the government. Offerors submit this offer by filling out Section B of the Uniform Contract Format when they submit their proposals. This discussion of cost to the government includes the amount to be paid to the contractor and other costs that the government might incur in procuring and using articles or services that are to be evaluated in dollar terms.

a. Amount to Be Paid to the Contractor

The amount to be paid to the contractor depends on the pricing arrangement to be used in the contract. When a firm-fixed-price contract is involved, the offeror's proposed price, not a mere estimate of the realistic cost, is the criterion that must be used in evaluating the proposal, *IBM Corp.*, Comp. Gen. Dec. B-299504, 2008

CPD ¶ 64; *Verestar Gov't Servs. Group*, Comp. Gen. Dec. B-291854, 2003 CPD ¶ 68; *Litton Sys., Inc.*, 63 Comp. Gen. 585 (B-215106), 84-2 CPD ¶ 317. This rule is followed because the contractor bears the risk of costs exceeding the price of a firm-fixed-price contract. However, an agency can evaluate whether a price is unrealistically low if it includes an evaluation factor in the RFP calling for such an evaluation. See *Pemco Aeroplex, Inc.*, Comp. Gen. Dec. B-310372.3, 2008 CPD ¶ 126, stating:

> Price realism is not ordinarily considered in the evaluation of proposals for the award of a fixed-price contract, because these contracts place the risk of loss upon the contractor. However, in light of various negative impacts on both the agency and the contractor that may result from an offeror's overly optimistic proposal, an agency may, as here, expressly provide that a price realism analysis will be applied in order to measure the offerors' understanding of the requirements and/ or to assess the risk inherent in an offeror's proposal. See, e.g., *Wackenhut Servs., Inc.*, B-286037, B-286037.2, Nov. 14, 2000, 2001 CPD ¶ 114 at 3; *Molina Eng'g, Ltd./Tri-J Indus., Inc. Joint Venture*, May 22, 2000, B-284895, 2000 CPD ¶ 86 at 4. Although the Federal Acquisition Regulation (FAR) identifies permissible price analysis techniques, FAR § 14.404-1, it does not mandate any particular approach; rather, the nature and extent of a price realism analysis, as well as an assessment of potential risk associated with a proposed price, are generally within the sound exercise of the agency's discretion. See *Legacy Mgmt. Solutions, LLC*, B-299981.2, Oct. 10, 2007, 2007 CPD ¶ 197 at 3; *Comprehensive Health Servs., Inc.*, B-310553, Dec. 27, 2007, 2007 CPD ¶ 9 at 8. In reviewing protests challenging an agency's evaluation of these matters, our focus is whether the agency acted reasonably and in a way consistent with the solicitation's requirements. See, e.g., *Grove Res. Solutions, Inc.*, B-296228, B-296228.2, July 1, 2005, 2005 CPD ¶ 133 at 4-5.

Thus, an agency may not adjust a fixed price if it doubts the offeror's ability to perform at the offered price, *IBM Corp.*, Comp. Gen. Dec. B-299504, 2008 CPD ¶ 64, but the low price may be addressed in the evaluation of non-price factors, such as performance risk, or as a matter of responsibility, *Pemco Aeroplex* (risk of low price properly evaluated because RFP called for evaluation of "proposal risk" by assessing "price realism"); *Alabama Aircraft Indus., Inc. – Birmingham v. United States*, 83 Fed. Cl. 666 (2008) (risk of low price in *Pemco Aeroplex* procurement not properly assessed because of flaws in agency reasoning); *Guam Shipyard*, Comp. Gen. Dec. B-311321, 2008 CPD ¶ 124 (low price properly assessed as "very high" risk when it was 23% under government estimate); *CSE Constr.*, Comp. Gen. Dec. B-291268.2, 2002 CPD ¶ 207 (where the RFP contains no relevant evaluation factor pertaining to price realism or understanding, a determination that an offeror's price on a fixed-price contract is a responsibility issue). Similarly, if the agency believes that the offeror's price indicates a lack of understanding of the work to be performed, this should be taken into consideration in the evaluation of capability or the determination of responsibility. See *Wackenhut Servs., Inc.*, Comp. Gen. Dec. B-286037, 2001 CPD ¶ 114 (low price of two offerors properly led to assessment of lack of understanding of the work but no requirement to make detailed assessment of elements of price of offeror with total price in line with other offerors); *Centech Group, Inc.*, Comp. Gen. Dec. B-278715, 98-1 CPD ¶ 108 (low option year prices indicated "an inherent lack of technical competence"). Furthermore, an agency may eliminate an offeror from the competitive range if it fails to submit information demonstrating that its low price is reasonable, *International Outsourcing Servs., LLC v. United States*, 69 Fed. Cl. 40 (2005). The GAO has taken note of the fact that there is no regulatory requirement for a price realism analysis because FAR 15.305(a)(1) merely provides that cost realism analyses may be used "in exceptional cases, on other competitive fixed-price-type contracts (see 15.404-1(d)(3))," *Team BOS/Naples − Gemmo S.p.A./DelJen*, Comp. Gen. Dec. B-298865.3, 2008 CPD ¶ 11. However, the GAO appears to be holding that price realism analysis will be required when the RFP states that the agency "may" make such an analysis, *Al Qabandi United Co.*, Comp. Gen. Dec. B-310600.3, 2008 CPD ¶ 112; *Computer Sciences Corp.*, Comp. Gen. Dec. B-298494.2, 2007 CPD ¶ 103.

There has been considerable confusion over the evaluation factor to be used with fixed-price incentive contracts, and the FAR does not address this issue. In the past the GAO stated that target cost should be used to evaluate the prices, *Televiso Elecs.*, 46 Comp. Gen. 631 (B-159922) (1967). See also *Serv-Air, Inc.*, 58 Comp. Gen. 362, 79-1 CPD ¶ 212, where the GAO held that the target price of one offeror could be contrasted with the ceiling price of another offeror in a "best case/worst case" comparison, and *Motorola, Inc.*, Comp. Gen. Dec. B-236294, 89-2 CPD ¶ 484, where the GAO condoned the use of the ceiling price to evaluate cost. The use of target prices alone might be logical if all offerors are proposing to use the same fixed-price incentive formula with the same ceiling. However, if the RFP permits offerors to proposed different formulas, it is better practice to use the ceiling price as the evaluation factor because this is the only element of the formula that is comparable for all offerors. With respect to realism of target cost proposals, FAR 15.305(a)(1) states that "Cost realism analyses may also be used on fixed-price incentive contracts" − apparently permitting use of probable target cost as an evaluation factor. The GAO reached this conclusion in *Eurest Support Servs.*, Comp. Gen. Dec. B-285813.3, 2003 CPD ¶ 139, holding that an agency must assess the realism of proposed target costs and adjust them for evaluation purposes if they are unrealistic. See also *Allied-Signal Aerospace Co.*, Comp. Gen. Dec. B-250822, 93-1 CPD ¶ 201, finding an agency decision to adjust target cost to reflect unrealistically low estimate "a prudent exercise of agency discretion;" and *Universal Techs., Inc.*, Comp. Gen. Dec. B-241157, 91-1 CPD ¶ 63, finding that the agency properly compared a realistic proposed target cost of one offeror with the proposed ceiling price of a competitor in making the source selection trade-off decision. If realistic target price is used as the evaluation factor, the target profit should be adjusted if a cost realism analysis indicates an adjustment of the target cost. However, the GAO has held that it is improper to adjust the ceiling price upward in connection with increasing the target cost based on a cost realism analysis, *Raytheon Co.*, Comp. Gen. Dec. B-242484.2, 91-2 CPD ¶ 131.

In cost-reimbursement contracts, both the realistic expected cost of performance and the proposed fee should be used as evaluation factors. FAR 15.305(a)(1) requires that a cost realism analysis be conducted "to determine what the Government should realistically expect to pay for the proposed effort," and FAR 15.404-1-(d)(i) states that the probable cost "shall be used for purposes of evaluation to determine the best value." This is consistent with GAO decisions, 50 Comp. Gen. 739 (B-171663) (1971); *DOT Sys., Inc.*, Comp. Gen. Dec. B-185558, 76-2 CPD ¶ 186; *Boeing Sikorsky Aircraft Support*, Comp. Gen. Dec. B-277263.2, 97-2 CPD ¶ 91. The GAO has held that where the RFP is amended to call for a cost-reimbursement rather than fixed-price contract, the agency should also amend the RFP to explicitly include cost realism as an evaluation factor and notify offerors that proposed costs may be adjusted accordingly, *Varian Assocs., Inc.*, Comp. Gen. Dec. B-209658, 83-1 CPD ¶ 658. In that case, the initial RFP had listed "Lowest Evaluated Cost to the Government" as a factor, but although the protest was denied the GAO stated that the better practice was to amend the solicitation.

The evaluation of fee depends on what type of cost-reimbursement contract is used. In a cost-plus-fixed-fee contract, the proposed fixed fee, rather than a realistic estimate of the fee, should be used as the evaluation factor because the former reflects a more reliable judgment, *Booz, Allen & Hamilton*, 63 Comp. Gen. 599 (B-213665), 84-2 CPD ¶ 329. In a cost-plus-award-fee contract, it is proper to use the offeror's proposed fee structure as the evaluation factor, *Management Servs., Inc.*, Comp. Gen. Dec. B-206364, 82-2 CPD ¶ 164. Thus, it is permissible to give a higher evaluation to an offeror that proposes a higher maximum fee on the theory that this will provide more incentive for good performance, *Boeing Sikorsky Aircraft Support*, Comp. Gen. Dec. B-277263.2, 97-2 CPD ¶ 91, or to an offeror that proposes to share its award fees with its employees on the theory that this will motivate them to perform better, *Cleveland Telecommunications Corp.*, 73 Comp. Gen. 303 (B-257294), 94-2 CPD ¶ 105. Compare *Research Triangle Inst.*, Comp. Gen. Dec. B-278254, 98-1 CPD ¶ 22, where an offeror was given a higher evaluation for proposing a low award fee.

b. Other Costs to the Government

Products or services purchased by the government, on either a fixed-price or cost-reimbursement basis, may result in the government incurring costs of acquisition or ownership that are not included in the contract price or cost. There is little clear guidance on the consideration of such costs as evaluation factors. The procurement statutes might be interpreted to require that other costs to the government be specified as evaluation factors. They state that solicitations "shall at a minimum include" evaluation factors, "including cost or price, cost-related or price-related factors and subfactors," 10 U.S.C. § 2305(a)(2)(A)(i) and 41 U.S.C. § 253a(b)(1)(A). However, the FAR does not repeat this language. FAR 15.304(c)(1) merely states: "Price or cost to the Government shall be evaluated in every source selection." The

GAO has not interpreted the statutes or the regulations as requiring the consideration of such costs in evaluating proposals, *Kastle Sys., Inc.*, Comp. Gen. Dec. B-231990, 88-2 CPD ¶ 415. See also *Sensis Corp.*, Comp. Gen. Dec. B-265790.2, 96-1 CPD ¶ 77 (life-cycle costs are not required to be evaluated as part of the cost/price evaluation). However, the failure to consider other costs to the government could lead to poor procurement decisions. As a matter of practice, other costs to the government are frequently used as evaluation factors or subfactors, whether objectively quantified or subjectively determined.

The most common cost of acquisition used as an evaluation criterion is transportation costs. This is one of the few areas in which evaluation of costs incurred by the government is mandated. FAR 47.305-2 provides that a solicitation for supplies will specify that offers may be f.o.b. origin, f.o.b. destination, or both, and that they will be evaluated on the basis of the lowest overall cost to the government. In such cases, the solicitation must require the offeror to furnish the government with applicable data necessary to compute transportation costs.

Costs incurred as a result of owning an item are part of what is known as "life cycle" costs, and, as discussed in Chapter 1, such costs should be considered during acquisition planning, FAR 7.105(a)(3)(i). FAR 7.101 defines life cycle costs as "the total cost to the Government of acquiring, operating, supporting, and (if applicable) disposing of the items being acquired." The magnitude of the costs beyond the original acquisition cost can greatly exceed the item's purchase price or production cost, but there are very few procurements that attempt to quantify life-cycle costs for evaluation purposes. See, for example, *Lockheed Missiles & Space Co. v. Dep't of the Treasury*, GSBCA 11776-P, 93-1 BCA ¶ 25,401, *aff'd*, 4 F.3d 955 (Fed. Cir. 1993), in which such costs resulted in awarding the contract to an offeror whose price totaled $1.4 billion over others whose prices were $900 and $700 million. Extensive agency analysis, quantified in dollar figures, illustrated the differences between the technical proposals and justified paying the price premium.

Quantification of life-cycle costs in dollar amounts in not required. Thus, life-cycle costs can be evaluated as a noncost evaluation factor. See *Ingalls Shipbuilding, Inc.*, Comp. Gen. Dec. B-275830, 97-1 CPD ¶ 180, stating:

> Ingalls argues that NAVSEA improperly failed to quantify probable LCC savings for each offer. Noting that the solicitation advised that the agency might be willing to pay a premium for the "approach that demonstrates the potential for greater life cycle cost reductions," Ingalls argues that NAVSEA "could not determine whether (or how much) to pay as a premium for a potentially greater life cycle cost saving, unless it had first determined how much potential saving was present in each offeror's proposed approach." NAVSEA explains that it was not possible to quantify the most likely LCC savings and the resulting most probable LCC for each proposal, given the early stage of the LPD 17 program and the information available to the agency.

Ingalls's argument is without merit. Ingalls's position fails to account for provisions of the solicitation providing that the agency would evaluate offerors' approaches to LCC cost reduction without actually quantifying LCC savings and the resulting most probable LCC for each proposal. In this regard, under the solicitation's statement of evaluation criteria, category 3 is entitled "Ownership Cost Reduction Approach," and category 3 proposals were to be "evaluated and assigned one of the following adjective ratings: (1) unacceptable, (2) marginal, (3) acceptable, (4) outstanding." At the same time, the RFP nowhere expressly stated that the agency would conduct a traditional most probable cost analysis with respect to LCC. Further, the solicitation's instructions for the preparation of proposals provided that:

> "Cost analyses required to support the Ship Propulsion Drive Train and Diesel Engines portion of the Offeror's proposal shall be the only portion of the Non-Price Proposal where dollars must be used.

> "The Offeror shall fully explain how it derives and establishes the baseline against which all savings are measured. All savings shall be shown with percentages only and not with dollars."

* * *

In our view, the solicitation supports NAVSEA's position that it was not required to quantify the most probable LCC reductions for each proposal and resulting most probable cost. Indeed, we believe that it was clear from the very use in the solicitation of such abstract language as "the highest likelihood" of reducing LCC and "the potential for" greater LCC reduction that the agency was not going to quantify the most probable LCC reductions and resulting most probable cost for each proposal.

However, quantification of life-cycle costs has been accomplished in several procurements. See, for example, *Sundstrand Corp.*, Comp. Gen. Dec. B-227038, 87-2 CPD ¶ 83 (life-cycle costs quantified by establishing "production price ceilings on future quantities . . . and sole-source components, spare and repair parts"); *American Airlines Training Corp.*, Comp. Gen. Dec. B-217421, 85-2 CPD ¶ 365 (cost of additional training added to proposed contract price for training to reflect retraining believed necessary to ensure that trainees were fully qualified).

DFARS PGI 207.105(b)(13)(i) states that the acquisition plan should describe "the extent of integrated logistics support planning, including total life cycle system management and performance based logistics." However, this apparently does not require the use of life-cycle costs as evaluation factors, as more definitive language contained in DAR 1-335 was not interpreted as imposing such a requirement, *Big Bud Tractors, Inc. v. United States*, 2 Cl. Ct. 188, *aff'd*, 727 F.2d 1118 (Fed. Cir. 1983); *Big Bud Tractors, Inc.*, Comp. Gen. Dec. B-209858, 83-1 CPD ¶ 127. The GAO found that although the regulation requires that life-cycle costs be considered as a factor during the procurement cycle, "we do not read the regulation as requiring that [life-cycle costs] be an evaluation factor for each award." Accord *Prudential-*

Maryland Joint Venture Co. v. Lehman, 590 F. Supp. 1390 (D.D.C. 1984). Whether to use life-cycle costs as evaluation factors in defense procurements is thus left to the discretion of the contracting officer. Other decisions affirming an agency decision not to evaluate life-cycle costs include *General Tel. Co. Of Cal.*, Comp. Gen. Dec. B-190142, Feb. 22, 1978, Unpub. (evaluation of the cost of government self-insurance would have been too "indefinite" and "speculative"); *Hawaiian Tel. Co.*, Comp. Gen. Dec. B-187871, 77-1 CPD ¶ 298 (evaluation of possible termination costs would be too speculative); *General Elec. Aerospace Sys.*, Comp. Gen. Dec. B-250514, 93-1 CPD ¶ 101 (no requirement to evaluate cost of limited rights in technical data).

If life cycle costs are not identified as an evaluation factor, they may not be evaluated, *Marquette Medical Sys., Inc.*, Comp. Gen. Dec. B-277827.5, 99-1 CPD ¶ 90 (agency improperly evaluated the savings from receiving new equipment versus the costs of receiving upgraded equipment). See also *Interspiro, Inc. v. United States*, 72 Fed. Cl. 672 (2006), holding that the agency properly did not evaluate life cycle costs because the RFP contained no statement they would be evaluated. Compare *Engineered Air Sys., Inc.*, Comp. Gen. Dec. B-283011, 99-2 CPD ¶ 63, where the GAO found that the agency properly evaluated extended warranties when the RFP merely stated that the agency would "give evaluation credit for proposed features that met or exceeded the stated objectives."

Agencies are given broad discretion in selecting the life cycle costs that will be evaluated. In *ViON Corp.*, Comp. Gen. Dec. B-256363, 94-1 CPD ¶ 373, the solicitation clearly set forth what factors would be considered in determining life cycle costs. The protester argued that the solicitation's model for evaluating life cycle cost was incomplete and unreasonable because it did not consider environmental costs, such as cooling, electricity, and space. The GAO denied the protest, stating that the agency properly decided not to consider environmental factors as part of life cycle costs because the agency's prior experience indicated that this was not a useful discriminator between technical solutions.

When the RFP states that life cycle costs are to be evaluated and requests data as to the costs that a proposed item will produce, the agency must use the data to assess the amount of life cycle costs to be attributed to each proposal, *Sikorsky Aircraft Co.*, Comp. Gen. Dec. B-299145, 2007 CPD ¶ 45. In that case, the GAO sustained a protest because the agency had obtained maintenance data for each proposed helicopter but had used a normalized number attributing the same maintenance costs to different helicopters. See also *Boeing Co.*, Comp. Gen. Dec. B-311344, 2008 CPD ¶ 114, sustaining a protest because the agency did not correctly use the data submitted by the protester to calculate the life cycle costs of proposed air tankers.

2. Non-Cost Offer Factors

Where the contractor is merely required to comply with specifications furnished by the government and the terms and conditions in the RFP, there will be no non-cost offer evaluation factors. However, in many procurements the government solicits or permits offerors to propose additions or alterations to the specifications or terms and conditions and treats these offers as evaluation factors. When such additions or alterations are used as evaluation factors, the agency is indicating to offerors that they are of value to the agency and that the agency will therefore consider paying a higher price to obtain that value. When this is done, the general practice is to subsequently rewrite the affected specifications or terms and conditions so that the awarded contract makes these offers contractually binding. However, agencies can treat these factors as capability factors and not incorporate them into the contract if they do not want to be contractually bound to them. See *DGR Assocs., Inc.*, Comp. Gen. Dec. B-285428, 2000 CPD ¶ 145, denying a protest asserting that the agency should not have assessed enhancements proposed by an offeror because they were not incorporated into the contract as promises.

The use of non-cost offer factors greatly complicates the task of offerors because they must attempt to anticipate the value that the agency will give to different amounts of enhanced performance or alteration of terms and conditions. To ease this problem, the best practice is for agencies to use such factors only when they can not specify their precise requirements in the RFP.

a. Enhancements

Probably the most common type of non-cost offer factor is enhancements to the work or results called for by the specifications. In such cases the specification generally will call for a minimum or target level of performance and the RFP will indicate that the agency will evaluate greater performance. The best practice is for the agency to clearly delineate the range of enhancements it is willing to consider so that offerors do not propose enhancements that are of no benefit to the agency. It is also good practice to obtain price proposals for different levels of enhancements to enable the agency to compare proposals at each level of performance. However, the use of general language stating that specified enhancements will be evaluated has been approved even when the offerors had to speculate as to the value of specific enhancements, *Telos Sys. Integration v. Administrative Office of the Courts*, GSBCA 13315-P, 96-1 BCA ¶ 27,990. See also *Lexis-Nexis*, Comp. Gen. Dec. B-260023, 95-1 CPD ¶ 14, where the GAO held that the RFP was sufficiently specific as to enhancements when it listed the areas where enhancements would be evaluated and gave some examples of features that were of value to the agency.

General statements in the RFP indicating that the agency was seeking superior performance have also been found to be sufficient to alert offerors that the agency was going to evaluate enhancements. See, for example, *Moreland Corp.*, Comp. Gen. Dec.

B-283685, 2002 CPD ¶ 4, rejecting a protest that the agency should not have evaluated certain enhancements in a competition for the design of a clinic, and stating:

> Where, as here, detailed technical proposals are sought and technical evaluation criteria are used to enable the agency to make comparative judgments about the relative merits of competing proposals, offerors are on notice that qualitative distinctions among the technical proposals will be made under the various evaluation factors. *Doss Aviation, Inc.; Dominion Aviation, Inc.*, B-275419 et al., Feb. 20, 1997, 97-1 CPD ¶ 117 at 8. Evaluation credit properly may be given, under these circumstances, where a proposal includes enhancements or features not specifically required by the solicitation. *Id.*

See also *IPlus, Inc.*, Comp. Gen. Dec. B-298020, 2006 CPD ¶ 90 (statement that award would be made to the "offeror whose proposal represented the best value" sufficient to alert offerors that agency would evaluate "innovations and creative approached"); *SGT, Inc.*, Comp. Gen. Dec. B-294722.4, 2005 CPD ¶ 151 (dedicated person to perform required job an enhancement when RFP evaluation factor was "comprehensiveness of the proposed approach, and likelihood of successfully meeting the solicitation requirements"); *Rome Research Corp.*, Comp. Gen. Dec. B-291162, 2002 CPD ¶ 209 (RFP sought "enhancements of value" in management proposals); *Engineering & Professional Servs., Inc.*, Comp. Gen. Dec. B-262179, 95-2 CPD ¶ 266 (RFP requirement that each offeror submit a matrix detailing where their systems met or exceeded the RFP requirements and desirable features alerted offeror that enhancements would be evaluated); and *Medical Dev. Int'l*, Comp. Gen. Dec. B-281484.2, 99-1 CPD ¶ 68 (RFP requirement for technical proposals indicated that enhancements would be evaluated).

If the RFP does not call for evaluation of enhanced performance, an agency is free to disregard proposed enhancements that it concludes do not benefit the agency, *U-Tech Servs. Corp.*, Comp. Gen. Dec. B-284183.3, 2002 CPD ¶ 78.

Enhancements have been used in procurements for a variety of products and services. See *Omega World Travel, Inc.*, Comp. Gen. Dec. B-276387.3, 98-2 CPD ¶ 73 (enhancements used in travel agency contract); *Technology Servs. Int'l, Inc.*, Comp. Gen. Dec. B-276506, 97-2 CPD ¶ 113 (enhancements used in grounds maintenance contract); *Canadian Commercial Corp./Polaris Inflatable Boats (Canada), Ltd.*, Comp. Gen. Dec. B-276945, 97-2 CPD ¶ 40 (enhancements used in inflatable boat contract); *Dube Travel Agency & Tours, Inc.*, Comp. Gen. Dec. B-270438.2, 96-1 CPD ¶ 141 (enhancements used in travel agency contract); *Holmes & Narver, Inc.*, Comp. Gen. Dec. B-266246, 96-1 CPD ¶ 55 (enhancements used in contract for design and construction of military housing); and *Cherry Hill Travel Agency, Inc.*, Comp. Gen. Dec. B-240386, 90-2 CPD ¶ 403 (agency may consider general and specific enhancements that are logically encompassed or related to stated evaluated criteria).

As discussed above, elements of the life-cycle cost of a product can also be evaluated as non-cost evaluation factors. See, for example, *Caterpillar, Inc.*, Comp. Gen. Dec. B-280362, 98-2 CPD ¶ 87, where the GAO found reasonable an agency's assessment that the awardee's vehicles had a higher capability to isolate and diagnose faults accurately, which, with the ease of access to problem areas as indicated by their lower maintainability index, had the potential to greatly reduce life-cycle costs.

b. *Technical Solutions*

It has been common practice to request technical proposals providing solutions to meet a government requirement. This originated in competitions for development contracts where an agency wanted to evaluate proposed designs of a new system to assess which was most likely to meet its needs. The technique has been carried over into service contracts where competing solutions to a need are sought. These solutions can be an offer factor if the technical proposal is incorporated into the contract as a promise to perform in accordance with the proposal. More often they are a capability factor where the contract does not make the solution mandatory but uses it to assess the capability of the offeror.

Making technical proposals contractually binding has the effect of making them the baseline against which to measure the contractor's performance. This will arguably benefit the government if the proposal contains performance requirements that are more demanding than the original government specification. In that case, the government will be able to hold the contractor bound to perform in accordance with its proposal (assuming that it contains promissory language), but it will have deprived the contractor of some of the flexibility that it would have had if it was performing to a government performance requirement. Alternatively, making the proposal contractually binding will harm the government if the proposal contains performance requirements that are less demanding than the original government specification. In that case, effort demanded by the government to meet its original performance requirements may well be construed as a contractual change for which the government will be required to give an equitable adjustment. See, for example, *Northrop Grumman Corp. v. United States*, 47 Fed. Cl. 20 (2000), holding that the contractor was not entitled to equitable adjustments for work not required by its technical proposal because the proposal was not incorporated into the contract.

Agencies vary widely in their practice of incorporating these technical proposals into their contracts and the practice usually cannot be discerned from protests involving this type of evaluation factor. However, there are many examples of protests involving competing technical solutions. See, for example, *Northrop Grumman Sys. Corp.*, Comp. Gen. Dec. B-298954, 2007 CPD ¶ 63 (evaluation of proposed radars in response to a government statement of objectives); *ViaSat, Inc.*, Comp. Gen. Dec.

B-291152, 2002 CPD ¶ 211 (evaluation of proposed communication satellite terminals to meet stated performance requirements); and *DRS Sys., Inc.*, Comp. Gen. Dec. B-289928.3, 2002 CPD ¶ 192 (evaluation of proposed thermal imaging systems against an agency purchase description).

c. Specific Products or Services

In some cases an agency will use a performance specification and evaluate specific products or services that will meet that specification. This technique is most practicable when there are a variety of products or services in the marketplace that will meet the agency's performance requirements and the agency will benefit by obtaining competitive prices for each product or service in order to identify the best value at the time of contract award. See, for example, *MD Helicopters, Inc.*, Comp. Gen. Dec. B-298502, 2006 CPD ¶ 164 (commercially available helicopters); and *Integrated Sys. Group*, Comp. Gen. Dec. B-272336, 96-2 CPD ¶ 144 (central processing units). This technique may not be practicable when the offered product or service has not been sold or provided, because in such cases the agency may have little ability to evaluate the feasibility of meeting a contract requirement to provide the offered product or service. The best practice is to perform a risk analysis in an attempt to ensure that the best value decision is based not only on the quality of the offered product or service, but also on the risk of being unable to perform as promised. See, for example, *Alliant Techsys., Inc.*, Comp. Gen. Dec. B-276162, 97-1 CPD ¶ 141, where the GAO denied a protest challenging the risk assessment of the technical feasibility of manufacturing the proposed product at the offered price. See also *Martin Marietta Corp.*, Comp. Gen. Dec. B-259823.4, 96-1 CPD ¶ 265, denying a protest that the agency had found that the protester's technical approach to meeting the specification was "unsatisfactory," and had awarded the contract to an offeror whose approach was rated "good."

d. Process or Techniques to Be Used

Another non-cost offer factor is the process or technique that the offeror intends to use to meet the government's performance requirements. This factor can be used in two ways. If it is used only to evaluate the offeror's understanding of the work or capability to perform the work, it is a capability factor. However, if the agency intends to incorporate the technique or process into the contract, making it contractually binding, it will be an offer factor. In most instances, where the agency determines that such a factor is necessary, the best practice is to treat this as a capability factor — giving the contractor the freedom to meet the performance requirements using some other technique or process; but there are some instances where an agency has determined that the specific technique or process has an identified value that will not be achieved by the use of any other technique or process. In such cases this should be treated as an offer factor.

When a proposed process or technique is used as an evaluation factor, it is good practice to evaluate the comparative risk of using different techniques. See, for example, *Robbins-Gioia, Inc.*, Comp. Gen. Dec. B-274318, 96-2 CPD ¶ 222, denying a protest that the agency had evaluated a proposal for the use of state-of-the-art software architecture as having moderate risk as compared to a proposal to use off-the-shelf software. In such cases the agency is conducting a form of design competition, requiring the evaluation of the potential effectiveness of the offered designs. See, for example, *AT&T Corp.*, Comp. Gen. Dec. B-261154.4, 96-1 CPD ¶ 232, where the GAO agreed that the agency's evaluation of competing designs was performed effectively.

e. Terms or Conditions

A fifth type of non-cost offer factor is the enhanced or specific term or condition. Enhanced terms and conditions should be treated in the same manner as other enhancements — the agency should state the minimum acceptable level and the range of enhanced performance that it considers to be of potential value. Specific terms and conditions that the agency requires to be filled out with explicit information should be clearly stated so that the offerors clearly understand the information that will be incorporated in the contract.

A common enhanced term or condition is a warranty clause where the agency solicits better warranty coverage than the minimum specified in the RFP. See *Integrated Sys. Group*, Comp. Gen. Dec. B-272336, 96-2 CPD ¶ 144, where offers were obtained for extended warranties of one and two years. A warranty evaluation factor can also be stated as an open-ended factor, allowing each offeror to propose the warranty offered. See *Eomax Corp.*, Comp. Gen. Dec. B-311391, 2008 CPD ¶ 130 (protester properly downgraded for proposing only a one year warranty on a high price product); *Scot, Inc.*, Comp. Gen. Dec. B-295569, 2005 CPD ¶ 66 (proposed extended warranty properly evaluated as providing only a small advantage when equipment was going to be stored for long periods); and *Landoll Corp.*, Comp. Gen. Dec. B-291381, 2003 CPD ¶ 40 (longer warranty properly evaluated as a strength).

Another common example of a specific term or condition is the Key Personnel clause that is used in many service procurements. As discussed below, key personnel is a frequently used as a capability factor, but when the names of the key personnel are incorporated into a Key Personnel clause, this factor becomes an offer factor because the contractor promises to use the specified personnel unless they become unavailable. Although the evaluation of key personnel can be a strong predictor of performance, it is completely valid only if the personnel proposed by the offer actually work on the contract. Yet, that is not the effect of a Key Personnel clause. Almost all the clauses in use call for the use of key personnel listed in the clause or equally qualified personnel approved by the contracting officer. This is, of course, a necessary part of the process because the contractor cannot guarantee that employees will stay with the company or be willing to work on the contract. The GAO has given contractors a substantial amount of freedom to operate under these clauses.

See, for example, *Laser Power Techs., Inc.*, Comp. Gen. Dec. B-233369, 89-1 CPD ¶ 267, where the protester argued that a competing offeror had to propose "permanent" employees to meet the key personnel requirements in the solicitation. The GAO denied the protest, stating:

> Laser Power essentially contends the RFP requires that proposed key personnel must be for permanent positions. However, the RFP, which contains the "key personnel" clause referenced above, does not require designated key personnel to be permanent, nor even that the contractor commence performance with the personnel listed in its proposal, so long as the contractor provides personnel as qualified as those listed in the proposal and obtains the Air Force's approval for all substituted key personnel. *A.B. Dick Co.*, B-233142, Jan. 31, 1989, 89-1 CPD ¶ [106]. Indeed, there is nothing unusual or inherently improper for an awardee to recruit and hire personnel employed by the incumbent contractor. *A.B. Dick Co.*, 233142, *supra*, at 5; *Applications Research Co.*, B-230097, May 25, 1988, 88-1 CPD ¶ 499.

On the other hand, the GAO will intervene if there is a substitution of lesser qualified personnel. See *KPMG Peat Marwick, LLP*, Comp. Gen. Dec. B-259479.2, 95-2 CPD ¶ 13, *recons. denied*, 95-2 CPD ¶ 26, where GAO stated the following rule:

> The agency asserts that under the RFP's "Key Personnel" clause, a standard provision which allows the contracting officer to authorize substitutions of personnel so long as the replacement personnel qualifications "are equal to or better [than] the qualifications of the personnel being replaced," it had unfettered authority to change [the contractor's] proposed personnel. Contrary to [the agency's] position, the RFP's key personnel clause cannot be used by the agency if the effect of the substitution is to significantly modify the contract awarded; such an interpretation would render meaningless the competition on the original solicitation requirements. *See Planning Research Corp. v. United States*, 971 F.2d 736 (Fed. Cir. 1992). Rather, the key personnel clause is simply intended to permit the natural turnover of personnel that tends to occur during the performance of a contract.

Thus, the GAO will find that the competition has not been fairly conducted if the Key Personnel clause is not enforced as written and will require that the procurement be recompeted. The same result was reached by the General Services Administration Board of Contract Appeals in *PSI Int'l, Inc. v. Dep't of Energy*, GSBCA 11521-P, 92-2 BCA ¶ 24,775, where it was held that it was improper to award a contract to an offeror that had not named its key personnel but had reserved the right to staff the contract with competent personnel.

f. Delivery or Completion Schedule

The agency may use the delivery or completion schedule as an offer factor. In such cases the RFP generally will state the time of performance that the agency must have and will permit offerors to propose shorter times of performance. This technique should never be used unless the agency has determined that it will benefit from faster performance, and the RFP should clearly state the amount of faster performance that will be of value. See *Rotair Indus., Inc.*, Comp. Gen. Dec. B-276435.2, 97-2 CPD ¶ 17, finding that the agency's selection of a higher-priced vendor with a shorter delivery schedule was reasonable because the agency determined that a longer delivery schedule would have a detrimental impact on the continuing back-order status of the critical application item being procured. Like other enhancements, it is also good practice to obtain price proposals on a stepladder basis so that offers can be rationally compared. When delivery is listed as an evaluation factor, offerors should understand that the agency will favorably evaluate faster delivery. See, for example, *Utility Tool & Trailer, Inc.*, Comp. Gen. Dec. B-310535, 2008 CPD ¶ 1 (proper to not pay significantly higher price for small delivery advantage); *Charles Kendall & Partners, Ltd.*, Comp. Gen. Dec. B-310093, 2007 CPD ¶ 210 (proper to pay significantly higher price for substantial delivery advantage); and *American Material Handling, Inc.*, Comp. Gen. Dec. B-297536, 2006 CPD ¶ 28 (proper to pay somewhat higher price for delivery advantage).

3. *Capability Factors*

"Capability factors" are those factors that are used to evaluate the relative ability of the competing offerors to perform the contract. These factors are never made part of the contract because they do not constitute contractual promises made by the offeror. However, as discussed above, they frequently include enhancements, technical solutions, or descriptions of a process or technique to be used that are included in technical or management proposals that are required to be submitted by each offeror. Whether such evaluation factors are offer factors or capability factors depends entirely on whether the agency intends to incorporate them into the contract as promises or merely use them to evaluate capability. When they are treated as capability factors, they will be discussed below as part of the "understanding the work" factor.

The evaluation of capability is essentially an assessment of the risk that an offeror will not successfully perform the proposed contract. Thus, performance risk is an inherent evaluation factor even though it is undisclosed in the RFP, *AHNTECH, Inc.*, Comp. Gen. Dec. B-299806, 2007 CPD ¶ 213; *AIA Todini-Lotos*, Comp. Gen. Dec. B-294337, 2004 CPD ¶ 211. Performance risk is most frequently assessed with regard to past performance. See *Lockheed Martin MS2 Tactical Sys.*, Comp. Gen. Dec. B-400135, 2008 CPD ¶ 157 (high performance risk proper based on poor past performance of major subcontractor); *Midwest Metals*, Comp. Gen. Dec. B-299805, 2007 CPD ¶ 131 (risk determined from past performance data system); *Boersma Travel Servs.*, Comp. Gen. Dec. B-297986.2, 2006 CPD ¶ 175 (moderate risk because agency could not understand information submitted by protester); and *TPL, Inc.*, Comp. Gen. Dec. B-297136.10, 2006 CPD ¶ 104 (moderately low risk because of "fair" past performance ratings on most comparable contracts). However, it can be used with regard to any evaluation factor. See, for example, *MCT JV*, Comp. Gen. Dec. B-311245.2, 2008 CPD ¶ 121, *recons. denied*, 2008 CPD ¶ 167 (significant risk from unrealistically capped overhead rates); *Fintrac, Inc.*, Comp. Gen. Dec. B-311462.2, 2008 CPD ¶ 191 (no perceived risk from lack of fixed fee in proposal); *Commercial Window Shield*, Comp. Gen. Dec. B-400154, 2008 CPD ¶ 134 (risk of vague staffing plan); *Global Solutions Network, Inc.*, Comp. Gen. Dec. B-298682.3, 2008 CPD ¶ 131 (risk of single person staffing two key positions); *Guam Shipyard*, Comp. Gen. Dec. B-311321, 2008 CPD ¶ 124 (high risk of unrealistically low price and mediocre past performance); *AT&T Corp.*, Comp. Gen. Dec. B-299542.3, 2008 CPD ¶ 65 (staffing plan created performance risk); *Raytheon Co.*, Comp. Gen. Dec. B-298626.2, 2007 CPD ¶ 185 (lack of data on product created high performance risk); and *Savantage Financial Servs., Inc.*, Comp. Gen. Dec. B-299798, 2007 CPD ¶ 214 (high performance risk based on evaluation of technical proposal submitted to demonstrate understanding of the work).

Air Force Mandatory Procedure 5315.305.5.2.2. describes this risk assessment as a "performance confidence assessment," which is applied to the evaluation of past performance using the evaluation technique described in the next section. This is an affirmative means of describing a risk assessment which has been accepted as rational, *CCITE/SC*, Comp. Gen. Dec. B-400782, 2008 CPD ¶ 216 (unknown confidence rating justified because of lack of relevant past performance); *United Paradyne Corp.*, Comp. Gen. Dec. B-297758, 2006 CPD ¶ 47 (technique acceptable but not used rationally). See also *Consolidated Eng'g Servs., Inc.*, Comp. Gen. Dec. B-311313, 2008 CPD ¶ 146, describing a Social Security Administration "confidence/performance risk" assessment covering both past performance and experience, and granting the protest because different assessments were given to the two final competitors even though they were both highly rated.

a. *Responsibility Determinations Distinguished*

Because these factors deal with the same matters that are considered in making responsibility determinations, it is important to distinguish between them. Agencies commonly evaluate factors and subfactors related to responsibility, notwithstanding the fact that a formal responsibility determination must ultimately be made before award of the contract. Such factors and subfactors frequently include experience, staffing, and past performance. This process does not officially constitute a responsibility determination as long as these factors are evaluated on a variable basis. Therefore, such evaluation does not conflict with the Small Business Administration's (SBA's) authority to resolve questions concerning the responsibility of small businesses. In *Electrospace Sys., Inc.*, 58 Comp. Gen. 415 (B-192574), 79-1 CPD ¶ 264, the GAO stated at 425:

> Since neither 10 U.S.C. § 2304(g) nor applicable regulations in any way restrict the "other factors" that may be used by agencies in selecting the proposal having the greatest value to the Government, we have not prohibited procuring agencies

from using responsibility-related factors in making relative assessments of the merits of competing proposals. There is no indication on the face of Public Law 95-89 or in the legislative history of the law that Congress intended to eliminate this long-standing practice as far as the evaluation of small business proposals are concerned. Thus, neither the cited precedent (40 Comp. Gen., *supra*) of advertised procurements nor the 1977 Public Law prevents the relative-assessment evaluation of responsibility-related information contained in small business proposals.

See also *Nomura Enters., Inc.*, Comp. Gen. Dec. B-277768, 97-2 CPD ¶ 148, where the protester, which was a small business concern, asserted that the evaluation of its past performance concerned a matter of its responsibility and was thus subject to SBA's Certificate of Competency (COC) procedures. The GAO disagreed, stating:

An agency may use traditional responsibility factors, such as experience or past performance, as technical evaluation factors, where, as here, a comparative evaluation of those areas is to be made. *Dynamic Aviation — Helicopters*, B-274122, Nov. 1, 1996, 96-2 ¶ 166 at 3. A comparative evaluation means that competing proposals will be rated on a scale relative to each other, as opposed to a pass/fail basis. *Id.* The record shows that the award here clearly was based on a comparative assessment of Nomura's and Defense's past performance records. Where a proposal is downgraded or found deficient pursuant to such an evaluation, the matter is one of relative technical merit, not nonresponsibility which would require a referral to the SBA.

In *T. Head & Co.*, Comp. Gen. Dec. B-275783, 97-1 CPD ¶ 169, the GAO held that an evaluation of capability factors that resulted in the conclusion that the offeror's proposal was "unacceptable" was not a determination of nonresponsibility because the evaluation had been arrived at in the course of a best value procurement where past performance was being evaluated on a variable basis and "unacceptable" was merely the lowest adjectival rating available. Compare *Phil Howry Co.*, Comp. Gen. Dec. B-291402.3, 2003 CPD ¶ 33, where the GAO ruled that refusing to award to the only company that had submitted a proposal because its past performance was rated "marginal/little confidence" was a nonresponsibility determination because there had been no comparative assessment (no other offeror to compare with). This appears to indicate that an agency will be required to allow a small business offeror to apply for a COC when it refuses to award to that offeror because of poor past performance when it is the only offer received.

It is improper to use responsibility-related factors or subfactors if the evaluation is merely to determine acceptability of a proposal, *Sanford & Sons Co.*, 67 Comp. Gen. 612 (B-231607), 88-2 CPD ¶ 266; *Angelo Warehouses Co.*, Comp. Gen. Dec. B-196780, 80-1 CPD ¶ 228. In *Sanford*, the agency determined that the offeror's past performance did not meet the minimum acceptable standard of performance. The GAO ruled that because this was tantamount to a determination that the protester was not responsible, Sanford, who was a small business, was entitled to request a Certificate of Competency from the Small Business Administration.

See also *Federal Support Corp.*, 71 Comp. Gen. 152 (B-245573), 92-1 CPD ¶ 81, and *Clegg Indus., Inc.*, 70 Comp. Gen. 679 (B-242204.3), 91-2 CPD ¶ 145, finding that an agency had improperly used responsibility factors to determine technical acceptability and pointed out that responsibility factors should be used only to make a comparative evaluation of the proposals. These cases could be read to preclude the use of responsibility factors or subfactors in any procurement where the award was to be made to the offeror that submitted the lowest-priced, technically acceptable proposal because any negative evaluation of responsibility could be used only to disqualify the offeror. However, there are other decisions of the GAO permitting rejection of proposals submitted by large businesses as being technically unacceptable based on responsibility-type factors related to the experience of the offeror, *Oak Ridge Associated Univ.*, Comp. Gen. Dec. B-245694, 92-1 CPD ¶ 86 (lack of experience required by RFP); *Aerostat Servs. Partnership*, Comp. Gen. Dec. B-244939.2, 92-1 CPD ¶ 71 (failure to propose staffing adequate to meet specifications); *Color Ad Signs & Displays*, Comp. Gen. Dec. B-241544, 91-1 CPD ¶ 154 (lack of required experience); *Sach Sinha & Assocs., Inc.*, 69 Comp. Gen. 108 (B-236911), 90-1 CPD ¶ 50 (personnel did not meet education and experience requirement of RFP). These decisions indicate that responsibility-type factors may be used to determine lack of acceptability of proposals from large businesses but not from small ones.

b. Past Performance

The Federal Acquisition Streamlining Act of 1994 (FASA) amended 10 U.S.C. § 2305(a) to require the use of past performance as an evaluation factor in source selection. This requirement is implemented in FAR 15.304(c), which provides:

> (3)(i) Except as set forth in paragraph (c)(3)(iii) of this section, past performance shall be evaluated in all source selections for negotiated competitive acquisitions expected to exceed the simplified acquisition threshold.
>
> > (ii) For solicitations involving bundling that offer a significant opportunity for subcontracting, the contracting officer must include a factor to evaluate past performance indicating the extent to which the offeror attained applicable goals for small business participation under contracts that required subcontracting plans (15 U.S.C. 637(d)(4)(G)(ii)).
>
> > (iii) Past performance need not be evaluated if the contracting officer documents the reason past performance is not an appropriate evaluation factor for the acquisition.

See also the OFPP publication, *Best Practices for Collecting and Using Current and Past Performance Information*, May 2000 (www.acqnet.gov/comp/seven_steps/library/OFPPbp-collecting.pdf), and the DOD publication, *A Guide to Collection and Use of Past Performance Information*, May 2003 (www.acq.osd.mil/dpap/Docs/PPI_Guide_2003_final.pdf)..

The evaluation of past performance reduces the emphasis on merely writing good proposals in favor of focusing on actual performance on prior contracts. Past performance can be evaluated as a separate evaluation factor or as a subfactor. Even before the FAR requirement, there was no question that this was a proper factor in the evaluation process, *Ferranti Int'l Defense Sys., Inc.*, Comp. Gen. Dec. B-237555, 90-1 CPD ¶ 239, even though it may give the incumbent contractor with a good performance record an advantage in the competition, *Bendix Field Eng'g Corp.*, Comp. Gen. Dec. B-241156, 91-1 CPD ¶ 44; *Eng'g & Computation, Inc.*, Comp. Gen. Dec. B-275180.2, 97-1 CPD ¶ 47.

While past performance can be used as either a factor or a subfactor, it is good practice to avoid using it as both simultaneously. For example, in *Center for Educ. & Manpower Resources*, Comp. Gen. Dec. B-191453, 78-2 CPD ¶ 21, it was held impermissible to evaluate past performance as a factor and also use past performance in the evaluation of technical and management factors. The GAO reasoned that this gave more weight to past performance than was indicated in the RFP. A similar result was reached in *Metric Sys. Corp.*, Comp. Gen. Dec. B-210218.2, 83-2 CPD ¶ 394. Compare *Global Assoc., Ltd.*, Comp. Gen. Dec. B-275534, 97-1 CPD ¶ 129, where the GAO rejected a protest that undue weight had been given to past performance. See also *Halter Marine, Inc.*, B-255429, 94-1 CPD ¶ 161, where the GAO found the evaluation to be unreasonable because the agency gave overwhelming emphasis to past performance by repeated consideration of that factor in both the technical merit and quality control capability factors. In *United Ammunition Container, Inc.*, Comp. Gen. Dec. B-275213, 97-1 CPD ¶ 58, the solicitation identified technical approach, management, and past performance as separate and independent evaluation factors. The protester asserted that the agency's evaluation of the awardee's proposal was flawed because the agency only considered the awardee's past performance record under the past performance factor but should have considered the awardee's past performance record under the other evaluation factors as well. The GAO denied the protest stating that this would have resulted in an exaggeration of the importance of the past performance factor.

The FAR guidance on past performance contains several references to the importance of the relevance of past performance, including the following statements in FAR 15.305(a)(2):

(i) . . . The currency and relevance of the information, source of the information, context of the data, and general trends in contractor's performance shall be considered

(ii) . . . The source selection authority shall determine the relevance of similar past performance information.

The GAO has interpreted these provisions are imposing a mandatory requirement on agencies to assess the relevance of past performance, *DRS C3 Sys., LLC*, Comp. Gen. Dec. B-310825, 2008 CPD ¶ 103; *Clean Harbors Envtl. Servs., Inc.*, Comp. Gen. Dec. B-296176.2, 2005 CPD ¶ 222.

While the regulation contains no explanation of the term "relevance of past performance information," it would appear to mean that an agency should give more weight to past performance on work that is like the work being procured (and conversely little or no weight to past performance of work that is dissimilar to the work being procured). Thus, the RFP should be clear that the offerors should refer their most relevant projects for consideration of past performance. This is particularly important because there are numerous instances where the GAO has ruled that agencies properly downgraded an offeror because of lack of relevant past performance even though it had very good past performance on dissimilar projects. In effect, such reasoning allows an agency to consider lack of comparable experience in the evaluation of past performance. For example, NASA uses an evaluation scheme that rates offerors' past performance in accordance with the relevance of their experience. Thus, to receive an "excellent" past performance rating, an offeror must have experience that is "highly relevant." GAO has accepted this scheme without comment in many protests including *ASRC Research & Tech. Solutions, LLC*, Comp. Gen. Dec. B-400217, 2008 CPD ¶ 202 (protest granted because scheme not followed); *Wackenhut Servs., Inc.*, Comp. Gen. Dec. B-400240, 2008 CPD ¶ 184 (protest denied because scheme followed). See also *AT&T Corp.*, Comp. Gen. Dec. B-299542.3, 2008 CPD ¶ 65 (to obtain "excellent" past performance rating, offeror had to have "highly relevant" experience); *Sherrick Aerospace*, Comp. Gen. Dec. B-310359.2, 2008 CPD ¶ 17 (agency determination that winning offeror had relevant experience justified low risk past performance evaluation); *JWK Int'l Corp.*, Comp. Gen. Dec. B-297758.3, 2006 CPD ¶ 142 (agency rating of little confidence justified when offeror had very good past performance on contract that was "somewhat relevant").

Agencies must use care in stating in the RFP what projects are relevant to the current project because the GAO has granted protests when an agency did not follow its own relevance guidelines. See, for example, *Clean Harbors Envtl. Servs., Inc.*, Comp. Gen. Dec. B-296176.2, 2005 CPD ¶ 222 (improper to fail to consider the lack of relevance of services that were smaller and less complex when RFP called for consideration of relevance); *Martin Elecs., Inc*, Comp. Gen. Dec. B-290846.3, 2003 CPD ¶ 6 (improper to fail to consider late deliveries on incomplete contract when RFP called for consideration of performance "occurring within the past three years to the date of the solicitation closing"). Compare *All Phase Envtl., Inc.*, Comp. Gen. Dec. B-292919.2, 2004 CPD ¶ 62, agreeing that pest control work was relevant to ground maintenance when the RFP called for relevant performance on "contracts of a similar size, scope, dynamic environment, and complexity." The GAO has also agreed that an agency is not bound by an experience relevance standard if the past performance relevance standard is stated in very general terms, *KIC Dev., LLC*, Comp. Gen. Dec. B-309869, 2007 CPD ¶ 184. In an unusual case, both the GAO and the Court of Federal Claims agreed that an agency properly considered large contracts not relevant to a procurement where most of the work would be on projects in the range of $15,000 to $1.7 million, *J.C.N. Constr. Co. v. United States*, 60 Fed. Cl. 400 (2004); *J.C.N. Constr. Co.*, Comp. Gen. Dec. B-293063, 2004 CPD ¶ 12.

In using past performance as an evaluation factor, the agency should state the scope of the factor in the RFP. See FAR 15.305(a)(2), which states:

(iii) The evaluation should take into account past performance information regarding predecessor companies, key personnel who have relevant experience, or subcontractors that will perform major or critical aspects of the requirement when such information is relevant to the instant acquisition.

When an agency sees that two companies have the same key person, the operations manager, it can reasonably attribute the past performance of one company to the other, *Daylight Tree Serv. & Equip., LLC*, Comp. Gen. Dec. B-310808, 2008 CPD ¶ 22. However, in spite of the seemingly mandatory requirement to evaluate key personnel, the GAO has ruled that it is proper to exclude key personnel from the evaluation of past performance, *JWK Int'l Corp.*, Comp. Gen. Dec. B-297758.3, 2006 CPD ¶ 142 (accepting explanation that information on skills of key personnel does not assist in evaluation of past performance of offeror). In addition, an agency may reasonably determine that prior experience of key personnel does not overcome lack of corporate experience, *Blue Rock Structures, Inc.*, Comp. Gen. Dec. B-287960, 2001 CPD ¶ 184.

With regard to subcontractors to be used by the offeror, the GAO has held that agencies can evaluate their past performance even though the RFP does not explicitly call for such evaluation, *AC Techs., Inc.*, Comp. Gen. Dec. B-293013, 2008 CPD ¶ 26; *Singleton Enters.*, Comp. Gen. Dec. B-298576, 2006 CPD ¶ 157; *Science & Tech., Inc.*, Comp. Gen. Dec. B-272748, 97-1 CPD ¶ 121. Thus, subcontractor performance is a frequent element of the past performance evaluation. See *Lockheed Martin MS2 Tactical Sys.*, Comp. Gen. Dec. B-400135, 2008 CPD ¶ 157 (high risk rating justified when 50% subcontractor had poor past performance); *STG, Inc.*, Comp. Gen. Dec. B-298543, 2006 CPD ¶ 166 (proper to limit subcontractor evaluations to work with government agencies); *Arora Group, Inc.*, Comp. Gen. Dec. B-297838.3, 2006 CPD ¶ 143 (proper to reduce performance rating because of mediocre subcontractor past performance); *Neal R. Gross & Co.*, Comp. Gen. Dec. B-275066, 97-1 CPD ¶ 30 (noting that the contractor always bears responsibility for the work of subcontractors); and *GZA Remediation, Inc.*, Comp. Gen. Dec. B-272386, 96-2 CPD ¶ 155 (good past performance rating properly based on a proposed subcontractor's prior contracts). Compare *USATREX Int'l, Inc.*, Comp. Gen. Dec. B-275592, 98-1 CPD ¶ 99, limiting past performance/experience to the offeror only. Agencies can properly assign a median rating when a proposed subcontractor has excellent past performance/experience but the offeror has no relevant past performance/experience, *Iplus, Inc.*, Comp. Gen. Dec. B-298020, 2006 CPD ¶ 90.

The current guidance on past performance is somewhat more detailed than that given in prior regulations. Under those regulations the GAO held that it was unreasonable to fail to obtain past performance information on the prior contract with the agency for the same services, *International Business Sys., Inc.*, Comp. Gen. Dec.

B-275554, 97-1 CPD ¶ 114, and that evaluators may use their personal knowledge in evaluating an offeror's past performance, *Omega World Travel, Inc.*, Comp. Gen. Dec. B-271126.2, 96-2 CPD ¶ 44. Agencies are generally given broad discretion on the information that is obtained. Random sampling has been permitted, *MilTech, Inc.*, Comp. Gen. Dec. B-275078, 97-1 CPD ¶ 208, and an agency has been permitted to contact a different number of sources for different offerors, *IGIT, Inc.*, Comp. Gen. Dec. B-275299.2, 97-2 CPD ¶ 7, or only a single reference, *Neal R. Gross & Co.*, Comp. Gen. Dec. B-275066, 97-1 CPD ¶ 30; *HLC Indus., Inc.*, Comp. Gen. Dec. B-274374, 96-2 CPD ¶ 214. Agencies also have considerable discretion in selecting the prior work that is relevant to the work being procured, *Roy F. Weston, Inc.*, Comp. Gen. Dec. B-274945, 97-1 CPD ¶ 92; and the GAO has denied protests when the agency determined that dissimilar work was relevant, *All Star Maint., Inc.*, Comp. Gen. Dec. B-271119, 96-1 CPD ¶ 278; *Hughes Missile Sys. Co.*, Comp. Gen. Dec. B-272418, 96-2 CPD ¶ 221. Compare *Ogden Support Servs., Inc.*, Comp. Gen. Dec. B-270012.2, 96-1 CPD ¶ 137, where the GAO granted a protest where the agency had considered dissimilar work relevant but the RFP had used an evaluation factor of "demonstrated successful performance on similar efforts." See also *PMT Servs., Inc.*, Comp. Gen. Dec. B-270538.2, 96-2 CPD ¶ 98, where the GAO granted a protest because an agency had rated an offeror's past performance as poor because it had no prior contracts of the same size as the current procurement, finding that complexity of the work on prior contracts was more important than dollar value of the contracts. Some agencies have used questionnaires to obtain past performance information, and this practice has been approved by the GAO, *Continental Serv. Co.*, Comp. Gen. Dec. B-274531, 97-1 CPD ¶ 9; *SWR, Inc.*, Comp. Gen. Dec. B-276878, 97-2 CPD ¶ 34. However, the GAO has ruled that it is improper to use surveys obtained from evaluations on prior procurements unless those surveys are based on comparable data and rating schemes, *Cooperativa Muratori Riunite*, Comp. Gen. Dec. B-294980, 2005 CPD ¶ 21.

The FAR requires that offerors be permitted to submit information on corrective action that has been taken to overcome past performance problems, but agencies have been given broad discretion in refusing to adjust past performance ratings to reflect such corrective action, *Laidlaw Envtl. Servs. (GS), Inc.*, Comp. Gen. Dec. B-271903, 96-2 CPD ¶ 75; *Macon Apparel Corp.*, Comp. Gen. Dec. B-272162, 96-2 CPD ¶ 95. In *Hughes Missile Sys., Co.*, Comp. Gen. Dec. B-272418, 96-2 CPD ¶ 221, the GAO denied a protest where the agency had adjusted a rating of one competitor based on corrective action but had refused to adjust the rating of another competitor that had overcome some of the problems encountered on a development contract by taking action on a follow-on production contract.

c. Experience

In most procurements the capability of an offeror cannot be determined accurately without considering the type and extent of its experience. FAR 15.304(c)

(2) suggests that agencies evaluate "prior experience." It appears to be a common belief that an evaluation of relevant past performance entails an evaluation of experience, but this is only an indirect way of assessing experience. In fact, while past performance and experience are both components of a contractor's capability that involve inquires into the past, their evaluation requires asking entirely different questions. To determine a contractor's experience the questions are: What have you done? and How many times or for how long have you done it? The question for past performance is: How well have you done it? To further complicate this issue, the protest decisions contain conflicting statements on the relationship of experience and past performance. See, for example, *Telcom Sys. Servs., Inc. v. Dep't of Justice*, GSBCA 13272-P, 95-2 BCA ¶ 27,849, where the board stated that experience must be considered when evaluating past performance. In that case the board stated: "It is unreasonable to suggest that past performance does not encompass experience." In contrast, in *Hughes Georgia, Inc.*, Comp. Gen. Dec. B-272526, 96-2 CPD ¶ 151, the GAO indicated that experience was not included in the evaluation of past performance. Other cases appear to indicate that there is a good deal of confusion on this issue. For example, many GAO decisions have allowed an agency to evaluate experience in the course of evaluating "relevant" past performance, *TPL, Inc.*, Comp. Gen. Dec. B-297136.10, 2006 CPD ¶ 104, while in *Ameriko, Inc.*, Comp. Gen. Dec. B-272989, 96-2 CPD ¶ 167, the GAO did not object to the consideration of past performance when the evaluation factor in the RFP was "experience." It has also been acceptable to treat corporate experience as a subfactor to past performance and "client satisfaction," *McGoldrick Constr. Servs. Corp.*, Comp. Gen. Dec. B-310340.3, 2008 CPD ¶ 120. In *Alpha Genesis, Inc.*, Comp. Gen. Dec. B-299859, 2007 CPD ¶ 167, the GAO provided the following summary of acceptable ways to assess experience:

> [A] solicitation may require the agency to evaluate "the extent, depth, and quality" of corporate experience. *JWK Int'l*, B-256609.4, Sept. 1, 1994, 95-1 CPD ¶ 166 at 9. Corporate experience may be combined with other factors such as "quality of work," *NWT, Inc.; PharmChem Labs., Inc.*, B-280988, B-280988.2, Dec. 17, 1998, 98-2 CPD ¶ 158 at 2, or past performance. *D.O.N. Protective Servs., Inc.*, B-249066, Oct. 23, 1992, 92-2 CPD ¶ 277 at 6-7. Agencies may make corporate experience an evaluation factor, with past performance as a subfactor. *Defense Tech., Inc.*, B-271682, July 17, 1996, 96-2 CPD ¶ 54 at 2.

See, however, *United Paradyne Corp.*, Comp. Gen. Dec. 297758, 2006 CPD ¶ 47, where the GAO disapproved factoring an average of an offeror's experience into its past performance rating (in effect reducing the past performance rating for experience on work that was not similar to the work to be performed on the proposed contract). The decision describes the improper technique as follows:

> After rating the relevance of each contract identified by the offeror in its proposal, the Air Force averaged these ratings to arrive at an overall "relevance" rating. It then integrated this rating with an overall past performance rating, also obtained by averaging the point scores on the performance questionnaires fur-

nished by the offeror's references. This process yielded an overall performance confidence rating. Thus, for example, an average relevance rating of "highly relevant" combined with an average past performance rating of "exceptional/high confidence" yielded an overall performance confidence rating of "exceptional/high confidence"; an average relevance rating of "relevant" combined with an average past performance rating of "exceptional/high confidence" yielded an overall performance confidence rating of "very good/significant confidence"; an average relevance rating of "somewhat relevant" combined with an average past performance rating of "exceptional/high confidence" yielded an overall performance confidence rating of "satisfactory/confidence"; and an average relevance rating of "not relevant" combined with an average past performance rating of "exceptional/high confidence" yielded an overall performance confidence rating of "neutral/unknown confidence."

Thus, it is highly desirable to evaluate past performance and experience separately. See *Executive Court Reporters, Inc.*, Comp. Gen. Dec. B-272981, 96-2 CPD ¶ 227, where the GAO stated that past performance and experience should be separate factors and evaluated separately. See also *Smart Innovative Solutions*, Comp. Gen. Dec. B-400323.3, 2008 CPD ¶ 220 (lack of "relevant experience" properly considered); *Engineering Constr. Servs., Inc.*, Comp. Gen. Dec. B-310311.2, 2008 CPD ¶ 6 ("relevant experience" properly evaluated as separate subfactor); *JAVIS Automation & Eng'g, Inc.*, Comp. Gen. Dec. B-290434, 2002 CPD ¶ 140 (past performance and experience evaluated together); *PW Constr., Inc.*, Comp. Gen. Dec. B-272248, 96-2 CPD ¶ 130 (evaluation of both experience and past performance properly performed).

The RFP should state whether the agency intends to evaluate corporate experience, experience of key personnel, or both. There is a great deal of discretion in making this determination and the GAO has held that the experience of key personnel can be evaluated under a "corporate experience" factor unless the RFP precludes such evaluation, *Data Mgmt. Servs. Joint Venture*, Comp. Gen. Dec. B-299702, 2007 CPD ¶ 139; *Dix Corp.*, Comp. Gen. Dec. B-293964, 2004 CPD ¶ 143. Nonetheless, it is better practice to state in the RFP precisely what experience is to be evaluated. See *Johnson Controls Sec. Sys., LLC*, Comp. Gen. Dec. B-296490.3, 2007 CPD ¶ 100 (corporate experience and experience of proposed staff); *Leader Communications Inc.*, Comp. Gen. Dec. B-298734, 2006 CPD ¶ 192 (experience of key personnel and corporate experience); *KIC Dev., LLC*, Comp. Gen. Dec. B-297425.2, 2006 CPD ¶ 27 (RFP stated that experience requirement could be met by experience of key personnel or subcontractors); *Sigmatech, Inc.*, Comp. Gen. Dec. B-271821, 96-2 CPD ¶ 101 (corporate experience plus "sufficient personnel with ample qualifications"). It has also been held to be proper to evaluate corporate experience and key personnel experience separately, giving a low rating on corporate experience even though the key personnel have good experience, *Population Health Servs., Inc.*, Comp. Gen. Dec. B-292858, 2003 CPD ¶ 217. In *Ashe Facility Servs., Inc.*, Comp. Gen. Dec. B-292218.3, 2004 CPD ¶ 80 the GAO granted a protest because the agency had considered the key personnel experience of the winning offeror but not of the protester, concluding that such information should have been considered because the RFP stated that the agency would consider "any information supplied by the offeror."

Once it has been determined that experience is to be evaluated, the types of experience relevant to the procurement must be determined. Often, RFPs merely indicate that experience on "similar" projects will be considered. There are many factors to be considered in determining similarity, including dollar value, complexity, and nature of the work. Some RFPs go into great detail specifying the types of experience considered important and, in some cases, their relative importance, *Vox Optima, LLC*, Comp. Gen. Dec. B-400451, 2008 CPD ¶ 212 ("40,000 annual billable hours in public affairs work"); *Burns and Roe Servs. Corp.*, Comp. Gen. Dec. B-296355, 2005 CPD ¶ 150 ("similar in complexity (i.e., type of work, size (contracts in excess of $5,000,000 per year) and volume"); *Planning Sys., Inc.*, Comp. Gen. Dec. B-292312, 2004 CPD ¶ 83 ("similar or directly related work experience within the past five years of similar scope, magnitude or complexity to that detailed in the SOW"); *Telestar Corp.*, Comp. Gen. Dec. B-275855, 97-1 CPD ¶ 150 (projects "of similar size and scope related to this effort"); *Sigmatech, Inc.*, Comp. Gen. Dec. B-271821, 96-2 CPD ¶ 101 (corporate experience plus "sufficient personnel with ample qualifications"), and agencies have been permitted to specify very limited types of relevant experience, *SKE Int'l, Inc.*, Comp. Gen. Dec. B-311383, 2008 CPD ¶ 111 (construction of multiple vertical construction multi-discipline projects simultaneously); *Zolon Tech, Inc.*, Comp. Gen. Dec. B-299904.2, 2007 CPD ¶ 183 (experience in specific technology to be used in design of information system – consultant's experience properly downgraded because he was not a subcontractor); *MELE Assocs., Inc.*, Comp. Gen. Dec. B-299229.4, 2007 CPD ¶ 140 (experience in four tasks to be performed); *Systems Application & Techs., Inc.*, Comp. Gen. Dec. B-270672, 96-1 CPD ¶ 182 (experience with contracting agency); *CAN Indus. Eng'g, Inc.*, Comp. Gen. Dec. B-271034, 96-1 CPD ¶ 279 (experience with the agency's system that was to be tested under the contract).

Even where solicitations use terms such as "similar" or "relevant" in describing the nature of the experience, the cases have been quite liberal in permitting the government to use specific discriminators that are not stated in the solicitation. See *EastCo Bldg.Servs., Inc.*, Comp. Gen. Dec. B-275334.2, 97-1 CPD ¶ 83, holding that the totality of the RFP will be considered in determining whether offerors were given appropriate notice of the factors to be considered, and stating

> EastCo argues that the agency improperly applied – and downgraded its proposal under the past performance/experience on similar projects factor based on – two undisclosed criteria: whether previously performed contracts were of at least a 3-year duration, and whether the areas of the buildings maintained under prior contracts had been at least 500,000 square feet.

> This argument is without merit. The RFP required offerors to list prior contracts, which would be evaluated for past performance/experience, and to indicate for

each contract (among other things) the type of facility, gross square footage, services performed, and duration. EastCo and the other offerors were on notice from these requirements that, in judging whether a prior contract would be deemed a "similar project," the agency would consider the similarity of the contracts to the RFP requirement in these areas, and reading these requirements together with the rest of the RFP should have put EastCo on notice of the agency's intent to consider these specific elements of its listed contracts. *See ORI Servs. Corp.*, B-261225, July 28, 1995, 95-2 CPD ¶ 55.

See also *Aviate L.L.C.*, Comp. Gen. Dec. B-275058.6, 97-1 CPD ¶ 162 (a factor used was the awardee's experience on "performance based contracting" although the RFP did not specifically call for that type of experience). Compare *Omniplex World Servs. Corp.*, Comp. Gen. Dec. B-290996.2, 2003 CPD ¶ 7, where the GAO held that it was improper to eliminate an offeror from the competition for not having experience running a detention facility when the RFP called for the evaluation of "'guard/custody officer' experience similar in size, scope and complexity to the RFP work requirements."

Experience of major subcontractors is usually considered relevant to an evaluation of an offeror's experience, *Kellogg Brown & Root Servs., Inc.*, Comp. Gen. Dec. B-298694.7, 2007 CPD ¶ 124, and, if the RFP includes a statement to this effect, the experience of proposed subcontractors must be included in the evaluation, *KC Dev., LLC*, Comp. Gen. Dec. B-297425.2, 2006 CPD ¶ 27.

In many procurements the agency can make a valid assessment of the capability of the offerors by using only the past performance and experience evaluation factors. When doing so, the agency should avoid the use of other capability factors that make the procurement more complex and costly. However, this decision will depend on the specific procurement. For example, in some manufacturing contracts, the agency may believe that it is essential to evaluate the facilities of each offeror. Some agencies believe it is crucial in service contracts to evaluate key personnel. Most agencies believe it is advantageous in research and development contracts to evaluate understanding of the work. It is important to select an array of factors that provide a balanced assessment of the capability of each offeror to perform the work called for by the contract but to limit the number of capability factors as much as practicable.

d. Key Personnel

One of the most commonly used evaluation factors in best value procurements is the key personnel that the offeror intends to use to perform the contract. It is an especially useful means of assessing the capability of offerors in research and development and service contracts, where the quality of the people will likely be a major determinant of the quality of the performance. However, this is so only if the contractor that wins the competition actually uses the key personnel that have been proposed. Many agencies attempt to make key personnel an offer factor by using key personnel clauses in solicitations requiring the offeror to use the personnel designated in the proposal (or equal personnel). This raises a question about the effectiveness of these clauses. See the discussion in Chapter 3.

Key personnel can be a useful evaluation factor if an agency obtains sufficient information to make a meaningful assessment of the qualifications of the people that are proposed. This generally requires obtaining more than merely resumes. See, for example, *Savannah River Alliance, LLC*, Comp. Gen. Dec. B-311126, 2008 CPD ¶ 88 (RFP required resumes, references, letters of commitment and participation in oral presentation); *Systems Res. & Applications Corp.*, Comp. Gen. Dec. B-299818, 2008 CPD ¶ 28 (RFP required evidence that personnel had experience with type of work being procured); and *Maden Techs.*, Comp. Gen. Dec. B-298543.2, 2006 CPD ¶ 167 (RFP required degree requirements and related experience for stated number of years). Nonetheless, agencies have been permitted to depend entirely on resumes. See *D&J Enters., Inc.*, Comp. Gen. Dec. B-310442, 2008 CPD ¶ 8 (protester properly excluded from competition range when it submitted experience of key personnel in lieu of required resumes); *Operational Res. Consultants, Inc.*, Comp. Gen. Dec. B-299131.1, 2007 CPD ¶ 38 (protester properly downgraded because resume of proposed project manager did not clearly show required type of experience); *Critical Incident Solutions, LLC*, Comp. Gen. Dec. B-298077, 2006 CPD ¶ 88 (quotation unacceptable because resume did not show required experience and agency not required to review other material which allegedly showed experience); *Tessada & Assocs., Inc.*, Comp. Gen. Dec. B-293942, 2004 CPD ¶ 170 (proposal properly downgraded because resume did not clearly show that person met experience requirement); and *Aerotek Scientific LLC*, Comp. Gen. Dec. B-293089, 2004 CPD ¶ 21 (resume improperly evaluated with regard to experience requirement). This reliance on resumes may be appropriate if the RFP calls for sufficient information in the resumes. See, for example, *Advanced Tech. Sys., Inc.*, Comp. Gen. Dec. B-296493.5, 2006 CPD ¶ 147 (resumes had to contain also been proposed for another contract being competed at the same time.

When this factor is used, the agency should decide which personnel are sufficiently important to the success of contract performance to be designated as key personnel. As a general rule, this should be a limited number of contractor employees. See, for example, *Dynamic Resources, Inc.*, Comp. Gen. Dec. B-277213, 97-2 CPD ¶ 100 (program manager, technical manager, senior reliability engineer, computer programmers, aircraft maintenance analysts, programmer/analyst, and software engineer are key personnel).

e. Facilities

Another evaluation factor that may be used in best value procurements is the evaluation of an offeror's facilities. See *The American Indian Center, Inc.*, Comp.

Gen. Dec. B-278678, 98-1 CPD ¶ 66 (proposal reasonably downgraded because location of clinic was not accessible by public transportation); *Voith Hydro, Inc.*, Comp. Gen. Dec. B-277051, 97-2 CPD ¶ 68 (proposal properly excluded from competitive range because unproven manufacturing facility posed unacceptable risk); *Conrex, Inc.*, Comp. Gen. Dec. B-266060.2, 96-1 CPD ¶ 46 (proposal reasonably downgraded because offeror failed to describe its facility adequately); and *Bannum, Inc.*, Comp. Gen. Dec. B-270640, 96-1 CPD ¶ 167 (agency reasonably excluded protester from competitive range because the facility that the protester proposed would require major renovations that could not be completed within the 60-day commencement time frame). An offeror's facility may also be evaluated as a subfactor. See *Schleicher Community Corrections, Inc.*, Comp. Gen. Dec. B-270499.3, 97-1 CPD ¶ 33.

f. Financial Capability

Earlier, there was considerable controversy over whether the financial ability of offerors should be used as an evaluation factor or subfactor. In *Delta Data Sys. Corp. v. Webster*, 744 F.2d 197 (D.C. Cir. 1984), the court followed the general rule that factors related to responsibility could be used for comparative purposes and applied this rule to permit the comparative evaluation of the financial condition of the offerors in a long-term contract. In arriving at this result, the court reversed a contrary conclusion of the GAO on the same case, *Delta Data Sys. Corp.*, Comp. Gen. Dec. B-213396, 84-1 CPD ¶ 430. The GAO continued to adhere to the premise that financial condition should be used as an evaluation factor only when there is some special justification for doing so. See *Flight Int'l Group, Inc.*, 69 Comp. Gen. 741 (B-238953.4), 90-2 CPD ¶ 257, where the GAO ruled that downgrading an offeror's management capabilities on the basis of financial weakness was actually a finding of nonresponsibility. However, there are cases where the GAO has permitted the use of financial condition as a specific evaluation factor, *Greyback Concession*, Comp. Gen. Dec. B-239913, 90-2 CPD ¶ 278 (no discussion of special justification used to justify evaluation of financial condition); *E.H. White & Co.*, Comp. Gen. Dec. B-227122.3, 88-2 CPD ¶ 41 (competition between small businesses). In the normal procurement situation there is little justification for making a comparative evaluation of financial condition, and generally this should be left to the responsibility determination.

g. Understanding the Work/Soundness of Approach

A common practice of agencies is to require the submission of technical and management proposals to assess each offeror's understanding of the work or the soundness of the approach of the offerors. As discussed above, such proposals can also be used to solicit non-cost elements of the offer such as enhancements, technical solutions, or processes or techniques to be used to perform the work. Some agencies make it mandatory to include such an evaluation factor. Thus, Air Force

Mandatory Procedure 5315.304.4.4.1.1 requires the factor "Mission Capability" on all procurements of $1 million or more (to assess "the offeror's capability to satisfy the government's requirements"), and NASA Source Selection Guide 1815.304-70 requires the factor "Mission Suitability" on all procurements of $50 million or more (optional on smaller procurements).

This factor assumes that an offeror's capability can be evaluated by requiring it to submit a preliminary design or a technical/management plan that describes, at some specified level of detail, how the contract will be performed. To the extent that these written submissions are created by the personnel that will ultimately perform the contract, this may be a valid assumption. Thus, in research and development procurements, as well as in design build competitions, where preliminary designs prepared by the offerors' own personnel are commonly used as a means of evaluating the capabilities of the competitors, the requirement for such designs is frequently believed to be a valid means of assessing the capability of the offerors. However, while such designs provide an agency with a considerable amount of information concerning the preliminary view of the offeror as to how the needs of the government can be best satisfied, they add a great amount of cost and time to the source selection process. In particular, the costs of the offerors are greatly increased because they are forced to create the preliminary design in order to participate in the competition, and the time required for the competition is greatly increased because the competitors must be given time to create the designs and the agency must allocate a significant period to evaluate the designs. Nonetheless, such design competitions have been accepted as a valid way of ascertaining the competence of the competitors. See, for example, *ITT Indus. Space Sys., LLC*, Comp. Gen. Dec. B-309964, 2007 CPD ¶ 217 (mission suitability properly evaluated in procurement of new land imaging instrument to be included in satellite); *Sikorsky Aircraft Co.*, Comp. Gen. Dec. B-299145, 2007 CPD ¶ 45 (mission capability properly evaluated but life-cycle cost improperly evaluated in procurement of new helicopter); *Compunetix, Inc.*, Comp. Gen. Dec. B-298489.4, 2007 CPD ¶ 12 (mission suitability properly evaluated in procurement of new mission voice systems). The requirement for a technical proposal describing the precise techniques that will be used to perform complex services has also been found to be an acceptable way to evaluate the offerors' capability. See, for example, *Savannah River Tank Closure, LLC*, Comp. Gen. Dec. B-400953, 2009 CPD ¶ 78 (method of cleaning tanks properly evaluated).

In service contracting, this design-competition technique has been emulated by calling for the submission of technical and management plans to assess the offerors' understanding of the work. Here there is far greater doubt as to the validity of the process because it is far less likely that the plans will be written by the personnel that will ultimately perform the work. In fact, it is well understood that many technical/management plans are prepared by specialized proposal-writing personnel. Furthermore, it is doubtful if such plans are a valid means of assessing capability, since there are numerous instances where fully capable offerors were found to be incapable because of badly written plans. For example, in *ManTech Int'l Corp.*,

Comp. Gen. Dec. B-311074, 2008 CPD ¶ 87, an incumbent contractor whose performance had been rated excellent was downgraded for not writing good responses to sample problems; in *HealthStar VA, PLLC*, Comp. Gen. Dec. B-299737, 2007 CPD ¶ 114, an incumbent contractor was downgraded because it left information out of its proposal; in *Management Tech. Servs.*, Comp. Gen. Dec. B-251612.3, 93-1 CPD ¶ 432, an incumbent contractor was downgraded in the scoring for failing to include in its plan the required information on how it intended to obtain and train its workforce; while in *Executive Security & Eng'g Techs., Inc.*, Comp. Gen. Dec. B-270518, 96-1 CPD ¶ 156, an incumbent contractor was downgraded for failing to provide information on its corporate experience. Successful incumbent contractors have also been excluded from the competitive range for poorly written technical/management plans, *Pedus Bldg. Servs., Inc.*, Comp. Gen. Dec. B-257271.3, 95-1 CPD ¶ 135 (sloppy technical proposal); *Premier Cleaning Sys., Inc.*, Comp. Gen. Dec. B-255815, 94-1 CPD ¶ 241 (omission of required documentation on capabilities of project manager currently managing the contract). See also *McAllister & Assoc., Inc.*, Comp. Gen. Dec. B-277029, 98-1 CPD ¶ 85, where an experienced contractor was dropped from the competitive range because it had submitted a poorly written technical proposal.

This type of assessment of understanding of the services to be performed through the use of technical/management plans is particularly questionable when the services being procured are routine, non-technical services. Nonetheless, there are numerous instances of offerors losing competitions for such services based on the evaluation of such plans. See, for example, *AHNTECH, Inc.*, Comp. Gen. Dec. B-299806, 2007 CPD ¶ 213 (food services); *Financial & Realty Servs., LLC*, Comp. Gen. Dec. B-299605.2, 2007 CPD ¶ 161 (warehouse operations and labor services); *Meeks Disposal Corp.*, Comp. Gen. Dec. B-299576, 2007 CPD ¶ 127 (refuse collection and recycling services set aside for small businesses); *Cortez, Inc.*, Comp. Gen. Dec. B-292178, 2003 CPD ¶ 184 (facility logistics services); *Philadelphia Produce Market Wholesalers, LLC*, Comp. Gen. Dec. B-298751, 2006 CPD ¶ 193 (fresh fruit and vegetable set aside for small businesses); *Leader Communications Inc.*, Comp. Gen. Dec. B-298734, 2006 CPD ¶ 192 (business support services); *Advanced Fed. Servs. Corp.*, Comp. Gen. Dec. B-298662, 2006 CPD ¶ 174 (administrative support for government facility set aside for 8(a) businesses); *Kola Nut Travel, Inc.*, Comp. Gen. Dec. B-296090.4, 2005 CPD ¶ 184 (travel services set aside for small businesses).

In spite of this evidence that the assessment of understanding of the work through the use of technical/management plans is a very questionable business practice in the service contracting area, there is no question that it is legally valid. See *Computerized Project Mgmt. Plus*, Comp. Gen. Dec. B-247063, 92-1 CPD ¶ 401, where the GAO stated:

> CPM complains here that the evaluators, who were familiar with CPM's performance, treated it "unfairly" because they scored its "[offer] within the four cor-

ners of the proposal," and did not "consider any knowledge they had of the work presently being performed by CPM" that was not reflected in its proposal. CPM adds that any informational deficiencies in its proposal should have been rectified by examining the performance of CPM on the predecessor contract and through "communication" with CPM.

CPM's reliance on its status as the incumbent is misplaced. A contracting activity's technical evaluation of a proposal is dependent upon the information furnished in the proposal. *All Star Maint., Inc.*, B-244143, Sept. 26, 1991, 91-2 CPD ¶ 294. There is no legal basis for favoring a firm with presumptions on the basis of the offeror's prior performance; rather, all offerors must demonstrate their capabilities in their proposals. *Id.* As CPM's sole objection to the evaluation of its technical proposal involves the activity's consideration of only the information furnished in CPM's proposal, and this manner of evaluation comports with the policy objectives in federal procurement statutes and regulations, we have no basis on which to conclude that the contracting activity acted unreasonably in its evaluation of CPM's proposal.

Notwithstanding this legal ruling, many agencies have concluded that the assessment of understanding of the work in service contracting procurements is of doubtful utility and that it adds significantly to the cost and time of the procurement process. Hence, this evaluation factor is being used less frequently than in the past.

It is proper to call for a risk assessment of the probability that a proposed management or technical plan will create performance problems. See Air Force Mandatory Procedure 5315.305.5.1.2. requiring the use of a "mission capability risk rating" and stating:

> The mission capability risk rating focuses on the weaknesses associated with an offeror's proposed approach. . . . Assessment of a mission capability risk considers potential for disruption of schedule, increased cost, or degradation of performance, the need for increased government oversight, and the likelihood of unsuccessful contract performance. . . . For any weakness identified, the evaluation shall address the offeror's proposed mitigation . . . and document why that approach is or is not acceptable. Whenever a strength is identified as part of the mission capability technical rating, (see 5.5.1.1 above), the evaluation shall assess whether the offeror's proposed approach would likely cause an associated weakness which may impact schedule, cost, or performance.

This technique has been upheld in *Trend Western Tech. Corp.*, Comp. Gen. Dec. B-275395.2, 97-1 CPD ¶ 201 (denying a protest that the agency had assessed a plan as having "moderate risk" because the staffing level was low); *Sensis Corp.*, Comp. Gen. Dec. B-265790.2, 96-1 CPD ¶ 77 (agency properly found moderate risk because the protester did not have a mature software development process); and *Hydro Eng'g, Inc. v. United States*, 37 Fed. Cl. 448 (1997) (agency properly found specific elements of a technical and management proposal created a risk of timely performance and technical compliance).

h. Price Realism

Price realism can be used to evaluate capability of an offeror by assessing its understanding of the work, its responsibility or the performance risk that is inherent in a low price. The use of such an evaluation is addressed only peripherally in FAR 15.404-1(d)(3), stating that "cost realism analysis" can be used on fixed-price incentive contracts, or "in exceptional cases, on other competitive fixed-price type contracts," but that, if it is used, prices cannot be adjusted upwards as a result of the analysis. See *IBM Corp.*, Comp. Gen. Dec. B-299504, 2008 CPD ¶ 64, granting a protest when the agency increased a contractor's prices in the evaluation process as a result of it's price realism analysis.

In spite of the sparse FAR coverage, the evaluation of price realism is a common practice with some procuring agencies. This use is limited by decisions of GAO holding that price realism can only be assessed if the solicitation contains an evaluation factor indicating that a proposal will be downgraded if the price is unrealistically low, *Possehn Consulting*, Comp. Gen. Dec. B-278579, 98-1 CPD ¶ 10 (where there is no RFP statement on the issue, price realism can only be used to evaluate responsibility of the offeror); *CSE Constr.*, Comp. Gen. Dec. B-291268.2, 2002 CPD ¶ 207 (price realism analysis not permitted when evaluation factors was "unbalanced or unreasonable price" – reasonableness indicates price is too high); *J.A. Farrington Janitorial Servs.*, Comp. Gen. Dec. B-296875, 2005 CPD ¶ 187 (price realism analysis not permitted when evaluation factor was "unreasonable as to price"); *Indtai, Inc.*, Comp. Gen. Dec. B-298432.3, 2007 CPD ¶ 13 (price realism analysis not permitted if not called for by RFP). See *Pemco Aeroplex, Inc.*, Comp. Gen. Dec. B-310372.3, 2008 CPD ¶ 126, stating:

> Price realism is not ordinarily considered in the evaluation of proposals for the award of a fixed-price contract, because these contracts place the risk of loss upon the contractor. However, in light of various negative impacts on both the agency and the contractor that may result from an offeror's overly optimistic proposal, an agency may, as here, expressly provide that a price realism analysis will be applied in order to measure the offerors' understanding of the requirements and/ or to assess the risk inherent in an offeror's proposal. See, e.g., *Wackenhut Servs., Inc.*, B-286037, B-286037.2 , Nov. 14, 2000, 2001 CPD ¶ 114 at 3; *Molina Eng'g, Ltd./Tri-J Indus., Inc. Joint Venture*, May 22, 2000, B-284895, 2000 CPD ¶ 86 at 4. Although the Federal Acquisition Regulation (FAR) identifies permissible price analysis techniques, FAR § 14.404-1, it does not mandate any particular approach; rather, the nature and extent of a price realism analysis, as well as an assessment of potential risk associated with a proposed price, are generally within the sound exercise of the agency's discretion. See *Legacy Mgmt. Solutions, LLC*, B-299981.2, Oct. 10, 2007, 2007 CPD ¶ 197 at 3; *Comprehensive Health Servs., Inc.*, B-310553, Dec. 27, 2007, 2007 CPD ¶ 9 at 8. In reviewing protests challenging an agency's evaluation of these matters, our focus is whether the agency acted reasonably and in a way consistent with the solicitation's requirements. See, e.g., *Grove Res. Solutions, Inc.*, B-296228, B-296228.2, July 1, 2005, 2005 CPD ¶ 133 at 4-5.

Evaluation factors that have supported the use of price realism analysis are "performance risk," *Trauma Serv. Group*, Comp. Gen. Dec. B-242902.2, 91-1 CPD ¶ 573; *Sabreliner Corp.*, Comp. Gen. Dec. B-284240.2, 2000 CPD ¶ 68; *Guam Shipyard*, Comp. Gen. Dec. B-311321, 2008 CPD ¶ 124, "management," *SEEMA, Inc.*, Comp. Gen. Dec. B-277988, 98-1 CPD ¶ 12 (low price indicated lack of understanding of the work by the offeror's management), and "understanding the requirements," *Consolidated Servs., Inc.*, Comp. Gen. Dec. B-276111.4, 98-1 CPD ¶ 14. A direct statement that price realism will be used to evaluate offers is also satisfactory. In *Team BOS/Naples – Gemmo S.p.A./DelJen*, Comp. Gen. Dec. B-298865.3, 2008 CPD ¶ 11, the RFP statement that "[u]nrealistic, unreasonable, or unbalanced pricing may cause a proposal to be determined unacceptable, or cause a reduction in price proposal rankings" was held to indicate that a price realism analysis would be made. See also *Centech Group, Inc.*, Comp. Gen. Dec. B-278715, 98-1 CPD ¶ 108, approving the price realism analysis and describing the RFP language as follows:

> The RFP emphasized that any proposal that was "unrealistically low in cost(s) and/or price [would] be deemed reflective of an inherent lack of technical competence [or] failure to comprehend the complexity and risk" of the requirements, justifying "rejection of the proposal."

IV. SCORING METHODS

The source selection plan should prescribe any scoring methods that are to be used to rate the proposals. When the procurement strategy calls for the selection of the acceptable source with the lowest price, the scoring system need only provide information on which offerors are acceptable. But when the tradeoff strategy is adopted, a scoring system may be used to convey more complex information. Agencies have generally prescribed such scoring methods for some of or all the evaluation factors as a means of summarizing the evaluations to assist the source selection authority in making the ultimate tradeoff decision between competing proposals. Scoring systems are no more than notational devices that provide a rough means of measuring differences between proposals.

There is no requirement that a scoring system be used. See FAR 15.305(a), which states:

> Evaluations may be conducted using any rating method or combination of methods, including color or adjectival ratings, numerical weights, and ordinal rankings.

Because scoring systems are primarily a means of aggregating complex information, they are of little use when there are a small number of evaluation factors or when the source selection team is composed of only a few people. In such cases the source selection decision can be made on the basis of the evaluations of the proposals without scores. For example, in a procurement where the only evaluation factors are price and offeror capability, no scores are needed to report the relative risk of the varying levels of capability and the differences in prices between the offerors. In contrast, when there are a large number of evaluation factors, scoring systems have generally been used as a means of summarizing the evaluations.

When an agency decides to use a notational scoring system for some of or all the factors, agencies are free to use any one of a wide variety of scoring systems as long as the system chosen has a rational basis, *Grey Advertising, Inc.*, 55 Comp. Gen. 1111 (B-184825), 76-1 CPD ¶ 325. Because all such systems, whether numerical, adjectival, color coding, or otherwise, convey essentially the same information, the selection of the system is not a critical element of the process. However, a system with a small number of gradations will not provide much discrimination between various levels of proficiency. The result is that systems limited to ratings of "pass/fail" or "excellent, good, fair, and poor" are less useful in communicating the differences between the proposals than systems with more gradations. Because the ultimate decision should be based on the actual strengths and weaknesses of the proposals, this should not be a serious defect in the source selection process. See, however, *Trijicon, Inc.*, 71 Comp. Gen. 41 (B-244546), 91-2 CPD ¶ 375, rejecting a color coding system that resulted in grades of blue for all elements of the proposal that were acceptable.

In most cases only some of the evaluation factors are scored. NASA scores technical and management ("mission suitability") but does not score cost to the government. See NFS 1815.304-70. The Naval Air Systems Command stated in NavAirInst 4200.27A, Feb. 12, 1985:

> The use of pre-established point systems is prohibited. A pre-established point system is one that is formulated and defined prior to receipt of the proposals. It represents an attempt by members of the SSEB [source selection evaluation board] to prejudge the relative importance of the many unidentified subelements of the selection criteria prior to knowing what all of those subelements are or exactly how they relate. Instead, quantitative factors (for example, speed, range, cost) shall be measured in their normal quantitative units of measure (that is, knots, nautical miles, dollars) and compared against the RFQ/P requirements, if established, and quantitative factors will be rated using descriptive terms.

The types of scoring systems that have been commonly used are discussed below.

A. Adjectival Ratings

Adjectival rating systems are widely used and generally call for a set of four or five ratings, such as excellent, good, fair, and poor; or outstanding, highly acceptable, acceptable, marginally acceptable, and unacceptable. These systems have the disadvantage of providing very few gradations to distinguish between proposals — making the scoring somewhat imprecise as a tool to measure the marginal differences between proposals. However, the GAO has accepted the use of these systems

— finding that they can give the source selection official a clear understanding of the relative merit of the proposals, *Dynamics Research Corp.*, Comp. Gen. Dec. B-240809, 90-2 CPD ¶ 471. See also *Metropolitan Contract Servs., Inc.*, Comp. Gen. Dec. B-191162, 78-1 CPD ¶ 435, *recons. denied*, 78-2 CPD ¶ 43, rejecting the argument that the use of an adjectival rating system precluded offerors from access to the rationale employed in the decision-making process, and *Akal Sec., Inc.*, Comp. Gen. Dec. B-261996, 96-1 CPD ¶ 33, where the GAO disagreed with the protester's contention that the use of the adjectival rating "acceptable" was too broad to allow for differences in technical superiority. The acceptance of such systems is justified because they do not form the basis for the ultimate source selection decisions. See *Able-One Refrigeration, Inc.*, Comp. Gen. Dec. B-244695, 91-2 CPD ¶ 384, where the GAO commented that adjectival scores "are useful only as guides to intelligent decision making, and are not generally controlling for award because they often reflect the disparate, subjective judgments of the evaluators." This reasoning has been stated many times such as in *Stateside Assocs., Inc.*, Comp. Gen. Dec. B-400670.2, 2009 CPD ¶ 120.

B. Color Coding

A scoring system very similar to adjectival scoring is the color coding system. See Air Force Mandatory Procedure 5315.305.5.1.1, which sets forth the following description of this type of system to be used to score mission capability:

Color	Rating	Description
Blue	Exceptional	Exceeds specified minimum performance or capability requirements in a way beneficial to the government. A proposal must have one or more strengths and no deficiencies to receive a blue.
Green	Acceptable	Meets specified minimum performance or capability requirements. A proposal must have no deficiencies to receive a green but may have one or more strengths.
Yellow	Marginal	There is doubt regarding whether an aspect of the proposal meets s specified minimum performance or capability requirements, but any such uncertainty is correctable.
Red	Unacceptable	Fails to meet specified performance or capability requirements. The proposal has one or more deficiencies and is not awardable.

Four colors serve essentially the same purpose as do four adjectives in that they provide minimal gradations to distinguish between proposals. However, the GAO has agreed with the use of color coding, holding that such a system does not produce "an artificial equality in the ratings," *Ferguson-Williams, Inc.*, 68 Comp. Gen. 25 (B-231827), 88-2 CPD ¶ 344. The GAO has also held that a color rating system does not prevent the agency from gaining a clear understanding of the relative merits of the proposals, *Bendix Field Eng'g Corp.*, Comp. Gen. Dec. B-241156, 91-1 CPD ¶ 44. See also *Peterson Bldrs., Inc.*, Comp. Gen. Dec. B-244614, 91-2 CPD ¶ 419, denying a protest that the color coding system obscured the fact that the technical proposals were essentially equal. However, the GAO has questioned a color coding system that rated all factors and subfactors as "green" that were acceptable, *Trijicon, Inc.*, 71 Comp. Gen. 41 (B-244546), 91-2 CPD ¶ 375. The GAO rejected this system because it did not differentiate between proposals that were merely acceptable and those with superior technical features — thus converting a tradeoff decisional scheme into a lowest-price, technically acceptable proposal scheme.

C. Risk Assessment Systems

Agencies have scored some evaluation factors in terms of risk. See, for example, Air Force Mandatory Procedure 5315.305.5.1.2, which calls for the use of "mission capability risk ratings" as follows:

Rating	Description
Low	Has little potential to cause disruption of schedule, increased cost or degradation of performance. Normal contractor effort and normal government monitoring will likely be able to overcome any difficulties.
Moderate	Can potentially cause disruption of schedule, increased cost or degradation of performance. Special contractor emphasis and close government monitoring will likely be able to overcome difficulties.
High	Likely to cause significant disruption of schedule, increased cost or degradation of performance. Extraordinary contractor emphasis and rigorous government monitoring may be able to overcome difficulties.
Unacceptable	The existence of a significant weakness or combination of weaknesses that is very likely to cause unmitigated disruption of schedule, drastically increased cost or severely degraded performance. Proposals with an unacceptable rating are not awardable.

This regulation also calls for the use of + and – markings to obtain better differentiation, as follows:

A plus "+" rating may be used as an option when risk is evaluated to be in the upper boundaries of a Mission Capability Risk Rating, but is not high enough to merit the next inferior rating. When assigning the risk rating, teams should endeavor to rate proposals as low, moderate, high, or unacceptable. However, if additional stratification within the Low, Moderate or High Risk ratings is desired, evaluators/teams may (optionally) annotate this by adding a plus "+" to the risk rating. For example, where in the judgment of the evaluator, an offeror has risk that approaches or is nearly rated as a Moderate risk, a Mission Capability Risk Rating of "Low +" could be assigned. Ensure, however, that the source selection record adequately addresses the rationale for assigning this inferior risk rating. The use of a (+) shall not apply to the "Unacceptable" risk rating.

In *Systems Eng'g & Mgmt. Co.*, Comp. Gen. Dec. B-275786, 97-1 CPD ¶ 133, the protester argued that the agency improperly evaluated the proposal risk of the awardee's proposal. Specifically, the protester claimed that because the awardee's wages were too low, it would not be able to retain qualified personnel over the course of contract performance. The GAO denied the protest, stating that the awardee's proposal acknowledged the low wages and provided a convincing rationale for its ability to offer such wages. In *Tecom, Inc.*, Comp. Gen. Dec. B-275518.2, 97-1 CPD ¶ 221, the GAO found reasonable an agency's determination that even though the agency gave the awardee proposal a "moderate risk" rating because of its minimum staffing numbers and protester had superior rating, the protester's proposal did not justify the higher cost. In *AlliedSignal, Inc.*, Comp. Gen. Dec. B-272290, 96-2 CPD ¶ 121, the awardee received an "outstanding/moderate" risk rating for a major weight component of its proposed product. The protester challenged the evaluation claiming that the "outstanding" element of the rating was not in accord with the evaluation criteria in the RFP. The GAO denied the protest, finding that the risk assessment, even if slightly out of line, did not impact significantly on the source selection decision.

The GAO will review an agency's evaluation of proposal risk to determine whether the judgment was reasonable. See *Trend Western Tech. Corp.*, Comp. Gen. Dec. B-275395.2, 97-1 CPD ¶ 201 (agency rating of proposal as "moderate risk" due to low staffing reasonable); *Robbins-Gioia, Inc.*, Comp. Gen. Dec. B-274318, 96-2 CPD ¶ 222 (agency rating of proposal as "moderate risk" reasonable because protester had limited systems engineering experience and lacked experience overseeing these processes as a general contractor).

Similarly, Air Force Mandatory Procedure 5315.305.5.2.2. uses the following rating system for past performance:

Rating	Definition
SUBSTANTIAL CONFIDENCE	Based on the offeror's performance record, the government has a high expectation that the offeror will successfully perform the required effort.
	Based on the offeror's performance record, the government has an expectation that the offeror will successfully perform the required effort.
LIMITEDCONFIDENCE	Based on the offeror's performance record, the government has a low expectation that the offeror will successfully perform the required effort.
NO CONFIDENCE	Based on the offeror's performance record, the government has no expectation that the offeror will be able to successfully perform the required effort.
UNKNOWN CONFIDENCE	No performance record is identifiable or the offeror's performance record is so sparse that no confidence assessment rating can be reasonably assigned.

D. Numerical Systems

Numerical systems typically assign points (on a scale of 100 or 1000) to the factors being scored. Most agencies that have used numerical scoring have scored only the non-price factors. However, a few agencies have used totally numerical systems — scoring price or cost as well as the other factors.

1. Partially Numerical Systems

The advantage of numerical scoring systems is that they generally contain a large number of gradations, which permits greater differentiation between proposals. However, the GAO has approved systems that reduce the number of gradations by prohibiting the use of certain scores. See *Hoffman Mgmt., Inc.*, 69 Comp. Gen. 579 (B-238752), 90-2 CPD ¶ 15 (10-5-0 scoring system with zero points given for meeting minimum requirements); *American Sys. Corp.*, Comp. Gen. Dec. B-247923.3, 92-2 CPD ¶ 158 (10-4-2-0 system); and *Joint Mgmt. & Tech. Servs.*, Comp. Gen. Dec. B-294229, 2004 CPD ¶ 208 (10-8-5-2-0 system). These systems tend to distort the differences between proposals, but the GAO has not seen the distortion as a serious problem — probably because the scores are not used as the basis of the source selection decision.

The apparent accuracy of numerical scoring can mislead source selection officials into believing that the total scores provide a precise overall assessment of the relative strengths and weaknesses of the proposals. See, for example, *Serco Inc. v.*

United States, 81 Fed. Cl. 463 (2008), where the court granted a protest because the agency had used a point scoring system that resulted in "false statistical precision." The flaw detected by the court was that the agency had scored subfactors adjectivally, converted these scores into whole numbers, averaged the whole number to arrive at a numerical value for each offeror that went to three decimal places, and then used this data to make the source selection decision. Similarly, in *Midland Supply, Inc.*, Comp. Gen. Dec. B-298720, 2007 CPD ¶ 2, the GAO sustained a protest because the source selection official had based the decision on "a mechanical comparison of the offerors' total point scores." Compare *Burchick Constr. Co.*, Comp. Gen. Dec. B-400342.3, 2009 CPD ¶ 102, where the source selection official made the decision on the strengths and weaknesses not the point scores, and *GAP Solutions, Inc.*, Comp. Gen. Dec. B-310564, 2008 CPD ¶ 26, where the source selection official properly ignored minor differences in numerical scores, determined that the offerors were "technically equal," and awarded to the low price offeror.

2. *Totally Numerical Systems*

Some agencies have used totally numerical scoring systems. Three systems of this nature have been commonly used: total point scoring, conversion to dollar value, and dollars per point.

a. *Total Point Scoring*

This system assigns point scores to each evaluation factor and makes the source selection decision based on the total point scores. In such a system all criteria, including price or cost, are numerically scored. Generally, price is scored by giving the lowest-price proposal the full number of points assigned to this criteria and computing the number of points for the other proposals in accordance with their relationship to the lowest price. This evaluation technique totally obscures the tradeoff between price and the other evaluation factors. An illustration of this problem is found in *Harrison Sys., Ltd.*, 63 Comp. Gen. 379 (B-212675), 84-1 CPD ¶ 572, where price was assigned 30 points and the proposals were:

A $1,150,782

B $1,392,293

Offeror A was given 30 points and Offeror B was given 24.79 points derived from the following formula:

$$\frac{\$1,150,782}{\$1,392,293} \times 30 = 24.79 \text{ points}$$

After completing the technical evaluation, the agency computed the results of the total evaluation as follows:

Proposal	Cost	Technical	Total
A	30 points	59.88 points	89.88 points
B	24.79 points	70 points	94.79 points

However, the source selection official was unwilling to blindly follow the RFP and award to Offeror B on the basis of the highest point score. The source selection official made an independent analysis and determined that the technical proposals were of equal merit. The contract was therefore awarded to Offeror A, based on its low price. The GAO upheld this decision on the theory that the source selection official had rescored the technical scores but stated that it would have granted the protest if the source selection official had independently analyzed whether the difference in technical merit was worth the difference in price.

The *Harrison Systems* case demonstrates the pitfalls inherent in the total point evaluation system. The summation of points to obtain a total score gives the appearance of mathematical exactitude, but there is no assurance that points assigned to one set of criteria have the same value to the government as points assigned to another set of criteria. Nonetheless, the GAO has accepted the conclusion that the offeror with the most points has properly been awarded the contract when the RFP has stated that would be the basis of the source selection. See *Securiguard/Group 4 Joint Venture*, Comp. Gen. Dec. B-280429, 98-2 CPD ¶ 118; *Barnard Constr. Co.*, Comp. Gen. Dec. B-271644, 96-1 CPD ¶ 18; and *Tulane Univ.*, Comp. Gen. Dec. B-259912, 95-1 CPD ¶ 210. In *Securiguard*, the GAO explained the reasoning as follows:

> The cost/technical tradeoff formula stated in the RFP already accounted for both technical merit and cost. Our Office has specifically recognized the permissibility of using such a formula in selecting an offeror....Because [the awardee's best and final offer] earned the highest combined cost/technical score under the specified formula, the agency was not required to perform any further cost/technical tradeoff analysis to justify the selection decision.

See also *Phoebe Putney Memorial Hospital*, Comp. Gen. Dec. B-311385, 2008 CPD ¶ 128, accepting the award to the offeror with the most points when the RFP stated that award would be "based on a scoring system." Like *Harrison Systems* this case illustrates the inherent irrationality of such a system because the assignment of points to prices on a geometric basis totally obscured the actual tradeoff between price and non-price factors.

Some agencies have used the total point evaluation system as a scoring technique but have not stated in the RFP that award would be made to the offeror earning the most points. In that situation it is proper to make a normal tradeoff analysis and award to the offeror with the best value, *DATEX, Inc.*, Comp. Gen. Dec. B-270268.2, 96-1 CPD ¶ 240; *Paxson Elec. Co. v. United States*, 14 Cl. Ct. 634 (1988). See *C&B Constr., Inc.*, Comp. Gen. Dec. B-401988.2, 2010 CPD ¶ 1, and *Midland Supply, Inc.*, Comp. Gen. Dec. B-298720, 2007 CPD ¶ 2, holding that the use of a normal tradeoff is required in this situation. Thus, it is not clear what is added to the evaluation process by giving point scores to price when a full tradeoff analysis is going to be made.

The use of numerical scoring methods that produce distorted scores has been discouraged. In *Custom Janitorial Serv.*, Comp. Gen. Dec. B-205023, 82-2 CPD ¶ 163, the GAO criticized the use of "spread scoring," in which the proposal with the lowest realistic cost received the maximum number of points and that with the highest cost received zero. The GAO concluded that this system produced distorted results when applied to the two offerors in the competitive range. See *Serco, Inc.*, 81 Fed. Cl. 463 (2008), where the court criticized the agency for "false statistical precision," describing the derivation of numerical scores for the non-cost evaluation factors at 486:

> GSA took the initial observations that it had accumulated in terms of past performance (PP) and the basic contract plans (BCP) and developed a composite technical score. . . . [T]he agency took slightly different paths in calculating the two numbers that were averaged to create that technical score, again enumerated as the "Weighted BCP/PP Average Score." In calculating the past performance component of that score, GSA first developed a consensus adjectival rating for each subfactor (*e.g.*, S), then converted those subfactors into whole numbers (*e.g.*, 4) and averaged them into an average PP score (*e.g.*, 4.50). Despite instructions to this effect in the SSP, GSA did not make use of consensus adjectival ratings in calculating the weighted BCP average score. Rather, it first assigned adjectival ratings to each of the elements that made up the three BCP subfactors (*e.g.*, S). It then converted those ratings into whole numbers and developed an average number for each element (*e.g.*, 4.25) and used those averages to calculate a value for each subfactor (*e.g.*, 4.21), which were then weighted to calculate the weighted average BCP score (*e.g.*, 3.125). The average PP score and the weighted average BCP score were then averaged, yet again, to produce the "Weighted BCP/PP Average Score," expressed in numbers carried out to three decimals (*e.g.*, 3.813).

After an extensive discussion of statistical writings, the court concluded that the small distinctions arrived at in making the source selection decision were not rational, stating at 488-89:

> [T]here are strong reasons to suspect that these comparisons were undermined by false precision, . . . For one thing, there is no indication that the initial numerical data generated in evaluating the offerors' proposals - data that, in the first instance, was captured in whole numbers (*e.g.*, 3, 4, or 5) - had anywhere near the level of accuracy reflected in the final evaluation scores (*e.g.*, 3.841). Indeed, in assigning adjectival scores to the various subfactors involved here, agency personnel effectively engaged in rounding (performing a computation with one digit in the operand) - they were, in other words, forced to choose one versus another adjectival

rating even when a fraction (*e.g.*, 3.8 rather than 4) would have been more accurate. Such imprecision and rounding is most evident in the evaluation of past performance, the accuracy of which depended, at the least, upon the following variables: (i) the accuracy associated with the scripts that were used by the contractor to query references; (ii) the accuracy of the contractor's various employees in interpreting and transcribing the answers received from the references; and (iii) the accuracy and potential rounding errors that occurred when the narrative answers recorded by the contractor were converted to adjectival scores and then to numbers. That the results of these observations were, by virtue of repeated calculations, eventually expressed in figures that were carried to three decimals gives those figures no more reliability than they had *ab initio*. Again, while repeated division creates decimals that can add an aura of precision, it does not actually increase accuracy.

See also *Tennessee Wholesale Drug Co.*, Comp. Gen. Dec. B-243018, 91-2 CPD ¶ 9, holding that a system that improperly reduced the importance of price as an evaluation factor unfairly distorted the scores. In *Lingtec, Inc.*, Comp. Gen. Dec. B-208777, 83-2 CPD ¶ 279, a form of mathematical analysis in which prices closest to the government estimate received maximum points and deviations from the estimate were penalized was held improper, as it penalized lower prices more than higher ones. It can be argued that any system that assigns scores by formula will potentially produce distorted results and, thus, should not be used.

b. Conversion to Dollar Values

Another completely numerical system determines the relative value of all evaluation factors according to their expected impact on the life-cycle cost of the item being procured. An example of this method is found in *Storage Tech. Corp.*, Comp. Gen. Dec. B-215336, 84-2 CPD ¶ 190, describing the method as follows:

> Section IV.3 of the RFP, "Evaluation of Proposals" . . . states that award will be "made to that responsible offeror whose proposal is in the best interests of the VA, cost and other factors considered." Section H.1.3 of the RFP lists the additional factors that the VA would consider. These factors were ranked in order of importance based on their maximum dollar impact on ESLC and listed in descending order of importance . . . . For each of these factors, the VA assigned a dollar credit or assessment commensurate with the cost savings/avoidance or added cost to be incurred by the VA with each proposal system. The VA indicates that the technical evaluation "dollars" are not intended to be precise indicators of actual value, but, rather, like a point score, will serve as a guide to the selecting official. The VA states that the dollar figures arrived at for these additional factors will be compared to the ESLC to determine which proposal is in the VA's best interests and award will be made on that basis.

See also *C.M.P., Inc.*, Comp. Gen. Dec. B-216508, 85-1 CPD ¶ 156, where the agency made the entire evaluation in dollars by assigning dollar amounts for the value of three years of previous performance, guarantee of performance, and remedial and preventive maintenance services.

Assigning dollar values to all evaluation factors is an extremely rare form of scoring. However, it is not uncommon to assign dollar values to some of the evaluation factors. See, for example, *Cessna Aircraft Co.*, Comp. Gen. Dec. B-261953.5, 96-1 CPD ¶ 132, where this occurred. The GAO indicated that it would accept the judgment of the agency in such cases, stating that life-cycle cost analysis involves the exercise of "informed judgment" and its use will not be questioned "unless it clearly lacks a reasonable basis."

c. Dollars per Point

The third totally numerical system is the dollars per point system. In this system all the criteria other than cost are scored numerically and the prices proposed are used to compute a mathematical relationship. An earlier version of DARCOM Pamphlet 715-3 described this system:

> (3) *Evaluation of lowest dollar per technical quality point ($/q.p.).* The concept of selecting the best technical proposal for the dollar is supportable by the dollar/technical point relationships. This factor can be determined by dividing the cost of the proposal by the total unweighted raw score developed for "technical." With the knowledge contained in the RFP that this relationship will be given consideration and will force offerors to tradeoff between cost and technical factors in order to prepare the best possible proposal at a fair and reasonable price, $/q.p. relationship by itself is not justification for selection; but is only considered an additional factor to offer to the SSA in making the decision. An example area is below:

Proposal	Cost	Technical	$/ q.p.
1	$30,000	374	$80.21
2	$28,500	355	$80.28
3	$42.500	385	$110.38
4	$32,670	362	$90.24

This technique gives an appearance of greater precision than is justified by the point scores assigned, because point scoring inherently is less precise than price, yet the use of a ratio between the scores assumes that they are of equal precision. However, it is an acceptable technique to make the initial evaluation of the proposals. See *Moran Assocs.*, Comp. Gen. Dec. B-240564.2, 91-2 CPD ¶ 495, where the agency did this and the GAO stated:

> We have recognized that such a cost/technical ratio formula can be a proper tool for the government to utilize in determining which proposal is the most advantageous to the government. See *Morrison-Knudsen Co., Inc.*, B-237800.2, 90-1 CPD ¶ 443. Here, the ratio was only one tool utilized to assure that the government was getting the best buys, given relative technical rankings and costs. The record shows that awards were not made to the offerors with the best ratios.

See also *Management Sys. Designers, Inc.*, Comp. Gen. Dec. B-244383.3, 91-2 CPD ¶ 310, where the GAO accepted the use of this technique as the sole basis for the source selection even though the RFP reserved the right to make an independent cost/technical tradeoff decision, *Frank E. Basil, Inc.*, Comp. Gen. Dec. B-208133, 83-1 CPD ¶ 91, allowing such an award even though the protester's price was significantly lower

E. Ranking

The direct ranking of proposals without the aid of scores has also been upheld, as numerical scoring does not "transform the technical evaluation into a more objective process," *Development Assocs., Inc.*, Comp. Gen. Dec. B-205380, 82-2 CPD ¶ 37. The GAO has even stated that "ranking proposals may be a more direct and meaningful method" than numerical scoring, *Maximus*, Comp. Gen. Dec. B-195806, 81-1 CPD ¶ 285. However, ranking is infrequently used because it is difficult to do when there are a number of evaluation factors. When an agency uses only a few evaluation factors, ranking becomes a much more feasible method.

V. DECISIONAL RULE

Along with the selection of the evaluation factors and scoring system, the agency must determine the fundamental basis that will be used to make the source selection decision. This discussion refers to the basis for making the decision as the "decisional rule." As discussed earlier, there are two fundamental decisional rules — the lowest-price, technically acceptable proposal rule and the tradeoff rule. However, FAR 15.100 permits the use of other decisional rules, and FAR 15.101 permits a decisional rule that combines the lowest-price, technically acceptable rule with the tradeoff rule.

When the tradeoff rule is adopted, the source selection decision will be made by comparing the marginal differences in the proposed costs or prices with the marginal differences in the non-cost factors. If an offeror has the lowest cost or price and is ranked highest on the non-cost factors, that offeror will be the winner. But in most procurements this will not be the case. Thus, when the proposal with the lowest cost or price is not given the highest ranking on the non-cost factors, the agency must decide whether the value of the marginal difference in the non-cost factors is worth the difference in price.

The GAO has ruled that it is legally permissible to avoid making a tradeoff analysis after proposal evaluation by adopting a decisional rule that the proposal achieving the highest number of points (when all evaluation factors are point scored) will be the winner. See *Barnard Constr., Co.*, Comp. Gen. Dec. B-271644, 96-2 CPD ¶ 18, which states:

Our Office has specifically recognized the propriety of using such a formula in selecting an offeror. See *Stone & Webster Eng'g Corp.*, B-255286.2, Apr. 12, 1994, 94-1 CPD ¶ 306; *Management Sys. Designers, Inc.*, B-244383.3, Sept. 30, 1991, 91-2 CPD ¶ 310. Because the awardee's proposal earned the highest combined price/technical score under the specified formula, the agency was not required to perform price/technical tradeoff analysis to justify the selection decision.

The same result was reached in *Tulane Univ.*, Comp. Gen. B-259912, 95-1 CPD ¶ 210, and *Securigard, Inc.*, Comp. Gen. Dec. B-248584, 92-2 CPD ¶ 156. This ruling is based on the questionable proposition that the agency has made the tradeoff at the time it constructed the point scoring system.

Using the same questionable reasoning, the GAO has also approved the use of a dollar per quality point system as the sole basis for source selection, *Shapell Gov. Hous., Inc.*, 55 Comp. Gen. 839 (B-183830), 76-1 CPD ¶ 161. See *Management Sys. Designers, Inc.*, Comp. Gen. Dec. B-244383.3, 91-2 CPD ¶ 310, accepting the use of this technique as the sole basis for the source selection even though the RFP reserved the right to make an independent cost/technical tradeoff decision. See also *Frank E. Basil, Inc.*, Comp. Gen. Dec. B-208133, 83-1 CPD ¶ 91, allowing such an award even though the protester's price was significantly lower. It is not clear why agencies have adopted these mechanical decisional rules in lieu of performing a tradeoff analysis after full evaluation of the competing proposals.

It has been common practice to believe that the statutorily required statement of relative importance is the decisional rule in tradeoff procurements. However, this statement does not state how the ultimate source selection will be made but rather gives the offerors an indication of the priorities of the agency in making the decision. Hence, a statement in the RFP that cost/price is more important than non-cost/price factors is merely a statement that the agency's priority is a low cost/price rather than high scores in the non-cost/price area. It is neither a statement that the agency will award to the offeror with the low cost/price nor a statement that the agency will not pay more to get a higher-rated offeror in the non-cost/price area. See Chapter 3 for a more complete discussion of the required statement of relative importance in the RFP and Chapter 9 for a complete discussion of how this statement impacts the source selection decision.

VI. OBTAINING INFORMATION FOR EVALUATION

The final issue to be addressed in the source selection plan is the technique that will be used to obtain the information necessary to evaluate the proposals. Three types of information are necessary in most competitively negotiated procurements: (1) pricing information, (2) technical information supporting offers, and (3) capability information.

A. Pricing Information

It is the government's policy that agencies should obtain the minimum amount of information necessary to determine the reasonableness of proposed prices or the realism of proposed costs. See FAR 15.402, which states:

15.402   Pricing policy.

Contracting officers shall —

(a) Purchase supplies and services from responsible sources at fair and reasonable prices. In establishing the reasonableness of the offered prices, the contracting officer —

(1) Shall obtain certified cost or pricing data when required by 15.403–4, along with data other than certified cost or pricing data as necessary to establish a fair and reasonable price; or

(2) When certified cost or pricing data are not required by 15.403–4, obtain data other than certified cost or pricing data as necessary to establish a fair and reasonable price, generally using the following order of preference in determining the type of data required:

(i) No additional data from the offeror, if the price is based on adequate price competition, except as provided by 15.403–3(b).

(ii) Data other than certified cost or pricing data such as —

(A) Data related to prices (e.g., established catalog or market prices, sales to non-governmental and governmental entities), relying first on data available within the Government; second, on data obtained from sources other than the offeror; and, if necessary, on data obtained from the offeror. When obtaining data from the offeror is necessary, unless an exception under 15.403–1(b)(1) or (2) applies, such data submitted by the offeror shall include, at a minimum, appropriate data on the prices at which the same or similar items have been sold previously, adequate for evaluating the reasonableness of the price.

(B) Cost data to the extent necessary for the contracting officer to determine a fair and reasonable price.

(3) Obtain the type and quantity of data necessary to establish a fair and reasonable price, but not more data than is necessary. Requesting unnecessary data can lead to increased proposal preparation costs, generally extend acquisition lead time, and consume additional contractor and

Government resources. Use techniques such as, but not limited to, price analysis, cost analysis, and/or cost realism analysis to establish a fair and reasonable price. If a fair and reasonable price cannot be established by the contracting officer from the analyses of the data obtained or submitted to date, the contracting officer shall require the submission of additional data sufficient for the contracting officer to support the determination of the fair and reasonable price.

(b) Price each contract separately and independently and not —

    (1) Use proposed price reductions under other contracts as an evaluation factor; or

    (2) Consider losses or profits realized or anticipated under other contracts.

(c) Not include in a contract price any amount for a specified contingency to the extent that the contract provides for a price adjustment based upon the occurrence of that contingency.

Additional guidance is provided in FAR 15.403-3:

15.403-3   Requiring data other than certified cost or pricing data.

(a)(1) In those acquisitions that do not require certified cost or pricing data, the contracting officer shall —

    (i) Obtain whatever data are available from Government or other secondary sources and use that data in determining a fair and reasonable price;

    (ii) Require submission of data other than certified cost or pricing data, as defined in 2.101, from the offeror to the extent necessary to determine a fair and reasonable price (10 U.S.C. 2306a(d)(1) and 41 U.S.C. 254b(d)(1)) if the contracting officer determines that adequate data from sources other than the offeror are not available. This includes requiring data from an offeror to support a cost realism analysis;

    (iii) Consider whether cost data are necessary to determine a fair and reasonable price when there is not adequate price competition;

    (iv) Require that the data submitted by the offeror include, at a minimum, appropriate data on the prices at which the same item or similar items have previously been sold, adequate for determining the reasonableness of the price unless an exception under 15.403–1(b)(1) or (2) applies; and

(v) Consider the guidance in section 3.3, chapter 3, volume I, of the Contract Pricing Reference Guide cited at 15.404–1(a)(7) to determine the data an offeror shall be required to submit.

(2) The contractor's format for submitting the data should be used (see 15.403–5(b)(2)).

(3) The contracting officer shall ensure that data used to support price negotiations are sufficiently current to permit negotiation of a fair and reasonable price. Requests for updated offeror data should be limited to data that affect the adequacy of the proposal for negotiations, such as changes in price lists.

(4) As specified in section 808 of the Strom Thurmond National Defense Authorization Act for Fiscal Year 1999 (Pub. L. 105–261), an offeror who does not comply with a requirement to submit data for a contract or subcontract in accordance with paragraph (a)(1) of this subsection is ineligible for award unless the HCA determines that it is in the best interest of the Government to make the award to that offeror, based on consideration of the following:

(i) The effort made to obtain the data.

(ii) The need for the item or service.

(iii) Increased cost or significant harm to the Government if award is not made.

(b) Adequate price competition. When adequate price competition exists (see 15.403–1(c)(1)), generally no additional data are necessary to determine the reasonableness of price. However, if there are unusual circumstances where it is concluded that additional data are necessary to determine the reasonableness of price, the contracting officer shall, to the maximum extent practicable, obtain the additional data from sources other than the offeror. In addition, the contracting officer should request data to determine the cost realism of competing offers or to evaluate competing approaches.

(c) Commercial items. (1) At a minimum, the contracting officer must use price analysis to determine whether the price is fair and reasonable whenever the contracting officer acquires a commercial item (see 15.404–1(b)). The fact that a price is included in a catalog does not, in and of itself, make it fair and reasonable. If the contracting officer cannot determine whether an offered price is fair and reasonable, even after obtaining additional data from sources other than the offeror, then the contracting officer shall require the offeror to submit data other than certified cost or pricing data to support further analysis (see 15.404–1). This data may include history of sales to non-governmental and governmental entities, cost data, or any other information the contracting officer requires to determine the price is fair and reasonable. Unless an exception under 15.403–1(b)(1) or (2) applies, the contracting officer shall require that the data submitted by the offeror include, at a minimum, appropriate data on the prices at which the same item or similar items have previously been sold, adequate for determining the reasonableness of the price.

(2) Limitations relating to commercial items (10 U.S.C. 2306a(d)(2) and 41 U.S.C. 254b(d)(2)). (i) The contracting officer shall limit requests for sales data relating to commercial items to data for the same or similar items during a relevant time period.

(ii) The contracting officer shall, to the maximum extent practicable, limit the scope of the request for data relating to commercial items to include only data that are in the form regularly maintained by the offeror as part of its commercial operations.

(iii) The Government shall not disclose outside the Government data obtained relating to commercial items that is exempt from disclosure under 24.202(a) or the Freedom of Information Act (5 U.S.C. 552(b)).

(3) For services that are not offered and sold competitively in substantial quantities in the commercial marketplace, but are of a type offered and sold competitively in substantial quantities in the commercial marketplace, see 15.403–1(c)(3)(ii).

1. *Price Reasonableness*

When the agency has decided to use a fixed-price-type contract, the contracting officer will have to have sufficient information to ensure that the contract price is reasonable. As indicated in the above FAR policy, when there is adequate price competition, the competitive prices submitted by the offerors will almost always provide sufficient information to determine that the price is reasonable. In such cases no pricing information need be obtained from the offerors. Indeed, when adequate price competition is present, 10 U.S.C. § 2306a and 41 U.S.C. § 254b, as implemented in FAR 15.403-1(b)(1), prohibit agencies from obtaining certified cost or pricing data.

Adequate price competition exists in a variety of circumstances. See FAR 15.403-1(c), which states:

(1) *Adequate price competition.* A price is based on adequate price competition if —

(i) Two or more responsible offerors, competing independently, submit priced offers that satisfy the Government's expressed requirement and if —

(A) Award will be made to the offeror whose proposal represents the best value (see 2.101) where price is a substantial factor in source selection; and

(B) There is no finding that the price of the otherwise successful offeror is unreasonable. Any finding that the price is unreasonable must be supported by a statement of the facts and approved at a level above the contracting officer;

(ii) There was a reasonable expectation, based on market research or other assessment, that two or more responsible offerors, competing independently, would submit priced offers in response to the solicitation's expressed requirement, even though only one offer is received from a responsible offeror and if —

(A) Based on the offer received, the contracting officer can reasonably conclude that the offer was submitted with the expectation of competition, e.g., circumstances indicate that —

(1) The offeror believed that at least one other offeror was capable of submitting a meaningful offer; and

(2) The offeror had no reason to believe that other potential offerors did not intend to submit an offer; and

(B) The determination that the proposed price is based on adequate price competition, is reasonable, and is approved at a level above the contracting officer; or

(iii) Price analysis clearly demonstrates that the proposed price is reasonable in comparison with current or recent prices for the same or similar items, adjusted to reflect changes in market conditions, economic conditions, quantities, or terms and conditions under contracts that resulted from adequate price competition.

If the agency determines that adequate price competition does not exist, it may have to obtain pricing information from the offerors. However, in such circumstances it is still the policy to obtain the minimum amount of information necessary to ensure that the price is reasonable. If the procurement is for a commercial item, FAR 15.404-3(c) imposes limitations on the amount of information that should be obtained. If the procurement is for a noncommercial item, FAR 15.403-1(c)(4) suggests limiting the amount of pricing data obtained by waiving the requirement for certified cost or pricing data, as follows:

Waivers. The head of the contracting activity (HCA) may, without power of delegation, waive the requirement for submission of certified cost or pricing data in exceptional cases. The authorization for the waiver and the supporting rationale shall be in writing. The HCA may consider waiving the requirement if the price can be determined to be fair and reasonable without submission of certified cost or pricing data. For example, if certified cost or pricing data were furnished on previous production buys and the contracting officer determines such data are sufficient, when combined with updated data, a waiver may be granted. If the HCA has waived the requirement for submission of certified cost or pricing data, the contractor or higher-tier subcontractor to whom the waiver relates shall be considered as having been required to provide certified cost or pricing data. Consequently, award of any lower-tier subcontract expected to exceed the certified cost or pricing data threshold requires the submission of certified cost or pricing data unless — (i) An exception otherwise applies to the subcontract; or (ii) The waiver specifically includes the subcontract and the rationale supporting the waiver for that subcontract.

If the procurement is for a commercial item, the key issue is whether there is adequate price competition – in which case the above procedure applies. If there is no competition, agencies must follow the guidance in FAR 15.402(c) above. That will general entail making a decision as to whether commercial prices will be required to be submitted or whether, as a last alternative, data other than certified cost or pricing data will be required. The Department of Defense has issued detailed guidance on obtaining sufficient data to determine that commercial item prices are fair and reasonable – particularly when there is little or no competition or the item has not yet been sold to commercial customers. DFARS PGI 215.403-1(c)(3)(A)(2) directs contracting officers to obtain "prior non-government sales data" on the precise item or the predecessor item if the item being procured has not yet been sold commercially but has evolved from a commercial item. DFARS PGI 215.403-3(1) states:

Sales data must be comparable to the quantities, capabilities, specifications, etc. of the product or service proposed. Sufficient steps must be taken to verify the integrity of the sales data, to include assistance from the Defense Contract Management Agency, the Defense Contract Audit Agency, and/or other agencies if required.

DFARS PGI 215.404-1(b)(i) points out that sometimes this type of sales data can be obtained through market research that finds data on commercial sales or in published catalogs or prices.

DFARS PGI 215.404-1(b)(ii) calls for obtaining "cost information" when sales data are not sufficient to demonstrate that the price is fair and reasonable:

In some cases, commercial sales are not available and there is no other market information for determining fair and reasonable prices. This is especially true when buying supplies or services that have been determined to be commercial but have only been "offered for sale" or purchased on a sole source basis with no prior commercial sales upon which to rely. In such cases, the contracting must require the offeror to submit whatever cost information is needed to determine price reasonableness.

The DOD guidance then makes it clear at DFARS PGI 215.404-1(c)(iii) that such "cost information" need not be submitted in accordance with the instructions in Table 15-2 of FAR 15.408 dealing with the submission of certified cost or pricing data but can be submitted in the contractor's format. See, however, the definition of "data other than certified cost or pricing data" in FAR 2.101 permitting agencies to require such data in accordance with Table 15-2 (without certification).

DFARS PGI 215.403-3(4) also contains a warning about relying on prior prices paid by the government:

> Before relying on a prior price paid by the Government, the contracting officer must verify and document that sufficient analysis was performed to determine that the prior price was fair and reasonable. Sometimes, due to exigent situations, supplies and services are purchased even though an adequate price or cost analysis could not be performed. The problem is exacerbated when other contracting officers assume these prices were adequately analyzed and determined to be fair and reasonable. The contracting officer also must verify that the prices previously paid were for quantities consistent with the current solicitation. Not verifying that a previous price analysis was performed, or the consistencies in quantity, has been a recurring issue on sole source commercial items reported by oversight organizations. Sole source commercial items require extra attention to verify that previous prices paid on Government contracts were sufficiently analyzed and determined to be fair and reasonable. At a minimum, a contracting officer reviewing price history shall discuss the basis of previous prices paid with the contracting organization that previously bought the item. These discussions shall be documented in the contract file.

2. Cost Realism

When the agency determines that a cost-reimbursement-type contract will be used or if it decides that price realism will be assessed in fixed-price- type contracts, it will have to obtain data to make this analysis. FAR 15.404-1 provides the following guidance on when cost realism analysis should be performed:

> (d) *Cost realism analysis.* (1) Cost realism analysis is the process of independently reviewing and evaluating specific elements of each offeror's proposed cost estimate to determine whether the estimated proposed cost elements are realistic for the work to be performed; reflect a clear understanding of the requirements; and are consistent with the unique methods of performance and materials described in the offeror's technical proposal.

>> (2) Cost realism analyses shall be performed on cost-reimbursement contracts to determine the probable cost of performance for each offeror.

>>> (i) The probable cost may differ from the proposed cost and should reflect the Government's best estimate of the cost of any contract that is most likely to result from the offeror's proposal.

The probable cost shall be used for purposes of evaluation to determine the best value.

(ii) The probable cost is determined by adjusting each offeror's proposed cost, and fee when appropriate, to reflect any additions or reductions in cost elements to realistic levels based on the results of the cost realism analysis.

(3) Cost realism analyses may also be used on competitive fixed-price incentive contracts or, in exceptional cases, on other competitive fixed-price-type contracts when new requirements may not be fully understood by competing offerors, there are quality concerns, or past experience indicates that contractors proposed costs have resulted in quality or service shortfalls. Results of the analysis may be used in performance risk assessments and responsibility determinations. However, proposals shall be evaluated using the criteria in the solicitation, and the offered prices shall not be adjusted as a result of the analysis.

The data that is necessary to make a cost realism analysis to determine probable cost in a cost-reimbursement-type contract is generally cost element breakdowns for major contract line items. In large contracts cost element breakdowns for subelements of the major contract line items may be called for. Such cost element breakdowns identify the essential cost information — purchased materials and subcontracts, labor hours, labor rates and indirect cost rates — that is necessary to assess the realism of the estimated costs. In many cases the agency can assess these estimates without obtaining cost or pricing data — with the assistance of government audit agencies or with pricing information available within the agency. If such information is not available, it may be necessary to obtain cost or pricing data. However, obtaining certified cost or pricing data is *prohibited* if adequate price competition has been obtained and the GAO has ruled that there is adequate price competition on cost-reimbursement contracts when cost is a substantial evaluation factor, *Dynalectron Corp.*, 52 Comp. Gen. 346 (B-176217) (1972) (cost to the government found to be a substantial factor in a cost-plus-award-fee contract even though it was 20% of the total evaluation); *U.S. Nuclear, Inc.*, 57 Comp. Gen. 185 (B-187716), 77-2 CPD ¶ 511 (adequate price competition found on a cost-plus-fixed-fee contract).

If a price realism analysis is going to be made on a fixed-price-type contract to assess the offerors' understanding of the work, even less data may be needed. In that circumstance the agency may need to assess only the labor hours proposed for major elements of the work, including labor hours to be incurred by subcontractors. Only labor hour estimates are needed to make such assessment. If the agency believes that the labor rates and indirect cost rates must also be assessed, cost element breakdowns can be obtained.

B. Technical Information Supporting Offers

Agencies have frequently required the submission of technical proposals as a major element of the information required for evaluation without making it clear whether the information in the proposal was to be used to evaluate offers or the capability of the offeror. However, it is good practice to distinguish these two types of technical proposals. The use of these proposals as a means of obtaining information to evaluate offeror capability will be discussed below. This section discusses the use of the technical proposal as a means of obtaining information to support the validity of technical offers.

When the agency solicits technical offers in addition to the price or cost offers, it must determine whether the offers will be understandable without explanation or whether they will need to be explained. For example, if the technical offers are merely to state what commercial products will be supplied to meet the contract requirements, the agency may need no information to assess the value of the offered products (if their characteristics are well known). Alternatively, available product literature may be all that is required. See FAR 12.205, which states:

> (a) Where technical information is necessary for evaluation of offers, agencies should, as part of market research, review existing product literature generally available in the industry to determine its adequacy for purposes of evaluation. If adequate, contracting officers shall request existing product literature from offerors of commercial items in lieu of unique technical proposals.

In contrast, if the technical offer is the design of a weapon system or a building, the agency may need technical information to assess the technical offer. In such cases the agency should call for a technical proposal providing all technical information necessary for the agency technical personnel to evaluate the risks that the offered product or building entails.

C. Capability Information

In almost all procurements the agency will assess the capability of the offerors as one of the evaluation factors. The information necessary to make this assessment will depend on the evaluation factors used and will be tailored to that factor. The major issues are found in obtaining information on past performance and experience and in demonstrating an understanding of the work.

1. Past Performance and Experience

Past performance information is obtained from two sources — agency data banks and references of agencies and companies for whom the offeror has previously worked. FAR 42.1502(a) requires agencies to compile data evaluating the contractor's performance on all contracts over $1 million, but this requirement has not been fully implemented. FAR 42.1503(e) limits the retention and use of the information to three years after the completion of contract performance. Under this regulation, contractors are given a minimum of 30 days to submit comments, rebut statements, or provide additional information. The completed evaluated information cannot be released to other than government personnel and the contractor whose performance is being evaluated during the period the information is being used for source selection purposes. It is generally believed that information that has been carefully reviewed by the contractor is more reliable than less formally developed information.

The earliest system of collecting performance information on contractors is the current system applicable to all construction contracts over $650,000, FAR 42.1502(e), and all architect-engineer contracts over $30,000, FAR 42.1502(f). These systems were all incorporated into the FAR in 1984. The Air Force adopted a system in 1988 called the Contractor Performance Assessment Reporting System (CPARS) to assess performance risk on current systems acquisitions greater than $5 million, AFSC Regulation 800-53, Aug. 11, 1988. CPARS is now used by most military services and is available on-line at www.defenselink.mil/dbt/cse_cpars.html. It is now implemented by the DOD Contractor Performance Assessment Reporting System (CPARS) Policy Guide, February 2009 (http://www.cpars.csd.disa.mil/cparsfiles/pdfs/DoD-CPARS-Guide.pdf). It rates contractor performance in one of the following categories:

Rating	Definition	Note
Dark Blue/Exceptional	Performance meets contractual requirements and exceeds many to the Government's benefit. The contractual performance of the element or sub-element being assessed was accomplished with few minor problems for which corrective actions taken by the contractor was highly effective.	To justify an Exceptional rating, identify multiple significant events and state how they were of benefit to the Government. A singular benefit, however, could be of such magnitude that it alone constitutes an Exceptional rating. Also, there should have been NO significant weaknesses identified.
Purple/Very Good	Performance meets contractual requirements and exceeds some to the Government's benefit. The contractual performance of the element or sub-element being assessed was accomplished with some minor problems for which corrective actions taken by the contractor was effective.	To justify a Very Good rating, identify a significant event and state how it was a benefit to the Government. There should have been no significant weaknesses identified.

Rating	Definition	Note
Green/Satisfactory	Performance meets contractual requirements. The contractual performance of the element or sub-element contains some minor problems for which corrective actions taken by the contractor appear or were satisfactory.	To justify a Satisfactory rating, there should have been only minor problems, or major problems the contractor recovered from without impact to the contract. There should have been NO significant weaknesses identified. Per DOD policy, a fundamental principle of assigning ratings is that contractors will not be assessed a rating lower than Satisfactory solely for not performing beyond the requirements of the contract.
Yellow/Marginal	Performance does not meet some contractual requirements. The contractual performance of the element or sub-element being assessed reflects a serious problem for which the contractor has not yet identified corrective actions. The contractor's proposed actions appear only marginally effective or were not fully implemented.	To justify Marginal performance, identify a significant event in each category that the contractor had trouble overcoming and state how it impacted the Government. A Marginal rating should be supported by referencing the management tool that notified the contractor of the contractual deficiency (e.g., management, quality, safety, or environmental deficiency report or letter).
Red/Unsatisfactory	Performance does not meet most contractual requirements and recovery is not likely in a timely manner. The contractual performance of the element or sub-element contains a serious problem(s) for which the contractor's corrective actions appear or were ineffective.	To justify an Unsatisfactory rating, identify multiple significant events in each category that the contractor had trouble overcoming and state how it impacted the Government. A singular problem, however, could be of such serious magnitude that it alone constitutes an unsatisfactory rating. An Unsatisfactory rating should be supported by referencing the management tools used to notify the contractor of the contractual deficiencies (e.g., management, quality, safety, or environmental deficiency reports, or letters).

The data collected are submitted to the contractor for review and comment before being entered into the system. Thereafter, evaluators use the data in accordance with their relevance to each specific procurement. The GAO has upheld the use of this system, *Rockwell Int'l Corp.*, Comp. Gen. Dec. B-261953.2, 96-1 CPD ¶ 34; *Questech, Inc.*, Comp. Gen. Dec. B-236028, 89-2 CPD ¶ 407; *Pan Am World Servs., Inc.*, Comp. Gen. Dec. B-235976, 89-1 CPD ¶ 283.

Because of the incomplete nature of agency data banks, data on past performance will have to be obtained from each offeror in most procurements. This will normally entail the obtaining of information on a specified number of recent contracts where the offeror has performed similar types of work. Generally, agencies request the names of key people that can be called as references and data as to the work done on the contract and problems encountered in its performance. See FAR 15.305(a)(2)(ii), stating:

> The solicitation shall describe the approach for evaluating past performance, including evaluating offerors with no relevant performance history, and shall provide offerors an opportunity to identify past or current contracts (including Federal, State, and local government and private) for efforts similar to the Government requirement. The solicitation shall also authorize offerors to provide information on problems encountered on the identified contracts and the offeror corrective actions..

Experience data can be obtained in the same manner as past performance information. Such information will focus on obtaining a sufficient description of the work performed on prior contracts to permit the agency to evaluate the degree of similarity of that work to the work called for by the instant procurement.

2. Understanding the Work

When an agency has decided to assess the capability of the offerors by assessing their understanding of the work, there are two ways to obtain the information — by calling for a written technical proposal or by scheduling oral presentations.

a. Technical and/or Management Proposals

As discussed earlier, agencies have commonly decided that each offeror should submit a "technical proposal" and/or a "management proposal" stating how it will perform each element of the work. This essay is then scored by technical evaluators to assess the offeror's understanding of the work. The reading and scoring of these proposals has added to the time required to conduct the competitive source selection, yet there is little indication that the scores achieved in this assessment are a very accurate indication of the offeror's capability to perform the contract. One reason for this imprecision is that these technical proposals can be written by professional proposal writers rather than by the personnel that will actually perform the work. Another problem is that the evaluation of these proposals is highly judgmental and may depend on the offeror's use of key terms or key concepts that are favored by the evaluators. As a result of these deficiencies, a number of agencies have decided that obtaining such technical proposals is not a valid means of assessing capability.

When such proposals are required, the RFP should contain very clear guidance on the information to be included and the format of the proposals. Minimal guidance is contained in FAR 15.204-5(b) as follows:

> Prospective offerors or respondents may be instructed to submit proposals or information in a specific format or severable parts to facilitate evaluation. The instructions may specify further organization of proposal or response parts, such as —
>
> (1) Administrative;
>
> (2) Management;
>
> (3) Technical;
>
> (4) Past performance; . . .

b. Oral Presentations

An alternative, and superior, way to assess understanding of the work is to schedule an oral presentation where the agency evaluators can discuss the performance of the contract with the key members of the offeror's staff that will be responsible for successful performance. Agencies began using oral presentations in lieu of technical proposals in the early 1990s and guidance on these presentations was included in the FAR Part 15 rewrite. See FAR 15.102, providing the following guidance on this technique:

> (a) Oral presentations by offerors as requested by the Government may substitute for, or augment, written information. Use of oral presentations as a substitute for portions of a proposal can be effective in streamlining the source selection process. Oral presentations may occur at any time in the acquisition process, and are subject to the same restrictions as written information, regarding timing (see 15.208) and content (see 15.306). Oral presentations provide an opportunity for dialogue among the parties. Pre-recorded videotaped presentations that lack real-time interactive dialogue are not considered oral presentations for the purposes of this section, although they may be included in offeror submissions, when appropriate.
>
> (b) The solicitation may require each offeror to submit part of its proposal through oral presentations. However, certifications, representations, and a signed offer sheet (including any exceptions to the Government's terms and conditions) shall be submitted in writing.
>
> (c) Information pertaining to areas such as an offeror's capability, past performance, work plans or approaches, staffing resources, transition plans, or sample tasks

(or other types of tests) may be suitable for oral presentations. In deciding what information to obtain through an oral presentation, consider the following:

> (1) The Government's ability to adequately evaluate the information;

> (2) The need to incorporate any information into the resultant contract;

> (3) The impact on the efficiency of the acquisition; and

> (4) The impact (including cost) on small businesses. In considering the costs of oral presentations, contracting officers should also consider alternatives to on-site oral presentations (e.g., teleconferencing, video teleconferencing).

When an agency decides to assess understanding of the work through an oral presentation in lieu of a technical proposal, it must decide on the time and format of the presentation.

FAR 15.102 provides detailed guidance on obtaining information, but not offers, through this process. This regulatory provision for obtaining information through the presentation process is consistent with prior practice. See *Intermagnetics Gen. Corp.*, Comp. Gen. Dec. B-255741.2, 94-1 CPD ¶ 302, holding that while an agency may limit its evaluation to information contained in written submissions, it also may decide to use other information, including that obtained in oral presentations:

> An agency may properly limit its evaluation to information contained in the four corners of a proposal, and [the protester] cites decisions in which we have denied protests alleging that the contracting agency should have used information from other sources, such as a pre-award survey, as a substitute for information that the solicitation directed offerors to include in their proposal. *See, e.g., Numax Elecs. Inc.*, B-210266, May 3, 1983, 83-1 CPD ¶ 470. [The protester] is also correct in noting that we have denied protests where the protester complained that the agency erred in not considering orally discussed changes to the protester's proposal, where the protester did not confirm the changes by incorporating them in its BAFO. *See, e.g., Recon Optical, Inc.*, B-232125, Dec. 1, 1988, 88-2 CPD ¶ 544.

> These decisions are not inconsistent with our denial of [the protester's] protest; they stand for the proposition that offerors act at their peril when they fail to include within the four corners of their proposals information required by the solicitation or requested by the agency during discussions, and that such proposals may properly be rejected. *See Abacus Enters.*, B-248969, Oct. 13, 1992, 92-2 CPD ¶ 242. However, we have also consistently held that, in evaluating proposals, contracting agencies may consider any evidence, even if that evidence is entirely outside the proposal (and, indeed, even if it contradicts statements in the proposal), so long as the use of the extrinsic evidence is consistent with established procurement practice. *See, e.g., Western Medical Personnel, Inc.*, 66 Comp. Gen. 699 (1987), 87-2 CPD ¶ 310; *AAA Eng'g & Drafting, Inc.*, B-250323, Jan. 26, 1993, 93-1 CPD ¶ 287.

See also *NW Ayer, Inc.*, Comp. Gen. Dec. B-248654, 92-2 CPD ¶ 154; and *Palmer Brown Cos.*, 70 Comp. Gen. 667 (B-243544), 91-2 CPD ¶ 134. In *Labat-Anderson, Inc.*, 71 Comp. Gen. 252 (B-246071), 92-1 CPD ¶ 193, the oral presentation resulted in a determination that the offeror lacked capability as it also did in *ARTEL, Inc.*, Comp. Gen. Dec. B-248478, 92-2 CPD ¶ 120, where the agency concluded from an oral presentation that there were serious doubts as to the quality and availability of the offeror's key personnel.

The most important part of an oral presentation is the dialog that occurs between the government technical personnel and the contractor's personnel that will be performing the contract. The present regulations make it clear that agency officials may ask questions and seek further detail during the oral presentation and this is consistent with prior decisions, *NAHB Research Found., Inc.*, Comp. Gen. Dec. B-219344, 85-2 CPD ¶ 248 (aggressive questioning permissible). However, both the Court of Federal Claims and the GAO have rejected protests that the agency did not use the oral presentation to obtain full information on the capability of an offeror. See *Bean Stuyvesant, L.L.C. v. United States*, 48 Fed. Cl. 303 (2000) (offeror properly downgraded for not discussing an issue – with no agency effort to raise the issue in the dialog); *Oceaneering Int'l, Inc.*, Comp. Gen. Dec. B-287325, 2001 CPD ¶ 95 (agency didn't raise omitted issue with offeror). Agencies that conduct oral presentations in this manner lose the full benefit of the technique.

Agencies may adopt reasonable rules governing the nature of the presentations, including limitations on the length and nature of the presentations, *American Sys. Corp.*, 68 Comp. Gen. 475 (B-234449), 89-1 CPD ¶ 537. They may also require that offerors meet mandatory requirements in an RFP before being eligible to make an oral presentation, *Inte-Great Corp.*, Comp. Gen. Dec. B-272780, 96-2 CPD ¶ 159. Some agencies have followed the questionable practice of requiring offerors to submit the slides that they will use in the oral presentation at the time the proposal is submitted. See *KSEND v. United States*, 69 Fed. Cl. 103 (2005), agreeing that an offeror that did not meet this requirement was properly dropped from the procurement. Compare *RGII Techs., Inc.*, Comp. Gen. Dec. B-278352.3, 98-1 CPD ¶ 130, where the GAO held that the slides were not subject to the late proposal rule when an offeror had submitted the slides late but copies had come with the written proposal.

Agencies may either preclude or permit discussions during the oral presentation, FAR 15.102(d)(6). However, if discussions occur, the agency must comply with the rules governing negotiations with all offerors in the competitive range, FAR 15.102(g). The GAO has not yet ruled that discussions occurred during an oral presentation. See *General Physics Federal Sys., Inc.*, Comp. Gen. Dec. B-275934, 97-1 CPD ¶ 171, where no ruling on this issue was made because there was no prejudice to the protester when the agency sought information on the commitment of proposed key personnel from all the offerors during the oral presentations. See also *Telestar Corp.*, Comp. Gen. Dec. B-275855, 97-1 CPD ¶ 150, finding that no discussions had occurred during an oral presentation; and *Development Alternatives, Inc.*, Comp. Gen. Dec. B-279920, 98-2 CPD ¶ 54, holding that requesting additional details concerning information in a proposal during an oral presentation did not constitute discussions. Compare *Global Analytic Information Tech. Servs., Inc.*, Comp. Gen. Dec. B-298840.2, 2007 CPD ¶ 57, holding that allowing an offeror to submit revised pricing *after* an oral presentation was a discussion. In *Sierra Military Health Servs., Inc.*, Comp. Gen. Dec. B-292780, 2004 CPD ¶ 55, GAO stated the rule as follows:

> The FAR generally anticipates "dialogue among the parties" in the course of an oral presentation, FAR § 15.102(a), and we see nothing improper in agency personnel expressing their view about vendors' quotations or proposals, in addition to listening to the vendors' presentations, during those sessions. Once the agency personnel begin speaking, rather than merely listening, in those sessions, however, that dialogue may constitute discussions. As we have long held, the acid test for deciding whether an agency has engaged in discussions is whether the agency has provided an opportunity for quotations or proposals to be revised or modified. *See, e.g., TDS, Inc.*, B-292674, Nov. 12, 2003, 2003 CPD ¶ 204 at 6; *Priority One Servs., Inc.*, B-288836, B-288836.2, Dec. 17, 2001, 2002 CPD ¶ 79 at 5. Accordingly, where agency personnel comment on, or raise substantive questions or concerns about, vendors' quotations or proposals in the course of an oral presentation, and either simultaneously or subsequently afford the vendors an opportunity to make revisions in light of the agency personnel's comments and concerns, discussions have occurred. *TDS, Inc., supra*, at 6; see FAR § 15.102(g).

D. Organizational Conflicts of Interest

FAR 9.504 requires that contracting officers identify potential organizational conflicts of interest (OCIs) before issuing an RFP, as follows:

> (a) Using the general rules, procedures, and examples in this subpart, contracting officers shall analyze planned acquisitions in order to —
>
>> (1) Identify and evaluate potential organizational conflicts of interest as early in the acquisition process as possible; and
>>
>> (2) Avoid, neutralize, or mitigate significant potential conflicts before contract award.
>
> (b) Contracting officers should obtain the advice of counsel and the assistance of appropriate technical specialists in evaluating potential conflicts and in developing any necessary solicitation provisions and contract clauses (see 9.506).
>
> (c) Before issuing a solicitation for a contract that may involve a significant potential conflict, the contracting officer shall recommend to the head of the contracting activity a course of action for resolving the conflict (see 9.506).

In addition, FAR 9.507-1 requires the inclusion of a solicitation provision in RFPs when the contracting officer determines that there is the possibility of an OCI:

As indicated in the general rules in 9.505, significant potential organizational conflicts of interest are normally resolved by imposing some restraint, appropriate to the nature of the conflict, upon the contractor's eligibility for future contracts or subcontracts. Therefore, affected solicitations shall contain a provision that —

> (a) Invites offerors' attention to this subpart;

> (b) States the nature of the potential conflict as seen by the contracting officer;

> (c) States the nature of the proposed restraint upon future contractor activities; and

> (d) Depending on the nature of the acquisition, states whether or not the terms of any proposed clause and the application of this subpart to the contract are subject to negotiation.

There is no standard solicitation provision in the FAR for this purpose.

If the contracting officer determines that a potential OCI can be avoided by the imposition of a restraint on the future conduct of the contractor, FAR 9.507-2 requires the use of both a solicitation provision and a contract clause:

> (a) If, as a condition of award, the contractor's eligibility for future prime contract or subcontract awards will be restricted or the contractor must agree to some other restraint, the solicitation shall contain a proposed clause that specifies both the nature and duration of the proposed restraint. The contracting officer shall include the clause in the contract, first negotiating the clause's final terms with the successful offeror, if it is appropriate to do so (see 9.508-1(d) of this subsection).

> (b) The restraint imposed by a clause shall be limited to a fixed term of reasonable duration, sufficient to avoid the circumstance of unfair competitive advantage or potential bias. This period varies. It might end, for example, when the first production contract using the contractor's specifications or work statement is awarded, or it might extend through the entire life of a system for which the contractor has performed systems engineering and technical direction. In every case, the restriction shall specify termination by a specific date or upon the occurrence of an identifiable event.

The FAR contains no solicitation provisions or clauses for this purpose. See, however, DEAR 952.209-72, containing the following required clause for contracts for advisory and assistance services:

> Organizational Conflicts of Interest (June 1997)

> (a) *Purpose.* The purpose of this clause is to ensure that the contractor (1) is not biased because of its financial, contractual, organizational, or other interests which relate to the work under this contract, and (2) does not obtain any unfair competitive advantage over other parties by virtue of its performance of this contract.

(b) *Scope.* The restrictions described herein shall apply to performance or participation by the contractor and any of its affiliates or their successors in interest (hereinafter collectively referred to as "contractor") in the activities covered by this clause as a prime contractor, subcontractor, cosponsor, joint venturer, consultant, or in any similar capacity. For the purpose of this clause, affiliation occurs when a business concern is controlled by or has the power to control another or when a third party has the power to control both.

(1) Use of Contractor's Work Product. (i) The contractor shall be ineligible to participate in any capacity in Department contracts, subcontracts, or proposals therefor (solicited and unsolicited) which stem directly from the contractor's performance of work under this contract for a period of (Contracting Officer see DEAR 9.507-2 and enter specific term) years after the completion of this contract. Furthermore, unless so directed in writing by the contracting officer, the Contractor shall not perform any advisory and assistance services work under this contract on any of its products or services or the products or services of another firm if the contractor is or has been substantially involved in their development or marketing. Nothing in this subparagraph shall preclude the contractor from competing for follow-on contracts for advisory and assistance services.

(ii) If, under this contract, the contractor prepares a complete or essentially complete statement of work or specifications to be used in competitive acquisitions, the contractor shall be ineligible to perform or participate in any capacity in any contractual effort which is based on such statement of work or specifications. The contractor shall not incorporate its products or services in such statement of work or specifications unless so directed in writing by the contracting officer, in which case the restriction in this subparagraph shall not apply.

(iii) Nothing in this paragraph shall preclude the contractor from offering or selling its standard and commercial items to the Government.

(2) Access to and use of information. (i) If the contractor, in the performance of this contract, obtains access to information, such as Department plans, policies, reports, studies, financial plans, internal data protected by the Privacy Act of 1974 (5 U.S.C. 552a), or data which has not been released or otherwise made available to the public, the contractor agrees that without prior written approval of the contracting officer it shall not:

(A) use such information for any private purpose unless the information has been released or otherwise made available to the public;

(B) compete for work for the Department based on such information for a period of six (6) months after either the completion of this contract or until such information is released or otherwise made available to the public, whichever is first;

(C) submit an unsolicited proposal to the Government which is based on such information until one year after such information is released or otherwise made available to the public; and

(D) release such information unless such information has previously been released or otherwise made available to the public by the Department.

(ii) In addition, the contractor agrees that to the extent it receives or is given access to proprietary data, data protected by the Privacy Act of 1974 (5 U.S.C. 552a), or other confidential or privileged technical, business, or financial information under this contract, it shall treat such information in accordance with any restrictions imposed on such information.

(iii) The contractor may use technical data it first produces under this contract for its private purposes consistent with paragraphs (b)(2)(i) (A) and (D) of this clause and the patent, rights in data, and security provisions of this contract.

(c) *Disclosure after award.* (1) The contractor agrees that, if changes, including additions, to the facts disclosed by it prior to award of this contract, occur during the performance of this contract, it shall make an immediate and full disclosure of such changes in writing to the contracting officer. Such disclosure may include a description of any action which the contractor has taken or proposes to take to avoid, neutralize, or mitigate any resulting conflict of interest. The Department may, however, terminate the contract for convenience if it deems such termination to be in the best interest of the Government.

(2) In the event that the contractor was aware of facts required to be disclosed or the existence of an actual or potential organizational conflict of interest and did not disclose such facts or such conflict of interest to the contracting officer, DOE may terminate this contract for default.

(d) *Remedies.* For breach of any of the above restrictions or for nondisclosure or misrepresentation of any facts required to be disclosed concerning this contract, including the existence of an actual or potential organizational conflict of interest at the time of or after award, the Government may terminate the contract for default, disqualify the contractor from subsequent related contractual efforts, and pursue such other remedies as may be permitted by law or this contract.

(e) *Waiver.* Requests for waiver under this clause shall be directed in writing to the contracting officer and shall include a full description of the requested waiver and the reasons in support thereof. If it is determined to be in the best interests of the Government, the contracting officer may grant such a waiver in writing.

See Chapter 4 for a complete discussion of the types of OCI and the restraints that have been found to be effective in mitigating the effects of OCIs.

CHAPTER 3

SOLICITING PROPOSALS

The aim of the solicitation process is to communicate an agency's needs to prospective offerors in such a manner as to provide for an efficient and fair competition so that the government's needs can be satisfied in a timely fashion and at a reasonable cost. Early notice of an agency's intent to procure articles or services benefits the government by giving potential offerors sufficient time to intelligently prepare their proposals and exercise their business judgment. The first required step in the process is the issuance of a procurement notice that gives advance notice that proposals will be requested. Thereafter, proposals, consisting of offers and information, are solicited through the issuance of a document called the request for proposals (RFP). FAR 15.203(a) sets forth the functions of RFPs and prescribes their minimum content as follows:

> Requests for proposals (RFPs) are used in negotiated acquisitions to communicate Government requirements to prospective contractors and to solicit proposals. RFPs for competitive acquisitions shall, at a minimum, describe the —
>
> (1) Government's requirement;
>
> (2) Anticipated terms and conditions that will apply to the contract:
>
> > (i) The solicitation may authorize offerors to propose alternative terms and conditions, including the contract line item number (CLIN) structure; and
> >
> > (ii) When alternative CLIN structures are permitted, the evaluation approach should consider the potential impact on other terms and conditions or the requirement (e.g., place of performance or payment and funding requirements) (see 15.206)
>
> (3) Information required to be in the offeror's proposal; and
>
> (4) Factors and significant subfactors that will be used to evaluate the proposal and their relative importance.

Clarity and completeness of the RFP are key factors in the competitive negotiation process. Prospective offerors must be able to understand what work is desired, what information is sought and how the competition will be conducted. Failure to issue an accurate and complete RFP will most likely result in less advantageous offers, the necessity for changes, delays, and the generation of protest costs.

I. FORMAT AND CONTENT OF THE RFP

RFPs are written to permit all offerors to compete on an equal basis, while preserving the flexibility of a contracting agency to allow offerors to propose different ways of satisfying its needs. They generally contain all the terms and conditions that the agency has decided to use in the contract so that contractual offers may be submitted in response to the RFP. They also lay the ground rules of the competition, including the information to be supplied by offerors and the closing date for the receipt of proposals.

FAR 15.204 requires that RFPs be prepared using the Uniform Contract Format but states that this format need not be used for:

(a) Construction and architect-engineer contracts (see part 36).

(b) Subsistence contracts.

(c) Supplies or services contracts requiring special contract formats prescribed elsewhere in this part that are inconsistent with the uniform format.

(d) Letter requests for proposals (see 15.203(e)).

(e) Contracts exempted by the agency head or designee.

The contract provisions in Parts I, II, and III of the Uniform Contract Format can constitute a complete contract except for the prices or costs and fee in Part B, which the offeror must fill out when the proposal is submitted. Thus, as in the case of sealed bidding, the government frequently writes an entire contract in the course of preparing the RFP. However, in negotiated procurement the RFP may solicit or permit additional or alternative offers that will vary the terms of the RFP and call for preparation of a final contract after negotiation has occurred. The Uniform Contract Format is specified in FAR 15.204-1(b) as follows:

Uniform Contract Format	
Part I — The Schedule	
Section	**Title**
A	Solicitation/contract form
B	Supplies or services and prices/costs
C	Description/specifications/statement of work
D	Packaging and marking
E	Inspection and acceptance
F	Deliveries or performance
G	Contract administration data
H	Special contract requirements

Part II Contract Clauses	
I	Contract clauses
Part III — List of Documents, Exhibits, and Other Attachments	
J	List of attachments
Part IV — Representations and Instructions	
K	Representations, certifications, and other statements of offerors or respondents
L	Instructions, conditions, and notices to offerors or respondents
M	Evaluation factors for award

This section of the chapter discusses the detailed elements of the RFP as set forth in each section of the format.

A. Solicitation Forms

FAR 15.204-2(a) provides that Standard Form 33 (Solicitation, Offer and Award), FAR 53.301-33, or Optional Form 308 (Solicitation and Offer — Negotiated Acquisition), FAR 53.302-308, may be used as the cover sheet for the RFP and will constitute Section A of the contract. See **Figure 3-1** and **Figure 3-2**, respectively. These forms contain a significant amount of key information, as well as blocks for the signatures of the prospective contractor. In addition, SF 33 contains a block for the signature of the contracting officer, which permits it to be used as an award form. SF 33 should be used when the contracting officer anticipates that award may be made on the basis of the solicitation without any changes. If changes or additions to the terms and conditions in the solicitation are anticipated, OF 308 can be used as the solicitation cover sheet — with OF 307 being used to award the contract. If these forms are not used, the information that they contain must be included in the RFP, FAR 15.204-2(a)(2).

The most important information in these forms is the time by which the proposal must be submitted and the requirement for signature of the proposal by an authorized representative of the contractor. The RFP must contain a specific closing date for the receipt of proposals. Offerors must be given sufficient time to submit proposals. FAR 5.203(c) implements the requirements of 41 U.S.C. § 416(a)(3)(iii) by stating that agencies must allow at least 30 days' response time from the date of issuance of the solicitation on all procurements that are over the simplified acquisition threshold and are not for commercial items. Protests of insufficient proposal preparation time are considered on the basis of all the facts pertaining to the procurement, but protesters must present specific facts as to why the time given is insufficient, *Cajar Defense Support Co.*, Comp. Gen. Dec. B-236892, 90-2 CPD ¶ 100, *recons. denied*, Comp. Gen. Dec. B-240477.2, 90-2 CPD ¶ 215. See *Control Data*

Corp., Comp. Gen. Dec. B-235737, 89-2 CPD ¶ 304, where a protest that the agency allowed insufficient time for preparation of proposals was denied because other offerors had not protested and several proposals had been submitted.

SOLICITATION, OFFER AND AWARD	1. THIS CONTRACT IS A RATED ORDER UNDER DPAS (15 CFR 7900)		RATING	PAGE	OF	PAGES

2. CONTRACT NUMBER	3. SOLICITATION NUMBER	4. TYPE OF SOLICITATION	5. DATE ISSUED	6. REQUISITION/PURCHASE NUMBER
		☐ SEALED BID (IFB) ☐ NEGOTIATED (RFP)		

7. ISSUED BY	CODE	8. ADDRESS OFFER TO *(If other than item 7)*

NOTE: In sealed bid solicitations "offer" and "offeror" mean "bid" and "bidder".

SOLICITATION

9. Sealed offers in original and _____ copies for furnishing the supplies or services in the Schedule will be received at the place specified in item 8, or if hand carried, in the depository located in _____ until _____ local time _____
(Hour)   (Date)

CAUTION - LATE Submissions, Modifications, and Withdrawals: See Section L, Provision No. 52.214-7 or 52.215-1. All offers are subject to all terms and conditions contained in this solicitation.

10. FOR INFORMATION CALL:	A. NAME	B. TELEPHONE *(NO COLLECT CALLS)*			C. E-MAIL ADDRESS
		AREA CODE	NUMBER	EXT.	

11. TABLE OF CONTENTS

(X)	SEC.	DESCRIPTION	PAGE(S)	(X)	SEC.	DESCRIPTION	PAGE(S)
		PART I - THE SCHEDULE				PART II - CONTRACT CLAUSES	
	A	SOLICITATION/CONTRACT FORM			I	CONTRACT CLAUSES	
	B	SUPPLIES OR SERVICES AND PRICES/COSTS				PART III - LIST OF DOCUMENTS, EXHIBITS AND OTHER ATTACH.	
	C	DESCRIPTION/SPECS./WORK STATEMENT			J	LIST OF ATTACHMENTS	
	D	PACKAGING AND MARKING				PART IV - REPRESENTATIONS AND INSTRUCTIONS	
	E	INSPECTION AND ACCEPTANCE			K	REPRESENTATIONS, CERTIFICATIONS AND OTHER STATEMENTS OF OFFERORS	
	F	DELIVERIES OR PERFORMANCE					
	G	CONTRACT ADMINISTRATION DATA			L	INSTRS., CONDS., AND NOTICES TO OFFERORS	
	H	SPECIAL CONTRACT REQUIREMENTS			M	EVALUATION FACTORS FOR AWARD	

OFFER *(Must be fully completed by offeror)*

NOTE: Item 12 does not apply if the solicitation includes the provisions at 52.214-16, Minimum Bid Acceptance Period.

12. In compliance with the above, the undersigned agrees, if this offer is accepted within _____ calendar days *(60 calendar days unless a different period is inserted by the offeror)* from the date for receipt of offers specified above, to furnish any or all items upon which prices are offered at the set opposite each item, delivered at the designated point(s), within the time specified in the schedule.

13. DISCOUNT FOR PROMPT PAYMENT *(See Section I, Clause No. 52.232-8)*	10 CALENDAR DAYS (%)	20 CALENDAR DAYS (%)	30 CALENDAR DAYS (%)	CALENDAR DAYS(%)

14. ACKNOWLEDGMENT OF AMENDMENTS *(The offeror acknowledges receipt of amendments to the SOLICITATION for offerors and related documents numbered and dated):*	AMENDMENT NO.	DATE	AMENDMENT NO.	DATE

15A. NAME AND ADDRESS OF OFFEROR	CODE	FACILITY	16. NAME AND THE TITLE OF PERSON AUTHORIZED TO SIGN OFFER *(Type or print)*

15B. TELEPHONE NUMBER			15C. CHECK IF REMITTANCE ADDRESS IS DIFFERENT FROM ABOVE - ENTER SUCH ADDRESS IN SCHEDULE.	17. SIGNATURE	18. OFFER DATE
AREA CODE	NUMBER	EXT.	☐		

AWARD *(To be completed by Government)*

19. ACCEPTED AS TO ITEMS	20. AMOUNT	21. ACCOUNTING AND APPROPRIATION

22. AUTHORITY FOR USING OTHER THAN FULL OPEN COMPETITION: ☐ 10 U.S.C. 2304 (c) ☐ 41 U.S.C. 253 (c)	23. SUBMIT INVOICES TO ADDRESS SHOWN IN *(4 copies unless otherwise specified)*	ITEM

24. ADMINISTERED BY *(If other than Item 7)*	25. PAYMENT WILL BE MADE BY	CODE

26. NAME OF CONTRACTING OFFICER *(Type or print)*	27. UNITED STATES OF AMERICA (Signature of Contracting Officer)	28. AWARD DATE

IMPORTANT - Award will be made on this Form, or on Standard Form 26, or by other authorized official written notice.

AUTHORIZED FOR LOCAL REPRODUCTION
Previous edition is unusable

STANDARD FORM 33 (REV,. 9-97)
Prescribed by GSA - Far (48 CFR) 53.214 (c)

Figure 3-1

SOLICITATION AND OFFER - NEGOTIATED ACQUISITION		PAGE	OF	PAGES

I. SOLICITATION

1. SOLICITATION NUMBER	2. DATE ISSUED	3. OFFERS DUE BY	4. OFFERS VALID FOR 60 DAYS UNLESS A DIFFERENT PERIOD IS ENTERED HERE

5. ISSUED BY	6. ADDRESS OFFER TO (If other than Item 5)

7. INFORMATION CALL (No collect calls)

A. NAME		B. TELEPHONE		C. E-MAIL ADDRESS
	AREA CODE	PHONE NUMBER		

8. BRIEF DESCRIPTION

9. TABLE OF CONTENTS

(X)	SEC.	DESCRIPTION	PAGE(S)	(X)	SEC.	DESCRIPTION	PAGE(S)
		PART I - THE SCHEDULE				PART II - CONTRACT CLAUSES	
	A	SOLICITATION/CONTRACT FORM			I	CONTRACT CLAUSES	
	B	SUPPLIES OR SERVICES AND PRICES/COSTS				PART III - LIST OF DOCUMENTS, EXHIBITS AND OTHER ATTACH.	
	C	DESCRIPTION/SPECS./WORK STATEMENT			J	LIST OF ATTACHMENTS	
	D	PACKAGING AND MARKING				PART IV - REPRESENTATIONS AND INSTRUCTIONS	
	E	INSPECTION AND ACCEPTANCE			K	REPRESENTATIONS, CERTIFICATIONS AND OTHER STATEMENTS OF OFFERORS	
	F	DELIVERIES OR PERFORMANCE					
	G	CONTRACT ADMINISTRATION DATA			L	INSTRS., CONDS., AND NOTICES TO OFFERORS	
	H	SPECIAL CONTRACT REQUIREMENTS			M	EVALUATION FACTORS FOR AWARD	

II. OFFER

The undersigned agrees to furnish and deliver the items or perform services to the extent states in this document for the consideration stated. The rights and obligations of the parties to the resultant contract shall be subject to and governed by this document and any documents attached or incorporated by reference.

10A. PERSONS AUTHORIZED TO NEGOTIATE	10B. TITLE	10C. TELEPHONE	
		AREA CODE	NUMBER

11. NAME AND ADDRESS OF OFFEROR	12A. SIGNATURE OF PERSON AUTHORIZED TO SIGN	
	12B. NAME OF SIGNER	
	12C. TITLE OF SIGNER	
	12D. DATE	12E. TELEPHONE
		AREA CODE / NUMBER

AUTHORIZED FOR LOCAL REPRODUCTION

OPTIONAL FORM 308 (9-97)
Prescribed by GSA - FAR (48 CFR) 53.215-1(f)

Figure 3-2

B. Contract Line Items

FAR 15.204-2(b) contains the following guidance on the information to be included in Section B of the RFP:

Include a brief description of the supplies or services; e.g., item number, national stock number/part number if applicable, nouns, nomenclature, and quantities. (This includes incidental deliverables such as manuals and reports.)

The purpose of this section is to give offerors a summary description of the contract requirements and provide a place for offerors to submit their proposed prices. Thus, the descriptions of the work in this section are very brief — with details left to Section C.

The number of line items is discretionary with the procuring agency. However, it is normal practice to include a separate line item whenever a different source of funds is used for the supplies or services being procured. This can result in fragmentation of the same work (such as a single product) into a number of line items in instances where the agency is buying that work for a number of different users or for different fiscal years.

There is a substantial variation in practice in setting forth line items for items such as manuals and other technical data. There is no guidance in the FAR on this issue, but DOD followed a practice for many years of providing that a contractor need not furnish data that was not listed on the Contract Data Requirements List, DD Form 1423, or called for by a contract clause required by the FAR or DFARS. While this practice is no longer stated in the DFARS, some DOD agencies continue to use a single line item for all data listed in DD Form 1423. Other agencies break out key data items, such as manuals and reports, as separate line items.

C. Specifications

Section C contains the detailed description of the work to be performed under the contract. Since decisions on how to write descriptions need to be made early in the procurement process, detailed guidance on writing work statements or specifications was included in Chapter 1. That section noted that the contract specification can be a detailed document that has evolved in an agency over a number of procurements or a new document written specifically for the procurement. In either case, the RFP must provide specific information to prospective offerors on the applicable specifications. However, the RFP need not actually contain the specifications except in certain situations. See FAR 11.201 for the following detailed guidance:

> (a) Solicitations citing requirements documents listed in the General Services Administration (GSA) Index of Federal Specifications, Standards and Commercial Item Descriptions, the DOD Streamlining and Standardization Information System (ASSIST), or other agency index shall identify each document's approval date and the dates of any applicable amendments and revisions. Do not use general identification references, such as "the issue in effect on the date of the solicitation." Contracting offices will not normally furnish these documents with the solicitation, except when —

(1) The requirements document must be furnished with the solicitation to enable prospective contractors to make a competent evaluation of the solicitation;

(2) In the judgment of the contracting officer, it would be impracticable for prospective contractors to obtain the documents in reasonable time to respond to the solicitation; or

(3) A prospective contractor requests a copy of a Government promulgated requirements document.

(b) Contracting offices shall clearly identify in the solicitation any pertinent documents not listed in the GSA Index of Federal Specifications, Standards and Commercial Item Descriptions or ASSIST. Such documents shall be furnished with the solicitation or specific instructions shall be furnished for obtaining or examining such documents.

(c) When documents refer to other documents, such references shall —

(1) Be restricted to documents, or appropriate portions of documents, that apply in the acquisition;

(2) Cite the extent of their applicability;

(3) Not conflict with other documents and provisions of the solicitation; and

(4) Identify all applicable first tier references.

(d)(1) The GSA Index of Federal Specifications, Standards and Commercial Item Descriptions, FPMR Part 101-29, may be purchased from the – General Services Administration, Federal Supply Service, Specifications Section, Suite 8100, 470 East L'Enfant Plaza, SW, Washington, DC 20407, Telephone (202) 619-8925.

(2) Most unclassified Defense specifications and standards may be downloaded from the following ASSIST websites:

(i) ASSIST (http://assist.daps.dla.mil).

(ii) Quick Search (http://assist.daps.dla.mil/quicksearch).

(iii) ASSISTdocs.com (http://assistdocs.com).

(3) Documents not available from ASSIST may be ordered from the Department of Defense Single Stock Point (DoDSSP) by – (i) Using the ASSIST Shopping Wizard (http://assist.daps.dla.mil/wizard);

(ii) Phoning the DoDSSP Customer Service Desk, (215) 697-2179, Mon-Fri, 0730 to 1600 EST; or

(iii) Ordering from DoDSSP, Building 4, Section D, 700 Robbins Avenue, Philadelphia, PA 19111-5094, Telephone (215) 697-2667/2179, Facsimile (215) 697-1462.

(4) The FIPS PUBS may be obtained from http://www.itl.nist.gov/fips-pubs/, or purchased from the Superintendent of Documents, U.S. Government Printing Office, Washington, DC 20402, Telephone (202) 512-1800, Facsimile (202) 512-2250; or National Technical Information Service (NTIS), 5285 Port Royal Road, Springfield, VA 22161, Telephone (703) 605-6000, Facsimile (703) 605-6900, Email: orders@ntis.gov.

(e) Agencies may purchase some nongovernment standards, including voluntary consensus standards, from the National Technical Information Service's Fedworld Information Network. Agencies may also obtain nongovernment standards from the standards developing organization responsible for the preparation, publication, or maintenance of the standard, or from an authorized document reseller. The National Institute of Standards and Technology can assist agencies in identifying sources for, and content of, nongovernment standards. DoD activities may obtain from the DoDSSP those nongovernment standards, including voluntary consensus standards, adopted for use by defense activities.

There are four mandatory solicitation provisions that inform potential offerors how to obtain the different types of specifications. See FAR 11.204 setting forth the following requirements:

(a) The contracting officer shall insert the provision at 52.211-1, Availability of Specifications Listed in the GSA Index of Federal Specifications, Standards and Commercial Item Descriptions, FPMR Part 101-29, in solicitations that cite specifications listed in the Index that are not furnished with the solicitation.

(b) The contracting officer shall insert the provision at 52.211-2, Availability of Specifications, Standards, and Data Item Descriptions Listed in the Acquisition Streamlining and Standardization Information System (ASSIST), in solicitations that cite specifications listed in the ASSIST that are not furnished with the solicitation.

(c) The contracting officer shall insert a provision substantially the same as the provision at 52.211-3, Availability of Specifications Not Listed in the GSA Index of Federal Specifications, Standards and Commercial Item Descriptions, in solicitations that cite specifications that are not listed in the Index and are not furnished with the solicitation, but may be obtained from a designated source.

(d) The contracting officer shall insert a provision substantially the same as the provision at 52.211-4, Availability for Examination of Specifications Not Listed in the GSA Index of Federal Specifications, Standards and Commercial Item Descriptions, in solicitations that cite specifications that are not listed in the Index and are available for examination at a specified location.

These provisions are intended to ensure that offerors can obtain specifications in a timely manner. For a case sustaining a protest due to an agency's failure to provide specifications properly, see *Pulse Elecs. Inc.*, Comp. Gen. Dec. B-244764, 91-2 CPD ¶ 468, where the GAO found that the Navy had improperly omitted information detailing the applicable revisions to military specifications and standards cited in the RFP, leaving offerors unable to prepare their proposals intelligently. Compare *Pulse Elecs., Inc.*, Comp. Gen. Dec. B-243769, 91-2 CPD ¶ 122, in which a similar protest by the same company was denied because the RFP in that procurement was not so complex as to require the inclusion of a Navy document. Offerors can be and have been awarded damages from the government due to reliance on misleading specifications and on RFPs that purposely omit pertinent information regarding contract performance. For a more detailed discussion of this topic, see Chapter 3 of Cibinic, Nagle & Nash, *Administration of Government Contracts* (4th ed. 2006).

D. Packaging and Marking

FAR 15.204-2(d) provides that Section D should contain packaging, packing, preservation, and marking provisions. Detailed guidance on this issue is left to agency regulations.

E. Inspection and Acceptance

Section E should contain the special clauses that the agency will use in inspecting and accepting the work. In most cases, the procuring agency will include the appropriate standard inspection clause from FAR 52.246, which includes the following clauses:

- -1   Contractor Inspection Requirements
- -2   Inspection of Supplies - Fixed-Price
- -3   Inspection of Supplies - Cost-Reimbursement
- -4   Inspection of Services - Fixed-Price
- -5   Inspection of Services - Cost-Reimbursement
- -6   Inspection - Time-and-Material and Labor-Hour
- -7   Inspection of Research and Development - Fixed-Price
- -8   Inspection of Research and Development - Cost-Reimbursement
- -9   Inspection of Research and Development (Short Form)
- -11   Higher-Level Contract Quality Requirement
- -12   Inspection of Construction
- -13   Inspection—Dismantling, Demolition, or Removal of Improvements
- -14   Inspection of Transportation
- -15   Certificate of Conformance

- -16   Responsibility for Supplies
- -17   Warranty of Supplies of a Noncomplex Nature
- -18   Warranty of Supplies of a Complex Nature
- -19   Warranty of Systems and Equipment under Performance Specifications or Design Criteria
- -20   Warranty of Services
- -21   Warranty of Construction
- -23   Limitation of Liability
- -24   Limitation of Liability - High-Value Items
- -25   Limitation of Liability-Services

FAR Subpart 46.2 contains detailed guidance on the selection of standard inspection clauses or other inspection clauses to minimize the costs to the government and utilize the contractor's inspection capabilities to the maximum extent, consistent with obtaining the necessary quality of work. FAR 46.201 contains the following general guidance:

(a) The contracting officer shall include in the solicitation and contract the appropriate quality requirements. The type and extent of contract quality requirements needed depends on the particular acquisition and may range from inspection at time of acceptance to a requirement for the contractor's implementation of a comprehensive program for controlling quality.

(b) As feasible, solicitations and contracts may provide for alternative, but substantially equivalent, inspection methods to obtain wide competition and low cost. The contracting officer may also authorize contractor-recommended alternatives when in the Government's interest and approved by the activity responsible for technical requirements.

(c) Although contracts generally make contractors responsible for performing inspection before tendering supplies to the Government, there are situations in which contracts will provide for specialized inspections to be performed solely by the Government. Among situations of this kind are —

(1) Tests that require use of specialized test equipment or facilities not ordinarily available in suppliers' plants or commercial laboratories (e.g., ballistic testing of ammunition, unusual environmental tests, and simulated service tests); and

(2) Contracts that require Government testing for first article approval (see Subpart 9.3).

(d) Except as otherwise specified by the contract, required contractor testing may be performed in the contractor's or subcontractor's laboratory or testing facility, or in any other laboratory or testing facility acceptable to the Government.

FAR 46.202 contains guidance on the types of quality assurance requirements that are used in government contracts. It states that, depending on the extent of quality assurance needed by the government for the acquisition involved, such requirements fall into four general categories: (1) commercial items where the government should rely on the contractor's existing system, (2) simplified acquisitions where the government should normally rely on the contractor to determine the level of inspection, (3) acquisitions using the standard requirement that the contractor have an inspection procedure acceptable to the government with reservation of the right of the government to also inspect the work, and (4) acquisitions of complex and critical items with higher-level contractor inspection requirements contained in specifications calling for additional documentation and verification of quality. FAR 46.203 then provides criteria for use of contract quality requirements:

> The extent of contract quality requirements, including contractor inspection, required under a contract shall usually be based upon the classification of the contract item (supply or service) as determined by its technical description, its complexity, and the criticality of its application.
>
> (a) *Technical description.* Contract items may be technically classified as—
>
> > (1) Commercial (described in commercial catalogs, drawings, or industrial standards); or
> >
> > (2) Military-Federal (described in Government drawings and specifications).
>
> (b) *Complexity.* (1) Complex items have quality characteristics, not wholly visible in the end item, for which contractual conformance must be established progressively through precise measurements, tests, and controls applied during purchasing, manufacturing, performance, assembly, and functional operation either as an individual item or in conjunction with other items.
>
> > (2) Noncomplex items have quality characteristics for which simple measurement and test of the end item are sufficient to determine conformance to contract requirements.
>
> (c) *Criticality.* (1) A critical application of an item is one in which the failure of the item could injure personnel or jeopardize a vital agency mission. A critical item may be either peculiar, meaning it has only one application, or common, meaning it has multiple applications.
>
> > (2) A noncritical application is any other application. Noncritical items may also be either peculiar or common.

F. Time and Place of Performance

Section F contains guidance on the time, place, and method of delivery or performance in accordance with FAR Subpart 11.4, which states:

11.401 General.

(a) The time of delivery or performance is an essential contract element and shall be clearly stated in solicitations. Contracting officers shall ensure that delivery or performance schedules are realistic and meet the requirements of the acquisition. Schedules that are unnecessarily short or difficult to attain —

(1) Tend to restrict competition,

(2) Are inconsistent with small business policies, and

(3) May result in higher contract prices.

(b) Solicitations shall, except when clearly unnecessary, inform bidders or offerors of the basis on which their bids or proposals will be evaluated with respect to time of delivery or performance.

(c) If timely delivery or performance is unusually important to the Government, liquidated damages clauses may be used.

*   *   *

12.403 Supplies and Services.

(a) The contracting officer may express contract delivery or performance schedules in terms of —

(1) Specific calendar dates;

(2) Specific periods from the date of the contract; i.e., from the date of award or acceptance by the Government, or from the date shown as the effective date of the contract;

(3) Specific periods from the date of receipt by the contractor of the notice of award or acceptance by the Government (including notice by receipt of contract document executed by the Government); or

(4) Specific time for delivery after receipt by the contractor of each individual order issued under the contract, as in indefinite delivery type contracts and GSA schedules.

(b) The time specified for contract performance should not be curtailed to the prejudice of the contractor because of delay by the Government in giving notice of award.

(c) If the delivery schedule is based on the date of the contract, the contracting officer shall mail or otherwise furnish to the contractor the contract, notice of award, acceptance of proposal, or other contract document not later than the date of the contract.

(d) If the delivery schedule is based on the date the contractor receives the notice of award, or if the delivery schedule is expressed in terms of specific calendar dates on the assumption that the notice of award will be received by a specified date, the contracting officer shall send the contract, notice of award, acceptance of proposal, or other contract document by certified mail, return receipt requested, or by any other method that will provide evidence of the date of receipt.

FAR 52.211-8 contains a number of alternate clauses that may be used in specifying the time of delivery as a firm contract requirement but permitting the offeror to propose earlier times of delivery. FAR 52.211-9 contains a number of alternate clauses that may be used in specifying desired and required times of delivery and permitting the offeror to propose alternate times of delivery. Paragraph (a) of all these clauses states that if the proposed delivery date is later than the specified or required delivery date, the offer "will be considered nonresponsive and rejected." This language applies only to sealed bid procurements and should be deleted from the clauses when they are used in negotiated procurements. In a negotiated procurement an offeror whose initial proposal does not comply with the required delivery schedules cannot receive award on the basis of its proposal but should still be considered for inclusion in the competitive range. Unlike sealed bid procurements, negotiated procurements permit giving offerors the opportunity to satisfy government requirements through discussions. Therefore, an offeror in a negotiated procurement that fails to comply with delivery times in its proposal should not be automatically labeled nonresponsive and rejected because this matter could easily be cleared up during discussions. See *Hollingsead Int'l*, Comp. Gen. Dec. B-227853, 87-2 CPD ¶ 372; *Xtek, Inc.*, Comp. Gen. Dec. 213166, 84-1 CPD ¶ 264; and *DPF Inc.*, Comp. Gen. Dec. B-180292, 74-1 CPD ¶ 303.

In some cases agencies use special "time of performance" clauses that make the time of performance, within a range, an evaluation factor. The GAO has sanctioned the use of time of performance as an evaluation factor, especially when the procurement is urgent. See *Shirley Constr. Corp.*, 70 Comp. Gen. 62 (B-240357), 90-2 CPD ¶ 380 (total time of performance one of four evaluation criteria); and *Hydroscience*, Comp. Gen. Dec. B-227989, 87-2 CPD ¶ 501 (offeror's proposal properly devalued due to uncertainty as to time of performance when swift performance was crucial).

FAR 52.211-10 contains mandatory clauses to be used in specifying the completion date for fixed-price construction contracts. FAR 52.211-11 and FAR 52.211-

12 contain liquidated damages clauses that may be used for various types of procurements.

G. Contract Administration Data

FAR 15.204-2(g) requires that Section G include accounting and appropriation data, as well as contract administration information or instructions other than those on the solicitation form. Standard Form 33 contains spaces for this data if it is simple. However, if the data is complex, it should be included in Section G. Optional Form 308 contains no spaces for this data.

Agencies that delegate contract administration functions to field offices should include this information in the solicitation. See FAR 42.202, which states:

(a) *Delegating functions.* As provided in agency procedures, contracting officers may delegate contract administration or specialized support services, either through interagency agreements or by direct request to the cognizant CAO listed in the Federal Directory of Contract Administration Services Components. The delegation should include —

(1) The name and address of the CAO designated to perform the administration (this information also shall be entered in the contract);

(2) Any special instructions, including any functions withheld or any specific authorization to perform functions listed in 42.302(b);

(3) A copy of the contract to be administered; and

(4) Copies of all contracting agency regulations or directives that are —

(i) Incorporated into the contract by reference; or

(ii) Otherwise necessary to administer the contract, unless copies have been provided previously.

(b) *Special instructions.* As necessary, the contracting officer also shall advise the contractor (and other activities as appropriate) of any functions withheld from or additional functions delegated to the CAO.

(c) *Delegating additional functions.* For individual contracts or groups of contracts, the contracting office may delegate to the CAO functions not listed in 42.302: *Provided* that —

(1) Prior coordination with the CAO ensures the availability of required resources;

(2) In the case of authority to issue orders under provisioning procedures in existing contracts and under basic ordering agreements for items and services identified in the schedule, the head of the contracting activity or designee approves the delegation; and

(3) The delegation does not require the CAO to undertake new or follow-on acquisitions.

(d) *Rescinding functions*. The contracting officer at the requesting agency may rescind or recall a delegation to administer a contract or perform a contract administration function, except for functions pertaining to cost accounting standards and negotiation of forward pricing rates and indirect cost rates (also see 42.003). The requesting agency must coordinate with the CAO to establish a reasonable transition period prior to rescinding or recalling the delegation.

(e) *Secondary delegations of contract administration*. (1) A CAO that has been delegated administration of a contract under paragraph (a) or (c) of this section, or a contracting office retaining contract administration, may request supporting contract administration from the CAO cognizant of the contractor location where performance of specific contract administration functions is required. The request shall —

(i) Be in writing;

(ii) Clearly state the specific functions to be performed; and

(iii) Be accompanied by a copy of pertinent contractual and other necessary documents.

(2) The prime contractor is responsible for managing its subcontracts. The CAO's review of subcontracts is normally limited to evaluating the prime contractor's management of the subcontracts (see Part 44). Therefore, supporting contract administration shall not be used for subcontracts unless —

(i) The Government otherwise would incur undue cost;

(ii) Successful completion of the prime contract is threatened; or

(iii) It is authorized under paragraph (f) of this section or elsewhere in this regulation.

(f) *Special surveillance*. For major system acquisitions (see Part 34), the contracting officer may designate certain high risk or critical subsystems or components for special surveillance in addition to requesting supporting contract administration. This surveillance shall be conducted in a manner consistent with the policy of requesting that the cognizant CAO perform contract administration functions at a contractor's facility (see 42.002).

The Department of Defense requires that most contracts be administered by the Defense Contract Management Agency. See DFARS 242.202 for a list of those contracts where DOD contracting activities may retain contract administration functions.

The FAR contains no guidance on specifying accounting and appropriations data. However, DFARS PGI 204.7107 requires contracting offices to use accounting classification reference numbers (ACRNs) in order to process certain contract data through the Military Standard Contract Administration Procedures (MILSCAP). MILSCAP uses the ACRNs to relate contract administration records to the long-line accounting classification used to obligate funds on the contract. NAPS 5232.792 repeats these requirements and adds that "accounting data shall also be shown on any change order or contract amendment to a contract that revises the accounting data for any item or increases or decreases the total amount of a contract."

H. Special Contract Requirements

FAR 15.204-2(h) provides that this section may contain any special contract requirements that are not contained in Section I. Although this gives procuring agencies almost total discretion on how to use this section, many agencies include clauses that are specially written for the procurement. When this is done, standard agency clauses will be included in Section I. This is a useful technique because it alerts offerors to specially written clauses that should be given close attention.

I. Contract Clauses

Section I contains most of the standard clauses for the proposed contract. Standard contract clauses are contained in FAR Part 52. The matrix in FAR 52.301 gives guidance on the clauses to be incorporated into the various types of contracts. Clauses are either (1) required, (2) required when applicable, or (3) optional. The matrix includes clauses for the following types of contracts:

Fixed-Price Supply

Cost-Reimbursement Supply

Fixed-Price Research and Development

Cost-Reimbursement Research and Development

Fixed-Price Service

Cost-Reimbursement Service

Fixed-Price Construction

Cost-Reimbursement Construction

Time-and-Materials/Labor-Hours

Leasing of Motor Vehicles

Communication Services

Dismantling, Demolition, or Removal of Improvements

Architect-Engineering

Facilities

Indefinite-Delivery

Transportation

Simplified Acquisition Procedures

Utility Services

Commercial Items

FAR 52.102(a) requires incorporation of clauses by reference to the maximum practical extent even if they —

(1) Are used with one or more alternates or on an optional basis;

(2) Are prescribed on a "substantially as follows" or "substantially the same as" basis, provided they are used verbatim;

(3) Require modification or the insertion by the Government of fill-in material (see 52.104); or

(4) Require completion by the offeror or prospective contractor. This instruction also applies to provisions completed as annual representations and certifications.

FAR 52.103 provides that when clauses are incorporated by reference, they are to be identified by FAR number, title, and date or by agency regulation number, title, and date. FAR 52.252-2 contains a clause giving clauses incorporated by reference the same effect as if they had been included verbatim.

The requirement to incorporate by reference clauses that must be filled in by one of the parties can result in an incomplete contract. See, for example, Alternate

I of the Rights in Data – General clause in FAR 52.227-14 which specifies a blank space for the uses that a government agency can make of limited rights technical data which is frequently incorporated in contracts without filling in the uses. FAR 52.104 contains the following guidance on filling in such clauses:

> (d) When completing blanks in provisions or clauses incorporated by reference, insert the fill-in information directly below the title of the provision or clause identifying to the lowest level necessary to clearly indicate the blanks being filled in.

If a clause that is incorporated by reference requires an offeror to fill in blanks, the offeror should print out the clause, fill in the blanks and submit the clause with its proposal. The only guidance on this procedure is the partial guidance in FAR 52.102(c) which requires contracting officers to identify, in special situations, such clauses in order to alert offerors that they must be filled in.

When an agency deviates from a standard clause, FAR 52.107(f) requires it to alert offerors to such deviation by including the following clause from FAR 52.252-6 in the RFP:

> (a) The use in this solicitation or contract of any Federal Acquisition Regulation (48 CFR Chapter 1) clause with an authorized deviation is indicated by the addition of (DEVIATION) after the date of the clause.
>
> (b) The use in this solicitation or contract of any [insert regulation name] (48 CFR ____) clause with an authorized deviation is indicated by the addition of (DEVIATION) after the name of the regulation.

Deviations are only effective if they are approved by an official with the authority to take such actions. This will be determined by the procurement regulations of the agency in question, but such authority is normally restricted to an agency official with responsibility for procurement. See *G.L. Christian & Assocs. v. United States*, 160 Ct. Cl. 1, 312 F.2d 418 (1963), where the government was not bound by a deviation from the regulations (deleting a mandatory standard clause) because the deviation had been approved by an Assistant Secretary of Defense without the proper authority.

Order of precedence clauses are also included in this section. FAR 15.209(h) requires insertion of the following standard Order of Precedence clause in FAR 52.215-8:

> ORDER OF PRECEDENCE — UNIFORM CONTRACT FORMAT (OCT 1997)
>
> Any inconsistency in this solicitation or contract shall be resolved by giving precedence in the following order:

(a) The Schedule (excluding the specifications).

(b) Representations and other instructions.

(c) Contract clauses.

(d) Other documents, exhibits, and attachments.

(e) The specifications.

This clause will obligate the contractor when two or more sections are in direct conflict. They have been applied against the government even when the contractor knew or should have known of a discrepancy prior to bidding as long as there is no overreaching, *Hensel Phelps Constr. Co. v. United States*, 886 F.2d 1296 (Fed. Cir. 1989). However, an order of precedence clause may not be applied automatically when there are obvious conflicts or errors, and strict application of the order of precedence clause would give rise to overreaching. In *Franchi Constr. Co. v. United States*, 221 Ct. Cl. 796, 609 F.2d 984 (1979), the court stated at 798:

> It is obvious that no careful writer of contracts would deliberately create a discrepancy, patent or latent, and then leave it to be resolved by the precedence clause. A discrepancy even with the precedence clause therefore indicates a probable mistake, which may be more or less serious. We would assume arguendo that a bidder, who noticed or should have noticed a serious mistake in the invitation or other of the contract documents, must divulge what he has or should have noticed to the government, and will not in equity be allowed to profit by not doing so, as it would be an instance of overreaching.

Construction contracts contain additional order of precedence language in the Specifications and Drawings clause in FAR 52.236-21, stating: "In case of difference between drawings and specifications, the specifications shall govern." For cases resolving controversies using this provision, see *Sletten Constr. Co.*, PSBCA 191, 76-2 BCA ¶ 11,990; *DeRalco, Inc.*, ASBCA 20630, 76-2 BCA ¶ 11,971; *J.R. Erickson*, AGBCA 333, 76-1 BCA ¶ 11,716; and *Bruce Anderson Co.*, ASBCA 29412, 89-2 BCA ¶ 21,872. Construction contracts also frequently contain provisions stating that large-scale drawings control over small-scale drawings. See, for example, *Rexach-HRH Constr. Corp.*, VACAB 721, 68-1 BCA ¶ 6924, in which it was held that the large-scale drawings would supersede the small-scale drawings in determining where to place a canopy.

The inclusion of these clauses has the advantage of permitting relatively mechanical resolution of a conflict, even though no assurance exists that the resulting decision will reflect the intent of the parties. See *John A. Volpe Constr. Co.*, VACAB 638, 68-1 BCA ¶ 6857, which illustrates this point.

J. List of Attachments

Section J contains a list of all attachments and exhibits to the contract. FAR 15.204-4 requires that the title, date, and number of pages be listed for each document. There is no provision permitting incorporation of these items by reference.

K. Certifications and Representations

The numerous solicitation provisions calling for certifications or representations by the offeror are contained in Section K. FAR 52.102(a)(4) indicates that such provisions should be incorporated by reference rather than being set forth in full text in the RFP. However, there is no guidance in the FAR as to how an offeror provides the required representation or certification when this is done. Nonetheless, offerors should print them out and submit them with the proposal if they are required to be filled in by each offeror.

The government uses these provisions to determine the status of the offeror and to ensure that the offeror will be in compliance with the socioeconomic requirements of the procurement. Thus, these provisions create a self-monitoring mechanism permitting offerors to establish their compliance by certification rather than by proving that certain requirements are met. In order to reduce the administrative burden on offerors, the government has adopted a policy of annual online representations and certifications using an Online Representations and Certifications Application (ORCA). All prospective contractors are required to participate in this system. See FAR 4.1201 stating:

(a) Prospective contractors shall complete electronic annual representations and certifications at http://orca.bpn.gov in conjunction with required registration in the Central Contractor Registration (CCR) database (see FAR 4.1102).

(b)(1) Prospective contractors shall update the representations and certifications submitted to ORCA as necessary, but at least annually, to ensure they are kept current, accurate, and complete. The representations and certifications are effective until one year from date of submission or update to ORCA.

(2) When any of the conditions in paragraph (b) of the clause at 52.219-28, Post-Award Small Business Program Rerepresentation, apply, contractors that represented they were small businesses prior to award of a contract must update the representations and certifications in ORCA as directed by the clause. Contractors that represented they were other than small businesses prior to award of a contract may update the representations and certifications in ORCA as directed by the clause, if their size status has changed since contract award.

(c) Data in ORCA is archived and is electronically retrievable. Therefore, when a prospective contractor has completed representations and certifications electronically via ORCA, the contracting officer must reference the date of ORCA verification in the contract file, or include a paper copy of the electronically-submitted representations and certifications in the file. Either of these actions satisfies contract file documentation requirements of 4.803(a)(11). However, if an offeror identifies changes to ORCA data pursuant to the FAR provisions at 52.204-8(d) or 52.212-3(b), the contracting officer must include a copy of the changes in the contract file.

This policy is implemented by inclusion in the RFP of the Annual Representations and Certifications solicitation provision in FAR 52.204-8 and the Central Contractor Registration clause in FAR 52.204-7. When this is done, FAR 4.1202 calls for the omission of the following provisions which would otherwise be included in many RFPs:

(a) 52.203-2, Certificate of Independent Price Determination.

(b) 52.203-11, Certification and Disclosure Regarding Payments to Influence Certain Federal Transactions.

(c) 52.204-3, Taxpayer Identification.

(d) 52.204-5, Women-Owned Business (Other Than Small Business).

(e) 52.209-5, Certification Regarding Responsibility Matters.

(f) 52.214-14, Place of Performance – Sealed Bidding.

(g) 52.215-6, Place of Performance.

(h) 52.219-1, Small Business Program Representations (Basic & Alternate I).

(i) 52.219-2, Equal Low Bids.

(j) 52.219-19, Small Business Concern Representation for the Small Business Competitiveness Demonstration Program.

(k) 52.219-21, Small Business Size Representation for Targeted Industry Categories Under the Small Business Competitiveness Demonstration Program.

(l) 52.219-22, Small Disadvantaged Business Status (Basic & Alternate. I)

(m) 52.222-18, Certification Regarding Knowledge of Child Labor for Listed End Products.

(n) 52.222-22, Previous Contracts and Compliance Reports.

(o) 52.222-25, Affirmative Action Compliance.

(p) 52.222-38, Compliance with Veterans' Employment Reporting Requirements.

(q) 52.222-48, Exemption from Application of the Service Contract Act to Contracts for Maintenance, Calibration, or Repair of Certain Equipment Certification.

(r) 52.222-52, Exemption from Application of the Service Contract Act to Contracts for Certain Services – Certification.

(s) 52.223-1, Biobased Product Certification.

(t) 52.223-4, Recovered Material Certification.

(u) 52.223-9, Estimate of Percentage of Recovered Material Content for EPA-Designated Items (Alternate I only).

(v) 52.223-13, Certification of Toxic Chemical Release Reporting.

(w) 52.225-2, Buy American Act Certificate.

(x) 52.225-4, Buy American Act – Free Trade Agreements – Israeli Trade Act Certificate (Basic, Alternate I & II).

(y) 52.225-6, Trade Agreements Certificate.

(z) 52.225-20, Prohibition on Conducting Restricted Business Operations in Sudan – Certification.

(aa) 52.226-2, Historically Black College or University and Minority Institution Representation.

(bb) 52.227-6, Royalty Information (Basic & Alternate I).

(cc) 52.227-15, Representation of Limited Rights Data and Restricted Computer Software.

There are two other clauses requiring certification during contract performance. The Requirements for Cost or Pricing Data or Information Other Than Cost or Pricing Data — Modifications clause in FAR 52.215-21 is inserted in most negotiated contracts. This clause requires the certification of cost or pricing data submitted in support of modifications over a specified dollar threshold. In addition, the Disputes clause in FAR 52.233-1, which is inserted in all contracts, requires certification of all claims over $100,000 stating that: (1) its claim is made in good faith, (2) supporting data are accurate and complete to the best of the contractor's knowledge and belief, (3) the amount requested accurately reflects the adjustment for which the contractor believes the government is liable, and (4) the official signing the certification is authorized to do so.

L. Instructions and Conditions

Section L contains those items that are generally referred to as solicitation provisions. See FAR 2.101, which defines a solicitation provision as "a term or condition used only in solicitations and applying only before contract award." This section contains standard provisions required by the FAR and specialized instructions relating to the specific procurement. It is common practice to include in Section L provisions giving detailed guidance as to the relevant information that must be submitted in order to permit the agency to evaluate the factors and subfactors included in Section M. The failure of Section L to give such guidance is one of the most common defects in the competitive negotiation process.

1. Standard Solicitation Provisions

FAR 15.209 requires the inclusion of a number of standard provisions in the RFP. FAR 15.209(a) requires that the FAR 52.215-1, Instructions to Offerors — Competitive Acquisition provision be included in all competitive solicitations where the government intends to award a contract without negotiations. Alternate I is to be used if the government has determined, in advance, that it will conduct negotiations. This provision also includes definitions and rules involving a number of matters, including modification and withdrawal of proposals, consideration of late proposals, acceptable restrictions on disclosure of information, and contract award. These matters were previously contained in a number of separate solicitation provisions. FAR 15.209(a)(2) also calls for the use of Alternate II to this solicitation provision when the government would be willing to accept alternate proposals. The use of this alternate allows the government to award a contract to an offeror submitting an alternate proposal without having to amend the RFP and provide all offerors the opportunity to compete on that alternate, *Litton Sys., Inc. v. Dep't of Transportation*, GSBCA 12911-P, 94-3 BCA ¶ 27,263. However, Alternate II "reserves the right" of the government to amend the RFP if the agency chooses to obtain competition on the alternate requirements.

FAR 15.209 provides guidance on a number of additional provisions that are commonly used in RFPs. FAR 15.209(b) requires the use of the FAR 52.215-2, Audit and Records — Negotiation provision or one of its alternate provisions in all negotiated procurements except for simplified acquisitions, acquisition of utility services at established rates, or acquisition of commercial items. FAR 15.209(e) requires the use of the FAR 52.215-5, Facsimile Proposals provision in all RFPs permitting the use of such proposals. FAR 15.209(f) requires use of the FAR 52.215-6, Place of Performance provision in all RFPs where the place of performance is not specified by the government.

FAR 15.209(h) requires the use of the FAR 52.215-8, Order of Precedence — Uniform Contract Format provision in all RFPs using the uniform contract format.

2. Award Procedures

While recognizing that award without negotiations would be preferable in many situations, Congress was concerned that competitors would not submit their best offers if they believed that the agency would likely conduct negotiations. Thus, 10 U.S.C. § 2305(a)(2)(B)(ii)(I) and 41 U.S.C. § 253a(b)(2)(B)(i) require that the solicitation indicate whether the agency intends to award without negotiations or intends to conduct negotiations, stating that the solicitation shall include —

> either a statement that the proposals are intended to be evaluated with, and award made after, discussions with the offerors, or a statement that the proposals are intended to be evaluated, and award made, without discussions with the offerors (other than discussions conducted for the purpose of minor clarification) unless discussions are determined to be necessary.

Neither the statutes nor the regulations provide any directions related to selecting the appropriate provision. FAR 15.209(a) merely requires that once this determination is made, the appropriate solicitation provision is to be adopted.

a. Without Negotiations Intended

Paragraph (f)(4) of the standard FAR 52.215-1 Instructions to Offerors — Competitive Acquisition solicitation provision permits award without negotiations as follows:

> The Government intends to evaluate proposals and award a contract without discussions with offerors (except clarifications as described in FAR 15.306(a). Therefore, the offeror's initial proposal should contain the offeror's best terms from a cost or price and technical standpoint. The Government reserves the right to conduct discussions if the Contracting Officer later determines them to be necessary. If the Contracting Officer determines that the number of proposals that would otherwise be in the competitive range exceeds the number at which an efficient competition can be conducted, the Contracting Officer may limit the number of proposals in the competitive range to the greatest number that will permit an efficient competition among the most highly rated proposals.

While indicating that award without negotiation is intended, this provision gives the agency the option to conduct negotiations when they are determined to be necessary. However, FAR 15.306(a)(2) requires that when such a determination is made, "the rationale for doing so shall be documented in the contract file." This provision apparently reflects the congressional concern that offerors might not make their best offers in their original submission if they expect negotiations to take place. Thus, the government should not avail itself of this option as a matter of course.

Incorporation of the substance of this notice into solicitations has been held to put offerors on notice that they should not expect to have an opportunity to revise their offers. See, e.g., *Robotic Sys. Tech.*, Comp. Gen. Dec. B-278195.2, 98-1 CPD ¶ 20, stating:

> [S]ince the RFP advised offerors that the agency intended to make award without discussions, RST could not reasonably presume that it would have a chance to improve its proposal through discussions. *Scientific-Atlanta, Inc.*, B-255343.2, B-255343.4, Mar. 14, 1994, 94-1 CPD ¶ 325 at 8–9.

An offeror does not have a right to award on the basis of an initial proposal, *Kisco Co.*, Comp. Gen. Dec. B-216953, 85-1 CPD ¶ 334.

b. Negotiations Intended

The nature of the specifications and the extent to which technical merit is to be considered in a tradeoff strategy procurement will be critical in determining whether to indicate in the solicitation that negotiations are intended. This was noted in H.R. Rep. 101-665, which stated:

> The committee believes that when technical characteristics that cannot be quantified in cost terms are so critical that they are weighed more than lowest overall cost, the government may need discussions to ensure a clear understanding by both the government and the contractor of what the government needs and can get.

When the agency has determined that it intends to conduct negotiations, the following Alternate I to the FAR 52.215-1 ¶ (f)(4) solicitation provision is to be used:

> The Government intends to evaluate proposals and award a contract after conducting discussions with offerors whose proposals have been determined to be within the competitive range. If the Contracting Officer determines that the number of proposals that would otherwise be in the competitive range exceeds the number at which an efficient competition can be conducted, the Contracting Officer may limit the number of proposals in the competitive range to the greatest number that will permit an efficient competition among the most highly rated proposals. Therefore, the offeror's initial proposal should contain the offeror's best terms from a price and technical standpoint.

When this provision is used, the government may not make award without negotiations, *American Native Med. Transport, LLC*, Comp. Gen. Dec. B-276873, 97-2 CPD ¶ 73.

3. Method of Submission of Offers and Information

Traditionally, the offer and information were submitted together in paper media in a sealed envelope. However, there are a growing number of procurements where facsimile or electronic submission is permitted or required. In addition, part of or all the required information may be submitted in an oral presentation.

a. Paper Media

Paragraph (c) of the Instructions to Offerors – Competitive Acquisition solicitation provision in FAR 52.215-1 provides guidance on the basic procedure to be followed in submitting offers and information:

> (1) Unless other methods (e.g., electronic commerce or facsimile) are permitted in the solicitation, proposals and modifications to proposals shall be submitted in paper media in sealed envelopes or packages (i) addressed to the office specified in the solicitation, and (ii) showing the time and date specified for receipt, the solicitation number, and the name and address of the offeror. Offerors using commercial carriers should ensure that the proposal is marked on the outermost wrapper with the information in paragraphs (c)(1)(i) and (c)(1)(ii) of this provision.
>
> (2) The first page of the proposal must show —
>
> > (i) The solicitation number;
> >
> > (ii) The name, address, and telephone and facsimile numbers of the offeror (and electronic address if available);
> >
> > (iii) A statement specifying the extent of agreement with all terms, conditions, and provisions included in the solicitation and agreement to furnish any or all items upon which prices are offered at the price set opposite each item;
> >
> > (iv) Names, titles, and telephone and facsimile numbers (and electronic addresses if available) of persons authorized to negotiate on the offeror's behalf with the Government in connection with this solicitation; and
> >
> > (v) Name, title, and signature of person authorized to sign the proposal. Proposals signed by an agent shall be accompanied by evidence of that agent's authority, unless that evidence has been previously furnished to the issuing office.

b. Facsimile or Electronic Submission

FAR 4.502(a) encourages the use of electronic commerce "whenever practicable or cost-effective." FAR 15.203(c) provides that when electronic commerce is an authorized means of submission, the RFP must "specify the electronic commerce method(s) that offerors may use (see Subpart (d))." There is no standard FAR solicitation provision specifying the method to be used – with the result that agencies are permitted to adopt different methods. FAR 4.502(b) contains the following general guidance:

(b) Agencies may exercise broad discretion in selecting the hardware and software that will be used in conducting electronic commerce. However, as required by Section 30 of the OFPP Act (41 U.S.C. 426), the head of each agency, after consulting with the Administrator of OFPP, shall ensure that systems, technologies, procedures, and processes used by the agency to conduct electronic commerce —

(1) Are implemented uniformly throughout the agency, to the maximum extent practicable;

(2) Are implemented only after considering the full or partial use of existing infrastructures;

(3) Facilitate access to Government acquisition opportunities by small business concerns, small disadvantaged business concerns, women-owned, veteran-owned, HUBZone, and service-disabled veteran-owned small business concerns;

(4) Include a single means of providing widespread public notice of acquisition opportunities through the Governmentwide point of entry and a means of responding to notices or solicitations electronically; and

(5) Comply with nationally and internationally recognized standards that broaden interoperability and ease the electronic interchange of information, such as standards established by the National Institute of Standards and Technology.

FAR 15.203(d) provides that proposals may be submitted by facsimile, giving the following guidance:

(1) In deciding whether or not to use facsimiles, the contracting officer should consider factors such as —

(i) Anticipated proposal size and volume;

(ii) Urgency of the requirement;

(iii) Availability and suitability of electronic commerce methods; and

(iv) Adequacy of administrative procedures and controls for receiving, identifying, recording, and safeguarding facsimile proposals, and ensuring their timely delivery to the designated proposal delivery location.

(2) If facsimile proposals are authorized, contracting officers may request offeror(s) to provide the complete, original signed proposal at a later date.

FAR 15.209(e) requires the contracting officer to include the following FAR 52.215-5 Facsimile Proposals provision in an RFP when submission by facsimile is authorized:

(a) Definition. Facsimile proposal, as used in this provision, means a proposal, revision or modification of a proposal, or withdrawal of a proposal that is transmitted to and received by the Government via facsimile machine.

(b) Offerors may submit facsimile proposals as responses to this solicitation. Facsimile proposals are subject to the same rules as paper proposals.

(c) The telephone number of receiving facsimile equipment is: [insert telephone number].

(d) If any portion of a facsimile proposal received by the Contracting Officer is unreadable to the degree that conformance to the essential requirements of the solicitation cannot be ascertained from the document —

(1) The Contracting Officer immediately shall notify the offeror and permit the offeror to resubmit the proposal;

(2) The method and time for resubmission shall be prescribed by the Contracting Officer after consultation with the offeror; and

(3) The resubmission shall be considered as if it were received at the date and time of the original unreadable submission for the purpose of determining timeliness, provided the offeror complies with the time and format requirements for resubmission prescribed by the Contracting Officer.

(e) The Government reserves the right to make award solely on the facsimile proposal. However, if requested to do so by the Contracting Officer, the apparently successful offeror promptly shall submit the complete original signed proposal.

The instructions for handling unreadable portions of facsimile or electronic submissions contained in this provision are set forth in FAR 15.207(c).

Offerors assume the risk of nonreceipt of their facsimile transmissions, *S.W. Elecs. & Mfg. Corp.*, Comp. Gen. Dec. B-249308, 92-2 CPD ¶ 320; *Microscope Co.*, Comp. Gen. Dec. B-257015, 94-2 CPD ¶ 157; *International Garment Processors*, Comp. Gen. Dec. B-299674, 2007 CPD ¶ 130. Offerors also assume the risk of nonreceipt of electronic transmissions, *Joint Venture Penauillie Italia S.p.A.; Cofathec S.p.A.; SEB.CO S.a.s.; CO.PEL.S.a.s.*, Comp. Gen. Dec. B-298865, 2007 CPD ¶ 7 (e-mail received by agency lacked required data); *Seven Seas Eng'g & Land Surveying*, Comp. Gen. Dec. B-294424.2, 2004 CPD ¶ 236 (e-mail final proposal revisions received late); *Sea Box, Inc.*, Comp. Gen. Dec. B-291056, 2002 CPD ¶ 181 (e-mail proposal late when received at agency initial point of entry on time but not received by contracting office until after required time); *Comspace Corp.*,

Comp. Gen. Dec. B-274037, 96-2 CPD ¶ 186 (quotation delivered to the offeror's government-approved Value Added Network but not transmitted to agency).

c. Oral Presentations or Interviews

Oral presentations or interviews, as discussed in Chapter 2, have been used for some time to enable procurement officials to obtain information leading to additional understanding of the offerors' capability and features of their offers. However, it was not until the FAR Part 15 rewrite that comprehensive coverage was adopted for these procedures. FAR 15.102 provides detailed guidance on obtaining information, but not offers, through this process. This regulatory provision for obtaining information through the presentation process is consistent with prior practice. See *Intermagnetics Gen. Corp.*, Comp. Gen. Dec. B-255741.2, 94-1 CPD ¶ 302, holding that while an agency may limit its evaluation to information contained in written submissions, it also may decide to use other information, including that obtained in oral presentations:

> An agency may properly limit its evaluation to information contained in the four corners of a proposal, and [the protester] cites decisions in which we have denied protests alleging that the contracting agency should have used information from other sources, such as a pre-award survey, as a substitute for information that the solicitation directed offerors to include in their proposal. *See, e.g., Numax Elecs. Inc.*, B-210266, May 3, 1983, 83-1 CPD ¶ 470. [The protester] is also correct in noting that we have denied protests where the protester complained that the agency erred in not considering orally discussed changes to the protester's proposal, where the protester did not confirm the changes by incorporating them in its BAFO. *See, e.g., Recon Optical, Inc.*, B-232125, Dec. 1, 1988, 88-2 CPD ¶ 544.

> These decisions are not inconsistent with our denial of [the protester's] protest; they stand for the proposition that offerors act at their peril when they fail to include within the four corners of their proposals information required by the solicitation or requested by the agency during discussions, and that such proposals may properly be rejected. *See Abacus Enters.*, B-248969, Oct. 13, 1992, 92-2 CPD ¶ 242. However, we have also consistently held that, in evaluating proposals, contracting agencies may consider any evidence, even if that evidence is entirely outside the proposal (and, indeed, even if it contradicts statements in the proposal), so long as the use of the extrinsic evidence is consistent with established procurement practice. *See, e.g., Western Medical Personnel, Inc.*, 66 Comp. Gen. 699 (1987), 87-2 CPD ¶ 310; *AAA Eng'g & Drafting, Inc.*, B-250323, Jan. 26, 1993, 93-1 CPD ¶ 287.

See also *NW Ayer, Inc.*, Comp. Gen. Dec. B-248654, 92-2 CPD ¶ 154; and *Palmer Brown Cos.*, 70 Comp. Gen. 667 (B-243544), 91-2 CPD ¶ 134. In *Labat-Anderson, Inc.*, 71 Comp. Gen. 252 (B-246071), 92-1 CPD ¶ 193, the oral presentation resulted in a determination that the offeror lacked capability as it also did in *ARTEL, Inc.*, Comp. Gen. Dec. B-248478, 92-2 CPD ¶ 120, where the agency concluded from an oral presentation that there were serious doubts as to the quality and availability of the offeror's key personnel.

If an agency decides to require oral presentations, the RFP should contain detailed guidance on their purpose — generally to assess the capability of the offerors. It should also contain guidance on their content and format. See FAR 15.102, which states:

> (d) When oral presentations are required, the solicitation shall provide offerors with sufficient information to prepare them. Accordingly, the solicitation may describe —
>
>> (1) The types of information to be presented orally and the associated evaluation factors that will be used;
>>
>> (2) The qualifications for personnel that will be required to provide the oral presentation(s);
>>
>> (3) The requirements for, and any limitations and/or prohibitions on, the use of written material or other media to supplement the oral presentations;
>>
>> (4) The location, date, and time for the oral presentations;
>>
>> (5) The restrictions governing the time permitted for each oral presentation; and
>>
>> (6) The scope and content of exchanges that may occur between the Government's participants and the offeror's representatives as part of the oral presentations, including whether or not discussions (see 15.306(d)) will be permitted during oral presentations.

There are several important issues that should be addressed in the RFP. First, it should state that the presentation is intended to address the key issues that are expected to arise during performance of the contract rather than general information demonstrating the capability of the offeror. These key issues can be specifically identified in the RFP or chosen by each offeror, at the discretion of the agency. The RFP should also state that the offeror's personnel attending the oral presentation should be the people that will be managing the performance of the key issue areas — whether they be employees of the offeror or of a prospective subcontractor. The RFP should then state the time allocated to an initial presentation by the offeror and the time allocated to dialog between the parties — in the form of a question and answer session, an interview, or the solution of a sample task. As a general proposition, it is good practice to devote more time to this dialog process than to the initial presentation.

An important element of the RFP guidance on oral presentations is whether they will either preclude or permit discussions during the oral presentation, FAR 15.102(d)(6). Very clear language should be included on this issue because, if discussions occur, the agency must comply with the rules governing negotiations with all offerors in the competitive range, FAR 15.102(g).

Agencies may adopt reasonable rules governing the nature of the presentations, including limitations on the length and nature of the presentations, *American Sys. Corp.*, 68 Comp. Gen. 475 (B-234449), 89-1 CPD ¶ 537. They may also require that offerors meet mandatory requirements in an RFP before being eligible to make an oral presentation, *Inte-Great Corp.*, Comp. Gen. Dec. B-272780, 96-2 CPD ¶ 159. Agencies have imposed two procedural requirements on oral presentations that have not enhanced the process. The first is the requirement that slides to be used must be submitted with the original proposal. While this requirement has been strictly enforced, *KSEND v. United States*, 69 Fed. Cl. 103 (2005), it is difficult to perceive how it reduces any advantage that might accrue to offerors that make their presentation later than other offerors. The second is the requirement restricting the nature of the media used in the presentation – such as requiring only black and white slides. Such a requirement merely precludes the use of media that is most effective in demonstrating the offeror's ability to deal with a potential area of difficulty – such as a color slide of a pie chart. These type requirements should not be called for in the RFP.

4. Specifying Information for Evaluation

In most procurements, much of the information for evaluation must be furnished by offerors. Thus, the RFP must advise offerors of the information that is to be included in proposals, FAR 15.203(a)(3). Instructions dealing with information to be furnished and its organization are included in Section L, FAR 15.204-5(b). The more specific the agency can be in these instructions, the more likely that offerors will submit relevant information. The RFP should state the specific types of information and how the information is to be organized and submitted. RFPs should require the submission of only information that is needed to evaluate the proposals.

a. Capability Information

Offerors should be requested to furnish information that will enable the agency to evaluate the relative capabilities of the offerors to perform the work. The amount and type of information will depend on the nature and complexity of the procurement.

(1) PAST PERFORMANCE INFORMATION

Data on past performance will have to be obtained from each offeror in most procurements. This will normally entail the obtaining of information on a specified number of recent contracts where the offeror has performed similar types of work. Generally, agencies request the names of key people that can be called as references and data as to the work done on the contract and problems encountered in its performance. See FAR 15.305(a)(2)(ii), which states:

> The solicitation shall describe the approach for evaluating past performance, including evaluating offerors with no relevant performance history, and shall provide offerors an opportunity to identify past or current contracts (including Federal, State, and local government and private) for efforts similar to the Government requirement. The solicitation shall also authorize offerors to provide information on problems encountered on the identified contracts and the offeror's corrective actions. . . .

The requirement that offerors be permitted to provide information on problems encountered and corrective actions is most readily met by requiring that each offeror submit a short self-assessment of its performance on each of the referenced contracts.

(2) EXPERIENCE REQUIREMENTS

The RFP should be clear as to the type and extent of experience required as discussed in Chapter 2. See *Telestar Corp.*, Comp. Gen. Dec. B-275855, 97-1 CPD ¶ 150 (experience required on projects "of similar size and scope related to this effort"), or on projects that are very closely related to the work called for by the proposed contract, *Systems Application & Techs., Inc.*, Comp. Gen. Dec. B-270672, 96-1 CPD ¶ 182 (experience with contracting agency); *CAN Indus. Eng'g, Inc.*, Comp. Gen. Dec. B-271034, 96-1 CPD ¶ 279 (experience with the agency's system that was to be tested under the contract). See also *Computer Sys. Dev. Corp.*, Comp. Gen. Dec. B-275356, 97-1 CPD ¶ 91, where the GAO noted the following description contained in the solicitation:

> Under the corporate experience factor, the RFP provided that consideration would be given to the "[b]readth (*i.e.*, variety or number of contracts) and significance (*i.e.*, size, complexity, participation) of corporate experience (including subcontractors and consultants of this proposal) in accomplishing efforts relevant to those described in the [statement of work]." The RFP also provided that "[w]hen cited contracts cover a variety of size and complexity, greater weight goes to relevant contracts of a size and complexity equal to or greater than this solicitation," and that "[p]articular emphasis shall be placed on contracts that provide [AIS] services in a dynamic environment . . . [such as] . . . [o]pen architecture or systems migration experience."

Generally, the information submitted to demonstrate past performance (references and self assessments) will be substantially the same as the information needed to demonstrate experience. However, when experience is going to be evaluated, the RFP should be very explicit in the precise information needed to meet the experience requirement.

(3) KEY PERSONNEL

When this factor is used, the agency should state in the RFP the jobs that are so important to the success of contract performance that the personnel filling then must be designated as key personnel. See *Dynamic Resources, Inc.*, Comp. Gen. Dec. B-277213, 97-2 CPD ¶ 100 (program manager, technical manager, senior reliability engineer, computer programmers, aircraft maintenance analysts, programmer/analyst, and software engineer); *DCT, Inc.*, Comp. Gen. Dec. B-261894.2, 95-2 CPD ¶ 237 (project manager, quality control officer, and persons responsible for major functional areas); *Global Assocs., Ltd.*, Comp. Gen. Dec. B-256277, 94-1 CPD ¶ 347 (personnel devoting 50% or more time to the contract); *Bannum, Inc.*, Comp. Gen. Dec. B-248169.2, 92-2 CPD ¶ 216 (facility manager, case manager, and counselor); and *T&M Joint Venture*, Comp. Gen. Dec. B-240747, 90-2 CPD ¶ 503 ("skilled/experienced professional and/or technical personnel").

The RFP must also require the submission of sufficient information to evaluate whether the key personnel proposed meet the requirements. At a minimum, this will require the submission of resumes but, as discussed in Chapter 2, relying on resumes alone is a questionable practice. Thus, it is better practice to require the submission of detailed information on the performance record of the key personnel that are proposed for the work. See, for example, *Systems Res. & Applications Corp.*, Comp. Gen. Dec. B-299818, 2008 CPD ¶ 28, where the RFP required evidence that personnel had experience with the type of work being procured. When the agency plans to conduct oral presentations, requiring the key personnel to participate in the presentation is a very good way of assessing the capability of those personnel. See, for example, *Savannah River Alliance, LLC*, Comp. Gen. Dec. B-311126, 2008 CPD ¶ 88, where the RFP required resumes, references, letters of commitment and participation in the oral presentation.

b. Cost/Price Information

The RFP should specifically identify the information that is required to evaluate price reasonableness or cost realism. As discussed in Chapter 2, it is the government's policy to obtain as little information as is necessary for this purpose.

Furthermore, there are now statutory prohibitions on the obtaining of certified cost or pricing data. As a result, there should be very few instances where the RFP calls for the submission of such data. However, the agency has considerable discretion in determining what information other than cost or pricing data is necessary to evaluate the proposed costs or prices.

FAR 15.403-5 contains the following guidance on the RFP language:

(a) Taking into consideration the policy at 15.402, the contracting officer shall specify in the solicitation (see 15.408 (l) and (m)) —

(1) Whether certified cost or pricing data are required;

(2) That, in lieu of submitting certified cost or pricing data, the offeror may submit a request for exception from the requirement to submit certified cost or pricing data;

(3) Any requirement for data other than certified cost or pricing data; and

(4) The requirement for necessary preaward or postaward access to offeror's records.

(b)(1) Format for submission of certified cost or pricing data. When certification is required, the contracting officer may require submission of certified cost or pricing data in the format indicated in Table 15–2 of 15.408, specify an alternative format, or permit submission in the contractor's format (See 15.408(l)(1)), unless the data are required to be submitted on one of the termination forms specified in subpart 49.6.

(2) Format for submission of data other than certified cost or pricing data. When required by the contracting officer, data other than certified cost or pricing data may be submitted in the offeror's own format unless the contracting officer decides that use of a specific format is essential for evaluating and determining that the price is fair and reasonable and the format has been described in the solicitation.

(3) Format for submission of data supporting forward pricing rate agreements. Data supporting forward pricing rate agreements or final indirect cost proposals shall be submitted in a form acceptable to the contracting officer.

FAR 15.408 provides a standard clause and four alternate clauses that can be used to implement this policy:

(l) Requirements for Certified Cost or Pricing Data and Data Other Than Certified Cost or Pricing Data. Considering the hierarchy at 15.402, the contracting officer shall insert the provision at 52.215–20, Requirements for Certified Cost or Pricing Data and Data Other Than Certified Cost or Pricing Data, in solicitations if it is reasonably certain that certified cost or pricing data or data other than certified cost or pricing data will be required. This provision also provides instructions to offerors on how to request an exception from the requirement to submit certified cost or pricing data. The contracting officer shall —

(1) Use the provision with its Alternate I to specify a format for certified cost or pricing data other than the format required by Table 15–2 of this section;

(2) Use the provision with its Alternate II if copies of the proposal are to be sent to the ACO and contract auditor;

(3) Use the provision with its Alternate III if submission via electronic media is required; and

(4) Replace the basic provision with its Alternate IV if certified cost or pricing data are not expected to be required because an exception may apply, but data other than certified cost or pricing data will be required as described in 15.403–3.

(1) Requiring Certified Cost or Pricing Data

If the contracting officer determines that certified cost or pricing data must be obtained and this standard provision is used with Alternate I, II, or III, the offeror is given the opportunity to defer the submission of cost or pricing data by claiming that either the "commercial-item" exception or the "prices set by law or regulation" exception applies. Alternatively, the contracting officer could insert a special provision calling for the submission of cost or pricing data to be certified at the completion of negotiations. However, it would be good practice to use the standard solicitation provision to ensure that certified cost or pricing data is not obtained unnecessarily.

(2) Requiring Data Other Than Certified Cost or Pricing Data

In the normal situation, where only data other than certified cost or pricing data is to be obtained, the contracting officer can use the Alternate IV solicitation provision. This form provision requires the contracting officer to state the precise information that is necessary:

Requirements for Cost or Pricing Data or Data Other Than Certified Cost or Pricing Data — Alternate IV (OCT 1997)

(a) Submission of certified cost or pricing data is not required.

(b) Provide data described below: [Insert description of the data and the format that are required, including access to records necessary to permit adequate evaluation of the proposed price in accordance with 15.403-3.]

The most common form of cost data of this nature will be cost element breakdowns for the work that is required by the contract. These breakdowns show the estimated dollar amounts of the various types of cost (material, labor, indirect costs, etc.) that the offeror anticipates will be required to perform the work. They are not cost or pricing data but are merely summary estimates that have been made by the offeror. However, they provide sufficient information to allow the contracting officer to perform a cost analysis — obtaining additional information (such as prior labor or indirect cost rates) from government auditors or from internal files documenting prior negotiations with the offeror. See *Research Mgmt. Corp.*, 69 Comp. Gen. 368 (B-237865), 90-1 CPD ¶ 352, for a case where this technique was used.

When contracting officers include a requirement for cost element breakdowns in the RFP, they should specify the level of the work breakdown structure that should be supported by such cost breakdowns. A work breakdown structure separates the contract work into its separate parts in a logical manner in order to ensure that all necessary tasks are considered in planning the job. See Military Standard (MIL-STD) 881B, Mar. 25, 1993, containing the following definition:

3.4 Work Breakdown Structure. A work breakdown structure (WBS) is a product-oriented family tree composed of hardware, software, services, data and facilities which results from systems engineering efforts during the acquisition of a defense materiel item. A work breakdown structure displays and defines the product(s) to be developed and/or produced and relates the elements of work to be accomplished to each other and to the end product(s). The work breakdown structures prescribed by this standard have been organized within the seven categories of defense materiel items and consist of the upper three levels of the work breakdown structure.

MIL-STD 881B calls for work breakdown structures to be organized into three levels:

Level 1: Level 1 is the entire defense materiel item; for example, the Minuteman ICBM System or the LHA Ship System. Level 1 is usually directly identified in the DOD programming/budget system either as an integral program element or as a project or subprogram within an aggregated program element.

Level 2: Level 2 elements are major elements of the defense material item and are subordinate to Level 1; for example, a ship, an air vehicle, a tracked vehicle, and aggregations of services (such as system test and evaluation, and systems engineering/program management) and data.

Level 3: Level 3 elements are elements subordinate to Level 2 major elements; for example, an electric plant, an airframe, the power package/drive train, or type of service (such as development test and evaluation, contractor technical support, training services), or type of data (such as technical publications). Lower levels follow the same process.

It can be seen that Level 1 corresponds, in general, to an entire contract and that Level 2 is normally used to identify the specific line items in a contract. Contractual documents do not normally contain any breakdowns that correspond to Level 3 in the DOD cost breakdown structure.

Cost breakdowns can be obtained for any level in the cost breakdown structure — with the understanding that the lower the level the more detailed the information that will be available to the contracting officer to use for evaluation purposes. In general, the size of the procurement will indicate which level is appropriate. Level 1, providing only a single cost element breakdown for the entire contract, will generally be sufficient for contracts with one major task. Level 2, providing cost element breakdowns for each contract line item, will be sufficient for almost all contracts sith multiple line items for different elements of work. Level 3 or lower, providing cost element breakdowns for parts of the work, will be called for in contracts for major systems, major construction projects, or complex services. See *Battelle Memorial Inst.*, Comp. Gen. Dec. B-278673, 98-1 CPD ¶ 107, for a case affirming the use of this technique for making a cost realism analysis. See also *Advanced Sys. Tech. & Mgmt., Inc.*, Comp. Gen. Dec. B-291529, 2002 CPD ¶ 219, where the agency used cost element breakdowns to evaluate estimates on a labor hour contract.

If adequate price competition on a fixed-price-type contract is anticipated, the contracting officer will usually be able to determine that the price is reasonable by analyzing the competitive prices or using pricing data obtained through market research or prior procurements. Hence, no supplementary data will need to be obtained from the offerors. In contrast, in cost-reimbursement contracts where there is adequate price competition, the contracting officer will generally need some cost data to evaluate the cost realism of the proposals. See the discussion in Chapter 2 as to the data that should be called for in this situation.

If the procurement is for commercial items, the contracting officer will have to specify the data that is needed for price analysis. If adequate price competition is anticipated, competitive prices will probably be sufficient. If no competition is anticipated, some pricing data will have to be obtained. See 10 U.S.C. § 2306a(d) (1) and 41 U.S.C. § 254b(d)(1), which state the following mandatory requirement to obtain data pertaining to commercial items in this situation:

Authority to Require Submission. When certified cost or pricing data are not required to be submitted under this section for a contract, subcontract, or modification of a contract or subcontract, the contracting officer shall require submission of data other than certified cost or pricing data to the extent necessary to determine the reasonableness of the price of the contract, subcontract, or modification of the contract or subcontract. Except in the case of a contract or subcontract covered by the exceptions [for adequate price competition and prices set by law or regulation], the data submitted shall include, at a minimum, appropriate information on the prices at which the same item or similar items have previously been sold that is adequate for evaluating the reasonableness of the price for the procurement.

Section 803 of the 1999 DOD Authorization Act, Pub. L. No. 105-261, provides:

(a) *Modification of Pricing Regulations for Certain Commercial Items Exempt from Cost or Pricing Data Certification Requirements* — (1) The Federal Acquisition Regulation issued in accordance with sections 6 and 25 of the Office of Federal Procurement Policy Act (41 U.S.C. 405, 421) shall be revised to clarify the procedures and methods to be used for determining the reasonableness of prices of exempt commercial items (as defined in subsection (d)).

    (2) The regulations shall, at a minimum, provide specific guidance on —

        (A) the appropriate application and precedence of such price analysis tools as catalog-based pricing, market-based pricing, historical pricing, parametric pricing, and value analysis;

        (B) the circumstances under which contracting officers should require offerors to exempt commercial items to provide —

            (i) information on prices at which the offeror has previously sold the same or similar items; or

            (ii) other information other than certified cost or pricing data;

        (C) the role and responsibility of Department of Defense support organizations in procedures for determining price reasonableness; and

        (D) the meaning and appropriate application of the term "purposes other than governmental purposes" in section 4(12) of the Office of Federal Procurement Policy Act (41 U.S.C. 403(12)).

10 U.S.C. § 2306a(d)(2) and 41 U.S.C. § 254b(d)(2) also require that the regulations contain limitations on the data that can be obtained when procuring a commercial item. These limitations are set forth in FAR 15.403-3(c):

(1) At a minimum, the contracting officer must use price analysis to determine whether the price is fair and reasonable whenever the contracting officer acquires a commercial item (see 15.404-1(b)). The fact that a price is included in a catalog does not, in and of itself, make it fair and reasonable. If the contracting officer cannot determine whether an offered price is fair and reasonable, even after obtaining additional data from sources other than the offeror, then the contracting of-

ficer shall require the offeror to submit data other than certified cost or pricing data to support further analysis (see 15.404–1). This data may include history of sales to non-governmental and governmental entities, cost data, or any other information the contracting officer requires to determine the price is fair and reasonable. Unless an exception under 15.403–1(b)(1) or (2) applies, the contracting officer shall require that the data submitted by the offeror include, at a minimum, appropriate data on the prices at which the same item or similar items have previously been sold, adequate for determining the reasonableness of the price.

> (2) Limitations relating to commercial items (10 U.S.C. 2306a(d)(2) and 41 U.S.C. 254b(d)(2)). (i) The contracting officer shall limit requests for sales data relating to commercial items to data for the same or similar items during a relevant time period.
>
> > (ii) The contracting officer shall, to the maximum extent practicable, limit the scope of the request for data relating to commercial items to include only data that are in the form regularly maintained by the offeror as part of its commercial operations.
> >
> > (iii) The Government shall not disclose outside the Government data obtained relating to commercial items that is exempt from disclosure under 24.202(a) or the Freedom of Information Act (5 U.S.C. 552(b)).
>
> (3) For services that are not offered and sold competitively in substantial quantities in the commercial marketplace, but are of a type offered and sold competitively in substantial quantities in the commercial marketplace, see 15.403–1(c)(3)(ii).

DFARS PGI 215.404-1(b)(iii)(B) requires contracting officers to request "non-Government sales data for quantities comparable to those in the solicitation" when purchasing a sole source commercial item. If no such data is available, this guidance requires obtaining sufficient "information other than cost or pricing data" to perform a price or cost analysis.

The RFP should call for data that meets these requirements. If no competition is anticipated, the contracting officer can fulfill the statutory requirement by using the following language in the Requirements for Certified Cost or Pricing Data or Data Other Than Certified Cost or Pricing Data solicitation provision at FAR 52.215-20:

> (ii) *Commercial item exception.* For a commercial item exception, the offeror shall submit, at a minimum, information on prices at which the same item or similar items have previously been sold in the commercial market that is adequate for evaluating the reasonableness of the price for this acquisition. Such information may include —

(A) For catalog items, a copy of or identification of the catalog and its date, or the appropriate pages for the offered items, or a statement that the catalog is on file in the buying office to which the proposal is being submitted. Provide a copy or describe current discount policies and price lists (published or unpublished), e.g., wholesale, original equipment manufacturer, or reseller. Also explain the basis of each offered price and its relationship to the established catalog price, including how the proposed price relates to the price of recent sales in quantities similar to the proposed quantities.

(B) For market-price items, the source and date or period of the market quotation or other basis for market price, the base amount, and applicable discounts. In addition, describe the nature of the market.

(C) For items included on an active Federal Supply Service Multiple Award Schedule contract, proof that an exception has been granted for the schedule item.

If the contracting officer anticipates that the offers will be for an item where the price is controlled by law or regulation, data should be obtained to verify that the proposed price is in accordance with the applicable law or regulation. The following language from the Requirements for Certified Cost or Pricing Data or Data Other Than Certified Cost or Pricing Data solicitation provision in FAR 52.215-20 can be used:

(i) *Identification of the law or regulation establishing the price offered.* If the price is controlled under law by periodic rulings, reviews, or similar actions of a governmental body, attach a copy of the controlling document, unless it was previously submitted to the contracting office.

If the contracting officer has obtained a waiver of certified cost or pricing data, the specific data needed will have to be specified in the solicitation. In this instance the contracting officer has almost complete discretion but should comply with the basic policy of obtaining as little data is necessary.

c. Technical Information

Offerors should specify any information that is required to determine the acceptability of articles or services. This may include brand name product descriptions or performance capabilities.

(1) FORMAT

Offerors should be given precise instructions on the format required for the submission of proposals. See FAR 15.204-5(b), which states:

Prospective offerors or respondents may be instructed to submit proposals or information in a specific format or severable parts to facilitate evaluation. The instructions may specify further organization of proposal or response parts, such as —

(1) Administrative;

(2) Management;

(3) Technical;

(4) Past performance; and

(5) Cost or pricing data (see Table 15-2 of 15.408) or information other than cost or pricing data.

In many cases, an agency following this guidance will call for the submission of separate sections of each proposal to correspond to the evaluation process that the agency intends to use. Thus, the RFP will frequently call for separate technical proposals and will often require a separate management proposal. Cost or pricing information is almost always required to be packaged separately from the other elements of the proposal.

More detailed instruction is contained in the Army Materiel Command, *Contracting for Best Value: A Best Practices Guide to Source Selection*, AMC-P 715-3 (Jan. 1, 1998):

Properly written proposal preparation instructions simplify the evaluators' job. That is, evaluators do not have to learn a new format for each proposal; they can evaluate the same requirements in each proposal in the same way. With a sufficient degree of structure in the proposal preparation requirements, you may be able to accept proposals in electronic form and use some automation in the evaluation process.

This guidance further provides:

The instructions for preparing and submitting proposals are critical to an acquisition using the tradeoff approach. There has to be a linkage between solicitation requirements, each evaluation factor and subfactor and the proposal preparation instructions.

Each evaluation factor and subfactor must correlate directly with the proposal preparation instructions.

If you cannot cross-walk the solicitation requirements, factors/subfactors and the proposal instructions, you have a conflict that you need to correct.

* * *

The information requested from offerors must correlate with the evaluation factors and subfactors. However, instructions that require voluminous information can cause potential offerors to forgo responding to the solicitation in favor of a less costly business opportunity. Furthermore, excessive size of proposals may increase the Government's costs to perform the evaluation and length of the evaluation period. In order to simplify the preparation of proposals and to make the evaluation easier, you may wish to consider imposing a realistic limit on the number of pages and foldouts to be submitted.

The instructions on the preparation and submission of proposals must:

Be clearly and precisely stated.

Be keyed to the evaluation factors and subfactors.

Describe the type, scope, content, and format of the information to be submitted.

Describe the order in which proposal responses and materials are to appear.

Be limited to the information needed to do the evaluation.

Although it is common practice to require the submission of technical and management proposals, there is very little guidance given to contracting officers on the instructions that should be included in the RFP to assist offerors in their preparation. The regulations are silent on this issue and most source selection manuals and handbooks contain very little assistance. The most complete guidance is contained in the Department of Commerce manual, Source Selection Procedures, Part 4, May 1989:

Proposal Format: The solicitation should contain specific instructions as to how the proposals should be organized and arranged to provide consistency with the evaluation factors to facilitate the evaluation process. This instruction should address the following:

A common numbering system for paragraphs and subparagraphs;

Major divisions to permit easy breakout by the evaluation teams;

Separate volumes for major divisions when the size of the acquisition warrants;

An executive summary which recapitulates the offer for the benefit of the SSO. This summary could include: work breakdown structure, synopsis of major features, and the advantages to the Government of this proposal.

A number of agencies, particularly NASA, include mandatory page limitations in their RFPs. See NFS 1815.204-70. These limitations are strictly enforced, and an agency may disregard all pages of a technical or management proposal in excess of the limitation, *Mathews Assocs., Inc.*, Comp. Gen. Dec. B-299305, 2007 CPD ¶ 47; *All Star Maint., Inc.*, Comp. Gen. Dec. B-244143, 91-2 CPD ¶ 294. Furthermore, page limitations have not been accepted as an excuse for lack of adequate detailed language in a technical proposal, *Professional Performance Dev. Group, Inc.*, Comp. Gen. Dec. B-311273, 2008 CPD ¶ 101 (35 page limitation); *Superior Landscaping Co.*, Comp. Gen. Dec. B-310617, 2008 CPD ¶ 33; *HealthStar VA, PLLC*, Comp. Gen. Dec. B-299737, 2007 CPD ¶ 114. If a page limitation is imposed, an agency must follow it during proposal evaluation, *ITT Electron Tech. Div.*, Comp. Gen. Dec. B-242289, 91-1 CPD ¶ 383; *Electronic Design, Inc.*, Comp. Gen. Dec. B-279662.2, 98-2 CPD ¶ 69. Compare *Global Solutions Network, Inc.*, Comp. Gen. Dec. B-298682.3, 2008 CPD ¶ 131, denying a protest that the agency waived the page limitation because the protester was not prejudiced, and *United Computer Sys., Inc.*, GSBCA 10303-P, 90-1 BCA ¶ 22,546, holding that RFPs that merely state that failure to conform with page limitations "*may* be cause for rejection" do not mandate rejection of nonconforming proposals. Page limitations will be interpreted as applying only to the substantive parts of the proposal unless otherwise specified, *Trident Sys., Inc.*, Comp. Gen. Dec. B-243101, 91-1 CPD ¶ 604 (cover page and table of contents of proposal properly excluded from limitation); *TRW, Inc.*, GSBCA 11309-P, 92-1 BCA ¶ 24,389 (illustrative handbooks not included in page limitation).

Imposing page limitations is a questionable practice because of the problems it can cause in the ensuing source selection process. See, for example, *IBM Corp.*, Comp. Gen. Dec. B-299504, 2008 CPD ¶ 64, where the protester was advised that it could avoid a page limitation in one part of the proposal by submitting information in another part but, when the agency refused to evaluate the information because it was in the wrong part, the GAO denied the protest. See also *Cerner Corp.*, Comp. Gen. Dec. B-293093, 2004 CPD ¶ 34, where the GAO denied a protest of unfair treatment when the agency waived a page limitation for the winning offeror because the ultimate source selection decision was based on final proposal revisions to which no page limitation had been applied, and *Bank of America*, Comp. Gen. Dec. B-287608, 2001 CPD ¶ 137, where a protest was granted because the agency did not clear up a patently ambiguous page limitation during discussions.

5. *Requiring Data for Modifications*

Similar procedures are prescribed for contract modifications. FAR 15.408(m) permits the contracting officer to insert the Requirements for Certified Cost or Pricing Data or Data Other Than Certified Cost or Pricing Data — Modifications clause in FAR 52.215-21 in contracts "if it is reasonably certain that [such] data will be required for modifications" to the contract. This clause also permits the contractor to apply for an exception in lieu of submitting certified cost or pricing data to support a modification over the statutory threshold and contains the same alternate provisions for varied submissions of data. Because some data will be required for modifications over the statutory threshold, it is anticipated that this clause will be used in all contracts where there is any possibility that a modification over $750,000 might be issued.

M. Evaluation Scheme

Section M should identify the procurement strategy that will be used in making the award. This entails the inclusion of a clear statement of whether the agency is using the tradeoff process, the lowest price, technically acceptable proposal process, some combination of these two, or any other strategy that the agency has selected. See Chapter 2 describing these strategies.

The instructions should also describe the type of contract that is to be used and the objectives that the agency has in the procurement. It is also helpful to include a description of the time that the agency intends to take to evaluate proposals and the intended date of award of the contract. Guidance of this nature is very beneficial to offerors in assisting them to allocate resources to the procurement.

It is also very helpful to offerors if the instructions include specific information on the evaluation process that will be followed. In particular, evaluation standards should be disclosed. See *Omniplex World Servs. Corp.*, Comp. Gen. Dec. B-290996.2, 2003 CPD ¶ 7; *RJO Enters., Inc.*, Comp. Gen. Dec. B-260126.2, 95-2 CPD ¶ 93, and *Sarasota Measurements & Controls, Inc.*, Comp. Gen. Dec. B-252406, 93-1 CPD ¶ 494, requiring the inclusion of evaluation standards in RFPs when they constituted government requirements. While the GAO has not required the disclosure of evaluation standards that merely give guidance to evaluators in assessing the relative value of factors or subfactors, *Computer Assocs. Int'l, Inc.*, Comp. Gen. Dec. B-292077.3, 2004 CPD ¶ 163; *Lexis-Nexis*, Comp. Gen. Dec. B-260023, 95-2 CPD ¶ 14, the inclusion of such standards in the RFP is good practice because it provides fuller information on the agency's acquisition strategy.

The evaluation factors and subfactors to be used and their relative importance must also be identified in Section M. FAR 15.204-5(c) provides minimal guidance, merely directing the agency to —

> Identify all significant factors and any significant subfactors that will be considered in awarding the contract and their relative importance (see 15.304(d)).

1. *Statement of Factors and Subfactors*

The FAR requirement for a statement of the factors and significant subfactors in the RFP is based on statutory requirements in 10 U.S.C. § 2305(a)(2)(A)(i) and 41 U.S.C. § 253a(b)(1)(A). However, neither the statutes nor the FAR contain any definition of "factor" or "subfactor." Hence, agencies have some latitude in characterizing the factors and subfactors. Nonetheless, the RFP should identify all issues that will be considered in the evaluation in order to ensure that the offerors fully understand the evaluation procedures that will be followed. See Chapter 2 for a complete discussion of the considerations to be taken into account in selecting factors and subfactors.

a. Factors

Agencies must include a clear statement of the factors in the RFP. As discussed in Chapter 2, there is no clear guidance on the classification of evaluation factors. However, considerable clarity can be achieved if they are divided into two classes — offer factors and capability factors.

(1) OFFER FACTORS

Offer factors are elements of the evaluation scheme that will be incorporated into the contract as binding promises. There is one mandatory offer factor — price or cost to the government — and there may be other offer factors when the agency decides to solicit other promises from the offerors.

(A) PRICE OR COST FACTORS

The price or cost to the government is submitted by the offerors when they fill out Section B of the solicitation, as discussed above. Normally, in fixed-price-type contracts, prices are solicited for each contract line item in Section B. Special instructions on providing these line item prices are usually included in Section B as well. In cost-reimbursement contracts, the agency may want line item estimated costs or a single estimated cost for the entire contract. The RFP should contain clear guidance in either Section B or Section M as to how the estimated costs are to be proposed.

On cost-reimbursement contracts, the RFP should state that probable cost, not proposed cost, will be the evaluation factor, and that a cost realism analysis will be used as the basis of determining the probable cost. The GAO has held that where the RFP is amended to call for a cost-reimbursement, rather than fixed-price, contract, the agency should also amend the RFP to explicitly state that it would analyze cost realism and notify offerors that proposed costs may be adjusted accordingly, *Varian Assocs., Inc.*, Comp. Gen. Dec. B-209658, 83-1 CPD ¶ 658. In this case the initial RFP had listed "Lowest Evaluated Cost to the Government" as a factor, but although the protest was denied, the GAO stated that the better practice was to amend the solicitation.

When life-cycle costs are an evaluation factor, it is unclear whether a general statement in the solicitation informing offerors that such costs are to be evaluated is adequate, or whether it is necessary to specify the particular costs to be evaluated. In *Lanier Bus. Prods., Inc.*, 60 Comp. Gen. 306 (B-223555), 81-1 CPD ¶ 188, *recons. denied ex rel., Dictaphone Corp.*, Comp. Gen. Dec. B-200695.2, 81-2 CPD ¶

511, resolicitation was recommended where the RFQ merely stated that life-cycle costing would be employed and did not adequately inform offerors of the specific evaluation factors to be used. The GAO stated at 307–08:

> We have often pointed out the need for agencies to provide in their solicitations a clear statement of the evaluation factors to be used so that fair and intelligent competition can be achieved. *See, e.g., Signatron, Inc.*, 54 Comp. Gen. 530 (1974), 74-2 CPD ¶ 368; *Frontier Broadcasting Co. d.b.a. Cable Colorvision*, 53 Comp. Gen. 676 (1974), 74-1 CPD ¶ 138. Therefore, when life cycle costs are to be evaluated, the solicitation must indicate that fact. *Eastman Kodak Company*, B-194584, August 9, 1979, 79-2 CPD ¶ 105. In addition, we believe that in most cases the particular elements of the life cycle cost evaluation should be disclosed since they may vary from procurement to procurement and from agency to agency. *See, e.g., Hasko-Air, Inc.*, B-192488, March 19, 1979, 79-1 CPD ¶ 190 (special inspection and repair costs were considered); *Eastman Kodak Company, supra* (maintenance and operating costs were considered); *Philips Business Systems, Inc.*, B-194477, April 9, 1980, 80-1 CPD ¶ 264 (telephone company rental charges were considered).

See also *Systemhouse Fed. Sys., Inc.*, GSBCA 9313-P, 88-2 BCA ¶ 20,603, granting a protest because the agency did not disclose the manner in which life-cycle cost analysis would be used (where it had a major impact on the evaluation). However, in *Southwestern Bell Tel. Co.*, Comp. Gen. Dec. B-200523.3, 82-1 CPD ¶ 203, the GAO stated:

> Where an agency makes it clear that its evaluation will be based on an analysis of expected system life-cycle costs without qualification, offerors may reasonably expect that all determinable elements of cost will be taken into account.

These cases illustrate the difficulties created by vague language describing the life-cycle costs that will be evaluated. The offerors clearly had difficulty ascertaining what costs would be evaluated, with the result that the ground rules of the competition were not clearly disclosed in the RFP. See also *AM Int'l*, Comp. Gen. Dec. B-200200, 81-1 CPD ¶ 258, stating: "When life-cycle costs are to be evaluated we believe that the solicitation should not only indicate the fact, but also the useful life period that will be utilized in the evaluation."

Care should be taken in specifying the life-cycle costs that are to be considered because the agency must consider the data furnished by each offeror during the evaluation, *Hughes STX Corp.*, Comp. Gen. Dec. B-278466, 98-1 CPD ¶ 52. See *Boeing Co.*, Comp. Gen. Dec. B-311344, 2008 CPD ¶ 114 (agency used data gathered before receipt of proposals containing specific data); and *Sikorsky Aircraft Co.*, Comp. Gen. Dec. B-299145, 2007 CPD ¶ 44 (agency used normalized dollar amount for different products).

(B) Non-Price or Non-Cost Factors

As discussed in Chapter 2, there are a variety of non-price or non-cost factors that can be used in the procurement process. Section M of the RFP must be clearly written to specifically identify these factors.

If the agency is calling for offers on potential enhancements, the RFP should be as specific as possible on the precise extent of enhancements that the agency desires. The best technique is to provide for prices on a step ladder basis using a form that can be filled out by each offeror. For example, if the agency is calling for prices for various amounts of hard drive in computers, the following form could be used:

Performance	Price
80 gbyts	
160 gbyts	
320 gbyts	
640 gbyts	

If the agency is soliciting offers for specific products or services or for a process or technique to be used, the RFP should require each offeror to identify the precise product that is being offered or the specific services that will be provided. In many cases the agency will want detailed information demonstrating that the product or service offered meets the agency's needs as described in the RFP. Since such information will not normally be incorporated into the contract document, the RFP should clearly state that this information should be submitted separately. This separation of the offer from information supporting the offer will assist the parties in drafting the final contractual document and will add clarity to that document.

(2) Capability Factors

As discussed in Chapter 2, there are a variety of capability factors that are commonly used in negotiated procurements. Past performance is the most commonly used capability factor, but experience and key personnel are also widely used. Understanding the work is also a frequently used factor to assess the offerors' capability.

When past performance is a factor, the RFP should clearly identify that it will be evaluated and should specify how the evaluation will be conducted. FAR 15.305(a)(2)(ii) contains the following detailed requirements when past performance is used as an evaluation factor:

The solicitation shall describe the approach for evaluating past performance including evaluating offerors with no relevant performance history, and shall provide offerors an opportunity to identify past or current contracts (including Federal, State, and local government and private) for efforts similar to the Government requirement. The solicitation shall also authorize offerors to provide information on problems encountered on the identified contracts and the offeror corrective actions. The Government shall consider this information, as well as information obtained from any other sources, when evaluating the offeror past performance. The source selection authority shall determine the relevance of similar past performance information.

The inclusion of a clear description of the method of evaluation will avoid any question of the agency's ability to make this type of evaluation. See *NITCO*, Comp. Gen. Dec. B-246185, 92-1 CPD ¶ 212, where the GAO rejected the use of past experience in manufacturing similar equipment when the RFP contained no indication of such a factor. Another case rejecting the use of past performance when it was not explicitly stated to be a factor is *Laser Power Techs., Inc.*, Comp. Gen. Dec. B-233369, 89-1 CPD ¶ 267, stating: "There is no legal basis for favoring a firm with presumptions on the basis of past performance; it must demonstrate capabilities in the proposal that were required by the RFP to be addressed."

When experience and key personnel are used as evaluation factors, they should also be clearly identified in the RFP and offerors should be advised as to how they will be used. Since these factors can be made a part of the evaluation of past performance, it is important that they be clearly defined. See Chapter 2 for a full discussion of the confusion in this area.

When understanding of the work is used as a factor, it should be clearly stated in the RFP. See *ENCORP Int'l, Inc.*, Comp. Gen. Dec. B-258829, 95-1 CPD ¶ 100, where consideration of an offeror's understanding of the work was held to be improper where there was no evaluation factor covering that issue. See also *Digital Equip. Corp.*, GSBCA 9131-P, 88-1 BCA ¶ 20,254, where a protest was granted because the RFP contained vague language describing the evaluation factors, which failed to indicate what characteristics in the computer system the agency was seeking; and *Storage Tech. Corp.*, GSBCA 8961-P, 87-2 BCA ¶ 19,953, granting a protest because of ambiguity in the description of an evaluation factor.

b. Subfactors

Significant subfactors must be listed in the RFP. If a subfactor will have an inordinate impact on the evaluation of a factor, it will be found to be a "significant" subfactor which must be identified in the RFP as having such impact, *Systemhouse Fed. Sys., Inc.*, GSBCA 9313-P, 88-2 BCA ¶ 20,603. See *Compuware Corp.*, GSBCA 8869-P, 87-2 BCA ¶ 19,781, where the agency was required to identify a subfactor that altered the focus of the evaluation scheme. See also *Devres, Inc.*, 66 Comp. Gen.

121 (B-224017), 86-2 CPD ¶ 652, where the GAO required listing of a subfactor for specific experience even though it was related to the "general experience" that had been listed. The specific experience subfactor was 60% of the general experience factor and 25% of the total scoring (it was larger than any other factor).

A subfactor that is not logically related to the stated factor may not be used if it is not separately listed See, for example, *Global Analytic Information Tech. Servs., Inc.*, Comp. Gen. Dec. B-298840.2, 2007 CPD ¶ 57, finding that the incumbent contractors' methods of improving their performance was not related to the "management approach" factor because it was an "incumbent-specific factor" that could not have been foreseen by the incumbents. However, there have been numerous protests where unlisted subfactors have been held to be logically related to a factor. For example, the requirement that the project director be available at the outset of the procurement was held to be logically related to the "Personnel Qualifications" evaluation factor, *Health Mgmt. Sys.*, Comp. Gen. Dec. B-200775, 81-1 CPD ¶ 255. Similarly, the subfactors "Compliance with Stated Minimum Requirements," "Additional Experience/Qualifications of Key Personnel," and "Experience in the Topical Area" were found to be sufficiently related to the "Personnel Qualifications" factor, *Management Sys. Designers, Inc.*, Comp. Gen. Dec. B-244383.4, 91-2 CPD ¶ 518. In *Telos Field Eng'g*, Comp. Gen. Dec. B-258805.2, 95-1 CPD ¶ 186, the protester contended that its proposal was improperly downgraded under the spare parts factor for proposing an inventory of older spare parts and on the ground that its current inventory did not consist of the optimal mix of equipment and was not organized in kits. The spare parts factor provided:

> "[D]oes the contractor have the ability to supply spare parts when needed? Does the contractor have an adequate reserve of parts and the means to quickly deliver them to the site? Could the contractor replace a complete piece of equipment if need be to incur maximum equipment uptime?"

In finding the evaluation reasonable, the GAO stated:

> [T]he type of inventory and the mix of parts reasonably could be expected to affect the ability to furnish parts for certain equipment, as well as the speed with which the contractor can furnish a part for a newer piece of equipment. Similarly, making parts available in kits, rather than individually, reasonably relates to the speed with which parts necessary for a certain repair can be ordered.

In other cases, cost management was held to be clearly related to past performance even though the RFP only listed "technical performance" and "schedule performance" as subfactors, *Bendix Field Eng'g Corp.*, Comp. Gen. Dec. B-241156, 91-1 CPD ¶ 44, and specific experience was held to be reasonably related to general experience, *Technical Servs. Corp.*, 64 Comp. Gen. 245 (B-214634), 85-1 CPD ¶ 152. In *JoaQuin Mfg. Corp.*, Comp. Gen. Dec. B-275185, 97-1 CPD ¶ 48, the GAO found that weight, number of footings, and visibility properly related to the suitability of design evaluation factor. In a very questionable decision, the GAO held that performance of work by segments of the company rather than by subcontractors was clearly related to the factor "Offeror's Ability to Provide Additional Effort," *Specialized Tech. Servs., Inc.*, Comp. Gen. Dec. B-247489.2, 92-1 CPD ¶ 510.

The GAO has consistently held that innovations and creative approaches need not be identified as subfactors because they are an integral element of evaluating the offeror's technical approach in a best value procurement, *ViroMed Labs., Inc.*, Comp. Gen. Dec. B-310747.4, 2009 CPD ¶ 32; *IAP World Servs., Inc.*, Comp. Gen. Dec. B-297084, 2005 CPD ¶ 199. See also *USGC, Inc.*, Comp. Gen. Dec. B-400184.2, 2009 CPD ¶ 9 ("disincentive plan" foregoing profit for tasks not meeting performance work statement requirements fell within technical approach factor); *AT&T Corp.*, Comp. Gen. Dec. B-299542.3, 2008 CPD ¶ 65 (being manufacturer of equipment related to factor assessing ability to provide equipment); *Apptis, Inc.*, Comp. Gen. Dec. B-299457, 2008 CPD ¶ 49 (proof of concept demonstration factor encompassed observations that company personnel were inefficient even though the demonstration was successful); *C. Young Constr., Inc.*, Comp. Gen. Dec. B-309740, 2007 CPD ¶ 198 (multiple-position personnel related to technical qualifications of key personnel factor); *Client Network Servs., Inc.*, Comp. Gen. Dec. B-297994, 2006 CPD ¶ 79 (knowledge of labor market related to staffing factor); *Ridoc Enter., Inc.*, Comp. Gen. Dec. B-292962.4, 2004 CPD ¶ 169 (management of subcontractors related to management plan factor); *Israel Aircraft Indus.*, Comp. Gen. Dec. B-274389, 97-1 CPD ¶ 41 (enhanced safety intrinsic to technical evaluation of equipment); *Myers Investigative & Security Servs., Inc.*, Comp. Gen. Dec. B-272947.2, 96-2 CPD ¶ 114 (solicitation clearly put offerors on notice that relevant experience would be evaluated under the past performance factor); and *Science & Tech., Inc.*, Comp. Gen. Dec. B-272748, 97-1 CPD ¶ 121 (offerors could not reasonably ignore factor left off the list of subfactors in section M but which was discussed in section L).

Subfactors need not be included on a separate list if they are described in a narrative form in the description of the factor, *Moran Assocs.*, Comp. Gen. Dec. B-240564.2, 91-2 CPD ¶ 495. In that case the GAO apparently believed that a diligent offeror would identify the subfactors from the narrative description. See also *ITT Electron Tech. Div.*, Comp. Gen. Dec. B-242289, 91-1 CPD ¶ 383, holding that there was no need to disclose an evaluation "checklist" when the items on the list were reasonably related to the evaluation factors. In *Stone Webster Eng'g Corp.*, Comp. Gen. Dec. B-255286.2, 94-2 CPD ¶ 306, the protester contended that the evaluation was improper because the agency evaluated proposals on a basis of an evaluation factor, "general strategy," that was not listed as an evaluation factor in the RFP. The agency stated that general strategy was not a separate evaluation criterion but was, however, considered as part of the evaluation of several factors that were set forth in the RFP. The GAO agreed, finding that the RFP did state that strategy formulation and selection of appropriate tactics would be a significant subfactor under the understanding the anticipated work evaluation factor.

Listed subfactors must include only elements that bear a relationship to the subfactor. The GAO has held that the financial condition of an offeror was not properly included in the subfactor "ability to meet the published schedule requirements of the Government at an acceptable level of risk," *Flight Int'l Group, Inc.*, 69 Comp. Gen. 741 (B-238953.4), 90-2 CPD ¶ 257.

c. Evaluation Standards

Some agencies create elaborate evaluation standards on their major procurements to ensure that evaluators make consistent evaluations. These standards provide detailed guidance on the scoring that will be given for specific proposals. There is no statutory or regulatory requirement that such standards be included in the RFP. However, without knowledge of such standards, offerors may be unable to determine how the source selection decision will be made. If that is the case, such standards should be stated in the RFP.

Evaluation standards that must be met to obtain a satisfactory score are considered to be significant subfactors which must be disclosed in the RFP. See *Sarasota Measurements & Controls, Inc.*, Comp. Gen. Dec. B-252406, 93-1 CPD ¶ 494, stating:

> It is fundamental that offerors must be advised of the bases upon which their proposals will be evaluated. *H.J. Group Ventures, Inc.*, B-246139, Feb. 19, 1992, 92-1 CPD ¶ 203; *Republic Realty Servs., Inc.*, B-242629, May 7, 1991, 91-1 CPD ¶ 446. In particular, contracting agencies are required by the Competition in Contracting Act of 1984 (CICA) to set forth in the solicitation, at a minimum, all significant evaluation factors and significant subfactors and their relative importance. 10 U.S.C. § 2305(a)(2)(A) (Supp. IV 1992); FAR 15.605(e) (FAC 90-7); *H.J. Group Ventures, Inc., supra.* While agencies are not required to specifically identify each element to be considered during the course of the evaluation where a particular element is intrinsic to the stated factors or subfactors, *Marine Animal Prods. Int'l, Inc.*, B-247150.2, July 13, 1992, 92-2 CPD ¶ 16, the solicitation must inform offerors of all minimum requirements that apply to evaluation factors and subfactors. FAR 15.605(e); see *W.B. Jolley*, 68 Comp. Gen. 444 (1989), 89-1 CPD ¶ 512. It is also fundamental that the contracting agency must treat all offerors equally, which includes providing a common basis for the preparation and the submission of proposals and not disparately evaluating offerors with respect to the same requirements. *AT&T Comm.*, 65 Comp. Gen. 412 (1986), 86-1 CPD ¶ 247; *Secure Servs. Tech., Inc.*, B-238059, Apr. 25, 1990, 90-1 CPD ¶ 429.

The same result was reached in *RJO Enters., Inc.*, Comp. Gen. Dec. B-260126.2, 95-2 CPD ¶ 93. This rule has not been applied to evaluation standards that contain only desirable features above the agency's minimum requirements, *Lexis-Nexis*, Comp. Gen. Dec. B-260023, 95-2 CPD ¶ 14. However, it is good practice to disclose such standards as well.

The GAO has also criticized the failure to disclose evaluation standards when they had a significant impact on the evaluation, *Postal Procurement: Eagle Air Hub Selection Not In Accordance With Solicitation*, Comp. Gen. Rep. GGD-92-127, Aug. 12, 1992. The undisclosed evaluation standard for completion of performance was as follows:

Days After Award	Points
305 or less	20
306 to 335	19
336 to 365	18
366 to 395	10
396 to 425	5
426 to 455	3

The GAO concluded that the RFP statement that completion within 365 days was "minimally acceptable" was an inadequate description of this scoring system — especially because this factor was the most important factor in the evaluation. Compare *P.E. Sys., Inc.*, Comp. Gen. Dec. B-249033.2, 92-2 CPD ¶ 409, where the GAO ruled that a "staffing model" used to assess the adequacy of proposed labor mixes and the offerors' understanding of the work need not be disclosed in the RFP.

2. Relative Importance

There are two aspects of the statutory requirement to provide a statement of relative importance in the RFP. At the highest level, there must be a statement of the relationship of cost/price to the non-price factors required by 10 U.S.C. § 2305(a)(3) (iii) and 41 U.S.C. § 253a(c)(1)(C). Below that level, there must be some indication of the relative importance of the factors and subfactors within the non-cost or price areas, 10 U.S.C. § 2305(a)(2)(A)(ii) and 41 U.S.C. § 253a(b)(1)(B).

a. Relationship of Cost/Price to Other Factors

The statutory requirement for a statement of relative importance between the cost/price factor and the non-price factors is implemented in FAR 15.304:

(e) The solicitation shall also state, at a minimum, whether all evaluation factors other than cost or price, when combined, are —

(1) Significantly more important than cost or price;

(2) Approximately equal to cost or price; or

(3) Significantly less important than cost or price (10 U.S.C. 2305(a)(3) (A)(iii) and 41 U.S.C. 253a(c)(1)(C)).

This requirement would appear to be applicable only when the tradeoff process was being used. Thus, when the lowest-price, technically acceptable proposal process is being used, the RFP would merely state that price would be the deciding factor in the second step of the process.

The GAO had ruled before the passage of these statutes that offerors were entitled to know the relative importance of price and the non-price factors. See *Signatron, Inc.*, 54 Comp. Gen. 530 (B-181782), 74-2 CPD ¶ 386, stating at 535:

> We believe that each offeror has a right to know whether the procurement is intended to achieve a minimum standard at the lowest cost or whether cost is secondary to quality. Competition is not served if offerors are not given any idea of the relative values of technical excellence and price.

Following the passage of the statutory requirements, the GAO held that in a procurement using the tradeoff process, the explicit words in this regulation need not be used if they do not accurately describe the relative importance. Hence, it was held that this requirement was met when the RFP contained an accurate statement that the non-price factor was "more important" than price, rather than "significantly more important," *Braswell Servs. Group*, Comp. Gen. Dec. B-276694, 97-2 CPD ¶ 18. However, when an agency uses the "more important" statement, it is improper to then treat the non-cost factors as significantly more important, *Johnson Controls Sec. Sys., LLC*, Comp. Gen. Dec. B-296490.3, 2007 CPD ¶ 100.

It is generally recognized that a bare statement of relative importance is not a description of how the source selection decision will actually be made but is only a statement of the importance of the factors to the agency in meeting its objectives. The statement that price is significantly more important than other factors does not mean that low price will win the competition but, rather, that the agency will not award to the offeror with a higher price unless it obtains a benefit worth the marginal difference in price. In order to make this clear to offerors and to avoid misleading them, many agencies provide more elaborate descriptions of the way that the source selection decision will be made. This usually consists of language stating, in some fashion, that the source selection decision will be based on an analysis of the *marginal difference* in the price and non-price factors to determine which proposal offers the best value to the government.

The following is provided, by way of illustration, as language that may be included in an RFP to meet the statutory requirement for a statement of relative importance, as well as stating how the source selection decision will be made:

> Award will be made to that offeror whose proposal contains the combination of those criteria offering the best overall value to the government. This will be determined by comparing differences in the value of non-cost features with differences in cost to the government. In making this comparison . . . (select the applicable alternative)

No. 1 (Non-cost features significantly more important) — the government is more concerned with obtaining superior technical or management performance than with making an award at the lowest overall cost to the government. However, the government will not make an award at a significantly higher overall cost to the government to achieve slightly superior technical or management performance.

No. 2 (Non-cost and cost to the government of equal importance) — the government is concerned with striking the most advantageous balance between technical and management performance and cost to the government.

No. 3 (Cost to the government significantly more important) — the government is more concerned with making an award at the lowest overall cost to the government than with obtaining superior technical or management performance. However, the government will not make an award based on a proposal offering significantly inferior technical or management performance in order to achieve a small savings in cost to the government.

This language attempts to tell offerors that the best value decision will ultimately be made on the basis of marginal differences between the competitors and that the agency will pay more or less for marginal differences in technical and management features but not a lot more for a marginal difference. This, of course, describes the essence of a tradeoff selection. For an example of actual language stating this process, see *DLM&A, Inc. v. United States*, 6 Cl. Ct. 329 (1984), where the RFP stated at 330:

[C]ost is not expected to be the controlling factor in the selection of a Contractor for this solicitation. The degree of importance of cost as a factor could become greater depending upon the equality of the proposals for other factors evaluated; where competing proposals are determined to be substantially equal, total cost and other cost factors would become the controlling factor.

Another example can be found in *EG&G Ortec*, Comp. Gen. Dec. B-213347, 84-1 CPD ¶ 182, *recons. denied*, 84-1 CPD ¶ 372, where the RFP contained the full point scoring system plus the following statement:

You are advised that paramount consideration shall be given to the evaluation of technical proposals rather than cost or price. It is pointed out, however, that should technical competence between offerors be considered approximately the same, then cost or price could become paramount.

In some cases, the GAO has held that this type of statement does not meet the requirement to state relative importance. See *Ogden Support Servs., Inc.*, Comp. Gen. Dec. B-270354, 96-1 CPD ¶ 175, where the RFP only stated that "cost would become more important as the difference in technical evaluation scores decreases and that cost 'may become' determinative when proposals are technically equal." The GAO stated that this scheme failed to state the relative importance of the cost factor.

Some agencies attempt to describe this source selection technique by describing the relative importance of the price and non-price factors and stating that award will be made to the proposal offering the best value, *Resource Mgmt. Int'l, Inc.*, Comp. Gen. Dec. B-278108, 98-1 CPD ¶ 29; *Modern Techs. Corp.*, Comp. Gen. Dec. B-278695, 98-1 CPD ¶ 81; or that is most advantageous to the government, *Tecom, Inc.*, Comp. Gen. Dec. B-275518.2, 97-1 CPD ¶ 221. Although this is legally sufficient, it does not give as clear an indication of the basis for the source selection as does the language recommended above.

Some agencies have used the term "relative weight" to describe "relative importance," and in some cases they have used percentage weights to assign points in a numerical scoring system. Stating relative weights meets the requirement to state relative importance. See, for example, *GC Servs. Ltd. Partnership*, Comp. Gen. Dec. B-298102, 2006 CPD ¶ 96 (past performance and experience weighted at 45%, technical approach weighted at 30% and management approach weighted at 25% of non-cost score); *Joint Mgmt. & Tech. Servs.*, Comp. Gen. Dec. B-294229, 2004 CPD ¶ 208 (technical approach — 35%, key/critical personnel — 25%, management approach — 20%, experience — 10%, past performance — 10%).

Failing to state relative "weights," when that term is used, will be found to be a failure to meet the requirement to state relative importance See *ENCORP Int'l, Inc.*, Comp. Gen. Dec. B-258829, 95-1 CPD ¶ 100, where the agency had explicitly refrained from stating the relative weights of the "more important" technical factors listed in the RFP. Instead, the RFP stated:

> When making tradeoff decisions during proposal preparation, offerors should remember that the Government prefers to obtain better offeror experience, past performance, and better savings. However, the relative influence that any of these factors will have on the source selection decision will ultimately depend on the marginal differences among the competing offerors, which will not be known until the proposals have been analyzed and compared to one another. Therefore, the Government has not assigned *weights* to these factors [emphasis added].

In a footnote the GAO stated that this statement failed to comply with the Competition in Contracting Act, which required, at a minimum, all evaluation factors and significant subfactors and their relative importance. See also *Bio-Rad Labs., Inc.*, Comp. Gen. Dec. B-297553, 2007 CPD ¶ 58 (no disclosure of relative weights of technical subfactors); and *SOS Interpreting, Ltd.*, Comp. Gen. Dec. B-293026, 2005 CPD ¶ 26 (no disclosure of relative weight of past performance or of technical subfactors).

b. Importance of Other Factors

There are a number of different methods of specifying the relative importance of factors other than cost or price.

(1) Listing Factors

A questionable technique for disclosing the relative importance of non-price/cost factors is merely to list the factors that will be evaluated in the RFP with no statement of relative importance. In such cases the offerors are expected to assume that all non-price/cosevaluation criteria are of approximately equal importance. See, for example, *Hyperbaric Techs., Inc.*, Comp. Gen. Dec. B-293047.2, 2004 CPD ¶ 87; *Maryland Office Relocators*, Comp. Gen. Dec. B-291092, 2002 CPD ¶ 198; *Carol Solomon & Assocs.*, Comp. Gen. Dec. B-271713, 96-2 CPD ¶ 28; *Computing & Software, Inc.*, 52 Comp. Gen. 686 (B-176763) (1973); *Dikewood Servs. Co.*, 56 Comp. Gen. 188 (B-186001), 76-2 CPD ¶ 520, where the GAO applied the presumption of equality in the absence of a contrary indication of relative importance in the RFP. Similarly, in *Fintrac, Inc.*, Comp. Gen. Dec. B-311462.2, 2008 CPD ¶ 191, and *Bio-Rad Labs., Inc.*, Comp. Gen. Dec. B-297553, 2007 CPD ¶ 58, a list of subfactors was presumed to have approximately equal importance.

(2) Descending Order of Importance

Another commonly used method of indicating relative order of importance of the non-price/cost factors is to list the factors or subfactors and state that they are listed in descending order of importance. The GAO has upheld use of this method where the evaluation scheme "reflects a reasonable downward progression of evaluation weights," *Optimum Tech., Inc.*, Comp. Gen. Dec. B-266339.2, 96-1 CPD ¶ 188. See also *Puglia Eng'g of Cal., Inc.*, Comp. Gen. Dec. B-297413, 2006 CPD ¶ 33; *Dawco Constr., Inc.*, Comp. Gen. Dec. B-278048.2, 98-1 CPD ¶ 32; *A&W Maint. Servs., Inc.*, Comp. Gen. Dec. B-255711.2, 95-1 CPD ¶ 24; and *North-East Imaging, Inc.*, Comp. Gen. Dec. B-256281, 94-1 CPD ¶ 332. However, a mere statement that the evaluation factors are listed in the order of their relative importance, without specifically assigning a degree of importance to each, is satisfactory so long as the differences between the importance assigned to any one factor and that assigned to the factors both immediately preceding and immediately following it are small. See *Sperry Rand Corp.*, Comp. Gen. Dec. B-179875, 74-2 CPD ¶ 158, stating that where one factor is to have predominant consideration over the other factors, this should be disclosed. In *BDM Servs. Co.*, Comp. Gen. Dec. B-180245, 74-1 CPD ¶ 237, the GAO stated that a predominant factor should have been identified in the RFP and added:

> Moreover, we believe the general relationship of the remaining factors to each other could have been described in narrative without violating the prohibition against disclosure of precise numerical weights in ASPR 3-501(D)(i). As a matter of sound procurement policy, the fullest possible disclosure of all of the evaluation factors and their relative importance is to be preferred to reliance on the reasonableness of the offeror's judgment as to the relative significance of the various evaluation factors.

See also *Finlen Complex, Inc.*, Comp. Gen. Dec. B-288280, 2001 CPD ¶ 167, holding that the 5% weight of past performance was required to be disclosed because offerors could have expected this subfactor to have a higher weight.

When factors are listed in descending order of importance, the agency must follow that scheme in making its source selection decision, *Boeing Co.*, Comp. Gen. Dec. B-311344, 2008 CPD ¶ 114. However, if the RFP states that the award will be made to the "best value" and lists the non-price factors in descending order of importance, it should not be interpreted as indicating that price will not be considered, *Banknote Corp. of Am., Inc. v. United States*, 365 F.3d 1345 (Fed. Cir. 2004). Further, an agency may not evaluate such a factor on a pass-fail basis because such a listing implies that all of the factors will be evaluated qualitatively, *Helicopter Transport Servs. LLC*, Comp. Gen. Dec. B-400295, 2008 CPD ¶ 180.

Where a solicitation lists non-price/cost evaluation factors and subfactors in descending order of importance, such an evaluation scheme does not indicate that the subfactors of lower-weighted factors are necessarily of less individual weight than subfactors of higher-weighted factors, *Brown & Root, Inc.*, Comp. Gen. Dec. B-270505.2, 96-2 CPD ¶ 143.

(3) ADJECTIVAL DESCRIPTIONS OF IMPORTANCE

Another technique for disclosing relative importance of the factors is to provide an adjectival description of the importance of each evaluation factor. It has been common practice to use such descriptions when the agency actually has firm weights for the non-cost factors. See, for example, *ITT Federal Servs. Int'l Corp.*, Comp. Gen. Dec. B-296783, 2007 CPD ¶ 43, where the RFP stated:

> The RFP advised that the price/cost and business/management/technical approach factors were equal in importance, and that each was significantly more important than past performance, and further, that the past performance and business/management/technical approach factors together were more important than price/cost.

These adjectival statements are also commonly used to describe complex source selection schemes. See, for example, *MD Helicopters, Inc.*, Comp. Gen. Dec. B-298502, 2006 CPD ¶ 178, where the GAO described the relationship of the factors as follows:

> The RFP provided for a "best value" evaluation of [Federal Aviation Administration] certification (which was evaluated as a "go/no go" criteria) and five other evaluation factors: price, technical, producibility/management (P/M), logistics, and past performance. Price was stated to be more important than technical, technical more important than P/M, and price and technical combined were significantly more important than P/M, logistics, and past performance. P/M and logistics were stated to be of equal importance and each was more important than past performance.

While these types of statements are difficult to decipher, they have been found to convey sufficient information to the offerors as to the relative importance of the factors.

Prior to the statutory requirement for a statement of the relationship between cost/price factor and the other factors, this was permitted with regard to the entire evaluation. See *Bayshore Sys. Corp.*, Comp. Gen. Dec. B-184446, 76-1 CPD ¶ 146, where the GAO found a mere statement that technical factors were more important than price was proper where the undisclosed technical-to-price ratio was 3 to 1. See also *Kirk-Mayer, Inc.*, Comp. Gen. Dec. B-208582, 83-2 CPD ¶ 288, where the GAO found satisfactory a statement that the weights attached to the four factors did not differ significantly, where the weights used in the evaluation were 25, 25, 20, and 30 points; and *Technical Servs. Corp.*, 64 Comp. Gen. 245 (B-214634), 85-1 CPD ¶ 152, where the GAO concurred with a statement that cost was "secondary" but "important" in a situation where cost was given a 20% weight and technical an 80% weight. However, the GAO has agreed that an award should be canceled and the RFP amended where the adjectival description is misleading as to the relative importance of a factor, *Unisys Corp.*, 67 Comp. Gen. 512 (B-230019.2), 88-2 CPD ¶ 35.

(4) NUMERICAL SYSTEMS

The relative importance of factors and subfactors may also be indicated by disclosing the numerical point score or percentage for each evaluation criterion in the RFP. An agency's RFP disclosures of its numerical systems must be sufficient to inform prospective offerors of how the rating system will apply to their proposals. In *National Capital Med. Found. Inc.*, Comp. Gen. Dec. B-215303.5, 85-1 CPD ¶ 637, the RFP failed to inform offerors that proposals would receive zero points out of a possible 110 allocated to "admission objectives" and 200 allocated to "quality objectives" if any one of the subcriteria under these objectives was rated less than acceptable, regardless of the merits of the others. The GAO found that application of such an undisclosed scoring scheme was arbitrary and inconsistent with the RFP requirements.

(5) SUBFACTORS

As with primary areas of the evaluation, an offeror may assume that all subfactors are of substantially equal importance in the absence of advice to the contrary, *North Am. Tel. Assoc.*, Comp. Gen. Dec. B-187239, 76-2 CPD ¶ 495; *Tracor, Inc.*, 56 Comp. Gen. 62 (B-186315), 76-2 CPD ¶ 386. However, if a subfactor is to play an important role in the source selection decision, that must be stated in the RFP. See, for example, *H. J. Group Ventures, Inc.*, Comp. Gen. Dec. B-246139, 92-1 CPD ¶ 203, finding improper heavy reliance on past performance when that factor had been listed as a "general consideration" but not included in the list of other factors that were stated in relative order of importance. See also *J.A. Jones Mgmt. Servs., Inc.*, Comp. Gen. Dec. B-254941.2, 94-1 CPD ¶ 244, where the agency improperly had greatly exaggerated the weight the RFP assigned to the key personnel evaluation factor; *University of Michigan*, 66 Comp. Gen. 538 (B-225756), 87-1 CPD ¶ 643, where it was improper to place heavy reliance on one factor when the RFP appeared to indicate that four technical factors were of relatively equal weight; and *Genasys Corp.*, GSBCA 8734-P, 87-1 BCA ¶ 19,556, where the RFP stated that one to three points would be given for technical enhancements to a proposed computer system but gave no indication which enhancements were of greater importance to the agency.

II. PUBLICIZING REQUIREMENTS AND SOLICITING COMPETITION

When the RFP has been drafted, the agency is ready to solicit proposals. However, prior to the issuance of the RFP, it must meet the statutory notice requirements. After the RFP is issued, amendments may be required or, in some circumstances, it may have to be canceled. This section discusses these issues in the sequence in which they occur.

A. Presolicitation Notices

The Small Business Act, 15 U.S.C. § 637(e), and the Office of Procurement Policy Act, 41 U.S.C. § 416(a), establish *minimum standards* for the development of competition by requiring that contracting officers publish a notice (synopsis) for each proposed procurement in excess of $10,000 and for proposed orders under basic agreements, basic ordering agreements, or similar arrangements exceeding $10,000. Procurement notices are intended to increase meaningful competition by explaining the government's requirements before issuance of an RFP. The agency may also use presolicitation notices or other techniques to develop competition well in advance of the prospective procurement.

The purposes served by this policy of publicizing proposed contract actions is stated in FAR 5.002 as follows:

Contracting officers must publicize contract actions in order to —

(a) Increase competition;

(b) Broaden industry participation in meeting Government requirements; and

(c) Assist small business concerns, veteran-owner small business concerns, service-disabled veteran-owner small business concerns, HUB-Zone small business concerns, small disadvantaged business concerns, and women-owned small business concerns in obtaining contracts and subcontracts.

1. Method of Publication

Although the statutes permit publication in the Commerce Business Daily (CBD) (the old publication method) or electronically, FAR 5.101(a)(1) has adopted the Governmentwide point of entry (GPE) as the standard method of publicizing contract actions expected to exceed $25,000. See FAR 2.101 containing the following description:

> Governmentwide point of entry (GPE) means the single point where Government business opportunities greater than $25,000, including synopses of proposed contract actions, solicitations, and associated information, can be accessed electronically by the public. The GPE is located at http://www.fedbizopps.gov.

FAR 5.101(a)(2) allows contract actions expected to exceed $10,000 but not expected to exceed $25,000 to be publicized by displaying a notice in a public place or "by any appropriate electronic means."

FAR 5.101(b) also allows additional method of publicizing contract actions as follows:

> In addition, one or more of the following methods may be used:
>
> (1) Preparing periodic handouts listing proposed contracts, and displaying them as in 5.101(a)(2).
>
> (2) Assisting local trade associations in disseminating information to their members.
>
> (3) Making brief announcements of proposed contracts to newspapers, trade journals, magazines, or other mass communication media for publication without cost to the Government.
>
> (4) Placing paid advertisements in newspapers or other communications media, subject to the following limitations:
>
>> (i) Contracting officers shall place paid advertisements of proposed contracts only when it is anticipated that effective competition cannot be obtained otherwise (see 5.205(d)).
>>
>> (ii) Contracting officers shall not place advertisements of proposed contracts in a newspaper published and printed in the District of Columbia unless the supplies or services will be furnished, or the labor performed, in the District of Columbia or adjoining counties in Maryland or Virginia (44 U.S.C. 3701).
>>
>> (iii) Advertisements published in newspapers must be under proper written authority in accordance with 44 U.S.C. 3702 (see 5.502(a)).

Notices are properly posted if they hyperlink from FedBizOpps to agency material, *LexisNexis, Inc.*, Comp. Gen. Dec. B-299381, 2007 CPD ¶ 73, or reference an agency web-site, *Wilcox Indus. Corp.*, Comp. Gen. Dec. B-287392, 2001 CPD ¶ 61. Notices are also properly posted if they require searching by geographic area, *Jess Bruner Fire Suppression*, Comp. Gen. Dec. B-296533, 2005 CPD ¶ 163. However, if the notice is misclassified, it will not meet the notice requirement, *TMI Mgmt. Sys., Inc.*, Comp. Gen. Dec. B-401530, 2009 CPD ¶ 191 (product code used when procurement was for services); *Gourmet Distributors*, Comp. Gen. Dec. B-259083, 95-1 CPD ¶ 130 (beverage vending services procurement classified using code for leasing or renting equipment).

2. *Mandatory Time Periods*

This publicizing policy gives potential competitors a short period to determine if they are capable of performing the proposed work and sufficient time to prepare a proposal. FAR 5.203 provides that solicitations may not be issued earlier than 15 days after publication of the notice except in the case of acquisitions of commercial items where the agency is permitted to use the combined synopsis/solicitation described in FAR 12.603. FAR 5.203(b) requires a reasonable response time for actions within the simplified acquisition threshold, and FAR 5.203(c) requires that the response time for actions over the simplified acquisition threshold, except for commercial item acquisitions, be at least 30 days after issuance of the solicitation. For research and development procurements, the required waiting period for the closing date for receipt of proposals is 45 days, FAR 5.203(e). These requirements set forth minimum periods only; many procuring agencies have found that extending the periods increases competition.

FAR 5.203(g) provides that contracting officers may, unless they have evidence to the contrary, presume that the notices are published one day after transmission to the GPE, but this presumption does not negate the statutory response times. See *AUL Instruments, Inc.*, 64 Comp. Gen. 871 (B-216543), 85-2 CPD ¶ 324, reaching this same conclusion under prior publication procedures. This FAR provision requires contracting officers, upon learning that the notice was not published within the one-day period, to consider whether the date for receipt of proposals should be extended or the notice requirement waived under FAR 5.202(a)(2). In *Shiloh Forestry, Inc.*, Comp. Gen. Dec. B-235449, 89-2 CPD ¶ 229, the GAO upheld a decision to waive the requirement based on the urgency of the procurement even though the notice was never published. See also *Electro-Methods, Inc.*, Comp. Gen. Dec. B-250931, 93-1 CPD ¶ 181, where the Air Force reasonably decided it had an urgent need for airplane engine duct supports and was therefore not required to synopsize the proposed acquisition. Similarly, in *JRW Mgmt. Co.*, Comp. Gen. Dec. B-260396.2, 95-1 CPD ¶ 276, the GAO held that the agency's need for shuttle bus services had been classified as urgent, and the procurement was consequently exempt from the FAR's general synopsis and time period requirements.

3. *Content of Notice*

According to 15 U.S.C. § 637(f) and 41 U.S.C. § 416(b), the following information must be contained in these notices:

(1) [an] accurate description of the property or services to be contracted for, which description (A) shall not be unnecessarily restrictive of competition, and (B) shall include, as appropriate, the agency nomenclature, National Stock Number or other part number, and a brief description of the item's form, fit, or function, physical dimensions, predominant material of manufacture, or similar information that will assist a prospective contractor to make an informed business judgment as to whether a copy of the solicitation should be requested;

(2) provisions that —

(A) state whether the technical data required to respond to the solicitation will not be furnished as part of such solicitation, and identify the source in the Government, if any, from which the technical data may be obtained; and

(B) state whether an offeror, its product, or service must meet a qualification requirement in order to be eligible for award, and, if so, identify the office from which the qualification requirement may be obtained;

(3) the name, business address, and telephone number of the contracting officer;

(4) a statement that all responsible sources may submit a bid, proposal, or quotation (as appropriate) which shall be considered by the agency;

(5) in the case of a procurement using procedures other than competitive procedures, a statement of the reason justifying the use of such procedures and the identity of the intended source; and

(6) in the case of a contract in an amount estimated to be greater than $25,000 but not greater than the simplified acquisition threshold, or a contract for the procurement of commercial items using simplified procedures —

(A) a description of the procedures to be used in awarding the contract; and

(B) a statement specifying the periods for prospective offerors and the contracting officer to take the necessary preaward and award actions.

See FAR 5.207 for detailed guidance on the format and content of these synopses.

4. Exemptions

A number of exemptions from the requirement for these notices are contained in 15 U.S.C. § 637(g) and 41 U.S.C. § 416(c). These are summarized in FAR 5.202:

The contracting officer need not submit the notice required by 5.201 when —

(a) The contracting officer determines that —

(1) The synopsis cannot be worded to preclude disclosure of an agency's needs and such disclosure would compromise the national security (e.g., would result in disclosure of classified information). The fact that a proposed solicitation or contract action contains classified information, or that access to classified matter may be necessary to submit a proposal or perform the contract does not, in itself, justify use of this exception to synopsis;

(2) The proposed contract action is made under the conditions described in 6.302-2 (or, for purchases conducted using simplified acquisition procedures, if unusual and compelling urgency precludes competition to the maximum extent practicable) and the Government would be seriously injured if the agency complies with the time periods specified in 5.203;

(3) The proposed contract action is one for which either the written direction of a foreign government reimbursing the agency for the cost of the acquisition of the supplies or services for such government, or the terms of an international agreement or treaty between the United States and a foreign government or international organizations, has the effect of requiring that the acquisition shall be from specified sources;

(4) The proposed contract action is expressly authorized or required by a statute to be made through another Government agency, including acquisitions from the Small Business Administration (SBA) using the authority of section 8(a) of the Small Business Act (but see 5.205(f)), or from a specified source such as a workshop for the blind under the rules of the Committee for the Purchase from the Blind and Other Severely Handicapped;

(5) The proposed contract action is for utility services other than telecommunications services and only one source is available;

(6) The proposed contract action is an order placed under Subpart 16.5;

(7) The proposed contract action results from acceptance of a proposal under the Small Business Innovation Development Act of 1982 (P.L. 97-219);

(8) The proposed contract action results from the acceptance of an unsolicited research proposal that demonstrates a unique and innovative concept (see 2.101) and publication of any notice complying with 5.207 would improperly disclose the originality of thought or innovativeness of the pro-

posed research, or would disclose proprietary information associated with the proposal. This exception does not apply if the contract action results from an unsolicited research proposal and acceptance is based solely upon the unique capability of the source to perform the particular research services proposed (see 6.302-1(a)(2)(i));

(9) The proposed contract action is made for perishable subsistence supplies, and advance notice is not appropriate or reasonable;

(10) The proposed contract action is made under conditions described in 6.302-3, or 6.302-5 with regard to brand name commercial items for authorized resale, or 6.302-7, and advance notice is not appropriate or reasonable;

(11) The proposed contract action is made under the terms of an existing contract that was previously synopsized in sufficient detail to comply with the requirements of 5.207 with respect to the current contract action;

(12) The proposed contract action is by a Defense agency and the contract action will be made and performed outside the United States and its outlying areas, and only local sources will be solicited. This exception does not apply to proposed contract actions covered by the World Trade Organization Government Procurement Agreement or a Free Trade Agreement (see Subpart 25.4);

(13) The proposed contract action –

> (i) Is for an amount not expected to exceed the simplified acquisition threshold;

> (ii) Will be made through a means that [provides access to the notice of proposed contract action through the GPE; and

> (iii) Permits the public to respond to the solicitation electronically; or

(14) The proposed contract action is made under conditions described in 6.302-3 with respect to the services of an expert to support the Federal Government in any current or anticipated litigation or dispute.

(b) The head of the agency determines in writing after consultation with the Administrator for Federal Procurement Policy and the Administrator of the Small Business Administration, that advance notice is not appropriate or reasonable.

It has also been held that the synopsis requirement is not directly applicable to reprocurements against defaulted contracts, *United States Pollution Control, Inc.,* Comp. Gen. Dec. B-225372, 87-1 CPD ¶ 96.

5. Effect of Improper Notice

The government's failure to publish the required notice properly may invalidate a procurement. See *RII*, Comp. Gen. Dec. B-251436, 93-1 CPD ¶ 223, where the GAO found cancellation and resolicitation of the procurement to be proper where the agency had misclassified a listing in the CBD as "research and development" instead of "professional, administrative, and management support services." The GAO stated that this error did not allow all potential offerors to compete and did not meet the requirement of full and open competition. See also *TMI Mgmt. Sys., Inc.*, Comp. Gen. Dec. B-401530, 2009 CPD ¶ 191; and *Gourmet Distributors*, Comp. Gen. Dec. B-259083, 95-1 CPD ¶ 130, sustaining protests where the agency misclassified procurements. In *Frank Thatcher Assocs.*, 67 Comp. Gen. 77 (B-228744), 87-2 CPD ¶ 480, the GAO ruled that misclassification of the notice was a statutory violation requiring the award of protest costs (the contract had been performed). See also *Pacific Sky Supply, Inc.*, Comp. Gen. Dec. B-225420, 87-1 CPD ¶ 206, holding that a notice not listing all the items to be procured from a single source was defective; and *United States Marshals Serv.*, Comp. Gen. Dec. B-224277.3, 87-1 CPD ¶ 430, holding that the agency had improperly failed to synopsize a procurement based on national security when it failed to include a full explanation of its use of this exception in the internal agency justification. Compare *Morris Guralnick Assocs.*, Comp. Gen. Dec. B-214751.2, 84-2 CPD ¶ 597, where the CBD notice appeared in the section for communications equipment rather than in the section on services, where it properly belonged. The GAO refused to cancel the contract because the statute contains no expression of congressional intent to require agencies to cancel otherwise proper awards where the exact letter of the statute was not followed. The GAO noted that the Navy complied with the spirit of the statute because notice was actually published and two firms were aware of the procurement. In *Pilkington Aerospace, Inc.*, Comp. Gen. Dec. B-259173, 95-1 CPD ¶ 180, the Air Force failed to publish an amended CBD synopsis increasing the quantity of goods from 35 to 325. The GAO agreed with the protester that the Air Force erred but denied the protest because the protester was not capable of meeting the increased needs. See also *Gott Corp.*, Comp. Gen. Dec. B-222586, 86-2 CPD ¶ 154, refusing to cancel the award for improper notice because the protester actually knew of the procurement in time to compete. Similarly, in *Space Vector Corp.*, Comp. Gen. Dec. B-253295.2, 93-2 CPD ¶ 273, the GAO held that, although the GPS receiver integration was a critical factor in the agency's sole source determination and should have been disclosed in the CBD synopsis, the protester was informed of this requirement during qualification discussions and was given the opportunity to demonstrate its capability.

6. Notice of Use of Other Than Competitive Procedures

One of the major functions of the notice is to alert potential competitors that an agency intends to conduct a procurement using other than competitive procedures.

Notices of procurements involving other than competitive procedures must contain a statement of the reason justifying such procedures and must identify the intended source, 41 U.S.C. § 416(b)(5); FAR 5.207(c)(14). The failure to comply with this publication requirement was held not to require termination of the resulting sole source award in *AUL Instruments, Inc.*, 64 Comp. Gen. 871 (B-216543), 85-2 CPD ¶ 324, because the GAO found no prejudice to the protester who did not appear able to meet the urgent requirements. However, the publication of this notice is mandatory; and when a potential contractor responds to such a notice, the agency must consider the response, 10 U.S.C. § 2304(f)(1)(C); 41 U.S.C. § 253(f)(1)(C). See *Masstor Sys. Corp.*, 64 Comp. Gen. 118 (B-215046), 84-2 CPD ¶ 598, holding that a sole source award was unreasonable because the agency rejected the responding offer for reasons not stated in the notice or otherwise made known to the offeror. See also *Standard Mfg. Co. v. United States*, 7 Cl. Ct. 54 (1984), where the court held that the protester's reply to a CBD notice stating that it was capable of performing the proposed work bound the government to an implied promise to fairly and honestly consider the response. Similarly, in *Magnavox Elec. Sys. Co. v. United States*, 26 Cl. Ct. 1373 (1992), the court held that the government's CBD market survey notice and prospective offeror's response resulted in an implied contract to give fair and impartial consideration to the response. But see *Motorola, Inc. v. United States*, 988 F.2d 113 (Fed. Cir. 1993), where the court stated that it is only the contractor's submission of a formal offer manifesting its intent to be bound by the solicitation's provision that justifies implying a reciprocal government commitment to fairly and honestly consider the offer. *Motorola* impliedly overrules *Standard* and *Magnavox* to the extent that those cases held that anything less than a formal, responsive offer can create an implied contract of fair and honest dealing. See *Infrastructure Def. Techs., LLC v. United States*, 81 Fed. Cl. 375 (2008), following *Motorola* in rejecting a protest because the company did not submit a proposal demonstrating that its product met the agency needs. Similarly, in *Pure Power!, Inc. v. United States*, 70 Fed. Cl. 739 (2006), a protest was dismissed because the company had only participated in a program testings its product (with no ensuing procurement). See also *Garchik v. United States*, 37 Fed. Cl. 52 (1996), where the Securities and Exchange Commission (SEC) published a notice in the CBD indicating its intent to enter into a sole source lease with its current landlord. The CBD notice invited property owners throughout the Washington, D.C. area to submit proposals, but stated that the SEC was only interested in leasing property located within a narrowly defined geographic area. The CBD notice also made clear that the request for proposals was not a request for competitive proposals and the information received "will normally be considered solely for the purpose of determining whether to conduct a competitive procurement." The plaintiffs submitted a proposal that was rejected by the SEC because it offered property outside the geographic area described in the CBD notice. The court held that it had no jurisdiction over the case because the plaintiffs did not submit a formal offer.

Mere inclusion in the notice of the identity of the intended source and the reason justifying the lack of competition are insufficient. These notices must also contain a sufficient description of the supplies or services being procured to allow potential competitors to assess their ability to meet the government's requirements, *M.D. Thompson Consulting, LLC*, Comp. Gen. Dec. B-297616, 2006 CPD ¶ 41 (notice to extend a sole-source contract inadequate); *Information Ventures, Inc.*, Comp. Gen. Dec. B-293518, 2004 CPD ¶ 76 (notice of intent to award a sole source contract inadequate). See also *Berkshire Computer Prods.*, Comp. Gen. Dec. B-240327, 91-1 CPD ¶ 464, indicating that the notice should contain sufficient information to permit prospective offerors to respond in a meaningful way with alternative approaches. In *Racal-Milgo*, 66 Comp. Gen. 430 (B-225681), 87-1 CPD ¶ 472, the GAO held that this did not require the inclusion of the agency's evaluation factors in the notice.

If a potential competitor fails to submit a timely expression of interest in response to a notice that other than competitive procedures will be used, it will be precluded from contesting the agency decision before the GAO. Thus, when the agency specified in the CBD notice that there was a 45-day period for the submission of expressions of interest in competing on a procurement, the GAO refused to rule on a protest from a firm that had not responded within that time, *Fraser-Volpe Corp.*, Comp. Gen. Dec. B-240499, 90-2 CPD ¶ 397. See also *Allerion, Inc.*, Comp. Gen. Dec. B-256986, 94-1 CPD ¶ 281 (protester must respond to CBD notices with a timely expression of interest in fulfilling the potential sole source requirement and must receive a negative agency response as a prerequisite to filing a protest challenging the agency's sole source decision). For procurements in excess of the simplified acquisition threshold, the 45-day period for the submission of responses to a published solicitation began with the date of publication of the notice in the printed version of the CBD — not the date of posting on the Internet (which may be earlier), *FN Mfg., Inc. v. United States*, 41 Fed. Cl. 186 (1998). When a potential competitor submits a timely expression of interest that is subsequently rejected, a protest will be untimely if it is not filed within 10 days of the rejection, *Keco Indus., Inc.*, Comp. Gen. Dec. B-238301, 90-1 CPD ¶ 490.

B. Solicitation of Offers

41 U.S.C. § 416(d) provides:

> An executive agency shall make available to any business concern, or the authorized representative of such concern, the complete solicitation package for any on-going procurement announced pursuant to a notice of solicitation under subsection (a). An executive agency may require the payment of a fee, not exceeding the actual cost of duplication, for a copy of such package.

The standard method of complying with this statutory requirement is to post solicitations of the GPE. See FAR 5.102 stating:

> (a)(1) Except as provided in paragraph (a)(5) of this section, the contracting officer must make available through the GPE solicitations synopsized through the

GPE, including specifications, technical data, and other pertinent information determined necessary by the contracting officer. Transmissions to the GPE must be in accordance with the interface description available via the Internet at http://www.fedbizopps.gov.

(2) The contracting officer is encouraged, when practicable and cost-effective, to make accessible through the GPE additional information related to a solicitation.

(3) The contracting officer must ensure that solicitations transmitted using electronic commerce are forwarded to the GPE to satisfy the requirements of paragraph (a)(1) of this section.

(4) When an agency determines that a solicitation contains information that requires additional controls to monitor access and distribution (e.g., technical data, specifications, maps, building designs, schedules, etc.), the information shall be made available through the Federal Technical Data Solution (FedTeDS) unless an exception in paragraph (a)(5) of this section applies. When FedTeDS is used, it shall be used in conjunction with the GPE to meet the synopsis and advertising requirements of this part.

(5) The contracting officer need not make a solicitation available through the GPE, or make other information available through FedTeDS as required in paragraph (a)(4) of this section, when –

(i) Disclosure would compromise the national security (e.g., would result in disclosure of classified information, or information subject to export controls) or create other security risks. The fact that access to classified matter may be necessary to submit a proposal or perform the contract does not, in itself, justify use of this exception;

(ii) The nature of the file (e.g., size, format) does not make it cost-effective or practicable for contracting officers to provide access to the solicitation through the GPE;

(iii) Agency procedures specify that the use of FedTeDS does not provide sufficient controls for the information to be made available and an alternative means of distributing the information is more appropriate; or

(iv) The agency's senior procurement executive makes a written determination that access through the GPE is not in the Government's interest.

When the agency has determined not to post a solicitation on the GPE, FAR 5.102(d) permits the agency to limit the solicitation technique to electronic commerce media (presumably internet or CDE-ROM). However, FAR 5.102(b) and (c) also provide procedures for making solicitations available in paper media as follows:

(b) When the contracting officer does not make a solicitation available through the GPE pursuant to paragraph (a)(5) of this section, the contracting officer –

(1) Should employ other electronic means (e.g., CD-ROM or electronic mail) whenever practicable and cost-effective. When solicitations are provided electronically on physical media (e.g., disks) or in paper form, the contracting officer must –

(i) Maintain a reasonable number of copies of solicitations, including specifications and other pertinent information determined necessary by the contracting officer (upon request, potential sources not initially solicited should be mailed or provided copies of solicitations, if available);

(ii) Provide copies on a "first-come-first-served" basis, for pickup at the contracting office, to publishers, trade associations, information services, and other members of the public having a legitimate interest (for construction, see 36.211); and

(iii) Retain a copy of the solicitation and other documents for review by and duplication for those requesting copies after the initial number of copies is exhausted; and

(2) May require payment of a fee, not exceeding the actual cost of duplication, for a copy of the solicitation document.

(c) In addition to the methods of disseminating proposed contract information in 5.101(a) and (b), provide, upon request to small business concerns, as required by 15 U.S.C. 637(b) –

(1) A copy of the solicitation and specifications. In the case of solicitations disseminated by electronic data interchange, solicitations may be furnished directly to the electronic address of the small business concern;

(2) The name and telephone number of an employee of the contracting office who will answer questions on the solicitation; and

(3) Adequate citations to each applicable major Federal law or agency rule with which small business concerns must comply in performing the contract.

1. *Agency Responsibility for Informing Potential Competitors*

Before the passage of the CICA, the GAO upheld awards if the government obtained "adequate competition" and held that the adequacy of competition did not depend upon whether every prospective offeror was afforded an opportunity to submit a proposal, *John Bransby Prods., Ltd.*, 60 Comp. Gen. 104 (B-198360), 80-2 CPD ¶ 419. This decision was based upon the government's reasonable efforts to inform offerors generally of the proposed procurement and upon the absence of probative evidence that the government had a conscious or deliberate intent to impede the participation of the prospective bidders. Even after the CICA required that all responsible sources be permitted to submit bids or proposals, the GAO did not require cancellation of a solicitation or an award merely because a prospective offeror was not furnished a copy of the solicitation, absent clear evidence of government fault. See *Price Waterhouse*, Comp. Gen. Dec. B-239525, 90-2 CPD ¶ 192, stating:

> A firm bears the risk of not receiving solicitation materials unless it is shown that the contracting agency made a deliberate effort to prevent the firm from competing, or that, even if not deliberate, the agency failed to provide the solicitation materials after the firm availed itself of every reasonable opportunity to obtain it. *Crown Management Servs., Inc.*, B-232431.4, Apr. 20, 1989, 89-1 CPD ¶ 393; *Uniform Rental Serv.*, B-228293, Dec. 9, 1987, 87-2 CPD ¶ 571.

See also *Sentinel Security & Patrol Servs.*, Comp. Gen. Dec. B-261018, 95-2 CPD ¶ 67 (inadvertent failure to provide solicitation amendment that set the revised bid opening date); *Lewis Jamison Inc. & Assocs.*, Comp. Gen. Dec. B-252198, 93-1 CPD ¶ 433 (inadvertent mailing of solicitation to wrong address); *International Ass'n of Fire Fighters*, Comp. Gen. Dec. B-220757, 86-1 CPD ¶ 31 (inadvertent failure to mail solicitation amendment); *Viktoria F.I.T., GmbH*, Comp. Gen. Dec. B-233125, 89-1 CPD ¶ 70 (inadvertent mailing of solicitation amendments to wrong address). In *Eagle Creek Archaeological Servs., Inc.*, Comp. Gen. Dec. B-258480, 95-1 CPD ¶ 43, the GAO found a series of errors by the agency to be inadvertent. Here, the protester had informed the agency of a change of address and had subsequently received a solicitation amendment at its new address. However, the contracting officer failed to update the mailing list with the result that a second amendment was mailed to the protester's former address and subsequently returned by mail to the agency rather than forwarded to the new address. Further, a personnel shortage resulted in the agency's failure to forward the amendment promptly to the protester. The protest was denied because these inadvertent errors did not show any deliberate attempt by the agency to exclude the protester.

This same reasoning has been carried over to the situation where the solicitation is posted electronically. See, for example, *Optelec U.S., Inc.*, Comp. Gen. Dec. B-400349, 2008 CPD ¶ 192, rejecting a protest where the company did not find the solicitation because it failed to monitor the GPE, stating:

> The Competition in Contracting Act of 1984 generally requires contracting agencies to obtain full and open competition through the use of competitive procedures, 10 U.S.C. § 2304(a)(1)(A) (2000), both to ensure that a procurement is open to all responsible sources and to provide the government with the opportunity to receive fair and reasonable prices. *Kendall Healthcare Prods. Co.*, B-289381, Feb. 19, 2002, 2002 CPD ¶ 42 at 6. In pursuit of these goals, a contracting agency has

the affirmative obligation to use reasonable methods to publicize its procurement needs and to timely disseminate solicitation documents to those entitled to receive them. However, concurrent with the agency's obligations in this regard, prospective contractors must avail themselves of every reasonable opportunity to obtain the solicitation documents. *Laboratory Sys. Servs., Inc.*, B-258883, Feb. 15, 1995, 95-1 CPD ¶ 90 at 2. Where a prospective contractor fails in this duty, we will not sustain its protest challenging the agency's failure to meet its solicitation dissemination obligations. *Wind Gap Knitwear, Inc.*, B-276669, July 10, 1997, 97-2 CPD ¶ 14 at 3. In considering such situations, we consider whether the agency or the protester had the last clear opportunity to avoid the protester's being precluded from competing. *Id.*

A protest was also denied when the company did not monitor the agency's website where the electronic posting of amendments to the solicitation was taking place, *Performance Constr., Inc.*, Comp. Gen. Dec. B-286192, 2000 CPD ¶ 180. This same reasoning was used when potential offerors received solicitations in paper form. See *Ervin & Assocs., Inc.*, Comp. Gen. Dec. B-278849, 98-1 CPD ¶ 92 (protest denied because the protester did not contact the agency when it did not receive an RFP on the date that the CBD notice of the procurement stated that it would be issued).

Agencies have been permitted to use questionable procedures without recourse of potential offerors. For example, in *Allied Materials & Equip. Co.*, Comp. Gen. Dec. B-293231, 2004 CPD ¶ 27, a protest was denied when the agency violated the FAR 5.102(a)(1) requirement that solicitations that are synopsized on the GPE also be available on the GPE by posting the solicitation on the agency website. The GAO reasoned:

> Allied learned of the solicitation through the July 18 [GPE] synopsis and, thus, as of that date, was aware of the August 20 anticipated closing time for the receipt of proposals. The protester nevertheless did not contact the agency prior to the closing time to inquire into the status of the solicitation, nor did it contact the agency shortly after the closing time to determine whether the closing time had been changed. Instead, the protester waited approximately 7 weeks after the closing time to inquire into the status of the procurement. This delay was unreasonable. While, as Allied notes, an anticipated closing time in a presolicitation notice may subsequently be extended, it nevertheless serves to establish the rough time frame during which a prospective offeror reasonably should expect to receive the announced solicitation. Prospective offerors cannot ignore the anticipated closing time when they are waiting to receive an announced solicitation — or, it follows, when they are awaiting the posting of a solicitation on a website. Rather, even where a prospective offeror has specifically requested a solicitation, see *Wind Gap Knitwear, Inc.*, [B-276669, July 10, 1997, 97-2 CPD ¶ 14], as the anticipated closing time approaches and then passes without its receiving the solicitation, the prospective offeror is reasonably expected to stop merely waiting and instead to take steps to actively seek the solicitation. We believe this principle necessarily extends to the circumstances here. While monitoring a website might initially be a reasonable approach to obtaining a solicitation that is to be posted there, we do not think it was reasonable for Allied to continue doing so as the closing time approached and passed, without at least attempting to obtain information

as to the status of the procurement; in this regard, as noted above, the synopsis included the names, telephone numbers, fax numbers, and e-mail addresses of both the contract specialist and the commodity business specialist involved with the solicitation.

2. Denial of Use of Paper Solicitations

Agencies can limit the solicitation technique to electronic means alone. In an early decision, *NuWestern USA Constructors, Inc.*, Comp. Gen. Dec. B-275514, 97-1 CPD ¶ 90, the GAO held that an agency's issuance of a solicitation only in electronic format (CD-ROM) was not unduly restrictive of competition or otherwise inconsistent with applicable law and regulation, stating:

> Federal agencies have traditionally issued their solicitations on paper and furnished paper copies to interested vendors, who then responded with paper proposals. With advances in the information technology field, however, agencies have found that the use of an electronic format, in place of a paper format, can be more efficient and economical. For example, submission of quotation prices on a floppy disk was required in *Latins American, Inc.*, 71 Comp. Gen. 436 (1992), 92-1 CPD ¶ 519, cost spreadsheets were required on disk in *D.O.N. Protective Servs., Inc.*, B-249066, Oct. 23, 1992, 92-2 CPD ¶ 277, and complete cost proposals on a disk were required in *W.B. Jolley*, 68 Comp. Gen. 443 (1989), 89-1 CPD ¶ 512. Further, in both *Continental Airlines, Inc.*, B-258271, B-258271.4, July 31, 1995, 95-1 CPD [¶ 5], and *Spectronics Corp.*, B-260924, July 27, 1995, 95-2 CPD ¶ 47, the agency furnished offerors with certain solicitation-related information on a computer disk, while in *Arcy Mfg. Co., Inc.*, et al., B-261538 et al., Aug. 14, 1995, 95-2 CPD ¶ 283, the agency conducted entire procurements electronically, posting solicitations on its electronic bulletin board and requiring electronic responses only. Moreover, with the enactment of the Federal Acquisition Streamlining Act of 1994, which called for the development and utilization of a federal acquisition computer network, 41 U.S.C. § 426 (1994), Congress clearly signaled its desire that agencies use electronic acquisition methods.

The solicitation was sent to 63 firms. The GAO found nothing in the procurement statutes or the Small Business Act that requires agencies to provide paper copies of solicitation documents on request. Requiring firms to have access to computerized CD-ROM printing equipment or incur a charge to have another company do the printing was found not unduly burdensome to prospective contractors.

3. Oral Solicitations

Oral solicitations are preferred for any procurement falling within the simplified acquisition threshold, but not exceeding $30,000, FAR 13.106-1(c). In addition, FAR 15.203(f) permits the use of oral solicitations for negotiated procurements:

> Oral RFPs are authorized when processing a written solicitation would delay the acquisition of supplies or services to the detriment of the Government and a no-

tice is not required under 5.202 (e.g., perishable items and support of contingency operations or other emergency situations). Use of an oral RFP does not relieve the contracting officer from complying with other FAR requirements.

(1) The contract files supporting oral solicitations should include —

(i) A description of the requirement;

(ii) Rationale for use of an oral solicitation;

(iii) Sources solicited, including the date, time, name of individuals contacted, and prices offered; and

(iv) The solicitation number provided to the prospective offerors.

(2) The information furnished to potential offerors under oral solicitations should include appropriate items from paragraph (e) of this section

C. Amendment or Cancellation of RFPs

When circumstances change or additional information is obtained after the issuance of the RFP, and before the receipt of proposals, the agency must determine whether to cancel or amend the solicitation. If there is a lack of funding or the requirements no longer exist, cancellation is the only option. However, if the procurement is to continue, the agency must decide whether to cancel the RFP and resolicit the requirement or to amend the RFP. See FAR 15.206(a), stating:

> When, either before or after receipt of proposals, the Government changes its requirements or terms and conditions, the contracting officer shall amend the solicitation.

Where the changes are very extensive, the choice might be to cancel and resolicit since this option would most likely reach the maximum number of offerors. However, the time required for resolicitation (mandatory presolicitation notices and the interval before RFP issuance) might not be acceptable. Thus, the decision to amend or resolicit must take these factors into consideration.

1. Issuance of Amendments

FAR 15.210(b) provides that Standard Form 30, Amendment of Solicitation/ Modification of Contract, or Optional Form 309, Amendment of Solicitation, may be used to amend solicitations. Prior to the FAR 15 rewrite, the use of Standard Form 30 was mandatory. Whether issued on these forms or otherwise in writing or electronically, the amendment must provide offerors sufficient information to determine the changed requirements. FAR 15.206(g) states that: "At a minimum, the following information should be included in each amendment:"

(1) Name and address of issuing activity.

(2) Solicitation number and date.

(3) Amendment number and date.

(4) Number of pages.

(5) Description of the change being made.

(6) Government point of contact and phone number (and electronic or facsimile address, if appropriate).

(7) Revision to solicitation closing date, if applicable.

FAR 15.206(f) permits oral notice of the amendment when "time is of the essence." It states that in such a case, "the contracting officer shall document the contract file and formalize the notice with an amendment." The importance of formalizing the notice in writing is illustrated in cases where the protester contends that it did not receive the notice that the agency claimed had been issued orally. In *Lockheed, IMS*, Comp. Gen. Dec. B-248686, 92-2 CPD ¶ 180, a protest was successful when the offeror denied that it received oral notice of the amendment, and the government did not follow up with an RFP amendment or other written confirmation. See also *CoMont, Inc.*, 65 Comp. Gen. 66 (B-219730), 85-2 CPD ¶ 555, sustaining a protest on the basis that the amendment was required to have been in writing, and *S3 Ltd*, Comp. Gen. Dec. B-287019.2, 2001 CPD ¶ 165, where the GAO stated that offerors could not reasonably rely on oral amendments not followed up in writing. However, in *AVL Books.Com, Inc.*, Comp. Gen. Dec. B-295780, 2005 CPD ¶ 46, a telephone call adding a requirement to the RFP was adequate when the time for issuance of the contract was only two weeks. See also *Family Stress Clinics of Am.*, Comp. Gen. Dec. B-270993, 96-1 CPD ¶ 223, where an oral amendment extending the closing date for submission of proposals indefinitely was given full effect even though it was not confirmed in writing. The GAO stated that the amendment was issued under exigent circumstances accompanying the shutdown of the contracting agency and the terms of the oral amendment were not in dispute.

2. Firms to Be Notified

FAR 15.206 specifies that amendments must be furnished as follows:

(b) Amendments issued before the established time and date for receipt of proposals shall be issued to all parties receiving the solicitation.

Even though the regulations provide that the amendment shall be sent to each prospective offeror, the GAO has consistently held that the offeror bears the risk of not receiving an amendment, assuming that full and open competition has been found and it has not been shown that there was a conscious and deliberate effort by the agency to exclude the offeror from participating in the competition, *CardioMetrix*, Comp. Gen. Dec. B-270701, 96-1 CPD ¶ 149; *CDA Inc.*, Comp. Gen. Dec. B-224971, 87-1 CPD ¶ 163. The underlying theory is that the agency discharges its legal responsibility when it issues and dispatches an amendment in sufficient time to permit all offerors to consider the amendment in formulating their offers. In *LexisNexis, Inc.*, Comp. Gen. Dec. B-299381, 2007 CPD ¶ 73, an amendment posted on the FedBizOpps website hyperlinked to the agency website did not excuse the protester's failure to find it. In *CompuServe*, Comp. Gen. Dec. B-192905, 79-1 CPD ¶ 63, an amendment issued to the offeror but addressed incorrectly provided no basis for extending the closing date for initial proposals even though the offeror's late acknowledgment was prompted by late receipt of the amendment. However, in *Andero Constr., Inc.*, 61 Comp. Gen. 253 (B-203898), 82-1 CPD ¶ 133, the GAO ignored the general rule that the offeror bears the risk of nondelivery of an amendment to the solicitation because the agency failed to establish affirmatively that it complied with DAR 2-208 (similar to FAR 14.208) where three of four offerors appeared not to have received the amendment in the mail. The agency never affirmatively stated that the amendments were mailed; thus, the GAO recommended that the agency cancel the solicitation and resolicit its requirements.

The failure to issue an amendment has been excused where the protesting offeror had actual notice of the change. See *General Offshore Corp.*, Comp. Gen. Dec. B-249601, 92-2 CPD ¶ 391, where the GAO held that the protester had received adequate notice of changed requirements through negotiations; and *Collins & Aikman Corp.*, Comp. Gen. Dec. B-247961, 92-2 CPD ¶ 41, stating in a footnote that an amendment was not required because the protester had knowledge of the change.

Failure to amend an RFP has also been excused where the protester was unable to demonstrate that it was prejudiced by the lack of notice. In *Saratoga Dev. Corp. v. United States*, 777 F. Supp. 29 (D.D.C. 1991), the court held that the test for prejudice is whether the protester would have altered its proposal to its competitive advantage and, further, that the protester has the burden of showing how it would have responded to notice of the change. No prejudice was found in *ALJU-CAR, LLC*, Comp. Gen. Dec. B-401249.4, 2009 CPD ¶ 165 (protester's price was so far out of line that no possibility it could have won had it known that contracting officer altered contract line items in evaluating prices); *Allied Materials & Equip. Co. v. United States*, 81 Fed. Cl. 448 (2008) (protester was not informed of a time extension on the submission of proposals but it did not submit concrete evidence of how it would have lowered its price had it known of the time extension); *Canberra Indus.*, Comp. Gen. Dec. B-271016, 96-1 CPD ¶ 269 (failure to amend a solicitation based on relaxed specifications but the protester did not present any evidence that it would have altered its proposal to its competitive advantage had it been given the opportunity to respond to the altered requirements); *Environmental Tectonics Corp.*,

Comp. Gen. Dec. B-209423, 83-1 CPD ¶ 81 (protester admitted that it could not have bettered its own proposed delivery time had it known of altered provision). The GAO will not overturn an award in which the agency has changed the evaluation criteria without notifying the offerors if the losers are not prejudiced by the change, *Akal Security, Inc.*, Comp. Gen. Dec. B-261996, 95-2 CPD ¶ 216; *Delta Dental Plan of Cal., Inc.*, Comp. Gen. Dec. B-260461, 95-1 CPD ¶ 293; *FKW Inc. Sys.*, Comp. Gen. Dec. B-235989, 89-2 CPD ¶ 370.

3. Time Extensions

There is no guidance in the FAR on granting time extensions for proposal submission when amendments are issued to the solicitation. However, additional time should be granted when amendments are issued close to the proposal submission date. In *ELCOM, Inc.*, Comp. Gen. Dec. B-209103, 83-2 CPD ¶ 80, the GAO denied a protest of insufficient time because of the protester's familiarity with the new requirement, the relatively small size of the purchase, and the fact that the protester merely showed it was inconvenienced by the receipt of the amendment on the date that proposals were due, not that it was prevented from responding or prejudiced in any manner. Similarly, the GAO denied a request for a time extension to respond to an amendment to an RFP where there was no evidence of a deliberate attempt to prevent the offeror from submitting a proposal and adequate competition was obtained, *Econ, Inc.*, Comp. Gen. Dec. B-198454, 80-2 CPD ¶ 60. In *Gel Sys., Inc.*, Comp. Gen. Dec. B-234283, 89-1 CPD ¶ 433, *recons. denied*, Comp. Gen. Dec. B-34283.2, 89-2 CPD ¶ 166, a protest was denied when the offerors were given only one working day to factor in three minor alterations to the agency's requirements.

CHAPTER 4

CONTRACTOR PROPOSAL DEVELOPMENT

Upon receiving notice of a proposed procurement, prospective contractors enter into an intensive period of analysis and writing in an effort to produce a proposal that will win the competition. In many, if not most, competitively negotiated procurements, the proposals submitted will be the primary basis for the selection of the source. Thus, proposal preparation is a key step in the source selection process.

This chapter discusses the process of obtaining information, analyzing the RFP, and submitting a proposal. The first section reviews activities of prospective contractors in obtaining information to be used in analyzing the government's requirements and in deciding on proposed strategies. It identifies practices that may seriously jeopardize their chances of success and possibly subject them to potential civil or criminal liability. It then deals with prohibited activities. The second section covers the analytical process conducted upon receipt of an RFP, followed by a discussion of the necessary contents of the proposal. The next sections address protests of RFP improprieties and the requirement for timely submission of proposals. The chapter concludes with a review of the rules regarding unsolicited proposals.

I. OBTAINING INFORMATION

Competitively negotiated procurements are required to be conducted in a manner that gives all competitors a fair and equal opportunity to win the competition. Conduct, on the part of either the government or the contractor, that is contrary to this policy is considered detrimental to the integrity of the procurement process. The result may be disqualification of the offeror on the particular procurement or criminal prosecution, depending on the nature of the conduct.

For many years, the specific types of conduct that were prohibited were not well defined. Rather, general standards of fair competition were relied on to a large extent to protect the integrity of the system. In addition, specific rules were identified in the course of protests to the GAO and the courts. Some specific types of conduct were discussed in the procurement statutes and regulations, as well as in criminal statutes. A set of more specific rules of conduct evolved in the 1960s and 1970s. As a result of the procurement scandals in the 1980s, this rather fragmented system was placed under congressional scrutiny. In 1988 Congress enacted 41 U.S.C. § 423 setting forth specific rules on procurement integrity. The Clinger-Cohen Act of 1996 amended the Procurement Integrity Act to streamline the provisions on disclosure of information. This statute is implemented by FAR 3.104. Although this statute did not provide a coherent statement of all the rules of conduct, it did further the evolution of these rules by providing additional guidance in several key areas. This section discusses the numerous rules that define the conduct of contractors during the procurement process — including the procurement integrity rules. 41 U.S.C. § 423(g) also provides that protests may no longer be filed based on an allegation that this statute has been violated unless the violation has been reported to the contracting agency within 14 days of learning of the violation. See *Omega World Travel, Inc. v. United States*, 82 Fed. Cl. 452 (2008), declining to rule on a contention that a contractor had obtained information improperly because the protester had not notified the agency of the alleged violation within 14 days. Compare *McKing Consulting Corp. v. United States*, 78 Fed. Cl. 715 (2007), holding that 41 U.S.C. § 423(g) does not apply to protests before the Court of Federal Claims.

A. Obtaining Information from the Government

The current Procurement Integrity Act, 41 U.S.C. § 423, consolidates and streamlines the rules pertaining to exchanges of information between potential offerors and contracting agencies. Paragraph (b) of that Act now prohibits a "person" from knowingly obtaining "contractor bid or proposal information" or "source selection information" before the award of the "Federal agency procurement" to which the information relates. See the discussion of these terms in Chapter 1. The Act imposes criminal penalties for its violation. See *United States v. Carlisle*, 2009 U.S. Dist. LEXIS 87687 (C.D. Cal. 2009). This Act applies the prohibition to any contractor, other business entity, or individual that obtains information even if that person is not participating in the procurement. It also seems to apply the prohibition without regard to the source of the information, with the result that it could arguably be a violation to obtain the information from a newspaper reporter or some other person not connected with the procurement. The only narrowing of the rule is that it is no longer a violation of the Act to solicit information if the information is not obtained. See FAR 3.104-4 for implementation of these requirements.

1. *Before Issuance of the RFP*

Because the time for proposal preparation is almost always quite short (typically 30 to 120 days), successful offerors frequently attempt to gain an advantage over their competitors by learning as much as possible about the procurement before the RFP is mailed. This enables them to assemble their proposal team, make their preliminary analysis of the procurement, and even begin drafting parts of the proposal before receipt of the RFP. While this is a sound strategy, it must be followed with great care to ensure that the rules governing procurement integrity and fair treatment of all offerors are not being violated. For example, in *Willamette-Western Corp.*, 54 Comp. Gen. 375 (B-179328), 74-2 CPD ¶ 259, the GAO sustained a protest where the successful offeror had received an advance copy of the RFP, which had not been furnished to other offerors. Similarly, in *Litton Sys., Inc.*, 68 Comp. Gen. 422

(B-234060), 89-1 CPD ¶ 186, *recons. denied*, 68 Comp. Gen. 677 (B-234060.2), 89-2 CPD ¶ 228, the GAO ordered a contractor disqualified for obtaining government information through a marketing consultant. See also *Spectrum Sciences & Software, Inc. v. United States*, 84 Fed. Cl. 716 (2008), where the court held the government liable for breach of contract when it used proprietary information to write a statement of work and disclosed some of the information to competitors.

FAR 15.201(f) permits the disclosure of "[g]eneral information about agency mission needs and future requirements" at any time. Thus, this information can be obtained from contracting, technical, or program personnel in a contracting agency as the requirements are identified. See *Lockheed Martin Sys. Integration — Owego — Costs*, Comp. Gen. Dec. B-287190.5, 2002 CPD ¶ 49, where the GAO regarded appearances before the agency to learn how a procurement was to be structured as market research activity which was permitted by FAR 15.201. However, potential contractors should be careful not to solicit or obtain information from agency source selection plans or technical evaluation plans because such information is prohibited "source selection information" under the Procurement Integrity Act. See FAR 3.104-3. In *Superlative Techs., Inc.*, Comp. Gen. Dec. B-310489, 2008 CPD ¶ 12, and Comp. Gen. Dec. B-310489.4, 2008 CPD ¶ 123, an agency cancelled a procurement because an incumbent subcontractor had learned about the details of an impending procurement – but then awarded the contract to that company under an interagency contract. The GAO ruled that this was an improper means of resolving a procurement integrity violation and recommended that the agency determine whether the company should be disqualified as a means of compensating for the unfair competitive advantage.

2. After Issuance of the RFP

Offerors also need information as to the details of a procurement after the RFP has been issued — to permit the most effective proposal preparation, conduct negotiations and the submission of a winning final proposal. Obtaining such information is good strategy. However, the procurement integrity and fair competition rules must be strictly followed to ensure that an offeror is not obtaining information that is barred by the Procurement Integrity Act. Particular care should be taken to avoid obtaining information on the details of proposals submitted by other contractors ("contractor bid or proposal information") or on the evaluation of proposals ("source selection information"). See FAR 3.104-4. Potential contractors must also ensure that they obtain the information in a manner that does not constitute criminal conduct. See *Miller-Holtzwarth, Inc. v. United States*, 44 Fed. Cl. 156 (1999), where the court sanctioned a contractor that had obtained information from the contracting officer indicating that it should lower its prices by 50% to beat out a competitor; and *AT&T Communications, Inc.*, GSBCA 9252-P, 88-2 BCA ¶ 20,805, where the board disqualified a contractor that had been given the range of its competitor's prices by a government employee with whom it had conducted employment discussions and to whom it had given gratuities.

FAR 15.201(f) provides that after the issuance of an RFP, information should be obtained from the contracting officer. Offerors should not query other agency personnel to obtain interpretation or explanation of parts of the RFP.

Even if a contractor has obtained information improperly, the GAO will not sustain a protest unless the contractor can demonstrate that it was competitively prejudiced, *Health Net Fed. Servs., LLC*, Comp. Gen. Dec. B-401652, 2009 CPD ¶ 213 (agency took information off of its website after one day and competitor stated it did not see it); *Kemron Envtl. Servs., Inc.*, Comp. Gen. Dec. B-299880, 2007 CPD ¶ 176 (contractor destroyed letter to other offeror when it saw it was misdirected).

A request for information to clarify the requirements of the solicitation is not a violation of the procurement integrity provisions, *Helmets Ltd.*, Comp. Gen. Dec. B-246301, 92-1 CPD ¶ 241. In that case the offeror requested the address and part numbers of a potential supplier of the parts. The GAO found that this was not source selection information and the request did not "jeopardize the integrity of the procurement."

B. Obtaining Information About Competitors

The techniques for gaining information about competitors are diverse, and some may not be proper. These techniques range from such benign activities as reading a competitor's sales brochure to such risky and potentially criminal practices as business espionage. For the company gathering information in the process of proposal preparation, it is good to consider the risks associated with each strategy to obtain information.

It is highly unlikely that valuable proposal information will be obtained knowingly and willingly from a competitor. Information obtained from or about a competitor usually comes from an individual. If the source of the information is a current or former employee of the competitor, special care is necessary. Information transmitted by a current employee with the authority to do so would generally present no problems. On the other hand, buying trade secrets or other proprietary information from a current or former employee would clearly entitle the aggrieved competitor to relief under the Uniform Trade Secrets Act, 14 U.L.A. § 437 (1980 and 1987 Supp.) or could constitute a tort or a crime. Even accepting a trade secret volunteered by a disgruntled current or former employee might be actionable under the Uniform Trade Secrets Act. In addition, an offeror can be disqualified from a procurement for obtaining vital information about a competitor during a competition, *Compliance Corp. v. United States*, 22 Cl. Ct. 193 (1990), *aff'd*, 960 F.2d 157 (Fed. Cir. 1992). In that case the offeror had approached employees of the incumbent contractor, who was competing for a follow-on services contract, to obtain information on the details of how the incumbent contractor was performing the work, as well as the contents of its proposal for the follow-on work. Upon learning of this conduct, the contracting officer disqualified the offeror, and the GAO sustained this action, *Compliance*

Corp., Comp. Gen. Dec. B-239252.3, 90-2 CPD ¶ 126, *recons. denied*, Comp. Gen. Dec. B-239252.3, 90-2 CPD ¶ 435. The Claims Court agreed with this decision, stating at 204:

> The court finds actual or attempted "industrial espionage" to be outside the realm of normal business practices, and the contracting officer is entitled to disqualify those who engage in such conduct, not only to protect the integrity of the contracting process, but also to deter others from similar conduct.

Similarly, in *Huynh Serv. Co.*, Comp. Gen. Dec. B-242297.2, 91-1 CPD ¶ 562, the GAO concurred with an agency decision to terminate a contract for the convenience of the government after it learned that the low bidder might have obtained a competitor's pricing information before it submitted its bid. In *Computer Tech. Assocs., Inc.*, Comp. Gen. Dec. B-288622, 2001 CPD ¶ 187, the GAO agreed that a competitor should be disqualified when it obtained and read e-mail transcripts of its competitors' oral presentations. The decision cites the Procurement Integrity Act provisions barring such conduct. See also *Litton Sys., Inc.*, 68 Comp. Gen. 422 (B-234060), 89-1 CPD ¶ 186, *recons. denied*, 68 Comp. Gen. 677 (B-234060.2), 89-2 CPD ¶ 228, disqualifying an offeror that had obtained source selection information through a marketing consultant; and *AT&T Communications, Inc.*, GSBCA 9252-P, 88-2 BCA ¶ 20,805, disqualifying an offeror that had been given the competitive range prices by a government employee. Compare *Systems Plus, Inc. v. United States*, 69 Fed. Cl. 757 (2006), overturning the disqualification of an offeror based on the appearance that it had improperly obtained a competitor's information because the contracting officer did not give the company an opportunity to respond to the charge. See also *McKing Consulting Corp. v. United States*, 78 Fed. Cl. 715 (2007) (holding that list of dental consultants used by protester was not proprietary because it had been posted on website for over a year); *Accent Serv. Co.*, Comp. Gen. Dec. B-299888, 2007 CPD ¶ 169 (holding that there was no impropriety in asking the incumbent contractor's employees questions about the staffing of the project during a site visit); *Avtel Servs., Inc. v. United States*, 70 Fed. Cl. 173 (2006), *appeal dismissed because of bankruptcy*, 501 F.3d 1259 (Fed. Cir. 2007) (finding that "much of the information on current staffing levels can be found in the public domain" or revealed through site visits to government facility); and *Rothe Dev., Inc.*, Comp. Gen. Dec. B-279839, 98-2 CPD ¶ 31 (protest denied because disclosure of incumbent staffing that government official derived by conducting "mental headcount" of contractor staff was not a trade secret).

Generally, if the government agency is not involved in the disclosure of information, the GAO will not rule on protests that one competitor acted improperly with regard to another competitor — stating that this is a private dispute to be resolved in the courts, *Telephonics Corp.*, Comp. Gen. Dec. B-401647, 2009 CPD ¶ 215 (allegation that one division of company improperly disclosed protester's proprietary information to another division); *Pemco Aeroplex, Inc.*, Comp. Gen. Dec. B-310372, 2008 CPD ¶ 2 (allegation that contractor had violated a nondisclosure agreement with its subcontractor that was now competing for follow-on contract); *Advanced Communications Sys., Inc.*, Comp. Gen. Dec. B-271040, 96-1 CPD ¶ 274 (allegation that competitor improperly obtained protester's proposal strategy and pricing information by hiring its employee); *Bildon, Inc.*, Comp. Gen. Dec. B-241375, 90-2 CPD ¶ 332 (allegation that company improperly obtained competitor's information by hiring employee who prepared proposal); *Garrett Corp.*, Comp. Gen. Dec. B-182991, 76-1 CPD ¶ 20 (allegation that competitor had obtained proprietary drawings by improper means); *York Indus., Inc.*, Comp. Gen. Dec. B-186958, 76-2 CPD ¶ 453 (allegation that competitor had used proprietary drawings in violation of license agreement).

The most difficult problems in this area are likely to arise where the company employs a competitor's former employee. Expertise, skill, and knowledge gained with one employer can be used without restriction in subsequent jobs. See *Electro-Craft Corp. v. Controlled Motion, Inc.*, 332 N.W.2d 890 (Minn. 1983), where the court stated: "The law of trade secrets will not protect talent or expertise, only secret information." However, use of trade secrets or proprietary information by a former employee may be restricted under the Uniform Trade Secrets Act and common law tort theories. Identifying information and knowledge that may be subject to such restrictions can be difficult. General knowledge about how a former employer prepares a proposal or goes about estimating a job is probably not protected. Specific knowledge about the contents of a pending proposal or the amount of a pending estimate in a competitive procurement probably cannot be disclosed or used. Former employees of a competitor should not be asked for such specific information nor be placed in a position where they are expected to use such information. See *Erskine & Branch v. Boeing Co.*, 2002 U.S. Dist. LEXIS 21819 (M.D. Fla. 2002), where the court found that a contractor had properly dismissed one employee that had brought his former employer's proprietary information to the contractor and another employee that had received the information without reporting it to the company, and *Air Prods. & Chemicals, Inc. v. Johnson*, 296 Pa. Super. 405, 442 A.2d 1114 (1982), where a company's bidding procedure, negotiating techniques, and cost and pricing methods were held to comprise trade secrets that should not have been disclosed by a former employee.

Information about a competitor's long-term marketing strategy for a particular product or service is valuable to the competitor and should not be requested from the competitor's former employees. See *Union Carbide Corp. v. UGI Corp.*, 731 F.2d 1186 (5th Cir. 1984), where marketing information and strategies were held to be trade secrets. However, a former employee cannot erase such knowledge from his or her mind, and it may be virtually impossible for an employee to perform his or her new job without consideration of knowledge about a prior employer's plans. See *Abbott Lab. v. Norse Chem. Corp.*, 33 Wis. 2d 445, 147 N.W.2d 529 (1967), where an employee's knowledge of a chemical production process was held to be "know-how or skill which cannot be blotted out of an employee's mind and cannot be labeled a trade secret." There is also the likelihood that the former employee has a specific contractual obligation to refrain from offering such assistance to competitors of a former employer.

As a general rule, information appearing in published sources may be used without restriction. See *McKay v. Communispond, Inc.*, 581 F. Supp. 801 (S.D.N.Y. 1983), where trade secret protection was denied for communications-skills instruction methods because much of the core program had been extensively described in publications. Information provided about competitors by third-party sources such as other contractors, subcontractors, or consultants generally can be used, although there are some limitations. If a consultant or subcontractor acts improperly in obtaining or using information about a competitor and shares that information with a client or prime contractor, the use of the information may be enjoined under the Uniform Trade Secrets Act even if the contractor using the information was not aware of, or involved in, the improper conduct. If the user either consented to or encouraged the improper conduct, punitive damages may be available to the competitor, and there may be criminal sanctions. In addition, the government might disqualify a contractor who has used such information from competing for a contract.

If a consultant or a subcontractor has obtained information from a competitor properly in connection with work done for that competitor and has agreed to hold the information confidential, the information should not be released to any other contractor. A contractor who uses such information, even without knowledge of its source, may be subject to injunctive action under the Uniform Trade Secrets Act and may also be disqualified from a particular contract.

C. Exchanging Information with Competitors

Offerors in fixed-price contracts are required by FAR 3.103-1 to certify that prices were arrived at independently without collusion between prospective contractors. This provision is implemented by the Certificate of Independent Price Determination solicitation provision in FAR 52.203-2. The contracting officer is directed to reject an offer if the certificate is altered, FAR 3.103-2(b).

Sanctions have been imposed on firms that entered into agreements on prices to be bid, *United States ex rel. Marcus v. Hess*, 317 U.S. 537 (1943). See *United States v. CFW Constr. Co.*, 649 F. Supp. 616 (D.S.C. 1986), *dismissed on other grounds*, 819 F.2d 1139 (4th Cir. 1987), imposing civil sanctions for bid rigging, and *United States v. Portsmouth Paving Corp.*, 694 F.2d 312 (4th Cir. 1982), imposing criminal sanctions for bid rigging. A debarment was upheld for collusively agreeing not to bid on a procurement, *Leitman v. McAusland*, 934 F.2d 46 (4th Cir. 1991). Collusive bidding will not be found unless there is proof of concerted action between two or more parties. In *Federal Trade Comm'n v. Lukens Steel Co.*, 454 F. Supp. 1182 (D.D.C. 1978), the court found no concerted action between Lukens and United States Steel Company in the pricing of steel plates for Navy ships when the two companies followed each other's published prices or prices obtained from the ship-builder. The court stated at 1193 that: "The actions of each defendant appear to be based upon independent judgment, a consideration of the defendant's own business interest, and an assessment of the competition."

The GAO usually will not rule on protests requesting that competing offerors be disqualified because of collusive bidding, *Shel-Ken Properties, Inc.*, Comp. Gen. Dec. B-261443, 95-2 CPD ¶ 139; *Seyforth Roofing Co.*, Comp. Gen. Dec. B-241719.2, 91-1 CPD ¶ 268; *Automated Datatron, Inc.*, Comp. Gen. Dec. B-184022, 75-2 CPD ¶ 153. However, in denying such protests the GAO has frequently stated that the alleged conduct was not improper. Thus, it has stated that it is not a violation of the independent pricing certificate for competitors to propose to use the same subcontractor, *McCombs Fleet Servs.*, Comp. Gen. Dec. B-278330, 98-1 CPD ¶ 24; for competitors to use a common subcontractor, *Ross Aviation, Inc.*, Comp. Gen. Dec. B-236952, 90-1 CPD ¶ 83; for affiliated firms to submit separate bids prepared by the same person, 51 Comp. Gen. 403 (B-174449) (1972); for a firm to bid as a joint venturer and also submit bids to competitors to perform work as a subcontractor, *Southern Maryland Gen. Contractors, Inc.*, 57 Comp. Gen. 277 (B-190270), 78-1 CPD ¶ 121; for partners sharing the same business address to submit separate bids, *Ace Reforestation, Inc.*, 65 Comp. Gen. 151 (B-220276), 85-2 CPD ¶ 704; or for a firm to mail letters to several potential competitors warning of possible legal action if they infringed patents, Comp. Gen. Dec. B-167152, Aug. 14, 1969, *Unpub.*

In many circumstances, however, information may legally be exchanged with competitors. Generally, if the prospective offeror legally obtains information directly from a competitor without any restriction on the ability to use that information, it is appropriate and legal to use that information in preparing proposals.

II. PROHIBITED ACTIVITIES

One of the most serious threats to the integrity of the procurement process is the possibility of conduct by contractors that will improperly influence the decisions of contracting officers and other government employees. To protect against this threat, there are a number of very strict criminal statutes.

A. Bribery and Gratuities

It is a crime for anyone to offer or give a bribe or gratuity to a federal employee or agent of the government, 18 U.S.C. § 201. Bribes are defined in 18 U.S.C. § 201(b) as giving something "with intent to influence any official act," "to influence" an official to commit "any fraud" or "to induce" an official to commit such an act. The courts have seen this as requiring a quid pro quo — the giving of something in exchange for action on the part of a government official, *United States v. Heffler*, 402 F.2d 924 (3d Cir. 1968), *cert. denied*, 394 U.S. 946 (1969); *United States v.*

Johnson, 621 F.2d 1073 (10th Cir. 1980). Most cases involving bribery under the statute concern cash payments, *United States v. Peleti*, 576 F.3d 377 (7th Cir. 2009) (cash payment for assistance in obtaining contract); United *States v. Kinter*, 235 F.3d 192 (8th Cir. 2000); (cash payment to technical employee advising contracting officer during source selection); *United States v. Johnson*, 621 F.2d 1073 (10th Cir. 1980) (cash payment offered to FAA procurement official); *United States v. Brasco*, 516 F.2d 816 (2d Cir.), *cert. denied*, 423 U.S. 860 (1975) (cash payments to Post Office officials to obtain contracts). However, a variety of other benefits have also been considered as value by courts in relation to bribery charges, *United States v McDade*, 28 F.3d 283 (3d Cir.1994) (travel expenses); *United States v. Harary*, 457 F.2d 471 (2d Cir. 1972) (prostitutes and cameras); *United States v. Ellenbogen*, 365 F.2d 982 (2d Cir. 1966), *cert. denied*, 386 U.S. 923 (1967) (an automobile).

In contrast, prohibited gratuities under the criminal code consist of giving something "for or because of any official act," 18 U.S.C. § 201(c). This can be proven without showing the quid pro quo such as by proving that the gift was merely to generally influence an official, *United States v. Campbell*, 684 F.2d 141, 221 App. D.C. 367 (D.C. Cir. 1982). However, the gift must be linked to a specific act that the employee has taken or can take to benefit the giver, *United States v. Sun-Diamond Growers of California*, 119 U.S. 1402 (1999). See *United States v. Neiderberger*, 580 F.2d 63 (3d Cir.), *cert. denied*, 439 U.S. 980 (1978), for a case affirming the conviction of a government employee for accepting five golfing trips even though there was no proof of any specific, identifiable act that the employee had done or had been requested to do. A variety of things of value have been held to violate this statute. See *United States v. Romano*, 583 F.2d 1 (1st Cir. 1978) (cash, meat, liquor, and clothing); *United States v. Hartley*, 678 F.2d 961 (11th Cir. 1982) (paid vacations); *United States v. Gorman*, 807 F.2d 1299 (6th Cir. 1986), *cert. denied*, 484 U.S. 815 (1987) (loans and promise of future employment); *United States v. McDade*, 827 F. Supp. 1153 (E.D. Pa. 1993), *aff'd*, 28 F.3d 283 (3d Cir. 1994) (many small gifts such as a golf jacket, a golf bag, and a golf umbrella); *United States v. Hoffmann*, No. 556 F.3d 871 (8th Cir. 2009) (golf clubs).

These statutes include things of value given to persons and companies assisting the government as well as government employees. Thus, persons that are in a position of public trust with regard to government funds are classified as public officials even though they are not directly employed by the federal government. See *United States v Kenney*, 185 F3d 1217 (11th Cir. 1999) (government contractor); *United States v Hang*, 75 F3d 1275 (8th Cir.1996) (employee of local housing authority); *United States v Strissel*, 920 F.2d 1162 (4th Cir. 1990) (director of local housing authority); *United States v. Kirby*, 587 F.2d 876 (7th Cir. 1978) (privately employed grain inspector licensed by the Department of Agriculture); *United States v. Griffin*, 401 F. Supp. 1222 (S.D. Ind. 1975), *aff'd without op.* 541 F.2d 284 (7th Cir. 1976) (privately employed broker under a HUD contract).

In light of these rules, potential contractors should be exceedingly cautious in giving anything of value to government employees connected with the procurement process. In addition to the specified criminal penalties for such conduct, offerors can be disqualified from a competition for giving a bribe. See, for example, *Howema Bau-GmbH*, Comp. Gen. Dec. B-245356, 91-2 CPD ¶ 214, where a competitor was properly excluded from competition for a suspected bribe, and *Litton Sys., Inc.*, 68 Comp. Gen. 422 (B-234060), 89-1 CPD ¶ 450, *recons. denied*, 68 Comp. Gen. 677 (B-234060.2), 89-2 CPD ¶ 228, directing an agency to terminate a major contract because a high-ranking official was bribed.

For additional guidance, see the standards of conduct of each procuring agency and the federal standards of conduct in 5 C.F.R. § 2635. These standards contain extensive guidance on gifts to federal employees in Subpart B, including exceptions permitting government employees to accept gifts of small dollar value in narrow circumstances. See also the Gratuities clause in FAR 52.203-3, which permits contract termination for the offering or giving of gratuities to obtain the contract or favorable treatment under the contract and calls for damages up to 10 times the amount of the gratuity on Department of Defense contracts pursuant to 10 U.S.C. § 2207. See, for example, *Erwin Pfister General-Bauunterhehmen*, ASBCA 43980, 01-2 BCA ¶ 31,431, where the government terminated the contracts, refused to pay for work performed, refused to pay for claimed extra work and assessed substantial exemplary damages. The board denied the contractor's appeal to recover the payments owed on the contract on the basis of the contractor's conviction of bribing a contract specialist. The same result was reached in *Andreas Boehm Malergrossbetrieb*, ASBCA 44017, 01-1 BCA ¶ 31,354; *Schneider Haustechnik GmbH*, ASBCA 43969, 01-1BCA ¶ 31,264; and *Schuepferling GmbH & Co., KG*, ASBCA 45567, 98-2 BCA ¶ 29,828. In these cases, the board rejected the argument that the government had ratified the contracts by allowing performance to continue after it learned of the bribes.

B. Employment Discussions

The original Procurement Integrity Act barred "competing contractors" from discussing employment with procurement officials during the conduct of a procurement. This provision was totally repealed in 1996, and the Act was rewritten to establish procedures to be followed if a procurement officer is contacted by an offeror regarding possible employment, 41 U.S.C. § 423(c). Government employees are also subject to criminal prosecution under 18 U.S.C. § 208 if they conduct employment negotiations with a company with which they are participating personally and substantially on a contract matter. 41 U.S.C. § 423(c)(4) calls for sanctions against offerors if they conduct employment discussions with government employees knowing that the employee has not complied with the Act.

The Procurement Integrity Act permits employment discussions with a procurement official if that official reports the contact and withdraws from the procurement:

(a) *Actions required of procurement officials when contacted by offerors regarding non-Federal employment.* (1) If an agency official who is participating personally and substantially in a Federal agency procurement for a contract in excess of the simplified acquisition threshold contacts or is contacted by a person who is a bidder or offeror in that Federal agency procurement regarding possible non-Federal employment for that official, the official shall —

(A) promptly report the contact in writing to the official's supervisor and to the designated agency ethics official (or designee) of the agency in which the official is employed; and

(B) (i) reject the possibility of non-Federal employment; or

(ii) disqualify himself or herself from further personal and substantial participation in that Federal agency procurement until such time as the agency has authorized the official to resume participation in such procurement, in accordance with the requirements of section 208 of title 18, United States Code, and applicable agency regulations on the grounds that —

(I) the person is no longer a bidder or offeror in that Federal agency procurement; or

(II) all discussions with the bidder or offeror regarding possible non-Federal employment have terminated without an agreement or arrangement for employment.

Under this Act the disqualification decision seems to be in the sole discretion of the official; but FAR 3.104-11(c) states that an official who "refuses to terminate employment discussions may be subject to agency administrative actions under 5 C.F.R. § 2635.604(d) if the official's disqualification from participation in a particular procurement interferes substantially with the individual's ability to perform assigned duties." Thus, an agency retains considerable control over this decision under the regulations. If an employee does decide to withdraw from a procurement, FAR 3.104-6(b) requires that a disqualification notice be promptly submitted to the head of the contracting activity, the contracting officer, the source selection authority, and the official's immediate supervisor. Thereafter, the official can resume work on the procurement only with the consent of the head of the contracting activity, FAR 3.104-6(c).

The new Act applies to contracts over the simplified acquisition threshold of $150,000 that are "federal agency procurements," which excludes sole source contracts and contract modifications. However, employment discussions during the negotiation of such transactions would be a violation of 18 U.S.C. § 208, 5 C.F.R. § 2635.603(b). The Act applies only to bidders and offerors, but FAR 3.104-5(a) states that the disqualification rules may apply to contacts with agents or intermediaries of the offeror.

Similar rules have been formulated in the implementation of 18 U.S.C. § 208, where seeking employment has been ruled to be a financial conflict of interest. The Standards of Ethical Conduct define "seeking employment" in 5 C.F.R. § 2635.603(b):

> An employee is seeking employment once he has begun seeking employment within the meaning of paragraph (b)(1) of this section and until he is no longer seeking employment within the meaning of paragraph (b)(2) of this section.
>
> (1) An employee has begun seeking employment if he has directly or indirectly:
>
> > (i) Engaged in negotiations for employment with any person. For these purposes, as for 18 U.S.C. § 208(a), the term negotiations means discussion or communication with another person, or such person's agent or intermediary, mutually conducted with a view toward reaching an agreement regarding possible employment with that person. The term is not limited to discussions of specific terms and conditions of employment in a specific position;
> >
> > (ii) Made an unsolicited communication to any person, or such person's agent or intermediary, regarding possible employment with that person. However, the employee has not begun seeking employment if that communication was:
> >
> > > (A) For the sole purpose of requesting a job application; or
> > >
> > > (B) For the purpose of submitting a resume or other employment proposal to a person affected by the performance or nonperformance of the employee's duties only as part of an industry or other discrete class. The employee will be considered to have begun seeking employment upon receipt of any response indicating an interest in employment discussions; or
> >
> > (iii) Made a response other than rejection to an unsolicited communication from any person, or such person's agent or intermediary, regarding possible employment with that person.

Once an employment discussion has commenced, it may be terminated by rejection of any possibility of employment. Terminating an immediate employment discussion will not be considered rejection of an offer of employment if the discussion is only deferred. See *Express One Int'l, Inc. v. United States Postal Serv.*, 814 F. Supp. 93 (D.D.C. 1992), where the court enjoined award of a contract because the employee of a consultant of the procuring agency had told the winning offeror "he would not be available for a personal meeting or to discuss a position until after [award of the contract]."

Negotiations for employment were found in *United States v Schaltenbrand*, 930 F.2d 1554 (11th Cir.1991), *cert. denied*, 502 U.S. 1005 (1991), where an Air Force reserve officer approached a prospective employer, filled out an application, came for an interview, discussed his qualifications and indicated a willingness to meet company officials, even though neither side made any formal offer until after he was finished with the project; *United States v Lord*, 710 F. Supp. 615 (E.D.Va. 1989), *aff'd*, 902 F2d 1567 (4th Cir.1990), where a government program manager discussed employment with a contractor; *United States v Gorman*, 807 F.2d 1299 (6th Cir.1986), *cert. denied*, 484 U.S. 815 (1987), where the government employee had an initial conversation with a company and gave them a list of conditions for employment. Compare *Air Line Pilots Assn., Int'l v. Dep't of Transportation*, 899 F.2d 1230 (D.C. Cir.1990), where no conflict was found when the Secretary of Transportation made a regulatory ruling at the time he was negotiating for employment with a law firm. The court based its conclusion of the fact that the law firm was not representing any of the parties to the regulatory ruling.

41 U.S.C. § 423(c) calls for civil penalties, contract termination or debarment for violations of these requirements by a contractor. In *AT&T Communications, Inc.*, GSBCA 9252-P, 88-2 BCA ¶ 20,805, an offeror was disqualified after receiving information from a government employee with whom it had discussed employment. Similarly, in *Four-Phase Sys., Inc.*, ASBCA 26794, 86-2 BCA ¶ 18,924, a contract modification was found to be unenforceable by the contractor because employment negotiations violating § 208 had occurred during its negotiation. This type of sanction will not be enforced unless the government employee plays a significant role in the contracting process. See *Chemonics Int'l Consulting Div.*, 63 Comp. Gen. 14 (B-210426), 83-2 CPD ¶ 426, where the GAO held that it was improper to withhold award from a firm that had offered employment to a government employee who had attended subsequent negotiations but had not participated in any significant way in those negotiations, and *CACI, Inc.-Fed. v. United States*, 1 Cl. Ct. 352, *rev'd*, 719 F.2d 1567 (Fed. Cir. 1983), where the court found no violation of § 208 when contract negotiations with a government employee occurred 16 months after an employment discussion had occurred.

C. Dealing with Agency Employees

Officers and employees of the government with a financial interest in an organization are prohibited from participating personally and substantially in any matter concerning that organization and the government, 18 U.S.C. § 208. This provision was intended to expand the proscriptions against employee participation with the private sector beyond the prior § 434, which merely prohibited certain transactions of business. Contracts that are tainted with this type of conflict of interest have been held to be void.

The Standards of Ethical Conduct contained in 5 C.F.R. § 2635, Subpart D, provide detailed guidance implementing this statutory proscription. The definition of "financial interest" is found at 5 C.F.R. § 2635.403(c):

> (1) Except as provided in paragraph (c)(2) of this section, the term financial interest is limited to financial interests that are owned by the employee or by the employee's spouse or minor children. However, the term is not limited to only those financial interests that would be disqualifying under 18 U.S.C. § 208(a) and § 2635.402. The term includes any current or contingent ownership, equity, or security interest in real or personal property or a business and may include an indebtedness or compensated employment relationship. It thus includes, for example, interests in the nature of stocks, bonds, partnership interests, fee and leasehold interests, mineral and other property rights, deeds of trust, and liens, and extends to any right to purchase or acquire any such interest, such as a stock option or commodity future. It does not include a future interest created by someone other than the employee, his spouse or dependent child or any right as a beneficiary of an estate that has not been settled.

> (2) The term financial interest includes service, with or without compensation, as an officer, director, trustee, general partner or employee of any person, including a nonprofit entity, whose financial interests are imputed to the employee under § 2635.402(b)(2)(iii) or (iv).

The Ethics in Government Act of 1978, 5 U.S.C. App. § 201 et seq., further requires the public disclosure of financial information by all political appointees and all civil service employees ranked GS-16 and above.

A financial interest is present if it is more than insubstantial, remote, or inconsequential. The Office of Government Ethics ruled in 83 OGE 1 (1983) that vested rights in a private corporation's pension plan constituted a financial interest. In another ruling, dated August 17, 1979, the office ruled that leaves of absence or reemployment rights with a former employer were financial interests in that company.

The leading case finding a contract void for a conflict of interest is *United States v. Mississippi Valley Generating Co.*, 364 U.S. 520 (1961). There the Court found that a statutory violation had occurred when the employee had both a financial stake in the outcome of the transaction and a sufficient contact with the transaction. In that case a temporary employee of the Bureau of the Budget, who served at the request of the bureau chief without pay, also served as an officer of a bank. An offeror on an RFP for construction of a power plant negotiated the early stages of the contract with the temporary employee and asked him to inquire into financing with bank officials. The temporary employee was not involved in the final contract negotiations but confidentially suggested revisions to the offeror's second proposal. The Court gave an expansive reading to the term "transacting business" as used in prior Section 434 and found that the employee's financial stake consisted of the potential business he had generated for another employer. It found sufficient contact with the transaction because he was involved in preliminary contract negotiations on behalf of both parties. Regarding the employee's financial stake, the Court held that positive corruption is not a prerequisite for violation of the conflicts statute and stated at 550: "[T]he statute is more concerned with what might have happened than with what actually happened." See also *Smith v. United States*, 305 F.2d 197 (9th Cir. 1962), where the court found a violation of § 434 even though the "transaction" consisted merely of an employee's failure to circumscribe the activities of subordinates who were involved in a conflict.

Although § 208 is much broader in scope than was § 434, the cases decided under this section do not appear to have given it as strict an interpretation as had been given to the prior statute. See, for example, *United States v. Ponnapula*, 246 F3d 576 (6th Cir. 2001) (no conflict where person acting for the Small Business Administration in sale of foreclosed property took a $5,000 retainer for future employment from buyer but had no substantial participation in transaction because her actions with regard to the sale were only ministerial); *Cexec, Inc. v. Dep't of Energy*, GSBCA 12909-P, 95-1 BCA ¶ 27,380 (no conflict when an employee, whose wife had a financial interest in the winning contractor, had only peripheral contact with the procurement); and *United States v. Tierney*, 947 F.2d 854 (8th Cir. 1991) (no conflict because the fact that prosecutor's husband was representing defendant's insurance company was too remote a connection). See also *Grassetti v. Weinberger*, 408 F. Supp. 142 (N.D. Cal. 1976), finding that an applicant for a grant had been improperly excluded from receiving a research grant on the grounds that members of the evaluation team were competing for grants. Though the team had sufficient contact with the transaction, the court stated that, although a conflict would arise where team members contributed to a decision as to whether to award themselves a grant, the allegation that a denial of a grant to another applicant would leave more money for the team was too remote to create a conflict. The cases that have enforced § 208 have dealt with considerably greater financial interests and contact than that in *Mississippi Valley* or *Smith*. See, for example, *United States v Bouchey*, 860 F Supp 890 (D.D.C. 1994) (alleged participation by government employee in conspiracy to pay inflated consulting fees); *United Tel. Co. of the Northwest*, GSBCA 10031-P, 89-3 BCA ¶ 22,108 (offeror disqualified because its subcontractor had used a government employee participating in the procurement as a consultant during the competition); *United States v. Irons*, 640 F.2d 872 (7th Cir. 1981) (affirming conviction of program officer for HEW who recommended to a contracting officer that an IFB be sent to a company he established for the purpose of receiving the IFB); *K & R Eng'g Co. v. United States*, 222 Ct. Cl. 340, 616 F.2d 469 (1980) (contract void where chief of a branch of the U.S. Army Corps of Engineers took kickbacks and profits from contracts awarded by his office to a particular contractor after giving contractor advance notice of the Invitation for Bids (IFB) and of the maximum amount the Corps would pay); and *United States v. Conlon*, 628 F.2d 150 (D.C. Cir. 1980) (indictment under § 208 reinstated where it was shown that the director of the Bureau of Engraving, who was also president of the American Bank Note Development Corp. (ABNC), participated in decision making regarding replacement of a Bureau signature system with one developed by ABNC).

D. "Revolving Door" Violations

There are two statutes prohibiting contractors from using former agency employees on subsequent work with the agency: 18 U.S.C. § 207 bars "officers and employees" from *representing* contractors, and 41 U.S.C. § 423(d) bars certain "officials" from *accepting compensation* from contractors.

1. 18 U.S.C. § 207

18 U.S.C. § 207 restricts officers and employees in the following circumstances:

- A former employee is prohibited for life from representing anyone else before the government on a particular matter the employee handled personally and substantially while a government official.
- A former employee is prohibited for two years from representing a party on a particular matter that had been under the employee's official responsibility during the last year of the employee's government service.
- A former employee is prohibited for one year from assisting others in trade or treaty negotiations the employee had been engaged in during the employee's final year of government service.
- A former senior-level employee is prohibited for one year from making any communication or appearance before the employee's former agency regardless of prior involvement in the matter.
- A former senior-level employee is prohibited for one year from assisting foreign entities before the government.
- A former "very senior level" employee is prohibited for one year from contacting employees of the executive branch of the government.

Criminal prosecutions under this statute are rare and a violation will not make invoices on a contract false claims, *United States ex rel. Siewick v. Jamieson Science & Eng'g, Inc.*, 214 F3d 1372 (D.C. Cir. 2000). However, alleged violations of this statute are sometimes raised in contesting the validity of contracts. The most egregious conduct falling within this provision is hiring government employees before the award of a contract when they have worked on the procurement. A contracting officer's disqualification of an offeror for such conduct was sustained in *NKF Eng'g, Inc. v. United States*, 805 F.2d 372 (Fed. Cir. 1986). In that case a former Navy civilian employee, who had participated substantially in the procurement process on a particular RFP, left federal employment to take a job with one of the offerors before the contract was awarded. That offeror subsequently submitted a price revision that was 33% lower than its earlier offer. The court upheld the disqualification of the offeror on the basis of an appearance of impropriety, even though the offeror claimed that it had carefully isolated the former government employee from its preparation of the final offer. The court agreed that the potential for an unfair competitive advantage so tainted the procurement process that the integrity of the process had been damaged.

a. Particular Matter

Violations of the first two restrictions require participation in a "particular matter" that was in the agency during the official's employment. Such a matter typically involves a "proceeding affecting legal rights" or transactions "between identifiable parties," 5 C.F.R. § 2637.201(c)(1). Excluded are formulation of general policy, rule making, and legislation. For a violation to occur, the subsequent representation must concern the same matter in which the employee participated during employment, 5 C.F.R. § 2637.201(c)(4). In *CACI, Inc.-Fed. v. United States*, 1 Cl. Ct. 352, *rev'd*, 719 F.2d 1567 (Fed. Cir. 1983), the Justice Department issued an RFP for ADPE services for the Information Systems Support Group (ISSG) of the department. Before award was made, an offeror who had provided these services for some time alleged that a conflict existed in that a vice president of a competitor had previously served as chief of the ISSG. In issuing an injunction barring award, the Claims Court found that the employee was involved in the same particular matter while working for the government, a criterion that satisfies either § 207(a) or § 207(b). The Federal Circuit reversed, holding that a follow-on service contract did not cover the same particular matter as the prior contract because the nature of the services had evolved and were broader than those on the earlier contract. The court appears to have read the statute narrowly in arriving at this conclusion. Contrast the *CACI* decision with *United States v. Medico Indus., Inc.*, 784 F.2d 840 (7th Cir. 1986), holding that a contract amendment adding a large quantity of units to an existing contract was sufficiently related to the original contract to be the same particular matter.

b. Personal and Substantial Participation

Violation of the first restriction occurs only when there has been a personal and substantial participation in the matter during employment, as stated at 5 C.F.R. § 2637.201(d)(1):

> *Basic requirements.* The restrictions of section 207(a) apply only to those matters in which a former Government employee had "personal and substantial participation," exercised "through decision, approval, disapproval, recommendation, the rendering of advice, investigation or otherwise." To participate "personally" means directly, and includes the participation of a subordinate when actually directed by the former Government employee in the matter. "Substantially" means that the employee's involvement must be of significance to the matter, or form a basis for a reasonable appearance of such significance. It requires more than of-

ficial responsibility, knowledge, perfunctory involvement, or involvement on an administrative or peripheral issue. A finding of substantiality should be based not only on the effort devoted to a matter, but on the importance of the effort. While a series of peripheral involvements may be insubstantial, the single act of approving or participation in a critical step may be substantial.

Review of a proposed notice of income tax deficiency and recommendation for its issuance constituted personal and substantial participation, *United States v. Nasser*, 476 F.2d 1111 (7th Cir. 1973). Preparing a memorandum and answering a legal question were also held to be such participation. Review of a patent application was held to be sufficient involvement in *Kearney & Trecker Corp. v. Giddings & Lewis, Inc.*, 452 F.2d 579 (7th Cir. 1971), *cert. denied*, 405 U.S. 1066 (1972).

c. Representation

The basic prohibition in 18 U.S.C. § 207(a)(1) is on representational activities carried out with the intent to influence. Representation may occur in the course of formal or informal appearances and in written or oral communications. Representation is defined in 5 C.F.R. § 2637.201(b) as "acting as agent or attorney, or other representative in an appearance, or communication with intent to influence." 5 CFR § 2637.201(b)(2) makes it clear that such representation can be by any former employee, stating:

> The statutory prohibition covers any other former employee, including managerial and technical personnel, who represents another person in an appearance or, by other communication, attempts to influence the Government concerning a particular matter in which he or she was involved. For example, a former technical employee may not act as a manufacturer's promotional or contract representative to the Government on a particular matter in which he or she participated. Nor could such employee appear as an expert witness against the Government in connection with such a matter.

5 CFR § 2637.201(b)(3) provides guidance on "appearances" and "communications," stating:

> An appearance occurs when an individual is physically present before the United States in either a formal or informal setting or conveys material to the United States in connection with a formal proceeding or application. A communication is broader than an appearance and includes, for example, correspondence or telephone calls.

The following example is set forth at 5 C.F.R. § 2637.201(b)(5):

> A Government employee, who participated in writing the specifications of a contract awarded to Q Company for the design of certain education testing programs, joins Q Company and does work under the contract. She is asked to accompany a company vice-president to a meeting to state the results of a series of trial tests,

and does so. No violation occurs when she provides the information to her former agency. During the meeting a dispute arises as to some terms of the contract, and she is called upon to support Q Company's position. She may not do so. If she had reason to believe that the contractual dispute would be a subject of the meeting, she should not have attended.

See *Robert E. Derecktor of R.I., Inc. v. United States*, 762 F. Supp. 1019 (D.R.I. 1991), where the court, interpreting the predecessor to § 207(a), held that a former employee's delivery of a bid package to his former agency did not constitute an appearance within the meaning of this restriction and that the employee did not deliver the bid with the intent to influence. See, however, *United States v. Coleman*, 805 F.2d 474 (3d Cir. 1986), where a former employee's presence at a meeting related to tax cases, which had been within the employee's supervisory responsibility before retiring, was found to constitute representation within the meaning of this restriction.

18 U.S.C. § 207(j)(5) permits "communications solely for the purpose of furnishing scientific or technological information" to the agency. See *J. L. Assocs.*, Comp. Gen. Dec. B-201331.2, 82-1 CPD ¶ 99, where this exception was applied by the Air Force to a briefing by a retired military officer concerning the same activity that he had commanded. The briefing concerned the contractor's experience on similar work with other agencies and occurred before issuance of an RFP.

Under a predecessor statute, participation in the preparation of a claim for reimbursement was held not to violate the statute because it did not amount to prosecution of a claim, *Acme Process Equip. Co. v. United States*, 171 Ct. Cl. 324, 347 F.2d 509 (1965), *rev'd on other grounds*, 385 U.S. 138 (1966).

d. Types of Employment or Contracting Permitted

Absent a violation of the specific provisions of 18 U.S.C. § 207, there is no general prohibition in this statute against employment of a former government employee by a contractor. 5 C.F.R. § 2637.101(c)(5) provides:

The provisions of 18 U.S.C. § 207 do not, however, bar any former Government employee, regardless of rank, from employment with any private or public employer after Government service. Nor do they effectively bar employment even on a particular matter in which the former Government employee had major official involvement except in certain circumstances involving persons engaged in professional advocacy. Former Government employees may be fully active in high-level supervisory positions whether or not the work is funded by the United States and includes matter in which the employee was involved while employed by the Government. The statutory provisions are not intended to discourage the movement of skilled professionals in Government, to and from positions in industry, research institutions, law and accounting firms, universities and other major sources of expertise. Such a flow of skills can promote efficiency and communication between the Government and private activities, and it is essential to the success of many Government programs. Instead, only certain acts which are detrimental to public confidence in the Government are prohibited.

For cases not applying this statute to mere employment, see *Perini/Jones, Joint Venture*, Comp. Gen. Dec. B-285906, 2002 CPD ¶ 68 (former employee that will serve as company's project manager who was in the procuring agency at time proposals were submitted and evaluated); *Medical Development Int'l*, Comp. Gen. Dec. B-281484.2, 99-1 CPD ¶ 68 (former employee that will serve as Associate Director of company and had policy position in agency); *Culp/Wesner/Culp*, Comp. Gen. Dec. B-212318, 84-1 CPD ¶ 17 (former agency employee in charge of preparing solicitation subsequently awarded subcontract); and *Bray Studios, Inc.*, Comp. Gen. Dec. B-207723, 82-2 CPD ¶ 373 (former agency employee now president of contractor and working in same area).

There is no general prohibition against entering into contracts with former government employees, *Sterling Med. Assocs.*, 62 Comp. Gen. 230 (B-209493), 83-1 CPD ¶ 215 (former employee of Veterans Administration awarded contract by the Department of the Navy); *Edward R. Jereb*, 60 Comp. Gen. 298 (B-200092), 81-1 CPD ¶ 178 (restriction prohibiting award of services contract to former agency employees held invalid); *Western Eng'g & Sales Co.*, Comp. Gen. Dec. B-205464, 82-2 CPD ¶ 277 (former employee awarded contract by agency based on proposal submitted after employment terminated). See, however, *Aviation Enters., Inc. v. Orr*, 29 Cont. Cas. Fed. (CCH) ¶ 82,053 (D.D.C. 1981), *vacated*, 716 F.2d 1403 (D.C. Cir. 1983), where a contract award to a company owned by a former military officer was enjoined because of a conflict of interest, without reference to the statute.

2. *41 U.S.C. § 423(d)*

A broader post-employment restriction applicable to specific former officials is set forth at 41 U.S.C. § 423(d). This new statute in § 4304 of the Clinger-Cohen Act of 1996 totally bars employment of a very limited number of officials for a one-year period, stating:

> (1) A former official of a Federal agency may not accept compensation from a contractor as an employee, officer, director, or consultant of the contractor within a period of one year after such former official —
>
> > (A) served, at the time of selection of the contractor or the award of a contract to that contractor, as the procuring contracting officer, the source selection authority, a member of the source selection evaluation board, or the chief of a financial or technical evaluation team in a procurement in which that contractor was selected for award of a contract in excess of $10,000,000;
> >
> > (B) served as the program manager, deputy program manager, or administrative contracting officer for a contract in excess of $10,000,000 awarded to that contractor; or

(C) personally made for the Federal agency —

> (i) a decision to award a contract, subcontract, modification of a contract or subcontract, or a task order or delivery order in excess of $10,000,000 to that contractor;

> (ii) a decision to establish overhead or other rates applicable to a contract or contracts for that contractor that are valued in excess of $10,000,000;

> (iii) a decision to approve issuance of a contract payment or payments in excess of $10,000,000 to that contractor; or

> (iv) a decision to pay or settle a claim in excess of $10,000,000 with that contractor.

(2) Nothing in paragraph (1) may be construed to prohibit a former official of a Federal agency from accepting compensation from any division or affiliate of a contractor that does not produce the same or similar products or services as the entity of the contractor that is responsible for the contract referred to in subparagraph (A), (B), or (C) of such paragraph.

FAR 3.104-3(d)(2) provides detailed guidance on the calculation of the one-year period. FAR 3.104-3(d)(3) states that the statute does not prohibit employment by a division or affiliate of a contractor that does not produce the same or similar products or services as the division with which the official had previous contact. FAR 3.104-6 contains guidance on obtaining advice from agency ethics officials on the application of these rules. 41 U.S.C. § 423(g) also provides that protests may no longer be filed based on an allegation that this statute has been violated unless the violation has been reported to the contracting agency within 14 days of learning of the violation. See *Honeywell Tech. Solutions, Inc.*, Comp. Gen. Dec. B-400771, 2009 CPD ¶ 49 (protest denied because protester did not file within 14 days of learning that winning offeror had hired an agency official as a consultant). However the GAO has ruled on protests alleging that a contractor had obtained an unfair competitive advantage through revolving door violations, *Day & Zimmermann Pantex Corp.*, Comp. Gen. Dec. B-286016, 2001 CPD ¶ 96 (no indication that hired official impacted award decision); *PRC, Inc.*, Comp. Gen. Dec. B-274698.2, 97-1 CPD ¶ 115, *recons. denied*, 97-2 CPD ¶ 10 (no impropriety in the employment of the former Commanding Officer of the procuring agency who had obtained an opinion that he was not a procurement official under the statute although he had concurred in the acquisition plan and appointed the source selection official).

This restriction replaces prior restrictions in 41 U.S.C. § 423(f) that became applicable when an employee's participation occurred during the conduct of a procurement. In that event the former procurement official was prohibited for two years from participating with a competing contractor in subsequent negotiations on that contract or from participating in the performance of that contract. Those restrictions also applied to first- and second-tier subcontractors with contracts in excess of $100,000, subcontractors that significantly assisted the prime contractor in negotiations of the prime contract, subcontractors specifically directed to the prime contractor by the procurement official, and subcontractors reviewed or approved by the procurement official. The GAO held that the interpretation and enforcement of the postemployment restrictions found in 41 U.S.C. § 423 are primarily matters for the procuring agency and the Department of Justice — with the result that protests will determine only "whether any action of the former government employee may have resulted in prejudice for, or on behalf of, the awardee," *Central Texas College*, 71 Comp. Gen. 164 (B-245233.4), 92-1 CPD ¶ 121. In *FHC Options, Inc.*, Comp. Gen. Dec. B-246793.3, 92-1 CPD ¶ 366, the GAO denied a protest based on the employment of a former government employee by the awardee's subcontractor because, although the former employee had assisted in the initial development of the performance work statement and the source selection plan for the solicitation, he had left the government before the RFP was issued, was not involved in the preparation of the awardee's proposal, and would not be involved in performing the contract.

There were also special purpose post-employment restrictions applicable only to defense or procurement personnel, 10 U.S.C. § 2397c. These provisions were repealed by § 4304(b)(1) of the Clinger-Cohen Act of 1996.

Formerly, a retired military officer was subject to two additional restrictions under 37 U.S.C. § 801 and 18 U.S.C. § 281. The Federal Acquisition Streamlining Act of 1994, Pub. L. No. 103-355, repealed 37 U.S.C. § 801. Under the provisions of that statute, a retired regular officer could not be paid from any appropriation for three years after retirement if the former officer was selling for himself or herself or for others or was contracting or negotiating to sell supplies or war materials to the DOD, the Coast Guard, NASA, or the Public Health Service. Section 4304(b)(3) of the Clinger-Cohen Act of 1996 repealed 18 U.S.C. § 281. This statute made it unlawful for a period of two years after retirement for a former military officer to be compensated for representing any person in the sale of goods or services to the military service from which the officer retired.

Section 4304(b)(6) of the Clinger-Cohen Act of 1996 also repealed 42 U.S.C. § 7216, prohibiting the Department of Energy from using employees of "energy concerns" in departmental matters involving that concern for a period of one year after employment. In *TRW Envtl. Safety Sys., Inc. v. United States*, 18 Cl. Ct. 33 (1989), award to an offeror was permanently enjoined when the court found a violation of that statute. In that case a former employee of a competitor had participated in drafting the statement of work and was appointed chairman of the source evaluation board within the one-year period.

E. Antitrust Violations

Actions of competitors who attempt to manipulate the market for government products and services may be sanctioned under the Sherman Act, 15 U.S.C. §§ 1–7 and the Clayton Act, 15 U.S.C. § 15. One such action would be an attempt to monopolize a market. See *Northrop Corp. v. McDonnell Douglas Corp.*, 705 F.2d 1030 (9th Cir.), *cert. denied*, 464 U.S. 849 (1983), where the court stated at 1057:

> At least two elements of proof are indispensable to make out a prima facie case of attempt to monopolize: (1) specific intent to control prices or destroy competition, and (2) predatory conduct designed to accomplish that unlawful purpose.

In this case the court made it clear that the antitrust laws apply to government markets, stating at 1055:

> The fact that the Government is the sole domestic purchaser and regulates foreign F-18 sales does not mean that no market exists which a competitor can attempt to monopolize. A manufacturer can attempt to monopolize a market by eliminating competition through predatory actions regardless of the product's sophistication and the limited number of its potential customers. The record does not indicate as a matter of law that the military aircraft industry enjoys some sort of natural monopoly that renders inapplicable the premise of the antitrust laws that competition will assure the customer the best product at the lowest price.

Predatory pricing, which is barred by 15 U.S.C. § 2, has also been found to be barred in government procurements in *Irvin Indus., Inc. v. Goodyear Aerospace Corp.*, 974 F.2d 241 (2d Cir. 1992). In that case the court found that predatory pricing would occur if an offeror submitted a price below its reasonably anticipated average variable cost of performing the work. On remand the district court found that no predatory pricing had occurred because the contractor had an honest belief that it was submitting a price that was above its average variable cost, *Irvin Indus., Inc. v. Goodyear Aerospace Corp.*, 803 F. Supp. 951 (S.D.N.Y. 1992). See also *Ovitron Corp. v. General Motors Corp.*, 364 F. Supp. 944 (S.D.N.Y. 1973), *aff'd*, 512 F.2d 442 (2d Cir. 1975), where the court found that predatory pricing had occurred through submission of a below-cost bid but awarded no damages because the competitor had failed to prove that it would have won the competition.

The procurement regulations contain little guidance on anticompetitive conduct. However, FAR 3.501-1 contains guidance on buying-in, which is defined as

> submitting an offer below anticipated costs, expecting to —

> > (a) Increase the contract amount after award (e.g., through unnecessary or excessively priced change orders); or

(b) Receive follow-on contracts at artificially high prices to recover losses incurred on the buy-in contract.

FAR 3.501-2 contains the following guidance on how a contracting officer should deal with buying-in:

(a) Buying-in may decrease competition or result in poor contract performance. The contracting officer must take appropriate action to ensure buying-in losses are not recovered by the contractor through the pricing of (1) change orders or (2) follow-on contracts subject to cost analysis.

(b) The Government should minimize the opportunity for buying-in by seeking a price commitment covering as much of the entire program concerned as is practical by using —

(1) Multiyear contracting, with a requirement in the solicitation that a price be submitted only for the total multiyear quantity; or

(2) Priced options for additional quantities that, together with the firm contract quantity, equal the program requirements (see Subpart 17.2).

(c) Other safeguards are available to the contracting officer to preclude recovery of buying-in losses e.g., amortization of non-recurring costs (see 15.408, Table 15-2, paragraph A., column (2) under "Formats for Submission of Line Item Summaries") and treatment of unreasonable price quotations (see 15.405).

The GAO has held that below-cost bidding is not illegal per se, and the decision whether to accept a below-cost offer is essentially a responsibility determination to be made by the contracting officer, *Little Susitna, Inc.*, Comp. Gen. Dec. B-244228, 91-2 CPD ¶ 6, or an assessment of the risk of awarding to an offeror that may not have the requisite technical competence because it does not understand the work, *SEEMA, Inc.*, Comp. Gen. Dec. B-277988, 98-1 CPD ¶ 12; *Centech Group, Inc.*, Comp. Gen. Dec. B-278715, 98-1 CPD ¶ 108. Although the GAO has held that an agency's acceptance of a below-cost offer is not grounds to sustain a protest, *Geophex, Ltd.*, Comp. Gen. Dec. B-246033, 92-1 CPD ¶ 186, it is unwise to submit an offer that is significantly below a reasonable estimated cost.

Very few reported cases have found anticompetitive conduct. See, however, *United States v. Perkins*, 596 F. Supp. 528 (E.D. Pa.), *aff'd*, 749 F.2d 29 (3d Cir. 1984), *cert. denied*, 471 U.S. 1015 (1985), where the court found that it was improper to set up six corporations to create the appearance of competition. The fact that this scheme had been carried out with the assistance of government personnel enabled the government to obtain convictions for bribery and gratuities under 18 U.S.C. § 201. Convictions were also obtained for false claims under 18 U.S.C. § 287, conspiracy under 18 U.S.C. § 371, wire fraud under 18 U.S.C. § 1343, and racketeering under 18 U.S.C. § 1961 et seq. See also *United States v. Bernard D. Reicher*, 983 F.2d 168

(10th Cir. 1992), where the court found an antitrust violation when an offeror induced another company to submit an offer to create the appearance of competition. The court held that a violation had occurred even though the second company was not capable of performing the contract.

Teaming agreements and joint ventures are frequently used in government contracting and do not violate the antitrust laws if they do not unduly restrict competition. See FAR 9.603, stating the general government policy as follows:

> The Government will recognize the integrity and validity of contractor team arrangements; provided, the arrangements are identified and company relationships are fully disclosed in an offer or, for arrangements entered into after submission of an offer, before the arrangement becomes effective. The Government will not normally require or encourage the dissolution of contractor team arrangements.

FAR 9.601 contains the following definition:

> "Contractor team arrangement" means an arrangement in which —

> (a) Two or more companies form a partnership or joint venture to act as a potential prime contractor; or

> (b) A potential prime contractor agrees with one or more other companies to have them act as its subcontractors under a specified Government contract or acquisition program.

Joint ventures are commonly used on construction contracts but are only rarely used on research and development or supply contracts. Teaming agreements between a prime contractor and one or more subcontractors are used frequently on development contracts and follow-on supply contracts. FAR 9.604 states that nothing in the regulation "authorizes contractor team arrangements in violation of antitrust statutes." These agreements can be independently challenged if they appear to violate such statutes. See the *Northrop Corp. v. McDonnell Douglas Corp.* case discussed above, where the court held that a teaming agreement containing future market restrictions was not illegal per se and that the agreement should be subjected to an antitrust "rule of reason" analysis to determine whether it violated 15 U.S.C. § 1. This analysis is used to determine whether the restraints can be justified as reasonable in light of their legitimate purposes and effects. The court indicated that factors to consider include the degree to which the arrangement increased competition by enabling participation in a market by one of the members that would otherwise be foreclosed from competing and the reasonableness of the restraints. Compare *COMPACT v. Metropolitan Gov't of Nashville & Davidson County*, 594 F. Supp. 1567 (M.D. Tenn. 1984), where the court refused to apply the rule of reason test to a joint venture of minority businesses in which the members had agreed not to pursue work in their individual capacities on projects that the joint venture had targeted for the submission of a joint venture proposal.

Certain agreements that restrict competition may be granted an exemption from the antitrust laws. For example, 15 U.S.C. § 638(d)(2) authorizes the Small Business Administration to approve agreements "between small business firms providing for a joint program of research and development, if the Administrator finds that the joint program proposed will maintain and strengthen the free enterprise system." Such approval may be granted after consultation with the chairman of the Federal Trade Commission and with the prior written approval of the Attorney General. Actions or omissions to act under such approved agreements are exempt from the antitrust laws and the Federal Trade Commission Act, 15 U.S.C. § 41 et seq. See also 15 U.S.C. § 640. Similarly, 50 U.S.C. App. § 2158(c)(1) provides exemption from the antitrust laws for defense production pools that support national defense "through the development of preparedness programs and the expansion of productive capacity and supply beyond levels needed to meet essential civilian demand." See FAR Subpart 9.7, which implements these statutes and permits contracting with these pools.

F. Payment of Contingent Fees

The government has a long-standing policy against the payment of contingent fees. This policy developed because of the government's concern that contingent fee arrangements expose government agencies to corrupting influences. It also reflects the government's recognition that such agreements could allow for the payment of exorbitant fees by contractors, leading to higher costs for the government, thereby resulting in an unnecessary waste of public funds. See *Quinn v. Gulf & Western Corp.*, 644 F.2d 89 (2d Cir. 1981). Thus, a clause is required by statute in negotiated contracts, 10 U.S.C. § 2306(b); 41 U.S.C. § 254(a), with the exception of contracts at or below the simplified acquisition threshold of $150,000 and contracts for the acquisition of commercial items, FAR 3.404. The clause to be used is contained in FAR 52.203-5:

COVENANT AGAINST CONTINGENT FEES (APR 1984)

(a) The Contractor warrants that no person or agency has been employed or retained to solicit or obtain this contract upon an agreement or understanding for a contingent fee, except a bona fide employee or agency. For breach or violation of this warranty, the Government shall have the right to annul this contract without liability or, in its discretion, to deduct from the contract price or consideration, or otherwise recover, the full amount of the contingent fee.

(b) "Bona fide agency," as used in this clause, means an established commercial or selling agency, maintained by a contractor for the purpose of securing business, that neither exerts nor proposes to exert improper influence to solicit or obtain Government contracts nor holds itself out as being able to obtain any Government contract or contracts through improper influence.

"Bona fide employee," as used in this clause, means a person, employed by a contractor and subject to the contractor's supervision and control as to time, place, and manner of performance, who neither exerts nor proposes to exert improper influence to solicit or obtain Government contracts nor holds out as being able to obtain any Government contract or contracts through improper influence.

"Contingent fee," as used in this clause, means any commission, percentage, brokerage, or other fee that is contingent upon the success that a person or concern has in securing a Government contract.

"Improper influence," as used in this clause, means any influence that induces or tends to induce a Government employee or officer to give consideration or to act regarding a Government contract on any basis other than the merits of the matter.

The covenant does not prohibit the payment of all contingent fees — only those made for the purpose of obtaining a contract. In *Browne v. R & R Eng'g Co.*, 264 F.2d 219 (3d Cir. 1959), the court held that contingent fee services in connection with a proposed contract that did not involve any dealings with officials responsible for the award of contracts were not prohibited. The GAO has followed this ruling. See *Holmes & Narver Servs., Inc.*, Comp. Gen. Dec. B-242240, 91-1 CPD ¶ 373, where an incumbent contractor offered to sell access to its employees and competitively useful contract information to potential offerors who agreed to purchase inventory and equipment at set prices if they won the contract. The GAO held that this was not a prohibited contingent fee arrangement because the payment would not be made for the purpose of soliciting or obtaining the contract at issue and the arrangement did not involve any dealings with government officials. See also *Kasler Elec. Co.*, DOTCAB 1425, 84-2 BCA ¶ 17,374, where a payment to a nonemployee estimator was contingent on award of the contract. The board held that the arrangement did not violate the covenant because the estimator's function was to price out a bid and not to solicit a government contract. Compare *Howard Johnson Lodge*, Comp. Gen. Dec. B-244302.2, 92-1 CPD ¶ 305, finding a violation of the covenant because the sales agent was directly contacting government agencies about potential contracts.

In addition, the covenant does not apply to "bona fide employees" or "bona fide selling agents." The factors to be considered in determining whether the recipient of a contingent fee is a bona fide selling agent in these exceptions are set forth at FAR 3.408-2(c), as follows:

(1) The fee should not be inequitable or exorbitant when compared to the services performed or to customary fees for similar services related to commercial business.

(2) The agency should have adequate knowledge of the contractor's products and business, as well as other qualifications necessary to sell the products or services on their merits.

(3) The contractor and the agency should have a continuing relationship or, in newly established relationships, should contemplate future continuity.

(4) The agency should be an established concern that has existed for a considerable period, or be a newly established going concern likely to continue in the future. The business of the agency should be conducted in the agency name and characterized by the customary indicia of the conduct of regular business.

(5) While an agency that confines its selling activities to Government contracts is not disqualified, the fact that an agency represents the contractor in Government and commercial sales should receive favorable consideration.

Established sales arrangements that are not confined to sales to the government do not violate the covenant, *Puma Indus. Consulting, Inc. v. Daal Assocs., Inc.*, 808 F.2d 982 (2d Cir. 1987). In *General Sales Agency*, Comp. Gen. Dec. B-247133.2, 92-1 CPD ¶ 544, a newly established arrangement with a sales organization for a 7 1/2% contingent fee was held proper because the parties anticipated that the arrangement would be long-standing and no improper influence had been exerted to obtain the contract. See also *Howard Johnson Lodge*, Comp. Gen. Dec. B-244302.2, 92-1 CPD ¶ 305, where a 10% contingent fee was held proper because there was "no hint" of improper influence in the arrangement, Similarly, in *Convention Mktg. Servs.*, Comp. Gen. Dec. B-245660.3, 92-1 CPD ¶ 144, no violation was found where contractors had entered into contingent fee arrangements with sales agents to assist in the acquisition and preparation of contracts but had not exerted improper influence to solicit or obtain the contracts. The GAO stated:

> The fact that an agent's fee is contingent upon the contractor receiving the contract award is insufficient to bring a fee arrangement under the contingent fee prohibition; rather, the regulation contemplates a specific demonstration that an agent is retained for the express purpose of contacting Government officials.

See also *Wickes Indus., Inc.*, ASBCA 17376, 75-1 BCA ¶ 11,180, for a decision in which the government was not allowed to cancel a contract when a contingency arrangement was considered bona fide because of the factors set forth in earlier regulations. See also Comp. Gen. Dec. B-157815, Jan. 21, 1966, *Unpub.*

The bona-fide employee exception focuses on the nature of the arrangement between the agent and the contractor, FAR 3.408-2(b). In *Quinn v. Gulf & Western Corp.*, 644 F.2d 89 (2d Cir. 1981), a contract was held to be unenforceable because the contingent fee arrangement between the turbine blade manufacturer and the owner of a consulting firm, who was also a special government employee, failed to satisfy the bona-fide employee criterion.

G. Accepting Kickbacks from Subcontractors

Contractors and subcontractors are prohibited from soliciting, accepting, or attempting to accept any kickback from their subcontractors by the Anti-Kickback Act of 1986, 41 U.S.C. §§ 51–58. This Act contains a broad definition of the term "kickback" as follows:

> The term "kickback" means any money, fee, commission, credit, gift, gratuity, thing of value, or compensation of any kind which is provided, directly or indirectly, to any prime contractor, prime contractor employee, subcontractor, or subcontractor employee for the purpose of improperly obtaining or rewarding favorable treatment in connection with a prime contract or in connection with a subcontract relating to a prime contract.

The purpose of this statute is to prevent payments that impede the competitive process. The typical kickback is paid to a purchasing agent of a contractor or subcontractor to obtain the award of a subcontract without having to participate in a fair competition. The purchasing agent, in turn, takes some action that distorts the competition. The presumption is that the government eventually pays the amount of the kickback through higher prices, and the Act permits the procuring agency to reduce the price by the amount of the kickback, 41 U.S.C. § 56. The Act also contains criminal and civil sanctions, 41 U.S.C. §§ 54 & 55.

The Act is implemented in FAR 3.502, and the Anti-Kickback Procedures clause at FAR 52.203-7. This clause requires the contractor to have internal procedures to detect and prevent kickbacks. It also requires the prompt reporting of kickbacks and cooperation with government agencies in the investigation of kickbacks. The clause is not applicable to contracts under $150,000 or to a contract for the acquisition of commercial items, FAR 3.502.3. However, such procurements are still subject to the Act.

There has been no significant litigation under this Act. However, see *Aalco Forwarding, Inc.*, Comp. Gen. Dec. B-277241.8, 97-2 CPD ¶ 110, holding that payment of commissions or rebates from tariff rates from carriers to brokers under government contract were not per se violations of the Act. See also *United States v Guthrie*, 64 F.3d 1510 (10th Cir. 1995), holding that contractors can be required to pay restitution for violations of the Act.

There was considerable litigation under a prior Act that was narrower in scope. There the courts required proof of specific intent and construed the value and intent elements of the kickback prohibition, following the cases on bribery, *Howard v. United States*, 345 F.2d 126 (1st Cir.), *cert. denied*, 382 U.S. 838 (1965). In addition, it was held that the government was not precluded from suing under both this Act and the False Claims Act, *United States v. General Dynamics Corp.*, 19 F.3d 770 (2d Cir. 1994).

III. ANALYSIS OF THE REQUEST FOR PROPOSALS

Upon receipt of an RFP, an offeror should immediately perform an analysis to decide whether it makes good business sense to submit a proposal. This analysis should not only focus on the evaluation factors set forth in the RFP, but should also extend to general business considerations of risk and potential benefits. Before expending substantial effort analyzing the RFP, the recipient should ascertain if it will be qualified to submit a proposal or receive an award. The RFP and its specifications must also be analyzed to ascertain whether there are impediments to winning the competition that can be corrected before the proposal is written. If so, they can be brought to the attention of the contracting officer or, in an extreme case, protested through the protest procedures. Finally, the offeror must carefully study the RFP to determine the government basis for awarding the contract. This will enable the offeror to prepare the proposal so that it contains all of the information needed by the government to perform its evaluation and offers the best value to the agency.

A. Offeror Qualification

It is the offeror's responsibility to ascertain whether it possesses the qualifications necessary to receive an award. In addition to provisions stated in the RFP, the offeror must assure itself that it meets general government contract eligibility requirements.

1. Eligibility

An offeror should take any necessary steps to ensure that it is eligible to perform the contract should it be selected for award. An offeror must be responsible at time of award. This means that a potential contractor must have the ability to perform as well as the determination to use this ability to complete the contract work in a satisfactory manner. In determining a potential contractor's ability to perform the contracting officer will consider a potential contractor's financial resources, its ability to comply with the delivery schedule, whether it has the necessary facilities and equipment, whether it has the necessary organization and experience, and whether it has obtained all required licenses and permits. Determining whether an offeror possesses the necessary will to perform involves evaluating the offeror's tenacity and perseverance and integrity. The responsibility of a prospective contractor is judged as of the time of award and not as of the time of submission of the offer, *CardioMetrix*, Comp. Gen. Dec. B-255748.2, 94-1 CPD ¶ 364; *Vulcan Eng'g Co.*, Comp. Gen. Dec. B-214595, 84-2 CPD ¶ 403; *Heli-Jet Corp. v. United States*, 2 Cl. Ct. 613 (1983). In negotiated procurement, these same responsibility criteria are used in evaluating the relative capability of the offerors. Thus, an offeror with marginal capability is not likely to receive an award in a competitive procurement.

Offerors that are debarred, suspended, or proposed for debarment are ineligible to receive award of a contract, FAR 9.404(a). FAR 9.405(d) contains the following procedures to ensure that the government does not deal with contractors that are listed on the List of Parties Excluded from Procurement Programs and Nonprocurement Programs:

> (1) After the opening of bids or receipt of proposals, the contracting officer shall review the List of Parties Excluded from Procurement Programs.

> * * *

> (3) Proposals, quotations, or offers received from any listed contractor shall not be evaluated for award or included in the competitive range, nor shall discussions be conducted with a listed offeror during a period of ineligibility, unless the agency head or a designee determines, in writing, that there is a compelling reason to do so. If the period of ineligibility expires or is terminated prior to award, the contracting officer may, but is not required to, consider such proposals, quotations, or offers.

> (4) Immediately prior to award, the contracting officer shall again review the List to ensure that no award is made to a listed contractor.

Under prior similar regulations, it was held that a contracting officer could properly refuse to award a contract to a bidder that had been proposed for debarment at the time of bid opening but had settled the issues (ending the debarment proceedings) at the time of award, *Instruments by Precision Ltd.*, Comp. Gen. Dec. B-235339, 89-2 CPD ¶ 138. Compare *Tracor Applied Sciences, Inc.*, Comp. Gen. Dec. B-221230.2, 86-1 CPD ¶ 189, holding that a contracting officer had discretion to award to a firm that was suspended or debarred at the time the offer was submitted, so long as it was not ineligible at the time of award, or to deny award even if the suspension or debarment was being reconsidered at the time of evaluation. The current FAR gives the contracting officer discretion to award to such a contractor when there is a "compelling reason," but it appears that agencies may be reluctant to find such compelling reasons. See *J.B. Kies Constr. Co.*, Comp. Gen. Dec. B-250797, 93-1 CPD ¶ 127, affirming a finding of no compelling reason where the bids were opened two days before the debarment ended and the debarment had been delayed for over two years because of "administrative oversight." In *TS Generalbau GmbH*, Comp. Gen. Dec. B-246034, 92-1 CPD ¶ 189, the GAO rejected the argument that the contractor had been arbitrarily suspended "just days before the bid opening and contract award," and in *Baxter Healthcare Corp.*, Comp. Gen. Dec. B-253455.3, 94-1 CPD ¶ 301, the protester was found ineligible for award where its suspension was not lifted until the afternoon after award and the contracting officer did not know that the suspension was about to end.

Each offeror must determine whether it qualifies as a small business. The initial determination of size is made by the small business, which is required to self-certify with its offer that it is small, 13 C.F.R. § 121.405(a). If, subsequently, an offeror is found not to be small by the Small Business Administration, the offeror may not, unless the SBA has issued a later decision finding the firm to be small, certify itself as small under the same or lower standards as those under which it had been found not to be small, 13 C.F.R. § 121.1009(g)(3); *Choctaw Mfg. Co. v. United States*, 761 F.2d 609 (11th Cir. 1985); *Propper Int'l, Inc.*, 55 Comp. Gen. 1188 (B-185302), 76-1 CPD ¶ 400. See *Timothy S. Graves*, Comp. Gen. Dec. B-253813, 93-2 CPD ¶ 244, *recons. denied*, 94-1 CPD ¶ 19, where award was denied to a firm that was in fact small at the time of award. In this case, the bidder on a timber sale had been determined not to be a small business by the SBA regional office. The bidder appealed the determination to the SBA's Office of Hearings and Appeals (OHA), and while the matter was being considered by the OHA, the bidder submitted a bid on a subsequent timber sale and certified itself to be a small business. Subsequently, the OHA reversed the regional office's determination on the previous contract, and the agency proposed to award the contract to the bidder. However, the award was appealed to the OHA, which held that the bidder could not qualify as small because the regional office determination had not been reversed at the time that the bidder signed its self-certification, even though by OHA's own determination, the bidder was small at the time. The GAO denied the subsequent protest on the grounds that the SBA size determination was conclusive.

Once a business is found to be other than small, it is required to recertify prior to bidding on any government procurement, 13 C.F.R. § 121.1010. In *Evans Cooperage Co.*, SIZ-94-11-2-145, May 5, 1995, *Unpub.*, the appellant was found to be other than small for the applicable 500-employee size standard in a particular solicitation. The appellant did not recertify but stated that it had intended to do so and that it now had fewer than 500 employees. The SBA found that this argument had no merit.

An offeror must also meet any prequalification requirements. An offeror seeking qualification must be promptly informed as to whether qualification is obtained and, if not attained, must be furnished specific information concerning the outcome, 41 U.S.C. § 253c; 10 U.S.C. § 2319. See Chapter 2 for a discussion of prequalification requirements.

A new eligibility requirement for contractors dealing with the Department of Defense is registration in the Central Contractor Registration (CCR) database. After May 31, 1998, prospective contractors must be registered in the CCR database prior to award of a contract, DFARS 204.7302.

2. Organizational Conflict of Interest

It is the policy of the government to avoid awarding contracts where the contractor would either have an actual or potential bias in making judgments required by contract performance or have an unfair competitive advantage in competing for future contracts, FAR 9.505. Such situations are called "organizational conflicts of interest" (OCIs). In implementing this policy, the contracting officer must decide whether to disqualify an offeror or to include a contract provision imposing restraints designed to avoid, neutralize, or mitigate the bias or competitive advantage, FAR 9.504(a)(2). The particular action the contracting officer should take depends on the nature of the conflict and the point in the procurement process at which it is identified. Offerors should analyze each solicitation – particularly those calling for the performance of services – to identify any potential OCIs and determine whether they will preclude award of future contracts or whether they can be dealt with by imposing contractual restraints on the offeror's future conduct.

FAR Subpart 9.5 contains a description of four scenarios where organizational conflicts of interest (OCIs) exist plus nine specific examples of applying the rules in this area. However, it leaves the determination of whether such a conflict exists and the preparation of appropriate contract language to each contracting officer. More detailed guidance must be obtained from the GAO decisions in this area. In that regard, the GAO concluded in *Aetna Gov. Health Plans, Inc.*, Comp. Gen. Dec. B-254397.15, 95-2 CPD ¶ 129, that there are three basic types of OCI – unequal access to information, setting biased ground rules, and impaired objectivity. See also Gordon, *Organizational Conflicts of Interest: A Growing Integrity Challenge*, 35 Pub. Cont. L.J. 25 (Fall 2005).

a. Unequal Access To Information

FAR 9.505 contains the following general guidance on this type of OCI:

(b) *Preventing unfair competitive advantage.* In addition to the other situations described in this subpart, an unfair competitive advantage exists where a contractor competing for award for any Federal contract possesses —

(1) Proprietary information that was obtained from a Government official without proper authorization; or

(2) Source selection information (as defined in [FAR] 2.101) that is relevant to the contract but is not available to all competitors, and such information would assist that contractor in obtaining the contract.

FAR 9.505-4 contains more explicit guidance as follows:

(a) When a contractor requires proprietary information from others to perform a Government contract and can use the leverage of the contract to obtain it, the contractor may gain an unfair competitive advantage unless restrictions are imposed. These restrictions protect the information and encourage companies to provide it when necessary for contract performance. They are not intended to protect information (1) furnished voluntarily without limitations on its use or (2) available to the Government or contractor from other sources without restriction.

(b) A contractor that gains access to proprietary information of other companies in performing advisory and assistance services for the Government must agree with the other companies to protect their information from unauthorized use or disclosure for as long as it remains proprietary and refrain from using the information for any purpose other than that for which it was furnished. The contracting officer shall obtain copies of these agreements and ensure that they are properly executed.

(c) Contractors also obtain proprietary and source selection information by acquiring the services of marketing consultants which, if used in connection with an acquisition, may give the contractor an unfair competitive advantage. Contractors should make inquiries of marketing consultants to ensure that the marketing consultant has provided no unfair competitive advantage.

This guidance describes the types of information covered by this rule as "proprietary information" and "source selection information." In *Aetna*, the GAO described the information covered as "nonpublic information." To fall in this category, the information must be *specific information* that gives a potential competitor a competitive advantage. However, it need not be proprietary information or source selection information. For example, in *Johnson Controls World Services, Inc.*, Comp. Gen. Dec. B-286714.2, 2001 CPD ¶ 20, GAO found this type of OCI when the awardee's proposed subcontractor for a maintenance contract was, under another contract, maintaining the agency's Executive Management Information System (EMIS) database, which provided detailed information on the agency's maintenance activities, reasoning:

> FAR 9.505(b) cites two kinds of information that can provide an offeror an unfair competitive advantage: proprietary information obtained from the government without proper authorization, and source selection information. However, the regulation recognizes that "conflicts may arise in situations not expressly covered in this section 9.505.... Each individual contracting situation should be examined on the basis of its particular facts and the nature of the proposed contract." FAR 9.505. The information principally in question here, EMIS data, does not fall within either category specified in the regulation, since it was presumably obtained with proper authorization and not in the course of the source selection process. However, if the information is as [the protester] alleges, it clearly could have provided the [awardee/subcontractor] team with an advantage in the competition. That advantage would be an unfair competitive advantage to the extent that the [awardee/subcontractor] team, and no other offeror, had relevant nonpublic information — beyond that which would be available to a typical incumbent installation logistics support contractor — that would assist it in obtaining the contract.

Potential OCIs of this type were found in *B.L. Harbert-Brasfield & Gorrie, JV*, Comp. Gen. Dec. B-402229, 2010 CPD ¶ 69, and *McCarthy/Hunt, JV*, Comp. Gen. Dec. B-402229.2, 2010 CPD ¶ 68 (parent company of consultant that had participate in planning procurement was negotiating to purchase subcontractor of selected contractor); *VRC, Inc.*, Comp. Gen. Dec. B-310100, 2007 CPD ¶ 202 (employee of a company that was a major stockholder in a proposed subcontractor worked directly for the contracting officer, had access to all source selection information, and was expected to assist the evaluators); *United States ex rel. Harrison v. Westinghouse Savannah River Co.*, 352 F.3d 908 (4th Cir. 2003) (employee of potential subcontractor had prepared internal documents justifying subcontracting training work); and *Ktech Corp.*, Comp. Gen. Dec. B-285330, 2002 CPD ¶ 77, 44 GC ¶ 247 (subcontractor had access to protester's technical information through its work in assisting the agency in monitoring the protester's performance on prior contract). However, most protests have been denied because the protester could not prove that the winning offeror had specific information that gave it a competitive advantage. See *Alabama Aircraft Indus., Inc. v. United States*, 83 Fed. Cl. 666 (2008), *aff'd*, 586 F.3d 1372 (Fed. Cir. 2009) (work on prior engineering services contract provided no specific information giving competitive advantage on aircraft maintenance contract); *Masai Techs. Corp. v. United States*, 79 Fed. Cl. 433 (2007) (contracting officer found that subcontractors to winning offeror did not have access to detailed information on program for which contract was awarded); *ARINC Eng'g Servs., LLC v. United States*, 77 Fed. Cl. 196 (2007) (work on prior contract was different and unrelated to work on new contract); *Chenega Fed Sys., LLC*, Comp. Gen. Dec. B-299310.2, 2007 CPD ¶ 196 (winning offeror hired government technical representative on prior contract but he had performed only "low-level administrative functions"); *Mechanical Equip. Co.*, Comp. Gen. Dec. B-292789.2, 2004 CPD ¶ 192 (prospective subcontractor working in the agency did not have access to critical information); *Perini/Jones, Joint Venture*, Comp. Gen. Dec. B-285906, 2002 CPD ¶ 68 (no proof that prospective project manager gained access to proprietary information when working for the agency at the time proposals were submitted); and *TRW, Inc.*, Comp. Gen. Dec. B-282162, 99-2 CPD ¶ 12 (no proof that subcontractor had gained access to proprietary information when serving as support service contractor). In *ARINC* the court stated at 203 - 04 that to prove this type of OCI, a protester would have to show that —

> (i) the awardee was so embedded in the agency as to provide it with insight into the agency's operations beyond that which would be expected of a typical government contractor; (ii) the awardee had obtained materials related to the specifications or statement of work for the instant procurement; or (iii) some other "preferred treatment or . . . agency action" has occurred.

It is clear that to prove this type of OCI, a protester must show evidence beyond the fact that the winning offeror has gained information because it has been the incumbent contractor. See *Systems Plus, Inc. v. United States*, 69 Fed. Cl. 757 (2006), where the court found no OCI when the winning offeror had worked with the agency in designing its information technology infrastructure and planning the process. Although the protester claimed that this gave the contractor a "superior understanding of [the agency's] network architecture, objectives, and requirements," the court found that the contractor did not have "the kind of specific, sensitive information that would create an OCI." The court noted that merely being an incumbent contractor did not generally create an OCI, stating at 771:

Incumbent status, without more, typically does not constitute "unequal access to information" for purposes of showing an OCI. See *Gulf Group, Inc. v. United States*, 56 Fed. Cl. 391, 398 & n.13 (2003) ("While an agency may not unduly tip the scales in favor of an incumbent, it certainly may weigh the competitive advantages offered by that incumbent via its relevant experience and performance with the contract subject matter."); *Winstar Commc'ns, Inc. v. United States*, 41 Fed. Cl. 748, 763 (1998) (citing *Matter of Versar, Inc.*, B-254464.3, 94-1 CPD ¶ 230, 1994 WL 120013, at *7 (GAO Feb. 16, 1994)) ("An offeror's competitive advantage gained through incumbency is generally not an unfair advantage that must be eliminated.").

See also *PAI Corp. v. United States*, 2009 U.S. Claims Lexis 320, *aff'd* 2010 U.S. App. Lexis 16201 (Fed. Cir. 2010); *Integrated Concepts & Research Corp.*, Comp. Gen. Dec. B-309803, 2008 CPD ¶ 117, and *Council for Adult & Experiential Learning*, Comp. Gen. Dec. B-299798.2, 2007 CPD ¶ 151.

This type of OCI does not exist with regard to information that has been furnished to an agency without proprietary legends. See *Snell Enters., Inc.*, Comp. Gen. Dec. B-290113, 2002 CPD ¶ 115, finding no OCI because the information had been furnished to the agency voluntarily with no proprietary markings.

This type of OCI can be overcome by disclosing the information in the RFP. See *KPMG Peat Marwick*, 73 Comp. Gen. 15 (B-251902.3), 93-2 CPD ¶ 272 (information obtained by Freedom of Information Act request during competition). Of course, this would be improper if the information was proprietary.

b. Setting Biased Ground Rules

Aetna describes this as a situation —

in which a firm, as part of its performance of a government contract, has in some sense set the ground rules for another government contract by, for example, writing the statement of work or the specifications. In these "biased ground rules" cases, the primary concern is that the firm could skew the competition, whether intentionally or not, in favor of itself. FAR 9.505-1, 9.505-2. These situations may also involve a concern that the firm, by virtue of its special knowledge of the agency's future requirements, would have an unfair advantage in the competition for those requirements.

FAR 9.505 describes two types of situations in which an OCI of this type is most likely to arise. The first situation is procurement of systems engineering and technical direction. FAR 9.505-1 contains the following bar when a contractor performs such work:

(a) A contractor that provides systems engineering and technical direction for a system but does not have overall contractual responsibility for its development, its integration, assembly, and checkout, or its production shall not (1) be awarded a contract to supply the system or any of its major components or (2) be a subcontractor or consultant to a supplier of the system or any of its major components.

(b) Systems engineering includes a combination of substantially all of the following activities: determining specifications, identifying and resolving interface problems, developing test requirements, evaluating test data, and supervising design. Technical direction includes a combination of substantially all of the following activities: developing work statements, determining parameters, directing other contractors' operations, and resolving technical controversies.

It has been held that "sustaining engineering" by a contractor on an aircraft program did not bar that contractor from performance of overhaul and maintenance contracts on the same aircraft because sustaining engineering was not the same as technical direction or systems engineering, *Hayes Int'l Corp. v. McLucas*, 509 F.2d 247 (5th Cir.), *cert. denied*, 423 U.S. 864 (1975). See also *Masai Techs. Corp. v. United States*, 79 Fed. Cl. 433 (2007), finding that work on prior contracts did not constitute systems engineering. Compare *MAR, Inc.*, Comp. Gen. Dec. B-215798, 85-1 CPD ¶ 121, where a contract for "scientific, engineering, analytical, technical and prototype-fabrication services" was held to involve a potential conflict of interest.

The second situation is the preparation of complete specifications for nondevelopmental items. See FAR 9.505-2 stating:

(a)(1) If a contractor prepares and furnishes complete specifications covering nondevelopmental items, to be used in a competitive acquisition, that contractor shall not be allowed to furnish these items, either as a prime contractor or as a subcontractor, for a reasonable period of time including, at least, the duration of the initial production contract. This rule shall not apply to —

      (i) Contractors that furnish at Government request specifications or data regarding a product they provide, even though the specifications or data may have been paid for separately or in the price of the product; or

      (ii) Situations in which contractors, acting as industry representatives, help Government agencies prepare, refine, or coordinate specifications, regardless of source, provided this assistance is supervised and controlled by Government representatives.

(2) If a single contractor drafts complete specifications for nondevelopmental equipment, it should be eliminated for a reasonable time from competition for production based on the specifications. This should be done in order to avoid a situation in which the contractor could draft specifications favoring its own products or capabilities. In this way the Government can be assured of getting unbiased advice as to the content of the specifications and can avoid allegations of favoritism in the award of production contracts.

* * *

(b)(1) If a contractor prepares, or assists in preparing, a work statement to be used in competitively acquiring a system or services-or provides material leading directly, predictably, and without delay to such a work statement — that contractor may not supply the system, major components of the system, or the services unless —

(i) It is the sole source;

(ii) It has participated in the development and design work; or

(iii) More than one contractor has been involved in preparing the work statement.

This situation may occur where the specifications contain substantial detail, *Nelson Erection Co.*, Comp. Gen. Dec. B-217556, 85-1 CPD ¶ 482 (specifications for repair of hangar door outlining specific repairs needed), as well as where the specifications are very general, *LW Planning Group*, Comp. Gen. Dec. B-215539, 84-2 CPD ¶ 531 (broad work statement for contract to revise a facility's master plan). This type of OCI has been found in a number of cases where the contractor played a major but not sole role in drafting a work statement. See *B.L. Harbert-Brasfield & Gorrie, JV*, Comp. Gen. Dec. B-402229, 2010 CPD ¶ 69, and *McCarthy/Hunt, JV*, Comp. Gen. Dec. B-402229.2, 2010 CPD ¶ 68 (parent company of consultant that had participate in preparation of design concept for hospital was negotiating to purchase subcontractor of selected contractor); *L-3 Services, Inc.*, Comp. Gen. Dec. B-400134.11, 2009 CPD ¶ 171 (OCI because contractor assisted in planning the procurement and writing the business case); *Lucent Techs. World Servs., Inc.*, Comp. Gen. Dec. B-295462, 2005 CPD ¶ 55, 47 GC ¶ 190 (OCI even though agency technical personnel participated in the preparation of the specifications by commenting on them as the contractor submitted drafts); *Basile, Baumann, Prost & Assocs., Inc.*, Comp. Gen. Dec. B-274870, 97-1 CPD ¶ 15 (OCI where offeror prepared statement of work and agency cost estimate); *Ressler Assocs., Inc.*, Comp. Gen. Dec. B-244110, 91-2 CPD ¶ 230 (OCI where protester had earlier prepared portions of the statement of work without contracting officer's knowledge); and *Network Solutions, Inc. v. Dep't of the Air Force*, GSBCA 11498-P, 92-3 BCA ¶ 25,083 (OCI where offeror, under an RFP for engineering of LANs, had previously installed the network on which a sample task set out in the RFP was based). Because most services, including construction, will be construed to involve nondevelopment work, contractors drafting specifications for such work will generally be excluded under this rule, e.g., *Danish Arctic Contractors*, Comp. Gen. Dec. B-212957, 84-1 CPD ¶ 131; *Ressler Assocs.*, Comp. Gen. Dec. B-244110, 91-2 CPD ¶ 230. Compare *Detica*, Comp. Gen. Dec. B-400523, 2008 CPD ¶ 217, where no OCI was found because an agency official hired by the winning offeror had not participated in preparing the final work statement; *Operational Resource Consultants, Inc.*, Comp. Gen. Dec. B-299131.1, 2007 CPD ¶ 38, where no OCI was found because the winning offeror had no role in drafting specifications; and *Analytic Sciences Corp.*, Comp. Gen. Dec. B-218074, 85-1 CPD ¶ 464, where the GAO questioned the exclusion of a company that had prepared a broad work statement because it was not clear whether the work statement involved existing software or software to be newly developed.

This type of OCI can exist even if the company assisting in the preparation of the specification believes that there will be no competition, *Energy Sys. Group*, Comp. Gen. Dec. B-402324, 2010 CPD ¶ 73. In that case, the company participated as a subcontractor in preparing a feasibility study for an energy saving contract believing that the utility contractor would be awarded the contract on a sole source basis. When the agency later decided to use a competitive procurement, the GAO ruled that the subcontractor had an OCI and could not participate in the competition.

No OCI will be found in this situation unless the offeror has a significant interest in the outcome of the competition. See *American Mgmt. Sys., Inc.* Comp. Gen. Dec. B-285645, 2000 CPD ¶ 163, holding that there was no OCI where a firm performing work for the agency, KPMG Peat Marwick, only had a "marketing alliance" with several of the competitors but had no relationship with regard to the procurement in question. The decision contains the following summary:

> We find the potential benefit to KPMG here is speculative and too remote from the present procurement to establish a significant organizational conflict of interest that the contracting agency must avoid, neutralize or mitigate pursuant to FAR Subpart 9.5. Compare *Professional Gunsmithing Inc.*, B-279048.2, Aug. 24, 1998, 98-2 CPD ¶ 49 at 3-4 (entitlement of consultant employed by the agency to help evaluate proposals to trademark royalties from awardee on products other than those to be provided under the contract is an interest that is speculative and too remote to create a significant conflict of interest) and *International Management and Communications Corp.*, B-272456, Oct. 23, 1996, 96-2 CPD ¶ 156 at 4 (awardee's interest in receiving repayment of debt owed to its affiliate organization by a potential recipient of advice and assistance under the awarded support services contract is not a significant conflict of interest because the relationship between the awardee/contract and the repayment of the debt is indirect) with *Aetna Gov't Health Plans, Inc.; Foundation Health Fed'l Servs., Inc.*, [Comp. Gen. Dec. B-254397.15, 95-2 CPD ¶ 129] at 13-17 (significant organizational conflict of interest exists where a corporate affiliate of a major subcontractor under one proposal evaluates proposals for the procuring agency).

The major exception to this type of OCI is for contractors that have designed a product under contract with the government. FAR 9.505-2 provides:

> (a)(3) In development work, it is normal to select firms that have done the most advanced work in the field. These firms can be expected to design and develop around their own prior knowledge. Development contractors can frequently start production earlier and more knowledgeably than firms that did not participate in the development, and this can affect the time and quality of production, both of which are important to the Government.

> In many instances the Government may have financed the development. Thus, while the development contractor has a competitive advantage, it is an unavoidable one that is not considered unfair; hence no prohibition should be imposed.

This exception was not applied in *SSR Engineers, Inc.* Comp. Gen. Dec. B-282244, 99-2 CPD ¶ 27, sustaining the agency's decision that an OCI blocked an architect-engineer from competing for a design-build project because it had prepared the master plan and the budget estimate for the project. The decision does not discuss why this prior effort was not permissible "design" effort. Other cases have refused to apply this exception because the work was not "developmental." See *LW Planning Group*, Comp. Gen. Dec. B-215539, 84-2 CPD ¶ 531, where an OCI was found when a contractor had prepared a work statement for a subsequent contract to revise a master plan, and *Basile, Baumann, Prost & Assocs., Inc.*, Comp. Gen. Dec. B-274870, 97-1 CPD ¶ 15, where an OCI was found when the contractor prepared a work statement for follow-on work during performance of a contract calling for the evaluation of government land for its suitability for recreational uses. In one unusual case, a development contractor was found to have an OCI barring it from competing for a follow-on contract for more design and development work because it has surreptitiously prepared a work statement for that contract, *Ressler Assocs., Inc.*, Comp. Gen. Dec. B-244110, 91-2 CPD ¶ 230. The GAO reasoned that the development contract exception applied only if the follow-on work called for the production of units. Compare *Analytic Sciences Corp.*, Comp. Gen. Dec. B-218074, 85-1 CPD ¶ 464, concluding that the development contract exception applied to a contract calling for the "design" of a technical support center.

c. Impaired Objectivity

FAR 9.505-3 contains a very short description of this type of OCI, stating:

> Contracts for the evaluation of offers for products or services shall not be awarded to a contractor that will evaluate its own offers for products or services, or those of a competitor, without proper safeguards to ensure objectivity to protect the Government's interests.

The definition of an OCI in FAR 2.101 contains additional guidance:

> Organizational conflict of interest means that because of other activities or relationships with other persons, a person is unable or potentially unable to render impartial assistance or advice to the Government, or the person's objectivity in performing the contract work is or might be otherwise impaired . . .

Aetna describes this as a situation —

> where a firm's work under one government contract could entail its evaluating itself, either through an assessment of performance under another contract or an

evaluation of proposals. FAR 9.505-3. In these "impaired objectivity" cases, the concern is that the firm's ability to render impartial advice to the government could appear to be undermined by its relationship with the entity whose work product is being evaluated.

Evaluation of this type of OCI requires detailed knowledge of the impact of the work called for by the prospective contract and the technical evaluation or consulting services of all divisions and subsidiaries of a competitor and its subcontractors that relate to the contract work. For example, OCIs were found in *The Analysis Group LLC*, Comp. Gen. Dec. B-401726, 2009 CPD ¶ 237, where the winning offeror would perform technical analysis of products of the same type as those it was selling, and in *Nortel Gov't Solutions, Inc.*, Comp. Gen. Dec. B-299522.5, 2009 CPD ¶ 10, where the winning offeror would review designs that it prepared on a prior contract. Similarly, in *Alion Science & Tech. Corp.*, Comp. Gen. Dec. B-297022, 2006 CPD ¶ 1, and Comp. Gen. Dec. B-297022.3, 2006 CPD ¶ 2, an OCI was found in two contracts for electromagnetic spectrum engineering services where the winning offeror had elements of its company and its subcontractors that made numerous spectrum dependent products. The GAO made a detailed analysis of the tasks on the proposed contract and determined that there was a risk of "impaired objectivity" because of this market position. In a subsequent decision, Comp. Gen. Dec. B-297022.4, 2006 CPD ¶ 146, the GAO agreed that the winning offeror had mitigated the OCI by contracting with "firewalled" subcontractors to perform the conflicted work. See also *Leboeuf v. Abraham*, 347 F.3d 315 (D.C. Cir. 2003), finding an OCI when the agency awarded a contract for legal advice on a project to a law firm that had previously provided legal advice to a contractor on the same project – on the theory that the new contract would require the law firm to review its prior work. In *LeBoeuf, Lamb, Greene & MacRae*, Comp. Gen. Dec. B-283825, 2000 CPD ¶ 35, the GAO had come to the opposite conclusion, finding no OCI because the work on the new contract did not require the contractor to review its work on the earlier contract. In *J&E Assocs., Inc.*, Comp. Gen. Dec. B-278771, 98-1 CPD ¶ 77, an OCI was found in allowing educational institutions to compete for a contract to counsel government employees on the appropriate educational institution to attend and to verify billing statements from their own institution. In *Washington Utility Group*, Comp. Gen. Dec. B-266333, 96-1 CPD ¶ 27, a proposed contractor and its major subcontractor were found unable to provide unbiased contracting and technical advice to the agency because they had numerous contacts with the industry being solicited. In *KPMG Peat Marwick*, Comp. Gen. Dec. B-255224, 94-1 CPD ¶ 111, an OCI was found where the protester would have been reviewing its own audits performed for the agency's predecessor. See also *Women's Energy, Inc.*, Comp. Gen. Dec. B-258785, 95-1 CPD ¶ 86. In *ICF Inc.*, Comp. Gen. Dec. B-241372, 91-1 CPD ¶ 124, a protester was excluded from a competition that would have involved its evaluation of the efficiency of sister corporations that had "response action" contracts with the Environmental Protection Agency. Similarly, in *Engineered Air Sys., Inc.*, Comp. Gen. Dec. B-230878, 88-2 CPD ¶ 77, it was proper to exclude the protester from a competition that would have required it to test and evaluate its own product, and in *Acumenics Research & Tech., Inc.*, Comp. Gen. Dec. B-211575, 83-2 CPD ¶ 94, the contractor properly was eliminated from the competition on a contract that would require the firm to evaluate the usefulness of its work under an earlier contract.

In an unusual impaired objectivity case, a contractor providing support services to the Nuclear Regulatory Commission that did not disclose that it was performing work for regulated companies at the same time it was assisting the agency in formulating policy was held to have violated the False Claims Act, *United States v. Science Applications Int'l Corp.*, 502 F. Supp. 2d 75 (D.D.C. 2007) (rejecting motion to dismiss), 653 F. Supp. 2d 87 (D.D.C. 2009) (denying motion for new trial following jury verdict) *remanded*, 2010 U.S. App. Lexis 24808 (D.C. Cir. 2010). The court affirmed the jury's determination that the damages were triple all of the payments on two contracts where the OCIs were not disclosed but the circuit court remanded for a new trial on whether any individual in the company knew of the offenses.

An OCI of this type will be found only when the contract calls for the application of judgment by the contractor. See *PURVIS Sys., Inc.*, Comp. Gen. Dec. B-293807.3, 2004 CPD ¶ 177, finding an OCI in a contract for analytical and technical support services for an agency in evaluating the performance of weapons manufactured by the contractor when the services being procured involved "analysis, evaluation and judgment." Compare *Overlook Sys. Techs., Inc.*, Comp. Gen. Dec. B-298099.4, 2006 CPD ¶ 185, finding that an OCI could be mitigated because only a small part of the work required the exercise of judgment, and *Computers Universal, Inc.*, Comp. Gen. Dec. B-292794, 2003 CPD ¶ 201, finding no OCI because the contract task of preparing a quality assurance program did not involve subjective judgment when the actual inspection of the company's work was to be done by others. Similarly, in *TDS, Inc.*, Comp. Gen. Dec. B-292674, 2003 CPD ¶ 204, no OCI was found when a subcontractor with an existing contract with the agency for "monitoring" work on new contracts did not have the task of "evaluating" the performance of the prospective contractor on the new contract. The GAO reasoned:

> [M]onitoring, standing alone, does not necessarily create the potential for impaired objectivity. Rather, as noted above, an impaired objectivity conflict typically arises where a firm is evaluating its own activities because the objectivity necessary to impartially evaluate performance may be impaired by the firm's interest in the entity being evaluated....While we do not exclude the possibility in a different context of monitoring activities resulting in an impaired objectivity OCI, here there is no evidence that [deleted] will be evaluating the performance of the help desk contractor, and there is nothing otherwise objectionable in the interrelationship of activities performed by [deleted] on the two contracts. Instead, the record shows that the help desk contractor's performance must at least meet the minimum standards outlined in the [Request for Quotations] and that the contracting officer's technical representative will be responsible for evaluating the adequacy of the firm's performance for purposes of assessing the firm's overall

performance, deciding whether or not to award option year requirements, and determining the firm's compensation under the [service level agreement].

See also *Wyle Labs., Inc.*, Comp. Gen. Dec. B-288892, 2002 CPD ¶ 12, finding no OCI where a contractor operated a top-level laboratory and several lower-level laboratories. The GAO accepted the agency's argument that government personnel would do the actual monitoring of performance of all of the laboratories. Similarly, in *Battelle Memorial Inst.*, Comp. Gen. Dec. B-218538, 85-1 CPD ¶ 726, a contract to prepare general methodologies to solve a technical program, including the summarization of technical data from past contract performance, was properly awarded to a contractor that was performing one of the prior contracts. The GAO reasoned that the contract did not require the assessment of the adequacy of its performance under the prior contract.

Neither will there be an OCI if the contractor has no financial interest in the application of its judgment on the new contract. See, for example, *Marinette Marine Corp.*, Comp. Gen. Dec. B-400697, 2009 CPD ¶ 16, finding no OCI when a consultant advised both the agency and the winning offeror because the consultant had no financial interest in the outcome of the competition. Similarly, in *Karrar Sys. Corp.*, Comp. Gen. Dec. B-310661, 2008 CPD ¶ 55, an OCI was avoided by severing the relationship between the winning offeror for administrative services and one of the competitors. See also *Teledyne-Commodore, LLC*, Comp. Gen. Dec. B-278408.5, 99-1 CPD ¶ 60, finding no OCI where an agency used a company to assist in evaluating proposals but the company had no financial interest in the outcome of the competition. The GAO rejected the contention that the company had an OCI because it would favor the technology that it had previously recommended. See also *CH2M Hill, Ltd.*, Comp. Gen. Dec. B-259511, 95-1 CPD ¶ 203, finding no conflict of interest when the president of a subcontractor chaired a community commission that was the focal point for relocation efforts caused by government downsizing. The GAO concluded that the commission had no control over the agency's efforts that would be facilitated by the contract. Compare *Greenleaf Constr. Co.*, Comp. Gen. Dec. B-293105.18, 2006 CPD ¶ 19, where a firm that had won a contract for home marketing and management services divested its interest in a firm that was the closing agent of the homes being managed. The GAO ruled that an OCI still existed because, while the firm had sold its interest in the closing firm, it had accepted compensation over a period covered by the contract — with the potential that it might make biased recommendations to keep that firm viable until it had been paid.

The GAO has also used this provision in determining whether there was impropriety in proposing the use of a government agency to assist in evaluating work when that agency had employees on the source selection team, *Battelle Memorial Inst.*, Comp. Gen. Dec. B-278673, 98-1 CPD ¶ 107. The GAO found that the agency had properly considered the matter and determined the conflict was not sufficient to require barring the offeror from the competition.

d. Fashioning A Remedy

When the contracting officer identifies a potential OCI, the offeror must be disqualified unless a restraint can be included in the contract to neutralize or mitigate the conflict. If the conflict results from past actions of the contractor, disqualification may be the only logical course of action. Such disqualification is mandatory with regard to contracts for products where the offeror has performed systems engineering or technical direction, FAR 9.505-1(a). See *Filtration Dev. Co. v. United States*, 60 Fed. Cl. 371 (2004) (disqualifying systems engineering contractor from providing components of system). It is also mandatory for a period of time it the offeror has drafted the specification for a nondevelopmental item, FAR 9.505-2(a). See *SSR Engineers, Inc.* Comp. Gen. Dec. B-282244, 99-2 CPD ¶ 27 (architect-engineer barred from competing for a design-build project because it had prepared the master plan and the budget estimate for the project); *Basile, Baumann, Prost & Assocs., Inc.*, Comp. Gen. Dec. B-274870, 97-1 CPD ¶ 1 (contractor that had prepared a work statement for follow-on work during performance of a contract calling for the evaluation of government land for its suitability for recreational uses barred from competing for follow-on contract); *Ressler Assocs., Inc.*, Comp. Gen. Dec. B-244110, 91-2 CPD ¶ 230 (a development contractor barred from competing for a follow-on contract for more design and development work when it has surreptitiously prepared a work statement for that contract); *LW Planning Group*, Comp. Gen. Dec. B-215539, 84-2 CPD ¶ 531 (protester disqualified from competing on work for which it had drafted the statement of work in performing a prior task order issued by the agency). Agencies have also included a clause in the original contract to prepare specifications barring the contractor from competing for production of the item, *Analytic Sciences Corp.*, Comp. Gen. Dec. B-218074, 85-1 CPD ¶ 464.

Disqualification under a current procurement may also be required in the other types of OCIs. In some unequal access to information cases, no other remedy is feasible because the risk of transmission of the information has already occurred. For example, in *VRC, Inc.*, Comp. Gen. Dec. B-310100, 2007 CPD ¶ 202, disqualification was found to be the only feasible course of action when a contracting officer did not learn until after receipt of proposals that a subcontractor had access to all of the agency's internal information about the procurement. See also *L-3 Servs., Inc.*, Comp. Gen. Dec. B-400134.11, 2009 CPD ¶ 171, where disqualification was required when the contractor had assisted in planning the procurement and a proposed mitigation plan was not submitted until after the work had been done, and *NKF Eng'g, Inc. v. United States*, 805 F.2d 372 (Fed. Cir. 1986), where a company was properly disqualified from a procurement when it hired a member of the agency's source selection board prior to the submission of best and final offers. Disqualification was also required in *Axion Resource Mgmt., Inc. v. United States*, 78 Fed. Cl. 576 (2007), rev'd, 564 F.3d 1374 (Fed. Cir. 2009), where the court found that information gained on one phase of a project would provide an undue competitive advantage in competing for the next phase. The GAO had concluded that disqualification was not required in *Axion Resource Mgmt., Inc.*, Comp. Gen. Dec. B-298870.3, 2007 CPD ¶ 117, and the Federal Circuit agreed because the Court of Federal Claims decision calling for disqualification was based on inadmissable new evidence outside of the administrative record before the agency and the was made by reviewing the decision of the agency de novo rather than on an arbitrary and capricious standard.

The same result frequently occurs in the impaired objectivity situations where the new contract requires the evaluation of work that a contractor has performed on a prior contract. For example, in *Leboeuf v. Abraham*, 347 F.3d 315 (D.C. Cir. 2003), a law firm was barred from competing when the contract required it to analyze legal opinions it had rendered on a prior contract. See also *Acumenics Research & Tech., Inc.*, Comp. Gen. Dec. B-211575, 83-2 CPD ¶ 94 (protester barred from competing for a contract that required it to evaluate the adequacy and applicability of specification that it had prepared under an earlier contract); *Cardiocare*, 59 Comp. Gen. 355 (B-195827), 80-1 CPD ¶ 237 (producer of medical equipment disqualified from competing for a contract to monitor the performance of that type equipment).

Disqualification under a current procurement can be avoided in some instances through the imposition of restraints. In such cases the solicitation and the contract must contain appropriate provisions, FAR 9.507-2.

In the unequal access to information situations, a fully effective restraint to prevent an OCI on future contracts would be a clause in the contract where the contractor obtained the information establishing a "firewall" prohibiting the dissemination of that information to any person that has not worked on the contract and precluding any of those personnel from participating in a procurement of follow-on work. See *LEADS Corp.*, Comp. Gen. Dec. B-292465, 2003 CPD ¶ 197, accepting a mitigation plan of this type on a task order contract where it was providing procurement services to the agency. The plan also included a provision where the contractor would notify the contracting officer of any task order for which it desired to compete so that the agency could avoid using the contractor's personnel on that task order. Similar plans have been accepted in *Research Analysis & Maint., Inc.* Comp. Gen. Dec. B-272261, 96-2 CPD ¶ 131 (delivery orders for which subcontractor had OCI would be given by agency to another delivery order contractor); and *Deloitte & Touche*, 69 Comp. Gen. 463 (B-238371), 90-1 CPD ¶ 486 (task orders where subcontractor had OCI would be performed by contractor). It is questionable whether an agency would accept even this type of broad restraint because of the fear that it was unenforceable. See, for example, ¶ (b)(2)(i)(B) of the DEAR 952.209-72 clause precluding competing for such work for a designated period. For partial implementation of such a restraint, see FAR 9.505-4(b) requiring contractors performing advisory and assistance services to "agree with other companies to protect their information from unauthorized use and disclosure." See *MAR, Inc.*, Comp. Gen. Dec. B-215798, 85-1 CPD ¶ 121, where the GAO agreed with the use of such a clause even though a protester contended that no competitors would disclose the data under such conditions.

In the impaired objectivity situations, the decisions arrive at different results with regard to the types of restraints that are appropriate. In *Aetna Gov. Health Plans, Inc.*, Comp. Gen. Dec. B-254397.15, 95-2 CPD ¶ 129, where a major subcontractor of an offeror was affiliated with a company giving advice to the agency on the selection of the source, the GAO ruled that no mitigation was possible where the subcontract was projected to be in the amount of $183 million and the company giving the advice was an integral part of the evaluation of proposals and the source selection process. The GAO concluded that a firewall between elements of a single company was not an effective mitigation technique. See also *Cahaba Safeguard Administrators, LLC*, Comp. Gen. Dec. B-401842.2, 2010 CPD ¶ 39, and *C2C Solutions, Inc.*, Comp. Gen. Dec. B-401106.5, 2010 CPD ¶ 38, where the GAO concluded that there was considerable doubt as to whether using a firewalled subcontractor for conflicted work was an effective remedy, and *First Coast Serv. Options, Inc.*, Comp. Gen. Dec. B-401429, 2010 CPD ¶ 6, where the GAO held that the agency had properly rejected a mitigation plan calling for a firewalled subcontractor. A similar result was reached in *Nortel Gov't Solutions, Inc.*, Comp. Gen. Dec. B-299522.5, 2009 CPD ¶ 10, where the GAO reasoned:

> SRA's proposal to separate its . . . personnel through use of a firewall appears to be of little, if any, help in resolving the OCI here. In this regard, the proposed firewall provides for SRA to manage the two contracts using "separate organizations with separate interests" and "distinct business objectives." It also prohibits SRA and subcontractor personnel working on one contract from providing support under the other contract, without written approval from the contracting officer. However, while a firewall arrangement may resolve and "unfair access to information" OCI, it is virtually irrelevant to an OCI involving potentially impaired objectivity. See *Aetna Gov't Health Plans* . . . This is because the conflict at issue pertains to the organization, and not the individual employees. Thus, while the firewall proposed by SRA may created the appearance of separation to mitigate the OCI, The fact remains that personnel under both contracts will be working for the same organization with an incentive ti benefit SRA overall.

On the other hand, a firewall between a contractor and its subcontractor has been accepted as an effective mitigation technique because it prevents the organization with the OCI from performing work for which it has previously performed services to the agency. See *Business Consulting Assocs., LLC*, Comp. Gen. Dec. B-299758.2, 2007 CPD ¶ 134 (contractor with OCI agreed to transfer work impacted by the OCI to firewalled subcontractor); *Alion Science & Tech. Corp.*, Comp. Gen. Dec. B-297022.4, 2006 CPD ¶ 146 (contractor with OCI agreed to transfer the one-third of work impacted by the OCI to a firewalled subcontractor); *Deutche Bank*, Comp. Gen. Dec. B-289111, 2001 CPD ¶ 210 (contractor with OCI agreed to transfer work impacted by the OCI to firewalled subcontractor that would report directly to agency); *Epoch Eng'g, Inc.*, Comp. Gen. Dec. B-276634, 97-2 CPD ¶ 72 (contractor agreed not to assign work impacted by a subcontractor's OCI to that firewalled subcontractor); *SC&A, Inc.*, Comp. Gen. Dec. B-270160.2, 96-1 CPD ¶ 197 (contractor agreed not to assign work impacted by a subcontractor's OCI to that firewalled subcontractor). In *Overlook Sys. Techs., Inc.*, Comp. Gen. Dec. B-298099.4, 2006 CPD ¶ 185, the GAO accepted a mitigation plan that included a number of elements — firewalling the subcontractor with an OCI, precluding assigning that subcontractor work impacted by the OCI, conducting regular OCI training, and requiring enhanced government oversight of the subcontractor with the OCI. See also *PRI, Inc.*, Comp. Gen. Dec. B-210714, 84-1 CPD ¶ 345, where the GAO denied a protest of bias concerning the overlapping roles of the awardee in separate contracts with the agency. It was held that potential bias could be avoided by having the agency monitor the placing of task orders to avoid such conflict.

e. Procedures

As discussed in Chapter 2, FAR 9.506(a) directs contracting officers to ascertain whether there will be a potential OCI when planning a procurement. FAR 9.502(b) states that OCIs are most likely to occur on service contracts where the contractor is performing work that supports the procurement efforts of an agency. In such cases, FAR 9.506(b) through (d) call for the inclusion of a solicitation provision warning of the potential OCI and a clause in such contracts defining the restraint that will be called for to overcome the OCI created by that contract. However, the absence of a clause in such a contract will not preclude disqualification of a contractor on a subsequent contract, if an OCI exists, *LW Planning Group*, Comp. Gen. Dec. B-215539, 84-2 CPD ¶ 531; *Research & Tech., Inc.*, Comp. Gen. Dec. B-211575, 83-2 CPD ¶ 94.

Offerors should not rely on the government agency to identify a potential OCI but should actively screen RFPs for these types of support services to identify the impact on their future business if performing the work will result on an OCI. When it is apparent that an OCI may be created, an offeror should either abstain from the competition, agree to a restraint from competing for future work blocked by the OCI, or propose a means of mitigation that will allow it to compete for future work. It can be argued that the contracting officer is required to attempt to negotiate a mitigation plan, when appropriate, before disqualifying an offeror because of an organizational conflict, FAR 9.504(e).

There is very little guidance in the FAR as to the course of action to be taken in considering the award of follow-on contracts that are impacted by an OCI on a prior or concurrent contract where the contractor is performing support services for the agency. If the prior or concurrent contract contains a clause prohibiting participation in the follow-on procurement, it is unlikely that the agency will consider a proposal and the contractor should probably forego the competition. However, even in that case, the contractor can submit a mitigation plan, which the contracting officer should consider. See FAR 9.504(e). See also *Informatics Corp. v. United States*, 40 Fed. Cl. 508 (1998), where the court granted a protest because the contracting officer had failed to consider a mitigation plan proposed by the offeror. The court also noted that FAR 9.504(d) requires that the decision of the contracting officer be documented in this situation. In *Orkand Corp.*, Comp. Gen. Dec. B-209662.2, 83-1 CPD ¶ 349, the GAO agreed with an agency determination that a contracting officer should have attempted to negotiate an appropriate contract clause.

If a competitor protests that the selected contractor has an OCI, the contracting officer must address the issue. See *J&E Assocs., Inc.*, Comp. Gen. Dec. B-278771, 98-1 CPD ¶ 77, where the GAO sustained a protest when the contracting officer totally failed to address a potential conflict.

B. Risk Analysis

The first issue in analyzing the RFP is determining whether the risks inherent in the procurement can be dealt with in a satisfactory manner. If they cannot, potential offerors should seriously consider avoiding the high cost of proposal preparation. Three risks must be analyzed. First, a potential offeror must make a realistic assessment of its prospect for winning the competition. Second, the offeror must determine what technical and management techniques will be required to perform the contract and the risks that are inherent in the potential inability to execute these techniques. Third, the offeror must assess its prospect of making a profit on the contract or deriving some other long-term benefit if it does win the competition.

1. Prospect of Winning

An offeror must assess its own capabilities in meeting the requirements of the RFP in comparison with the capabilities of all potential competitors. The first step in this assessment is to determine the key factors that will be used to select the source for the procurement. As discussed in Chapter 3, these will normally be set forth in Section M of the RFP and will generally be broken into technical, management, and cost/price. A significant element of the capability assessment will generally consist of an evaluation of each offeror's past performance and experience.

In many procurements technical considerations are so important that they may be considered controlling — in the sense that an offeror will conclude that award will not be made to a competitor that does not demonstrate strong technical capabilities through proposal evaluation and assessment of past performance/experience. This requires a highly competent technical team that has the ability to convey its capabilities to the procuring agency and can demonstrate good past performance. If the RFP calls for a technical proposal, a successful offeror must submit a well-written technical approach to performing the work. If the RFP calls for an oral presentation, a successful offeror will have to bring in a team that can credibly discuss and assess the technical difficulties that are expected to be encountered during contract performance. Potential offerors must first assess the ability of their own technical personnel and then review the possibility of using subcontractors to provide technical capabilities that they do not have in sufficient strength to meet these requirements. In procurements where technical factors are important, a proposal should not be submitted if the offeror cannot assemble a strong technical team.

Management factors are also of great importance in many procurements. Many agencies look for assurance that a contractor will have a strong management team performing the contract. In some cases this will be determined by the quality of the offeror's personnel as demonstrated by its management proposal or an oral presentation; in others it will be more heavily influenced by the past performance of the offeror. Potential offerors must determine the basis that the agency will use to evaluate management capability and must assess their ability to obtain a strong evaluation in this area.

When the RFP indicates that the agency will assess past performance and experience, an offeror must review its relevant projects and make a realistic assessment of the ratings that its past customers will provide. If it is concluded that some customers will give negative assessments, the offeror should determine if it can provide sufficient information to persuade the procuring agency that the assessments are incorrect or to demonstrate that it has taken steps to overcome the problems that were encountered. It should be recognized that it is very difficult to demonstrate remedial steps if the negative assessments are on recent work. When a potential offeror concludes that it cannot counter negative past performance assessments, it should recognize that there is little likelihood of winning the competition unless it can offer a significant benefit to the agency in some other aspect of the evaluation.

Cost/price factors are considered in every procurement and should be considered to be of significance in all cases. Even if the RFP states that technical and management factors are predominant, cost/price will become paramount if the technical and management proposals are evaluated as being equal or very close. In addition, most procurements ultimately involve a tradeoff between cost/price and the technical and management factors — with the result that a strong technical and management proposal with a high cost/price may not be selected. Thus, offerors must determine if they can submit a proposal that is competitive in the cost/price area. If not, they will have little realistic chance of winning the competition unless they can convince the agency that their technical or management superiority is worth the difference in cost or price.

Evaluation of the prospect of winning the competition depends to a great degree on a realistic assessment of the other companies competing for the contract. Even if a potential offeror submits a proposal that is evaluated highly, it will win the competition only if its proposal is the best in comparison with the other proposals. Most companies would decide to submit a proposal if they have the requisite level of excellence to ensure high scores in all areas of the evaluation. There will undoubtedly be some situations where the correct business decision is not to submit a proposal because one or more other competitors have an overwhelming advantage in the particular procurement.

2. Feasibility of Technical and Management Promises

In many procurements the RFP will require the offeror to provide a detailed plan setting forth the techniques that will be used to accomplish the end results called for by the contract. This plan will be part of the technical and management proposals to be submitted or may be included in an oral presentation. In formulating such a plan, the offeror must assess the risk that it will be unable to carry out the plan as described in the proposal. The impact of this risk will be considerably greater if the plan is incorporated into the contract as part of the promises made by the contractor.

The initial step in this risk analysis is to determine the feasibility of the plan. If the plan is composed of work that the offeror has done in the past and experienced personnel are available to work on the contract, the risks will be low. If the plan calls for innovative approaches or work that has never been done in the past, the risks will be considerably higher. In either case the offeror must include sufficient labor hours in its cost or price proposal to perform the planned work. Obviously, the fewer the labor hours, the higher the risk.

The second step in this risk analysis is to determine if the plan will be made part of the contract. When it is not part of the contract, the contractor will have far greater flexibility in altering the plan if the original plan is not entirely feasible. If it is part of the contract, the agency may insist that the work be done in accordance with the plan or may demand consideration for a deviation from the plan. Unfortunately, many RFPs do not state whether the plan will be part of the contract. In such cases the offeror will have to assess this risk by looking to past practice of the agency and any indications of the agency's intention that can be gleaned from the RFP. If this is a critical issue, a question should be submitted to the contracting officer asking whether the plan will be made part of the contract.

3. Profitability

It should be a truism that it is senseless to win a contract that does not lead to either immediate profit or some long-term benefit to the company. A firm must therefore make a careful analysis of the potential profitability of any procurement before submitting an offer. Factors that must be considered in this analysis include the following:

- Probability of the level and consistency of government funding of the contemplated program
- Potential for follow-on work and program growth and the probability that such work will be awarded to the contractor winning the present contract

- Prospect for making a profit on the entire program considering the type of contract being used and the level of price that will be required to win the award
- Prospect for the program to employ key personnel of the contractor who would not otherwise remain available for future work
- Possibility that the program will provide benefits other than profit in the form of technological innovations that can be used in other areas

C. Problem Analysis

One of the first steps in preparing a proposal is to review the RFP to identify any flaws or ambiguities. This review encompasses the evaluation criteria, the type of contract, and the statement of work and/or specifications. If there are ambiguities in the specifications or other parts of the RFP, clarification or explanation should be requested from the contracting officer as quickly as possible. There is no guidance in the standard RFP provisions as to how potential contractors can obtain explanations or interpretations of RFP during the proposal process. However, prior to the FAR Part 15 rewrite, the following standard solicitation provision was included in FAR 52.215-14:

EXPLANATION TO PROSPECTIVE OFFERORS (APR 1984)

Any prospective offeror desiring an explanation or interpretation of the solicitation, drawings, specifications, etc., must request it in writing soon enough to allow a reply to reach all prospective offerors before the submission of their offers. Oral explanations or instructions given before the award of the contract will not be binding. Any information given to a prospective offeror concerning a solicitation will be furnished promptly to all other prospective offerors as an amendment of the solicitation, if that information is necessary in submitting offers or if the lack of it would be prejudicial to any other prospective offerors.

This provision established a procedure requiring contracting officers to review all requests for explanations and to furnish the answers to all potential competitors in writing. In spite of the deletion of this provision from the FAR, it can be expected that many agencies will continue to provide such explanations and interpretations at the request of offerors. In many instances such interpretations and explanations may be given orally only to the offeror raising the question, because the contracting officer determines that the issue is clearly dealt with in the RFP. It would appear that the receipt of such information is proper, but the GAO has ruled that offerors rely on such explanations at their peril, *Hugo Key & Son, Inc.*, Comp. Gen. Dec. B-251053.4, 93-2 CPD ¶ 21; *Jensen Corp.*, 60 Comp. Gen. 543 (B-200277.2), 81-1 CPD ¶ 524; *Blue Ridge Sec. Guard Serv., Inc.*, Comp. Gen. Dec. B-208605.2, 82-2 CPD ¶ 464. Whenever an offeror receives an oral explanation of any part of the RFP that appears to be obscure or ambiguous, it should request the contracting officer to follow up the oral communication with a written confirmation sent to all potential offerors.

Requests for explanations and interpretations should be submitted as soon as possible in order to provide sufficient time for responses to be issued to the offerors so that they can submit timely proposals. See *National Customer Eng'g*, Comp. Gen. Dec. B-254950, 94-1 CPD ¶ 44, sustaining the refusal of a contracting officer to answer questions asked two and three days prior to the proposal submission date.

D. Analysis of Evaluation Scheme

The first step in the analysis of the evaluation scheme is to determine whether the agency is using the low-price technically acceptable proposal process, the tradeoff process, or some other scheme (as discussed in Chapter 2). This will determine the sequence of proposals and the method of selection of the winning contractor. If the low-price technically acceptable proposal process is called for by the RFP, the offeror will know that the ultimate selection will be based on low price alone. If a number of offerors are potentially able to submit acceptable proposals, it will be unwise to compete unless there is some assurance that a low-price solution to the agency's needs can be proposed.

In the majority of instances, the agency will be using the tradeoff process. In that case a close analysis of the source selection scheme is required. As discussed in Chapter 3, Section M of the RFP should include a statement of the evaluation factors and subfactors that will be considered and the relative importance of the price and non-price factors. It should also contain guidance on the relative importance of the subfactors. If the RFP states that low price is a major consideration, the offeror should make every effort to propose technical and management approaches that can be performed economically and efficiently. Overly elaborate technical efforts or management systems should be avoided because they will inevitably lead to a noncompetitive price. On the other hand, if the RFP states that the agency's major interest is in technical excellence, the offeror should strive for technical excellence even if somewhat more costly. Even in this case, however, excessively high costs must be avoided because almost all RFPs permit award on the basis of lower price when the differential between offered prices is significant.

E. Identifying Mandatory Requirements

Most RFPs contain mandatory requirements that must be met in order to qualify for award. These must be identified, and the offeror must decide whether to agree to these requirements or to request an alternate specification or contract clause. It is also very risky to take exception to a mandatory requirement when the procurement uses the low-price technically acceptable proposal process, because in that type procurement a proposal taking exception to a mandatory technical requirement can be rejected as being unacceptable, *Green Shop, Inc.*, Comp. Gen. Dec. B-278125, 97-2 CPD ¶ 154; *Ericsson, Inc.*, Comp. Gen. Dec. B-274668, 97-1 CPD ¶ 33.

When the tradeoff procedure is being used but it is anticipated that the agency is going to award on the basis of the initial proposals without entering into negotiations, it is very risky to submit a proposal that does not agree to meet all of the mandatory requirements because in such circumstances award will be possible only if the agency enters into discussions. Thus, agencies can reject a proposal that does not comply with the requirements without any further communication with the offeror, *Advanced Designs Corp.*, Comp. Gen. Dec. B-275928, 98-1 CPD ¶ 100 (agency properly rejected proposal that took exception to RFP requirements and did not propose firm fixed prices as required); *Integration Techs. Group. Inc.*, Comp. Gen. Dec. B-274288.5, 97-1 CPD ¶ 214 (agency not required to request verification of possible error that went to the substance of the required characteristics of the product offered); and *Scientific-Atlanta Inc.*, Comp. Gen. Dec. B-255343.2, 94-1 CPD ¶ 325 (agency properly rejected proposal that took exception to material terms of the solicitation).

If it is anticipated that award will not be made until after negotiations have been conducted, it is less risky to submit a proposal that takes exception to a mandatory requirement. Nonetheless, in those circumstances there is still the possibility that the agency will not place the proposal in the competitive range. See, for example, *Orbit Advanced Techs., Inc.*, Comp. Gen. Dec. B-271293, 96-1 CPD ¶ 254 (offeror eliminated from competitive range because proposed product did not meet technical requirements).

If the RFP calls for the submission of data demonstrating that an offeror can meet a mandatory requirement, great care should be exercised in submitting data that clearly demonstrates the offeror's capabilities. If the data is not satisfactory to the agency, a proposal can be rejected for failing to meet the mandatory requirement, *Working Alternatives, Inc.*, Comp. Gen. Dec. B-276911, 97-2 CPD ¶ 2 (failure to submit documentation showing right to use facility); *JEOL USA, Inc.*, Comp. Gen. Dec. B-277160, 97-2 CPD ¶ 3 (failure to submit descriptive literature); *CHI Fabrication Servs.*, Comp. Gen. Dec. B-275079, 97-1 CPD ¶ 40 (failure to submit drawings showing that design requirement was met); *Premier Cleaning Sys., Inc.*, Comp. Gen. Dec. B-255815, 94-1 CPD ¶ 241 (failure to submit letter of intent and resume on project manager). Statements in cover letters that raise doubts as to the offeror's intent to meet a mandatory requirement can also be grounds for rejection of a proposal, *Potomac Elec. Corp.*, Comp. Gen. Dec. B-313060, 2008 CPD ¶ 63 (statement in letter that motor would be a "form, fit and function replacement" of specified motor not a clear statement that it would meet all specified salient characteristics).

In all cases, when an offeror proposes to deviate from mandatory requirements of the RFP, it should include a clear statement explaining why the deviation is necessary or desirable. It should also propose a clear alternative with adequate explanation to demonstrate to the agency that the alternative meets its needs or provides a better solution than called for by the RFP. It should be recognized, however, that procuring agencies have considerable discretion in evaluating such explanations and rejecting them if they are not persuaded that the deviation is desirable.

F. Identifying Information to Submit

Winning proposals are carefully structured to provide the information necessary to permit evaluation of all elements of the evaluation scheme and to obtain high evaluations in each area. Thus, an evaluation must be made of what information the agency is seeking, as well as the type of information that will earn high scores. When an agency requests written technical and/or management proposals, offerors must understand that it is their responsibility to affirmatively demonstrate in the proposal that they can meet the contract requirements. See *Government Telecommunications, Inc.*, Comp. Gen. Dec. B-299542.2, 2007 CPD ¶ 136, rejecting the contention that the agency evaluators should have sought more information before concluding that the offered products were not available on the market, stating:

> GTI's argument here reflects a fundamental misunderstanding of the proposal process. It is an offeror's responsibility to submit a well-written proposal, with adequately detailed information, which clearly demonstrates compliance with the solicitation requirements and allows for a meaningful review by the procuring agency. *CACI Techs., Inc.*, B-296946, Oct. 27, 2005, 2005 CPD ¶ 198 at 5. An offeror is responsible for affirmatively demonstrating the merits of its proposal and risks the rejection of its proposal if it fails to do so. *HDL Research Lab, Inc.*, B-294959, Dec. 21, 2004, 2005 CPD ¶ 8 at 5. Here, since it was GTI's responsibility to establish the timely availability of its proposed IP telephones — not, as the protester argues, the evaluators' responsibility to establish unavailability — and GTI admittedly failed to do so, we find the agency's evaluation to be entirely reasonable.

The first step in identifying the types of information being sought for evaluation is to carefully analyze Section L of the RFP. This section spells out all the instructions for submitting a proposal, and most agencies include the instructions on the format and content of proposals in this section. See FAR 15.204-5(b), giving the following guidance to contracting officers:

> Insert in this section solicitation provisions and other information and instructions not required elsewhere to guide offerors or respondents in preparing proposals or responses to requests for information. Prospective offerors or respondents may be instructed to submit proposals or information in a specific format or severable parts to facilitate evaluation. The instructions may specify further organization of proposal or response parts, such as —
>
> (1) Administrative;
>
> (2) Management;

(3) Technical;

(4) Past performance; and

(5) Certified cost or pricing data (see Table 15-2 of 15.408) or data other than certified cost or pricing data.

When the RFP calls for the submission of an offer in severable parts, it is very important to comply exactly with the instructions on the content of each part. Otherwise, the agency may be unable to evaluate the proposal in accordance with its internal procedures.

Unfortunately, many RFPs do not contain complete guidance on the desired content of proposals in Section L. Therefore, a prospective offeror should also make a thorough analysis of the evaluation scheme set forth in Section M to determine if there are items of information that are logically necessary to perform the evaluation called for that are not required by Section L. If so, such information should be included in the proposal. In this regard, offerors should be overly cautious. They should not rely only on Section L but should independently determine what information will be needed by agency personnel to perform the evaluation described in Section M.

G. Protests of RFP Improprieties

The opportunity to protest against RFP improprieties to the GAO will be lost if the protest is not raised before the closing date for receipt of proposals. Thus, if a potential offeror finds an impropriety in the RFP that prejudices its prospect of winning the competition, a protest should be filed well ahead of the time of submission of proposals. Initially, such protest should be made to the contracting officer, who is required to consider it, FAR 33.102. Such a protest must be received by the contracting officer before the time for submission of proposals, *Microwave Solutions, Inc.*, Comp. Gen. Dec. B-245963, 92-1 CPD ¶ 169. See also 4 C.F.R. § 21.2(a)(1). This requirement will be strictly enforced, *Mead Data Central*, 70 Comp. Gen. 371 (B-242598), 91-1 CPD ¶ 330 (facsimile protest received one minute after closing time rejected as being late). Protests filed with the proposal do not meet this requirement, *Darome Connection*, Comp. Gen. Dec. B-230629, 88-1 CPD ¶ 461.

Normally protests received by the contracting officer before the closing date will result in the prevention of contract award until the protest is resolved. See FAR 33.103(f), which states:

Action upon receipt of protest. (1) Upon receipt of a protest before award, a contract may not be awarded, pending agency resolution of the protest, unless award is justified, in writing, for urgent and compelling reasons or is determined, in writing to be in the best interest of the Government. Such justification or determination shall be approved at a level above the contracting officer, or by another official pursuant to agency procedures.

If award is withheld pending agency resolution of the protest, the contracting officer will inform the offerors whose offers might become eligible for award of the contract. If appropriate, the offerors should be requested, before expiration of the time for acceptance to avoid the need for resolicitation. In the event of failure to obtain such extension of offers, consideration should be given to proceeding with award pursuant to paragraph (f)(1) of this section.

Many types of improprieties must be protested prior to the closing date for receipt of proposals:

- Challenge to automated best value model score, *Dayton-Granger, Inc.*, Comp. Gen. Dec. B-279553.3, 98-2 CPD ¶ 90
- Challenge that solicitation experience evaluation provisions are restrictive or otherwise defective, *High Country Contracting*, Comp. Gen. Dec. B-278649, 98-1 CPD ¶ 39
- Challenge to the RFP's award criteria — arguing that agency should have used the basis of the lowest-priced technically acceptable offer technique not the tradeoff technique, *Compania De Asesoria Y Comercio, S.A.*, Comp. Gen. Dec. B-278358, 98-1 CPD ¶ 26
- Challenge that award criteria were ambiguous, *Dix Corp.*, Comp. Gen. Dec. B-293964, 2004 CPD ¶ 143
- An evaluation scheme that is defective or prejudicial, *Neal R. Gross & Co.*, Comp. Gen. Dec. B-275066, 97-1 CPD ¶ 30; *DynCorp*, 70 Comp. Gen. 38 (B-240980.2), 90-2 CPD ¶ 310
- Use of RFQ rather than RFP or IFB, *Lynwood Mach. & Eng'g, Inc.*, Comp. Gen. Dec. B-285696, 2001 CPD ¶ 113
- Challenge to solicitation scoring scheme, *The Leader Mortgage Co.*, Comp. Gen. Dec. B-274110.2, 97-1 CPD ¶ 187, or to relative importance of evaluation factors, *Cherokee Information Servs., Inc.*, Comp. Gen. Dec. B-291718, 2003 CPD ¶ 49
- Lack of specific provision in RFP on how price was to be evaluated, *Neal R. Gross & Co.*, Comp. Gen. Dec. B-275066, 97-1 CPD ¶ 30
- Insufficient time for performance or delivery, *Topley Realty Co.*, 65 Comp. Gen. 510 (B-221459), 86-1 CPD ¶ 398
- RFP provided for only revised business proposals precluding revised technical proposals, *S. C. Myers & Assocs., Inc.*, B-286297, 2001 CPD ¶ 16
- The inclusion of the protester's proprietary information in the RFP, *Austin Co., Advanced Tech. Sys.*, Comp. Gen. Dec. B-212792, 84-1 CPD ¶ 257
- The inclusion of proposal page limitations in the RFP, *Community Partnership LLC*, Comp. Gen. Dec. B-286844, 2001 CPD ¶ 38; *EAI Corp.*, Comp. Gen. Dec. B-239231.10, 90-2 CPD ¶ 325
- Inclusion in RFP that security clearance was not required, *Triple Canopy, Inc.*, Comp. Gen. Dec. B-310566.4, 2008 CPD ¶ 207

- RFP statement that government personnel would be available during contract work, *IBM Global Business Servs.*, Comp. Gen. Dec. B-298833.4, 2007 CPD ¶ 82

A protest, if successful, may result in a GAO recommendation either to cancel or to cancel and resolicit the procurement, *Pemco Aeroplex, Inc.*, Comp. Gen. Dec. B-280397, 98-2 CPD ¶ 79 (cancel and resolicit); *Satellite Servs.*, Comp. Gen. Dec. B-280945, 98-2 CPD ¶ 125 (cancel).

IV. CONTENTS OF PROPOSALS

The key to winning most competitively negotiated procurements is the submission of a clear and coherent proposal. In the past, the term "proposal" has been used broadly to refer to an offeror's entire submission in response to an RFP, consisting of both an offer which can be accepted by the government and information to be considered by the government in evaluating proposals. The term has also been used to describe separate parts of the submission. Thus, RFPs often requested offerors to organize submissions into separate portions called "Technical Proposals," "Management Proposals," and "Cost Proposals." Although the distinction between the offer and information was recognized in a number of provisions in drafts of FAR Part 15 during the rewriting process, the final rewrite eliminated most of these distinctions. Thus, it is necessary to determine whether the final rewrite's use of the term "proposal" in a particular provision is intended to refer to the offer or information or both. Some contracting officers have recognized the distinction between these two portions of the submission and have drafted their RFPs so that the offer and information in the offeror's submission can be readily distinguished. However, in most cases, the RFP may not clearly distinguish the offer from information that is necessary for evaluation. The following discussion uses the term "proposal" to refer to the total submission in response to an RFP and the terms "offer" and "information" to distinguish between the two components of the submission.

Proposals that do not demonstrate a present intent to be bound upon acceptance by the government without further discussion or negotiations are not eligible for award, and an offeror submitting such a proposal could lose a contract by failing to comply with the RFP. In many cases the government will not award the contract without written or oral discussions, and such discussions permit the offeror the opportunity to cure technical defects in the proposal if such proposal is found to be within the competitive range. However, to ensure that the proposal is not rejected where the agency decides to award without discussions, offerors should complete the solicitation documents as required by the RFP as the initial step in competing for a negotiated procurement.

Proposals must include all information requested by the RFP; the offeror should not assume any prior knowledge on the part of the evaluators. In many procurements the evaluators are instructed to base their evaluation only on the information in the proposal, and this procedure has been affirmed by the GAO. See, for example, *Computerized Project Mgmt. Plus*, Comp. Gen. Dec. B-247063, 92-1 CPD ¶ 401, stating:

> [The protester] complains here that the evaluators, who were familiar with [the protester's] performance, treated it "unfairly" because they scored its "[offer] within the four corners of the proposal," and did not "consider any knowledge they had of the work presently being performed by [the protester]" that was not reflected in its proposal. [The protester] adds that any informational deficiencies in its proposal should have been rectified by examining the performance of [the protester] on the predecessor contract and through "communication" with [the protester].

> [The protester's] reliance on its status as the incumbent is misplaced. A contracting activity's technical evaluation of a proposal is dependent upon the information furnished in the proposal. *All Star Maint., Inc.*, B-244143, Sept. 26, 1991, 91-2 CPD ¶ 94. There is no legal basis for favoring a firm with presumptions on the basis of the offeror's prior performance; rather, all offerors must demonstrate their capabilities in their proposals. *Id.* As [the protester's] sole objection to the evaluation of its technical proposal involves the activity's consideration of only the information furnished in [the protester's] proposal, and this manner of evaluation comports with the policy objectives in federal procurement statutes and regulations, we have no basis on which to conclude that the contracting activity acted unreasonably in its evaluation of [the protester's] proposal.

Offerors should follow the RFP instructions precisely — providing all information called for even if it appears unnecessary. See, for example, *Management Tech. Servs.*, Comp. Gen. Dec. B-251612.3, 93-1 CPD ¶ 432, where an incumbent contractor was given low scores on its proposal because it did not provide required information on its plan to obtain and train its work force. The GAO paid no attention to its plea that there was no need for an incumbent contractor to submit such a plan because it had a work force in place. See also *Executive Security & Eng'g Techs., Inc.*, Comp. Gen. Dec. B-270518, 96-1 CPD ¶ 156, denying a protest of an incumbent contractor that was downgraded for not furnishing required information on its corporate experience.

The necessity for exercising great care in the preparation of proposals cannot be overemphasized. There are hundreds of protests that have been denied because the agency was found to have strictly evaluated a proposal and rejected it for lack of clarity, cohesion, organization, etc. See *Avue Techs. Corp.*, Comp. Gen. Dec. B-298380.4, 2008 CPD ¶ 182, stating:

> [I]t is an offeror's responsibility to submit an adequately written proposal with sufficient information for the agency to evaluate and determine compliance with the solicitation's requirements. *Interstate Gen. Gov't Contractors, Inc.*, B-290137.2, June 21, 2002, 2002 CPD ¶ 105 at 5; *Better Serv.*, B-256498.2, Jan. 9, 1995, 95-1 CPD ¶ 11 at 2. With regard to the role of the agency, our Office has held that in evaluating a proposal, an agency is under no obligation "to decipher a poorly organized proposal," *Shumaker Trucking and Excavating Contractors, Inc.*,

B-290732, Sept. 25, 2002, 2002 CPD ¶ 169 at 5, or to reach favorable conclusions regarding the merits of a proposal or the compliance of the proposal with a solicitation's requirements where the information supporting such conclusions is "not readily apparent," *DATEX, Inc*, B-270268.2, Apr. 15, 1996, 96-1 CPD ¶ 240 at 6, "not clearly delineated," *Joint Mgmt. & Tech. Servs.*, B-294229; B-294229.3, Sept. 22, 2004, 2004 CPD ¶ 208 at 5, or not set forth with the requisite degree of precision required by the RFP. *Ace Info. Sys.*, B-295450.2, Mar. 7, 2005, 2005 CPD ¶ 75 at 8; *United Def. LP*, B-286925.3 et al., Apr. 9, 2001, 2001 CPD ¶ 75 at 19. Nor is an agency required to "deduce []" that a proposal meets certain requirements where the proposal lacks the level of detail the RFP requires, *SOS Interpreting, Ltd.*, B-287505, June 12, 2001, 2001 CPD ¶ 104 at 11-12, or accept a proposal that the agency finds is unclear or ambiguous regarding its merits or compliance with the solicitation's requirements. *Ace Info. Sys., supra* at 7; *Innovative Commc's Techs., Inc.*, B-291728; B-291728.2, Mar. 5, 2003, 2003 CPD ¶ 58 at 5-7; *JAVIS Automation & Eng'g, Inc.*, B-290434; B-290434.2, Aug. 5, 2002, 2002 CPD ¶ 140 at 6 (it is not the agency's obligation to fill in gaps in an offeror's proposal during the evaluation process).

A. Offer

The offer describes what the contractor is willing to agree to, and its terms become part of the contract when accepted by the government. See FAR 2.101, which contains the following definition of "offer":

> "Offer" means a response to a solicitation that, if accepted, would bind the offeror to perform the resultant contract.

1. Contents of Offer

In the typical negotiated contract, the offer consists of the terms specified in the RFP (specifications, clauses, and so on, contained in Parts I, II, and III of the Uniform Contract Format) and the prices or estimated costs specified by the offeror in Section B. FAR 15.204-2(a)(1) provides for the use of Optional Form (OF) 308, Solicitation and Offer — Negotiated Acquisition, or Standard Form (SF) 33, Solicitation, Offer and Award, to submit proposals. These forms reference the various sections of the RFP that will become part of the contract, refer to the prices that are offered, and provide spaces for a signature and for the "offer date." FAR 15.204-2-(a)(2)(ix) requires that the solicitation include the "offer expiration date" when the forms are not used.

a. Price

In submitting price proposals, the contractor must determine the prices to be offered and submit them in the form requested. Because offers may be accepted by an agency without discussions, the initial price should be such that the contractor will be able to perform the work satisfactorily for that price. Generally, an initial proposal should include the price for each item that reflects the contractor's actual cost plus a profit for that item. Contractors should use common business sense in formulating prices and should structure a proposal around the stated evaluation criteria so that a proposal promises to complete the work required in the RFP for the lowest commercially acceptable price for the contractor. As discussed earlier, there are several restrictions on that discretion. The FAR requires that prices be determined independently to prevent collusive pricing. Though a contractor may submit a proposal that represents no profit, or even a loss, to the contractor, certain types of below-cost offers are prohibited under the antitrust laws. The FAR also prohibits materially unbalanced pricing and provides for correction of certain types of errors in proposed prices.

(1) INDEPENDENT PRICING

The Certificate of Independent Price Determination solicitation provision at FAR 52.203-2(a), which is included in all RFPs, states the following:

The offeror certifies that —

(1) The prices in this offer have been arrived at independently, without, for the purposes of restricting competition, any consultation, communication, or agreement with any other offeror or competitor relating to (i) those prices . . . or (iii) the methods or factors used to calculate the prices offered . . .

An offeror may gather data for pricing from any in-house source, from producers or distributors of supplies or services required for the contract, or from subcontractors, but should be wary of using data gathered from other outside sources and industry representatives in formulating prices. The GAO will not review a claim that an offeror has violated the certificate of independent price determination because such a determination is a matter of responsibility that is within the discretion of the contracting officer, *U-Liners Contracting Co.*, Comp. Gen. Dec. B-245179.2, 91-2 CPD ¶ 370.

(2) UNBALANCED OFFERS

Where the solicitation contains multiple items or work over multiple periods, offerors may seek to obtain a competitive advantage by unbalancing the prices. Paragraph (f)(8) of the FAR 52.215-1 Instructions to Offerors — Competitive Acquisition provision warns offerors that their offers may be rejected if the prices are materially unbalanced, stating:

The Government may determine that a proposal is unacceptable if the prices proposed are materially unbalanced between line items or subline items. Unbalanced pricing exists when, despite an acceptable total evaluated price, the price of one or more contract line items is significantly overstated or understated as indicated by the application of cost or price analysis techniques. A proposal may be rejected if the Contracting Officer determines that the lack of balance poses an unacceptable risk to the Government.

Although the majority of protests alleging unbalanced pricing occur in sealed bidding cases, the concept of unbalanced pricing has also been applied to negotiated procurements, *Litton Sys., Inc.*, Comp. Gen. Dec. B-239123.3, 90-2 CPD ¶ 276. The GAO has held that a proposed price may not be accepted by a contracting agency if the proposed price in the offer is found to be materially unbalanced, *International Transport, S.A.*, Comp. Gen. Dec. B-244853, 91-2 CPD ¶ 489. The contracting officer may reject such a proposal without discussions, *Ocean Habitability, Inc.*, Comp. Gen. Dec. B-227304, 87-2 CPD ¶ 265, or may seek to remedy the unbalanced price through discussions, *Dynamic Science, Inc.*, Comp. Gen. Dec. B-270448.3, 96-1 CPD ¶ 236.

The current FAR replaces this rule with a discretionary rule stating that an unbalanced proposal may be rejected if the contracting officer determines that the lack of balance "poses an unacceptable risk to the Government," FAR 15.404-1(g)(3). For cases affirming the contracting officer's acceptance of unbalanced prices because of no unacceptable risk, see *Accumark, Inc.*, Comp. Gen. Dec. B-310814, 2008 CPD ¶ 68 (estimated quantity of the high priced line item was reasonably accurate); *Scot, Inc.*, Comp. Gen. Dec. B-295569, 2005 CPD ¶ 66 (price of most likely quantity to be purchased lower than competitors); and *Semont Travel, Inc.*, Comp. Gen. Dec. B-291179, 2002 CPD ¶ 200 (price of high price base year was not out of line even if lower priced option years were not exercised). See also *Cherokee Painting LLC*, Comp. Gen. Dec. B-311020.3, 2009 CPD ¶ 18, where no unacceptable risk was found by analyzing past prices which had not resulted in undue costs to the government, and *Citywide Managing Servs. of Port Washington, Inc.*, Comp. Gen. Dec. B-281287.12, 2001 CPD ¶ 6, rejecting a protest even though the agency had not analyzed the risk of unbalanced prices because the protester did not submit evidence that the government would pay higher prices. For a case agreeing that an offer should be rejected because of undue risk, see *L. W. Matteson, Inc.*, Comp. Gen. Dec. B-290224, 2002 CPD ¶ 89.

Prior to the FAR Part 15 rewrite, unbalanced pricing in competitive proposals was treated in the same manner as in sealed bidding, requiring that to reject an offer it had to be both mathematically unbalanced and materially unbalanced. See *Astrosystems, Inc.*, Comp. Gen. Dec. B-260399.2, 95-2 CPD ¶ 18 (protester failed to show reasonable doubt for material unbalancing); *Laidlaw Envtl. Servs., Inc.*, Comp. Gen. Dec. B-261603, 95-2 CPD ¶ 171 (no evidence of enhanced prices); and *Allstate Van & Storage, Inc.*, Comp. Gen. Dec. B-270744, 96-1 CPD ¶ 191 (no basis in record to conclude mathematical unbalancing).

b. Delivery Terms

The RFP may request that the offeror agree to specific delivery or completion terms. In such cases the RFP will state the time of performance that the agency must have and will permit offerors to propose shorter times of performance.

c. Articles or Services to Be Furnished

The RFP may require or permit the offeror to specify the specific article or service to be provided. For example, this may mean offering a brand-name or equal product.

2. Intention To Perform

An offeror can be held liable for fraud if it makes the government an offer that it does not intent to keep. In *United States ex rel. Hendow v. University of Phoenix*, 461 F.3d 1166 (9th Cir. 2006), *cert. denied*, 550 U.S. 903 (2007), the court used the term "promissory fraud" to explain that an offeror could be liable for false claims if it intentionally made a promise that it did not intend to keep in performing the contract. The court cited *United States ex rel. Main v. Oakland City Univ.*, 426 F.3d 914 (7th Cir. 2005), *cert. denied*, 547 U. S. 1071 (2006), in support of this theory. In two instances, the government has been unable to prove to the court that it did not intend to perform as promised. See *United States ex rel. Laird v. Lockheed Martin Eng'g & Science Servs. Co.*, 491 F.3d 254 (5th Cir. 2007), where the government was unable to show that the contractor did not intend to use the proposed workforce although it used a higher skilled workforce in performing the contract. See also *United States ex rel. Bettis v. Odebrecht Contractors of California, Inc.*, 393 F.3d 1321 (D.C. Cir. 2005), where the court rejected the application of this theory to a situation where the contractor allegedly intentionally submitted a price that was significantly less that its expected costs of performance. The court reasoned that, since this was a firm fixed price contract, the contractor bore the risk of losing money and there was no proof that it intended to not perform or assert fraudulent claims to recover its losses.

3. Offer Strategy

A number of strategies may be available to an offeror. These include deciding on the pricing and other aspects of the offer, whether to make an offer on all the items covered by the RFP, and whether to submit alternate or multiple offers.

a. Best Terms

One of the most difficult decisions to make is whether to submit an offer containing the best possible offer the firm can make or one reserving some improvements for the later stages of the process. The problem is that in a competitive environment, the offeror may not get an opportunity to make concessions and improve the offer.

In this regard, ¶ (f)(4) of the FAR 52.215-1 Instructions to Offerors — Competitive Acquisition provision warns offerors that:

> The Government intends to evaluate proposals and award a contract without discussions with offerors (except clarifications described in FAR 15.306(a)). Therefore, the offeror's initial proposal should contain *the offerors best terms* from a cost or price and technical standpoint. [Emphasis supplied.]

See *Advanced American Diving Serv., Inc.*, Comp. Gen. Dec. B-274766, 97-1 CPD ¶ 1, stating:

> [The protester] argues that the agency should have held discussions to permit it to correct any deficiencies in its proposal. However, there generally is no requirement that an agency hold discussions when the solicitation advises offerors that the agency intends to make award without discussions. Federal Acquisition Regulation 15.610(a)(3) (FAC 90-31); *Triple P Servs., Inc.*, B-271777, July 24, 1996, 96-2 CPD ¶ 39. Since the solicitation advised offerors that the agency intended to make award without discussions, [the protester] could not presume that it would have a chance to improve its proposal through discussions. The burden was on [the protester] to submit an initial proposal containing sufficient information to demonstrate its merits, and the protester ran the risk of having its proposal rejected by failing to do so. *Scientific-Atlantic, Inc.*, B-255343.2; B-255343.4, Mar. 14, 1994, 94-1 CPD ¶ 325.

Even where the solicitation indicates that the government plans to undertake discussions with offerors within the competitive range, an offer at less than the best possible terms runs the risk of being found to be outside the competitive range.

In view of the new policies encouraging the award of more contracts without discussions and the limiting of the competitive range when discussions are to be held (as discussed in Chapter 7), the best strategy is to include the best terms in the initial offer. This will limit the ability of the offeror to make concessions during negotiations but will provide the greatest likelihood that the offeror will win the competition.

b. Items Offered

Where the RFP calls for a number of severable items and the solicitation does not specifically require that offers be made on all the items, the offeror must decide whether to submit an offer on all the items or on only some of them. The only FAR provision dealing with this issue is contained in ¶ (c)(4) of the FAR 52.215-1 Instructions to Offerors — Competitive Acquisition solicitation provision: "Unless otherwise specified in the solicitation, the offeror may propose to provide any item or combination of items." If it decides to submit an offer covering all the items, the offeror should consider whether to condition its offer on award of all the items. This condition, termed an "all-or-none" offer, would insure that the offeror would not receive partial awards. In such a case the all-or-none prices will be compared with the price combinations for all the items offered by other offerors without an all-or-none condition, *Banknote Corp. of Am., Inc.*, Comp. Gen. Dec. B-245528.2, 92-1 CPD ¶ 53. If no such condition is contained in the offer, ¶¶ (f)(5) and (f)(6) of the FAR 52.215-1 Instructions to Offerors — Competitive Acquisition solicitation provision permit the government to award multiple contracts for all or a part of any contract line items.

c. Alternate or Multiple Offers

Offerors may want to consider submitting more than one offer. This may be particularly desirable when the specifications permit the offeror to determine the way that the work will be performed, such as in a performance or functional specification. See also FAR 11.002(e) permitting agencies to identify performance levels as targets rather than as fixed or minimum requirements. In other cases an offeror may conclude that a non-specification offer will have sufficient advantages for the government to consider amending the specifications to permit its consideration. Each of these two situations has been referred to as an "alternate proposal." This term has been used to describe the case where an offeror submits two or more offers each meeting the RFP requirements. It has also been used in the case where the offeror submits one offer meeting the requirements and another that does not, or merely submits one offer that does not conform to the RFP. The FAR does not provide comprehensive directions as to the treatment to be given the offers when an offeror elects to follow one of these strategies, but it would appear that agencies have substantial discretion in evaluating such offers and conducting the procurement to obtain the best value for the government. However, an agency that conducts "discussions" in order to understand an alternate proposal may not award the contract on the basis of that proposal without conducting discussions with all other offerors in the competitive range, *Integrated Sys Group*, Comp. Gen. Dec. B-272336, 96-2 CPD ¶ 144.

(1) Nonconforming Offers

If an offeror submits an alternate offer that deviates from the requirements of the RFP, the government may not award to that offeror but must revise the RFP to permit other offerors to propose to the deviation, FAR 15.206(d). See *Labat-Anderson, Inc.*, 71 Comp. Gen. 252 (B-246071.5), 92-1 CPD ¶ 193, holding that it was improper to accept an offer that deviated from a staffing level required by the RFP, and *International Data Sys., Inc.*, Comp. Gen. Dec. B-277385, 97-2 CPD ¶ 96, sustaining a protest when the agency awarded a contract with a substitute product for one called for by the RFP. The proper course of action was followed in *Simmonds Precision Prods., Inc.*, Comp. Gen. Dec. B-244559.3, 93-1 CPD ¶ 483, where, upon receipt of a deviating offer containing terms that were more attractive than those required by the RFP, other offerors were given the opportunity to submit revised offers.

An offer is not nonconforming, however, if the RFP states that the agency reserves the right to award to a proposal that does not meet all the mandatory requirements of the solicitation, *Litton Sys., Inc. v. Dep't of Transportation*, GSBCA 12911-P, 94-3 BCA ¶ 27,263. In that case the board held that the agency was not required to amend the RFP to permit award to an alternate offer that did not conform to the mandatory requirements because all the offerors had been informed that the agency might follow that procedure.

The only provision dealing with this issue is FAR 15.209(a)(2), which directs that language similar to the following Alternate II to the FAR 52.215-1 Instructions to Offerors — Competitive Acquisition provision be incorporated into the RFP if the government would be willing to accept alternate proposals:

> (9) Offerors may submit proposals that depart from stated requirements. Such proposals shall clearly identify why the acceptance of the proposal would be advantageous to the Government. Any deviations from the terms and conditions of the solicitation, as well as the comparative advantage to the Government, shall be clearly identified and explicitly defined. The Government reserves the right to amend the solicitation to allow all offerors an opportunity to submit revised proposals based on the revised requirements.

While the presence of this provision appears to indicate that nonconforming offers will be considered, such offers can be accepted only if the solicitation is amended to give other competitors the opportunity to make offers to the revised specifications.

The absence of the Alternate II language does not necessarily mean that offers that deviate from the RFP must be rejected. The sealed bid concept of responsiveness does not apply to negotiated procurements, *Gardiner, Kamya & Assocs., P.C.*, Comp. Gen. Dec. B-258400, 95-1 CPD ¶ 191. Thus, the contracting officer has the discretion to include such an offer in the competitive range and seek to have a nonconformity cured through discussions or to amend the solicitation as required by FAR 15.206(g). However, the offeror takes the risk that the offer will be rejected and the offeror excluded from the competitive range. See *Bencor-Petrifond*, Comp. Gen. Dec. B-254205, 93-2 CPD ¶ 208 (proposal departed from RFP's construction schedule); and *Discount Mach. & Equip., Inc.*, Comp. Gen. Dec. B-241444, 90-2 CPD ¶ 474 (offeror unable to meet technical provisions). Which course of action will be taken by the contracting officer will depend on the number and nature of conforming offers received and the benefits offered by the nonconforming offer. However, an offer that is totally out of compliance with the RFP may not be considered, *Best W. Quantico Inn/Conference Ctr.*, Comp. Gen. Dec. B-209500, 83-1 CPD ¶ 164. In that case the offeror responded to an RFP with only a contract pricing proposal when the RFP required a technical proposal.

It is not improper to submit a noncompliant alternate offer to ensure that an agency does use ambiguous RFP language to award on a seemingly improper basis.

See *Power Connector, Inc.*, Comp. Gen. Dec. B-285395, 2000 CPD ¶ 152, rejecting the contention that an alternate offer of a foreign product was unlawful when the RFP called for a domestic product but contained a description of how foreign products would be evaluated.

(2) MULTIPLE CONFORMING OFFERS

The present FAR, like its predecessor, does not deal with the submission of multiple conforming offers. Nevertheless, the GAO has held that there is no need for the solicitation to contain a provision authorizing multiple offers for them to be considered, *Educational Media, Inc.*, Comp. Gen. Dec. B-225457.2, 87-1 CPD ¶ 498, and *Federal Computer Corp.*, 66 Comp. Gen. 139 (B-223932), 81-2 CPD ¶ 665. See also 33 Comp. Gen. 499 (B-119646) (1954); and 39 Comp. Gen. 892 (B-142957) (1960), holding that the submission of multiple offers are appropriate competitive techniques. For an instance where an alternate offer was selected for contract award, see *OK Produce*, Comp. Gen. Dec. B-299058, 2007 CPD ¶ 31.

To be valid, alternate offers must conform to the terms of the solicitation. See *Aeroflex Test Solutions*, Comp. Gen. Dec. B-295380, 2005 CPD ¶ 51, holding that the contracting officer properly did not consider an alternate offer that did not contain fixed prices as required by the RFP, and *Americom Gov't Servs., Inc.*, Comp. Gen. Dec. B-292242, 2003 CPD ¶ 163, holding that an alternate offer was properly considered unacceptable when it stated that its proposed satellite services were "subject to availability." See also *P.G. Elecs., Ltd.*, Comp. Gen. Dec. B-261883, 95-2 CPD ¶ 202, where the agency could not evaluate an alternate offer of an extended warranty because its terms were unclear, and *Head, Inc.*, Comp. Gen. Dec. B-299523, 2007 CPD ¶ 109, where an alternate offer was not dealt with because of lack of supporting documentation. Compare *Citrus College*, Comp. Gen. Dec. B-293543, 2004 CPD ¶ 104, where the GAO rejected the contention that the agency accepted an alternate proposal that did not comply with the RFP requirements because the protester did not prove prejudice.

Although the receipt of multiple offers can be of value to the government, they do require additional evaluation. This could be unduly burdensome in cases where substantial evaluation effort is required, such as where many different approaches are proposed or there are a large number of multiple proposals. See, for example, *Moreland Corp.*, Comp. Gen. Dec. B-291086, 2002 CPD ¶ 197, where five offerors submitted 14 offers and alternate offers, and *Banknote Corp. of Am., Inc.*, Comp. Gen. Dec. B-245528.2, 92-1 CPD ¶ 53, where the evaluation was complicated and delayed by the fact that one offeror submitted four separate price offers and another submitted ten. Thus, agencies can properly preclude multiple offers by including a provision in the solicitation prohibiting more than one offer, *ACS State Healthcare, LLC*, Comp. Gen. Dec. B-292981, 2004 CPD ¶ 57; *Dale Stevens Constr.*, Comp. Gen. Dec. B-242234, 91-1 CPD ¶ 354. However, such a provision will not necessarily prevent separate offers from being submitted by separate but affiliated firms. In *Robbins — Gioia, Inc.*, Comp. Gen. Dec. B-274318, 96-2 CPD ¶ 222, the RFP stated that (1) "an offeror may submit a maximum of one fully compliant proposal," (2) "no alternate proposals will be accepted," and (3) "if an offeror submits more than one proposal, all proposals will be returned without evaluation." The GAO denied the protest against consideration of offers from affiliated firms, holding that the general rule is that contracting agencies may accept bids and offers from affiliated firms unless doing so would prejudice the government's interests or give the affiliated offerors an unfair advantage over other offerors.

B. Information

The typical RFP will require the offeror to furnish a considerable amount of information. Much of the information will deal with the offeror's capability to perform, including such subjects as past performance, experience, facilities and equipment, financial capacity, and key personnel. Requests for information dealing with how the offeror intends to perform the work and what techniques it will use in managing the work often call for the offeror to include this information in what have been called "technical proposals" and "management proposals," which are used to assess the offeror's capability. Such requests for information have been criticized as creating essay contests, and many agencies have stopped requiring them. They should be distinguished from RFP provisions which require the offeror to include in the offer details of the work or explanations of the offer that will be incorporated into the contract. When such technical information is to be incorporated into the contract, great care should be taken to ensure that the language is clear and concise, in order to avoid disputes as to its meaning.

1. Technical Information

Offerors may be required to furnish technical information that will be used in assessing the offeror's know-how or the degree of risk involved in the way the offeror intends to perform. When such information is required, offerors should devote full attention to ensuring that their information describes sound technical solutions and contains thorough documentation. Proposals with significant informational deficiencies are excluded as a matter of course, *Kahn Instruments, Inc.*, Comp. Gen. Dec. B-277973, 98-1 CPD ¶ 11; *McAllister & Assocs., Inc.*, Comp. Gen. Dec. B-277029.3, 98-1 CPD ¶ 85; *University Sys., Inc.*, GSBCA 10924-P, 91-1 BCA ¶ 23,617; *Integrated Microcomputer Sys., Inc.*, Comp. Gen. Dec. B-239126.4, 90-2 CPD ¶ 195; and submissions that are not supported with sufficient technical information may be excluded from the competitive range, *Hamilton Sundstrand Power Sys. v. United States*, 75 Fed. Cl. 512 (2007); *Hamilton Sundstrand Power Sys.*, Comp. Gen. Dec. B-298757, 2006 CPD ¶ 209; *LaBarge Prods., Inc.*, Comp. Gen. Dec. B-287841, 2001 CPD ¶ 177; *American Oversees Book Co.*, Comp. Gen. Dec. B-266297, 96-1 CPD ¶ 60; *Millar Elevator Indus., Inc.*, Comp. Gen. Dec. B-250992.2, 93-1 CPD

¶ 212; *KCI, Inc.*, Comp. Gen. Dec. B-244690, 91-2 CPD ¶ 395; *Wyle Lab.*, Comp. Gen. Dec. B-239671, 90-2 CPD ¶ 231. Page limitations on the length of technical proposals are not accepted as an excuse for insufficient technical information, *Professional Perf. Dev. Group, Inc.*, Comp. Gen. Dec. B-311273, 2008 CPD ¶ 101 (35 page limitation with 10 of 12 offerors deemed to have submitted unacceptable proposals). See *AHNTECH, Inc.*, Comp. Gen. Dec. B-299806, 2007 CPD ¶ 213, stating the basic rule as follows:

> An offeror must submit a proposal that is adequately written and that affirmatively establishes its merits or run the risk of having the proposal rejected as technically unacceptable. *Source AV, Inc.*, B-234521, June 20, 1989, 89-1 CPD ¶ 578 at 3. In reviewing whether a proposal was properly rejected as technically unacceptable for informational deficiencies, we examine the record to determine, among other things, whether the RFP called for detailed information and the nature of the informational, deficiencies, for example, whether they tended to show that the offeror did not understand what it would be required to do under the contract. *BioClean Med. Sys., Inc.*, B-239906, Aug. 17, 1990, 90-2 CPD ¶ 142 at 3; *DRT Assocs., Inc.*, B-237070 Jan. 11, 1990, 90-1 CPD ¶ 47 at 3. The evaluation of technical proposals is a matter within the discretion of the contracting agency. *Marine Animal Prods. Int'l, Inc.*, B-247150.2, July 13, 1992, 92-2 CPD ¶ 16 at 9. We will not reevaluate a proposal but, rather, will consider whether the agency's evaluation was reasonable and consistent with the evaluation scheme in the RFP. *Communications Int'l, Inc.*, B-238810, B-238810.2, July 3, 1990, 90-2 CPD ¶ 3 at 3.

If the RFP calls for a specific description of how the work will be performed, the offeror can be downgraded for not supplying such information, *Northwestern Travel Agency, Inc.*, Comp. Gen. Dec. B-244592, 91-2 CPD ¶ 363. Merely repeating portions of the RFP ("parroting" the RFP) is a poor strategy, *Paragon Dynamics, Inc.*, Comp. Gen. Dec. B-251280, 93-1 CPD ¶ 248. See *Government Telecommunications, Inc.*, Comp. Gen. Dec. B-299542.2, 2007 CPD ¶ 136; *Bannum, Inc.*, Comp. Gen. Dec. B-271075, 96-1 CPD ¶ 248, and *Supreme Automation Corp.*, Comp. Gen. Dec. B-224158, 87-1 CPD ¶ 83, where offerors were eliminated from the competitive range because they repeated back portions of the specification without affirmatively demonstrating the merits of their technical approach. Similarly, merely promising to meet the requirements in the RFP will almost invariably lead to a poor evaluation, *IVI Corp.*, Comp. Gen. Dec. B-310766, 2008 CPD ¶ 21 (blanket offer to submit an "equal" product not sufficient to show that it would meet salient characteristics); *Hubbell Elec. Heater Co.*, Comp. Gen. Dec. B-289098, 2002 CPD ¶ 15 (blanket promise to conform to ISO 9000 insufficient to demonstrate ability to do so); *Eastern Tech. Enters., Inc.*, Comp. Gen. Dec. B-259844, 95-1 CPD ¶ 232 (blanket offers of compliance are not adequate substitutes for detailed technical information); *Inter-Con Sec. Sys., Inc.*, Comp. Gen. Dec. B-235248, 89-2 CPD ¶ 148 (exclusion from competitive range proper when proposal merely made a "blanket promise" to comply with RFP). Compare *Moxon, Inc.*, Comp. Gen. Dec. B-179160, 74-1 CPD ¶ 134, where the GAO held that discussions should have been held to determine what the protester was offering. See *Corporate Jets, Inc.*, GSBCA 11049-P, 91-2 BCA ¶ 23,998, *recons. denied*,

91-2 BCA ¶ 23,999, where it was held proper to eliminate an incumbent contractor from the competitive range because it failed to submit detailed technical information and merely stated that it would continue to perform as it had been performing on the current contract. For similar reliance on past performance and subsequent rejection from the competitive range, see *InterAmerica Research Assocs., Inc.*, Comp. Gen. Dec. B-253698.2, 93-2 CPD ¶ 288.

If the RFP requires the submission of test data to show that an offered product meets the specifications, an offer can be rejected for failing to submit compete test data, *General Dynamics C4 Sys., Inc.*, Comp. Gen. Dec. B-299675.2, 2008 CPD ¶ 122. Technical information may also be necessary to instruct an agency on how to conduct the test of a sample. See *L-3 Communications EOTech, Inc.*, Comp. Gen. Dec. B-311453, 2008 CPD ¶ 139, denying a protest where an agency did not properly use a sample because of lack of information on how to tighten a locking nut.

If an RFP calls for the submission of a sample task response, care must be used to submit a full description of the offeror's approach to performing the task. See *Veterans Tech., LLC*, Comp. Gen. Dec. B-310303.2, 2008 CPD ¶ 31 (response failed to include technical approach or demonstration of competence of personnel).

A misrepresentation as to the technical capabilities of a proposed product can be construed as a false statement under 31 U.S.C. § 1001, subjecting the offeror to civil liability under the False Claims Act, 31 U.S.C. § 3729, *United States ex rel. Westrick v. Second Chance Body Armor, Inc.*, No 04-280 (RWR) (D.D.C. 2010). See *Harrison v. Westinghouse Savannah River Co.*, 176 F.3d 776 (4th Cir. 1999), holding that false statements about how a contract will be performed could be false claims, stating that "estimates" can be false claims at 792:

> Finally [the contractor] argues that [it's] statements cannot create False Claims Act liability because they were only estimates. Expressions of opinion are not actionable as fraud; fraud may only be found in expressions of fact which "(1) admit[] of being adjudged true or false in a way that (2) admit[] of empirical verification." *Presidio Enters., Inc. v. Warner Bros. Distributing Corp.*, 784 F.2d 674, 679 (5th Cir. 1986). *See also Boisjoly v. Morton Thiokol, Inc.*, 706 F. Supp. 795, 810 (D. Utah 1988) (no False Claims Act liability for statement "clearly not a statement of fact that can be said to be either true or false"). The fact that cost figures are clearly marked as estimates might affect their ability to influence agency decision-making under the [*United States ex rel. Berge v. Bd. of Trustees of Univ. of Ala.*, 104 F.3d 1453, 1458 (4th Cir.), *cert. denied*, 139 L. Ed. 2d 232, 522 U.S. 916, 118 S. Ct. 301 (1997)] materiality standard. However, an opinion or estimate carries with it "an implied assertion, not only that the speaker knows no facts which would preclude such an opinion, but that he does know facts which justify it." W. Page Keeton, *et al.*, Prosser & Keeton on the Law of Torts § 109, at 760 (5th ed. 1984). [The plaintiff] has alleged that [the contractor] knew each of these statements was false. The [government agency] could have been influenced by each of them under the legally reasonable belief that [the contractor] did not know its own estimates were false.

2. Management Information

The offeror may be called on to explain how it plans to manage the work to attain the promised technical solution. Whereas technical information focuses on how the work will be performed, management information focuses on whether the offeror's organization will manage its resources to achieve those results. The offeror will be required to show the government what personnel and material resources it will use and how it will organize and control those resources to bring the contract work to a successful conclusion. As is the case with technical proposals, lack of detail in management proposals will generally result in lower scores and general statements will not suffice, *SPAAN Tech., Inc.*, Comp. Gen. Dec. B-400406, 2009 CPD ¶ 46 (management proposal contained little rationale for proposed organizational structure); *DIY, Inc.*, Comp. Gen. Dec. B-293105.13, 2005 CPD ¶ 50 (insufficient description of methods of conducting management and marketing services for homes); *Science & Tech., Inc.*, Comp. Gen. Dec. B-272748, 97-1 CPD ¶ 121 (management proposal contained statements such as "our managers who are incumbent personnel understand Fort Huachuca's mission"). See also *Joint Threat Servs.*, Comp. Gen. Dec. B-278168, 98-1 CPD ¶ 18 (staffing cuts in option years were only implied in protester's management proposal, notwithstanding fact that cost proposal promised an in-depth analysis of the reduction plan in its management proposal); *Global Eng'g & Constr. (J.V.)*, Comp. Gen. Dec. B-275999.4, 97-2 CPD ¶ 125 (agency reasonably downgraded offeror's management proposal because it did not submit a clear management structure); and *Quality Elevator Co.*, Comp. Gen. Dec. B-271899, 96-2 CPD ¶ 89 (lower grade justified because protester's management proposal failed to describe the differing management needs of the various work tasks). In *Avue Techs. Corp.*, Comp. Gen. Dec. B-298380.4, 2008 CPD ¶ 182, a proposal was rejected for failing to demonstrate that the offeror was agreeing to the agency's requirements regarding proprietary information.

3. Representations and Certifications

Section K of the RFP will contain a number of representations and certifications that must be filled out by the offeror. Offerors are properly excluded from the competition if they submit a false representation or certification, *Southwestern Bell Tel. Co.*, Comp. Gen. Dec. B-292476, 2003 CPD ¶ 177; *Hedgecock Elec., Inc.*, Comp. Gen. Dec. B-274776.2, 97-1 CPD ¶ 51. See *Universal Techs. Inc.*, Comp. Gen. Dec. B-248808.2, 92-2 CPD ¶ 212, holding that a firm need not be disqualified if the agency determines that the false certification was not made in bad faith. Compare *Tiger Enters., Inc.*, Comp. Gen. Dec. B-292815.3, 2004 CPD ¶ 19, recommending immediate termination of a contract that was awarded based on a false certification that the offeror met the small business size standard. However, the contracting agency is not required to investigate a certification to determine if it is false unless it has information so indicating. See *E.D.I., Inc.*, Comp. Gen. Dec. B-251750, 93-1 CPD ¶ 364, stating:

When a bidder or offeror represents that it will furnish end products of designated or qualifying countries, it is obligated under the contract to comply with that representation. If prior to award an agency has reason to believe that a firm will not provide compliant products, the agency should go beyond a firm's representation of compliance with the Trade Agreements Act; however, where the contracting officer has no information prior to award which would lead to such a conclusion, the contracting officer may properly rely upon an offeror's representation without further investigation. See *Oliver Prods. Co.*, B-245672, Jan. 7, 1992, 92-1 CPD ¶ 33 (Buy American Act certification); *General Sales Agency*, B-247529.2, Aug. 6, 1992, 92-2 CPD ¶ 80 (contingent fee representation similar to end product certification); cf. *Manufacturing Tech. Assocs. Inc.*, B-251759, Apr. 5, 1993, 93-1 CPD ¶ __ (with regard to a bidder's certification of compliance with the restriction on the acquisition of foreign machine tools, an agency's investigation into the country of origin of product offered in response to a protester's pre-award complaint satisfied an agency's duty of inquiry).

Offerors have been held liable for false claims for submitting false certifications. See *United States ex rel. Fallon v. Accudyne Corp.*, 880 F. Supp. 636 (W.D. Wis. 1995) (false certifications with respect to compliance with environmental standards); *United States v. Incorporated Village of Island Park*, 888 F. Supp. 419 (E.D.N.Y. 1995) (false certifications of compliance with the non-discrimination requirements of the Fair Housing Act and with an affirmative action plan); *United States ex rel. Thompson v. Columbia/HCA Healthcare Corp.*, 125 F.3d 899 (5th Cir. 1997), and *United States ex rel. Pogue v. American Healthcorp., Inc.*, 914 F. Supp. 1507 (M.D. Tenn. 1996) (false certifications of compliance with the Medicare anti-kickback and anti-self-referral statutes); and *Ab-Tech Constr., Inc. v. United States*, 31 Fed. Cl. 429 (1994), *aff'd*, 57 F.3d 1084 (Fed. Cir. 1995) (false certifications of compliance with rules for continuing adherence to the requirements of a Small Business Administration minority contracting program).

4. *Capability Information*

Most RFPs call for the submission of information showing the offeror's capabilities as part of the technical or management proposal or as separate information. The most important types of capability information deal with experience, past performance, and the personnel who will perform the contract. As a general rule, submission of specific information is far more effective than the mere inclusion of general statements on the abilities of the organization, *Honolulu Marine, Inc.*, Comp. Gen. Dec. B-245329, 91-2 CPD ¶ 586; *EAP Consultants*, Comp. Gen. Dec. B-238103, 90-1 CPD ¶ 358. See *Prudent Techs., Inc.*, Comp. Gen. Dec. B-297425, 2006 CPD ¶ 16, where a proposal was correctly rated unacceptable because the protester did not furnish specific capability information in the form required by the RFP, and *Carpetmaster*, Comp. Gen. Dec. B-294767, 2004 CPD ¶ 226, where the proposal was properly downgraded when the protester did not supply contract numbers and other detailed information. See also *MIL Corp.*, Comp. Gen. Dec. B-297508, 2006 CPD ¶ 34 stating:

It is the responsibility of a firm competing for a government contract to provide an adequately written submission, and an agency may downgrade a submission for the lack of requested information. *Incident Catering Servs., LLC*, B-296435.2 et al., Sept. 7, 2005, 2005 CPD ¶ 193 at 7; *Formal Mgmt. Sys., Inc.*, B-259824, May 3, 1995, 95-1 CPD ¶ 227 at 3. Here, MIL's quotation failed to provide any specific examples of flexibility or timely task completion, as required by the RFQ. In fact, the only parts of its quotation to which the protester points as evidencing flexibility and timeliness are statements which merely repeat the past performance evaluation subfactors. In light of the fact that MIL's quotation does no more than "parrot back" the stated evaluation criteria, we find the agency's evaluation here to be both reasonable and consistent with the solicitation. See *Wahkontah Servs., Inc.*, B-292768, Nov. 18, 2003, 2003 CPD ¶ 214 at 7.

Offerors should exercise care in the assertions that they make concerning their capability. See *United States ex rel. Longhi v. Lithium Power Techs., Inc.*, 530 F. Supp. 2d 888 (S.D. Tex. 2008), *aff'd*, 575 F.3d 468 (5th Cir. 2009), *cert. denied*, 130 S. Ct. 2092 (2010), assessing triple the contract price as damages because the contractor misrepresented its prior experience, its arrangements with another firm and the extent of its facilities in its proposal. See also *Dual, Inc.*, Comp. Gen. Dec. B-280719, 98-2 CPD ¶ 133, where the protester argued that the winning offeror had been guilty of misrepresentation by stating that it would perform the work at a particular division when, in fact, it was negotiating the sale of that division to another company while the procurement was being conducted. The GAO sustained the protest, agreeing with the protester that Dual had an obligation to advise the Air Force of its negotiations and that its failure to do so was a misrepresentation which affected the evaluation process. Similarly, in *Greenleaf Constr. Co.*, Comp. Gen. Dec. B-293105.18, 2006 CPD ¶ 19, the GAO sustained a protest because the winning offeror had not informed the agency that two of the designated key personnel had stated they would not work on contract.

a. Experience and Past Performance

Information concerning an offeror's experience and past performance record will be required to be furnished in almost all procurements. Experience deals with the types of work that the offeror or its employees have performed, and past performance deals with how well the work was performed. Although the request may not clearly distinguish between the two, information on both types of background will be important. See *Telcom Sys. Servs., Inc. v. Dep't of Justice*, GSBCA 13272-P, 95-2 BCA ¶ 27,849 ("unreasonable to suggest that past performance does not encompass experience").

In addition to complying with the RFP's specific requests for past performance and experience information, the offeror should offer additional information that would explain or supplement the information furnished. Thus, the offeror should provide a thorough analysis of its experience and past performance on contracts that are similar to the procurement in question and should demonstrate that those contracts are relevant to the evaluation of its performance for the current effort. If the RFP requires offerors to obtain questionnaires from references, it is the offeror's responsibility to ensure that the questionnaires are submitted, *Capitol Drywall Supply, Inc.,* Comp. Gen. Dec. B-400721, 2009 CPD ¶ 17; *American Floor Consultants, Inc.,* Comp. Gen. Dec. B-294530.7, 2006 CPD ¶ 97, and that they are submitted by an independent source, *Metro Mach. Corp.,* Comp. Gen. Dec. B-295744, 2005 CPD ¶ 112 (evaluation by offeror of subcontractors did not meet RFP requirement for independent evaluation). Where there have been instances of poor or unsuccessful past performance, the offeror should provide any factual information that would establish extenuating circumstances. Factual information on steps taken to correct or avoid such occurrences should also be supplied. See *Del-Jen Int'l Corp.,* Comp. Gen. Dec. B-297960, 2006 CPD ¶ 81 (protest denied when protester did not demonstrate that it had corrected past deficiencies in performing as incumbent contractor); *Hanley Indus., Inc.,* Comp. Gen. Dec. B-295318, 2005 CPD ¶ 20 (low rating of past performance justified when protester did not take opportunity to submit evidence of corrective action); *Si-Nor, Inc.,* Comp. Gen. Dec. B-292748.2, 2004 CPD ¶ 10 (low rating of past performance justified when agency was given only partial evidence of corrective action).

When information on experience is requested, a detailed description of past efforts should be provided, *Sunbelt Properties, Inc.,* Comp. Gen. Dec. B-245729.3, 92-1 CPD ¶ 278. See *M. Erdal Kamisli, Ltd.,* Comp. Gen. Dec. B-291522, 2003 CPD ¶ 19, stating:

> An agency's evaluation is dependent upon information furnished in a proposal, and it is the offeror's burden to submit an adequately written proposal for the agency to evaluate. *Chant Eng'g Co., Inc.,* B-279049, B-279049.2, Apr. 30, 1998, 98-2 CPD ¶ 65 at 7. It was ERKA's responsibility to provide sufficient information in its proposal, as was required by the RFP, regarding the nature of the listed project experience to enable a meaningful review of the offeror's experience. ERKA failed to do so, and our Office will not entertain the protester's complaint that it was entitled to evaluation credit simply because it believes that the agency should have been aware of the omitted information.

In some cases the RFP may require information on the experience of both the offeror and its personnel, *General Physics Fed. Sys., Inc.,* Comp. Gen. Dec. B-275934, 97-1 CPD ¶ 171 (personnel experience and corporate experience); and *Global Assocs., Ltd.,* Comp. Gen. Dec. B-275534, 97-1 CPD ¶ 129 (corporate experience and personnel qualifications and experience). Where an offeror has not had the specific experience required, the lack of corporate experience may be overcome by the experience of employees, *Consultants on Family Addiction,* Comp. Gen. Dec. B-274924.2, 97-1 CPD ¶ 80 (nothing improper in evaluating an offeror's capacity to perform services based on the experience of those who will perform those services); and *EBA Eng'g, Inc.,* Comp. Gen. Dec. B-275818, 97-1 CPD ¶ 127 (a competitor for a service contract was entitled to use the experience of the incumbent employees). In addition, the past performance of a parent company may be used if the offeror can show that the parent will participate in performing the prospective contract, *Frontier Sys. Integrators, LLC*, Comp. Gen. Dec. B-298872.3, 2007 CPD ¶ 46.

b. Key Personnel

The personnel that the offeror intends to use in performing the contract are of prime importance in many procurements. Resumes of key personnel are frequently required and should probably be submitted even when they have not been requested. The importance of complying with resume requirements is demonstrated by *Verizon Federal, Inc.*, Comp. Gen. Dec. B-293527, March 26, 2004, *Unpub.*, where an offeror was rated unacceptable because of missing and incomplete resumes even though it was rated outstanding in past performance. See also *Inter-Con Sec. Sys., Inc.*, Comp. Gen. Dec. B-235248, 89-2 CPD ¶ 148, where an incumbent contractor was properly eliminated from the competitive range of the follow-on procurement because it failed to provide resumes of key personnel and other requested information. For a similar result, see *Lakeside Escrow & Title Agency, Inc.*, Comp. Gen. Dec. B-310331.3, 2008 CPD ¶ 14; *Pyramid Servs., Inc.*, Comp. Gen. Dec. B-257085.2, 94-2 CPD ¶ 79. Compare *Global Solutions Network, Inc.*, Comp. Gen. Dec. B-298682.3, 2008 CPD ¶ 131, denying a protest that the agency allowed the winning offeror to submit resumes exceeding the RFP page limitation – because the protester was not prejudiced. The GAO used similar reasoning in granting a protest where the agency had improperly downgraded a proposal because the resumes did not include information that it had learned during discussions, *Arora Group*, Comp. Gen. Dec. B-293102, 2004 CPD ¶ 61.

Offerors have also been disqualified from the competition because of inaccuracies in listing key personnel, *Electronic Data Sys. Fed. Corp.*, GSBCA 9869-P, 89-2 BCA ¶ 21,655, *recons. denied*, 89-2 BCA ¶ 21,778, *aff'd in part, vacated in part sub. nom. Planning Research Corp. v. United States*, 971 F.2d 736 (Fed. Cir. 1992) (submission of 101 resumes with no intention to use the personnel); *Ultra Tech. Corp.*, Comp. Gen. Dec. B-230309.6, 89-1 CPD ¶ 42 (proposing person as lead technician without obtaining his permission); *ManTech Advanced Sys. Int'l, Inc.*, Comp. Gen. Dec. B-255719.2, 94-1 CPD ¶ 326 (misrepresenting availability of incumbent personnel). Compare *Patriot Contract Servs., LLC v. United States*, 388 F. Supp. 2d 1010 (N.D. Cal. 2005), holding that the winning offeror had not clearly known that most of the key personnel would not be available when the contract was awarded a year after their names had been submitted, and *Orion Int'l Techs. v. United States*, 66 Fed. Cl. 569 (2005), holding that there was no misrepresentation when an employee of the incumbent contractor had signed a noncompete agreement but appeared willing to work for the offeror. In *CBIS Fed., Inc.*, 71 Comp. Gen. 319 (B-245844.2), 92-1 CPD ¶ 308, the GAO stated that when an offeror finds that proposed personnel are no longer available, the offeror should withdraw the names and propose substitutes in the best and final offer.

The offeror may be required to furnish evidence that the listed key personnel will be available for performance if the offeror receives the award. In such cases the GAO has ruled that award would be improper if the offeror does not supply information ensuring that key personnel would be available to perform the contract, *ManTech Field Eng'g Corp.*, Comp. Gen. Dec. B-245886.4, 92-1 CPD ¶ 309. Thus, failure to do so will result in the submission being held to be unacceptable or downgraded, *Native American Indus. Distributors, Inc.*, Comp. Gen. Dec. B-310737.3, 2008 CPD ¶ 76 (signed non-disclosure agreements not substitutes for required letters of commitment); *Xeta Int'l Corp.*, Comp. Gen. Dec. B-255182, 94-1 CPD ¶ 109 (failure to provide required letters of commitment for proposed key personnel). In *Scientific Mgmt. Assocs., Inc.*, Comp. Gen. Dec. B-238913, 90-2 CPD ¶ 27, the RFP stated that proposed personnel with nonbinding hiring agreements would not be evaluated as highly. The GAO held that the protester was properly excluded from the competitive range because of conditional hiring agreements for several key personnel. Similarly, in *IMR Servs. Corp.*, Comp. Gen. Dec. B-230586, 88-1 CPD ¶ 548, the proposed program manager was also committed to work as a site manager at another location. The GAO held that it was not unreasonable for the agency to downgrade a proposal in which a proposed manager would be stationed at a location different from the center of contract activity.

5. *Information in Support of Price*

Care must be exercised in submitting accurate information when an offeror is requested to describe how the estimated prices have been arrived at. See, for example, *United States v. United Techs. Corp.*, No. 3:99-cv-093 (S.D. Ohio 2008), *rev'd on other grounds*, 626 F.3d 313 (6th Cir. 2010), where the contractor was found guilty of fraud for inaccurately describing the estimating procedures that had been used to arrive at the proposed prices. See also *United States v. White*, 765 F.2d 1469 (11th Cir. 1985), finding fraud when the contractor submitted estimates that deviated substantially from actual costs that had been incurred but stated in negotiations that the estimates were based on costs. There are also several cases indicating that a contractor can be liable for not disclosing that amounts have been inappropriately added to the estimated costs because they do not then constitute its "best estimate." This "best estimate" requirement originated in the certification at the bottom of the DD Form 633 and was carried over to the since-eliminated Standard Form 1411 — the cover pages for the submission of cost or pricing data. In *United States v. Singer Co.*, 889 F.2d 1327 (4th Cir. 1989), the court ruled that not disclosing that contingency costs had been added to an estimate to provide for "negotiating loss" created False Claims Act liability. This ruling came in the context of bankruptcy proceedings and was followed up in *In re Bicoastal Corp.*, 124 B.R. 598, 37 CCF ¶ 76075 (M.D. Fla. 1991), and 134 B.R. 50, 37 CCF ¶ 76243 (M.D. Fla. 1991). A similar result occurred in *United States v. Leo*, 941 F.2d 181 (3d Cir. 1991), affirming a criminal conviction for telling subcontractors to pad their proposed cost estimates that were then submitted to the government.

It is common practice for agencies to request pricing information on a specified spreadsheet so that all offerors' information can be compared readily. When the RFP contains such a requirement, offerors must be careful to follow the instructions precisely. See *Capitol Supply, Inc.*, Comp. Gen. Dec. B-309999.3, 2008 CPD ¶ 35, where a quotation was properly rejected because the company's price could not be compared because they were not submitted in accordance with the instructions in the RFQ.

As discussed in Chapter 3, it is the government's policy to obtain as little data as possible to support the proposed costs or prices. The goal of this policy is to avoid the submission of cost or pricing data in order to shorten the evaluation period and minimize the resources used by the government agency to evaluate costs or prices, FAR 15.402(a)(3). In order to carry out this policy, agencies are instructed in FAR 15.408(l) to use the Requirements for Certified Cost or Pricing Data or Data Other Than Certified Cost or Pricing Data solicitation provision in FAR 52.215-20 when it is determined that data will be necessary to support cost or price proposals. Alternate provisions are to be used to elaborate on the specific data that is needed. This provision allows offerors to apply for an exception to submitting certified cost or pricing data as follows:

(a) Exceptions from certified cost or pricing data. (1) In lieu of submitting certified cost or pricing data, offerors may submit a written request for exception by submitting the information described in the following subparagraphs. The Contracting Officer may require additional supporting information, but only to the extent necessary to determine whether an exception should be granted, and whether the price is fair and reasonable.

(i) Identification of the law or regulation establishing the price offered. If the price is controlled under law by periodic rulings, reviews, or similar actions of a governmental body, attach a copy of the controlling document, unless it was previously submitted to the contracting office.

(ii) Commercial item exception. For a commercial item exception, the offeror shall submit, at a minimum, information on prices at which the same item or similar items have previously been sold in the commercial market that is adequate for evaluating the reasonableness of the price for this acquisition. Such information may include —

(A) For catalog items, a copy of or identification of the catalog and its date, or the appropriate pages for the offered items, or a statement that the catalog is on file in the buying office to which the proposal is being submitted. Provide a copy or describe current discount policies and price lists (published or unpublished), e.g., wholesale, original equipment manufacturer, or reseller. Also explain the basis of each offered price and its relationship to the established catalog price, including how the proposed price relates to the price of recent sales in quantities similar to the proposed quantities;

(B) For market-priced items, the source and date or period of the market quotation or other basis for market price, the base amount, and applicable discounts. In addition, describe the nature of the market;

(C) For items included on an active Federal Supply Service Multiple Award Schedule contract, proof that an exception has been granted for the schedule item.

(2) The offeror grants the Contracting Officer or an authorized representative the right to examine, at any time before award, books, records, documents, or other directly pertinent records to verify any request for an exception under this provision, and the reasonableness of price. For items priced using catalog or market prices, or law or regulation, access does not extend to cost or profit information or other data relevant solely to the offeror's determination of the prices to be offered in the catalog or marketplace.

This provision calls for the submission of certified cost or pricing data if no exception is applied for and it contains no mention of the adequate price competition exception. Thus, if an offeror does not believe that the procurement falls under the commercial item exception or the prices set by law or regulation exception but that it is a competitive procurement, clarification must be obtained from the contracting officer as to what data should be submitted. This clarification should be obtained immediately after receipt of the RFP in order to provide time to prepare the data.

Although agencies may call for a variety of types of data to support the cost or price proposal, three major types of data may be called for — (i) commercial item data, (ii) data to permit a cost realism analysis, and (iii) certified cost or pricing data. These three types will be discussed in this section.

a. Commercial Item Data

The government has a clear policy that certified cost or pricing data may not be obtained when a commercial item is being procured, FAR 15.403-1(b)(3). Thus, agencies must determine reasonableness of the price of commercial items using some other type of data. In the case where there are competing commercial items, it can be expected that the agency will use the competitive prices to analyze their reasonableness and no other data will be needed. If there are no competitive alternatives to the commercial item, the agency will have to obtain data to ascertain price reasonableness. FAR 15.403-3(c) states the policy on obtaining such data by stating that contracting officers may obtain the following type of data:

(c) *Commercial items.* (1) At a minimum, the contracting officer must use price analysis to determine whether the price is fair and reasonable whenever the contracting officer acquires a commercial item (see 15.404–1(b)). The fact that a price is included in a catalog does not, in and of itself, make it fair and reasonable. If the contracting officer cannot determine whether an offered price is fair and reasonable, even after obtaining additional data from sources other than the offeror, then the contracting officer shall require the offeror to submit data other than certified cost or pricing data to support further analysis (see 15.404–1). This data may include history of sales to non-governmental and governmental entities, cost data, or any other information the contracting officer requires to determine the price is fair and reasonable. Unless an exception under 15.403–1(b)(1) or (2) applies, the contracting officer shall require that the data submitted by the offeror include, at a minimum, appropriate data on the prices at which the same item or similar items have previously been sold, adequate for determining the reasonableness of the price.

This policy attempts to encourage agencies to seek data supporting commercial prices from sources other than the offeror. However, in most cases it can be anticipated that data will be sought from the offeror. FAR 15.403-3(c) provides the limitations on such requests:

(2) *Limitations relating to commercial items (10 U.S.C. 2306a(d)(2) and 41 U.S.C. 254b(d)).* (i) The contracting officer shall limit requests for sales data relating to commercial items to data for the same or similar items during a relevant time period.

(ii) The contracting officer shall, to the maximum extent practicable, limit the scope of the request for information relating to commercial items to include only data that is in the form regularly maintained by the offeror as part of its commercial operations.

(iii) The Government must not disclose outside the Government data obtained relating to commercial items that is exempt from disclosure under 24.202(a) or the Freedom of Information Act (5 U.S.C. 552(b)).

See also DFARS PGI 215.403-1(c)(3)(A)(2) directing contracting officers to obtain "prior non-government sales data" on the precise item or the predecessor item if the item being procured has not yet been sold commercially but has evolved from a commercial item. PGI 215.403-3(1) states:

Sales data must be comparable to the quantities, capabilities, specifications, etc. of the product or service proposed. Sufficient steps must be taken to verify the integrity of the sales data, to include assistance from the Defense Contract Management Agency, the Defense Contract Audit Agency, and/or other agencies if required.

Offerors submitting proposals for commercial items can anticipate that the RFP may not be in accord with these policies but may ask for considerable data to support the commercial price. In such case the offeror should immediately ask the contracting officer whether adequate price competition is expected and, if so, should request that the RFP be amended to delete the requirement for data. If it is found that adequate price competition is not expected but the offeror believes that competitive prices will be submitted, the contracting officer should be requested to defer the requirement for submission of data until the proposals have been received. If the agency insists on the submission of data, attempts should be made to limit the required amount of data. All these steps must be taken before the submission of the proposal.

If no relief can be obtained from an overly broad RFP data submission requirement, the offeror should submit sufficient current data to demonstrate that the price proposed is in line with recent sales of comparable quantities of the commercial item under similar conditions. To the extent that the RFP imposes different conditions than commercial sales, the costs of these conditions should be explained in demonstrating that the price offered is in line with prior sales. If the commercial item being offered to the government has not been sold previously, data on the sales of similar items should be provided with an explanation of the methodology used to arrive of the price of the new item.

b. Cost Realism Data

If the procurement calls for a cost-reimbursement contract, the agency will have to make a cost realism analysis during the evaluation process and will need data for that purpose. Generally, this will be accomplished by including Alternate IV to the Requirements for Cost or Pricing Data or Information Other Than Cost or Pricing Data solicitation provision in FAR 52.215-20 in the RFP and specifying the data required. This provision states the following:

> (a) Submission of certified cost or pricing data is not required.

> (b) Provide data described below: [Insert description of the data and the format that are required, including access to records necessary to permit an adequate evaluation of the proposed price in accordance with 15.403-3.]

Generally, the agency will request cost element breakdowns as discussed in Chapter 3. These breakdowns will provide detailed information on the resources (types and amount of labor and materials and subcontracts) estimated to be required in performing various tasks or line items plus the rates (labor rates and indirect cost rates) that are being proposed.

Offerors should exercise great care to ensure that the resources to be used on each contract task are sufficient to perform the work required by the RFP or described in the technical proposal. If the technical proposal has more labor hours than does the cost proposal, it can be expected that the agency will arrive at a probable cost higher than the proposed costs, *EDO Corp.*, Comp. Gen. Dec. B-296861, 2005 CPD ¶ 196; *TechDyn Sys. Corp.*, Comp. Gen. Dec. B-237618, 90-1 CPD ¶ 264; *Complere, Inc.*,

Comp. Gen. Dec. B-227832, 87-2 CPD ¶ 254. If the technical proposal has fewer resources than does the cost proposal, it can be expected that the agency will downgrade the technical proposal because the offeror does not understand the work. In either instance, the agency is required to resolve the discrepancy between the two proposals, *Earl Indus., LLC,* Comp. Gen. Dec. B-309996, 2007 CPD ¶ 203; *Serco, Inc.,* Comp. Gen. Dec. B-298226, 2006 CPD ¶ 120. If both the technical proposal and the cost proposal have too few resources, agencies can be expected to downgrade the technical proposal and arrive at a probable cost higher than the proposed costs, *Joint Threat Servs.,* Comp. Gen. Dec. B-278168, 98-1 CPD ¶ 18; *IT Facilities Servs.,* Comp. Gen. Dec. B-279585, 98-2 CPD ¶ 16. If a significant amount of the work is to be subcontracted, it may be necessary to provide information on the labor hours that will be incurred by the major subcontractors in order to permit the agency to analyze the realism of the costs for those tasks. See, for example, *BAE Sys. Norfolk Ship Repair, Inc.,* Comp. Gen. Dec. B-297879, 2006 CPD ¶ 75, where the agency properly disregarded subcontractor quotations that did not included estimated labor hours, *Robotic Sys. Tech.,* Comp. Gen. Dec. B-278195.2, 98-1 CPD ¶ 20, where the offeror was properly eliminated from the competitive range because it did not provide sufficient subcontractor information to permit a cost realism analysis, and *Litton Sys., Inc., Amecon Div.,* Comp. Gen. Dec. B-275807.2, 97-1 CPD ¶ 170, where upward adjustment to proposed subcontract costs was approved because they were logical based on the sparse information provided by the offeror.

If the offeror proposes fewer labor hours than are indicated by past experience, it should include an explanation in the proposal as to how the efficiencies are to be achieved. See *Hernandez Eng'g, Inc.,* Comp. Gen. Dec. B-286336, 2001 CPD ¶ 89 (unsubstantiated labor hour estimate lower than historical levels justified cost realism adjustment); *Scientific & Commercial Sys. Corp.,* Comp. Gen. Dec. B-283160, 99-2 CPD ¶ 78 (staffing level adjusted because agency knew past attempts to reduce staff had failed). When an offeror provides a reasonable explanation of the techniques that will be used to achieve efficiencies, an agency is entitled to rely on that explanation, *NHIC Corp.,* Comp. Gen. Dec. B-310801, 2008 CPD ¶ 67, even though it is based on a small amount of actual experience, *Palmetto GBA, LLC,* Comp. Gen. Dec. B-298962, 2007 CPD ¶ 25.

Offerors will also generally be required to provide information on the labor and indirect cost rates that they used to estimate the costs of performance. Agencies can be expected to obtain verification of the rates used from the cognizant government auditors and to adjust the rates during the cost realism analysis if they appear to be low in comparison to prior rates, *SGT, Inc.,* Comp. Gen. Dec. B-294722.4, 2005 CPD ¶ 151 (labor rates); *Radian, Inc.,* Comp. Gen. Dec. B-256313.2, 94-1 CPD ¶ 299 (labor rates); *Polaris, Inc.,* Comp. Gen. Dec. B-220066, 85-2 CPD ¶ 669 (indirect cost rates), or market rates, *Magellan Health Servs.,* Comp. Gen. Dec. B-298912, 2007 CPD ¶ 81 (labor rates): *Roy F. Weston, Inc.,* Comp. Gen. Dec. B-274945, 97-1 CPD ¶ 92 (labor rates). Thus, if the offeror uses rates lower than incurred rates in its cost estimates, it should include a very comprehensive explanation of the way that it will achieve the reduction. For cases where protests were denied because this explanation was regarded as adequate, see *Summit Research Corp.*, Comp. Gen. Dec. B-287523, 2001 CPD ¶ 176; *Booz-Allen & Hamilton, Inc.*, Comp. Gen. Dec. B-275934.2, 97-1 CPD ¶ 222; *Signal Corp.*, Comp. Gen. Dec. B-241849, 91-1 CPD ¶ 218, and *Purvis Sys., Inc.*, Comp. Gen. Dec. B-245761, 92-1 CPD ¶ 132.

Detailed explanations are also needed to support any other cost that may appear to be low for the level of work required. See, for example, *Centra Tech., Inc.*, Comp. Gen. Dec. B-274744, 97-1 CPD ¶ 35, where the GAO held that an agency had properly adjusted travel costs upward to match the costs incurred by the incumbent contractor where the offeror's proposal did not explain the low estimate of travel costs.

c. Certified Cost or Pricing Data

As discussed above, the submission of certified cost or pricing data should be called for in very few competitively negotiated procurements. If the RFP calls for such data and an offeror believes that adequate competition will be obtained, it should immediately ask the contracting officer to defer the requirement for certified cost or pricing data until after proposals have been submitted.

If the submission of certified cost or pricing data is required, offerors must exercise great care to ensure that they fully meet the stringent submission requirements. Detailed guidance on these requirements is set forth in Table 15-2 of FAR 15.408. Instruction 4 of Table 15-2 calls for the submission to be organized by contract line item as follows:

D. You must show the relationship between contract line item prices and the total contract price. You must attach cost-element breakdowns for each proposed line item, using the appropriate format prescribed in the "Formats for Submission of Line Item Summaries" section of this table. You must furnish supporting breakdowns for each cost element, consistent with your cost accounting system.

This guidance thus requires the submission of cost element breakdowns for each line with supporting data for each cost element breakdown. The guidance on the supporting data states:

C. As part of the specific information required, you must submit, with your proposal —

(1) Certified cost or pricing data (as defined at FAR 2.101). You must clearly identify on your cover sheet that certified cost or pricing data are included as part of the proposal.

(2) Information reasonably required to explain your estimating process, including —

(i) The judgmental factors applied and the mathematical or other methods used in the estimate, including those used in projecting from known data; and

(ii) The nature and amount of any contingencies included in the proposed price.

* * *

F. Whenever you have incurred costs for work performed before submission of a proposal, you must identify those costs in your cost/price proposal.

G. If you have reached an agreement with Government representatives on use of forward pricing rates/factors, identify the agreement, include a copy, and describe its nature.

Paragraph C calls for the submission of both factual data and judgmental data. However, there is a significant difference between these two types of data. There is no legal liability for the submission of inaccurate judgmental data. But 10 U.S.C. § 2306a(e) and 41 U.S.C. § 254b(e) require contracts to contain a price reduction clause for defective certified cost or pricing data and 10 U.S.C. § 2306a(f) and 41 U.S.C. § 254b(f) call for interest on overpayments because of defective data and double recovery in the event the offeror knowingly submitted defective data.

The factual data to be submitted are called "certified cost or pricing data" and will vary in amount depending on the element of cost being considered and the work being procured. The statutory requirement for the submission of this data is to ensure that both parties base their negotiations on the same data as to prior incurred costs and management decisions. The offeror's judgmental projections will also be the subject of analysis and negotiations; but it is likely that the government team will make independent projections of future costs, and much of the ultimate price negotiation will consist of a comparison and evaluation of these different projections.

The offeror's estimate is normally broken down into categories of cost, such as labor, material, and indirect costs, that are listed in the cost element breakdowns. In accordance with Cost Accounting Standard 401, 48 C.F.R. § 99.401, each contractor's estimating practices must be consistent with its cost accounting practices used in accumulating and reporting actual costs. Although each contractor has substantial freedom in establishing its cost accounting system, the costs accumulated must be directly related to the cost elements in estimates. Table 15-2 reflects this freedom by prescribing no specific cost breakdown by elements of cost. The following discussion addresses the requirement for the submission of certified cost or pricing data, the broad types of costs that are common to almost all systems, and the requirement that such data be certified at the conclusion of negotiations.

d. Definition of Cost or Pricing Data

The regulations contain a comprehensive definition of "cost or pricing data," emphasizing that such data are factual in nature but including some illustrations that are less than clear. See FAR 2.101, which states:

> Cost or pricing data (10 U.S.C. 2306a(h)(1) and 41 U.S.C. 254b) means all facts that, as of the date of price agreement, or, if applicable, an earlier date agreed upon between the parties that is as close as practicable to the date of agreement on price, prudent buyers and sellers would reasonably expect to affect price negotiations significantly. Cost or pricing data are factual, not judgmental; and are verifiable. While they do not indicate the accuracy of the prospective contractor's judgment about estimated future costs or projections, they do include the data forming the basis for that judgment. Cost or pricing data are more than historical accounting data; they are all the facts that can be reasonably expected to contribute to the soundness of estimates of future costs and to the validity of determinations of costs already incurred. They also include, but are not limited to, such factors as — (1) Vendor quotations; (2) Nonrecurring costs; (3) Information on changes in production methods and in production or purchasing volume; (4) Data supporting projections of business prospects and objectives and related operations costs; (5) Unit-cost trends such as those associated with labor efficiency; (6) Make-or-buy decisions; (7) Estimated resources to attain business goals; and (8) Information on management decisions that could have a significant bearing on costs.

The statutes contain a much shorter definition at 10 U.S.C. § 2306a(i) and 41 U.S.C. § 254b(i):

> [T]he term "cost or pricing data" means all facts that, as of the date of agreement on the price of a contract (or the price of a contract modification) or, if applicable consistent with subsection (e)(1)(B) [requiring the data to be as close to the data of agreement on price "as is practicable"], another date agreed upon between the parties, a prudent buyer or seller would reasonably expect to affect price negotiations significantly. Such term does not include information that is judgmental, but does include the factual information from which a judgment was derived.

It has been very difficult to arrive at a precise distinction between factual data and judgmental information. However, it is very clear that recorded costs are factual — with the result that they are cost or pricing data. Thus, the term includes labor rates paid in prior periods, *Boeing Co.*, ASBCA 32753, 90-1 BCA ¶ 22,270, *recons. denied*, 90-1 BCA ¶ 22,426; *Kaiser Aerospace & Elecs. Corp.*, ASBCA 32098, 90-1 BCA ¶ 22,489, *recons. denied*, 90-2 BCA ¶ 22,695; incurred labor hours, *Grumman Aerospace Corp.*, ASBCA 35188, 90-2 BCA ¶ 22,842; and incurred indirect costs, *Norris Indus., Inc.*, ASBCA 15442, 74-1 BCA ¶ 10,482. Information in the offeror's purchasing department relating to the prices of materials to be used to perform the contract is also factual in nature. Thus, the term includes purchase orders, *Grumman Aerospace Corp.*, ASBCA 35188, 90-2 BCA ¶ 22,842, and vendor quotations, *Cutler-Hammer, Inc. v. United States*, 189 Ct. Cl. 76, 416 F.2d 1306 (1969). Accounting adjustments to actual cost data are also cost or pricing data, *Hughes Aircraft Co.*, ASBCA 46321, 97-1 BCA ¶ 28,972.

Accounting information on the costs of prior work on different projects may also be cost or pricing data if the information is sufficiently relevant to be usable in the analysis of proposed costs. Thus, prices paid for "similar" items were held to be cost or pricing data, *Hardie-Tynes Mfg. Co.*, ASBCA 20717, 76-2 BCA ¶ 12,121.

In some cases a mixture of factual data and judgmental information has been held to be cost or pricing data. For example, in *Lambert Eng'g Co.*, ASBCA 13338, 69-1 BCA ¶ 7663, labor-hour estimates derived from actual information were held to be cost or pricing data even though they were technically not actual cost data. In *Aerojet-General Corp.*, ASBCA 12264, 69-1 BCA ¶ 7664, *modified*, 70-1 BCA ¶ 8140, the underlying factual data in an internal company report analyzing a sub-contractor's pricing proposal were held to be cost or pricing data. See also *Grumman Aerospace Corp.*, ASBCA 27476, 86-3 BCA ¶ 19,091, holding that an internal company report analyzing a subcontractor's proposal was cost or pricing data, *Texas Instruments, Inc.*, ASBCA 23678, 87-3 BCA ¶ 20,195, holding that a computer-generated report containing an estimate of the costs of future work that was derived from actual cost data but manipulated using complex estimating formulas was cost or pricing data, and *Black River Limited Partnership*, ASBCA 46790, 97-2 BCA ¶ 29,077, holding that computer models spreading the costs of performance of the contract, as well as the internal memoranda and reports explaining and justifying their validity, were cost or pricing data. All these cases seem to find that a document is cost or pricing data because it is the most readily available document and contains some factual data.

A contractor's management decisions are cost or pricing data if (1) they have a substantial relationship to a cost element and (2) they are made by an official with the authority to approve the action under consideration, *Lockheed Corp.*, ASBCA 36420, 95-2 BCA ¶ 27,722. In *Lockheed*, the board found that a decision to adopt a new strategy in collective bargaining negotiations met the first test because it would have a substantial effect on wage rates to be paid in the future. The board found, however, that this decision did not meet the second test because it had not been approved by se-nior corporate management as required by the policies of the company. In *Motorola, Inc.*, ASBCA 41528, 94-2 BCA ¶ 26,596, and *Motorola, Inc.*, ASBCA 48841, 96-2 BCA ¶ 28,465, a manufacturing policy memorandum directing that certain costs not be charged to government contracts was held to be cost or pricing data. In *Aerojet Ordnance Tenn.*, ASBCA 36089, 95-2 BCA ¶ 27,922, a management decision to proceed "with all possible haste" to close a waste containment pond was not cost or pricing data because the cost consequences of the decision could not be determined until the action was approved by the state of Tennessee. In contrast, *Millipore Corp.*, GSBCA 9453, 91-1 BCA ¶ 23,345, held that a decision to change the company's discount policy did constitute cost or pricing data. The board did not address the question of whether a decision to alter the discount policy had been made at a level of management with the authority to approve the decision. It would seem that to fall within the scope of this rule, the decision would have to impact the resources expected to be used to perform the work, such as a decision to change work methods or to buy from a different vendor. It is doubtful that a management decision to project costs differently would fall within this rule because such a decision is purely judgmental.

Factual data submitted by a subcontractor on a prior contract to support the prices of long-lead items were held to be cost or pricing data on a current contract because the items were transferred to the current contract, *General Dynamics Corp.*, ASBCA 39866, 94-1 BCA ¶ 26,339. Similarly, a cost analysis made by a subcontractor to test the validity of the price of a sub-subcontractor was cost or pricing data when it demonstrated that the subcontractor's quoted price, which had been submitted to the government, was too high, *McDonnell Aircraft Co.*, ASBCA 44504, 97-1 BCA ¶ 28,977.

Data containing only judgments are not cost or pricing data. In *Litton Sys., Inc.*, ASBCA 36509, 92-2 BCA ¶ 24,842, the board held that the estimated standard labor hours (ESLH) used by the contractor were not cost or pricing data even though there were internal reports listing these hours for parts manufactured by the contractor. The board found that the reports were not in themselves factual in nature because they contained no facts. The board distinguished these reports from documents containing mixed fact and judgment, stating at 123,944–45:

> The ESLH report is not mixed fact and judgment. In this appeal, we have no underlying document that is verifiable. The ESLH report is based on estimates made by [the contractor's] industrial engineers or test engineers and, as we have found above, no two industrial engineers or test engineers would estimate either the task or the frequency of the task the same. The ESLH report is therefore pure judgment and is, accordingly, not data and need not be disclosed.

Internal data showing how the contractor arrived at the estimated costs has been held to be cost or pricing data. For example, in *United Techs. Corp.*, ASBCA 51410, 04-1 BCA ¶ 32,556, *aff'd*, 463 F.3d 1261 (Fed. Cir. 2006), the board found defective data, stating at 161,025:

> At the time it was putting together its BAFO, appellant created documents entitled "Material Standards for FEC BAFO" (the Bible Sheet), and "Summary of ECP's." These documents showed the costs that flowed into appellant's BAFO price. Appellant did not disclose these documents to the AT as part of its cost or pricing data prior to award. Clearly, these documents related to the cost and pricing of the BAFO. We conclude that they were cost or pricing data under TINA and should have been timely disclosed to the government prior to award. These nondisclosed pieces of data provided the government with an understanding of the significance of appellant's data as it related to appellant's BAFO which became the contract price - and which understanding it did not have prior to award without the benefit of these documents. The cost or pricing data provided by ap-

pellant were not fully and meaningfully disclosed, were inaccurate and were defective under TINA.

See also *United States v. United Techs. Corp.*, No. 3:99-cv-093, 2008 WL 3007997 (S.D. Ohio 2008), *rev'd on other grounds*, 626 F.3d 313 (6th Cir. 2010), where the court found false statements, in some data supporting a BAFO, where the contractor made assertions as to how it had arrived at the BAFO price that were untrue. These statements were different than the undisclosed estimating material described above by the board and were directly pertinent to the estimating techniques that had been used by the contractor.

e. Insignificant Data

In a few cases contractors have escaped liability for nonsubmission of certified cost or pricing data by demonstrating that the data were not the type that prudent buyers and sellers would have believed to have a significant effect on the pricing. For example, in *Plessey Indus., Inc.*, ASBCA 16720, 74-1 BCA ¶ 10,603, a rejected vendor quotation was found not to be significant, and in *Boeing Co.*, ASBCA 20875, 85-3 BCA ¶ 18,351, incurred labor costs at the beginning of the contract were held to be the type of information that would not have been used by prudent buyers and sellers in the pricing process. The same logic would apply to old information in the nature of cost or pricing data. For example, contractors have labor rate and overhead rate information going back many years. Only the data relating to recent years are useful in estimating future costs. Reasonable buyers and sellers might disagree over how many years' information is significant, but all would agree that obsolete information would be of no use. The rule that all significant data must be disclosed has on occasion been interpreted very strictly. In *Sylvania Elec. Prods., Inc. v. United States*, 202 Ct. Cl. 16, 479 F.2d 1342 (1973), the Court of Claims held that if there is a "logical nexus between the nondisclosed pricing data and the possibility of a lower negotiated contract price, then the data is to be considered significant and subject to disclosure." Offerors should exercise care in deciding to use this logic to withhold data that the government may believe are necessary to evaluate the proposed costs.

f. Submission Techniques

A note in Table 15-2 provides that two techniques are acceptable for the submission of cost or pricing data: physical submission and specific identification:

Note 1: There is a clear distinction between submitting certified cost or pricing data and merely making available books, records, and other documents without identification. The requirement for submission of certified cost or pricing data is met when all accurate certified cost or pricing data reasonably available to the offeror have been submitted, either actually or by specific identification, to the Contracting Officer or an authorized representative. As later data comes into your possession, it should be submitted promptly to the Contracting Officer in a manner that clearly shows how the data relates to the offeror's proposal. The requirement for submission of certified cost or pricing data continues up to the time of agreement on price, or an earlier data agreed upon between the parties if applicable.

There is little guidance in the regulations or the litigated cases as to how specific identification of data is accomplished, but, at a minimum, the location of each element of the data should be stated. See *M-R-S Mfg. Co. v. United States*, 203 Ct. Cl. 551, 492 F.2d 835 (1974), requiring communication of the specific data that are relevant to the pricing action. Instruction 2 in Table 15-2 contains guidance on the preparation of an index of data that may meet part or all of this requirement:

> B. In submitting your proposal, you must include an index, appropriately referenced, of all the certified cost or pricing data and information accompanying or identified in the proposal. In addition, you must annotate any future additions and/ or revisions, up to the date of agreement on price, or an earlier date agreed upon by the parties, on a supplemental index.

While these specific identification requirements are somewhat cryptic, there is a clear rule that merely making the data available without specific identification is insufficient. Thus, giving complete access to all contractor data does not meet the submission requirement if the government employees are not made specifically aware of the significance of the data, *Hughes Aircraft Co.*, ASBCA 46321, 97-1 BCA ¶ 28,972 (making cost ledgers available for audit); *Aerojet-General Corp.*, ASBCA 12873, 69-1 BCA ¶ 7585 (submitting data to the government plant representative); *McDonnell Douglas Corp.*, ASBCA 12786, 69-2 BCA ¶ 7897 (making data available to government auditor and resident price analyst); *Grumman Aerospace Corp.*, ASBCA 35188, 90-2 BCA ¶ 22,842 (giving contractor complete access to subcontractor data but not identifying relevant data). However, if the government pricing personnel have actual knowledge of the data, the submission requirement is satisfied, *Texas Instruments, Inc.*, ASBCA 23678, 87-3 BCA ¶ 20,195 (data was delivered to the government auditor and analyzed by both the auditor and the price analyst); *Boeing Co.*, ASBCA 32753, 90-1 BCA ¶ 22,270, *recons. denied*, 90-1 BCA ¶ 22,426 (government price analyst had informed other government personnel of new rates); *Litton Sys., Inc.*, ASBCA 34435, 93-2 BCA ¶ 25,707 (contractor submitted monthly actuals of indirect costs to resident DCAA auditor); *Martin Marietta Corp.*, ASBCA 48223, 98-1 BCA ¶ 29,592 (submitting quarterly reports of actual G&A rates to cognizant auditor). In one case, *Motorola, Inc.*, ASBCA 41528, 94-2 BCA ¶ 26,596, the board inferred that current indirect cost data of a subcontractor had been submitted to a resident auditor because that auditor gave the contractor a recommendation for an overhead rate that was apparently based on knowledge of that data.

g. Explaining the Significance of the Data

In a number of cases, submission of certified cost or pricing data without an explanation of their significance has been held to be a failure to meet the statutory requirement. Thus, a contractor must make efforts to tell the government pricing personnel how the data are relevant to the cost estimate in instances when this is not readily apparent. This obligation occurs in two distinct situations: when the data are complex or unusual in nature and when they are submitted to update previously submitted data.

Complexity of the data is determined on a case-by-case basis. For example, in *Grumman Aerospace Corp.*, ASBCA 35188, 90-2 BCA ¶ 22,842, the subcontractor had not explained the significance of labor-hour data submitted to the contractor in computerized form. The board determined that the relevance of the data was not readily apparent to the contractor's pricing personnel and that the subcontractor had failed to meet the submission requirement when it did not explain the data. In contrast, in *Boeing Co.*, ASBCA 32753, 90-1 BCA ¶ 22,270, *recons. denied*, 90-1 BCA ¶ 22,426, the contractor was found to have met the submission requirement when it submitted raw data on labor rates without explanation. The board found that the government personnel were fully able to use the data in their raw form and, therefore, that no further explanation of the data was required. Similarly, in *Rosemount, Inc.*, ASBCA 37520, 95-2 BCA ¶ 27,770, the contractor was found to have met the submission requirement when it gave the government its incurred labor hours for the product being procured. The board rejected the argument that the contractor was required to plot the hours on a learning curve in order to meet the submission requirement, finding that the agency's negotiators could easily have plotted the data. These cases illustrate the basic proposition that the Truth in Negotiations Act does not require the offeror to perform routine analysis of cost or pricing data for the government.

This rule requiring explanation of the data will also apply if the data contain information that is unusual in nature. For example, in *Grumman*, the subcontractor submitted information on an interdivisional order but did not disclose that the price of the order included profit. The board ruled that this nondisclosure was a failure to meet the submission requirement because the subcontractor knew that the inclusion of profit in such orders was generally against government policy.

The rule is also applied in cases where the contractor updates prior data. For example, in *Singer Co. v. United States*, 217 Ct. Cl. 225, 576 F.2d 905 (1978), the court held that the contractor's mailing of monthly labor-hour reports to government field pricing personnel and auditors did not meet the submission requirement. The court was critical of the offeror's failure to identify the specific relationship of this information to the cost estimate. Similarly, cost or pricing data submitted in connection with other procurements do not meet the submission requirement on a contract to which the data have not been related, *Sylvania Elec. Prods., Inc. v. United States*, 202 Ct. Cl. 16, 479 F.2d 1342 (1973).

h. Currency of the Data

Until 1995 the certificate required to be executed by the offeror before award of the contract stated that the date of currency of the data was to be the date when price negotiations were concluded. See *Arral Indus., Inc.*, ASBCA 41493, 96-1 BCA ¶ 28,030, where the board found that the date when price negotiations were concluded was best determined by the date on the certificate. This made the data used in the negotiation defective because they had not been updated.

To preclude this result offerors performed "sweeps," making a total review of their cost or pricing data after the conclusion of price negotiations and submitting all new data to the contracting officer. This delayed the award of the contract and led to difficult decisions as to what the Government should do with the new data.

In 1995 the FAR was revised to permit the parties to agree on variable dates of currency. See FAR 15.403-4(b)(2) and Note 1 to Table 15-2. The Certificate of Current Cost or Pricing Data, in FAR 15.406-2(a), was also revised to contain the following instruction on the date of currency of the data:

> ** Insert the day, month, and year when price negotiations were concluded and price agreement was reached or, if applicable, an earlier date agreed upon between the parties that is as close as practicable to the date of agreement on price.

In addition, FAR 15.406-2(c) contains the following guidance:

> The contracting officer and contractor are encouraged to reach a prior agreement on criteria for establishing closing or cutoff dates when appropriate in order to minimize delays associated with proposal updates. Closing or cutoff dates should be included as part of the data submitted with the proposal and, before agreement on price, data should be updated by the contractor to the latest closing or cutoff dates for which the data are available. Use of cutoff dates coinciding with reports is acceptable, as certain data may not be reasonably available before normal periodic closing dates (e.g., actual indirect costs). Data within the contractor's or a subcontractor's organization on matters significant to contractor management and to the Government will be treated as reasonably available. What is significant depends upon the circumstances of each acquisition.

This new policy reflects the fact that in order to be in compliance with the currency requirement, the offeror must continually update the data until the price is agreed upon, and this requirement may not be waived by a government employee, *Singer Co. v. United States*, 217 Ct. Cl. 225, 576 F.2d 905 (1978). If there is insufficient time to compile the data in a usable form, the requirement can arguably be met by submitting raw data as they exist in the contractor's records, *Conrac Corp. v. United States*, 214 Ct. Cl. 561, 558 F.2d 994 (1977); *Lambert Eng'g Co.*, ASBCA 13338, 69-1 BCA ¶ 7663.

The best way to ensure that the currency requirement is met is for the contracting officer and the offeror to agree on the closing dates for various types of data at the conclusion of the negotiation and to attach this agreement to the certificate. In most cases these closing dates correspond to the labor rate and indirect cost rate information already furnished to the government. The offeror then conducts a sweep to check for any material cost or labor-hour information that has been accumulated during the negotiation. Such information would be furnished to the contracting officer with the signed certificate. By following this procedure, the offeror fully complies with the currency requirement of the Truth in Negotiations Act.

In the absence of an agreement on cutoff dates, there is a significant question as to whether an offeror is permitted any lag time for the transmission of cost or pricing data within the corporate structure. In *Sylvania Elec. Prods., Inc. v. United States*, 202 Ct. Cl. 16, 479 F.2d 1342 (1973), the Court of Claims established a strict rule that the data must be current as of the time of the price negotiation. The court held that data received by the contractor's purchasing government. This decision raises the question as to whether any period of time is permitted for processing the information through a company. The original board decisions allowed such a time lag, *American Bosch Arma Corp.*, ASBCA 10305, 65-2 BCA ¶ 5280, and one later case permitted a substantial time lag (as much as six months) in a situation where the contracting officer concurred in the nonsubmission of current data, *LTV Electrosystems, Inc.*, ASBCA 16802, 73-1 BCA ¶ 9957, *recons. denied*, 74-1 BCA ¶ 10,380. However, it is clear from the language in *Sylvania* that the court will not tolerate a time lag of any significant length. See, however, *Boeing Co.*, ASBCA 20875, 85-3 BCA ¶ 18,351, where the board permitted a three-week lag in the preparation of labor-cost data because this was the period required by the contractor's accounting system. In *Aerojet Ordnance Tenn.*, ASBCA 36089, 95-2 BCA ¶ 27,922, labor-hour information through February 28 was required to be submitted for a negotiation completed on the following March 2.

C. Signature of the Proposal

Paragraph (c) of the Instructions to Offerors — Competitive Acquisition solicitation provision in FAR 52.215-1 contains guidance making signature of the proposal mandatory:

(2) The first page of the proposal must show —

* * *

(v) Name, title, and signature of person authorized to sign the proposal. Proposals signed by an agent shall be accompanied by evidence of that agent's authority, unless that evidence has been previously furnished to the issuing office.

The GAO has held that a proposal must be rejected if it does not contain a signature, and the RFP contemplates award on the basis of initial proposals, *SWR, Inc.*, Comp. Gen. Dec. B-278415, 97-2 CPD ¶ 166; *Valencia Tech. Servs., Inc.*, Comp. Gen. Dec. B-223288, 86-2 CPD ¶ 40. In these cases the GAO relied on cases dealing with unsigned sealed bids and found that it would be unfair to other offerors if a contracting officer permitted an offeror to sign its offer after the time proposals were opened. The GAO also rejected the argument that lack of a signature was a minor informality. In effect, this is an application of the responsiveness requirement to competitive proposals even though this rule is generally not applicable in negotiated procurement. Neither decision contains any recognition of the significant differences between sealed bidding and competitive negotiation. It would appear that unsigned offers could be considered if the RFP included Alternate I to the Instructions to Offerors — Competitive Acquisition provision in FAR 52.215-1, precluding the agency from making an award on the basis of the initial proposals.

FAR 4.502(d) permits the use of electronic signatures when a proposal is to be submitted electronically. In *Tishman Constr. Corp.*, Comp. Gen. Dec. B-292097, 2003 CPD ¶ 94, the agency was required to honor a timely signed electronic proposal even though the required paper proposal was not submitted on time. The GAO concluded that the late submission of the paper proposal was a "minor, immaterial deviation from the solicitation requirements."

The GAO has also followed sealed bidding cases when competitive proposals are signed by agents. Thus, evidence of an agent's authority may be submitted after opening of proposals, but proof that an offeror submitting a proposal in its own name was acting as an agent may not be submitted after opening. See *Hay-Holland Co.*, Comp. Gen. Dec. B-233002, 89-1 CPD ¶ 102, where the agency properly rejected an offer that was signed and subscribed by an agent without mention of the agent-principal relationship. The GAO rejected the protester's contention that the incorrect signature was a clerical error that should have been corrected through discussions. In *WorldWide Parts, Inc.*, Comp. Gen. Dec. B-244793, 91-2 CPD ¶ 156, the GAO held that an agent who submits a proposal listing itself as the offeror may not submit evidence after the closing date for receipt of proposals to show the agent-principal relationship because to do so would constitute an improper transfer of a proposal. See also *American Mat'l Handling, Inc.*, Comp. Gen. Dec. B-253818, 93-2 CPD ¶ 246 (award to an entity other than that named in original offer is improper).

A proposal that is properly signed by one offeror may be transferred or assigned to another firm only if such a transfer is affected by operation of law, which is interpreted to include a merger, a corporate reorganization, a sale of an entire business or that portion of a business embraced by a proposal, or other means not barred by anti-assignment statutes, *Numax Elecs., Inc.*, 54 Comp. Gen. 580 (B-181670), 75-1 CPD ¶ 21.

D. Format and Style of the Proposal

The format and style of a submission are intangible considerations in winning competitions. A good submission is organized and written so that it can be read by government evaluators of many different functional and technical disciplines such as management, contracting, engineering, legal, accounting, and others. Features the offeror will want to consider in developing its proposal include the following:

- Inclusion of an executive summary to highlight the salient aspects. A good summary may be read by the source selection official and other agency officials too busy to read the entire document.
- An index that cross-references the statement of work to the information and the offer. This can be valuable in showing the Government exactly how the offer matches the evaluation factors expressed in the RFP.
- The organization of the submission should indicate that the offeror is orderly, thorough, and effective. It should be made easy to break out into component parts for evaluation by technical, business, and pricing personnel.

The way in which a submission is presented can have a significant effect on its evaluation. See *Professional Software Eng'g, Inc.*, Comp. Gen. Dec. B-272820, 96-2 CPD ¶ 193 (proposal downgraded for typographical errors); *Engineering & Envtl., Inc.*, Comp. Gen. Dec. B-271868.3, 96-2 CPD ¶ 182 ("many typographical errors and misspelling" and "inattention to detail"); *Triple P Servs., Inc.*, Comp. Gen. Dec. B-271777, 96-2 CPD ¶ 39 (proposal downgraded for typographical errors and inappropriate language that had been taken from other proposals); *SC&A, Inc.*, Comp. Gen. Dec. B-270160.2, 96-1 CPD ¶ 197 (proposal downgraded because it was disorganized and superficial); and *Pannesma Co.*, Comp. Gen. Dec. B-251688, 93-1 CPD ¶ 333 ("sloppy proposal" reflecting a "casual approach").

1. Completeness and Coherence

It is the offeror's responsibility to ensure its submission is, in all respects, a complete document, *Westvold & Assocs.*, Comp. Gen. Dec. B-201032, 81-1 CPD ¶ 354. It should also be a coherent document — both within each section and among sections. One of the most common failings is the inclusion of conflicting data and information in the technical, management, and cost sections. See, for example, *Earle Palmer Brown Cos.*, 70 Comp. Gen. 667 (B-243544) 91-2 CPD ¶ 134, where the agency properly adjusted the contractor's price upward upon determining that the contractor could not pay the salary of required personnel for the cost offered in its proposal; and *AmerInd, Inc.*, Comp. Gen. Dec. B-248324, 92-2 CPD ¶ 85, where the agency properly determined that the costs offered by the protester bore no relation to the cost of personnel for whom the protester submitted resumes.

Whenever data can be summarized in graphic form, it is wise to include such charts and graphs. They are particularly important when page limitations make it necessary to present information in the most concise form. However, such charts and graphs should be simple and direct. Although the FAR Part 15 rewrite eliminated the Unnecessarily Elaborate Proposals or Quotations solicitation provision, it is still sound advise not to submit unnecessarily elaborate brochures or other presentations beyond those sufficient to present a complete and effective response to a solicitation. In *Professional Data Servs., Inc.*, Comp. Gen. Dec. B-220002, 33 Cont. Cas. Fed. (CCH) ¶ 74,331, *Unpub.*, Dec. 13, 1985, the agency rejected the protester's offer because it was overly elaborate and the GAO upheld that decision, stating:

> [O]ne reason that [the protester] did not receive higher scores for Technical Understanding and Approach was because [the protester] submitted an unnecessarily elaborate proposal that in part was confusing regarding what was being offered. An offeror has the burden of submitting an adequately written proposal permitting the agency to make an intelligent evaluation, and failure to do so justifies lowering the proposal's score.

Conversely, when a proposal has been rejected because it lacks detail or specifics, the GAO has routinely rejected the argument that the proposal could not be more detailed without violating the unnecessarily elaborate proposal prohibition. In *TLC Sys.*, Comp. Gen. Dec. B-243220, 91-2 CPD ¶ 37, the GAO stated that none of the unnecessarily elaborate provisions "can be read to obviate the clearly expressed requirements to submit specified information with the proposal." See also *Global Valuation Serv.*, Comp. Gen. Dec. B-230753, 88-1 CPD ¶ 604, rejecting the protester's assertion that its "rather limited proposal" was justified by the RFP's caution against submitting overly elaborate proposals. Thus, offerors must strike a balance between clear and coherent explanation of their proposed method of performance and unduly elaborate detailing.

Paragraph (c)(iv) of the Instructions to Offerors — Competitive Acquisition solicitation provision in FAR 52.215-1 contains a further formal requirement — that offerors must provide the names, titles, and telephone and facsimile numbers of persons authorized to negotiate on the offeror's behalf. While there is no indication that a proposal can be rejected for failure to comply with this requirement, the information should be furnished as a matter of course in each proposal.

2. Cover Letters

It is not good practice to include a cover letter with a proposal because any statements in the cover letter may be found to have conditioned the offer being made by the offeror. In this regard, the GAO has followed the sealed bidding rule making conditioned bids nonresponsive. See, for example, *New Dimension Masonry, Inc.*, Comp. Gen. Dec. B-258876, 95-1 CPD ¶ 102. Thus, a contracting officer was found entitled to reject a proposal where a cover letter stating that its product was a "fit, form and function replacement" of the product described in the RFP, *Potomac Elec. Corp.*, Comp. Gen. Dec. B-311060, 2006 CPD ¶ 63. The GAO concluded that the contracting officer had properly concluded that this statement could indicate that the product did not meet all of the salient characteristics that were included in the RFP. A similar result was reached in *INDUS Tech., Inc.*, Comp. Gen. Dec. B-297800.13, 2007 CPD ¶ 116, where cover letters accompanying the proposals provided for an acceptance period of 180 days, and the solicitation required a minimum acceptance period of 350 days and specifically stated that proposals providing less than the minimum acceptance period would be rejected.

3. Page Limitations

Another formal requirement in many solicitations is a page limitation for some or all of the sections of the proposal. Page limitations are strictly enforced, *Client Network Servs., Inc.*, Comp. Gen. Dec. B-297994, 2006 CPD ¶ 79 (agency properly downgraded proposal that did not follow formatting requirements in RFP); *Electronic Design, Inc.*, Comp. Gen. Dec. B-279662.2, 98-2 CPD ¶ 69 (agency improperly permitted offeror to include material greatly exceeding page limitations in BAFO without informing other offerors); *Management & Indus. Tech Assocs.*, Comp. Gen. Dec. B-257656, 94-2 CPD ¶ 134 (agency properly rejected pages in excess of limitation); *U.S. Envtl. & Indus., Inc.*, Comp. Gen. Dec. B-257349, 94-2 CPD ¶ 51 (smaller typeface created excess pages and improper competitive advantage); *All Star Maint., Inc.*, Comp. Gen. Dec. B-244143, 91-2 CPD ¶ 294 (single spacing, instead of double spacing created excess pages and improper competitive advantage). However, the GAO has ruled that it is proper to exclude the cover sheet and table of contents from the page limitation when the RFP is silent on this issue, *Trident Sys., Inc.*, Comp. Gen. Dec. B-243101, 91-1 CPD ¶ 604. Compare *Centech Group, Inc.*, Comp. Gen. Dec. B-278904.4, 98-1 CPD ¶ 149, holding that it was proper to include coversheets, dividers and table of contents pages in the page count because that was required by the RFP.

The GAO has also ruled that it is not proper to evaluate a long appendix to a proposal that exceeded the page limitation in the RFP, *ITT Electron Tech. Div.*, Comp. Gen. Dec. B-242289, 91-1 CPD ¶ 383. The General Services Board held that it was proper to exclude a Contract Start-Up Handbook and a Task Leader Handbook from the page limitation on technical proposals, *TRW, Inc.*, GSBCA 11309-P, 92-1 BCA ¶ 24,389. The board stated that this exclusion was reasonable because the handbooks were not used in scoring the proposal — although they were used to "ameliorate . . . concerns about [the offeror's] ability to effect a smooth transition in the event [the offeror] was awarded the contract." In *Macfadden & Assocs., Inc.*, Comp. Gen. Dec. B-275502, 97-1 CPD ¶ 88, the GAO reasoned that whether an agency can automatically reject an entire proposal that exceeds a page limit rather than evaluate only the proposal pages within the limit depends on the language of the solicitation, stating:

If the solicitation provides that a proposal exceeding a specified page limit will be rejected and an offeror, without protesting that provision, chooses to compete in accordance with the RFP's terms but nevertheless submits a proposal that exceeds the limit, rejection of the proposal, at least in general, would seem to be unobjectionable. Where, however, the solicitation states that a proposal exceeding a page limit may be excluded from consideration, we think offerors are reasonably put on notice that rejection for exceeding the page limit will not be automatic but instead will occur only if there is a reasonable basis for such action.

In *HSQ Tech.*, Comp. Gen. Dec. B-277048, 97-2 CPD ¶ 57, the RFP stated that noncompliance with the stated page limitation "could result in elimination of the offer from the proposal process." The GAO followed the logic in *Macfadden* stating that "could" meant that such a proposal could not automatically be rejected but, rather, may properly be rejected only if there was a reasonable basis for the rejection. The GAO found that the agency reasonably concluded that the proposal without the excess pages was unacceptable because it lacked material sections of the technical proposal and the entire price proposal.

4. *Proprietary Information*

FAR 15.207(b) provides that proposals must be "safeguarded from unauthorized disclosure throughout the source selection process." This provision merely instructs the contracting officer on the protections that are required to be used in handling the data. Offerors are permitted to place proprietary markings on their proposals to ensure that such protection is given. Paragraph (e) in the Instructions to Offerors — Competitive Acquisition provision in FAR 52.215-1 implements this regulation:

> Offerors that include in their proposals data that they do not want disclosed to the public for any purpose, or used by the Government except for evaluation purposes, shall —
>
> (1) Mark the title page with the following legend:
>
>> This includes data that shall not be disclosed outside the Government and shall not be duplicated, used, or disclosed — in whole or in part — for any purpose other than to evaluate this proposal. If, however, a contract is awarded to this offeror as a result of — or in connection with — the submission of this data, the Government shall have the right to duplicate, use, or disclose the data to the extent provided in the resulting contract. This restriction does not limit the Government's right to use information contained in this data if it is obtained from another source without restriction. The data subject to this restriction are contained in sheets [insert numbers or other identification of sheets]; and
>
> (2) Mark each sheet of data it wishes to restrict with the following legend:

> Use or disclosure of data contained on this sheet is subject to the restriction on the title page of this proposal.

This provision permits offerors to mark all data in the proposal — whether technical, management, or financial data — with the prescribed legend and requires government agencies to protect such data during the source selection process, and thereafter for the losing offerors. However, if the contract is awarded, this provision states that the government's obligation to protect the data of the winning offeror ceases, and thereafter, the government's right to disclose the information is governed by the clauses of the contract. With regard to properly marked technical data submitted to civilian agencies, protection would be granted by the Rights in Data — General clause in FAR 52.227-14 when it is included in the resulting contract. If this clause is not included in the contract, there may well be no government promise to protect proprietary technical data. Even if the clause is included in the contract, it contains no government promise to protect management and financial data. Thus, offerors dealing with civilian agencies desiring to protect such data should request that a clause be included in the contract for that purpose. With regard to proposal data submitted to the Department of Defense, 10 U.S.C. § 2305(g) prohibits disclosure of this data unless it is incorporated into the contract by reference. This statute would appear to override the language in the solicitation provision stating that there is no protection for the winning contractor after award of the contract. To the extent that the data was incorporated into the contract, the only protection would be that granted to properly marked technical data under the Rights in Technical Data — Noncommercial Items clause in DFARS 252.227-7013 when it is included in contracts of the Department of Defense.

FAR 15.609 provides instructions on the protection of data in unsolicited proposals. Paragraph (a) contains a legend that must be placed on the title page of the proposal and ¶ (b) requires that each page of the proposal containing proprietary information must contain a short legend specified therein. However, if the submitter does not place a legend on the proposal, ¶ (d) requires the "agency point of contact" to place a cover sheet on the proposal cautioning government personnel that they should not disclose the information to unauthorized persons. Furthermore, FAR 15.608(a) prohibits use of any data in the unsolicited proposal as the basis for a solicitation or negotiations with another firm. Paragraph (e) provides that the notice on the cover sheet is not to be used to justify withholding the information if there is a Freedom of Information Act request for it. In that case, the agency must independently determine if it meets one of the exceptions of the Act. Submitters of unsolicited proposals should carefully mark their unsolicited proposals as required by this regulation because they cannot rely on the guidance to agency personnel to protect and not use unmarked information. See *Xerxe Group, Inc. v. United States*, 278 F.3d 1357 (Fed. Cir. 2002), ruling that an agency had properly disclosed information on unmarked pages of the proposal even though the proper legend had been placed on the title page of the proposal. Compare *Wesleyan Co. v. United States*, 454 F.3d 1375 (Fed. Cir. 2006), holding that the submitter of an unsolicited proposal might have proprietary rights when it sold prototypes "for evaluative or demonstrative purposes" with tags that contained proprietary markings.

E. Acknowledging Receipt of Amendments

Offerors are required to acknowledge the receipt of amendments to the solicitation either upon receipt or on the cover sheet of the proposal. Paragraph (b) of the Instructions to Offerors — Competitive Acquisition solicitation provision in FAR 52.215-1 provides:

> If this solicitation is amended, all terms and conditions that are not amended remain unchanged. Offerors shall acknowledge receipt of any amendment to this solicitation by the date and time specified in the amendment(s).

If a contracting officer posts a set of questions and answers to a solicitation on its website but does not designate them as an amendment, they will be treated as an amendment because they have a significant impact on the terms of the procurement, *Linguistic Sys., Inc.*, Comp. Gen. Dec. B-296221, 2005 CPD ¶ 104.

The failure to acknowledge receipt of a material amendment precludes award to that offeror on the basis of the initial proposal, *Nomura Enter., Inc.*, Comp. Gen. Dec. B-277768, 97-2 CPD ¶ 148. Agencies are also permitted to reject an offer where a material amendment has not been acknowledged, *ECI Defense Group*, Comp. Gen. Dec. B-400177, 2008 CPD ¶ 141; *Skyline ULTD, Inc.*, Comp. Gen. Dec. B-297800.3, 2006 CPD ¶ 128; *Integrated Bus. Solutions, Inc.* Comp. Gen. Dec. B-292239, 2003 CPD ¶ 122. However, a contracting officer may establish a competitive range and permit the offeror to acknowledge the amendment in negotiations, *Grove Resource Solutions, Inc.*, Comp. Gen. Dec. B-296228, 2005 CPD ¶ 133; *International Filter Mfg. Corp.*, Comp. Gen. Dec. B-235049, 89-1 CPD ¶ 586; *Galaxy Aircraft Instruments Co.*, Comp. Gen. Dec. B-194356, 80-1 CPD ¶ 364. The choice of which alternative to follow will depend on the degree of competition and the value of the offer in relation to the other offers. The failure to acknowledge an amendment does not preclude award, however, where the amendment is reflected in the terms of the offer, *Language Servs. Assocs., Inc.*, Comp. Gen. Dec. B-297392, 2006 CPD ¶ 20 (quotation); *Pitney Bowes, Inc.*, Comp. Gen. Dec. B-294868, 2005 CPD ¶ 10 (quotation); where "the offeror is otherwise obligated to perform in accordance with the terms of the solicitation," *E. Frye Enters., Inc.*, Comp. Gen. Dec. B-258699.2, 95-1 CPD ¶ 64; or where the amendment does not contain material provisions, *International Data Sys., Inc.*, Comp. Gen. Dec. B-277385, 97-2 CPD ¶ 96 (failure to acknowledge amendment waived as minor informality).

The mere fact that an offeror does not receive an amendment is no excuse for failure to acknowledge the amendment where full and open competition and reasonable prices are obtained and the agency did not deliberately exclude the offeror from competition, *CDA, Inc.*, Comp. Gen. Dec. B-224971, 87-1 CPD ¶ 163, and *O.J. Best Servs., Inc.*, Comp. Gen. Dec. B-276954, 97-1 CPD ¶ 231 (of 21 offers received, 19 acknowledged receipt of the amendments).

V. ORAL PRESENTATIONS

As discussed in Chapter 2, it has become common practice for agencies to obtain some of the information to be used in the evaluation process through oral presentations. In most cases such presentations will be focused on the capability of the offeror to perform the contract, and the material presented will be used to assess the offeror's understanding of the work. However, because oral presentations can be used for other purposes as well, offerors should carefully read the RFP to determine the scope of the oral presentation. If the RFP is not clear as to the content and format of the oral presentation, the offeror should contact the contracting officer to obtain more information on the requirements of the agency.

A. Content of the Presentation

The offeror should use the oral presentation to demonstrate that it is fully capable of performing the critical tasks on the proposed contract. This is usually best done by discussing these tasks and identifying key problems that are anticipated and proposed methods of dealing with those problems. Lengthy discussion of the general capabilities of the offeror is generally not as effective as specific identification of the capability to perform key tasks. See *Client Network Servs., Inc.*, Comp. Gen. Dec. B-297994, 2006 CPD ¶ 79, where an offeror was downgraded because it covered general capability in the oral presentation rather than addressing the issues involved in the procurement for which it was competing.

Offerors should ensure that the key personnel that they propose to use will be available to attend the oral presentation. See *Sandi Group, Inc.*, Comp. Gen. Dec. B-401218, 2009 CPD ¶ 123, holding that the protester was properly denied the opportunity to make an oral presentation (or to compete for the work) when its project manager left the company after the proposal had been submitted and the agency refused to permit substitution of another person because that would constitute a late proposal revision.

Offerors should exercise care in the assertions that they make in their oral presentations. See *Johnson Controls Security Sys.*, Comp. Gen. Dec. B-296490, 2007 CPD ¶102, where an offeror was faced with potential disqualification because it misrepresented in its oral presentation that it was taking required actions to qualify its personnel. Compare *EBA Eng'g, Inc.*, Comp. Gen. Dec. B-275818, 97-1 CPD ¶ 127, where the protester argued that the winning offeror had been guilty of misrepresentation by stating that it would hire all necessary incumbent employees to perform the service contract that was the subject of the competition, but the GAO held that this was not a defect in the procurement because the offeror had inserted a statement in its BAFO correcting this overly broad statement.

B. Format of the Presentation

The RFP should identify the process that the agency will require offerors to follow in making the oral presentation. See FAR 15.102(d). If this is not clear, an offeror should immediately request more explicit guidance from the contracting officer.

1. Offeror's Team

The offeror's team should be composed of key personnel who will perform or personally direct the work if awarded the contract, such as project managers, task leaders, and other in-house staff. If a significant amount of the work will be subcontracted, members of the subcontractor staff should make the relevant presentation. The offeror's team must demonstrate that it has the expertise to satisfy the requirement. Compare *ARTEL, Inc.*, Comp. Gen. Dec. B-248478, 92-2 CPD ¶ 120, where the agency concluded from an oral presentation that there were serious doubts as to the quality and availability of the offeror's key personnel, and *Planning & Dev. Collaborative Int'l*, Comp. Gen. Dec. B-299041, 2007 CPD ¶ 28, where an offeror was downgraded because its team did not work well together during an oral presentation, with *Savannah River Alliance, LLC*, Comp. Gen. Dec. B-311126, 2008 CPD ¶ 88, where the agency selected a contractor based, to large measure, on the fact that its team functioned very well in solving problems during the oral presentation,. It can be seen that one of the most important aspects of an oral presentation is the ability of the offeror's participants to function well as a team. As another example, in *Labat-Anderson, Inc.*, 71 Comp. Gen. 252 (B-246071), 92-1 CPD ¶ 193, the oral presentation resulted in a determination that the offeror lacked capability. The GAO stated:

> The TEC [technical evaluation committee] stated that although the protester submitted a "strong original proposal," the TEC's review of the BAFO (including the oral presentation/interviews and written proposal) submitted by "Labat-Anderson — particularly the interview and discussion sessions — raised serious questions regarding their understanding of the overall project concept and their ability to field a cohesive implementation team." Specifically, the TEC found that at the oral presentation and interviews "the individual Labat-Anderson team members displayed a lack of consensus and at times even confusion regarding BICSN's primary purpose." The TEC found that "the firm's disappointing performance during the oral presentations and interviews was a surprise" and believed that the "poor quality" of Labat-Anderson's oral presentation resulted from an apparent lack of dialogue between the protester's South African candidates and its American team members prior to the oral presentation.

The offeror's team should carefully read the RFP to ensure that it understands the ground rules for the oral presentation and contact the agency if there is anything that it does not understand. For instance, if the agency is planning to use a pop quiz during the presentation, the offeror should know in advance whether it will be permitted to caucus with other members of its team or contact an outside source by cell phone before answering.

2. Material to be Used

The offeror's team may use visual aids such as slides, flip charts, and multimedia computer screen shows to enhance its oral presentation. The oral presentation should not replicate information already requested in the written proposal. Visual aids should not be overly detailed or too technical. See the Army Materiel Command guidance in *Contracting for Best Value: A Best Practices Guide to Source Selection*, AMC-P 715-3 (Jan. 1, 1998), which states:

> Presenters should not include overly detailed, technical information on slides. Attempting to put a written technical proposal on presentation slides makes it difficult for evaluators to read and follow.

Visual aids may be required to be submitted before the actual presentation. See *RGII Techs., Inc.*, Comp. Gen. Dec. B-278352.2, 98-1 CPD ¶ 130, where the RFP stated:

> In order to ensure the integrity of the source selection process, the offeror must use the overhead slides submitted to the Government with its offer when making its Oral Presentation, without any alteration. The technical evaluation team may review the copies of the slides prior to the presentation. The offeror may submit no other written documentation for its Oral Presentation. When evaluating the offeror's Oral Presentation, the Government will consider only those overhead slides that were actually projected and addressed by the offeror during its presentation.

It has been common practice for agencies to require the submission of slides to be used in the oral presentation at the time the original proposal is submitted. This requirement has been strictly enforced, *KSEND v. United States*, 69 Fed. Cl. 103 (2005) (proposal properly rejected when transparencies were not submitted with offer). See also *Innovative Mgmt., Inc.*, Comp. Gen. Dec. B-291375, 2003 CPD ¶ 11, finding no basis for a protest when the agency lost the transparencies with the result that the protester had to use copies during the presentation.

If materials are incorrect, a proposal may be downgraded. In *Modern Techs. Corp.*, Comp. Gen. Dec. B-278695, 98-1 CPD ¶ 81, the protester argued that its oral presentation charts erroneously stated that the team leader would be selected upon award of the task order. The Air Force evaluators preferred that an offeror's team leader be identified prior to the issuance of an order and assessed a weakness against the proposal. The protester asserted, and the agency confirmed, that the protester's presenter orally stated that the word "select" should be "confirm" when showing chart 87. The GAO failed to see how the agency's conclusion that the proposal was unclear about when a team leader would be selected was unreasonable, stating that the chart itself and both words "select" and "confirm" leave room for a reasonable conclusion that the agency could award an order and then learn the identity of the awardee's team leader.

3. Time Limitations

The solicitation will generally state a firm time limit for each presentation. There is no ideal length allowed for a presentation; the length will depend on the complexity of the acquisition, as well as the agency's past experience or lessons learned in previously conducted oral presentations. See *Information Sys. Tech. Corp.*, Comp. Gen. Dec. B-280013.2, 98-2 CPD ¶ 36 (two hours permitted for oral presentation).

The AMC guidance states:

> It is not advisable to limit the time for individual topics or sections within the presentation. As with the proposal itself, this detail is the responsibility of the presenter.

Thus, the offeror team should monitor its time carefully to ensure that all of the designated tasks be addressed during the oral presentation. See *T Square Logistics Servs. Corp.*, Comp. Gen. Dec. B-291851, 2003 CPD ¶ 160, requiring the downgrading of an oral presentation that did not address some of the specified subelements of the work

4. Exchanges with Government Team

The present regulations make it clear that agency officials may ask questions and seek further detail. This is consistent with prior decisions, *NAHB Research Found., Inc.*, Comp. Gen. Dec. B-219344, 85-2 CPD ¶ 248 (aggressive questioning permissible). Offerors have been properly downgraded because they did not give convincing responses to questions during an oral presentation. See *Zolon Tech, Inc.*, Comp. Gen. Dec. B-299904.2, 2007 CPD ¶ 183 (no member of offeror's team could answer a question about a critical aspect of the proposed work); *Advanced Tech. Sys., Inc.*, Comp. Gen. Dec. B-296493.5, 2006 CPD ¶ 147, (team responded that it had not yet decided on what management tool to use). See also *Systems Research & Applications Corp.*, Comp. Gen. Dec. B-299818, 2008 CPD ¶ 28, where a protest was granted, in part, because the agency failed to ask the protester to explain a term used in the oral presentation and then downgraded the protester because it did not understand the term.

Agencies may also adopt reasonable rules governing the nature of the presentations, including limitations on the length and nature of the presentations, *American Sys. Corp.*, 68 Comp. Gen. 475 (B-234449), 89-1 CPD ¶ 537. They may also require that offerors meet mandatory requirements in an RFP before being eligible to make an oral presentation, *Inte-Great Corp.*, Comp. Gen. Dec. B-272780, 96-2 CPD ¶ 159.

Agencies may either preclude or permit discussions during the oral presentation, FAR 15.102(d)(6). However, if discussions occur, the agency must comply with the rules governing negotiations with all offerors in the competitive range, FAR 15.102(g). See *Global Analytic Info. Tech. Servs., Inc.*, Comp. Gen. Dec. B-298840.2, 2007 CPD ¶ 57, holding that a discussion had occurred when an agency asked for more detailed pricing information during the oral presentation and the offeror subsequently submitted the information using revised pricing logic. See also *General Physics Federal Sys., Inc.*, Comp. Gen. Dec. B-275934, 97-1 CPD ¶ 171, where no ruling on this issue was made because there was no prejudice to the protester when the agency sought information on the commitment of proposed key personnel from all of the offerors during the oral presentations. Most protests on this issue have found that no discussions occurred during the oral presentation, *Sierra Military Health Servs., Inc.*, Comp. Gen. Dec. B-292780, 2004 CPD ¶ 55 (probing staffing information in original presentation not discussion); *Development Alternatives, Inc.*, Comp. Gen. Dec. B-279920, 98-2 CPD ¶ 54 (question and answer session not discussions). In the former decision, the GAO stated the rule as follows:

> The FAR generally anticipates "dialogue among the parties" in the course of an oral presentation, FAR § 15.102(a), and we see nothing improper in agency personnel expressing their view about vendors' quotations or proposals, in addition to listening to the vendors' presentations, during those sessions. Once the agency personnel begin speaking, rather than merely listening, in those sessions, however, that dialogue may constitute discussions. As we have long held, the acid test for deciding whether an agency has engaged in discussions is whether the agency has provided an opportunity for quotations or proposals to be revised or modified. See, e.g., *TDS, Inc.*, B-292674, Nov. 12, 2003, 2003 CPD ¶ 204 at 6; *Priority One Servs., Inc.*, B-288836, B-288836.2, Dec. 17, 2001, 2002 CPD ¶ 79 at 5. Accordingly, where agency personnel comment on, or raise substantive questions or concerns about, vendors' quotations or proposals in the course of an oral presentation, and either simultaneously or subsequently afford the vendors an opportunity to make revisions in light of the agency personnel's comments and concerns, discussions have occurred. *TDS, Inc., supra*, at 6; see FAR § 15.102(g).

VI. SUBMITTING PROPOSALS

The RFP will specify the method of submitting offers and information and the format that must be observed. Failure to follow these instructions may result in the submission being rejected. See *Environmental Control Div., Inc.*, Comp. Gen. Dec. B-255181, 94-1 CPD ¶ 115, where the GAO found that the agency properly rejected a protester's BAFO, which had been transmitted by facsimile in response to the agency's facsimile transmitted request for BAFOs, because the solicitation did not allow for offers or modifications to be transmitted by facsimile.

A. Method of Submission

The basic method of submission of offers and information is in paper media in a sealed envelope. However, there are a growing number of procurements where facsimile or electronic submission is permitted or required. In addition, part of or the required information may be submitted in an oral presentation.

1. Paper Media

Paragraph (c) of the Instructions to Offerors — Competitive Acquisition solicitation provision in FAR 52.215-1 provides guidance on the basic procedure to be followed in submitting offers and information:

(1) Unless other methods (e.g., electronic commerce or facsimile) are permitted in the solicitation, proposals and modifications to proposals shall be submitted in paper media in sealed envelopes or packages (i) addressed to the office specified in the solicitation, and (ii) showing the time and date specified for receipt, the solicitation number, and the name and address of the offeror. Offerors using commercial carriers should ensure that the proposal is marked on the outermost wrapper with the information in paragraphs (c)(1)(i) and (c)(1)(ii) of this provision.

(2) The first page of the proposal must show —

(i) The solicitation number;

(ii) The name, address, and telephone and facsimile numbers of the offeror (and electronic address if available);

(iii) A statement specifying the extent of agreement with all terms, conditions, and provisions included in the solicitation and agreement to furnish any or all items upon which prices are offered at the price set opposite each item;

(iv) Names, titles, and telephone and facsimile numbers (and electronic addresses if available) of persons authorized to negotiate on the offeror's behalf with the Government in connection with this solicitation; and

(v) Name, title, and signature of person authorized to sign the proposal. Proposals signed by an agent shall be accompanied by evidence of that agent's authority, unless that evidence has been previously furnished to the issuing office.

2. Facsimile or Electronic Submission

FAR 15.203(c) provides that when electronic commerce is an authorized means of submission, the RFP must "specify the electronic commerce method(s) that offerors may use (see Subpart 4.5)." FAR 15.209(e) requires the contracting officer to include the following FAR 52.215-5 Facsimile Proposals provision in an RFP when submission by facsimiles is authorized:

(a) Definition. Facsimile proposal, as used in this provision, means a proposal, revision or modification of a proposal, or withdrawal of a proposal that is transmitted to and received by the Government via facsimile machine.

(b) Offerors may submit facsimile proposals as responses to this solicitation. Facsimile proposals are subject to the same rules as paper proposals.

(c) The telephone number of receiving facsimile equipment is: [insert telephone number].

(d) If any portion of a facsimile proposal received by the Contracting Officer is unreadable to the degree that conformance to the essential requirements of the solicitation cannot be ascertained from the document —

(1) The Contracting Officer immediately shall notify the offeror and permit the offeror to resubmit the proposal;

(2) The method and time for resubmission shall be prescribed by the Contracting Officer after consultation with the offeror; and

(3) The resubmission shall be considered as if it were received at the date and time of the original unreadable submission for the purpose of determining timeliness, provided the offeror complies with the time and format requirements for resubmission prescribed by the Contracting Officer.

(e) The Government reserves the right to make award solely on the facsimile proposal. However, if requested to do so by the Contracting Officer, the apparently successful offeror promptly shall submit the complete original signed proposal.

The instructions for handling unreadable portions of facsimile or electronic submissions contained in this provision are also set forth in FAR 15.207(c).

Offerors assume the risk of having their facsimile or electronic transmissions considered, *S.W. Elecs. & Mfg. Corp.*, Comp. Gen. Dec. B-249308, 92-2 CPD ¶ 320. For electronic transmission, delivery to the offeror's government approved Value Added Network (VAN) was not sufficient, *Comspace Corp.*, Comp. Gen. Dec. B-274037, 96-2 CPD ¶ 186 (involving a request for quotations).

B. Timely Submission Required

Although earlier drafts had proposed liberalizing the rule concerning late proposals, the final FAR Part 15 rewrite adopted the "late is late" rule. Thus, offerors must use great care to ensure the timely submission of offers, modifications or revisions. This strict rule, with very limited exceptions, is contained in ¶ (3) the

FAR 52.215-1 Instructions to Offerors – Competitive Acquisition solicitation provision as follows:

(i) Offerors are responsible for submitting proposals, and any modifications or revisions, so as to reach the Government office designated in the solicitation by the time specified in the solicitation. If no time is specified in the solicitation, the time for receipt is 4:30 p.m., local time, for the designated Government office on the date that proposal or revision is due.

(ii)(A) Any proposal, modification, or revision received at the Government office designated in the solicitation after the exact time specified for receipt of proposals is "late" and will not be considered unless it is received before award is made, the Contracting Officer determines that accepting the late proposal would not unduly delay the acquisition; and –

(1) If it was transmitted through an electronic commerce method authorized by the solicitation, it was received at the initial point of entry to the Government infrastructure not later than 5:00 p.m. one working day prior to the date specified for receipt of proposals; or

(2) There is acceptable evidence to establish that it was received at the Government installation designated for receipt of proposals and was under the Government's control prior to the time set for receipt of proposals; or

(3) It is the only proposal received.

(B) However, a late modification of an otherwise successful proposal that makes its terms more favorable to the Government, will be considered at any time it is received and may be accepted.

(iii) Acceptable evidence to establish the time of receipt at the Government installation includes the time/date stamp of that installation on the proposal wrapper, other documentary evidence of receipt maintained by the installation, or oral testimony or statements of Government personnel.

(iv) If an emergency or unanticipated event interrupts normal Government processes so that proposals cannot be received at the office designated for receipt of proposals by the exact time specified in the solicitation, and urgent Government requirements preclude amendment of the solicitation, the time specified for receipt of proposals will be deemed to be extended to the same time of day specified in the solicitation on the first work day on which normal Government processes resume.

Essentially the same language is contained in FAR 15.208.

The government's determination of the time of receipt is binding unless it is clearly unreasonable. Thus, a contracting official's reliance on the time/date clock will generally be found to be reasonable, *Haskell Co.*, Comp. Gen. Dec. B-292756, 2003 CPD ¶ 202 (reasonable reliance on time/date clock that turned to 14:01 shortly after proposal received); *States Roofing Corp.*, Comp. Gen. Dec. B-286052, 2000 CPD ¶ 182 (reasonable reliance on time/date clock rather than wall clock in same room); *Pat Mathis Constr. Co.*, Comp. Gen. Dec. B-248979, 92-2 CPD ¶ 236 (reasonable reliance on time/date clock showing offer's proposal to be one minute late rather than on clock in conference room adjoining the proposal delivery point). If the agency does not record the time of receipt of proposals, a Federal Express receipt signed by an agency employee may be used to establish that a proposal was timely received, *M.J.S., Inc.*, Comp. Gen. Dec. B-244410, 91-2 CPD ¶ 344.

The late rule has been enforced strictly and the offer must be received by the government exactly on time and at the place specified in the RFP. See, for example, *Logistics Mgmt. Inst.*, Comp. Gen. Dec. B-276143, 97-1 CPD ¶ 186 (7 minutes late). See also *Med-National, Inc.*, Comp. Gen. Dec. B-277430, 97-2 CPD ¶ 67 (offeror could not show by a preponderance of evidence that its hand-carried proposal was "in the proper place by the proper time"); *Koba Assocs., Inc.*, Comp. Gen. Dec. B-265854, 95-2 CPD ¶ 212 (hand-carried proposal delivered to the depository office three minutes after time specified for receipt of proposals late); *Hallcrest Sys., Inc.*, Comp. Gen. Dec. B-215328, 84-2 CPD ¶ 334 (hand-carried proposal received one minute late rejected); and *Priest & Fine, Inc.*, Comp. Gen. Dec. B-213603, 84-1 CPD ¶ 358 (hand-delivered proposal received two minutes late not considered).

When submission of offers by facsimile is authorized by inclusion in the RFP of the Facsimile Proposals clause in FAR 52.215-5, the offeror must prove that the complete proposal was received by the closing time. See *GROH GmbH*, Comp. Gen. Dec. B-291980, 2003 CPD ¶ 53, holding that a proposal was late when the agency claimed it had not received the fax transmission and the RFP included the agency fax number but not the clause. Even if the fax is transmitted before opening, it must get to the place designated in the solicitation on time, *Instrument Assocs.*, Comp. Gen. Dec. B-256814, 94-2 CPD ¶ 52 (bid was rejected where both sender's and agency's fax activity reports showed fax was transmitted on time but did not get to opening on time); *Microscope Co.*, Comp. Gen. Dec. B-257015, 94-2 CPD ¶ 157 (proposal was rejected even though offeror's telephone records showed timely transmission where agency provided sworn statement by contract specialist responsible for checking fax machine that proposal was not received on time); and *R.C. Constr. Co.*, Comp. Gen. Dec. B-250037.2 (Feb. 24, 1993) (bid modification received by fax three minutes before closing in room connected to bid opening room was rejected when received in opening room four minutes after opening). Further, the entire message must be received before the time for submission, *Cyber Digital, Inc.*, Comp. Gen. Dec. B-270107, 96-1 CPD ¶ 20; *Radar Devices, Inc.*, Comp. Gen. Dec. B-249118, 92-2 CPD ¶ 287 (where transmission began before closing but completed after closing, contracting officer could only consider preclosing transmission). However, the date/time notation on a facsimile has been used as evidence that a BAFO was timely received when the agency did not apply its own date/time stamp upon actual receipt, *Essex Electro Eng'rs, Inc.*, Comp. Gen. Dec. B-238207, 90-1 CPD ¶ 438. The fact that the government's fax machine is out of order, out of paper, or busy will not excuse the failure to meet the required time, *Brookfield Dev., Inc.*, Comp. Gen. Dec. B-255944, 94-1 CPD ¶ 273 (BAFO due at 4 00 p.m. rejected where transmission began at 3:50 and was not completed until 4:16 because the government's fax machine was busy).

When the RFP required submission of both paper and electronic proposals, failure of the paper version to arrive on time after timely receipt of the electronic version was a minor informality that should have been waived by the contracting officer, *Tishman Constr. Corp.*, Comp. Gen. Dec. B-292097, 2003 CPD ¶ 94.

C. Circumstances Permitting Acceptance of Late Offers

The GAO ruled for a number of years that contracting officers could avoid the late-is-late rule by extending the closing time for proposals or final proposal revisions when they found out that a late proposal or revision was about to be submitted or had been submitted. See *Ivy Mech. Co.*, Comp. Gen. Dec. B-272764, 96-2 CPD ¶ 83; *Geo-Seis Helicopters, Inc.*, Comp. Gen. Dec. B-299175, 2007 CPD ¶ 135. However, in *Geo-Seis Helicopters, Inc. v. United States*, 77 Fed. Cl. 633 (2007), the Court of Federal Claims ruled that the FAR late-is-late provision pertaining to both proposals and final proposal revisions is binding on the contracting officer and prohibits extending the closing time after the time has passed, reasoning at 642-43:

> As part of a larger effort to revise the FAR's Part 15, Contracting by Negotiation, the FAR Council issued proposed rules that would have amended the "late is late" rule. Federal Acquisition Regulation; Part 15 Rewrite — Phase I, 61 Fed. Reg. 48,380, 48,380-81 (Sept. 12, 1996). The FAR Council explained that the proposed rule changes involved "[m]ajor policy shifts," including "[r]evision of the rules governing late proposals for negotiated acquisitions to make the offeror responsible for timely delivery of its offer, and to allow late offers to be considered if doing so is in the best interests of the Government." *Id.* at 48,380-81. As proposed, the "late is late" rule would have stated in relevant part: "Offers, and requested revisions to them, that are received in the designated office after the time for receipt are 'late' *and shall be considered at the Source Selection Authority's discretion.*"

*   *   *

> On September 30, 1997, the Civilian Agency Acquisition Council and the Defense Acquisition Regulations Council ("the Councils") issued a final rule revising FAR Part 15. *See* Federal Acquisition Regulation; Part 15 Rewrite; Contracting by Negotiation and Competitive Range Determination, 62 Fed. Reg. 51,224 (Sept. 30, 1997). Both proposals for modifying the "late is late" rule — proposed FAR § 52.215-1(c)(3) and proposed FAR § 15.207(b) — were rejected in the final

version of the FAR revisions. *Id.* at § 51,235, § 51,259. The Councils explained that the final rule reflected a decision to "[r]eestablish . . . the 'late is late' rule for receipt of proposals, responses to requests for information, and modifications." *Id.* at 51,224.

* * *

In light of this regulatory history, reading FAR § 52.215-1(c)(3)(ii)(A) – by omission – to permit the [agency's extension of the closing time after it had passed] is unwarranted. As Geo-Seis points out, a standard rule of statutory construction – and one equally applicable to interpreting regulations – is that a court must not give an enactment a construction that has been specifically considered and rejected. *See Immigration & Naturalization Serv. v. Cardoza-Fonseca,* 480 U.S. 421, 442-443, 107 S. Ct. 1207, 94 L. Ed. 2d 434 (1987) ("Few principles of statutory construction are more compelling than the proposition that Congress does not intend *sub silentio* to enact statutory language that it has earlier discarded in favor of other language.")

In *Allied Materials & Equip. Co. v. United States,* 81 Fed. Cl. 448 (2008), the court held that this decision does not preclude extending the closing time before it has occurred. Thus, it appears that the only grounds for accepting a late proposal are those stated in the above rules.

1. *Electronic Submission*

The FAR has adopted a special rule for a late electronically submitted proposals, stating that they will only be acceptable if they are "received at the initial point of entry to the Government infrastructure not later than 5:00 p.m. one working day prior to the date specified for receipt of proposals." There is no explanation for this unusually strict rule but the GAO has held that the correct reading of the FAR is that this rule is the exclusive rule for electronically submitted proposals, *Sea Box, Inc.,* Comp. Gen. Dec. B-251056, 2002 CPD ¶ 181. Thus, it held in that case that the rule on government mishandling of proposals and revisions did not apply when they were submitted electronically, reasoning:

> While the second exception may be broad enough to encompass situations involving electronic commerce delivery methods, we do not read the regulation as providing two alternative means for determining whether a late electronically transmitted proposal may be accepted.

> The first exception applies, by its express terms, to situations where a proposal has been submitted by an electronic commerce method, and unqualifiedly permits such a late proposal to be considered for award only if it was received at the initial point of entry to the government infrastructure no later than 5:00 p.m. the preceding working day. Although not expressly stated in the regulation, we think the second exception necessarily applies only to proposals delivered by other than electronic means. This is so because, under the protester's alternative interpreta-

tion, late electronically transmitted proposals could be considered for award under the second exception whether or not they were received at the initial point of entry by the preceding working day; this would essentially render the first exception a nullity. Since the first exception expressly applies to electronically transmitted proposals, there is no reason to assume that such a result was intended. Moreover, such an interpretation would be inconsistent with the fundamental principle that statutes and regulations must be read and interpreted as a whole, thereby giving effect to all provisions. See *Waste Mgmt. of North Am.*, B-225551, B-225553, Apr. 24, 1987, 87-1 CPD ¶ 435 at 5.

The late-is-late rule is strictly enforced with regard to electronically submitted proposals or final proposal revisions. See *Symetrics Indus., LLC*, Comp. Gen. Dec. B-298759, 2006 CPD ¶ 154, where proposals were due by 3:00 pm, Symetrics' electronically submitted final proposal revision was received by the agency's server at 2:57:41 p.m. but did not reach the contracting office until 3:01 p.m. Because the contracting office was the designated place for submission of proposals, the GAO ruled that the late-is-late rule applied and the contracting officer was correct in rejecting the proposal. Further, the GAO ruled that the exception for government mishandling of proposals did not apply. See also *Urban Title, LLC*, Comp. Gen. Dec. B-311437.3, 2009 CPD ¶ 311 (electronically submitted final proposal revision late even though it was transmitted 12 minutes before closing time because it arrived at agency five weeks later); *Conscoop - Consorzia Fra Coop. Di Prod. E Lavoro v. United States*, 62 Fed. Cl. 219 (2004) (electronically submitted proposal late even though it was transmitted two minutes before the closing time because it arrived at agency over an hour later); *PMTech, Inc.*, Comp. Gen. Dec. B-291082, 2002 CPD ¶ 172 (electronically submitted proposal late even though it was transmitted 13 minutes before closing time). In *Integrated Business Solutions, Inc.*, Comp. Gen. Dec. B-292239, 2003 CPD ¶ 122, an electronically submitted proposal was late when it was received two minutes late and the RFP did not permit the submission of proposals electronically. The same result was reached in *Integrated Business Solutions, Inc. v. United States*, 58 Fed. Cl. 420 (2003). Similarly, in *Adirondack Constr. Co.*, Comp. Gen. Dec. B-280015.2, 98-2 CPD ¶ 55, the electronically submitted proposal was found to be late because it was not received by the agency by the closing time and had been transmitted only 13 minutes before that time. In *Labatt Food Serv., Inc. v. United States*, 84 Fed. Cl. 50 (2008), the court overlooked the late electronic submission of a final proposal revision and ruled that the procurement should be redone because the RFP required proposals to be submitted by fax and all business had been conducted electronically. The GAO had reached the opposite result in *Labatt Food Serv., Inc.*, Comp. Gen. Dec. B-310939.6, 2008 CPD ¶ 162.

Once electronic commerce is adopted as the means for publicizing RFPs and submitting proposals, offerors are responsible for monitoring the website for RFPs and amendments. Thus, failure to see an RFP when it is posted is not an excuse for late submission of a proposal, *Optelec U.S., Inc.*, Comp. Gen. Dec. B-400349, 2008 CPD ¶ 192. In that case, the protester had registered on the FedBizOpps website and applied for automatic notification of proposals but had failed to notice that the website had discontinued this practice, resulting in late receipt of the RFP and late submission of the proposal.

2. *Offers Submitted By Other Means That Are "Under The Control" Of The Government*

The only excuse for offers, revisions and modifications that do not arrive at the designated office by the closing time is provided in ¶ (c)(3)(ii)(A)(2) of the FAR 52.215-1 provision, which indicates that they can be accepted if they are "received at the Government installation designated for receipt" and "under the Government's control" by the closing time. This appears to be a less stringent test than under the prior regulation which provided that offers, revisions and modifications submitted by regular mail, facsimile or hand-carried that did not arrive at the designated office by the closing time could be considered only if the lateness was due primarily to government mishandling. However, in order to avail itself of the current rule an offeror must show that the proposal was both "received" and "under the control." Thus, a proposal delivered to the agency at the wrong address would be "under the control" of the agency but would not have been "received" because it was not delivered to the "designated" office, *Shirlington Limousine & Transportation, Inc.*, Comp. Gen. Dec. B-299241.2, 2007 CPD ¶ 68. Similarly, a proposal that was time-stamped by a security guard and then taken to the contracting office by the offeror was not "under the control" of the government until final delivery, *Immediate Sys. Resources, Inc.*, Comp. Gen. Dec. B-292856, 2003 CPD ¶ 227.

Under the prior rule, mishandling by the U.S. Postal Service did not constitute "Government mishandling," *California State Univ., Fullerton*, Comp. Gen. Dec. B-243020.2, 91-1 CPD ¶ 452. See also *Northwest Heritage Consultants*, Comp. Gen. Dec. B-299547, 2007 CPD ¶ 93, where, under the current rule, the GAO found that a Postal Service tracking record was found to be insufficient proof of delivery.

Causes for late delivery that are outside of the government's control have never been recognized as an excuse for late delivery of an offer. See, for example, *Ironhorse Ltd.*, Comp. Gen. Dec. B-256582, 94-1 CPD ¶ 76 (severe weather); *University of Kansas*, Comp. Gen. Dec. B-222329, 86-1 CPD ¶ 369 (bad weather and congested air traffic); *Unitron Eng'g Co.*, 58 Comp. Gen. 748 (B-194707), 79-2 CPD ¶ 155 (common carrier closed its offices during emergency at nearby nuclear electric power generating plant).

An offeror can not meet the requirement that the government has "received" the proposal on time if it fails to follow the instructions for delivery in the RFP. See, for example, *Sector One Security Solution*, Comp. Gen. Dec. B-400728, 2008 CPD ¶ 224, where the agency refused delivery of a proposal sent by UPS messenger. The

GAO denied the protest because the offeror had not made special arrangements for hand-carried proposals as required by the RFP, stating:

> It is the responsibility of each firm to deliver its proposal to the proper place at the proper time, and late delivery generally requires rejection of the submission. *Sencland CDC Enters.*, B-252796, B-252797, July 19, 1993, 93-2 CPD ¶ 36 at 3. Where late receipt results from the failure of a vendor to reasonably fulfill its responsibility for ensuring timely delivery to the specified location, the late offer may not be considered. *Aztec Dev. Co.*, B-256905, July 28, 1994, 94-2 CPD ¶ 48 at 3. An offer that arrives late may only be considered if it is shown that the paramount reason for late receipt was improper government action, and where consideration of the proposal would not compromise the integrity of the competitive procurement process. *Caddell Constr. Co., Inc.*, B-280405, Aug. 24, 1998, 98-2 CPD ¶ 50 at 6. Improper government action in this context is affirmative action that makes it impossible for the offeror to deliver the proposal on time. *Id.*

See also *Castle Group*, Comp. Gen. Dec. B-297853, 2006 CPD ¶ 55 (offeror did not use the full address required by the RFP); *InfoGroup Inc.*, Comp. Gen. Dec. B-294610, Sept. 30, 2004, 2004 U.S. Comp. Gen. LEXIS 199 (offeror failed to use room number provided in RFP); *Environmental, Inc.,* Comp. Gen. Dec. B-294057, 2004 CPD ¶ 138 (offerors delivered courier-delivered proposals to address for mailed proposals). The same result was reached under prior regulations. See *Social Eng'g Tech.*, Comp. Gen. Dec. B-187194, 77-1 CPD ¶ 234, where the offer was found to be late even though it had been delivered to the HUD mail room on time. The GAO reached this conclusion because the mail room was not the office designated for hand-delivered proposals. The same result was arrived at in *CSLA, Inc.*, Comp. Gen. Dec. B-255177, 94-1 CPD ¶ 63.

Under the "mishandling" rule it was extremely difficult for offerors to establish that the lateness was due to improper government action. In *Vikonics, Inc.*, Comp. Gen. Dec. B-222423, 86-1 CPD ¶ 419, a protester alleged that its hand-carried proposal was late because it was delayed in getting a base pass and the receptionist gave incorrect directions. The GAO denied the protest stating that delays in gaining access to government buildings are not unusual and should be expected. See also *Einhorn Yaffee Prescott*, Comp. Gen. Dec. B-259552, 95-1 CPD ¶ 153, where the protester's BAFO was logged in at 1:05, five minutes after the time set for receipt. In denying the protester's claim of improper government action, the GAO reasoned that the paramount cause of the lateness was that the offeror's messenger attempted to make the delivery only 5 minutes before the closing time. This same reasoning is used by the GAO in ruling on protests under the new rule. See, for example, *Kesser Int'l*, Comp. Gen. Dec. B-296294, 2005 CPD ¶ 127, holding that a 20 minute security delay on a military base should have been foreseen by the offeror and was not the "paramount" cause of the late delivery, and *Hospital Klean of Texas, Inc.*, Comp. Gen. Dec. B-295836, 2005 CPD ¶ 185, holding that the fact that the designated building was locked was the "paramount" cause of the protester's inability to deliver the proposal.

Government mishandling was found in *Brazos Roofing, Inc.*, Comp. Gen. Dec. B-275113, 97-1 CPD ¶ 43 (lateness caused by inoperable government equipment); *Timber-Mart Southwest, Inc.*, Comp. Gen. Dec. B-274677, 97-1 CPD ¶ 38 (failure to check mailbox until after time for receipt); *Wand Elec.*, Comp. Gen. Dec. B-250576, 93-1 CPD ¶ 59 (bid depository was not checked within a reasonable time before offers were due); and *Space Ordinance Sys.*, 63 Comp. Gen. 482 (B-214079), 84-2 CPD ¶ 61 (telegraphic proposal modification received two and one-half hours prior to closing, but not delivered to the proper office until two days later).

An even earlier version of the government mishandling exception required that the late receipt be due "solely" to the government's mishandling. Under that regulation the GAO dealt with cases involving joint responsibility for lateness by using a "paramount" cause rationale. See *Bergen Expo Sys., Inc.*, Comp. Gen. Dec. B-236970, 89-2 CPD ¶ 540 (government at fault for restricting access to bid depository but paramount cause was Federal Express courier's failure to wait or to return on time); *Gulls, Inc.*, Comp. Gen. Dec. B-232599, 89-1 CPD ¶ 74 (bid delivered two minutes late could not be considered even though front door of government installation was locked and blocked by construction since bidder's failure to allow sufficient time to deliver bid was the paramount cause); *Bullard & Danbury Auto Processing*, Comp. Gen. Dec. B-226841, 87-2 CPD ¶ 8 (government officials' failure to redirect misdelivered bid was incidental, rather than paramount, cause of lateness); *Scherr Constr. Co. v. United States*, 5 Cl. Ct. 249 (1984) (government failure to answer telephone during normal business hours due to flex time was not paramount cause since subsequent action by bidder's delivery agent could have resulted in timely delivery). These cases should be compared with *Rocky Mountain Trading Co.*, GSBCA 8671-P, 87-1 BCA ¶ 19,406, where a properly addressed submission was found to be timely even though a United Parcel Service (UPS) courier took it to the shipping and receiving facility instead of the specified room. There, the government agency unbeknown to bidders, had an arrangement with UPS to deliver all packages to the shipping and receiving facility.

When government actions prior to the receipt of the bid or proposal cause the lateness, it has been held proper to consider the offer under the current regulation. See *Weeks Marine, Inc.*, Comp. Gen. Dec. B-292758, 2003 CPD ¶ 183, holding that it was proper to accept a late bid when the IFB listed the wrong room for delivery of the bid and the bid was delivered one minute late. Compare *O.S. Sys., Inc.*, Comp. Gen. Dec. B-292827, 2003 CPD ¶ 211, holding that a late proposal was properly rejected even though the delivery instructions in the RFP did not indicate the difficulty that was encountered because of base security. Cases under the mishandling rule followed the same logic. See *Richards Painting Co.*, Comp. Gen. Dec. B-232678, 89-1 CPD ¶ 76, finding that a bid, which arrived in the bid opening room three minutes late, should be considered where the bid opening room was different from the room designated for the receipt of hand-carried bids and the latter room was not staffed when the bidder attempted to deliver the bid prior to the time for opening. In addition, the front door was locked and blocked by construction and the bidder had to go around to the rear of the building. See also *I&C Constr. Co.*, Comp. Gen. Dec. B-186766, 76-2 CPD ¶ 139, where the designated building for delivery was locked while all government employees were attending a retirement luncheon; and *United Teleplex*, Comp. Gen. Dec. B-237160.2, 90-1 CPD ¶ 146, finding that the solicitation failed to accurately indicate the place of delivery and agency personnel misdirected the offeror upon arrival.

Mishandling was generally not found if the proposal did not contain the time and date specified for receipt and the solicitation number, as required by ¶ (c)(3) (iii) of the FAR 52.215-1 provision. Thus, no mishandling was found in *Human Resources Consulting Serv.*, Comp. Gen. Dec. B-232338, 88-2 CPD ¶ 340, where a proposal not containing the solicitation number or time for receipt was delivered over eight hours before submission time but was misrouted by the agency. The GAO concluded the primary cause of the lateness was the contractor's lack of diligence. In *Alpha Tech. Servs., Inc.*, Comp. Gen. Dec. B-243322, 91-2 CPD ¶ 56, proposals were delivered via U.S. mail's express mail delivery service two hours before time set for receipt of proposals. However, the proposals were not routed to the contracting officer until after closing time. The GAO held that lack of identification markings rather than agency mishandling caused the late deliveries. See also *Secure Applications, Inc.*, Comp. Gen. Dec. B-261885, 95-2 CPD ¶ 190, finding no government mishandling where the offeror had failed to identify its submission as a proposal or otherwise mark the submission with an identifying solicitation number or closing date deadline and time; and had allowed only one day for delivery.

The GAO would not consider the government mishandling exception to the late proposal rule until the offeror established, with documented evidence, that the proposal was actually received by the government prior to the closing date *Southeastern CAD/CAM*, 71 Comp. Gen. 78 (B-244745), 91-2 CPD ¶ 453 (drawings were allegedly transmitted by facsimile but no proof of receipt); *Microscope Co.*, Comp. Gen. Dec. B-257015, 94-2 CPD ¶ 157 (revised proposal was allegedly transmitted by facsimile but no proof of receipt).

3. Modifications to "Otherwise Successful" Proposals

Under FAR 15.208(b)(2), the contracting officer can accept a modification to an "otherwise successful" proposal if it makes the terms of the offer more favorable to the government. However, this rule deals only with modifications to offers that have already been determined to be winning offers. Thus, the rule cannot be used to accept a final proposal revision that is late. See *Sunrise Medical HHG, Inc.*, Comp. Gen. Dec. B-310230, 2008 CPD ¶ 7, stating:

> [A]n offeror cannot make itself the "otherwise successful offeror" by submitting a late proposal modification; instead the offeror must already be the offeror in line for award prior to the time the late proposal modification is submitted.

Phyllis M. Chestang, B-298394.3, Nov. 20, 2006, 2006 CPD ¶ 176 at 5 n.3. In this regard, an offeror cannot avail itself of the late proposal submission provision where the agency has not already identified an "otherwise successful offeror." *Global Analytic Info. Tech. Servs., Inc.*, B-298840.2, Feb. 6, 2007, 2007 CPD ¶ 57 at 5-6.

See also *Masai Techs. Corp. v. United States*, 79 Fed. Cl. 433 (2007), where the protester's late proposal modifications were properly rejected because it had been told previously that its proposal was unacceptable; and *Omega Sys., Inc.*, Comp. Gen. Dec. B-298767, 2006 CPD ¶ 170, where the protesters late proposal revisions were properly rejected because it had been told in discussions that it was not in line for award. Compare *NCR Gov't Sys. LLC*, Comp. Gen. Dec. B-297959, 2006 CPD ¶ 82, holding that it was proper to accept a late addition to the winning offeror's final proposal revisions because the addition was not instrumental in the award decision.

4. Emergencies or Unanticipated Events

The "emergency or unanticipated event" exception in ¶ (3)(iv) applies only if the event impacts the operations of the government agency. See *CFS-INC, JV*, Comp. Gen. Dec. B-401809.2, 2010 CPD ¶ 85 (government agency was conducting "normal Government processes" even though agency was open on a "2-hour delayed arrival/unscheduled leave" basis after the agency had been shut down for almost a week); *Conscoop - Consorzia Fra Coop. Di Prod. E Lavoro v. United States*, 62 Fed. Cl. 219 (2004) (government electronic mail system fully functional and five proposals received in spite of regional power failure); *Educational Planning & Advice, Inc.*, Comp. Gen. Dec. B-274513, 96-2 CPD ¶ 173 (four bidders submitted timely bids and agency proceeded to bid opening in spite of hurricane emergency); and *Unitron Eng'g Co.*, 58 Comp. Gen. 748 (B-194707), 79-2 CPD ¶ 155 (mail deliveries were normal and five bids received in spite of blizzard).

D. Oral Presentations

FAR 15.102(a) states that oral presentations "are subject to the same restrictions as written information, regarding timing (see 15.208) . . . ." While the meaning of this provision is unclear, it appears that it will be enforced with regard to information regarding an oral presentation that is required to be submitted with the proposal. See *RGII Techs., Inc.*, Comp. Gen. Dec. B-278352.2, 98-1 CPD ¶ 130, where the winning offeror did not submit the originals of its oral presentation slides until after the initial proposal due date. The GAO held that this did not constitute a late proposal because the offeror had submitted copies of the slides on time, stating:

> Offerors are responsible for submitting offers, and any modifications to them, so as to reach the government office designated in the solicitation on time. FAR 15.412(b) (June 1997). Proposals, and modifications to them, that are received in the designated government office after the exact time specified are "late," and

shall be considered only if received before award and the circumstances meet the specific requirements of the provision at FAR 52.215-10. FAR 15.412(c). This rule regarding late proposals also applies to proposals which are received in part prior to the deadline, but where material portions of the proposal are not received until after the deadline. *See Inland Serv. Corp., Inc.*, B-252947.4, Nov. 4, 1993, 93-2 CPD ¶ 266 at 4 (proposal was late and not acceptable where the technical proposal was received on time but the price proposal was late); *Radar Devices, Inc.*, B-249118, Oct. 27, 1992, 92-2 CPD ¶ 287 at 3 (proposal sent by fax was late where, even though delivery began before the deadline, the majority of the proposal was not received prior to the deadline).

However, even where not all of the information which a solicitation requires is submitted prior to the deadline, the proposal may not be considered late if the information received by the deadline is sufficient to constitute a complete proposal, such that the offeror submitting the proposal did not obtain an unfair competitive advantage. *See Abt Assocs., Inc.*, 66 Comp. Gen. 460, 462–63 (1987), 87-1 CPD ¶ 513 at 2–3 (where a solicitation required the submission of multiple copies of a proposal, the submission of fewer copies by the deadline was not a late proposal because, even absent the copies, the content of the proposal was complete); see also *Wetlands Research Assocs., Inc.*, 71 Comp. Gen. 289, 292 n.7 (1992), 92-1 251 at 5 n.7 (timely submitted proposal which omitted a required photograph and drawing was not late where the proposal otherwise demonstrated the offeror's corresponding technical ability). Under such circumstances, the failure to submit all requested information is a waivable informality or irregularity. *Abt Assocs., Inc., supra*, 87-1 CPD ¶ 513 at 3.

E. Modification, Revision, and Withdrawal

The RFP forms specify the time within which the government may accept offers. Block 12 of Standard Form (SF) 33 provides that the offeror agrees to perform the work "if this offer is accepted within 60 calendar days unless a different date is inserted by the offeror." Block 4 of Optional Form (OF) 308, in turn, states: "Offers valid for 60 days unless a different period is entered here." Neither of these provisions prohibit the offeror from modifying, revising, or withdrawing the offer prior to its acceptance. While the relevant FAR sections cited below speak in terms of modification, revision and withdrawal of "proposals," it is evident from the context that they are referring to "offers" and not "information." See, for example, FAR 15.208 which is titled, "Submission, modification, revision, and withdrawal of *proposal*" but which states in ¶ (a), "Offerors are responsible for submitting *offers*, and any revisions and modifications to them."

1. Modification

FAR 15.001 defines a modification as follows:

Proposal modification is a change made to a proposal before the solicitation closing date and time, or made in response to an amendment, or made to correct a mistake at any time before award.

This definition indicates that the term "proposal modification" is intended to cover the narrow situation where the offeror desires to modify its offer before it is contacted by the agency. By its terms, the definition precludes such modifications after the solicitation closing date and time unless the modification is made in response to an amendment to the solicitation. However, the definition also includes the situation where the offeror desires to correct a mistake in its offer after the closing date of the solicitation. This issue of mistake correction will be discussed in Chapter 5. FAR 15.508 provides that mistakes discovered after award are to be processed substantially in accordance with the mistake in bid procedures set forth in FAR 14.407-4.

2. Revision

FAR 15.001 uses the term "revision" to cover the situation where an offeror changes the terms of its offer after the solicitation closing date and time. It defines a revision as follows:

> Proposal revision is a change to a proposal made after the solicitation closing date, at the request of or as allowed by a contracting officer, as the result of negotiations.

This definition permits offers to be revised only as a result of negotiations, and negotiations are to take place only after a competitive range has been established. See FAR 15.307. The subject of offer revisions will be covered in the discussion of negotiations in Chapter 8.

3. Withdrawal

Offers may be withdrawn by an offeror at any time prior to acceptance. See ¶ (c) of the Instructions to Offerors — Competitive Acquisition solicitation provision at FAR 52.215-1, which states:

> (3)(v) Proposals may be withdrawn by written notice received at any time before award. Oral proposals in response to oral solicitations may be withdrawn orally. If the solicitation authorizes facsimile proposals, proposals may be withdrawn via facsimile received at any time before award, subject to the conditions specified in the provision at 52.215-5, Facsimile Proposals. Proposals may be withdrawn in person by an offeror or an authorized representative, if the identity of the person requesting withdrawal is established and the person signs a receipt for the proposal before award.

* * *

> (8) Proposals may be withdrawn at any time before award. Withdrawals are effective upon receipt of notice by the Contracting Officer.

A similar provision is contained in FAR 15.208(e), which also contains the internal government procedures for disposing of withdrawn proposals, including electronically submitted proposals. Although this FAR 52.215-1 provision contains no guidance on the withdrawal of electronically submitted proposals, it can be assumed that they can be withdrawn electronically as long as the electronic transmission is received by the agency before acceptance of the proposal.

The broad right of withdrawal before award in the present FAR is consistent with previous FAR provisions, and the GAO has consistently accepted the FAR provision as governing and has held that a signed offer is revocable before acceptance and, therefore, is not a firm offer, *Pedestrian Bus Stop Shelters, Ltd.*, 63 Comp. Gen. 265 (B-212570), 84-1 CPD ¶ 331. The Armed Services Board of Contract Appeals has described an offeror's right to withdraw its offer prior to award as a "fundamental protection," *Toyad Corp.*, ASBCA 26785, 85-3 BCA ¶ 18,354.

VII. UNSOLICITED PROPOSALS

When a business firm anticipates a government need for a product, a service, or research, it may submit a proposal without having been solicited. Unsolicited proposals may be based on knowledge gained through several means, such as from performance of work under an existing contact, a government agency general statement of needs, or independent research within the company. FAR 15.603 emphasizes the advantages of unsolicited proposals to the government, stating:

> Unsolicited proposals allow unique and innovative ideas or approaches that have been developed outside the Government to be made available to Government agencies for use in accomplishment of their missions.

Unsolicited proposals containing new and innovative ideas should be submitted only after it has been determined that there is no other agency procedures for receiving proposals. See FAR 15.602, stating:

> It is the policy of the Government to encourage the submission of new and innovative ideas in response to Broad Agency Announcements, Small Business Innovation Research topics, Small Business Technology Transfer Research topics, Programs Research and Development Announcements, or any other Government-initiated solicitation or program. When the new and innovative ideas do not fall under topic areas publicized under those programs or techniques, the ideas may be submitted as unsolicited proposals.

This guidance will preclude the separate evaluation of unsolicited research proposals in most agencies because they award research contracts using one or more of these techniques.

Many firms have submitted unsolicited proposals in the hope of obtaining a sole source procurement. In this regard, the Competition in Contracting Act, 10 U.S.C. § 2304(d)(1)(A) and 41 U.S.C. § 253(d)(1)(A), provides:

> [I]n the case of a contract for property or services to be awarded on the basis of acceptance of an unsolicited research proposal, the property or services shall be considered to be available from only one source if the source has submitted an unsolicited research proposal that demonstrates a unique and innovative concept the substance of which is not otherwise available to the United States . . . .

However, as discussed in Chapter 1, this language is being interpreted as permissive rather than mandatory. Further, it only applies to unsolicited proposals for research work. Unsolicited proposals for other types of work are generally subject to the requirement for full and open competition. Thus, firms should not consider unsolicited proposals as a means of obtaining a contract without competition.

Despite the fact that unsolicited proposals do not guarantee sole source procurement, their submission can serve a beneficial purpose under some circumstances. For example, in *Astron*, Comp. Gen. Dec. B-236922.2, 90-1 CPD ¶ 441, a firm submitted an unsolicited proposal to furnish a quantity of nondevelopmental items for test and evaluation to demonstrate that they met an urgent Army requirement. Based on the knowledge gained from the proposal, the contracting officer published a *Commerce Business Daily* notice soliciting competitive nondevelopmental items, evaluated two responses, and justified a sole source procurement on the basis of a determination that no other firm could furnish a nondevelopmental item meeting the requirement. The GAO ruled that this was a proper procedure. See also *Fraser-Volpe Corp.*, Comp. Gen. Dec. B-240499, 90-2 CPD ¶ 397, where a firm used an unsolicited proposal to demonstrate to a procuring agency that it had the necessary qualifications to perform certain work. Unfortunately, the GAO agreed with the agency that the proposal had been submitted too late to be considered for an ongoing procurement, but the agency promised to consider the firm in the future. Most of the recent protests in this area have been similar — where the unsolicited proposal is being used as a marketing device rather than as a means to obtain a sole source contract. However, it is a good marketing device and can be used successfully in this way.

An unsolicited proposal may include data that the offeror does not want disclosed except for purposes of evaluation. In these circumstances it is essential for the offeror to appropriately mark the proposal with a legend clearly limiting the use of the proposal information. Such legends are set out in FAR 15.609.

CHAPTER 5

COMMUNICATIONS TO FACILITATE EVALUATION

Following the submission of offers, there are many occasions when communications between the government and one or more of the offerors are necessary in order to arrive at a full understanding of the proposals. After the receipt of initial offers, such communications can assist the government in determining whether to make an award on the basis of the initial proposals or in deciding which offerors should be included in the competitive range. Communications can also be helpful if questions arise after the submission of final revised proposals. In these situations, communications may also be necessary when mistakes are suspected or alleged. However, if these communications become "discussions," the government loses the right to award without conducting meaningful discussions with all offerors in the competitive range.

This limitation on the ability of an agency to communicate with offerors during proposal evaluation places contracting officials in a dilemma. To maximize efficiency, they want to award contracts on the basis of the initial proposals as frequently as possible, and if they establish a competitive range and conduct discussions, they want to award a contract based on the final proposal revisions that are received thereafter. Yet, in both of these situations, they do not want to award a contract without fully understanding the proposals of the competitors. Thus, they may need to communicate with one or more offerors. Limited communications, called "clarifications," are permissible, but they must always be conscious of the need to avoid conducting discussions. Unfortunately, the statutes, regulations, and decisions in this area have not been very helpful in assisting contracting officials in deciding what communications with one or more offerors would preclude award without discussions or would require discussion with all other offerors within the competitive range. However, there seems to be agreement that a major purpose of the FAR Part 15 rewrite was to permit more freedom in these communications.

The fundamental policy reason for limiting communications in this manner is to ensure that competing offerors are treated fairly. There has been a continuing concern by some that contracting officials will give some offerors an unfair advantage by conducting extensive communications regarding their proposals whereas other offerors will not have the same opportunity to explain or enhance their proposals. This concern was addressed by the FAR Council in its comments on the FAR Part 15 rewrite at 62 Fed. Reg. 51226 (1997):

> Some respondents expressed concern that the increased exchanges between the Government and industry throughout the acquisition process increased the risk of

unfair practices. The final rule encourages earlier and more meaningful exchanges of information between the Government and potential contractors to achieve a better understanding of the Government's requirements and the offerors' proposals. This rule contains limits on exchanges that preclude favoring one offeror over another, revealing offerors' technical solutions, revealing prices without the offerors' permission, and knowingly furnishing source selection information.

It should be clear that even though the communications rules are written in order to ensure fairness, there is also a fundamental requirement that offerors be treated fairly at every stage of the procurement process. See FAR 1.102-2(c)(1), stating:

> An essential consideration in every aspect of the System is maintaining the public's trust. Not only must the System have integrity, but the actions of each member of the Team must reflect integrity, fairness, and openness. The foundation of integrity within the System is a competent, experienced, and well-trained, professional workforce. Accordingly each member of the Team is responsible and accountable for the wise use of public resources as well as acting in a manner which maintains the public's trust. Fairness and openness require open communication among team members, internal and external customers, and the public.

The concept of equal treatment and fairness was discussed in *General Physics Federal Sys., Inc.*, Comp. Gen. Dec. B-275934, 97-1 CPD ¶ 171:

> Our decisions sustaining protests that an agency held discussions with only one offeror — a scenario found in a minority of our meaningful discussions cases, which usually present distinctions between clarifications and discussions or challenges to the adequacy of discussions the agency intended to hold — have generally focused on the inherent unfairness of agency actions that fail to provide unsuccessful offerors the same opportunity as the awardee to improve their relative standing in a negotiated competition. *Raytheon Co.*, B-261959.3, Jan. 23, 1996, 96-1 CPD ¶ 37, at 11–12; *Paramax Sys. Corp.; CAE-Link Corp.*, B-253098.4; B-253098.5, Oct. 27, 1993, 93-2 CPD ¶ 282, at 6. In such cases, we generally conclude that if the protester had been given the opportunity to address evaluator concerns during discussions it would have submitted a materially revised proposal, and the outcome of the competition might have been changed. *Raytheon Co., supra*, at 12, n. 11.

Thus, it appears that in close questions as to the classification of communications, the decision will be based on considerations of whether an offeror has been treated unfairly or whether another offeror has been given more favorable treatment.

This chapter will address the issue of communications during the evaluation process in two sections. The first section will review the rules that evolved under the FAR language prior to the FAR Part 15 rewrite in order to provide an understanding of the limitations that the FAR Council perceived as inhibiting efficient procurement. The second section will analyze the scope of the supposedly more liberal communication rule that is contained in the FAR Part 15 rewrite. The conduct of discussions with offerors in the competitive range will be covered in Chapter 8.

I. PRE-FAR PART 15 REWRITE RULE

Prior to the FAR Part 15 rewrite, the permissible communications during proposal evaluation were described as "clarifications." It was also understood that "discussions" could not be conducted without losing the right to award on the basis of the initial proposals and that, once a "discussion" had occurred, the agency was required to establish a competitive range and conduct discussions with all offerors in the range. The rule focused on the dichotomy between these two terms. They were derived from the procurement statutes, defined in the regulations, and interpreted in numerous protest decisions.

A. Development of Statutory Language

The initial statute did not use the term "clarification." However, the term "discussions" was originally incorporated into 10 U.S.C. § 2304 by Pub. L. No. 87-653 on Sept. 10, 1962, providing for oral or written discussions with all offerors within the competitive range and permitting award on initial proposals without discussions. The term was not defined in the statute, but the GAO interpreted these provisions as requiring discussions with all offerors in the competitive range "if negotiations (i.e., discussions) be conducted with one of the offerors," 46 Comp. Gen. 191 (B-158686), 1966 CPD ¶ 76. In 1984, this concept was incorporated in the Competition in Contracting Act, Pub. L. No. 98-369, which provided that "discussions conducted for the purpose of minor clarification" would not prohibit award without discussions. The same terminology is now contained in 10 U.S.C. § 2305(b)(4)(A), as follows:

> The head of an agency shall evaluate competitive proposals in accordance with paragraph (1) and may award a contract —
>
> > (i) after discussions with the offerors, provided that written or oral discussions have been conducted with all responsible offerors who submit proposals within the competitive range; or
> >
> > (ii) based on the proposals received, without discussions with the offerors (other than discussions conducted for the purpose of minor clarification) provided that the solicitation included a statement that proposals are intended to be evaluated, and award made, without discussions, unless discussions are determined to be necessary.

Essentially the same language is contained in 41 U.S.C. § 253b(d)(1). Neither statute defines the terms "discussions," "clarification" or "minor clarification."

B. Procurement Regulations

There was no guidance on this issue in the procurement regulations until 1974 when the Armed Services Procurement Regulation was amended to contain the following provision in ASPR 3-805.1:

(b) For the sole purpose of eliminating minor uncertainties or irregularities, such as discussed in 2-405 [the sealed bidding provision on minor informalities], an inquiry may be made to an offeror concerning his proposal. Such inquiries and resulting clarification furnished by the offeror shall not constitute discussions within the meaning of this paragraph 3-805. If the clarification prejudices the interest of other offerors, award may not be made without discussion with offerors in the competitive range.

This guidance was deleted from the ASPR in 1976.

When the Federal Acquisition Regulation was promulgated in April 1984, it restated the guidance on this issue by providing in FAR 15.610(a)(3) that award could be made to the "most favorable initial proposal" if "in fact" there had been no "written or oral discussion with any offeror." In addition, FAR 15.611(c) provided that discussion should not be reopened after the receipt of best and final offers, but if it was, all offerors in the competitive range should be included. The FAR also defined "clarifications" and "discussions" in FAR 15.601:

"Clarification," as used in this subpart, means communication with an offeror for the sole purpose of eliminating minor irregularities, informalities, or apparent clerical mistakes in the proposal. It is achieved by explanation or substantiation, either in response to Government inquiry or as initiated by the offeror. Unlike discussion (see definition below), clarification does not give the offeror an opportunity to revise or modify its proposal, except to the extent that correction of apparent clerical mistakes results in a revision.

"Discussion," as used in this subpart, means any oral or written communication between the Government and an offeror (other than communications conducted for the purpose of minor clarification), whether or not initiated by the Government, that (a) involves information essential for determining the acceptability of a proposal, or (b) provides the offeror an opportunity to revise or modify its proposal.

These definitions remained in effect until they were removed by the FAR Part 15 rewrite. The FAR also contained detailed guidance on the treatment of mistakes in proposals that were discovered before award. This guidance in FAR 15.607 permitted limited correction of mistakes in the clarification process and unlimited correction of mistakes in the discussion process. This entire provision was removed in the rewrite.

C. Protest Interpretation

The issue of the limitations on communications arose in the early protests of negotiated procurements in the GAO where the agency enunciated the distinction between discussions and clarifications and ruled on many cases where it was necessary to interpret the meaning of these terms. These rulings occurred prior to the issuance of the FAR in 1984 and continued after the FAR adopted the basic concepts that had been laid out in the prior GAO decisions.

1. Early Evolution of the Rule

The early decisions of the GAO were very clear in regard to communications relating to the actual offer made by an offeror, but were not as clear with regard to communications relating to information provided by an offeror to facilitate evaluation of proposals. With regard to offers, the GAO ruled that a communication that permitted an offeror to alter its offer or clear up an ambiguity in its offer was a discussion, precluding award without conducting discussions with other offerors in the competitive range. Improper discussions were found when an offeror reduced its price, 51 Comp. Gen. 479 (B-173703) (1972); when an offeror acknowledged an addendum to the RFP after the date for submission of proposals, 50 Comp. Gen. 202 (B-170751) (1970); when an agency issued an amendment to the RFP with an extension of time for submitting revised proposals, 50 Comp. Gen. 246 (B-169148) (1970); when an agency requested a new price based on deletion of the first-article testing requirement, 48 Comp. Gen. 663 (B-165084) (1969); when an offeror withdrew exceptions it had taken to the RFP, 53 Comp. Gen. 139 (B-178212) (1973); when the contracting officer accepted a late price increase from the successful offeror, *Corbetta Constr. Co.*, 55 Comp. Gen. 201 (B-182979), 75-2 CPD ¶ 144, *modified*, 55 Comp. Gen. 972, 76-1 CPD ¶ 240; and when an offeror explained its ambiguous price proposal, *PRC Info. Sciences Co.*, 56 Comp. Gen. 768 (B-188305), 77-2 CPD ¶ 11.

In contrast, the GAO ruled that no discussion had occurred when the agency merely obtained additional information to assist in the evaluation of proposals but did not permit the offeror to alter its proposal. No discussions were found in Comp. Gen. Dec. B-170989, Nov. 17, 1971, *Unpub.*, where there had been a meeting between the awardee and the contracting officer to explain the awardee's lowered price; 52 Comp. Gen. 358 (B-176182) (1972), where the agency had made a plant visit to obtain information to make a cost realism analysis; and *Fechheimer Bros., Inc.*, Comp. Gen. Dec. B-184751, 76-1 CPD ¶ 404, where an offeror was requested to submit a second sample product and to certify that the original sample met the specifications. *Ensign Bickford Co.*, Comp. Gen. Dec. B-180844, 74-2 CPD ¶ 97, is illustrative of the reasoning of these early decisions. There the agency contacted the offerors after receipt of proposals to clarify the requirements for government-furnished material, but neither offeror claimed the right to amend their proposed price. The GAO found that there had been no discussions, because it appeared that both offerors had submitted their original prices based on the clarification issued by the agency.

These early cases finding no discussion when the agency obtained information to assist in the evaluation process appear to be cases where the information was not required to be submitted by the RFP. However, when additional information was requested because the offeror had not provided all the information requested in the RFP or because the evaluators did not understand the information provided in response to an RFP requirement for information, the GAO held that obtaining such information constituted discussions. See, for example, *Centro Corp.*, Comp. Gen. Dec. B-186842, 77-1 CPD ¶ 75, where the GAO agreed with the procuring agency that a request for clarification of proposals lacking in necessary information was a discussion because it sought information that "went to the heart of [the] proposals and had a substantial effect on the Government's determination of acceptability." The information sought was additional material to demonstrate an understanding of the work, additional information on the personnel to be used to perform the work, and a description of the offeror's plan of action. This rule that discussions occurred when the agency sought information "essential for determining the acceptability of a proposal" was followed in numerous cases. See *Human Resources Co.*, Comp. Gen. Dec. B-187153, 76-2 CPD ¶ 459 (submission of considerable information elaborating on original technical proposal); *New Hampshire-Vermont Health Serv.*, 57 Comp. Gen. 347 (B-189603), 78-1 CPD ¶ 202 (submission of detailed explanation of proposed changes that was required by RFP but not included in original proposal); *MAR, Inc.*, Comp. Gen. Dec. B-194631, 79-2 CPD ¶ 116 (submission of additional data on the experience of proposed subcontractors as required by the RFP); *John Fluke Mfg. Co.*, Comp. Gen. Dec. B-195091, 79-2 CPD ¶ 367 (submission of data to show that an "equal" product met the contract specifications where RFP stated that "a substitute item shall not be used without prior testing and approval"); *ABT Assoc., Inc.*, Comp. Gen. Dec. B-196365, 80-1 CPD ¶ 362 (explanation of method of performing the work in view of staff reductions proposed by offeror where the acceptability of the proposal was dependent on a satisfactory explanation); and *Raytheon Serv. Co.*, 59 Comp. Gen. 316 (B-194928), 80-1 CPD ¶ 214 (additional information on whether work would be done by contractor or subcontractor to enable agency to make a cost realism analysis). It was also held that seeking information that was in addition to that originally called for by the RFP was a discussion, *Amram Nowak Assocs., Inc.*, Comp. Gen. Dec. B-187253, 76-2 CPD ¶ 454.

At the same time that these rules were being formulated, the GAO continued to rule that no discussions occurred if the agency obtained information that was not required to be submitted by the RFP. See, for example, *General Kinetics, Inc.*, Comp. Gen. Dec. B-190359, 78-1 CPD ¶ 231 (meeting with offeror to resolve doubts of agency technical personnel that offeror had capability to perform when contracting officer had determined that offeror was capable and RFP required no submission of information to demonstrate capability); *International Business Investments, Inc.*, 60 Comp. Gen. 275 (B-198894), 81-1 CPD ¶ 125 (communication to ensure that offeror had adequate equipment to perform work); *ConDiesel Mobile Equip. Div.*, Comp. Gen. Dec. B-201568, 82-2 CPD ¶ 294 (request that offeror demonstrate technical capability to perform work after questions had been raised in preaward survey, but no such information had been required by RFP). These cases were based on the rationale that no discussion had occurred because there had been no change to the offeror's proposal. It seems apparent that the GAO was defining the word "proposal" to include both the offer and the information required to be submitted to permit evaluation. Thus, whether obtaining information constituted discussions was highly dependent on whether the information was called for by the RFP.

2. Interpretation of the Original FAR

After the issuance of the FAR in 1984, adopting the definition of discussions to include "information essential for determining the acceptability of a proposal," the GAO continued to follow its earlier reasoning. The clearest cases were those holding that communications leading to a change to an offer or clearing up an ambiguity in an offer were discussions. See, for example, *Industrial Lift Truck Co. of N.J., Inc.*, 67 Comp. Gen. 525 (B-230921), 88-2 CPD ¶ 61 (question to offeror as to whether it intended to offer a noncompliant time of delivery); *Federal Data Corp.*, 69 Comp. Gen. 196 (B-236265.2), 90-1 CPD ¶ 104 (substitution of several line items because line items in offer did not meet the contract requirements); *Dresser-Rand Co.*, Comp. Gen. Dec. B-237342, 90-1 CPD ¶ 179 (substitution of item to be delivered to meet newly discovered agency requirement); *Microlog Corp.*, Comp. Gen. Dec. B-237486, 90-1 CPD ¶ 227 (reduction of prices to reflex current contract); *Canadian Commercial Corp.*, Comp. Gen. Dec. B-246311, 92-1 CPD ¶ 233 (information addressing one aspect of the offer that did not comply with the contract specifications); *HFS, Inc.*, Comp. Gen. Dec. B-248204.2, 92-2 CPD ¶ 188 (obtaining detailed pricing information that was to be incorporated into the contract); *4th Dimension Software, Inc.*, Comp. Gen. Dec. B-251936, 93-1 CPD ¶ 420 (submission of information in response to inquiry as to whether offeror was proposing work that did not meet the contract specifications); *Paramax Sys. Corp.*, Comp. Gen. Dec. B-253098.4, 93-2 CPD ¶ 282 (reducing maximum fee from 12% to 9%); *Raytheon Co.*, Comp. Gen. Dec. B-261959.3, 96-1 CPD ¶ 37 (communications clearing up the data rights that were being offered); *Global Assocs., Ltd.*, Comp. Gen. Dec. B-271693, 96-2 CPD ¶ 100 (submission of document clearing up ambiguity as to whether offeror complied with Limitations on Subcontracting clause); *Integrated Sys. Group*, Comp. Gen. Dec. B-272336, 96-2 CPD ¶ 144 (submission of letters explaining ambiguous pricing terms of alternate proposals); and *Tri-State Gov't Servs., Inc.*, Comp. Gen. Dec. B-277315.2, 97-2 CPD ¶ 143 (communication to obtain offeror's agreement that prices proposed covered quantities above the estimated quantities in the RFP). One exception to this rule that altering the offer is a discussion was a reduction in price by the winning offeror. See *Saco Defense, Inc.*, Comp. Gen. Dec. B-240603, 90-2 CPD ¶ 462, finding that there could be no possible prejudice to the protester when the offeror reduced its price below the price that had been evaluated when it won the competition. Similarly, in *Hawaii Int'l Movers, Inc.*, Comp. Gen. Dec. B-248131, 92-2 CPD ¶ 67, an inquiry as to which line item a price reduction applied to was a proper clarification.

Communications to obtain information required by the RFP for evaluation of proposals continued to be held to be discussions. See, for example, *Motorola, Inc.*,

66 Comp. Gen. 519 (B-225822), 87-1 CPD ¶ 604 (submission of supplemental information to original technical proposal); *Corporate America Research Assocs., Inc.*, Comp. Gen. Dec. B-228579, 88-1 CPD ¶ 160 (providing letters of commitment from key employees as required by RFP); *McManus Security Sys.*, 67 Comp. Gen. 534 (B-231105), 88-2 CPD ¶ 68 (submission of significant technical information on proposed security system); *University of South Carolina*, Comp. Gen. Dec. B-240208, 90-2 CPD ¶ 249 (substitution of key personnel); *Crestmont Cleaning Serv. & Supply Co.*, Comp. Gen. Dec. B-252490, 93-2 CPD ¶ 2 (obtaining information demonstrating ability to obtain qualified personnel); and *Working Alternatives, Inc.*, Comp. Gen. Dec. B-276911, 97-2 CPD ¶ 2 (submission of formal document showing right to use facility as required by RFP). These cases generally reasoned that permitting one offeror to provide supplemental information that was to be used to evaluate its proposal provided it with an unfair advantage over other offerors that were not given a similar opportunity.

An exception to the rule regarding information required by the RFP was information needed to demonstrate the responsibility of the offeror where the GAO followed the sealed bidding rule that such information may be submitted after the proposal even if it is required to be included in the proposal, *Alan Scott Indus., Grieshaber Mfg. Co.*, 63 Comp. Gen. 610 (B-212703), 84-2 CPD ¶ 349 (letter confirming the characteristics of samples that were furnished pursuant to an RFP provision stating that they were submitted only for the purpose of demonstrating the offeror's capability); *Edgewater Mach. & Fabricators, Inc.*, Comp. Gen. Dec. B-219828, 85-2 CPD ¶ 630 (preaward survey); *Advance Gear & Mach. Corp.*, Comp. Gen. Dec. B-228002, 87-2 CPD ¶ 519 (identity of supplier of critical material); *A.B. Dick Co.*, Comp. Gen. Dec. B-233142, 89-1 CPD ¶ 106 (inquiry as to details of small and disadvantaged business subcontracting plan); *Eagle Tech., Inc.*, Comp. Gen. Dec. B-236255, 89-2 CPD ¶ 468 (furnishing names of additional sources of credit to demonstrate financial ability); *Thermal Reduction Co.*, Comp. Gen. Dec. B-236724, 89-2 CPD ¶ 527 (inquiry probing whether offeror of low price fully understood specifications); *Cajar Defense Support Co.*, Comp. Gen. Dec. B-239297, 90-2 CPD ¶ 76 (explanation of labor rates that appeared to be very low and thus raised question of offeror's ability to perform contract); and *Kahn Instruments, Inc.*, Comp. Gen. Dec. B-277973, 98-1 CPD ¶ 11 (inquiry concerning small business subcontracting plan).

Communications obtaining information that was not required by the RFP and did not significantly alter the evaluation of proposals were held not to be discussions. See *Alan Scott Indus.*, 63 Comp. Gen. 610 (B-212703), 84-2 CPD ¶ 349 (obtaining name of supplier to confirm that certification of domestic product was correct); *Northern Virginia Serv. Corp.*, Comp. Gen. Dec. B-258036.2, 95-1 CPD ¶ 36 (verification from offeror that it would pay laborers the amounts in the wage determination); *Sociometrics, Inc.*, Comp. Gen. Dec. B-261367.2, 95-2 CPD ¶ 201 (explanation of deleted labor hours in best and final offer); *Assets Recovery Sys., Inc.*, Comp. Gen. Dec. B-275332, 97-1 CPD ¶ 67 (communication involving different use of payments offered by winning offeror but not altering the amount to be paid); *Robotic Sys. Tech.*, Comp. Gen. Dec. B-278195.2, 98-1 CPD ¶ 20 (explanation of methodology used in computing costs to aid agency's cost analyst in confirming that cost data was consistent with proposed price); and *WECO Cleaning Specialists, Inc.*, Comp. Gen. Dec. B-279305, 98-1 CPD ¶ 154 (obtaining cost or pricing data to demonstrate that offeror's price was not excessively low). See also *Aquidneck Sys. Int'l, Inc.*, Comp. Gen. Dec. B-257170.2, 94-2 CPD ¶ 122, holding that no discussion occurred when an agency obtained information confirming the validity of a proposal that had been misevaluated by the technical evaluators. In almost all these cases, the agency had selected the offeror as the winner of the competition but had sought additional information to allay doubts as to some aspect of the offer, such as a possible low price or lack of compliance with a contract requirement.

Discussions were also found not to have occurred when the communication clarified a minor informality. In *E. Frye Enters., Inc.*, Comp. Gen. Dec. B-258699, 95-1 CPD ¶ 64, clarifications, but not discussions, occurred when offerors were allowed to correct certifications, acknowledge nonmaterial amendments to the RFP, and correct obvious mistakes in extended prices. See also *Advance Gear & Mach. Corp.*, Comp. Gen. Dec. B-228002, 87-2 CPD ¶ 519 (obtaining correct certifications); *Loral Infrared & Imaging Sys., Inc.*, Comp. Gen. Dec. B-247127.3, 92-2 CPD ¶ 52 (communications to persuade offeror to delete proprietary legends from pages of proposal to which the agency already had unlimited rights); *CDA Investment Techs., Inc.*, Comp. Gen. Dec. B-272093, 97-1 CPD ¶ 102 (communications to ensure that offeror intended to perform in accordance with its proposal); and *BE, Inc.; PAI Corp.*, Comp. Gen. Dec. B-277978, 98-1 CPD ¶ 80 (obtaining additional information that was "not substantial" regarding past performance and experience). Similarly, merely obtaining a missing page from a proposal was held not to constitute discussions, *KOH Sys., Inc.*, GSBCA 9388-P, 88-2 BCA ¶ 20,690.

Correction of mistakes was also permitted in the clarification process as long as the mistake was clerical, FAR 15.607(a), or the offer intended was provable by clear and convincing evidence on the face of the proposal, FAR 15.607(c)(3). See *International Business Sys., Inc.*, Comp. Gen. Dec. B-270632.2, 96-1 CPD ¶ 276, holding that a mistake clear on the face of the proposal could be corrected without reopening discussions. See also *Stacor Corp.*, Comp. Gen. Dec. B-231095, 88-2 CPD ¶ 9 (omitted price corrected when the amount intended was obvious from prior negotiations); *A.B. Dick Co.*, Comp. Gen. Dec. B-233142, 89-1 CPD ¶ 106 (line item total prices corrected to correspond to unit prices when RFP provided that unit prices prevailed); *Action Serv. Corp.*, Comp. Gen. Dec. B-246413, 92-1 CPD ¶ 267 (unit price corrected to correspond to total price when it was obviously wrong from face of offer); *Dataproducts New England, Inc.*, Comp. Gen. Dec. B-246149.3, 92-1 CPD ¶ 231 (bar chart showing noncomplying delivery schedule corrected when there was no other indication in offer that offeror did not intend to comply with contractual delivery requirement); *PHP Healthcare Corp.*, Comp. Gen. Dec. B-251799, 93-1 CPD ¶ 366 (unit price corrected to conform to total price when unit price clearly out of line with other offers); and *Joint Threat Servs.*,

Comp. Gen. Dec. B-278168, 98-1 CPD ¶ 18 (price increased to reflect obvious error in computation of subcontractor costs). This correction rule could not be used to alter elements of a proposal that were intended by the offeror but later found to be disadvantageous, because in that situation, there was no mistake. See *Contact Int'l Corp.*, Comp. Gen. Dec. B-237122.2, 90-1 CPD ¶ 481; *McGhee Constr. Inc.*, Comp. Gen. Dec. B-255863, 94-1 CPD ¶ 254; and *Star Detective & Security Agency, Inc. & E.L.A. Security, Inc., a Joint Venture*, Comp. Gen. Dec. B-260948.2, 95-2 CPD ¶ 90. For cases finding that mistakes could not be corrected through clarification because they were not apparent in the proposal, see *Pulau Elecs. Corp.*, Comp. Gen. Dec. B-254443, 93-2 CPD ¶ 326; *Communications Int'l Inc.*, Comp. Gen. Dec. B-246076, 92-1 CPD ¶ 194; *ES, Inc.*, Comp. Gen. Dec. B-258911.2, 95-1 CPD ¶ 168; *Integration Techs. Group, Inc.*, Comp. Gen. Dec. B-274288.5, 97-1 CPD ¶ 214; and *Matrix Int'l Logistics, Inc.*, Comp. Gen. Dec. B-272388.2, 97-2 CPD ¶ 89. See also *ALM, Inc.*, 65 Comp. Gen. 405 (B-221230.3), 86-1 CPD ¶ 240, holding that mistakes could not be corrected without conducting discussions when the correction permitted the offeror to materially change its pricing by increasing the estimated costs of the contract 19% above the amount used to evaluate the offer for source selection purposes.

Even when there had been improper discussions, protests were not granted if the protester was not prejudiced. See *National Medical Staffing, Inc.*, Comp. Gen. Dec. B-242585.3, 91-2 CPD ¶ 1 (substitution of key person did not effect the relative standing of the offerors); *Strategic Analysis, Inc.*, Comp. Gen. Dec. B-270075, 96-1 CPD ¶ 41 (obtaining required letter of commitment from key person not prejudicial when protester could not demonstrate that it could have improved its competitive position through discussions); *EastCo Bldg. Servs., Inc.*, Comp. Gen. Dec. B-275334, 97-1 CPD ¶ 83 (permitting revised proposal with higher price not prejudicial when winning offeror was rated substantially better on both price and technical evaluation); and *USATREX Int'l, Inc.*, Comp. Gen. Dec. B-275592, 98-1 CPD ¶ 99 (obtaining information necessary to evaluate cost proposal not prejudicial because discussions with protester would not have placed in line for award).

II. COMMUNICATIONS UNDER THE FAR PART 15 REWRITE

Post-submission communications are now addressed under FAR 15.306 entitled, "Exchanges with offerors after receipt of proposals." Three types of exchanges are covered: (1) communications and award without discussion, (2) communications prior to establishing the competitive range, and (3) negotiations with offerors within the competitive range. The following material discusses the first two types of communications, which are exchanges with offerors to facilitate the evaluation of proposals. It also discusses the treatment of mistakes alleged before award. Negotiations with offerors within the competitive range will be discussed in Chapter 8.

A. Communications and Award Without Discussions

FAR 15.306(a) contains the following coverage of communications (termed clarifications) prior to award without discussions:

(a) Clarifications and award without discussions. (1) Clarifications are limited exchanges, between the Government and offerors, that may occur when award without discussions is contemplated.

(2) If award will be made without conducting discussions, offerors may be given the opportunity to clarify certain aspects of proposals (e.g., the relevance of an offeror's past performance information and adverse past performance information to which the offeror has not previously had an opportunity to respond) or to resolve minor or clerical errors.

The comments accompanying the publication of the FAR Part 15 rewrite indicate that the deletion of the previous definitions and the adoption of the above language was intended to permit increased exchanges of information while still complying with the statutory requirements for award without discussions. See 62 Fed. Reg. 51228 (1997), stating:

Clarifications. We drafted the rule to allow as much free exchange of information between offerors and the Government as possible, while still permitting award without discussions and complying with applicable statutes. The proposed rule did not differentiate between exchanges of information when award without discussions was contemplated versus when a competitive range would be established. Public comment pointed out that the proposed rule language may allow exchanges beyond what is permitted by applicable statute when making award without discussions. In drafting the second proposed rule, we limited these exchanges. The resulting language still permits more exchange of information between offerors and the Government than the current FAR. This policy is expected to help offerors, especially small entities that may not be familiar with proposal preparation, by permitting easy clarification of limited aspects of their proposals.

An earlier draft would have enabled the government to obtain "relevant information (in addition to that submitted in the offeror's proposal) needed to understand and evaluate the offeror's proposal." It further provided that: "The nature and extent of communications between the Government and offerors is a matter of contracting officer judgment."

The statutory term "minor clarification" and the regulatory term "limited exchanges" are not in themselves meaningful in distinguishing between clarifications and discussions. In determining the extent to which the final rewrite permits more exchange of information than the prior FAR rules, it is necessary to consider the purpose of the exchange. If the exchange is intended to obtain a revision in the offer, oral or written discussions and final revised proposals will be required. Conversely, it would appear that information exchanges that are conducted with all offerors that are similarly situated and do not vary the terms of their offers should not preclude award without discussions. Some decisions of the GAO and the Court of Federal Claims have looked outside of FAR 15.306(a) to arrive at this interpretation of the permissible scope of clarifications. See *Antarctic Support Assocs. v. United States*, 46 Fed. Cl. 145 (2000); *Cubic Defense Sys., Inc. v. United States*, 45 Fed. Cl. 450 (1999); and *MG Indus.*, Comp. Gen. Dec. B-283010.3, 2000 CPD ¶ 17, looking to the FAR 15.306(d) rule on "discussions" and reasoning that if a discussion pursuant to that definition did not occur, the agency must have been conducting clarifications. Using different reasoning, the court in *Information Tech. & Applications Corp. v. United States*, 51 Fed. Cl. 340 (2001), affirmed in a 2 to 1 decision, 316 F. 3d 1312 (Fed. Cir. 2003), held that the additional information sought by the contracting officer was better described by the rule in FAR 15.306(b) but that, since it did not fall within the rule in FAR 15.306(d), it was a permissible clarification. This reasoning is understandable because exchanges that occur during the initial evaluation of proposals are simultaneously covered by the rules in both FAR 15.306(a) and (b). However, the GAO decisions discussed below do not always follow this seemingly logical distinction between "clarifications" and "discussions."

1. Communications Constituting Offer Revisions

A major problem with the statutory and regulatory coverage of discussions and clarifications has been the ambiguous use of the word "proposal" — sometimes referring to the entire submission and other times referring to the offer. Although any changes or additions to information may result in a revision to the information that is included in a proposal, such changes or additions should be distinguished from offer revisions. Revisions are defined in FAR 15.001, as follows:

> *Proposal revision* is a change to a proposal made after the solicitation closing date, at the request of or as allowed by a contracting officer, as the result of negotiations.

While the term "proposal" is used in this definition, a reasonable interpretation is that it refers to offers as opposed to information. This is so because the definition indicates that revisions result from negotiations, and it is not likely that the contracting officer would negotiate over information. Negotiations are conducted over the terms of the offer, which will be incorporated into the contract. Such revisions would result from changes in the price, time for performance, description of the work, or other terms of the contract.

However the word "proposal" is interpreted, it is clear that changes to the offer made in a proposal can not be considered to be clarifications. See, for example, *Manthos Eng'g, LLC*, Comp. Gen. Dec. B-401751, 2009 CPD ¶ 216 (mandatory option prices could not be obtained through a clarification); *Kellogg Brown & Root Servs., Inc.*, Comp. Gen. Dec. B-400614.3, 2009 CPD ¶ 50 (offeror's "assumption" attached to its cost proposal that raised question whether it would comply with mandatory technical specification could only be cleared up by discussions); *C. Young Constr., Inc.*, Comp. Gen. Dec. B-309740, 2007 CPD ¶ 198 (offeror's proposal to staff job that did not comply with mandatory specification could only be cleared up by discussions); *Nu-Way, Inc.*, Comp. Gen. Dec. B-296435.5, 2005 CPD ¶ 195 (ambiguity in offeror's proposal as to whether its equipment met mandatory requirement could only be resolved by discussions); *Cooperativa Maratori Riuniti-Anese*, Comp. Gen. Dec. B-294747, 2004 CPD ¶ 210 (allowing offeror to revise offer to meet required completion data could only be done through discussions); *DynCorp Int'l LLC*, Comp. Gen. Dec. B-294232, 2004 CPD ¶ 187 (allowing offeror to explain inadequacies in mandatory staffing plan would have required discussions); *Priority One Servs., Inc.*, Comp. Gen. Dec. B-288836, 2002 CPD ¶ 79 (changes to cost proposal); *International Resources Group*, Comp. Gen. Dec. B-286663, 2001 CPD ¶ 35 (email containing a list of "technical and cost comments"); *Dubinsky v. United States*, 43 Fed. Cl. 243 (1999) (telephone call discussion to "clear up" specification compliance and warranties); and *Wellco Enters., Inc.*, Comp. Gen. Dec. B-282150, 99-1 CPD ¶ 107 (allowing offeror to clear up proposed deviations to the contract specifications would have been a discussion). Compare *S4, Inc.*, Comp. Gen. Dec. B-299817, 2007 CPD ¶ 164, holding that a request that the offeror confirm that it would comply with contract requirement was not a discussion because it did not allow the offeror to alter the offer.

In *Language Servs. Assocs., Inc.*, Comp. Gen. Dec. B-297392, 2006 CPD ¶ 20, the GAO did not follow this reasoning but held that a "clarification" of the quoted prices stating that the offeror "would like to reserve the right to negotiate with the [agency] an adjustment in pricing" if the agency's estimated quantities were incorrect was not a discussion, reasoning:

> In this case, the communications that took place between [the offeror] and the agency do not appear to have led to a material revision of the vendor's quotation; in any event, these communications had no effect on the acceptability of [the offeror's] quotation and [the offeror's] competitive position remained the same.

2. Communications Concerning Information

Although it is clear that communications constituting revisions to offers are not permitted when award is to be made without discussions, information exchanges that do not concern changes to offers may be appropriate in the clarification process. However, it is useful to distinguish between information concerning the capability of the offeror and information relating to the features of the offer. Whereas the former should clearly be clarifications under FAR 15.206(a), past decisions dealing with information relating to the offer make inclusion of this type of communication more problematic.

As noted above, the distinction between clarifications and discussions is particularly difficult because the GAO decisions use the ambiguous word "proposal" in ruling on this issue. For many years, the GAO has stated, as in *Government Tele-communications, Inc.*, Comp. Gen. Dec. B-299542.2, 2007 CPD ¶ 136:

> The "acid test" for deciding whether discussions have been held is whether it can be said that an offeror was provided the opportunity to modify its proposal. *National Beef Packing Co.*, B-296534, Sept. 1, 2005, 2005 CPD ¶ 168 at 11; *Pak Tower Mgmt. Ltd.*, B-295589, B-295589.2, Mar. 22, 2005, 2005 CPD ¶ 77 at 7.

As discussed below, the question of whether the communication gave the offeror an "opportunity to modify its proposal" is decided on a case-by-case basis. While the GAO decisions are somewhat confusing, they generally indicate that obtaining information to make a proposal "acceptable" is a discussion, while information supporting a proposal that has already been determined to be "acceptable" is a clarification.

a. Capability Information

Capability information deals with the offeror's ability to perform as promised, as opposed to information pertaining to what has been promised. FAR 15.306(a)(2) recognizes that this is an appropriate area of communication, identifying past performance information as an example of the class of information that should be subject to clarification. This distinction was also recognized under prior regulations where communications were permitted to ensure that the winning offeror was *responsible*. In *Hercules, Inc.*, Comp. Gen. Dec. B-167643, Jan. 20, 1970, *Unpub.*, the GAO stated:

> [W]e conclude that an offeror's responsibility or ability to perform may be discussed without foreclosing the right of the contracting officer to invoke the exception to the requirement for conducting written or oral discussions. Any other conclusion would either deprive the government of the right to make award on the basis of initial proposals or allow such an award only at the peril of dealing with nonresponsible contractors.

See also *Edgewater Mach. & Fabricators, Inc.*, Comp. Gen. Dec. B-219828, 85-2 CPD ¶ 630, stating:

> Although we recognize that a successful negotiated procurement requires both an acceptable proposal and a capable contractor, we find no substance to Edgewater's argument that the determination of the acceptability of the proposal and the capability of the prospective contractor are inextricably intertwined. The FAR, at 48 C.F.R. §§ 15.610 and 15.611, clearly relates to the discussions necessary to determine the acceptability of a proposal and the best and final offers that must follow such discussions. FAR, 48 C.F.R. § 9.100, clearly indicates that the purpose of a preaward survey is to evaluate the capability of the prospective contractor to perform the contract. *See Saxon Corp.*, B-216148, Jan. 23, 1985, 85-1 CPD ¶ 87. Thus, the determinations as to the acceptability of a proposal and the capability of an offeror involve distinct functions for different purposes usually performed

at different times by different people. Moreover, the record here demonstrates that the survey team did not step outside the bounds of its responsibility evaluation. This is illustrated by Edgewater's statement that the survey included:

> ". . . a physical survey of the manufacturing facilities, its equipment, the quality control program, what subcontracting programs were envisaged, inquiries as to quotations from seller of long lead items and all of the other matter which go into a sound manufacturing operation. Before and after the actual day of this visit of the pre-award survey team, [Edgewater] had been supplying financial data to DCAAS in Orlando as a part of the pre-award survey."

These are all appropriate matters on which to base a responsibility determination and are consistent with the requirements of FAR, 48 C.F.R. § 9.104, that set forth the general and special standards to be applied by the survey team in its evaluations.

See *Kitco, Inc.*, Comp. Gen. Dec. B-221386, 86-1 CPD ¶ 321 (requesting and furnishing information regarding background and capability of proposed subcontractor did not preclude award without discussions); *Dynamic Resources, Inc.*, Comp. Gen. Dec. B-277213, 97-2 CPD ¶ 100 (preaward survey not improper discussions); and *UNICCO Gov't Servs., Inc.*, Comp. Gen. Dec. B-277658, 97-2 CPD ¶ 134 (site visit to offeror's facility and inspection of equipment did not constitute discussions).

FAR 15.306(a) is not clear as to whether these decisions allowing communications to determine responsibility of the offeror as part of the clarification process permit the same amount of communication when an agency intends to evaluate the capability of the offerors on a relative basis, as is normally done in a tradeoff procurement. However, the Federal Circuit appears to have concluded that similar reasoning should be followed in ascertaining the scope of FAR 15.306(a). See *Information Tech. & Applications Corp. v. United States*, 316 F.3d 1312 (Fed. Cir. 2003), holding that requests for information (ENs) about the qualifications of subcontractors and the amount of work they would perform were clarifications not discussions, stating at 1322-23:

> The communications in question in this case, ENs 0001, 0002 and 0002a, were for the purpose of obtaining additional information about the subcontractors that RSIS had listed in its proposal. Specifically, the ENs asked RSIS to provide "additional relevant past performance information, to further describe the lead role for [the subcontractors]." EN 0002. In its response, RSIS explained which parts of the project each subcontractor would support and detailed their relevant experience with regard to those tasks. The government argues that these communications constituted clarifications, and not discussions. We agree for two reasons.

> First, these communications were not discussions. As explained above, the new regulation contemplates discussions as occurring in the context of negotiations. 48 C.F.R. § 15.306(d) (2002). As such, when discussions are opened, bidders have the opportunity to revise their proposals, in order "to maximize the Govern-

ment's ability to obtain the best value." *Id.* at § 15.306(d)(2). In this case, the government did not give RSIS the opportunity to revise its proposal, and RSIS did not change the terms of its proposal to make it more appealing to the government. Under these circumstances, it is clear that ENs 0001, 0002 and 0002a, and RSIS's response to them, did not constitute discussions.

Second, the Air Force's request was merely a request for clarification of the relevant experience of RSIS's subcontractors, as permitted by the regulation. The regulation provides that "offerors may be given the opportunity to clarify certain aspects of proposals." 48 C.F.R. § 15.306(a)(2) (2002). One example that the regulation provides of such a clarification is "the relevance of an offeror's past performance information . . . ." *Id.* We can discern no distinction between this clear example in the regulation and the Air Force's request for clarification of the subcontractors' relevant experience in this case. We therefore conclude that the challenged communications, ENs 0001, 0002 and 0002a, were merely requests for clarification.

We reject appellant's argument that the ENs could not be clarifications because they "requested additional information." Any meaningful clarification would require the provision of information, and the example of a clarification given in the regulation, "the relevance of an offeror's past performance information," requires the provision of information. *Id.* The appellant also contends that a clarification cannot call for new information if the information is "necessary to evaluate the proposal." There is no requirement in the regulation that a clarification not be essential for evaluation of the proposal. As one commentary has observed, under the new regulations, "'clarifications' by one offeror could lead to an increase in its past performance score or perhaps tilt the award in its favor." John S. Pachter *et al.*, *The FAR Part 15 Rewrite*, 98-05 Briefing Papers 1, 6 (1998). Appellant's cramped conception of "clarification" is, moreover, not in harmony with the stated purpose of the 1997 amendments, which was to "support[] more open exchanges between the Government and industry, allowing industry to better understand the requirement [sic] and the Government to better understand industry proposals." 62 Fed. Reg. at 51,224.

Even were the regulations not clear, we give deference to an agency's permissible interpretation of its own regulations. *United States v. Cleveland Indians Baseball Co.*, 532 U.S. 200, 218-19, 149 L. Ed. 2d 401, 121 S. Ct. 1433 (2001); *Am. Express Co. v. United States*, 262 F.3d 1376, 1382 (Fed. Cir. 2001). The agency designated the ENs as "FAR 13.306(a) clarifications" and included the notice, "please note that this clarification does not constitute oral discussions with the offeror." EN 0002 (referring to 48 C.F.R. § 15.306(a)). It was a reasonable interpretation of the acquisition regulations to view the ENs as clarifications, and we defer to that interpretation. We recently emphasized that "the [acquisition] regulations entrust the contracting officer with especially great discretion, extending even to his application of procurement regulations." *Am. Tel. & Tel. Co. v. United States*, 307 F.3d 1374, 1379 (Fed. Cir. 2002). The appellant here has not shown that the contracting officer misconstrued the regulations or that the procurement was not in accordance with the law.

This decision indicates that weight should be given to the intent of the agency in communication with the offerors. Hence, when an agency intends to probe capability information in the clarification process, this should be clearly stated in the RFP. Furthermore, all offerors should be treated in the same manner when this type of clarification is conducted. This will ensure that no offeror is given a preference prior to award without discussions by being given the opportunity to supplement or explain its capability while a competitor is not given the same opportunity.

The GAO had reached the same result in *Information Tech. & Applications Corp.*, B-288510, 2002 CPD ¶ 28, reasoning that this subcontractor information pertained to the relevance of the offeror's past performance. Several court decisions have also followed similar reasoning. See *Antarctic Support Assocs. v. United States*, 46 Fed. Cl. 145 (2000) (obtaining the names of references to vouch for the fact that a proposed subcontractor would continue to operate in the face of a declaration of bankruptcy); and *Forestry Surveys & Data v. United States*, 44 Fed. Cl. 493 (1999) (several offerors queried about aspects of their performance on prior contracts). See also *Griffy's Landscape Maint., LLC v. United States*, 46 Fed. Cl. 257 (2000), holding that an agency was *obligated* to verify a lack of required information relating to an offeror's insurance coverage in its proposal. The court reasoned that not including such information was a mistake that was apparent to the contracting officer and, therefore, should have led to a verification request. The court held that such a verification request was in the nature of a clarification not a discussion. This decision has been interpreted as being applicable only to "clerical errors," *Camden Shipping Corp. v. United States*, 89 Fed. Cl. 433 (2009); *C.W. Over & Sons v. United States*, 54 Fed. Cl. 514 (2002).

Subsequent GAO decisions have not followed the broad reasoning of the court in *Information Technology*. See, for example, *Computer Sciences Corp.*, Comp. Gen. Dec. B-298494.2, 2007 CPD ¶ 103, where the GAO explicitly rejected the argument that subcontracting plans could be made acceptable through the clarification process. In reaching this conclusion, it stated that its prior decisions holding that improvement of a subcontracting plan during an assessment of responsibility of the offeror was not a discussion did not apply when capability of the offerors was to be determined on a comparative basis, stating:

> The agency contends, however, citing a number of decisions of our Office, that exchanges regarding the acceptability of a required small business subcontracting plan — even the submission of a revised plan — relate to an offeror's responsibility and therefore are not discussions. See *General Dynamics-Ordnance & Tactical Sys., Inc.*, B-295987, B-295987.2, May 20, 2005, 2005 CPD ¶ 114 at 9-10; *AmClyde Engineered Prods. Co., Inc.*, B-228271.2, June 21, 1999, 99-2 CPD ¶ 5 at 8; *Kahn Instruments*, B-277973, Dec. 15, 1997, 98-1 CPD ¶ 11 at 10-11; *A.B Dick Co.*, B-233142, Jan. 31, 1989, 89-1 CPD ¶ 106 at 3; *Southeastern Center for Electrical Eng'g Educ.*, B-230692, July 6, 1988, 88-2 CPD ¶ 13 at 5-6.
>
> It is true that in each of the cases cited by [the agency] we found that exchanges concerning an offeror's small business subcontracting plan were not discussions

because those plans were only evaluated as part of the agency's responsibility determination. See, e.g., *General Dynamics-Ordnance & Tactical Sys., Inc., supra*, at 10 ("A request for, or providing of, information that relates to offeror responsibility, rather than proposal evaluation, does not constitute discussions and thus does not trigger the requirement to hold discussions with other competitive range offerors.") (footnote omitted). However, in each of these cases, unlike the RFP at issue here, the solicitation did not include a technical evaluation factor under which the comparative merits of offerors' small business subcontracting plans would be considered to determine which proposal represented the best value to the government and thus entitled to award. Thus, under the circumstances of each of these cases, the assessment of offerors' small business subcontracting plans could only be done as part of the agency's responsibility determination.

Nonetheless, the GAO has sometimes found that capability information can be obtained through the clarification process. See, for example, *Environmental Quality Mgmt., Inc.*, Comp. Gen. Dec. B-402247.2, 2010 CPD ¶ 75 (verifying that referenced contracts met the RFP relevance requirement); *Kuhana-Spectrum Joint Venture, LLC*, Comp. Gen. Dec. B-400803, 2009 CPD ¶ 36 (missing certifications and representations can be corrected during clarification); *USGC, Inc.*, Comp. Gen. Dec. B-400184.2, 2009 CPD ¶ 9 (explanations of composition of labor in acceptable technical proposals properly obtained through clarifications); *United Medical Sys.-DE, Inc.*, Comp. Gen. Dec. B-298438, 2006 CPD ¶ 148 (obtaining information showing that offeror had necessary equipment to perform work promised by the offer was proper clarification); *Park Tower Mgmt. Ltd.*, Comp. Gen. Dec. B-295589, 2005 CPD ¶ 77, and *Park Tower Mgmt. Ltd. v. United States*, 67 Fed. Cl. 548 (2005) (checking with offeror to determine whether it still intended to hire incumbent contractor's personnel was proper clarification); *AHNTECH, Inc.*, Comp. Gen. Dec. B-293582, 2004 CPD ¶ 113 (52 "clarification requests" seeking more information on how offeror would perform the work were proper clarifications); *Citrus College*, Comp. Gen. Dec. B-293543, 2004 CPD ¶ 104 (obtaining explanation of manning chart a proper clarification).

Other GAO decisions reach the opposite conclusion holding that capability information can only be obtained through discussions when the information is obtained to determine the "acceptability" of a proposal. See *General Injectables & Vaccines, Inc.*, Comp. Gen. Dec. B-298590, 2006 CPD ¶ 173 (clearing up inadequate responses to a significant number of the system security plan questions not proper clarification when offeror had to submit an acceptable plan to qualify for award); *T.J. Lambrecht Constr., Inc.*, Comp. Gen. Dec. B-294425, 2004 CPD ¶ 198 (obtaining experience information that offeror had omitted from proposal could not be done through clarification process); *Verizon Federal, Inc.*, Comp. Gen. Dec. B-293527, 2004 CPD ¶ 186 (obtaining resumes required to be submitted with proposal would have constituted discussions); *ACS State Healthcare, LLC*, Comp. Gen. Dec. B-292981, 2004 CPD ¶ 57 (amplifying poorly written aspects of technical proposal could not have been done through obtaining clarifications); *Ballast Ham Dredging BV*, Comp. Gen. Dec. B-291848, 2003 CPD ¶ 76 (obtaining required information on capability to schedule work would have constituted discussions); *Priority One Servs., Inc.*, Comp. Gen. Dec. B-288836, 2002 CPD ¶ 79 (allowing offeror to substitute key personnel for those that were unavailable or unacceptable was a discussion); and *J.A.Jones/IBC J.V.*, Comp. Gen. Dec. B-285627, 2000 CPD ¶ 161 (obtaining additional information about the qualifications of offerors design team would have been a discussion).

FAR 15.306(a) also allows the correction of "minor or clerical errors" as part of the clarification process. See *Galen Med. Assocs., Inc. v. United States*, 369 F.3d 1324 (Fed. Cir. 2004), permitting an offeror to raise its price to correct a mathematical error prior to award without discussions.

If the agency is evaluating the capability of the offerors through technical proposals that are used to assess their understanding of the work, interpreting the new FAR to permit supplementing or clarifying such technical proposals prior to award without discussions is directly contrary to the pre-FAR Part 15 rewrite interpretation, as discussed above. Hence, in such circumstances the agency should clearly describe its procedure in the RFP and should take great care to give all offerors an opportunity to supplement or clarify their proposals.

The provision in FAR 15.306(a)(2) that offerors "may" be given an opportunity to comment on adverse past performance information is permissive and, hence, a contracting officer may award without discussions to another offeror without obtaining such comments, *NMS Mgmt., Inc.*, Comp. Gen. Dec., B-286335, 2000 CPD ¶ 197; *U.S. Constructors, Inc.*, Comp. Gen. Dec. B-282776, 99-2 CPD ¶ 14; *Inland Servs. Corp.*, Comp. Gen. Dec. B-282272, 99-1 CPD ¶ 113; *Rohmann Servs., Inc.*, Comp. Gen. Dec. B-280154.2, 98-2 CPD ¶ 134. See *A.G. Cullen Constr., Inc.*, Comp. Gen. Dec. B-284049.2, 2000 CPD ¶ 45, holding that clarifications would be required in this situation if it was an abuse of discretion to fail to seek the offeror's comments, as follows:

> With regard specifically to clarifications concerning adverse past performance information to which the offeror has not previously had an opportunity to respond, we think that, for the exercise of discretion to be reasonable, the contracting officer must give the offeror an opportunity to respond where there clearly is a reason to question the validity of the past performance information, for example, where there are obvious inconsistencies between a reference's narrative comments and the actual ratings the reference gives the offeror. In the absence of such a clear basis to question the past performance information, we think that, short of acting in bad faith, the contracting officer reasonably may decide not to ask for clarifications.

See *United Coatings*, Comp. Gen. Dec. B-291978.2, 2003 CPD ¶ 146, applying this standard but finding no abuse of discretion because the agency had no reason to question the validity of the adverse information; *General Dynamics-Ordnance & Tactical Sys.*, Comp. Gen. Dec. B-295987, 2005 CPD ¶ 114, finding no abuse of discretion because agency had first-hand knowledge of the adverse information; and

Bannum, Inc., Comp. Gen. Dec. B-298281.2, 2006 CPD ¶ 163, finding no prejudice in failing to discuss adverse past performance information because protester had received high rating in spite of adverse information.

b. Information About Offers

Early decisions dealing with offer information made a distinction between obtaining information explaining the features of an offer and revisions to the offer that would preclude award without discussions. See *Amram Nowak Assocs., Inc.*, Comp. Gen. Dec. B-187253, 76-2 CPD ¶ 454, stating:

> The question of what constitutes discussions depends on whether an offeror has been given a chance to revise or modify its proposal. 51 Comp. Gen. 479, 481, *supra*. Thus, we have held that a requested "clarification" which resulted in a price reduction constituted discussions. 48 Comp. Gen. 663 (1969). However, an explanation by an offeror of the basis of its price reduction without an opportunity to change its proposal was held not to constitute discussions. B-170989, B-170990, November 17, 1971.

See also *Keco Indus., Inc.*, Comp. Gen. Dec. B-170990, Nov. 17, 1971, *Unpub.*, stating:

> In B-167643, November 14, 1969, we stated that the discussions contemplated by the statute relate to proposals within the competitive range but not to discussions relating to an offeror's responsibility or the ability to perform. In B-170751, September 23, 1970, 50 Comp. Gen. [202], cited by Keco's counsel, one of the offerors failed to acknowledge an addendum which changed the specifications and thereby affected the price. This offeror orally acknowledged the amendment subsequent to the closing time for receipt of proposals. In the written confirmation of the oral acknowledgment requested by the procuring activity, the offeror confirmed that the price offered was based on the specifications as changed by the amendment. It was held that this exchange constituted negotiations and that award could no longer be made on the basis of the initial proposals.
>
> The meeting with Trane on August 21, 1970, was intended only as an opportunity for Trane to explain its price reductions and was in fact so limited. Presumably there was no opportunity for Trane to make any change in its proposal or for the government representatives to effect any change in the solicitation provisions. Therefore, we do not believe that the meeting constitutes a basis for invalidating the award.

However, as the GAO broadened the definition of discussions and this interpretation was incorporated in the former FAR 15.601, communications were found to be discussions even though the terms of the offer were not changed. The theory of these holdings was that a discussion occurred if there was a communication involving "information essential for determining the acceptability of a proposal." See, for example, *International Resources Group*, Comp. Gen. Dec. B-286663, 2001 CPD

¶ 35 (a discussion had occurred when the contracting officer gave the winning of-feror a list of technical and cost comments regarding its proposal and permitted it to submit revisions to its proposal); *Integration Tech. Group, Inc.*, Comp. Gen. Dec. B-274288.5, 97-1 CPD ¶ 214 (identification of components to be furnished); and *Strategic Analysis, Inc.*, Comp. Gen. Dec. B-270075.4, 96-1 CPD ¶ 41 (inquiry of employment status of designated key employee where RFP required letters of intent for proposed key personnel not currently employees). In such cases the GAO found that discussions would have been required to alter or supplement information that had been part of the required proposal of the offeror. Nonetheless, the GAO continued to hold, in some cases, that obtaining explanations of a proposal were not discussions because no proposal revision had occurred. See *Houston Air, Inc.*, Comp. Gen. Dec. B-292382, 2003 CPD ¶ 144, finding no discussions where agency sought correc-tions to weight and balance information; *SRS Techs.*, Comp. Gen. Dec. B-291618.2, 2003 CPD ¶ 70, finding no discussions where the agency obtained information on how accounting systems accounted for uncompensated overtime; *WECO Cleaning Specialists, Inc.*, Comp. Gen. Dec. B-279305, 98-1 CPD ¶ 154, finding no discus-sions where the agency obtained cost or pricing data to ensure that the offeror's price was realistic; and *Robotic Sys. Tech.*, Comp. Gen. Dec. B-278195.2, 98-1 CPD ¶ 20, finding no discussions where the offeror explained its cost proposal but did not add any information that was not included in the original proposal. See also *Develop-ment Alternatives, Inc.*, Comp. Gen. Dec. B-279920, 98-2 CPD ¶ 54, holding that obtaining additional information to explain an offeror's technical proposal was not a discussion, stating:

> [T]he record shows that the questions asked are in the nature of clarifications — they merely request additional detail concerning information already presented in [the offeror's] proposal as revised by its written BAFO. For example, in its BAFO, [the offeror] reduced by ten the number of Bosnian lending professionals that it would use under the contract. During the oral interview the firm was asked to describe any changes that this reduction would require in the way the lending staff was deployed and organized. Other questions included requests for elabora-tion on the reasons for selecting particular personnel and on arguments made and positions taken in the BAFO to support a particular approach. Contrary to [the protester's] position, the fact that some of its scores changed as a result of the oral interview does not show that it was allowed to revise its proposal, but that its explanations of what was already proposed became more clear, at times to the firm's detriment and at times to its benefit.

There continue to be a variety of decisions under the current FAR 15.306(a). In general, obtaining information to explain an offeror's proposed costs or prices has been held to be a proper clarification as long as the offeror does not alter the pro-posed cost or price. See *VMD Sys. Integrators, Inc.*, Comp. Gen. Dec. B-401037.4, 2009 CPD ¶ 252 (request for each offeror to show that pricing rates had been au-dited); *Career Training Concepts, Inc. v. United States*, 83 Fed. Cl. 215 (2008), and *Career Training Concepts, Inc.*, Comp. Gen. Dec. B-311429, 2009 CPD ¶ 97 (request for the elements of the offeror's price and an explanation of the escalation rate used to determine the price); *Colson Servs. Corp.*, Comp. Gen. Dec. B-310971, 2008 CPD ¶ 85 (request as to whether offered rebates were on a monthly or annual basis a proper clarification because it did not represent "a meaningful opportunity to revise pricing"); *NCR Gov't Sys. LLC*, Comp. Gen. Dec. B-297959, 2006 CPD ¶ 82 (request for a revised catalog of prices when the offer contained all of the required prices with the catalog being merely a backup document); *SecureNet Co. v. United States*, 72 Fed. Cl. 800 (2006) (obtaining price realism analysis from DCAA was not a discussion); *SRS Techs.*, Comp. Gen. Dec. B-291618.2, 2003 CPD ¶ 70 (request for information on how accounting system dealt with uncompensated overtime); *Northeast MEP Servs., Inc.*, Comp. Gen. Dec. B-285963.9, 2001 CPD ¶ 66 (obtaining assurance that estimated costs covered all required services when some government evaluators thought the technical proposal might have indicated otherwise); *MG Indus.*, Comp. Gen. Dec. B-283010.3, 2000 CPD ¶ 17 (obtaining assurance that proposed price covered solicitation requirements); *Northeast MEP Servs., Inc.*, Comp. Gen. Dec. B-285963.9, 2001 CPD ¶ 66 (requesting "clarification" whether some of the services discussed in the technical proposal as "fee-based" services would result in additional costs to the government), and *MG Indus.*, Comp. Gen. Dec. B-283010.3, 2000 CPD ¶ 17 (asking the offeror to affirm that its statement that its price was based on furnishing the "total supply" of gas did not mean that the price did not apply to the indefinite delivery/indefinite quantity contract for which the offer had been submitted). These decisions frequently stated that the exchange is a clarification because the information was not required to determine the acceptability of the proposal.

The decisions vary with regard to obtaining information as to other elements of an offer. Most decisions hold that obtaining explanations about an offered product or service is a discussion. See *4D Security Solutions, Inc.*, Comp. Gen. Dec. B-400351.2, 2009 CPD ¶ 5 (explanation of characteristics of offered product could not be obtained during clarifications because this would allow the company to "materially alter or explain its quotation by having the agency consider information not contained within the four corners of its initial quotation"); *Government Telecommunications, Inc.*, Comp. Gen. Dec. B-299542.2, 2007 CPD ¶ 136 (obtaining information to determine whether offered products were available on the market could not be done through clarifications because this "would have involved material changes to the offeror's proposal"); *Gemmo-CCC*, Comp. Gen. Dec. B-297447.2, 2006 CPD ¶ 182 (obtaining required information describing the offered product would constitute discussions because it "would involve submission of information necessary to make the proposal acceptable"); *Southern California Eng'g, Inc.*, Comp. Gen. Dec. B-296244, 2005 CPD ¶ 134 (obtaining missing pump specifications needed to determine acceptability of product could only be done through discussions); *QuickHire, LLC*, Comp. Gen. Dec. B-293098, 2004 CPD ¶ 33 (clearing up vague or incomplete technical description of product offered would have required discussions); *ProMar*, Comp. Gen. Dec. B-292409, 2003 CPD ¶ 187 (obtaining missing product literature showing compliance with specifications would have required discussions); and *eMind*, Comp. Gen. Dec. B-289902, 2002 CPD ¶ 82 (obtaining required course descriptions nor permissible through clarifications). Compare *Houston Air, Inc.*, Comp. Gen. Dec. B-292382, 2003 CPD ¶ 144 (obtaining updated information on product not a discussion when offeror had already submitted acceptable information); *Firearms Training Sys., Inc. v. United States*, 41 Fed. Cl. 743 (1998) (demonstration of offered computer-operated simulator does not bar award without discussions).

The GAO has also followed prior decisions in holding that requiring an offeror to verify its online representations and certifications was a clarification not a discussion, *Kuhana-Spectrum Joint Venture, LLC*, Comp. Gen. Dec. B-400803, 2009 CPD ¶ 36.

It can be seen that there is a lack of clarity in the decisions regarding the distinction between clarifications and discussions when the government obtains additional information regarding offers. With the deletion of the FAR 15.601 definitions of discussions and clarification, and the stated intent of the drafters of the FAR Part 15 rewrite, it is arguable that agencies should be permitted to seek explanations of offers before award without discussions. This would be in accord with earlier holdings of the GAO prior to the adoption of the FAR.

If an agency adopts this interpretation of the FAR Part 15 rewrite, it should clearly state in the RFP that it reserves the right to seek information clarifying any element of an offer prior to award without discussions. Thereafter, in following this procedure, it should exercise great care to ensure that all offerors are treated even-handedly. Thus, if any offeror is permitted to clarify its offer, all other offerors whose offers are not fully understood should also be given an opportunity to clarify or explain their offers.

3. The Permissive Nature Of Clarifications

Because FAR 15.306(a) is permissive rather than mandatory, most decisions hold that contracting officers have a great deal of discretion in determining whether to ask for clarification of some element of a proposal. See *Gulf Group, Inc. v. United States*, 61 Fed. Cl. 338 (2004), where the agency evaluation team stated that clarification of the protester's experience was necessary but the source selection official proceeded to award to a competitor without obtaining the clarification. The court denied the protest, stating at 360:

> In support of its argument that the Corps's failure to exercise its discretionary authority was itself an abuse of discretion, Gulf Group notes the announced goal of the clarifications policy: "This policy is expected to help offerors, especially small entities that may not be familiar with proposal preparation, by permitting easy clarification of limited aspects of their proposals." Gulf Group argues that it is exactly the sort of business this regulation was intended to benefit. But the benefit that was created, if it could even be characterized as such, was not the *right* to clarify information in proposals. The benefit, instead, is that whenever the contracting officials think a clarification of certain aspects of a proposal would be helpful, *they* have

the discretion to seek such a clarification, even when discussions with all bidders would not occur. The FAR allows, but does not require, such exchanges to take place. As this Court has found, "an agency representative has broad discretion to decide whether to communicate with a firm concerning its performance history." *JWK International Corp v United States*, 52 Fed Cl 650, 661 (2002).

Compare *L-3 Communications Eotech, Inc. v. United States*, 83 Fed. Cl. 643 (2008), granting a protest when the agency did not seek clarification of unclear information on conducting a test procedure but established a competitive range of one with a competitor with the intention of allowing that company to work out issues of noncompliance with the specifications during discussions.

The discretionary clarification rule has resulted in a number of decisions holding that an agency is not required to permit an offeror to submit information explaining or rebutting adverse past performance information on which it has had no previous opportunity to comment. See *SKE Int'l, Inc.*, Comp. Gen. Dec. B-311383, 2008 CPD ¶ 111; *JWK Int'l Corp. v. United States*, 52 Fed. Cl. 650 (2002); *NMS Mgmt., Inc.*, Comp. Gen. Dec. B-286335, 2000 CPD ¶ 197. In *General Dynamics — Ordnance & Tactical Sys.*, Comp. Gen. Dec. B-295987, 2005 CPD ¶ 114, the GAO indicated that giving an offeror such an opportunity would be required "where there clearly is a reason to question the validity of the past performance information" being used by the agency.

The discretionary clarification rule has also resulted in a number of decisions holding that clarifications can be conducted with only one offeror. See *DynCorp Int'l LLC v. United States*, 76 Fed. Cl. 528, 540 (2007), holding that it was proper to clear up minor issues with one offeror without clarifying the information submitted by the protester. See also *General Dynamics-Ordinance & Tactical Sys.*, Comp. Gen. Dec. B-295987, 2005 CPD ¶ 114, stating:

> [C]larifications, in contrast to discussions, do not trigger a requirement that the agency seek clarifications from other offerors. See *Landoll Corp.*, B-291381 et al., Dec. 23, 2002, 2003 CPD ¶ 40 at 8; *Priority One Servs., Inc.*, B-288836, B-288836.2, Dec. 17, 2001, 2002 CPD ¶ 79 at 5; *Global Assocs. Ltd.*, B-271693, B-271693.2, Aug. 2, 1996, 96-2 CPD ¶ 100 at 4. While we recognize that there may be a rare situation where it would be unfair to request clarification from one offeror but not from another, the mere fact that an agency requests clarification from one offeror and not another, does not constitute unfair treatment.

Similarly, in *INDUS Tech., Inc.*, Comp. Gen. Dec. B-297800.13, 2007 CPD ¶ 116, it was proper to not clarify whether a cover letter statement was intended to indicate that the offeror would not comply with a mandatory requirement even though the agency had clarified issues in other proposals, and in *Landoll Corp.*, Comp. Gen. Dec. B-291381, 2003 CPD ¶ 40, it was proper not to clarify issues because such action would not have changed the protester's competitive position. Thus, only when clarification with only one offeror is perceived as resulting in unfair treatment to another offeror, will such action be held to be improper.

B. Communications Prior to Establishing the Competitive Range

The previous FAR did not deal with the subject of communications with parties prior to the establishment of the competitive range. The initial proposed rewrite of FAR Part 15 in 61 Fed. Reg. 48380, Sept. 12, 1996, contained an excellent rule that would have allowed contracting agencies to fully understand proposals before making the decision to award without discussions or establish a competitive range:

15.407 — Communications with offerors.

(a) Competition on other than price alone and the source selection process necessarily involve communications between the Government and competing offerors. Open communications support the goal of efficiency in Government procurement (10 U.S.C. 2304(j) and 41 U.S.C. 253(h)) by providing the Government with relevant information (in addition to that submitted in the offeror's initial proposal) needed to understand and evaluate the offeror's proposal. The nature and extent of communications between the Government and offerors is a matter of contracting officer judgment.

(b) *Communication with offerors prior to establishment of the competitive range.* Communication with offerors after receipt of proposals, but prior to establishment of the competitive range (or award, if award is to be made without discussions), is encouraged to obtain information to facilitate the Government's decision either to award without discussions or determine the competitive range. Information received during this phase of communications may provide context to the proposal in that it allows the Government to understand the offeror's intent. Consequently, it may be used in proposal evaluation. Communications conducted pursuant to this paragraph-

(1) Are not "discussions" (see 15.409(c));

(2) Do not permit changes in an offeror's proposal other than correction of mistakes;

(3) Are conducted to obtain information that explains or resolves ambiguities or other concerns (e.g., perceived errors, perceived omissions, or perceived deficiencies) in the offeror's proposal. However, a willingness by the offeror to correct any perceived errors, perceived omissions, perceived deficiencies, or other concerns does not require that the offeror be placed in the competitive range;

(4) Shall only be initiated if authorized by the contracting officer; and

(5) Need not be conducted with all offerors. For example, when trying to determine the competitive range, the Government could limit communications to those offerors, whose proposals, on initial evaluation, would be

neither clearly "in" nor clearly "out" of the competitive range. Similarly, when trying to decide whether or not to award without discussions, the Government could limit communications to the offeror(s), based on initial evaluation, deemed to have the greatest likelihood of award.

As discussed earlier, adverse comments on this proposed rule led to the promulgation of separate rules for "clarifications" that could occur before award without discussions and "communications" that could occur before establishing a competitive range. The pre-competitive range rule was incorporated into FAR 15.306(b) by the FAR Part 15 rewrite as follows:

(b) Communications with offerors before establishment of the competitive range. Communications are exchanges, between the Government and offerors, after receipt of proposals, leading to establishment of the competitive range. If a competitive range is to be established, these communications —

(1) Shall be limited to the offerors described in paragraphs (b)(1)(i) and (b)(1)(ii) of this section and —

(i) Shall be held with offerors whose past performance information is the determining factor preventing them from being placed within the competitive range. Such communications shall address adverse past performance information to which an offeror has not had a prior opportunity to respond; and

(ii) May only be held with those offerors (other than offerors under paragraph (b)(1)(i) of this section) whose exclusion from, or inclusion in, the competitive range is uncertain;

(2) May be conducted to enhance Government understanding of proposals; allow reasonable interpretation of the proposal; or facilitate the Government's evaluation process. Such communications shall not be used to cure proposal deficiencies or material omissions, materially alter the technical or cost elements of the proposal, and/or otherwise revise the proposal. Such communications may be considered in rating proposals for the purpose of establishing the competitive range;

(3) Are for the purpose of addressing issues that must be explored to determine whether a proposal should be placed in the competitive range. Such communications shall not provide an opportunity for the offeror to revise its proposal, but may address —

(i) Ambiguities in the proposal or other concerns (e.g., perceived deficiencies, weaknesses, errors, omissions, or mistakes (see 14.407)); and

(ii) Information relating to relevant past performance; and

(4) Shall address adverse past performance information to which the offeror has not previously had an opportunity to comment.

The promulgation comments indicate that these provisions were adopted to assuage the concerns of small businesses. See 62 Fed. Reg. 51229 (1997):

> Public comments indicated that the second proposed rule did not establish a "bright line" distinction between when communications conducted in order to establish a competitive range end, and when discussions begin. Small businesses were concerned that the Government may conduct inappropriate communications with selected offerors prior to the establishment of the competitive range to the detriment of small businesses. We revised the final rule to accommodate this concern by clearly defining when discussions begin. We adopted this alternative to preclude the occurrence of the inappropriate communications that concerned small businesses.

While these provisions seem unnecessary, because there is little harm in conducting discussions before establishing a competitive range rather than after the range is established, they do serve the purpose of encouraging contracting agencies to obtain necessary information in order to make a valid competitive range determination. Thus, they give the contracting officer considerable discretion in seeking both offer and capability information on offerors when their inclusion in the competitive range is uncertain. Seeking such information permits the agency to make the competitive range determination based on a full understanding of the proposal — furthering the goal of establishing a competitive range consisting of only those offerors that are most highly rated. The only limitation on such communications is that the proposals may not be revised, FAR 15.306(b)(2) and (3). The only way to carry out the intent of this provision of facilitating the competitive range determination is to interpret the term "proposal" to mean "offer."

Where the evaluation indicates, with certainty, that an offer is outside the competitive range, communication is required for past performance information that the offeror has not had an opportunity to address, FAR 15.306(b)(1)(i). However, communications concerning other issues with the proposal are discretionary with the agency. See *L-3 Communications EOTech, Inc.*, Comp. Gen. Dec. B-311453, 2008 CPD ¶ 139 (no requirement that agency ask offeror whether its test procedure was correctly written when the offered product had failed the procedure); *Professional Performance Development Group, Inc.*, Comp. Gen. Dec. B-311273, 2008 CPD ¶ 101 (no requirement that agency give protester the opportunity to correct significant informational deficiencies); *Americom Gov't Servs., Inc.*, Comp. Gen. Dec. B-292242, 2003 CPD ¶ 163 136 (no requirement to allow protester to cure deficiencies); and *The Cmty. Partnership LLC*, Comp. Gen. Dec. B-286844, 2001 CPD ¶ 38 (protester properly excluded from competitive range without communication because decision not uncertain and past performance not determining factor). See *Government Telecommunications, Inc.*, Comp. Gen. Dec. B-299542.2, 2007 CPD ¶ 136, stating:

[C]ommunications are limited exchanges between the agency and offerors after receipt of proposals leading to the establishment of the competitive range. An agency is required to hold communications with offerors whose past performance information is the determining factor preventing their proposals from being placed in the competitive range; otherwise, an agency may, but is not required to, engage in communications with offerors whose exclusion from, or inclusion in, the competitive range is uncertain. FAR § 15.306(b)(1); *Americom Gov't. Servs., Inc.*, [Comp. Gen. Dec. B-292242, 2003 CPD ¶ 163] at 6. As with clarifications, communications are not to be used to cure proposal deficiencies or material omissions, materially alter the technical or cost elements of the proposal, and/or otherwise revise the proposal. FAR § 15.306(b)(2).

The decisions on correcting mistakes prior to establishing the competitive range are somewhat contradictory. See *CSE Constr.*, Comp. Gen. Dec. B-291268.2, 2004 CPD ¶ 207, holding that FAR 15.306(b) required the contracting officer to verify whether a mistake had been made. See also *U.S. Facilities, Inc.*, Comp. Gen. Dec. B-293029, 2004 CPD ¶ 17, ruling that the contracting officer had properly requested that a company verify whether it had made a mistake in its prices. Compare *Battelle Memorial Inst.*, Comp. Gen. Dec. B-299533, 2007 CPD ¶ 94, holding that there was no requirement that an offeror be allowed to correct an alleged mistake that its option prices were not clearly stated, reasoning:

> Battelle argues that the agency improperly rejected its initial proposal based on Battelle's omission of the option year pricing. Battelle contends that the agency should have suspected that Battelle had made a "mistake or clerical error" in its proposal and had a "duty to verify" Battelle's proposal and conduct "clarifications" to allow Battelle to correct the omission. In support of its argument, Battelle cites FAR § 15.306(a)(2), which permits clarifications to "resolve minor or clerical errors," and FAR § 15.306(b)(3)(i), which permits communications before the establishment of the competitive range to address proposal ambiguities such as "errors, omissions, or mistakes."

> An offeror bears the burden of submitting and adequately written proposal that contains all of the information required under a solicitation, *Sam Facility Mgmt, Inc.*, B-292237, July 22, 2003, 2003 CPD ¶ 147 at 5, and an agency may reject a proposal that omits required pricing. *Joint Venture Penauillie Italia S.p.A; Co-fathec S.p.A; SEB.CO S.a.s; CO.PEL.S.a.s.*, B-298865, B-298865.2, Jan. 3, 2007, 2007 CPD ¶ 7 at 6. Although, in an appropriate case, an agency may allow an offeror to correct a mistake or clerical error in a cost or price proposal through clarifications (as opposed to discussions), when it does so, both the existence of the mistake or error and the amount intended by the offeror must be apparent from the face of the proposal. *Id.* at 8. Here, although the existence of Battelle's error was clear from the face of its proposal, it was not obvious what pricing Battelle intended to propose for the missing option years. Although, as Battelle points out, the initial proposal referred to "inflation adjustment[s]" in the narrative portion of the proposal, these vague references do not explain Battelle's intended pricing for the option years. That is, Battelle's option year pricing, as reflected in the 24 pages of pricing spreadsheets and additional narrative that Battelle provided to

the agency in its agency protest, could not be gleaned from Battelle's references to inflation adjustments in the initial proposal submission, and did not constitute "minor or clerical errors" as contemplated by the FAR. Thus, we find that the omission of Battelle's option year pricing could not be corrected through clarification or verification. See *University of Dayton Research Inst.*, B-296946.6, June 15, 2006, 2006 CPD ¶ 102 at 8.

Regarding Battelle's argument that "errors, omissions, or mistakes" can be corrected by communications before the establishment of the competitive range, FAR § 15.306(b)(2) specifically provides that communications under this section "shall not be used to cure proposal deficiencies or material omissions, materially alter the technical or cost elements of the proposal, and/or otherwise revise the proposal." See also FAR § 15.306(b)(3) ("communications shall not provide an opportunity for the offeror to revise its proposal"). Again, we agree with the agency that Battelle's omission of the option year pricing is material, given the RFP's requirements to provide detailed option year pricing for evaluation, and any attempt to cure this omission would necessitate submission of a revised proposal and would constitute discussions.

See also *Aeronautical Instrument & Radio Co.*, Comp. Gen. Dec. B-298582.2, 2007 CPD ¶ 10, where mistake correction was refused because the protester did not furnish the required evidence of the mistake, and *U.S. Reconstruction & Development Corp.*, Comp. Gen. Dec. B-296195, 2005 CPD ¶ 126, where proposing nonconforming work was not the type of mistake subject to correction.

With respect to offers that are clearly within the competitive range, there is no need for communications prior to the conduct of negotiations.

C. Oral Presentations

Oral presentations were incorporated into FAR 15.102 by the rewrite. FAR 15.102(a) states that oral presentations can occur at any time during the acquisition process. Presentations that occur during the discussion process following the establishment of the competitive range will be controlled by the negotiation rules in FAR 15.306(d), which will be discussed in Chapter 8. This section is concerned with communications during oral presentations prior to award without discussions and prior to the establishment of the competitive range.

The new regulations appear to indicate that oral presentations conducted prior to award without discussions can encompass both capability information and information explaining offers, but may not be used to permit an offeror to alter its offer. It is clear that these regulations authorize broadened exchange of information when oral presentations are conducted. FAR 15.102 does not use the term "clarification," and the FAR 15.102(c) suggested subjects for presentations consist of both capability and offer information. FAR 15.102(a) indicates that such presentations may "substitute for, or augment, written information" and that they are "subject to the same restrictions as written information." Thus, is appears that oral presentations should be subject to the same rules as written information. See also FAR 15.102(g) stating:

> If, during an oral presentation, the Government conducts discussions (see 15.306(d)), the Government must comply with 15.306 and 15.307.

This provision, by its reference to FAR 15.306(d), indicates that award on initial offers would be precluded only where the communications are the negotiations described in FAR 15.306(d).

One way to reconcile these provisions is to treat oral presentations as the final part of the proposal — eliciting only information that is not covered in the written proposal and limiting the exchange of information during any interview or question and answer session to that scope of information. See FAR 15.102(a) and (b) describing oral presentations as a means for each offeror to submit "portions" or "part" of its proposal through such presentations. In such circumstances, the entire oral presentation process can be regarded as the initial obtaining of information to be used for evaluation of each offeror's capability and there can be no issue of proposal revision since all information submitted would be initial proposal information. This interpretation will be effective as long as the agency does not elicit information during the oral presentation that significantly varies information contained in the written proposal. See *Aliron Int'l, Inc.*, Comp. Gen. Dec. B-285048.2, 2000 CPD ¶ 125, denying a protest that discussions had occurred during an oral presentation. The GAO noted that the RFP had provided that the oral presentation was part of the proposal and concluded:

> We also find factually unsupported Aliron's contention that the agency engaged in discussions during the oral presentations. The agency denies that it did anything more during those presentations than seek clarifications of the proposals, and Aliron's protest — alleging essentially that the questions asked were minor — in fact supports the agency's position. In Aliron's words, the agency was "seeking amplification of certain aspects of Aliron's proposal" at the oral presentation. These essentially undisputed facts constitute clarifications, not discussions.

Whatever interpretation of the new FAR is arrived at, it should be clear that the very nature of oral presentations involves the exchange of information. It might be expected that a broader range of communications would be permitted where the presentations involve all offerors submitting acceptable offers. The government made this argument in *General Physics Federal Sys., Inc.*, Comp. Gen. Dec. B-275934, 97-1 CPD ¶ 171. There, award was made after oral presentations, including a question and answer session, without a call for best and final offers. The protester provided information that was used by the government in downgrading its ranking. It argued that the oral presentations process constituted discussions and that it should have been given an opportunity to submit a best and final offer. The GAO found that the protester was not prejudiced because the presentation process conducted by the government did not result in unfair treatment and resolved the protest on those grounds. However, it declined to rule on the issue of whether the oral presentation process should be treated differently from other communications, stating:

> Given our conclusion — discussed in detail below — that General Physics was not prejudiced by the Navy's actions, we conclude that this is not the appropriate case for a substantive ruling on whether the question and answer session constituted discussions. Until such time as this matter is raised by a party with a stake in the outcome, we will hold in abeyance our views on whether this approach is consistent with current statutory and regulatory requirements.

See also *PEMCO World Air Servs.*, Comp. Gen. Dec. B-284240.3, 2000 CPD ¶ 71 (no discussion in reconciling seemingly inconsistent information); *Universal Bld'g Maint., Inc.*, Comp. Gen. Dec. B-282456, 99-2 CPD ¶ 32 (agency should not have considered information in oral presentation that offeror's parent organization would be part of the team performing the contract); and *Caterpillar, Inc.*, Comp. Gen. Dec. B-280362, 98-2 CPD ¶ 87 (no discussion in probing warranty administration procedures when no change made to offered warranty). In *Telestar Corp.*, Comp. Gen. Dec. B-275855, 97-1 CPD ¶ 150, the GAO found that no discussions had occurred during an oral presentation where the agency asked questions to "clarify written materials," "amplify areas not adequately explained," and "probe the qualifications and abilities of the key personnel proposed," explaining in a footnote:

> To the extent that the protester may have misconstrued the interview phase of the proposal process as oral discussions, the RFP explicitly advised that the interviews were not intended to be discussions and that offerors would not be entitled to submit revised offers upon their conclusion.

The same result was reached in *Development Alternatives, Inc.*, Comp. Gen. Dec. B-279920, 98-2 CPD ¶ 54. Similarly, in *BE, Inc.; PAI Corp.*, Comp. Gen. Dec. B-277978, 98-1 CPD ¶ 80, the GAO denied a protest that discussions had occurred during an oral presentation. The agency had asked the offeror to elaborate on the work it had done on prior contracts and to provide additional information on the qualifications of one of its proposed managers. The GAO stated:

> These questions were in the nature of clarifications — they merely sought additional detail concerning past performance information already presented in [the winning offeror's] proposal. The information was not substantial — the first question merely sought the identity of a defense programs organization, and the second sought information on only one presentation out of the several contract tasks. The information requested in no way can be said to have been necessary to establish the acceptability of [the winning offeror's] proposal.[3]

> [3] Indeed, we note that the current version of the FAR considers an opportunity to address "the relevance of an offeror's past performance information" to be in the same category as an opportunity "to resolve minor or clerical errors"; both are suitable for undertaking during clarifications. FAR 15.306(a)(2) (FAC 97-02).

[The protester] also cites a question posed by [the agency] to [the winning offeror] concerning its proposed Performance Assessment Division (PAD) Task Manager: "Slide 2.2.4-Please clarify [DELETED] years in DOE Programs . . . as it pertains to the required experience." However, the record indicates that [the agency's] question did not involve information essential for determining the acceptability of [the winning offeror's] proposal or otherwise afford [the winning offeror] an opportunity to revise its proposal. As noted by the agency, while [the agency's] question cited a brief entry on a chart in [the winning offeror's] slides which listed its proposed key personnel, [the winning offeror's] written proposal included a detailed 2-page resume for [the winning offeror's] proposed PAD task manager; according to the agency, this detailed resume clearly established the compliance of the proposed PAD task manager with the solicitation's minimum experience requirements for that position.

While these cases do not interpret the post-FAR Part 15 rewrite language, a similar result was reached in *Sierra Military Health Servs., Inc.*, Comp. Gen. Dec. B-292780, 2004 CPD ¶ 55, where GAO found that information provided in an oral presentation before the agency personnel had asked any questions "could not have been the result of discussions" because it was part of the initial presentation. In addition, the GAO held that a question about the scope of the offeror's experience was a clarification request not a discussion. See also *Synoptic Sys. Corp.*, Comp. Gen. Dec. B-290789.4, 2003 CPD ¶ 42, where the GAO treated an oral presentation as a means of obtaining information about the lines of communication within the offeror's organization. On the other hand, allowing an offeror to change its offer as a result of the exchange during an oral presentation has been held to be a discussion, *Global Analysis Information Tech. Servs., Inc.*, Comp. Gen. Dec. B-298840.2, 2007 CPD ¶ 57 (offeror changed option prices); *TDS, Inc.*, Comp. Gen. Dec. B-292674, 2003 CPD ¶ 204 (offeror changed price and technical proposal).

In any event, the decisions appear to indicate that agencies have considerable discretion in permitting a broad scope of communication about information in conducting oral presentations prior to award without discussions if they do not permit offeror's to revise their offers. Note, however, that in *TDS, Inc.*, the GAO stated a rule that could be interpreted as broadening this distinction between obtaining information and permitting a change to an offer:

> The FAR anticipates "dialogue among the parties" in the course of an oral presentation, FAR § 15.102(a), and we see nothing improper in agency personnel expressing their view about vendors' quotations or proposals, in addition to listening to the vendors' presentations, during those sessions. Once the agency personnel begin speaking, rather than merely listening, in those sessions, however, that dialogue may constitute discussions. As we have long held, the acid test for deciding whether an agency has engaged in discussions is whether the agency has provided an opportunity for quotations or proposals to be revised or modified. See, e.g., *Priority One Servs., Inc.*, B-288836, B-288836.2, Dec. 17, 2001, 2002 CPD ¶ 79 at 5. Accordingly, where agency personnel comment on, or raise substantive questions or concerns about, vendors' quotations or proposals in the course of an oral presentation, and either simultaneously or subsequently afford

the vendors an opportunity to make revisions in light of the agency personnel's comments and concerns, discussions have occurred. See FAR § 15.102(g).

Thus, it is clear that agencies will be required to follow the procedure for an oral presentation described in the RFP and will also be required to treat all offerors evenhandedly in conducting oral presentations.

If an agency has decided to establish a competitive range, the oral presentations would normally be scheduled after the range had been established. Then oral presentations would be conducted only with those offerors in the competitive range, and it would not matter if discussions occurred during the oral presentation or later in the process. See, for example, *L&M Techs., Inc.*, Comp. Gen. Dec. B-278044.5, 98-1 CPD ¶ 131, finding that the agency had followed proper procedures in conducting an oral presentation with offerors in the competitive range, conducting discussions immediately thereafter, obtaining and evaluating best and final offers, and obtaining another set of best and final offers without conducting additional oral presentations. The GAO concluded that there was no impropriety with this procedure because all offerors had been given the same opportunity to revise their proposals. See also *RTF/TCI/EAI J.V.*, Comp. Gen. Dec. B-280422.3, 98-2 CPD ¶ 162, where oral presentations were conducted only with offerors in the competitive range.

If oral presentations were conducted in order to determine which offerors should be placed in the competitive range, the rules in FAR 15.306(b) would apply, but there would appear to be little or no harm if discussions occurred at this time because the offerors would be requested to submit final proposal revisions after the conclusion of discussions. See, for example, *Dynamic Resources, Inc.*, Comp. Gen. Dec. B-277213, 97-2 CPD ¶ 100.

FAR 15.102 contains the following additional guidance on the procedures to be followed when oral presentations are required:

> (e) The contracting officer shall maintain a record of oral presentations to document what the Government relied upon in making the source selection decision. The method and level of detail of the record (e.g., videotaping, audio tape recording, written record, Government notes, copies of offeror briefing slides or presentation notes) shall be at the discretion of the source selection authority. A copy of the record placed in the file may be provided to the offeror.

> (f) When an oral presentation includes information that the parties intend to include in the contract as material terms or conditions, the information shall be put in writing. Incorporation by reference of oral statements is not permitted.

While this regulation gives the contracting officer the choice of the method of documentation, the GAO has granted protests when the documentation did not indicate the content of the presentation that led to a reduced score for the protester, *Checchi & Co. Consulting, Inc.*, Comp. Gen. Dec. B-285777, 2001 CPD ¶ 132. In that case there was conflicting evidence as to what subjects the protester had covered in its presentation and no "contemporaneous record" of the presentation. See also *Johnson Controls Security Sys.*, Comp. Gen. Dec. B-296490, 2007 CPD ¶ 102 (agency criticized for lack of any documentation or presentation); *e-LYNXX Corp.*, Comp. Gen. Dec. B-292761, 2003 CPD ¶ 219 (lack of documentation required hearing that produced conflicting testimony which did not resolve the protest); *J & J Maint., Inc.*, Comp. Gen. Dec. B-284708.2, 2000 CPD ¶ 106 (evaluators' notes on the presentation held insufficient because they did not summarize the presentation); and *Future-Tec Mgmt. Sys., Inc.*, Comp. Gen. Dec. B-283793.5, 2000 CPD ¶ 59 (lack of any documentation led to the granting of the protest). These cases indicate that some recording of the presentation should be made in order to create the type of evidence required by the GAO.

D. Mistakes

The statutes do not deal with the subject of mistakes discovered or alleged prior to award. Prior to the FAR rewrite, FAR 15.607 contained detailed procedures directing contracting officers to examine proposals for mistakes. Where communications were considered to prejudice "the interest of other offerors" or where correction of a mistake would require reference "to documents, worksheets, or other data outside the solicitation and proposal," the mistake could be corrected only through oral or written discussions with all offerors within the competitive range. These provisions were removed in the final rewrite, and the FAR now contains only fragmentary procedures for correction of mistakes.

Under the FAR rewrite, as was the case under the prior regulations, allegations of error and requests for verification and subsequent verifications that mistakes have not been made are not discussions but may be conducted as necessary to clarify whether a mistake has been made, *U.S. Facilities, Inc.*, Comp. Gen. Dec. B-293029, 2004 CPD ¶ 17; *R&B Rubber & Eng'g, Inc.*, Comp. Gen. Dec. B-214299, 84-1 CPD ¶ 595. Similarly, because a proposal may be withdrawn freely, communications resulting in withdrawal do not require discussions with all offerors. However, the FAR contains no explicit requirement that a contracting officer request verification when a mistake is suspected (as is the case in sealed bidding under FAR 14.407-1). Nonetheless, in *Griffy's Landscape Maint. LLC v. United States*, 46 Fed. Cl. 257 (2000), a contracting officer was required to verify whether a mistake had been made when the offeror failed to provide the name and telephone number of a point of contact for its insurer — a failure which the court concluded was a "clerical mistake." Similarly, in *CSE Constr.*, Comp. Gen. Dec. B-291268.2, 2004 CPD ¶ 207, the GAO held that FAR 15.306(b) required the contracting officer to verify whether a mistake had been made.

The deletion of the pre-rewrite FAR 15.607 and its requirements for correction of mistakes through the discussion process raises the question of what types of mistakes may be corrected without requiring discussions with all offerors. It appears that the authors of the FAR Part 15 rewrite intended to adopt the rule applicable to sealed bidding when they indicated in FAR 15.001 that a "proposal modification" is a change made to a proposal "to correct a mistake at any time before award." This would allow correction of mistakes prior to award without discussions as is done in sealed bidding procurements. See FAR 14.407 and the discussion in Chapter 5, Section IV of Cibinic & Nash, *Formation of Government Contracts* (3d ed. 1998). Application of these rules would require that the contracting officer request verification of an offer whenever a mistake was suspected and would permit correction of a mistake at any time that it met the requirements of the regulation. This would permit the contracting officer to deal with mistakes as they were identified or disclosed without losing the right to award the contract without discussions. See *U.S. Facilities, Inc.*, Comp. Gen. Dec. B-293029, 2004 CPD ¶ 17, holding that asking the offeror to verify its price or request correction of a mistake did not constitute discussions. Correction of a mistake to an *offer* should not be treated as a clarification because it is clear that offerors cannot be altered during the clarification process. Rather, correction of a mistake is a distinct process that should routinely occur as an agency is evaluating a proposal. Stated differently, correction of a mistake in an offer is the only alteration to an offer that can properly occur prior to award without discussions – as occurs regularly in the sealed bidding process.

However, FAR 15.306(a) only includes communications to "resolve minor or clerical errors" under the description of "clarifications." See *Galen Med. Assocs., Inc. v. United States*, 369 F.3d 1324 (Fed. Cir. 2004), permitting an offeror to raise its price to correct a mathematical error prior to award without discussions. In contrast, the GAO has followed the prior rule significantly limiting the correction of mistakes in the clarification process. See *Joint Venture Penauillie Italia S.p.A.; Cofathec S.p.A.; SEB.CO S.a.s.; CO.PEL.S.a.s.*, Comp. Gen. Dec. B-298865, 2007 CPD ¶ 7, where the GAO ruled that the omission of option year pricing was not a correctable mistake during the clarification process, stating:

> An agency may allow an offeror to correct a clerical error in a cost or price proposal through clarifications, as opposed to discussions, where the existence of the mistake and the amount intended by the offeror is clear from the face of the proposal. *Joint Threat Servs.*, B-278168, B-278168.2, Jan. 5, 1998, 98-1 CPD ¶ 18 at 12-13; see also FAR § 15.306. However, both the existence of an error and the intended pricing must be apparent from the face of the proposal. *CIGNA Gov't Servs.*, LLC, May 4, 2006, B-297915.2, 2006 CPD ¶ 74 at 9.

This same narrow rule has been followed in *Paraclete Contracts*, Comp. Gen. Dec. B-299883, 2007 CPD ¶ 153 (improper to obtain clarification of ambiguous prices by using mistake correction procedures because the prices were not "apparent on the face of its offer"); *Battelle Memorial Inst.*, Comp. Gen. Dec. B-299533, 2007 CPD ¶ 94 (decision not to obtain clarification of omitted option prices by using mistake correction procedures proper because the prices "were not apparent on the face of the proposal"); *CIGNA Gov't Servs., LLC*, Comp. Gen. Dec. B-297915.2, 2006 CPD ¶ 74 (improper to obtain clarification of level of effort in final proposal revision when correct level was not apparent it revision's face); and *Omega World Travel, Inc.*, Comp. Gen. Dec. B-283218, 2002 CPD ¶ 5 (correcting erroneous application of discount rate could only be done through discussions). In *IPlus, Inc.*, Comp. Gen. Dec. B-298020, 2006 CPD ¶ 90, it was proper to correct contract line item prices to match sub line item prices and to delete the price from a contract line item that called for no price because these were clerical errors that could be seen from the face of the proposal. Similarly, in *National Beef Packing Co.*, Comp. Gen. Dec. B-296534, 2005 CPD ¶ 168, it was proper to correct the labeling of a product (changing "case ready ground beef" to "course ground beef") because the specifications clearly called for course ground beef.

FAR 15.306(b)(3)(i) includes "errors, omissions, or mistakes (see 14.407)" as items which might be addressed prior to the establishment of the competitive range. This appears to indicate that there is more discretion to correct mistakes prior to establishing the competitive range – permitting an agency to correct a mistake that kept an offeror out of the competitive range. However, it has been held that this is not a mandatory procedure with the result that offerors can be excluded from the competitive range without having the opportunity to correct a mistake, *Battelle Memorial Inst.*, Comp. Gen. Dec. B-299533, 2007 CPD ¶ 94 (omitting option prices from proposal); *Aeronautical Instrument & Radio Co.*, Comp. Gen. Dec. B-298582.2, 2007 CPD ¶ 10 (insufficient evidence of mistake furnished by protester); *U.S. Reconstruction & Dev. Corp.*, Comp. Gen. Dec. B-296195, 2005 CPD ¶ 126 (proposing nonconforming work not the type of mistake than is correctable under FAR 15.306(b)).

CHAPTER 6

EVALUATION AND RANKING OF PROPOSALS

Evaluation is an ongoing process that starts upon the receipt of proposals, continues during communications and negotiations, and concludes with the evaluation of final proposal revisions. The purpose of evaluation is to assess the quality of each offer and to determine the capability of each offeror. However, this may be done only by evaluating proposals in terms of the evaluation factors set forth in the Request for Proposals (RFP). The results of proposal evaluation are explained in narrative comments of the evaluators and are generally summarized in some type of scoring system. FAR 15.305(a) states the basic rules for proposal evaluation as follows:

> Proposal evaluation is an assessment of the proposal and the offeror's ability to perform the prospective contract successfully. An agency shall evaluate competitive proposals and then assess their relative qualities solely on the factors and subfactors specified in the solicitation. Evaluations may be conducted using any rating method or combination of methods, including color or adjectival ratings, numerical weights, and ordinary rankings. The relative strengths, deficiencies, significant weaknesses, and risks supporting proposal evaluation shall be documented in the contract file.

I. EVALUATION PROCESS

Because there is no guidance in the FAR on the methodology used by agencies to evaluate proposals, they are free to perform the evaluation in any manner that ensures fairness and objectivity. In performing the evaluation, agencies may first screen the proposals to determine whether they are so deficient as to not require evaluation. Thereafter, agencies should evaluate all remaining proposals.

A. Treatment of Proposals Not Meeting Mandatory Requirements

The first step in the evaluation process is the screening of all proposals to determine whether any are not in compliance with the mandatory requirements of the RFP. Because award of the contract cannot be made on the basis of a proposal that does not meet the material requirements of the RFP, the agency must eliminate such proposals from consideration if award is to be made without discussions. Even when a competitive range is to be established, proposals not meeting mandatory requirements can generally be dropped from the competition. Alternatively, if the agency decides that the offeror is a viable competitor, it can amend the RFP to adopt the deviation from the requirement and allow all offerors to compete on that basis or include the proposal in the competitive range and permit the offeror to correct the noncompliance during the negotiation process. The issue of whether to include an offeror with a proposal that does not meeting a mandatory requirement in the competitive range is discussed in Chapter 7.

The rule that award cannot be made on the basis of a materially noncomplying proposal is firmly established. See *Hawkins & Powers Aviation, Inc.*, Comp. Gen. Dec. B-244360, 91-2 CPD ¶ 313, stating:

> In negotiated procurements any proposal that fails to conform to material terms and conditions of the solicitation should be considered unacceptable and may not form the basis for an award. *See Bridge Street Acquisition Corp.*, B-239121.3, Nov. 13, 1990, 90-2 CPD ¶ 388; *Martin Marietta Corp.*, B-233742.4, 69 Comp. Gen. 214 (1990), 90-1 CPD ¶ 132. An offeror must write its proposal so that it clearly demonstrates that it meets the material requirements of the RFP, otherwise the offeror runs the risk of having the proposal rejected. *See Mannesmann Tally Corp.*, B-238790.4, Oct. 16, 1990, 90-2 CPD ¶ 293.

See also *S.M. Stoller Corp.*, Comp. Gen. Dec. B-400937, 2009 CPD ¶ 193 (agency cannot waive RFP requirement that contractor prepare two documents for each sub-project); *Trammell Crow Co.*, Comp. Gen. Dec. B-311314.2, 2008 CPD ¶ 129 (agency cannot waive RFP requirement that building amenities be in place at time of occupancy of leased building); *Essex Corp.*, Comp. Gen. Dec. B-246536.3, 92-2 CPD ¶ 170 (award improper when offeror did not submit required letters of intent from key personnel); *National Medical Staffing, Inc.*, 69 Comp. Gen. 500 (B-238694), 90-1 CPD ¶ 530 (award improper when offeror failed to submit evidence of license, resume, and statement of experience of key personnel as required by RFP).

The GAO has permitted an agency to waive a noncompliant proposal and has denied a protest when the protester was not prejudiced by the waiver, *Safety-Kleen Corp.*, Comp. Gen. Dec. B-274176, 96-2 CPD ¶ 200 (failure to submit required insurance certificates); *Brown & Root, Inc. & Perini Corp., a joint venture*, Comp. Gen. Dec. B-270505.2, 96-2 CPD ¶ 143 (failure of member of winning joint venture to obtain security clearance by required date); *Warren Pumps, Inc.*, Comp. Gen. Dec. B-258710, 95-1 CPD ¶ 79, *recons. denied*, 95-2 CPD ¶ 20 (improperly included requirement that source be approved prior to date of RFP); *Sabreliner Corp.*, Comp. Gen. Dec. B-248640.4, 92-2 CPD ¶ 222 (requirement that contractor be a domestic company); *Corporate Jets, Inc.*, Comp. Gen. Dec. B-246876.2, 92-1 CPD ¶ 471 (experience requirement for key person).

1. *Identifying a Mandatory Requirement*

The Court of Federal Claims has not permitted proposals to be excluded from the competition for failure to meet a mandatory requirement unless the requirement is clearly stated in the RFP. See *Mantech Telecommunications & Info. Sys. Corp. v. United States*, 49 Fed. Cl. 57 (2001), *aff'd*, 30 Fed. Appx. 995 (Fed. Cir. 2002), stating at 67:

> A mandatory minimum requirement must be clearly identified as such within the solicitation so as to "put offerors on notice" of the serious consequences of failing to meet the requirement. *Isratex, Inc. v. United States*, 25 Cl. Ct. 223, 229 (1992). *See also Cubic Def. Sys., Inc. v. United States*, 45 Fed. Cl. 450, 460 (1999). As discussed by this court in *Israetex, Inc.*, 25 Cl. Ct. at 229-30, language used to provide such notice typically emphasizes that a proposal must meet the requirement in order to be eligible for evaluation or, conversely, that failure to comply with the requirement will lead to outright rejection of the proposal.

See also *NEQ, LLC v. United States*, 88 Fed. Cl. 38 (2009) (requirement for notice of commitment from "team subcontractors" did not apply to specialty subcontractors); *Omniplex World Servs. Corp.*, Comp. Gen. Dec. B-290996, 2003 CPD ¶ 7 (requirement for "'guard/custody officer' experience similar in size, scope and complexity to the RFP work requirements" did not call for direct corporate experience in performing detention/custody services); *Cubic Defense Sys., Inc. v. United States*, 45 Fed. Cl. 450 (1999) (requirement for demonstration plan does not make elements of demonstration mandatory).

Proposals that do not agree to the terms and conditions which the RFP states will be part of the contract are clearly not in compliance because they do not make the offer that has been solicited by the government. See, for example, *Hawkins & Powers Aviation, Inc.*, Comp. Gen. Dec. B-244360, 91-2 CPD ¶ 313 (reservation of right not to comply with mandatory technical orders of agency); *Martin Marietta Corp.*, 69 Comp. Gen. 214 (B-233742.4), 90-1 CPD ¶ 132, *recons. denied*, 69 Comp. Gen. 445 (B-233742.5), 90-1 CPD ¶ 469 (offered computer workstations not in compliance with contract specifications); *Instruments S.A., Inc.*, Comp. Gen. Dec. B-238452, 90-1 CPD ¶ 476 (failure to agree to furnish source code to any software written under contract); *Joanell Labs., Inc.*, Comp. Gen. Dec. B-242415, 91-1 CPD ¶ 424 (offered product noncompliant with technical specifications); *AT&T*, Comp. Gen. Dec. B-250516.3, 93-1 CPD ¶ 276, *recons. denied*, 93-2 CPD ¶ 111 (offered product not currently available as required by RFP); *International Sales, Ltd.*, Comp. Gen. Dec. B-253646, 93-2 CPD ¶ 146 (statement in best and final offer that offeror could not unequivocally state that its building met the specification requirements); *Paramax Sys. Corp.*, Comp. Gen. Dec. B-253098.4, 93-2 CPD ¶ 282 (offer of 12% maximum fee when RFP limited it to 9%); *Brooks Towers, Inc.*, Comp. Gen. Dec. B-255944.2, 94-1 CPD ¶ 289 (offered lease space not in compliance with floor/loading requirement); *Vertiflite, Inc.*, Comp. Gen. Dec. B-256366, 94-1 CPD ¶ 304 (offer proposed different payment terms); *Scientific-Atlanta, Inc.*, Comp. Gen. Dec. B-255343.2, 94-1 CPD ¶ 325 (proposal took exception to several terms and conditions including statement "all other terms will be subject to mutual agreement prior to contract award"); *Martin Warehousing & Distribution, Inc.*, Comp. Gen.

Dec. B-270651.2, 96-1 CPD ¶ 205 (proposal conditioned on award of "primary" indefinite-quantity contract only, when RFP precluded such offers); *Team One USA, Inc.*, Comp. Gen. Dec. B-272382, 96-2 CPD ¶ 129 (offered product noncompliant with specifications that established minimum requirements, not design preferences); *Harris Corp.*, Comp. Gen. Dec. B-274566, 96-2 CPD ¶ 205 (offer conditioned option prices on continuity of production between base and option quantities); *Ericsson, Inc.*, Comp. Gen. Dec. B-274668, 97-1 CPD ¶ 33 (offered product noncompliant with technical specifications); and *Tri-State Gov't Servs., Inc.*, Comp. Gen. Dec. B-277315.2, 97-2 CPD ¶ 143 (offer split line items with different prices for initial quantity and following quantity).

2. *Amending the RFP*

Agencies have broad discretion to amend an RFP after reviewing proposals in order to enhance the competition. For example, if a noncompliant proposal offers to perform the work in a more desirable way, the agency has the option of amending the RFP and soliciting offers from all prospective contractors remaining in the competition. See FAR 15.206(d), stating:

> If a proposal of interest to the Government involves a departure from the stated requirements, the contracting officer shall amend the solicitation, provided this can be done without revealing to the other offerors the alternate solution proposed or any other information that is entitled to protection (see 15.207(b) and 15.306(e)).

See *EP Productions, Inc. v. United States*, 63 Fed. Cl. 220 (2004), permitting an amendment to allow three noncompliant competitors to remain in the competition and describing the broad discretion of the contracting officer as follows at 224-25:

> FAR § 15.206(a) states that "when, either before or after the receipt of proposals, the government changes its requirements or terms and conditions, the contracting officer shall amend the solicitation." Numerous cases indicate that this provision may - indeed, must - be invoked where "after a solicitation is issued, [the agency] determines that a noncompliant proposal represents the best value to the Government." *Beta Analytics [Int'l, Inc. v. United States]*, 44 Fed. Cl. [131 (1999)] at 139; *see also MVM Inc. v. United States*, 46 Fed. Cl. 126, 131-32 (2000); *Candle Corp. v. United States*, 40 Fed. Cl. 658, 663 (1998). Amendments under this provision may also be appropriate "to avoid award decisions not based on the agency's most current view of its needs." *NV Servs.*, B-284119.2, 2000 CPD ¶ 64, at 12 (Comp. Gen. 2000); *see also ManTech Telecomm. & Info. Sys. Corp. v. United States*, 49 Fed. Cl. 57, 74-75 (2001). Indeed, most cases in which agencies have run afoul of this FAR provision involve situations in which evaluation requirements were changed without the requisite formal amendment. *See Gentex Corp. v. United States*, 58 Fed. Cl. 634, 653 (2003); *Beta Analytics*, 44 Fed. Cl. at 139.

See also *Argencord Mach. & Equip., Inc. v. United States*, 68 Fed. Cl. 167 (2005) (agency could have amended the RFP to permit alternate material proposed by one offeror); *Digital Techs., Inc.*, Comp. Gen. Dec. B-291657, 2004 CPD ¶ 235 (amendment of RFP rather than award to next offeror permissible when original winner was not a small business but requirements had changed in the interim); *Simmonds Precision Prods., Inc.*, Comp. Gen. Dec. B-244559, 93-1 CPD ¶ 483 (upon receipt of offer with more attractive terms than required by RFP, agency properly amended RFP to give all offerors opportunity to submit revised offers).

Agencies have been permitted to amend the RFP to revise the evaluation criteria if the initial evaluation demonstrates that the criteria are flawed. See *L-3 Communications EOTech, Inc. v. United States*, 83 Fed. Cl. 643 (2008), permitting the issuance of new test criteria after initial product testing revealed the original criteria were too stringent. The court stated at 657:

> Amendments to evaluation criteria after evaluation procedures have begun, are not, by themselves, indicative of reversible error by the government. *See Pacer Sys., Inc.*, B-215999, 84-2 CPD ¶ 645 (Comp. Gen. Dec. 10, 1994) ("[GAO] has held that the contracting officer can amend the RFP after the proposal closing date. For example, reopening competition following the closing date and receipt of 'best and final offers' is appropriate when an ambiguity in the solicitation is apparent.") (citation omitted). However, many of the decisions approving of post-bid submission amendments rely upon other factors ensuring adequate competition, such as an opportunity for offerors to submit revised proposals, or the fact that more than one offeror became eligible for award because of an amended requirement. *See, e.g., id.; see also ManTech Telecomms. & Info. Sys. Corp. v. United States,* 49 Fed. Cl. 57, 73-76 & n.25 (citing cases for the proposition that amending a solicitation requirement and then considering revised offers is generally permissible); *Sea Containers Am., Inc.,* B-243228, 91-2 CPD ¶ 45 (Comp. Gen. July 11, 1991) (noting that three offerors would have been eliminated from the competition but for the relaxed solicitation requirement provided by the amendment, and that revised offers were then solicited from all offerors).

The mandatory amendment rule in FAR 15.206(a), discussed in *EP Productions*, applies to situations where the agency's requirements have changed to a significant extent. See *Global Solutions Network, Inc.*, Comp. Gen. Dec. B-298682.2, 2007 CPD ¶ 223, stating:

> Where an agency's requirements change materially after a solicitation has been issued, it must issue an amendment notifying offerors of the change and affording them an opportunity to respond. Federal Acquisition Regulation § 15.206(a); *Northrop Grumman Info. Tech., Inc., et al.*, B-295526, Mar. 16, 2005, 2005 CPD ¶ 45 at 13; *Symetrics Indus., Inc.*, B-274246.3 et al., Aug. 20, 1997, 97-2 CPD ¶ 59 at 6. This rule applies even after the submission of final proposal revisions, up until the time of award. *Northrop Grumman Info. Tech., Inc. et al., supra; Digital Techs., Inc.*, B-291657.3, Nov. 18, 2004, 2004 CPD ¶ 235 at 3; *NV Servs.*, B-284119.2, Feb. 25, 2000, 2000 CPD ¶ 64 at 17. Amending the solicitation provides offerors an opportunity to submit revised proposals on a common basis that reflects the agency's actual needs. *Multimax, Inc., et al.* B-298249.6, et al., Oct. 24, 2006, 2006 CPD ¶ 165 at 6.

See also *Systems Mgmt., Inc.,* Comp. Gen. Dec. B-287032.3, 2001 CPD ¶ 85 (amendment of RFP required when agency relaxed mandatory certification requirement for weather observation system); and *MVM. Inc. v. United States,* 46 Fed. Cl. 126 (1999) (amendment of RFP required when agency significantly reduced amount of work).

When an agency finds that an offeror has failed to comply with a mandatory requirement of the RFP, in lieu of amending the RFP, it can generally continue to deal with that offeror if it establishes a competitive range and corrects the noncompliance during negotiations. See Chapter 7 for a full discussion of the process that must be followed in that situation. However, if the proposal is unsigned, the agency *must* reject the proposal, *SWR, Inc.,* Comp. Gen. Dec. B-278415, 97-2 CPD ¶ 166.

B. Exclusion of Deficient Proposals

Once the evaluation process has begun, an agency may drop a proposal from the process before completion of its evaluation if it so deficient that further evaluation would be fruitless. This rule is not stated in the FAR but is included in NFS 1815.305-70, as follows:

> Identification of unacceptable proposals.
>
> (a) The contracting officer shall not complete the initial evaluation of any proposal when it is determined that the proposal is unacceptable because:
>
> > (1) It does not represent a reasonable initial effort to address the essential requirements of the RFP or clearly demonstrates that the offeror does not understand the requirements;
> >
> > (2) In research and development acquisitions, a substantial design drawback is evident in the proposal, and sufficient correction or improvement to consider the proposal acceptable would require virtually an entirely new technical proposal; or
> >
> > (3) It contains major technical or business deficiencies or omissions or out-of-line costs which discussions with the offeror could not reasonably be expected to cure.
>
> (b) The contracting officer shall document the rationale for discontinuing the initial evaluation of a proposal in accordance with this section.

See *L-3 Communications EOTech, Inc.,* Comp. Gen. Dec. B-311453, 2008 CPD ¶ 139, denying a protest that the agency dropped an offeror from the competition when its product failed a required test. The RFP had stated:

> A failure in any one or more of the essential criteria as stated shall be cause for elimination from further consideration for award and [the] offeror[']s submission will not be further evaluated.

For other cases where the RFP permitted dropping of offerors before the completion of the evaluation process, see *USIA Underwater Equip. Sales Corp.*, Comp. Gen. Dec. B-292827.2, 2004 CPD ¶ 32 (sample product's test failure eliminated need for further agency evaluation of proposal); *Pride Mobility Prods. Corp.*, Comp. Gen. Dec. B-291878, 2003 CPD ¶ 80 (poor rating on one test requirement permitted dropping of offeror without further evaluation); *Sun Chem. Corp.*, Comp. Gen. Dec. B-288466, 2001 CPD ¶ 185 (offeror with sample product that did not meet safety standard properly dropped from competition before completion of testing); *LaBarge Prods., Inc.*, Comp. Gen. Dec. B-287841, 2001 CPD ¶ 177 (lack of "support and elaboration" on system to be furnished); *Good Food Serv., Inc.*, Comp. Gen. Dec. B-277145, 98-1 CPD ¶ 102 ("numerous and extensive informational deficiencies"); *Advanced Design Corp.*, Comp. Gen. Dec. B-275928, 98-1 CPD ¶ 100 (agency properly dropped a completely nonconforming proposal from the competition without scoring it); *W&D Ships Deck Works, Inc. v. United States*, 39 Fed. Cl. 638 (1997) ("grossly deficient" proposal); *Dimensions Int'l/QSOFT, Inc.*, Comp. Gen. Dec. B-270966, 96-1 CPD ¶ 257 (RFP called for no further evaluation of proposals if sample task submissions were unsatisfactory).

It is also permissible to use an RFP provision excluding offerors that do not meet a mandatory requirement from making an oral presentation, *Inte-Great Corp.*, Comp. Gen. Dec. B-272780, 96-2 CPD ¶ 159.

C. Overcoming Noncompliant Proposals

Agencies have not been permitted to accept blanket statements from an offeror that it would comply with all mandatory requirements when the proposal itself does not demonstrate compliance. See *Red River Holdings, LLC v. United States*, 87 Fed. Cl. 768 (2009), holding that an agency cannot ignore failure of a proposal to demonstrate that it meets mandatory requirements based on offeror's assertions that it would meet such requirements. See *International Data Prods., Inc.*, Comp. Gen. Dec. B-275480.2, 97-1 CPD ¶ 179, where the agency contended that by signing the solicitation's global certification of compliance, and taking no exception to the specifications, the awardees established the technical acceptability of their proposals irrespective of the contents of their proposals. The GAO disagreed, stating:

> While an agency can properly provide for a certification of compliance and based on such certification accept a proposal that does not affirmatively establish compliance with the specifications, an offeror's blanket certification or promise of compliance is insufficient to establish compliance where the agency has reason to question the characteristics of the products being offered. *See generally Lappen Auto Supply Co., Inc.*, B-261475, Aug. 14, 1995, 95-2 CPD ¶ 68 at 4 (although "brand name" offeror was not required to submit descriptive literature, its unsolicited literature could not be disregarded to the extent that it clearly qualified the bid by describing an item that did not satisfy a specified salient characteristic); *SeaBeam Instruments, Inc.*, B-253129, Aug. 19, 1993, 93-2 CPD ¶ 106 at 7 (certification of compliance with Appropriations Act domestic manufacture restriction may not be

accepted where the proposal suggests noncompliance); *Mine Safety Appliances Co.; Interspiro, Inc.*, B-247919.5; B-247919.6, Sept. 3, 1992, 92-2 CPD ¶ 150 at 3 (even where a solicitation does not require a showing of compliance with each solicitation requirement, a proposal that does not explicitly show compliance with a requirement may not be accepted where there is reason to doubt that the offeror is agreeing to meet that requirement). Thus, notwithstanding the existence of a signed global certification, our Office will still review protests that the agency had reason to question the characteristics of the products being offered.

See also *International Data Prods. Corp.*, Comp. Gen. Dec. B-274654, 97-1 CPD ¶ 34, where it was held proper for an agency to reject a proposal as noncompliant when technical literature conflicted with the offeror's statement that its product would comply with the specifications, and *Eigen*, Comp. Gen. Dec. B-249860, 92-2 CPD ¶ 426, holding that an agency improperly accepted a blanket offer of compliance with requirements without submitting required information demonstrating that requirements would be met.

The GAO has also held that an agency may not clear up proposal statements that its offer is conditioned by awarding a contract excluding the proposal from the contract documents and containing a clear statement that the offeror will comply with the RFP. See *Barents Group, L.L.C.*, Comp. Gen. Dec. B-276082, 97-1 CPD ¶ 164, where the winning offeror had placed conditions on its offered labor rates. The GAO sustained a protest against award to that offeror, stating:

> [The agency] also argues that [the winning offeror] signed a contract document, which was the exclusive written agreement memorializing all of the terms and conditions, and which stated:
>
>> "The rights and obligations of the parties to this contract shall be subject to and governed by the following documents: (a) this award/ contract, (b) the solicitation, if any, and (c) such provisions, representations, certifications, and specifications as are attached or incorporated by reference herein."
>
> Apparently, based on this provision, it is [the agency's] position that since [the offeror's] proposal did not become a part of the contract, the objectionable language in that proposal is not part of the contract and therefore had no impact on the award. According to [the agency], because the contract includes [the winning offeror's] maximum fixed daily labor rates and multipliers, [that offeror] cannot charge the government more than those fixed rates and multipliers under the contract.
>
> We do not agree. Even though an awarded contract may not incorporate all aspects of a proposal, the contract may not materially vary the terms of the offer. *The Orkand Corp.*, B-224541, Dec. 31, 1986, 86-2 CPD ¶ 723 at 8; *Computer Network Corp. et al. — Request for Recon.*, B-186858, June 13, 1977, 77-1 CPD ¶ 422 at 6. Moreover, in negotiated procurements, any proposal that fails to conform to material terms and conditions of a solicitation should be considered unacceptable and may not form the basis for an award. *Martin Marietta Corp.*, 69 Comp. Gen.

214, 219 (1990), 90-1 CPD ¶ 32 at 7; *L & E Assocs., Inc.*, B-258808.4, June 22, 1995, 95-1 CPD ¶ 288 at 4. Any other rule would be inconsistent with the government's obligation to treat all offerors fairly and to provide a common basis for the competition. Since [the winning offeror's] proposal included conditions on its multipliers, no award could be made based on that proposal.

D. Evaluation Procedures

The FAR contains no guidance on the procedures to be followed in evaluating proposals. Agencies are free to follow any procedure that results in fair evaluation. See FAR 1.102-2(c)(3) stating that " [a]ll . . . prospective contractors shall be treated fairly and impartially but need not be treated the same." It is permissible for the entire source selection team to evaluate all elements of the proposal, but it has been common practice to require the proposal to be submitted in separate parts in order to permit specialists to evaluate their part of the proposal. See FAR 15.204-5(b). In this situation the technical elements of the proposal will be evaluated by technical personnel, the cost or price elements will be evaluated by contracting personnel, and the capability elements (past performance, experience, key personnel, etc.) may be evaluated jointly.

When an agency intends to separate the cost and technical evaluations, it has been common practice to withhold the cost information from technical personnel, with the result that the technical package describes the work to be done but may not include a description of the resources (labor hours and amount of subcontracted effort) needed to perform the various tasks on the contract. Without such resource information, the technical evaluation will be imprecise at best. The FAR Part 15 rewrite addressed this problem by providing in FAR 15.305(a)(4) that: "Cost information may be provided to members of the technical evaluation team." A well-written RFP requires that such information as to resources to be applied be included in the technical package. If the RFP does not contain this data, the agency should extract the information from the cost proposal and provide it to the technical evaluators. This will permit them to arrive at an accurate assessment of the offerors' technical understanding of the requirements as well as their ability to perform the work described in the RFP. See *AmerInd, Inc.*, Comp. Gen. Dec. B-248324, 92-2 CPD ¶ 85, where the GAO affirmed the contracting officer's adjustment of an offeror's cost proposal to reflect the salaries of personnel discussed in the technical proposal. See also *Satellite Servs., Inc.*, Comp. Gen. Dec. B-286508, 2001 CPD ¶ 30, where a protest was sustained because the winning offeror's low estimate of resources in its price proposal was not used by the technical evaluators to assess its understanding of the work.

Objectivity is generally sought by having the same evaluators review each proposal or portion of a proposal. However, if it is impractical to do so, proposals can be evaluated by different personnel. See *Design Concepts, Inc.*, Comp. Gen. Dec. B-186125, 76-2 CPD ¶ 365 (30 proposals divided among the evaluators); *T.V. Travel,*

Inc., 65 Comp. Gen. 109 (B-218198), 85-2 CPD ¶ 640 (37 proposals evaluated in six groups); *Innovative Logistics Techniques, Inc.*, Comp. Gen. Dec. B-275786.2, 97-1 CPD ¶ 144 (one evaluator reviewed both proposals and two evaluators each reviewed one proposal). Oral presentations can also be evaluated by different personnel, *Quality Elevator Co.*, Comp. Gen. Dec. B-276750, 97-2 CPD ¶ 28. The key question is whether the evaluation fairly reflects the strengths and weaknesses of each proposal.

Agencies may change evaluators during the course of a procurement, and changes have been permitted even when the RFP stated the composition of the evaluation team. See *PADCO, Inc.*, Comp. Gen. Dec. B-270445, 96-1 CPD ¶ 142, stating:

> Generally, the composition of a technical evaluation board or committee is within the discretion of the contracting agency, and we will not question the composition of the board or committee unless there is evidence of fraud, bad faith, conflict of interest, or actual bias. *MGM Land Co.*; *Tony Western*, B-241169; B-241169.2, Jan. 17, 1991, 91-1 CPD ¶ 50. Further, even the fact that the composition of the evaluation committee or board changes during the course of a procurement does not automatically indicate anything improper, so long as the underlying evaluation is reasonable and consistent with the evaluation criteria. *See Space Applications Corp.*, B-233143.3, Sept. 21, 1989, 89-2 CPD ¶ 255.

Thus, initial proposals may be evaluated by one set of evaluators, and final proposal revisions by another, *Data Flow Corp.*, 62 Comp. Gen. 506 (B-209499), 83-2 CPD ¶ 57. Similarly, an agency may reevaluate proposals using a more experienced group of evaluators, *WR Sys., Ltd*, Comp. Gen. Dec. B-287477, 2001 CPD ¶ 118; *SOS Interpreting, Ltd.*, Comp. Gen. Dec. B-287505, 2001 CPD ¶ 104; *Pro-Mark, Inc.*, Comp. Gen. B-247248, 92-2 CPD ¶ 124. New evaluators may also be used after the agency has lost a protest, *Burchick Constr. Co.*, Comp. Gen. B-400342.3, 2009 CPD ¶ 102; *PRC, Inc.*, 71 Comp. Gen. 530 (B-233561.8), 92-2 CPD ¶ 215, or has decided to take corrective action to forestall a protest, *Domain Name Alliance Registry*, Comp. Gen. B-310803.2, 2008 CPD ¶ 168. See *Matrix Int'l Logistics, Inc.*, Comp. Gen. Dec. B-277208, 97-2 CPD ¶ 94, for a case where the GAO did not object to the fact that a different team of evaluators arrived at significantly different evaluations. However, most agencies attempt to use the same evaluation personnel throughout the procurement.

Frequently, the same factors are evaluated by a number of evaluators who arrive at a different assessment of the merits of the proposals and different scores. The GAO has stated: "Since evaluating proposals involves subjective as well as objective judgments, it is not unusual for individual evaluators to reach disparate conclusions," *Mounts Eng'g*, 65 Comp. Gen. 476 (B-218489.4), 86-1 CPD ¶ 358. Similarly, in *Systems Research & Applications Corp.*, Comp. Gen. Dec. B-299818, 2008 CPD ¶ 28, the GAO stated: "We recognize that it is not unusual for individual evaluator ratings to differ from one another, or to differ from the consensus ratings eventually assigned." In *Group GPS Multimedia*, Comp. Gen. Dec. B-310716, 2008 CPD ¶ 34, it was proper for the source selection official to make the final evaluation when two technical evaluators could not agree, and in *EBA Ernest Bland Assocs.*, Comp. Gen. Dec. B-270496, 96-1 CPD ¶ 148, the GAO found nothing unusual or improper in the fact that two individual agency evaluators gave widely divergent scores to the same proposal. Therefore, disparities in evaluator scores alone do not suffice to show improper or irrational evaluations, even if the final scores are averaged. See *Cube-All Star Servs. (J.V.)*, Comp. Gen. Dec. B-291903, 2003 CPD ¶ 145 (all evaluators did not identify same technical deficiencies); *Arsenault Acquisition Corp.*, Comp. Gen. Dec. B-276959, 97-2 CPD ¶ 74 (low score of one of four evaluators based on different assessment); *Arthur Anderson & Co.*, 71 Comp. Gen. 233 (B-245903), 92-1 CPD ¶ 168 (consensus score of 27 after initial scores of 25, 25, and 30); *Syscon Servs.*, 68 Comp. Gen. 698 (B-235647), 89-2 CPD ¶ 258 (evaluations ranged from unacceptable to acceptable to better than acceptable); and *Monarch Enters., Inc.*, Comp. Gen. Dec. B-233303, 89-1 CPD ¶ 222 (scores from different evaluation panels varied significantly). On the other hand, if factor scores are averaged or added, the agency must make sure that offers are not unreasonably downgraded for notations that are meant to be neutral. See *Inlingua Schools of Language*, Comp. Gen. Dec. B-229784, 88-1 CPD ¶ 340, finding unfairness in a point-adding system that scored questions answered as "not applicable" with zeros, thereby penalizing the protester for meaningless data. Similarly, consensus evaluations must be supported by rational conclusions, *Magnum Medical Personnel, A Joint Venture,* Comp. Gen. Dec. B-297687.2, 2006 CPD ¶ 99.

There is no requirement that agencies develop consensus scores in order to reconcile disparate evaluations. See *Smart Innovative Solutions*, Comp. Gen. Dec. B-400323.3, 2008 CPD ¶ 220, stating:

> [W]e are aware of no statute or regulation that requires an agency to create a consensus report in evaluating proposals, nor is there any requirement that every individual evaluator's scoring sheet track the final evaluation report. See *Andrulis Corp.*, B-281002.2, June 2, 1999, 99-1 CPD ¶ 105 at 5 (a consensus score need not be the same score as initially scored by the individual evaluators). In short, these matters alone will not lead our office to conclude that there was an impropriety in the agency's evaluation or a violation of procurement law or regulation.

Nonetheless, it is good practice for agencies to develop consensus scores in order to reconcile disparate scores and ensure that the evaluators have not made obvious mistakes in their evaluation. See *Resource Applications, Inc.*, Comp. Gen. Dec. B-274943.3, 97-1 CPD ¶ 137, where the GAO described the flexibility given consensus procedures to achieve this result:

> There is nothing inherently objectionable in an agency's decision to develop a consensus rating. *Appalachian Council, Inc.*, B-256179, May 20, 1994, 94-1 CPD ¶ 319. The fact that the evaluators individually rated TechLaw's proposal for [certain] subfactors less favorably than they did on a consensus basis for those subfactors, and individually rated RAI's proposal for [certain] subfactors more favorably than they did on a consensus basis for those subfactors does not, by

itself, warrant questioning the final evaluation results. *See Syscon Servs., Inc.*, 68 Comp. Gen. 698 (1989), 89-2 CPD ¶ 258; *Dragon Servs., Inc.*, B-255354, Feb. 25, 1994, 94-1 CPD ¶ 151. Agency evaluators may discuss the relative strengths and weaknesses of proposals in order to reach a consensus rating, which often differs from the ratings given by individual evaluators, since such discussions generally operate to correct mistakes or misperceptions that may have occurred in the initial evaluation. *Schweizerr Aircraft Corp.*, B-248640.2; B-248640.3, Sept. 14, 1992, 92-2 CPD ¶ 200; *The Cadmus Group, Inc.*, B-241372.3, Sept. 25, 1991, 91-2 CPD ¶ 271. Thus, a consensus score need not be the score of the majority the evaluators initially awarded — the score may properly be determined after discussions among the evaluators. *GZA Remediation, Inc.*, B-272386, Oct. 3, 1996, 96-2 CPD ¶ 155 (note 3). In short, the overriding concern in the evaluation process is that the final score assigned accurately reflects the actual merits of the proposals, not that it be mechanically traceable back to the scores initially given by the individual evaluators. *Id.*; *Dragon Servs., Inc., supra.*

See *Bering Straits Tech. Servs., LLC*, Comp. Gen. Dec. B-401560.3, 2009 CPD ¶ 201 (proper consensus of "good" when three evaluators rated proposal "excellent" and one rated it "good"); *Domain Name Alliance Registry*, Comp. Gen. Dec. B-310803.2, 2008 CPD ¶ 168 (proper consensus of "minor weakness" when two evaluators found no weakness and one found major weakness); *Systalex Corp.*, Comp. Gen. Dec. B-400109, 2008 CPD ¶ 148 (strength found by one evaluator need not be reflected in consensus score); *Veterans Tech., LLC*, Comp. Gen. Dec. B-310303.2, 2008 CPD ¶ 31 (consensus evaluation can vary from evaluation of all evaluators); *General Injectables & Vaccines, Inc.*, Comp. Gen. Dec. B-298590, 2006 CPD ¶ 173 ("pressure" on evaluators to reach consensus did not demonstrate irrational evaluation).

Consensus evaluations have been held to be rational and reliable even when the agency has destroyed the evaluation records of individual evaluators, *Government Acquisitions, Inc.*, Comp. Gen. Dec. B-401048, 2009 CPD ¶ 137; *Alliance Tech. Servs., Inc.*, Comp. Gen. Dec. B-311329, 2008 CPD ¶ 108; *Joint Mgmt. & Tech. Servs.*, Comp. Gen. Dec. B-294229, 2004 CPD ¶ 208, merely averaged the individual scores, *Trusted Base, LLC*, Comp. Gen. Dec. B-401670, 2009 CPD ¶ 218; or the individual evaluators have not recorded their evaluations, *Dellew Corp.*, Comp. Gen. Dec. B-298233.2, 2006 CPD ¶ 144.

In *United Int'l Investigative Servs., Inc. v. United States*, 41 Fed. Cl. 312 (1998), the court held that the agency had acted improperly in failing to permit the evaluators to discuss their evaluations in an effort to arrive at a consensus when the source selection plan called for such a "group discussion." This decision is unusual because it has generally been held that agencies are not bound by their internal source selection plans.

E. Retention Of Evaluation Documents

Agencies should retain all of the evaluation documents created during the evaluation process. FAR 4.801(a) requires agencies to establish contract files "containing the records of all contractual transactions." FAR 4.801(b) requires these filed "constitute a complete history of the transaction for the purpose of – (4) Furnishing essential facts in the event of litigation or congressional inquiries." In *Pitney Bowes Gov't Solutions, Inc. v. United States*, 93 Fed. Cl. 327 (2010), the court held that destruction of evaluators' worksheets violated this requirement, stating at 335:

> [T]he destruction of the individual TEP [technical evaluation panel] members' score sheets is barred by the FAR provisions. The current contract file for the challenged procurement does not "constitute a *complete* history of the transaction," FAR § 4.801(b) (emphasis added), nor does it "[f]urnish[] essential facts in the event of litigation. FAR § 4.801(b)(4). FAR § 4.801(b) expressly refers to § 4.803, which provides "examples of the records normally contained . . . in contract files." FAR § 4.803. Specifically, the record as submitted does not contain all "[s]ource selection documentation," as required by FAR § 4.803(a)(13). It was foreseeable that the individual rating sheets could well become relevant to issues arising in a bid protest, particularly in a situation where, as here, the bias of one or more of the panel members is alleged. No preturnatural clairvoyance would be required to envision that possibility. Although the ratings of the individual members of the TEP presumably were taken into account by, and wrapped into, the consensus report of the TEP, without the separate score sheets of the individual panel members, the court is unable to assess any divergence in the ratings which produced that consensus, or in turn, determine whether there existed personal bias in favor of [the winning contractors] on the part of one or more of the panel members. The argument by the government and the intervenor that the individual members' rating sheets were in effect no more than drafts of the final consensus report of the [TEP] is not supportable. The consensus report necessarily represented an amalgam of the views of the panel members and would have tended to suppress individual views.

In this case, the court ruled that the protester could depose each member of the evaluation panel in order to determine his or her individual views in the initial evaluation. It also noted that the contracting officer responsible for destroying the worksheets might be subject to sanctions for spoilation of evidence. No sanctions were imposed, however, because the agency found the evaluator's worksheets. 94 Fed. Cl. 1 (2010).

The GAO has reached the opposite conclusion, holding in numerous decisions that it does not object to the destruction of the worksheets of individual evaluators as long as a consensus evaluation supports the source selection decision. See *Joint Mgmt. & Tech. Servs.*, Comp. Gen. Dec. B-294229, 2004 CPD ¶ 208, stating:

> Where, as here, the agency has destroyed individual evaluation materials, its actions are unobjectionable provided that the consensus evaluation materials relied on by the agency support the agency's judgments regarding the relative merits of the proposals. *Global Eng'g and Constr., LLC*, B-290288.3, B-290288.4, Apr. 3, 2003, 2003 CPD ¶ 180 at 3 n.3.

Nonetheless, on occasion the GAO has held a hearing in order to determine the substantive conclusions reached by each individual evaluator. See *Dynalantic Corp.*, Comp. Gen. Dec. B-274944.2, 97-1 CPD ¶ 101, where such a hearing was held and the agency was directed to pay the protester for the cost of the hearing when the protest was granted on other grounds.

II. DISCRETIONARY NATURE OF THE EVALUATION PROCESS

Agencies are granted a considerable degree of discretion in the evaluation of proposals. An evaluation made by a procuring agency will not be disturbed unless it is arbitrary or in violation of procurement statutes or regulations, *Pacific Consultants*, Comp. Gen. Dec. B-198706, 80-2 CPD ¶ 129. See *Buffalo Organization for Social & Tech. Innovation, Inc.*, Comp. Gen. Dec. B-196279, 80-1 CPD ¶ 107, where the GAO enunciated its traditional position in this area:

> The determination of the relative merits of proposals is the responsibility of the procuring agency since it must bear the burden of any difficulties incurred by reason of a defective evaluation. In light of this, we have held that procuring officials enjoy a reasonable degree of discretion in the evaluation of proposals and such discretion must not be disturbed unless shown to be arbitrary or in violation of the procurement statutes and regulations.

In more recent decisions, the GAO has summarized this position as follows in *Lakeside Escrow & Title Agency, Inc.*, Comp. Gen. Dec. B-310331.3, 2008 CPD ¶ 14:

> In reviewing [protests of an agency's evaluation], we do not conduct a new evaluation or substitute our judgment for that of the agency, but examine the record to determine whether the agency's judgment was reasonable and in accordance with the terms of the solicitation and applicable procurement statutes and regulations. *Wahkontah Servs., Inc.*, B-292768, Nov. 18, 2003, 2003 CPD ¶ 214 at 4. An offeror's mere disagreement with the agency's evaluation is not sufficient to render the evaluation unreasonable. *Ben-Mar Enters., Inc.*, B-295781, Apr. 7, 2005, 2005 CPD ¶ 68 at 7.

See also *Matrix Int'l Logistics, Inc.*, Comp. Gen. Dec. B-272388.2, 97-2 CPD ¶ 89; *PRC, Inc.*, Comp. Gen. Dec. B-274698.2, 97-1 CPD ¶ 115; and *Main Bldg. Maint., Inc.*, Comp. Gen. Dec. B-260945, 95-2 CPD ¶ 214. Nonetheless, when an evaluator has personal knowledge of an offeror's experience, it is improper to disregard such experience in the evaluation, *Safeguard Maint. Corp.*, Comp. Gen. Dec. B-260983.3, 96-2 CPD ¶ 116. See also *Arctic Slope World Servs., Inc.*, Comp. Gen. Dec. B-284481, 2000 CPD ¶ 75 (assessment that incumbent's project manager was not a "team player"); and *The Futures Group Int'l*, Comp. Gen. Dec. B-281274.2, 2000 CPD ¶ 147 (evaluators used knowledge of offeror's performance on prior contracts).

Agencies have broad discretion in the evaluation process. Despite this broad discretion, evaluations must be able to withstand scrutiny as to their reasonableness and must be made in accordance with the evaluation scheme described in the RFP. Agency evaluations have been overturned if they are irrational, arbitrary, or not based on evidence in the record. However, erroneous evaluations will not be overturned if they are based on errors which are merely minor or nonprejudicial.

A. Irrational Evaluations

Irrational evaluations involve evaluation decisions that are inherently erroneous and could not be followed even if specifically outlined in the RFP. For example, in *Dynalantic v. United States*, 945 F.2d 416 (Fed. Cir. 1991), the offeror's significantly less expensive offer was rejected based on an unreasonable assumption that Dynalantic was ignorant of industry standards. Expert testimony illustrated that the Air Force itself lacked such knowledge. In *Programmatics, Inc.*, Comp. Gen. Dec. B-228916.2, 88-1 CPD ¶ 35, the GAO deemed an evaluation irrational where two of five evaluators significantly reduced the protester's technical scores during a second evaluation without having any reason for doing so. See also *Humana Military Healthcare Servs.*, Comp. Gen. Dec. B-401652.2, 2009 CPD ¶ 219 (unreasonable to not reflect protester's prior practice of obtaining discounts in evaluation of cost proposal); *Engineering Mgmt. & Integration, Inc.*, Comp. Gen. Dec. B-400356.4, 2009 CPD ¶ 114 (unreasonable to downgrade offeror for not providing required percentage of certified employees when it provided the raw number of such employees); *Honeywell Tech. Solutions, Inc.*, Comp. Gen. Dec. B-400771, 2009 CPD ¶ 49 (unreasonable to conclude that past performance on a very small contract was relevant to work called for by contract being competed); *Sikorsky Aircraft Co.*, Comp. Gen. Dec. B-299145, 2007 CPD ¶ 45 (irrational to normalize life-cycle cost evaluation when RFP called for data from each offeror on past programs); *Systronics, Inc.*, Comp. Gen. Dec. B-293102, 2006 CPD ¶ 15 (irrational to give noncomplying quotation a high score); *Arora Group*, Comp. Gen. Dec. B-297346, 2004 CPD ¶ 61 (unreasonable to downgrade offeror because required certifications were not listed on resume when they were included in response to discussion question); *T Square Logistics Servs. Corp.*, Comp. Gen. Dec. B-291851, 2003 CPD ¶ 160 (unreasonable to give high scores to areas not covered in oral presentation); *Eurest Support Servs.*, Comp. Gen. Dec. B-285813.3, 2003 CPD ¶ 139 (unreasonable evaluation of realism of quantity of labor needed to perform fixed price incentive contract); *Dismas Charities, Inc.*, Comp. Gen. Dec. B-292091, 2003 CPD ¶ 125 (unreasonable to fail to consider all information submitted in proposal); *M&S Farms, Inc.*, Comp. Gen. Dec. B-290599, 2002 CPD ¶ 174 (unreasonable to give high past performance score because agency received more questionnaires); *PADCO, Inc. — Costs*, Comp. Gen. Dec. B-289096.3, 2002 CPD ¶ 135 (unreasonable to accept, without analysis, proposed indirect cost rates far below incurred rates); *Perini/Jones, (J.V.)*, Comp. Gen. Dec. B-285906, 2002 CPD ¶ 68 (unreasonable to give company credit for experience for affiliated company that would not perform work on contract); *OSI Collection Servs.*, Inc., Comp. Gen. Dec. B-286597, 2001 CPD ¶ 18 (irrational to base past performance evaluation on numerical scores detailing number of failures where offerors had disparate amount of work); *Summit Research Corp.*, Comp. Gen. Dec. B-287523, 2001 CPD ¶ 176 (irrational to exclude small business offeror from evaluation of small business participation); *Green Valley Transp., Inc.*, Comp. Gen. Dec. B-285283, 2000 CPD ¶ 133 (irrational to assess number of performance problems when offerors had disparate amounts of work); *AIU North Am., Inc.*, Comp. Gen. Dec. B-283743.2, 2000 CPD ¶ 39 (unreasonable to fail to consider resources of corporation that acquired offeror when evaluating such resources); *Consolidated Eng'g Servs., Inc.*, Comp. Gen. Dec. B-279565.2, 99-1 CPD ¶ 75 (irrational to downgrade offeror because of inadequate description of subcontractor's experience when another offeror provided information on same subcontractor); *SCIENTECH, Inc.*, Comp. Gen. Dec. B-277805.2, 98-1 CPD ¶ 33 (irrational to exclude from the past performance evaluation the offeror's efforts as the incumbent contractor and its major subcontractors); *HG Properties A, L.P.*, Comp. Gen. Dec. B-277572, 97-2 CPD ¶ 123 (unreasonable to give awardee 225 points of the 250 points available for efficient layout when the awardee's layout was inconsistent with the stated evaluation factors); *Technology Servs. Int'l, Inc.*, Comp. Gen. Dec. B-276506, 97-2 CPD ¶ 113 (unreasonable to give awardee the highest rating under a significant quality control technical subfactor when it did not submit a detailed work scheduling scheme as contemplated by this subfactor); *ST Aerospace Engines Pte., Ltd.*, Comp. Gen. Dec. B-275725, 97-1 CPD ¶ 161 (irrational to evaluate negative past performance of affiliate when it will play no role in contract performance); *International Bus. Sys., Inc.*, Comp. Gen. Dec. B-275554, 97-1 CPD ¶ 114 (irrational to ignore the past performance of the incumbent contractor because the agency technical person had not filled out the past performance questionnaire); *Cygnus Corp.*, Comp. Gen. Dec. B-275181, 97-1 CPD ¶ 63 (unreasonable to ignore additional information contained in BAFO); *PMT Servs., Inc.*, Comp. Gen. Dec. B-270538.2, 96-2 CPD ¶ 98 (irrational to evaluate only the size of prior projects when the evaluation factor called for a review of projects with "similar complexity" to the subject procurement); *Access Logic, Inc.*, Comp. Gen. Dec. B-274748, 97-1 CPD ¶ 36 (unreasonable to evaluate offered product as unacceptable for failing to meet a requirement not specified in RFP); *Safeguard Maint. Corp.*, Comp. Gen. Dec. B-260983.3, 96-2 CPD ¶ 116 (irrational to give a low score to a proposal for not furnishing required information when the evaluators had personal knowledge of the information); *RJO Enters., Inc.*, Comp. Gen. Dec. B-260126.2, 95-2 CPD ¶ 93 (unreasonable to downgrade a proposal for not furnishing sufficient resumes when they were not called for in the RFP); *ManTech Envtl. Tech., Inc.*, Comp. Gen. Dec. B-271002, 96-1 CPD ¶ 272 (unreasonable to perform cost realism analysis based only on inadequate DCAA audit); *TRESP Assocs., Inc.*, Comp. Gen. Dec. B-258322.5, 96-1 CPD ¶ 8 (unreasonable not to raise protester's scores when it successfully addressed all weaknesses in BAFO); *L.K. Comstock, Inc.*, Comp. Gen. Dec. B-261711.5, 96-1 CPD ¶ 4 (unreasonable to evaluate price using offered discounts that are based on quantities that are far higher than prior agency experience); *NITCO*, Comp. Gen. Dec. B-246185, 92-1 CPD ¶ 212 (unreasonable to evaluate past performance in manufacturing a product when there was no indication in the RFP that this would be a consideration); and *DynCorp*, Comp. Gen. Dec. B-232999, 89-1 CPD ¶ 152 (irrational to find two proposals technically equal where one contained many obvious weaknesses not apparent in the other). Similarly, in *Inlingua Schools of Languages*, Comp. Gen. B-229784, 88-1 CPD ¶ 340, questions answered by an offeror's reference as "not applicable" were irrationally scored as zeros, and in *SDA, Inc.*, Comp. Gen. Dec. B-248528.2, 93-1 CPD ¶ 320, rating past experience by the percentage of past projects that were similar in size to the contract work was inherently irrational. In the latter case the GAO commented that the rating scheme gave the highest rating to the offeror that listed the fewest irrelevant past projects. Such a system was seen to be inherently illogical, and the protest was sustained. In *CBIS Fed., Inc. v. Dep't of the Interior*, GSBCA 12092-P, 93-2 BCA ¶ 25,643, the board criticized evaluations that gave maximum scores to proposals that met the minimum requirements where the procurement was clearly a best value procurement.

B. Arbitrary Evaluations

Evaluations are occasionally overturned because they are purely arbitrary. For example, the General Services board rejected a technical evaluation that reduced the score of one offeror simply because the contracting officer did not know the proposed project manager, *Compuware Corp.*, GSBCA 9533-P, 88-3 BCA ¶ 21,109. The board commented that the person in question had excellent credentials and that it was unfair to penalize an offeror for such arbitrary reasons. See also *Intown Properties, Inc.*, Comp. Gen. Dec. B-262236.2, 96-1 CPD ¶ 89, where the agency did not even consider different personnel included in a BAFO because the agency had found the originally proposed personnel to be weak.

Evaluations are also likely to be found to be arbitrary when offerors are not treated equally in the evaluation process. Such situations develop when offerors that are similarly situated are given different scores or one offeror is given an unfair advantage during the evaluation process. *J.M. Cashman, Inc.*, Comp. Gen. Dec. B-233733, 89-1 CPD ¶ 380, is a good example of such arbitrary evaluation. In that case the GAO found that downgrading one offeror's score due to a lack of experience without doing the same for a similar offeror was unjustified. Likewise, in *Contingency Mgmt. Group, LLC*, Comp. Gen. Dec. B-309752, 2008 CPD ¶ 83, unequal treatment was found where one offeror was permitted to base its proposal on assumptions about a sample task scenario that did not match the RFP and were not available to the other offerors. See also *Ahtna Support & Training Servs., LLC*, Comp. Gen. Dec. B-400947.2, 2009 CPD ¶ 119 (crediting only one offeror with experience of subcontractor unequal treatment); *ITT Federal Servs. Int'l Corp.*, Comp. Gen. Dec. B-296783, 2007 CPD ¶ 43 (using one competitor's staffing approach to adjust the costs of protester an unfair practice); *Magnum Med. Personnel, A Joint Venture*, Comp. Gen. Dec. B-297687.2, 2006 CPD ¶ 99 (disparate evaluations of capability); *BAE Tech. Servs., Inc.*, Comp. Gen. Dec. B-296699, 2006 CPD ¶ 91 (using different standard to evaluate offerors' proposed initiatives to reduce staffing); *PGBA, LLC v. United States*, 60 Fed. Cl. 196 (2004) (downgrading one offeror for lack of specificity without applying same standard to other offerors); *Ashe Facility Servs., Inc.*, Comp. Gen. Dec. B-292218.3, 2004 CPD ¶ 80 (giving credit for experience of key personnel in evaluating corporate experience only to awardee); *Southwestern Bell Tel. Co.*, Comp. Gen. Dec. B-292476, 2003 CPD ¶ 177 (equal evaluations when awardee had ethical problems); *Preferred Sys. Solutions, Inc.*, Comp. Gen. Dec. B-292322, 2003 CPD ¶ 166 (same ratings where evaluation showed differences); *Kathryn Huddleston & Assocs., Ltd.*, Comp. Gen. Dec. B-289453, 2002 CPD ¶ 57 (different treatment of quotations failing to meet solicitation requirement); *Myers Investigations & Sec. Servs., Inc.*, Comp. Gen. Dec. B-288468, 2001 CPD ¶ 189 (different evaluations of past performance when data was similar); *York Bldg. Servs., Inc.*, Comp. Gen. Dec. B-282887.10, 2000 CPD ¶ 141 (key personnel not meeting requirement rated differently); *Saco Defense Corp.*, Comp. Gen. Dec. B-283885, 2000 CPD ¶ 34 (winning offeror given same score as protester when it submitted very sparse information on its quality system); *CRAssocs., Inc.*, Comp. Gen. Dec. B-282075.2, 2000 CPD ¶ 63 (disparate scores when two offerors made same statement); *Electronic Design, Inc.*, Comp. Gen. Dec. B-279662.2, 98-2 CPD ¶ 69 (one offeror permitted to add to its BAFO 1,700 page attachment to initial proposal that exceeded page limitation although no other offerors were told that such detailed information was permissible for inclusion in BAFO); *Aerospace Design & Fabrication, Inc.*, Comp. Gen. Dec. B-278896.2, 98-1 CPD ¶ 139 (one offeror permitted to submit more past performance references than another offeror); *U.S. Property Mgmt. Serv. Corp.*, Comp. Gen. Dec. B-278727, 98-1 CPD ¶ 88 (two offerors with a similar lack of experience given very disparate scores); *New Breed Leasing Corp.*, Comp. Gen. Dec. B-259328, 96-2 CPD ¶ 84 (evaluation comments indicated that the protester had addressed all the agency's concerns in its BAFO and had "enhanced" its proposal, but the protester's scores were not raised); *Main Bldg. Maint., Inc.*, Comp. Gen. Dec. B-260945.4, 95-2 CPD ¶ 214 (protester evaluated as having none of the six "strengths" of the winning offeror when, in fact, it had four); *Deployable Hosp. Sys., Inc.*, Comp. Gen. Dec. B-260778, 95-2 CPD ¶ 65 (two technical proposals rated as equal because both offerors had the same experience, but the GAO found that the protester had significantly more experience than the winning offeror); *Arco Mgmt. of Washington, D.C., Inc.*, Comp. Gen. Dec. B-248653, 92-2 CPD ¶ 173 (winning offeror's BAFO scores were increased based on very "conclusionary" information whereas the protester's BAFO scores were not increased after the submission of substantive responses to issues raised in discussions); and *United Int'l Eng'g, Inc.*, 71 Comp. Gen. 177 (B-245448.3), 92-1 CPD ¶ 122 (contracting officer raised one offeror's labor cost estimate without doing the same for a competitor with a similar estimate).

An extreme form of arbitrary evaluation is evident in situations where the procuring agency purposely favors one offeror over another. For example, in *Xerox Corp. v. United States*, 21 Cl. Ct. 278 (1990), the agency displayed an unethical and even criminal bias toward the awardee. It changed the RFP to omit a requirement that the awardee could not satisfy. It also met secretly with the awardee, after BAFOs had been submitted, to allow it to improve its evaluation by correcting a mistake in its proposal without allowing other offerors to change their proposals. The entire procurement was eventually voided, and Xerox obtained reimbursement for all costs. See also *Lockheed Martin Corp.*, Comp. Gen. Dec. B-295402, 2005 CPD ¶ 24, where the source selection official changed the RFP technical requirements to favor a contractor with which she was negotiating future employment. Similarly, in *Lockheed Martin Corp.*, Comp. Gen. Dec. B-295401, 2005 CPD ¶ 41, the source selection official pressured the evaluators into changing their evaluations and then awarded the contract to the contractor with which she was negotiating future employment.

C. Evaluations Not Based on Evidence

Evaluation decisions must be based on tangible evidence to support an agency's decision. In *Amtec Corp.*, Comp. Gen. Dec. B-240647, 90-2 CPD ¶ 482, *recons. denied*, 91-2 CPD ¶ 473, the GAO overturned a "marginal" technical evaluation because the agency record contained no evidence supporting such a grading. Similarly, in *Radiation Oncology Group of WNY, PC*, Comp. Gen. Dec. B-310354.2, 2009 CPD ¶ 136, a protest was sustained because the agency concluded two proposals were technically equal but had no evidence demonstrating that their unequal evaluations were incorrect. See also *Spherix, Inc.*, Comp. Gen. Dec. B-2945723, 2005 CPD ¶ 3 (agency "projected" offeror's staffing level with no evidence to support projection); *National City Bank of Indiana*, Comp. Gen. Dec. B-287608.3, 2002 CPD ¶ 190 (no evidence to support conclusion low staffing was adequate); *DynCorp Int'l, LLC*, Comp. Gen. Dec. B-289863, 2002 CPD ¶ 83 (no evidence to support rejection of technical evaluators' concern of inadequate staffing); *Meredian Mgmt.*, Comp. Gen. Dec. B-281287.10, 2001 CPD ¶ 5 (inadequate staffing not factored into evaluation); *SWR, Inc.*, Comp. Gen. Dec. B-286161.2, 2001 CPD ¶ 32 (lack of experience not demonstrated by information provided by protester); *One-Source Energy Servs., Inc.*, Comp. Gen. Dec. B-283445, 2000 CPD ¶ 109 (report of telephone conversation with references not a fair reflection of conversation); *Maritime Berthing, Inc.*, Comp. Gen. Dec. B-284123.3, 2000 CPD ¶ 89 (evaluation that offeror met specification requirement when evidence in proposal and known to agency proved otherwise); *Future-Tec Mgmt. Sys., Inc.*, Comp. Gen. Dec. B-283793.5, 2000 CPD ¶ 59 (cost realism adjustment based on misunderstanding of the cost proposal); *L-3 Communications Corp.*, Comp. Gen. Dec. B-281784.3, 99-1 CPD ¶ 81 (cost realism analysis using unaudited indirect cost information which was rescinded by protester); *Matrix Int'l Logistics, Inc.*, Comp. Gen. Dec. B-272388.2, 97-2 CPD ¶ 89 (no evidence to support changing of winning contractor's scores from "good" to "excellent" in evaluating BAFO); *NavCom Defense Elecs., Inc.*, Comp. Gen. Dec. B-276163, 97-1 CPD ¶ 189 (no evidence to support finding that winning contractor's past performance was for work similar to contract work); *Henschel, Inc.*, Comp. Gen. Dec. B-275390.5, 97-1 CPD ¶ 184 (no evidence to support agency determination that offered product was equal to brand name product); *JW Assocs., Inc.*, Comp. Gen. Dec. B-275209, 97-1 CPD ¶ 57 (no evidence to support evaluation of technical proposals); *Ogden Support Servs., Inc.*, Comp.

Gen. Dec. B-270012.2, 96-1 CPD ¶ 177 (no evidence to support excellent past performance scores of winning offeror); *TRESP Assoc.*, Comp. Gen. Dec. B-258322.5, 96-1 CPD ¶ 8 (contracting officer relied on three supposed discriminators, none of which accurately reflected terms of protester's proposal); *Engineering & Computation, Inc.*, Comp. Gen. Dec. B-261658, 95-2 CPD ¶ 176 (no evidence to support evaluation that protester's proposal posed performance risks); *Telos Field Eng'g*, Comp. Gen. Dec. B-253492.6, 94-2 CPD ¶ 240 (no evidence to support higher scores for winning offeror's BAFO); *TRW, Inc.*, Comp. Gen. Dec. B-254045.2, 94-1 CPD ¶ 18 (high evaluation of selected offeror not supported when questions raised by lower-level evaluators regarding the selected firm's technical proposal and substantial "unquantified" concerns about that firm's evaluated cost were not resolved); *HSI-CCEC*, Comp. Gen. Dec. B-240610, 90-2 CPD ¶ 465 (low evaluation of skills of subcontractors not supported by information submitted by the offeror; low evaluation of minority subcontracting unjustified when offeror stated intention to use minority firms that were part of its joint venture); *Asbestos Mgmt., Inc.*, Comp. Gen. Dec. B-237841, 90-1 CPD ¶ 325 (evaluation of key consultant improper when agency had lost qualification statement submitted with proposal); and *Coastal Science & Eng'g, Inc.*, 69 Comp. Gen. 66 (B-236041), 89-2 CPD ¶ 436 (evaluation not substantiated by the record when two competitors received relatively equal technical scores even though one was found to be "sufficiently technically superior to warrant payment of [a significant] cost premium").

Evaluations will also be held to be improper if the agency ignores evidence. See, for example, *Intercon Assocs., Inc.*, Comp. Gen. Dec. B-298282, 2006 CPD ¶ 121, where the GAO sustained a protest because the "evaluation judgments are, in many instances, either factually incorrect, internally contradictory, or so cryptic that we are unable to discern the basis for the evaluators' concerns." See also *MMI Federal Marketing Serv. Corp.*, Comp. Gen. Dec. B-297537, 2006 CPD ¶ 38 (evaluation that offeror met Berry Amendment requirement when evidence indicated it did not); *Cogent Sys., Inc.*, Comp. Gen. Dec. B-295990.4, 2006 CPD ¶ 179 (evaluators ignored different product offered in final proposal revision); *Locus Tech., Inc.*, Comp. Gen. Dec. B-293012, 2004 CPD ¶ 16 (evaluators ignored significant portion of final proposal revision).

Evaluations will also be overturned when it becomes apparent that the evaluators do not understand the data available to them. For example, in *Computer Sys. & Resources, Inc.*, GSBCA 9176-P, 88-1 BCA ¶ 20,331, an evaluation was overturned when, among other things, the chief evaluator admitted validating a critical portion of a proposal without understanding it. The board questioned how she could approve an offer without knowing if it satisfied the necessary requirements. Another evaluation was overturned when the evaluators "extrapolated" successful performance after the offeror had failed the required tests, *Mine Safety Appliance Co.*, 69 Comp. Gen. 562 (B-238597.2), 90-2 CPD ¶ 11. The GAO concluded that the agency should not have proceeded with the procurement without determining why the item did not perform properly. See also *Haworth, Inc.*, Comp. Gen. Dec. B-297077, 2005 CPD ¶

215 (evaluators did not see that descriptive literature concerning product indicated that it did not meet specifications).

D. Immaterial and Nonprejudicial Errors in Evaluation

Even if an agency has improperly evaluated a proposal, a protest will not be granted unless the protester can demonstrate that the improper evaluation would have affected the outcome of the competition. See *CDA Investment Techs., Inc.,* Comp. Gen. Dec. B-272093.3, 97-1 CPD ¶ 103, stating:

> To demonstrate prejudice, the protester must show or it must otherwise be evident from the record before us that there is a reasonable possibility that but for the alleged agency error, the protester would have otherwise been selected for award. *Global Assocs. Ltd.,* B-271693; B-271693.2, Aug. 2, 1996, 96-2 CPD ¶ 100, at 6.

Generally, the decision as to whether prejudice occurred is made by assessing the standing of the competitors after correcting the evaluation error. If the protester's proposal after correction of the evaluation error would not have had a chance of winning the competition, the protest will be denied. See, for example, *Electro-Voice, Inc.,* Comp. Gen. Dec. B-278319, 98-1 CPD ¶ 23 (erroneous evaluation of one technical feature of offered product did not overcome fact that winning contractor's product was superior); *International Data Prods. Corp.,* Comp. Gen. Dec. B-274654, 97-1 CPD ¶ 34 (erroneous evaluation of one technical feature of proposed computer system did not effect relative standing of offerors); *Northport Handling, Inc.,* Comp. Gen. Dec. B-274615, 97-1 CPD ¶ 3 (erroneous omission of data on incumbent's past performance not prejudicial because its past performance had been rated as low risk and would not have changed significantly if data had been included); *Optimum Tech., Inc.,* Comp. Gen. Dec. B-266339.2, 96-1 CPD ¶ 188 (equal weighting of evaluation factors when RFP called for unequal weights not prejudicial when protester benefited by incorrect weighting); *Executive Security & Eng'g Techs., Inc.,* Comp. Gen. Dec. B-270518, 96-1 CPD ¶ 156 (failure to score experience as incumbent contractor not prejudicial because adding the score that should have been given would not have made the protester the winner); *Deployable Hospital Sys., Inc.,* Comp. Gen. Dec. B-260778.2, 96-1 CPD ¶ 113 (erroneous evaluation of one technical subfactor not prejudicial because even reversing scores on this subfactor between protester and winning contractor would not change outcome); and *Tracor, Inc.,* 56 Comp. Gen. 62 (B-186315), 76-2 CPD ¶ 386 (failure by the agency to follow stated evaluation criteria not a basis for upsetting the award because proper evaluation would not have significantly modified the assigned scores).

Agencies have attempted to show that evaluation errors were nonprejudicial by rescoring the protester's proposal during the protest process. However, the GAO has been skeptical of such an argument and has tended to consider the protest on the basis of the original scoring. See *Mechanical Contractors, S.A.,* Comp. Gen. Dec. B-277916, 97-2 CPD ¶ 121, stating:

Regarding the PCC's reevaluation of the proposals to correct errors identified by the protester, while we consider the entire record, including statements and arguments made in response to a protest in determining whether a selection decision is supportable, we accord much greater weight to contemporaneous source selection materials than to judgments, such as the selection officials' reevaluation here, made in response to protest contentions. *Dyncorp*, 71 Comp. Gen. 129, 134 n.12 (1991), 91-2 CPD ¶ 575 at 7 n.13; *Southwest Marine, Inc.; American Sys. Eng'g Corp.*, B-265865.3, B-265865.4, Jan. 23, 1996, 96-1 CPD ¶ 56 at 10. This reflects our concern that reevaluations and redeterminations prepared in the heat of an adversarial process may not represent the fair and considered judgment of the agency, which is a prerequisite of a rational evaluation and source selection process. *Boeing Sikorsky Aircraft Support*, B-277263.2, B-277263.3, Sept. 29, 1997, 97-2 CPD [¶ 91 at 15].

The protest is sustained.

We recommend that both proposals be reevaluated, that the reevaluation be documented, and that a new selection decision be made.

Compare *Dube Travel Agency & Tours, Inc.*, Comp. Gen. Dec. B-270438, 96-1 CPD ¶ 141, where the GAO permitted the agency to rescore to correct a purely mathematical error and used the rescoring to find that no prejudice had occurred.

III. FOLLOWING THE RFP EVALUATION SCHEME

Evaluations will be found to be improper if the evaluators do not comply with the evaluation scheme set forth in the RFP. This requires that the evaluation process be completed during the source selection – issues cannot be left for resolution after contract award, *Sabreliner Corp.*, Comp. Gen. Dec. B-290515, 2003 CPD ¶ 4.

In most best value procurements, the RFP will call for a comparative assessment of various aspects of the proposals and this requires the agency evaluators to identify and assess the relative merits of the proposals. Thus, merely finding that disparate proposals are satisfactory or acceptable will be found to fail to comply with the RFP requirements. See, for example, *Systems Research & Applications Corp.*, Comp. Gen. Dec. B-299818, 2008 CPD ¶ 28, where the GAO stated:

Where, as here, the RFP states a best value evaluation plan — as opposed to selection of the lowest priced, technically acceptable offer — evaluation of proposals is not limited to determining whether a proposal is merely technically acceptable; rather, proposals should be further differentiated to distinguish their relative quality under each stated evaluation factor by considering the degree to which technically acceptable proposals exceed the stated minimum requirements or will better satisfy the agency's needs. See *The MIL Corp.*, B-294836, Dec. 30, 2004, 2005 CPD ¶ 29 at 8; *Johnson Controls World Servs., Inc., Meridian Mgmt. Corp.*, B-281287.5 et al., June 21, 1999, 2001 CPD ¶ 3 at 8.

See also *Northrop Grumman Information Tech., Inc.*, Comp. Gen. Dec. B-400134.10, 2009 CPD ¶ 167 (substantially different proposals given the same rating); *Boeing Co.*, Comp. Gen. Dec. B-311344, 2008 CPD ¶ 114 (no indication that evaluation considered the fact that the protester satisfied significantly more requirements than the selected offeror); *Earl Indus., LLC*, Comp. Gen. Dec. B-309996, 2007 CPD ¶ 203 (no indication of assessment of relative technical merit of offerors).

FAR 15.305(a) follows the language in 10 U.S.C. § 2305(b)(1) and 41 U.S.C. § 253(b), in stating a narrower requirement – that evaluations shall be based solely on the factors and subfactors specified in the RFP. Thus, the GAO has stated that it is generally improper to add or substitute evaluation criteria after proposals have been submitted unless the RFP is amended. See *Grey Advertising, Inc.*, 55 Comp. Gen. 1111 (B-184825), 76-1 CPD ¶ 325, stating that "once offerors are informed of the criteria against which proposals will be evaluated, it is incumbent upon the procuring activity to adhere to those criteria." Unless the solicitation has been amended, the entire evaluation must be based on the stated factors throughout the competitive negotiation process. See also *T-C Transcription, Inc.*, Comp. Gen. Dec. B-401470, 2009 CPD ¶ 172 (improper to downgrade protester for not submitting resumes of personnel when RFP had no such requirement); *EPW Closure Servs., LLC*, Comp. Gen. Dec. B-294910, 2006 CPD ¶ 3 (improper evaluation where agency failed to assess stated factor in evaluation); *Priority One Servs., Inc.*, Comp. Gen. Dec. B-288836, 2002 CPD ¶ 79 (no determination of probable cost of offers in cost reimbursement contract); *CSE Constr.*, Comp. Gen. Dec. B-291268.2, 2002 CPD ¶ 207 (evaluation of understanding of work when that was not a stated factor); *Olympus Bldg. Servs., Inc.*, Comp. Gen. Dec. B-285351, 2000 CPD ¶ 178 (using undisclosed standards to evaluate experience, staffing and management approach); *Wachenhut Int'l, Inc.*, Comp. Gen. Dec. B-286193, 2001 CPD ¶ 8 (failure to make "comprehensive review of compensation plans" as called for by RFP); *Ogden Support Servs., Inc.*, Comp. Gen. Dec. B-270012.2, 96-1 CPD ¶ 177, Comp. Gen. Dec. B-270012.4, 96-2 CPD ¶ 137 (noncompliant evaluation where agency evaluated past performance on dissimilar work although the RFP called for "successful performance on similar efforts").

Evaluation techniques specified in the RFP must also be followed. See, for example, *Ashbury Int'l Group, Inc.*, Comp. Gen. Dec. B-401123, 2009 CPD ¶ 140, where the GAO granted a protest because the agency had not tested the product sample of the selected offeror as required by the RFP. See also *General Dynamics Information Tech.*, Comp. Gen. Dec. B-299873, 2007 CPD ¶ 194 (improper evaluation when agency used labor rates proposed by an offeror in one table when the RFP stated that the rates in another table would be used if there was an inconsistency); *KIC Dev., LLC*, Comp. Gen. Dec. B-297425.2, 2006 CPD ¶ 27 (improper to determine offeror did not meet experience requirement when RFP allowed subcontractor experience to meet requirement); *Clean Harbors Envt'l Servs., Inc.*, Comp. Gen. Dec. B-296176.2, 2005 CPD ¶ 222 (improper to treat all past performance as equally relevant when RFP called for assessing varying degrees of relevance); *Lockheed Martin Corp.*, Comp.

Gen. Dec. B-293679, 2004 CPD ¶ 115 (unreasonable to determine that proposal met RFP requirement to fully describe design features of product based on evaluator's knowledge of subcontractor's competence); *Computer Information Specialist, Inc.*, Comp. Gen. Dec. B-293049, 2004 CPD ¶ 1 (improper evaluation where agency relied on blanket statements of compliance when RFP called for submission of specific information showing compliance); *Johnson Controls World Servs., Inc.*, Comp. Gen. Dec. B-281287.5, 2001 CPD ¶ 3 (giving no credit for proposals with greater technical merit); *Saco Defense Corp.*, Comp. Gen. Dec. B-283885, 2000 CPD ¶ 34 (rating proposal low risk when offeror did not provide detailed information required by RFP to make the assessment); *ENMAX Corp.*, Comp. Gen. Dec. B-281965, 99-1 CPD ¶ 102 (rating proposal acceptable when offeror did not submit required information); *Technology Servs. Int'l, Inc.*, Comp. Gen. Dec. B-276506, 97-2 CPD ¶ 113 (improper evaluation where agency gave the highest rating under a significant quality control technical subfactor even though the awardee's proposal did not submit a detailed work scheduling scheme as contemplated by this subfactor).

A. Scope of Evaluation

Notwithstanding the requirement that only stated factors may be evaluated, agencies have been permitted to broaden the scope of the evaluation by considering all issues that are related to a factor and to narrow the scope of the evaluation by only considering those issues that are perceived to be relevant to the factor.

1. Broadening the Scope

The evaluation of a factor may consider all matters that offerors would reasonably have believed to be within the scope of the factor. See *Bank Street College of Educ.*, 63 Comp. Gen. 393 (B-213209), 84-1 CPD ¶ 607, stating at 400:

> As far as consistency with the evaluation criteria is concerned, while the source selection official may not judge the merits of the proposals based on criteria that offerors were not advised would be considered, the official may properly take into account specific, albeit not expressly identified, matters that are logically encompassed by or related to the stated criteria.

This relationship will be found if a consideration is not listed in Section M but is discussed in Section L of the RFP, *J.A. Jones Grupo de Servicios, SA*, Comp. Gen. Dec. B-283234, 99-2 CPD ¶ 80; *Science & Tech., Inc.*, Comp. Gen. Dec. B-272748, 97-1 CPD ¶ 121. See also *NEQ, LLC v. United States*, 88 Fed. Cl. 38 (2009), where it was found proper to evaluate the presence of the offerors' personnel in listed cities when they were required to submit charts and maps showing the location of their personnel, and *Forestry, Surveys & Data*, Comp. Gen. Dec. B-276802.3, 97-2 CPD ¶ 46, where experience was properly evaluated when it was not listed as a factor in the solicitation, but experience questionnaires were required to be submitted.

Agency evaluation personnel are given considerable discretion in determining which matters are "logically encompassed by or related to" an evaluation factor. This discretion has been very broad when factors involving the capability of the offerors are being evaluated. For example, in *Homequity, Inc.*, Comp. Gen. Dec. B-223997, 86-2 CPD ¶ 685, it was held proper for evaluators to consider the cumulative experience of the offerors' key personnel in evaluating the "organization and experience" factor, and in *Cygnus Corp.*, Comp. Gen. Dec. B-275957, 97-1 CPD ¶ 202, evaluation of the experience of key personnel was proper when the evaluation factor was "corporate experience." See also *NEQ, LLC v. United States*, 88 Fed. Cl. 38 (2009) (metropolitan presence of offerors' offices properly considered in evaluating quick response time requirement); *Professional Perf. Development Group, Inc.*, Comp. Gen. Dec. B-311273, 2008 CPD ¶ 101 ("tested relationships" with required personnel properly considered under RFP calling for evaluation of how offeror would respond to "temporary staffing surges"); *Savannah River Alliance, LLC*, Comp. Gen. Dec. B-311126, 2008 CPD ¶ 88 (diverse experience of key personnel properly considered in evaluating innovative approaches and broad experience); *Matthews Mfg., Inc.*, Comp. Gen. Dec. B-299518, 2007 CPD ¶ 110 (producing the identical product properly considered in evaluating "existing manufacturing capabilities"); *Base Techs., Inc.*, Comp. Gen. Dec. B-293061.2, 2004 CPD ¶ 31 (length of relevant experience of key personnel properly considered in evaluating "qualifications" of key personnel); *Network Eng'g, Inc.*, Comp. Gen. Dec. B-292996, 2004 CPD ¶ 23 (use of incumbent personnel properly considered in evaluating "relevant staff experience"); *Gentex Corp. – Western Operations*, Comp. Gen. Dec. B-291793, 2003 CPD ¶ 66 (funding profile properly considered in evaluating offeror's ability to meet program objectives including development effort "within cost and schedule constraints"); *IBP, Inc.*, Comp. Gen. Dec. B-289296, 2002 CPD ¶ 39 (special consideration for performance as incumbent contractor considered under "experience" factor); *NCLN20, Inc.*, Comp. Gen. Dec. B-287692, 2001 CPD ¶ 136 (organizational structure and transaction plan considered under staffing plan); *Oceaneering Int'l, Inc.*, Comp. Gen. Dec. B-287325, 2001 CPD ¶ 95 (contingency of lack of availability of mobilization port considered under mobilization factor); *MCA Research Corp.*, Comp. Gen. Dec. B-278268.2, 98-1 CPD ¶ 129 (number of employees with security clearances and retention rates of personnel properly considered under management and personnel factors); *Cygnus Corp.*, Comp. Gen. Dec. B-275957, 97-1 CPD ¶ 202 (evaluation of the experience of key personnel proper when the evaluation factor was "corporate experience"); *EastCo Bldg. Servs., Inc.*, Comp. Gen. Dec. B-275334, 97-1 CPD ¶ 83 (evaluation of past performance of only contracts of a similar size proper even though the RFP did not mention this limitation); *Myers Investigative & Security Servs., Inc.*, Comp. Gen. Dec. B-272947.2, 96-2 CPD ¶ 114 (solicitation clearly put offerors on notice that relevant experience would be evaluated under the past performance factor); *Omega World Travel, Inc.*, Comp. Gen. Dec. B-271262.2, 96-2 CPD ¶ 44 (evaluators permitted to use their personal knowledge regarding negative aspects of an offeror's past performance to downgrade that offeror's proposal even though this was not mentioned in the RFP); *American Dev. Corp.*, Comp. Gen. Dec. B-251876.4, 93-2 CPD ¶ 49 (consideration of the relevance of prior contracts was proper when the evaluation factor was past performance); *Quantum Research, Inc.*, Comp. Gen. Dec. B-242020, 91-1 CPD ¶ 310 (proper to downgrade a proposal calling for extended work weeks when the evaluation factors called for evaluation of the quality of personnel and their ability to provide services);*Western Medical Personnel, Inc.*, 66 Comp. Gen. 699 (B-227991), 87-2 CPD ¶ 310 (offerors were on notice of the agency's intention to evaluate past performance when the RFP contained an evaluation factor entitled "References"); *S.C. Jones Servs., Inc.*, Comp. Gen. Dec. B-223155, 86-2 CPD ¶ 158 (experience of a predecessor firm with the same key personnel was properly used to evaluate the factor of "organizational experience and past performance"); *Technical Servs. Corp.*, 64 Comp. Gen. 245 (B-214634), 85-1 CPD ¶ 152 (specific experience was held to be reasonably related to general experience); and *Courseware, Inc.*, Comp. Gen. Dec. B-200731, 81-1 CPD ¶ 133 (proper evaluation found when the agency gave a considerably higher score to offerors proposing the use of two experts rather than one when the evaluation factor called for evaluation of expertise in a subject area). In very questionable decisions, cost management was held to be clearly related to past performance even though the RFP listed only "technical performance" and "schedule performance" as subfactors, *Bendix Field Eng'g Corp.*, Comp. Gen. Dec. B-241156, 91-1 CPD ¶ 44, and performance of work by segments of the company rather than by subcontractors was clearly related to the factor "Offeror's Ability to Provide Additional Effort," *Specialized Tech. Servs., Inc.*, Comp. Gen. Dec. B-247489.2, 92-1 CPD ¶ 510.

An evaluation issue has also been found to be within the scope of the RFP because it was raised during discussions with the offerors, *Intermagnetics Gen. Corp.*, Comp. Gen. Dec. B-286596, 2001 CPD ¶ 10. There, the GAO held that the agency had properly evaluated the compatibility of offered products with other products because this question had been asked during discussions. See also *Interstate Elec. Corp.*, Comp. Gen. Dec. B-286466, 2001 CPD ¶ 29, where an unlisted evaluation factor was found proper because it was identified in an oral presentation as well as in Section L of the RFP.

Considerable discretion has also been granted to agencies in determining which considerations are related to offers. For example, in *International Bus. Machs. Corp. v. Dep't of the Treasury*, GSBCA 11777-P, 92-3 BCA ¶ 25,401, *aff'd, Lockheed Missiles & Space Co. v. Bentsen*, 4 F.3d 955 (Fed. Cir. 1993), the board held that the agency properly evaluated the productivity of the proposed computer systems in the technical and cost evaluation even though productivity was not mentioned in the list of factors. The board stated that the protesters should not have been surprised that the agency would be concerned about productivity because it was inherent in the evaluation of computer systems for use by government agencies. In this regard, agencies can evaluate the extent that an offeror proposes to exceed the agency's requirement when it evaluates the offer. See *IAP World Servs., Inc.*, Comp. Gen. Dec. B-297084, 2005 CPD ¶ 199, stating:

[In a best value procurement,] the agency is not limited to determining whether a proposal is merely technically acceptable; rather, proposals may be evaluated to distinguish their relative quality by considering the degree to which they exceed the minimum requirements or will better satisfy the agency's needs. *Israel Aircraft Indus., Ltd., MATA Helicopters Div.*, B-274389 et al., Dec. 6, 1996, 97-1 CPD ¶ 41 at 5-6; *Meridian Corp.*, B-246330.3, July 19, 1993, 93-2 CPD ¶ 29 at 6-7.

See also *USGC, Inc.*, Comp. Gen. Dec. B-400184.2, 2009 CPD ¶ 9 (innovative disincentive plan offered agency a way to reduce risk); *Cerner Corp.*, Comp. Gen. Dec. B-293093, 2004 CPD ¶ 34 (selection of approach that agency evaluated as best meeting RFP's performance goals); *Preferred Sys. Solutions*, Comp. Gen. Dec. B-291750, 2003 CPD ¶ 56 (transition plan and resumes of key personnel demonstrated that management plan offered lower risk even though such information was not required by RFP); *Israel Aircraft Indus., Ltd.*, Comp. Gen. Dec. B-274389, 97-1 CPD ¶ 41 (enhanced safety of aircraft subsystem intrinsic to stated evaluation factors covering performance and usability of subsystem); *Hydro Eng'g, Inc. v. United States*, 37 Fed. Cl. 448 (1997) (efficiency, reliability and maintainability of equipment properly considered in evaluating design of equipment); and *JoaQuin Mfg. Corp.*, Comp. Gen. Dec. B-275185, 97-1 CPD ¶ 48 (weight, number of footings, and visibility properly related to the suitability of design evaluation factor).

In spite of the breadth of the rules permitting significant leeway in interpreting the scope of the listed evaluation factors, an agency may not evaluate an issue that has no relationship to the factors contained in the RFP. The GAO has stated that there must be a "clear nexus between the stated (evaluation) criteria and the unstated criteria," *Global Analytic Information Tech. Servs., Inc.*, Comp. Gen. Dec. B-298840.2, 2007 CPD ¶ 57. See *T-C Transcription*, Comp. Gen. Dec. B-401470, 2009 CPD ¶ 172 (improper to downgrade proposal for lack of resumes when RFP did not call for their submission); *Consolidated Eng'g Servs., Inc.*, Comp. Gen. Dec. B-311313, 2008 CPD ¶ 146 (improper to evaluate whether offeror had performed all services in a single past contract when factor was experience of "size, scope and complexity" of proposed work); *Meridian Mgmt. Corp.*, Comp. Gen. Dec. B-285127, 2000 CPD ¶ 121 (maintenance and repair of specialized laboratory equipment not within scope of services for laboratories when offerors were not permitted to see laboratories before proposing and no specialized equipment mentioned in RFP); *NITCO*, Comp. Gen. Dec. B-246185, 92-1 CPD ¶ 212 (improper to evaluate past experience in manufacturing a product when there was no indication in the RFP that this would be a consideration); *Flight Int'l Group, Inc.*, 69 Comp. Gen. 741 (B-238953.4), 90-2 CPD ¶ 257 (financial condition was not within the scope of subfactor "ability to meet the published schedule requirements of the government at an acceptable level of risk"); and *J.M. Cashman, Inc.*, Comp. Gen. Dec. B-233733, 89-1 CPD ¶ 380 (improper to downgrade an offeror for proposing to subcontract work when there was no mention of the issue in the evaluation factors).

Agencies have encountered problems in attempting to include price realism as a consideration when it is not listed as a factor. See *Possehn Consulting*, Comp. Gen. Dec. B-278579, 98-1 CPD ¶ 10, where the GAO held that price realism did not fall within the past performance, experience, or key personnel factors. The GAO stated that price realism would have been a legitimate consideration if there had been a factor encompassing the offerors' understanding of the work. Compare *SEEMA, Inc.*, Comp. Gen. Dec. B-277988, 98-1 CPD ¶ 12, where consideration of price realism was found to be within the scope of the factors because the RFP included a factor evaluating management. The GAO found that price realism was within the scope of this factor because the RFP description of what would be evaluated in the management area included the evaluation of understanding of the work. Price realism has also been held to fall under other factors, *Centech Group, Inc.*, Comp. Gen. Dec. B-278715, 98-1 CPD ¶ 108 (technical competence factor); and *Arora Group, Inc.*, Comp. Gen. Dec. B-277674, 98-1 CPD ¶ 64 (proposal risk factor).

2. Narrowing the Scope

Agencies have also been permitted to evaluate only those considerations that they perceive to be relevant to an evaluation factor. See, for example, *EastCo Bldg. Servs., Inc.*, Comp. Gen. Dec. B-275334, 97-1 CPD ¶ 83, where evaluation of past performance of only contracts of a similar size was considered proper even though the RFP did not mention this limitation, and *AVIATE L.L.C.*, Comp. Gen. Dec. B-275058.6, 97-1 CPD ¶ 162, where a factor used in selecting the source was the awardee's experience on performance-based contracting although the RFP did not specifically call for that type of experience. See also *AWD Techs., Inc.*, Comp. Gen. Dec. B-250081.2, 93-1 CPD ¶ 83 (experience in the specific work called for by the contract was properly given heavy weight when the evaluation factor was denominated "past project experience").

B. Failure to Evaluate a Stated Factor

Once an evaluation factor has been included in the RFP, the agency may not ignore that factor. In *Cardkey Sys., Inc.*, Comp. Gen. Dec. B-239433, 90-2 CPD ¶ 159, an evaluation was found improper because it did not consider a feature of the system being procured that had been designated as desirable in the RFP. The GAO found that the protester had increased its price to provide the feature and was prejudiced by the fact that the feature was not considered during the evaluation. See also *General Dynamics Information Tech.*, Comp. Gen. Dec. B-299873, 2007 CPD ¶ 194 (improper evaluation when agency used labor rates proposed by an offeror in one table when the RFP stated that the rates in another table would be used if there was an inconsistency); *Advanced Sys. Dev., Inc.*, Comp. Gen. Dec. B-298411, 2006 CPD ¶ 137 (improper evaluation when agency did not evaluate price proposals for "completeness" of supporting data when RFP stated it would be evaluated); *Low & Assocs., Inc.*, Comp. Gen. Dec. B-297444.2, 2006 CPD ¶ 76 (RFP on-site performance requirement ignored in evaluation); *KIC Dev., LLC*, Comp. Gen. Dec. B-297425.2, 2006 CPD ¶ 27 (improper to determine offeror did not meet experience require-ment when RFP allowed subcontractor experience to meet requirement); *EPW Clo-sure Servs., LLC*, Comp. Gen. Dec. B-294910, 2006 CPD ¶ 3 (improper evaluation where agency failed to assess stated factor in evaluation); *Lockheed Martin Corp.*, Comp. Gen. Dec. B-293679, 2004 CPD ¶ 115 (unreasonable to determine that pro-posal met RFP requirement to fully describe design features of product based on evaluator's knowledge of subcontractor's competence); *Computer Information Spe-cialist, Inc.*, Comp. Gen. Dec. B-293049, 2004 CPD ¶ 1 (improper evaluation where agency relied on blanket statements of compliance when RFP called for submis-sion of specific information showing compliance); *CSE Constr.*, Comp. Gen. Dec. B-291268.2, 2002 CPD ¶ 207 (evaluation of understanding of work when that was not a stated factor); *Priority One Servs., Inc.*, Comp. Gen. Dec. B-288836, 2002 CPD ¶ 79 (no determination of probable cost of offers in cost reimbursement con-tract); *Wachenhut Int'l, Inc.*, Comp. Gen. Dec. B-286193, 2001 CPD ¶ 8 (failure to make "comprehensive review of compensation plans" as called for by RFP); *Saco Defense Corp.*, Comp. Gen. Dec. B-283885, 2000 CPD ¶ 34 (rating proposal low risk when offeror did not provide detailed information required by RFP to make the assessment); *ENMAX Corp.*, Comp. Gen. Dec. B-281965, 99-1 CPD ¶ 102 (rating proposal acceptable when offeror did not submit required information); *E.L. Hamm & Assocs., Inc.*, Comp. Gen. Dec. B-280766.3, 99-1 CPD ¶ 85 (failure to adjust la-bor rates in cost realism analysis to conform to wage determination); *Labat-Ander-son*, 71 Comp. Gen. 252 (B-246071), 92-1 CPD ¶ 193 (institutional experience and quality of proposal not evaluated); and *Cenci Powder Prods., Inc.*, 68 Comp. Gen. 387 (B-234030), 89-1 CPD ¶ 381 (seven factors not considered).

The same rule applies to past performance. When it is designated as an evalu-ation factor, a source selection official may not ignore information regarding poor past performance of an offeror, *G. Marine Diesel*, 68 Comp. Gen. 577 (B-236622), 89-2 CPD ¶ 101 (agency failed to use data within agency regarding poor perfor-mance of ongoing contract), or good past performance, *Univox California, Inc.*, Comp. Gen. Dec. B-210941, 83-2 CPD ¶ 395 (agency failed to use data furnished by offeror); *Inlingua Schools of Languages*, Comp. Gen. Dec. B-229784, 88-1 CPD ¶ 340 (agency failed to use data within agency relating to performance as incumbent contractor). Neither may it treat all past performance as equally relevant when RFP called for assessing varying degrees of relevance, *Clean Harbors Envt'l Servs., Inc.*, Comp. Gen. Dec. B-296176.2, 2005 CPD ¶ 222.

C. Subfactors

When a subfactor is specified in the RFP, it is subject to the same rule applying to factors — it may not be ignored in the evaluation. Thus, it was improper for an agency to fail to consider six of 12 specified evaluation subfactors where the effect was to increase the relative importance of price from 30% to 50%, *Dynalectron*

Corp., Comp. Gen. Dec. B-187057, 77-1 CPD ¶ 95. If subfactors are listed without any indication of relative importance, they will be treated as equally important. Giving such a subfactor predominance is improper, *Isratex, Inc. v. United States*, 25 Cl. Ct. 223 (1992). See also *Lloyd H. Kessler, Inc.*, Comp. Gen. Dec. B-284693, 2000 CPD ¶ 96, sustaining a protest where a subfactor was given very heavy importance without notice in the RFP.

When a subfactor is not specified in the RFP, it may be used in the evaluation of offers if it meets the relationship rule discussed above. The GAO has been liberal in applying this rule. See, for example, *Bendix Field Eng'g Corp.*, Comp. Gen. Dec. B-241156, 91-1 CPD ¶ 44, where the past performance factor listed two subfactors, technical performance and schedule performance, yet the GAO ruled that it was proper to downgrade past performance because of a cost overrun on a prior contract. See also *Barnes & Reinecke, Inc.*, Comp. Gen. Dec. B-236622, 89-2 CPD ¶ 572, where past efforts in designing tracked vehicles were found to be reasonably related to a subfactor covering "knowledge of Tracked Armored Vehicles." In *Stewart-Warner Elecs. Corp.*, Comp. Gen. Dec. B-235774.3, 89-2 CPD ¶ 598, the GAO permitted the evaluation of 31 technical subfactors where the RFP called for "paying appropriate premiums for measured increments of quality."

The requirement to list significant subfactors has been liberally interpreted to permit the nondisclosure of subfactors that are logically and reasonably related to the stated evaluation factors, *Buffalo Organization for Social & Tech. Innovation, Inc.*, Comp. Gen. Dec. B-196279, 80-1 CPD ¶ 101. See *Thomas G. Gebhard, Jr., P.E., Ph.D.*, Comp. Gen. Dec. B-196454, 80-1 CPD ¶ 115, stating:

> We have held that each evaluation subcriterion need not be disclosed in the solicitation so long as offerors are advised of the basic criteria. *Genasys Corporation*, 56 Comp. Gen. 835 (1977), 77-2 CPD ¶ 60. Additional factors may be used in an evaluation where there is sufficient correlation between an additional subcriterion and the generalized criteria in the RFP so that offerors are on reasonable notice of the evaluation criteria to be applied to their proposals. *Littleton Research and Engineering Corp.*, B-191245, June 30, 1978, 78-1 CPD ¶ 466.

There have been numerous protests where unlisted subfactors have been held to be logically related to a factor. For example, the requirement that the project director be available at the outset of the procurement was held to be logically related to the personnel qualifications evaluation factor, *Health Mgmt. Sys.*, Comp. Gen. Dec. B-200775, 81-1 CPD ¶ 255. Similarly, the subfactors "Compliance with Stated Minimum Requirements," "Additional Experience/Qualifications of Key Personnel," and "Experience in the Topical Area" were found to be sufficiently related to the personnel qualifications factor, *Management Sys. Designers, Inc.*, Comp. Gen. Dec. B-244383.4, 91-2 CPD ¶ 518. In *Telos Field Eng'g*, Comp. Gen. Dec. B-258805.2, 95-1 CPD ¶ 186, the protester contended that its proposal was improperly downgraded under the spare parts factor for proposing an inventory of older spare parts and on the ground that its current inventory did not consist of the optimal mix of equipment and was not organized in kits. The spare parts factor stipulated the following criteria:

> "[D]oes the contractor have the ability to supply spare parts when needed? Does the contractor have an adequate reserve of parts and the means to quickly deliver them to the site? Could the contractor replace a complete piece of equipment if need be to incur maximum equipment uptime?"

In finding the evaluation reasonable, the GAO stated:

> [T]he type of inventory and the mix of parts reasonably could be expected to affect the ability to furnish parts for certain equipment, as well as the speed with which the contractor can furnish a part for a newer piece of equipment. Similarly, making parts available in kits, rather than individually, reasonably relates to the speed with which parts necessary for a certain repair can be ordered.

Subfactors need not be included on a separate list if they are described in a narrative form in the description of the factor, *Moran Assocs.*, Comp. Gen. Dec. B-240564.2, 91-2 CPD ¶ 495. In that case the GAO apparently believed that a diligent offeror would identify the subfactors from the narrative description. See also *ITT Electron Tech. Div.*, Comp. Gen. Dec. B-242289, 91-1 CPD ¶ 383, holding that there was no need to disclose an evaluation checklist when the items on the list were reasonably related to the evaluation factors. In *Stone Webster Eng'g Corp.*, Comp. Gen. Dec. B-255286.2, 94-2 CPD ¶ 306, the protester contended that the evaluation was improper because the agency evaluated proposals on a basis of "general strategy," which was not listed as an evaluation factor in the RFP. The agency stated that general strategy was not a separate evaluation criterion but was, however, considered as part of the evaluation of several factors that were set forth in the RFP. The GAO agreed, finding that the RFP did state that strategy formulation and selection of appropriate tactics would be a significant subfactor under the understanding the anticipated work evaluation factor.

If a subfactor will have an inordinate impact on the evaluation of a factor, it will be found to be a significant subfactor and must be identified in the RFP as having such impact, *Systemhouse Fed. Sys., Inc.*, GSBCA 9313-P, 88-2 BCA ¶ 20,603. See *Compuware Corp.*, GSBCA 8869-P, 87-2 BCA ¶ 19,781, where the agency was required to identify a subfactor which altered the focus of the evaluation scheme. See also *Devres, Inc.*, 66 Comp. Gen. 121 (B-224017), 86-2 CPD ¶ 652, requiring listing of a subfactor for specific experience even though it was related to the general experience that had been listed. The specific experience subfactor was 60% of the general experience factor and 25% of the total scoring (it was larger than any other factor).

IV. CHANGING FACTORS OR SUBFACTORS

FAR 15.206 provides specific guidance governing changes to government requirements. These rules also apply to changes to the evaluation factors. If an agency determines during the evaluation process that different evaluation factors will yield a more sound source selection decision, it may amend the RFP to ensure that the offerors have an opportunity to respond to the new evaluation factors. For example, the GAO has held that changes in evaluation factors are ordinarily permitted during the course of a negotiated procurement so long as the offerors are given the opportunity to respond to them, *Consulting & Program Mgmt.*, 66 Comp. Gen. 229 (B-225369), 87-1 CPD ¶ 229 (recommending a resolicitation relaxing experience requirements so as not to deprive any offeror of a chance of award). Similarly, in *H.J. Group Ventures, Inc.*, Comp. Gen. Dec. B-246139.3, 92-2 CPD ¶ 116, it was found proper to add an evaluation factor for performance risk and permit new proposals.

One result of this rule is that a relaxation of requirements for the winning offeror without informing the other competitors is improper, *Courtland Mem'l Hosp.*, Comp. Gen. Dec. B-286890, 2001 CPD ¶ 48 (disregard of "preferences" in RFP); *ACS Gov't Solutions Group, Inc.*, Comp. Gen. Dec. B-282098, 99-1 CPD ¶ 106 (relaxation of specification guidance on use of in-house system); *Barents Group, L.L.C.*, Comp. Gen. Dec. B-276082, 97-1 CPD ¶ 164 (relaxation of requirement to submit resumes in specific labor category); *Armour of America, Inc.*, Comp. Gen. Dec. B-237690, 90-1 CPD ¶ 304 (relaxation of technical specifications); *MTS Sys. Corp.*, Comp. Gen. Dec. B-238137, 90-1 CPD ¶ 434 (relaxation of domestic source requirement) In *Minnesota Mining & Mfg. Co. v. Shultz*, 583 F. Supp. 184 (D.D.C. 1984), the court found an improper deviation from the technical requirements by the offeror that had been selected for award and noted that any change in factors must be communicated to every offeror. See also *Paper Corp. of the U.S.*, Comp. Gen. Dec. B-229785, 88-1 CPD ¶ 388, where the agency was found to have improperly relaxed a testing requirement in evaluating the sample submitted by the awardee, and *Management Sys. Designers, Inc.*, Comp. Gen. Dec. B-244383.4, 91-2 CPD ¶ 518, where the agency was required to inform offerors of a significant change in quantity. In extreme cases substantial and significant changes in the evaluation factors will require an amended solicitation in order to allow other offerors the opportunity to submit proposals, *United Tel. Co.*, Comp. Gen. Dec. B-246977, 92-1 CPD ¶ 374.

The requirement that offerors be advised of changes in evaluation factors does not apply to changes in subfactors that are reasonably related to stated evaluation factors but that are not themselves listed in the RFP, *Dynalectron Corp.*, Comp. Gen. Dec. B-199741, 81-2 CPD ¶ 70. In that case the GAO held that the unlisted subcriterion which was changed "was devised in order to assist the technical evaluators in their internal deliberations."

The same procedures must be used when an agency changes the evaluation scheme. Thus, it is not improper for an agency to issue an amended solicitation altering the relative importance of the evaluation factors, *Unisys Corp.*, 67 Comp. Gen. 512 (B-230019.2), 88-2 CPD ¶ 35 (clarifying the importance of cost), or the overall evaluation scheme, *Galler Assocs., Inc.*, Comp. Gen. Dec. B-210204, 83-1 CPD ¶ 515 (changing from low-cost acceptable offer scheme to tradeoff scheme); *American Lawn Serv., Inc.*, Comp. Gen. Dec. B-267715, 95-2 CPD ¶ 278 (changing from tradeoff scheme to lowest-priced, technically acceptable basis). It is also proper to amend the evaluation scheme in the solicitation to accommodate a method of performance suggested by an offeror, *Loral Terracom*, 66 Comp. Gen. 272 (B-224908), 87-1 CPD ¶ 182 (different technical approach). Of course, such changes are only permissible if all offerors still under consideration are informed of the change, *Labat-Anderson Inc.*, 71 Comp. Gen. 252 (B-246071), 92-1 CPD ¶ 193 (change required by issuance of amendment to RFP or by raising issue in discussions); *Hughes STX Corp. v. NASA*, GSBCA 11665-P, 92-3 BCA ¶ 25,035 (change only allowed with amendment).

The GAO will not overturn an award in which the agency has changed the evaluation criteria without notifying the offerors if the losers are not prejudiced by the change, *FKW Inc. Sys.*, Comp. Gen. Dec. B-235989, 89-2 CPD ¶ 370; *Akal Security, Inc.*, Comp. Gen. Dec. B-261996, 96-1 CPD ¶ 33; *Mc Rae Indus., Inc.*, Comp. Gen. Dec. B-287609.2, 2001 CPD ¶ 127.

V. DISQUALIFICATION OF OFFERORS

There is a growing body of law holding that an offeror should be disqualified from the procurement if the agency learns during the evaluation that the offeror has violated a criminal statute or committed some other serious impropriety. Such disqualification is not a determination of lack of responsibility and thus need not be referred to the Small Business Administration if the offeror is a small business, *NKF Eng'g, Inc. v. United States*, 805 F.2d 372 (Fed. Cir. 1986); *Compliance Corp. v. United States*, 22 Cl. Ct. 193 (1990), *aff'd*, 960 F.2d 157 (Fed. Cir. 1992). The result of this rule is that an offeror may be immediately dropped from the competition without further evaluation when the agency learns of the impropriety.

One type of violation that has led to such disqualification is fraud in the form of material misrepresentation. See, for example, *ACS Gov't Servs., Inc.*, Comp. Gen. Dec. B-293014, 2004 CPD ¶ 18, where the GAO ruled that an offeror should be disqualified when it falsely represented that three key personnel had agreed to work for the firm. Other cases disqualifying offerors for material misrepresentation include *Patriot Contract Services — Advisory Opinion*, Comp. Gen. Dec. B-294777.3, 2005 CPD ¶ 97 (submission of resumes without discussing salary as required by RFP and misstatements as to reasons why they subsequently rejected employment); *S.C. Myers & Assocs., Inc.*, Comp. Gen. Dec. B-286297, 2001 CPD ¶ 16 (submission of name of key person with knowledge that that person would only remain on job during initial phase of contract); *ManTech Advanced Sys. Int'l, Inc.*, Comp. Gen. Dec. B-255719.2, 94-1 CPD ¶ 326 (submission of resumes of personnel with no intent to use those workers); *University Sys., Inc. v. Dep't of Health & Human Servs.*, GSB-CA 12039-P, 93-2 BCA ¶ 25,646 (false certification that tested product was same as product called for by specifications); *PPATHI, Inc.*, Comp. Gen. Dec. B-249182.4, 93-1 CPD ¶ 64 (multiple nondisclosures and false certifications); *Electronic Data Sys. Fed. Corp.*, GSBCA 9869-P, 89-2 BCA ¶ 21,655, *recons. denied*, 89-2 BCA ¶ 21,778, *aff'd sub. nom. Planning Research Corp. v. United States*, 971 F.2d 736 (Fed. Cir. 1992) (submission of resumes of 101 personnel to be employed on contract with no intent to use those workers); *Ultra Tech. Corp.*, Comp. Gen. Dec. B-230309.6, 89-1 CPD ¶ 42 (proposing person as lead technician without obtaining his permission); and *Informatics, Inc.*, 57 Comp. Gen. 217 (B-188566), 78-1 CPD ¶ 53 (misstating the availability of proposed personnel). See also *Biospherics, Inc.*, Comp. Gen. Dec. B-253891.2, 93-2 CPD ¶ 333, where the GAO agreed that an offeror should be disqualified when it did not disclose that a number of the personnel proposed for the contract had also been proposed for another contract being competed at the same time.

The GAO has held that the degree of misrepresentation will establish whether an offeror must be barred from the procurement. See *Aerospace Design & Fabrication, Inc.*, Comp. Gen. Dec. B-278896.2, 98-1 CPD ¶ 139, holding that the agency was not required to disqualify an offeror that had falsely stated that it had commitments from three of its five key personnel, stating:

> In attempting to fashion the appropriate remedy here, we begin with [the protester's] assertion that [the winning offeror] should be barred from further participation in this procurement based on its misrepresentation of the availability of its proposed key personnel, following our holding in *Informatics, Inc., supra*. While the preliminary clearance process [the winning offeror] used here did not rise to the level of a commitment between it and its proposed key personnel, we do not find the same level of disregard for the truth that we found in the *Informatics* case. In that case, the awardee responded to an agency question during discussions asking the nature of the commitments received from the incumbent personnel. The awardee asserted that it had surveyed 60 of 95 incumbent personnel to ascertain their availability, and — in a detailed written explanation of the results of that survey — claimed that a substantial percentage of those employees were either committed or would probably join the company. In fact, our review showed that 59 of the employees had not even been contacted by the awardee during the period the awardee claimed to have conducted its survey. [The winning offeror's] misrepresentations, in contrast, were less pervasive in nature, and were compounded by agency actions during the evaluation. Under these circumstances, we do not believe it would be appropriate to bar [the winning offeror] from further participation in this competition.

Disqualification is not proper when the misrepresentation is inadvertent rather than intentional, *Johnson Controls Security Sys.*, Comp. Gen. Dec. B-296490, 2007 CPD ¶ 102 (no recommendation to disqualify offeror when agency recorded false statement but record of oral presentation did not clearly indicate that statement had been made); *Integration Techs. Group, Inc.*, Comp. Gen. Dec. B-291657, 2003 CPD ¶ 55 (no recommendation to disqualify offeror that had misrepresented the role of important subcontractor); *Tucson Mobilephone, Inc.*, Comp. Gen. Dec. B-258408.3, 95-1 CPD ¶ 267 (record did not support a finding that offeror intentionally misrepresented that it had lead technician's permission to use his credentials); *Universal Techs., Inc.*, Comp. Gen. Dec. B-248808.2, 92-2 CPD ¶ 212 (false certification not made in bad faith). In *ManTech Field Eng'g Corp.*, Comp. Gen. Dec. B-245886.4, 92-1 CPD ¶ 309, *recons. denied*, 92-2 CPD ¶ 89, although the offeror made no attempt to determine whether personnel were available prior to submitting its BAFO, the GAO did not find an intentional misrepresentation and recommended that discussions be reopened.

It is unlikely that a misrepresentation will be found when an offeror makes statements about events that will occur in the future. For example, no misrepresentation was found when an offeror stated that its product was a nondevelopmental item but numerous changes were required to meet requirements, *Northrop Grumman Corp. v. United States*, 50 Fed. Cl. 443 (2001). See also *R&D Maint. Servs., Inc.*, Comp. Gen. Dec. B-292342, 2003 CPD ¶ 162 (disqualification not required when company subcontracted work that was proposed to be performed in-house); *Ann Riley & Assocs., Ltd*, Comp. Gen. Dec. B-271741.3, 97-1 CPD ¶ 122 (violation of subcontracting limitation due to events during performance).

The Court of Federal Claims has held that there is no misrepresentation if the offeror learns after submission of its final proposal revisions that its key personnel will not be available but does not inform the government, *OAO Corp. v. United States*, 49 Fed. Cl. 478 (2001). The court reasoned that it was not clear that there was a legal duty to update a proposal in this manner. Compare *Dual, Inc.*, Comp. Gen. Dec. B-280179, 98-2 CPD ¶ 133, holding that there had been a misrepresentation when an offeror sold a division employing the listed personnel after submitting its proposal but did not inform the agency of the sale.

Offerors have also been disqualified for violating or appearing to violate the conflict of interest laws barring retired government employees from participating in certain government procurements, 18 U.S.C. § 207 (barring representation of contractor in matter where there has been substantial prior involvement). See, for example, *Guardian Techs. Int'l*, Comp. Gen. Dec. B-270213, 96-1 CPD ¶ 104 (recommending disqualification of company whose president had access to inside information because he was former employee of procuring agency); and *Naddaf Int'l Trading Co.*, Comp. Gen. Dec. B-238768.2, 90-2 CPD ¶ 316 (ruling that the contracting officer had properly disqualified an offeror that employed a retired military officer who had contacted the Small Business Administration to argue for the issuance of a Certificate of Competency). Compare *CNA Corp. v. United States*, 81 Fed. Cl. 722 (2008), holding that a company should not be disqualified because its principal investigator had not participated "substantially" in program before he left the agency. Offerors have also been disqualified for conducting employment discussions with a current government employee, 18 U.S.C. § 208 (barring engaging in discussion of future employment while participating in a matter in which the potential employer is involved); 41 U.S.C. § 423 (barring engaging in any discussion of future employment during a procurement). For example, in *NKF Eng'g, Inc. v. United States*, 805 F.2d 372 (Fed. Cir. 1986), the court ruled that the contracting officer had properly disqualified an offeror who hired a member of the Navy source selection board after the initial evaluation and prior to the submission of the best and final offer. The contracting officer had concluded that this gave an appearance of impropriety even though the offeror claimed that the government employee had been carefully screened from the people in the company handling the procurement.

Conflicts of interest involving current government employees will disqualify offerors from the procurement, 18 U.S.C. § 208 (barring participation in procurement involving offeror in which employee had financial interest); FAR Subpart 3.6 (barring award of contract to company owned or controlled by government employee). For example, in *United Tel. Co.*, GSBCA 10031-P, 89-3 BCA ¶ 22,108, an offeror was disqualified because its subcontractor had used a government employee participating in the procurement as a consultant during the competition. Similarly, in *Revnet Env't & Analytical Lab., Inc.*, Comp. Gen. Dec. B-221002.2, 86-2 CPD ¶ 102, the contracting officer disqualified an offeror that had submitted an offer developed by a government employee who had attempted to disassociate himself from his company by turning it over to his wife.

The responsibility for determining whether an offeror should be disqualified due to a conflict of interest rests with the agency and will be upheld by the GAO so long as the decision is reasonable, *Cygnus Corp.*, Comp. Gen. Dec. B-275957, 97-1 CPD ¶ 202. In *Cygnus*, the protester asserted that the offeror should have been disqualified from the competition because the offeror's spouse was a government employee. The protester argued that by virtue of having vested marital property rights, the government employee possessed substantial ownership or control of the offeror such that the matter constituted a conflict of interest. The GAO denied the protest finding no evidence of substantial control or interest such as to warrant disqualification.

Offerors are also properly disqualified because of an organizational conflict of interest, *DSD Lab., Inc. v. United States*, 46 Fed. Cl. 467 (2000). There the court sustained a disqualification because the company had given advice to the agency on structuring the procurement and participated in writing the work statement. See also *Lucent Techs. World Servs. Inc.*, Comp. Gen. Dec. B-295462, 2005 CPD ¶ 55 (protester properly disqualified because it prepared specification for commercial-type item); *Aetna Gov't Health Plans, Inc.*, Comp. Gen. Dec. B-254397.15, 96-2 CPD ¶ 129 (protester should have been disqualified because of impaired objectivity); *QualMED, Inc. v. Office of Civilian Health & Med. Program of the Uniformed Services*, 934 F. Supp. 1227 (D. Col. 1996) (agreeing that GAO had power to make recommendation in *Aetna*). In *L-3 Services, Inc.*, Comp. Gen. Dec. B-400134.11, 2009

CPD ¶ 171, the GAO recommended that a subcontractor with an OCI be excluded from the competition but that the agency could reopen the competition allowing the contractor to obtain a new subcontractor.

Improperly obtaining information during the procurement process will also serve as a grounds for disqualifying offerors. For example, in *Kellogg Brown & Root Servs., Inc.*, Comp. Gen. Dec. B-400787.2, 2009 CPD ¶ 54, the protester was properly disqualified from competing for two task orders when its employee had received an email from the contracting officer containing proprietary information and had not immediately deleted it from his computers. The GAO held that the contracting officer had cause to disqualify the protester because of an appearance of impropriety even though the employee stated that he had not read the document. See also *Computer Tech. Assocs., Inc.*, Comp. Gen. Dec. B-288622, 2001 CPD ¶ 187 (reasonable to disqualify protester whose employees had seen transcripts of competitors' oral presentations); *Litton Sys., Inc.*, 68 Comp. Gen. 422 (B-234060), 89-1 CPD ¶ 450, *recons. denied*, 68 Comp. Gen. 677 (B-234060.2) 89-2 CPD ¶ 228 (ordering a contractor disqualified for obtaining government information through a marketing consultant); *AT&T Communications, Inc.*, GSBCA 9252-P, 88-2 BCA ¶ 20,805 (disqualifying an offeror that had been given the range of its competitor's prices by a government employee with whom it had conducted employment discussions and to whom it had given gratuities). Similarly, in *Compliance Corp.*, Comp. Gen. Dec. B-239252, 90-2 CPD ¶ 126, *recons. denied*, 90-2 CPD ¶ 435, the contracting officer properly disqualified an offeror who had obtained government information from an incumbent service contractor through the use of industrial espionage. The Federal Circuit agreed with this decision in *Compliance Corp. v. United States*, 22 Cl. Ct. 193 (1990), *aff'd*, 960 F.2d 157 (Fed. Cir. 1992), holding that industrial espionage was a valid ground for disqualification (even though no government personnel were involved) because such activity puts the integrity of the procurement system at risk.

In reviewing the reasonableness of an agency's decision on disqualification, the GAO will examine both the nature of the information to which the offeror had access, *Textron Marine Sys.*, Comp. Gen. Dec. B-255580.3, 94-2 CPD ¶ 63 (information disclosed did not give an unfair competitive advantage), and the conditions under which access was gained, *KPMG Peat Marwick*, Comp. Gen. Dec. B-251902.3, 93-2 CPD ¶ 272, *recons. denied*, 94-1 CPD ¶ 201 (offeror received information through Freedom of Information Act). For example, in *IGIT, Inc.*, Comp. Gen. Dec. B-271823, 96-2 CPD ¶ 51, the GAO sustained a protest challenging a contracting officer's decision to disqualify the protester from the competition on the basis that the protester had possessed a page from the installation's solicitation register that included a lump-sum government estimate for the cost of the solicited work. The GAO found that there was no basis to conclude that the offeror obtained the information improperly. The information was taped to the offeror's door apparently to advise IGIT of the agency's decision to resolicit the laundry services rather than to exercise the options. The GAO also found that the information could be given to the other offerors to ameliorate any competitive advantage.

Offerors that give bribes or gratuities to government employees will be disqualified. See *Litton Sys., Inc.*, 68 Comp. Gen. 422 (B-234060), 89-1 CPD ¶ 450, *recons. denied*, 68 Comp. Gen. 677 (B-234060.2), 89-2 CPD ¶ 228, ordering termination of a major contract due to bribery of a high-ranking government employee by the awardee. See also *Howema Bau-GmbH*, Comp. Gen. Dec. B-245356, 91-2 CPD ¶ 214 (excluding protester from contract consideration due to suspected bribery of government officials); and *National Roofing & Painting Corp.*, ASBCA 36,551, 90-2 BCA ¶ 22,936 (voiding contract because it was "tainted with fraud from its inception as well as during performance").

VI. RANKING PROPOSALS AND DOCUMENTING THE EVALUATION

FAR 15.305(a) contains the following statement on the evaluation process:

> Evaluations may be conducted using any rating method or combination of methods, including color or adjectival ratings, numerical weights, and ordinal rankings. The relative strengths, deficiencies, significant weaknesses, and risks supporting proposal evaluation shall be documented in the contract file.

The first sentence contains a permissive procedure allowing agencies to use a notational scoring or ranking technique as part of the evaluation process. Almost all agencies follow such a procedure by requiring some sort of scoring or ranking in their source selection plan. The second sentence contains a mandatory procedure requiring agencies to document "relative strengths, significant weaknesses, and risks" that have been identified during the evaluation of proposals. The general rule is that the source selection decision must be based on the documented "relative strengths, significant weaknesses, and risks" – not on the scores or rankings. See *JW Assocs., Inc.*, Comp. Gen. Dec. B-275209, 97-1 CPD ¶ 57, stating:

> While both adjectival ratings and point scores are useful as guides to decision-making, they generally are not controlling, but rather, must be supported by documentation of the relative differences between proposals, their weaknesses and risks, and the basis and reasons for the selection decision.

A. Notational Scoring Systems

Scoring systems are notational devices that provide a rough means of measuring differences between proposals. The three most common systems call for the assignment of adjectival, color or numerical scores to the some or all of the factors and subfactors and it is common for an agency to use two of these systems simultaneously – such as an adjectival system that is converted to color scores. Since the source selection decision is expected to be made ultimately on the "relative strengths, significant weaknesses, and risks" that have been identified in the proposals, it is questionable whether the scoring systems provide any benefit to the contracting agency.

In general, an agency's scoring system cannot be challenged, *MINACT, Inc.*, Comp. Gen. Dec B-400951, 2009 CPD ¶ 76 (adjectival rating permissible when RFP called for numerical scoring); *Trajen, Inc.*, Comp. Gen. Dec. B-296334, 2005 CPD ¶ 153 (use of three adjective system instead of five called for by RFP not grounds for protest); *BRC Assocs., Inc.*, Comp. Gen. Dec. B-237156, 90-1 CPD ¶ 145 (numerical scoring of subfactors permitted even though the RFP stated that subfactors did not have assigned points). Compare *Lithos Restoration, Ltd.*, 71 Comp. Gen. 367 (B-247003.2), 92-1 CPD ¶ 379, where the RFP stated that technical factors were more important than price, technical subfactors were listed in descending order of importance, and the first of four technical subfactors listed would be evaluated on a "go, no-go" basis. The GAO held that failing to score the first evaluation subfactor in these circumstances was a violation of the RFP evaluation scheme because the evaluation procedure could only be reasonably interpreted as requiring point scoring of the most important technical subfactor in making the price/technical tradeoff.

In addition, agency evaluators are given considerable discretion in assigning scores to proposals. See *MiTech, Inc.*, Comp. Gen. Dec. B-275078, 97-1 CPD ¶ 208, stating:

> The evaluation and scoring of proposals is a matter primarily within the discretion of the contracting activity since it is responsible for defining its needs and for determining the best methods of accommodating those needs, and technical evaluators have considerable latitude in assigning ratings which reflect their subjective judgments of a proposal's relative merits. *Bunker Ramo Corp.*, 56 Comp. Gen. 712 (1977), 77-1 CPD ¶ 427; *Met-Pro Corp.*, B-250706.2, Mar. 24, 1993, 93-1 CPD ¶ 263; *Abt Assocs., Inc.*, B-237060.2, Feb. 26, 1990, 90-1 CPD ¶ 223. In reviewing an agency's technical evaluation, we will not rescore proposals but rather will review the agency's evaluation to ensure that it was reasonable and in accordance with the RFP criteria. *Abt Assocs., Inc.*, *supra*. A protester's mere disagreement with the particular point scores awarded to its proposal does not render the evaluation unreasonable. *DBA Sys., Inc.*, B-241048, Jan. 15, 1991, 91-1 CPD ¶ 36.

Thus, when source selection decisions are based on the strengths, weakness, and risks in the proposals, protests of incorrect scoring are routinely denied. See, for example, *Blackwater Lodge & Training Ctr., Inc. v. United States*, 86 Fed. Cl. 488 (2009) ("Courts should look beyond the adjectival ratings because proposals awarded the same adjectival ratings are not necessarily equal in quality."); *Karrar Sys. Corp.*, Comp. Gen. Dec. B-310661.3, 2008 CPD ¶ 55 ("focus on the adjectival ratings . . . misplaced"); *Pemco Aeroplex, Inc.*, Comp. Gen. Dec. B-310372, 2008 CPD ¶ 2 (proposals with same adjectival rating "not necessarily of equal quality"); *Raymond Assocs., LLC*, Comp. Gen. Dec. B-299496, 2007 CPD ¶ 107 (purportedly irrational averaging of subfactor ratings not relevant when decision considered strengths and weaknesses); *DeTekion Sec. Sys., Inc.*, Comp. Gen. Dec. B-298235, 2006 CPD ¶ 130 ("adjectival ratings and point scores are . . . tools to assist source selection officials in evaluating proposals; they do not mandate automatic selection of a particular proposal"); *Mechanical Equip. Co.*, Comp. Gen. Dec. B-292789.2, 2004 CPD ¶ 192 ("the protesters' disagreement over the actual adjectival ratings is essentially inconsequential"); This reasoning has been followed by the GAO even when the protester had alleged that the scoring system called for by the RFP misled the protester in deciding what effort to propose, *Northrop Grumman Tech. Servs., Inc.*, Comp. Gen. Dec. B-291506, 2003 CPD ¶ 25. There the agency had used a computerized system that gave the same point score to "good" and "excellent" but had not actually relied on the system in making the final source selection decision.

Most scoring systems do not score all the factors and subfactors. Technical and management factors appear to be the most frequently scored, while price or cost is the least frequently scored. This is logical because the marginal difference in price or cost between the proposals, which will be used to make the source selection decision, is clearly apparent in dollar amounts and scoring tends to obscure rather than illuminate this difference. However, the GAO has held that it is proper to give adjectival scores to life cycle costs, *Raytheon Co.*, Comp. Gen. Dec. B-298626.2, 2007 CPD ¶ 185.

Scoring systems are particularly useful when there are a large number of evaluation factors and subfactors. However, as the number of factors decreases, there is less need for scoring. For example, the only factors in a number of procurements are past performance and price. In such cases there would appear to be no need to score the proposals.

Any system can be used as long as it provides meaningful distinctions among proposals of various merit. The most frequently used systems are those identified in FAR 15.305(a): adjectival rating systems, color coding, numerical scoring, and ranking.

1. *Adjectival Ratings*

Adjectival rating systems generally call for the use of four or five ratings such as excellent, good, fair, and poor; or outstanding, highly acceptable, acceptable, marginally acceptable, and unacceptable. In spite of the fact that such systems provide the evaluators very few scores to differentiate between proposals, the GAO has accepted the use of these systems — finding that they can give the source selection official a clear understanding of the relative merit of the proposals, *Dynamics Research Corp.*, Comp. Gen. Dec. B-240809, 90-2 CPD ¶ 471. See also *Akal Security, Inc.*, Comp. Gen. Dec. B-261996, 96-1 CPD ¶ 33, rejecting the argument that an adjectival system that scored compliant proposals as either "acceptable" or "exceptional" did not properly reflect technical superiority. The GAO reasoned that such a system was satisfactory because it was "only a guide" to assist in the evaluation process. See also *Stateside Assocs., Inc.*, Comp. Gen. Dec. B-400670.2, 2009 CPD ¶ 120, rejecting the contention that a cumulative adjectival score was misleading, stating:

Whether assigned to each factor or to a proposal overall, adjectival ratings are not binding on the source selection official but, rather, serve only as a guide to intelligent decision making. *Chapman Law Firm*, LPA, B-293105.6 et al., Nov. 15, 2004, 2004 CPD ¶ 233 at 5. The essence of the evaluation is reflected in the evaluation record itself, not the adjectival ratings. The record here shows that the SSB evaluated each factor individually, included a detailed discussion of each strength and weakness, and based its tradeoff recommendation on the relative strengths and weaknesses of the proposals, not the overall adjectival ratings.

Some of these decisions indicate that evaluators must exercise care in providing narrative comments, noting instances where the same adjectival rating has been given to proposals of different merit. See *Command Mgmt. Servs., Inc.*, Comp. Gen. Dec. B-310261, 2008 CPD ¶ 29, stating:

The evaluation of proposals and assignment of adjectival ratings should generally not be based upon a simple count of strengths and weaknesses, but on a qualitative assessment of the proposals consistent with the evaluation scheme; thus, to the extent that CMS's arguments are based on merely counting weaknesses, they do not provide a basis to challenge the reasonableness of the evaluation. *Kellogg Brown & Root Servs., Inc.*, B-298694.7, June 22, 2007, 2007 CPD ¶ 124 at 5. In any case, since adjectival scores are merely guides for intelligent decision making in the procurement process, they do not necessarily mandate selection of a particular proposal for award. *KBM Group, Inc.*, B-281919, B-281919.2, May 3, 1999, 99-1 CPD ¶ 118 at 11. The more important consideration is whether the evaluation record and source selection decision show that the agency reasonably assessed the relative merits of the proposals in accordance with the stated evaluation criteria.

In a few instances the GAO has rejected adjectival ratings that distort the relationship between the proposals. See, for example, *Redstone Tech. Servs.*, Comp. Gen. Dec. B-259222, 95-1 CPD ¶ 181, sustaining a protest finding that the contracting officer had mechanically applied the adjectival scoring system without documenting whether the relative differences represented any meaningful qualitative differences justifying award to a higher-technically rated, significantly higher-cost offeror. See also *Deployable Hosp. Sys., Inc.*, Comp. Gen. Dec. B-260778, 95-2 CPD ¶ 65, sustaining a protest when two offerors with significantly different levels of experience were scored as acceptable. Compare *Wackenhut Servs., Inc.*, Comp. Gen. Dec. B-400240, 2008 CPD ¶ 184, denying a protest that the agency had not given it a higher rating because it had more good adjectival scores, stating that such scores "should not be mechanically derived or applied." The opposite result was reached in *Wackenhut Servs., Inc. v. United States*, 85 Fed. Cl. 273 (2009), where the court enjoined the procurement, in part because the agency had been arbitrary and capricious in scoring the proposals without adequate documentation of how the scores were arrived at. See also *Femme Comp Inc. v. United States*, 83 Fed. Cl. 704 (2008), where the court found that the agency's scoring was flawed but that the flaw amounted to "harmless error." Similarly, in *Information Sciences Corp. v. United States*, 80 Fed. Cl. 759 (2008), the court granted a protest, in part because of inaccurate scoring.

Evaluators should make sure that their adjectival ratings are in accord with their narrative comments. See, for example, *New Breed Leasing Corp.*, Comp. Gen. Dec. B-259328, 96-2 CPD ¶ 84, where the GAO sustained a protest because the adjectival ratings given to the source selection official did not reflect the actual evaluation results.

2. Color Ratings

Most color rating systems are very similar to adjectival scoring in the fact that they have very few scores. Thus, the notational system, in itself, does not provide very clear gradations between proposals. See, for example, the Air Force system discussed in Chapter 2, which distinguishes categories only as blue, green, yellow, and red. In spite of such minimal gradation, the GAO has agreed with the use of color rating, holding that such a system does not produce "an artificial equality in the ratings," *Ferguson-Williams, Inc.*, 68 Comp. Gen. 25 (B-231827), 88-2 CPD ¶ 344. The GAO has also held that a color scoring system does not prevent the agency from gaining a clear understanding of the relative merits of the proposals, *Gracon Corp.*, Comp. Gen. Dec. B-293009, 2004 CPD ¶ 58, and *Bendix Field Eng'g Corp.*, Comp. Gen. Dec. B-241156, 91-1 CPD ¶ 44. See also *Peterson Bldrs., Inc.*, Comp. Gen. Dec. B-244614, 91-2 CPD ¶ 419, denying a protest that the color rating system obscured the fact that the technical proposals were essentially equal, and *Hogar Crea, Inc.*, Comp. Gen. Dec. B-311265, 2008 CPD ¶ 107, denying a protest that since the offerors were given the same color scores, they should have been treated as equal.

These decisions are based on the view that the color coding will not be the basis of the source selection decision, but that the source selection official will be provided with an analysis of the relative strengths and weaknesses of the proposals. See *Precision Mold & Tool*, Comp. Gen. Dec. B-400452.4, 2009 CPD ¶ 84, stating that, when strengths and weaknesses are used to make the source selection decision, "the color rating assigned is inconsequential in the analysis." See also *Cherry Road Techs.*, Comp. Gen. Dec. B-296915, 2005 CPD ¶ 197, rejecting the argument that the color rating scheme "lacked coherent standards" and that the assigned colors were inconsistent with the evaluation. Thus, when such scoring does not differentiate between proposals of unequal merit, great care should be exercised to ensure that the differences between the proposals are documented. See *Trijicon, Inc.*, 71 Comp. Gen. 41 (B-244546), 91-2 CPD ¶ 375, rejecting the use of a green-yellow-red scoring system that was used without differentiating between proposals that were merely acceptable and those with superior technical features — thus converting a tradeoff decisional scheme into a low-price, technically acceptable proposal scheme.

3. Numerical Systems

Numerical systems can be considerably more accurate in reflecting differences between proposals because they generally contain a large number of gradations, which permits greater differentiation. However, this apparent accuracy can mislead source selection officials into believing that the total scores provide a precise overall assessment of the relative strengths and weaknesses of the proposals. See, for example, *Serco Inc. v. United States*, 81 Fed. Cl. 463 (2008), where the court granted a protest because the agency had used a point scoring system that resulted in "false statistical precision." The flaw detected by the court was that the agency had scored subfactors adjectivally, converted these scores into whole numbers, averaged the whole number to arrive at a numerical value for each offeror that went to three decimal places, and then used this data to make the source selection decision. Similarly, in *Midland Supply, Inc.*, Comp. Gen. Dec. B-298720, 2007 CPD ¶ 2, the GAO sustained a protest because the source selection official had based the decision on "a mechanical comparison of the offerors' total point scores." Compare *GAP Solutions, Inc.*, Comp. Gen. Dec. B-310564, 2008 CPD ¶ 26, where the source selection official properly ignored minor differences in numerical scores, determined that the offerors were "technically equal," and awarded to the low price offeror.

A number of protests have been granted because the evaluators have not assigned the same numerical grades to proposals with the same degree of merit. See, for example, *Century Envtl. Hygiene, Inc.*, Comp. Gen. Dec. B-279378, 98-1 CPD ¶ 164, where the GAO granted a protest because the agency identified weaknesses in proposals but gave different scores to the competitors without any explanation of the differences. See also *Ogden Servs., Inc.*, Comp. Gen. Dec. B-270012.2, 96-1 CPD ¶ 177 (no explanation of why awardee received a near perfect score under past performance factor when proposal did not demonstrate mail/service or similar experience as required by RFP); *Engineering & Computation,* Inc., Comp. Gen. Dec. B-261658, 95-2 CPD ¶ 176 (no documentation explaining protester's low scores where it appeared to have addressed a perceived weakness in its BAFO); *DNL Properties, Inc.*, Comp. Gen. Dec. B-253614.2, 93-2 CPD ¶ 301 (no explanation of different scores for different proposals that appear to be similar); *Arco Mgmt. of Washington, D.C., Inc.*, Comp. Gen. Dec. B-248653, 92-2 CPD ¶ 173 (no explanation of why protester's BAFO was given no additional points although it responded to all discussion questions whereas the winning offeror's BAFO was rescored upward in same circumstances).

Numerical scores assigned to proposals must be inherently rational. In *SDA, Inc.*, Comp. Gen. Dec. B-248528.2, 93-1 CPD ¶ 320, the GAO granted a protest because the numerical scores given for experience were irrational. The agency used a system where an offeror was given a zero score if over half the prior projects it listed were under an undisclosed size — even if many of the projects indicated substantial experience. In *SIMCO, Inc.*, Comp. Gen. Dec. B-229964, 88-1 CPD ¶ 383, a cost evaluation was overturned for using an all-or-nothing point system not specified in the RFP and for failing to weigh price as 20% of the total score as promised. Similarly, a technical evaluation scheme giving no credit for partially unsatisfactory proposals was held noncompliant in *National Capital Med. Found., Inc.*, Comp. Gen. Dec. B-215303.5, 85-1 CPD ¶ 637, because such a grading system was not outlined in the RFP. Compare *Home & Family Servs., Inc.*, Comp. Gen. Dec. B-182290, 74-2 CPD ¶ 366, allowing such a scoring system because it was described in the RFP.

4. Ranking

The direct ranking of proposals, without the aid of scores, has been upheld. The reasoning for this is that numerical scoring does not "transform the technical evaluation into a more objective process," *Development Assocs., Inc.*, Comp. Gen. Dec. B-205380, 82-2 CPD ¶ 37. The GAO has even stated that "ranking proposals may be a more direct and meaningful method" than numerical scoring, *Maximus*, Comp. Gen. Dec. B-195806, 81-1 CPD ¶ 285. However, ranking is infrequently used because it bypasses the scoring of proposals in terms of how well they meet the RFP requirements. To overcome this potential difficulty, an agency can use initial scoring but then provide overall ranking to the source selection official to aid in the decision, *Cerner Corp.*, Comp. Gen. Dec. B-293093, 2004 CPD ¶ 34. However, ranking is done, it does not overcome the necessity of identifying the strengths, weaknesses and risks in the proposals.

B. Assessment of Strengths, Weaknesses, and Risks

The most important part of the evaluation process is the assessment of the strengths, deficiencies, significant weaknesses, and risks of each proposal and the assessment of their relative qualities. Prior to the rewrite of FAR Part 15, this assessment was required only on "formal source selections." However, FAR 15.305(a) now requires this assessment to be made on all competitively negotiated procurements. This is the critical information that is used to make the source selection decision and serves as an essential part of the documentation supporting that decision. The FAR contains no guidance on who should make these assessments or when they should be made, but it has been common practice to direct evaluators to assess each proposal's quality in meeting the requirements of the RFP and its evaluation factors first and then to have the evaluators or some other group assess the relative merits of the competing proposals. In a case where the Air Force regulation required this two-step procedure, the Court of Federal Claims held that permitting the evaluators to make the comparative assessment during their initial evaluation was a "harmless regulatory violation," *Aero Corp. v. United States*, 38 Fed. Cl. 237 (1997). See also *Food Servs. of Am.*, Comp. Gen. Dec. B-276860, 97-2 CPD ¶ 55, and *ASR Mgmt. & Tech. Servs.*, Comp. Gen. Dec. B-244862.3, 92-1 CPD ¶ 383, where the GAO noted that comparative assessments were made by technical evaluators but did not comment on the use of the procedure. Thus, it appears that agencies can either use the two-step process or make a comparative assessment in the initial evaluation. Whichever method is used, it should be clear that the end result is a comparative assessment of the relative merits of the proposals, because that must be the basis for the ultimate source selection decision, FAR 15.308.

1. Documenting the Assessment

FAR 15.305(a) requires documentation as follows:

The relative strengths, deficiencies, significant weaknesses, and risks supporting proposal evaluation shall be documented in the contract file.

This documentation is generally prepared in narrative form simultaneously with the scoring and describes the reasons for the scores that the evaluators assigned to the proposal. Thus, these narratives identify the "strengths, deficiencies, significant weaknesses, and risks" of each proposal that have led to the score that has been assigned. A fully documented evaluation will contain narratives for each score — generally at the lowest level of scoring in the evaluation scheme. It is very helpful if these narratives contain a reference to the specific pages of the proposal that contain the information on which the evaluation is based.

These narrative statements can be prepared by each evaluator or as a summary evaluation by all the evaluators that have assessed the element of the proposals being evaluated. Preparation of these narratives at the same time the proposals are scored provides an excellent discipline for the evaluators because it forces them to justify their scores. If the narratives are prepared by the entire evaluation team, this will also force evaluators to reconcile disparate scores or at least to focus on the reason for disparities. Thus, the preparation of narratives reflecting the consensus of the evaluation team can improve the scoring as well as flow valuable information to the source selection official. When a consensus evaluation document is prepared, it is important that it include sufficient explanation of the assessment so that it can be reviewed in the event of a protest, *DGR Assocs., Inc.*, Comp. Gen. Dec. B-285428, 2000 CPD ¶ 145.

Although the FAR gives no guidance on the extent of documentation required, it is clear that the GAO demands sufficient documentation to permit consideration of a protest asserting that the agency has not followed the evaluation scheme in the RFP. See *Satellite Servs., Inc.*, Comp. Gen. Dec. B-286508, 2001 CPD ¶ 30, stating:

> In reviewing an agency's evaluation of proposals and source selection decision, we examine the record to determine whether the agency acted reasonably and consistent with the stated evaluation factors as well as applicable statutes and regulations. *PRC, Inc.*, B-274698.2, B-274698.3, Jan. 23, 1997, 97-1 CPD ¶ 115 at 4. Implicit in the foregoing is that the evaluation must be documented in sufficient detail to show that it was reasonable and bears a rational relationship to the announced evaluation factors. FAR §§ 15.305(a), FAR 15.308. . . .

This appears to be a flexible requirement based on the complexity of each source selection. In *Champion-Alliance, Inc.*, Comp. Gen. Dec. B-249504, 92-2 CPD ¶ 386, the GAO held that relatively little documentation was required from the agency because the requirements under the RFP were fairly unambiguous and the proposals were very similar. See also *Quality Elevator Co.*, Comp. Gen. Dec. B-276750, 97-2 CPD ¶ 28, where inadequate documentation was overlooked because the proposals were very similar. See *Apex Marine Ship Mgmt. Co., LLC*, Comp. Gen. Dec. B-278276.25, 2000 CPD ¶ 164, stating:

> [A]n agency must document its judgments in sufficient detail to show that they are not arbitrary. *U.S. Defense Sys., Inc.*, B-245563, Jan. 17, 1992, 92-1 CPD ¶89

at 3. The amount and detail of documentation necessary to demonstrate that an agency's judgments were reasoned and rational will vary from procurement to procurement, and there is no absolute requirement that evaluation records must include narrative explanations for every score assigned. See *Delta Dental Plan of Cal. v. Perry*, 1996 WL 83881 (N.D. Cal. 1996) at 15, citing *Champion-Alliance, Inc.*, B-249504, Dec. 1, 1992, 92-2 CPD ¶ 6 at 6-7 (contemporaneous summary evaluation narrative and post-protest amplification sufficient documentation).

However, even when the technical scores of the top two offerors were within one percentage point of each other, the GAO sustained a protest because the scores were not adequately supported by written narratives, *Universal Shipping Co.*, Comp. Gen. Dec B-223905.2, 87-1 CPD ¶ 424. For other protests that have been sustained because of insufficient documentation, see *Radiation Oncology Group of WNY, PC*, Comp. Gen. Dec. B-310354.2, 2009 CPD ¶ 136 (agency record contained no "comprehensive assessment or listing of the proposals' strengths and weaknesses"); *Panacea Consulting, Inc.*, Comp. Gen. Dec. B-299307.4, 2007 CPD ¶ 141 (no statement of strengths or weaknesses supporting numerical scores); *Pemco Aeroplex, Inc.*, Comp. Gen. Dec. B-310372, 2007 CPD ¶ 2, recons. denied, 2008 CPD ¶ 24 (no documentation supporting element of price realism analysis); *Systems Research & Applications Corp.*, Comp. Gen. Dec. B-299818, 2008 CPD ¶ 28 (evaluators worksheets contained no explanation of scoring); *Intercon Assocs., Inc.*, Comp. Gen. Dec. B-298282, 2006 CPD ¶ 121 (evaluator documents "factually incorrect, internally contradictory," or "cryptic"); *Keeton Corrections, Inc.*, Comp. Gen. Dec. B-293348, 2005 CPD ¶ 44 (no evidence that source selection official was presented with details of evaluation); *National City Bank of Indiana*, Comp. Gen. Dec. B-287608.3, 2002 CPD ¶ 190 (no documentation explaining why staffing reductions would allow offeror to meet technical requirements); *Bank of Am.*, Comp. Gen. Dec. B-287608, 2001 CPD ¶ 137 ("virtually no evaluator worksheets" showing the basis for cost realism calculations and adjustments); *BAE Sys.*, Comp. Gen. Dec. B-287189, 2001 CPD ¶ 86 (no indication that a "potential strength" included in the protester's technical proposal was considered by the agency evaluators); *J & J Maint., Inc.*, Comp. Gen. Dec. B-284708.2, 2000 CPD ¶ 106 (no narratives showing how numerical scores were reconciled); *Future-Tec Mgmt., Sys., Inc.*, Comp. Gen. Dec. B-283793.5, 2000 CPD ¶ 59 (insufficient documentation of evaluation to understand source selection decision); *MCR Fed., Inc.*, Comp. Gen. Dec. B-280969, 99-1 CPD ¶ 8 (no documentation showing that technical proposals were equal when they were scored differently); *Matrix Int'l Logistics, Inc.*, Comp. Gen. Dec. B-272388.2, 97-2 CPD ¶ 89 (summary evaluation results with no narrative supporting changed scores on BAFOs); *J.A. Jones Mgmt. Servs., Inc.*, Comp. Gen. Dec. B-276864, 97-2 CPD ¶ 47 (no explanation in "cursory narratives" of seemingly irrational scores given to protester); *JW Assocs., Inc.*, Comp. Gen. Dec. B-275209, 97-1 CPD ¶ 57 (one-paragraph summary of each proposal with no supporting narrative for low scores); *Engineering & Computation, Inc.*, Comp. Gen. Dec. B-261658, 95-2 CPD ¶ 176 (summary decision memorandum but no narrative for individual subfactors where significant risks had been found); *Deployable Hospital Sys., Inc.*,

Comp. Gen. Dec. B-260778, 95-2 CPD ¶ 65 (preaward survey showed significant distinctions between the two offerors that did not support an equal rating on their quality control factors and subfactors and the ratings were not otherwise explained or justified); *Arco Mgmt. of Washington, D.C., Inc.*, Comp. Gen. Dec. B-248653, 92-2 CPD ¶ 173 (no narratives supporting point scores); *Northwest EnviroService, Inc.*, 71 Comp. Gen. 453 (B-247380.2), 92-2 CPD ¶ 38 (no documentation to support evaluation that competing offerors were equal in past performance); and *Beckman Instruments, Inc.*, Comp. Gen. Dec. B-246195.3, 92-1 CPD ¶ 365 (no documentation showing that agency evaluated changes in BAFO). When the agency's source selection apparently deviates in any way from the stated evaluation criteria, the GAO will require comprehensive documentation explaining the apparent deviation, *Dewberry & Davis*, Comp. Gen. Dec. B-247116, 92-1 CPD ¶ 421 (award to low-priced, technically acceptable offer where evaluation scheme provided that technical merit was more important than price).

In a rare case, *Helicopter Transport Servs. LLC*, Comp. Gen. Dec. B-400295, 2008 CPD ¶ 180, where the agency arrived at an evaluation of an offeror's past performance by a discussion by a group of evaluators providing their experience working with the offerors, the GAO granted the protest because of lack of documentation, stating:

> In an evaluation that takes into account the agency's own knowledge of offerors' performance, the fundamental requirement that evaluation judgments be documented in sufficient detail to show that they are reasonable and not arbitrary must still be met. *Omega World Travel, Inc.*, B-271262.2, July 25, 1996, 96-2 CPD ¶ 44 at 4.

Prior to the FAR Part 15 rewrite, which added the requirement in FAR 15.305(a) that this documentation be included in the contract file, agencies were permitted to destroy the worksheets of individual evaluators if the documentation that was retained was sufficient to justify the source selection decision or if the decision could be supported by explanations created after the protest was filed. See *Dimensions Int'l/QSOFT, Inc.*, Comp. Gen. Dec. B-270966, 96-1 CPD ¶ 257, stating:

> While an agency is not required to retain every document or worksheet generated during its evaluation of proposals, the agency's evaluation must be sufficiently documented to allow review of the merits of a protest. *Southwest Marine, Inc.*; *American Sys. Eng'g Corp.*, [Comp. Gen. Dec. B-265865.3, 96-1 CPD ¶ 56; *KMS Fusion, Inc.*, B-242529, May 8, 1991, 91-1 CPD ¶ 447. In this regard, evaluators' notes and workpapers may or may not be necessary to determine the reasonableness of the agency's evaluation. *KMS Fusion, Inc.*, *supra*; *see Department of the Army-Recon.*, B-240647.2, Feb. 26, 1991, 91-1 CPD ¶ 211. Where an agency fails to document or retain evaluation materials, it bears the risk that there is inadequate supporting rationale in the record for the source selection decision and that we will not conclude that the agency had a reasonable basis for the decision. *Southwest Marine, Inc.*; *American Sys. Eng'g Corp.*, *supra*; *Engineering and Computa-*

tion, Inc., B-261658, Oct. 16, 1995, 95-2 CPD ¶ 176; *American President Lines, Ltd.*, B-236834.3, July 20, 1990, 90-2 CPD ¶ 53. We find no basis to object to the Navy's evaluation and subsequent rejection of Dimension's proposal. While we think the Navy's destruction of the individual evaluators' worksheets may have been premature, this is insufficient reason to disturb a procurement where, as here, the protest record is otherwise adequate for our review.

See also *Dynalantic Corp.*, Comp. Gen. Dec. B-274944.2, 97-1 CPD ¶ 101, permitting the agency to attempt to justify the evaluation of the protester in a hearing after it had destroyed the evaluators' work papers. In sustaining the protest because of the lack of rationale supporting the decision, the GAO granted protest costs and noted that they were higher because of the need for a hearing. It was also noted that the agency had decided to discontinue the practice of destroying work papers.

Since the FAR Part 15 rewrite the GAO has continued to allow agencies considerable flexibility in handling the evaluation documentation. See, for example, *Government Acquisitions, Inc.*, Comp. Gen. Dec. B-401048, 2009 CPD ¶ 137, denying a protest that the evaluation worksheets had been destroyed, stating:

> Although an agency must document its evaluation judgments in sufficient detail to show that they are not arbitrary, the necessary amount and level of detail will vary from procurement to procurement. *U.S. Defense Sys., Inc.*, B-245563, Jan. 17, 1992, 92-1 CPD ¶ 89 at 3; *Champion-Alliance, Inc.*, B-249504 , Dec. 1, 1992, 92-2 CPD ¶ 386 at 6-7. For example, there is no requirement that the evaluation record must include narrative explanations for every rating assigned. *Apex Marine Ship Mgmt. Co., LLC; American V-Ships Marine, Ltd.*, B-278276.25, B-278276.28, Sept. 25, 2000, 2000 CPD ¶ 164 at 8-9. Similarly, there is no requirement that an agency retain individual evaluator's notes or worksheets, provided the agency's final evaluation documentation reasonably explains the basis for the agency's judgments. *Global Eng'g and Constr. LLC*, B-290288.3, B-290288.4, Apr. 3, 2003, 2003 CPD ¶ 180 at 3 n.3.

See also *The Community Partnership LLC*, Comp. Gen. Dec. B-286844, 2001 CPD ¶ 38, and *Structural Preservation Sys., Inc.*, Comp. Gen. Dec. B-285085, 2000 CPD ¶ 131, denying protests because the "surviving record" was sufficient to show that the evaluation was reasonable. Compare *Pitney Bowes Gov't Solutions, Inc. v. United States*, 93 Fed. Cl. 327 (2010), finding this practice improper.

2. Comparison of Proposals

FAR 15.305(a) also requires that agencies "assess [the] relative qualities" of the proposals. As noted above, this comparison of the proposals is generally done as a second step in the evaluation process and is frequently done by an evaluation board or the evaluation team leaders. In many ways this is the most important part of the narratives because it summarizes the information needed by the source selection official to make the selection decision.

This comparison should be prepared in sufficient detail to identify each area of significant difference between proposals. Ideally, the narrative will contain a concise description of the difference and an assessment of the *value of the difference* or the *impact* that the difference will have on the procuring agency. This value/impact statement in the technical and management areas provides the key information needed by the source selection official in making the tradeoff with the cost/price differences among offerors. Thus, such narratives provide the source selection official clear information concerning the relative advantages or disadvantages of proposals in a way that scores (such as numbers, colors, or adjectives) obviously cannot.

Agencies are permitted considerable discretion in identifying the values and impacts of competing proposals during this comparative assessment. See *Alliant Techsystems, Inc.*, Comp. Gen. Dec. B-276162, 97-1 CPD ¶ 141, stating:

> Evaluating the relative merits of competing proposals is a matter within the discretion of the contracting agency since the agency is responsible for defining its needs and the best method of accommodating them, and it must bear the burden resulting from a defective evaluation. *Advanced Tech. And Research Corp.*, B-257451.2, Dec. 9, 1994, 94-2 CPD ¶ 230 at 3. Consequently, in reviewing an evaluation we will not reevaluate proposals but instead will examine the agency's evaluation to ensure that it was reasonable and consistent with the stated evaluation criteria.

See also *Suncoast Assocs., Inc.*, Comp. Gen. Dec. B-265920, 95-2 CPD ¶ 268, holding that the agency's explanation of why it determined two proposals to be technically equivalent, despite the protester's two-point advantage in technical scoring, was reasonable and consistent with the documentation, which showed the relative strengths and weaknesses of the proposals. In *Juarez & Assocs., Inc.*, Comp. Gen. Dec. B-265950.2, 96-1 CPD ¶ 152, the protester contended that the contracting officer limited his determination that the proposals were technically equal to a review of the point scores alone. The GAO disagreed, stating that the contracting officer's determination statement concluding that the proposals were essentially technically equal cited the slight point differential and provided a reasoned analysis pointing out that although the protester's proposal was rated higher in the least important technical evaluation factor, the awardee's proposal was rated higher under the most important technical evaluation factor. Compare *Northwest EnviroService, Inc.*, 71 Comp. Gen. 453 (B-247380.2) 92-2 CPD ¶ 38, sustaining a protest because the record lacked sufficient documentation to show that the source selection was reasonably based on the announced evaluation criteria.

VII. EVALUATION OF SPECIFIC FACTORS

A number of evaluation factors are commonly used in most competitively negotiated procurements. These factors have been subject to such numerous protests that there is extensive guidance on the pitfalls that can be encountered in their evaluation.

A. Cost or Price to the Government

Price or cost to the government is an evaluation factor in every procurement, FAR 15.304(c)(1). In fixed-price-type contracts the agency must make a price reasonableness determination as part of the evaluation process to ensure that the proposed prices are not too high, FAR 15.402(a), FAR 15.404-1(a). Agencies are also permitted to make price realism analyses to assess performance risk by measuring an offeror's understanding of the work or technical capability, FAR 15.404-1(d)(3). In cost-reimbursement-type contracts the evaluation factor must be probable cost to the government that must be determined by making a cost realism analysis using cost analysis techniques, FAR 15.404-1(d)(2).

There is no guidance in the FAR on the analytical technique that is to be used for time-and-materials and labor-hour contracts. It can be argued that the proposed fixed labor rates should be subject to a price reasonableness type analysis or a price realism analysis. See, for example, *General Dynamics Information Tech.*, Comp. Gen. Dec. B-299873, 2007 CPD ¶ 194, granting a protest where the agency stated that it would evaluate fixed labor rates multiplied by estimated quantities of labor on a price analysis basis but did not follow the RFP scheme in computing the labor rates of the winning offeror. On the other hand, although cost realism analysis is not required, it might be concluded that an agency should make such analysis to adjust proposed costs upward to reflect probable costs if it concludes that an offeror has proposed insufficient labor hours to perform the work in a sample task. See *Ball Aerospace & Techs. Corp.*, Comp. Gen. Dec. B-402148, 2010 CPD ¶ 37, stating:

> [T]here is no requirement that an agency conduct a cost realism analysis for a solicitation that provides for the award of a time-and-materials contract with fixed-price burdened labor rates, in the absence of a solicitation provision requiring such an analysis. *Resource Consultants, Inc.*, B-290163, B-290163.2, June 7, 2002, 2002 CPD ¶ 94 at n.1; *General Atomics*, B-287348, B-287348.2, June 11, 2001, 2001 CPD ¶ 169 at 7.

1. Price Analysis

When a fixed-price-type contract is to be awarded using competitive procedures, price analysis is generally used to ascertain whether the proposed prices are fair and reasonable. This is the normal procedure in lieu of cost analysis because agencies are prohibited from obtaining certified cost or pricing data when there is adequate price competition, FAR 15.403-1(b)(1). Price analysis is also the preferred technique when fixed prices are being evaluated because it is faster and requires much less accumulation of detailed data by both parties, FAR 15.402(a)(3). See *Gap Solutions, Inc.*, Comp. Gen. Dec. B-310564, 2008 CPD ¶ 26, and *Citywide Managing Servs. of Port Washington, Inc.*, Comp. Gen. Dec. B-281287.12, 2001 CPD ¶ 6, rejecting the contention that the agency was required to evaluate the cost elements of each offerors' proposal in order to determine that the prices were reasonable and realistic.

FAR 15.404-1(b) defines "price analysis" as follows:

(1) Price analysis is the process of examining and evaluating a proposed price without evaluating its separate cost elements and proposed profit.

The price analysis techniques that are usable in this process are described in FAR 15.404-1(b)(2):

(2) The Government may use various price analysis techniques and procedures to ensure a fair and reasonable price. Examples of such techniques include, but are not limited to, the following:

(i) Comparison of proposed prices received in response to the solicitation. Normally, adequate price competition establishes a fair and reasonable price (see 15.403–1(c)(1)).

(ii) Comparison of the proposed prices to historical prices paid, whether by the Government or other than the Government, for the same or similar items. This method may be used for commercial items including those "of a type" or requiring minor modifications.

(A) The prior price must be a valid basis for comparison. If there has been a significant time lapse between the last acquisition and the present one, if the terms and conditions of the acquisition are significantly different, or if the reasonableness of the prior price is uncertain, then the prior price may not be a valid basis for comparison.

(B) The prior price must be adjusted to account for materially differing terms and conditions, quantities and market and economic factors. For similar items, the contracting officer must also adjust the prior price to account for material differences between the similar item and the item being procured.

(C) Expert technical advice should be obtained when analyzing similar items, or commercial items that are "of a type" or requiring minor modifications, to ascertain the magnitude of changes required and to assist in pricing the required changes.

(iii) Use of parametric estimating methods/application of rough yardsticks (such as dollars per pound or per horsepower, or other units) to highlight significant inconsistencies that warrant additional pricing inquiry.

(iv) Comparison with competitive published price lists, published market prices of commodities, similar indexes, and discount or rebate arrangements.

(v) Comparison of proposed prices with independent Government cost estimates.

(vi) Comparison of proposed prices with prices obtained through market research for the same or similar items.

(vii) Analysis of data other than certified cost or pricing data (as defined at 2.101) provided by the offeror.

Price analysis is generally based on data obtained from sources other than the prospective contractor. See the preferences set forth in FAR 15.403-3. This information is gathered by the government negotiating team from as many sources as possible and should be accumulated as a product or service is repeatedly purchased. Generally, to assure that the proposed contract price is reasonable and/or realistic, a sound price analysis will be based on several different types of data. See, for example, *Navistar Defense, LLC*, Comp. Gen. Dec. B-401865, 2009 CPD ¶ 258, where the agency used a variety of techniques to make a thorough analysis to determine that seemingly low were realistic. However, when strong competition is obtained, the primary element of price analysis will be the competitive prices that have been submitted to the agency.

Very few protest cases discuss the use of price analysis for negotiated procurements. However, there is considerable guidance on this topic in protests involving sealed bid procurements where the contracting officer has used price analysis to make a determination as to the reasonableness of the price. Almost all these cases deny the protest that the agency has performed an improper price analysis, finding instead that there is great discretion in this area. See *Family Realty*, Comp. Gen. Dec. B-247772, 92-2 CPD ¶ 6, stating that: "The depth of an agency's price analysis is a matter within the sound exercise of the agency's discretion." But see *Crawford Labs.*, Comp. Gen. Dec. B-277069, 97-2 CPD ¶ 63, where the GAO sustained a protest finding that the agency provided no rational basis for its determination of price reasonableness of contract awards for primer coatings at prices more than double the award prices under the prior procurement for the same items.

There is a large degree of discretion when a contracting officer does a thorough price analysis and determines that a price is reasonable in spite of its being higher than other prices. See, for example, *Ashland Sales & Serv. Co./Macon Garment, Inc., a Joint Venture*, Comp. Gen. Dec. B-400466, 2008 CPD ¶ 196, denying a protest that a HUBZone set-aside should have been withdrawn because the price was 30% higher than the price of the small business protester. The GAO reasoned:

> Here, the record indicates that the contracting officer conducted a thorough price analysis of [the HUBZone contractor's] offer. This price analysis explicitly made a comparison between [that] price and the price offered by [the protester] on [an earlier] small business set-aside, and noted the 30.7 percent price differential. The price analysis also considered that there was adequate price competition in the HUBZone set-aside solicitation in the form of offers from five different HUBZone firms, three of which were included in the competitive range; during discussions, all three firms were advised to review their proposed prices. Ultimately, the con-

tracting officer determined that [the HUBZone contractor's] price was fair and reasonable based on adequate price competition, and discounted the price differential between [the two companies] as a product of the three times greater quantity under the small business set-aside solicitation.

Based on our review of the record, we cannot conclude that the contracting officer's conclusion was unreasonable. That all offers received in response to the HUBZone set-aside solicitation were higher in price than the offer submitted by the protester on the prior solicitation can reasonably be interpreted (as the contracting officer did) to indicate that the difference in volume between the two solicitations had a material impact on price. In light of that factor, we find the contracting officer's decision to discount the differential between solicitations in determining reasonable price, relying on the price competition achieved on the particular solicitation at issue, to be unobjectionable.

Price analysis is also useful in detecting mistakes. See FAR 14.407-1 requiring contracting officers to examine all bids for mistakes immediately after bid opening and requiring a request for verification of the bid if a mistake is suspected. FAR Part 15 has no similar explicit requirement when conducting a negotiated procurement but it is good practice to follow the same procedure. See, however, *University of Dayton Research Inst.*, Comp. Gen. Dec. B-296946.6, 2006 CPD ¶ 102, holding that a significant mistake could not be corrected during clarifications.

Price analysis can be done at different levels of work depending on the complexity of the procurement. In the case of procurements with multiple contract line items, prices will usually be solicited for each line item and price analysis will be performed for each line item. See, for example, *Comprehensive Health Servs., Inc.*, Comp. Gen. Dec. B-310553, 2008 CPD ¶ 9, upholding the price analysis of line item prices. It is improper, however, to determine that an offeror's proposed prices are unreasonable because a single line item price is high when its total price is similar to other total prices, *R&G Food Serv., Inc.*, Comp. Gen. Dec. B-296435.4, 2005 CPD ¶ 194 (high mileage rate for delivering food not dispositive when food prices are reasonable). In procurements for complex work, prices can be required to be submitted for segments of the work – allowing price analysis for each segment. This is commonly done on construction contracts where prices are required for each element of a building, using standard construction breakdowns of the work (excavation, foundations, structure, electrical, plumbing, etc.).

Although price analysis is also done to evaluate fixed-price labor hour rates – particularly in evaluating proposals for IDIQ contracts – it is of questionable value in this area. The difficulty is that, while price analysis can indicate whether the proposed labor rate is high or low in comparison with other rates, it cannot account for the productivity of the labor that is being offered. Thus, the use of price analysis to evaluate fixed labor rates can lead to a false assessment of the costs that the government will actually pay for work that is awarded to an offeror with low labor rates on a cost-reimbursement, time-and-materials, or labor hours basis.

The various techniques used to perform a price analysis are discussed below.

a. Competitive Prices

Prices proposed by competitors are the most important data used in price analysis. They are based on the identical specifications for the work and are submitted in the same time period, thus reflecting current economic conditions. Competitors' prices are particularly useful when the contract will be fixed-price or fixed-price with economic price adjustment. In these cases the competitors are motivated to estimate their costs accurately, yet are subject to competitive pressures to propose a price that is low enough to win the competition. Thus, reliance on comparison of the competitive prices to ensure reasonableness of the price may be all that is necessary. See, for example, *HSG-SKE*, Comp. Gen. Dec. B-274769, 97-1 CPD ¶ 20, where the GAO denied a protest alleging inadequate price analysis when the contracting officer had compared the competitive prices for each contract line item and had checked these prices against the independent government estimate. See also *Cube Corp.*, Comp. Gen. Dec. B-277353, 97-2 CPD ¶ 92 (price analysis fully adequate when contracting officer used competitive prices, independent government estimate and limited cost data); *Ameriko-OMSERV*, Comp. Gen. Dec. B-252879.5, 94-2 CPD ¶ 219 (price analysis adequate where agency performed a line-item-by-line-item comparison of awardee's prices to those of its competitors); and *Management Tech. Servs.*, Comp. Gen. Dec. B-251612.3, 93-1 CPD ¶ 432 (no basis to question the agency's price analysis where agency compared awardee's price to the government estimate and to the prices submitted by the other offerors).

Competitive prices have also been used to determine that a price was unreasonable. For example, it has been held proper to cancel invitations for bids (IFBs) based on unreasonableness of prices (1) when the price of a nonresponsive bidder was significantly lower than the lowest responsive bid, *McCarthy Mfg. Co.*, 56 Comp. Gen. 369 (B-186550), 77-1 CPD ¶ 116; and (2) when the prices in a post-bid opening quotation were lower than the timely bids, *Mil-Base Indus.*, Comp. Gen. Dec. B-218015, 85-1 CPD ¶ 421. In *Mil-Base*, the GAO recognized that such a situation could establish price unreasonableness but questioned the reliability of the quote under the facts of that case. Similarly, prices from small businesses have been found unreasonable (and set-asides canceled) based on proposed prices from large business firms, *Nutech Laundry & Textiles, Inc.*, Comp. Gen. Dec. B-291739, 2003 CPD ¶ 34; *Hughes & Sons Sanitation*, Comp. Gen. Dec. B-270391, 96-1 CPD ¶ 119; *Western Filter Corp.*, Comp. Gen. Dec. B-247212, 92-1 CPD ¶ 436; *Stacor Corp.*, 57 Comp. Gen. 234 (B-189987), 78-1 CPD ¶ 68; on proposed prices from other small businesses, *Frontier Transportation, Inc.*, Comp. Gen. Dec. B-400345, 2008 CPD ¶ 165 (HUBZone preference not followed in cascaded set-aside); and on prices from foreign companies, *General Metals, Inc.*, Comp. Gen. Dec. B-248446.3, 92-2 CPD ¶ 256. But see *Airborne Servs., Inc.*, Comp. Gen. Dec. B-221894, 86-1 CPD ¶ 523, where the GAO held that an informal telephone quotation from a firm was not sufficiently reliable to support a determination of unreasonable price.

The mere presence of competition is not always adequate to ensure that the prices proposed are fair and reasonable. For example, if the low offeror has such a decided advantage gained from past performance of the work that it is practically immune from competition, other competitive prices would not provide a valid basis for comparison. Similarly, competitive prices may be suspect when there are a very limited number of competitors. In such cases the relative experience and sophistication of the offerors must be closely scrutinized. The contracting officer must also assess whether the market conditions are the same for the various competitors. In a period of high economic activity when the competitors are working close to their levels of capacity, competitive prices are not nearly as good an indicator of reasonable price as are prices submitted when competitors are actively seeking more work.

b. Prior Prices

The second type of information that can be used to assess proposed prices is pricing information from prior procurements. Both contract prices and other available price information should be reviewed. See, for example, *General Dynamics - Ordnance & Tactical Sys.*, Comp. Gen. Dec. B-401658, 2009 CPD ¶ 217 (prior prices paid by agency showed prices were realistic); *Paraclete Contracts*, Comp. Gen. Dec. B-299883, 2007 CPD ¶ 153 (prior prices paid by agency showed price was reasonable); *Motorola, Inc.*, Comp. Gen. Dec. B-277862, 97-2 CPD ¶ 155 (prices and sales data from prior contracts demonstrated the reasonableness of prices for option quantity); *Crawford Labs.*, Comp. Gen. Dec. B-277069, 97-2 CPD ¶ 63 (prices double those of prior procurement unreasonable); *TAAS Israel Indus., Ltd.*, Comp. Gen. Dec. B-260733, 95-2 CPD ¶ 23 (prior prices paid to other contractors on recent competitive procurements showed that price was reasonable); *California Scaffold Corp.*, Comp. Gen. Dec. B-220082.2, 85-2 CPD ¶ 729 (prior prices of an incumbent contractor were used to show unreasonable price); and *Century Metal Parts Corp.*, Comp. Gen. Dec. B-194421.3, 79-2 CPD ¶ 437 (past procurement history demonstrated that price was reasonable). In some cases prior prices have been used along with the government estimate to demonstrate that the price was unreasonable, *Quality Inn & Suites Conference Center*, Comp. Gen. Dec. B-283468, 99-2 CPD ¶ 72; *Western Filter Corp.*, Comp. Gen. Dec. B-247212, 92-1 CPD ¶ 436; *Freund Precision, Inc.*, Comp. Gen. Dec. B-207426, 82-2 CPD ¶ 509; *Society Brand, Inc.*, 55 Comp. Gen. 475 (B-183963), 75-2 CPD ¶ 327.

Several variables must be accounted for when using prior pricing information. One of the most important of these variables is changes in economic conditions between the times of the prior procurements and the current procurement. See *Honolulu Disposal Serv., Inc. — Recons.*, 60 Comp. Gen. 642 (B-200753.2), 81-2 CPD ¶ 126, finding a price unreasonable because it was 14% higher than prior years' prices, whereas the agency believed a 3% inflation adjustment was reasonable. This type of adjustment is particularly important in a period of sharply rising prices. Another important variable is differences in quantity. As a general rule, it is expected that higher quantities will yield lower prices, but this may not hold true when a company is exceeding its capacity. It is also important to determine the total quantities involved when the product or service is being produced or performed for other customers as well as the procuring agency. A third factor is the inclusion of nonrecurring costs in the prices. If the offeror has been forced to discontinue the work since the performance of the prior contract, startup costs may necessarily be included in the new price. This raises the question of whether nonrecurring costs were included in the prior prices. In order to make a fair comparison, such nonrecurring costs should be removed from both prices and assessed separately. See *General Fire Extinguisher Corp.*, 54 Comp. Gen. 416 (B-181796), 74-2 CPD ¶ 278, where prior prices from a contractor were used to demonstrate reasonableness of prices including startup costs. The source of the prior price may also be a factor. See *W.H. Compton Shear Co.*, Comp. Gen. Dec. B-208626.2, 83-2 CPD ¶ 404, where the fact that the prior price was obtained from a foreign company was validly considered in finding reasonableness of price.

If the same work has not been done in the past, comparative prices of *similar work* can be used as a rough means of price analysis. In such cases adjustments must be made to account for the dissimilarities between the two types of work. If the differences in the work are minor, such adjustments may not be too difficult to determine. However, at a minimum, this will require a detailed analysis of the product or services to ascertain its specific differences from prior products or services. See *Family Realty*, Comp. Gen. Dec. B-247772, 92-2 CPD ¶ 6, where prices received on another solicitation for similar services were used, along with the competitive prices on the instant procurement and the government estimate, to determine whether the proposed price was reasonable.

When data is available for several years, price analysis can be very valuable. Detailed analysis will disclose pricing trends that may indicate that significant learning has occurred and should be expected to continue through the current purchase. This type of information is a valuable cross-check for the competitive pricing information discussed above.

c. Parametric Data

Some industries compile and use very general data relating prices of products to characteristics of the product such as weight, electrical or electronic circuits, or other units of measurement. One of the oldest types of this information is the data compiled by the aircraft manufacturing industry relating labor hours in manufacturing to aircraft weight. Such data is useful in making a price analysis — especially if the database is sufficiently large to demonstrate a consistent relationship. There is considerable guidance on the use of parametric data in the DCAA Contract Audit Manual (DCAM) 7640.1 (www.dcaa.mil/cam.html). Paragraph 9-1003.2 contains five criteria for judging the reliability of this type of data when submitted by a contractor:

> Do the procedures clearly establish guidelines for when parametric techniques would be appropriate?

Are there guidelines for the consistent application of estimating techniques?

Is there proper identification of sources of data and the estimating methods and rationale used in developing cost estimates?

Do the procedures ensure that relevant personnel have sufficient training, experience, and guidance to perform estimating tasks in accordance with the contractor's established procedures?

Is there an internal review of and accountability for the adequacy of the estimating system, including the comparison of projected results to actual results and an analysis of any differences?

If these criteria are met, parametric data submitted by contractors can provide another indication of the reasonableness of a proposed price. Such data can also be compiled and used by government agencies in analyzing prices. Supplementary guidance on parametric cost estimating is contained in the NASA *Parametric Cost Estimating Handbook* (2d ed. 2009) (http://cost.jsc.nasa.gov/pcehg.html). See also the International Society of Parametric Analysts' *Parametric Estimating Handbook* (4th ed. 2008) (www.galorath.com/images/uploads/ISPA_PEH_4th_ed_Final.pdf).

Agencies have also used statistical techniques to evaluate prices. See, for example, *PWC Logistics Servs., Inc.*, Comp. Gen. Dec. B-299820, 2007 CPD ¶ 162, upholding the use of a "best case" and "worst case" analysis of material prices based on changes in prices over the past ten years. Compare *Boeing Co.*, Comp. Gen. Dec. B-311344, 2008 CPD ¶ 114, where a protest was granted because the agency improperly used a "Monte Carlo" simulation to adjust prices for realism. The defect identified by the GAO was that the agency used data on government costs of total weapon systems to determine possible variations in costs of nonrecurring engineering (only one small element of total cost variations). See also *EPW Closure Servs., LLC*, Comp. Gen. Dec. B-294910, 2006 CPD ¶ 3, criticizing an agency for accepting a contingency allowance included in a proposed price based on a "Monte Carlo" simulation performed by the offeror.

d. Published Prices

If the product or service is sold to the public, the offeror may have published prices or standard pricing techniques that are used for these sales. Such information will frequently demonstrate that the price is reasonable — especially if the product or service is sold in a competitive market. For example, in *Logics, Inc.*, Comp. Gen. Dec. B-237412, 90-1 CPD ¶ 189, a protest was sustained where the agency failed to consider pricing information contained in a government catalog that indicated that the fair market prices of an item in question were much higher than the agency estimates. With this type of information, care must be used in determining what discounts are given for quantity purchases and what other types of special arrangements are made for preferred customers. See *Interscience Sys., Inc.*, 59 Comp. Gen. 658 (B-195773), 80-2 CPD ¶ 106, where the GAO found that discounts were not sufficiently large to permit a determination of reasonableness based on market prices. The volume of sales to the general public will also be a factor in assessing the validity of this type of data. Thus, a large volume of sales at a published price in a competitive market would make such data highly reliable, while a low volume of sales in a narrow market would render the data less reliable.

Published prices for similar products or services may also be useful in performing a price analysis. Of course, adjustments have to be made to reflect dissimilarities, but if the differences are minor, this may be a valid source of information. See, for example, *Eclipse Sys., Inc.*, Comp. Gen. Dec. B-216002, 85-1 CPD ¶ 267, where reasonableness of price was determined based on a market survey of prices of comparable products.

e. Independent Government Cost Estimates

Although the current FAR contains no requirement that agencies prepare an independent cost estimate for each procurement, this has been very common practice. Prior to the FAR Part 15 rewrite, FAR 15.803(b) required the development of such an estimate as follows:

> Before issuing a solicitation, the contracting officer shall (when it is feasible to do so) develop an estimate of the proper price level or value of the supplies or services to be purchased. Estimates can range from simple budgetary estimates to complex estimates based on inspection of the product itself and review of such items as drawings, specifications, and prior data.

The only mandatory requirements for the preparation of such estimates are in FAR 36.203 (construction procurements) and FAR 36.605 (architect/engineering services).

Paragraph 3.5.1 of DOD Regulation 5000.2-R, *Mandatory Procedures for Major Defense Acquisition Programs (MDAPs) and Major Automated Information System (MAIS) Acquisition Programs* (Mar. 15, 1996), also required life-cycle cost estimates for all major programs in the Department of Defense. This requirement is not included in the current regulation.

Such independent estimates are based on all the types of data that are discussed above plus any cost or pricing data that may be available from past procurements. They represent the agency's best estimate of the most reasonable current price for the products or services being procured. Thus, they can serve as a sound basis for finding a price unreasonable, *Division Laundry & Cleaners, Inc.*, Comp. Gen. Dec. B-311242, 2008 CPD ¶ 97 (upholding cancellation of set-aside when two small businesses were over 35% above government estimate); *Overstreet Elec. Co.*, Comp. Gen. Dec. B-284691, 2000 CPD ¶ 79 (approving cancellation of solicitation when low bid exceeded government estimate by 32%); *Trebor Indus., Inc.*, Comp. Gen. Dec. B-228906, 87-2 CPD ¶ 446 (denying protest of cancellation when the sole bidder's price was 38% higher than a government estimate based on data from a reliable incumbent supplier); *Kinetic Structures Corp. v. United States*, 6 Cl. Ct. 387 (1984) (permitting cancellation of IFB because all prices were unreasonable when compared to government estimate); *Northern Va. Van Co. v. United States*, 3 Cl. Ct. 237 (1983) (approving cancellation of solicitation because of a large discrepancy between the bid and the government estimate because the cancellation would prevent "a misapplication of public funds"); and *Clark Bros. Contractors*, Comp. Gen. Dec. B-189625, 78-1 CPD ¶ 11 (upholding cancellation of IFB because sole bid was 13.67% higher than government estimate). When offerors propose different products to meet an agency's requirements, it is reasonable for the agency to make a separate independent cost estimate for each product and determine that a higher priced product is reasonably priced based on that estimate, *Marinette Marine Corp.*, Comp. Gen. Dec. B-400697, 2009 CPD ¶ 16.

Because government estimates are made early in the procurement process, it may be necessary to update them for use in the price analysis. See, for example, *Legacy Mgmt. Solutions, LLC*, Comp. Gen. Dec. B-299981.2, 2007 CPD ¶ 197, where the government estimate was revised downward in order to determine that seemingly low prices were realistic. See also *Adam Elec. Co.*, Comp. Gen. Dec. B-207782, 82-2 CPD ¶ 576, where all bid prices were determined to be unreasonable based on a government estimate that was revised after bid opening. The GAO upheld the cancellation of the IFB even though the bid prices were lower than the original government estimate. Of course, the competitive prices that are proposed may also demonstrate that market conditions have overridden the basic logic used in making the government estimate. The proper procedure is to consider both the government estimates and other proposed prices. See *Academy Facilities Mgmt.*, Comp. Gen. Dec. B-401094.3, 2009 CPD ¶ 139 (whether government estimate was flawed not considered because agency also used competing prices and analysis of cost elements to determine that price was realistic); *Hawkeye Glove Mfg., Inc.*, Comp. Gen. Dec. B-299237, 2007 CPD ¶ 49 (government estimate and other small business prices used to determine price reasonableness); *Synectic Solutions, Inc.*, Comp. Gen. Dec. B-299086, 2007 CPD ¶ 36 (three acceptable proposals were lower than the government estimate); *Mindleaf Techs., Inc.*, Comp. Gen. Dec. B-294242, 2004 CPD ¶ 157 (price realistic because, although it was somewhat lower than competitors' prices, it was higher than government estimate); *Hughes Advanced Sys. Co.*, GSBCA 9601-P, 89-1 BCA ¶ 21,276 (government estimate used to suggest price reasonableness and competitive prices supported the decision); *Mid-Atlantic Forestry Servs., Inc.*, Comp. Gen. Dec. B-217334, 85-2 CPD ¶ 279 (competitive prices and the government estimate used to demonstrate that the proposed price was not only reasonable but also quite low); and *Francis & Jackson, Assocs.*, 57 Comp. Gen. 244 (B-190023), 78-1 CPD ¶ 79 (price found reasonable by comparing it to both the government estimate and competitive prices). Compare *National Projects, Inc.*, Comp. Gen. Dec. B-283887, 2000 CPD ¶ 16, where all five competitive prices significantly exceeded the government estimate but the agency still concluded that the government estimate was accurate, cancelled the IFB, and conducted a negotiated procurement. In one interesting case an agency was allowed to cancel a procurement after a specification change rendered the government estimate unreliable and left the contracting officer uncertain as to the reasonableness of the protester's price, *Adrian Supply Co.*, Comp. Gen. Dec. B-241502, 91-1 CPD ¶ 138. Verifying the price would have required an audit, which could not have been completed before the end of the fiscal year, when the funds for the project expired.

f. Market Prices

Prices of the same or similar items that are available in the commercial market provide an excellent comparison to prices proposed for government contracts. See *Operational Support & Servs.*, Comp. Gen. Dec. B-299660.2, 2007 CPD ¶ 182, upholding a determination of fair market price based on the labor rates on Federal Supply Schedule contracts and salaries listed on web sites. See also *Sea-Land Serv., Inc.*, Comp. Gen. Dec. B-246784.6, 93-2 CPD ¶ 84, where the GAO agreed with the use of this type of information for price analysis before this category was added to the FAR in 1995. In *Tiger Truck, LLC*, Comp. Gen. Dec. B-400685, 2009 CPD ¶ 19, the GAO rejected a contention that the agency should not have used the price of foreign-made vehicles in determining whether a price was fair and reasonable, stating:

> Tiger also complains that the agency misevaluated price by considering Chinese-made vehicles as a basis of price comparison. We find nothing in the [Trade Agreements Act] or its implementing regulations that prohibits the consideration of these prices as one aspect of determining whether a quoted price is fair and reasonable. We note that in analogous situations, agencies are permitted to use the prices of ineligible offerors as a basis of comparison when determining price reasonableness. See *American Imaging Servs.*, B-238969, B-238971, July 19, 1990, 90-2 CPD ¶ 51 at 3 (in a procurement set aside for small business, prices from ineligible large businesses may be considered in evaluating the reasonableness of a small business' price); see also FAR § 25.105 (in Buy American Act procurements, domestic product prices may be compared to foreign prices, albeit, unlike with TAA procurements, domestic prices in Buy American Act procurements are considered reasonable only if they do not exceed certain identified percentages). Furthermore, the FAR broadly provides that an agency may use a variety of techniques or procedures in determining price reasonableness, including, but not limited to, comparing prices received in response to a solicitation; comparing prices previously proposed for the same or similar items; comparing published market prices; and comparing proposed prices to an independent government estimate. FAR § 15.404-1(b).

Care must be exercised in using this type of information because of the large differences that may exist between commercial transactions and government procurements. In some cases the undue complexity of government procurements may justify a significantly higher price than that being offered in the commercial market.

On the other hand, there may be situations where the government is buying such large quantities of the supplies or services that it will expect to pay a lower price than the commercial market price. Similarly, lower prices would be called for if the commercial price was for just-in-time delivery but the government was buying a product to be placed in its supply system.

g. Information Submitted By Offeror

Occasionally, the solicitation will require offerors to submit detailed pricing information and a price can be determined unreasonable if that information demonstrates such unreasonableness. For example, in *Concepts Bldg. Sys., Inc.*, Comp. Gen. Dec. B-281995, 99-1 CPD ¶ 95, the agency solicited information on the markup that vendors would add to commercial prices. The GAO agreed that the agency properly rejected a proposal calling for a markup of 13% because the agency's negotiation objective was a 7% markup.

Information in a technical proposal as to how an offeror will perform the work can also bear on the validity of a price analysis if the details of the offeror's pricing information do not match the technical proposal. See *Resource Consultants, Inc.*, Comp. Gen. Dec. B-293073.3, 2005 CPD ¶ 131, granting a protest on the basis that the winning offeror's price was not in line with its proposed method of accomplishing the work – which had unfairly earned it a high technical evaluation.

2. Cost Realism Analysis

Cost realism analysis is used to determine the *probable cost* of each competing offeror for a cost-reimbursement contract, FAR 15.404-1(d)(2); *KPMG Peat Marwick, LLP*, Comp. Gen. Dec. B-259479.2, 95-2 CPD ¶ 13. It is very clear that cost realism analysis is mandatory on cost-reimbursement contracts. See FAR 15.404-1(d)(2)(i) and *Tidewater Constr. Corp.*, Comp. Gen. Dec. B-278360, 98-1 CPD ¶ 103, where the agency merely compared the costs proposed by the competing offerors. The GAO granted the protest stating that this was a price analysis not a cost realism analysis because the agency did not analyze the individual cost elements of the offerors for realism. Neither may an agency avoid updating the cost realism analysis if the procurement is extended as a result of a sustained protest, *The Futures Group Int'l*, Comp. Gen. Dec. B-281274.5, 2000 CPD ¶ 148, or when an offeror has altered its proposed costs in its best and final offer, *ITT Fed. Servs. Int'l Corp.*, Comp. Gen. Dec. B-283307, 99-2 CPD ¶ 76. Further, an agency risks being found to have conducted an improper cost realism analysis if the contracting officer makes an adjustment based on a guess as to the cost methodology used by the offeror and the guess proves to be incorrect, *Future-Tec Mgmt. Sys., Inc.*, Comp. Gen. Dec. B-283793.5, 2000 CPD ¶ 59. An agency must also adequately document its cost realism analysis or risk having an award be overturned, *National City Bank of Indiana*, B-287608.3, 2002 CPD ¶ 190.

The primary inquiry in making a cost realism analysis is whether the offeror's estimate of the cost of performance contains sufficient costs to permit accomplishment of the work. See the following definition in FAR 15.404-1(d):

> (1) Cost realism analysis is the process of independently reviewing and evaluating specific elements of each offeror's proposed cost estimate to determine whether the estimated proposed cost elements are realistic for the work to be performed; reflect a clear understanding of the requirements; and are consistent with the unique methods of performance and materials described in the offeror's technical proposal.

In order to determine this probable cost, the contracting officer must determine why any cost element is apparently lower than the actual cost that will be incurred. If the contracting officer determines that the cost element is intentionally unrealistically low or it is low because the offeror does not understand the work, it should be adjusted to a realistic probable cost for the purpose of evaluating the offer. However, if the cost element is low because the offeror has a better way to perform the work, no adjustment is required. Careful analysis is required to determine why the submitted costs appear to be low.

There are a few GAO decisions holding that when an agency concludes in its cost realism analysis that an offeror's costs are *too high*, it should use a probable cost lower than the offeror's estimated costs. See *S.M. Stoller Corp.*, Comp. Gen. Dec. B-400937, 2009 CPD ¶ 193, stating:

> The FAR states that a cost realism evaluation must consider the probable cost to the government for each offeror's proposal, and that agencies must evaluate offerors' probable cost by "evaluating specific elements of each offeror's proposed cost estimate to determine whether the estimated proposed cost elements are realistic for the work to be performed," FAR § 15.404-1(d)(1). The agency must then "adjust[] each offeror's proposed cost, and fee when appropriate, to reflect any additions or reductions in cost elements to realistic levels based on the results of the cost realism analysis." FAR § 15.404-1(d)(2)(ii). We have held that agencies should make downward adjustments to an offeror's evaluated cost where the proposal shows a misunderstanding of the requirements in a manner which would cause the government to incur a lower cost than that identified in the proposal. See *Priority One Servs., Inc.*, B-288836, B-288836.2, Dec. 17, 2001, 2002 CPD ¶ 79 at 3-4 (protest sustained where agency concludes that protester misunderstood the requirements for other direct costs; most probable cost should have been reduced to reflect agency's judgment as to costs actually to be incurred); *Kellogg Brown & Root Servs., Inc.*, B-298694 et al., Nov. 16, 2006, 2006 CPD ¶ 160 at 5-8 (agency properly made downward adjustment to protester's probable cost where indirect cost rates were overstated).

The specific cost elements of each proposal are reviewed using cost analysis techniques, but as discussed in Chapter 2, certified cost or pricing data should generally not be obtained on competitively negotiated cost-reimbursement contracts because adequate price competition is usually present. Thus, the cost analysis performed in this circumstance will consist of analysis of the cost elements without detailed cost or pricing data. FAR 15.404-1(c)(1) defines "cost analysis" as follows:

> Cost analysis is the review and evaluation of the separate cost elements and profit in an offeror's or contractor's proposal (including cost or pricing data or information other than cost or pricing data), and the application of judgment to determine how well the proposed costs represent what the cost of the contract should be, assuming reasonable economy and efficiency.

Cost analysis differs intrinsically from price analysis in that cost analysis focuses on the reasonableness of the estimated costs of performance, not the reasonableness of the contract price. Cost analysis reviews each element of cost to ascertain whether the contractor's estimate contains an accurate and reasonable prediction of the costs that will be incurred during performance of the work. Cost analysis requires a complete review of the offeror's proposed costs to assure that they reflect an accurate projection of the costs of performance of the work to be placed under the contract. The elements of cost analysis are described in FAR 15.404-1(c) as follows:

> (2) The Government may use various cost analysis techniques and procedures to ensure a fair and reasonable price, given the circumstances of the acquisition. Such techniques and procedures include the following:
>
>> (i) Verification of cost or pricing data and evaluation of cost elements, including —
>>
>>> (A) The necessity for, and reasonableness of, proposed costs, including allowances for contingencies;
>>>
>>> (B) Projection of the offeror's cost trends, on the basis of current and historical cost or pricing data;
>>>
>>> (C) Reasonableness of estimates generated by appropriately calibrated and validated parametric models or cost-estimating relationships; and
>>>
>>> (D) The application of audited or negotiated indirect cost rates, labor rates, and cost of money or other factors.
>>
>> (ii) Evaluating the effect of the offeror's current practices on future costs. In conducting this evaluation, the contracting officer shall ensure that the effects of inefficient or uneconomical past practices are not projected into the future. In pricing production of recently developed complex equipment, the contracting officer should perform a trend analysis of basic labor and materials, even in periods of relative price stability.
>>
>> (iii) Comparison of costs proposed by the offeror for individual cost elements with —

(A) Actual costs previously incurred by the same offeror;

(B) Previous cost estimates from the offeror or from other offerors for the same or similar items;

(C) Other cost estimates received in response to the Government's request;

(D) Independent Government cost estimates by technical personnel; and

(E) Forecasts or planned expenditures.

(iv) Verification that the offeror's cost submissions are in accordance with the contract cost principles and procedures in Part 31 and, when applicable, the requirements and procedures in 48 CFR Chapter 99 (Appendix of the FAR loose-leaf edition), Cost Accounting Standards.

(v) Review to determine whether any cost or pricing data necessary to make the contractor's proposal accurate, complete, and current have not been either submitted or identified in writing by the contractor. If there are such data, the contracting officer shall attempt to obtain them and negotiate, using them or making satisfactory allowance for the incomplete data.

(vi) Analysis of the results of any make-or-buy program reviews, in evaluating subcontract costs (see 15.407-2).

Note that (i) and (v) of this guidance are not applicable when cost or pricing data are not obtained. However, the balance of the guidance is applicable to cost realism analysis. Because cost or pricing data will not be used in most cost realism analyses, the rules pertaining to the obtaining and use of such data will not be discussed in this chapter. See Chapter 9 of Cibinic & Nash, *Formation of Government Contracts* (3d ed. 1998) for complete coverage of this type of cost analysis.

The contracting officer enjoys considerable discretion in deciding how to use available cost data in making a cost realism analysis. See *Palmetto GBA, LLC*, Comp. Gen. Dec. B-298962, 2007 CPD ¶ 25, describing the required degree of precision as follows:

An agency is not required to conduct an in-depth cost analysis, see FAR § 15.404-1(c), or to verify each and every item in assessing cost realism; rather, the evaluation requires the exercise of informed judgment by the contracting agency. *Cascade Gen., Inc.*, B-283872, Jan. 18, 2000, 2000 CPD ¶ 14 at 8. Further, an agency's cost realism analysis need not achieve scientific certainty; rather, the methodology employed must be reasonably adequate and provide some measure of confidence that the rates proposed are reasonable and realistic in view of other cost information reasonably available to the agency as of the time of its evaluation. See *SGT, Inc.*, B-294722.4, July 28, 2005, 2005 CPD ¶ 151 at 7; *Metro*

Mach. Corp., B-295744; B-295744.2, Apr. 21, 2005, 2005 CPD ¶ 112 at 10-11. Because the contracting agency is in the best position to make this determination, we review an agency's judgment in this area only to see that the agency's cost realism evaluation was reasonably based

See also *Allied-Signal Aerospace Co.*, Comp. Gen. Dec. B-249214.4, 93-1 CPD ¶ 109, where the GAO held that an agency was not required to make a comparative analysis of each element of each offeror's detailed cost estimates, stating that instructing the offerors to submit cost estimates at the work breakdown level did not obligate the agency to analyze that information "in any greater detail than was necessary to assure the realism of the cost proposals." Similarly, in *Communications Int'l, Inc.*, Comp. Gen. Dec. B-246076, 92-1 CPD ¶ 194, the sum of work element cost estimates, rather than the total cost estimate, was properly used in the evaluation, and the contracting officer was not required to reopen discussions to reconcile disparity between the two.

a. Basic Requirements

Agencies must perform a cost realism analysis in sufficient depth to arrive at a reasonable probable cost for each offeror based on the way they propose to perform the contract. It is improper merely to compare the total cost estimate of the offerors to the government estimate because they may have found a more effective way to accomplish the proposed work. See *Tidewater Constr. Co.*, Comp. Gen. Dec. B-278360, 98-1 CPD ¶ 103, stating:

> While the agency in its report argues that it performed a cost realism analysis "consistent with the techniques suggested by FAR 15.805-3," the agency could not have done so because it did not require offerors to provide or identify elements of cost and did not in any case analyze such costs in determining cost realism. Rather, the record establishes that the agency's evaluation was a "price analysis" that is only intended to "ensure a fair and reasonable price," and is not intended to be used, nor can it reasonably be used, to ascertain the cost realism of a cost reimbursement proposal. *See* FAR 15.805-2; *see KPMG Peat Marwick, L.L.P.*, B-259479.2, May 9, 1995, 95-2 CPD ¶ 13 at 7–10.

* * *

> The [agency's] comparison of the various work item costs in the government estimate to the offerors' target costs for the same line items cannot suffice as a sufficient analysis of cost realism where the agency has not considered the offerors' individual technical approaches or determined whether the offerors' proposals are consistent with the technical and cost parameters that were reflected in the government estimate. *See ManTech Envtl. Tech., Inc.*, B-271002 et al., June 3, 1996, 96-1 CPD ¶ 272 at 4–5, 8–12; *The Jonathan Corp., Metro Mach. Corp.*, [B-251698.3, May 17, 1993, 93-2 CPD ¶ 175], at 11–13. As indicated above, the agency made no attempt to determine the offerors' technical approaches.

The same result was reached in *Boeing Sikorsky Aircraft Support*, Comp. Gen. Dec. B-277263.2, 97-2 CPD ¶ 91.

Agencies are accorded substantial discretion in making a cost realism analysis, but they must meet the test of *rationality*. See *Science Applications Int'l Corp.*, Comp. Gen. Dec. B-238136.2, 90-1 CPD ¶ 517, stating:

> [A]n agency is not required to conduct an in-depth cost analysis or to verify each and every item in conducting its cost realism analysis. Rather, the evaluation of competing cost proposals requires the exercise of informed judgment by the contracting agency involved, since it is in the best position to assess "realism" of cost and technical approaches and must bear the difficulties of additional expenses resulting from a defective cost analysis. *Burns & Roe Indus. Servs. Co.*, B-233561, Mar. 7, 1989, 89-1 CPD ¶ 250. Since the cost realism analysis is a judgmental function on the part of the contracting agency, our review is limited to a determination of whether an agency's cost evaluation was reasonably based. *OptiMetrics, Inc.; NU-TEK Precision Optical Corp.*, [68 Comp. Gen. 714], B-235646; B-235646.2, Sept. 22, 1989, 89-2 CPD ¶ 266.

See *Halifax Tech. Servs., Inc. v. United States*, 848 F. Supp. 240 (D.D.C. 1994), and *Program Resources, Inc.*, GSBCA 8879-P, 87-2 BCA ¶ 19,816, following the same standard of rationality. Thus, adjustments must be made if an offeror includes no cost estimate for work that is required by the contract work statement, *NV Servs.*, Comp. Gen. Dec. B-284119.2, 2000 CPD ¶ 64. In that case, the agency made no adjustments when the winning offeror left out costs for employee training, safety equipment and phaseout costs. Similarly, an adjustment was required where an offeror had included significant costs that were not necessary for contract performance, *Priority One Servs., Inc.*, Comp. Gen. Dec. B-288836, 2001 CPD ¶ 79. Furthermore, when cost realism adjustments are made, offerors must be afforded equal treatment, *DynCorp Int'l LLC*, Comp. Gen. Dec. B-289863, 2002 CPD ¶ 83. Thus, a cost realism analysis finding an offeror's costs to be realistic will not be sustained if those costs are based on an interpretation of the work statement that is unreasonable, *S.M. Stoller Corp.*, Comp. Gen. Dec. B-400937, 2009 CPD ¶ 193. Finally, the adjustments that are made must be supported by sufficient data to permit analysis of the validity of the adjustments, *Day & Zimmermann Servs. v. United States*, 38 Fed. Cl. 591 (1997).

A cost realism analysis need not identify every adjustment that might be made to an offeror's cost of performance. In *Raytheon Support Servs. Co.*, 68 Comp. Gen. 566 (B-234920), 89-2 CPD ¶ 84, the GAO found that the agency's cost realism analysis was satisfactory even though it did not make some possible adjustments. In a footnote the GAO stated:

> We find no merit to Raytheon's argument that the Navy should have made downward adjustments to its cost proposal for Raytheon's "inadvertent" failure to take into consideration any "productivity" or "learning curve" reductions in its cost proposal. The burden is on the offeror to submit a cost proposal that takes into

consideration all aspects of its technical approach and the agency has no duty to prepare or revise an offeror's proposal.

See also *PAE GmbH Planning & Constr.*, 68 Comp. Gen. 358 (B-233823), 89-1 CPD ¶ 336, denying a protest that the contracting officer should have seen a mistake in the offeror's cost proposal in the process of making the cost realism analysis. The GAO concluded that the mistake was neither readily apparent in the data included in the protester's proposal nor made any clearer by comparison with other proposals. Compare *Environmental Affairs Mgmt., Inc.*, Comp. Gen. Dec. B-277270, 97-2 CPD ¶ 93, finding that is was proper to add an estimate of the award fee to an offeror's estimate when the agency concluded that the offeror had omitted the fee from the proposal by mistake, and *Litton Sys., Inc., Amecon Div.*, Comp. Gen. Dec. B-275807.2, 97-1 CPD ¶ 170, finding that it was proper to correct an apparent mistake by adding in labor hours that had been subtracted in the cost estimate but had been explained in the BAFO narrative as having been added.

In order to be rational, the cost realism analysis has to be performed on a contractor-by-contractor basis. The contracting officer must consider both the work the contractor proposes to do and the contractor's cost structure in order to determine whether the proposed costs are an accurate projection of the costs of that work. Thus, a mechanical approach that applies the same factors to all offerors is likely to fail the test of rationality. In *Jonathan Corp.*, Comp. Gen. Dec. B-251698.3, 93-2 CPD ¶ 174, the protesters argued that the Navy's cost realism analysis was arbitrary and irrational because it mechanically adjusted the offerors' proposed labor-hour and material cost estimates based on an undisclosed government estimate. The GAO summarized the Navy approach as follows:

> The computer was programmed to accept an offeror's labor hour and material costs for a work item if the number was within plus or minus [deleted] percent of the government's estimate for that item.

> For those work items where an offeror's proposed labor hour and material cost estimates were outside the [deleted] percent range, the source selection plan proposed a two-pronged approach. The first approach provided that if an "offeror's estimate is not adequately supported with data and rationale," the estimate would be rejected and the government's labor hour or material cost estimate would be used instead to calculate the projected cost to the government. The second approach provided that if an "offeror's estimate is well supported with an equal probability of [g]overnment or [o]fferor being correct," the following predetermined mathematical formula would be used to determine an adjusted labor hour or material cost estimate:

>> "One half of the difference between the [g]overnment estimate and the offeror's proposed cost [will be] added to (or subtracted from) the offeror's estimate after first reducing or increasing the [g]overnment estimate by [deleted] % in the direction of the difference (reduce the difference) in order to establish projected cost and adjustment dollars."

In other words, the computer program approximately "split the difference" between the government's labor hour or material cost estimate and the offeror's proposed labor hours and material cost for each of the 100 work items in the notional package.

The GAO sustained the protest, finding that the agency failed to consider each offeror's individualized approach and instead mechanically adjusted costs. The GAO stated that the agency's cost evaluation "did not satisfy the requirement for an independent analysis of each offeror's cost proposal based upon its particular approach, personnel, and other circumstances." The Court of Claims reached the same conclusion in *Day & Zimmermann Serv. v. United States,* 38 Fed. Cl. 591 (1997). See also *Metro Mach. Corp.*, Comp. Gen. Dec. B-297879.2, 2006 CPD ¶ 80; *Information Ventures, Inc.*, Comp. Gen. Dec. B-297276.2, 2006 CPD ¶ 45; and *Honeywell Tech. Solutions, Inc.*, B-292354, 2005 CPD ¶ 107, granting protests when the agency used the its own estimate of labor hours to adjust the offered labor hours without evaluating the techniques the offerors proposed to perform the work. See also *Hughes STX Corp.*, Comp. Gen. Dec. B-278466, 98-1 CPD ¶ 52, finding an improper cost realism analysis of labor rates because the agency used the incumbent contractor's historical labor rates as the probable cost without considering the offeror's specific technical approach to performing the work. The GAO called this a "mechanical" approach that was precluded by *United Int'l Eng'g, Inc.*, 71 Comp. Gen. 177 (B-245448.3), 92-1 CPD ¶ 122. Similarly, in *SRS Techs.*, Comp. Gen. Dec. B-291618.2, 2003 CPD ¶ 70, the GAO held that it was unreasonable to increase the rates for the protester who planned to use uncompensated overtime when the other offeror did not plan to use uncompensated overtime, reasoning that the protester was entitled to use the advantage of the lower rates since there was no prohibition on the use of uncompensated overtime and there was no indication that the protester would not use uncompensated overtime.

Normalization is proper if there is no logical reason to believe that the offerors' costs will be different for some element of the work. See *Univ. Research Co., LLC v. United States*, 65 Fed. Cl. 500 (2005), stating at 509:

> This Court and the GAO have recognized that normalization is appropriate when there is no logical basis for differences in approach, or there is insufficient information available in the proposals. See, e.g.,[*Computer Sciences Corp. v. United States*, 51 Fed. Cl. 297, 316 (2002)] at 316; *General Research Corp.*, 70 Comp. Gen. 279, B-241569 (1991). Thus, in general, the purpose of the cost realism analysis "is to segregate cost factors which are 'company unique' — depending on variables resulting from dissimilar company policies — from those which are generally applicable to all offerors and therefore subject to normalization." *Computer Sciences Corp.*, 51 Fed. Cl. at 316 (citing *SGT, Inc.*, B-281773 (1999)).

See also *ASRC Research & Tech. Solutions, LLC*, Comp. Gen. Dec. B-400217, 2008 CPD ¶ 202, holding that it was proper to use the same fixed labor rates for all offerors that intended to hire the incumbent workforce (a normalization logic). However, the GAO granted the protest because the agency had increased the protester's probable cost with no proof that it's proposed fixed labor rates were lower than the incumbent's rates. The GAO also ruled that it was improper to downgrade the protester in the evaluation of its management plan because it had proposed low labor costs when the agency did not have precise data on the incumbent's labor rates.

Cost realism adjustments are also improper if they alter an offeror's standard accounting practices. See *Kellogg Brown & Root Servs., Inc.*, Comp. Gen. Dec. B-298694, 2006 CPD ¶ 160, granting a protest when the agency deleted an element of cost from the offeror's indirect costs, thereby not accepting the offeror's approved accounting system. The GAO reasoned:

> CAS 401 – which is applicable to [the offeror] – requires a contractor's practices in estimating costs for a proposal to be consistent with cost accounting practices used by the contractor in accumulating and reporting costs. 48 C.F.R. § 9904.401-20 (2005). This requirement is imposed because "[c]onsistency in the application of cost accounting practices is necessary to enhance the likelihood that comparable transactions are treated alike," so that, among other things, there is "financial control over costs during contract performance." *Id.* More significantly, CAS 402 – also applicable to [the offerro] – states:
>
> > All costs incurred for the same purpose, in like circumstances, are either direct costs only or indirect costs only with respect to final cost objectives. No final cost objective shall have allocated to it as an indirect cost any cost, if other costs incurred for the same purpose, in like circumstances, have been included as a direct cost of that or any other final cost objective. Further, no final cost objective shall have allocated to it as a direct cost any cost, if other costs incurred for the same purpose, in like circumstances, have been included in any indirect cost pool to be allocated to that or any other final cost objective.
>
> 48 C.F.R. § 9904.402-40. Because of these requirements, [the offeror] was and will be required to account for its costs in a manner consistent with its established accounting practices during the course of this contract performance. *General Research Corp.*, B-241569, Feb. 19, 1991, 91-1 CPD ¶ 183 at 9; *CACI, Inc.– Fed.*, B-216516, 84-2 CPD ¶ 542 at 10-13. Consequently, in determining [the offeror's] evaluated probable cost for performing this contract, the agency could not reclassify costs that [the offeror] treats as indirect costs in its accounting system as direct costs.

If an offeror places a contractually binding cap on an element of cost, that amount can be determined by a cost realism analysis to be the probable cost of performance, *BNF Techs., Inc.*, Comp. Gen. Dec. B-254953.3, 94-1 CPD ¶ 274 (contracting officer improperly adjusted capped overhead and G&A costs above the amount of the cap); *Unisys Corp. v. National Aeronautics & Space Admin.*, GSBCA 13247-P, 95-2 BCA ¶ 27,818 (contracting officer properly used cap on phase-out costs but was entitled to adjust cap on overhead based on information in proposal); *Halifax Tech. Servs., Inc. v. United States*, 848 F. Supp. 240 (D.D.C. 1994) (contracting officer properly used capped labor costs in making cost realism analysis). However, if the contracting officer concludes that a realistic estimate of the rates to be incurred is below the cap, that estimate can be used in lieu of the cap, *Delta Research Assocs., Inc.*, Comp. Gen. Dec. B-254006.2, 94-1 CPD ¶ 47. Similarly, if the contracting officer reasonably concludes that the cap will only be partially effective, other costs can be adjusted to a realistic amount, *University Research Co., LLC*, Comp. Gen. Dec. B-294358.8, 2006 CPD ¶ 61. When the capped costs are used as the probable costs, the contracting officer must still consider whether the amount imposes a constraint on the offeror significant enough to hamper its ability to perform the work under contract, creating a performance risk, *MCT JV*, Comp. Gen. Dec. B-311245.2, 2008 CPD ¶ 121, *recons. denied*, 2008 CPD ¶ 167; *Cubic Field Servs., Inc.*, Comp. Gen. Dec. B-247780, 92-1 CPD ¶ 525.

b. *Guidance on Cost Elements*

The cost realism analysis is normally done by analyzing each major cost element: material, direct labor, indirect costs, and other direct costs.

(1) MATERIAL

This category encompasses all work to be purchased by the offeror from raw materials to major subcontracts. Most of the cost realism analysis of material costs appears to occur in reviewing the proposed subcontracts in competing offers. See, for example, *BAE Sys. Norfolk Ship Repair, Inc.*, Comp. Gen. Dec. B-297879, 2006 CPD ¶ 75, agreeing that it was reasonable to use prior labor costs rather than fixed-price quotations from subcontractors to determine the realistic costs of performance. The contracting officer had concluded that the quotations were not a good indication of the price that would ultimately be paid to the subcontractors. See also *Electronic Data Sys. Fed. Corp.*, Comp. Gen. Dec. B-207311, 83-1 CPD ¶ 264, where the offeror's proposed subcontract costs were found to be too low because they did not reflect the need for a subcontractor during the entire life of the contract. Subcontractors' labor and indirect cost rates should also be checked for cost realism when the subcontracts will be performed on a cost-reimbursement basis, *General Marine Indus. of N.Y., Inc.*, Comp. Gen. Dec. B-240059, 90-2 CPD ¶ 311; *OptiMetrics, Inc.*, 68 Comp. Gen. 714 (B-235646), 89-2 CPD ¶ 266. See also *Dayton T. Brown, Inc.*, Comp. Gen. Dec. B-229664, 88-1 CPD ¶ 321, where material costs were determined to be realistic even though they appeared low; the reasoning was that the material costs would not impact the ultimate cost to the government because they were included in indirect costs of performance. In *GEC-Marconi Elec. Sys. Corp.*, Comp. Gen. Dec. B-276186, 97-2 CPD ¶ 23, the GAO found reasonable an agency's determination that the protester's proposed material costs were unrealistically low. The agency had found 30 material cost deviations. The agency considered 17 of the deviations to be substantiated by the protester's explanation that the reduction in material costs was due to a new source of supply or an increase in quantity to be ordered. The agency rejected as unsubstantiated those reductions that the protester stated were due merely to an audit or correction to the pricing bill of material without further explanation. Similarly, in *Litton Sys., Inc., Amecom Div.*, Comp. Gen.

Dec. B-275807.2, 97-1 CPD ¶ 170, the GAO found it proper to add subcontract labor hours where the offeror had included no labor hours because the subcontractors had stated that they would perform the work at no cost. The agency's rationale was that the offeror had no binding agreement with the subcontractors.

(2) DIRECT LABOR

Cost realism analysis of direct labor costs is performed by reviewing the labor hours proposed by the offeror, as well as the labor rates that will be applied to the various categories of direct labor to be used.

Perhaps the major area where discrepancies are found in proposals is the estimated number of labor hours required for performance. One commonly used cost realism analysis technique is to compare the labor hours in the cost proposal with the labor hours in the technical proposal. If they vary, it is logical to conclude that the cost proposal is incorrect and to rely on the hours in the technical proposal, *TechDyn Sys. Corp.*, Comp. Gen. Dec. B-237618, 90-1 CPD ¶ 264; *Complere, Inc.*, Comp. Gen. Dec. B-227832, 87-2 CPD ¶ 254. In *Earl Indus., LLC*, Comp. Gen. Dec. B-309996, 2007 CPD ¶ 203, a protest was granted when the agency used the hours in the cost proposal rather than adjusting them upwards to reflect the technical proposal. See, however, *DLM&A, Inc. v. United States*, 6 Cl. Ct. 329 (1984), where this type of discrepancy in the two proposals was resolved during the analysis. See also *ITT Fed. Servs. Int'l Corp.*, Comp. Gen. Dec. B-283307, 99-2 CPD ¶ 76, where the GAO sustained a protest because the agency had failed to analyze the technical approach of the offeror in concluding that the labor costs were too low.

The cases have sustained other reasons for determining that labor-hour estimates are incorrect. See, for example, *Lumetra v. United States*, 84 Fed. Cl. 542 (2008) (prior performance of work with substantially more hours required upward adjustment of labor hours); *Westech Int'l, Inc. v. United States*, 79 Fed. Cl. 272 (2007) (hours added based on agency judgment that they were needed to provide sufficient staff to perform required tasks); *ITT Indus. Space Sys., LLC*, Comp. Gen. Dec. B-309964, 2007 CPD ¶ 217 (proposed techniques for performing work required adjusting labor hours); *EDO Corp.*, Comp. Gen. Dec. B-296861, 2005 CPD ¶ 196 (lack of explanation of low amounts of labor for specific tasks justified upward adjustment); *United Payors & United Providers Health Servs. v. United States*, 55 Fed. Cl. 323 (2003) (underestimate of required work led to adjusted costs); *Hernandez Eng'g, Inc.*, Comp. Gen. Dec. B-286336, 2001 CPD ¶ 89 (unsubstantiated labor hours lower than "historical" levels not realistic); *Scientific & Commercial Sys. Corp.*, Comp. Gen. Dec. B-283160, 99-2 CPD ¶ 78 (staffing level low because past attempts to reduce staff had failed); *Joint Threat Servs.*, Comp. Gen. Dec. B-278168, 98-1 CPD ¶ 18 (reduced labor hours for option years not realistic when no work reduction was anticipated in those years); *TRW Inc.*, Comp. Gen. Dec. B-234558.2, 89-2 CPD ¶ 560 (use of new personnel would require more labor hours than estimated); and *Range Tech. Servs.*, 68 Comp. Gen. 81 (B-231968), 88-2 CPD ¶ 474 (past staffing levels indicated that the labor hours were underestimated). See also *Aircraft Porous Media, Inc.*, Comp. Gen. Dec. B-241665.2, 91-1 CPD ¶ 356, where it was held proper to conclude that the estimate of labor hours was too low when the offeror had reduced the labor hours in its BAFO because of savings that could be achieved through simultaneous performance of similar work on another contract. The GAO found that the contracting officer had the discretion to question the offeror's ability to achieve such savings. In *Fairchild Weston Sys., Inc.*, Comp. Gen. Dec. B-229568.2, 88-1 CPD ¶ 394, the agency was permitted to make major changes in the labor hours proposed by both offerors based on the technical expertise of agency personnel. See, however, *Aurora Assocs., Inc.*, Comp. Gen. Dec. B-215565, 85-1 CPD ¶ 470, finding improper an assumption that all offerors' direct costs would be the same, despite the agency's claim that this assumption was necessary: the contracts were indefinite-quantity contracts for the design and evaluation of agricultural projects, and the agency did not know what tasks each contractor would be asked to perform or for what period of time. In a very questionable decision, *Aerospace Design & Fabrication, Inc.*, Comp. Gen. Dec. B-278896.2, 98-1 CPD ¶ 139, the GAO found rational an adjustment of the incumbent contractor's labor hours to a higher number than it had incurred for the same work on the prior contract. The adjustment was based on the agency's conclusion that the offeror would incur 2,080 hours per man-year even though it had incurred fewer hours per man-year on the prior contract by using some part-time employees.

A number of cases support an agency's conclusion that apparently low estimates of labor hours are realistic because it has determined that the offeror's approach to the work will likely require fewer hours than have been used in the past, *S.M. Stoller Corp.*, Comp. Gen. Dec. B-400937, 2009 CPD ¶ 193; *Palmetto GBA, LLC*, Comp. Gen. Dec. B-298962, 2007 CPD ¶ 25; *Cascade Gen., Inc.*, Comp. Gen. Dec. B-283872, 2000 CPD ¶ 14; *Consolidated Safety Servs., Inc.*, Comp. Gen. Dec. B-252305.2, 93-2 CPD ¶ 225; *Research Analysis & Maint., Inc.*, Comp. Gen. Dec. B-239223, 90-2 CPD ¶ 129; *SRS Techs.*, Comp. Gen. Dec. B-238403, 90-1 CPD ¶ 484; *OptiMetrics, Inc.*, 68 Comp. Gen. 714 (B-235646.2), 89-2 CPD ¶ 266. See also *Unisys Corp. v. National Aeronautics & Space Admin.*, GSBCA 13247-P, 95-2 BCA ¶ 27,818, where the board agreed that the agency had made a valid analysis of the staffing levels required for support services even though they were lower than the incumbent contractor's staffing levels, and *CIGNA Gov't Servs., LLC*, Comp. Gen. Dec. B-297915, 2006 CPD ¶ 73, where the GAO agreed that the agency properly did not adjust seemingly low labor hours because the agency's review of past performance of the offeror indicated that it had done the work more efficiently than other contractors. Compare *PRC Kentron, Inc.*, Comp. Gen. Dec. B-230212, 88-1 CPD ¶ 537, where the GAO did not object to a solicitation provision calling for automatic adjustment of labor hours that did not conform to the agency's prescribed staffing levels, with *ELS, Inc.*, Comp. Gen. Dec. B-283236, 99-2 CPD ¶ 92, where the GAO agreed that the agency was not required to adjust a proposal to reflect the amount of effort that the agency had included in its budget estimate.

Labor rates can also be questioned when the rates included in a proposal are not realistic. For example, in *Hernandez Eng'g, Inc.*, Comp. Gen. Dec. B-286336, 2001 CPD ¶ 89; and *Computer Sciences Corp.*, Comp. Gen. Dec. B-210800, 84-1 CPD ¶ 422, the agency properly concluded that the offeror's proposed labor rates were too low because they were below the rates being paid by an incumbent service contractor. The agency assumed that the winning contractor would hire most of the incumbent employees at their current salaries. Rates have been properly adjusted upward because they were low in *Wyle Labs., Inc.*, Comp. Gen. Dec. B-311123, 2009 CPD ¶ 96 (adjustment proper because it was based on rates proposed by offeror for prior contract); *A. T. Kearney, Inc.*, Comp. Gen. Dec. B-237731, 90-1 CPD ¶ 305 (adjustment proper because rates were under the current average rates being paid on a similar contract); and *Associates in Rural Dev., Inc.*, Comp. Gen. Dec. B-238402, 90-1 CPD ¶ 495 (both salaries and fringe benefits were properly found low by comparing them to earlier costs). Similarly, in *Booz-Allen & Hamilton, Inc.*, Comp. Gen. Dec. B-275934.2, 97-1 CPD ¶ 222, an upward adjustment of labor rates was sustained even though the offeror based its proposed rates on actual averages. The agency concluded that the offeror could not retain competent personnel at the proposed rates. In *E.L. Hamm & Assocs., Inc.*, Comp. Gen. Dec. B-280766.3, 99-1 CPD ¶ 85, a protest was granted when the agency failed to make an upward adjustment to labor rates that were for personnel that were not qualified to perform the proposed work. In *Magellan Health Servs.*, Comp. Gen. Dec. B-298912, 2007 CPD ¶ 81, and in *ManTech Envtl. Tech., Inc.*, Comp. Gen. Dec. B-271002, 96-1 CPD ¶ 272, protests were granted when the agency failed to adjust very low labor rates and it was doubtful the offeror would be able to hire qualified personnel at those rates. See also *ITT Fed. Servs. Int'l Corp.*, B-289863.4, 2002 CPD ¶ 216. In *Radian, Inc.*, Comp. Gen. Dec. B-256313.2, 94-1 CPD ¶ 299, it was proper to make an upward adjustment in labor rates based on a "rate check" furnished by the cognizant DCAA auditors. See also Boeing *Sikorsky Aircraft Support*, Comp. Gen. Dec. B-277263.2, 97-2 CPD ¶ 91, *Sabre Sys., Inc.*, Comp. Gen. Dec. B-255311, 94-1 CPD ¶ 129, and *NKF Eng'g, Inc.*, Comp. Gen. Dec. B-232143, 88-2 CPD ¶ 497, where labor rates after the first year of performance were found to be low because they did not reflect normal escalation, and *Bendix Field Eng'g Corp.*, Comp. Gen. Dec. B-230076, 88-1 CPD ¶ 437, where rates were found low because they were under the rates prescribed by the Service Contract Act. Compare *Information Network Sys., Inc.*, Comp. Gen. Dec. B-284854, 2000 CPD ¶ 104 (no adjustment found reasonable because the agency concluded that the offeror could probably hire employees at labor rates that were lower than those of the incumbent contractor); *Advanced Communications Sys., Inc.*, Comp. Gen. Dec. B-283650, 2000 CPD ¶ 3 (no adjustment found reasonable because the impact of a few of the labor rates that were slightly lower than Bureau of Labor Statistics rates in the area was less than 1%); and *Ares Corp.*, Comp. Gen. Dec. B-275321, 97-1 CPD ¶ 82 (adjustment of only 1% for future years found reasonable based on analysis of the specific company). See also *Telos Corp.*, Comp. Gen. Dec. B-279493.3, 98-2 CPD ¶ 30, where low rates were not adjusted because the offeror had signed letters of commitment from the employees and the offeror was paying similar rates to other employees. In *Unified Indus. Inc.*, Comp. Gen. Dec. B-237868,

90-1 CPD ¶ 346, it was held improper not to question proposed wages that were less than the required wage rates under the Service Contract Act.

It is improper to question labor rates based on past experience without making a detailed analysis of the offeror's specific approach to performance and the personnel expected to be hired, *United Int'l Eng'g, Inc.*, 71 Comp. Gen. 177 (B-245448.3), 92-1 CPD ¶ 122. In that case the contracting officer had mechanically questioned the labor rates without making such an analysis. See *Bendix Field Eng'g Corp.*, Comp. Gen. Dec. B-246236, 92-1 CPD ¶ 227, where the GAO also ruled that a labor rate adjustment was improper when the agency's application of a projected inflation factor resulted in labor rates in excess of those called for by the collective bargaining agreement that the offeror had with its union. The GAO also rejected adjustments to management salaries because they were made mechanically without considering the specifics of the offeror's situation. See also *Hughes STX Corp.*, Comp. Gen. Dec. B-278466, 98-1 CPD ¶ 52, finding the cost realism evaluation unreasonable where the evaluators had mechanically compared the protester's and incumbent's proposed labor rates to the historical labor rates without considering the particular offeror's technical approach or other information in the proposal. Compare *Booz-Allen & Hamilton, Inc.*, Comp. Gen. Dec. B-275934.2, 97-1 CPD ¶ 222, agreeing with the use of the agency's estimated labor rates in lieu of the offeror's rates, which were stated to be at the average rate of the employees to be used in performing the contract. The GAO found the adjustment rational because the offeror had not provided a narrative, as required by the RFP, stating how it could meet the requirements at such low rates. See also *Roy F. Weston, Inc.*, Comp. Gen. Dec. B-274945, 97-1 CPD ¶ 92, finding it proper to adjust an offeror's labor rates to a composite rate used by all the offerors. It is proper to accept rates that appear to be low when the agency determines that they are the rates being paid by the incumbent offeror that is competing for the work, *Kalman & Co.*, Comp. Gen. Dec. B-287442.2, 2002 CPD ¶ 63, are the rates currently being paid by the offeror and its major subcontractor, *Advanced Communications Sys., Inc.*, Comp. Gen. Dec. B-283650, 2000 CPD ¶ 3, are supported by commitments from personnel to work at those rates, *Telos Corp.*, Comp. Gen. Dec. B-279493.3, 98-2 CPD ¶ 30, or are the rates being currently paid to employees that will work on the contract, *ATLIS Fed. Servs., Inc.*, Comp. Gen. Dec. B-275065.2, 97-1 CPD ¶ 84.

When labor rates are questioned, the contracting officer must be certain that the adjustments are based on the offeror's accounting practices. For example, an adjustment of rates to reflect a 40-hour work week was overturned in *General Research Corp.*, Comp. Gen. Dec. B-241569, 91-1 CPD ¶ 183, because the offeror had an established accounting practice (disclosed in its Cost Accounting Standards disclosure statement) that charged for labor based on the full hours worked by each employee. The GAO stated that the contracting officer should not have relied on the incorrect advice of the Defense Contract Audit Agency (DCAA) auditor, who stated that the disclosure statement did not deal with this issue, but should have been familiar with the offeror's accounting practices. Compare *PAI, Inc.*, 67 Comp. Gen. 516 (B-230610), 88-2 CPD ¶ 36, sustaining a protest that the contracting officer had not adjusted labor rates to comply with a solicitation provision prohibiting use of rates based on uncompensated overtime. The GAO did not address the issue of whether such rates were in accordance with the offeror's accounting practices. Similarly, in *Hardman (J.V.)*, Comp. Gen. Dec. B-224551, 87-1 CPD ¶ 162, the GAO agreed with an adjustment to remove the effect of uncompensated overtime, pursuant to a solicitation provision, without addressing the accounting practices of the offeror. Compare *Systems Integration & Research, Inc.*, Comp. Gen. Dec. B-279759.2, 99-1 CPD ¶ 54, where labor rates based on uncompensated overtime were properly accepted where the solicitation did not prohibit the use of such rates, and *SRS Techs.*, Comp. Gen. Dec. B-291618.2, 2003 CPD ¶ 70, where it was improper to adjust the rates for uncompensated overtime since the solicitation did not prohibit its use.

In *Compuware Corp.*, GSBCA 9533-P, 88-3 BCA ¶ 21,109, the board rejected an upward adjustment of labor rates that conflicted with the findings of the auditor reviewing the proposals. The auditor had determined that the contractor reasonably concluded that an imminent turnover in employees would lower its labor costs because the new workers would be paid less than those with seniority. The board found that the contracting officer had no evidence that the audit finding was incorrect. Compare *SGT, Inc.*, Comp. Gen. Dec. B-294722.4, 2005 CPD ¶ 151, where the GAO held that the agency properly made an independent analysis of labor rates when the DCAA audit of the rates was inconclusive.

(3) INDIRECT COSTS

Contracting officers also frequently question proposed costs in the indirect cost area. In *Polaris, Inc.*, Comp. Gen. Dec. B-220066, 85-2 CPD ¶ 669, the GAO held that an agency was correct in concluding that the offeror's proposed overhead rates were too low. The offeror had projected a gradual reduction in overhead rates over a five-year period, but the agency had rejected this possibility based on the recommendations of the DCAA. Similarly, in *Coleman Research Corp.*, Comp. Gen. Dec. B-278793, 98-1 CPD ¶ 111, the contracting officer properly used prior-year indirect cost rates when the offeror had included substantially lower rates in the proposal based on its theory that additional work would reduce its rates without submitting sufficient evidence to support this theory. See also *Mandex, Inc.*, Comp. Gen. Dec. B-241841, 91-1 CPD ¶ 253, *recons. denied*, 91-2 CPD ¶ 83, where an offeror's G&A rate was found to be low because it was based on an accounting system change that had not been fully approved by the administrative contracting officer at the time of award (the change had been approved by the DCAA subject to correction of deficiencies in the accounting system). Compare *Aurora Assocs., Inc.*, Comp. Gen. Dec. B-215565, 85-1 CPD ¶ 470, where a conclusion that the rate was too low was found to be improper because the agency used only the highest indirect cost multiplier when three different multipliers, corresponding to different categories of employees, were applicable to the proposed costs. In *Hanford Envtl. Health Found.*, Comp. Gen. Dec. B-292858.2, 2004 CPD ¶ 164, acceptance of a fringe benefit rate that was lower than the incumbent contractor's rate was proper when the lower rate was comparable to local rates.

Some contracting officers have avoided the detailed analysis of indirect costs by merely comparing proposed overhead rates to prior rates. While this is a rather imprecise technique, it has been affirmed as a proper basis for a cost realism analysis. See *Signal Corp.*, Comp. Gen. Dec. B-241849, 91-1 CPD ¶ 218, and *Purvis Sys., Inc.*, Comp. Gen. Dec. B-245761, 92-1 CPD ¶ 132, where it was held proper to determine a probable cost using prior-year indirect cost rates when the offeror had included substantially lower rates in the proposal based on its theory that additional work would reduce its rates but had failed to submit sufficient evidence to support this theory. Protests have been granted because the contracting officer did not adjust rates that were below current rates, *E.L. Hamm & Assocs., Inc.*, Comp. Gen. Dec. B-280766.3, 99-1 CPD ¶ 85 (rate substantially below the DCAA approved rate); *The Futures Group Int'l*, Comp. Gen. Dec. B-281274.2, 2000 CPD ¶ 147 (rates were significantly below the most recent rates). Compare *Booz-Allen & Hamilton, Inc.*, Comp. Gen. Dec. B-275934.2, 97-1 CPD ¶ 222, where it was found proper to use the five months experienced rates to project annual rates when the offeror had revised its accounting system. In that case, the contracting officer had rejected the DCAA auditor's analysis that suggested using average rates.

If an offeror agrees to place a "cap" on its indirect cost rates, it is proper to use those rates in determining the probable cost in making the cost realism analysis, *E.L. Hamm & Assocs., Inc.*, Comp. Gen. Dec. B-280766.5, 2000 CPD ¶ 13 (capped G&A rate); *MAR, Inc.*, Comp. Gen. Dec. B-255309.4; 94-2 CPD 19 (capped overhead rate); *Technical Resources, Inc.*, Comp. Gen. Dec. B-253506, 93-2 CPD 176 (capped overhead rate); *Vitro Corp.*, Comp. Gen. Dec. B-247734.3, 92-2 CPD ¶ 202 (capped G&A rate). It has also been held that it is improper to disregard capped rates in determining the probable cost, *Veda, Inc.*, Comp. Gen. Dec. B-278516.2, 98-1 CPD ¶ 112; *BNF Techs., Inc.*, Comp. Gen. Dec. B-254953.3, 94-1 CPD ¶ 274. However, if the contracting officer concludes that a realistic estimate of the rates to be incurred is below the cap, that estimate can be used in lieu of the cap, *Delta Research Assocs., Inc.*, Comp. Gen. Dec. B-254006.2, 94-1 CPD ¶ 47. If the capped rates are unrealistically low, the agency should consider the risk that performing at a low rate will impact the contractor's financial condition, *MCT JV*, Comp. Gen. Dec. B-311245.2, 2008 CPD ¶ 121, *recons. denied*, 2008 CPD ¶ 167 (protest granted because agency did not consider risk of capped rates when RFP warned of such risk).

In making the cost realism analysis of indirect costs, the contracting officer may rely entirely on the computations of the cognizant auditor, *Summit Research Corp.*, Comp. Gen. Dec. B-287523, 2001 CPD ¶ 176; *ELS, Inc.*, Comp. Gen. Dec. B-283236, 99-2 CPD ¶ 92; *SRS Techs.*, Comp. Gen. Dec. B-238403, 90-1 CPD ¶ 484. See also *Geo-Centers, Inc.*, Comp. Gen. Dec. B-276033, 97-1 CPD ¶ 182, where an agency correctly accepted a new overhead structure that had been approved by the DCAA, and *Polaris, Inc.*, Comp. Gen. Dec. B-220066, 85-2 CPD ¶ 669, where an agency was found to have correctly concluded that the offeror's projected gradual reduction in overhead rates over a five-year period led to unduly low overhead rates, based on the recommendations of the DCAA. Conversely, an auditor's recommendations may be disregarded entirely if the contracting officer disagrees with the analysis, *Booz-Allen & Hamilton, Inc.*, Comp. Gen. Dec. B-275934.2, 97-1 CPD ¶ 222, or believes that the information is invalid, *Electronic Warfare Integration Network*, Comp. Gen. Dec. B-235814, 89-2 CPD ¶ 356.

A cost realism adjustment will not be sustained if it is based on incorrect advice from the DCAA, *General Research Corp.*, Comp. Gen. Dec. B-241569, 91-1 CPD ¶ 183. In addition, reliance on unaudited information obtained from a government auditor has been found to be unjustified where the information proves to be unreliable, *L-3 Communications Corp.*, Comp. Gen. Dec. B-281784.3, 99-1 CPD ¶ 81. Compare *Intermetrics, Inc.*, Comp. Gen. Dec. B-259254.2, 95-1 CPD ¶ 215, and *Radian, Inc.*, Comp. Gen. Dec. B-256313.2, 94-2 CPD ¶ 104, sustaining cost realism adjustments based on unaudited rate checks by DCAA auditors that were based on current data.

FAR 15.407-3(b) requires contracting officers to use forward pricing rates as the basis for pricing "all contracts" during the period an agreement on such rates is in effect unless the ACO determines that a "changed condition invalidates the agreement." It is proper to use such labor and indirect cost rates in performing a cost realism analysis, *Hoboken Shipyards, Inc.*, Comp. Gen. Dec. B-219428, 85-2 CPD ¶ 416, *recons. denied*, 85-2 CPD ¶ 582. In *Jonathan Corp.*, Comp. Gen. Dec. B-230971, 88-2 CPD ¶ 133, the contracting officer used such rates in concluding that the estimated costs were too low even though the offeror attempted to demonstrate that the forward pricing rates were invalid due to changed conditions. The GAO agreed with the contracting officer's conclusion, finding that the offeror had not clearly demonstrated that the rates were invalid. Similarly, in *Coleman Research Corp.*, Comp. Gen. Dec. B-278793, 98-1 CPD ¶ 111, the contracting officer properly relied on recently negotiation forward pricing rates as well as rates incurred on a prior contract in rejecting low proposed rates.

(4) OTHER DIRECT COSTS

Cost realism analysis has been used to question other direct costs proposed by offerors. For example, in *Amtec Corp.*, Comp. Gen. Dec. B-240647, 90-2 CPD ¶ 482, the contracting officer properly found the estimate of travel costs too low because the discount fares proposed by an offeror would probably not be obtainable during performance. Similarly, in *CWIS, LLC*, Comp. Gen. Dec. B-287521, 2001 CPD ¶ 119, travel costs were properly adjusted upward to reflect a requirement for trips on short notice, and in *Centra Tech., Inc.*, Comp. Gen. Dec. B-274744, 97-1 CPD ¶ 35, the agency properly adjusted an offeror's travel costs based on the costs incurred on the current contract. See also *Priority One Servs., Inc.*, Comp. Gen. Dec. B-288836, 2002 CPD ¶ 79, sustaining a protest where the agency failed to reduce costs of equipment which protester had included in its estimate because it misunderstood the requirements. Compare *Abt Assocs.*, Comp. Gen. Dec. B-294130.2, 2004 CPD ¶ 220, where the agency made no adjustments to travel and per diem costs because they were in line with past experience, and *Cygnus Corp.*, Comp. Gen. Dec. B-275957, 97-1 CPD ¶ 202, finding that it was proper to use the same other direct costs for all offerors by "normalizing" this cost element. See also *Science Applications Int'l Corp.*, Comp. Gen. Dec. B-238136.2, 90-1 CPD ¶ 517, where it was found proper to accept a low rate for other direct costs when the agency, after discussions, agreed with the offeror's rationale for the low rate.

3. Price Realism Analysis

As discussed in Chapter 2, agencies can also make a price realism analysis in a competition for fixed-price contracts to determine if the proposed price is unrealistically low. When the RFP states that such an analysis will be made, the agency has considerable discretion in selecting the technique that will be used. See, for example, *Navistar Defense, LLC*, Comp. Gen. Dec. B-401865, 2009 CPD ¶ 258, where the agency used both price analysis and cost analysis techniques to determine that seemingly low prices were realistic. See also *G4S Gov't Servs.*, Comp. Gen. Dec. B-401694, 2009 CPD ¶ 236, rejecting the contention that the agency made an inadequate price realism analysis, stating "an agency has considerable discretion in determining the nature and extent of required price realism and proposal risk assessments."

Although the FAR refers only to cost realism analysis, greater clarity is achieved by calling it "price realism analysis." This signifies that such analysis *cannot be used to adjust the offered prices* but may only be used to make a responsibility determination, a performance risk assessment, or an analysis of whether the offeror understands the work. Contracting officers have considerable discretion in deciding whether to call for such analysis in the RFP. See *American Techs., Inc.*, Comp. Gen. Dec. B-401445, 2009 CPD ¶ 178, stating:

> In general, there is no requirement that a price realism analysis be performed when award of a fixed-price contract is contemplated. *Phoebe Putney Mem'l Hosp.*, B-311385, June 19, 2008, 2008 CPD ¶ 128 at 2. As was the case here, however, a solicitation for a fixed-price contract may provide for a price realism analysis for the purpose of assessing offerors' understanding of the requirements or the risk inherent in offerors' proposals. *PHP Healthcare Corp.*, B-251933, May 13, 1993, 93-1 CPD ¶ 381 at 5. The nature and extent of a price realism analysis ultimately are matters within the exercise of the agency's discretion, and our review of such an evaluation is limited to determining whether it was reasonable and consistent with the solicitation's evaluation criteria. *Northrop Grumman Info. Tech., Inc. et al.*, B-295526 et al., Mar. 16, 2005, 2005 CPD ¶ 45 at 19.

Price realism analysis can be used to make a performance risk assessment or to analyze understanding of the work only when it relates to an express evaluation factor in the RFP. See *Possehn Consulting*, Comp. Gen. Dec. B-278579, 98-1 CPD ¶ 10, where the contracting officer rejected an offer for being unrealistically low when there was no evaluation factor for performance risk or understanding the work. The GAO granted the protest, stating:

> A determination that an offeror's price on a fixed-price contract is too low generally concerns the offeror's responsibility, *i.e.*, the offeror's ability and capacity to successfully perform the contract at its offered price. *Cromartie Constr. Co.*, B-271788, July 30, 1996, 96-2 CPD ¶ 48 at 5; *Envirosol, Inc.*, B-254223, Dec. 2, 1993, 93-2 CPD ¶ 295 at 5; *Ball Technical Products Group*, B-224394, Oct. 17, 1986, 86-2 CPD ¶ 465 at 2. As part of the technical evaluation, an agency may assess the reasonableness of a low price to evaluate an offeror's understanding of the solicitation requirements, so long as the RFP provides for evaluation of offeror understanding as part of the technical evaluation. *Cromartie Constr. Co., supra; Envirosol, Inc., supra.*

> In this case, however, there was no technical evaluation criterion or proposal requirement addressing an offeror's understanding of requirements. Instead, the RFP examined only experience, past performance, and personnel qualifications. This being so, the agency's concern about the reasonableness of Possehn's low prices could not be considered other than as a responsibility matter. *Cromartie Constr. Co., supra*; *Envirosol, supra*, at 6. Since Possehn is a small business, the agency was required to refer any finding of nonresponsibility to the Small Business Administration (SBA) for review. 15 U.S.C. § 637(b)(7) (1994); Federal Acquisition Regulation § 19.602-1(a); *Cromartie Constr. Co., supra; Envirosol, supra*. Accordingly, we sustain Possehn's challenge in this area.

Similarly, in *Arora Group, Inc.*, Comp. Gen. Dec. B-277674, 98-1 CPD ¶ 64, the agency had stated in the RFP that price realism was an element of the past performance evaluation factor but had evaluated a low price as a performance risk even though there was no such evaluation factor. The GAO granted the protest, stating:

> The protester also argues that the agency evaluation was improper because it made price realism a separate and determinative evaluation factor, when the RFP stated that price realism was to be part of the past performance evaluation. We agree. The RFP specifically provided, under the price evaluation factor, that a price realism analysis would be conducted and that any suspected unrealistic pricing which result in a suspected understatement of the costs or misunderstanding of the requirements would be addressed in the evaluation of the offeror's past performance. While the protester's proposal consistently received a rating of "Good" for past performance, the protester's failure to provide for salary escalation was considered to present a risk of nonperformance that the agency was not willing to accept. Clearly, the [agency] did not evaluate price realism as provided for by the solicitation, that is, within the context of [the protester's] past performance rating, which the [agency] rated as "Good." In this regard, the RFP provided for award to the offeror with the best combination of past performance and price. [The protester] received a "Good" rating on past performance, as did [the winning offeror], and proposed a price that was more than $[deleted] lower than that proposed by

[the winning offeror]. Rather than making a tradeoff determination on the basis of these evaluations, as called for by the RFP, the agency business clearance memorandum states that "[the protester] was not considered for award due to the price realism concerns associated with their offer." In essence, the [agency] ignored the stated evaluation criteria.

When the RFP calls for making a price realism analysis to evaluate performance risk, this becomes an evaluation factor which must be used in making the source selection decision, *Pemco Aeroplex, Inc.*, Comp. Gen. Dec. B-310372, 2008 CPD ¶ 2, *recons. denied*, 2008 CPD ¶ 24. See *Al Qabandi United Co.*, Comp. Gen. Dec. B-310600.3, 2008 CPD ¶ 112, finding that the RFP statement that award would be made to the "lowest realistically priced" offeror required the agency to make a price realism analysis.

Although the contracting officer has considerable discretion in determining that a contractor's low price constitutes a performance risk, the GAO will grant a protest if the risk is minimal. See, for example, *Joint Venture Penauille/BMAR & Assocs., LLC*, Comp. Gen. Dec. B-311200, 2008 CPD ¶ 118. Compare *Team BOS/Naples – Gemmo S.p.A./DelJen*, Comp. Gen. Dec. B-298865.3, 2008 CPD ¶ 11, upholding a contracting officer's analysis indicating that a low price did not constitute a performance risk.

When the RFP calls for a price realism analysis, the agency must perform the analysis in a competent manner. See *Health Net Fed. Servs., LLC*, Comp. Gen. Dec. B-401652.3, 2009 CPD ¶ 220, granting a protest because the agency made the analysis using total staffing rather than the staffing that was proposed for each element of the work. In this case, the price realism analysis was impeded by the fact that the agency did not correlate the technical proposal with the cost proposal. See also *Joint Venture Penauille/BMAR & Assocs., LLC*, Comp. Gen. Dec. B-311200, 2008 CPD ¶ 118, concluding that low indefinite-quantity pricing for minor work was not a reasonable indication of overall low pricing risk. In general, however, the GAO has been reluctant to grant protests that the agency did not properly perform a price realism analysis. See *New Breed, Inc.*, Comp. Gen. Dec. B-400554, 2009 CPD ¶ 4 (no requirement that agency obtain cost or pricing data to perform analysis); *Accumark, Inc.*, Comp. Gen. Dec. B-310814, 2008 CPD ¶ 68 (comparison of prices and government estimate adequate basis for making analysis); *Systems Research & Applications Corp.*, Comp. Gen. Dec. B-299818, 2008 CPD ¶ 28 (comparison of labor rates with industry statistics adequate analysis); *Legacy Mgmt. Solutions, LLC*, Comp. Gen. Dec. B-299981.2, 2007 CPD ¶ 197 (comparing proposed prices to government estimate and other proposed prices and ensuring that prices reflected labor categories and hours specified in solicitation constituted reasonable analysis); *Navarro Research & Eng'g, Inc.*, Comp. Gen. Dec. B-299981, 2007 CPD ¶ 195 (comparing proposed prices to government estimate and other proposed prices and ensuring that prices reflected labor categories and hours specified in solicitation was reasonable analysis); *Foresight Science & Tech., Inc.*, Comp. Gen. Dec.

B-297910.2, 2006 CPD ¶ 187 (review of labor rates and skill mix required for tasks adequate analysis).

While price realism can be used to assess performance risk when the RFP calls for such an assessment, a low price does not necessarily lead to the conclusion that there are risks. Each offeror must be assessed based on its specific offer. See *New Breed, Inc.*, Comp. Gen. Dec. B-400554, 2009 CPD ¶ 4, affirming a price realism analysis where the contracting officer reviewed the specific costing format used by each offeror and found the prices realistic, and *DIGICON Corp.*, Comp. Gen. Dec. B-275060, 97-1 CPD ¶ 64, affirming a price realism analysis where the contracting officer found that low labor rates for one offeror did not pose a significant risk, whereas lower labor rates for the protester was found to pose a significant risk. See also *Pacific Ship Repair & Fabrication, Inc.*, Comp. Gen. Dec. B-279793, 98-2 CPD ¶ 29 (low labor rates and low prices on two line items posed performance risk); *Sarasota Measurements & Controls, Inc.*, Comp. Gen. Dec. B-252406.3, 94-2 CPD ¶ 32 (low price posed risk that offeror could not complete work); *Newport News Shipbuilding & Drydock Co.*, Comp. Gen. Dec. B-254969, 94-1 CPD ¶ 198 (low price poses performance risk even if offeror is capable of absorbing the potential loss); *Trauma Serv. Group*, Comp. Gen. Dec. B-242902.2, 91-1 CPD ¶ 573 (low rates of compensation created risk of inadequate performance); *Culver Health Corp.*, Comp. Gen. Dec. B-242902, 91-1 CPD ¶ 556 (low rates of compensation of proposed employees created risk of poor performance); *Computer Based Sys., Inc.*, 70 Comp. Gen. 172 (B-240963), 91-1 CPD ¶ 14 (low price indicated that offeror had chosen a high-risk technical approach); *Modern Techs. Corp.*, Comp. Gen. Dec. B-236961.4, 90-1 CPD ¶ 301 (extended workweek created substantial risk offeror would be unable to hire and retain stable workforce); *Systems Processes & Eng'g Corp.*, Comp. Gen. Dec. B-234142, 89-1 CPD ¶ 441, *recons. denied*, 89-2 CPD ¶ 191 (unexplained price reduction in BAFO resulted in low price, which poses a significant performance risk). Compare *Harris Corp. v. United States*, 628 F. Supp. 813 (D.D.C. 1986), where the court held that it was improper to downgrade a proposal merely because the offeror had made a decision to absorb some costs of performance. See also *DMS-All Star Joint Venture*, Comp. Gen. Dec. B-310932.6, 2009 CPD ¶ 212 (agency entitled to accept a below-cost proposal for fixed-price contract); *EBA Eng'g, Inc.*, Comp. Gen. Dec. B-275818, 97-1 CPD ¶ 127 (contracting officer properly found that there was not significant risk in a seemingly low indirect cost rate of the winning offeror); and *VSE Corp.*, Comp. Gen. Dec. B-247610.2, 92-2 CPD ¶ 81 (contracting officer acted properly in not downgrading an offeror's technical and management proposal where proposed labor rates were lower than the government's estimate but analysis indicated that they did not detract from the offeror's ability to perform the work). It has also been held proper to find a performance risk when the offeror does not submit data explaining a low price. See *General Elec. Co.*, 55 Comp. Gen. 1450 (B-186372), 76-2 CPD ¶ 269, where the source selection official concluded that there was performance risk because the contractor had not submitted detailed cost data supporting the reduced price in its BAFO.

Price realism is also frequently treated as a means of assessing whether an offeror understands the work, and this is proper if that is an evaluation factor. See, for example, *Team BOS/Naples-Gemmo S.p.A./DelJen*, Comp. Gen. Dec. B-298865.3, 2008 CPD ¶ 11; and *Tecom, Inc.*, Comp. Gen. Dec. B-275518.2, 97-1 CPD ¶ 221, affirming assessments that offerors with a low price understood the work. The agency had made a careful review of their proposals and determined that they demonstrated understanding even though the prices was quite low. See also *Boersma Travel Servs.*, Comp. Gen. Dec. B-297986.2, 2006 CPD ¶ 175 (evaluators had "limited concerns" about low prices but concluded that offeror understood the work); *Consolidated Servs., Inc.*, Comp. Gen. Dec. B-276111.4, 98-1 CPD ¶ 14 (cursory assessment of low prices satisfactory to reach conclusion that offeror understood the work); *East/West Indus., Inc.*, Comp. Gen. Dec. B-278734.4, 98-1 CPD ¶ 143 (price realism analysis persuaded agency that awardee understood the contract requirements, notwithstanding its low price); *HSG-Holzmann Technischer Servs. GmbH; HSG-GeBe*, Comp. Gen. Dec. B-274992.2, 97-1 CPD ¶ 87 (agency reasonably concluded that although rates were low, this did not evince a lack of understanding of the contract requirements); *Triple P Servs., Inc.*, Comp. Gen. Dec. B-271629.3, 96-2 CPD ¶ 30 (provision announcing intent to perform a cost realism analysis in an RFP for a fixed-price contract is unobjectionable where the RFP states that the analysis is for the limited purpose of aiding the agency in measuring the offerors' understanding of the work and the RFP includes as part of evaluation of technical proposals an assessment of the offerors' understanding of the technical requirements); and *EC Corp.*, Comp. Gen. Dec. B-266165.2, 96-1 CPD ¶ 153 (price realism analysis demonstrated an acceptable level of understanding under the work accomplishment and methodology factor).

Price realism can also be used to assess an offeror's responsibility. Because this is done outside of the evaluation scheme, no evaluation factor is needed for this use of price realism. See *Computer Sys. Int'l, Inc.*, Comp. Gen. Dec. B-276955, 97-2 CPD ¶ 49, where although the RFP indicated that price realism would be considered a matter of responsibility, the contracting officer found that an offeror with a low price was still responsible. Similarly, in *SAIC Computer Sys.*, Comp. Gen. Dec. B-258431.2, 95-1 CPD ¶ 156, the GAO denied a protest that the agency unreasonably failed to assess the technical risk in the awardee's offer of allegedly low prices, stating that where the solicitation contemplated the award of a fixed-price contract and there were no stated criteria for price realism analysis or the evaluation of offerors' understanding, the reasonableness of an offeror's low price concerns the offeror's responsibility. See also *Oshkosh Truck Corp.*, Comp. Gen. Dec. B-252708.2, 93-2 CPD ¶ 115 (low-price offeror was responsible).

4. *Obtaining Field Pricing Assistance*

In many cases the contracting officer will request assistance from field personnel and audit agencies to confirm the reasonableness of proposed prices or the realism of the proposed costs. However, the obtaining of such assistance is at the discretion of the contracting officer. See FAR 15.404-2, which states:

(a) Field pricing assistance. (1) The contracting officer should request field pricing assistance when the information available at the buying activity is inadequate to determine a fair and reasonable price. Such requests shall be tailored to reflect the minimum essential supplementary information needed to conduct a technical or cost or pricing analysis.

(2) Field pricing assistance generally is directed at obtaining technical, audit, and special reports associated with the cost elements of a proposal, including subcontracts. Information on related pricing practices and history may also be obtained. Field pricing assistance may also include information relative to the business, technical, production, or other capabilities and practices of an offeror. The type of information and level of detail requested will vary in accordance with the specialized resources available at the buying activity and the magnitude and complexity of the required analysis.

(3) When field pricing assistance is requested, contracting officers are encouraged to team with appropriate field experts throughout the acquisition process, including negotiations. Early communication with these experts will assist in determining the extent of assistance required, the specific areas for which assistance is needed, a realistic review schedule, and the information necessary to perform the review.

When the agency has contract administration personnel in the field, they may be called upon to assess and verify the material costs and labor hours in the offerors' proposed costs. In many cases the only assistance that will be needed from audit agencies is verification of the labor and indirect cost rates that have been used to each offeror. See *Battelle Memorial Inst.*, Comp. Gen. Dec. B-278673, 98-1 CPD ¶ 107, for a case where the GAO affirmed this limited use of field audit assistance.

Obtaining field pricing assistance can slow the evaluation process. Hence, FAR 15.404-2(b) provides for techniques to expedite the flow of information as follows:

(b) Reporting field pricing information. (1) Depending upon the extent and complexity of the field pricing review, results, including supporting rationale, may be reported directly to the contracting officer orally, in writing, or by any other method acceptable to the contracting officer.

(i) Whenever circumstances permit, the contracting officer and field pricing experts are encouraged to use telephonic and/or electronic means to request and transmit pricing information.

(ii) When it is necessary to have written technical and audit reports, the contracting officer shall request that the audit agency concurrently forward the audit report to the requesting contracting officer and the administrative contracting officer (ACO). The

> completed field pricing assistance results may reference audit information, but need not reconcile the audit recommendations and technical recommendations. A copy of the information submitted to the contracting officer by field pricing personnel shall be provided to the audit agency.
>
> (2) Audit and field pricing information, whether written or reported telephonically or electronically, shall be made a part of the official contract file (see 4.807(f)).

On occasion, the agency will receive a cost proposal that is so deficient in information that analysis is not practicable. FAR 15.404-2(d) contains the following guidance on this situation:

> (d) Deficient proposals. The ACO or the auditor, as appropriate, shall notify the contracting officer immediately if the data provided for review is so deficient as to preclude review or audit, or if the contractor or offeror has denied access to any records considered essential to conduct a satisfactory review or audit. Oral notifications shall be confirmed promptly in writing, including a description of deficient or denied data or records. The contracting officer immediately shall take appropriate action to obtain the required data. Should the offeror/contractor again refuse to provide adequate data, or provide access to necessary data, the contracting officer shall withhold the award or price adjustment and refer the contract action to a higher authority, providing details of the attempts made to resolve the matter and a statement of the practicability of obtaining the supplies or services from another source.

B. Past Performance

Past performance has become one of the most significant evaluation factors because it is mandatory on all procurements over $150,000 and is used on many procurements of lesser amount. There has also been a trend toward using past performance as the only non-cost evaluation factor. Thus, the fair and evenhanded evaluation of past performance has become a critical necessity, *Myers Investigative & Security Servs., Inc.*, Comp. Gen. Dec. B-288468, 2001 CPD ¶ 189 (similar data on two offerors treated differently); *Beneco Enters., Inc.*, Comp. Gen. Dec. B-283512, 2000 CPD ¶ 175, B-283512.3, 2000 CPD ¶ 176 (ratings did not correspond to information in the contract file). There have been numerous recent protests challenging past performance assessments.

In spite of the many challenges to past performance evaluations, the GAO has accorded agencies considerable discretion in the evaluation of contractor past performance. See *HLC Indus., Inc.*, Comp. Gen. Dec. B-274374, 96-2 CPD ¶ 214, stating:

> Evaluation of an offeror's past performance is a matter within the discretion of the contracting agency, and we will not substitute our judgment for the agency's, so long as the rating is reasonably based and documented. *PMT Servs., Inc.*, B-270538.2, Apr. 1, 1996, 96-2 CPD ¶ 98. Mere disagreement with the agency's

evaluation does not itself render the evaluation unreasonable, *Macon Apparel Corp.*, B-272162, Sept. 4, 1996, 96-2 CPD ¶ 95.

See *Master Lock Co., LLC*, Comp. Gen. Dec. B-309982.2, 2009 CPD ¶ 2, denying a protest that a contractor with highly satisfactory past performance had only been rated "good," and *ITT Indus. Space Sys.*, LLC, Comp. Gen. Dec. B-309964, 2007 CPD ¶ 217, denying a protest that the agency had not properly considered a variety of performance information. However, broad discretion does not permit use of an irrational evaluation system, *Green Valley Trans, Inc.*, Comp. Gen. Dec. B-285283, 2000 CPD ¶ 133. There the GAO granted a protest because the agency, in assessing past performance, had used the total number of instances of defective performance without regard to the volume of work of the competitors.

A similar degree of discretion is accorded by the Court of Federal Claims, *Akal Security, Inc. v. United States*, 87 Fed. Cl. 311 (2009); *Gulf Group Inc. v. United States,* 61 Fed. Cl. 338 (2004); *Maintenance Engineers v. United States*, 50 Fed. Cl. 399 (2001).

This broad discretion permits agencies to refuse to accept an offeror's explanation for a poor past performance rating, *H.F. Henderson Indus.*, Comp. Gen. Dec. B-275017, 97-1 CPD ¶ 27; *Continental Serv. Co.*, Comp. Gen. Dec. B-274531, 97-1 CPD ¶ 9. In *Precision Echo, Inc.*, Comp. Gen. Dec. B-276740, 97-2 CPD ¶ 114, the GAO found that the agency had properly concluded that difficulties in using the offeror's equipment, although primarily due to user error, were also due to the design of the equipment. See also *S3 Ltd.*, Comp. Gen. Dec. B-288195, 2001 CPD ¶ 164 (agency acted properly in finding some performance risk after evaluating somewhat conflicting assessments of several people that had worked on a contract where the protester had encountered problems); *KELO, Inc.*, Comp. Gen. Dec. B-284601.2, 2000 CPD ¶ 110 (agency rejected explanations of performance problems); *MAC's General Contractor*, Comp. Gen. Dec. B-276755, 97-2 CPD ¶ 29 (agency could give a poor evaluation based on a default termination that was still in litigation – stating that such an evaluation may be based on a "reasonable perception of inadequate prior performance"). Agencies may also exercise their discretion to downgrade an offeror that does not submit the past performance information called for by the RFP, *Al Andalus General Contracts Co. v. United States*, 86 Fed. Cl. 252 (2009). On the other hand, agencies can accept an offeror's explanation that it did not cause the performance problems. See *MCR Eng'g Co.*, Comp. Gen. Dec. B-287164, 2001 CPD ¶ 82 (agency accepted explanation that problems were caused by the government); *Millar Elevator Serv. Co.*, Comp. Gen. Dec. B-284870.5, 2001 CPD ¶ 34 (agency accepted explanation that performance problem was caused by late award of contract); *Dynacs Eng'g Co.*, Comp. Gen. Dec. B-284234, 2000 CPD ¶ 50 (agency accepted explanations of performance problems).

One of the major tasks in evaluating contractor past performance information is to distinguish between one or a few instances of performance problems and a significant record of inferior performance. For example, in *Marinette Marine Corp.*, Comp. Gen. Dec. B-400697, 2009 CPD ¶ 16, the agency closely reviewed a single case of inferior performance and concluded that it would not impact the work on the contract to be awarded. See also *MCT JV*, Comp. Gen. Dec. B-311245.2, 2008 CPD ¶ 121 (agency reasonably found "outstanding" past performance even though offeror had encountered some problems in the past); *SKE Int'l, Inc.*, Comp. Gen. Dec. B-311383, 2008 CPD ¶ 111 (agency reasonably found "very good" past performance although there were a few poor ratings in the data base); *BFI Waste Sys. of Nebraska, Inc.*, Comp. Gen. Dec. B-278223, 98-1 CPD ¶ 8 (contracting officer reasonably found that awardee's performance overall during the past five to six years overcame alleged deficiencies its performance under the incumbent contract); and *Cubic Applications, Inc.*, Comp. Gen. Dec. B-274768, 97-1 CPD ¶ 98 (contracting officer reasonably evaluated the performance reports on the competitors, considered the negative comments, but concluded that the overall positive nature of the reports indicated that the winning offeror was entitled to an excellent rating). However, when contracting officers have received a significant number of negative comments on an offeror's past performance, it has properly been given lower ratings. See, for example, *AAC Assocs., Inc.*, Comp. Gen. Dec. B-274928, 97-1 CPD ¶ 55, where the contracting officer gave a moderate past performance rating based on a number of negative comments from references; and *SEAIR Transport Servs., Inc.*, Comp. Gen. Dec. B-274162, 96-2 CPD ¶ 198, where the contracting officer concluded that the overall ratings given by references adequately reflected the severity of the problems that they had identified. In *Quality Fabricators, Inc.*, Comp. Gen. Dec. B-271431, 96-2 CPD ¶ 22, there were so many past performance problems that the contracting officer properly dropped the offeror out of the competitive range.

Care must also be exercised in determining responsibility for past performance problems. See *CDA Investment Techs., Inc.*, Comp. Gen. Dec. B-272093, 97-1 CPD ¶ 102, affirming the evaluation of a contractor and a subcontractor on a prior contract that were competing for a new contract and there had been performance problems on the prior contract. The evaluators took the time to make a careful analysis of which problems should be attributable to each of the two companies and gave them past performance ratings in accordance with this assignment of responsibility. Similarly, in *Pemco Aeroplex, Inc.*, Comp. Gen. Dec. B-310372, 2008 CPD ¶ 2, the agency properly gave an offeror a rating of "satisfactory confidence" after carefully assessing the cause of prior performance difficulties, and in *Sumaria Sys., Inc.*, Comp. Gen. Dec. B-299517, 2007 CPD ¶ 122, the agency properly rechecked with the personnel on a referenced contract to obtain more current information on the cause of the problem. Compare *Sikorsky Aircraft Co.*, Comp. Gen. Dec. B-299145.4, 2007 CPD ¶ 78, where the protester was downgraded based on a negative report from the program manager on an ongoing contract where significant problems had been encountered. Although the GAO ruled that this was proper, there was little indication that the agency had investigated to determine whether the problems were caused by the government or the contractor and four other customers of the protester reported very good past performance. It is also proper to defer the assessment of responsibility for a prior problem when an agency investigation is still underway, *Metson Marine Servs., Inc.*, Comp. Gen. Dec. B-299705, 2007 CPD ¶ 159.

1. Sources and Reliability of Past Performance Information

Most agencies have obtained the information from offerors and from references submitted by the offerors or other organizations that have dealt with the offeror. FAR 15.305(a)(2)(ii) requires that offerors be permitted to identify all organizations to whom they have sold similar goods or services. Agencies must carefully assess this information to ensure that it is a reliable measure of the past performance of the offeror. Although there may be some question as to the reliability of such information, the practice of calling references and other organizations for whom the offeror has worked has not been challenged. However, care must be exercised to ensure that offerors are given the same opportunity to submit reference information. See *Aerospace Design & Fabrication, Inc.*, Comp. Gen. Dec. B-278896.2, 98-1 CPD ¶ 139, sustaining a protest because one offeror had been permitted to submit more reference information than was permitted by the RFP. In *Serco, Inc. v. United States*, 81 Fed. Cl. 463 (2008), the court held that the method of data collection was unreliable, summarizing the requirement for reliable information as follows at 483:

> [T]here is nothing inherently wrong with an agency using a survey, telephone interview, or questionnaire to elicit information regarding past performance. To the contrary, a review of agency regulations, *see, e.g.*, 48 C.F.R. § 1815.304-70-(d)(3) (1999), not to mention the decisional law, suggests that such surveying has been frequently employed without objection.[28] Nonetheless, such surveys must satisfy FAR § 15.305(a)(2), which requires an agency to consider "[t]he currency and relevance of [past performance] information, source of the information, context of the data, and general trends in contractor's performance." Reflecting these requirements, cases examining the use of surveys have focused on whether they were reasonably designed to generate information of sufficient reliability to support the evaluation methodology to be used in assessing past performance. *See Redcon, Inc.*, 2000 CPD ¶ 188, at 6 (2000); *ENMAX Corp.*, 99-1 CPD ¶ 102, at 5 (1999); *Pacific Ship Repair and Fabrication, Inc.*, 98-2 CPD ¶ 29, at 3 (1998). Those cases suggests that the presence *vel non* of the following indicia aids in assessing that reliability: (i) whether the questions are specific enough to elicit information responsive to evaluation criteria; (ii) whether the definitions of adjectival ratings were made available either to the surveyors or the references; (iii) whether the surveys are conducted by personnel otherwise knowledgeable regarding the procurement; and (iv) whether steps were taken to verify the accuracy of the survey responses.[29] The "key question," as the GAO has noted, is whether the survey is such that "the past performance information is accurately conveyed." *Redcon*, 2000 CPD ¶ 188, at 6.

---

[28] For cases discussing procurements in which surveys were used, *see, e.g., Southern Foods, Inc. v. United States*, 76 Fed. Cl. 769, 779 (2007); *Day & Zimmermann Servs., a Div. of Day & Zimmermann, Inc. v. United States*,

38 Fed. Cl. 591, 609 (1997); *S3 LTD*, 2001 CPD ¶ 165, at 5 (2001); *Beneco Enters., Inc.*, 2000 CPD ¶ 175, 2-3 (1999); *Cont'l Serv. Co.*, 97-1 CPD ¶ 9, 2-3 (1996); *see also* Ralph C. Nash & John Cibinic, "Postscript IV: Past Performance Evaluations," 16 No. 3 Nash & Cibinic Rep. P 14 (2002) ("Data can be obtained from references by questionnaire or telephone interview."). Indeed, the Office of Federal Procurement Policy (OFPP) has provided guidance on how such surveys should be conducted. *See* Office of Mgmt. & Budget, OFPP, Best Practices for Collecting and Using Past Performance Information (2000) ("If adequate documentation is not readily available . . . then a brief survey with follow up calls, or phone interviews should be used to verify past performance."); *id.* at Appendix I (providing a sample survey form).

[29] *See, e.g.*, *Cooperativa Muratori Riuiniti*, 2005 CPD ¶ 21, at 6 (2005) (survey that was not geared to the evaluation criteria held to be arbitrary and capricious); *FC Construction Co., Inc.*, 2001 CPD ¶ 76, at 5 (2001) (telephone survey not arbitrary capricious, where conducted by contract administrator who read references twenty-six questions, provided the references with the definitions for adjectival ratings, and allowed references to review completed questionnaires); *Dismas Charities, Inc.*, 2003 CPD ¶ 125, at 4 (2003) (questionnaires were "materially flawed" and contrary to the FAR when the agency did not provide references with instructions on how to score offeror's past performance); *ENMAX Corp.*, 99-1 CPD ¶ 102, at 5 (survey was reasonable where it includes seventeen questions that were designed to correspond with the three technical evaluation factors and required the reference to rate the offeror as "above average," "average," "below average," or "not observed"); *see also Maint. Engrs. v. United States*, 50 Fed. Cl. 399, 421 (2002); *S3 LTD*, 2001 CPD ¶ 165, at 5.

In using references, random sampling has been permitted, *MilTech, Inc.*, Comp. Gen. Dec. B-275078, 97-1 CPD ¶ 208, and there is no requirement that stringent efforts be made to contact references, *Guam Shipyard*, Comp. Gen. Dec. B-311321, 2008 CPD ¶ 124, or that all references given by the offeror be contacted, *Sunrise Medical HHG, Inc.*, Comp. Gen. Dec. B-310230, 2008 CPD ¶ 7; *U.S. Tech. Corp.*, Comp. Gen. Dec. B-278584, 98-1 CPD ¶ 78. Furthermore, agencies may contact a different number of sources for different offerors, *IGIT, Inc.*, Comp. Gen. Dec. B-275299.2, 97-2 CPD ¶ 7. Although contacting only a single reference would not appear to yield an inadequate sample, this questionable practice has also been permitted, *Neal R. Gross & Co.*, Comp. Gen. Dec. B-275066, 97-1 CPD ¶ 30; *HLC Indus., Inc.*, Comp. Gen. Dec. B-274374, 96-2 CPD ¶ 214. Thus, adverse past performance assessments have been considered to be reliable when they were based on a single contract, *Compania De Asesoria Y Comercio, S.A.*, Comp. Gen. Dec. B-278358, 98-1 CPD ¶ 26 (seven deficiency reports on prior contract); *ECC Int'l Corp.*, Comp. Gen. Dec. B-277422, 98-1 CPD ¶ 45 (significant difficulties on prior production contract). If the references can not be contacted with reasonable efforts, an agency may give an offeror a poor past performance rating, *Consolidated Eng'g Servs., Inc.*, Comp. Gen. Dec. B-277273, 97-2 CPD ¶ 86.

Some agencies have had the offerors obtain and submit letters of recommendation from past buyers of their services. This can lead to the appearance of unfairness if some of the offerors obtain more extensive letters. See *Mid-Atlantic Design & Graphics*, Comp. Gen. Dec. B-276576, 98-1 CPD ¶ 132, denying a protest that the winning offeror had been permitted to obtain very thorough letters describing the relevant work that had been done on past projects, reasoning that a prudent offeror would have obtained such detailed letters.

Some agencies have used questionnaires to obtain past performance information, and this practice has been approved by the GAO, *Continental Serv., Co.*, Comp. Gen. Dec. B-274531, 97-1 CPD ¶ 9; *SWR, Inc.*, Comp. Gen. Dec. B-276878, 97-2 CPD ¶ 34. Although this is a questionable practice, use of scores on questionnaires without supporting information or commentary has also been approved, *Pacific Ship Repair & Fabrication, Inc.*, Comp. Gen. Dec. B-279793, 98-2 CPD ¶ 29; *Boeing Sikorsky Aircraft Support*, Comp. Gen. Dec. B-277263.2, 97-2 CPD ¶ 91.

It is proper to use the ratings on cost-plus-award-fee contracts in the assessment of past performance, *Oceaneering Int'l, Inc.*, Comp. Gen. Dec. B-278126, 98-1 CPD ¶ 133.

The other major way to obtain past performance information is through data collection systems. In an effort to improve the reliability of past performance information, FAR 42.1502(a) requires the preparation of performance evaluation reports on all contracts over $150,000. Contractors must be given the opportunity to include comments on these evaluations, and agencies must make a final review attempting to reconcile disagreements, FAR 42.1503(b). These evaluations are then available for use by all agencies, FAR 42.1503(c), and there is little question that such information can be used in the evaluation process, *American Constr. Co.*, Comp. Gen. Dec. B-401493.2, 2009 CPD ¶ 214; *Precision Mold & Tool*, Comp. Gen. Dec. B-400452.4, 2009 CPD ¶ 84. The Department of Defense has implemented these requirements by adopting a detailed performance rating system. See "A Guide to Collection and Use of Past Performance Information," May 2003. This system classifies contracts into eight areas: systems, services, information technology, operations support, health care, fuels, construction and architect-engineer services, and science and technology. In each of these areas, specified elements of performance will be assessed and placed in an automated data bank for use in the source selection process.

Another source of past performance information is agency personnel that have dealt with the offeror in the past. FAR 15.305(a)(2)(ii) states that the agency "shall consider . . . information obtained from any other sources, when evaluating past performance." The GAO rejected the contention that such information should not be used in *Paragon Sys., Inc.*, Comp. Gen. Dec. B-299548.2, 2007 CPD ¶ 178, finding it proper to contact personnel on a referenced contract that were not included in the offeror's information, stating:

[A]n agency is generally not precluded from considering any relevant information, and is not limited to considering only the information provided within the
"four corners" of vendor's quotation when evaluating past performance. See
FAR § 15.305(a)(2)(ii); *Weidlinger Assocs., Inc.*, [B-299433, B-299433.2, May
7, 2007, 2007 CPD ¶ 91]; *Forest Regeneration Servs.* B-290998, Oct. 30, 2002,
2002 CPD ¶ 187 at 6.

Thus, agencies can seek information from a variety of sources in order to assess the past performance of an offeror. It is proper to use information within the
government as well as the information obtained from references, *PHT Supply Corp.
v. United States*, 71 Fed. Cl. 1 (2006). Thus, it is proper to consider a past default
termination of the offeror, *Precision Prosthetics, Inc.*, Comp. Gen. Dec. B-401023,
2009 CPD ¶ 83. In rating past performance with the same agency, it is proper for the
evaluators to use their personal knowledge of an offeror's performance of contracts
with the agency. See *TEAM Support Servs., Inc.*, Comp. Gen. Dec. B-279379.2,
98-1 CPD ¶ 167; *Omega World Travel, Inc.*, Comp. Gen. Dec. B-271262.2, 96-2
CPD ¶ 44; and *HLC Indus., Inc.*, Comp. Gen. Dec. B-274374, 96-2 CPD ¶ 214.
In these cases the GAO commented that the agency was, in effect, using itself as a
reference. It is also proper to give heavier weight to work for the same agency than
work for private buyers, *Court Copies & Images, Inc.*, Comp. Gen. Dec. B-277268,
97-2 CPD ¶ 85. In *Systems Integration & Dev., Inc.*, Comp. Gen. Dec. B-271050,
96-1 CPD ¶ 273, the GAO also denied a protest claiming that using the past performance of an incumbent gave the incumbent an unfair competitive advantage. As
discussed below, when such information is highly relevant to the instant procurement, it is required to be used.

The subjectivity of some past performance information has led to questions about
its reliability. FAR 42.1501 defines "past performance information" as follows:

Past performance information is relevant information, for future source selection
purposes, regarding a contractor's action under previously awarded contracts. It
includes, for example, the contractor's record of conforming to contract requirements and to standards of good workmanship; the contractor's record of forecasting and controlling costs; the contractor's adherence to contract schedules,
including the administrative aspects of performance; the contractor's history of
reasonable and cooperative behavior and commitment to customer satisfaction;
the contractor's record of integrity and business ethics, and generally, the contractor's business-like concern for the interest of the customer.

Although the elements of this definition dealing with "reasonable and cooperative
behavior" and "customer satisfaction" allow a great deal of subjectivity in the evaluations, the GAO has denied a protest that these elements permit contracting officers
to rely on "gossip and innuendo," *RMS Indus.*, Comp. Gen. Dec. B-247229, 92-1
CPD ¶ 451. In that procurement the agency used the FAR definition but changed
"history of" to "reputation for." The GAO stated:

[W]e find nothing unlawful in the agency's taking into account, as one element of past performance, an offeror's reputation for reasonable and cooperative behavior and commitment to customer satisfaction. In the context of this [request for proposals], we understand the term "reputation" to refer to fact-based evaluations rather than mere hearsay. We note that [the protester] does not challenge the propriety of the agency's seeking references from prior contracts. Indeed, where, as here, the solicitation informs offerors that the references will be considered as part of the evaluation process, relying on such references is a common and proper part of proposal evaluation.

2. Relevance of the Data

FAR 15.305(a)(2)(i) requires agencies to consider the relevance of past performance information. Thus, it is improper to give performance on less relevant work the same weight as performance on highly relevant work. See *United Paradyne Corp.*, Comp. Gen. Dec. B-297758, 2006 CPD ¶ 47, granting a protest because the agency had averaged the past performance evaluations for highly relevant work and far less relevant work. See also *ASRC Research & Tech. Solutions, LLC*, Comp. Gen. Dec. B-400217, 2008 CPD ¶ 202 (evaluation unreasonable when agency did not consider the substantial difference in size between the awardee's past performance references and the size of the contemplated contract, as required by the solicitation); *DRS C3 Sys., LLC*, Comp. Gen. Dec. B-310825, 2008 CPD ¶ 103 (evaluation unreasonable when agency ignored assessment of poor performance on highly relevant contract); *Harbors Envtl. Servs., Inc.*, Comp. Gen. Dec. B-296176.2, 2005 CPD ¶ 222 (evaluation unreasonable when agency gave incumbent contractor and awardee identical ratings, although awardee's references were for services smaller and less complex than service being procured); *KMR, LLC*, Comp. Gen. Dec. B-292860, 2003 CPD ¶ 233 (evaluation unreasonable when solicitation stated evaluation would be based on performance of "same or similar" work and awardee's references were for different work).

Agencies have considerable discretion in determining what prior work will yield a meaningful assessment of the competence of the offeror to perform the contract being awarded, *ManTech Int'l Corp.*, Comp. Gen. Dec. B-311074, 2008 CPD ¶ 87; *Roy F. Weston, Inc.*, Comp. Gen. Dec. B-274945, 97-1 CPD ¶ 92. See *Apptis, Inc.*, Comp. Gen. Dec. B-299457, 2008 CPD ¶ 49, finding it proper to give more relevance to the amount of work with the agency itself. See also *Jason Assocs. Corp.*, Comp. Gen. Dec. B-278689, 98-1 CPD ¶ 67, holding that the source selection official had acted properly in reading reference questionnaires to ascertain which work was relevant. It has been held proper to base the entire past performance evaluation on the single most relevant contract, ignoring other work, *Braswell Servs. Group, Inc.*, Comp. Gen. Dec. B-278921.2, 98-2 CPD ¶ 10. The GAO has also denied protests when the agency determined that dissimilar work was relevant, *All Star Maint., Inc.*, Comp. Gen. Dec. B-271119, 96-1 CPD ¶ 278; *Hughes Missile Sys. Co.*, Comp. Gen. Dec. B-272418, 96-2 CPD ¶ 221. Similarly, a protest was denied when the agency considered the quality of prior work more relevant than the small size of the contracts on which the work was done, *SP Sys., Inc. v. United States,* 86 Fed. Cl. 1 (2009). Compare *Ogden Support Servs., Inc.,* Comp. Gen. Dec. B-270012.2, 96-1 CPD ¶ 137, granting a protest where the agency had considered dissimilar work relevant when the RFP had used an evaluation factor of "demonstrated successful performance on similar efforts." See also *PMT Servs., Inc.,* Comp. Gen. Dec. B-270538.2, 96-2 CPD ¶ 98, granting a protest because the agency had scored an offeror's past performance poor because it had no prior contracts of the same size as the current procurement. The GAO found that complexity of the work on prior contracts was more relevant than dollar value of the contracts. In one unusual situation, an agency properly determined that work on smaller projects was more relevant than work on larger projects because the contract to be awarded would require work on small projects, *J.C.N. Constr. Co. v. United States,* 60 Fed. Cl. 400 (2004); *J.C.N. Constr Co.,* Comp. Gen. Dec. B-293063, 2004 CPD ¶ 12.

The GAO has required that agencies consider past performance on work that is "too close at hand" to the current procurement. Thus, the GAO held that it was unreasonable to fail to obtain past performance information on the prior contract with the agency for the same services, *International Bus. Sys., Inc.,* Comp. Gen. Dec. B-275554, 97-1 CPD ¶ 114. The GAO granted the protest in part because of the fact that the contracting officer had also been the contracting officer on the prior contract and had recently written a letter stating that the offeror's performance on the prior contract had been "exemplary." The GAO stated the rule that "some information is simply too close at hand to require offerors to shoulder the inequities that spring from an agency's failure to obtain, and consider, the information." The same result was reached in *East-West Indus., Inc.,* Comp. Gen. Dec. B-297391.2, 2006 CPD ¶ 161 (prior contract with agency); *International Resource Recovery, Inc. v. United States,* 64 Fed. Cl. 150 (2005) (settlement agreement with agency replacing a default termination); *Seattle Security Servs., Inc. v. United States,* 45 Fed. Cl. 560 (2000) (prior contract with agency for same work); and *SCIENTECH, Inc.,* Comp. Gen. Dec. B-277805.2, 98-1 CPD ¶ 33 (recent contract with agency for same services).

This rule will not apply if the agency personnel conducting the procurement do not know of the offeror's past performance. See *MIL Corp.,* Comp. Gen. Dec. B-297508, 2006 CPD ¶ 34, stating:

> In those narrow instances where we have applied the "simply too close at hand" principle, we have required the protester to demonstrate that the outside information bearing on the offeror's proposal was not just known by the agency generally, but rather, that the information was known to the specific agency employees involved in the source selection process. For example, in *International Bus. Sys., Inc.,* the protester demonstrated that the contracting officer had first-hand knowledge of the protester's past performance of the required work; in *GTS Duratek,* [B-280511.2, Oct. 19, 1998, 98-2 CPD ¶ 130], the protester demonstrated that the agency failed to consider the offeror's performance of a prior contract where the contracting officer's technical representative

for the incumbent contract had personal knowledge of the offeror's prior performance and was a member of the technical evaluation team for the subject solicitation.

See also *Shaw-Parsons Infrastructure Recovery Consultants, LLC; Vanguard Recovery Assistance, Joint Venture*, Comp. Gen. Dec. B-401679.4, 2010 CPD ¶ 77 (rule was not violated when the evaluators did not know about incumbent's performance, even though the COTR for the incumbent contract was an advisor to the evaluation board); *Firestorm Wildfire Suppression, Inc.*, Comp. Gen. Dec. B-3120136, 2007 CPD ¶ 218 (rule did not apply when evidence did not show evaluators knew of report prepared by different agency, even though the report was provided to official of their own agency); *Paragon Sys., Inc.*, Comp. Gen. Dec. B-299548.2, 2007 CPD ¶ 178 ("too close" rule did not apply where comments written by agency inspectors critical of selectee's performance under previous task order had been lost, were not referred to in evaluation file, and were unknown to source selection authority, although known to the evaluators). Thus, GAO has not applied the rule on grounds that the agency should have known about the information.

It is common practice to describe what work is relevant in the RFP and agencies are required to follow that description in the evaluation process. In numerous procurements, the RFP states that references should be provided for "the same or similar work" as that being procured with guidance on the size of contracts that were performed. When such a description is included in the RFP, the agency will be required to apply it in the evaluation process. See *Honeywell Tech. Solutions, Inc.*, Comp. Gen. Dec. B-400771, 2009 CPD ¶ 49 (evaluation unreasonable when agency gave "excellent" rating when prior contracts were much smaller than proposed contract and RFP called for evaluation of "similar" work); *Continental RPVs*, Comp. Gen. Dec. B-292768.2, 2004 CPD ¶ 56 (evaluation unreasonable when agency gave the awardee the same low risk rating for past performance as it gave the incumbent, even though it appeared that the awardee had not done as much of the "same or similar" work as the incumbent); *Southwestern Bell Tel. Co.*, Comp. Gen. Dec. B-292476, 2003 CPD ¶ 177 (evaluation unreasonable when agency failed to consider awardee's record of integrity and business ethics, as required by RFP, and the awardee's record was problematical); *Martin Elecs., Inc.*, Comp. Gen. Dec. B-290846.3, 2003 CPD ¶ 6 (evaluation unreasonable when agency failed to consider negative past performance information with respect to contracts that were "recent" as defined by RFP); *Sonetronics, Inc.*, Comp. Gen. Dec. B-289459.2, 2002 CPD ¶ 48 (evaluation unreasonable when RFP contemplated evaluation on basis of "at least" three completed contracts for similar work and agency gave awardee perfect score for past performance based on only one completed contract for similar work); *Finlen Complex, Inc.*, Comp. Gen. Dec. B-288280, 2001 CPD ¶ 167 (agency gave past performance far less weight than indicated in solicitation); and *Meridian Mgmt. Corp.*, Comp. Gen. Dec. B-285127, 2000 CPD ¶ 121 (agency downgraded offeror for failure to submit references that were not required by RFP). However, a "same or similar" description does not require agency to review only identical work, *Tiger Truck LLC*, Comp. Gen. Dec. B-310759, 2008 CPD ¶ 44; *DGR Assocs., Inc.*, Comp. Gen. Dec. B-285428, 2000 CPD ¶ 145.

FAR 15.305(a)(2)(iii) states that agencies "should take into account . . . predecessor companies, key personnel . . . or subcontractors" when assessment of their performance is relevant. Prior to this regulation the GAO permitted agencies to include key personnel on the past performance assessment, *Technical Resources, Inc.*, Comp. Gen. Dec. B-253506, 93-2 CPD ¶ 176, or to exclude them from the assessment, *Hard Bodies, Inc.*, Comp. Gen. Dec. B-279543, 98-1 CPD ¶ 172. Under the current regulation key personnel can be evaluated even when this is not listed as an evaluation factor, *SDS Int'l v. United States*, 48 Fed. Cl. 742 (2001); *DRA Software Training*, Comp. Gen. Dec. B-289128, 2002 CPD ¶ 11. It is proper to evaluate a new company solely on the basis of the past performance of its key personnel, *JSW Maint., Inc.*, Comp. Gen. Dec. B-400581.5, 2009 CPD ¶ 182. See also *Lynwood Mach. & Eng'g, Inc.*, Comp. Gen. Dec. B-287652, 2001 CPD ¶ 138 (proper to evaluate past performance of "special project manager"); *General Atomics*, Comp. Gen. Dec. B-287348, 2001 CPD ¶ 169 (proper to evaluate past performance of a group of key personnel that had worked on project when the contract was held by another company); *SDS Int'l*, Comp. Gen. Dec. B-285822, 2000 CPD ¶ 167 (proper to evaluate past performance of one key person of newly formed company). On the other hand, it is also proper not to evaluate key personnel separately, *KIRA, Inc.*, Comp. Gen. Dec. B-287573, 2001 CPD ¶ 152, 43 GC ¶ 367; *Urban-Meridian Joint Venture*, Comp. Gen. Dec. B-287168, 2001 CPD ¶ 91; *SWR, Inc.*, Comp. Gen. Dec. B-286044.2, 2000 CPD ¶ 174.

It has also been held proper to evaluate past performance of subcontractors in evaluating a contractor, *Triad Logistics Servs. Corp.*, Comp. Gen. Dec. B-296511.3, 2005 CPD ¶ 189 (proper to rate contractor with no past performance record "very good" when major subcontractor had excellent ratings); *Information Tech. & Applications Corp. v. United States*, 51 Fed. Cl. 340 (2001) (even subcontractors performing minor elements of work may be evaluated); *Neal R. Gross & Co.*, Comp. Gen. Dec. B-275066, 97-1 CPD ¶ 30 (adverse performance rating proper even though poor performance was attributable to some extent to subcontractors, because the prime contractor always bears responsibility for the work of subcontractors); *Battelle Memorial Inst.*, Comp. Gen. Dec. B-278673, 98-1 CPD ¶ 107 (good past performance rating proper even though good performance was entirely the result of subcontractor effort).

Although the FAR is silent on the issue, agencies have also been permitted to evaluation the performance of parent companies and affiliates when their resources will be used to perform the contract. See *Humana Military Healthcare Servs.*, Comp. Gen. Dec. B-401652.2, 2009 CPD ¶ 219, stating:

> An agency properly may attribute the experience or past performance of a parent or affiliated company to an offeror where the firm's proposal demonstrates that the resources of the parent or affiliate will affect the performance of the offeror. *Perini/Jones, Joint Venture*, B-285906, Nov. 1, 2000, 2002 CPD ¶ 68 at 4. The relevant consideration is whether the resources of the parent or affiliated company – its workforce, management, facilities or other resources – will be provided or

relied upon for contract performance such that the parent or affiliate will have meaningful involvement in contract performance. *Ecompex, Inc.*, B-292865.4 et al., June 18, 2004, 2004 CPD ¶ 149 at 5.

See, however, *Health Net Fed. Servs., LLC*, Comp. Gen. Dec. B-401652.3, 2009 CPD ¶ 220, granting a protest because the agency gave credit for past performance of a parent company and affiliates without proof of what prior contracts they had performed or what work they would do on current contract. See also *Daylight Tree Serv. & Equip., LLC*, Comp. Gen. Dec. B-310808, 2008 CPD ¶ 23 (information on affiliated company at same address as offeror is relevant). If the agency finds no evidence that the resources of the parent or affiliate organization will be used and there is not other relevant past performance, it is proper to assign a neutral rating to the offeror, *Bering Straits Tech. Servs. LLC*, Comp. Gen. Dec. B-401560.3, 2009 CPD ¶ 201.

A number of agencies have used the questionable logic of treating the relevance of past performance as an assessment of the offeror's experience by giving offerors without much relevant work lower scores on their past performance evaluation, and this has been accepted by the GAO. See *ACS State Healthcare, LLC*, Comp. Gen. Dec. B-292981, 2004 CPD ¶ 57 (lower past performance rating justified by less relevant experience); *Five-R Co.*, Comp. Gen. Dec. B-288190, 2001 CPD ¶ 163 (proper to give only "satisfactory/confidence" score to protester because its past projects were not like work being procured); *Gulf Group, Inc.*, Comp. Gen. Dec. B-287697, 2001 CPD ¶ 135 (score lowered because relevance of past work was "limited"); *J.A. Jones Mgmt. Servs., Inc.*, Comp. Gen. Dec. B-284909.5, 2001 CPD ¶ 64 (assessment reduced because of less relevant past performance); *Birdwell Bros. Painting & Refinishing*, Comp. Gen. Dec. B-285035, 2000 CPD ¶ 129 (score lowered because no past work of the size and complexity of the instant contract); *Marathon Constr. Corp.*, Comp. Gen. Dec. B-284816, 2000 CPD ¶ 94 (score lowered because no work of the type called for by the instant contract); *Molina Eng'g, Ltd./Tri-J Indus., Inc. Joint Venture*, Comp. Gen. Dec. B-284895, 2000 CPD ¶ 86 (score of "amber/ high risk" based on lack of contracts of similar size and scope as instant contract); *Dellew Corp.*, Comp. Gen. Dec. B-284227, 2000 CPD ¶ 52 (assessment of higher performance risk than winning offeror because of lack of relevant work); *Clean Venture, Inc.*, Comp. Gen. Dec. B-284176, 2000 CPD ¶ 47 (score of "fair" for very good performance on contracts of less complexity than instant contract); *Champion Serv. Corp.*, Comp. Gen. Dec. B-284116, 2000 CPD ¶ 28 (higher performance risk because of less relevant work than winning contractor). Compare *Airwork Limited-Vinnell Corp. (a Joint Venture)*, Comp. Gen. Dec. B-285247, 2000 CPD ¶ 150, where the GAO agreed with the agency that it was not required to give the protester a higher past performance rating because it had more relevant work experience. A clearer way to evaluate the amount of experience of an offeror is to treat "experience" as a separate evaluation factor.

One way to ensure relevance is to evaluate past performance on only those contracts that were performed by the group that is proposed for the current procurement and that were for similar work. See, for example, *Robbins-Gioia, Inc.*, Comp. Gen. Dec. B-274318, 96-2 CPD ¶ 222, where the agency only considered contracts performed by the same division of the company; and *TESCO*, Comp. Gen. Dec. B-271756, 96-1 CPD ¶ 284, where the scope of work was narrowly defined. Similarly, in *Israel Aircraft Indus.*, Comp. Gen. Dec. B-274389, 97-1 CPD ¶ 41, the RFP stated that the agency would focus its evaluation of past performance risk on the offerors' and proposed subcontractors' histories of past performance relevant to the proposed effort, and stated detailed instructions regarding the information that offerors were to provide. In *EastCo Bldg. Servs., Inc.*, Comp. Gen. Dec. B-275334, 97-1 CPD ¶ 83, the GAO denied a protest where the agency had limited its evaluation of past performance to contracts of a comparable size to the procurement being undertaken. Compare *Computer Sys. Dev. Co.*, Comp. Gen. Dec. B-275356, 97-1 CPD ¶ 91, denying a protest where the agency gave the winning offeror high past performance ratings based on contracts much smaller than the one under consideration.

3. Corrective Action

FAR 15.305(a)(2)(ii) requires that offerors be permitted to submit information on corrective action that has been taken to overcome past performance problems, and agencies have lost protests for failure to tell an offeror that corrective action is necessary to cure a past performance problem, *Alliant Techsystems, Inc.*, Comp. Gen. Dec. B-260215.4, 95-2 CPD ¶ 79.

Agencies have been given broad discretion in assessing whether corrective action will overcome prior performance problems. See, for example, *Lockheed Martin MS2 Tactical Sys.*, Comp. Gen. Dec. B-400135, 2008 CPD ¶ 157, and *Parmatic Filter Corp.*, Comp. Gen. Dec. B-285288.3, 2001 CPD ¶ 71, where the agency determined that the corrective action of one offeror was more effective than the corrective action of the protester. There are numerous instances where the refusal to adjust past performance ratings to reflect corrective action has been upheld, *Day & Zimmermann Pantex Corp.*, Comp. Gen. Dec. B-286016, 2001 CPD ¶ 96 (agency discounted protester's claim that it had rectified poor prior performance); *GEC-Marconi Elec. Sys. Corp.*, Comp. Gen. Dec. B-276186, 97-2 CPD ¶ 23 (evaluators not convinced that on-time delivery on recent contracts demonstrated that offeror had corrected problems that led to late delivery on earlier contracts); *Laidlaw Envtl. Servs. (GS), Inc.*, Comp. Gen. Dec. B-271903, 96-2 CPD ¶ 75 (evaluators not convinced that corrective action would be effective); *Macon Apparel Corp.*, Comp. Gen. Dec. B-272162, 96-2 CPD ¶ 95 (evaluators not convinced that corrective action was sufficient to solve problems). In *Hughes Missile Sys. Co.*, Comp. Gen. Dec. B-272418, 96-2 CPD ¶ 221, the GAO denied a protest where the agency had adjusted a rating of one competitor based on corrective action but had refused to adjust the rating of another competitor that had overcome some of the problems encountered on a development contract by taking action on a follow-on productions contract. Compare *Trifax Corp.*, Comp. Gen. Dec. B-279561, 98-2 CPD ¶ 24, where a protest was granted because the agency had not properly rescored a proposal after it learned that prompt corrective action had been taken by the protester. See also *Savannah River Tank Closure,LLC*, Comp. Gen. Dec. B-400953, 2009 CPD ¶ 78, denying a protest where the agency had determined that the corrective action "adequately addressed the agency's concerns" but still view the prior problems as "unfavorable data."

The GAO and the Court of Federal Claims have also affirmed agency decisions to accept the corrective action taken by an offeror as curing the performance problems. See *Blackwater Lodge & Training Center, Inc. v. United States*, 86 Fed. Cl. 488 (2009), and *Blackwater Lodge & Training Center, Inc.*, Comp. Gen. Dec. B-311000.2, 2009 CPD ¶ 66, where the agency had assessed the performance risk as "low" after considering the offeror's new procedures to correct safety problems on past contracts. See also *CWIS, LLC*, Comp. Gen. Dec. B-287521, 2001 CPD ¶ 119 (winning offeror's score was reasonably increased based on corrective action); *Proteccion Total/Magnum Security, S.A.*, Comp. Gen. Dec. B-278129.4, 98-1 CPD ¶ 137 (agency had found that an offeror's prompt response to a cure notice demonstrated that its past performance was good); and *Chemical Demilitarization Assocs.*, Comp. Gen. Dec. B-277700, 98-1 CPD ¶ 171 (agency had found that past poor performance was based on poor specifications and the offeror had no further problems after the specifications were corrected).

4. Offerors with No Past Performance

41 U.S.C. § 405 states the following rule with regard to evaluating offerors where the agency has no past performance information:

> (j)(2) In the case of an offeror with respect to which there is no information on past contract performance or with respect to which information on past contract performance is not available, the offeror may not be evaluated favorably or unfavorably on the factor of past contract performance.

Initially the FAR implemented this statute by requiring that evaluation of past performance in this situation result in a rating of "neutral." However, the FAR Part 15 rewrite altered the FAR to adopt the statutory language. FAR 15.305(a)(2)(iv) now provides:

> In the case of an offeror without a record of relevant past performance or for whom information on past performance is not available, the offeror may not be evaluated favorably or unfavorably on past performance.

There are numerous cases affirming an agency's assigning a "neutral" rating because the offeror has no contracts or similar size or complexity. See, for example, *Commissioning Solutions Global, LLC*, Comp. Gen. Dec. B-401553, 2009 CPD ¶ 210 (all three referenced contracts much smaller than instant procurement); *CMC & Maint., Inc.*,

Comp. Gen. Dec. B-292081, 2003 CPD ¶ 107 (referenced contracts smaller and dissimilar from instant procurement); *Kalman & Co.*, Comp. Gen. Dec. B-287442.2, 2002 CPD ¶ 63 (no contracts of similar size or similarity with instant procurement); *MCS of Tampa, Inc.*, Comp. Gen. Dec. B-288271.5, 2002 CPD ¶ 52 (two referenced contracts were smaller and no information could be obtained on only similar contract). Similarly, the GAO has affirmed "neutral" ratings when an offeror has no contracts that have been completed within a reasonable time of the competition. See *Futurecom, Inc.*, Comp. Gen. Dec. B-400730.2, 2009 CPD ¶ 42 ("neutral" rating appropriate when offeror has no relevant contracts that have been completed in last three years). In a questionable decision, the GAO affirmed the use of a "neutral" rating on one reference for which no information could be obtained although information was received from two other references, *Chicataw Constr., Inc.*, Comp. Gen. Dec. B-289592, 2002 CPD ¶ 62.

This rule covers not only offerors with no relevant past performance but also offerors where the agency is unable to obtain data. See *Advanced Data Concepts, Inc.*, Comp. Gen. Dec. B-277801.4, 98-1 CPD ¶ 145, holding that it was proper to give an offeror a "neutral" rating when offices in the same agency failed to complete reference questionnaires, stating:

> [T]here is no legal requirement that all past performance references be included in a valid review of past performance. *Dragon Servs., Inc.*, B-255354, Feb. 25, 1994, 94-1 CPD ¶ 151 at 8; *Questech, Inc.*, B-236028, Nov. 1, 1989, 89-2 CPD ¶ 407 at 3. For our Office to sustain a protest challenging the failure to obtain or consider a reference's assessment of past performance, a protester must show unusual factual circumstances that convert the failure to a significant inequity for the protester. *International Bus. Sys., Inc.*, B-275554, Mar. 3, 1997, 97-1 CPD ¶ 114 at 5. The record here shows that the agency contacted each of [the protester's] references, and made at least an initial attempt to obtain the information properly identified by [the protester] in its proposal. When the agency did not receive responses, the agency followed the RFP-described procedure of assigning a neutral rating in this area.

See *Bering Straits Tech. Servs., LLC*, Comp. Gen. Dec. B-401560.3, 2009 CPD ¶ 201, affirming a "neutral" rating when the protester did not show that affiliated companies would perform any part of the work and proposed a project manager that had only worked on a small contract that required similar work to the instance procurement. See also *Herley Indus., Inc.*, Comp. Gen. Dec. B-400736.2, 2009 CPD ¶ 48, holding it proper to give an offeror a "neutral" rating when it had not furnished past performance information on two of the three elements of the work. However, a neutral rating should not be assigned if an offeror intentionally fails to submit required past performance information. See *Forest Regeneration Servs. LLC*, Comp. Gen. Dec. B-290998, 2002 CPD ¶ 187, stating:

> [A]n offeror cannot simply choose to withhold past performance information — and thereby obtain a neutral rating — where the solicitation expressly states that the information should be furnished, and where the information is readily available to the offeror. *Menendez-Donnell & Assocs.*, B-286599, Jan. 16, 2001, 2001 CPD ¶ 15 at 4.

The GAO has accorded agencies wide discretion in assessing the impact of lack of relevant past performance. Thus, the GAO has agreed that an "excellent" rating on past performance can be considered superior to a "neutral" rating, *Engineering & Computation, Inc.*, Comp. Gen. Dec. B-275180.2, 97-1 CPD ¶ 47. The GAO also stated that an evaluation of "good" past performance may be considered to be superior to an evaluation of "neutral" past performance. See *Excalibur Sys., Inc.*, Comp. Gen. Dec. B-272017, 96-2 CPD ¶ 13, stating:

> Thus, where an RFP identifies past performance and price as the evaluation criteria and indicates that an offeror with good past performance can expect a higher rating than an offeror without such a record of performance, proposals must be evaluated on that basis, and ultimately the selection official must decide, if the offeror with the better past performance rating is not the low-cost offeror, whether the more costly offeror represents the best value to the government in light of the better past performance rating.
>
> In general, we do not view RFP evaluation schemes that specify a "neutral" rating for vendors with no past performance record, *see, e.g., Quality Fabricators, Inc.*, B-271431; B-271431.3, June 25, 1996, 96-2 CPD [¶ 22]; *Caltech Serv. Corp.*, B-261044.4, Dec. 14, 1995, 95-2 CPD ¶ 285, as precluding this same type of source selection decision-making. That is, we think that the use of a neutral rating approach, to avoid penalizing a vendor without prior experience and thereby enhance competition, does not preclude, in a best value procurement, a determination to award to a higher-priced offeror with a good past performance record over a lower-cost vendor with a neutral past performance rating. Indeed such a determination is inherent in the concept of best value.

Unfortunately, in the *Excalibur* procurement, the contracting officer had stated in the RFP that offerors with no past performance record would be evaluated "solely on the basis of price." The GAO did not object to this questionable evaluation technique but affirmed the agency's award on the basis of price alone.

The GAO has rejected the contention that a contract should not be awarded to an offeror with a neutral rating based on no relevant past performance, *M&M Ret. Enters., LLC*, Comp. Gen. Dec. B-297282, 2005 CPD ¶ 224. The GAO has also affirmed giving an offeror with no performance record a "good" rating when that rating connoted "adequately sufficient," *Oceaneering Int'l, Inc.*, Comp. Gen. Dec. B-278126, 98-1 CPD ¶ 133. The GAO explained that "good" in the rating scheme was not substantively different from "neutral" when it meant merely adequate. See also *HoveCo*, Comp. Gen. Dec. B-298697, 2006 CPD ¶ 171, holding that there was little difference between a rating of "unknown confidence" and a rating of "little confidence." However, it is clearly improper to give an offeror with no performance record a "red" rating, *MIL Corp.*, Comp. Gen. Dec. B-294836, 2005 CPD ¶ 29.

When agencies evaluate past performance in terms of performance risk, there is some question as to how an offeror with no record of past performance should be scored. See *Phillips Indus., Inc.*, Comp. Gen. Dec. B-280645, 98-2 CPD ¶ 74, where the protester questioned the legality of a finding that such an offeror posed a performance risk but the GAO denied the protest because the contract had been awarded to a higher-priced offeror with excellent past performance, stating:

> We share the protester's concern with the language in the selection decision documentation that Phillips and Landscapers Supply, vendors with no performance histories, pose a "performance risk" or a "great risk" for award. As the protester argues, a company like Phillips which may be new to government contracting should not be disqualified from award merely because it lacks a performance history. As the agency recognizes, such an approach would be inconsistent with the FAR and the RFP. FAR § 15.305(a)(2)(iv) provides that, for past performance evaluations, in the case of an offeror without a record of relevant past performance or for whom information on past performance is not available, the offeror may not be evaluated favorably or unfavorably on past performance. The RFP ABVM clause also states that lack of performance history is not grounds for disqualification for award. . . . Nonetheless, as explained above, the contracting officer's decision to award to the slightly higher-priced firm with an established excellent performance history, rather than a lower-priced vendor with no performance history with the agency, was permissible and reasonable.

C. Experience

As noted above, the experience of the offerors is evaluated either as part of the evaluation of past performance or as a separate evaluation factor. The latter practice is superior because it allows the agency to make a separate assessment of whether the offeror's have performed work that is similar to the work being procured and to use the fact that they have such experience in determining the risk that they will not successfully accomplish the work. When experience is stated as a separate factor, the agency must demonstrate that it actually evaluated this factor, *Bio-Rad Labs., Inc.*, Comp. Gen. Dec. B-297553, 2007 CPD ¶ 58. However, if an offeror fails to provide the information on experience requested by the RFP, the agency can drop the offeror from the competition, *Prudent Techs., Inc.*, Comp. Gen. Dec. B-297425, 2006 CPD ¶16. See also *Sam Facility Mgmt., Inc.*, Comp. Gen. Dec. B-292237, 2003 CPD ¶ 147, where the agency properly downgraded the protester because it had no provided the required details on past contracts in the experience section of its proposal – even though the details were in the past performance section. The GAO commented that "agencies evaluating one section of a proposal are not obligated to go in search of needed information." See also *JAVIS Automation & Eng'g, Inc.*, Comp. Gen. Dec. B-290434, 2002 CPD ¶ 140 (offeror downgraded for lack of details required by RFP).

When experience is to be evaluated, the standard to be used is normally stated in the RFP and agencies must adhere to this description. See *Consolidated Eng'g Servs., Inc.*, Comp. Gen. Dec. B-311313, 2008 CPD ¶ 146, sustaining a protest where the agency downgraded the protester because it had not obtained its experience on a single contract when the RFP contained no "one contract" standard. See also *Doyon-Am. Mech., JV; NAJV, LLC*, Comp. Gen. Dec. B-310003, 2008 CPD ¶ 50 (sustaining a protest because the agency evaluated experience of parent/affiliated companies when RFP stated only projects on which offeror served as prime contractor or teaming partner would be considered); *GlassLock, Inc.*, Comp. Gen. Dec. B-299931, 2007 CPD ¶ 216 (sustaining a protest because the agency gave double credit for good experience by including it in the evaluation of a proposed project plan factor as well as the experience factor); *Data Mgmt. Servs. Joint Venture*, Comp. Gen. Dec. B-299702, 2007 CPD ¶ 139 (agency improperly considered experience on smaller projects when RFP required experience of projects of "similar" magnitude but protest denied for lack of prejudice); Court of Federal Claims held agency interpreted RFP properly in *Data Mgmt. Servs. Joint Venture v. United States*, 78 Fed. Cl. 366 (2007); *L-3 Communications Titan Corp.*, Comp. Gen. Dec. B-299317, 2007 CPD ¶ 66, *recons. denied*, 2007 CPD ¶ 121 (sustaining a protest because the agency concluded offerors had equal experience when one had more and the RFP stated that more credit would be given "the greater the extent" of experience); *KIC Dev., LLC*, B-297425.2, 2006 CPD ¶ 27 (sustaining a protest because the agency did not evaluate the experience of subcontractors and key personnel as permitted by RFP); *Myers Investigative & Security Servs., Inc.*, Comp. Gen. Dec. B-288468, 2001 CPD ¶ 189 (agency improperly evaluated only experience with agency when there was no such RFP statement); *Mechanical Contractors, S.A.*, Comp. Gen. Dec. B-277916, 97-2 CPD ¶ 121 (sustaining a protest because the agency gave no weight to industry certifications as demonstrating experience although the RFP required information as to such certifications). This requirement to follow the RFP description is enforced loosely by reading the description broadly. See *RCL Components, Inc.*, Comp. Gen. Dec. B-400175, 2009 CPD ¶ 98, finding the agency had properly evaluated experience because the RFP description of the past performance evaluation included a statement that relevancy would be determined by the "magnitude of effort and complexities."

As in the case of past performance, agencies are accorded considerable discretion in assessing the relevance of past work to the work to be performed on the contract. See *K-Mar Indus., Inc.*, Comp. Gen. Dec. B-400487, 2009 CPD ¶ 159, stating:

> The evaluation of proposals is a matter within the discretion of the contracting agency since the agency is responsible for defining its needs and the best method of accommodating them. In reviewing an agency's evaluation, we will not reevaluate proposals, but instead will examine the agency's evaluation to ensure that it was reasonable and consistent with the solicitation's evaluation criteria. *Dual, Inc.*, 98-1 CPD ¶ 146 at 3. Where a solicitation requires the evaluation of the offerors' experience, an agency has broad discretion to determine whether a particular contract is relevant to an evaluation of experience. See *All Phase Envtl., Inc.*, B-292919 et al., Feb. 4, 2004, 2004 CPD ¶ 62 at 3. An offeror's mere disagreement with the agency does not render the evaluation unreasonable. *Dual, Inc., supra*.

See *Zolon Tech, Inc.*, Comp. Gen. Dec. B-299904.2, 2007 CPD ¶ 183, where the GAO denied a protest when the agency surprisingly downgraded the protester on experience because it intended to use a consultant with experience rather than having employees with the requisite experience. See also *Alpha Genesis, Inc.*, Comp. Gen. Dec. B-299859, 2007 CPD ¶ 167 (agency was free to evaluate only the amount of experience not the quality of the experience when the RFP narrowly stated the evaluation factor); *Financial & Realty Services, LLC*, Comp. Gen. Dec. B-299605.2, 2007 CPD ¶ 161 (agency properly downgraded protester because it did not comply with RFP requirement to match its experience with each contract task); *MarLaw-Arco MFPD Mgmt.*, Comp. Gen. Dec. B-291875, 2003 CPD ¶ 85 (agency properly did not give experience with agency work higher value that experience with other comparable work); *M. Erdal Kamisli, Ltd.*, Comp. Gen. Dec. B-291522, 2003 CPD ¶ 19 (agency permitted to give higher experience rating to offeror that listed the most projects on which it had comparable experience). However, the GAO will grant a protest if the evaluation is irrational. See, for example, *Cooperativa Muratori Riuniti*, Comp. Gen. Dec. B-294980, 2005 CPD ¶ 21, where the GAO granted a protest when the agency downgraded the protester because no single referenced contract was of the magnitude of the current procurement but that procurement called for multiple items of work and the protester had numerous prior contracts whose work cumulated to the magnitude being procured. Similarly, in *Olympus Bldg. Servs., Inc.*, Comp. Gen. Dec. B-285351, 2000 CPD ¶ 178, a protest was granted when the agency gave experience ratings on the basis of the size of buildings that had been managed and averaged the ratings, but did not inform the offerors of this scoring method, with the result that the protester submitted more projects than required, yielding a lower experience assessment.

Agencies frequently evaluate the experience of prospective subcontractors and this is proper when there is some indication in the RFP that it will be done, *PAI Corp. v. United States*, 2009 U.S. Claims Lexis 320, *aff'd*, 614 F.3d 1347 (Fed. Cir. 2010). The GAO has gone further and held that subcontractor experience can be evaluated even when the RFP does not provide for such evaluation. See *Kellogg Brown & Root Servs., Inc.*, Comp. Gen. Dec. B-298694.7, 2007 CPD ¶ 124, stating:

> An agency may base the evaluation of corporate experience on the experience of subcontractors when the subcontractors are to do the work to which the experience is applicable, so long as the solicitation allows for the use of subcontractors and does not prohibit the consideration of a subcontractor's experience in the evaluation. *Loral Sys. Co.*, B-270755, Apr. 17, 1996, 96-1 CPD ¶ 241 at 5; *Seair Transport Servs., Inc.*, B-252266, June 14, 1993, 93-1 CPD ¶ 458 at 5.

This reasoning has also been applied to the evaluation of the experience of key personnel when the RFP does not specifically state that such information would be considered in the evaluation of the offeror's experience, *Dix Corp.*, Comp. Gen. Dec. B-293964, 2004 CPD ¶ 143. However, there is no requirement that an agency evaluate key personnel as part of the evaluation of corporate experience, *Blue Rock Structures, Inc.*, Comp. Gen. Dec. B-287960.2, 2001 CPD ¶ 184.

When an offeror has no experience but intends to use subcontractors with good experience, an agency can reach a balanced evaluation of the overall experience. See *IPlus, Inc.*, Comp. Gen. Dec. B-298020, 2006 CPD ¶ 90, stating:

> There is no requirement, however, that an agency must directly "credit" or otherwise substitute a subcontractor/mentor's experience or past performance for a prime contractor/protege that lacks past performance of its own. Instead, an agency may consider the prime contractor/protege's lack of experience and past performance and balance that information against the subcontractor/mentor's experience and past performance. *J.A. Farrington Janitorial Servs.*, B-296875, Oct. 18, 2005, 2005 CPD ¶ 187 at 5.

This same reasoning applies when a agency is evaluating the experience of key personnel that is gained working for another contractor. See *STEM Int'l, Inc.*, Comp. Gen. Dec. B-295471, 2005 CPD ¶ 19, where the GAO concurred with the agency's balancing of good experience of key personnel with no experience of the protester.

Where a solicitation indicates that experience will be evaluated, the agency may evaluate the extent to which an offeror's specific experience is directly related to the work required by the contract even when there is no statement in the RFP to that effect. See *International Bus. & Tech. Consultants, Inc.*, Comp. Gen. Dec. B-310424.2, 2008 CPD ¶ 185, where the agency properly considered whether the offerors had experience performing the precise work called for by the contract. See also *American Artisan Productions, Inc.*, Comp. Gen. Dec. B-293801.2, 2004 CPD ¶ 127 (proper to evaluate whether offerors had experience in setting up specific types of exhibits called for by RFP); *High Country Contracting*, Comp. Gen. Dec. B-278649, 98-1 CPD ¶ 39 (contracting officer reasonably determined that the protester's proposal posed a moderate risk because it had limited relevant construction experience); *Dual, Inc.*, Comp. Gen. Dec. B-279295, 98-1 CPD ¶ 146 (agency reasonably determined that protester did not have relevant corporate experience in a required area); *ECG, Inc.*, Comp. Gen. Dec. B-277738, 97-2 CPD ¶ 153 (agency reasonably determined that although experience on one small project was not similar in size, scope, or complexity to that described in the RFP, experience of proposed subcontractors had corporate experience on projects similar in size, scope, and complexity to that described in the RFP). See also *WECO Cleaning Specialists, Inc.*, Comp. Gen. Dec. B-279305, 98-1 CPD ¶ 154 (protester's proposal failed to elaborate on the scope and complexity of its prior experience, and the information provided "was very vague"); *Centra Tech., Inc.*, Comp. Gen. Dec. B-274744, 97-1 CPD ¶ 35 (protester's experience was rated as only "fair" and awardee's rating was "excellent" because protester and its proposed subcontractors had limited experience compared to the incumbent awardee); *EastCo Bldg. Servs., Inc.*, Comp. Gen. Dec. B-275334, 97-1 CPD ¶ 83 (protester's proposal downgraded based on lack of certain experience under three-year contracts); *Engineering & Computation, Inc.*, Comp. Gen. Dec. B-275180.2, 97-1 CPD ¶ 47 (incumbent contractor was rated "excellent" for relevant corporate experience as opposed to the protester, a new corporate entity, which was rated "neutral" for this evaluation factor because it had no prior corporate experience).

Proposals must be treated equally under the experience evaluation factor. Unequal treatment was found in *Ahtna Support & Training Servs., LLC*, Comp. Gen. Dec. B-400947.2, 2009 CPD ¶ 119 (agency assessed the experience of sub-contractor of one offeror but not of protester); *Ashe Facility Servs., Inc.*, Comp. Gen. Dec. B-292218.3, 2004 CPD ¶ 80 (agency assessed the experience of key personnel of one offeror, but not the protester, in its evaluation of experience). Similarly, in *U.S. Property Mgmt. Serv. Corp.*, Comp. Gen. Dec. B-278727, 98-1 CPD ¶ 88, the GAO found that the agency unequally evaluated the experience of the protester and the awardee where both firms were newly formed corporations, yet the agency did not downgrade the awardee's proposal, as it did protester's, for not evidencing significant corporate experience. See also *Aerospace Design & Fabrication, Inc.*, Comp. Gen. Dec. B-278896.2, 98-1 CPD ¶ 139, finding that ambiguous terms in the solicitation resulted in an unequal competition. Based on RFP limitations of five pages discussing the offeror's relevant experience and past performance and two references on forms supplied within the solicitation for each prime and subcontractor participating in the proposal, the protester included two references for itself and two references for each of its subcontractors and used its five-page discussion to expand on the information related to its two references and those of its subcontractors. In contrast, the awardee, which did not propose to use subcontractors, included the two required references but used its five-page discussion to expand on those two references and on its experience with six other related contracts.

D. Key Personnel

When a agency decides to evaluate key personnel as a separate factor, it should assess the experience of the personnel rather than merely reviewing resumes. See, for example, *Savannah River Alliance, LLC*, B-311126, 2008 CPD ¶ 88, where the agency evaluated resumes, made reference checks, reviewed letters of commitment and then required the key personnel to attend an oral presentation where they worked sample tasks. The GAO rejected the protester's contention that the evaluation was not correctly done when the agency concluded that the protester's personnel were not as experienced as the winning offeror. See also *PAI Corp.*, Comp. Gen. Dec. B-298349, 2006 CPD ¶ 124, where the GAO agreed with the agency's determination that certain experience of a key person did not qualify as the type of experience required by the RFP; and *Base Techs., Inc.*, Comp. Gen. Dec. B-293061.2, 2004 CPD ¶ 31, where the GAO denied a protest arguing that the experience of key personnel should not have been considered because it was not explicitly stated in the RFP. The disadvantage of only reviewing resumes is seen in *DEI Consulting*, Comp. Gen. Dec. B-401258, 2009 CPD ¶ 151, where the agency downgraded the protester because of lack of full information in the resume. The GAO denied a protest of this procedure but it is apparent that the agency acted without adequate information as to the qualifications of the key person in arriving at this result. Compare *Trammell Crow Co.*, Comp. Gen. Dec. B-311314.2, 2008

CPD ¶ 129, holding that the agency was required to disclose the downgrading of key personnel in discussions because they were significant weaknesses.

It is proper to evaluate a key person even if the agency knows that he will not be assigned to the contract for its full duration, *U.S. Facilities, Inc.*, Comp. Gen. Dec. B-293029, 2004 CPD ¶ 17 (project manager had been promoted but was committed to stay with project until a suitable replacement was found). Conversely, it is within the discretion to drop a competitor when an agency finds that the project manager will leave the company after the contract work has commenced successfully, *S. C. Myers & Assocs., Inc.*, Comp. Gen. Dec. B-286297, 2001 CPD ¶ 16. See also *MCR Eng'g Co.*, Comp. Gen. Dec. B-287164, 2001 CPD ¶ 82, where it was found proper to ignore the fact that former key employees had assisted the offeror in achieving good past performance because it had continued to perform well after they left the company.

E. Technical and Management Plans

Agencies have very broad discretion in evaluating technical and management plans. See *Hernandez Eng'g, Inc.*, Comp. Gen. Dec. B-286336, 2001 CPD ¶ 89, stating:

> The evaluation of technical proposals is primarily the responsibility of the contracting agency. Our Office will not make an independent determination of the merits of technical proposals; rather, we will examine the record to ensure that the agency's evaluation was reasonable and consistent with the stated evaluation criteria. *Litton Sys., Inc.*, B-237596.3, Aug. 8, 1990, 90-2 CPD ¶ 115 at 8. A protester's mere disagreement with the agency's evaluation does not render the evaluation unreasonable. *SWR Inc.*, B-286044.2, B-286044.3, Nov. 1, 2000, 2000 CPD ¶ 174 at 3.

As discussed in Chapter 2, there are two distinct types of technical and management plans that are used as evaluation factors. The first type is the description of the work that is being *offered* to meet the agency's needs. The second type is the description of the processes that will be used that demonstrates that the offeror has the *capability* to perform the work. This latter type of plan is generally submitted under an evaluation factor described as "understanding the work" or "soundness of approach."

1. Description of Work

The evaluation of the work that an offeror proposes to do to meet the requirements of the RFP is primarily within the province of the technical staff of the agency. Thus, neither the GAO nor the Court of Federal Claims will overturn such a technical evaluation unless it is clearly irrational. See, for example, *Savannah River Tank Closure, LLC*, Comp. Gen. Dec. B-400953, 2009 CPD ¶ 78 (winner proposed superior technical approach); *Savannah River Alliance, LLC*, Comp. Gen. Dec. B-311126, 2008 CPD ¶ 88 (winner offered superior key personnel); *Wackenhut*

Int'l, Inc., Comp. Gen. Dec. B-299022, 2007 CPD ¶ 44 (excessively long work-week); *Smiths Detection, Inc.*, Comp. Gen. Dec. B-298838, 2007 CPD ¶ 5 (inferior software design); *Gemma-CCC*, Comp. Gen. Dec. B-297447.2, 2006 CPD ¶ 182 (failure to submit required data showing that proposed product met agency requirements); *Integrate, Inc.*, Comp. Gen. Dec. B-296526, 2005 CPD ¶ 154 (failure to show that proposed software met RFP requirements); *TDF Corp.*, Comp. Gen. Dec. B-288392, 2001 CPD ¶ 178 (inadequate staffing); *SOS Interpreting, Ltd.*, Comp. Gen. Dec. B-287505, 2001 CPD ¶ 104 (inadequate system for handling sensitive information); *United Defense LP*, Comp. Gen. Dec. B-286925.3, 2001 CPD ¶ 75 (offered product inferior in a number of ways to that of competitor); *ABIC, Ltd.*, Comp. Gen. Dec. B-286460, 2001 CPD ¶ 46 (insufficient staffing and inadequate staff coverage of key work); *Coastal Drilling, Inc.*, Comp. Gen. Dec. B-285085.3, 2000 CPD ¶ 130 (offered product did not meet a mandatory requirement); *AMS Mech. Sys., Inc.*, Comp. Gen. Dec. B-281136, 99-2 CPD ¶ 59 (offered product did not appear to meet requirements and offeror did not furnish supporting information to demonstrate that it did); *Joint Threat Servs.*, Comp. Gen. Dec. B-278168, 98-1 CPD ¶ 18 (inadequate staffing). Compare *Meridian Mgmt. Corp.*, Comp. Gen. Dec. B-281287.10, 2001 CPD ¶ 5, where a protest was sustained because the agency had given a high rating to a technical proposal that did not contain employees with skills necessary for the job; *OneSource Energy Servs., Inc.*, Comp. Gen. Dec. B-283445, 2000 CPD ¶ 109, where a protest was sustained because a low rating for inadequate staffing was based on the agency's estimate of staffing needs without analysis of the proposal to determine if it was based on a "unique approach" or skilled staff; *ATA Defense Indus., Inc.*, Comp. Gen. Dec. B-282511, 99-2 CPD ¶ 33, where a protest was sustained because the agency gave the winning offeror a high technical rating that was not supported by the facts; and *Consolidated Eng'g Servs., Inc.*, Comp. Gen. Dec. B-279565.2, 99-1 CPD ¶ 75, where a protest was sustained because the agency did not give the protester credit for beneficial features in its technical proposal.

It is proper to make a risk assessment of the probability that a proposed management or technical approach will create performance problems. See, for example, *Trend Western Tech. Corp.*, Comp. Gen. Dec. B-275395.2, 97-1 CPD ¶ 201, denying a protest that the agency had assessed a plan as having moderate risk because the staffing level was low. In *TEAM Support Servs., Inc.*, Comp. Gen. Dec. B-279379.2, 98-1 CPD ¶ 167, the agency downgraded the protester's proposal because the protester did not propose to use permanent employees for general on-site labor. The GAO found reasonable the evaluator's assessment that the management approach created the risk that maintenance and operation tasks would be unacceptably delayed because the local construction industry would be competing for the same laborers and the evaluator believed it unlikely that the protester could obtain local labor in a timely manner. See also *Ultra Elecs. Ocean Sys., Inc.*, Comp. Gen. Dec. B-400219, 2008 CPD ¶ 183 (proposed revisions to the design of product created potential performance risk); *Compunetix, Inc.*, Comp. Gen. Dec. B-298489.4, 2007 CPD ¶ 12 (significant modification needed for product posed a technical risk); *Sensis Corp.*, Comp. Gen. Dec. B-265790.2, 96-1 CPD ¶ 77 (moderate risk because the protester did not have a mature software development process); and *Hydro Eng'g, Inc. v. United States*, 37 Fed. Cl. 448 (1997) (specific elements of a technical and management proposal created a risk of timely performance and technical compliance).

When an agency evaluates the actual product to be delivered, it is highly unlikely that a protest will be successful. See, for example, *MD Helicopters, Inc.*, Comp. Gen. Dec. B-298502, 2006 CPD ¶ 164, denying a protest where the agency based its technical evaluation on four hours of flight testing of competitive helicopters.

2. Understanding the Work

A less rational, but common, type of evaluation of technical and management plans assesses whether the offeror has proven that it has the requisite capability by demonstrating an understanding of the work in the way the plan is written. Agencies also have wide latitude in making this subjective type of evaluation. See, for example, *Government Acquisitions, Inc.*, Comp. Gen. Dec. B-401048, 2009 CPD ¶ 137 (offeror failed to submit resumes required in management plan); *Kuhana/Spectrum Joint Venture, LLC*, Comp. Gen. Dec. B-400803, 2009 CPD ¶ 36 (management plan misdescribed mentor/protégé program and omitted key personnel); *LOGMET, LLC*, Comp. Gen. Dec. B-400355.2, 2008 CPD ¶ 175 (proposed staffing plan showed lack of understanding of requirements); *Professional Performance Dev. Group, Inc.*, Comp. Gen. Dec. B-311273, 2008 CPD ¶ 101 (numerous informational deficiencies in plans); Comp. Gen. Dec. B-309964, 2007 CPD ¶ 217 (inadequate coverage of required technical maturation plans); *Operational Resource Consultants, Inc.*, Comp. Gen. Dec. B-299131.1, 2007 CPD ¶ 38 (technical proposal failed to discuss some required areas); *Bernard Cap Co.*, Comp. Gen. Dec. B-297168, 2005 CPD ¶ 204 (manufacturing approach not as sound as winning offeror); *TekStar, Inc.*, Comp. Gen. Dec. B-295444, 2005 CPD ¶ 53 (technical and management proposals did not demonstrate capability); *LifeCare, Inc.*, Comp. Gen. Dec. B-291672, 2003 CPD ¶ 95 (poorly written and incomplete technical proposal); *Chart Indus., Inc.*, Comp. Gen. Dec. B-288248, 2001 CPD ¶ 174 (technical plan very general, lacking sufficient detail); *Strategic Resources, Inc.*, Comp. Gen. Dec. B-287398, 2001 CPD ¶ 131 (management plan lacked detail in dealing with staffing issues); *Fisherman's Boat Shop, Inc.*, Comp. Gen. Dec. B-287592, 2001 CPD ¶ 123 (required network schedule omitted option items and merely added start and finish dates to items listed in RFP); *Evolving Resources, Inc.*, Comp. Gen. Dec. B-287178, 2001 CPD ¶ 83 (management plan failed to adequately describe its process for managing task orders); *ITT Fed. Sys. Int'l Corp.*, Comp. Gen. Dec. B-285176.4, 2001 CPD ¶ 45 (lack of sufficient detail in technical proposal); *Calian Tech. (US), Ltd.*, Comp. Gen. Dec. B-284814, 2000 CPD ¶ 85 (technical plan showed lack of understanding of work to be performed); *Rotech Med. Corp.*, Comp. Gen. Dec. B-283295.2, 99-2 CPD ¶ 86 (technical proposal "disorganized, confusing, and largely bereft of narrative detail"); *Scientific & Commercial Sys. Corp.*, Comp. Gen. Dec. B-283160, 99-2 CPD ¶ 78 (technical proposal lacked detail in discussion of one task); *Manufacturing Eng'g Sys., Inc.*, Comp. Gen. Dec. B- 287074, 99-2 CPD ¶ 58 (technical proposal lacked complete explanation of approach); *Johnson Controls, Inc.*, Comp. Gen. Dec. B-282326, 99-2 CPD ¶ 6 (some pages of proposal unreadable); *Companie De Asesoria Y Comercio, S.A.*, Comp. Gen. Dec. B-278358, 98-1 CPD ¶ 26 (technical proposal lacked specific details and descriptions); *Intown Properties, Inc.*, Comp. Gen. Dec. B-272524, 96-2 CPD ¶ 149 (management plan merely repeated solicitation without providing specific information); *Quality Elevator Co.*, Comp. Gen. Dec. B-271899, 96-2 CPD ¶ 89 (management plan lacked detail).

The great latitude accorded to agency in this area is demonstrated by the cases that deny protests even though the agency has awarded the contract to a company that did not submit a plan with the detail required by the RFP. See, for example, *GTE Hawaiian Tel. Co.*, Comp. Gen. Dec. B-276487.2, 97-2 CPD ¶ 21, where the agency had required each offeror to address compliance with more than 1,300 technical requirements but had imposed an 800-page limit on technical proposals. The GAO denied a protest that the winning offeror had not addressed all the requirements. See also *JW Assocs., Inc.*, Comp. Gen. Dec. B-275209, 97-1 CPD ¶ 57, where the GAO initially granted a protest, in part because the agency had not documented its evaluation of a technical plan, but subsequently denied the protest when the agency reevaluated the technical plan of the winning offeror and determined that it was adequate even though it contained far less detail than the plan of the protester, and *SDS Int'l, Inc.*, Comp. Gen. Dec. B-279361, 98-2 CPD ¶ 7, affirming an agency's evaluation of a technical proposal as acceptable even though it did not describe the technical approach to be used as called for in the RFP, reasoning that the offeror had complied with the RFP by stating that it was capable of performing and that the contract specification was so detailed that there was little room for describing a technical approach different from that specification.

Disparate scoring has not generally been grounds for protest. See *Matrix Int'l Logistics, Inc.*, Comp. Gen. Dec. B-272388.2, 97-2 CPD ¶ 89, where the agency had evaluated one proposal as "excellent" and "clearly superior" to another in the initial procurement but had evaluated the same proposal as "good" and the other proposal as "excellent" in a resolicitation following a sustained protest. The GAO did not comment on the disparity in evaluations in denying the protest on the resolicitation. Compare *Dynalantic Corp.*, Comp. Gen. Dec. B-274944.2, 97-1 CPD ¶ 101, where the GAO made a detailed review of the agency's evaluation of the protester's technical and management proposal and determined that the identified deficiencies were easily correctable and, thus, that the protester should not have been dropped from the competitive range. See also *ITT Federal Servs. Int'l Corp.*, Comp. Gen. Dec. B-296783, 2007 CPD ¶ 43 (protest granted where staffing plan was downgraded because it had less staff than irrational government estimate); *Engineering Mgmt. & Integration, Inc.*, Comp. Gen. Dec. B-291672, 2003 CPD ¶ 95 (protest granted where offeror was rejected for not furnishing required staffing information but had actually furnished more complete information in a different form).

When an agency is evaluating understanding of the work in a cost-reimbursement procurement, it should correlate the evaluation of the technical and management proposal with the evaluation of cost realism. See Comp. Gen. Dec. B-298266, 2006 CPD ¶ 120, stating:

> Typically, where an agency concluded in the course of a cost realism analysis that an offeror's proposed staffing levels are unrealistically low, but the corresponding technical approach is evaluated as appropriate, the agency must reconcile these conclusions.

> * * *

> [T]he Navy's failure to evaluate [the offeror's] proposal in light of it's cost realism adjustments was contrary to the RFP. As relevant here, under the RFP cost realism language, the Navy was required "to verify the offeror's understanding of the requirements." In addition, the amended RFP requesting FPRs stated that the Navy would require offerors to "demonstrate that offerors fully understood the specific and unique requirements of the efforts" in their sample task responses, and that the Navy would "evaluate each offeror's depth of understanding and knowledge of the solicitation requirements and [the offeror's] demonstrated ability to perform tasks set forth in the Solicitation Statement of Work."

In some cases, this type of evaluation drops offerors that are known to be capable from the competition. See, for example, *Raloid Corp.*, Comp. Gen. Dec. B-297176, 2005 CPD ¶ 205, denying a protest by a company that had successfully manufactured a product in the past but was downgraded because it did not state precisely how the product would be manufactured as required by the RFP. Similarly, in *Ideamatics, Inc.*, Comp. Gen. Dec. B-297791.2, 2006 CPD ¶ 87, the company that had created a computerized system was determined to have only had a fair understanding of that system and a fair ability to maintain and enhance the system because of its inadequate description of these functions in its technical proposal. Successful incumbents (where the agency has explicit knowledge of their capabilities) frequently lose competitions for failure to write good technical or management proposals. See *ManTech Int'l Corp.*, Comp. Gen. Dec. B-311074, 2008 CPD ¶ 87 (poor response to sample task); *HealthStar VA, PLLC*, Comp. Gen. Dec. B-299737, 2007 CPD ¶ 114 (incomplete information because of page limitations); *BAE Sys. Norfolk Ship Repair, Inc.*, Comp. Gen. Dec. B-297879, 2006 CPD ¶ 75 (downgrading of management approach satisfactory even though offeror had successfully managed prior projects); *International Resource Recovery, Inc. v. United States*, 60 Fed. Cl. 1 (2004) (failure to submit mobilization plan for work it was currently performing); *Executive Security & Eng'g Techs., Inc.*, Comp. Gen. Dec. B-270518, 96-1 CPD ¶ 156 (no information on corporate experience); *Pedus Bldg. Servs., Inc.*, Comp. Gen. Dec. B-257271.3, 95-1 CPD ¶ 135 (sloppily written technical proposal); *Management Tech. Servs.*, Comp. Gen. Dec. B-251612.3, 93-1 CPD ¶ 432 (minimal information on obtaining and training workforce). See *Computerized Project Mgmt. Plus*, Comp. Gen. Dec. B-247063, 92-1 CPD ¶ 401, stating the long-standing rule with regard to protests of this type of evaluation:

[The protester] complains here that the evaluators, who were familiar with [the protester's] performance, treated it "unfairly" because they scored its "[offer] within the four corners of the proposal," and did not "consider any knowledge they had of the work presently being performed by [the protester]" that was not reflected in its proposal. [The protester] adds that any informational deficiencies in its proposal should have been rectified by examining the performance of [the protester] on the predecessor contract and through "communication" with [the protester].

[The protester's] reliance on its status as the incumbent is misplaced. A contracting activity's technical evaluation of a proposal is dependent upon the information furnished in the proposal. *All Star Maint., Inc.,* B-244143, Sept. 26, 1991, 91-2 CPD ¶ 294. There is no legal basis for favoring a firm with presumptions on the basis of the offeror's prior performance; rather, all offerors must demonstrate their capabilities in their proposals. *Id.* As [the protester's] sole objection to the evaluation of its technical proposal involves the activity's consideration of only the information furnished in [the protester's] proposal, and this manner of evaluation comports with the policy objectives in federal procurement statutes and regulations, we have no basis on which to conclude that the contracting activity acted unreasonably in its evaluation of [the protester's] proposal.

Protests have been granted when the agency does not evenhandedly evaluate such proposals. See, for example, *Northrop Grumman Information Tech., Inc.,* Comp. Gen. Dec. B-400134.10, 2009 CPD ¶ 167, granting a protest where the agency had given the same evaluation to proposals offering different levels of subcontracting. See also *Tidewater Homes Realty, Inc.,* Comp. Gen. Dec. B-274689, 96-2 CPD ¶ 241 (agency had given the protester low scores for lack of detail but had given the winning offeror high scores for a proposal containing a similar level of detail). In *Electronic Design, Inc.,* Comp. Gen. Dec. B-279662.2, 98-2 CPD ¶ 69, a protest was sustained on the basis that the agency conducted the competition on an unequal basis by permitting the awardee to include in its BAFO a 1,700 page appendix that had been rejected initially because it exceeded the page limitation on the management/technical proposals. The GAO found that this was unfair to the protester who had no way of determining that such an extensive addition to its management/technical plan would be accepted or expected.

VIII. REJECTION OF ALL PROPOSALS

The government is not necessarily bound to award a contract to any offeror after receiving and evaluating proposals. The agency has broad authority to reject all proposals received in response to a solicitation. FAR 15.305(b) states:

> The source selection authority may reject all proposals received in response to a solicitation, if doing so is in the best interest of the Government.

The pre-FAR Part 15 rewrite version provided more detailed guidance on the grounds for rejecting all proposals received in response to a solicitation. Specifically, FAR 15.506(b) stated:

All proposals received in response to a solicitation may be rejected if the agency head determines in writing that —

(1) All otherwise acceptable proposals received are at unreasonable prices;

(2) The proposals were not independently arrived at in open competition, were collusive, or were submitted in bad faith (see Subpart 3.3 for reports to be made to the Department of Justice);

(3) A cost comparison as prescribed in OMB Circular A-76 and Subpart 7.3 shows that performance by the Government is more economical; or

(4) For other reasons, cancellation is clearly in the Government's best interest.

Rejection of all proposals and cancellation of the procurement have been permitted by the GAO with few limitations. See Chapter 8 for a discussion of the rules regarding cancellation after the receipt of proposals with the intent to conduct another competition. In this regard the FAR 14.404-1(a) "compelling reason" basis for cancellation of an IFB after bid opening is not applicable. In *CFM Equip. Co.*, Comp. Gen. Dec. B-251344, 93-1 CPD ¶ 280, the GAO held that an agency needs only a "reasonable basis" to cancel an RFP. In discussing the difference between the standards for canceling an RFP or IFB, the GAO stated:

> Under FAR 15.608(b)(4), a procuring agency may reject all proposals received in response to an RFP if cancellation is clearly in the government's interest. Thus, as a general rule, in a negotiated procurement the contracting agency need only demonstrate a reasonable basis to cancel a solicitation after receipt of proposals, as opposed to the "cogent and compelling" reason required to cancel an IFB where sealed bids have been opened. *Xactex Corp.*, B-241739, May 5, 1992, 92-1 CPD ¶ 423. The standards differ because in procurements using sealed bids, competitive positions are exposed as a result of the public opening of bids, while in negotiated procurements there is no public opening. *ACR Elecs., Inc.*, B-232130.2; B-232130.3, Dec. 9, 1988, 88-2 CPD ¶ 577. The question presented by this protest is whether the agency's second thoughts about its procurement strategy have a reasonable basis.

See also *Pemco Aeroplex, Inc.*, Comp. Gen. Dec. B-275587.9, 98-2 CPD ¶ 17, stating:

> In a negotiated procurement, the contracting officer has broad authority to decide whether to cancel the solicitation; there need be only a reasonable basis for the cancellation. *Cantu Servs., Inc.*, B-219998.9, B-233697, Mar. 27, 1989, 89-1 CPD ¶ 306 at 2. So long as there is a reasonable basis for doing so, an agency may cancel a solicitation no matter when the information precipitating the cancellation first surfaces or should have been known, even if the solicitation is not canceled until after proposals have been submitted and evaluated, *Peterson-Nunez Joint Venture*, B-258788, Feb. 13, 1995, 95-1 CPD ¶ 73 at 4; *Nomura Enter. Inc.*, B-251889.2, May 6 1993, 93-1 CPD ¶ 490 at 3–4; after contract award, see *Atlantic Scientific & Tech. Corp.*, B-276334.2, Oct. 27, 1997, 97-2 CPD ¶ 116 at 2; or after the an-

nouncement of a different course of action in response to a GAO protest. *Id*. at 1–2. In addition, although we will consider a protester's contention that an agency's actual motivation in canceling a solicitation is to avoid awarding a contract or is in response to the filing of a protest, see *Griffin Servs., Inc.*, B-237268.2 et al., June 14, 1990, 90-1 CPD ¶ 558 at 3, *recon. denied*, B-237268.3 et al., Nov. 7, 1990, 90-2 CPD ¶ 369, if there is a reasonable basis for the cancellation, notwithstanding some element of personal animus, we will not object to the cancellation. *Dr. Robert J. Telepak*, B-247681, June 29, 1992, 92-2 CPD ¶ 4 at 4.

An agency may reject all proposals if the prices proposed are unreasonable. Usually this occurs when only one technically acceptable offer is received and that offeror's price is unreasonable. See *Bahan Dennis, Inc.*, Comp. Gen. Dec. B-249496.3, 94-1 CPD ¶ 184; *Selecta Corp.*, Comp. Gen. Dec. B-252182, 93-1 CPD ¶ 421; and *Adrian Supply Co.*, Comp. Gen. Dec. B-241502, 91-1 CPD ¶ 138.

In *R. & W. Flammann GmbH*, Comp. Gen. Dec. B-278486, 98-1 CPD ¶ 40, the GAO found no reasonable basis for cancellation of a procurement. The contracting officer had decided to cancel the procurement and resolicit after improprieties in the procurement process had been alleged. However, the GAO found that the protester, who had submitted the low price and was in line for award, had played no part in the alleged improprieties, and no other offeror would be prejudiced by an award. See also *Griffin Servs. Inc.*, Comp. Gen. Dec. B-237268.2, 90-1 CPD ¶ 558, where it was held that prior poor performance of a small business plus the fact that only one offer was received were not reasonable bases for cancellation. The GAO concluded that the purported agency decision to perform the work in-house was a pretext for not referring the matter to the Small Business Administration for a determination of nonresponsibility, stating:

> As a general matter, we do not review agency decisions to cancel solicitations because the work is to be performed in-house, since these decisions are matters of executive branch policy. E.g., *RAI, Inc.*, B-231889, July 13, 1988, 88-2 CPD ¶ 48 (allegation that decision to perform services in-house failed to comply with Office of Management and Budget Circular No. A-76). Where, as here, the protester argues that the agency's rationale is a pretext — that the agency's actual motivation was to avoid awarding it a contract, we will examine the reasonableness of the agency's justification. *H. David Feltoon*, B-232418, Jan. 5, 1989, 89-1 CPD ¶ 10; *Judith White*, B-233853.2, June 9, 1989, 89-1 CPD ¶ 544.

Agencies have considerable discretion in deciding to reject all proposals and cancel the procurement without any intention to resolicit. This has been held proper when the agency determines that it no longer has a requirement for the items or services, *Rotary Furnishing Co.*, Comp. Gen. Dec. B-277704, 97-2 CPD ¶ 140; *Total Design Servs.*, Comp. Gen. Dec. B-257128.2, 94-2 CPD ¶ 142; when use of an existing contract is perceived to be more advantageous, *Lasmer Indus., Inc.*, Comp. Gen. Dec. B-400866.2, 2009 CPD ¶ 77; *Borenstein Group, Inc.*, Comp. Gen. Dec. B-309751, 2007 CPD ¶ 174; *CAT Flight Servs., Inc.*, Comp. Gen. Dec. B-294186, 2004 CPD

¶ 178; when an interagency agreement is found to be preferable, *RN Expertise, Inc.*, Comp. Gen. Dec. B-401020, 2009 CPD ¶ 63; when Congressional inquiries make the need for the work questionable, *Kenco Assocs., Inc.*, Comp. Gen. Dec. B-297503, 2006 CPD ¶ 24; when the agency decides to procure from Federal Prison Industries, *Management Solutions, L.C.*, Comp. Gen. Dec. B-298883, 2006 CPD ¶ 197; when an agency decides to perform the work with its own forces, *Aleut Facilities Support Servs.,LLC*, Comp. Gen. Dec. B-401925, 2009 CPD ¶ 202; *Cattlemen's Meat Co.*, Comp. Gen. Dec. B-296616, 2005 CPD ¶ 167; *Southwest Anesthesia Servs.*, Comp. Gen. Dec. B-279176.2, 98-2 CPD ¶ 28; when the agency determines that the specifications and evaluation factors were drafted by a potential competitor, *e-Management Consultants, Inc.*, Comp. Gen. Dec. B-400585.2, 2009 CPD ¶ 39; or when the agency anticipates closing the facility in which the contract would be performed, *Lake Region Office Supply, Inc.*, Comp. Gen. Dec. B-243934, 91-1 CPD ¶ 502. In *Global Solutions Network, Inc.*, Comp. Gen. Dec. B-299424, 2007 CPD ¶ 76, cancellation was justified when the agency issued an RFP for five years of work under a franchise fund but before award established a process to review whether it would continue to support the fund. Cancellation was also held proper in order to avoid litigation, *All Seasons Apparel, Inc.*, Comp. Gen. Dec. B-401805, 2009 CPD ¶ 221. In that case, the RFP was cancelled because the GAO and the Department of Justice had issued conflicting decisions on whether Historically Underutilized Business Zone small business concerns had priority over 8(a) shall business firms and the agency concluded that either decision it reached could be challenged.

Agencies properly cancel RFPs if they determine that a small business set-aside has not yielded reasonable prices. See *Division Laundry & Cleaners, Inc.*, Comp. Gen. Dec. B-311242, 2008 CPD ¶ 97 (prices over 35% above government estimate); *Ystueta, Inc.*, Comp. Gen. Dec. B-296628.4, 2006 CPD ¶ 46 (prices exceeded agency cost estimate); *Rice Servs., Inc.*, Comp. Gen. Dec. B-293861, 2004 CPD ¶ 167 (all proposals rated "marginal"); *Sunshine Kids Serv. Supply Co.*, Comp. Gen. Dec. B-292141, 2003 CPD ¶ 119 (only proposal had unreasonable price and was technically unacceptable); *Nutech Laundry & Textiles, Inc.*, Comp. Gen. Dec. B-291739, 2003 CPD ¶ 34 (offered price was almost double price of large business).

In many instances, offerors have expended significant amounts of money in competing for the work only to find the procurement cancelled. An egregious example of this is *VSE Corp.*, Comp. Gen. Dec. B-290452.2, 2005 CPD ¶ 111, where the procurement had been conducted over a five year period during with the agency had gone through a reorganization and new officials had decided to significantly alter the acquisition plan.

CHAPTER 7

AWARD WITHOUT NEGOTIATIONS/
COMPETITIVE RANGE DECISION

Upon the completion of the evaluation of offers, the agency must decide whether to make an award without negotiations or to establish a competitive range and conduct negotiations with all the offerors within the competitive range. Whether award without negotiations is permissible depends on a number of factors, including the provisions included in the solicitation, the offers received, and the nature of communications between the agency and the offerors. Within these parameters, the agency has broad discretion in deciding whether to award or to negotiate. It also has broad discretion in establishing the competitive range. The statutory and regulatory requirements concerning the exercise of these discretionary determinations have evolved over the years.

Although the statutes use the phrase "award without discussions," the phrase "award without negotiations" is more descriptive of the concept and avoids use of the same term to describe two different types of communications. The statutory provisions authorizing award "based on the proposals received" give two different meanings to the word "discussions." It is used to describe both the communications that are permitted prior to award on the basis of proposals received and the communications that are to occur after the competitive range is established. See 10 U.S.C. § 2305(b)(4)(A)(ii) and 41 U.S.C. § 253b(d)(1)(B), which state that award can be made on the basis of proposals received "without discussions with the offerors (other than discussions conducted for the purpose of minor clarifications)." The same different meanings of "discussions" are contained in 10 U.S.C. § 2305(a)(2)(B)(ii)(I) and 41 U.S.C. § 253a(b)(2)(B)(i). In addition, the FAR Part 15 rewrite removed the definition of "discussions" that had previously appeared in the FAR. It envisions that the exchanges between the agency and the offerors after establishment of the competitive range will constitute "negotiations" that "may include bargaining," FAR 15.306(d).

I. POLICY

The government policy concerning whether to award without negotiations or to establish a competitive range and conduct discussions has changed several times over the years. The original statutory standard permitted award on an "initial proposal . . . where it can be clearly demonstrated from the existence of adequate competition or accurate prior cost experience that acceptance of an initial proposal without discussion would result in fair and reasonable prices," 10 U.S.C. § 2304(g) (1964). However, the Competition in Contracting Act (CICA) changed this standard, substituting "full and open competition" for "adequate competition" and "lowest overall cost to the Government" for "fair and reasonable prices." These changes were interpreted by the GAO to mean that award on the basis of the initial proposals could be made only to the offeror with the lowest evaluated price among the technically acceptable proposals. In effect, this precluded price/quality/ capability tradeoffs at this stage of the process. See, for example, *Information Spectrum, Inc.*, Comp. Gen. Dec. B-233208, 89-1 CPD ¶ 187. Subsequently, Congress recognized that the "lowest overall cost" standard was too restrictive, causing unnecessary competitive range determinations, thereby increasing the cost and time of procurements. In 1990 it removed the "lowest overall cost" language and made related changes for defense contracts, § 802 of the National Defense Authorization Act for 1991, Pub. L. No. 101-510. Four years later the same changes were adopted for non-defense agencies by the Federal Acquisition Streamlining Act of 1994, Pub. L. No. 103-355.

These final statutory changes removed all standards governing when an agency could award without negotiations but required agencies to include language in the solicitation stating which procedure would be followed. Thus, as discussed in Chapter 3, 10 U.S.C. § 2305(a)(2)(B)(ii)(I) and 41 U.S.C. § 253a(b)(2)(B)(i) require that the solicitation include

> either a statement that the proposals are intended to be evaluated with, and award made after, discussions with the offerors, or a statement that the proposals are intended to be evaluated, and award made, without discussions with the offerors (other than discussions conducted for the purpose of minor clarification) unless discussions are determined to be necessary.

Neither the statutes nor the regulations, provide any guidance on selecting the appropriate provision. However, it can be anticipated that most requests for proposals (RFPs) will call for award without negotiations, because ¶ (f)(4) of the standard FAR 52.215-1 Instructions to Offerors — Competitive Acquisition solicitation provision permits award without negotiations as follows:

> The Government intends to evaluate proposals and award a contract without discussions with offerors (except clarifications as described in FAR 15.306(a). Therefore, the offeror's initial proposal should contain the offeror's best terms from a cost or price and technical standpoint. The Government reserves the right to conduct discussions if the Contracting Officer later determines them to be necessary. If the Contracting Officer determines that the number of proposals that would otherwise be in the competitive range exceeds the number at which an efficient competition can be conducted, the Contracting Officer may limit the number of proposals in the competitive range to the greatest number that will permit an efficient competition among the most highly rated proposals.

While indicating that award without negotiation is intended, this provision gives the agency the option to conduct negotiations when they are determined to be "necessary." There is no regulatory guidance on when negotiations would be necessary, but FAR 15.306(a)(2) requires that when such a determination is made, "the rationale for doing so shall be documented in the contract file." This provision apparently reflects congressional concern that offerors might not make their best offers in their original submissions if they expect negotiations to take place. Thus, when this standard solicitation provision is used, the agency should conduct the procurement with the goal of awarding without negotiations.

As discussed in Chapter 3, if the agency has determined that it intends to conduct negotiations, it will include Alternate I to the FAR 52.215-1(f)(4) solicitation provision in the RFP. In that case the agency will have no choice of awarding on the basis of initial proposals because when this provision is used, the government may not make award without negotiations. See *American Native Medical Transport, LLC*, Comp. Gen. Dec. B-276873, 97-2 CPD ¶ 73, where the GAO stated that award on the basis of initial proposals was improper when the RFP called for discussions, but refused to grant the protest because the protester could not prove that it was prejudiced by the failure to conduct negotiations. See also *Christie Constructors, Inc.*, Comp. Gen. Dec. B-271759, 96-2 CPD ¶ 87, where the agency awarded the contract without negotiations but the solicitation contained both provisions (calling for award without negotiations and for negotiation with all offerors in the competitive range). The GAO denied the protest of failure to establish a competitive range because the conflicting provisions should have been protested prior to the submission of proposals.

II. DECIDING WHETHER TO AWARD OR NEGOTIATE

As discussed above, when the standard solicitation provision is used, neither the statutes nor the FAR specify criteria for determining whether to hold negotiations. 10 U.S.C. § 2305(b)(4)(A) merely states:

> The head of an agency shall evaluate competitive proposals in accordance with paragraph (1) and may award a contract —
>
>> (i) after discussions with the offerors, provided that written or oral discussions have been conducted with the responsible offerors who submit proposals within the competitive range; or
>>
>> (ii) based on the proposals received, without discussions with the offerors (other than discussions conducted for the purpose of minor clarification) provided that the solicitation included a statement that proposals are intended to be evaluated, and award made, without discussions, unless discussions are determined necessary.

Substantially the same language is contained in 41 U.S.C. § 253b(d)(1).

Under the CICA standard, negotiations appeared to have been the favored procedure. However, the statutory changes have served to make award without negotiations, at least an equally appropriate procedure. House Report 101-665, 101st

Cong., 2d Sess. (accompanying Pub. L. No. 101-510) discussed some of the factors to consider in making the selection. However, it did not go so far as indicating a preference for either procedure, stating: "The committee does not recommend a preference for conducting discussions or not conducting discussions, believing that this is more appropriately dealt with in regulation." The FAR has not adopted any guidance implementing these statutes. The lack of statutory or regulatory direction leaves the agency with broad discretion in determining whether or not negotiations should be conducted.

A. Award Without Negotiations

Award without negotiations is one of the most important techniques that agencies have adopted to streamline their procurements. House Report 101-665 recognized the advantages of this process by noting the following benefits of making awards without negotiations:

- Significant reduction of acquisition lead time
- Permitting award on technical superiority when discussions are not needed
- Lessening the chances of wrongful disclosure of source selection information
- Reduction of the government's overall acquisition costs by reducing the amount a contractor is spending on bid and proposal costs

An additional benefit is the avoidance of final proposal revisions that include arbitrary price reductions. Such reductions have resulted in excessively low prices that can create serious difficulties during contract performance.

1. Agency Discretion

Under the current statutes, award without negotiations is highly discretionary. It is clear that an offeror does not have a *right* to award on the basis of an initial proposal. See *Kisco Co.*, Comp. Gen. Dec. B-216953, 85-1 CPD ¶ 334, establishing this rule under earlier statutes.

In *International Data Prods. Corp.*, Comp. Gen. Dec. B-274654.5, 97-1 CPD ¶ 34, the GAO recognized the broad discretion the statutes and the FAR afford the agency:

> With respect to the general decision to award without discussions, we addressed this issue in response to IDP's protest and need not revisit it here. However, we will address two of Dunn's contentions that unique factors here required the agency to open discussions. First, Dunn argues that our prior decision in *The Jonathan Corp.; Metro Machine Corp.*, B-251698.3; B-251698.4, May 17, 1993, 93-2 CPD

¶ 174, *recon. denied, Moon Eng'g Co., Inc.*, B-251698.6, Oct. 19, 1993, 93-2 CPD ¶ 233, mandates overturning the agency's decision not to hold discussions in this case. Dunn claims that the agency and intervenor failed to distinguish this case because it cannot be distinguished. We disagree.

As an initial matter, Dunn correctly notes that a contracting officer's decision to make award on initial proposals is not unfettered. *The Jonathan Corp.; Metro Machine Corp.*, *supra* at 14. We will review the exercise of such discretion to ensure that it was reasonably based on the particular circumstances of the procurement, including consideration of the proposals received and the basis for the selection decision. *Lloyd-Lamont Design, Inc.*, B-270090.3, Feb. 13, 1996, 96-1 CPD ¶ 71 at 6; *Facilities Management Co., Inc.*, B-259731.2, May 23, 1995, 95-1 CPD ¶ 274 at 8. On the other hand, this discretion is quite broad, and in recent years has been expanded. For example, Congress has deleted the requirement originally set forth in the Competition in Contracting Act that an agency could only make award without discussions to the offeror with the lowest price or evaluated cost. Compare 10 U.S.C. § 2305(b)(4)(A)(ii) (1988) with 10 U.S.C. § 2305(b)(4)(A)(ii) (1994) (showing deletion of requirement applicable to defense agencies) and 41 U.S.C. § 253b(d)(1)(B) (1988) with 41 U.S.C. § 253(d)(1)(B) (1994) (showing deletion of requirement applicable to civilian agencies). In addition, the FAR now provides that once the government has stated its intent to award without discussions, "the rationale for reversal of this decision shall be documented in the contract file." FAR 15.610(a)(3) (FAC 90-31, Oct. 1, 1995).

See also *Synectic Solutions, Inc.*, Comp. Gen. Dec. B-299086, 2007 CPD ¶ 36; *Colmek Sys. Eng'g*, Comp. Gen. Dec. B-291931.2, 2003 CPD ¶ 123; *J.A. Jones/IBC J.V.*, Comp. Gen. B-285627, 2000 CPD ¶ 161; *Bulova Techs. LLC*, Comp. Gen. Dec. B-281384, 99-1 CPD ¶ 99; *Inter-Con Sec. Servs., Inc.*, Comp. Gen. Dec. B-270828, 96-1 CPD ¶ 233; *Faison Office Prods. Co.*, Comp. Gen. Dec. B-260259, 95-2 CPD ¶ 116; *Energy & Envtl. Research Corp.*, Comp. Gen. Dec. B-261422, 95-2 CPD ¶ 81; and *Professional Safety Consultants Co.*, Comp. Gen. Dec. B-247331, 92-1 CPD ¶ 404.

Arguments that discussion is required in order to permit offerors to improve their proposals have been uniformly rejected. See, for example, *Infotec Dev., Inc.*, Comp. Gen. Dec. B-258198, 95-1 CPD ¶ 52, stating:

[The protester] also contends that the agency's determination not to conduct discussions was unreasonable because the agency "has produced no evidence that discussions would have involved any undue burden," and the lack of discussions essentially mandated that award be made to [the winning offeror]. [The protester] further contends that the agency was required to conduct discussions in order to provide [the protester] with the opportunity to improve its proposal such that it would receive higher color/adjectival ratings under certain evaluation subfactors, and to provide the protester with an opportunity to justify its proposed costs.

* * *

There is no requirement in law or regulation that an agency, which has included [the provision calling for award without negotiations] in a solicitation, show that the conduct of discussions would cause it "undue burden" prior to making award based upon initial proposals without discussions. See 10 U.S.C. § 2305(b)(4)(A)(ii) (Supp. V 1993); FAR 15.610 and 52.115-16, Alternate III. Nor is there anything improper in an agency's making award based upon initial proposals where only one offeror submits an offer which the agency determines acceptable. See *Analytical Chemists, Inc.*, B-256037, Apr. 29, 1994, 94-1 CPD ¶ 283; *Benton Corp.*, B-249092, Oct. 21, 1992, 92-2 CPD ¶ 264. Finally, there is no requirement that the agency afford an offeror, such as [the protester], the opportunity to improve its proposal such that it would receive a higher color/adjectival rating in the agency's evaluation, or to justify proposed costs determined unreasonable by the agency in its evaluation of initial proposals. See *Scientific-Atlanta, Inc.*, B-255343.2; B-255343.4, Mar. 14, 1994, 94-1 CPD ¶ 325; *A Plus Serv., Unlimited,* [B-255198.2, Jan. 31, 1994, 94-1 CPD ¶ 52]. Since the solicitation advised offerors that the agency intended to make award without discussions, [the protester] could not presume that it would have a chance to improve its proposal through discussions. *Scientific-Atlanta, Inc., supra*. The burden was on [the protester] to submit an initial proposal that adequately demonstrated its own merits, and the protester ran the risk of not receiving award by failing to do so. *Id*. Based on our review, we find reasonable the agency's decision to make award based upon initial proposals without discussions. See *TRI-COR Indus., Inc.,* [B-252366.3, Aug. 25, 1993, 93-2 CPD ¶ 137].

2. Lack of Discussions

The rule was established many years ago that once a discussion was held with one offeror, the agency could no longer award on the basis of initial proposals but was required to establish a competitive range and conduct discussions with all offerors within the range, 50 Comp. Gen. 202 (B-170751) (1970). However, communications in the form of clarifications were permissible prior to award on the basis of the initial proposals, *CompuServe Data Sys., Inc.*, 60 Comp. Gen. 468 (B-195982.2), 81-1 CPD ¶ 374. See Chapter 5 for a complete discussion of the difference between discussions and clarifications.

In applying this rule, it does not appear to matter which party initiated the communication that led to a discussion. See, for example, *CDA Investment Techs., Inc.*, Comp. Gen. Dec. B-272093, 97-1 CPD ¶ 102, *recons. denied*, 97-1 CPD ¶ 103, where the agency selected one of the offerors on the basis of its initial proposal and sent it a contract document incorporating the full proposal by reference. The offeror signed the document and returned it to the agency with a cover letter noting that it would perform the contract using a few personnel and subcontractors different than it had proposed. In several subsequent exchanges, the contracting officer stated that the offeror could not change its proposal and the offeror stated that it would abide by the "material terms and conditions" of its original proposal. The GAO concluded that award on the basis of the original proposal was proper because there had been no discussion, stating:

[T]he record does not show that [the winning offeror] made any material changes to its initial proposal with respect to the use of subcontractors through the May 2 letter, or through subsequent communications with the [agency]. As noted above, [the winning offeror's] proposal stated that the firm was considering the use of a subcontractor for keying in the Form 13F filings; the record indicates that it is not an uncommon practice for the contractor to supplement its work force during the peak periods corresponding to the regulatory quarterly filing deadlines. The May 2 letter, with its general reference to the use of subcontractors, cannot reasonably be read as materially changing the approach set out in [the winning offeror's] proposal. To the extent the May 2 letter raised any uncertainty about [the winning offeror's] intent, the record shows that, in light of the responses to his inquiries, the contracting officer reasonably concluded that the awardee did not make any material changes to its proposal.

* * *

Based on our review of the record, we conclude that the contracting officer properly determined that award was made on the basis of [the winning offeror's] proposal as it was evaluated and selected, and that the May 2 letter made no material changes to the proposal. Accordingly, there is no basis for us to conclude that the [agency] conducted improper discussions with [the winning offeror] such that it was required to give the other offerors an opportunity to revise their proposals before making award.

3. Best Value Determination

Award without negotiations should be made when the agency can determine that one of the offerors has submitted a proposal that clearly represents the best value to the government. The GAO has denied protests of awards on the basis of initial proposals when the agency can demonstrate that the award was made to the offeror that offered the best value. In such cases the mere possibility that lower prices or better technical solutions might result from negotiations is not sufficient to overcome the agency's determination that negotiations are not necessary. See, for example, *Bannum, Inc.*, Comp. Gen. Dec. B-400928.2, 2009 CPD ¶ 144 (reasonable to award without discussions to technically superior offeror with slightly higher price); *Chem-Spray-South, Inc.*, Comp. Gen. Dec. B-298281.2, 2006 CPD ¶ 163 (reasonable to award without discussions to lower priced proposal even when higher technically rated offeror stated informally that it would lower its price); *General Dynamics – Ordnance & Tactical Sys.*, Comp. Gen. Dec. B-295987, 2005 CPD ¶ 114 (proper to not allow offeror to comment on adverse performance evaluation when awarding without negotiations); *HDL Research Lab, Inc.*, Comp. Gen. Dec. B-294959, 2005 CPD ¶ 8 (reasonable to drop protester that had numerous informational deficiencies when award was made without negotiations); *ACC Constr. Co.*, Comp. Gen. Dec. B-288934, 2001 CPD ¶ 190 (reasonable to award without discussions to technically superior offeror with 3.8% higher price); *Olympus Bldg. Servs., Inc.*, Comp. Gen. Dec. B-285351.3, 2001 CPD ¶ 115 (award on initial proposals reasonable when offeror has low price and best technical evaluation); *Carlson WagonLit Travel*, Comp. Gen. Dec. B-287016, 2001 CPD ¶ 49 (award to only acceptable proposal); *PEMCO World Air Servs.*, Comp. Gen. Dec. B-284240.3, 2000 CPD ¶ 71 (award could not be made to protester because of questions as to whether it could meet contract requirements); *Sabreliner Corp.*, Comp. Gen. Dec. B-284240.2, 2000 CPD ¶ 68 (award to acceptable offeror when protester's 25% lower price was unrealistically low); *Inland Servs. Corp.*, Comp. Gen. Dec. B-282272, 99-1 CPD ¶ 113 (award without discussions even though protester had no opportunity to comment on adverse past performance information); *TEAM Support Servs., Inc.*, Comp. Gen. Dec. B-279379.2, 98-1 CPD ¶ 167 (reasonable to award to technically superior proposal even though protester's technically unacceptable proposal had lower price); *Robotic Sys. Tech.*, Comp. Gen. Dec. B-278195.2, 98-1 CPD ¶ 20 (reasonable to award to offeror with superior technical proposal even though protester's unacceptable proposal was capable of being made acceptable and its price was one half of price of awardee); *Richard M. Milburn High School*, Comp. Gen. Dec. B-277018, 97-2 CPD ¶ 53 (reasonable to award without negotiations to offeror whose proposal contains a reasonable price and is technically superior); *Harry A. Stroh Assocs., Inc.*, Comp. Gen. Dec. B-274335, 97-1 CPD ¶ 18 (award without negotiations to offeror submitting technically superior proposal at a fair price reasonable even though protester argued that a possibility existed that its inferior proposal could become best value through discussions); *Lloyd-Lamont Design, Inc.*, Comp. Gen. Dec. B-270090.3, 96-1 CPD ¶ 71 (award without negotiations to offeror with technically superior proposal at slightly higher cost reasonable where awardee was best value); *Cornet, Inc.*, Comp. Gen. Dec. B-270330, 96-1 CPD ¶ 189 (award without negotiations reasonable given technical superiority of awardee's proposal and determination that no other offeror could improve its proposal to the level of awardee's); *Southwest Marine, Inc.*, Comp. Gen. Dec. B-265865.3, 96-1 CPD ¶ 56 (award without negotiations reasonable where proposal was evaluated as clearly best value); *Facilities Mgmt.Co.*, Comp. Gen. Dec. B-259731.2, 95-1 CPD ¶ 274 (award without negotiations reasonable when awardee with lowest probable cost was highest ranked technically); *Information Spectrum, Inc.*, Comp. Gen. Dec. B-256609.3, 94-2 CPD ¶ 251 (award without negotiations to offeror with best technical proposal at higher price reasonable when agency determined it constituted the best value); and *Federal Sys. Group*, GSBCA 11461-P, 92-1 BCA ¶ 24,591 (award without discussions to offeror with best technical proposal at slightly higher price reasonable where contracting officer concluded that protester's low price would increase when deficiencies were corrected). In *Battelle Memorial Inst.*, Comp. Gen. Dec. B-299533, 2007 CPD ¶ 94, the GAO held that the agency properly dropped the protester from the competition without discussing lack of required option year prices when the RFP stated that a competitive range would be established on the basis of only the technical proposals. The GAO reasoned that since the agency had decided to award without negotiations, the RFP provision reserving price negotiations to offerors in the competitive range did not come into play.

The GAO has also recognized that an agency may consider the need for early commencement of performance and the cost of continuing the procurement process in deciding to award without negotiations. See *Charleston Marine Containers, Inc.*, Comp. Gen. Dec. B-283393, 99-2 CPD ¶ 84, denying a protest where the contracting officer awarded the contract to the best value offeror without discussions in order to ensure that the delivery schedule would be met, and *Tomco Sys., Inc.*, Comp. Gen. Dec. B-275551, 97-1 CPD ¶ 130, denying a protest where the agency had cited these considerations in awarding to a technically strong proposal at a slightly higher price than the protester had proposed. See also *Federal Sys. Group*, GSBCA 11461-P, 92-1 BCA ¶ 24,591, where the General Services Board recognized that the need for quick award of a contract was a valid consideration in making the decision to award without negotiations.

The GAO has also denied protests of award without negotiations when the award was to be made to the lowest-price, technically acceptable proposal, *Advanced American Diving Serv., Inc.*, Comp. Gen. Dec. B-274766, 97-1 CPD ¶ 1. In that case it was held that the agency was not required to conduct discussions with an offeror that had submitted an unacceptable proposal even though its price was the lowest. Award to a reasonably priced acceptable proposal was sustained. See also *LOGMET, LLC*, Comp. Gen. Dec. B-400355.2, 2008 CPD ¶ 175, where award without negotiations was found proper when there were a number of acceptable proposals, and *Integrated Techs. Group, Inc.*, Comp. Gen. Dec. B-274288.5, 97-1 CPD ¶ 214, where award without negotiations was found proper where there were two technically acceptable proposals and discussions would have been required to correct an obvious mistake in the protester's proposal that could not be corrected through clarifications under the FAR prior to the Part 15 rewrite.

Award without negotiations has been held to be improper if the agency cannot make a clear determination as to which offeror has proposed the best value without discussions. See, for example, *Jonathan Corp.*, Comp. Gen. Dec. B-251698.3, 93-2 CPD ¶ 174, *recons. denied*, 93-2 CPD ¶ 233, where the agency had determined that competing technical proposals were essentially equal and had awarded without negotiations to the offeror with the lowest probable cost. The GAO found that the agency's cost realism analysis was flawed, with the result that it was unclear which proposal represented the best value to the government. Where negotiations were necessary to ascertain the probable costs of the competing offerors, the GAO held that award without negotiations was improper. This reasoning was followed by the Court of Federal Claims in *Day & Zimmermann Servs. v. United States*, 38 Fed. Cl. 591 (1997), where the agency had conducted a flawed cost realism analysis in a procurement where the competing offerors had been evaluated as being very close on the other evaluation factors. The court held that it was improper to award without negotiations when discussions were needed to determine an accurate probable cost in order to make a rational tradeoff decision. See also *Computer Literacy World, Inc. v. Dep't of the Air Force*, GSBCA 13438-P, 96-1 BCA ¶ 28,119, where the board held in a 2-to-1 decision that negotiations were required when five offerors with prices lower than the winning offeror's had very minor defects in their proposals that could have been "easily corrected." The majority concluded that the agency could not award without negotiations when lower prices were a "virtual certainty" if negotiations were conducted. The dissenting judge disagreed, arguing that because there was no violation of statute or regulation in awarding without negotiations, this was a matter within the discretion of the agency. Compare *Silynx Communications, Inc.*, Comp. Gen. Dec. B-310667, 2008 CPD ¶ 36, holding that award without negotiations was proper because there was a clear basis for distinguishing between the technical merits of the proposals.

B. Decision to Negotiate

Where the solicitation indicates that award without negotiations is anticipated, the agency must balance the possibility of obtaining a better contract through negotiations against the risk that offerors on future procurements will not submit their best proposals initially if the agency does not act in accordance with the solicitation provisions. In general, this balance can be achieved if the agency conducts negotiations only if circumstances indicate that the government can obtain a significantly better bargain. This would be the case where one or more otherwise favorable offers contain defects. This is particularly so where the defects are readily correctable as occurred in *Computer Literacy World, Inc. v. Dep't of the Air Force*, GSBCA 13438-P, 96-1 BCA ¶ 28,119. In such cases the agency will have to predict the improvement in the bargain that can be achieved from negotiations, recognizing that this may be a highly discretionary decision. However, it is unlikely that a decision to conduct negotiations to achieve a better bargain would be overturned in the protest process.

In addition, an agency may find it necessary to conduct negotiations to clear up ambiguities in proposals or to arrive at a fair evaluation of proposals. See *Day & Zimmermann Servs. v. United States*, 38 Fed. Cl. 591 (1997), where the court held that negotiations were necessary for these purposes. See also *Veda Inc. v. United States*, Civ. Action No. 93-0518-LFO (D.D.C. 1993), where the court found that the decision to conduct discussions was reasonable because the contracting officer had serious problems with Veda's Small Business and Small Business Subcontracting Plan and deemed it unacceptable. Negotiations may also be called for when the agency finds it necessary to make major adjustments to the offeror's cost proposal to arrive at the probable cost of performance, *Jonathan Corp.*, Comp. Gen. Dec. B-251698.3, 93-2 CPD ¶ 174, *recons. denied*, 93-2 CPD ¶ 233. In deciding whether to negotiate in such situations, the agency should balance the delay and expense involved in conducting negotiations with the potential benefits that might be obtained. It should also consider the effect on competitors, such as unduly increasing bid and proposal expense.

III. DETERMINING THE COMPETITIVE RANGE

Determination of the competitive range is of extreme importance to both the government and competitors. Nevertheless, neither of the statutes provided any guidance for contracting agencies in establishing the range. Former FAR 15.609(a) contained the following statement:

> The competitive range shall be determined on the basis of cost or price and other factors that were stated in the solicitation and shall include all proposals that have a reasonable chance of being selected for award. When there is doubt as to whether a proposal is in the competitive range, the proposal should be included.

Following this guidance many agencies were including a large number of offerors in the competitive range with the result that they were unable to conduct meaningful negotiations with these offerors. This practice also increased the costs of the competition by requiring many competitors to continue to participate in the process when only one would be awarded a contract. In one case such a competitor recovered the costs of remaining in the competition because it was placed in the competitive range without any real chance for award, *SMS Data Prods. Group, Inc.*, GSBCA 8589-P, 87-1 BCA ¶ 19,496. These negative effects of broad inclusion of offerors in the competitive range were recognized as detrimental to the competitive negotiation process, and in 1995 Congress was requested to amend the procurement statutes to permit more limited competitive range determinations.

The statutes and regulations now contain completely different standards for determining the competitive range. As a result, the large number of decisions dealing with this issue are either no longer applicable or are of questionable authority.

A. Standards for Inclusion

The standards for inclusion in the competitive range and for determining its size were changed significantly with the passage of the Clinger-Cohen Act of 1996, Pub. L. No. 104-106, and the promulgation of the FAR Part 15 rewrite.

1. Statutory Changes

In passing the Clinger-Cohen Act, Congress recognized that the inclusion of a large numbers of offers in the range can unnecessarily increase the time and cost of procurements and considered a number of ways in which the size of the range could be limited. Alternatives aimed at replacing the requirement for full and open competition were rejected because of concerns that they would lead to noncompetitive practices. However, two provisions were adopted – resulting in the current FAR standard for determining inclusion in the competitive range. First, 10 U.S.C. § 2304(j) and 41 U.S.C. § 253(h) require that full and open competition be conducted "efficiently" as follows:

> The Federal Acquisition Regulation shall ensure that the requirement to obtain full and open competition is implemented in a manner that is consistent with the need to efficiently fulfill the Government's requirements.

More specifically, 10 U.S.C. § 2305(b)(4)(B) and 41 U.S.C. § 253b(d)(2) permit the contracting officer to limit the competitive range:

If the contracting officer determines that the number of offerors that would otherwise be included in the competitive range . . . exceeds the number at which an efficient competition can be conducted, the contracting officer may limit the number of proposals in the competitive range, in accordance with the criteria specified in the solicitation, to the greatest number that will permit an efficient competition among the offerors rated most highly in accordance with the criteria.

2. FAR Part 15 Rewrite

The FAR Part 15 rewrite significantly changed the standards for inclusion in the competitive range and implemented the statutory authority for limiting the size for purposes of efficiency. The FAR had required that an offer be included in the competitive range if it had a "reasonable chance of being accepted for award" and had stated: "When there is doubt as to whether a proposal is in the competitive range, the proposal should be included." These standards were removed and replaced with what appears to be a two-step process. First, the agency is required to establish a competitive range, which is to include "all of the most highly rated proposals," FAR 15.306(c)(1). Then, the agency must decide if the number of such proposals is too large for an efficient competition. If so, FAR 15.306(c)(2) permits the number to be limited as follows:

After evaluating all proposals in accordance with 15.305(a) and paragraph (c) (1) of this section, the contracting officer may determine that the number of most highly rated proposals that might otherwise be included in the competitive range exceeds the number at which an efficient competition can be conducted. Provided the solicitation notifies offerors that the competitive range can be limited for purposes of efficiency (see 52.215-1(f)(4)), the contracting officer may limit the number of proposals in the competitive range to the greatest number that will permit an efficient competition among the most highly rated proposals (10 U.S.C. § 2305(b)(4) and 41 U.S.C. § 253b(d)).

The FAR Councils explained this revised language in 62 Fed. Reg. 51226, as follows:

The competitive range guidance in the final rule indicates that contracting officers shall establish a competitive range comprised of only those proposals most highly rated. In contrast, the current FAR advises contracting officers "when there is doubt as to whether a proposal is in the competitive range, the proposal should be included." We considered retaining the existing FAR standard for inclusion in the competitive range, but ultimately rejected it because there are readily discernible benefits from including only the most highly rated offers in the competitive range. First, those included will know that they have a good chance of winning the competition — making it in their best interests to compete aggressively. Second, those eliminated from the range are spared the cost of pursuing an award they have little or no chance of winning. Retaining marginal offers in the range imposes additional, and largely futile, effort and cost on both the Government and industry. We also note that comments received from Government agencies indicate that award is nearly always made to one of the three most highly rated offerors in the competitive range. Therefore, including an offeror that is not most highly rated in the competitive range would not likely impact the final award decision. This final rule ensures that offerors with little probability of success are advised early on that their competitive position does not merit additional expense in a largely futile attempt to secure the contract.

This knowledge will benefit both large and small entities, but will be especially beneficial to small entities that have constrained budgets. These entities will be able to conserve scarce bid and proposal funds and employ their resources on more productive business opportunities. In addition, the new standard has the derivative benefit of encouraging offerors to submit better, more robust initial proposals in recognition of the fact that only the most highly rated proposals will be included in the competitive range.

3. Most Highly Rated Proposals and Efficient Competition

Neither the statutes nor the final FAR Part 15 rewrite attempts to define these terms. Draft versions of the rewrite had listed factors to be considered in limiting the competitive range, but these factors were deleted from the final rewrite to permit "the facts of the instant acquisition to guide the contracting officer" in limiting the competitive range, 62 Fed. Reg. 51228 (1997). Similarly, the rewrite does not contain a definition of "efficiency." However, the promulgation comments make it clear that the cost and time involved in conducting negotiations were the primary factors in rejecting the prior "when in doubt leave them in" rule.

The determination of which proposals are the most highly rated will depend on the facts and circumstances of each procurement. Under the FAR rewrite, as under the prior regulations, the determination will be based on a comparison of the offers and the capability of the offerors. If there is a break or gap in the evaluation scores, this would be a rational basis for determining the most highly rated proposals. See *Community Partnership LLC*, Comp. Gen. Dec. B-286844, 2001 CPD ¶ 38, and *Arsenault Acquisition Corp.*, Comp. Gen. Dec. B-276959, 97-2 CPD ¶ 74, affirming the use of this technique. For other protests denying exclusion from the competitive range, see *Orion Mgmt., LLC*, Comp. Gen. Dec. B-400680.2, 2009 CPD ¶ 21 (lowest rated of three proposals excluded); *Computer & Hi-Tech Mgmt., Inc.*, Comp. Gen. Dec. B-293235.4, 2004 CPD ¶ 45 (agency has discretion to determine which proposals are most highly rated); *Aliron Int'l, Inc.*, Comp. Gen. Dec. B-285048.2, 2000 CPD ¶ 125 (lowest rated of four proposals excluded); *Northwest Procurement Inst., Inc.*, Comp. Gen. Dec. B-286345, 2000 CPD ¶ 192 (two highly rated proposals included — protester's lower rated proposal excluded); and *Wilson 5 Servs. Co.*, Comp. Gen. Dec. B-285343.2, 2000 CPD ¶ 157 (top two offerors included based on break in scores even though excluded protester had lower price). Compare *ABIC Ltd.*, Comp. Gen. Dec. B-286460, 2001 CPD ¶ 46, where an agency included six offerors in the range even though there was a clear gap after the third offeror.

This comparative approach to determining the competitive range generally precludes the use of a predetermined cutoff score as a means of determining the range, *DOT Sys., Inc.*, Comp. Gen. Dec. B-186192, 76-2 CPD ¶ 3. In 50 Comp. Gen. 59 (B-169645) (1970), the RFP contained a minimum score, 75, below which proposals would be deemed outside the competitive range. As a result of this cutoff score, five proposals with point scores between 71.4 and 74.8 were excluded. The GAO held that these five proposals could not be excluded from the competitive range solely because they fell below the cutoff score. In *National Veterans Law Ctr.*, 60 Comp. Gen. 223 (B-198738), 81-1 CPD ¶ 58, the contracting agency established an evaluation score of 80 points, arguing that this was only a "qualifying" score meant to inform the offerors of the relative importance of each area of evaluation. The GAO found no difference between this qualifying score and a predetermined cutoff score that establishes the competitive range and reiterated the impropriety of its use. Nevertheless, the GAO has upheld the exclusion of an offeror based on a predetermined cutoff score when the score of the excluded proposal was so low in comparison with scores on other proposals that no prejudicial effect could be said to exist, 52 Comp. Gen. 382 (B-174870) (1972); *PRC Computer Ctr., Inc.*, 55 Comp. Gen. 60 (B-178205), 75-2 CPD ¶ 35; *Monarch Enters., Inc.*, Comp. Gen. Dec. B-233303, 89-1 CPD ¶ 222.

Although the FAR uses the term "most highly rated proposals," an agency is permitted to include only one proposal in the competitive range if no other proposal has a reasonable chance of being selected for award, *SDS Petroleum Prods., Inc.*, Comp. Gen. Dec. B-280430, 98-2 CPD ¶ 59. In this decision, the GAO rejected the argument that the agency was required to keep the top rated proposals in the competition because of the new language in the FAR and the deletion of the prior language stating that the competitive range should include "all proposals with a reasonable chance for award." See also *Firearms Training Sys., Inc. v. United States*, 41 Fed. Cl. 743 (1998), where the court held that the new FAR language permitted a competitive range of one. In that case, the court also held that the new FAR gave the agency broad discretion in determining when to establish the competitive range — allowing the agency to conduct a demonstration of proposed products before establishing the competitive range.

Reduction of the competitive range on the basis of efficiency is more problematic. As seen from the above comment, the FAR Councils appear to have concluded that, as a general rule, no more than three offerors should be included in the competitive range. Nonetheless, the FAR contains no such guidance. See, however, NFS 1815.306, which contains the following statement:

> (c)(2) A total of no more than three proposals shall be a working goal in establishing the competitive range. Field installations may establish procedures for approval of competitive range determinations commensurate with the complexity or dollar value of an acquisition.

It seems clear that elimination of proposals that have been determined to be among those most highly rated would be likely to subject an agency to protests of unfair treatment. Thus, elimination of such proposals should be done very cautiously. Where negotiations are not anticipated to be complex or time-consuming, a relatively large number of offerors might not result in inefficiency, and a greater number of proposals could be retained in the competitive range. In contrast, where the nature of the procurement and the offers require substantial negotiations and complex offer revisions, limiting the competitive range would be desirable. In such cases the agency should carefully document the differences between the proposals and endeavor to eliminate those proposals that do not have a good chance of winning the competition. If, as the FAR seems to indicate, reduction requires the elimination of proposals that are essentially equal in merit and, hence, most highly rated, it is difficult to see what rationale would support the elimination of offerors from the competitive range when other offerors that had similar evaluations were included in the range. It would be sounder practice to include all of the most highly rated offerors in the range. See, however, *Kathpal Techs., Inc.*, Comp. Gen. Dec. B-283137.3, 2000 CPD ¶ 6, where the GAO suggested that using this technique might have been a way to limit the number of competitors in a situation where the agency had received over 200 proposals. Compare *Meridian Mgmt. Corp.*, Comp. Gen. Dec. B-285127, 2000 CPD ¶ 121, granting a protest where the agency achieved an efficient number of competitors by dropping all proposals with low scores or high prices. The GAO reasoned that the agency had not considered the protester's low prices in dropping it because of a questionable poor evaluation of its nonprice factors.

B. Discretion to Include or Exclude

Under the FAR Part 15 rewrite, as under the prior regulations, the agencies have broad discretion in determining whether to include an offer in or exclude it from the competitive range. Thus, such decisions will not be disturbed unless they are clearly shown to be arbitrary or unreasonable. See, for example, *W&D Ships Deck Works, Inc. v. United States*, 39 Fed. Cl. 638 (1997), where the court stated that it would not overrule a competitive range decision unless it was "clearly unreasonable." See *L&M Techs., Inc.*, Comp. Gen. Dec. B-278044.5, 98-1 CPD ¶ 131, stating:

> The determination of whether a proposal is in the competitive range is principally a matter within the contracting agency's discretion, since agencies are responsible for defining their needs and for deciding the best method of meeting them. *Engineering & Env't, Inc.*, B-271868.3, Sept. 3, 1996, 96-2 CPD ¶ 182 at 3. In determining the competitive range, it is an acceptable practice to compare the evaluation scores and consider an offeror's relative standing among its competitors, and to exclude a proposal that is technically acceptable, when, relative to other acceptable offers, it is determined to have no reasonable chance of being selected for award. *Information Sys. & Networks Corp.*, [B-237687, Feb. 22, 1990, 90-1 CPD ¶ 203]. A protester's mere disagreement with the agency's judgment is not sufficient to establish that the agency acted unreasonably in this regard. *Delta Ventures*, B-238655, June 25, 1990, 90-1 CPD ¶ 588 at 4.

Accord, *Impresa Construzioni Geom. Domenico Garufi v. United States*, 44 Fed. Cl. 540 (1999), *aff'd*, 238 F.3d 1324 (Fed. Cir. 2001). This same broad discretion is being accorded under the new "most highly rated" standard, *Medical Staffing Joint Venture, LLC*, Comp. Gen. Dec. B-400705.2, 2009 CPD ¶ 71; *EAA Capital Co., L.L.C.*, Comp. Gen. Dec. B-287460, 2001 CPD ¶ 107. See, for example, *Outdoor Venture Corp.*, Comp. Gen. Dec. B-401351.2, 2009 CPD ¶ 194, allowing exclusion of an offeror whose deficiencies were "of greater magnitude" than the deficiencies of the offeror placed in the competitive range.

Nonetheless, contracting officers must treat all offerors fairly. Thus, they are not free to treat similarly situated offerors differently. See *Isometrics, Inc. v. United States*, 5 Cl. Ct. 420 (1984), where the exclusion of a proposal that might legitimately have been excluded due to a failure to comply with RFP requirements was held to be improper because a similarly situated offeror was included in the competitive range and given an opportunity to cure the problems. See also *Columbia Research Corp.*, Comp. Gen. Dec. B-284157, 2000 CPD ¶ 158, holding that an offeror was improperly excluded when comparison of its technical proposal to the higher scored proposals revealed no material differences in either the quantity or magnitude of the weaknesses and its cost proposal was the lowest. Compare *Outdoor Venture Corp.*, Comp. Gen. Dec. B-401351.2, 2009 CPD ¶ 194, finding no unequal treatment when one offeror with deficiencies in its technical proposal was included and the protester with deficiencies in its technical proposal was excluded because its deficiencies were "of greater significance."

Offerors have also been found to have been improperly excluded from the competitive range when the exclusion is based on an unjustified evaluation. See *Trifax Corp.*, Comp. Gen. Dec. B-279561, 98-2 CPD ¶ 24 (offeror improperly excluded based on improper scoring of its past performance).

The discretion to include or exclude offerors from the competitive range permits agencies to include marginal proposals in the competitive range in order to broaden the competition. See, for example, *440 East 62nd Street Co.*, Comp. Gen. Dec. B-276058.2, 98-1 CPD ¶ 73, denying a protest asserting that it should have been excluded from the competitive range because it was weak on several evaluation factors. The GAO stated:

> [A]n agency may broaden the competitive range to maximize the competition and provide fairness to the various offerors. *Avondale Tech. Servs., Inc.*, B-243330, July 18, 1991, 91-2 CPD ¶ 72 at 3. Here, the protester was fully aware when it submitted its offer that the [solicitation's] evaluation criteria would favor an offeror with closer proximity to public transportation, smaller floor plate sizes, and a more modern office building which projected a desired professional image. The protester was therefore cognizant that it would be in an "uphill battle" to have a chance at award. See *Deskin Research Group, Inc.*, B-254487.2, Feb. 22, 1994, 94-1 CPD ¶ 134 at 5. Yet the protester chose to aggressively pursue competing for this requirement. Under these circumstances, the protester cannot reasonably

claim that it somehow was misled by its inclusion in the competitive range. In sum, we find nothing improper in the agency's establishing a competitive range of three proposals that included [the protester's].

1. Factors to Consider

The statutes require that the competitive range be established "solely on the factors specified in the solicitation," 10 U.S.C. § 2305(b)(1) and (4)(A) and 41 U.S.C. § 253b(a) and (d). This requirement is repeated in the final rewrite, FAR 15.306(c) (1) and FAR 15.305(a). Previously, the regulations required that "cost or price and other factors" be considered in establishing the competitive range, pre-rewrite FAR 15.609(a). The same language was included in an early draft of FAR 15.306(c)(1), but it was removed from the final draft.

The deletion of the language concerning consideration of cost does not necessarily mean that cost is not to be considered. Cost, with all the other evaluation factors, would ordinarily be considered in establishing the range. However, in some instances a complete evaluation of each element of each offer would not appear to be necessary prior to determining the competitive range. If any aspects of an offer are so inferior to those of other offers as to make it unlikely that it could be improved through negotiations, it would not be reasonable to invest more time and effort in continuing to evaluate that offer. See NFS 1815.305-70, Identification of Unacceptable Proposals, stating:

(a) The contracting officer shall not complete the initial evaluation of any proposal when it is determined that the proposal is unacceptable because:

(1) It does not represent a reasonable initial effort to address the essential requirements of the RFP or clearly demonstrates that the offeror does not understand the requirements;

(2) In research and development acquisitions, a substantial design drawback is evident in the proposal, and sufficient correction or improvement to consider the proposal acceptable would require virtually an entirely new technical proposal; or

(3) It contains major technical or business deficiencies or omissions or out-of-line costs which discussions with the offeror could not reasonably be expected to cure.

(b) The contracting officer shall document the rationale for discontinuing the initial evaluation of a proposal in accordance with this section.

There is support for this interpretation in decisions under the prior rules. Under the pre-rewrite rules (requiring consideration of cost), it was held to be proper to exclude offers without considering price or cost when the technical proposal was clearly unacceptable, *Regional Envtl. Consultants*, 66 Comp. Gen. 67 (B-223555), 86-2 CPD ¶ 476, *recons. denied*, 66 Comp. Gen. 388 (B-223555.2), 87-1 CPD ¶ 428; *Aid Maint. Co.*, Comp. Gen. Dec. B-255552, 94-1 CPD ¶ 188; *Telestar Corp.*, Comp. Gen. Dec. B-275855, 97-1 CPD ¶ 150. For an analysis of this rule, see *Paul & Gordon*, 52 Comp. Gen. 382 (B-174870) (1972), explaining that the procedure was compatible with the prior statutory requirement in 10 U.S.C. § 2304(g) that "proposals, including price, shall be solicited." However, technically inferior but acceptable proposals may not be rejected without considering cost or price, *Arc-Tech, Inc.*, Comp. Gen. Dec. B-400325.3, 2009 CPD ¶ 53; *Femme Comp, Inc. v. United States*, 83 Fed. Cl. 704 (2008); *Information Sciences Corp. v. United* States, 73 Fed. Cl. 70 (2006); Columbia *Research Corp.*, Comp. Gen. Dec. B-284157, 2000 CPD ¶ 158; *Kathpal Techs., Inc.*, Comp. Gen. Dec. B-283137.3, 2000 CPD ¶ 6; *Possehn Consulting*, Comp. Gen. Dec. B-278579.2, 98-2 CPD ¶ 33; *HSI-CCEC*, Comp. Gen. Dec. B-240610, 90-2 CPD ¶ 465; *Bay Tankers, Inc.*, 69 Comp. Gen. 403 (B-238162), 90-1 CPD ¶ 389. See *SCIENTECH, Inc.*, Comp. Gen. Dec. B-277805.2, 98-1 CPD ¶ 33, holding it improper to exclude an acceptable offer without considering cost, stating:

> Cost or price must be considered as a factor; it is improper to exclude an offeror from the competitive range solely on the basis of technical considerations, unless the proposal is technically unacceptable. *S&M Property Management*, B-243051, June 28, 1991, 91-1 CPD ¶ 615 at 4; *HCA Gov't Servs., Inc.*, B-224434, Nov. 25, 1986, 86-2 CPD ¶ 611 at 3–4.

> The failure to consider cost in competitive range and award decisions is improper. Agencies must consider cost to the government in evaluating competing proposals. 41 U.S.C. § 253a(b)(1) (1994). Agencies have considerable discretion in determining the appropriate method for taking cost into account; they do not have discretion, however, not to consider cost at all, as happened here. *Health Servs. Int'l, Inc.*; *Apex Envtl., Inc.*, B-247433, B-247433.2, June 5, 1992, 92-1 CPD ¶ 493 at 4.

See also *Global, A 1" Flagship Co.*, Comp. Gen. Dec. B-297235, 2006 CPD ¶ 14, holding that it was improper to exclude a company with an acceptable technical proposal from the competitive range because it was 15% higher in cost. Compare *The Cmty. Partnership LLC*, Comp. Gen. Dec. B-286844, 2001 CPD ¶ 38, holding it proper to exclude an acceptable offer without considering cost when the competition was for the first phase of a project with each winner to receive a fee of $350,000 to perform the work in that phase.

A technically acceptable proposal may be properly determined to be outside the competitive range because the contracting officer believes that the prospective costs of performance are too high and cannot be reduced sufficiently without detracting from the proposal's technical acceptability, *Tracor Marine, Inc.*, Comp. Gen. Dec. B-222484, 86-2 CPD ¶ 150 (denying protest even though protester's technical score was highest). See also *Telos Corp.*, Comp. Gen. Dec. B-279493.3, 98-2 CPD ¶ 30 (76% higher probable cost than other offeror); *Radio Sys., Inc.*, Comp. Gen. Dec. B-255080, 94-1

CPD ¶ 9 (350% higher price than the low offeror); *Everpure, Inc.*, Comp. Gen. Dec. B-226395.2, 88-2 CPD ¶ 264 (sustaining exclusion of higher-priced proposal even though that left only one offeror in the competitive range); *Systems Integrated*, Comp. Gen. Dec. B-225055, 87-1 CPD ¶ 114 (30% higher proposed costs); and *Jack Faucett Assocs.*, Comp. Gen. Dec. B-224414, 86-2 CPD ¶ 310 (35% higher costs).

A technically acceptable proposal may also be properly determined to be outside the competitive range because the contracting officer believes that the proposed price is unrealistically low. See *International Outsourcing Servs., LLC*, Comp. Gen. Dec. B-295959, 2006 CPD ¶ 6, stating:

> The protester . . . argues that under the solicitation its proposal cannot be rejected as unacceptable because its price was considered unrealistically low. However, . . . the solicitation expressly provided that "[p]roposals will be evaluated to determine whether offered prices are realistic," and specifically informed offerors that the analysis would include the distinct queries of whether the prices were realistic "in relation to the work to be performed, reflect a clear understanding of the requirements, and are consistent with other portions of the offeror's proposal." . . Accordingly, this is no an instance such as pointed to by the protester in *Possehn Consulting*, B-278759, Jan. 9, 1988, 98-1 CPD ¶ 10, where the rejection of a proposal because its pricing was found to be unrealistic was determined to be a matter of responsibility due to the solicitations's lack of ayn evaluation factor or criteria related to price realism.

The lower the technical rating, the less the cost differential must be to properly exclude an offeror from the competitive range. See, for example, *Bollam, Sheedy, Torani & Co.*, Comp. Gen. Dec. B-270700, 96-1 CPD ¶ 185 (agency properly excluded proposal because it was ranked tenth out of 34 and the price was higher than seven of the eight proposals with higher technical scores); and *Emerald Maint., Inc.*, Comp. Gen. Dec. B-221353, 86-1 CPD ¶ 308 (offeror with a probable cost only 14% higher properly excluded when its technical rating was 30% lower).

A low cost proposal is not guaranteed inclusion in the competitive range by virtue of its low cost. See, for example, *D S, Inc.*, Comp. Gen. Dec. B-289676, 2002 CPD ¶ 58 (proposal contained insufficient costs to perform the work); *Molina Eng'g, Ltd./Tri-J Indus., Inc. J.V.*, Comp. Gen. Dec. B-284895, 2000 CPD ¶ 86 (proposal with unrealistically low price); *McDonald Constr. Servs., Inc.*, Comp. Gen. Dec. B-285980, 2000 CPD ¶ 183 (proposal was approximately 10% lower in price but was much lower rated on technical factors); and *Hydroscience, Inc.*, Comp. Gen. Dec. B-227989, 87-2 CPD ¶ 501 (proposal with three major technical deficiencies even though it was considerably lower in cost).

2. Comparative Nature of Decision

The competitive range determination is generally made by comparing the competing proposals in order to determine whether any proposal has a reasonable chance of winning the competition. See, for example, *Atlantic Coast Contracting, Inc.*, Comp. Gen. Dec. B-270645.2, 96-1 CPD ¶ 252, stating:

> In determining the competitive range, it is an acceptable practice to compare the evaluation scores and consider an offeror's relative standing among its competitors and to exclude a proposal that is capable of being made technically acceptable when, relative to other offers, it is determined to have no reasonable chance of being selected for award.

In reviewing the comparative assessment of the agency, the GAO noted that the protester had received a score far below that of higher-ranked offerors and found that the low scores were adequately supported in the evaluation documentation. For other cases affirming the comparative method of determining which proposals should be included in the competitive range, see *Medical Dev. Int'l, Inc. v. United States*, 89 Fed. Cl. 691 (2009) (protester's low comparative rating on price justifies exclusion even though it had slightly higher technical rating); *Government Telecommunications, Inc.*, Comp. Gen. Dec. B-299542.2, 2007 CPD ¶ 136 (substantial difference in rating of protester and two most highly rated proposals); *Erinys Iraq Ltd. v. United States*, 78 Fed. Cl. 518 (2007) (unduly high comparative price properly excluded protester); *Information Sys. Tech. Corp.*, Comp. Gen. Dec. B-291747, 2005 CPD ¶ 76 (one proposal rated far higher than other two acceptable proposals); *Northwest Procurement Inst., Inc.*, Comp. Gen. Dec. B-286345, 2000 CPD ¶ 192 (nonprice score far below other two offerors); *Arsenault Acquisition Corp.*, Comp. Gen. Dec. B-276959, 97-2 CPD ¶ 74 (proposal scored "good" but was not comparable to best proposals); *Consolidated Eng'g Servs., Inc.*, Comp. Gen. Dec. B-277273, 97-2 CPD ¶ 86 (three proposals with top scores properly included in competitive range when there was a significant break with lower scored proposals); *Techniarts Eng'g*, Comp. Gen. Dec. B-271509, 96-2 CPD ¶ 1 (protester's technically acceptable proposal was inferior to several other proposals); and *Interactive Communication Tech., Inc.*, Comp. Gen. Dec. B-271051, 96-1 CPD ¶ 260 (technically acceptable proposal rated much lower than other proposals properly excluded from competitive range).

Comparative assessments can even be used to reduce the competitive range to a single offeror. See *DuVALL Servs. Co.*, Comp. Gen. Dec. B-265698.2, 96-1 CPD ¶ 133, stating:

> Even a proposal that is technically acceptable as submitted need not be included in the competitive range when, relative to other acceptable offers, it is determined to have no reasonable chance of being selected for award. *Wordpro, Inc.*, B-242100.2, Apr. 24, 1991, 91-1 CPD ¶ 404; see *Hummer Assocs.*, B-236702, Jan. 4, 1990, 90-1 CPD ¶ 12. This "relative" approach to determining the competitive range, that is, comparing one offeror's proposal to those of other offerors, may be used even where it results in a competitive range of one. *Everpure, Inc.*, [B-226395.2, Sept. 20, 1988, 88-2 CPD ¶ 264]; *Systems Integrated*, B-225055, Feb. 4, 1987, 87-1 CPD ¶ 114.

3. Inclusion of Defective or Unacceptable Offers

Because negotiations are conducted for the purpose of giving offerors the opportunity to cure weaknesses or deficiencies or to modify other aspects of their proposals, an offer need not be excluded from the competitive range solely because it fails to conform to the RFP. In this respect the competitive range decision is very different from the "nonresponsiveness" determination in sealed bid contracting. See *Construcciones Aeronauticas, S.A.*, Comp. Gen. Dec. B-244717, 91-2 CPD ¶ 461, where the GAO stated that "the concept of competitive range — whether the proposal is or can be readily made acceptable — is incompatible with responsiveness." See also *DeMat Air, Inc. v. United States*, 2 Cl. Ct. 197 (1983). In *AVIATE L.L.C.*, Comp. Gen. Dec. B-275058.6, 97-1 CPD ¶ 162, the GAO stated:

> Contrary to [the protester's] apparent belief, there is no per se prohibition against the inclusion of a technically unacceptable proposal in the competitive range. Rather, a fundamental purpose in conducting discussions is to determine whether deficient proposals are reasonably susceptible of being made acceptable through discussions. *Construcciones Aeronauticas, S.A.*, 71 Comp. Gen. 82, 85-86 (1991), 91-2 CPD ¶ 461 at 6–7; *Scan-Optics, Inc.*, B-211048, Apr. 24, 1984, 84-1 CPD ¶ 464 at 4–5. An unacceptable proposal that is reasonably susceptible of being made acceptable through discussions and which the agency reasonably determines has a reasonable chance of being selected for award properly is included in the competitive range. See *SAIC Computer Sys.*, B-258431.2, Mar. 13, 1995, 95-1 CPD ¶ 156 at 4.

Similarly, in *Carahsoft Tech. Corp. v. United States*, 86 Fed. Cl. 325 (2009), the Court of Federal Claims stated at 341-42:

> [U]nlike a non-responsive bid in sealed bidding where there is neither a competitive range determination, nor subsequent rounds of discussions and offer revisions, a technically unacceptable proposal may be considered for award if the proposal would otherwise be competitive and if its technically unacceptable terms can be cured by the offeror in a revised proposal. *See Birch & Davis Int'l, Inc. v. Christopher*, 4 F.3d 970, 974 (Fed. Cir. 1993) ("'[A] proposal must generally be considered in the competitive range unless it is so technically inferior or out of line as to price, as to render discussions meaningless.'") (quoting *M.W. Kellogg Co. v. United States*, 10 Cl.Ct. 17, 23 (1986)); *Labat-Anderson, Inc. v. United States*, 42 Fed. Cl. 806, 841 (1999) ("[T]echnically unacceptable proposals must generally be considered to be within the competitive range if capable of being made technically acceptable and if the proposal's cost or price term is competitive.").

In *National Ass'n of State Directors of Special Educ., Inc.*, Comp. Gen. Dec. B-227989, 89-1 CPD ¶ 189, the GAO affirmed a contracting officer's decision to keep a technically unacceptable proposal in the competitive range because it was one of only two proposals. See also *Grove Resource Solutions, Inc.*, Comp. Gen. Dec. B-296228, 2005 CPD ¶ 133; and *SWR, Inc.*, Comp. Gen. Dec. B-286229, 2000 CPD

¶ 196, noting that the purpose of establishing a competitive range is to cure deficiencies. In a decision that is at variance with the regulatory and decisional principles for establishing the competitive range, the GAO held that the Army should have rejected a proposal that substantially failed to conform to the RFP, *Computer Mach. Corp.*, 55 Comp. Gen. 1151 (B-185592), 76-1 CPD ¶ 358. In that decision the GAO stated that when an agency uses the term "responsive" in its RFP, the offeror should understand that any terms referenced thereby are considered to be material requirements and that a proposal failing to conform to such terms will be considered unacceptable.

4. Exclusion for Offer Deficiencies

Although proposals with significant offer deficiencies may be included in the competitive range, they may also be excluded if the contracting officer determines that the offeror does not stand a reasonable chance of winning the competition. Contracting officers have been given broad discretion in making this determination. See, for example, *All Computer Consulting, Inc.*, Comp. Gen. Dec. B-401204, 2009 CPD ¶ 132 (exclusion proper where proposal did not demonstrate that proposed product met specification requirements); *L-3 Comms. EOTech, Inc.*, Comp. Gen. Dec. B-311453, 2008 CPD ¶ 130 (exclusion proper where bid sample failed tests – Court of Federal Claims reached opposite result in *L-3 Comms. EOTech, Inc. v. United States*, 83 Fed. Cl. 643 (2008)); *Pacific Lock Co.*, Comp. Gen. Dec. B-309982, 2007 CPD ¶ 191 (exclusion proper where proposal did not clearly prove that product was "U.S. made"); *Kolob Canyons Air Serv.*, Comp. Gen. Dec. B-398240.2, 2006 CPD ¶ 106 (exclusion proper where proposal did not demonstrate that aircraft contained required avionics); *Integration Techs. Group, Inc.*, Comp. Gen. Dec. B-295958, 2005 CPD ¶ 99 (exclusion proper where offered product did not meet specifications); *CliniComp, Int'l*, Comp. Gen. Dec. B-294059, 2004 CPD ¶ 209 (product not commercially available as required by RFP); *Wahkontah Servs., Inc.*, Comp. Gen. Dec. B-292768, 2003 CPD ¶ 214 (exclusion proper where proposal merely parroted back RFP requirements); *Americom Gov't Servs., Inc.*, Comp. Gen. Dec. B-292242, 2003 CPD ¶ 163 (exclusion proper when proposal included conditions on contract requirements); *B.E. Meyers & Co.*, Comp. Gen. Dec. B-283796, 2000 CPD ¶ 9 (exclusion proper when proposal was very short and incomplete); *Novavax, Inc.*, Comp. Gen. Dec. B-286167, 2000 CPD ¶ 202 (proper to exclude offeror that took exception to important requirement of RFP); *Wirt Inflatable Specialists, Inc.*, Comp. Gen. Dec. B-282554, 99-2 CPD ¶ 34 (exclusion proper when product failed test even though offeror could have easily corrected problem); *Clean Serv. Co.*, Comp. Gen. Dec. B-281141.3, 99-1 CPD ¶ 36 (exclusion proper when winning proposal was subsequently reevaluated without pages exceeding page limitation and found unacceptable); and *Cache Box, Inc.*, Comp. Gen. Dec. B-279892, 98-2 CPD ¶ 146 (exclusion proper when proposal offered product that either did not meet specification or was ambiguous as to its ability to meet specification). It is clearly proper to exclude from the competitive range a proposal that could be made acceptable only if major modifications or revisions were undertaken, *Orincon Corp.*, Comp.

Gen. Dec. B-276704, 97-2 CPD ¶ 26 (failure to propose small business subcontractors sufficient to meet the contractual subcontracting requirement); *Orbit Advanced Techs., Inc.*, Comp. Gen. Dec. B-271293, 96-1 CPD ¶ 254 (numerous deficiencies in explaining how its proposed product met the contract specifications and in justifying its costs); *Hines-Ike Co.*, Comp. Gen. Dec. B-270693, 96-1 CPD ¶ 158 (proposed technique of performing one segment of work that did not meet the specifications plus numerous informational deficiencies); *Eastern Tech. Enters., Inc.*, Comp. Gen. Dec. B-259844, 95-1 CPD ¶ 232 (no description of techniques to be used to perform the work as required by the solicitation); and *Pyramid Servs., Inc.*, Comp. Gen. Dec. B-257085, 94-2 CPD ¶ 79 (proposal failed to propose sufficient staffing, proposed using older, used equipment, and offeror lacked experience). A proposal was also properly excluded where the offeror informed the agency that it needed more time to resolve a zoning deficiency with the local authorities, *Dismas Charities, Inc.*, Comp. Gen. Dec. B-284754, 2000 CPD ¶ 84.

A proposal was found properly excluded when the offeror did not respond to a request for clarification of the technically unacceptable proposal in a timely manner, *Data Resources, Inc.*, 65 Comp. Gen. 125 (B-220079), 85-2 CPD ¶ 670. The exclusion of a proposal that was not "grossly deficient" was upheld where inclusion would not have enhanced competition, as the protester was the sole offeror, *Magnavox Advanced Prods. & Sys. Co.*, Comp. Gen. Dec. B-215426, 85-1 CPD ¶ 146. The agency decided to exclude the proposal from the competitive range and resolicited with relaxed specifications.

5. Informational Deficiencies

Many RFPs require the submission of information relating to the offeror's capability to perform or to establish that the products or services offered meet the specifications. Contracting agencies have been permitted to exclude offers from the competitive range for material failures to provide such information. In determining whether an informational deficiency is material, the GAO has considered (1) the detail called for in the RFP, (2) whether the omissions make the proposal unacceptable or merely inferior, (3) the scope and range of omissions, and (4) whether the proposal offers significant cost savings, *XYZTEK Corp.*, Comp. Gen. Dec. B-214704, 84-2 CPD ¶ 204. Offerors have been held to bear the risk of submitting proposals that do not comply with the RFP's informational requirements, *Pace Data Sys., Inc.*, Comp. Gen. Dec. B-236083, 89-2 CPD ¶ 429. Compare *Birch & Davis Int'l, Inc. v. Christopher*, 4 F.3d 970 (Fed. Cir. 1993), finding an offeror improperly excluded from the competitive range based on informational deficiencies because it had a reasonable chance for award.

Proposal page limitations are not an excuse for failing to provide required information. In *Infotec Dev., Inc.*, Comp. Gen. Dec. B-238980, 90-2 CPD ¶ 58, a proposal was properly excluded for lack of information after the agency rejected

49 pages of the proposal that exceeded the page limitations in the RFP. Similarly, in *Management & Indus. Techs. Assocs.*, Comp. Gen. Dec. B-257656, 94-2 CPD ¶ 134, an RFP had a 20-page limit and the protester submitted more than 200 pages of material. The agency removed the pages that exceeded the page limit, found the remaining pages deficient, and excluded the protester from the competitive range. See also *HSQ Tech.*, Comp. Gen. Dec. B-277048, 97-2 CPD ¶ 57, finding it proper to exclude a proposal that exceeded the overall 300-page limitation with the result that none of its price proposal was included in the evaluation; and *Integrated Tech. Works, Inc. — Telara, Inc.*, Comp. Gen. Dec. B-286769.5, 2001 CPD ¶ 141, where the refusal to evaluate pages exceeding the 30-page limitation made an offeror technically unacceptable.

Where the information that is not submitted is for the purpose of verifying whether the offered products or services conform to specifications, exclusion from the competitive range has been held to be justified. See *Hamilton Sundstrand Poser Sys. v. United States*, 75 Fed. Cl. 512 (2007) (lack of narrative description as to how product complies with purchase description); *TMC Design Corp.*, Comp. Gen. Dec. B-296194.3, 2005 CPD ¶ 158 (lack of details about product's capabilities – exclusion proper even though testing of product was to be conducted prior to award decision); *Consultants in Continual Improvement*, Comp. Gen. Dec. B-289351, 2002 CPD ¶ 40 (proposal did not give details of the offeror's proprietary method of performing the work); *Speegle Constr., Inc.*, Comp. Gen. Dec. B-286063, 2000 CPD ¶ 190 (offeror that had not provided the technical solutions required by the RFP); and *Working Alternatives, Inc.*, Comp. Gen. Dec. B-276911, 97-2 CPD ¶ 2 (offeror failed to provide mandatory documentation demonstrating that it had a right to use its proposed prison facility). In *Amperif Corp.*, Comp. Gen. Dec. B-211992, 84-1 CPD ¶ 409, the exclusion of a proposal was upheld where the proposal "parroted" the specifications and merely stated it would meet or exceed the minimum requirements. The solicitation required detailed discussion of plans for satisfying or taking exception to the requirements, although it also cautioned that "unnecessarily elaborate brochures" or other representations might be taken as evidence of a lack of cost consciousness. The GAO stated that where the solicitation includes specific instructions to address mandatory requirements, "offerors are put on notice that they risk rejection if they fail to do so." See also *Ensign-Bickford Co.*, Comp. Gen. Dec. B-211790, 84-1 CPD ¶ 439; and *S&Q Corp.*, Comp. Gen. Dec. B-219420, 85-2 CPD ¶ 471, *recons. denied*, 85-2 CPD ¶ 628, where proposals were excluded from the competitive range for failing to include detailed information establishing the feasibility of the proposed approach.

Information related to the capability of the offeror has also been held to be material, and the failure to furnish such information has been held to be a valid reason for exclusion from the competitive range. Thus, informational deficiencies in technical or management proposals used to assess the offerors' understanding of the work also constitute valid reasons for exclusion of an offeror from the competitive range. See *D&J Enters., Inc.*,Comp. Gen. Dec. B-310442, 2008 CPD ¶ 8 (insufficient information on key personnel and organizational structure); *Profes-*

sional Performance Dev. Group, Inc., Comp. Gen. Dec. B-311273, 2008 CPD ¶ 101 (information provided either parroted back RFP's requirements or stated intent to comply with RFP); *Femme Comp, Inc. v. United States*, 83 Fed. Cl. 704 (2008) (information was in wrong volume of proposal as delineated in RFP); *C. Martin Co.*, Comp. Gen. Dec. B-299382, 2007 CPD ¶ 74 (proposal appeared to use old information not responding to current requirements); *B&S Transport, Inc.*, Comp. Gen. Dec. B-299144, 2007 CPD ¶ 16 (insufficient information on management and operational approach); *Sigma One Corp.*, Comp. Gen. Dec. B-294719, 2005 CPD ¶ 49 ("overly general" treatment of required information); *Wahkontah Servs., Inc.*, Comp. Gen. Dec. B-292768, 2003 CPD ¶ 214 (information provided either parroted back in whole or part RFP's requirements or lacked sufficient information and detail to determine that offeror understood work required); *DSC Cleaning, Inc.*, Comp. Gen. Dec. B-292125, 2003 CPD ¶ 118 (no references provided); *LaBarge Prod., Inc.*, Comp. Gen. Dec. B-287841, 2001 CPD ¶ 177 (insufficient information on experience and qualifications as well as insufficient technical information); *EAA Capital Co., L.C.C.*, Comp. Gen. Dec. B-287460, 2001 CPD ¶ 107 (insufficient information on management capability, technical plan and prior experience); *Essex Electro Eng'rs, Inc.*, Comp. Gen. Dec. B-284149, 2000 CPD ¶ 72 (poorly written proposal parroting RFP); *Matrix Gen., Inc.*, Comp. Gen. Dec. B-282192, 99-1 CPD ¶ 108 (insufficient capability information); *Ervin & Assocs., Inc.*, Comp. Gen. Dec. B-280993, 98-2 CPD ¶ 151 (poorly written proposal was "technically unacceptable"); *RAMCOR Servs. Group Inc.*, Comp. Gen. Dec. B-276633.2, 98-1 CPD ¶ 121 (major defects in management, preventative maintenance and quality control plans); *Chant Eng'g Co.*, Comp. Gen. Dec. B-257125.2, 94-2 CPD ¶ 247 (informational deficiencies rendered proposal so deficient that it would require a major rewrite in order to be made acceptable); and *Pace Data Sys., Inc.*, Comp. Gen. Dec. B-236083, 89-2 CPD ¶ 429 (poor draftsmanship). In *Aliron Int'l, Inc.*, Comp. Gen. Dec. B-285048.2, 2000 CPD ¶ 125, it was held proper to exclude an offeror based on an inferior oral presentation that did not cover the required information.

Offerors have been properly excluded from the competitive range for informational deficiencies demonstrating their understanding of the work even when the agency knows that they are fully capable of performing. See *HealthStar VA, PLLC*, Comp. Gen. Dec. B-299737, 2007 CPD ¶ 114, stating:

> An offeror's technical evaluation is dependent upon the information furnished; there is no legal basis for favoring a firm with presumptions on the basis of its incumbent status. It is the offeror's burden to submit an adequately written proposal; an offeror, including an incumbent contractor, must furnish, within its proposal, all information that was requested or necessary to demonstrate its capabilities in response to the solicitation. *Computerized Project Mgmt. Plus*, B-247063, Apr. 28, 1992, 92-1 CPD ¶ 401 at 3.

Thus, incumbent contractors have been excluded from the competitive range for informational deficiencies, *SPAAN Tech, Inc.*, Comp. Gen. Dec. B-400406, 2009

CPD ¶ 46 (failure to provide information on quality assurance plan); *International Resource Recovery, Inc. v. United States*, 60 Fed. Cl. 1 (2004) (failure to submit mobilization plan for work currently being performed); *Interactive Communication Tech., Inc.*, Comp. Gen. Dec. B-271051, 96-1 CPD ¶ 260 (incumbent's technical proposal lacked detailed information on technical approach and staffing); *Pedus Bldg. Servs., Inc.*, Comp. Gen. Dec. B-257271.3, 95-1 CPD ¶ 135 (sloppy technical proposal did not demonstrate that incumbent contractor understood how to perform the work); *Premier Cleaning Sys., Inc.*, Comp. Gen. Dec. B-255815, 94-1 CPD ¶ 241 (failure to submit resume and signed letter of intent of incumbent project manager was a significant deficiency that supported elimination from competitive range). See also *McAllister & Assocs., Inc.*, Comp. Gen. Dec. B-277029.3, 98-1 CPD ¶ 85, where an offeror with significant experience in performing work like that called for by the contract was held to be properly excluded from the competitive range because of a poorly written technical proposal. An incumbent contractor has also been excluded from the competitive range for failing to meet an RFP require-ment as to how the work is to be performed even though they have successfully performed the work a different way, *Saftey-Kleen (Pecatonica), Inc.*, Comp. Gen. Dec. B-290838, 2002 CPD ¶ 176.

Given the increased latitude provided by the FAR Part 15 rewrite, the contract-ing agencies will continue to have broad discretion in this area. In exercising this discretion, the number and nature of the other proposals should be considered. If the substantive portions of the proposal (the offer) place it within the proposals "most highly rated," the failure to provide material information would not call for exclusion unless the number of proposals is to be limited for purposes of efficiency. In exercis-ing the authority to reduce the size of the range for purposes of efficiency, the agency must treat the offerors fairly. Thus, it would be improper to exclude such an offer if other offers included in the reduced range had similar informational deficiencies.

6. Competitive Range of One

Prior to the new rules on establishing the competitive range, an agency's deci-sion to include only one offeror in the competitive range was subject to close scru-tiny due to the elimination of competition, *Birch & Davis Int'l, Inc. v. Christopher*, 4 F.3d 970 (Fed. Cir. 1993); *Besserman Corp.*, Comp. Gen. Dec. B-237327, 90-1 CPD ¶ 191; *Apt Corp.*, GSBCA 9237-P, 88-1 BCA ¶ 20,411. A competitive range of one was overturned in a number of cases. See *Dynalantic Corp.*, Comp. Gen. Dec. B-274944.2, 97-1 CPD ¶ 101 (deficiencies of eliminated proposal were mi-nor and easily correctable and price was lower); *Coastal Gov't Servs., Inc.*, Comp. Gen. Dec. B-250820, 93-1 CPD ¶ 167 (inadequacies were minor and could have been easily resolved during discussions); *Stay, Inc.*, Comp. Gen. Dec. B-247606, 92-1 CPD ¶ 481 (reasons for exclusion of protester were minor and some deficien-cies were also found in awardee's proposal); *Corporate Strategies, Inc.*, Comp. Gen. Dec. B-239219, 90-2 CPD ¶ 99 (lower priced proposals that were eliminated were rated excellent or good and had weaknesses that could have been resolved by discussions).

Based on the new competitive range rules, the GAO no longer follows this rule. Thus, since the FAR now uses the term "most highly rated proposals," an agency is permitted to include only one proposal in the competitive range if no other proposal has a reasonable chance of being selected for award, *TekStar, Inc.*, Comp. Gen. Dec. B-295444, 2005 CPD ¶ 53; *Information Sys. Tech. Corp.*, Comp. Gen. Dec. B-291747, 2003 CPD ¶ 72; *SDS Petroleum Prods., Inc.*, Comp. Gen. Dec. B-280430, 98-2 CPD ¶ 59, or if all other proposals have deficiencies, *General Atomics Aeronautical Sys., Inc.*, Gen. Dec. B-311004, 2008 CPD ¶ 105 (protester's proposal would have required major revisions); *M&M Investigations, Inc.*, Gen. Dec. B-299369.2, 2007 CPD ¶ 200 (protester's proposal was 30% higher in price and not rated best technically); *SOS Interpreting, Ltd.*, Comp. Gen. Dec. B-287505, 2001 CPD ¶ 104 (TEP rated proposal conditionally acceptable overall, which meant proposal did not meet all requirements); *Clean Serv. Co.*, Comp. Gen. Dec. B-281141.3, 99-1 CPD ¶ 36 (protester's proposal exceeded page limitations); *Wirt Inflatable Specialists, Inc.*, Comp. Gen. Dec. B-282554, 99-2 CPD ¶ 34 (protester's product leaked during preaward test). In the *SDS* decision, the GAO rejected the argument that the agency was required to keep the top rated proposals in the competition because of the new language in the FAR and the deletion of the prior language stating that the competitive range should include "all proposals with a reasonable chance for award." See also *Firearms Training Sys., Inc. v. United States*, 41 Fed. Cl. 743 (1998), where the court held that the new FAR language permitted a competitive range of one. In that case, the court also held that the new FAR gave the agency broad discretion in determining when to establish the competitive range — allowing the agency to conduct a demonstration of proposed products before establishing the competitive range. Compare *Bean Stuyvesant, L.L.C. v. United States*, 48 Fed. Cl. 303 (2000), upholding a determination that only one offeror was in the competitive range but stating that "strict scrutiny" should continue to be given to such determinations under the new FAR.

Even under the old policy, the GAO upheld such a decision to establish a competitive range of one when it was reasonably made. For cases upholding the decision to include only one offeror within the competitive range, see *Quality Fabricators, Inc.*, Comp. Gen. Dec. B-271431, 96-2 CPD ¶ 22 (offeror with third lowest price but exceptional score on past performance only one of six offerors included in competitive range because past performance was the predominant evaluation factor); *Cobra Techs., Inc.*, Comp. Gen. Dec. B-272041, 96-2 CPD ¶ 73 (other two offerors were scored far lower than single offeror in competitive range); *Resource Applications, Inc.*, Comp. Gen. Dec. B-271079, 96-1 CPD ¶ 244 (only other proposal properly excluded because it contained significant deficiencies that would have required a substantial rewrite); *EER Sys. Corp.*, Comp. Gen. Dec. B-256383, 94-1 CPD ¶ 354 (proposal was substantially inferior in demonstrating an understanding of requirements and no appreciable cost difference between the two proposals to justify inclusion in competitive range); *Novel Pharmaceutical, Inc.,* Comp. Gen. Dec. B-255374, 94-1 CPD ¶ 149 (proposal had no reasonable chance for award because it did not show that protester had the required experience or capability to perform the contract); *HITCO,* 68 Comp. Gen. 10 (B-232093), 88-2 CPD ¶ 337 (excluded proposal had numerous informational deficiencies rated unacceptable); *Rice Servs., Ltd.,* 68 Comp. Gen. 112 (B-232610), 88-2 CPD ¶ 514 (lack of required explanatory information after clarification request); *Optical Data Sys. — Tex., Inc.,* Comp. Gen. Dec. B-227755, 87-2 CPD ¶ 393 (protester's proposal not close to being acceptable and deficiencies not easily correctable); *Systems Integrated,* Comp. Gen. Dec. B-225055, 87-1 CPD ¶ 114 (protester's proposal priced 30% higher and offered no technical advantages); *Commission on Professional & Hosp. Activities,* Comp. Gen. Dec. B-228924, 87-2 CPD ¶ 637 (protester's proposal did not contain essential required information and was quite inferior); and *Regional Envtl. Consultants,* 66 Comp. Gen. 67 (B-223555), 86-2 CPD ¶ 476, *recons. denied,* 66 Comp. Gen. 388 (B-223555.2), 87-1 CPD ¶ 428 (protester's technical proposal significantly inferior even though scores quite similar).

C. Changes in the Competitive Range

The competitive range is dynamic rather than static. Thus, as an agency learns more about an offeror, through communications, negotiations or reevaluation, the competitive range may be altered to reflect the current status of the offerors.

1. Removal from the Competitive Range

Procuring agencies are not bound by initial determinations to include offers within the competitive range, *Intown Properties, Inc.,* Comp. Gen. Dec. B-250232, 93-1 CPD ¶ 43. In this regard FAR 15.306(c)(3) provides that an offer originally included in the competitive range may be removed, as follows:

> If the contracting officer, after complying with paragraph (d)(3) of this section, decides that an offeror's proposal should no longer be included in the competitive range, the proposal shall be eliminated from consideration for award. Written notice of this decision shall be provided to unsuccessful offerors in accordance with 15.503.

If, after or during discussions, it becomes clear that a proposal should not have been included, or no longer belongs, in the competitive range, the offeror may be precluded from further written or oral discussions, *Shel-Ken Properties, Inc.,* Comp. Gen. Dec. B-277250, 97-2 CPD ¶ 79; *MAR Inc.,* Comp. Gen. Dec. B-246889, 92-1 CPD ¶ 367; *Scientific Mgmt. Assocs., Inc.,* Comp. Gen. Dec. B-238913, 90-2 CPD ¶ 27. In *Travel Co.,* Comp. Gen. Dec. B-249560.2, 93-1 CPD ¶ 76, the protester was initially found to be within the competitive range, but after the agency requested and received supplementary and clarifying information, it determined that the protester was only at a minimally acceptable level and, therefore, no longer within the competitive range. Similarly, in *Hamilton Sundstrand Power Sys.*, Comp. Gen. Dec. B-298757, 2006 CPD ¶ 194; *Worldwide Primates, Inc.*, Comp. Gen. Dec. B-294481, 2004 CPD ¶ 206; *Outdoor Venture Corp.*, Comp. Gen. Dec. B-288894.2, 2002 CPD ¶ 13, *PeopleSoft USA, Inc.*, Comp. Gen. Dec. B-283497, 2000 CPD ¶ 25, and *Novavax, Inc.*, Comp. Gen. Dec. B-286167, 2000 CPD ¶ 202, proposals with significant deficiencies were included in the competitive range but dropped when discussions did not clear up the deficiencies. Compare *Symtech Corp.*, Comp. Gen. Dec. B-289332, 2002 CPD ¶ 43, holding that the agency had no reasonable basis for dropping a proposal from the competitive range because of its response to discussion questions. See also *Impresa Construzioni Geom. Domenico Garufi v. United States*, 44 Fed. Cl. 540 (1999), *aff'd*, 238 F.3d 1324 (Fed. Cir. 2001) (proper to exclude offeror from competitive range when answers to discussion questions show lack of understanding of work); *Dismas Charities, Inc.*, Comp. Gen. Dec. B-284754, 2000 CPD ¶ 84 (proper to drop an offeror when necessary information was not included in BAFO); *Labat — Anderson, Inc. v. United States*, 42 Fed. Cl. 806 (1999) (proper exclusion when BAFO was technically unacceptable); *Magnum Prods., Inc.*, Comp. Gen. Dec. B-277917, 97-2 CPD ¶ 160 (offeror properly dropped after its BAFO did not cure a major deficiency pointed out during discussions); *Shel-Ken Properties, Inc.*, Comp. Gen. Dec. B-277250, 97-2 CPD ¶ 79 (offeror properly excluded when there were five BAFOs rated higher technically and three of these had lower prices); and *Herley Indus., Inc.*, Comp. Gen. Dec. B-237960, 90-1 CPD ¶ 364, *recons. denied*, 90-2 CPD ¶ 173 (proper to drop offeror when there remained "significant deficiencies" after the first round of discussions. Compare *Voith Hydro, Inc.*, Comp. Gen. Dec. B-277051, 97-2 CPD ¶ 68, holding that an offeror was improperly dropped from the competitive range based on deficiencies in its BAFO when the deficiencies had been apparent in a question and answer session during oral presentations but had not been identified by the agency during negotiations.

An offeror may be dropped from the competitive range once negotiations have begun without affording the offeror an opportunity to submit a revised offer. See FAR 15.306(d)(4), which states:

> If, after discussions have begun, an offeror originally in the competitive range is no longer considered to be among the most highly rated offerors being considered for award, that offeror may be eliminated from the competitive range whether or not all material aspects of the proposal have been discussed, or whether or not the offeror has been afforded an opportunity to submit a proposal revision (see 15.307(a) and 15.503(a)(1)).

Conducting discussions with all offerors does not obligate the agency to conduct further discussions with all offerors or to allow all to submit further proposal revisions, *OMV Med., Inc.*, Comp. Gen. Dec. B-281490, 99-1 CPD ¶ 38; *All State Boiler Work, Inc.*, Comp. Gen. Dec. B-277362, 97-2 CPD ¶ 144; *ALM, Inc.*, Comp. Gen. Dec. B-217284, 85-1 CPD ¶ 433; *Informatics Gen. Corp.*, Comp. Gen. Dec. B-210709, 83-2 CPD ¶ 47, *recons. denied*, 83-2 CPD ¶ 580. In *A. T. Kearney, Inc.*,

Comp. Gen. Dec. B-237731, 90-1 CPD ¶ 305, an offeror was properly dropped from the competitive range when additional cost realism analysis indicated that its probable costs were not as low as originally thought and its technical score was far below the other offeror. In *Systems Integrated*, Comp. Gen. Dec. B-225055, 87-1 CPD ¶ 114, it was held proper to drop one of two competitors with almost equal technical scores from the competitive range because its cost proposal was almost 30% higher. See also *DuVALL Servs. Co.*, Comp. Gen. Dec. B-265698.2, 96-1 CPD ¶ 133, finding proper an agency's decision to drop a protester from the revised competitive range because it did not have a reasonable chance for award. The protester's explanation and analysis of the staffing requirement during discussions indicated to the contracting officer that it would not be likely to perform well. Similarly, in *HSQ Tech.*, Comp. Gen. Dec. B-279707, 98-2 CPD ¶ 13, *Akal Security, Inc.*, Comp. Gen. Dec. B-271385, 96-2 CPD ¶ 77, and *L&M Techs., Inc.*, Comp. Gen. Dec. B-278044.5, 98-1 CPD ¶ 131, offerors were properly eliminated from the competitive range after several rounds of discussions and BAFOs because the agency concluded that they no longer had a reasonable chance for award.

2. Addition or Reinstatement to the Competitive Range

Offerors excluded or removed from the competitive range are required to be given prompt preaward notice of exclusion, FAR 15.503(a)(1) and may request a preaward debriefing, FAR 15.505. Following notice or debriefing, the agency may discover that the offer was mistakenly excluded. Under such circumstances, it would be appropriate for the agency to include or reinstate the offer in the range. See *Jason Assocs. Corp.*, Comp. Gen. Dec. B-278689, 98-1 CPD ¶ 67, and *Joint Threat Servs.*, Comp. Gen. Dec. B-278168, 98-1 CPD ¶ 18, where, after agency-level protests, the protesters were placed back in the competitive range, and *Industrial Property Mgmt.*, Comp. Gen. Dec. B-291336.2, 2003 CPD ¶ 205, where an offeror was placed in the competitive range after initially being excluded. In *Textron, Inc. v. United States*, 74 Fed. Cl. 277 (2006), two offerors were placed back into the competitive range after filing suit in the Court of Federal Claims. See also *E.L. Hamm & Assocs., Inc.*, Comp. Gen. Dec. B-280766.3, 99-1 CPD ¶ 85, where, after a protest to the GAO, the agency added the protester and other offerors with comparable scores to the competitive range. However, the inclusion would have to be based on the offer as originally submitted. FAR 15.307(a) prohibits the agency from accepting or considering revisions to offers once they are excluded:

> If an offeror's proposal is eliminated or otherwise removed from the competitive range, no further revisions to that offeror's proposal shall be accepted or considered.

A similar provision was in the pre-rewrite FAR (FAR 15.603). Although this provision affords the agency protection against having to cope with a flurry of proposal revisions and a never ending evaluation process, there may be circumstances where consideration of a revision would be desirable. It is difficult to see the harm in considering an unsolicited revision that did not require significant evaluation effort and did not result in unfair treatment of the other offerors.

CHAPTER 8

NEGOTIATIONS

The procurement statutes require "written or oral discussions" with all offerors in the competitive range. However, they do not indicate the purpose of the discussion process, the matters to be discussed, or the procedures to be followed in conducting negotiations. The pre-rewrite FAR was also silent on the purpose of discussions. In addition, under the pre-rewrite rules, contracting agencies were significantly limited in the type of exchanges that could take place in the discussion process (former FAR 15.610). The rewrite made a number of substantial changes in the rules for discussions. Among the stated purposes of the rewrite were to increase the scope of discussions, 62 Fed. Reg. 51225 (1997). The aim was to "require a more robust exchange of information during discussions," which would consist of "negotiations" that include bargaining with the view to "allowing the offeror to revise its proposal," 62 Fed. Reg. 51229 (1997). This goal of the rewrite was expressed by adopting new terminology, using the word "negotiations" to describe the process that had previously been called "discussions." Thus, FAR 15.306(d)(3), was rewritten to state:

> *Exchanges with offerors after establishment of the competitive range.* Negotiations are exchanges, in either a competitive or sole source environment, between the Government and offerors, that are undertaken with the intent of allowing the offeror to revise its proposal. These negotiations may include bargaining. Bargaining includes persuasion, alteration of assumptions and positions, give-and-take, and may apply to price, schedule, technical requirements, type of contract, or other terms of a proposed contract. When negotiations are conducted in a competitive acquisition, they take place after establishment of the competitive range and are called discussions.

This new description of the process of discussions with offerors in the competitive range encourages contracting officers to conduct in-depth negotiations with each offeror and appears to permit bargaining to alter all elements of the procurement. However, the guidance is somewhat misleading because if such negotiations alter the mandatory contract requirements or terms and conditions included in the RFP, all offerors still in the competition must be informed of the alteration by an amendment to the RFP, FAR 15.206(a) and (c). See, for example, *Red River Holdings, LLC v. United States*, 87 Fed. Cl. 768 (2009) (protest sustained because agency relaxed mandatory specification requirements); *Trammell Crow Co.*, Comp. Gen. Dec. B-311314.2, 2008 CPD ¶ 129 (protest sustained because agency altered key evaluation factor); *OTI America, Inc. v. United States*, 68 Fed. Cl. 646 (2005) (protest sustained because agency used internal evaluation criteria inconsistently without amending RFP to inform offerors of criteria); *Northrop Grumman Information Tech., Inc.*, Comp. Gen. Dec. B-295526, 2005 CPD ¶ 45 (protest sustained because agency significantly changed its approach to exercising options after receipt of final proposal revisions); *Systems Mgmt., Inc.*, Comp. Gen. Dec. B-287032, 2001 CPD ¶ 85 (protest sustained because agency relaxed mandatory solicitation requirement); *Mangi Envtl. Group, Inc. v. United States*, 47 Fed. Cl. 10 (2000) (protest sustained because agency relaxed mandatory requirements); *International Data Sys., Inc.*, Comp. Gen. Dec. B-277385, 97-2 CPD ¶ 96 (protest sustained because winning offeror was permitted to furnish product with newer technology than that in specifications); *Symetrics Indus., Inc.*, Comp. Gen. Dec. B-274246.3, 97-2 CPD ¶ 59 (protest sustained because agency made significant changes to the estimated quantities in an IDIQ solicitation); and *Dairy Maid Dairy, Inc.*, Comp. Gen. Dec. B-251758.3, 93-1 CPD ¶ 404 (protest sustained because agency changed proposed requirements contract to definite quantity contract prior to award). Furthermore, if the alteration is "so substantial as to exceed what prospective offerors reasonably could have anticipated," the contracting officer must cancel the solicitation and issue a new one, FAR 15.206(e). See *AirTrak Travel*, Comp. Gen. Dec. B-292101, 2003 CPD ¶ 117, recommending reopening the competition to all vendors when the agency had issued an amendment to the RFP that significantly altered the risk imposed on contractors by the original RFP. Compare *The New Jersey & H Street Limited Partnership*, Comp. Gen. Dec. B-288026, 2001 CPD ¶ 125, ruling that an offeror that had been excluded from the competitive range was not entitled to receive an amendment to the RFP because the amendment was not substantial, and *Government Contract Servs. Co.*, Comp. Gen. Dec. B-294367, 2004 CPD ¶ 215, ruling that an offeror that had not competed was not entitled to cancellation of the solicitation because the amendment to the RFP did not substantially alter it.

This chapter first considers the rules governing negotiations as expressed in the revised FAR and the decisions of the GAO and the Court of Federal Claims. It then deals with the matters to be addressed in negotiating to obtain more favorable proposals. Negotiation procedures and improper negotiation practices are then covered. The chapter concludes with the coverage of the process of obtaining proposal revisions and actions which follow the receipt of final revisions.

I. RULES GOVERNING NEGOTIATIONS

The FAR rewrite contained revised guidance on the matters that should be covered in the negotiation. However, it divided the guidance into a *mandatory rule* and a *permissive rule* encouraging robust negotiations – apparently recognizing that if it contained a broad requirement for extensive negotiations, that would create an undesirable basis for protests.

A. The Mandatory Rule

There have been several different FAR descriptions of the mandatory rule in the past two decades. In addition, the GAO has formulated its own requirement for "meaningful discussions" without regard to the language in the FAR. The result has been considerable confusion on the precise mandatory requirements that must be met in order to meet the minimum standards for the conduct of negotiations.

1. Pre-Rewrite Rule

In pre-rewrite FAR 15.610(c)(2) the only mandatory requirement was that the contracting officer "advise the offeror of deficiencies" and "deficiency" was narrowly defined in FAR 15.601 as "any part of a proposal that fails to satisfy the Government's requirements." However, the GAO did not accept this narrow statement of the mandatory rule but held in a number of cases that discussions had to be "meaningful." The most striking case of this type was *Eldyne, Inc.*, Comp. Gen. Dec. B-250158, 93-1 CPD ¶ 430, finding inadequate discussions where the contracting officer failed to discuss areas of an offeror's technical and management proposals where it had received low scores because of lack of detail in the proposal. The GAO explained this ruling in *Dep't of the Navy — Recons.*, Comp. Gen. Dec. B-250158.4, 93-1 CPD ¶ 422, as follows:

> The Navy's contention that contracting officers are never required to discuss aspects of a proposal that do not make it unacceptable is simply wrong. As we stated in our decision sustaining Eldyne's protest, discussions conducted with offerors in the competitive range must be meaningful. FAR 15.610; *Jaycor*, B-240029.2 et al., Oct. 31, 1990, 90-2 CPD ¶ 354. The FAR explicitly recognizes that, in conducting meaningful discussions, a contracting officer must use his or her judgment based on the facts of each acquisition (except that deficiencies and other matters listed in FAR 15.610(c) must always be discussed). Substitution of the mechanical approach suggested by the Navy for this exercise of judgment can, as it did in this case, frustrate the fundamental requirement of the Competition in Contracting Act of 1984 (CICA), 41 U.S.C. § 253b(d)(2) (1988), for meaningful discussions. As reflected in FAR 15.610, CICA effectively requires agencies to point out *weaknesses, deficiencies or excesses in proposals necessary for an offeror to have a reasonable chance of being selected for award*, which is, after all, the basis for including a proposal in the competitive range in the first place. See FAR 15.609(a); *Price Waterhouse*, B-222562, Aug. 18, 1986, 86-2 CPD ¶ 190. (Italics added)

Following this decision, the GAO stated that agencies "must point out weaknesses that, unless corrected, would prevent an offeror from having a reasonable chance for award," *Gutierrez-Palmenberg, Inc.*, Comp. Gen. Dec. B-255797.3, 94-2 CPD ¶ 158; *Docusort, Inc.*, Comp. Gen. Dec. B-254852, 94-1 CPD ¶ 38. See also *Alliant Techsys., Inc.*, Comp. Gen. Dec. B-260215.4, 95-2 CPD ¶ 79, finding that the agency could not avoid its obligation to conduct discussions by labeling significant weaknesses as something less than a deficiency. However, in other decisions, the GAO did not require disclosure of areas in which the offer was acceptable but contained an approach that was relatively less desirable than the approach proposed by another offeror, *Data Sys. Analysts, Inc.*, Comp. Gen. Dec. B-255684, 94-1 CPD ¶ 209. See *Fairchild Space & Defense Corp.*, Comp. Gen. Dec. B-243716, 91-2 CPD ¶ 190, stating:

[T]here is no requirement on the part of an agency to identify relative weaknesses in a proposal which is technically acceptable, but presents a relatively less desirable approach than others received.

2. Initial Rewrite Rule

The FAR Part 15 rewrite appeared to adopt the GAO rule by requiring in FAR 15.306(d)(3) the disclosure in negotiations of not only "deficiencies" but also "significant weaknesses" and "other aspects of its proposal that could . . . be altered or explained to enhance materially the proposal's potential for award." FAR 15.301 defined "deficiency" and "significant weakness" as follows:

"Deficiency," as used in this subpart, is a material failure of a proposal to meet a Government requirement or a combination of significant weaknesses in a proposal that increases the risk of unsuccessful contract performance to an unacceptable level.

"Weakness," as used in this subpart, is a flaw in the proposal that increases the risk of unsuccessful contract performance. A "significant weakness" in the proposal is a flaw that appreciably increases the risk of unsuccessful contract performance.

Coupled with the broad endorsement of bargaining in FAR 15.306(d), these changes appeared to make it clear that contracting officers were expected to have relatively robust negotiations with offerors in the competitive range.

While the FAR rewrite and the GAO decisions seemingly enunciated a clear mandatory rule, its scope was obscured by subsequent decisions. In *MCR Fed., Inc.*, Comp. Gen. Dec. B-280969, 99-1 CPD ¶ 8, a protest was denied where the agency had failed to discuss the fact that a technical evaluation was scored as "acceptable" because it met all of the solicitation requirements. The GAO stated, "We do not read the revised Part 15 language to change the legal standard so as to require discussion of all proposal areas where ratings could be improved." Similarly, in *Du & Assocs., Inc.*, Comp. Gen. Dec. B-280283.3, 98-2 CPD ¶ 156, the GAO stated:

We view the statutory and regulatory mandate for discussions with all competitive range offerors, which was not changed in the FAR Part 15 rewrite, as requiring that such discussions must be meaningful, equitable and not misleading. See 41 U.S.C. § 253b(d)(1)(A) (1994); FAR 15.306(d)(1). At issue here is whether the FAR Part 15 rewrite altered the rules governing the content of discussions in a way relevant to the outcome of this protest. We recognize that the FAR rewrite could be read to limit the discretion of the contracting officer by requiring discussion of all aspects of the proposal "that could, in the opinion of the contracting officer, be altered or explained to enhance materially the proposal's potential for award." We do not believe, however, that it was the intention of the rewrite to limit the contracting officer's discretion in this manner. Cf. *SDS Petroleum Prods., Inc.* B-280430, Sept. 1, 1998, 98-2 CPD ¶ 59 at 5 (intent of Part 15 rewrite was to give contracting officers discretion to establish a more limited competitive range than was permitted previously). Consequently, we do not view the rewrite as having changed the prior legal requirements governing discussions in a manner which affects this case. See *MCR Fed., Inc.*, B-280969, Dec. 14, 1998, 98-2 CPD ¶ at 10-11. The rule thus remains that, while an agency is required to conduct meaningful discussions leading an offeror into the areas of its proposal requiring amplification or revision, the agency is not required to "spoon-feed" an offeror as to each and every item that could be revised so as to improve its proposal. See *Applied Cos.*, B-279811, July 24, 1998, 98-2 CPD ¶ 52 at 8. This is especially the case where, as here, the RFP evaluation criteria and instructions to offerors on proposal preparation are detailed and clear with respect to the problem areas. *Id.*

Subsequent decisions also permitted limited discussions. Thus, the GAO ruled in a number of cases that there is no need to discuss the fact that an offeror's price is high, *MarLaw-Arco MFPD Mgmt.*, Comp. Gen. Dec. B-291875, 2003 CPD ¶ 85 (although price was "significantly" higher than awadee, it was "reasonable" and only somewhat higher than government estimate); *Cherokee Info. Servs.*, Comp. Gen. Dec. B-287270, 2001 CPD ¶ 77 (although price was over 15% over winning offeror, it was "competitive and not unrealistically high"); *Hydraulics Int'l, Inc.*, Comp. Gen. Dec. B-284684, 2000 CPD ¶ 149 (although price was 70% higher than winning offeror, it was not "inherently unreasonable" when the technical proposal was considered); *Biospherics, Inc.*, Comp. Gen. Dec. B-285065, 2000 CPD ¶ 118 (although price was considerably higher, it was within 200% of winning offeror and thus not subject to discussion under agency's rule); *AJT & Assocs.*, Inc., Comp. Gen. Dec. B-284305, 2000 CPD ¶ 60 (contracting officer did not consider 24% higher price too high). In other cases, very limited discussion of a high price have been held to be sufficient, *WorldTravelService*, Comp. Gen. Dec. B-284155.3, 2001 CPD ¶ 68 (protester told that is should "take a look" at its prices because they were "way too high"); *Wackenhut Int'l, Inc.*, Comp. Gen. Dec. B-286193, 2001 CPD ¶ 8 (suggestion that protester "revise its price to make it more favorable"); *WinStar Fed. Servs.*, Comp. Gen. Dec. B-284617, 2000 CPD ¶ 92 (protester told to "review sharpening [its] pencil" and that numerous prices "significantly exceed" the government's estimate). The GAO also ruled that there is no need to discuss somewhat negative performance ratings if they are not identified as "significant weaknesses," *Digital Sys. Group, Inc.*, Comp. Gen. Dec. B-286931, 2001 CPD ¶ 50 ("marginal" ratings); *ITT Fed. Servs. Int'l Corp.*, Comp. Gen. Dec. B-283307, 99-2 CPD ¶ 76 ("good" rating). The Court of Federal Claims followed this reasoning and permitted very limited discussions of past performance issues, *JWK Int'l Corp. v. United States*, 49 Fed. Cl. 371 (2001), *aff'd*, 279 F.3d 985 (2002) (sufficient discussion when contracting officer identified an "unsatisfactory" rating in a "discussion letter"); *Cubic Defense Sys., Inc. v. United States*, 45 Fed. Cl. 450 (1999) (adequate notification of poor past performance when agency posed the issue of "management weaknesses" without identifying the contracts from which that conclusion was derived). Some cases held that only "material" problems need be discussed. See *Cube Corp. v. United States*, 46 Fed. Cl. 368 (2000), where the court reasoned at 384:

> Plaintiff has not convinced the court that the disadvantages which were not shared with Cube meet these somewhat stringent definitions [of "deficiency" and

"significant weakness"]. The disadvantages listed above do not rise to the level of "material failures," rendering the risk of unsuccessful contract performance unacceptable, or constitute flaws of such magnitude that appreciably increase the risk of unsuccessful contract performance, or even provide an opportunity to enhance "materially" the chance for award. Plaintiff has not demonstrated how disadvantages on the order of [DELETED] would have improved materially Cube's chance for award.

See also *Ryder Move Mgmt., Inc. v. United States*, 48 Fed. Cl. 380 (2001) (no discussions required to address the interpretation of data that could not be altered in another proposal); *J.A. Jones/Bell, J.V.*, Comp. Gen. Dec. B-286458, 2001 CPD ¶ 17 (not discussing one area of concern permitted because the protester did not show how it could have improved its proposal); *Arctic Slope World Servs., Inc.*, Comp. Gen. Dec. B-284481, 2000 CPD ¶ 75 (not discussing two areas of concern proper because they were viewed by the agency "simply as weaknesses"); *Consolidated Eng'g Servs., Inc.*, Comp. Gen. Dec. B-279565.5, 99-1 CPD ¶ 76 (no need to discuss the fact that an offered "optional initiative" was of no value to the agency because it did not have an impact on price); and *ACRA, Inc. v. United States*, 44 Fed. Cl. 288 (1999) (although it was a "close question," there was no requirement to tell an offeror that it's failure to propose an "enhancement" had led to a reduced score). In rare cases, material deficiencies were found and a protest was granted. See, for example, *CRAssociates, Inc.*, Comp. Gen. Dec. B-282075.2, 2000 CPD ¶ 63, where two unidentified material deficiencies were not discussed and the protester won. See also *Dismas Charities, Inc.*, Comp. Gen. Dec. B-284754, 2000 CPD ¶ 84, where lack of proof of zoning for a building was identified as a material deficiency but the protest was denied because of lack of proof of prejudice, and *ACS Gov't Solutions Group, Inc.*, Comp. Gen. Dec. B-282098, 99-1 CPD ¶ 106, finding a lack of adequate discussions where the agency did not inform the protester that it was concerned with the fact that option year prices were higher than the base year price. This latter decision relied on the GAO's pre-FAR Part 15 rewrite rule rather than the FAR language. Thus, it states that discussions "cannot be meaningful unless they lead an offeror into those weaknesses, excesses or deficiencies of its proposal that must be addressed in order for it to have a reasonable chance of being selected for award." Similarly, in *Cotton & Co., LLP*, Comp. Gen. Dec. B-282808, 99-2 CPD ¶ 48, the GAO found a lack of meaningful discussions when the agency did not inform the protester of the major deficiency in its technical proposal as well as its concern regarding the qualifications and experience of its proposed staff. See also *OMV Med., Inc.*, Comp. Gen. Dec. B-281388, 99-1 CPD ¶ 53, implying that failing to tell the protester that its labor rates are high is an inadequate discussion but denying the protest because there was no prejudice from such failure.

3. 2001 FAR Change

In December 2001 the FAR was changed to narrow the mandatory rule to conform to the decisions of the GAO subsequent to the FAR Part 15 rewrite. The current rule in FAR 15.306(d)(3) now reads:

At a minimum, the contracting officer must, subject to paragraphs (d)(5) and (e) of this section and 15.307(a), indicate to, or discuss with, each offeror still being considered for award, *deficiencies, significant weaknesses, and adverse past performance information to which the offeror has not yet had an opportunity to respond.* The contracting officer also is encouraged to discuss other aspects of the offeror's proposal that could, in the opinion of the contracting officer, be altered or explained to enhance materially the proposal's potential for award. However, the contracting officer is not required to discuss every area where the proposal could be improved. The scope and extent of discussions are a matter of contracting officer judgment. (Italics added)

It can be seen that elements of a proposal that could "be altered or explained to enhance materially the proposal's potential for award" have been taken out of the mandatory rule and made permissive discussion items. The FAR Council explained this change in 66 Fed. Reg. 65368 as follows:

This final rule amends FAR 15.306(d) to clarify that the contracting officer is not required to discuss every area where the proposal could be improved. The rule explains that discussions of offerors' proposals beyond deficiencies and significant weaknesses are a matter of contracting officer judgment. GAO has already interpreted the previous FAR language consistently with this clarification in *MRC Federal, Inc.* (B-280969, December 14, 1998), and *Du & Associates* (B-280283.3, December 22, 1998). The rule encourages the contracting officer to discuss other aspects of an offeror's proposal that have the potential, if changed, to materially increase the value of the proposal to the Government (B-280283.3). However, the rule makes clear that whether these discussions would be worthwhile is within the contracting officer's discretion.

Further explanation is contained in 66 Fed. Reg. 65349, as follows:

The rule amends FAR 15.306(d) to clarify that, although the contracting officer must discuss deficiencies, significant weaknesses, and adverse past performance information to which the offeror has not yet had an opportunity to respond and is encouraged to discuss other aspects of the offeror's proposal, the contracting officer is not required to discuss every area where the proposal could be improved. This clarifies the existing policy that any discussions beyond the minimum elements stated in the FAR are a matter of contracting officer judgment.

In *Base Techs., Inc.*, Comp. Gen. Dec. B-293061.2, 2004 CPD ¶ 31, the GAO noted the discretion accorded by the new FAR 15.306(d):

While discussions must address at least deficiencies and significant weaknesses identified in proposals, the scope and extent of discussions are largely a matter of the contracting officer's judgment. Federal Acquisition Regulation (FAR) 15.306(d)(3); *Northrop Grumman Info. Tech., Inc.*, B-290080 *et a*l., June 10, 2002, 2002 CPD ¶ 136 at 6. In this regard, we review the adequacy of discussions to ensure that agencies point out weaknesses that, unless corrected, would prevent an offeror from having a reasonable chance for award. *Northrop Grumman Info.*

Tech., Inc., supra. An agency is not required to afford offerors all-encompassing discussions, or to discuss every aspect of a proposal that receives less than the maximum score, and it is not required to advise an offeror of a weakness that is not considered significant, even if the weakness subsequently becomes a determinative factor in choosing between two closely ranked proposals.

In spite of this narrowing of the mandatory discussion rule, conducting limited discussions is not sound policy. Particularly, attempting to draw distinctions between "deficiencies" and "weaknesses" and to determine when a "weakness" is "significant," would be difficult, at best, and of questionable benefit. Rather, contracting officers should fully explore the offers that are in the competitive range and conduct meaningful negotiations on all elements of the proposal which could be altered to improve the chance of the offeror winning the competition.

B. The Permissive Rule

As currently written, the FAR thus gives contracting officers a great deal of discretion under the permissive rule to carry out the goal of conducting robust negotiations. However, as discussed earlier, there is little doubt that one of the major goals of the rewrite was to induce contracting officers to have more thorough negotiations. Hence, there are a number of indications in the FAR that contracting officers are strongly encouraged to assist offerors to make the best offer possible in order to ensure that the government awards to the offeror with the best value. For example, FAR 15.306(d)(2) states that the major purpose of negotiations is to obtain best value for the government:

> The primary objective of discussions is to maximize the Government's ability to obtain best value, based on the requirement and the evaluation factors set forth in the solicitation.

In addition, the "technical leveling" prohibition was removed from the FAR. Under the pre-rewrite rules, agencies were prohibited from "helping an offeror" to improve its proposal under certain conditions (former FAR 15.610(d) precluding "technical leveling"). However, this prohibition was rewritten in FAR 15.306(e)(1) to merely preclude favoring one offeror over another. Furthermore, FAR 15.306(d) (4) now encourages technical leveling by stating:

> In discussing other aspects of the proposal, the Government may, in situations where the solicitation stated that evaluation credit would be given for technical solutions exceeding any mandatory minimums, negotiate with offerors for increased performance beyond any mandatory minimums, and the Government may suggest to offerors that have exceeded any mandatory minimums (in ways that are not integral to the design), that their proposals would be more competitive if the excesses were removed and the offered price decreased.

GAO has recognized that helping offerors improve their proposals is an integral part of the negotiation process. See *First Preston Housing Initiatives, LP*, Comp. Gen. Dec. B-293105.2, 2004 CPD ¶ 221, stating:

> There was nothing improper in the agency's actions. Rather, as outlined by the protester, the agency provided [the winning offeror] with discussions that pointed out, and provided the firm an opportunity to respond to, the proposal weaknesses and deficiencies identified in its proposal during the evaluation. This is what agencies are required to do when conducting discussions. See FAR § 15.306(d) (3); see also *SWR, Inc.*, B-286161.2, Jan. 24, 2001, 2001 CPD ¶ 32 at 6-7 n.7 (discussions should be as specific as practicable under the circumstances). We note that First Preston likewise was afforded detailed discussions in which the agency identified 8 weaknesses and provided the firm some 12 detailed discussion questions. The fact that [the winning offeror's] responses to the questions resulted in an improved evaluation rating does [not] evidence some impropriety; rather, such improvement is precisely what the discussion process envisions.

This is consistent with the view previously expressed by the GAO that discussions should be conducted "to the end that competition is maximized and the government is assured of receiving the most favorable contract," 51 Comp. Gen. 621 (B-173677) (1972). See also 52 Comp. Gen. 466 (B-177008) (1973), stating at 468:

> Since one of the primary purposes of conducting negotiations with offerors is to raise to an acceptable status those proposals which are capable of being made acceptable, and thereby increase competition for the procurement, we believe it is incumbent upon Government negotiators to be as specific as practical considerations will permit in advising offerors of the corrections required in their proposals.

FAR 15.307(b) also appears to contemplate negotiations until understanding is reached with each offeror in the competitive range. Thus, it would appear that assistance to offerors is appropriate if all offerors are treated fairly, the rules against improper disclosure of source selection information and bid and proposal information are observed, and the assistance is not a response to an offeror's incompetence. Care should be taken to ensure that the assistance does not result in a superior offer from an offeror with inferior capabilities, *Raytheon Ocean Sys. Co.*, Comp. Gen. Dec. B-218620.2, 86-1 CPD ¶ 134. Award to an incapable or less capable offeror would not be in the government's interest.

II. NEGOTIATING TO OBTAIN BEST VALUE

Negotiations are not an end in themselves. The purpose of the policy favoring robust negotiations is to obtain the most favorable contract for the government. See FAR 15.306(d)(2), which states that the primary purpose of negotiations is to obtain best value for the government. Obtaining best value does not necessarily mean negotiating the lowest possible price and imposing the greatest possible risk on the contractor. While the contracting officer is required to ensure that the government does not pay a higher price than is necessary, it is also incumbent on the contracting officer to make certain that the price is not so low as to impede performance. See FAR 9.103(c) which indicates the various problems that can result from a price which is too low:

> The award of a contract to a supplier based on lowest evaluated price alone can be false economy if there is subsequent default, late deliveries, or other unsatisfactory performance resulting in additional contractual or administrative costs. While it is important that Government purchases be made at the lowest price, this does not require an award to a supplier solely because that supplier submits the lowest offer.

It is also important that the appropriate contract type be selected so that too great a risk is not imposed on the contractor. See FAR 16.103(a):

> Selecting the contract type is generally a matter for negotiation and requires the exercise of sound judgment. Negotiating the contract type and negotiating prices are closely related and should be considered together. The objective is to negotiate a contract type and price (or estimated cost and fee) that will result in reasonable contractor risk and provide the contractor with the greatest incentive for efficient and economical performance.

The following material contains a detailed analysis of the legal rules distinguishing between mandatory and permissive negotiations, which are identified in the GAO and Court of Federal Claims decisions as the requirement for "meaningful discussions." Contracting officer must be aware of these rules but should recognize that they do not identify a clear line of demarcation. In the face of this lack of clarity, it is not good business practice to attempt to limit the issues raised during negotiations to the smallest number that will satisfy the legal rules. Rather, contracting officers should err on the side of robust negotiations where all elements of a proposal that have been downgraded are identified and explained to each offeror in the competitive range.

A. Discretion

Contracting agencies have broad discretion in conducting negotiations. See FAR 15.306(d)(3) stating that "the scope and extent of discussions are a matter of contracting officer judgment." See also *Quality Elevator Co.*, Comp. Gen. Dec. B-271899, 96-2 CPD ¶ 89, stating:

> Contracting agencies have wide discretion in determining the nature and scope of negotiations. While discussions must provide offerors with an equal opportunity to revise their proposals, the content and extent of discussions are within the discretion of the contracting officer. *See Tritech Field Eng'g, Inc.*, B-255336.2, Apr. 13, 1994, 94-1 CPD ¶ 261. Since the number and type of deficiencies, if any, will vary among proposals, there is no requirement that all offerors receive the same number or type of discussion questions. *Textron Marine Sys.*, B-255580.3, Aug.

2, 1994, 94-2 CPD ¶ 63. Rather, the agency should individualize the evaluated deficiencies of each offeror in its conduct of discussions. *Pan Am World Servs., Inc., et al.*, B-231840 *et al.*, Nov. 7, 1988, 88-2 CPD ¶ 446. Because the degree of deficiencies in proposals will vary, the amount of specificity or detail of discussions will also vary among the offerors. *Pope Maintenance Corp.*, B-206143.3, Sept. 9, 1982, 82-2 CPD ¶ 218.

However, within this discretion, negotiations must be meaningful and must be conducted in a way that offerors are treated fairly. See 51 Comp. Gen. 621 (B-173677) (1972); and *Wetlands Research Assocs., Inc.*, Comp. Gen. Dec. B-246342, 92-1 CPD ¶ 251. The "burden to conduct meaningful discussions is on the contracting officer and not on individual offerors," *Teledyne Lewisburg Okl. Aerotronics, Inc.*, Comp. Gen. Dec. B-183704, 75-2 CPD ¶ 228. See *LB&B Assocs., Inc.*, Comp. Gen. Dec. B-281706, 99-1 CPD ¶ 74, stating:

> The statutory and regulatory requirement for discussions with all competitive range offerors (41 U.S.C. § 253b (d)(1)(A) (1994); FAR 15.306(d)(1)) means that such discussions must be meaningful, equitable, and not misleading. *Du & Assocs., Inc.*, B-280283.3, Dec. 22, 1998, 98-2 CPD ¶ 156 at 7; *I.T.S. Corp.*, B-280431, Sept. 29, 1998, 98-2 CPD ¶ 89 at 6. For discussions to be meaningful, they must lead offerors into the areas of their proposals requiring amplification or revision; the agency is not required to "spoon-feed" an offeror as to each and every item that could be revised so as to improve its proposal, however. *Du & Assocs., Inc., supra*, at 7-8; *Applied Cos.*, B-279811, July 24, 1998, 98-2 CPD ¶ 52 at 8.

The Court of Federal Claims has adopted the same reasoning as to the extent of and limitations on the discretion of contracting officers in determining the extent of negotiations. See *Advanced Data Concepts, Inc. v United States*, 43 Fed. Cl. 410 (1999), *aff'd*, 216 F.3d 1054 (Fed. Cir. 2000), agreeing that the contracting officer has broad discretion in conducting discussions and quoting pre-rewrite FAR 15.610(b) which stated "the content and extent of the discussions is a matter of the contracting officer's judgment, based on the particular facts of each acquisition."

B. Dealing With Deficiencies and Weaknesses

The terms "deficiency" and "weakness" have been at the center of much confusion in the discussion process. Under the pre-rewrite FAR, "deficiency" was defined in FAR 15.601 and contracting officers were directed to "advise the offeror of deficiencies" in FAR 15.610(c)(2); but no statement requiring notice of "weaknesses" was present. The only reference to "weaknesses" was in a provision directing the contracting officer not to engage in "technical leveling (i.e., helping an offeror to bring its proposal up to the level of other proposals . . . by pointing out weaknesses," FAR 15.610(d)). This language was generally interpreted as not requiring disclosure of areas in which the offer was acceptable but contained an approach that was relatively less desirable than the approach proposed by another offeror, *Research for Better Schools, Inc.*, Comp. Gen. Dec. B-270774.3, 96-2 CPD ¶ 41; *Data Sys.*

Analysts, Inc., Comp. Gen. Dec. B-255684, 94-1 CPD ¶ 209. See, however, *Voith Hydro, Inc.*, Comp. Gen. Dec. B-277051, 97-2 CPD ¶ 68, holding that an agency could not avoid the meaningful discussion requirement by citing the technical leveling prohibition when the weakness was material and had a significant impact on the protester's chance of winning the procurement, and *Professional Servs. Group, Inc.*, Comp. Gen. Dec. B-274289.2, 97-1 CPD ¶ 54, holding that an agency cannot find that a defect in a proposal is a relative weakness if it results in a score in the deficient range based on the conclusion that the offeror did not meet minimum requirements. See also *Global Indus., Inc.*, Comp. Gen. Dec. B-270592.2, 96-2 CPD ¶ 85, ruling that the agency was required to discuss a weakness that was identified as being a "serious concern" and "of major importance" in the evaluation of the proposal. The GAO also ruled that weaknesses need not be disclosed if they are not significant." The test seemed to be whether the weakness had a significant impact on the source selection decision. See *Development Alternatives, Inc.*, Comp. Gen. Dec. B-279920, 98-2 CPD ¶ 54, stating:

> We review the adequacy of discussions to ensure that agencies point out weaknesses that, unless corrected, would prevent an offeror from having a reasonable chance for award. *Department of the Navy — Recon.*, B-250158.4, May 28, 1993, 93-1 CPD ¶ 422 at 4 n.2. Agencies need not discuss every aspect of the proposal that receives less than the maximum score or identify relative weaknesses in a proposal that is technically acceptable but presents a less desirable approach than others. *SeaSpace Corp.*, B-252476.2, June 14, 1993, 93-1 CPD ¶ 462 at 15, *recon. denied*, B-252476.3, Oct. 27, 1993, 93-2 CPD ¶ 251.

> As explained above, in evaluating [the protester's] initial proposal two evaluators believed that the experience of [the protester's] banking subcontractor gave it a more limited ability to significantly supplement [the protester's] capabilities than might appear, and downgraded it by 4 and 5 points, respectively. While this matter was not one of the discussion questions listed in [the protester's] BAFO request letter, there is no evidence that the firm's use of this bank was considered a significant weakness. In addition to the fact that relatively few points were deducted from its score for this reason, neither the TEC [technical evaluation committee] memorandum on the evaluation of initial proposals nor the TEC memorandum on the evaluation of BAFOs mentions this matter. Moreover, it is clear that the existence of this weakness did not keep [the protester] from having a reasonable chance for award; the firm was very much in the competition and was ultimately not selected for other reasons. Since the principal concerns about its proposal were brought to its attention, and since this concern did not prevent [the protester] from having a reasonable chance for award, [the agency's] failure to point it out did not deprive [the protester] of meaningful discussions. *Fluor Daniel, Inc.*, B-262051, B-262051.2, Nov. 21, 1995, 95-2 CPD ¶ 241 at 5.

The FAR rewrite addressed the confusion in this area by requiring in FAR 15.306(d)(3) negotiations disclose not only deficiencies but also "significant weaknesses." In addition, the prohibition against technical leveling was removed. However, contracting officers must still distinguish between deficiencies and weaknesses and then decide whether a weakness is "significant." The cases since the rewrite indicate that attempting to draw these distinctions is difficult at best and of questionable benefit. See, for example, *Trammell Crow Co.*, Comp. Gen. Dec. B-311314.2, 2008 CPD ¶ 129, where the agency argued that it was not required to discuss its perception that the protester's key personnel lacked qualifications because this was only a "weakness." The GAO granted the protest, concluding that the weakness was significant because it led to a significant downgrading of the protester's proposal. See also *Lockheed Martin Simulation, Training & Support*, Comp. Gen. Dec. B-292836.8, 2005 CPD ¶ 27, holding that numerous areas where protester was downgraded, leading to a "marginal/high risk" rating, were cumulatively significant weaknesses. Compare *Structural Assocs., Inc./Comfort Sys. USA (Syracuse) Joint Venture v. United States*, 89 Fed. Cl. 735 (2009), holding that lack of experience resulting in a rating of "good" rather than "excellent" was neither a deficiency not a significant weakness; *Planning & Dev. Collaborative Int'l*, Comp. Gen. Dec. B-311314.2, 2007 CPD ¶ 28, concluding, after a detailed review of the facts, that a weakness was not significant, and *PAI Corp.*, Comp. Gen. Dec. B-298349, 2006 CPD ¶ 123, finding high price and lower rated key personnel not to be weaknesses. See *DMS All-Star Joint Venture v. United States*, 90 Fed. Cl. 653 (2010), following the GAO reasoning on this issue. However, if the agency characterizes a weakness as significant, it is highly likely that it will be regarded as significant in a protest, *Spherix, Inc.*, Comp. Gen. Dec. B-294572, 2005 CPD ¶ 3.

It is also problematic for the contracting officer to conclude that weaknesses need not be discussed because the offeror can do nothing to correct the problem. See *Burchick Constr. Co.*, Comp. Gen. Dec. B-400342, 2008 CPD ¶ 203, where the contracting officer failed to discuss weaknesses in the technical proposal based on this conclusion. The GAO granted the protest because the weaknesses pertained primarily to lack of information which could have been furnished had the protester been informed of the weaknesses. See also *T Square Logistics Servs. Corp. – Costs*, Comp. Gen. Dec. B-297790.4, 2006 CPD ¶ 78, finding lack of meaningful discussions when the agency failed to inform the protester that its had insufficient experience in one part of the work. The GAO reasoned that this was a correctable weakness because the protester could have obtained a subcontractor with the requisite experience.

It can be concluded that the best course of action for contracting officers is to fully explore the offers that are in the competitive range and conduct meaningful negotiations on all elements of the proposal that could be altered to improve the chance of the offeror winning the competition.

1. Specific Identification

The GAO has stated that "it is incumbent upon Government negotiators to be as specific as practical considerations will permit in advising offerors of the corrections required in their proposals," 52 Comp. Gen. 466 (B-177008) (1973). Thus, at a minimum, discussions must lead the offeror "into the areas of [its] proposal which require amplification," *Price Waterhouse*, Comp. Gen. Dec. B-222562, 86-2 CPD ¶ 190. See also *TRS Research*, Comp. Gen. Dec. B-274845, 97-1 CPD ¶ 6; *Creative Mgmt. Tech., Inc.*, Comp. Gen. Dec. B-266299, 96-1 CPD ¶ 61; and *Research Analysis & Maint., Inc.*, Comp. Gen. Dec. B-242836.4, 91-2 CPD ¶ 387. In evaluating whether there has been sufficient disclosure of deficiencies, the primary focus is on whether there has been a reasonable communication of specific deficiencies rather than requiring any specific form of communication.

The agency must disclose any matters which would result in the proposal being unacceptable or would not be considered for award, *Columbia Research Corp.*, Comp. Gen. Dec. B-247631, 92-1 CPD ¶ 539. A failure to hold meaningful discussions was found where several offerors were not told during discussions that various proposed personnel were considered unqualified, 52 Comp. Gen. 466 (B-177008) (1973). See also *Creative Info. Tech., Inc.*, Comp. Gen. Dec. B-293073.10, 2005 CPD ¶ 110 (agency's statement that price was "overstated" did not inform protester that it had grossly overestimated the level of effort anticipated by the agency); *ACS Gov't Solutions Group, Inc.*, Comp. Gen. Dec. B-280098, 99-1 CPD ¶ 106 (agency did not inform offeror of concern over high prices in option years); *CitiWest Properties, Inc.*, Comp. Gen. Dec. B-274689.4, 98-1 CPD ¶ 3 (agency failed to inform protester of its deficiency in not submitting required form); *International Data Sys., Inc.*, Comp. Gen. Dec. B-277385, 97-2 CPD ¶ 96 (agency failed to tell an offeror that it had proposed a noncompliant delivery schedule); *Delta Data Sys. Corp. v. Webster*, 240 App. D.C. 182, 744 F.2d 197 (D.C. Cir. 1984) (agency did not inform the offeror that it had concluded that the proposal evidenced insufficient financing for the contract); and *General Elec. Co. v. Seamans*, 340 F. Supp. 636 (D.D.C. 1972) (offeror was not informed that its price was considered unrealistically low).

When a competitive range offeror's proposal indicates that it does not understand the evaluation scheme, the agency must raise this issue, *Lockheed Martin Corp.*, Comp. Gen. Dec. B-293679, 2004 CPD ¶ 115. There the agency did not inform the protester that it had rejected proposed manufacturing cost savings if a product the protester was proposing to design was manufactured in its facilities because it planned to compete the production work.

Vague statements that do not identify a specific issue have also been held to be inadequate discussions. In *Matrix Int'l Logistics, Inc.*, Comp. Gen. Dec. B-272388.2, 97-2 CPD ¶ 89, inadequate discussions were found when the agency identified a particular material line item whose price was either grossly excessive or mistaken but only gave the offeror a general statement that its overall price was too high. See also *New Jersey & H Street, LLC*, Comp. Gen. Dec. B-311314.3, 2008 CPD ¶ 133 (general statement to all competitors that evaluation factor was important but no indication to protester of specific issues with its compliance); *AT&T Corp.*, Comp. Gen. Dec. B-299542.3, 2008 CPD ¶ 65 (reference to lack of information on staffing plan but no indication that agency believed it contained too few personnel); *Lockheed Martin Simulation, Training*

& *Support*, Comp. Gen. Dec. B-292836.8, 2005 CPD ¶ 27 (statement that protester was responsible for making proposal "responsive, clear and accurate" and that responses should be "strategic, not just tactical" insufficient to alert protester to specific weaknesses). In *Advanced Sys. Dev., Inc.*, Comp. Gen. Dec. B-298411, 2006 CPD ¶ 137, the agency's statement that the offeror had violated the RFP's price target led the protested to reduce its price when the agency's concern was that the price was too low. The GAO sustained the protest after the protester had been awarded the contract at the low price.

The GAO has also stated that, in general, once discussions are opened, the agency is required to point out all deficiencies in the offeror's proposal, not merely selected areas, *CRAssociates, Inc.*, Comp. Gen. Dec. B-282075.2, 2000 CPD ¶ 63; *TM Sys., Inc.*, Comp. Gen. Dec. B-228220, 87-2 CPD ¶ 573. Partial discussions have been found inadequate. For example, in *Multimax, Inc.*, Comp. Gen. Dec. B-298249.6, 2006 CPD ¶ 165, offerors were misled when agency identified some labor rates as high but did not identify other labor rates that were also high. See also *Tracor Marine, Inc.*, Comp. Gen. Dec. B-207285, 83-1 CPD ¶ 604, where it was found improper to disclose to the offeror that its proposed schedule was unrealistic, while disclosing only one out of five bases for this conclusion. Offerors should not be left with the impression that there are no remaining problem areas. See *E-Systems, Inc.*, Comp. Gen. Dec. B-191346, 79-1 CPD ¶ 192, stating:

> We have regarded as deficient negotiations which led an offeror reasonably to believe that a problem area had been cleared up during oral discussions because of the lack of specific identification of a proposal weakness.

In *Dynalectron Corp.*, Comp. Gen. Dec. B-193604, 79-2 CPD ¶ 50, the GAO found that Dynalectron had not been sufficiently alerted to remaining deficiencies in its proposal when, after revisions had been made, it was shown a list of five deficiencies with the words "cleared by amendment" written after the first three deficiencies. Dynalectron misinterpreted this to mean these deficiencies had been cleared up by its revisions and made no further changes in these areas.

If agency personnel recognize that an offeror does not understand their concern over some aspect of the proposal, they must clearly identify the issue. See *Cotton & Co., LLP*, Comp. Gen. Dec. B-282808, 99-2 CPD ¶ 48, stating:

> In view of Cotton's opportunity to revise its proposal, the oral discussions, and the provisions of the SOW, the [Technical Evaluation Panel] chair concluded that it was not his place to challenge Cotton's approach. However, his conclusion ignores the reality of the conduct of the oral discussions. While oral discussions can serve as a valuable negotiating tool, agency negotiators need to keep in mind that their reaction, or failure to react, to an offeror's position during oral discussions risks misleading the offeror. See, e.g., *Voith Hydro, Inc.*, [B-277051, Aug. 22, 1997, 97-2 CPD ¶ 68] (agency failed to advise offeror of major weakness in proposal despite being specifically asked during oral discussions whether the agency had concerns in that area). Here, in light of the obliqueness of the agency's written

and oral communications on the matter (as well as the unusual nature of the distinction that the agency was making between disbursements and procurements), it was reasonable for Cotton to conclude, at the end of the oral discussions, that it had addressed the agency's concern. Yet, in those discussions, the TEP chair recognized that the offeror had not understood the agency's concern about the firm's proposal and had, instead, conveyed its intention to continue to propose an audit approach which would not satisfy the agency. While agency negotiators are not required to repeat concerns once they have been clearly laid out or to "spoon-feed" an offeror, see *Applied Cos.*, [B-279811, July 24, 1998, 98-2 CPD ¶ 52], here the TEP chair's silence essentially misled the firm; at the least, the agency had an obligation to advise Cotton that the firm's response had not addressed the agency's concern.

2. Express Notification Excused

When a protester asserts that the agency has not specifically identified areas where proposals should be amplified or changed, the Court of Federal Claims or the GAO will carefully examine the content of the negotiations to determine if the contracting officer has identified the deficiency or weakness. The decisions conducting such examination appear to give agencies considerable deference in this regard. However, agencies should err on the side of greater communication rather than relying on these rulings to win a protest.

a. Identification of Problem Sufficiently Clear

A lack of specific identification will not be fatal if the offeror has been given sufficient information to provide notice of the deficiency. In *Broomall Indus., Inc.*, Comp. Gen. Dec. B-193166, 79-1 CPD ¶ 467, the GAO found that a broad request that the offeror "discuss in detail" one aspect of the required work was sufficient to disclose that the proposal was deficient in that area, stating:

> We have held that requests for clarification or amplification or other statements made during discussions which lead offerors into areas of their proposals that are unclear are sufficient to alert offerors to deficiencies in their proposals. *Serv-Air, Inc.*, B-189884, September 25, 1978, 78-2 CPD ¶ 223; *Houston Films, Inc.*, B-184402, December 22, 1975, 75-2 CPD ¶ 404.

Similarly, where the agency was concerned about the analytic model used by the protester and questioned the protester's low proposed level of effort, which was primarily attributable to the model, this was enough to alert the protester of the real concern, *CRC Sys., Inc.*, Comp. Gen. Dec. B-207847, 83-1 CPD ¶ 462. See also *Kerr Contractors, Inc. v. United States*, 89 Fed. Cl. 312 (2009) (asking protester to address "risk" of work at proposed level sufficient to indicate that agency considered level too low); *Academy Facilities Mgmt. v. United States*, 87 Fed. Cl. 441 (2009) (use of term "overstated" when price appeared high and "significantly overstated" when price appeared both high and unbalanced was sufficient indication of government concerns); *SelectTech Bering Straits Solutions JV*, Comp. Gen. Dec. B-400964, 2009 CPD ¶ 100 (statement that staffing levels were low sufficient without identifying that only some were low and others were high); *New Breed, Inc.*, Comp. Gen. Dec. B-400554, 2009 CPD ¶ 4 (no requirement to identify specific weaknesses when protester told that its risk management and quality control plans were weak); *Karrar Sys. Corp.*, Comp. Gen. Dec. B-310661, 2008 CPD ¶ 51 (request to confirm that prices were based on RFP data sufficient to indicate that prices were considered high); *Mechanical Equip. Co.*, Comp. Gen. Dec. B-292789.2, 2004 CPD ¶ 192 (statement that manning was "inadequate" sufficient without indicating how low the estimate was); *Hanford Envtl. Health Found.*, Comp. Gen. Dec. B-292858.2, 2004 CPD ¶ 164 (no need to tell protester staffing was considered high when agency told it to more effectively describe staffing); *T-L-C Sys.*, Comp. Gen. Dec. B-287452, 2001 CPD ¶ 106 (general warning that proposal did not meet RFP requirement for full documentation sufficient to alert protester to lack of clarity of product literature); *J.A. Jones/Bell, J.V.*, Comp. Gen. Dec. B-286458, 2001 CPS ¶ 17 (request for reasoning to support use of technique sufficient to indicate that agency was critical of technique); *Information Network Sys., Inc.*, Comp. Gen. Dec. B-284854, 2000 CPD ¶ 104 (question as to adequacy of labor rates sufficient to indicate concern with workforce retention risk); *Professional Performance Dev. Group, Inc.*, Comp. Gen. Dec. B-279561.2, 99-2 CPD ¶ 29 (question as to responsibilities of two levels of management sufficient to indicate view that they were redundant); *SEEMA, Inc.*, Comp. Gen. Dec. B-277988, 98-1 CPD ¶ 12 (stating that price was significantly below the government estimate and that its cost savings measures were not supported by data sufficient to lead the protester into the area of the deficiency); *Centech Group, Inc.*, Comp. Gen. Dec. B-278715, 98-1 CPD ¶ 108 (advising protester that composite labor category prices for services contract were either too high or two low sufficient even though the agency did not specify which categories were high and which were low); *EastCo Bldg. Servs., Inc.*, Comp. Gen. Dec. B-275334, 97-1 CPD ¶ 83 (advising protester that staffing for mechanical requirements appear to be inadequate sufficient without detailed analysis because the RFP contained detailed specifications covering all work required to be performed); and *Quachita Mowing, Inc.*, Comp. Gen. Dec. B-276075, 97-1 CPD ¶ 167 (pointing out that protester's work year was based on 1,992 hours rather than the standard 2,080 hours sufficient to indicate the agency's general concern that proposed hours were too low). In *Voices R Us*, Comp. Gen. Dec. B-274802.2, 97-2 CPD ¶ 170, the GAO found that the agency was not required to provide offerors with verbatim comments regarding all past performance surveys received but was required to impart sufficient information to afford offerors a fair and reasonable opportunity to respond to problems identified.

When the purpose of an evaluation factor is to determine whether offerors understand the work required to meet the agency's needs, the requirement for identification of a deficiency is reduced. See *ITT Fed. Sys. Int'l Corp.*, Comp. Gen. Dec. B-285176.4, 2001 CPD ¶ 45, stating:

[T]he requirement for meaningful discussions does not require [giving] the off-eror the opportunity to learn each and every weakness associated with its proposal during discussions, particularly where as here one aspect of the evaluation was to test the offerors' technical understanding.

b. Minor Weaknesses

Although meaningful discussions require disclosure of deficiencies, there is considerable discretion in deciding which aspects of a proposal are of sufficient significance to warrant disclosure and discussion. The GAO has frequently stated that an agency "is under no obligation to discuss every aspect of the proposal which received less than the maximum score," *ADP Network Servs., Inc.*, Comp. Gen. Dec. B-200675, 81-1 CPD ¶ 157; *Communications Int'l, Inc.*, Comp. Gen. Dec. B-246076, 92-1 CPD ¶ 194. The Court of Federal Claims is in accord with this view, *Dynacs Eng'g Co. v. United States*, 48 Fed. Cl. 124 (2000). See *ManTech Sec. Techs. Corp.*, Comp. Gen. Dec. B-297133.3, 2006 CPD ¶ 77, stating:

> An agency is not required to afford offerors all-encompassing discussions, or to discuss every aspect of a proposal that receives lower than the maximum score, and is not required to advise an offeror of a minor weakness that is not considered significant, even where the weakness subsequently becomes a determinative fac-tor in choosing between two closely ranked proposals. *American Ordnance, LLC*, B-292847, et al., Dec. 5, 2004, 2004 CPD ¶ 3 at 4-5.

See also *SEAIR Transport Servs.*, Inc., Comp. Gen. Dec. B-274436, 96-2 CPD ¶ 224, holding that the protester was not entitled to discussions that would essen-tially have been conducted solely to permit it to achieve a perfect score in all areas. In *TRW, Inc.*, Comp. Gen. Dec. B-243450.2, 91-2 CPD ¶ 160, the GAO stated this rule very liberally, holding that the agency was required to disclose elements of subfactors that had been downscored only when the subfactor had received a score of less than four on a 10-point rating scale. This ruling was based on the fact that the agency defined a score of four as "satisfactory" and designated such problems as "disadvantages," not "deficiencies." Compare *Technical & Mgmt. Servs. Corp.*, Comp. Gen. Dec. B-242836.3, 91-2 CPD ¶ 101, where the protester received ac-ceptable ratings in every category despite receiving unacceptable ratings in several subcategories because high scores in other subcategories raised the averages. The GAO held that the agency must discuss every rating that is less than acceptable and hence was required to discuss these inadequate ratings. Minor weaknesses were also found in *International Business & Tech. Consultants, Inc.*, Comp. Gen. Dec. B-310424.2, 2008 CPD ¶ 185 (weakness that agency itself considered minor in the evaluation); *Cornell Cos.*, Comp. Gen. Dec. B-310548, 2007 CPD ¶ 212 (weak-ness that did not prevent protester from having a reasonable chance to win); *PWC Logistics Servs., Inc.*, Comp. Gen. Dec. B-299820, 2007 CPD ¶ 162 (criticisms of risk management plan when it was rated "at the low end" of "highly acceptable"); *IAP World Servs., Inc.*, Comp. Gen. Dec. B-297084, 2005 CPD ¶ 199 (agency not required to discuss all areas where protester did not receive "highest possible rating"); *American Ordnance, LLC*, Comp. Gen. Dec. B-292847, 2004 CPD ¶ 3 (only minor weaknesses when proposal was rated "good"); *4-D Neuroimaging*, Comp. Gen. Dec. B-286155.2, 2001 CPD ¶ 183 (relative disadvantages in comparison to competitor); *KIRA, Inc.*, Comp. Gen. Dec. B-287573, 2001 CPD ¶ 152 (lack of experience of subcontractor that was not considered material); *SDOS Interpreting, Ltd.*, Comp. Gen. Dec. B-287477.2, 2001 CPD ¶ 84 (higher price that was considered reasonable); *Digital Sys. Group, Inc.*, Comp. Gen. Dec. B-286931, 2001 CPD ¶ 50 (two marginal past performance ratings that were not considered significant weaknesses); *AJT & Assocs., Inc.*, Comp. Gen. Dec. B-284305, 2000 CPD ¶ 60 (higher price that was believed to have resulted from technical approach of protester); *PRB Assocs., Inc.*, Comp. Gen. Dec. B-277994, 98-1 CPD ¶ 13 (proposal areas were rated "good" but not "excellent"); *American Combustion Indus., Inc.*, Comp. Gen. Dec. B-275057.2, 97-1 CPD ¶ 105 (issues that did not "strongly influence" the source selection decision); *Software Eng'g, Inc.*, Comp. Gen. Dec. B-272820, 96-2 CPD ¶ 193 (instances that result from the offeror's own lack of diligence, such as typographical errors in the proposal); and *TRI-COR Indus., Inc.*, Comp. Gen. Dec. B-259034.2, 95-1 CPD ¶ 143 (instances in which the protester's proposal exhibited a lack of technical understanding).

The GAO has also stated that there is no requirement to discuss minor weaknesses that later become critical to the source selection decision. See *Volmar Constr., Inc.*, Comp. Gen. Dec. B-270364, 96-1 CPD ¶ 139, stating:

> An agency is not required during discussions to discuss elements of a proposal that are not deficient and need not conduct discussions in an area where an offeror is acceptable in order to bring the proposal up to the level of other proposals. See *Biloxi-D'Iberville Press*, B-243975.2, Sept. 27, 1991, 91-2 CPD ¶ 301; *Martin Advertising Agency, Inc.*, B-225347, Mar. 13, 1987, 87-1 CPD ¶ 285. Nor is an agency required to advise an offeror of a minor weakness that is not considered significant, even where it subsequently becomes the determinative factor when two closely-ranked proposals are compared. *Booz, Allen & Hamilton, Inc.*, B-249236.2 et al., Mar. 5, 1993, 93-1 CPD ¶ 209; *Training and Management Resources, Inc.*, B-220965, Mar. 12, 1986, 86-1 CPD ¶ 244.

C. Adverse Past Performance Information

Prior to the December 2001 revision, FAR 15.306(d)(3) required discussion of such adverse past performance information only if it was a "significant weakness" or a "deficiency." This led to the GAO denying protests of lack of discussion of such information, *Digital Sys. Group, Inc.*, Comp. Gen. Dec. B-286931, 2001 CPD ¶ 50. However, the current FAR requires that, to the extent that past performance information has not been discussed with an offeror prior to establishing the competitive range, negotiations must address adverse past performance information to which the offeror has not previously had an opportunity to comment, FAR 15.306(b)(4). Once such a discussion occurs, the agency must follow the requirement that meaningful discussions be held with all offerors in the competitive range, *Gulf Copper Ship Repair, Inc.*, Comp. Gen. Dec. B-293706.5, 2005 CPD ¶ 5108.

When the offeror is told of adverse past performance information, the agency may not reveal the names of individuals providing the adverse information, FAR 15.306(e)(4). This prohibition does not appear to preclude revealing the name of the contractor or government agency from whom the information was obtained or the contract or project that the information relates to, and indeed, such information would be necessary in order to permit the offeror to provide its comments rebutting the information or explaining the steps that it had taken to ensure that the problem would not recur.

In *Dismas Charities, Inc.*, Comp. Gen. Dec. B-292091, 2003 CPD ¶ 125, and *Biospherics, Inc.*, Comp. Gen. Dec. B-278278, 98-1 CPD ¶ 161, discussions were found inadequate where the agency did not inform the offeror of adverse past performance information. See also *ST Aerospace Engines Pte. Ltd.*, Comp. Gen. Dec. B-275725, 97-1 CPD ¶ 161 (agency improperly downgraded protester's proposal based on the protester's affiliate company's poor past performance when the agency should have verified the relationship between the two companies during discussions with the firm). In contrast, adequate discussions have been found in a number of cases. See *JWK Int'l Corp. v. United States*, 49 Fed. Cl. 371 (2001), *aff'd*, 279 F.3d 985 (2002) (an "unsatisfactory" rating was identified in a discussion letter); *Davies Rail & Mech. Works, Inc.*, Comp. Gen. Dec. B-283911.2, 2000 CPD ¶ 48 (past problems were listed in a discussion letter); *Cubic Defense Sys., Inc. v. United States*, 45 Fed. Cl. 450 (1999) (agency stated there were reported management deficiencies without identifying the contracts where they were reported); and *IGIT, Inc.*, Comp. Gen. Dec. B-275299.2, 97-2 CPD ¶ 7 (agency sent the protester a discussion question asking if it had any information from a contractor showing that its subcontract had not been terminated for poor performance). See also *Voices R Us*, Comp. Gen. Dec. B-274802.2, 97-2 CPD ¶ 170, stating:

> In conducting adequate discussions in the past performance area, agencies are not required to provide offerors with verbatim comments regarding all past performance surveys received; rather, agencies are required to impart sufficient information to afford the offeror a fair and reasonable opportunity to respond to the problems identified. *Pacific Architects & Eng'rs, Inc.*, B-274405.2, B-274405.3, Dec. 18, 1996, 97-1 CPD ¶ 42 at 4. An agency discharges its obligation where it simply identifies categories of past performance problems that relate to the specific problems found in the past performance surveys. *Id.* at 4–5.

When past performance issues are "well documented," no discussion of adverse past performance information is necessary. See *Stateside Assocs., Inc.*, Comp. Gen. Dec. B-400670.2, 2009 CPD ¶ 120 (adverse performance had been addressed during performance of task orders); *Del-Jen Int'l Corp.*, Comp. Gen. Dec. B-297960, 2006

CPD ¶ 81 (adverse performance had been addressed during contract administration); *PharmChem, Inc.*, Comp. Gen. Dec. B-292408.2, 2004 CPD ¶ 60 (adverse performance had been addressed during contract administration). Neither is there a requirement to discuss such information when it was not material in deciding not to award to the company. See *Standard Communications, Inc.*, Comp. Gen. Dec. B-296972, 2005 CPD ¶ 200 (no requirement to discuss relevance of information when it is clear to the agency); *Maytag Aircraft Corp.*, Comp. Gen. Dec. B-287589, 2001 CPD ¶ 121 (discussions would not have changed the facts); *Digital Sys. Group, Inc.*, Comp. Gen. Dec. B-286931, 2001 CPD ¶ 50 (marginal ratings would not have enhanced potential for award); *ABIC, Ltd.*, Comp. Gen. Dec. B-286460, 2001 CPD ¶ 46 (low ratings were not the determinative factor in eliminating protester from competitive range); *ITT Fed. Servs. Int'l Corp.*, Comp. Gen. Dec. B-283307, 99-2 CPD ¶ 76 ("good" ratings were not significant weaknesses).

D. Obtaining Additional Information

In many cases, the agency may conclude that it has insufficient information to determine exactly what performance is being offered or what information is being submitted to demonstrate that the offeror has the requisite capability. This may result from an offeror's failure to provide required information or from questions as to the meaning of statements in the proposal. As discussed earlier, there are many instances where an agency has properly excluded a competitor from the competitive range for such lack of information. However, if such a competitor is included in the competitive range, these matters should be addressed in the negotiation.

1. Discussion Mandatory

Calling for submission of necessary information is mandatory when the offeror has not submitted information that is needed by the agency to evaluate the proposal but was not explicitly called for by the RFP, *Ashbury Int'l Group, Inc.*, Comp. Gen. Dec. B-401123, 2009 CPD ¶ 140. Similarly, when this informational inadequacy results from a lack of clarity in the RFP, discussion of the matter is required. In *Logistic Sys. Inc.*, 59 Comp. Gen. 548 (B-196254), 80-1 CPD ¶ 442, *recons. denied*, 80-2 CPD ¶ 313, the GAO stated at 553:

> Where, as here, a proposal in the competitive range is informationally inadequate so that the agency evaluators cannot determine the extent of the offeror's compliance with its requirements, the agency should use the discussion process to attempt to ascertain exactly what the offeror is proposing. In this connection, we have recognized that where a solicitation specifically calls for certain information, the agency should not be required to remind the offeror to furnish the necessary information with its final proposal. *Value Engineering Company*, Comp. Gen. Dec. B-182421, July 3, 1975, 75-2 CPD ¶ 10. But here the solicitation was not so specific in calling for information on the offeror's personnel and laboratory facilities.

See also *Sperry Corp.*, 65 Comp. Gen. 195 (B-220521), 86-1 CPD ¶ 28, where discussions of price alone were held improper because there were correctable informational deficiencies in lower-priced offers. See also *Bank of Am.*, Comp. Gen. Dec. B-287608, 2001 CPD ¶ 137 (agency required to discuss numerous instances of lack of detail where protester could have improved proposal); *CRAssociates, Inc.*, Comp. Gen. Dec. B-282075.2, 2000 CPD ¶ 263 (agency required to identify missing information and information it did not understand); and *Mechanical Contractors, S.A.*, Comp. Gen. Dec. B-277916.2, 98-1 CPD ¶ 68 (perceived informational gaps in proposal). Because it is frequently difficult to determine whether an informational deficiency is due to lack of clear guidance in the RFP, contracting officers should normally point out such deficiencies during discussions.

Inadequate discussions have also been found when the agency needs additional information to fully evaluate an offeror's proposal. See *Tiger Truck, LLC*, Comp. Gen. Dec. B-400685, 2009 CPD ¶ 19 (agency failed to obtain sufficient information to determine whether offered product complied with the Trade Agreements Act); *Cogent Sys., Inc.*, Comp. Gen. Dec. B-295990.4, 2005 CPD ¶ 179 (agency failed to seek information on whether product met requirements); *Boeing Sikorsky Aircraft Support*, Comp. Gen. Dec. B-277263.2, 97-2 CPD ¶ 91 (request for verification of proposed costs not sufficiently specific when the agency had a detailed concern with the format used to display the costs); and *International Underwriters, Inc.*, Comp. Gen. Dec. B-198109, 80-2 CPD ¶ 410 (agency failed to inform the offeror that it was unable to contact the offeror's references).

2. Information Clearly Required in RFP

When the solicitation contains a clear requirement for information, the agency has a very low disclosure requirement in the negotiation process. See, for example, *MTP (JV)*, Comp. Gen. Dec. B-276903, 97-2 CPD ¶ 38, where the RFP required a resume showing that the proposed project manager met experience requirements in terms of years of performance of specified tasks. The GAO stated that the agency's expressed concern over the proposed project manager's experience and its question as to whether he had a high school diploma met the discussion requirement because the protester should have been alerted that the resume did not state the years of experience in various jobs, reasoning:

> As an initial matter, the failure to provide any dates for the candidate's experience reflects gross carelessness by [the protester], frustrating any attempt to determine whether the candidate met the RFP requirements. Further, having made the error in its initial proposal, even a cursory review prior to the submission of BAFOs should have alerted [the protester] to the omission of information relative to the candidate's qualifications. In addition, in the discussions letter the agency specifically advised the protester of the omission ("insufficient information was provided to review the qualifications of the proposed Project Manager") and, overall, the RFP itself sets the requirements out very simply and very specifi-

cally. (As noted above, they include, in addition to the high school diploma, the community college degree (or experience), 3 years food service experience, and 2 years supervisory experience.) Moreover, during discussions the agency issued an amendment to the RFP which required submission of the PDF, a form which specifically calls for offerors to provide the kind of information missing from [the protester's] proposal.

Under the circumstances here, we cannot conclude that a reasonably prudent offeror, reviewing the agency's question in conjunction with the material that it had submitted with its proposal, could have failed to recognize the need to provide the basic information necessary for evaluation of its proposal. *See Textron Marine Sys.*, B-243693, Aug. 19, 1991, 91-2 CPD ¶ 162 at 8 (although agency orally ascribed a deficiency to the wrong key employee proposed by protester, a reasonably prudent offeror would have ensured that each of its proposed key personnel met the requirements of the RFP, given the specificity of the RFP requirements for education and experience, and general written guidance and oral advice from the agency regarding key personnel qualifications). Given this conclusion — that [the protester] received sufficient notice that its proposed project manager did not meet the RFP requirements — we see no basis to conclude that the agency failed to hold meaningful discussions with [the protester] because it did not more specifically identify the omissions in [the protester's] proposal.

See also *Wade Perrow Constr.*, Comp. Gen. Dec. B-255332.2, 94-1 CPD ¶ 266, where the protester asserted that the agency should have told it during discussions that it had not furnished the required details concerning subcontract provisions and number and type of tests to be performed to assure quality performance. In denying the protest, the GAO stated:

[The protester] challenges the adequacy of discussions with respect to its omission of certain required information from its proposal. In describing the required project management plan to be submitted by offerors with their proposals, section L of the solicitation, "Solicitation Instructions and Conditions," referred to the criteria under the project management plan factor as set forth in section M, "Evaluation Factors for Award." These included criteria for (1) "[p]roposed method for controlling quality of subcontracted work (include contract provisions to be included in subcontracts)," and (2) "[n]umber and type of tests to be performed to assure quality of work segments." Although [the protester] generally discussed in its proposal its approach to quality control, it did not furnish details concerning subcontract provisions and numbers and types of tests to be performed, which were required by the solicitation, and its BAFO apparently was downgraded accordingly. The Corps did not raise its concerns with respect to subcontract provisions and the number and type of tests to be performed during discussions and [the protester] argues that this failure was improper. However, where, as here, certain information is specifically requested in the solicitation, the offeror is already on notice of what it must do to submit an adequate proposal, and the agency is not required to specifically remind an offeror during discussions to submit that information. *See Dynamic Sys. Technology, Inc.*, B-253957, Sept. 13, 1993, 93-2 CPD ¶ 158; *Delta Food Serv.*, B-245804.2, Feb. 11, 1992, 92-1 CPD ¶ 172.

See also *Trajen, Inc.*, Comp. Gen. Dec. B-296334, 2005 CPD ¶ 153, finding adequate discussions when the agency requested the submission of information already required by the RFP. Compare *Burchick Constr. Co.*, Comp. Gen. Dec. B-400342, 2008 CPD ¶ 203, sustaining a protest where the agency did not discuss weaknesses in a technical proposal that were based on inadequate information that was required by the RFP. The GAO reasoned that the informational deficiencies were significant weaknesses that could have been corrected if the protester had been informed of them.

E. Resolution of Uncertainties

Agencies should resolve uncertainties in order to avoid rejection or downgrading of a proposal because of lack of understanding of its terms. See *Analytical Servs., Inc.*, Comp. Gen. Dec. B-202473, 82-1 CPD ¶ 214, *recons. denied*, 82-2 CPD ¶ 502, in which discussions were found inadequate where the protester was not informed that the agency could not ascertain the extent to which research associate services were included in the proposal's indirect cost pool and, consequently, could not accurately compare the protester's proposed costs with those of other offerors. See also *Cotton & Co. LLP*, Comp. Gen. Dec. B-282808, 99-2 CPD ¶ 48 (inadequate discussion when the agency did not clear up issues where it was clear protester misunderstood solicitation); *Voith Hydro, Inc.*, Comp. Gen. Dec. B-277051, 97-2 CPD ¶ 68 (discussions inadequate where the agency determined that the protester's plan to use a new plant to manufacture the required items was an unacceptable risk but failed to discuss this deficiency with the protester); *American Combustion Indus.*, Comp. Gen. Dec. B-275057.2, 97-1 CPD ¶ 105 (agency improperly downgraded the protester when the agency, without discussing the matter with the protester, assumed that one of the protester's personnel would initially substitute for the proposed project manager); *Peter N.G. Schwartz Cos. Judiciary Square Ltd.*, Comp. Gen. Dec. B-239007.3, 90-2 CPD ¶ 353, *aff'd*, Civ. Action No. 90-2951 (D.D.C. 1991) (improper to downgrade a proposal based on a lack of clarity of the role of certain employees when the matter could have been cleared up through discussions).

A call for best and final offers (now final proposal revisions) alone does not constitute meaningful discussions when there are still unresolved uncertainties concerning the proposals, *Decision Sciences Corp.*, 60 Comp. Gen. 36 (B-196100), 80-1 CPD ¶ 357.

Agencies have also been required to resolve uncertainties as to whether an offeror is submitting an alternate proposal. See *Peirce-Phelps, Inc.*, Comp. Gen. Dec. B-238520.2, 91-1 CPD ¶ 385, stating:

> Where there are uncertainties with respect to proposals, attempts should be made to resolve the problem with meaningful discussions which point out the uncertainties and give the offeror an opportunity to resolve them. . . . The requirement for meaningful discussions extends to alternate, acceptable proposals within the competitive range. *San/Bar Corp.*, B-219644.3, Feb. 21, 1986, 86-1 CPD ¶ 183.

Agencies should also resolve ambiguities in the solicitation that can be seen from information in a proposal. For example, in *Bank of Am.*, Comp. Gen. Dec. B-287608, 2001 CPD ¶ 137, the RFP contained a very ambiguous page limitation requirement that the protester interpreted as limiting the technical proposal to 100 pages. A protest was sustained when the agency criticized the proposal for lack of sufficient detail but did not tell the protester that the limit was 200 pages. See also *Government of Harford County, Maryland*, Comp. Gen. Dec. B-283259, 99-2 CPD ¶ 81, finding inadequate discussions in failing to resolve a solicitation ambiguity but denying the protest for lack of prejudice.

F. Sample Tasks

An agency may limit discussions of a deficiency when the deficient score relates to the offeror's general understanding of the technical aspects of the work as demonstrated by its submission of a solution to a sample task, *Syscon Servs., Inc.*, 68 Comp. Gen. 698 (B-235647), 89-2 CPD ¶ 258. In *Technology Applications, Inc.*, Comp. Gen. Dec. B-238259, 90-1 CPD ¶ 451, the GAO stated:

> Where an offeror's responses to sample tasks are used to test its understanding of the technical requirements of a contemplated contract, as opposed to being used to evaluate the adequacy of its technical approach to the contract work, an agency need not specify during discussions all identified deficiencies in the offeror's approach to the tasks.

The GAO reasoned that if the purpose of the task is to determine whether the offeror has the background and understanding to identify and resolve the technical issues that would arise during contract performance, to require the agency to discuss weak sample task results would defeat the purpose of using the response to a sample task to determine the offeror's understanding of the work. See also *Fluor Daniel, Inc.*, Comp. Gen. Dec. B-262051, 95-2 CPD ¶ 241, finding no need to discuss weakness in "limited scenerio" submitted by offerors to show understanding of work; *Delany, Siegel, Zorn & Assocs., Inc.*, Comp. Gen. Dec. B-258221.2, 95-2 CPD ¶ 7, finding no need to discuss "sample report;" and *NDI Eng'g Co.*, Comp. Gen. Dec. B-245796, 92-1 CPD ¶ 113, upholding the agency's decision not to discuss low scores on responses to a sample task when the responses were used to determine the offerors' understanding of the contract work. In *MCR Fed., Inc.*, Comp. Gen. Dec. B-280969, 99-1 CPD ¶ 8, the GAO found no requirement to discuss an "acceptable" sample task rating when the agency had discussed a "marginal" sample task rating with the winning offeror.

Although discussions of sample task responses are not generally required, an agency may open discussions in order to better understand the response. However, if that occurs, the discussions must be meaningful. See *Integrated Concepts & Research Corp.*, Comp. Gen. Dec. B-309803, 2008 CPD ¶ 117 (informing offeror that amount of labor in sample task appeared high sufficient to alert protester that its price was high);

Serco, Inc., Comp. Gen. Dec. B-298266, 2006 CPD ¶ 120 (discussions elicited more information from offerors but agency misused information in evaluation process); *Delphinus Eng'g, Inc.*, Comp. Gen. Dec. B-298266, 2006 CPD ¶ 7 (discussions requested explanation of low price but protester provided in explanation in final proposal revision); *American Sys. Corp.*, Comp. Gen. Dec. B-292755, 2003 CPD ¶ 225 (evaluation notice sufficient to alert protester to issues even though it was misunderstood).

G. Product Demonstrations

When the agency requires offerors to demonstrate their product as part of the evaluation and then conducts discussions with the offerors still in the competitive range, it must discuss any perceived weaknesses revealed in the demonstration. In *Apptis, Inc.*, Comp. Gen. Dec. B-299457, 2008 CPD ¶ 49, the agency claimed that there was no such requirement because the demonstration revealed difficulty in using the product which could not be corrected (arguing that the sample task reasoning applied). The GAO rejected this argument, stating:

> [E]ven though Apptis could not change the events that transpired at its . . . demonstration, the agency was nevertheless required to point out the weaknesses it observed and provide the firm with an opportunity to address them. Thus, for example, Apptis's discussion responses and/or FPR could have refuted the agency's purported observations, provided explanations as to why the events occurred, or proposed methods by which to address the agency's associated concerns.

Compare *Cerner Corp.*, Comp. Gen. Dec. B-293093, 2004 CPD ¶ 34, holding that there was no requirement that a contractor be advised that its product used an approach that was considered to be less effective than a competing product, and *SeaArk Marine, Inc.*, Comp. Gen. Dec. B-292195, 2003 CPD ¶ 108, holding that there was no requirement for discussions after a product demonstration when the RFP precluded such discussions.

H. Cost and Price Negotiations

Under the pre-rewrite FAR, there was a hesitancy on the part of some agencies to conduct meaningful cost or price negotiations. This was caused partly by the admonition in pre-rewrite FAR 15.610(e)(2) that the contracting officer not use

> Auction techniques, such as —
>
> > (i) Indicating to an offeror a cost or price that it must meet to obtain further consideration;
> >
> > (ii) Advising an offeror of its price standing relative to another offeror (however, it is permissible to inform an offeror that its cost or price is considered by the Government to be too high or unrealistic); and

(iii) Otherwise furnishing information about other offerors' prices.

The reference to auction techniques and subsections (i) and (ii) were removed in the rewrite and replaced with the following language in FAR 15.306(e):

Government personnel engaged in the acquisition shall not engage in conduct that —

(3) Reveals an offeror's price without that offeror's permission. However, the contracting officer may inform an offeror that its price is considered by the Government to be too high, or too low, and reveal the results of the analysis supporting that conclusion. It is also permissible, at the Government's discretion, to indicate to all offerors the cost or price that the Government's price analysis, market research, and other reviews have identified as reasonable (41 U.S.C. 423(h)(1)(2)).

In addition, FAR 15.306(d) includes price among examples of issues that are subject to negotiations. Thus, the FAR now permits full price negotiation with each offeror in the competitive range. The best guidance has been issued by NASA in NFS 1815.306, stating:

(d)(3)(A) The contracting officer shall identify any cost/price elements that do not appear to be justified and encourage offerors to submit their most favorable and realistic cost/price proposals, but shall not discuss, disclose, or compare cost/price elements of any other offeror. The contracting officer shall question inadequate, conflicting, unrealistic, or unsupported cost information; differences between the offeror's proposal and most probable cost assessments; cost realism concerns; differences between audit findings and proposed costs; proposed rates that are too high/low; and labor mixes that do not appear responsive to the requirements. No agreement on cost/price elements or a "bottom line" is necessary.

See *MCT JV*, Comp. Gen. Dec. B-311245.2, 2008 CPD ¶ 121, holding that the agency was required to indicate to the protester that there was a significant disparity between the allocation of the labor hours in its cost and technical proposals. See also *Price Waterhouse*, 65 Comp. Gen. 205 (B-220049), 86-1 CPD ¶ 54, sustaining a protest because the agency failed to inform the protester during discussions that its estimated level of effort and proposed price were considered unreasonably high. Compare *Metro Mach. Corp.*, Comp. Gen. Dec. B-295744, 2005 CPD ¶ 112, where an adequate discussion occurred when the agency asked for an explanation of the proposed labor rates without telling the protester that it concluded they were unrealistically low, and *Engineering Servs. Unlimited, Inc.*, Comp. Gen. Dec. B-291275, 2003 CPD ¶ 15, where no violation of the FAR was found when the agency told the protester that its labor rates were significantly lower than incumbent rates.

Even when auctioning was prohibited, the practice was narrowly defined as occurring when there was "direct price bidding between two competing offerors,"

Washington School of Psychiatry, Comp. Gen. Dec. B-192756, 79-1 CPD ¶ 178. See also 52 Comp. Gen. 425 (B-176334) (1973); and *General Eng'g Serv., Inc.*, Comp. Gen. Dec. B-242618.2, 92-1 CPD ¶ 266. Because the language prohibiting auctions was removed, it would not be improper for the agency to conduct an auction provided that it received the permission of all offerors to have their prices disclosed, FAR 15.306(e)(3). Whether such permission could be obtained and whether it would be wise to conduct auctions are another matter.

Under the pre-rewrite rules, agencies were permitted to reveal their own conception of price reasonableness to all offerors by disclosing the amount of funds available for the project, *M.W. Kellogg Co./Siciliana Appalti Costruzioni, S.p.A., J.V. v. United States*, 10 Cl. Ct. 17 (1986); disclosing the government estimate, *A.T.F. Constr. Co.*, Comp. Gen. Dec. B-228060, 87-2 CPD ¶ 436; or disclosing current contract prices, *Bethlehem Steel Corp., Baltimore Marine Div.*, Comp. Gen. Dec. B-231923, 88-2 CPD ¶ 438. In *Ikard Mfg. Co.*, 63 Comp. Gen. 239 (B-213891), 84-1 CPD ¶ 266, the contracting officer reopened negotiations after both best and final offers contained prices considered too high and told both offerors that the Army's negotiating goal was a $1,740 unit price. The GAO indicated that this procedure was proper because the point of the auction prohibition was to prevent direct price bidding between offerors, not to prevent the government from negotiating price when it had not otherwise disclosed the competitive standing of offerors. See also *Printz Reinigung GmbH*, Comp. Gen. Dec. B-241510, 91-1 CPD ¶ 143, where the GAO considered the disclosure of a desired price range to be a permissible negotiation tool for achieving a fair and reasonable price.

Agencies must disclose unreasonably high prices in discussions, *Tiger Truck, LLC*, Comp. Gen. Dec. B-400685, 2009 CPD ¶ 19; *Creative Info. Tech., Inc.*, Comp. Gen. Dec. B-293073.10, 2005 CPD ¶ 110. However, the GAO has *not* required agencies to discuss price with offerors whose prices are not unreasonably high, *Integrated Concepts & Research Corp.*, Comp. Gen. Dec. B-309803, 2008 CPD ¶ 117; *Synergetics, Inc.*, Comp. Gen. Dec. B-299904, 2007 CPD ¶ 168; *DeTekion Sec. Sys,, Inc.*, Comp. Gen. Dec. B-298235, 2006 CPD ¶ 130; *MarLaw-Arco MFPD Mgmt.*, Comp. Gen. Dec. B-291875, 2003 CPD ¶ 85; *Jacobs Serv. Co.*, Comp. Gen. Dec. B-262088.3, 97-1 CPD ¶ 220. Similarly, in *Akal Security, Inc.*, Comp. Gen. Dec. B-271385, 96-2 CPD ¶ 77, there was no need to advise an offeror that its price was above that of other offerors, as well as the government estimate when the agency had concluded that the price was reasonable. The GAO stated:

> Although an agency may inform an offeror during discussions that its price is considered to be too high or unrealistic where otherwise appropriate, FAR 15.610(e)(2)(ii), the government has no responsibility to do so where the offeror's price is not considered excessive or unreasonable. *Weeks Marine, Inc./Bean Dredging Corp., a Joint Venture*, 69 Comp. Gen. 108 (1989), 89-2 CPD ¶ 505; *Applied Remote Technology, Inc.*, B-250475, Jan. 22, 1993, 93-1 CPD ¶ 58; *Warren Elec. Constr. Corp.*, B-236173.4; B-236173.5, July 16, 1990, 90-2 CPD ¶ 34. Further,

an agency is not required to conduct price discussions with an offeror solely because its price is higher than that of other offerors; on the contrary, an agency is generally constrained not to advise an offeror of its price standing relative to other offerors. FAR 15.610(e)(2).

Here, the agency performed a price analysis of the proposals and determined that [the protester's] price was competitive and not unrealistically high. Accordingly, the agency had no duty to advise [the protester] that its price was high. *See Weeks Marine, Inc./Bean Dredging Corp., a Joint Venture, supra.*

The Court of Federal Claims has followed the GAO reasoning on this issue. See *DMS All-Star Joint Venture v. United States*, 90 Fed. Cl. 653 (2010), stating at 669:

As to discussions regarding an offeror's costs, unless an offeror's costs constitute a significant weakness or deficiency in its proposal, the contracting officer is not required to address in discussions costs that appear to be higher than those proposed by other offerors. *SOS Interpreting, Ltd.,* B-287477.2, 2001 CPD ¶ 84, at 3 (Comp. Gen. May 16, 2001) (citation omitted). In other words, "if an offeror's costs are not so high as to be unreasonable and unacceptable for contract award, the agency may conduct meaningful discussions without raising the issue of the offeror's costs." *Yang Enters., Inc.; Santa Barbara Applied Research, Inc.,* B-294605.4, B-294605.5, B-294605.6, 2005 CPD ¶ 65, at 9 (Comp. Gen. April 1, 2005) (citation omitted). In essence, it is mandatory for the agency to discuss costs or pricing when the prices submitted in a firm's proposal "would preclude award to the firm." *Gen. Dynamics-Ordnance & Tactical Sys.,* B-401658, B-401658.2, 2009 CPD ¶ 217, at 5 (Comp. Gen. Oct. 26, 2009) (*General Dynamics*) (citation omitted). In *General Dynamics,* the Comptroller General determined that the protestor's pricing was not unreasonable, so as to require discussions, where high-priced items and favorable prices combined to produce a reasonable offer well within an acceptable overall bid price range. *Id.* Because the protestor was not precluded from winning the contract because of its costs, no discussions of the protestor's costs were necessary. *Id.*

Compare *WorldTravelServ. v. United States*, 49 Fed. Cl. 431 (2001), holding that an agency must disclose during discussions that it has concluded that a price is "too high." The court made it clear, however, that there was no requirement to tell the offeror how much it was too high.

Neither has the GAO required that offerors be specifically told that their price was unrealistically low as long as they were informed that the agency was looking at this issue. See *SEEMA, Inc.*, Comp. Gen. Dec. B-277988, 98-1 CPD ¶ 12, denying a protest where the agency did not tell the protester that its price was considered unrealistic but told it that its price was significantly below the government estimate and not supported by the cost-savings data included in its proposal. Compare *Robinson's Lawn Servs., Inc.*, Comp. Gen. Dec. B-299551.5, 2009 CPD ¶ 45, denying a protest that the price discussions had induced the protester to raise its prices resulting in loss of the competition where the agency told both offerors that their prices were unrealistically low. In contrast, in *Advanced Sys. Dev., Inc.*, Comp. Gen. Dec. B-298411, 2006 CPD ¶ 137, the GAO held that an unfair discussion had occurred when the agency induced a competitor to lower its price by not disclosing that it corrected an error to raise the price and telling the competitor that its price violated a price target – resulting in award to the competitor.

The government may have different price objectives for each offer. See *Racal Guardata, Inc.*, 71 Comp. Gen. 218 (B-245139.2), 92-1 CPD ¶ 159, where the GAO reasoned that no unfairness occurred where the price objectives were based on the technical proposals of each competitor and were not stated as mandatory figures. In *Griggs & Assocs., Inc.*, Comp. Gen. Dec. B-205266, 82-1 CPD ¶ 458, the GAO upheld the agency's disclosure of individual cost objectives developed for each offeror's proposal based on separate appraisals of each offeror's costs as a valid basis for negotiations. In *Newport News & Drydock Co.*, Comp. Gen. Dec. B-254969, 94-1 CPD ¶ 198, the GAO stated:

> NNS and Ingalls contend that the agency improperly coached NASSCO by providing that firm during written discussions with the government estimate, including both the overall estimated overrun ([deleted]) and the estimate in critical areas (e.g., "your proposed manhours for SWBS groups 100 and 500 are unrealistically low by approximately 40%, and 50% respectively"), such that NASSCO knew by how much it had to increase its price and profit in order to avoid having its price be found unrealistically low. NNS and Ingalls note that, in contrast, NAVSEA never advised them of the detailed government estimate for their proposals.

> A contracting agency properly may disclose a price objective to an offeror as a negotiation tool for reaching an agreement as to a fair and reasonable price, *Racal Guardata, Inc.*, 71 Comp. Gen. 219 (1992), 92-1 CPD ¶ 159, although where the agency discloses the Government estimate to only some offerors it runs the risk that the discussions will be rendered unfair and prejudicial to the other offerors. *Cf. Bank Street College of Education*, 63 Comp. Gen. 393 (1984), 84-1 CPD ¶ 607 (not improper to discuss government cost estimate with awardee but not protester where only the awardee's proposed costs were above the government estimate).

> Here, even if NNS and Ingalls are correct that it was improper to inform only NASSCO of the detailed government estimate, had the agency provided NNS and Ingalls with the equivalent information for their proposals, the outcome would have been the same. In this regard, the benefit NASSCO arguably obtained from the specific information it received was being able — unlike NNS and Ingalls — roughly to calculate the price at which its proposal would be found unrealistically low. Based on this figure, it was able to modify (i.e., increase) its BAFO target price precisely enough that the agency would not find the price unreasonably low and thus discard that price and use the higher "Estimated Final Price to the Government" in evaluating NASSCO's proposal. If the protesters had been furnished equivalent information, it would have provided them with the same benefit — it would have allowed them roughly to calculate the price below which their proposals would be deemed unrealistically low. Since (the record shows) the lowest realistic prices for the protesters under the original government estimate were

higher than NASSCO's BAFO price (because both protesters' costs of perfor-mance were inherently higher than NASSCO's), neither would have moved into line for award basing their BAFO prices on this calculation. *See Racal Guardata, Inc., supra* (where alleged improper discussions did not prejudice the protester, protest will not be sustained).

I. Correction of Mistakes

Prior to the FAR rewrite, most mistakes in proposals were corrected during oral or written discussions. See pre-rewrite FAR 15.607(c). The rewrite deleted this guid-ance and covered mistakes in a very cursory way, mentioning that they could be corrected prior to establishing a competitive range with offerors whose exclusion or inclusion in the competitive range was uncertain. The FAR is silent on correction of mistakes during negotiations, but it seems apparent that the contracting officer should notify offerors of suspected mistakes if they have not been identified previously.

In *Fidelity Techs. Corp.*, Comp. Gen. Dec. B-276425, 97-1 CPD ¶ 197, the pro-test was sustained where the protester's proposal included an apparently erroneous small disadvantaged business (SDB) certification and the contracting officer failed to provide the protester an opportunity to correct it. In refuting the Navy's argument that it did not have to provide the protester notice of possible error during negotia-tions, the GAO stated:

> The Navy argues that it could only consider information within the four corners of that proposal. This argument is unpersuasive, both because the inconsistencies within the proposal itself put the contracting officer on notice of the apparent error and because an agency may take into account its knowledge in evaluating proposals and making an award. *TRESP Assocs., Inc.; Advanced Data Concepts, Inc.,* B-258322.5; B-258322.6, Mar. 9, 1995, 96-1 CPD ¶ 8 at 6–7. Indeed, some information is simply too close at hand for the agency not to consider it. *International Bus. Sys., Inc.,* B-275554, Mar. 3, 1997, 97-1 CPD ¶ 114 at 5.

> Here, the Navy made no attempt to resolve the protester's SDB status, even though it could have done so through the clarification process. *See Jimmy's Ap-pliance,* 61 Comp. Gen. 4444, 446 (1982), 82-1 CPD ¶ 542 at 2–4. Moreover, de-spite conducting discussions with the offerors, it did not mention the SDB status question in its discussions with Fidelity. Because discussions were held, we need not decide whether the agency would have been required to clarify Fidelity's SDB status if award had been made on the basis of initial proposals. When discussions are held, they are required to be meaningful. *See Ashland Sales & Serv., Inc.,* B-255159, Feb. 14, 1994, 94-1 CPD ¶ 108 at 3. Here, this meant that the Navy had an obligation to raise the SDB status question in its discussions with Fidelity, in light of the inconsistencies within the firm's proposal, the significance of the 10-percent evaluation preference under the program whose purpose is to assist small disadvantaged firms, and the agency's apparent knowledge of the inaccuracy of the SDB representations in the proposal. See FAR § 15.610(c)(4) (FAC 90-44) (during discussions, contracting officer shall resolve any suspected mistakes by

calling them to offeror's attention). Accordingly, we conclude that, because of the specific circumstances present in this instance, the agency acted improperly by not resolving the question of Fidelity's SDB status before award.

See also *American Mgmt. Sys., Inc.*, Comp. Gen. Dec. B-215283, 84-2 CPD ¶ 199, sustaining a protest where the offeror's proposal indicated a unit charge for tape storage of $2.50 per tape per day in one area and $2.50 per tape per year in another and the contracting officer failed to resolve the discrepancy during discussions. Similarly, in *Dep't of the Air Force*, 67 Comp. Gen. 372 (B-229059.2), 88-1 CPD ¶ 357, the GAO modified its recommendation of an earlier opinion, admitting that it had overlooked the fact that a contracting officer had failed to clarify or correct a significant price error in one offeror's BAFO that increased the offered price significantly. In the earlier opinion, *Centel Business Sys.*, 67 Comp. Gen. 156 (B-229059), 87-2 CPD ¶ 629, the GAO sustained the protest and recommended that the offer be reevaluated as if the protester had not made the error. In this case the GAO looked at the facts again and conceded that some ambiguity in Centel's price proposal still existed. Recommending that discussions be reopened, the GAO stated at 375:

> Although to reopen negotiations at this juncture would create an auction situation, in our view, the importance of correcting the error through further negotiations overrides any harmful effect on the integrity of the competitive procurement system.

Compare *American Elec. Lab., Inc.*, 65 Comp. Gen. 62 (B-219582), 85-2 CPD ¶ 545, holding that prohibition of price auctioning outweighs benefits of reopening discussions, and *International Business Machs., Corp.*, GSBCA 11324-P, 92-1 BCA ¶ 24,439, holding that it was improper, after the award, to correct its price, which had been incorrectly computed because of an ambiguity in the RFP. The GSBCA reasoned that no mistake had occurred and that reopening discussions in this situation was tantamount to an auction. See also *Contel Information Sys., Inc.*, Comp. Gen. Dec. B-220215, 86-1 CPD ¶ 44, finding that an agency had no obligation to correct a mistake that was the fault of the offeror and could not be easily detected by the contracting officer.

If the contracting officer resolves a potential mistake through a reasonable interpretation of the proposal, there will be no obligation to raise the issue during discussions with the offeror. In *Timeplex, Inc.*, Comp. Gen. Dec. B-220069, 85-2 CPD ¶ 651, there was a large discrepancy between the B- and L-tables. The Air Force assumed that the protester had merely miscalculated the various cost summaries in the L-table, which served only as a summary of the prices listed in the B-table, and therefore did not request verification of the protester's bid. The protester, however, had calculated the L-table first and then had intended to structure those cost summaries back into the B-table. The GAO held that the government's assumption was reasonable, given that the normal procedure would have been to calculate the L-table summaries from the various pricing elements in the B-table. Compare *PAE GmbH*

Planning & Constr., 68 Comp. Gen. 358 (B-233823), 89-1 CPD ¶ 336, holding that minor irregularities or clerical errors apparent on the face of the proposal had to be corrected during discussions if the agency opened discussions.

There is no obligation to correct mistakes in discussions if an offeror could not win the competition with the corrected offer. See *Engineering & Professional Servs.*, Comp. Gen. Dec. B-219657, 85-2 CPD ¶ 621, holding that failure to reopen discussions was not prejudicial because the protester would not have been found responsible.

III. NEGOTIATION PROCEDURES

In conducting negotiations with offerors in the competitive range, an agency has broad discretion in selecting the specific procedure — as long as it meets the fundamental requirement that deficiencies and significant weaknesses be disclosed to the maximum extent possible. The potential procedures available to the contracting officer range from detailed negotiations in which terms to be included in the final proposal revision are agreed upon to a more arm's-length process in which the contracting officer merely notifies the offerors of problems with their proposals and each offeror then attempts to improve those areas in the proposal revision. In the procurement of major systems and information technology it is common practice to send out evaluation notices and/or clarification requests during the evaluation as questions arise as to the specifics in a proposal. This procedure is highly effective when there is little doubt that all of the competitors will be placed in the competitive range with the result that there is no concern as to whether a discussion has occurred. There have been no protests challenging whether such a procedure probes areas that are not covered by FAR 15.306(b), dealing with permissible exchanges before the establishing of the competitive range.

A. Preparing for Negotiations

The only guidance in the FAR on the preparation needed to conduct negotiations is with regard to the negotiation of contract prices. FAR 15.406-1 requires that the contracting officer do sufficient analysis to formulate prenegotiation objectives, as follows:

(a) The prenegotiation objectives establish the Government's initial negotiation position. They assist in the contracting officer's determination of fair and reasonable price. They should be based on the results of the contracting officer's analysis of the offeror's proposal, taking into consideration all pertinent information including field pricing assistance, audit reports and technical analysis, fact-finding results, independent Government cost estimates and price histories.

(b) The contracting officer shall establish prenegotiation objectives before the negotiation of any pricing action. The scope and depth of the analysis supporting the objectives should be directly related to the dollar value, importance, and complexity of the pricing action. When cost analysis is required, the contracting officer shall document the pertinent issues to be negotiated, the cost objectives, and a profit or fee objective.

There is no guidance in the FAR on the preparation needed to negotiate other elements of competitive proposals. However, ¶ 15.4-3, Attachment A, of the Department of Energy Acquisition Guide, while focusing primarily and negotiation of cost or price, contains the following guidance on other issues that should be covered in negotiations:

(B) Other Negotiation Objectives and Issues

Identify non-pricing related issues that must be addressed as part of the negotiation. Examples include:

1. Delivery or performance issues

2. Proposed special provisions.

3. Any deviations to regulations and the required approvals.

4. Contractor assumptions.

5. Any solicitation provisions that have been challenged by the Offeror or to which they have taken exception.

6. Discussion of unique features of the contract, e.g., pensions, contractor human resource management, transition issues, cost sharing, options, Government furnished facilities, property, or equipment not provided for in the contract.

7. Conflict of interest issues.

See also ¶ 604.03 of the Department of Commerce *Source Selection Procedures* stating:

Before conducting discussions, it is important to have a meeting [within the agency] to develop a written agenda for the discussions. At this meeting, the CO [contracting officer] will define the role of each attendee and tell them when they will be allowed to enter into the discussions. The actual conduct of the discussions will at all times be under the control of the CO.

This guidance makes it clear that it is important to have a clear agenda for discussions and suggests that this agenda be furnished to the offeror in advance to ensure that discussions are as meaningful as possible. None of the agency handbooks address whether an offeror should be permitted to add items to this agenda, but this should be standard practice. One of the purposes of discussions is to ascertain whether each offeror fully comprehends the needs of the agency as expressed in the RFP, and an excellent way to determine this is to encourage each offeror to raise questions during the discussions. Offerors' questions, however, should be disclosed to the agency in advance of the actual discussions. This permits the agency to fully consider the issue raised and have personnel at the discussion who are prepared to deal with the issue.

B. Form of Negotiations

The form of negotiations is not addressed in the FAR but they should be structured to permit sufficient communication to ensure that offerors are fairly and equally informed of information necessary to decide whether to revise their offers. The actual form of negotiations will not be questioned as long as it achieves these objectives. Thus, discussions in the form of written questions have been permitted. See *Fort Carson Support Servs. v. United States*, 71 Fed. Cl. 571 (2006), finding a list of discussion questions designated either "weaknesses" or "deficiencies" adequate to inform protester of areas to be addressed in its final proposal revisions. See also *DRS C3 Sys., LLC*, Comp. Gen. Dec. B-310825, 2008 CPD ¶ 103 (letter listing "discussion questions" and calling for written response); *Interstate Elec. Corp.*, Comp. Gen. Dec. B-286466, 2001 CPD ¶ 29 (telecopied "evaluation notices" identifying specific concerns met discussion requirement); *SRS Techs.*, Comp. Gen. Dec. B-270341.2, 96-1 CPD ¶ 120 (two written discussion items reasonably led the protester into the areas of its proposal that needed amplification); *Gutierrez-Palmenberg, Inc.*, Comp. Gen. Dec. B-255797.3, 94-2 CPD ¶ 158 (written list of items sufficiently alerted the protester to specific areas of its proposal considered weak or requiring further explanation); *Johnson, Basin & Shaw, Inc.*, Comp. Gen. Dec. B-240265, 90-2 CPD ¶ 371 (sufficient discussion in the form of written questions submitted to the offeror); and *American Dist. Tel. v. Dep't of Energy*, 555 F. Supp. 1244 (D.D.C. 1983) (list of requested "explanations" and "clarifications" would have alerted a reasonable offeror that the items were deficiencies). In *Joule Tech. Corp.*, Comp. Gen. Dec. B-197249, 80-2 CPD ¶ 231, the GAO commented on this written listing of deficiencies as follows:

> The real question here is not whether the October 19 letter, standing alone, described the deficiencies perceived in Joule's proposal in such intimate detail that there could be no doubt as to their identification and nature, but whether the letter imparted sufficient information to Joule to afford it a fair and reasonable opportunity in the context of this procurement to identify and correct the deficiencies in its proposal. We believe that it did.

See also *KPMG Peat Marwick*, Comp. Gen. Dec. B-258990, 95-1 CPD ¶ 116, holding that there was no requirement that the agency conduct face-to-face discussions in addition to, or in lieu of, written discussions; and *Austin Elecs.*, 54 Comp. Gen. 60 (B-180690), 74-2 CPD ¶ 61, rejecting the protester's assertion that the agency was required to conduct give-and-take oral discussions. The GAO held that the agency's decision to disclose deficiencies by letter was not an abuse of discretion.

In spite of the numerous decisions permitting written discussions, it is doubtful that this procedure is an adequate form of communication when there are significant deficiencies or weaknesses. See *Logistic Sys., Inc.*, 59 Comp. Gen. 548 (B-196254), 80-1 CPD ¶ 442, finding that there had been inadequate communication of the deficiencies when the agency sent the offeror an elaborate list of deficiencies and conducted no oral discussions. See also *Hughes STX Corp.*, Comp. Gen. Dec. B-278466, 98-1 CPD ¶ 52, where very brief written discussion questions were held to have misled the offeror as to the level of concern the agency had as to the realism of the proposed labor costs.

Oral discussions can be held over the telephone, Comp. Gen. Dec. B-157156, Nov. 8, 1965, *Unpub.*, by teleconference, *ITT Corp., Sys. Div.*, Comp. Gen. Dec. B-310102.6, 2010 CPD ¶ 12, or in a face-to-face meeting. However, meetings are normally called for in procurements where there are significant deficiencies or weaknesses. The information conveyed orally should be carefully documented to ensure that the offeror fully understands the issue. See *New Jersey & H St., LLC*, Comp. Gen. Dec. B-311314.3, 2008 CPD ¶ 133, sustaining a protest when the protester asserted that it had never been told of a weakness that the agency claimed it had disclosed. When meetings are held, there is no requirement that agreement be reached on each issue. See 52 Comp. Gen. 161 (B-176223) (1972), stating at 164:

> The duration per se of a negotiation session is by no means determinative of whether meaningful discussions have been held. Moreover, while recognizing that the term negotiation (which we equate to discussions) generally implies a series of offers and counter-offers we have not concluded that the presence of such offers and counter-offers is essential for compliance with 10 U.S.C. § 2304(g).

The descriptions in FAR 15.306(d) of negotiation as including bargaining and in FAR 15.307(b) of negotiating until the parties reach understanding make it clear that the FAR Councils believed that discussions would include more face-to-face meetings where the contracting officer and the offeror conduct negotiations until they reach an understanding of the best offer that each offeror can make. However, it does not appear from the description in protest decisions that this has occurred. Rather, there continue to be numerous instances of pro forma discussions where the agency merely sends offerors a list of deficiencies and significant weaknesses. While it is doubtful whether this type of negotiation is a satisfactory communication device, it has not been questioned by either the GAO or the Court of Federal Claims. See, for example, *Kerr Contractors, Inc. v. United States*, 89 Fed. Cl. 312 (2009) (discussion letters sent to all offerors); *Korrect Optical, Inc.*, Comp. Gen. Dec. B-288128, 2001 CPD ¶ 171 (letter with list of "significant deficiencies"); *Davies Rail & Mech. Works, Inc.*, Comp. Gen. Dec. B-283911.2, 2000 CPD ¶ 48 (letter with list of "deficiencies and weaknesses").

C. Reaching Agreement on Final Proposal

In adopting the term "negotiations" to describe the discussion process, the FAR rewrite appears to have embraced the concept that negotiations should result in agreement between the parties as to the final proposal that will be submitted by the offeror. Thus, FAR 15.307(b) calls for proposal revisions to "document understandings reached during negotiations." FAR 15.001 amplifies this concept with the following definition:

> Proposal revision is a change to a proposal made after the solicitation closing date, at the request of or as allowed by a contracting officer, as the result of negotiations.

This concept has been adopted by the Army in *Contracting for Best Value: A Best Practices Guide to Source Selection*, AMC-P 715-3 (Jan. 1, 1998), which states:

> During discussions, our objective should be to reach complete agreement between and understanding by the Government and the offeror regarding all of the basic requirements in the solicitation. In essence, obtaining a contract that demonstrates the greatest promise of meeting the solicitation's requirements and no surprises after award is the goal of both the Government and the offeror.

Similar guidance is contained in NFS 1815.306(d)(3):

> (B) The contracting officer shall discuss contract terms and conditions so that a "model" contract can be sent to each offeror with the request for final proposal revisions. If the solicitation allows, any proposed technical performance capabilities above those specified in the RFP that have value to the Government and are considered proposal strengths should be discussed with the offeror and proposed for inclusion in that offeror's "model" contract. These items are not to be discussed with, or proposed to, other offerors. If the offeror declines to include these strengths in its "model" contract, the Government evaluators should reconsider their characterization as strengths.

The goal of reaching agreement with each competing offeror during the negotiation places a significant burden on the contracting officer because such "agreements" can not guarantee to any offeror that it will win the competition. During negotiations of this type, the agency personnel must work with each offeror to assist it to make the best offer it is capable of but, at the same time, must alert each offeror to the fact that the ultimate selection decision will be based on analysis of the relative merits of the competing offers. Throughout such negotiations, the offerors must be treated in an evenhanded fashion with regard to the information revealed. Furthermore, agency personnel must exercise great care not to reveal elements of one offer to any other offeror.

Care must be exercised to ensure that interim revisions to offers are documented in writing and are understood to supersede the original offer. See *CCL, Inc.*, Comp.

Gen. Dec. B-251527, 93-1 CPD ¶ 354, *recons. denied*, 93-2 CPD ¶ 178, ruling that although revised prices submitted by an offeror during negotiations revoked the original offer, they were not new offers that served the purpose of keeping the offer open for 60 days as called for by the Standard Form 33 cover sheet of the original offer. The GAO reached this conclusion because the letter submitting the revised prices contained no indication that the offeror intended to keep them open for 60 additional days.

IV. IMPROPER NEGOTIATIONS

Negotiation practices that result in unequal treatment of offerors must be avoided. They destroy the integrity of the competitive system and may be grounds for successful protests. In addition, some practices are prohibited by statute and regulation. This section deals with these improper negotiating practices and considers those situations where a lack of prejudice may be grounds for dismissal of a protest.

A. Unequal Treatment

The proper operation of a competitive system depends upon offerors who have faith in the integrity of the system. The belief of offerors that they will receive fair treatment is a cornerstone of effective competition, Thus, ensuring that all offerors are treated fairly is a major concern when conducting negotiations. In 51 Comp. Gen. 621 (B-173677) (1972), the GAO stated at 622:

> [T]he statute [now 10 U.S.C. § 2305(b)(4)(A)] should not be interpreted in a manner which discriminates against or gives preferential treatment to any competitor. Any discussion with competing offerors raises the question as to how to avoid unfairness and unequal treatment.

The Court of Federal Claims identified the fact that fairness continues to be an integral part of the negotiation/discussion process in *Dynacs Eng'g Co. v. United States*, 48 Fed. Cl. 124 (2000), where it found unfair discussions when, during reopened discussions, the agency identified "weaknesses" that had been identified in the first round of discussions, but not addressed, with one offeror but not with the protester.

Fairness requires the agency to ensure that offerors compete on an equal basis. The GAO held in *Perkin-Elmer Corp.*, Comp. Gen. Dec. B-204082, 82-1 CPD ¶ 315, that where the specifications are ambiguous and it becomes clear during discussions that offerors are proposing on different bases, the agency has a duty to conduct further discussions to assure competition on the same basis. In *MSI, Div. of Bionetics Corp.*, Comp. Gen. Dec. B-233090, 89-1 CPD ¶ 185, discussions were required where the proposals indicated that the offerors did not understand the quantity of work required.

One of the most common examples of unequal treatment is where the agency gives information to one or more offerors but fails to provide the same information to other offerors who might be able to use it to their advantage. See *Kerr Contractors, Inc. v. United States*, 89 Fed. Cl. 312 (2009), stating at 329:

> The government, when conducting discussions with offerors in the competitive range, may not "engage in conduct that . . . [f]avors one offeror over another." 48 C.F.R. § 15.306(e) (2008). This regulation does not permit a procuring agency to engage in unequal discussions, where a crucial and advantageous piece of information is withheld from some but not all offerors remaining in the competition. *See, e.g., Metcalf Constr. Co. v. United States,* 53 Fed. Cl. 617, 634-35 (2002) (holding, in that case, that "the bidders were treated unequally where one bidder was advised, in no uncertain terms, not to exceed the budget ceilings, and a second bidder under identical circumstances was not"). Nonetheless, "agencies are not required to conduct identical discussions with each offeror." *Femme Comp [Inc. v. United States]*, 83 Fed. Cl. [704 (2008)] at 735 (citing *WorldTravelService v. United States,* 49 Fed. Cl. 431, 440 (2001)). Rather, the procuring agency should tailor discussions to each offeror's proposal. *WorldTravelService,* 49 Fed. Cl. at 440.

See, for example, *SeaSpace*, 70 Comp. Gen. 268 (B-241564), 91-1 CPD ¶ 179, where the agency improperly suggested that one offeror use a more powerful computer that had recently come on the market without providing the same suggestion to other offerors. See also *Ashbury Int'l Group, Inc.*, Comp. Gen. Dec. B-401123, 2009 CPD ¶ 140 (improper to tell only one offeror that management plan should be submitted); *TDS, Inc.*, Comp. Gen. Dec. B-292674, 2003 CPD ¶ 204 (agency gave two competitors far more detailed questions than those given protester); *CitiWest Properties, Inc.*, Comp. Gen. Dec. B-274689.4, 98-1 CPD ¶ 3 (unfair to point out insufficient information in a prescribed form to one offeror but not to another); and *Cylink Corp.*, Comp. Gen. Dec. B-242304, 91-1 CPD ¶ 384 (improper to inform only one competitor that the agency would accept performance that seemed to be out of compliance with the specifications).

Unfairness was found where an agency asked one offeror to demonstrate that an affiliated company's experience should be attributed to it without informing the protester that it had informational deficiencies in its experience information, *Core Tech Int'l Corp. – Costs*, Comp. Gen. Dec. B-400047.2, 2009 CPD ¶ 59. See also *American K-9 Detection Servs., Inc.*, Comp. Gen. Dec. B-400464.6, 2009 CPD ¶ 107 (agency allowed one offeror to correct deficiency making proposal technically acceptable without telling protester that its option prices created a "performance risk"); *Boeing Co.*, Comp. Gen. Dec. B-311344, 2008 CPD ¶ 114 (in continuing discussions, agency told protester it had met requirement and did not reveal that it had altered this conclusion while continuing to work with competitor to ensure that it met the requirement); *Advanced Sys. Dev., Inc.*, Comp. Gen. Dec. B-298411, 2006 CPD ¶ 137 (agency induced competitor to lower its price by misleading discussions and then selected competitor based on low price); *Martin Elecs., Inc.*, Comp. Gen.

Dec. B-290846.3, 2003 CPD ¶ 6 (agency discussed delivery deficiencies with only one offeror); *Morrison Knudsen Corp.*, Comp. Gen. Dec. B-270703, 96-2 CPD ¶ 86 (agency did not adequately inform the protester that it needed to list the equipment that would be used but explicitly told the awardee that it should list such equipment); *Management Sys. Designers, Inc.*, Comp. Gen. Dec. B-244383.4, 91-2 CPD ¶ 518 (agency told only one offeror that it had decided to delete a significant portion of the work); *EMS Dev. Corp.*, 70 Comp. Gen. 459 (B-242484), 91-1 CPD ¶ 427, *recons. denied*, 91-2 CPD ¶ 131 (agency provided clarifications of the solicitation requirements to an offeror under a sole source solicitation but did not provide the same clarifications to the protester when the solicitation was resolicited on a competitive basis); *Grumman Data Sys. Corp. v. Stone*, 37 Cont. Cas. Fed. (CCH) ¶ 76,179 (D.D.C. 1991) (agency answered questions of one offeror but disclosed answers without the corresponding questions to the other offerors); and *Northwest Regional Educ. Lab.*, Comp. Gen. Dec. B-213464, 84-1 CPD ¶ 357 (agency inaccurately informed all offerors how much higher their proposed costs were than the government estimate and the information given to the protester involved a significantly larger percentage error than the mistaken figures provided to other offerors).

While fairness requires equal treatment of offerors with similar deficiencies, it does not require the agency to spend an equal amount of time with all offerors or to discuss the same areas. The Court of Federal Claims has recognized that the content and extent of negotiations with each offeror will be determined by the deficiencies in the particular proposal, *Drexel Heritage Furnishings, Inc. v. United States*, 7 Cl. Ct. 134 (1984). See FAR 15.306(d)(1):

> Discussions are tailored to each offeror's proposal, and shall be conducted by the contracting officer with each offeror within the competitive range.

See *Lockheed Martin Corp.*, Comp. Gen. Dec. B-293679, 2004 CPD ¶ 115, where the GAO responded to an agency evaluator's statement that he was told that, to be fair, he had to ask the same questions of each offeror by stating:

> This advice is directly contrary to the FAR, which provides that discussions should be "tailored to each offeror's proposal." FAR § 15.306(d)(1).

See also *Trident Sys., Inc.*, Comp. Gen. Dec. B-243101, 91-1 CPD ¶ 604, where the GAO made the following observations concerning tailoring the negotiations:

> [I]nsofar as Trident alleges the Navy did not hold equal discussions because the offerors were not asked the same questions, the only additional question Trident was asked concerned its relationship with its subcontractor; SPA was not asked this question because SPA did not propose to use a subcontractor. In any case, in order for discussions to be meaningful, contracting agencies must furnish information to all offerors in the competitive range as to the areas in which their proposals are believed to be deficient so that the offerors have a chance to revise their proposals to fully satisfy the agency requirements. *Pan Am World Servs.,*

Inc.; *Base Maintenance Support Group; Holmes & Narver Servs, Inc.*, B-231840 et al., Nov. 7, 1988, 88-2 CPD ¶ 446. In other words, since the number and type of proposal deficiencies will vary among offerors the agency should tailor the discussions for each offeror, based on the offerors' evaluated deficiencies. *Holmes & Narver, Inc.*, B-239469.2; B-239469.3, Sept. 14, 1990, 90-2 CPD ¶ 210.

Thus, an agency may properly conduct "extensive discussions with offerors whose initial proposals contain technical deficiencies while conducting more limited discussions with offerors whose proposals contain fewer weaknesses or deficiencies," *Pacific Architects & Eng'rs, Inc.*, Comp. Gen. Dec. B-236432, 89-2 CPD ¶ 494. Hence, it is proper to conduct detailed discussions with offerors whose proposals contain technical deficiencies while affording those with technically acceptable proposals only an opportunity to submit a final proposal, *Weinschel Eng'g Co.*, 64 Comp. Gen. 524 (B-217202), 85-1 CPD ¶ 574. The agency may also reveal the government's cost estimate to an offeror proposing a cost considered too high without disclosing the estimate to an offeror submitting an acceptable proposed cost, *Bank Street College of Educ.*, 63 Comp. Gen. 393 (B-213209), 84-1 CPD ¶ 607, *recons. denied*, 84-2 CPD ¶ 445. See also *Biospherics, Inc.*, Comp. Gen. Dec. B-285065, 2000 CPD ¶ 118, finding no unequal discussions where the agency discussed low price with one offeror but did not discuss high price with protester, and *Ralph G. Moore & Assoc.*, Comp. Gen. Dec. B-270686, 96-1 CPD ¶ 118, holding that an agency did not conduct unequal discussions when it discussed the awardee's unreasonably low price and did not discuss the protester's reasonable price. See also *Pharm-Chem, Inc.*, Comp. Gen. Dec. B-291725.3, 2003 CPD ¶ 148 (clearing up role of one required employee proper when no such discussion was necessary with incumbent protester); *WorldTravelService*, Comp. Gen. Dec. B-284155.3, 2001 CPD ¶ 68 (proper to identify technical deficiencies with one offeror only when the other offerors have no such deficiencies); *Ann Riley & Assocs., Ltd.*, Comp. Gen. Dec. B-271741.2, 97-1 CPD ¶ 120, *recons. denied*, 97-1 CPD ¶ 122 (more discussion with one offeror proper because its proposal contained more weaknesses); *Quality Elevator Co.*, Comp. Gen. Dec. B-271899, 96-2 CPD ¶ 89 (more questions posed to higher-rated offeror proper when questions were tailored to proposals); *CBIS Fed. Inc.*, 71 Comp. Gen. 319 (B-245844.2), 92-1 CPD ¶ 308 (more extensive discussions with one offeror proper because that offeror's proposal contained more deficiencies); *Holmes & Narver, Inc.*, Comp. Gen. Dec. B-239469.2, 90-2 CPD ¶ 210 (issues to be discussed vary among proposals).

Under the FAR Part 15 rewrite the rules regarding fairness were somewhat altered. Thus, in *Synetics, Inc. v. United States*, 45 Fed. Cl. 1 (1999), the court ruled that it was fair to tell an offeror a precise way to improve its proposal, citing the removal of the prohibition of technical leveling in FAR 15.306(e) as well as the encouragement to "enhance materially the proposal's potential for award," in FAR 15.306(d)(3). See also *Mantech Telecommunications & Info. Sys. Corp. v. United States*, 49 Fed. Cl. 57 (2001), where the court held that it was fair to conduct multiple rounds of discussions, noting that the FAR Part 15 rewrite had eliminated the limitations on multiple rounds as well as the prohibition of technical leveling.

B. Misleading Communications

In addition to treating offerors equally, an agency may not mislead an offeror during negotiations, *Hughes STX Corp.*, Comp. Gen. Dec. B-278466, 98-1 CPD ¶ 52. In that case the discussions suggested two separate cost concerns and appear to have induced Hughes not only to escalate its first-year direct labor rates, but also to then increase these rates across the board. The GAO found that the discussion questions materially overstated the agency's relatively limited concern about the Hughes rates and were thus misleading. See also *Spherix, Inc.*, Comp. Gen. Dec. B-294572.3, 2005 CPD ¶ 183 (agency misled protester by implying that RFP requirements were firm while accepting an alternate solution from a competitor); *Cygnus Corp.*, Comp. Gen. Dec. B-292649.3, 2004 CPD ¶ 162 (agency misled protester by stating that the discussions "resulted in agreement of all technical and cost issues raised during negotiations" when it had identified a number of undiscussed weaknesses); *Biospherics, Inc.*, Comp. Gen. Dec. B-278278, 98-1 CPD ¶ 161 (agency misled protester during discussions by failing to inform it that its cost/pricing was considered unrealistically low and, instead, twice encouraging protester to reduce its proposed price); *SRS Techs.*, Comp. Gen. Dec. B-254425.2, 94-2 CPD ¶ 125 (agency misled protester where the agency considered the protester's initial proposal to be deficient for proposing cost discounts without adequate supporting information and not only failed to advise the protester of this deficiency during discussions but instructed the protester not to discount costs); *Price Waterhouse*, Comp. Gen. Dec. B-254492.2, 94-1 CPD ¶ 168 (agency misled protester when it questioned level pricing of options in the initial discussions, inducing the offeror to propose lower levels of effort for option years, and subsequently did not inform the offeror that it had determined internally lower levels of effort in option years were not called for). Compare *American Medical Professionals, Inc.*, Comp. Gen. Dec. B-275784, 97-1 CPD ¶ 134, holding that it was not misleading to ask an offeror to verify that it could perform at the quoted prices. For another case where the GAO found that the agency did not conduct misleading discussions, see *Analytical & Research Tech., Inc.*, Comp. Gen. Dec. B-276064, 97-1 CPD ¶ 200. There the GAO found that the protester unreasonably interpreted the agency's explanation regarding staffing requirements as permitting an approach that was inconsistent with the solicitation requirements. Similarly, in *Ideal Electronic Security Co.*, Comp. Gen. Dec. B-298221, 98-2 CPD ¶ 14, the GAO held that the agency had not misled the protester into offering only a small price reduction by stating that its price was competitive and its escalation ratios appeared reasonable.

C. Prohibited Conduct

The FAR Part 15 rewrite made significant changes in specifying the conduct that is improper. FAR 15.306(e) provides the following limitations on communications:

Government personnel involved in the acquisition shall not engage in conduct that —

(1) Favors one offeror over another;

(2) Reveals an offeror's technical solution, including unique technology, innovative and unique uses of commercial items, or any information that would compromise an offeror's intellectual property to another offeror;

(3) Reveals an offeror's price without that offeror's permission. However, the contracting officer may inform an offeror that its price is considered by the Government to be too high, or to low, and reveal the results of the analysis supporting that conclusion. It is also permissible, at the Government's discretion, to indicate to all offerors the cost or price that the Government's price analysis, market research, and other reviews have identified as reasonable (41 U.S.C. 423(h)(1)(2));

(4) Reveals the names of individuals providing reference information about an offeror's past performance; or

(5) Knowingly furnishes source selection information in violation of 3.104 and 41 U.S.C. 423(h)(1)(2).

The first three prohibitions were substantially rewritten in the FAR Part 15 rewrite to reduce their scope. Thus, as discussed earlier, the "technical leveling" prohibition was eliminated and the "auction" prohibition was narrowed. The second prohibition of revealing another offeror's technical solution, previously described as "technical transfusion," was not significantly altered from the prior FAR. The fourth prohibition was added by the rewrite. The fifth prohibition refers to a portion of the Procurement Integrity Act.

1. Favoring One Offeror

The first prohibition covered "technical leveling" in the pre-rewrite FAR. Thus, prior to the rewrite, agencies were prohibited from coaching offerors to bring them up to the level of a competitor. However, there were no protests finding that such coaching had actually occurred. As discussed earlier, such coaching is now encouraged as long as it does not involve providing information from a competitor's proposal.

The GAO is now citing the first prohibition barring favoring one offeror in holding that agencies have engaged in unfair treatment, *Boeing Co.*, Comp. Gen. Dec. B-311344, 2008 CPD ¶ 114 (agency misled protester into believing that it had met performance objective); *Sytronics, Inc.*, Comp. Gen. Dec. B-297346, 2006 CPD ¶ 15 (winning offeror was told its price was "excessive" while protester with similar price was told that its price was "high"); *Martin Elecs., Inc.*, Comp. Gen. Dec. B-290846.3, 2003 CPD ¶ 6 (winning offeror was "favored" because its poor past performance was probed while the protester's was not); and *Chemonics Int'l, Inc.*, Comp. Gen. Dec. B-282555, 99-2 CPD ¶ 61 (personnel which the agency believed were unsuitable were probed in one offer but not the other). See also *Knightsbridge Constr.*, Comp. Gen. Dec. 291475.2, 2003 CPD ¶ 5, finding unfair treatment in providing information to only one offeror but dismissing the protest for lack of prejudice.

2. Technical Transfusion

Helping an offeror to improve its proposal through the use of information gained from another offer was described in the pre-FAR rewrite as "technical transfusion." It is now described in the second prohibition as revealing information that is "unique" or "intellectual property." In addition to being illegal, there is a procurement policy reason for refraining from such conduct. In 51 Comp. Gen. 621 (B-173677) (1972), the GAO enunciated this reason for avoidance of this practice, stating that if the government disclosed technical innovations to other offerors, offerors would tend to hold back technical innovation from the negotiation process. Thus, the government would lose the benefits accruing from contractor innovation during negotiation. See also 52 Comp. Gen. 870 (B-177542) (1973), stating at 872:

> However, in 51 Comp. Gen. 621 (1972), we recognized that the statute should not be interpreted in a manner which discriminates against or gives preferential treatment to a competitor and that the disclosure to other offerors of one offeror's innovative solution to a problem is unfair. Thus, where there is a research and development procurement and the offeror's independent approach to solving a problem is the essence of the procurement, technical negotiations must be curtailed to the extent necessary to avoid technical "transfusion."

It has been very difficult for a protester to establish that technical transfusion has taken place because the GAO requires proof "that the contracting agency either directly or indirectly disclosed one offeror's technical approach to another offeror," *Northwest Regional Educ. Lab.*, Comp. Gen. Dec. B-222591.3, 87-1 CPD ¶ 74. Thus, even if the protester can prove similarities to its technical approach in a competitor's final proposal, the lack of actual evidence of disclosure will lead to a denial of the protest, *Le Don Computer Servs., Inc.*, Comp. Gen. Dec. B-225451.2, 87-1 CPD ¶ 441. Similarly, speculative protests of possible technical transfusion are summarily denied, *Sparta, Inc.*, Comp. Gen. Dec. B-228216, 88-1 CPD ¶ 37. A lack of technical transfusion has been found in *Ashe Facility Servs., Inc.*, Comp. Gen. Dec. B-292218.3, 2004 CPD ¶ 80 (asking about equipment to be used for ground maintenance work); *WorldTravelServ.*, Comp. Gen. Dec. B-284155.3, 2001 CPD ¶ 68 (asking about use of interpreters where RFP required special treatment for patients speaking different languages); *Voith Hydro, Inc.*, Comp. Gen. Dec. B-277051, 97-2 CPD ¶ 68 (advising offeror to use proven manufacturing facility); *Creative Mgmt. Tech., Inc.*, Comp. Gen. Dec. B-266299, 96-1 CPD ¶ 61 (asking offeror to provide specific documents showing capability when such documents were not called for by RFP but had been provided by competitor). In *Gentex Corp. — Western Operations,*

Comp. Gen. Dec. B-291793, 2003 CPD ¶ 66, the protester contended that since its initial proposal contained variation in quantity and warranty clauses and its competitor's did not, transfusion occurred when the clauses appeared in the competitor's revised proposal. The protester argued that the transfusion resulted when the agency asked the competitor whether it would "consider putting a variation clause in the contract" and what were its "[t]houghts on warranty." The GAO ruled that "technical transfusion" had not occurred since there was not a "disclosure of a unique or ingenious technical solution from a competitor's proposal." It also ruled that the questions were not improper because they were "neutral."

If one offeror proposes a technical approach not permitted by the RFP but that the agency would like to consider, it is not improper to disclose to other offerors that the agency is willing to consider alternative approaches (as long as the specific technical approach proposed is not disclosed), *Rix Indus., Inc.*, Comp. Gen. Dec. B-241498, 91-1 CPD ¶ 165; *Loral Terracom*, 66 Comp. Gen. 272 (B-224908), 87-1 CPD ¶ 182. In addition, if the procuring agency is aware of a technical concept prior to the submission of a proposal incorporating that concept, conveying the concept to another offeror is not technical transfusion, *Dynalectron Corp.*, Comp. Gen. Dec. B-216201, 85-1 CPD ¶ 525. See also *Litton Sys., Inc.*, Comp. Gen. Dec. B-239123, 90-2 CPD ¶ 114, finding no technical transfusion when the procuring agency discussed with all offerors the need for testing that was first identified by the protester. The GAO accepted the procuring agency's explanation that all the offerors had identified the need to verify that the various proposed techniques met the contract requirement and that the discussions of specific testing flowed from this mutual identification of a gap in the RFP. It is also not improper to permit an offeror for a follow-on service contract to visit the government site where the incumbent contractor is performing the work, *Contact Int'l Corp.*, 70 Comp. Gen. 115 (B-237122.3), 90-2 CPD ¶ 442.

3. Revealing Prices

Prior to the FAR rewrite, the third prohibition banned "auctions." However, it was narrowed considerably in the FAR rewrite so that it now prohibits only the disclosure of prices without consent. See *Strand Hunt Constr., Inc.*, Comp. Gen. Dec. B-292415, 2003 CPD ¶ 167, noting that the auction prohibition was removed from the FAR. In addition, this provision permits disclosure of government estimates of reasonable costs or prices. This rewritten language has been interpreted to allow agencies to reveal a considerable amount of pricing information to offerors. There is general agreement that it allows an agency to tell an offeror that its price is considered to be "high," *Dynacs Eng'g Co. v. United States*, 48 Fed. Cl. 124 (2000). Other decisions permitting disclosure of information include *Chenega Fed. Sys., LLC*, Comp. Gen. Dec. B-299310.2, 2007 CPD ¶ 196 (revealing detailed government analysis of offeror's probable costs); *Kaneohe Gen. Servs., Inc.*, Comp. Gen. Dec. B-293097.2, 2004 CPD ¶ 50 (disclosing government estimate to all offerors in second round of discussions permissible); *Engineering Servs. Unlimited, Inc.,* Comp. Gen. Dec. B-291275, 2003 CPD ¶ 15 (questioning the low level of labor rates in proposal not within the scope of this prohibition); *Korrect Optical, Inc.,* Comp. Gen. Dec. B-288128, 2001 CPD ¶ 171 (revealing average prices of five offerors in competitive range fits within permission to reveal a government estimate); and *OMV Medical, Inc. v. United States,* 219 F.3d 1337 (Fed. Cir. 2000) (stating that proposed salaries were below "current average annual salaries" did not reveal incumbent's salaries).

It might be argued that this provision precludes the use of reverse auction procedures where prices are electronically posted without disclosing the company submitting the price. There is no decision on whether FAR 15.306(e)(3) bears on this issue, but the GAO ruled in *MTB Group, Inc.,* Comp. Gen. Dec. B-295463, 2005 Comp. Gen. ¶ 40, that reverse auctions do not violate the procurement statutes when used in simplified acquisitions, stating:

> Regarding MTB's specific objection — that the reverse auction here is impermissible because it will result in disclosure of its price — we find no basis for objecting to the agency's approach. MTB is correct that the Act prohibits government officials and those acting on behalf of the government from knowingly disclosing contractor quotation or proposal information before award. 41 U.S.C. § 423(a). However, that prohibition is not absolute. Rather, the Act specifically provides that it does not "restrict the disclosure of information to, or its receipt by, any person or class of persons authorized in accordance with applicable agency regulations or procedures, to receive the information," 41 U.S.C. § 423(h)(1), and does not "restrict a contractor from disclosing its own quote or proposal information or the recipient from receiving that information." 41 U.S.C. § 423(h)(2). We think the price disclosure under HUD's reverse auction procedures falls within the exception language, although we are aware of no judicial or other authoritative interpretation of these provisions. First, under the procedure the agency has established, vendors actually will disclose their own prices — albeit, as a condition of competing — by entering the prices on the auction website; as noted, a vendor's disclosing its own price is not prohibited under the Act. n3 Moreover, even if the price disclosure were considered to be by government officials due to its nature as a precondition to a vendor's competing, the disclosure is pursuant, and integral, to the reverse auction procurement procedures established by the agency; we thus would view the disclosure as being to persons authorized by agency procedures to receive the information, consistent with the exception language. See generally *DGS Contract Serv., Inc. v. United States,* 43 Ct. Cl. 227, 236 (1999); *Ocean Servs., LLC.,* B-292511.2, Nov. 6, 2003, 2003 CPD ¶ 206 at 5 (neither the Act nor the FAR establishes an absolute prohibition against disclosure of price information, and both make clear that prices can be disclosed under certain circumstances).

4. Procurement Integrity

The statutory reference to conduct prohibited by this provision is the Procurement Integrity Act, 41 U.S.C. § 423, which includes a prohibition on the disclosure of "contractor bid or proposal information" which is not included in this FAR provision. See Chapter 1 for a discussion of the Procurement Integrity Act. In addition, a criminal statute, 18 U.S.C. § 1905, broadly prohibits the disclosure of proprietary information. Violation of these statutory provisions could result in criminal liability. See *Panafax Corp.*, Comp. Gen. Dec. B-201176, 81-1 CPD ¶ 515, *recons. denied*, 81-2 CPD ¶ 220, where a disclosure to another offeror of Panafax's identity as an offeror and the fact that Panafax was offering a newly developed machine enabled the offeror to lower its price 27%, $1 below Panafax's price. A referral was made to the Department of Justice, and the GAO sustained the protest, stating that the disclosure of information enabled the other offeror to determine what equipment its competitor was offering and at approximately what price.

D. Procedure Following Improper Disclosure

When there has been an improper disclosure of pricing or technical information, the contracting officer must decide on a course of action to minimize the harm. The general rule stated by the GAO is that the requirement for full and open competition overrides the prohibitions against improper disclosure — with the result that the proper course of action may be to reopen the competition permitting all offerors to compete. See *Pan Am Support Servs., Inc.*, 66 Comp. Gen. 457 (B-225964.2), 87-1 CPD ¶ 512, stating at 460:

> [C]oncerns as to technical leveling or technical transfusion do not necessarily overcome the need to remedy a procurement which has failed to satisfy the statutory requirement for full and open competition. See *Roy F. Weston, Inc. — Request for Reconsideration*, B-221863.3, Sept. 29, 1986, 86-2 CPD ¶ 324. Similarly, the risk of an auction is generally viewed as secondary to the preservation of the integrity of the competitive procurement system through the taking of appropriate corrective action. *Environmental Tectonics Corp. — Reconsideration*, B-225474.2 et al., Apr. 9, 1987, 87-1 CPD ¶ [96].

This rule has been followed in *Logicon, Inc. v. United States*, 22 Cl. Ct. 776 (1991), and *IMS Servs., Inc. v. United States*, 33 Fed. Cl. 167 (1995). In both cases the court emphasized the difficult burden — not met by either plaintiff — of showing that an offeror's individual prejudice resulting from the disclosure of pricing information before the protest outweighed the harm to the procurement process that would occur if the agency were denied the ability to take corrective action by reopening the solicitation. However, there is generally no requirement to disclose the prices submitted by all offerors when the competition is reopened. See *SYMVION-ICS, Inc.*, Comp. Gen. Dec. B-293824.2, 2004 CPD ¶ 204, and *Alatech Healthcare, LLC*, Comp. Gen. Dec. B-289134.3, 2002 CPD ¶ 73, where the protester argued that it should be provided with a competitor's unit prices since its unit prices had been disclosed in a debriefing. The GAO noted that while such a technique might be acceptable where prices have been *improperly* disclosed, it was not required in this case since disclosure of prices in a debriefing is *not* improper. See also *BNF Techs., Inc.*, Comp. Gen. Dec. B-254953.4, 94-2 CPD ¶ 258 (stating that "the possibility that a contract may not be awarded based upon true competition is more harmful to the integrity of the competitive procurement system than the risk of an auction"); *Unisys Corp.*, 67 Comp. Gen. 512 (B-230019.2), 88-2 CPD ¶ 35 (holding that "where the reopening of negotiations is properly required, the prior disclosure of an offeror's proposal does not preclude reopening"); *Faxon Co.*, 67 Comp. Gen. 39 (B-227835.3), 87-2 CPD ¶ 425 (reopening negotiations after an improper award was neither technical leveling nor an improper auction, although original awardee's proposal had been disclosed). An exception to this rule occurs when the offeror obtains information by illegal means. See *Litton Sys., Inc.*, 68 Comp. Gen. 422 (B-234060), 89-1 CPD ¶ 450, *recons. denied*, 68 Comp. Gen. 677, 89-2 CPD ¶ 228, ordering the termination of a contract because of evidence that the contractor had obtained proprietary information concerning the procurement through bribery of a government official.

In following the general rule, the GAO has approved actions in which the agency did not attempt to remedy the effects of the improper disclosure. For example, in *Computer Sciences Corp.*, Comp. Gen. Dec. B-231165, 88-2 CPD ¶ 188, negotiations were continued with an offeror that had inadvertently been given access to another offeror's costing data. The GAO stated that the agency would be justified in removing the offeror from the procurement if its BAFO indicated that it had made use of the data. See also *Lockheed Martin Maritime Sys. & Sensors*, Comp. Gen. Dec. B-299766, 2008 CPD ¶ 116, where the GAO approved of the agency's reopening of the competition including the offeror that had received a competitor's technical information.

In contrast to the rule on pricing information, an agency is required to disclose to all competitors detailed information on solicitation requirements that has been disclosed to one offeror in the debriefing process, *SYMVIONICS, Inc.*, Comp. Gen. Dec. B-293824.2, 2004 CPD ¶ 204.

When prices have been revealed to one offeror, several methods have been used to avert an unfair competitive advantage. A commonly used method is for the agency to make an award on the basis of initial proposals and permit no modifications, Comp. Gen. Dec. B-171015, July 13, 1971, *Unpub.* For instance, in *M. Bennett, Ltd.*, Comp. Gen. Dec. B-198316, 80-1 CPD ¶ 363, the GAO recommended that an award on initial proposals be made where the offerors' prices were improperly revealed at a public opening of proposals. See also *American Elec. Labs., Inc.*, 65 Comp. Gen. 62 (B-219582), 85-2 CPD ¶ 545, concurring with award on BAFOs where pricing information had been revealed in a protest because reopening negotiations would constitute auctioning, which would impugn the integrity of the competitive system.

Another method of averting unfairness is to solicit revisions to the non-price aspects of the competing proposals but to deny the opportunity to revise prices. This is appropriate when the new negotiations are necessary to correct some aspect of the procurement that is not likely to have an impact on the competing prices. See *Krueger Int'l, Inc.*, Comp. Gen. Dec. B-260953.4, 96-1 CPD ¶ 235, stating:

[W]here the reopening of discussions is due, not to the addition of a new solicitation requirement or a change in an existing requirement, but to the need to correct an informational deficiency in a technical proposal, the correction of which is unlikely to have a cost impact, an agency may limit proposal revisions to revisions in technical proposals. *See Pacific Architects and Engineers, Inc. — Recon.*, B-232500.4, Mar. 3, 1989, 89-1 CPD ¶ 231; *see generally Eldyne, Inc.*, B-250158 et al., Jan. 14, 1993, 93-1 CPD ¶ 430, *recon. denied, Dept. of the Navy — Recon.*, B-250158.4, May 28, 1993, 93-1 CPD ¶ 422; *System Planning Corp.*, B-244697.4, June 15, 1992, 92-1 CPD ¶ 516; *URS Int'l, Inc., and Fischer Eng'g & Maintenance Co., Inc.; Global-Knight, Inc.*, B-232500; B-232500.2, Jan. 10, 1989, 89-1 CPD ¶ 21. We find that the reopening of discussions here is necessary only to correct informational deficiencies in the technical proposals, the correction of which is unlikely to have a significant cost impact, and that therefore [the agency] was not required to permit revisions to offerors' prices.

See also *ST Aerospace Engines Pte., Ltd.*, Comp. Gen. Dec. B-275725.3, 97-2 CPD ¶ 106, holding that negotiations were properly reopened to clear up only past performance evaluation issues and BAFOs were properly limited to past performance information. The same result was reached in *Honeywell Tech. Solutions, Inc.*, Comp. Gen. Dec. B-400771.6, 2009 CPD ¶ 240, where the GAO rejected the protester's argument that the entire competition should be reopened because all of the information was out of date.

Another technique is to cancel the RFP after an improper disclosure has been made, *Neomed, Inc.*, Comp. Gen. Dec. B-186930, 76-2 CPD ¶ 434; *Ford Aerospace & Communications Corp.*, Comp. Gen. Dec. B-224421.2, 86-2 CPD ¶ 582. Compare *Apex Int'l Mgmt. Servs., Inc.*, 60 Comp. Gen. 172 (B-200008), 81-1 CPD ¶ 24, finding it improper for the agency to have canceled a solicitation due to an improper award, but because low prices had been disclosed, recommending reinstatement of the solicitation and award based on a new responsibility determination. In *Franklin Inst.*, 55 Comp. Gen. 280 (B-182560), 75-2 CPD ¶ 194, an employee of one competitor was allowed to sit in on discussions conducted with another offeror. The GAO recommended that the agency either revise its RFP to eliminate possible advantages or, if a revision would be detrimental to the agency's needs, exclude the recipient of the information from the competition.

The GAO has also approved the disclosure of all prices to eliminate an improper advantage one offeror may have as a result of its knowledge of the winning price. For instance, in *T M Sys., Inc.*, 55 Comp. Gen. 1066 (B-185715), 76-1 CPD ¶ 299, one offeror submitted a revised price, claiming a mistake on its initial proposal, after it was erroneously informed of the only other offeror's initial price. It was held that it was proper for the contracting officer to disclose both offerors' proposed prices and call for BAFOs. See also *Federal Data Corp.*, GSBCA 9732-P, 89-1 BCA ¶ 21,414, *aff'd*, 911 F.2d 699 (Fed. Cir. 1990), finding that the government's disclosure of all competitors' prices after one offeror's price was prematurely disclosed was a good-faith effort to place all competitors on an equal footing during the second round of

BAFOs, and any auction concerns were overridden by the need for such corrective action. Compare *University Sys., Inc. v. Defense Nuclear Agency*, GSBCA 11813-P, 92-3 BCA ¶ 25,173, where the board sustained the agency's decision not to reveal all prices after the winning offeror's price had been disclosed in the notice of award. The board reasoned that there was no need to reveal all prices to equalize the competition because the revealed price had been the high price and, thus, the other offerors' knowledge of the price did not pose a significant competitive harm. See also *International Bus. Machs. Corp.*, GSBCA 11324-P, 92-1 BCA ¶ 24,439, holding that this technique of disclosing all information is not allowed to be used if the improper disclosure was not the result of a procurement error but occurred during a debriefing. It is highly questionable whether this type of mass disclosure of pricing information is proper in view of the Procurement Integrity Act, 41 U.S.C. § 423(a), as amended in 1996.

E. Prejudice

Even if there is an impropriety in the conduct of negotiations, a protest will not be sustained unless the protester shows that it has been prejudiced, *Statistica, Inc. v. Christopher*, 102 F.3d 1577 (Fed. Cir. 1996). See *Kling Corp.*, Comp. Gen. Dec. B-309930.2, 2008 CPD ¶ 102 (no demonstration that protester would have reduced prices or cured past performance issues sufficient to win award); *OfficeMax, Inc.*, Comp. Gen. Dec. B-299340.2, 2007 CPD ¶ 158 (protester did not provide the required service and no indication that it would); *Puglia Eng'g of Cal., Inc.*, Comp. Gen. Dec. B-297413, 2006 CPD ¶ 33 (discussions would have led to increase in proposed price – making offer less desirable); *Abt Assocs., Inc.*, Comp. Gen. Dec. B-295449, 2005 CPD ¶ 54 (improving evaluation in areas not discussed would not have enhanced technical score sufficiently to win competition); *Orca Northwest Real Estate Servs. v. United States*, 65 Fed. Cl. 1 (2005) (price differential between winning offeror and protester was so great that higher technical score through reopened discussions would not have changed outcome); *Consolidated Eng'g Servs., Inc. v. United States*, 64 Fed. Cl. 617 (2005) ("highly improbable" that lack of meaningful discussion in one small area would have changed source selection decision); *DuRette Constr. Co.*, Comp. Gen. Dec. B-294379, 2004 CPD ¶ ___ (disclosure of unique saving suggestion did not impact competition because neither offeror used suggestion in final proposal revision); *Cerner Corp.*, Comp. Gen. Dec. B-293093, 2004 CPD ¶ 34 (waiver of page limitation for winning offeror had little impact when decision was made on the basis of product demonstration); *Knightsbridge Constr. Corp.*, Comp. Gen. Dec. B-291475.2, 2003 CPD ¶ 5 (fairly informing offeror of lack of information would not have elicited experience that met RFP requirement); *Sytel, Inc.*, Comp. Gen. Dec. B-277849.2, 98-1 CPD ¶ 21 (no indication that offeror would have reduced its labor rates to a sufficient level to win competition); *Ricards Int'l, Inc.*, Comp. Gen. Dec. B-277808, 98-1 CPD ¶ 2 (speculative that protester might have lowered its fee had agency informed it that it must use the higher indirect cost rates contained in the firm's current rate agreement); *ABB Power Generation,*

Inc., Comp. Gen. Dec. B-272681, 96-2 CPD ¶ 183 (even if protester's proposal had received the maximum score in an evaluation area associated with an allegedly inadequately discussed issue, it still would not have been in line for award); *Continental Serv., Co.*, Comp. Gen. Dec. B-271754, 96-2 CPD ¶ 65 (submission of explanation of adverse past performance information would not have raised scores sufficiently to place protester in line for award); *McDonald-Bradley*, Comp. Gen. Dec. B-270126, 96-1 CPD ¶ 54 (no indication that protester would have lowered wage rates further in its BAFO had the discussions not been what they were); *Northrop Worldwide Aircraft Servs., Inc.*, Comp. Gen. Dec. B-262181, 95-2 CPD ¶ 196 (impropriety in discussions could have only improved the technical rating of the protester's proposal to the level of awardee's but would not have affected its inferior current and past performance ratings, which were pivotal in award decision); and *TRW, Inc.*, Comp. Gen. Dec. B-243450.2, 91-2 CPD ¶ 160 (protester's high price would have precluded award even if it had received maximum score on corrected deficiencies that were not disclosed).

V. PROPOSAL REVISIONS

Under the pre-rewrite FAR, changes to proposals following negotiations were termed "best and final offers" (BAFOs). The rewrite changed this terminology to deal with both "proposal revisions" and "final proposal revisions." FAR 15.001 defines "proposal revision" as a revision that occurs "as a result of negotiations:"

> "Proposal revision" is a change to a proposal made after the solicitation closing date, at the request of or as allowed by a contracting officer, as the result of negotiations.

Thus, such revisions of proposals will occur only during or after negotiations with offerors within the competitive range. FAR 15.307(b) contains the following coverage of such proposal revisions and also addresses "final proposal revisions:"

> The contracting officer may request or allow proposal revisions to clarify and document understandings reached during negotiations. At the conclusion of discussions, each offeror still in the competitive range shall be given an opportunity to submit a final proposal revision. The contracting officer is required to establish a common cut-off date only for receipt of final proposal revisions. Requests for final proposal revisions shall advise offerors that the final proposal revisions shall be in writing and that the Government intends to make award without obtaining further revisions.

Thus, this guidance deals with two types of proposal revisions: those agreed to during the negotiation process and final proposal revisions.

The first type of proposal revision is made to "clarify and document understandings reached during negotiations." This language appears to deal with alterations to the original *offer* made by the offeror since it is unlikely that the contracting officer would reach an "understanding" regarding information submitted by the offeror to demonstrate its capability or to support its offer. Thus, this new FAR appears to permit contracting agencies to request an offeror to put revisions to its offer in writing in order to ensure that the parties have reached a clear understanding on the terms of the potential contract they have negotiated. This practice has been followed by some contracting agencies in the past — especially on relatively complex procurements. See NFS 1815.306(d)(3)(C), calling for reaching agreement on a "model contract" with each offeror during negotiations. Under the FAR rewrite, contracting agencies may adopt this procedure if they believe that it will enhance the competitive negotiation process.

The second type of proposal revision is the "final proposal revision." Obtaining such revisions is mandatory, and all offerors in the competitive range must be permitted to submit their proposal revisions on a common cutoff date. In the initial draft of the FAR rewrite, obtaining such revisions was permissive and no common cutoff date was required. However, there were major objections to this change to the process, with the result that the FAR Councils withdrew the proposal and adopted a final rule essentially the same as the prior BAFO rule. Because the protest decisions in this area had focused on this mandatory BAFO process, they are equally applicable to the new rule.

Final proposal revisions, like BAFOs, can include alterations to the original offer as well as revisions to any part of the original proposal. Thus, offerors can submit additional information to enhance their capability assessment or to support their offers. For example, it has been common practice to propose different personnel or to revise a technical proposal that is being used to assess the offeror's understanding of the work. BAFOs have also included additional information supporting offered prices or technical performance. The amount of information submitted will depend on the number of weaknesses and deficiencies identified in the negotiations, but it should be clear that the offeror has the full opportunity to address all such weaknesses and deficiencies in its proposal revision.

A. Requesting Final Proposal Revisions

If the negotiations with the offerors in the competitive range have not been carried to the point of agreement between the parties, the request for final proposal revisions will be essentially the same as a request for BAFOs. Assuming that the negotiations have been thorough and meaningful, all that is required is that the offeror be clearly informed of the common cutoff date for submission of the final proposal. There is no need for a statement that negotiations are concluded or for a statement that award may be made without further discussions, *Spectrum Sciences & Software, Inc.*, Comp. Gen. Dec. B-282373, 99-1 CPD ¶ 114. It is good practice to warn offerors that significant changes in their proposals that have not been discussed may lead to a rescoring of the proposal to their detriment and will not generally require additional negotiations. See *Jacobs Serv. Co.*, Comp. Gen. Dec. B-262088.3, 97-1 CPD ¶ 220, finding that the agency had not misled an offeror when it warned that changes to the staffing allocations could result in a finding that the proposal was unacceptable.

Oral requests for final proposal revisions may be necessary in some procurements and are not prohibited by the FAR. However, they should be followed up in writing to ensure that there is no misunderstanding. See *Woodward Assocs., Inc.*, Comp. Gen. Dec. B-216714, 85-1 CPD ¶ 274, where under prior regulations, the protester misinterpreted an ambiguous oral request for a second round of BAFOs as a request for reconfirmation of its price. The GAO ruled that another round of discussions should be held to correct the confusion that had occurred as a result of the unclear nature of the oral request and the lack of a written confirmation. When an oral request for BAFOs was followed up by a written confirmation, no relief was granted if an offeror misconstrued the request, *KMS Fusion, Inc.*, Comp. Gen. Dec. B-242529, 91-1 CPD ¶ 447; *Israel Aircraft Indus., Ltd.*, Comp. Gen. Dec. B-239211, 90-2 CPD ¶ 84. It has also been held that if an amendment does not specifically request offerors to submit BAFOs, "language giving notice to all offerors of a common cutoff date for receipt of offers has the intent and effect of a request for BAFOs," *Cleveland Telecommunications Corp. v. National Aeronautics & Space Admin.*, GSBCA 12586-P, 94-2 BCA ¶ 26,620.

If the negotiations have been carried to the point of agreement with each offeror in the competitive range, the agency may expect the final proposal revisions to reflect that agreement. However, under FAR 15.307(b), offerors can submit a final offer that varies from such agreement in any way that they desire. Final offers that vary substantially from the prior agreement can lead to difficulties in the procurement process because they require the agency to expend resources in evaluating the new offer and create the risk of misunderstandings between the parties. In some cases they have led to the need for additional negotiations and a new set of final proposals. Thus, some agencies have attempted to reduce the number of unforeseen changes to the offers by including specific guidance in the request for final revisions, including the agreement that has been reached. See, for example, NFS 1815.307, stating:

> (b)(i) The request for final proposal revisions (FPRs) shall also:
>
> > (A) Instruct offerors to incorporate all changes to their offers resulting from discussions, and require clear traceability from initial proposals;
> >
> > (B) Require offerors to complete and execute the "model" contract, which includes any special provisions or performance capabilities the offeror proposed above those specified in the RFP;
> >
> > (C) Caution offerors against unsubstantiated changes to their proposals; and

(D) Establish a page limit for FPRs.

For a case agreeing that it is proper to require offerors to substantiate changes to their proposals that alter prices, as required by subparagraph (C) above, see *Cessna Aircraft Co.*, Comp. Gen. Dec. B-261953.5, 96-1 CPD ¶ 132. See also *Sutron Corp.*, Comp. Gen. Dec. B-270456, 96-1 CPD ¶ 143, agreeing with an agency's evaluation that an unexplained BAFO price reduction posed a high performance risk that rendered the protester's proposal unacceptable.

In any case, the aim should be to receive a proposal from each competitor that the agency fully understands and can accept if it is determined to be most advantageous to the government. This is achievable under the FAR rewrite because full communication is permitted in the negotiation process.

Generally, the request for proposal revisions is open-ended in permitting alterations to the original proposals. However, in limited circumstances it is permissible to limit the scope of such revisions. Thus, the GAO will review the record to see if the agency has a "reasonable basis for restricting the scope of revisions," *Computer Assocs. Int'l, Inc.*, Comp. Gen. Dec. B-292077.2, 2003 CPD ¶ 157. See *Honeywell Tech. Solutions, Inc.*, Comp. Gen. Dec. B-400771.6, 2009 CPD ¶ 240 (limiting revisions to past performance information needed to overcome prior protest); *Rel-Tek Sys. & Design, Inc.*, Comp. Gen. Dec. B-280463.7, 99-2 CPD ¶ 1 (limiting revisions to areas that had been identified in prior protest as being ambiguous); *Krueger Int'l, Inc.*, Comp. Gen. Dec. B-260953.4, 96-1 CPD ¶ 235 (limiting revisions to the submission of samples and additional technical information but prohibited new prices); and *Metron Corp.*, Comp. Gen. Dec. B-227014, 87-1 CPD ¶ 642 (limiting revisions to only costs and prices). When a request for final proposals contains restrictions on the permissible alterations, the agency must abide by those restrictions and not consider additional alterations submitted by offerors, *DynaLantic Corp.*, 68 Comp. Gen. 413 (B-234035), 89-1 CPD ¶ 421 (technical alterations should not have been considered when agency had called for "best and final price and delivery schedule" and had stated "negotiations have been concluded").

B. Reasonable Time

To foster fair competition, the established common cutoff date should allow sufficient time for all offerors in the competitive range to submit their final proposal revisions. When discussions are conducted sequentially, this means that the closing date should give adequate time to the last offeror with whom discussions have been conducted. However, the amount of time is highly dependent on the circumstances. See *Morris Guralnick Assocs., Inc.*, Comp. Gen. Dec. B-218353, 85-2 CPD ¶ 50 (one day for submission of BAFOs reasonable when both competitors were able to submit proposals within that time period); *Evergreen Landscaping, Inc.*, Comp. Gen. Dec. B-239241, 90-2 CPD ¶ 36 (six days reasonable for submission of BAFOs where both offerors were given the same amount of time and both offerors were located in the same city); *FRC Int'l, Inc.*, Comp. Gen. Dec. B-255345, 94-1 CPD ¶ 125 (two and one quarter hours reasonable for submission of BAFOs where there was decreasing availability and increasing price of the item needed and the offerors' proposals were scheduled to expire within two days – noting that because the offerors revised their proposals quickly during discussion it was reasonable for the agency to presume that the offerors could quickly submit BAFOs).

When negotiations have been carried to the point of agreement with each of the competitors, it would appear that less time is required for the preparation of final proposal revisions. In that case each offeror might need to do no more than verify that its negotiated agreement is still valid. However, additional time should be allowed if it is clear that offerors will submit proposal revisions dealing with informational deficiencies or weaknesses.

C. Common Cutoff Date

The FAR 15.307(b) requirement for a common cutoff date for the receipt of final revisions has been justified as necessary to preserve the integrity of the competition in order to minimize the possibility of information in one proposal "leaking" to another offeror with a later closing date. See *Federal Data Corp.*, Comp. Gen. Dec. B-236265.4, 90-1 CPD ¶ 504; and *Kleen-Rite Corp.*, Comp. Gen. Dec. B-209474, 83-1 CPD ¶ 512, stressing the need for such a common cutoff date as an essential part of the competitive negotiation process. The purpose of establishing a common cutoff date is to prevent offerors from being treated unfairly or being prejudiced. See *Comprehensive Health Servs., Inc. v. United States*, 70 Fed. Cl. 700 (2006), stating at 730-31:

> Had NASA considered new information supplied after the cut-off date, as a revision to the offeror's proposal, the agency would have violated FAR 15.307(b) and such conduct reasonably could have been viewed as according CHS with preferential treatment. *See Integrated Bus. Solutions v. United States*, 58 Fed. Cl. 420, 428 (Fed. Cl. 2003) ("Here, as GAO recognized, it would have been unfair to require the other offerors to submit FRPs by the March 13 deadline but permit IBS to confirm its initial proposal days later."); *Dubinsky v. United States*, 43 Fed. Cl. 243, 263-64 (Fed. Cl. 1999) ("[B]y providing a common cut-off date, it sets a level playing field on which [the offerors] may compete for the contract."); *see also In re G.D. Searle & Co.*, B-247077, B-247146, 92-1 CPD ¶ 406, at 2-3 (Comp. Gen. Apr. 30, 1992) ("[A]gencies are required to provide all offerors the same information in order to ensure that the acquisition is conducted on an equal basis for all competing firms. . . . In the absence of written notice to all offerors, it would have been unfair and improper to consider Searle's proposal, since the other offerors were not provided the same information and opportunity regarding the submission of their offers.").

However, prejudice does not necessarily occur because there is no common cutoff date. See *Gas Turbine Corp.*, Comp. Gen. Dec. B-251265, 93-1 CPD ¶ 400, stating:

We agree that the Coast Guard's failure to set a common cut-off date caused no prejudice here. There is no allegation that any aspect of GTC's proposal was disclosed to Turbo. Moreover, as noted above, there is no basis to conclude that, even if the agency had afforded GTC the few extra days provided to Turbo, the protester could have obtained the seven parts which it did not propose to provide in its BAFO. On the current record, it appears implausible that an additional few days would have enabled GTC to obtain the missing seven parts from the OEM (Turbo) or any other source. Accordingly, GTC was not prejudiced by the absence of a common cut-off date for the submission of BAFOs, and we therefore deny this ground of protest.

See also *Atlantic Terminal Co.*, Comp. Gen. Dec. B-160976, May 29, 1967, *Unpub.* (no prejudice, although the successful offeror was permitted to revise its price on February 6, and the unsuccessful offeror was last contacted regarding its price on January 31); *Canaveral Port Servs., Inc.*, Comp. Gen. Dec. B-211627.3, 84-2 CPD ¶ 358 (no prejudice where the agency used staggered closing dates but kept all offers sealed until a common opening date); and *Special Operations Group, Inc.*, Comp. Gen. Dec. B-287013, 2001 CPD ¶ 73 (lack of common date noted but not cited as basis for sustaining protest). Mistaken notification to one offeror of a common closing date one week in advance of the date supplied to other offerors was not prejudicial because the government offered to extend the offeror's time to enable resubmission of the BAFO, *Alan-Craig, Inc.*, Comp. Gen. Dec. B-202432, 81-2 CPD ¶ 263. In *B.F. Goodrich Co.*, Comp. Gen. Dec. B-230674, 88-1 CPD ¶ 471, the GAO criticized the agency for not establishing a common cutoff date but denied the protest. In *Amcare Medical Servs., Inc.*, Comp. Gen. Dec. B-271595, 96-2 CPD ¶ 10, the GAO ruled that a protest claiming the lack of a common cutoff date was untimely because it was apparent on the face of the RFP. The common cutoff date applies to written proposals, or written confirmation of oral proposals, unless oral BAFOs are authorized in the RFP, *Gregory A. Robertson*, Comp. Gen. Dec. B-213351, 84-1 CPD ¶ 592.

The contracting officer may extend the closing date for receipt of final proposal revisions if such extension will enhance competition, *Solar Resources, Inc.*, Comp. Gen. Dec. B-193264, 79-1 CPD ¶ 95. In *Institute for Advanced Safety Studies*, Comp. Gen. Dec. B-221330.2, 86-2 CPD ¶ 110, it was held proper to extend the closing date for BAFOs by three days because none of the offerors were prejudiced by this extension. In addition, an agency may extend the closing date for BAFOs upon request of an offeror. See also *Fort Biscuit Co.*, Comp. Gen. Dec. B-247319, 92-1 CPD ¶ 440, where extension of the closing date was proper to permit a competitor to submit a proposal that otherwise would not have been submitted, and *TRS Design & Consulting Servs.*, Comp. Gen. Dec. B-218668.2, 85-2 CPD ¶ 370, where the agency properly extended the closing date after it misinformed one of two offerors, causing it to miss the original closing date. The decision to extend the closing date to accept late BAFOs is within the contracting officer's discretion and will not be reviewed by the GAO, *Scientific Sys., Inc.*, Comp. Gen. Dec. B-225574, 87-1 CPD ¶ 19.

D. Late Proposal Revisions

The Instructions to Offerors — Competitive Acquisition solicitation provision at FAR 52.215-1 defines late proposals, modifications, or final revisions as those received after the designated time for receipt. Thus, late final proposal revisions are normally rejected unless they meet one of the exceptions to these rules.

Under the late proposal rules contained in ¶ (c)(3)(ii) of the standard solicitation provision in FAR 52.215-1, a late final proposal revision is subject to the same strict rules that are applied to late proposals. See Chapter 4 for a complete discussion of these rules.

The GAO has strictly construed the FAR definition of lateness. For example, the GAO held that a BAFO that was received six minutes late was properly rejected where none of the exceptions to the late proposal rule applied, *Potomac Sys. Resources, Inc.*, Comp. Gen. Dec. B-219896, 85-2 CPD ¶ 393. In *Einhorn Yaffee Prescott*, Comp. Gen. Dec. B-259552, 95-1 CPD ¶ 153, the GAO found no agency mishandling when a courier arrived at the agency at five minutes before the closing time but could not make contact with agency personnel until five minutes after the closing time. In *Fishermen's Boat Shop, Inc.*, Comp. Gen. Dec. B-223366, 86-2 CPD ¶ 389, the GAO held that a BAFO received in the agency's central mail depot 25 minutes before the closing time was properly rejected as late because receipt at the mail depot does not constitute receipt at the designated contracting facility, and an agency cannot reasonably be expected to convey the mail to the contracting facility in 25 minutes.

When a final proposal is submitted by facsimile transmission, the facsimile must be received in its entirety by the agency with a reasonable time remaining for it to carry the proposal from the facsimile room to the contracting office, *Phoenix Research Group, Inc.*, Comp. Gen. Dec. B-240840, 90-2 CPD ¶ 514. Thus, an offer that is received in the facsimile room several minutes before the deadline may still be rejected if the agency can not reasonably relay the proposal to the contracting office before the deadline. See also *Cyber Digital, Inc.*, Comp. Gen. Dec. B-270107, 96-1 CPD ¶ 20 (where entire BAFO was not received until after deadline, agency was not required to consider that portion of the BAFO received before the deadline because it did not constitute the entire proposal).

When a final proposal is submitted electronically, it must arrive at the designated office within the time specified, *Symetrics Indus., LLC*, Comp. Gen. Dec. B-298759, 2006 CPD ¶ 154. In that case, the final proposal arrived at the agency server on time but was delayed in arriving at the contracting office. The GAO held that the rule in FAR 15.215-1(c)(3)(ii)(A)(2), permitting acceptance if it arrived at the government installation on time, did not apply to electronically submitted final proposal revisions.

The GAO has applied the late proposal revision rule to a situation where the agency called for the submission of responses to "items for negotiation" by a specified date even though the request did not use the term "final proposal revision," *Seven Seas Eng'g & Land Surveying*, Comp. Gen. Dec. B-294424.2, 2004 CPD ¶ 236.

FAR 52.215-1(c)(6) allows offerors to submit modifications at any time before award if the modification is made in response to an amendment or for the purpose of correcting a mistake. The government may elect to consider a late BAFO that modifies an otherwise acceptable low offer, and other offerors may not complain because their relative standing is not affected, *Woodward Assocs., Inc.*, Comp. Gen. Dec. B-216714, 85-1 CPD ¶ 274.

Although a late final offer generally may not be considered for award, it has been held to be a revocation of the original offer precluding award on the basis of the original offer, *Touchstone Textiles, Inc.*, Comp. Gen. Dec. B-272230.4, 96-2 CPD ¶ 107 (higher-priced late BAFO manifested intent to modify and replace original offer); *Dep't of the Army — Recons.*, Comp. Gen. Dec. B-251527.3, 93-2 CPD ¶ 178 (late BAFO was "evidence that [offeror] no longer intended [its earlier prices] to be available for acceptance"). In *Integrated Business Solutions, Inc.*, Comp. Gen. Dec. B-292239, 2003 CPD ¶ 122, the submission of an unauthorized electronic revision and a late hard copy revision operated to revoke the initial offer.

VI. ACTIONS FOLLOWING RECEIPT OF FINAL REVISIONS

After receipt of final proposal revisions, the agency must reevaluate the proposals as quickly as possible. It is then in a position to proceed to source selection and award of a contract. However, under some circumstances it may be necessary to reopen negotiations. An agency can obtain clarification of final proposal revisions, *VMD Sys. Integrators, Inc.*, Comp. Gen. Dec. B-401037.4, 2009 CPD ¶ 252; *IPlus, Inc.*, Comp. Gen. Dec. B-298020, 2006 CPD ¶ 90; *Antarctic Support Assocs. v. United States*, 46 Fed. Cl. 145 (2000), or correct a mistake in a final proposal revision, *Joint Threat Servs.*, Comp. Gen. Dec. B-178168, 98-1 CPD ¶ 18, but, if it enters into negotiations/discussions with one offeror, it must reopen discussions with all offerors in the competitive range, *International Resources Group*, Comp. Gen. Dec. B-286663, 2001 CPD ¶ 35, unless there has been no prejudice to the protester, *USATREX Int'l, Inc.*, Comp. Gen. Dec. B-275592, 98-1 CPD ¶ 99.

A. Reevaluation

The first step after receipt of final proposal revisions is the reevaluation of each proposal to determine its current status in the competition. The failure to correctly assess the changes an offeror made in a proposal can lead to the granting of a protest, *Jaycor*, Comp. Gen. Dec. B-240029.2, 90-2 CPD ¶ 354. See, for example, *Ashbury Int'l Group, Inc.*, Comp. Gen. Dec. B-401123, 2009 CPD ¶ 140 (agency failed to test article submitted with final proposal revisions); *Contingency Mgmt. Group, LLC*, Comp. Gen. Dec. B-309752, 2008 CPD ¶ 83 (agency's acceptance of nonconforming assumption of requirements in offeror's final proposal revision gave it unfair advantage over others); *Johnson Controls Security Sys.*, Comp. Gen. Dec. B-296490, 2007 CPD ¶ 102 (agency based award on material misrepresentation in final proposal revisions); *ITT Fed. Servs. Int'l Corp.*, Comp. Gen. Dec. B-296783, 2007 CPD ¶ 43 (agency ignored requirement that offeror explain basis for reduced labor hours); *Advanced Sys. Dev., Inc.*, Comp. Gen. Dec. B-298411, 2006 CPD ¶ 137 (agency lack of understanding of awardee's revised prices led to irrational decision); *YORK Bldg. Servs., Inc.*, Comp. Gen. Dec. B-296948.2, 2005 CPD ¶ 202 (agency only evaluate final proposal revisions for acceptability); *Spherix, Inc.*, Comp. Gen. Dec. B-294572.3, 2005 CPD ¶ 183 (unfair evaluation of final proposal revisions); *Lockheed Martin Information Sys.*, Comp. Gen. Dec. B-292836, 2003 CPD ¶ 230 (significant evaluation errors); *Matrix Int'l Logistics, Inc.*, Comp. Gen. Dec. B-272388.2, 97-2 CPD ¶ 89 (agency could not explain its rationale for upgrading one offeror from good to excellent and finding technical equality with protester); *Intown Properties, Inc.*, Comp. Gen. Dec. B-262236.2, 96-1 CPD ¶ 89 (agency unreasonably evaluated BAFO where protester, in response to discussions about lack of qualifications of certain personnel, proposed different personnel in its BAFO but the agency did not consider this); and *Jack Faucett Assocs.*, Comp. Gen. Dec. B-233224, 89-1 CPD ¶ 115, *recons. denied*, 89-1 CPD ¶ 551 (agency could not explain its failure to upgrade a BAFO when the offeror included more manpower in response to an agency statement that too little manpower was a deficiency). Compare *General Sec. Servs. Corp.*, Comp. Gen. Dec. B-280388, 99-1 CPD ¶ 49, where the rescoring was unexplained but the final score was justified. This reevaluation must, of course, follow the original evaluation criteria in the RFP, *Hattal & Assocs.*, 70 Comp. Gen. 632 (B-243357), 91-2 CPD ¶ 90.

Agency evaluators have the same discretion in evaluating final proposal revisions that they have in evaluating original proposals. Thus, an agency may use information in a cost proposal to downgrade a technical proposal, *Cygna Project Mgmt.*, Comp. Gen. Dec. B-236839, 90-1 CPD ¶ 21. Similarly, a BAFO may be downgraded for failing to specifically elaborate on how the work will be performed, *Northwestern Travel Agency, Inc.*, Comp. Gen. Dec. B-244592, 91-2 CPD ¶ 363, or how its costs have been estimated, *Labat-Anderson, Inc.*, Comp. Gen. Dec. B-287091, 2001 CPD ¶ 79. In *Fintrac, Inc.*, Comp. Gen. Dec. B-311462.2, 2008 CPD ¶ 191, the GAO found that the agency had properly altered the weights of evaluation subfactors to correct an error in the original evaluation. Final proposal revision changes may also be disregarded if the agency concludes that they do not effect the initial evaluation, *Cobra Techs., Inc.*, Comp. Gen. Dec. B-280475, 98-2 CPD ¶ 98. In *SelectTech Bering Straits Solutions JV*, Comp. Gen. Dec. B-400964, 2009 CPD ¶ 100, the agency properly downgraded an offeror when it did not include initially proposed enhancements in the model contract submitted with its final proposal revisions; the agency correctly reasoning that the enhancement would not be contractually binding.

In assessing the impact of final proposal revisions, the agency can totally re-evaluate the proposals, *Information Sys. Tech. Corp.*, Comp. Gen. Dec. B-288490.2, July 3, 2002, *Unpub.*, or reevaluate only the changes from the original proposal, *Ecology & Env't, Inc.*, Comp. Gen. Dec. B-277061.2, 97-2 CPD ¶ 65. It has been found proper for agency evaluators to assess the changes that revisions have made to the original proposal and report them to the source selection official, *Northwest Regional Educ. Lab.*, Comp. Gen. Dec. B-222591.3, 87-1 CPD ¶ 74; *VSE Corp.*, Comp. Gen. Dec. B-224397, 86-2 CPD ¶ 392, or to take the changes into consideration when making the source selection decision, *Marinette Marine Corp.*, Comp. Gen. Dec. B-400697, 2009 CPD ¶ 16; *Palmetto GBA, LLC*, Comp. Gen. Dec. B-298962, 2007 CPD ¶ 25; *Ebon Research Sys.*, Comp. Gen. Dec. B-261403.2, 95-2 CPD ¶ 152; *Scientex Corp.*, Comp. Gen. Dec. B-238689, 90-1 CPD ¶ 597. See also *Aircraft Porous Media, Inc.*, Comp. Gen. Dec. B-241665.2, 91-1 CPD ¶ 356, *recons. denied*, 91-1 CPD ¶ 613, finding that it was proper for an agency not to bother rescoring because the changes in the BAFO could not have altered the original determination that two proposals were technically equal; *Cygnus Corp.*, Comp. Gen. Dec. B-275957, 97-1 CPD ¶ 202, finding that the agency had acted properly in deciding that no technical rescoring was necessary when the competitors had made only minor changes to proposals that had been evaluated as excellent in the original scoring; and *Health Mgmt. Resources, Inc.*, Comp. Gen. Dec. B-270185, 96-1 CPD ¶ 23, finding that rescoring was not required because the agency found that each offeror "had improved to the same degree." However, a lack of documentation showing that BAFOs have been evaluated will lead to a sustained protest, *Biospherics, Inc.*, Comp. Gen. Dec. B-278508.4, 98-2 CPD ¶ 96.

There is no requirement that the final proposals be evaluated by the same evaluators that scored the original proposals, *Data Flow Corp.*, 62 Comp. Gen. 506 (B-209499), 83-2 CPD ¶ 57. However, the reevaluation must be reasonable in applying the evaluation criteria, *Bauer Assocs., Inc.*, Comp. Gen. Dec. B-229831.6, 88-2 CPD ¶ 549. The GAO has stated that the fact that new evaluators reached different conclusions than the original evaluators does not automatically indicate an impropriety, *Chemonics Int'l*, Comp. Gen. Dec. B-222793, 86-2 CPD ¶ 161. See also *Magnavox Advanced Prods. & Sys. Co.*, Comp. Gen. Dec. B-215426, 85-1 CPD ¶ 146 (finding differences among individual evaluators as insufficient to discredit a technical evaluation).

B. Reopening Negotiations

Reopening negotiations is not a desirable course of action. It adds time and expense to the procurement and extends the time when information may be improperly disclosed. See *Mine Safety Appliances Co.*, Comp. Gen. Dec. B-242379.5, 92-2 CPD ¶ 76, holding that the conduct of another round of negotiations in the absence of a valid reason tends to undermine the integrity of the competitive negotiation process. Pre-rewrite FAR 15.611(c) stated that negotiations should not be reopened "unless it is clearly in the Government's best interests to do so." In addition, DFARS 215.611 prohibited contracting officers from reopening negotiations unless higher-level approval was obtained. However, the FAR Part 15 rewrite removed this coverage, leaving the matter to the contracting officer's discretion under the circumstances surrounding each procurement. In *Dynacs Eng'g Co.*, Comp. Gen. Dec. B-284234, 2000 CPD ¶ 50, the GAO noted this change in holding that the agencies use of multiple rounds of discussions was not improper. Similarly, DOD requirement for higher approval has been deleted from the DFARS. See, however, NFS 1815.307(b)(ii), requiring the approval of the Associate Administrator for Procurement to reopen discussions on procurements of $50 million or more and the approval of the procurement officer of the procuring activity to reopen discussions on smaller procurements.

Agencies are required to reopen discussions if the evaluation of the offeror's final proposal identifies significant weaknesses or deficiencies that were not identified in the original evaluation and hence not discussed in the original discussion, *Al Long Ford*, Comp. Gen. Dec. B-297807, 2006 CPD ¶ 68; *Consolidated Eng'g Servs., Inc. v. United States*, 64 Fed. Cl. 617 (2005); *DevTech Sys., Inc.*, Comp. Gen. Dec. B-284860.2, 2001 CPD ¶ 11. See *Carahsoft Tech. Corp. v. United States*, 86 Fed. Cl. 325 (2009), holding that it is proper to reopen discussions in such circumstances even if the deficiency makes the proposal unacceptable. Furthermore, if discussions are reopened with one offeror in the competitive range, they must be reopened with all other offerors still in the range, *Cigna Gov't Servs., LLC*, Comp. Gen. Dec. B-297915.2, 2006 CPD ¶ 74; *Lockheed Martin Aeronautics Co.*, Comp. Gen. Dec. B-295401, 2005 CPD ¶ 41.

It is proper to reopen discussions if substantial questions requiring discussions are raised by one of the proposal revisions, *Ocean Tech., Inc.*, Comp. Gen. Dec. B-183749, 75-2 CPD ¶ 262; a question of contract compliance is raised during reevaluation, *AmClyde Engineered Prods. Co.*, Comp. Gen. Dec. B-282271, 99-1 CPD ¶ 5; previously existing ambiguities are not discovered until after submission of BAFOs, 52 Comp. Gen. 409 (B-176913) (1973), *Swedlow, Inc.*, 53 Comp. Gen. 564 (B-178212), 74-1 CPD ¶ 55; there is a substantial cost disparity between offerors, *Telos Corp.*, Comp. Gen. Dec. B-279493.3, 98-2 CPD ¶ 30; additional technical information is needed to evaluate the proposals, *Introl Corp.*, Comp. Gen. Dec. B-194570, 80-1 CPD ¶ 41; government estimates are discovered to be in error, *Dyneteria, Inc.*, Comp. Gen. Dec. B-181707, 75-1 CPD ¶ 86; government requirements change, *ACS Sys. & Eng'g, Inc.*, Comp. Gen. Dec. B-275439.2, 97-1 CPD ¶ 126; *Simulators Ltd., Inc.*, Comp. Gen. Dec. B-208418, 82-2 CPD ¶ 473; incorrect information has been provided to one offeror during discussions, *Computer Related Servs., Inc.*, Comp. Gen. Dec. B-244638, 91-2 CPD ¶ 420; specifications are not clear, *ES, Inc.*, Comp. Gen. Dec. B-258911.2, 95-1 CPD ¶ 168; or the agency discovers that it has failed to identify a deficiency in the initial negotiations, *Dube Travel Agency & Tours, Inc.*, Comp. Gen. Dec. B-270438, 96-1 CPD ¶ 141. Also upheld was a decision to reopen discussions and request a second round of BAFOs after the recommended awardee's place of performance had become unavailable and the quality of materials required by the government had changed, *Hayes Int'l Corp. v. United States*, 7 Cl. Ct. 681 (1985). See also *M.W. Kellogg Co./Siciliana Appalti Costruzioni S.p.A. (J.V.) v. United States*, 10 Cl. Ct. 17 (1986), and *Meridian Mgmt. Corp.*, Comp. Gen. Dec. B-278099, 97-2 CPD ¶ 157, permitting multiple BAFOs.

If discussions are reopened, it is proper to raise issues that were brought to an offeror's attention in the initial discussions, *Dynacs Eng'g Co.*, Comp. Gen. Dec. B-284234, 2000 CPD ¶ 50. The GAO stated that this was an acceptable means of "maximizing the Government's ability to obtain best value" as called for by FAR 15.306(d)(2) in the FAR rewrite. The GAO also noted that there had been previous rulings to this effect, stating:

> We note that, even under the prior version of the FAR, a procuring agency properly could reopen discussions to discuss a previously raised item when the agency felt such action was necessary to resolve its concerns before making an award. See *Telos Corp.*, B-279493.3, July 27, 1998, 98-2 CPD ¶ 30 at 9-11; *Prospective Computer Analysts, Inc.*, B-275262.2, Feb. 24, 1997, 97-2 CPD ¶ 22 at 3-5.

While the agency has the discretion to call for another round of proposals, it also has the discretion to refuse to do so. See *Textron, Inc. v. United States*, 74 Fed. Cl. 277 (2006), where the agency was not required to reopen negotiations when it asked for additional test data during the original discussions and concluded that the new data indicated a deficiency in the proposed ship without giving the protester the opportunity to explain the data. Thus, the agency is not obligated to bring up deficiencies remaining from the initial proposal when the offeror has already been informed of the deficiency, *LIS, Inc.*, Comp. Gen. Dec. B-400646.4, 2010 CPD ¶ 40; *ITT Indus. Space Sys., LLC,* Comp. Gen. Dec. B-309964, 2007 CPD ¶ 217; *Ideamatics, Inc.*, Comp. Gen. Dec. B-297791.2, 2006 CPD ¶ 87; *Si-Nor, Inc.*, Comp. Gen. Dec. B-290150.4, 2003 CPD ¶ 45; *Metcalf Constr. Co.*, Comp. Gen. Dec. B-289100, 2002 CPD ¶ 31; *Phoenix Safety Assocs., Ltd.*, Comp. Gen. Dec. B-216504, 84-2 CPD ¶ 621.

It is also proper not to conduct further negotiations to clarify or amplify newly introduced aspects of its final proposal revision. See *RCA Serv. Co.*, Comp. Gen. Dec. B-197752, 80-1 CPD ¶ 407, concurring in the decision of the procuring agency not to reopen discussions with an offeror that had included a cost ceiling in its BAFO on a cost-plus-award-fee support services contract. The agency awarded the contract to another offeror because of grave doubts raised by the cost ceiling proposal without discussing it with the protester. The GAO stated:

> In reviewing whether the Army acted properly in not reopening discussions with offerors, we cannot ignore the length of time that this procurement was in process — more than 1 year from the issuance of the RFP to receipt of best and final offers. Clearly, the time for innovative suggestions and approaches was over when RCA presented its price ceiling proposal. In this regard, our decision in *Electronic*

Communications, Inc., 55 Comp. Gen. 636 [B-183677] (1976), 76-1 CPD ¶ 15, cited by the Army, presented a similar situation. There, an offeror's best and final offer appeared to be inconsistent with the RFP and its initial acceptable offer. We held that the contracting officer's determination not to reopen discussions with all offerors in the competitive range was proper as not being in the best interests of the Government. We also noted that when an offeror submits in its best and final offer unexplained or incomplete revisions to its otherwise acceptable proposal, it has the burden of affirmatively demonstrating the acceptability of its proposal. Here, RCA did not meet its burden.

The same result was arrived at in *Akal Security, Inc.*, Comp. Gen. Dec. B-401469, 2009 CPD ¶ 183 (agency concluded reduced staffing was a weakness); *Honeywell Tech. Solutions, Inc.*, Comp. Gen. Dec. B-400771, 2009 CPD ¶ 49 (agency concluded that protester demonstrated lack of understanding of requirement in responding to prior discussed weaknesses); *DRS C3 Sys., LLC*, Comp. Gen. Dec. B-310825, 2008 CPD ¶ 103 (agency found design submitted in response to discussions inferior); *L-3 Communications Corp.*, Comp. Gen. Dec. B-299227, 2007 CPD ¶ 83 (agency concluded protester's substitution of another product indicated a lack of technical competence); *MD Helicopters, Inc.*, Comp. Gen. Dec. B-298502, 2006 CPD ¶ 164 (agency concluded level pricing over long contract posed a risk); *Air Products Healthcare*, Comp. Gen. Dec. B-298293, 2006 CPD ¶ 123 (new information on sufficiency of services judged not to meet agency requirements); *Mechanical Equip. Co.*, Comp. Gen. Dec. B-292789.2, 2004 CPD ¶ 192 (lack of supporting data in final proposal revisions); *Cube-All Star Servs., Joint Venture*, Comp. Gen. Dec. B-291903, 2003 CPD ¶ 145 (proposal revision made proposal unacceptable); *NLX Corp.*, Comp. Gen. Dec. B-288785, 2001 CPD ¶ 198 (agency properly assessed a low price as imposing a risk when the price was significantly reduced in the proposal revision); *Litton Sys., Inc., Amecon Div.*, Comp. Gen. Dec. B-275807.2, 97-1 CPD ¶ 170 (agency properly adjusted the probable cost of an offeror's proposal without further discussions when it increased the labor hours estimated to be necessary to perform the work); *Serv-Air, Inc.*, Comp. Gen. Dec. B-258243, 96-1 CPD ¶ 267 (agency found deficiency or weakness that had been introduced in the BAFO); and *Saco Defense, Inc.*, Comp. Gen. Dec. B-252066, 93-1 CPD ¶ 395 (agency not required to conduct new tests on a redesigned item that was proposed as a solution to deficiencies identified in discussions). See also *Joint Threat Servs.*, Comp. Gen. Dec. B-278168, 98-1 CPD ¶ 18, where it was held proper not to reopen negotiations to point out a staffing deficiency in the BAFO that had not been made a part of the original discussions because it had been considered a minor weakness. The GAO found that the agency had acted correctly because it was the staff reductions in the BAFO that turned the weakness into a deficiency. Thus, an offeror takes the risk that aspects of its proposal included in the final proposal revisions for the first time will be found unacceptable by the agency, *Global Solutions Network, Inc.*, Comp. Gen. Dec. B-298682.3, 2008 CPD ¶ 131 (single employee filling two key positions); *Suntron Corp.*, Comp. Gen. Dec. B-270456, 96-1 CPD ¶ 143 (unexplained cost reduction); *Logicon RDA*, Comp. Gen. Dec. B-261714.2, 95-2 CPD ¶ 286 (unsupported cost reduction introduced for first time in BAFO); *Aircraft Porous Media, Inc.*, Comp. Gen. Dec. B-241665.2,

91-1 CPD ¶ 356 (reduced cost adjusted upward because not realistic and rationale for reduction not sufficiently explained); *Management & Tech. Servs. Co.*, Comp. Gen. Dec. B-209513, 82-2 CPD ¶ 571 (new management technique).

This rule was carried to the extreme under the pre-rewrite FAR 15.311(c) in holding that an agency need not reopen discussions to permit correction of a mistake in the BAFO, *Standard Mfg. Co.*, 65 Comp. Gen. 451 (B-220455), 86-1 CPD ¶ 304; *American Elec. Lab., Inc.*, 65 Comp. Gen. 62 (B-219582), 85-2 CPD ¶ 545. Compare *FCC.O&M, Inc.*, Comp. Gen. Dec. B-238610.2, 91-1 CPD ¶ 26, where it was found proper to conduct another round of discussions in order to correct a mistake in the winning offeror's proposal. Thus, an agency may, but is not required to, reopen discussions after submission of final proposal revisions, and the agency's decision will not be disturbed unless it is found to be unreasonable.

The rule permitting the contracting officer not to reopen discussions when an offeror has included newly introduced material in a final proposal does not apply to information which the agency learns from other sources that appears to modify a proposal. See *AAA Eng'g & Drafting, Inc.*, Comp. Gen. Dec. B-250323, 93-1 CPD ¶ 287, where the contracting officer gave a BAFO a low evaluation based on a manning table obtained in a preaward survey that appeared to conflict with the manning table that had been included in the BAFO. The GAO ruled that the contracting officer should have sought clarification because the offeror did not state that the new manning table modified its BAFO.

VII. AMENDMENT AND CANCELLATION OF THE RFP

When the needs or circumstances change or when new information or defects in the RFP are discovered, the agency may be required to amend or cancel the RFP. Cancellations resulting from the government no longer having a need for the procurement or from lack of funds are not at issue. Furthermore, cancellation is proper if the source selection authority determines that no offer meets the agency's needs. See Chapter 9. However, where the government still intends to continue on with the procurement, the RFP must be amended. See FAR 15.206(a), which states:

> When, either before or after receipt of proposals, the Government changes its requirements or terms and conditions, the contracting officer shall amend the solicitation.

Whether the changes require or permit cancellation and resolicitation or can be implemented by amending the RFP depends on the nature and timing of the changes. Although cancellation followed by a resolicitation with a new RFP and an amendment without cancellation each involve amended RFPs, the latter action permits the government to continue with the procurement. Thus, it may be more attractive to procurement officials because it saves both time and administrative effort. Conversely, resolicitation may expand the field of competition and result in a more advantageous deal for the government.

A. Cancellation and Resolicitation

The only FAR provision dealing with cancellation and resolicitation is FAR 15.206(e), which states:

> If, in the judgment of the contracting officer, based on market research or otherwise, an amendment issued after offers are received is so substantial as to exceed what prospective offerors reasonably could have anticipated, so that additional sources likely would have submitted offers had the substance of the amendment been known to them, the contracting officer shall cancel the original solicitation and issue a new one, regardless of the stage of the acquisition.

The pre-FAR 15 rewrite version of this regulation had an additional provision that directed that the new solicitation be furnished to all firms originally solicited and any added to the original list. Although the normal rules of full and open competition would require that the new solicitation be publicized, it would seem appropriate for the government also to resolicit those firms originally solicited.

Cancellation of an RFP after offerors have expended the effort to prepare proposals is not a desirable course of action. In *Loral Fairchild Corp.*, Comp. Gen. Dec. B-242957.2, 91-2 CPD ¶ 218, the GAO stated that the changes would have to "significantly alter the purpose or nature of the contract" or change the "field of competition" in order to require a cancellation. See *Denwood Properties Corp.*, Comp. Gen. Dec. B-251347.2, 93-1 CPD ¶ 380, where the changes involved a reduction in the amount of space to be leased and the agency's desire to open the competition to consider build-to-suit facilities. The GAO stated that "it would not have been proper" to simply amend the specifications because the changes were substantial and would likely increase the field of competition.

The GAO has stated that generally cancellation is appropriate where changes to the solicitation are expected to result in increased competition or lower prices. See *Blue Rock Structures, Inc.*, Comp. Gen. Dec. B-400811, 2009 CPD ¶ 26 (rewriting specifications to obtain better prices through increased competition); *North Shore Medical Labs, Inc.*, Comp. Gen. Dec. B-311070, 2008 CPD ¶ 144 (original RFP did not promote effective competition); *SEI Group, Inc.*, Comp. Gen. Dec. B-299108, 2007 CPD ¶35 (agency decided to revise procurement strategy to reduce costs); *Glen/Mar Constr., Inc.*, Comp. Gen. Dec. B-298355, 2006 CPD ¶ 117 (proposed prices were much higher than agency budget); *Goode Constr., Inc.*, Comp. Gen. Dec. B-288655.4, 2002 CPD ¶ 25 (adopting a different construction schedule); *Noelke GmbH*, Comp. Gen. Dec. B-278324.2, 98-1 CPD ¶ 46 (updating requirements and improving evaluation scheme to obtain increased competition); *Robertson Leasing Corp.*, Comp. Gen. Dec. B-275152, 97-1 CPD ¶ 49 (relaxing the specifications). Compare *Pro-Fab*, Comp. Gen. Dec. B-243607, 91-2 CPD ¶ 128, refusing to allow the contracting officer to cancel the solicitation because there was no reason to believe that any added competition would result from a resolicitation, nor was there any real prospect for additional cost savings.

Whether the field of competition would be increased by competition depends on the facts and circumstances of each individual case. A number of cases have held that cancellation and resolicitation was not required even though significant changes were made. For example, in *Atkins Enters., Inc., Comp. Gen. Dec. B-241047, 91-1 CPD ¶ 42*, a change from a 690-day, eight-phase construction schedule to one of 630 days with two phases was found not to be an appreciable change. See also *Defense Group, Inc.*, Comp. Gen. Dec. B-253795, 94-1 CPD ¶ 196, where a 12.3% increase in overall contract effort was not considered a substantial change to the basic nature of the contemplated contract. For other cases finding that cancellation of a solicitation was not required because the change was not substantial, see *SMS Data Prods. Group v. Austin*, 940 F.2d 1514 (Fed. Cir. 1991) (changing the solicitation by advancing the commercial availability date of laptop computers); *Corporate Jets, Inc.*, GSBCA 11049-P, 91-2 BCA ¶ 23,998 (adding option with a potential to increase the number of helicopters from 26 to 75); *Cape Fear Paging Co.*, Comp. Gen. Dec. B-252160.2, 93-1 CPD ¶ 347 (elimination of separate line item and combining prices into remaining item); *Di Frances Co.*, Comp. Gen. Dec. B-245492, 91-2 CPD ¶ 323 (5.9% decrease in the requirements); *Goodway Graphics of Virginia, Inc.*, Comp. Gen. Dec. B-236386, 89-2 CPD ¶ 491 (change affecting only five of 71 items); *Chromatics, Inc.*, Comp. Gen. Dec. B-224515, 87-1 CPD ¶ 171 (deletion of design requirements from specification); and *Hughes Aircraft Co.*, Comp. Gen. Dec. B-222152, 86-1 CPD ¶ 564 (elimination of one of two alternative technical approaches).

Cancellation with the intent to resolicit is also proper if the agency finds that it had not done a good job in stating its requirements. See *Applied Resources, Inc.*, Comp. Gen. Dec. B-400144.7, 2009 CPD ¶ 161 (prolonged protests led to reassessment of requirements); *Optimum Servs., Inc.*, Comp. Gen. Dec. B-401051, 2009 CPD ¶ 85 (program funding reduced after protest of original procurement); *Knight's Armament Co.*, Comp. Gen. Dec. B-299469, 2007 CPD ¶ 85 (offered products did not meet agency needs requiring revision of specifications); *ELEIT Tech., Inc.*, Comp. Gen. Dec. B-294193.2, 2004 CPD ¶ 203 (agency decided to bundle work into larger package); *Surgi-Textile*, Comp. Gen. Dec. B-289370, 2002 CPD ¶ 38 (specifications found to be inadequate); *Nidek, Inc.*, Comp. Gen. Dec. B-272255, 96-2 CPD ¶ 112 (medical staff needed time to develop an accurate statement of its needs, when all firms could submit an offer); *Chant Eng'g Co.*, Comp. Gen. Dec. B-270149.2, 96-1 CPD ¶ 96 (government needs were overstated and the agency determined that enhanced competition would result from a relaxation of the requirements); *JRW Mgmt. Co.*, Comp. Gen. Dec. B-260396.2, 95-1 CPD ¶ 276 (cancellation because agency received only one response and recognized that it could meet its needs with an alternate approach that presented an opportunity for increased competition).

Cancellation and resolicitation is also appropriate where necessary to ensure fair competition, *IT Corp.*, Comp. Gen. Dec. B-289517.3, 2002 CPD ¶ 123. In an unusual situation, cancellation was appropriate in order to avoid protests based on a disagreement between GAO and the Executive Branch over the priority that should be given the HUBZone contractors, *All Seasons Apparel, Inc.*, Comp. Gen.

Dec. B-401805, 2009 CPD ¶ 221. See also *Kenco Assocs., Inc.*, Comp. Gen. Dec. B-297503, 2006 CPD ¶ 24, where cancellation was found a proper response to Congressional criticism of the procurement.

Cancellation and resolicitation are also proper if an agency finds a better procurement strategy. See *Starlight Corp.*, Comp. Gen. Dec. B-297904.2, 2006 CPD ¶ 65 (RFP needed to be rewritten to clarify experience requirement); *Logistics Solutions Group, Inc.*, Comp. Gen. Dec. B-294604.7, 2005 CPD ¶ 141 (RFP no longer reflected agency needs); *VSE Corp.*, Comp. Gen. Dec. B-290452.2, 2005 CPD ¶ 111 (almost five years had passed since original proposals); *Best Foam Fabricators, Inc.*, Comp. Gen. Dec. B-259905.3, 95-1 CPD ¶ 275 (cancellation to obtain the items from the organization designated by the Committee for Purchase from the Blind and Other Severely Handicapped rather than another offeror under the solicitation); *General Projection Sys.*, 70 Comp. Gen. 345 (B-241418.2), 91-1 CPD ¶ 308 (cancellation because item was solicited in the RFP on a "brand name" rather than on a "brand name or equal" basis and an acceptable equal item was proposed); *Independent Bus. Servs., Inc.*, 69 Comp. Gen. 51 (B-235569.4), 90-1 CPD ¶ 207 (cancellation where no offerors proposed compliant products, and the agency determined that if it resolicited under less restrictive specifications, it would increase competition). However, cancellation was found unreasonable when the RFP had called for a price-only competition and the agency intended to reopen the competition on a sealed bidding basis, *Rand & Jones Enters. Co.*, Comp. Gen. Dec. B-296483, 2005 CPD ¶ 142.

B. Amendment without Cancellation

Even if the agency decides not to cancel the RFP, an amendment is required if changes would have a significant impact on competition, *Joint Action in Community Serv., Inc.*, Comp. Gen. Dec. B-214564, 84-2 CPD ¶ 228; *Computek, Inc.*, 54 Comp. Gen. 1080 (B-182576), 75-1 CPD ¶ 384. A significant impact on competition occurs when (1) mandatory specifications or terms and conditions are changed and (2) offerors not receiving notice of the changes would be prejudiced. In *Management Sys. Designers, Inc.*, Comp. Gen. Dec. B-244383.8, 92-1 CPD ¶ 496, prejudice was found where an offeror showed that it might have revised its proposal.

An amendment is called for where the relative importance of the evaluation factors is altered, *Unisys Corp.*, 67 Comp. Gen. 512 (B-230019.2), 88-2 CPD ¶ 35 (clarifying the importance of cost), or the overall evaluation scheme is changed, *Galler Assocs., Inc.*, Comp. Gen. Dec. B-210204, 83-1 CPD ¶ 515 (changing from lowest-cost, technically acceptable offer scheme to best-value scheme). See also *Occu-Health, Inc.*, Comp. Gen. Dec. B-270228.3, 96-1 CPD ¶ 196, requiring amending the RFP when the agency decides not to evaluate options. When such an amendment alters the evaluation scheme, the best procedure is to allow the offerors to submit new proposals. See *Cooperativa Muratori Riuniti*, Comp. Gen. Dec. B-294980.5, 2005 CPD ¶ 144, stating:

Where, as here, an agency decides to amend a solicitation after closing and permit offerors to revise their proposals in response, however, we think that offerors should be permitted to revise any aspect of their proposals, including those that were not the subject of the amendment, unless the agency offers evidence that the amendment could not reasonably have any effect on other aspects of proposals, or that allowing such revisions would have a detrimental impact on the competitive process.

See also *Lockheed Martin Sys. Integration-Owego*, Comp. Gen. Dec. B-299145.5, 2007 CPD ¶ 155, granting a protest because the agency did not allow the offerors to submit completely new proposals when the amendment made a major change in how support costs would be evaluation.

FAR 15.206(d) permits an amendment to take advantage of an offer that deviates from the RFP:

If a proposal of interest to the Government involves a departure from the stated requirements, the contracting officer shall amend the solicitation, provided this can be done without revealing to the other offerors the alternate solution proposed or any other information that is entitled to protection (see 15.207(b) and 15.306(e)).

See *IRT Corp.*, Comp. Gen. Dec. B-246991, 92-1 CPD ¶ 378 (deviation in specifications for x-ray machine); *Loral Terracom*, 66 Comp. Gen. 272 (B-224908), 87-1 CPD ¶ 182 (different technical approach suggested by an offeror).

Amendments are not required if the claimed deviation is from a provision that is not mandatory, *Howard Cooper Corp. v. United States*, 763 F. Supp. 829 (1991). In *AEL Defense Corp.*, Comp. Gen. Dec. B-251376, 93-1 CPD ¶ 256, the protester alleged that the agency improperly awarded the contract to a firm whose proposal did not conform to a design referenced in a RFP document. The protester asserted that the design was mandatory and, therefore, the RFP should have been amended. The GAO denied the protest, stating that the design was not mandatory under the hierarchy established in the specification. Similarly, a contracting officer was not required to issue an amendment to an RFP after changing specified computer systems where the government provided all equipment necessary for performance of the contract and the change brought about no cost savings to offerors, *Optimum Sys., Inc.*, Comp. Gen. Dec. B-194984, 80-2 CPD ¶ 32. See also *Litton Sys., Inc. v. Dep't of Transportation*, GSBCA 12911-P, 94-3 BCA ¶ 27,263.

1. Issuance of Amendments

FAR 15.210(b) provides that Standard Form 30, Amendment of Solicitation/ Modification of Contract, or Optional Form 309, Amendment of Solicitation, may be used to amend solicitations. Prior to the FAR 15 rewrite, the use of Standard Form 30 was mandatory. Whether issued on these forms or otherwise in writing or electronically, the amendment must provide offerors sufficient information to determine the changed requirements. FAR 15.206(g) states that: "At a minimum, the following information should be included in each amendment:"

(1) Name and address of issuing activity.

(2) Solicitation number and date.

(3) Amendment number and date.

(4) Number of pages.

(5) Description of the change being made.

(6) Government point of contact and phone number (and electronic or facsimile address, if appropriate).

(7) Revision to solicitation closing date, if applicable.

FAR 15.206(f) permits oral notice of the amendment when "time is of the essence." It states that in such a case, "the contracting officer shall document the contract file and formalize the notice with an amendment." The importance of formalizing the notice in writing is illustrated in cases where the protester contends that it did not receive the notice that the agency claimed had been issued orally. See *Lockheed, IMS*, Comp. Gen. Dec. B-248686, 92-2 CPD ¶ 180 (protest successful when offeror denied that it received oral notice of the amendment); and *I.E. Levick & Assocs.*, Comp. Gen. Dec. B-214648, 84-2 CPD ¶ 695 (failure to issue a written amendment is a procedural defect whenever an offeror effectively denies having been advised orally).

In *Labat-Anderson Inc.*, 71 Comp. Gen. 252 (B-246071), 92-1 CPD ¶ 193, the GAO suggested that notification of changes might be accomplished by either raising the issue in discussions with all offerors within the competitive range or issuing an amendment to the RFP. It would appear that the discussion method would be appropriate only for relatively simple changes.

2. Firms to Be Notified

FAR 15.206 specifies that amendments should be furnished as follows:

(b) Amendments issued before the established time and date for receipt of proposals shall be issued to all parties receiving the solicitation.

(c) Amendments issued after the established time and date for receipt of proposals shall be issued to all offerors that have not been eliminated from the competition.

Although an amendment may not be made after submission of proposals so as to intentionally preclude further competition, agencies may amend the solicitation after submission of proposals to take advantage of terms being offered by a particular offeror if other offerors are given the opportunity to respond to the change, *Cel-U-Dex Corp.*, Comp. Gen. Dec. B-195012, 80-1 CPD ¶ 102; *Sub-Sea Sys, Inc.*, Comp. Gen. Dec. B-195741, 80-1 CPD ¶ 123. See *Zublin Delaware, Inc.*, Comp. Gen. Dec. B-227003.2, 87-2 CPD ¶ 149, in which an amendment containing new government needs was permitted even though it excluded some offerors because it was done in the public interest. Similarly, an agency may amend an RFP after the closing date to set aside the procurement exclusively for small business if such action has a reasonable basis, *Gill Mktg. Co.*, Comp. Gen. Dec. B-194414.3, 80-1 CPD ¶ 213. It has also been held that an agency need not issue an amendment after qualifying additional parties to a qualified products list (QPL), even though the RFP lists only one source on the *QPL*, Comp. Gen. Dec. B-196242, Mar. 5, 1980, *Unpub.*

Once a competitive range has been established, agencies are not required to issue amendments to offerors outside the competitive range so long as the amendment is not directly related to the reason for the excluded offeror's rejection, *Amperif Corp.*, Comp. Gen. Dec. B-211992, 84-1 CPD ¶ 409. This is the case even where the change is significant, *Labat-Anderson Inc.*, B-246071, 92-1 CPD ¶ 193. For instance, no amendment is required where a contract is amended from a cost-type to a fixed-price contract, *Westinghouse Elec. Corp.*, Comp. Gen. Dec. B-197768, 80-1 CPD ¶ 378. See also *Loral Terracom, Marconi Italiana*, Comp. Gen. Dec. B-224908, 87-1 CPD ¶ 182, where an amendment recognizing alternative methods of satisfying the agency's requirements was properly limited to offerors within the competitive range. Compare *Information Ventures, Inc.*, Comp. Gen. Dec. B-232094, 88-2 CPD ¶ 443, where an amendment relaxing the specifications was required to be sent to an excluded offeror because it directly related to the reasons for exclusion. See also *Hamilton Tool Co.*, Comp. Gen. Dec. B-218260.1, 85-1 CPD ¶ 566, where resolicitation of all offerors was required when different requirements were arrived at with the only offeror in the competitive range. In *Lobar Inc.*, Comp. Gen. Dec. B-247843.3, 92-2 CPD ¶ 139, the GAO found that the agency had acted properly when, after determining that the specifications exceeded the government's minimum needs, it amended the RFP and reopened with all offerors, both those within and outside the competitive range.

CHAPTER 9

SOURCE SELECTION

Upon completion of the evaluation of the proposals, the agency is prepared to select the winning contractor(s). FAR 15.302 states: "The objective of source selection is to select the proposal that represents the best value." When the FAR 15.101-2 lowest-price technically acceptable source selection process is used, the selection decision can be made quite quickly because it does not involve tradeoffs. The only matters for determination are whether the lowest priced offer is technically acceptable and whether that offeror is responsible. Thus, there is not even a need to evaluate the technical acceptability of higher priced offerors. In FAR 15.101-2 tradeoff procurements, offers other than the lowest priced or other than the highest technically rated may be selected. Depending upon the evaluation factors and the evaluation scheme, this can be a more difficult decision requiring a significant degree of judgment to be exercised in selecting the source.

I. SOURCE SELECTION AUTHORITY

While the procurement statutes provide that the agency, 41 U.S.C. § 253b(d)(3), or the head of the agency, 10 U.S.C. § 2305(b)(4)(C), shall award the contract, the FAR provisions focus on the individual who will make the selection and award decisions. This individual is called the source selection authority (SSA). FAR 15.303(a) provides that the contracting officer is the SSA "unless the agency head appoints another individual for a particular acquisition or group of acquisitions." In many agencies, particularly in large-dollar procurements, the SSA is a high-level agency official.

A. Responsibilities

The source selection responsibilities of the SSA are set out in FAR 15.303(b), as follows:

(4) Ensure that proposals are evaluated based solely on the factors and subfactors contained in the solicitation (10 U.S.C. 2305(b)(1) and 41 U.S.C. 253b(d)(3));

(5) Consider the recommendations of advisory boards or panels (if any); and

(6) Select the source or sources whose proposal is the best value to the Government (10 U.S.C. 2305(b)(4)(B) and 41 U.S.C. 253b(d)(3)).

In addition, the SSA must make a determination of whether to award without negotiation or whether to award after receiving final proposal revisions or to call for further revisions.

B. Independent Judgment

FAR 15.308 requires that, while the SSA may use the analyses of other participants in the process, the source selection decision must represent the SSA's independent judgment:

> The source selection authority's (SSA) decision shall be based on a comparative assessment of proposals against all source selection criteria in the solicitation. While the SSA may use reports and analyses prepared by others, the source selection decision shall represent the SSA's independent judgment.

The information furnished to the SSA can vary in nature and detail. It may consist only of evaluation results or may also contain further analyses and recommendations for award. The SSA must make an assessment of the information and determine whether it conforms to the evaluation factors specified in the solicitation and whether it is sufficient to make a rational selection for award. If not, the SSA must see that corrective action is taken.

In fulfilling his or her obligations, the SSA can become deeply involved in all aspects of the procurement. See *Digital Sys. Group, Inc.*, Comp. Gen. Dec. B-286931, 2001 CPD ¶ 50, rejecting a protest that the contracting officer, acting as the SSA, had approved the source selection plan, conducted discussions, served as a member of the evaluation board and the cost team. The decision states that "While it is conceivable that a CO's active participation in multiple stages of the evaluation process could compromise that process, that clearly is not the case here." See also *JW Holding Group & Assocs., Inc.*, Comp. Gen. Dec. B-285882.3, 2003 CPD ¶ 126, denying a protest that the SSA served as the head of the price evaluation team. Compare *Wackenhut Servs., Inc. v. United States*, 85 Fed. Cl. 273 (2008), suggesting that it may have been improper for the SSA to influence the evaluators during the evaluation process.

A suggestion from the contracting officer that the SSA "beef up" the explanations for arriving at the source selection decision did not indicate that the SSA had not exercised independent judgment, *Microware Outsourcing, Inc. v. United States*, 72 Fed. Cl. 694 (2006).

1. Using Evaluations or Recommendations

In smaller procurements the SSA (generally the contracting officer) may participate in the entire evaluation process with the result that there is no need to communicate the results of the evaluation to the SSA. However, in larger procurements there will be such a need because the SSA has not participated in the evaluation. In that situation agencies generally require the preparation of written documentation summarizing the results of the evaluation and often require briefings of the SSA. See, for example, the Army guidance in *Contracting for Best Value: A Best Practices Guide to Source Selection*, AMC-P 715-3 (Jan. 1, 1998), stating:

Documentation explaining the final results of the evaluation should be prepared for the source selection authority to use in making the selection decision. This documentation should include the technical and/or past performance evaluation results, the cost/price evaluation, and the comparative value analysis, if applicable, for each proposal in the competitive range. The documentation should also include other considerations such as the results of negotiations. For more complex source selections, this is accomplished by means of a formal report that is provided to the source selection authority. For less complex source selections, the documentation may be included as part of the Price Negotiation Memorandum. It should be simple but concise and should cross-reference rather than repeat information in existing documents as much as possible (e.g., the source selection plan, evaluation team consensus report). The analysis and comparisons in this documentation should be used as an aid to the source selection authority's judgment — not as a substitute for judgment.

For guidance on briefing the SSA, see NFS 1815.370 requiring the following procedure when source evaluation boards (SEBs) have done the evaluation:

(h) SEB presentation. (1) The SEB Chairperson shall brief the SSA on the results of the SEB deliberations to permit an informed and objective selection of the best source(s) for the particular acquisition.

(2) The presentation shall focus on the significant strengths, deficiencies, and significant weaknesses found in the proposals, the probable cost of each proposal, and any significant issues and problems identified by the SEB. This presentation must explain any applicable special standards of responsibility; evaluation factors, subfactors, and elements; the significant strengths and significant weaknesses of the offerors; the Government cost estimate, if applicable; the offerors' proposed cost/price; the probable cost; the proposed fee arrangements; and the final adjectival ratings and scores to the subfactor level.

(3) Attendance at the presentation is restricted to people involved in the selection process or who have a valid need to know. The designated individuals attending the SEB presentation(s) shall:

(i) Ensure that the solicitation and evaluation processes complied with all applicable agency policies and that the presentation accurately conveys the SEB's activities and findings;

(ii) Not change the established evaluation factors, subfactors, elements, weights, or scoring systems; or the substance of the SEB's findings. They may, however, advise the SEB to rectify procedural omissions, irregularities or inconsistencies, substantiate its findings, or revise the presentation.

(4) The SEB recorder will coordinate the formal presentation including arranging the time and place of the presentation, assuring proper attendance, and distributing presentation material.

Procedures, such as these, that communicate summaries of the evaluations to the SSA have been sustained as fully adequate to ensure rational source selection decisions. See, for example, *Sabreliner Corp.*, Comp. Gen. Dec. B-242023, 91-1 CPD ¶ 326, stating:

> The SSA is not required to personally review the proposals or the complete evaluation documentation, but can rely upon a briefing that presents the results of the proposal evaluation. *See Systems & Processes Eng'g Corp.*, B-234142, May 10, 1989, 89-1 CPD ¶ 441. Here, the SSA, in addition to receiving a technical evaluation briefing, reviewed the proposal analysis report, which set forth, among other things, a description of the evaluation standards and criteria; a description of the competing proposals; a comparative evaluation analysis of the proposal; the offerors' proposed prices/costs; and the performance risk assessment.

In most cases the SSA can rely on the scores of the evaluators and the evaluation board's conclusions. See *Wyle Labs., Inc.*, Comp. Gen. Dec. B-311123, 2009 CPD ¶ 96 (SSA based decision on SSEB's overriding of evaluators judgment of risk); *MD Helicopters, Inc.*, Comp. Gen. Dec. B-298502, 2006 CPD ¶ 164 (SSA based decision on detailed discussions with SSEB, SSAC and users or product being procured); *Metro Mach. Corp.*, Comp. Gen. Dec. B-295744, 2005 CPD ¶ 112 (SSA accepted evaluation assessments of three evaluation committees); *Computer Sciences Corp. v. United States*, 51 Fed. Cl. 297 (2001) (SSA based decision on evaluators comparative assessment of offerors' past performance); *Keane Fed. Sys., Inc.*, Comp. Gen. Dec. B-280595, 98-2 CPD ¶ 132 (SSA based decision on detailed comparison of offers by "best value working group"); *Development Alternatives, Inc.*, Comp. Gen. Dec. B-279920, 98-2 CPD ¶ 54 (SSA relied on assessment of majority of evaluators); *KRA Corp.*, Comp. Gen. Dec. B-278904, 98-1 CPD ¶ 147 (SSA based decision on oral and written evaluation reports plus questions of evaluators); *International Data Prods. Corp.*, Comp. Gen. Dec. B-274654, 97-1 CPD ¶ 34 (SSA based selection decision on detailed analysis in SSEB report); *Allied Tech. Group, Inc.*, Comp. Gen. Dec. B-271302, 96-2 CPD ¶ 4 (SSA based selection decision on contract evaluation board findings and discussion with board); *ICF Kaiser Eng'rs*, Comp. Gen. Dec. B-271079, 96-2 CPD ¶ 15 (SSA based award decision on information set forth in the SEB and TEP reports). It is also proper for the SSA to obtain and rely on legal advice from an agency lawyer, *Creative Apparel Assocs.*, Comp. Gen. Dec. B-275139, 97-1 CPD ¶ 65.

When there is disagreement among the evaluators or within an evaluation board, the SSA may have a heightened responsibility to explain his or her reliance on the evaluation report. See *Information Sciences Corp. v. United States*, 73 Fed. Cl. 70 (2006), *amended*, 75 Fed. Cl. 406 (2007), sustaining a protest where the SSA adopted a minority report almost verbatim in the source selection decision. The court held that this did not demonstrate the exercise of independent judgment – apparently because the SSA did not explain why the minority view was correct.

2. Reliance Not Justified

The SSA is not entitled to rely on faulty evaluations. See, for example, *Programmatics, Inc.*, Comp. Gen. Dec. B-228916.2, 88-1 CPD ¶ 35, where a review of the narrative statements prepared by two evaluators indicated that there was no rational support for the scores given by the evaluators and adopted by the source selection official. Thus the SSA is ultimately responsible for any mistakes made in the evaluation process. In *J.A. Jones Mgmt. Servs., Inc.*, Comp. Gen. Dec. B-276864, 97-2 CPD ¶ 47, the GAO observed:

> While an agency's initial review of proposals may be done independently, it is necessary for the agency at some point to make a rational comparison of the relative merits of directly competing proposals. The agency's SSA cannot make a rational comparison where the evaluators' point scores do not accurately reflect the relative strengths and weaknesses of the competing proposals and the record lacks adequate documentation in support of such technical point scores. Here, the dearth of evaluation narratives or other explanations in this evaluation record and the SSA's summary reliance on the point scores, which have been sufficiently shown by the protester to be inaccurate in numerous areas, lead us to the conclusion that the SSA could not and did not make a reasonable selection decision. *See Adelaide Blomfield Management Co.,* [72 Comp. Gen. 335 (B-253128.2), 93-2 CPD ¶ 197], at 4–6. In sum, on the evaluation record furnished to our Office — consisting of point scores and cursory narratives — we find the absence of a consistent, reasonable and accurate evaluation scoring as well as the absence of supporting narrative documentation; moreover, the agency has offered no substantive response to the protester's concerns in response to the protest, and our review shows none. Here, we simply are unable to assess the reasonableness of the agency's selection decision. Accordingly, we sustain the protest.

Protests have been granted when the SSA made the selection decision based on the conclusions of the evaluators but it was later determined that the conclusions were unsupported by the evaluation documentation. See *Health Net Fed. Servs., LLC*, Comp. Gen. Dec. B-401652.3, 2009 CPD ¶ 220 (SSA relied on evaluator's conclusion that corporate parent of offeror met experience requirement when neither had investigated role of parent); *Contingency Mgmt. Group, LLC*, Comp. Gen. Dec. B-309752, 2008 CPD ¶ 83 (decision based on responses to scenario in RFP where evaluators did not consider impact of proposals that altered the assumptions in the scenario with the result that they were able to propose lower prices); *Apptis, Inc.*, Comp. Gen. Dec. B-299457, 2008 CPD ¶ 49 (SSA relied on SSEB's improper use of past performance to evaluate risk of technical solution); *Keeton Corrections, Inc.*, Comp. Gen. Dec. B-293348, 2005 CPD ¶ 44 (SSA relied on misleading narrative supporting contracting officer's evaluation of past performance); *SDS Int'l, Inc.*, Comp. Gen. Dec. B-291183, 2003 CPD ¶ 137 (SSA based decision on evaluators' misreading of technical proposal); *Ashland Sales & Serv. Co.*, Comp. Gen. Dec. B-291206, 2003 CPD ¶ 36 (SSA relied on contracting officer document that contained factual errors); *Shumaker Trucking & Excavating Contractors, Inc.*, Comp.

Gen. Dec. B-290732, 2002 CPD ¶ 169 (SSA endorsed contracting officer's conclusion that was based on higher point score with no consideration of strengths and weaknesses); *Green Valley Trans., Inc.*, Comp. Gen. Dec. B-285283, 2000 CPD ¶ 133 (SSA followed the evaluators' theory that past performance should be rated on the basis of the number of late deliveries without considering the volume of shipments); *CRAssociates, Inc.*, Comp. Gen. Dec. B-282075.2, 2000 CPD ¶ 63 (SSA relied on faulty technical evaluation and mathematical scoring mistakes); *Saco Defense Corp.*, Comp. Gen. Dec. B-283885, 2000 CPD ¶ 34 (SSA relied on an evaluation that the prospective winning offeror had furnished sufficient information to demonstrate that its quality system was adequate); *ITT Fed. Servs. Int'l Corp.*, Comp. Gen. Dec. B-283307, 99-2 CPD ¶ 76 (SSA determined that the protester's costs were unrealistic when the cost evaluation team had made no cost realism analysis to determine the probable costs of performance); and *JW Assocs., Inc.*, Comp. Gen. Dec. B-275209, 97-1 CPD ¶ 57 (evaluation report contained only the prices, point scores of the non-price evaluation factors, and a one-paragraph narrative giving summary conclusions without explaining the different scores given to the competing offerors). See also *Century Envtl. Hygiene, Inc.*, Comp. Gen. Dec. B-279378, 98-1 CPD ¶ 164, where the SSA improperly determined that the low-priced offeror was not among the technically best qualified offerors based on evaluation conclusions that were not supported by the evaluation documentation; and *New Breed Leasing Corp.*, Comp. Gen. Dec. B-259328, 96-2 CPD ¶ 84, where the selection decision was based on uncorrected errors in scoring, an inaccurate assessment of the past performance of one of the offerors, and assessments of technical differences between the proposal that were inconsistent with the evaluation record and the proposals.

3. Ordering Reevaluation

The SSA can order a complete reevaluation if there are doubts about the validity of the initial evaluation, *PRC, Inc.*, Comp. Gen. Dec. B-233561.8, 92-2 CPD ¶ 215. In that case a new evaluation panel was constituted after questions were raised about the propriety of the initial evaluation. The GAO stated:

> Contracting officials in negotiated procurements have broad discretion to take corrective action where the agency determines that such action is necessary to ensure fair and impartial competition. *Oshkosh Truck Corp.; Idaho Norland Corp.*, B-237058.2; B-237058.3, Feb. 14, 1990, 90-1 CPD ¶ 274. An agency may convene a new selection board and conduct a new evaluation where the record shows that the agency made the decision in good faith, without the specific intent of changing a particular offeror's technical ranking or avoiding an award to a particular offeror. *Burns & Roe Servs. Corp.*, B-248394, Aug. 25, 1992, 92-2 CPD ¶ [124]; *Loschky, Marquardt & Nesholm*, B-222606, Sept. 23, 1986, 86-2 CPD ¶ 336. We will not object to proposed corrective action where the agency concludes that award was not necessarily made on a basis most advantageous to the government, so long as the corrective action taken is appropriate to remedy the impropriety. See *Oshkosh Truck Corp.; Idaho Norland Corp., supra*; *Power Dynatec Corp.*, B-236896, Dec. 6, 1989, 89-2 CPD ¶ 522.

See also *Team BOS/Naples — Gemmo S.p.A./DelJen*, Comp. Gen. Dec. B-298865.3, 2008 CPD ¶ 11 (GAO did not question reevaluation when SSA found errors in initial evaluation); *East/West Indus., Inc.*, Comp. Gen. Dec. B-278734.4, 98-1 CPD ¶ 143 (GAO did not question reconvening the evaluators to perform a more detailed evaluation of the proposals); *EBA Eng'g, Inc.*, Comp. Gen. Dec. B-275818, 97-1 CPD ¶ 127 (GAO found proper an agency's decision to replace panel members in order to avoid the appearance of impropriety); and *Pro-Mark, Inc.*, Comp. Gen. Dec. B-247248, 92-1 CPD ¶ 448 (GAO affirmed a decision of an agency to reevaluate proposals using a more experienced evaluation panel).

4. Rescore or Conduct Own Evaluation

The SSA is not bound by the rankings, scores, or recommendations of either the evaluators or boards or other intermediate groups, as long as the official has a rational basis for the differing evaluation. In some cases source selection officials merely ignore the scores and make the source selection decision based on the narratives. However, in some instances an attempt is made to make the scores an accurate reflection of the merits of the proposals.

There have been numerous protest decisions upholding reevaluation or rescoring by source selection officials, either explicitly or implicitly. See *Grey Advertising, Inc.*, 55 Comp. Gen. 1111 (B-184825), 76-1 CPD ¶ 325, stating at 1120:

> [W]hile point scores, technical evaluation narratives, and adjective ratings may well be indicative of whether one proposal is technically superior to another and should therefore be considered by source selection officials, *see EPSCO, Incorporated*, B-183816, November 21, 1975, 75-2 CPD ¶ 338, we have recognized that selection officials are not bound by the recommendations made by evaluation and advisory groups. *Bell Aerospace Company*, 55 Comp. Gen. 244 (1975), 75-2 CPD ¶ 168; *Tracor Jitco, Inc., supra*; 51 Comp. Gen. 272 (1971); B-173137(1), *supra*. This is so even though it is the working level procurement officials and evaluation panel members who may normally be expected to have the technical expertise relevant to the technical evaluation of proposals. Accordingly, we have upheld source selection officials' determinations that technical proposals were essentially equal despite an evaluation point score differential of 81 out of 1000, *see* 52 Comp. Gen. 686, *supra*, and despite contracting officer recommendations that award be made to the offeror with the highest technical rating. *See* 52 Comp. Gen. 738, *supra*.

It is appropriate for the SSA to use "personal experience" in making the evaluation, *Raytheon Co.*, Comp. Gen. Dec. B-291449, 2003 CPD ¶ 54.

Reevaluation or rescoring is often performed by the SSA to correct errors or poor judgment of subordinate evaluation personnel. In the *Grey* case, for instance, Navy officials determined that two proposals were technically equal, although the evaluation panel rated the protester's technical proposal 47 points higher (on a scale of 1,000 points). The GAO found this judgment had a rational basis, as the officials had concluded that the protester's higher score was based too much on the advantages of incumbency rather than actual technical superiority. Similarly, in *Polaris, Inc.*, Comp. Gen. Dec. B-220066, 85-2 CPD ¶ 669, the GAO approved a rescoring by an SSA based on his view that the evaluation panel had misinterpreted the RFP requirement; and in *L&E Assocs.*, Comp. Gen. Dec. B-224448, 86-2 CPD ¶ 568, the contracting officer properly altered the protester's technical score when he found that the evaluating committee had based their technical evaluations solely on cost and later had performed only cursory and insufficient analysis in the reevaluation. See also *TPL, Inc.*, Comp. Gen. Dec. B-297136.10, 2006 CPD ¶ 104 (SSA disagreed with evaluators' assessment of program management subfactor); *University Research Co.*, Comp. Gen. Dec. B-294358.6, 2005 CPD ¶ 83 (contracting officer disregarded assessments of evaluator and found technical proposals equal); *Synoptic Sys. Corp.*, Comp. Gen. Dec. B-290789.4, 2003 CPD ¶ 42 (SSA reevaluated proposals after outcome prediction by GAO); *Sayed Hamid Behbehani & Sons, WLL*, Comp. Gen. Dec. B-288818.6, 2002 CPD ¶ 163 (SSA reevaluated proposals without reference to original evaluations); *R.C.O. Reforesting*, Comp. Gen. Dec. B-280774.2, 98-2 CPD ¶ 119 (contracting officer properly reduced past performance score because of default termination not known to evaluators); and *Pro-Mark, Inc.*, Comp. Gen. Dec. B-247248, 92-1 CPD ¶ 448 (contracting officer properly lowered incongruous quality control scores given by an inexperienced review panel).

When an SSA makes an independent assessment, it will be subject to scrutiny for reasonableness. See *Consolidated Eng'g Servs.Inc.*, Comp. Gen. Dec. B-311313, 2008 CPD ¶ 146 (SSA changed experience evaluation based on issues not in RFP); *AT&T Corp.*, Comp. Gen. Dec. B-299542.3, 2008 CPD ¶ 65 (no explanation of how SSA arrived at different conclusion than evaluators regarding the impact of over-staffing); *IDEA Int'l, Inc. v. United States*, 74 Fed. Cl. 129 (2006) (SSA awarded to low price without considering evaluators' conclusion that protester had "slightly stronger proposal"); *DynCorp Int'l LLC*, Comp. Gen. Dec. B-289863, 2002 CPD ¶ 83 (SSA discounted weaknesses in awardee's proposal without explaining rationale for decision); *AIU North Am., Inc.*, Comp. Gen. Dec. B-283743.2, 2000 CPD ¶ 39 (SSA's determination that technical proposals were equal was neither supported by contemporaneous documentation nor satisfactorily explained during the protest); *Chemical Demilitarization Assocs.*, Comp. Gen. Dec. B-277700, 98-1 CPD ¶ 171 (SSA had made an improper determination that two technical proposals were of equal technical merit when the evaluation documentation rated the protester's proposal considerably higher in merit and the SSA could not explain why this assessment of the evaluators was inaccurate); *Morrison Knudsen Corp.*, Comp. Gen. Dec. B-270703, 96-2 CPD ¶ 86 (SSA's conclusion that selected offeror had superior subcontract approach unreasonable when the two proposals were not fundamentally different in this regard); *TRESP Assocs., Inc.*, Comp. Gen. Dec. B-258322.5, 96-1 CPD ¶ 8 (SSA's independent assessment of the capability of the offeror was not backed up by any specific facts but was based on general impressions).

In a number of cases, a source selection decision has been upheld on the basis that the SSA implicitly rescored some aspect of the evaluation. For example, in *PRC Kentron, Inc.*, Comp. Gen. Dec. B-230212, 88-1 CPD ¶ 537, rescoring was permitted to overcome the over-reliance on incumbency by the evaluators, but "no formal rescoring was performed." See also *GTE Hawaiian Tel. Co.*, Comp. Gen. Dec. B-276487.2, 97-2 CPD ¶ 21 (SSA acted rationally in ignoring a significant difference in technical scores that seemed to greatly overstate the actual difference between the offerors); *NKF Eng'g, Inc.*, Comp. Gen. Dec. B-232143, 88-2 CPD ¶ 497 (contracting officer properly considered the protester's score an exaggeration of its technical superiority because the evaluation committee did not consider relevant factors in management and employee transition when giving the scores); and *CRC Sys., Inc.*, Comp. Gen. Dec. B-207847, 83-1 CPD ¶ 462 (contracting officer implicitly lowered the protester's high score because its offer did not satisfy all the RFP requirements). In an unusual case, *Bank St. College of Educ.*, 63 Comp. Gen. 393 (B-213209), 84-1 CPD ¶ 607, *recons. denied*, 84-2 CPD ¶ 445, the agency director overturned a finding of technical superiority made by a technical evaluation panel without actually altering the technical scores. The GAO approved this intervention into the selection process finding that the director properly concluded that the awardee's proposal was actually technically superior because the level of effort in the protester's proposal deviated significantly from the RFP's estimated level of effort. Implicit rescoring is not sound practice and should be avoided. When the source selection official concludes that rescoring is necessary, the contract file should contain a clear indication of the rescoring that has occurred and the justification for that rescoring.

The SSA is also permitted to conduct a completely independent evaluation if the original evaluation is not acceptable, *Benchmark Sec., Inc.*, Comp. Gen. Dec. B-247655.2, 93-1 CPD ¶ 133. In that case the GAO affirmed the decision of the SSA after he completely altered the evaluation of the offerors, determined that two best proposals were technically equal and that costs of performance would be equivalent, and selected the incumbent contractor – commenting that the evaluation and source selection were well reasoned and thoroughly documented. See also *Fort Carson Support Servs. v. United States*, 71 Fed. Cl. 571 (2006) (upholding SSA's reassessment of past performance of protester); *Jason Assocs. Corp.*, Comp. Gen. Dec. B-278689, 98-1 CPD ¶ 67 (upholding SSA's reevaluation of sample writings when it became known that they had been previously accepted by the agency); *EBA Eng'g, Inc.*, Comp. Gen. Dec. B-275818, 97-1 CPD ¶ 127 (upholding SSA's independent assessment when the evaluation panel was severely divided); *LTR Training Sys., Inc.*, Comp. Gen. Dec. B-274996, 97-1 CPD ¶ 71 (upholding SSA's decision to bypass the evaluations and make a completely independent assessment of the proposals determining that they were technically equal in merit); *Ryan Assocs., Inc.*, Comp. Gen. Dec. B-274194, 97-1 CPD ¶ 2 (upholding SSA's independent cost/technical tradeoff differing from the technical evaluators' tradeoff analysis based on criticism of the contracting officer); *Loral Aeronutronic*, Comp. Gen. Dec. B-259857.2, 95-2 CPD ¶ 213 (upholding the SSAC's change of a risk assessment and a technical rating based on an analysis of the SSEB's findings); and *Calspan Corp.*, Comp. Gen. Dec. B-258441, 95-1 CPD ¶ 28 (upholding SSA's decision to raise the awardee's score on past performance based on the knowledge of agency personnel familiar with the prior successful performance of the awardee).

The SSA is permitted to use information in one segment of a proposal to alter an evaluation of another segment. For example, in a procurement that precluded the technical evaluators from seeing the pricing proposal, the source selection evaluation board made substantial adjustments to the technical evaluation based on information in the pricing proposal. The GAO denied the protest ruling that this procedure was entirely proper, *Cygna Project Mgmt.*, Comp. Gen. Dec. B-236839, 90-1 CPD ¶ 21. Failure to correlate the information in the segments of an offeror's proposal can lead to an irrational evaluation or at least to a poor selection of the source. Hence, SSAs should ensure that such correlation is made, with commensurate adjustments to the scores, before the source selection decision is made.

5. Rejection of All Proposals and Cancellation of Solicitation

One of the responsibilities of the SSA is to determine, after the completion of proposal evaluation, whether to reject all proposals and cancel the solicitation. When none of the offers provide value to the government, it would not be appropriate to continue a procurement and make an award. In this regard, the procurement statutes provide that "all . . . proposals . . . may be rejected if the head of the agency determines that such action is in the public interest," 10 U.S.C. § 2305(b)(2) and 41 U.S.C. § 253b(b). FAR 15.305(b) vests the authority to make this determination in the SSA. Pre-rewrite FAR 15.608(b) dealt with this subject and contained a number of examples where rejection of all offers would be justified. It also required a determination, in writing, that one of the identified factors was present. However, this provision was deleted in the rewrite which merely authorizes rejection if the SSA determines rejection to be in the "best interest" of the government. The SSA has broad discretion in making such determinations. See *Lasmer Indus., Inc.*, Comp. Gen. Dec. B-400866.2, 2009 CPD ¶ 77, permitting cancellation when the SSA found that it was more advantageous to procure the part from an existing contract and stating:

> An agency has broad authority to cancel an RFP or RFQ, and needs only a reasonable basis to do so. *Deva & Assocs. PC*, B-309972.3, Apr. 29, 2008, 2008 CPD ¶ 89 at 3 (RFQ); *A-Tek, Inc.*, B-286967, Mar. 22, 2001, 2001 CPD ¶ 57 at 2 (RFP). Moreover, an agency may properly cancel a solicitation no matter when the information precipitating the cancellation first surfaces or should have been known. *Daston Corp.*, B292583, B-292583.2, Oct. 20, 2003, 2003 CPD ¶ 193 at 3. Where a protester has alleged that an agency's rationale for cancellation is pretextual, that is the agency's actual motivation is to avoid awarding a contract on a competitive basis or to avoid resolving a protest, we will closely examine the

bases for the agency's actions.., B-310489, B-310489.2, Jan. 4, 2008, 2008 CPD ¶ 12 at 7; *Gonzales-McCaulley Inv. Group, Inc.*, B-299936.2, Nov. 5, 2007, 2007 CPD ¶ 192 at 5. Notwithstanding such closer scrutiny and even if it can be shown that personal animus or pretext may have supplied at least part of the motivation to have the RFP canceled, the reasonableness standard applicable to cancellation of a solicitation remains unchanged. *e-Management Consultants, Inc.; Centech Group, Inc.*, B-400585.2, B-400585.2, Feb. 3, 2009, 2009 CPD ¶ 39 at 5; *Dr. Robert J. Telepak*, B-247681, June 29, 1992, 92-2 CPD ¶ 4 at 4. Cancellation of a solicitation is reasonable where the agency determines that it no longer has a requirement for the item solicited, *Peterson-Nunez Joint Venture*, B-258788 , Feb. 13, 1995, 95-1 CPD ¶ 73 at 4, or where the agency discovers an existing contract for its requirement would be more advantageous to the government than continuing with the procurement. *Brian X. Scott*, B-310970; B-310970.2, Mar. 26, 2008, 2008 CPD ¶ 59 at 3.

One of the primary reasons for rejection of all proposals and cancellation is when it is determined that it is not in the best interest of the government to award to any of the offerors. See *North Shore Medical Labs, Inc.*, Comp. Gen. Dec. B-311070, 2008 CPD ¶ 144 (no acceptable proposals and stringent RFP requirement limited competitors); *Knight's Armament Co.*, Comp. Gen. Dec. B-299469, 2007 CPD ¶ 85 (none of the offered products met agency needs); *Glen/Mar Constr., Inc.*, Comp. Gen. Dec. B-298355, 2006 CPD ¶ 117 (all offered prices much higher than agency budget); *Sunshine Kids Serv. Supply Co.*, Comp. Gen. Dec. B-292141, 2003 CPD ¶ 119 (cancellation proper when only HUBZone competitor submitted unacceptable proposal); *Nutech Laundry & Textiles, Inc.*, Comp. Gen. Dec. B-291739, 2003 CPD ¶ 34 (small business price was much higher than government estimate); *D&K Constr. Co.*, Comp. Gen. Dec. B-281244.3, 99-2 CPD ¶ 57 (cancellation appropriate when protester's final proposal was noncompliant and other offeror's final proposal was submitted late); and *Rotary Furnishing Co.*, Comp. Gen. Dec. B-277704, 97-2 CPD ¶ 140 (cancellation appropriate when one offeror submitted a high price and the other offeror was nonresponsible). Cancellation and resolicitation is proper where the lowest price can not be determined to be reasonable, *Razorcom Teleph & Net, LLC v. United States*, 56 Fed. Cl. 140 (2003); *Process Control Techs. v. United States*, 53 Fed. Cl. 71 (2002), and *Interstate Rock Prods., Inc. v. United States*, 50 Fed. Cl. 349 (2001).

Another proper basis for cancellation is when the agency determines that there is another source for the product or service. See *Klinge Corp. v. United States*, 83 Fed. Cl. 773 (2008) (agency used Federal Supply Schedule after mistakenly concluding that protester's offer was noncompliant with the Trade Agreements Act); *Borenstein Group, Inc.*, Comp. Gen. Dec. B-309751, 2007 CPD ¶ 174 (agency found that existing contract could be used); *Management Solutions, L.C.*, Comp. Gen. Dec. B-298883, 2006 CPD ¶ 197 (agency found item was required to be procured from Federal Prison Industries); and *CAT Flight Servs., Inc.*, Comp. Gen. Dec. B-294186, 2004 CPD ¶ 178 (agency found existing contract). See also *FFTF Restoration Co. LLC v. United States*, 86 Fed. Cl. 226 (2009), where cancellation was found proper when the agency encountered delays in awarding the contract, faced budget limitations and concluded that the remaining work could be more effectively performed by the incumbent contractor. Although the plaintiff small business had expended several hundred thousand dollars competing for the procurement, the court noted that the SSA has broad discretion in arriving at a decision to cancel the procurement. See also *DCMS-ISA, Inc. v. United States*, 84 Fed. Cl. 501 (2008), permitting cancellation of a small business set aside procurement because none of the competitors had sufficient experience.

However, rejection of all offers and cancellation of the solicitation is a serious matter, particularly where substantial effort has been expended in the submission and evaluation of offers. Thus, rejection and cancellation would not be appropriate where concerns with the procurement could be addressed through negotiations, *A&W Flamar GmbH*, Comp. Gen. Dec. B-278486, 98-1 CPD ¶ 40. Cancellation was held to be improper where prices had been disclosed and the agency intended to move to a sealed bid procurement, *Rand & Jones Enters. Co.*, Comp. Gen. Dec. B-296483, 2005 CPD ¶ 142, where the winning small business was found nonresponsible without referring the matter to the Small Business Administration, *Phil Howry Co.*, Comp. Gen. Dec. B-291402.3, 2003 CPD ¶ 33, where a determination of excessive price was not warranted, *Nutech Laundry & Textile, Inc. v. United States*, 56 Fed. Cl. 588 (2003), and where the sole reason was to avoid contracting with a bidder, *Parcel 49C Ltd. Partnership v. United States*, 31 F.3d 1147 (Fed. Cir. 1994), and *126 Northpoint Plaza Ltd. Partnership v. United States*, 34 Fed. Cl. 105 (1995).

The decision to continue with the procurement will also be upheld if the SSA has a reasonable basis for continuing. See *XTRA Lease, Inc. v. United States*, 50 Fed. Cl. 612 (2001), where the agency decided to delay award and request offerors to extend proposals rather than recompete the procurement. See also *ACC Constr. Co.*, Comp. Gen. Dec. B-289167, 2002 CPD ¶ 21; and *Baltimore Gas & Elec.Co. v. United States*, 133 F. Supp. 2d 721 (D. Md. 2001). However, cancellation and resolicitation may be required where the cost realism or price analysis is not properly accomplished, *United Payors & United Providers Health Servs., Inc. v. United States*, 55 Fed. Cl. 323 (2003), and *Al Ghanim Combined Group Co. v. United States*, 56 Fed. Cl. 502 (2003). In *R&W Flammann GmbH v. United States*, 53 Fed. Cl. 647 (2002), the cancellation was required when prices were released to a competitor.

C. Allegations of Bias

Offerors are entitled to fair and impartial treatment in the source selection process and have a right to an unbiased determination of which source should receive the award. In a number of cases, charges have been made that the selection was based on favoritism. It has been very difficult to overcome a source selection decision through the allegation of bias of the SSA. In *Avtel Servs., Inc. v. United States*, 70 Fed. Cl. 173 (2005), the court held that a protester must overcome the presumption that government officials act in good faith in order to prove bias. In *Conax Fla. Corp. v. United States*, 641 F. Supp. 408 (D.D.C. 1986), *aff'd*, 824 F.2d 1124 (D.C. Cir. 1987), the court held that even if a protester establishes some degree of bias, it cannot win unless it can show that the source selection decision was unreasonable. In addition, in *Howard Cooper Corp. v. United States*, 763 F. Supp. 829, 841 (E.D. Va. 1991), the court, quoting *Arrowhead Metals, Ltd. v. United States*, 8 Cl. Ct. 703, 712 (1985), stated that claims of bias must be established by "well-nigh irrefragable proof." In *GE Gov't Servs., Inc. v. United States*, 788 F. Supp. 581 (D.D.C. 1992), a protester attempted to establish bias by providing statements about the SSA that demonstrated he was prejudiced against the protester. The protester also submitted evidence of sexual improprieties with a contractor employee. The court denied any relief because there was no proof that the source selection decision was affected by any alleged bias. It based its decision, to a large extent, on the fact that other agency officials that had participated in the procurement had also arrived at the decision that the selected contractor had offered the best value to the government.

The GAO also requires very clear evidence of bias with the result that there are almost no decisions finding bias. See *Crescent Helicopters*, Comp. Gen. Dec. B-283469.2, 99-2 CPD ¶ 107, stating:

> [B]ecause government officials are presumed to act in good faith, we do not attribute unfair or prejudicial motives to them on the basis of inference or supposition. *Ameriko Maintenance Co.*, B-253274, B-253274.2, Aug. 25, 1993, 93-2 CPD ¶ 121 at 5. Thus, where a protester alleges bias on the part of government officials, the protester must provide credible evidence demonstrating a bias against the protester or for the awardee and that the agency's bias translated into action that unfairly affected the protester's competitive position. *Advanced Sciences, Inc.*, B-259569.3, July 3, 1995, 95-2 CPD ¶ 52 at 17; *E.J. Richardson Assocs., Inc.*, B-250951, Mar. 1, 1993, 93-1 CPD ¶ 185 at 6.

For example, in *Centra Tech., Inc.*, Comp. Gen. Dec. B-274744, 97-1 CPD ¶ 35, the GAO found no evidence that the personal relationship between the director of the Johnson Space Center and the president of the awardee firm improperly influenced the SSA's decision because the SSA was in a subordinate position to the director. The GAO pointed out that although the director appointed the SSA, the director was not involved in the evaluation nor was there any evidence that the director had any contact with the source selection team during the course of the procurement. Similarly, in *Warvel Prods., Inc.*, Comp. Gen. Dec. B-281051.5, 99-2 CPD ¶ 13, the GAO found no conclusive evidence of bias from internal documents indicating that high agency officials believed that the ultimate winning contractor had submitted the best value proposal and would win a procurement that had been delayed by litigation. See also *TruLogic, Inc.*, Comp. Gen. Dec. B-297252.3, 2006 CPD ¶ 29 (failure to follow recommendation of evaluation panel not evidence of bias); *Millar Elevator Serv. Co.*, Comp. Gen. Dec. B-284870.5, 2001 CPD ¶ 34 (no proof of bias in letter written to a competitor by the project manager on a previous project, who was serving as an evaluator, suggesting that it could win this procurement by performing well on that project); and *J.A. Jones Grupo d Servicios, SA*, Comp. Gen. Dec. B-283234, 99-2 CPD ¶ 80 (no bias when contracting officer advised the incumbent contractor to make its oral presentation as if it were a new contractor and not rely on fact that it was the incumbent).

The GAO will not grant a protest because of bias unless it is demonstrated that the bias resulted in unfair treatment of the protester. See *ABIC, Ltd.*, Comp. Gen. Dec. B-286460, 2001 CPD ¶ 46, stating:

> [E]ven if bias were apparent, as indicated above, the ultimate inquiry is whether any bias translated into action that unfairly affected the protester's competitive position in the procurement. In this regard, the mere fact that evaluators or source selection personnel may have been involved adversarially with competing offerors in past procurements, without more, does not establish that the agency acted out of bias against an offeror. See, e.g., *Arctic Slope World Servs., Inc.*, B-284481, B-284481.2, Apr. 27, 2000, 2000 CPD ¶ 75 at 12-13 (evidence that contracting officer did not expeditiously handle protester's claims under incumbent contract and held negative views regarding the protester's past performance, did not indicate bias); *TEAM Support Servs., Inc.*, B-279379.2, June 22, 1998, 98-1 CPD ¶ 167 at 6 (project officer's disagreement with protester over contract administration matters under prior contract did not show that the officer was biased against protester during evaluation in current procurement); *Southern California Eng'g Co., Inc.*, B-232390, Oct. 25, 1988, 88-2 CPD ¶ 391 at 3 (alleged disparate actions in prior procurements are not evidence that agency failed to act in good faith in protested procurement).

In several instances the GAO has dealt with source selection decision effected by bias when the SSA admitted bias toward the Boeing Co. See *Lockheed Martin Aeronautics Co.*, Comp. Gen. Dec. B-295401, 2005 CPD ¶ 41 (protest sustained when biased SSA required technical ratings be changed and discussions to be reopened to favor Boeing); *Lockheed Martin Corp.*, Comp. Gen. Dec. B-295402, 2005 CPD ¶ 24 (protest sustained when biased senior procurement official deleted a requirement and its evaluation factor to favor Boeing). See also *Ball Aerospace & Techs. Corp.*, Comp. Gen. Dec. B-298522, 2006 CPD ¶ 113, rejecting a protest because it was not timely filed after the public admission of bias.

Although the GAO normally rejects allegations of bias, it has recommended, in the face of protests of unfair treatment of an offeror, that the agency appoint a new source selection team to reevaluate the proposals. See, for example, *Meridian Mgmt. Corp.*, Comp. Gen. Dec. B-281287.10, 2001 CPD ¶ 5 (unequal treatment of offerors "makes it advisable to convene a new source selection team"). Agencies have also appointed new personnel as a means of overcoming allegations of bias. See *U-Tech Servs. Corp.*, Comp. Gen. Dec. B-284183.3, 2002 CPD ¶ 78 (entirely new team); *RTF/TCI/EAI J.V.*, Comp. Gen. Dec. B-280422.3, 98-2 CPD ¶ 162 (new evaluators); and *EBA Eng'g, Inc.*, Comp. Gen. Dec. B-275818, 97-1 CPD ¶ 127 (chairman of evaluation panel).

II. SELECTION DECISION

Neither the procurement statutes nor the FAR specify detailed standards for the source selection decision. The statutes merely require that the award is to be made "to the responsible source whose proposal is most advantageous to the United States, considering only cost or price and the other factors included in the solicitation," 10 U.S.C. § 2305(b)(4)(c) and 41 U.S.C. § 253b(d)(3). The FAR adds little, simply stating that the selection decision "shall be based upon a comparative assessment of proposals against all source selection criteria in the solicitation," FAR 15.308. Thus, the rules governing the source selection decision have been derived from decisions in contract award controversies.

The elements of the source selection decision are the comparative assessment of the proposals against the evaluation criteria and the ultimate tradeoff decision if the lowest-price proposal is not rated most highly on the non-price factors. The SSA has broad discretion in making the tradeoff decision but must make the decision consistent with the description of the evaluation factors and evaluation scheme in the solicitation.

A. Consistency with Solicitation

Despite having a great deal of discretion in making the ultimate tradeoff decision, the SSA must follow the guidance in the RFP as to the way the selection decision will be made. However, the majority of decisions hold that there is no requirement that the SSA comply with the source selection plan adopted by the agency in formulating the procurement, *Manson Constr. Co. v. United States*, 79 Fed. Cl. 16 (2007); *Delta Dental of Cal.*, Comp. Gen. Dec. B-296307, 2005 CPD ¶ 152; *DTH Mgmt. JV*, Comp. Gen. Dec. B-283239, 99-2 CPD ¶ 68; *Allied Signal, Inc.*, Comp. Gen. Dec. B-272290, 96-2 CPD ¶ 121; *Johnson Controls World Servs., Inc.*, 72 Comp. Gen. 91 (B-249643.2), 93-1 CPD ¶ 72. Compare *Fort Carson Support Servs. v. United States*, 71 Fed. Cl. 571 (2006), holding that an agency's failure to adhere to its source selection plan made its source selection decision arbitrary.

1. Consideration of All Factors

The SSA must consider all evaluation factors as called for by the RFP and may not introduce new factors or subfactors into the process. See *Halter Marine, Inc.*, 73 Comp. Gen. 99 (B-255429), 94-1 CPD ¶ 161, sustaining a protest because the agency failed to consider a number of the enumerated evaluation factors. See also *Navistar Defense, LLC*, Comp. Gen. Dec. B-401865, 2009 CPD ¶ 258 (improper to fail to consider risk of lack of key tooling when RFP stated that existing production capability would be evaluated for risk); *Apptis, Inc.*, Comp. Gen. Dec. B-299457, 2008 CPD ¶ 49 (past performance improperly used to evaluate risk of technical solution); *ProTech Corp.*, Comp. Gen. Dec. B-294818, 2005 CPD ¶ 73 ("better-ments" not given consideration called for by RFP); *KIRA, Inc.*, Comp. Gen. Dec. B-287573, 2001 CPD ¶ 152 (improper to consider possible bankruptcy of subcontractor because financial ability was not a factor); *Courtland Mem'l Hosp.*, Comp. Gen. Dec. B-286890, 2001 CPD ¶ 48 (one factor not given the importance stated in the RFP and another factor ignored); *Wackenhut Int'l, Inc.*, Comp. Gen. Dec. B-286193, 2001 CPD ¶ 8 (improper to not consider full compensation plan when RFP called for comprehensive review of plans); *Meridian Mgmt. Corp*, Comp. Gen. Dec. B-285127, 2000 CPD ¶ 121 (improper to consider experience in performing specialized work when RFP gave no indication that such work was required); *Lloyd H. Kessler, Inc.*, Comp. Gen. Dec. B-284693, 2000 CPD ¶ 96 (improper to consider undesignated special experience that was treated as 40% of total nonprice evaluation); *AIU North Am., Inc.*, Comp. Gen. Dec. B-283743.2, 2000 CPD ¶ 39 (agency did not consider the "availability of corporate resources" factor); *Marquette Med. Sys., Inc.*, Comp. Gen. Dec. B-277827.5, 99-1 CPD ¶ 90 (improper to consider agency's internal savings for use of items when no indication of life cycle cost factor in RFP); and *FC Business Sys., Inc.*, Comp. Gen. Dec. B-278730, 98-2 CPD ¶ 9 (SSA ignored one of the evaluation factors).

The evaluation criteria in the RFP must be followed even if this produces an irrational result. See *Unified Indus., Inc.*, Comp. Gen. Dec. B-237868, 90-1 CPD ¶ 346, *recons. denied*, 90-2 CPD ¶ 120, where the agency was required to follow the RFP statement that all offerors would be evaluated using "the same number of hours" even though this meant evaluating the incumbent contractor on labor hours that it would not incur in performing the proposed contract. The GAO dismissed the Navy's argument that this would be irrational and unrealistic, holding that the rule requiring evaluation in accordance with the RFP was firm. Clearly, in this case the agency should have amended the evaluation criteria in the RFP when it found that the stated criteria produced an irrational result.

As discussed in Chapter 6, this rule does not prevent evaluation using any matters within the scope of the factors and subfactors set forth in the RFP, and there are numerous cases giving a broad interpretation of scope.

2. Follow Selection Scheme

The SSA must follow the decisional scheme described in the RFP. For example, if the RFP states that award will be made to the proposal with the best value based on a tradeoff analysis, the agency may not select the lowest-priced offer among those proposals that are technically acceptable, *Special Operations Group, Inc.*, Comp. Gen. Dec. B-287013, 2001 CPD ¶ 73; *Technical Support Serv., Inc.*, Comp. Gen. Dec. B-279665, 98-2 CPD ¶ 126; *Akal Security, Inc.*, Comp. Gen. Dec. B-261996, 96-1 CPD ¶ 33; *American Lawn Serv., Inc.*, Comp. Gen. Dec. B-267715, 95-2 CPD ¶ 278; and *DynCorp*, 71 Comp. Gen. 129 (B-245289), 91-2 CPD ¶ 575. Neither may an agency evaluate one of the non-price factors on a pass/fail basis when the RFP lists it as a factor to be used in making a tradeoff decision, *Helicopter Transport Servs., LLC*, Comp. Gen. Dec. B-400295, 2008 CPD ¶ 180. See also *Beacon Auto Parts*, Comp. Gen. Dec. B-287483, 2001 CPD ¶ 116, where a protest was sustained because the agency awarded to the offeror with the best technical score after determining that it had proposed a "fair and reasonable" price. The GAO concluded that no tradeoff had been made in these circumstances even though the source selection decision stated that the winning offeror's proposal was "considered the best value to the government based on past performance and technical capability."

In a tradeoff procurement, an SSA may not select the offeror with the best technical proposal from among only those offerors that submitted good prices. See *Electronic Design, Inc.*, Comp. Gen. Dec. B-279662.2, 98-2 CPD ¶ 69, where the agency chose the best technical offer from those that were priced within the agency budget. The GAO granted the protest, stating:

> An evaluation and source selection which fails to give significant consideration to cost or price is inconsistent with CICA and cannot serve as a reasonable basis for award. . . . Cost or price has not been accorded significant consideration if the agency's evaluation and source selection decision so minimizes the potential impact of cost or price as to make it a nominal evaluation factor. *Coastal Science and Eng'g, Inc.*, B-236041, Nov. 7, 1989, 89-2 CPD ¶ 436 at 3.

> Here, the agency states that price was considered only to determine whether a proposal was eligible for award. Proposals with prices greater than the budget were not eligible for, nor considered for award. Once three of the proposals were determined eligible for award based on price, the Navy states that it did not consider the relative differences in price among the proposals, and did not perform a price/technical tradeoff; rather, technical merit was the sole consideration in the selection decision. Thus, to the extent the agency did consider price in this procurement, it was solely to determine basic eligibility for award. Such a consideration of price is nominal; indeed, anything less would be to ignore price completely.

Conversely, an agency must include in its tradeoff analysis any lower-priced offeror that submits an acceptable proposal, *Finlen Complex, Inc.*, Comp. Gen. Dec. B-288280, 2001 CPD ¶ 167. See also *Coastal Environments, Inc.*, Comp. Gen. Dec. B-401889, 2009 CPD ¶ 261 (agency made improper tradeoff analysis between the two offerors that had been rated "good" on the non-price factors, omitting consideration of lower offerors that had been rated "acceptable"); *T-C Transcription, Inc.*, Comp. Gen. Dec. B-401470, 2009 CPD ¶ 172 (contracting officer improperly made tradeoff decision between offeror rated "excellent" on non-price factors and lowest priced offeror rated "good" – omitting other offerors rated "good"); *Universal Bldg. Maint., Inc.*, Comp. Gen. Dec. B-282456, 99-2 CPD ¶ 32 (contracting officer improperly considered only the four highest ranked technical proposals with the result that no tradeoff analysis was made of the protester's lowest price proposal) See also *A & D Fire Protection, Inc.*, Comp. Gen. Dec. B-288852, 2001 CPD ¶ 201, where a protest was sustained when the agency made no tradeoff analysis on proposals that were not "sufficiently technical capable to perform the project." The GAO found that the agency had determined that the protester's proposal was technically acceptable and therefore was required to include it in the tradeoff analysis. This rule does not apply to technically unacceptable proposals, which need not be subjected to a tradeoff analysis, *SBC Fed. Sys.*, Comp. Gen. Dec. B-283693, 2000 CPD ¶ 5.

When making multiple awards, an agency must perform a tradeoff analysis between all of the offerors with acceptable offers. Thus, it is improper to drop the highest rated technical proposal because it contains such a high price that it does not win against the lowest price proposal, *Beneco Enters., Inc.*, Comp. Gen. Dec. B-283154, 2000 CPD ¶ 69. The GAO reasoned that the protester might have won against the two other awardees that had higher prices even though they had higher technical evaluations than the lowest price proposal.

See also *Boeing Sikorsky Aircraft Support*, Comp. Gen. Dec. B-277263.2, 97-2 CPD ¶ 91, ruling that probable cost was a mandatory element of the source selection decision in a procurement involving a cost-reimbursement contract, and *Geo-Centers, Inc.*, Comp. Gen. Dec. B-276033, 97-1 CPD ¶ 182, holding that the offerors' costs to perform sample tasks had to be considered in making a source selection decision on a cost-reimbursement contract. In *MIS Farms, Inc.*, Comp. Gen. Dec. B-290599, 2002 CPD ¶ 174, the GAO held that it was improper to deduct points when an offeror met a mandatory minimum requirement.

B. Numerical Formulas

When the RFP states that the source selection decision will be based on a numerical formula, the source selection official must follow the formula in making the source selection decision. However, as discussed in Chapter 3, agencies rarely rely on such formulas but merely state that the decision will be based on a tradeoff analysis (best value analysis) or a low price technical acceptable determination. Thus, the degree of discretion in this area depends on the degree of specificity of this statement in the RFP.

1. Award on Basis of Highest Points

Although it is questionable whether completely mathematical scoring formulas will yield rational tradeoffs, agencies have been permitted to avoid this tradeoff analysis and use mathematical formulas to make the source selection decision. For example, when an agency uses a decisional scheme where all evaluation factors, including price, are point scored, it has been held proper to award to a higher-priced offeror without analyzing whether the difference in technical scores is worth the difference in price. See *Barnard Constr. Co.*, Comp. Gen. Dec. B-271644, 96-1 CPD ¶ 18, stating:

[T]o the extent [the protester] challenges the agency's tradeoff decision on the ground that the point difference between its and [the winning offeror's] proposals does not warrant the price premium, the protest is without merit. The formula stated in the RFP already accounted for both technical merit and price. Our Office has specifically recognized the propriety of using such a formula in selecting an offeror . . . . Because the awardee's proposal earned the highest combined price/technical score under the specified formula, the agency was not required to perform any further price/technical tradeoff analysis to justify the selection decision.

The use of a total point formula has been permitted when the RFP states that the offeror with the most points will be selected for award, *Stone & Webster Eng'g Corp.*, Comp. Gen. Dec. B-255286.2, 94-1 CPD ¶ 306; *Securigard, Inc.*, Comp. Gen. Dec. B-248584, 92-2 CPD ¶ 156, and where the RFP warned offerors that the agency might not use the formula but, instead, might award on the basis of a tradeoff decision, *Management Sys. Designers, Inc.*, Comp. Gen. Dec. B-244383.3, 91-2 CPD ¶ 310. Compare *National Toxicology Labs., Inc.*, Comp. Gen. Dec. B-281074.2, 99-1 CPD ¶ 5, where the SSA performed a thorough tradeoff analysis to ensure that the offeror with the most points actually was offering the best value.

While a total point formula must be used to make the source selection decision, this does not prevent the source selection official from rescoring the proposals. See *Harrison Sys., Ltd.*, 63 Comp. Gen. 379 (B-212675), 84-1 CPD ¶ 572, permitting award to the offeror with the second highest number of points because the SSA had implicitly rescored the technical proposal based on his determination that the offer gave the agency the best value.

This strict rule does not apply to procurements where total numerical scores are computed for each offeror but the RFP gives the SSA discretion to make a best value decision. In that case, the SSA must perform a normal tradeoff analysis assessing the strengths, weaknesses and risks of the proposals. See *Medical Dev. Int'l*, Comp. Gen. Dec. B-281484.2, 99-1 CPD ¶ 68, stating:

Not only do we disagree with [the protester's] argument that source selection officials must mechanically award contracts to the offeror whose proposal receives the highest number of points merely because the solicitation's evaluation approach scores both cost and technical factors, *Resource Management. Int'l, Inc.*, B-278108, Dec. 22, 1997, 98-1 CPD ¶ 29 at 4-5, but, as we recently held, we view mechanical reliance on a purely mathematical price/technical tradeoff methodology as improper. *Opti-Lite Optical*, B-281693, Mar. 22, 1999, 99-1 CPD ¶ at 5. Thus, we disagree with the protester's claim that the agency improperly abandoned a preestablished tradeoff scheme.[7]

[7] While we will not foreclose the possibility that an agency could structure a mathematical tradeoff formula in such a manner which encompasses a reasoned cost/technical tradeoff, id. at 5 n.4, we generally consider unwise such restrictions on the discretion of source selection officials to make tradeoff decisions. See *Harrison Sys. Ltd.*, [B-212675, May 25, 1984, 84-1

CPD ¶ 572] at 5. In any event, there is no evidence of any such formula in the solicitation here.

See also *Burchick Constr. Co.*, Comp. Gen. Dec. B-400342, 2008 CPD ¶ 2o3, stating that a mechanical comparison of point scores "is not a valid substitution for the qualitative assessment of the technical differences of the proposals or of the benefits associated with a proposal's additional cost." The same result was reached in *Midland Supply, Inc.*, Comp. Gen. Dec. B-298720, 2007 CPD ¶ 2; *Schaeffer Eye Center*, Comp. Gen. Dec. B-284268, 2000 CPD ¶ 53, and *Resource Mgmt. Int'l, Inc.*, Comp. Gen. Dec. B-278108, 98-1 CPD ¶ 29. Previously, the GAO affirmed a source selection decision in a procurement with this type of evaluation scheme where the SSA merely awarded to the offeror with the highest point score without making a tradeoff analysis, *Management Sys. Designers, Inc.*, Comp. Gen. Dec. B-244383.3, 91-2 CPD ¶ 310. See also *Halifax Sec. Servs., Inc.*, Comp. Gen. Dec. B-248584, 92-2 CPD ¶ 156; and *Tulane Univ.*, Comp. Gen. Dec. B-259912, 95-1 CPD ¶ 210.

2. *Dollars-Per-Point*

A dollars-per-point formula may also be used to make the source selection decision. See *Frank E. Basil, Inc.*, Comp. Gen. Dec. B-208133, 83-1 CPD ¶ 81, and *Shappell Gov't Housing, Inc.*, 55 Comp. Gen. 839 (B-183830), 76-1 CPD ¶ 161. See also *General Offshore Corp. — Riedel Co., a Joint Venture*, Comp. Gen. Dec. B-271144.2, 96-2 CPD ¶ 42, where the GAO approved of a source selection based on a variable ratio between technical scores and cost scores, stating:

> While evaluation point scores or adjectival ratings alone are not indicative of the relative value of proposals, and generally should be used as a guideline for intelligent decision-making, such that a selection decision should reflect the procuring agency's considered judgment of the significance of the difference in scores or ratings, *M.D. Oppenheim & Co., P.A.*, 70 Comp. Gen. 213 (1991), 91-1 CPD ¶ 98, we have consistently upheld source selection decisions which rely solely on mathematical cost/technical tradeoff methodologies where the application of such a methodology is consistent with the source selection scheme stated in the RFP. *See, e.g., Douglas County Aviation, Inc., et al.*, 64 Comp. Gen. 888 (1985), 85-2 CPD ¶ 345; *Tulane Univ.*, B-259912, Apr. 21, 1995, 95-1 CPD ¶ 210.

C. Requirement for Best Value Decision

In tradeoff procurements, the SSA is required to make the source selection decision by comparing the differences in non-price factors with the differences in prices. See FAR 15.308 calling for a "comparative assessment of proposals against all source selection criteria in the solicitation." In almost all cases this means that the scores assigned to the proposals should not be used, by themselves, to make the source selection decision. See *JW Assocs., Inc.*, Comp. Gen. Dec. B-275209, 96-2 CPD ¶ 18, stating:

While both adjectival ratings and point scores are useful as guides to decision-making, they generally are not controlling, but rather, must be supported by documentation of the relative differences between proposals, their weaknesses and risks, and the basis and reasons for the selection decision.

See *Allied Signal, Inc.*, Comp. Gen. Dec. B-272290, 96-2 CPD ¶ 121, stating that "a selection should reflect the procuring agency's considered judgment of whether significant technical differences exist in the proposals that identify a particular proposal as technically superior regardless of close scores or ratings among proposals." See also *Wackenhut Servs., Inc. v. United States*, 85 Fed. Cl. 273 (2008) (no tradeoff between price and non-price factors); *Shumaker Trucking & Excavating Contractors, Inc.*, Comp. Gen. Dec. B-290732, 2002 CPD ¶ 169 (higher point score on technical not justification for selection of higher price offer); *DevTech Sys., Inc.*, Comp. Gen. Dec. B-284879, 2000 CPD ¶ 200 (based on detailed analysis, 6% higher technical score does not indicate superior technical proposal). In *Computer Tech. Servs., Inc.*, Comp. Gen. Dec. B-271435, 96-1 CPD ¶ 283, the GAO approved the SSA's probing of the evaluation team to determine the significance of differences in point scores, stating:

Selection officials must decide whether the point scores show technical superiority and what that difference may mean in terms of contract performance. *See Grey Advertising, Inc.*, 55 Comp. Gen. 1111 (1976) 76-1 CPD ¶ 325.

* * *

Source selection officials in appropriate circumstances properly may conclude that a numerical scoring advantage based primarily on incumbency does not indicate an actual technical superiority that would warrant paying a higher price, *Sparta, Inc.*, B-228216, Jan. 15, 1988, 88-1 CPD ¶ 37; *see also Northern Virginia Serv. Corp.*, B-258036.2; B-258036.3, Jan. 23, 1995, 95-1 CPD ¶ 36, n. 5 (citing *NUS Corp.; The Austin Co.*, B-221863; B-221863.2, June 20, 1986, 86-1 CPD ¶ 574), and we see nothing unreasonable about the SSA's conclusion here. Accordingly, we think that the SSA's conclusion that [the protester's] numerical rating advantage did not reflect an actual technical superiority that would warrant paying its higher price also was a reasonable exercise of the SSA's discretion.

This logic was approved by the Federal Circuit in *Lockheed Missiles & Space Co. v. Bentsen*, 4 F.3d 955 (Fed. Cir. 1993), where the court stated at 960:

Neither the FAR nor the broad language of the RFP requires that evaluation points be proportional to cost. Accordingly, a proposal which is one point better than another but costs millions of dollars more may be selected if the agency can demonstrate within a reasonable certainty that the added value of the proposal is worth the higher price. Here, as we have already noted, the [agency] tradeoff analysis revealed that the dollar value of the two technical subfactors together with the value of the nonquantified discriminators justified the additional price to the [winning offeror's] proposal.

Accord, *Grumman Data Sys. v. Dalton*, 88 F.3d 990 (Fed. Cir. 1996). Thus, the selection will be upheld so long as there is a coherent and reasonable explanation for the selection, *Latecoere Int'l, Inc. v. Dep't of the Navy*, 19 F.3d 1342 (11th Cir. 1994).

1. Improper Reliance on Scores

Since the tradeoff decision must be made on the basis of the relative strengths, weaknesses and risks of the proposals, a bare comparison of point scores will not demonstrate that the agency has made a rational source selection decision. See *Shumaker Trucking & Excavating Contractors, Inc.*, Comp. Gen. Dec. B-290732, 2002 CPD ¶ 169, where the source selection decision stated:

> It was the recommendation of the technical evaluation board that the URS Group has presented the best value based on its overall technical evaluation and price. It received the highest technical evaluation, scoring 134 points, verses 93 points for Shumaker Trucking. This represents a technical difference of 44 percent (134/93=1.44). Also the difference on item 3, which is the technical approach to perform the work, the difference was even greater, being 20 points for Shumaker Trucking and 43 points for URS. This represents over 100 percent difference in this important aspect.

> The URS Group's bid, while being below the Government Estimate, is within 2 percent. The URS Group was selected for recommendation of award as they offer the best overall value to the Government. This is based on their technical score and the price being fair and reasonable. While they are somewhat higher than the second rated firm (Shumaker Trucking) the Technical Evaluation Board and the Contracting Officer felt the difference in cost of $395,739.05 is justified based on the superior scoring on past performance and technical approach provided in their proposal.

The GAO sustained the protest, stating:

> The record contains no evidence that the agency compared the advantages of the awardee's proposal to those of Shumaker's proposal, or considered why any advantages of the awardee's proposal were worth the approximately $400,000 higher price. As we have previously stated, point scores are but guides to intelligent decision making. *Ready Transp., Inc.*, B-285283.3, B-285283.4, May 8, 2001, 2001 CPD ¶ 90 at 12. In this case the [agency's] tradeoff is inadequate because its mechanical comparison of the offerors' point scores was not a valid substitute for a qualitative assessment of the technical differences between the offers from URS and Shumaker, so as to determine whether URS's technical superiority justified the price premium involved.

There are several GAO decisions finding a source selection unreasonable because it was based on a "mechanical comparison" of scores. See *Midland Supply, Inc.*, Comp. Gen. Dec. B-298720, 2007 CPD ¶ 2 (decision based on total points without any tradeoff analysis); *Johnson Controls World Servs., Inc.*, Comp. Gen.

Dec. B-289942, 2002 CPD ¶ 88 (decision based solely on number of "outstanding" and "highly satisfactory" ratings); *Opti-Lite Optical*, Comp. Gen. Dec. B-281693, 99-1 CPD ¶ 61 (decision based solely on point scores for technical and price when RFP did not state award would be made to offeror with most points); and *Teltara Inc.*, Comp. Gen. Dec. B-280922, 98-2 CPD ¶ 124 (decision based on percentage differences in price and technical scores). In *Wackenhut Servs., Inc.*, Comp. Gen. Dec. B-400240, 2008 CPD ¶ 184, the protester argued that its proposal was superior because it received more "strengths" than the winning offeror. The GAO denied the protest concluding that the protester was asking for a "mathematical or mechanical consideration" of the scores which was not the correct way to make the source selection decision. The Court of Federal Claims reached the opposite conclusion in *Wackenhut Servs., Inc. v. United States*, 85 Fed. Cl. 273 (2008), concluding that the source evaluation board's increase of point scores was arbitrary because it was not adequately justified. This may indicate that the court is more willing to grant relief when there are disparities in scoring – even though the scores are not the ultimate basis for the source selection decision.

2. *General Statements*

General statements as to the merits of the various proposals are also insufficient to demonstrate that a satisfactory tradeoff analysis has been made. See *Serco, Inc. v. United States*, 81 Fed. Cl. 463 (2008), stating at 496-97:

> [FAR 15.308] requires the agency to make a business judgment as to whether the higher price of an offer is worth the technical benefits its acceptance will afford. *See, e.g., TRW, Inc.*, 98 F.3d at 1327; *Dismas Charities, Inc.*, 61 Fed. Cl. at 203. Doing this, the decisional law demonstrates, obliges the agency to do more than simply parrot back the strengths and weaknesses of the competing proposals - rather, the agency must dig deeper and determine whether the relative strengths and weaknesses of the competing proposals are such that it is worth paying a higher price. Second, in performing the tradeoff analysis, the agency need neither assign an exact dollar value to the worth associated with the technical benefits of a contract nor otherwise quantify the non-cost factors. FAR § 15.308 ("the documentation need not quantify the tradeoffs that led to the decision"); *Widnall v. B3H Corp.*, 75 F.3d 1577, 1580 (Fed. Cir. 1996). But, this is not to say that the magnitude of the price differential between the two offers is irrelevant - logic suggests that as that magnitude increases, the relative benefits yielded by the higher-priced offer must also increase. *See Beneco Enters., Inc.*, 2000 CPD ¶ 69 at 5 (1999). To conclude otherwise, threatens to "minimize[] the potential impact of price" and, in particular, to make "a nominal technical advantage essentially determinative, irrespective of an overwhelming price premium." *Coastal Sci. and Eng'g, Inc.*, 89-2 CPD ¶ 436 at 2 (1989); *see also Lockheed Missiles & Space Co.*, 4 F.3d at 959-60. Finally - and many cases turn on this point - the agency is compelled by the FAR to document its reasons for choosing the higher-priced offer. Conclusory statements, devoid of any substantive content, have been held to fall short of this requirement, threatening to turn the tradeoff process into an empty exercise. Indeed, apart from the regulations, generalized statements that fail to reveal the agency's tradeoff calculus deprive this

court of any basis upon which to review the award decisions. *See Johnson Controls World Servs.*, 2002 CPD ¶ 88 at 6; *Satellite Servs., Inc.*, 2001 CPD ¶ 30 at 9-11; *Si-Nor, Inc.*, 2000 CPD ¶ 159 at 3 (1999).

See also *Blue Rock Structures, Inc.*, Comp. Gen. Dec. B-293134, 2004 CPD ¶ 63, sustaining a protest where the source selection decision merely concluded that the protester's higher rated proposal was essentially equal to the winning proposals without any discussion or analysis of the differences in the proposals. The GAO stated:

> A tradeoff analysis that fails to furnish any explanation as to why a higher-rated proposal does not in fact offer technical advantages or why those technical advantages are not worth a price premium does not satisfy the requirement for a documented tradeoff rationale, particularly where, as here, price is secondary to technical considerations under the RFP's evaluation scheme.

See also *LIS, Inc.*, Comp. Gen. Dec. B-400646.2, 2010 CPD ¶ 5 (general statement that selected offeror addressed all agency concerns without any analysis of strength, weaknesses or risks in proposals); *Systems Research & Applications Corp.*, Comp. Gen. Dec. B-299818, 2008CPD ¶ 28 (no qualitative assessment of strengths of competing proposals to satisfy agency requirements using different approaches); *Preferred Sys. Solutions, Inc.*, Comp. Gen. Dec. B-292322, 2003 CPD ¶ 166 (general statement that the proposals had "nearly equivalent ratings in non-cost areas" inadequate explanation of why protester's highly rated proposal was not worth its higher costs and prices); *Johnson Controls World Servs., Inc.*, Comp. Gen. Dec. B-289942, 2002 CPD ¶ 88 (general statement that higher scored proposal contained "no discernible benefits" inadequate demonstration of tradeoff analysis); *Si-Nor, Inc.*, Comp. Gen. Dec. B-282064, 2000 CPD ¶ 159 (bare statement that better past performance was worth over 10% more); *Lloyd H. Kessler, Inc.*, Comp. Gen. Dec. B-284693, 2000 CPD ¶ 96 (mere statement that "concerns arising from reports of adverse past performance" justified paying a higher cost); *Beneco Enters., Inc.*, Comp. Gen. Dec. B-283154, 2000 CPD ¶ 69 (statement that "the benefits and advantages" of the protester's higher-rated technical proposal did not justify "payment of the significant additional price" and is not "in the best interest of the Government" insufficient proof of rational tradeoff analysis); and *TRW, Inc.*, 68 Comp. Gen. 511 (B-234558), 89-1 CPD ¶ 584 ("Monte Carlo" risk analysis, computing potential costs of improving proposal with low ratings not a demonstration that tradeoff analysis considered differences in evaluations).

3. Determinations of Equality

There are a large number of cases where the SSA exercises discretion by ignoring differences in technical scoring by evaluators and determining that the technical merit of competing offers is relatively equal, thus allowing contracts to be awarded to the lower-cost offeror. In *Verify, Inc.*, 71 Comp. Gen. 158 (B-244401.2), 92-1 CPD ¶ 107, for example, the contracting personnel and evaluators agreed that the original technical scores given to Verify were an overstatement of merit and that rescoring was necessary to achieve accuracy. The final score given by the contracting officer was actually lower than the original score and supported a finding of technical equality between Verify and the lower cost awardee. Similarly, in *Resource Mgmt. Int'l, Inc.*, Comp. Gen. Dec. B-278108, 98-1 CPD ¶ 29, the SSA made a careful assessment of the evaluations and determined that the slightly higher technical score of the protester was not significantly different from that of a lower-priced offeror.

In most cases such determinations of equality are made without explicitly re-scoring the proposals. For example, in *Jack Faucett Assocs. — Request for Recons.*, Comp. Gen. Dec. B-233224.2, 89-1 CPD ¶ 551, the contracting officer properly awarded the contract to the low-priced offeror after concluding that Faucett's high-er-price offer, with a technical score of 8.63 out of 10 points, was substantially equal to the lower-priced offeror's technical score of 8.22. See also *RONCO Consulting Corp.*, Comp. Gen. Dec. B-280113, 98-2 CPD ¶ 41 (technical evaluation committee advised the contracting officer that it had no preference among three offerors with different technical scores); *EBA Eng'g, Inc.*, Comp. Gen. Dec. B-275818, 97-1 CPD ¶ 127 (SSA determined that the technical proposals were basically equal even though the source selection panel rated the protester higher on every evaluation factor); *LTR Training Sys., Inc.*, Comp. Gen. Dec. B-274996, 97-1 CPD ¶ 71 (contracting officer found the proposals technically equal although the evaluators had scored the protester's proposal substantially higher); *Juarez & Assocs., Inc.*, Comp. Gen. Dec. B-265950.2, 96-1 CPD ¶ 152 (contracting officer found the proposals technically equal when the evaluators had scored the protester's proposal somewhat higher); *General Offshore Corp.*, Comp. Gen. Dec. B-246824, 92-1 CPD ¶ 335 (contracting officer properly found that a 9% higher technical score did not represent any actual technical superiority and awarded to the lower-cost offeror); and *Systems Integrated*, Comp. Gen. Dec. B-225055, 87-1 CPD ¶ 114 (low-priced awardee's technical score of 66.7 out of 80 points was properly considered by the contracting officer to be equal to the 68.1 technical score of the higher-priced offer).

Such a determination of equality has also been supported in a case where the RFP called for precise numerical scores for technical and cost factors and stated that award would be made to the offeror with the highest number of points. The GAO stated that the source selection official would not have been permitted to alter the cost/technical tradeoff announced in the RFP but was entitled to rescore the propos-als by determining that the technical proposals were equal, *Harrison Sys., Ltd.*, 63 Comp. Gen. 379 (B-212675), 84-1 CPD ¶ 572. See also *Crowley Maritime Salvage*, Comp. Gen. Dec. B-234555, 89-1 CPD ¶ 555 (award to lower point total permis-sible where contracting officer determined that a 14.4% difference in technical score was not significant).

The GAO has permitted determinations of equality even though the technical fac-tors are weighted more heavily than cost, *E.J. Richardson Assocs., Inc.*, Comp. Gen. Dec. B-250951, 93-1 CPD ¶ 185 (technical scores of 93.3 and 90.0 found substantially equal when technical factor "slightly more important" than cost); *WB, Inc.*, Comp. Gen.

Dec. B-250954, 93-1 CPD ¶ 173 (technical scores of 88 and 87 found essentially equal when technical factor was "primary" and price/cost was "least important"); *Systems Research Corp.*, Comp. Gen. Dec. B-237008, 90-1 CPD ¶ 106 (technical scores of 48.15 and 54.63 found equal where technical factors had weight of 60%); *DDL Omni Eng'g*, Comp. Gen. Dec. B-220075, 85-2 CPD ¶ 684 (technical scores of 6.61 and 6.96 found equal where the technical score was "of paramount importance" but variable).

A finding of equality of technical scores is frequently upheld where technical evaluators can give no cogent reasons explaining the technical point differential between two proposals. This was permitted in *DLM&A, Inc. v. United States*, 6 Cl. Ct. 329 (1984), where the selection official determined on this basis that the proposals were "substantially equal" and, therefore, awarded to the low cost proposal.

Determinations of equality will be overturned if they are not supported by reasoned analysis. See, for example, *Radiation Oncology Group of WNY, PC*, Comp. Gen. Dec. B-310354.2, 2009 CPD ¶ 136 (no support for contracting officer's conclusion that offerors with different point scores were equal); *DynCorp*, Comp. Gen. Dec. B-232999, 89-1 CPD ¶ 152 (no rational explanation for ignoring evaluators' concerns); *University Found., Cal. State Univ., Chico*, Comp. Gen. Dec. B-200608, 81-1 CPD ¶ 54 (no indication given as to why the evaluation point scores were not followed in awarding the contract). See also *Tracor Jitco, Inc.*, 54 Comp. Gen. 896 (B-182213), 75-1 CPD ¶ 253, where the source selection was based on the conclusion of one evaluator that the proposals were technically equal, but no reasoning was advanced to support the conclusion and it conflicted with the factually supported views of two other evaluators and the technical evaluation committee. The selection decision was later found to be supportable, after a review of the selection process by the procuring agency showed that the evaluator had judged the proposals technically equal on the basis of additional information from the awardee that cleared up deficiencies, *Tracor Jitco, Inc.*, 55 Comp. Gen. 499 (B-182213), 75-2 CPD ¶ 344.

The selection official is not required to find the proposals equal when the point differential is small. See *Super Teams Operating Co.*, Comp. Gen. Dec. B-260100, 95-1 CPD ¶ 246, where the protester received a technical score of 83.3, the awardee received a score of 86.7, and a third (high-cost) offeror received a technical score of 91.1. The source selection official considered the 86.7 and 91.1 scores to be technically equal. The protester argued that if a difference of 4.4 points makes two proposals technically equal, the smaller difference of 2.9 points must make its proposal equal to the awardee's technical proposal. The GAO denied the protest, stating that "closeness of point scores does not necessarily indicate that proposals are essentially equal." The source selection official determined that there were significant differences in the technical merit between the proposals and this difference was reflected in the narrative summaries. See also *Bell & Howell Corp.*, Comp. Gen. Dec. B-196165, 81-2 CPD ¶ 49, upholding the decision that close technical scores were not equal, stating "[t]he dispositive element in a case such as this is not the technical scores per se but the considered judgment of the procuring agency concerning the significance of that difference."

C. Impact of Statement of Relative Importance

In procurements where the source selection official is given discretion to select the offeror proposing the best value, the statement of relative importance in the RFP does not play a significant rule in the source selection decision. This is because the tradeoff between price/cost and non-price/cost factors made by the selection official must still be based on the established criteria and the ultimate decision will be based on an assessment of whether the difference in the non-price/cost factors is worth the difference in price. For example, if the RFP states that non-price factors are significantly more important than price, award would rationally be made to the low price offer when the difference in the non-price factors was small. Conversely, if the RFP states that price is significantly more important than the non-price factors, award would rationally be made to the a higher priced offer when there was a significant difference in the non-price factors. Thus, as illustrated below, whatever the statement of relative importance, a reasonable tradeoff between price/cost and the other factors is generally supported.

1. Non-Price/Cost More Important Than Price

If the RFP states that non-price/cost factors are more important than price, the SSA is permitted to select an offeror that has proposed a significantly higher price if the benefits in the non-price/cost factors can be identified. See *Comprehensive Health Servs., Inc.*, Comp. Gen. Dec. B-310553, 2008 CPD ¶ 9 (RFP stated that technical approach, management capability and past performance significantly more important than price); *Textron, Inc. v. United States*, 74 Fed. Cl. 277 (2006) (RFP stated that management, systems engineering, mission effectiveness, and support significantly more important than price in contract to design and manufacture boats); *Puglia Eng'g of Cal., Inc.*, Comp. Gen. Dec. B-297413, 2006 CPD ¶ 33 (RFP stated that five non-price factors were significantly more important than price); *Remington Arms Co.*, Comp. Gen. Dec. B-297374, 2006 CPD ¶ 32 (RFP stated that bid sample and technical proposal significantly more important than price); *Standard Communications, Inc.*, Comp. Gen. Dec. B-296972, 2005 CPD ¶ 200 (RFP stated that mission capability, past performance and risk significantly more important than price); *Chenega Tech. Products, LLC*, Comp. Gen. Dec. B-295451.5, 2005 CPD ¶ 123 (RFP stated that past performance significantly more important than price); *Continental RPVs*, Comp. Gen. Dec. B-292768.6, 2004 CPD ¶ 103 (RFP made non-price factors more important than price); *Information Network Sys., Inc.*, Comp. Gen. Dec. B-284854, 2000 CPD ¶ 104 (better prospect of workforce retention worth slightly higher probable cost); *Compania De Asesoria Y Comercio, S.A.*, Comp. Gen. Dec. B-278358, 98-1 CPD ¶ 26 (RFP stated that management was more important than either technical or quality control, which were of equal importance, and price was the least important); *EDG Eng'g of Texas, Inc.*, Comp. Gen. Dec. B-218540, 85-2 CPD ¶ 32 (RFP stated that primary emphasis would be placed on technical factors, a lesser degree of importance would be placed on the management/personnel area, and an even lesser degree on the cost/

price area); and *Fairchild Weston Sys., Inc.*, Comp. Gen. Dec. B-218470, 85-2 CPD ¶ 39 (RFP stated that technical proposals "were significantly more important" than cost proposals). In *Suddath Van Lines, Inc.*, Comp. Gen. Dec. B-274285.2, 97-1 CPD ¶ 204, the GAO affirmed a decision to award a contract for moving services to an offeror with higher technical ratings at a price 18% and 31% above the respective prices of the protesters. See also *Seedburo Equip. Co.*, Comp. Gen. Dec. B-278659, 98-1 CPD ¶ 65, where the SSA selected an offeror with prices 9% to 18% higher than those of an offeror whose technical proposal was slightly lower rated; and *Israel Aircraft Indus., Inc.*, Comp. Gen. Dec. B-274389, 97-1 CPD ¶ 41, where the SSA selected an offeror with higher technical scores and lower performance risk even though its price was approximately $4 million more than the protester's offer to perform for $23 million. The most striking decision of this type is *Lockheed Missile & Space Co. v. Dep't of the Treasury*, GSBCA 11776-P, 93-1 BCA ¶ 25,401, *aff'd*, 4 F.3d 995 (Fed. Cir. 1993), where the board affirmed the award to an offeror that had submitted a superior technical proposal at a price of $1.4 billion, which was more than $500 million higher than its next competitor. The board would not affirm the award until the agency had submitted a detailed analysis of the discriminators between the proposals — showing that the difference in technical merit was worth the difference in price by quantifying some of the major technical factors.

Award to the higher-priced offeror has been overturned in a few cases where the benefits could not be demonstrated or the evaluation was flawed. See *Sturm, Ruger & Co.*, Comp. Gen. Dec. B-250193, 93-1 CPD ¶ 42, where the GAO overturned a $1,366,550 award to an offeror receiving a technical score of 94 points when the protester had received a score of 89 points and had proposed a price of $768,012. The GAO rejected the agency's contention that price should only be considered when the technical scores were equal and held that in such a best value procurement, award to the higher-priced offer "should be supported by a specific, documented determination that the technical superiority of the higher-priced offer warrants the additional cost involved, even where, as here, cost is stated to be the least important factor." Similarly, in *System Dev. Corp.*, Comp. Gen. Dec. B-213726, 84-1 CPD ¶ 605, the GAO found an award to a technically higher-rated, higher-price firm to have been improper where the awardee's offer was scored only eight points higher than the protester's proposal (on a scale of 100 points), but the awardee's proposed price was more than 50% higher and the record contained no justification for paying a much greater cost for a proposal only slightly better in terms of quality. See also *ITT Fed. Servs. Int'l Corp.*, Comp. Gen. Dec. B-296783, 2007 CPD ¶ 43 (unreasonable evaluation made decision to pay higher price questionable); *YORK Bldg. Servs., Inc.*, Comp. Gen. Dec. B-296948.2, 2005 CPD ¶ 202 (flawed evaluation made decision to pay higher price questionable); *Spherix, Inc.*, Comp. Gen. Dec. B-294572.3, 2005 CPD ¶ 183 (failure to consider relative similarities and differences in the two proposals made decision to pay higher price questionable); *Beautify Prof. Servs. Corp.*, Comp. Gen. Dec. B-291954.3, 2003 CPD ¶ 178 (award to highest rated past performance without considering that it was 25% higher in price not proper); *CRAssocs., Inc.*, Comp. Gen. Dec. B-282075.2, 2000 CPD ¶ 63 (inadequate documentation and potential evaluation errors made decision to pay significantly higher costs questionable); *Ball Tech. Prods. Group*, Comp. Gen. Dec. B-224394, 86-2 CPD ¶ 465 (improper to award to offeror with "excellent" technical proposal when its price was 53% higher than another offeror with "acceptable" technical proposal). It appears that protests were sustained in these cases because the agency did not present detailed evaluations of the technical benefits that justified paying the higher prices.

Selection of a lower-priced proposal is justified if the SSA determines that the nonprice/cost benefits offered by the high priced offeror are not worth the higher cost. See, for example, *United Eng'rs & Constructors, Inc.*, Comp. Gen. Dec. B-240691, 90-2 CPD ¶ 490, where the GAO agreed with a decision to award to an offeror that was $11 million lower in probable cost even though a competitor had submitted a clearly superior technical and management proposal. The RFP had stated that management and technical factors were more important than cost, but that award would be made to the most advantageous proposal. The GAO stated:

> [E]ven if cost is the least important evaluation criterion, an agency may properly award to a lower-cost, lower-scored offeror if it determines that the cost premium involved in awarding to a higher-rated, higher-cost offeror is not justified given the acceptable level of technical competence available at the lower cost. *Carrier Joint Venture*, B-233702, Mar. 13, 1989, 89-1 CPD ¶ 268, *aff'd*, B-233702.2, June 23, 1989, 89-1 CPD ¶ 594. The determining element is not the difference in technical merit, per se, but the contracting agency's judgment concerning the significance of the difference. *Dayton T. Brown, Inc.*, B-229664, Mar. 30, 1988, 88-1 CPD ¶ 321. Cost/technical tradeoffs may be made, and the extent to which one may be sacrificed for the other is governed only by the test of rationality and consistency with the established evaluation criteria.

Similarly, in *Ecology & Env't, Inc.*, Comp. Gen. Dec. B-209516, 83-2 CPD ¶ 229, the GAO held that a selection official, finding a particular percentage differential in technical scores insignificant, was not compelled to find a lower percentage cost differential insignificant, stating: "Contracting agencies generally need a degree of discretion in weighing the significance of the relationship between technical scores and cost differentials, and reserve to themselves such discretion by not including rigid evaluation formulas in the RFP." See also *Karrar Sys. Corp.*, Comp. Gen. Dec. B-310661.3, 2008 CPD ¶ 55 (rational to award at significantly lower price when nonprice differential between offerors was small); *First Preston Housing Initiatives, LP*, Comp. Gen. Dec. B-293105.2, 2004 CPD ¶ 221 (award at lower price justified when non-price factors were evaluated as essentially equal); *Mechanical Equip. Co.*, Comp. Gen. Dec. B-292789.2, 2004 CPD ¶ 192 (rational to award at significantly lower price when either company could perform contract); *E.L. Hamm & Assocs., Inc.*, Comp. Gen. Dec. B-280766.5, 2000 CPD ¶ 13 (rational to award to lower cost because technical benefits not worth difference); *Randolph Eng'g Sunglasses*, Comp. Gen. Dec. B-280270, 98-2 CPD ¶ 39 (reasonable to award at lower price to offeror evaluated as "good" on past performance rather than to higher-priced offeror evaluated as "excellent"); *East/West Indus., Inc.*, Comp. Gen. Dec. B-278734.4, 98-1 CPD ¶ 143 (reasonable to award to low-priced proposal with medium risk rather than to the higher-priced proposal with low risk); *U.S. Tech. Corp.*, Comp. Gen. Dec. B-278584, 98-1 CPD ¶ 78 (reasonable to award to offeror with a lower price and "satisfactory" past performance rather than to offeror with "exceptional" past performance); *Research Triangle Inst.*, Comp. Gen. Dec. B-278254, 98-1 CPD ¶ 22 (rational to determine that the differences in technical merit were not worth the higher price of protester); *Crown Clothing Corp.*, Comp. Gen. Dec. B-277505.2, 97-2 CPD ¶ 127 (affirming award to low-price offeror because the difference in technical scores, even if the protest of an improper evaluation was sustained, would not be worth the difference in price); *PRC, Inc.*, Comp. Gen. Dec. B-274698.2, 97-1 CPD ¶ 115 (award to the lower-cost proposal reasonable even though protester's proposal was scored higher on all technical factors); *Creative Apparel Assocs.*, Comp. Gen. Dec. B-275139, 97-1 CPD ¶ 65 (award rational when SSA determined that slightly higher price was not worth the modest difference in technical rating); *Ares Corp.*, Comp. Gen. Dec. B-275321, 97-1 CPD ¶ 82 (award to lower-cost offeror reasonable when protester had a slightly higher technical rating); *ERC Envtl. & Energy Servs. Co.*, Comp. Gen. Dec. B-241549, 91-1 CPD ¶ 155 (award to low-cost proposal rational when the difference in price was significant and the difference in technical factors was relatively small); and *Wyle Lab., Inc.*, 69 Comp. Gen. 648 (B-239113), 90-2 CPD ¶ 107 (reasonable determination that the difference in technical merit not worth the difference in price).

Award to a lower-priced offeror will be overturned if the source selection official cannot state a reasonable basis for giving up the technical benefits offered by the higher-priced, technically superior offeror. For instance, in *Dewberry & Davis*, Comp. Gen. Dec. B-247116, 92-1 CPD ¶ 421, a protest was sustained because the agency did not provide justification of its selection of the lower-priced proposal where the RFP had stated that technical was more important than cost. The GAO stated that it would uphold such a decision only if the agency provided a "cogent rationale" in the documentation for such a decision. Similarly, in *PharmChem Lab., Inc.*, Comp. Gen. Dec. B-244385, 91-2 CPD ¶ 317, the GAO sustained a protest where the source selection official had determined two technical proposals equal and awarded to the low-cost offeror in the face of evaluations that indicated that the higher-cost offeror was clearly superior, reasoning that the small difference in cost savings was not worth the difference in technical merit and recommended award to the higher-cost, technically superior offeror. See also *Hattal & Assocs.*, 70 Comp. Gen. 632 (B-243357), 91-2 CPD ¶ 90, where an award was overturned because it was made to a lower-cost offeror when the two competitors had both been determined to be technically acceptable. The GAO stated at 637:

> When an RFP provides that the technical factors will be considered more important than cost, a procuring agency may not make its award decision as though the RFP provided for award to the lowest cost, technically acceptable offeror. *RCA Serv. Co.*, B-219406.2, Sept. 10, 1986, 86-2 CPD ¶ 278. It is improper for an agency to induce an offeror to prepare and submit a proposal emphasizing technical excellence, than fail to consider technical factors and award solely on

the basis of cost. Such action clearly disregards the RFP's evaluation criteria. . . . *Kempter-Rossman Int'l*, B-220772, Feb. 4, 1986, 86-1 CPD ¶ 127; *Applied Financial Analysis, Ltd.*, B-194388.2, Aug. 10, 1979, 79-2 CPD ¶ 113.

In some cases involving cost-reimbursement contracts, the GAO has stressed the "extremely strong justification" necessary to support award to a lower-cost proposal that is ranked lower in technical and management. For example, in *DLI Eng'g Corp.*, Comp. Gen. Dec. B-218335, 85-1 CPD ¶ 742, *recons. denied*, 65 Comp. Gen. 34 (B-218335.2), 85-2 CPD ¶ 468, the GAO indicated that, where the selection official does not rescore proposals or otherwise indicate that the technical point differential is not an accurate measure of the difference in technical quality of the proposals, primary emphasis may not be placed on cost in the selection decision when the RFP stated that cost was the least important criterion. The Navy justified selection of the lower-cost offeror by claiming that although the lower-cost proposal was technically inferior, the inferiority could be overcome by the application of additional contractor and government hours and also that the total government expenditure would still be less after these additional amounts were added to the awardee's costs. The GAO, however, found that the awardee would not be able to offer several unique technical features offered by the protester even with the additional hours, and thus, the selection was inconsistent with the RFP criteria. See also *RCA Serv. Co.*, Comp. Gen. Dec. B-219406.2, 86-2 CPD ¶ 278, where it was found improper to award to a lower-cost proposal with only an adequate technical rating where technical merit was the most important criteria. Similarly, in *AAA Eng'g & Drafting, Inc.*, Comp. Gen. Dec. B-202140, 81-2 CPD ¶ 16, the GAO upheld a protest where the agency recommended award to the low-cost offeror submitting the lowest rated technical proposal when the RFP stated that the evaluation criteria were listed in descending order of importance and cost was ranked third out of four evaluation factors. The GAO concluded that cost could not account for more than 20 to 25% of the total evaluation.

2. Price/Cost More Important Than Non-Price/Cost

When the RFP states that price is more important than the other factors, the SSA can award the contract to the offeror with the lowest price as long as the price advantage outweighs the technical advantage of higher-priced offerors, *GTE Hawaiian Tel. Co.*, Comp. Gen. Dec. B-276487.2, 97-2 CPD ¶ 21. See also *Geo-Seis Helicopters, Inc.*, Comp. Gen. Dec. B-299175, 2007 CPD ¶ 135 (rational to award at lower price when price was more important than past performance and difference in past performance was "exceptional" versus "neutral"); *MD Helicopters, Inc.*, Comp. Gen. Dec. B-298502, 2006 CPD ¶ 164 (rational to award at lower price when price was more important than non-price factors).

In this situation the SSA is also permitted to award the contract to an offeror with a higher price if the differences in technical and management merit are worth paying the higher costs. In *Frequency Eng'g Lab. Corp.*, Comp. Gen.

Dec. B-225606, 87-1 CPD ¶ 393, award at a price of $57.6 million was permitted when the protester had offered a price of $51.2 but had proposed to use less qualified personnel whom the agency evaluated as posing a much higher risk that performance would not be successfully accomplished. See also *Univ. of Kansas Medical Ctr.*, Comp. Gen. Dec. B-278400, 98-1 CPD ¶ 120 (award at significantly higher price justified by superior approach to quality management and more convenient locations for medical care); *Centex Constr. Co.*, Comp. Gen. Dec. B-238777, 90-1 CPD ¶ 566 (award to offeror with slightly higher price justified by strong technical rating); *Oklahoma Aerotronics, Inc.*, Comp. Gen. Dec. B-237705.2, 90-1 CPD ¶ 337 (award to an offeror with 2% higher price justified by the lower technical risk obtained); and *F.A.S. Sys. Corp.*, Comp. Gen. Dec. B-236344, 89-2 CPD ¶ 512 (award to offeror with $1.1 million higher price justified when detailed agency evaluation indicated significantly stronger technical ability).

3. Price and Non-Price Equal

When the price factor and the non-price factors are stated to be equal, the source selection official has full discretion to make a best value source selection decision. In 52 Comp. Gen. 686 (B-176763) (1973), the GAO held that under the RFP, cost could be deemed equally as important as technical merit and that the agency had discretion to assess cost ceilings and cost realism considerations in determining which offer was most advantageous to the government. In *440 East 62nd Street Co.*, Comp. Gen. Dec. B-276058.2, 98-1 CPD ¶ 73, and *EER Sys. Corp.*, 69 Comp. Gen. 207 (B-237054), 90-1 CPD ¶ 123, selection decisions for higher-priced, higher-technically rated offerors were affirmed because they provided the best value to the government. The protester's offer was found to represent inferior personnel and quality of work and was judged to be not worth the monetary difference. See also *J.C.N. Constr. Co.*, Comp. Gen. Dec. B-293063, 2004 CPD ¶ 12 (award at higher price because of higher technical rating); *Kay & Assocs., Inc.*, Comp. Gen. Dec. B-291269, 2003 CPD ¶ 12 (award at higher price because of better past performance); *Dawco Constr., Inc.*, Comp. Gen. Dec. B-278048.2, 98-1 CPD ¶ 32 (award at "somewhat" higher price to offeror with a much higher-rated proposal); *SWR, Inc.*, Comp. Gen. Dec. B-276878, 97-2 CPD ¶ 34 (award to a higher-priced offer to obtain better past performance); and *Martech USA, Inc.*, Comp. Gen. Dec. B-250284.2, 93-1 CPD ¶ 110 (award at 15% higher price when protester had been rated lowest technically because of poor past performance). However, the tradeoff that is made between cost and technical/management proposals must still be justified as being rational. See, for example, *Kempter-Rossman Int'l*, Comp. Gen. Dec. B-220772, 86-1 CPD ¶ 127, finding it unreasonable to award to a 2% lower-priced offer when the competing offer had a 25% technical superiority and the RFP gave equal weight to the price and technical factors. Similarly, in *Mechanical Contractors, S.A.*, Comp. Gen. Dec. B-277916, 97-2 CPD ¶ 121, a protest was sustained when the GAO found multiple errors in the evaluation that was used by the SSA to make the selection decision.

D. Documentation

Agencies must prepare documentation demonstrating that the source selection decision was reasonable and consistent with the solicitation. Prior to the FAR rewrite, the FAR required only fragmentary documentation to support selection decisions, with FAR 15.608(a)(3) requiring some documentation of technical evaluations and FAR 15.612(d)(2) requiring documentation of source selection decisions on "formal source selections." However, the GAO required agencies to submit documentation when awards were protested. See *Quality Elevator Co.*, Comp. Gen. Dec. B-276750, 97-2 CPD ¶ 28, stating:

> While judgments concerning the evaluation of proposals are by their nature subjective, they must be reasonable; such judgments must bear a rational relationship to the announced criteria upon which proposals were to be evaluated. *Management Technology, Inc.*, B-257269.2, Nov. 8, 1994, 95-1 CPD ¶ 248 at 6–7. Implicit in the foregoing is that the rationale for these judgments must be documented in sufficient detail to show that they are not arbitrary and that there was a reasonable basis for the selection decision. *Id.* Federal Acquisition Regulation (FAR) 15.608(a)(3) requires documentation to support the evaluation of proposals, including the basis for evaluation and an analysis of the technically acceptable and unacceptable proposals, an assessment of each offeror's ability to accomplish the technical requirement, and a summary of findings. FAR 15.612(d)(2) requires supporting documentation for the source selection decision, stating the basis and reasons for the decision and showing the relative differences among proposals and their strengths, weaknesses, and risks in terms of the evaluation criteria. Numerical point scores, while useful as guides to decision-making, do not of themselves supply the basis and reason for the award decision. *U.S. Defense Sys., Inc.*, B-245563, Jan. 17, 1992, 92-1 CPD ¶ 89 at 3; *S&M Property Management*, B-243051, June 28, 1991, 91-1 CPD ¶ 615 at 4. Where there is inadequate supporting documentation for an award decision, we cannot conclude that the agency had a reasonable basis for the decision. *Hattal & Assocs.*, 70 Comp. Gen. 632, 637 (1991), 91-2 CPD ¶ 90 at 7.

The FAR rewrite adopted a more rigorous documentation requirement following the guidance established by the GAO. See FAR 15.308, stating the following requirement:

> The source selection decision shall be documented, and the documentation shall include the rationale for any business judgments and tradeoffs made or relied on by the SSA, including benefits associated with additional costs. Although the rationale for the selection decision must be documented, that documentation need not quantify the tradeoffs that led to the decision.

See also FAR 15.305(a), which includes the following statement:

> (3) *Technical evaluation.* When tradeoffs are performed (see 15.101-1), the source selection records shall include —

(i) An assessment of each offeror's ability to accomplish the technical requirements; and

(ii) A summary, matrix, or quantitative ranking, along with appropriate supporting narrative, of each technical proposal using the evaluation factors.

The documentation need not be contained in the ultimate award decision, but it must be present in the record. See *All Star-Cabaco Enter. (JV)*, Comp. Gen. Dec. B-290133, 2002 CPD ¶ 127, and *Allied Tech. Group, Inc.*, Comp. Gen. Dec. B-282739, 99-2 CPD ¶ 45, where the SSA accepted the recommendation of the Source Selection Evaluation Board, and the qualitative tradeoff documentation in the Board's recommendation was held to be sufficient. However, merely accepting evaluators' recommendations that do not contain such tradeoff analyses is insufficient, *Universal Bld'g Maint., Inc.*, Comp. Gen. Dec. B-282456, 99-2 CPD ¶ 32.

1. Rationale for Business Judgment

If an agency's documentation does not demonstrate that the source selection decision is rational, a protest will be granted. See *Matrix Int'l Logistics, Inc.*, Comp. Gen. Dec. B-272388.2, 97-2 CPD ¶ 89, where the determination of the SSA that two technical proposals were "essentially equal" was not supported in the documentation submitted by the agency. The GAO sustained the protest, stating:

An agency which fails to adequately document its evaluation of proposals or [the] source selection decision bears the risk that its determinations will be considered unsupported, and absent such support, our Office may be unable to determine whether the agency had a reasonable basis for its determinations.

See also *Navistar Defense, LLC*, Comp. Gen. Dec. B-401865, 2009 CPD ¶ 258 (no documentation to support rating of "good" past performance (rather than "excellent") which agency stated was based on negative comments that had been inadvertently destroyed); *Radiation Oncology Group of WNY, PC*, Comp. Gen. Dec. B-310354.2, 2009 CPD ¶ 136 (no documentation showing that contracting officer considered strengths and weaknesses of competing proposals – merely a statement that offerors with different point scores were equal); *ACCESS Sys., Inc.*, Comp. Gen. Dec. B-400623.3, 2009 CPD ¶ 56 (no documentation showing that agency made meaningful tradeoff analysis); *AT&T Corp.*, Comp. Gen. Dec. B-299542.3, 2008 CPD ¶ 65 (no documentation showing how SSA arrived at different conclusion than evaluators regarding the impact of overstaffing); *Apptis, Inc.*, Comp. Gen. Dec. B-299457, 2008 CPD ¶ 49 (no documentation to support findings regarding demonstration of proposed solution); *Systems Research & Applications Corp.*, Comp. Gen. Dec. B-299818, 2008 CPD ¶ 28 (no documentation showing that SSA made a qualitative assessment of strengths of competing proposals to satisfy agency requirements using different approaches); *Panacea Consulting, Inc.*, Comp. Gen. Dec. B-299307.4, 2007 CPD ¶ 141 (no documentation showing that agency made meaningful tradeoff analysis – only numerical scores); *Bank of Am.*, Comp. Gen. Dec. B-287608, 2001 CPD ¶ 137 (documents contained multiple errors and reflected various mistakes and/or omissions); *Beacon Auto Parts*, Comp. Gen. Dec. B-287483, 2001 CPD ¶ 116 (documentation contained no indication that a cost/technical tradeoff had been made); *Cortland Mem'l Hosp.*, Comp. Gen. Dec. B-286890, 2001 CPD ¶ 48 (documentation did not show that agency followed evaluation criteria); *J&J Maint., Inc.*, Comp. Gen. Dec. B-284708.2, 2000 CPD ¶ 106 (no adequate documentation of oral presentation or strengths, weaknesses or risks of proposals); *Opti-Lite Optical*, Comp. Gen. Dec. B-281693, 99-1 CPD ¶ 61 (point scores alone inadequate to explain tradeoff decisions); *MCR Fed., Inc.*, Comp. Gen. Dec. B-280969, 99-1 CPD ¶ 8 (no documentation showing a comparison of the proposals or a discussion of their technical differences); *J.A. Jones Mgmt. Servs., Inc.*, Comp. Gen. Dec. B-276864, 97-2 CPD ¶ 47 (inadequate documentation to support decision when agency submitted "point scores and cursory narratives" with no "consistent, reasonable and accurate evaluation scoring" nor "supporting narrative documentation"); *J.W. Assocs., Inc.*, Comp. Gen. Dec. B-275209, 97-1 CPD ¶ 57 (point scores and one-paragraph "evaluation summary" inadequate to explain the evaluation of technical proposals); *Cygnus Corp.*, Comp. Gen. Dec. B-275181, 97-1 CPD ¶ 63 (documentation contained only point scores for technical factors with no explanation of basis for scores); *TRW, Inc.*, Comp. Gen. Dec. B-260788.2, 96-1 CPD ¶ 11 (no explanation of why award was made to higher-priced offeror when technical proposals appear to be almost the same); *Engineering & Computation, Inc.*, Comp. Gen. Dec. B-261658, 95-2 CPD ¶ 176 (no explanation of agency analysis that protester's proposal posed risks); *Arco Mgmt. of Wash., D.C., Inc.*, 72 Comp. Gen. 258 (B-248653), 92-2 CPD ¶ 173 (no documentation explaining rescoring of BAFOs); and *U.S. Defense Sys., Inc.*, Comp. Gen. Dec. B-245563, 92-1 CPD ¶ 89 (final technical scores, accompanied by no narrative explanation of any kind, inadequate to justify selection decision).

The GAO has not demanded that the documentation cover every element of the selection decision as long as it supports the overall rationale used by the SSA. See *SEAIR Transport Servs., Inc.*, Comp. Gen. Dec. B-274436, 96-2 CPD ¶ 224, stating:

> SEAIR challenges the agency's documentation of its award decision, characterizing the record as "devoid of any real rationale for the decision to award the contract to EAST," and alleging that the source selection decision does not address the relative differences between SEAIR's and EAST's proposals. While the selection official's judgment must be documented in sufficient detail to show it is not arbitrary, *KMS Fusion, Inc.*, B-242529, May 8, 1991, 91-1 CPD ¶ 447, a source selection official's failure to specifically discuss every detail regarding the relative merit of the proposals in the selection decision document does not affect the validity of the decision if the record shows that the agency's award decision was reasonable. See *McShade Gov't Contracting Servs.*, B-232977, Feb. 6, 1989, 89-1 CPD ¶ 118. Here, the record documents the evaluation process, the color coding, and the risk assessments, concluding with the agency's determination that SEAIR's and EAST's proposals were essentially equal technically. The source

selection document refers to this determination and concludes that, taking price into consideration, EAST's lower-priced offer represented the best overall value to the government. We see no basis to object to the source selection document, which very clearly sets forth the basis for the agency's award decision.

The documentation need not comply literally with the requirement of the FAR that it contain a statement of the "strengths, weaknesses and risks" as long as it explains the selection decision. See *Matrix Int'l Logistics, Inc.,* Comp. Gen. Dec. B-272388.2, 97-2 CPD ¶ 89, stating:

> The form of the documentation is not important if it supports the source selection decision. Thus, sketches of proposed designs were adequate documentation in lieu of narratives where aesthetics was a relevant factor in the construction of a scenic footbridge, *Bell Free Contractors, Inc.*, Comp. Gen. Dec. B-227576, 87-2 CPD ¶ 418.

See also *PRC, Inc.*, Comp. Gen. Dec. B-274698.2, 97-1 CPD ¶ 115, where the documentation was found adequate because it identified all of the "significant discriminators" between the proposals even though it did not record strengths and weaknesses of the individual proposals.

2. Post-Protest Documentation

While documentation compiled contemporaneously with the evaluation and the source selection decision is required by the FAR, the lack of contemporaneous documentation will not be fatal in a protest if the evaluation and selection can be shown to be reasonable and in conformance with the evaluation criteria. Thus, documentation supporting the source selection decision may be created by the agency after the filing of a protest. See *Remington Arms Co.*, Comp. Gen. Dec. B-297374, 2006 CPD ¶ 32, stating:

> While we generally give little weight to reevaluations prepared in the heat of the adversarial process, post-protest explanations that provide a detailed rationale for contemporaneous conclusions, as is the case here, simply fill in previously unrecorded details, and will generally be considered in our review of the rationality of selection decisions, so long as those explanations are credible and consistent with the contemporaneous record. *NWT, Inc.: PharmChem Labs., Inc.*, B-280988, B-280988.2, Dec. 17, 1998, 98-2 CPD ¶ 158 at 16.

Thus, documentation supporting the source selection decision may be provided by the agency after the filing of a protest as long as that documentation is consistent with the rationale used in making the original decision, *Ideal Elec. Sec. Co.*, Comp. Gen. Dec. B-283398, 99-2 CPD ¶ 87; *MCR Fed., Inc.*, Comp. Gen. Dec. B-280969, 99-1 CPD ¶ 8. See also *TLT Constr. Corp.*, Comp. Gen. Dec. B-286226, 2000 CPD ¶ 179 (agency's post-protest explanation of its determination to use negotiated procedures held to be consistent with the evaluation plan); *Pickering Firm,*

Inc., Comp. Gen. Dec. B-277396, 97-2 CPD ¶ 99 (source selection decision affirmed based on evaluator worksheets and consensus ratings created after protest to support a "sparse" memorandum prepared at time of selection decision), *Environmental Affairs Mgmt., Inc.*, Comp. Gen. Dec. B-277270, 97-2 CPD ¶ 93 (source selection decision affirmed based on "legal brief, a contracting officer's statement, and declarations made by the SSA and the chairman of the [source evaluation committee]," all prepared after the protest was filed); *AT&T Corp.*, Comp. Gen. Dec. B-260447.4, 96-1 CPD ¶ 200 (source selection decision affirmed based on the agency protest report, which presented extensive and detailed narratives concerning the strengths of the awardee's technical and management proposals when this information was consistent with the less detailed contemporaneous documentation); *Sociometrics, Inc.*, Comp. Gen. Dec. B-261367.2, 95-2 CPD ¶ 201 (although the details of the cost realism analysis were not spelled out in a contemporaneous document, the contracting officer adequately explained the details of the analysis in an agency protest report); and *Hydraudyne Sys. & Eng'g B.V.*, Comp. Gen. Dec. B-241236, 91-1 CPD ¶ 88 (source selection decision sustained based on its after-the-fact explanations of the scoring of individual evaluators after the documentation created by these evaluators had been discarded). In *Universal Shipping Co.*, Comp. Gen. Dec. B-223905.2, 87-1 CPD ¶ 424, *recons. denied*, 87-2 CPD ¶ 125, the protester won the initial protest based on a finding of inadequate documentation but ultimately lost the protest on the basis of documentation created by the agency after the initial decision by the GAO.

The GAO has refused to rely on post-protest explanations of the source selection decision that have been prepared by the agency's legal counsel, *Radiation Oncology Group of WNY, PC*, Comp. Gen. Dec. B-310354.2, 2009 CPD ¶ 136. In that case the SSA had only stated that she determined the offerors were "essentially technically equal" with no further explanation.

The Court of Federal Claims has also admitted documentation filed after the plaintiff has lost a GAO protest, *Wackenhut Servs., Inc. v. United States*, 85 Fed. Cl. 273 (2008).

A common technique for remedying insufficient documentation has been for the GAO to hold a hearing where agency officials can explain the evaluation and source selection decision. A number of protests have been denied on the basis of such information See *Manassas Travel, Inc.*, Comp. Gen. Dec. B-294867.3, 2005 CPD ¶ 113 (testimony providing more details regarding strengths of winning offeror); *SOS Interpreting, Ltd.*, Comp. Gen. Dec. B-287505, 2001 CPD ¶ 104 (testimony providing detailed rationale for selection decision held to be credible and consistent with contemporaneous record); *Northeast MEP Servs., Inc.*, Comp. Gen. Dec. B-285963.5, 2001 CPD ¶ 28 (chairman of evaluation board explained the basis for determining that protester had weaknesses); *Draeger Safety, Inc.*, Comp. Gen. Dec. B-285366, 2000 CPD ¶ 139 (testimony of evaluator after evaluation documentation was destroyed accepted as providing acceptable contemporaneous documentation supporting selection decision); *Simborg Dev., Inc.*, Comp. Gen. Dec. B-283538, 2000 CPD ¶ 12 (testimony gave credible explanation of selection decision); *NWT, Inc.*, Comp. Gen. Dec. B-280988.2, 98-2 CPD ¶ 158 (based on transcript and hearing, GAO concluded that "while not recorded at the time, the agency did compare performance levels"); *Pacifica Servs., Inc.*, Comp. Gen. Dec. B-280921, 98-2 CPD ¶ 137 (detailed rationale given in declaration and hearing was held to "simply fill in unrecorded details") and *Jason Assocs. Corp.*, Comp. Gen. Dec. B-278689, 98-1 CPD ¶ 67 (source selection affirmed based on testimony). In contrast, the hearing may confirm that the agency has made a flawed source selection decision, *Keeton Corrections, Inc.*, Comp. Gen. Dec. B-293348, 2005 CPD ¶ 44 (hearing showed SSA had been given faulty information on past performance); *Preferred Sys. Solutions, Inc.*, Comp. Gen. Dec. B-292322, 2003 CPD ¶ 166 (hearing showed that SSA did not make independent decision); *Sabreliner Corp.*, Comp. Gen. Dec. B-288030, 2001 CPD ¶ 170 (testimony repeated "errors" and "inconsistencies" in documentation supporting sole source procurement).

The GAO has also permitted such later explanations — even in the extreme case where the agency has destroyed the original documentation. See *Southwest Marine, Inc.*, Comp. Gen. Dec. B-265865.4, 96-1 CPD ¶ 56, stating:

> In determining the rationality of an agency's evaluation and award decision, we do not limit our review to contemporaneous evidence, but consider all the information provided, including the parties' arguments, explanations, and hearing testimony. *Benchmark Sec., Inc.*, [Comp. Gen. Dec. B-247655, 93-1 CPD ¶ 133]; *KMS Fusion, Inc.*, [Comp. Gen. Dec. B-242529, 91-1 CPD ¶ 447]; *Hydraudyne Sys. and Eng'g B.V.*, [Comp. Gen. Dec. B-241236, 91-1 CPD ¶ 88]. While we consider the entire record, including the parties' later explanations and arguments, we accord greater weight to contemporaneous evaluation and source selection material than to arguments and documentation prepared in response to protest contentions. *DynCorp*, 71 Comp. Gen. 129 (1991), 91-2 CPD ¶ 575.

> Here, the Navy's destruction of the evaluators' notes and workpapers left a written record that did not meet the requirements of FAR 15.608(a)(3)(ii). The contemporaneous documentation retained by the Navy — the TEC's final report, the TEC chair's cost/technical tradeoff document, and source selection decision — did not adequately explain why BAV's proposal was judged to be technically superior to SWM's and AMSEC's. Specifically, while the TEC report described BAV's proposal's strengths and advantages to justify its "highly acceptable" rating, it did not explain why the protesters' proposals, which appeared from this document to have similar strengths, were not essentially technically equivalent. Accordingly, the retained documentation was not sufficient to support the evaluation results. Indeed, a hearing was convened at our request, in part, because of the inadequacy of the evaluation documentation in the record, which did not fully explain the agency's evaluation . . . and the hearing testimony revealed that a number of identified strengths and weaknesses for all offerors' proposals were not recorded in the TEC's final evaluation report. . . .

> While the Navy's document destruction was improper, we will not disrupt an agency's procurement on this basis alone where the protest record is otherwise

adequate for our review. *See Hydraudyne Sys. and Eng'g B.V., supra.* SWM and AMSEC assert that the evaluators' notes and workpapers are necessary here to allow for our review of the procurement; they correctly note that the evaluators could not recall in their hearing testimony all the details of the lengthy evaluation process and that there were some minor inconsistencies in the evaluators' testimony. This, however, does not establish the inadequacy of the protest record. The testimony of the agency's evaluators, TEC chair, and SSA explained the basis of the agency's evaluation conclusions, and, more specifically, why BAV's proposal was determined to be technically superior to SWM's and AMSEC's; they agreed on the major aspects of the evaluation and the evaluated differences among the parties' proposals. Looking at the record as a whole, we believe that it adequately explains the agency's actions so as to allow the parties to present their arguments concerning the reasonableness of the agency's source selection and to allow our Office to effectively review the matter. *Id.*

From our detailed review of this record, we conclude that the agency's evaluation of technical proposals and its cost/technical tradeoff decision were reasonable.

There is some disagreement on the weight to be accorded to documentation that is created after a protest has been filed. One judge in the Court of Federal Claims has stated that it should be accorded the "same deference" given to documentation created at the time the selection decision was made, *Tech Sys., Inc. v. United States*, 50 Fed. Cl. 216 (2001). Another judge treated such documentation as mere "argument," *Cubic Applications, Inc. v. United States*, 37 Fed. Cl. 339 (1997). The GAO accords "greater weight to contemporaneous source selection materials rather than documents . . . prepared in response to protest contentions," *DynCorp*, 71 Comp. Gen. 129 (B-245289), 91-2 CPD ¶ 575. Thus, documentation that offers new justifications for the selection decision rather than amplifying the original justification will be highly suspect. See *Boeing Sikorsky Aircraft Support,* Comp. Gen. Dec. B-277263.2, 97-2 CPD ¶ 91, refusing to rely on the agency's mock source selection decision based on the assumption that all the protester's complaints were valid, stating:

> While we consider the entire record, including statements and arguments made in response to a protest in determining whether an agency's selection decision is supportable, we accord greater weight to contemporaneous source selection materials rather than judgments, such as the selection officials' reevaluation here, made in response to protest contentions. *Dyncorp*, 71 Comp. Gen. 129, 134 n.12 (1991), 91-2 CPD ¶ 575 at 7 n.13; *Southwest Marine, Inc.; American Sys. Eng'g Corp.*, B-265865.3, B-265865.4, Jan. 23, 1996, 96-1 CPD ¶ 56 at 10. As pointed out above, the agency does not acknowledge that it erred. Rather, we are faced with an agency's efforts to defend, in the face of a bid protest, its prior source selection through submission of new analyses, which the agency itself views as merely hypothetical and which are based on information that the agency continues to argue is not accurate. The lesser weight that we accord these post-protest documents reflects the concern that, because they constitute reevaluations and redeterminations prepared in the heat of an adversarial process, they may not represent the fair and considered judgment of the agency, which is a prerequisite of a rational evaluation and source selection process.

This logic was followed in *United Int'l Eng'g, Inc.*, 71 Comp. Gen. 177 (B-245448.3), 92-1 CPD ¶ 122, in which the source selection official's post-selection testimony regarding his reluctance to award to the protester was inconsistent with the evaluation criteria and contemporaneous evidence. The GAO sustained the protest "giving due weight to the contemporaneous source selection documents." In *ManTech Envt'l Research Servs. Corp.*, Comp. Gen. Dec. B-292602, 2003 CPD ¶ 221, the GAO rejected post-protest reevaluation because it was performed by the same personnel defending the protest. See also *Systems Research & Applications Corp.*, Comp. Gen. Dec. B-299818, 2008 CPD ¶ 28 (granting protest because agency officials showed at hearing that they did not qualitatively assess the merits of the proposals); *Si-Nor, Inc.*, Comp. Gen. Dec. B-292748.2, 2004 CPD ¶ 10 (rejecting argument that dissimilar prior contract was not used to evaluate experience); *Dismas Charities, Inc.*, Comp. Gen. Dec. B-292091, 2003 CPD ¶ 125 (rejecting post-protest reevaluation of past performance); *Johnson Controls World Servs., Inc.*, Comp. Gen. Dec. B-289942, 2002 CPD ¶ 88 (rejecting sufficiency of post-protest addendum that still did not contain comparative assessment of strength of protester's technical proposal); *Wackenhut Servs., Inc.*, Comp. Gen. Dec. B-286037, 2001 CPD ¶ 114 (rejecting justification for selection decision that was not reflected in contemporaneous record); *BAE Sys.*, Comp. Gen. Dec. B-287189, 2001 CPD ¶ 86 (rejecting explanation of evaluation that was inconsistent with record); *Farmland Nat'l Beef*, Comp. Gen. Dec. B-286607, 2001 CPD ¶ 31 (rejecting undocumented testimony that telephone call occurred); *CRAssociates, Inc.*, Comp. Gen. Dec. B-282075.2, 2000 CPD ¶ 63 (post-protest documentation does not overcome contemporaneous record showing improper evaluation); *Maritime Berthing, Inc.*, Comp. Gen. Dec. B-284123.3, 2000 CPD ¶ 89 (rejecting documentation using new date from offeror not contained in original proposal); *Possehn Consulting*, Comp. Gen. Dec. B-278579.2, 98-2 CPD ¶ 33 (rejecting argument that if agency had included protester's proposal in the competitive range, it still would not have won the competition); *Arora Group, Inc.*, Comp. Gen. Dec. B-277674, 98-1 CPD ¶ 64 (rejecting post-protest justifications of clearly erroneous price realism analysis); and *Mechanical Contractors, S.A.*, Comp. Gen. Dec. B-277916, 97-2 CPD ¶ 121 (rejecting statement in protest report that agency had given favorable consideration to a certification of a subcontractor because there was no indication of such consideration in contemporaneous evaluation documents).

3. Quantification of Non-Price Factors

Quantification of technical ratings is not required when a tradeoff decision is made, FAR 15.308. This rule was established by the Court of Appeals for the Federal Circuit in *Lockheed Missiles & Space Co. v. Bentsen*, 4 F.3d 955 (Fed. Cir. 1993). See also *EG&G Team*, Comp. Gen. Dec. B-259917, 95-2 CPD ¶ 175, stating that "the source selection authority has discretion to determine how to balance cost and technical advantages in making an award decision in a best value procurement." Quantification was not required in *MD Helicopters, Inc.*, Comp. Gen. Dec. B-298502, 2006 CPD ¶ 164; *Basic Contracting Servs., Inc.*, Comp. Gen. Dec. B-284649, 2000 CPD ¶ 120; *A.G. Cullen Constr., Inc.*, Comp. Gen. Dec. B-284049.2, 2000 CPD ¶ 45; *Allied*

Tech. Group, Inc., Comp. Gen. Dec. B-282739, 99-2 CPD ¶ 45; *KRA Corp.*, Comp. Gen. Dec. B-278904, 98-1 CPD ¶ 147; *Research Triangle Inst.*, Comp. Gen. Dec. B-278254, 98-1 CPD ¶ 22; *Sudath Van Lines, Inc.*, Comp. Gen. Dec. B-274285.2, 97-1 CPD ¶ 204; *Ingalls Shipbuiding, Inc.*, Comp. Gen. Dec. B-275830, 97-1 CPD ¶ 180; and *Kay & Assocs., Inc.*, Comp. Gen. Dec. B-258243.7, 96-1 CPD ¶ 266.

When quantification of the benefit of making an award to a higher-priced offer is practical, the tradeoff should be justified in terms of dollars. See, for example, *Continental Airlines, Inc.*, Comp. Gen. Dec. B-258271.4, 97-1 CPD ¶ 81, holding that the agency had made a valid tradeoff decision by quantifying most of the non-price evaluation factors; and *Global Assocs., Ltd.*, Comp. Gen. Dec. B-275534, 97-1 CPD ¶ 129, where quantification of many of the non-price factors was found to be proper. See *Satellite Servs., Inc.*, Comp. Gen. Dec. B-286508, 2001 CPD ¶ 30, stating:

> While quantification of the value of technical differences is not required, a source selection official may quantify the value of technical differences in dollar terms as part of a cost/technical tradeoff; the quantification, however, must be rationally based and consistent with the RFP. *University of Kansas Med. Ctr.*, B-278400, Jan. 26, 1998, 98-1 CPD ¶ 120 at 6.

See *Olin Corp.*, Comp. Gen. Dec. B-283401, 99-2 CPD ¶ 88, finding that the SSA properly rejected the quantification of one offeror's litigious record of past performance because there was no way to accurately predict its future behavior.

It is also proper to quantify in-house costs necessitated by an offeror's proposed method of performance in order to determine the full cost of award to that offeror, *Cerner Corp.*, Comp. Gen. Dec. B-293093, 2004 CPD ¶ 34 (additional costs in using protester's software and following protester's deployment schedule).

III. POST-SELECTION COMMUNICATION

Neither the procurement statutes nor the FAR deal with the subject of communications between the agency and the selected offeror after selection has been made and before award. However, in many cases it is necessary to clear up uncertainties or to resolve remaining issues before award can be made. In other cases the agency may wish to negotiate more favorable terms or prices with the selected source. It is essential to determine whether such communications constitute negotiations, which would require the agency to negotiate with all those who submitted offers (if award was being made on the basis of initial proposals) or with all those remaining in the competitive range (if final offer revisions have been requested).

A. Negotiations Not Permitted

The general rule is that negotiation with only one offeror is prohibited. Such negotiations would occur if an offeror were given the opportunity to revise its offer or to establish that the offer is acceptable. See *SmithKline Beecham Pharmaceuticals, N.A.*, Comp. Gen. Dec. B-252226.2, 93-2 CPD ¶ 79, stating:

> It is a fundamental principle of federal procurement that all offerors must be treated equally. *Loral Terracom*; *Marconi Italiana*, 66 Comp. Gen. 272 (1987), 87-1 CPD ¶ 182. Thus, the conduct of discussions with one offeror generally requires that discussions be conducted with all offerors whose offers are within the competitive range and that offerors have an opportunity to submit revised offers. *Microlog Corp.*, B-237486, Feb. 26, 1990, 90-1 CPD ¶ 227. This rule applies even to post-selection negotiations that do not directly affect the offerors' relative standing, because all offerors are entitled to an equal opportunity to revise their proposals. *PRC Information Sciences Co.*, 56 Comp. Gen. 768 (1977), 77-2 CPD ¶ 11.

See also *Priority One Servs., Inc.*, Comp. Gen. Dec. B-288836, 2002 CPD ¶ 79 (offeror required to replace personnel not found to be acceptable and raising salary levels for some personnel); *The Futures Group Int'l*, Comp. Gen. Dec. B-281274.5, 2000 CPD ¶ 148 (agreeing to cap on indirect cost rates during a protest a material change in offer requiring discussions with all competitors in competitive range); and *Global Assocs., Ltd.*, Comp. Gen. Dec. B-271693.2, 96-2 CPD ¶ 100 (offer as received could not have been accepted). See also *Hunt Bldg. Co. v. United States*, 61 Fed. Cl. 243 (2004), finding improper post-selection negotiations that made significant changes to the basis for the competition. In *Matrix Int'l Logistics, Inc.*, Comp. Gen. Dec. B-272388.2, 97-2 CPD ¶ 89, the GAO held that correction of a mistake in awardee's price after receipt of best and final offers required discussions with all offerors where the intended price was not ascertainable from the offer and the solicitation. In assessing the post-selection communication cases, the GAO focuses on whether there is a "reasonable possibility of prejudice" to the other offerors, *Labat-Anderson Inc.*, 71 Comp. Gen. 252 (B-246071.2), 92-1 CPD ¶ 193.

B. Clarifications and Nonmaterial Changes

Communications in the nature of clarifications that would be permissible under FAR 15.306(a) do not require communications with other offerors. See Chapter 5 for a discussion of this type of communications. Thus, "touch up negotiations" have been permitted, *Medical Care Dev., Inc.*, Comp. Gen. Dec. B-227848.3, 87-2 CPD ¶ 371. In addition, discussing or requiring changes in nonmaterial aspects of an offer would not require negotiations with other offerors. See *Acepex Mgmt. Corp.*, Comp. Gen. Dec. B-283080, 99-2 CPD ¶ 77 (obtaining comments on the validity of a protest not a change to the offer); *Assets Recovery Sys., Inc.*, Comp. Gen. Dec. B-275332, 97-1 CPD ¶ 67 (change in payment provision did not increase or decrease overall value of offer); *Optimum Sys., Inc.*, Comp. Gen. Dec. B-194984, 80-2 CPD ¶ 32 (substitution of computer would have had same effect on all offerors); and *Information Sys. & Networks Corp.*, Comp. Gen. Dec. B-220661, 86-1 CPD ¶ 30 (negotiations to obtain a small reduction in price). See also *L.G. Lefler v. United States*, 6 Cl. Ct. 514 (1984), where the offer would have been lowest even without the negotiated price change.

It appears that communications of this type are contemplated by the guidance in FAR 15.504, which states:

> The contracting officer shall award a contract to the successful offeror by furnishing the executed contract or other notice of the award to that offeror.

> (a) If the award document includes information that is different than the latest signed proposal, as amended by the offeror's written correspondence, both the offeror and the contracting officer shall sign the contract award.

This provision apparently permits the contracting officer to include information in the final contract that is different from the prior documentation in the proposal and proposal revisions. Such information would be the likely result of post-selection communications to clear up minor problems.

C. Negotiations Permitted

There are several situations in which negotiations with only the selected source will be permitted.

1. Alternate Selection Procedures

In the past, several agencies adopted alternate source selection procedures that permitted a significant amount of negotiation with only the selected offeror. These procedures were authorized by pre-rewrite FAR 15.613, as follows:

> (a) The National Aeronautics and Space Administration (NASA) and the Department of Defense (DOD) have developed, and use in appropriate situations, source selection procedures that limit discussions with offerors during the competition and that differ from other procedures described in Subpart 15.6. The procedures are the NASA Source Evaluation Board procedures and the DOD "Four Step" Source Selection Procedures. Detailed coverage of these procedures is in the respective agency acquisition regulations.

> (b) Other agencies may use either the NASA or DOD procedures as a model in developing their own procedures, including applicability criteria, consistent with mission needs.

Under the NASA procedure and the DOD four-step procedure set forth in DFARS 215.613-70, the agency conducted limited communications with all offerors within the competitive range and then negotiated the final contract price, terms, and conditions with the selected offeror. However, the negotiations could not permit any changes in the government's requirements or the offer that would affect the source selection decision. The GAO recognized that such procedures met the statutory requirements for conducting oral or written discussions with all offerors within the competitive range. See *Ogden Logistics Servs.*, Comp. Gen. Dec. B-257731.3, 95-1 CPD ¶ 3, stating:

[T]he FAR expressly acknowledges that NASA and DOD have developed alternate "source selection procedures that limit discussions with offerors during the competition, and that differ from other procedures prescribed in [FAR] Subpart 15.6." FAR 15.613(a). In essence, NASA's alternate procedures, set forth at 48 C.F.R. § 18-15.613-71, limit discussions to clarification of proposals. Our Office has recognized NASA's alternate procedures as one legitimate approach to the statutory requirement for holding discussions with competitive range offerors. *Taft Broadcasting Corp.*, B-222818, July 29, 1986, 86-2 CPD ¶ 125; *Support Sys. Assocs., Inc.*, B-215421, Sept. 4, 1984, 84-2 CPD ¶ 249; *Program Resources, Inc.*, B-192964, Apr. 23, 1979, 79-1 CPD ¶ 281.

See also *Sperry Rand Corp.*, 54 Comp. Gen. 408 (B-181460), 74-2 CPD ¶ 276; *Dynalectron Corp.*, 54 Comp. Gen. 562 (B-181738), 75-1 CPD ¶ 17; *Management Servs., Inc.*, 55 Comp. Gen. 715 (B-184606), 76-1 CPD ¶ 74; *GTE Sylvania*, 57 Comp. Gen. 715 (B-188272), 77-2 CPD ¶ 422; and *Taft Broadcasting Corp.*, Comp. Gen. Dec. B-222818, 86-2 CPD ¶ 125.

The GAO has also recognized the validity of similar procedures adopted by the Department of Energy, *Holmes & Narver, Inc.*, Comp. Gen. Dec. B-239469.2, 90-2 CPD ¶ 210, *recons. denied*, 91-1 CPD ¶ 51. Compare *Airco, Inc. v. Energy Res. & Dev. Admin.*, 528 F.2d 1294 (7th Cir. 1975), rejecting the contention that these procedures should be applied retroactively.

The Department of Health and Human Services alternate procedure at HHSAR 315.370 provides:

> (a) After selection of the successful proposal, the Contracting Officer may finalize details with the selected offeror, if necessary. However, the Contracting Officer shall not introduce any factor that could have an effect on the selection process after the common cutoff date for receipt of final proposal revisions, nor shall the finalization process in any way prejudice the competitive interest or rights of the unsuccessful offerors. The Contracting Officer shall restrict finalization of details with the selected offeror to definitizing the final agreement on terms and conditions, assuming none of these factors were involved in the selection process.

In *Prospect Assocs., Inc.*, Comp. Gen. Dec. B-260696, 95-2 CPD ¶ 53, the agency, using this procedure, conducted negotiations with the selected offeror on labor and indirect cost rates and other "minor issues." The negotiations resulted in a "relatively minor reduction" in the offered cost. The GAO held that there was no need to negotiate with other offerors because the purpose of the negotiation was to "definitize" the terms, "not to obtain more competitive pricing." That case should be contrasted with *SmithKline Beecham Pharmaceuticals, N.A.*, Comp. Gen. Dec. B-252226.2, 93-2 CPD ¶ 79, where the agency negotiated a concession from the selected offeror and the GAO held that this required negotiations with other offerors, based on the rationale that the agency was reluctant to award a contract to the selected source without the concession.

The former FAR 15.613 authorizing these alternative procedures was removed in the FAR Part 15 rewrite. However, FAR 15.101 permits agencies considerable latitude in designing source selection methods:

> An agency can obtain best value in negotiated acquisitions by using any one or a combination of source selection approaches.

The Department of Defense has indicated that FAR 15.101 permits contracting agencies to develop selection procedures that permit negotiation after source selection. See 62 Fed. Reg. 63050 (1997), stating:

> DFARS guidance on the four-step source selection process and the alternate source selection process have been removed, as the new guidance at FAR 15.101, best value continuum, clearly allows such source selection processes.

This removal of the four-step procedure indicates that alternative procedures can be adopted by contracting officers without the necessity of regulatory coverage. However, in doing so the procedures to be followed must be spelled out in the solicitation so that offerors will be able to compete on a common basis. In addition, negotiations must not (1) change the government's requirements, (2) make an unacceptable offer acceptable, (3) change the basis for selection, or (4) otherwise prejudice other offerors. See *SAMS El Segundo, LLC*, Comp. Gen. Dec. B-291620.3, 2003 CPD ¶ 48, where the agency adopted a phased selection procedure calling for negotiations with the selected offeror. See also *Northrop Grumman Tech. Servs., Inc.*, Comp. Gen. Dec. B-291506, 2003 CPD ¶ 25, where the agency added an item of government-furnished property before award – following a procedure specified in the RFP.

2. Competitive Range of One

Post-selection negotiations have been held to be appropriate where only one offeror was found to be in the competitive range. See *HITCO*, 68 Comp. Gen. 10 (B-232093), 88-2 CPD ¶ 337 (all but one offeror excluded from the competitive range when others were found to have deficiencies*); Rice Servs., Ltd.*, 68 Comp. Gen. 112 (B-232610), 88-2 CPD ¶ 514 (the sum of both major and minor deficiencies in the protester's offer justified its exclusion from the competitive range, which was narrowed to one); and *Regional Envtl. Consultants*, 66 Comp. Gen. 67 (B-223555), 86-2 CPD ¶ 476, *recons. denied*, 66 Comp. Gen. 388 (B-22355.2), 87-1 CPD ¶ 428 (one of two offerors excluded from the competitive range because of its undesirable approach to the contracted-for work). However, in these cases, however, the GAO made it clear that source selection decisions that result in competitive ranges of one would be carefully scrutinized in the interest of achieving full and open competition.

The statutory and regulatory changes in describing the competitive range have made competitive ranges of one more acceptable. See *Clean Serv. Co.*, Comp. Gen. Dec. B-281141.3, 99-1 CPD ¶ 36, stating:

> [T]he FAR Part 15 rewrite provides that "based on the ratings of each proposal against all evaluation criteria, the contracting officer shall establish a competitive range comprised of all of the most highly rated proposals." FAR 15.306(c)(1); see *SDS Petroleum Prods., Inc.*, [B-280430, Sept. 1, 1998, 98-2 CPD ¶ 59]. We have concluded that the Part 15 rewrite does not require that agencies retain a proposal in the competitive range simply to avoid a competitive range of one; conducting discussions and requesting best and final offers from offerors with no reasonable chance of award would benefit neither the offerors nor the government. *Id*. at 6; see also 62 Fed. Reg. 51,224, 51,226 (1997) (retaining marginal offers in competitive range imposes additional and largely futile effort and cost on government and industry).

See also *L-3 Communications EOTech, Inc.*, Comp. Gen. Dec. B-311453, 2008 CPD ¶ 139 (protester eliminated for failing to meet essential requirement); *General Atomics Aeronautical Sys., Inc.*, Comp. Gen. Dec. B-311004, 2008 CPD ¶ 105 (protester eliminated based on significant deficiencies); *M&M Investigations, Inc.*, Comp. Gen. Dec. B-299369.2, 2007 CPD ¶ 200 (protester did not have reasonable chance for award); *Brian X. Scott*, Comp. Gen. Dec. B-298568, 2006 CPD ¶ 156 (protester required change in contract terms); *TekStar, Inc.*, Comp. Gen. Dec. B-295444, 2005 CPD ¶ 53 (protester eliminated based on materially deficient proposal); *National Shower Express, Inc.*, Comp. Gen. Dec. B-293970, 2004 CPD ¶ 140 (protester's proposal stated only that it would comply with requirements); *Information Sys. Tech. Corp.*, Comp. Gen. Dec. B-291747, 2003 CPD ¶ 72 (protester did not have reasonable chance for award); *SOS Interpreting, Ltd.*, Comp. Gen. Dec. B-287505, 2001 CPD ¶ 104 (protester eliminated based on several deficiencies); *Novavax, Inc.*, Comp. Gen. Dec. B-286167, 2000 CPD ¶ 202 (offeror eliminated from second round of discussions); *Dismas Charities, Inc.*, Comp. Gen. Dec. B-284754, 2000 CPD ¶ 84; and *Firearms Training Sys., Inc. v. United States*, 41 Fed. Cl. 743 (1998). In *Outdoor Venture Corp.*, Comp. Gen. Dec. B-401351.2, 2009 CPD ¶ 194, the GAO concurred with the agency decision to put one unacceptable offeror in the competitive range while excluding another unacceptable offeror that had more deficiencies. Compare *Global, A 1st Flagship Co.*, Comp. Gen. Dec. B-297233, 2006 CPD ¶ 14, finding an improper competitive range of one where the agency included awardee's technically unacceptable proposal and excluded protester's "highly acceptable" technical proposal, on the basis that protester's evaluated cost/price was 15% higher than the awardee's. These cases indicate that a competitive range of one is appropriate when one offeror is clearly superior.

CHAPTER 10

AWARD AND DEBRIEFING

The culmination of the competitive negotiation process is forming a binding contract with the selected contractor. However, before award is made, the contracting officer is required to give preaward notices and, under certain circumstances, give a debriefing to firms not selected. In most cases, award is made by accepting the offer that is most advantageous to the government. In other cases, this may require preparation of an integrated agreement and having that document signed by the contractor. This chapter considers the various steps that are involved in these functions.

I. AWARD

Once a source selection decision has been made, the contracting officer is to make the award with "reasonable promptness" by transmitting the notice of award "in writing or by electronic means," 10 U.S.C. § 2305(b)(4)(c) and 41 U.S.C. § 253b(d)(3). Additional procedures for making awards are outlined in FAR 15.504:

> The contracting officer shall award a contract to the successful offeror by furnishing the executed contract or other notice of the award to that offeror.
>
> (a) If the award document includes information that is different than the latest signed proposal, as amended by the offeror's written correspondence, both the offeror and the contracting officer shall sign the contract award.
>
> (b) When an award is made to an offeror for less than all of the items that may be awarded and additional items are being withheld for subsequent award, each notice shall state that the Government may make subsequent awards on those additional items within the proposal acceptance period.

In some cases the notice of award might constitute an acceptance by the government of an offer contained in a final proposal revision or initial proposal. This would occur, for example, in a situation where the government was fully in agreement with all the terms of that offer and merely desired to enter into a binding contract immediately. However, in many cases the contracting officer will want to prepare an integrated contractual document and obtain the signature of both parties to that document, as described in FAR 15.504(a) above. In such cases the notice of award may merely notify the offeror that it has been selected for award and that the integrated document will be forwarded in due course. Offerors should be aware that there are varying procedures used in this area and should ensure that they have a legally binding document before beginning work.

Statutory and regulatory requirements for a notice of award to be "in writing or by electronic means" raise the question of whether the contracting officer can form a contract by giving an oral notice of award. There is sparse litigation dealing with this subject, but the cases that do exist suggest strongly that an oral notice would not be effective. See, for example, *R.J. Crowley, Inc.*, ASBCA 28730, 86-1 BCA ¶ 18,739. In addition, the GAO has enforced the FAR requirement that award of the contract be in written form. See *Litton Sys., Inc.*, Comp. Gen. Dec. B-229921, 88-1 CPD ¶ 448, holding that the protester's argument that partial award had been made orally over the phone was irrelevant in light of an actual written award made to another offeror, as was required. In *G. McMillan & Co.*, Comp. Gen. Dec. B-239805, 90-2 CPD ¶ 214, the GAO stated, in reference to an argument that a protester was due expenses it incurred in anticipation of receiving a contract award, that "[s]ince the law and regulations require written notice of award, we think it unlikely that the protester could establish that a contract resulted from the alleged oral advice." The GAO generally will not consider protests as to the "adequacy" of the award because that is a "procedural matter,"*Al Hamra Kuwait Co.*, Comp. Gen. Dec. B-288970, 2001 CPD ¶ 208.

When award is made by obtaining the signature of both of the parties, it is usually made on one of the standard forms prescribed by the government. If the government is merely accepting an offer without alteration by awarding on the basis of the initial proposals or final proposal revisions that have not changed the original offer, it can accomplish this by signing Standard Form (SF) 33, FAR 53.301-33, or SF 1442, FAR 53.301-1442, if these have been used as the cover page for the solicitation.

If Optional Form (OF) 308, FAR 53.302-308, has been used in transmitting the solicitation, this is not possible because that form has no place for signature by the contracting officer. If there have been alterations to the request for proposals (RFP) during the procurement process, the agency can use either SF 26, FAR 53.301-26, or OF 307, FAR 53.302-307, as the cover page to the integrated contract. Alternatively, an agency can create its own award cover page as long as it complies with FAR 15.504 as follows:

> (c) If the Optional Form (OF) 307, Contract Award, Standard Form (SF) 26, Award/Contract, or SF 33, Solicitation, Offer and Award, is not used to award the contract, the first page of the award document shall contain the Government's acceptance statement from Block 15 of that form, exclusive of the Item 3 reference language, and shall contain the contracting officer's name, signature, and date. In addition, if the award document includes information that is different than the signed proposal, as amended by the offeror's written correspondence, the first page shall include the contractor's agreement statement from Block 14 of the OF 307 and the signature of the contractor's authorized representative.

Telegraphic notices of award were frequently used by the government to speed up the award process. In 49 Comp. Gen. 295 (B-167473) (1969), where an offeror was notified of award of a negotiated contract telegraphically and only later sent the formal contract documents, the GAO remained silent on the issue as to what point the government was bound. In many cases involving sealed bidding, however, the GAO has explicitly held that the government was bound by telegraphic notices of award. See *S.J. Groves*, 55 Comp. Gen. 936 (B-184260), 76-1 CPD ¶ 205, holding that because Groves protested after the agency had sent a telegraphic notice of award to the winner, its protest was a postaward protest. In *Wolverine Diesel Power Co.*, 57 Comp. Gen. 468 (B-189789), 78-1 CPD ¶ 375, telegraphic notices of award of two contracts were sent several days before the awardee attempted to withdraw its erroneous bids. The GAO held that the telegrams made the contract effective and, therefore, that the awardee had made its allegations of mistake in bidding after award. See also *Niedenthal Corp.*, ASBCA 48159, 96-2 BCA ¶ 28,572, where the agency sent facsimile notice of award to the offeror on July 20, 1994. Niedenthal informed the agency of a mistake in its bid on July 26 and later tried to claim that award could not be made by facsimile. The board held that the mistake-in-bid claim was a postaward claim under the Contract Disputes Act. Although these cases primarily refer to sealed bid procurements, their reasoning would be applicable to negotiated procurements where the telegraphic notice was framed in terms of acceptance of an offeror's final proposal revisions or initial proposal with no alteration in terms.

As discussed above, award can be made by signing the cover page of the offer on one of the standard forms prescribed by the government. However, if there have been alterations to the contractual language in the RFP during the procurement process, this can lead to confusion. See *F & F Lab., Inc.*, ASBCA 33007, 89-1 BCA ¶ 21,207, where the contracting officer signed SF 26 after the contractor had stated in its offer that it would supply a candy bar at variance with that called for by the specifications. The board held the government bound on the theory that the offer was incorporated by reference into the contract by the terms of the standard form. The listing of provisions on the standard form can also have consequences when these forms are used for acceptance. For example, in *Codex Corp.*, GSBCA 8186-P, 86-1 BCA ¶ 18,590, the contracting officer and the awardee signed the cover page of SF 26, where the table of contents indicated which sections of the contract were to be incorporated. In actuality, one of the sections was missing from the contract due to a clerical error. The board found that the parties had entered into a binding contract and that, despite its absence from the actual contract, the section in question was incorporated into the contract by reference on the cover page.

As a general rule, when written or oral discussions have been held and new offers requested, award is made by acceptance of the new offer (in one of the forms described above). However, award has been permitted on the basis of an original offer where the offeror did not submit a BAFO in response to the request for BAFOs, *MR&S/AME*, Comp. Gen. Dec. B-250313.2, 93-1 CPD ¶ 245. In that case the GAO reasoned that the offeror had agreed to an extension that kept its original offer open beyond the award date and the submission of a BAFO was permissible, not mandatory. The GAO also ruled that contacting the offeror to find out why no BAFO had been submitted was not a post-BAFO discussion. Award has not been permitted on the basis of the initial offer where the offeror submitted its BAFO late, *Touchstone Textiles, Inc.*, Comp. Gen. Dec. B-272230.4, 96-2 CPD ¶ 107. In that case the GAO reasoned that the agency could not ignore the intent conveyed by the submission of a modified proposal and, thus, the late BAFO constituted a revocation of the initial offer. Revocation of the original offer was also found when an offeror submitted its final proposal revisions in unauthorized electronic form that arrived late, *Integrated Bus. Solutions, Inc.*, Comp. Gen. Dec. B-292239, 2003 CPD ¶ 122; *Integrated Bus. Solutions, Inc. v. United States*, 58 Fed. Cl. 203 (2003).

A. Contents of Contract

The contracting parties should ensure that the award document is clear as to the contents of the contract. If award is made by signing SF 33 or SF 1442, the parties will have agreed that the contract consists of the documents referred to on those forms plus any amendments to the solicitation. This would appear to exclude any parts of the offeror's proposal that were submitted in separate documents, including any cover letter to the proposal. However, if the contractor includes contract language conflicting with the RFP, it may create an ambiguity which should be cleared up. See, for example, *Catel, Inc.*, ASBCA 52224, 02-1 BCA ¶ 31,731, holding the contractor bound when it attempted to exclude work that was required by the specifications but was held bound to the specifications because its language was vague. See also *Ferguson-Williams, Inc.*, ENGBCA 6482, 99-1 BCA ¶ 30,731, where the contractor's statement in Part B that home office overhead was included in its price conflicted with a special contract clause in Part I. The board ruled that the contractor was not entitled to be reimbursed its home office overhead because a solicitation provision stated that "financial data submitted with an offer . . . will [not] form a part of the resulting contract." Apparently, in neither case did either party recognize their lack of agreement on the terms of the contract — with the contractor being penalized for not clearly up the problem.

When SF 33 or SF 1442 are used and an offeror conditions the offer by altering the solicitation requirements in a material way, the award would not be binding on the offeror because the government's acceptance would not match the offer. Thus, the issue must be addressed before award. When the agency wants to incorporate material in the contract that is not part of the solicitation, then SF 26, OF 307, or an agency form should be used. In such cases the contracting officer should clearly indicate what documents are part of the contract. When SF 26 is used, the contracting officer can rewrite the contract documents, check block 17 on the form, and send the new contract to the offeror for signature. The offeror's proposal will not be part of the contract unless it is specifically listed, *Loral Aerospace Corp.*, ASBCA 46373, 97-2 BCA ¶ 29,128, but, if it is listed, it will be part of the contract, *Ervin & Assocs., Inc. v. United States*, 59 Fed. Cl. 267 (2004), *aff'd*, 120 Fed. Appx. 353 (Fed. Cir. 2005). Alternatively, the contracting officer can incorporate the offeror's proposal in the contract, sign the form, and check block 18. In either case the form should clearly identify what is part of the contract in order to avoid confusion on this issue. See the discussion of *F & F Lab., Inc.* and *Codex Corp.*, above.

OF 307 ameliorates the problem of potential confusion in using SF 26 by omitting blocks 17 and 18 and providing in block 14 that the contract will consist of "this document and any documents attached or incorporated by reference." However, the clarity of the document is still dependent on a clear statement of the contents of the contract.

The most troublesome issue in determining what is part of the contract is the question of whether proposals are part of the contract. Because the typical proposal contains considerable material that is in the nature of information or other non-promissory type material, it is generally not good practice to incorporate the entire proposal in the contract. Furthermore, the proposal may contain detailed data that conflicts with the contract specifications. The lack of clarity as to the contents of the contract can easily lead to litigation. See *Singer-General Precision, Inc.*, ASBCA 13241, 73-2 BCA ¶ 10,258, where the board had to resolve the question of whether the specifications or the conflicting technical proposal embodied the agreement of the parties. It gave no general rule but stated:

> [The contractor] was not free to ignore clearly-stated contractual requirements merely because the Government found the technical proposal acceptable and incorporated it into the contract. On the other hand, the Government could not with immunity require [the contractor] to perform work which was contrary to stated details, design and concepts in the proposal. When consideration is given to the specific claims, we will if applicable and necessary to decide a particular claim give further consideration to the contentions of the parties as presented in this general issue.

The board then analyzed each claim of the contractor for an equitable adjustment to determine what the parties had agreed to. See also *TRW, Inc.*, ASBCA 27299, 87-3 BCA ¶ 19,964, where the contracting officer incorporated the proposal into the contract to the extent it did not deviate from the government specifications. The board held that one aspect of the proposal was binding because it was promissory and another aspect was not binding because it was not promissory. Compare *Omni Corp. v. United States*, 41 Fed. Cl. 585 (1998), holding that a contractor was not bound to perform work in accordance with a technique described in its technical proposal which was not incorporated (the agency had unsuccessfully attempted to bind the contractor to perform such work by vague language in Section M of the RFP).

Silence on the status of proposals has also led to difficulties. See, for example, *Johnson Controls, Inc.*, ASBCA 25714, 82-1 BCA ¶ 15,779, holding the government bound to the terms of a technical proposal that was not clearly incorporated into the contract because it clearly stated that the contractor was offering to perform the work in a way that deviated with a detailed specification statement. In contrast, in *Northrop Grumman Corp. v. United States*, 47 Fed. Cl. 20 (2000), the court held that the contractor's proposal was not the baseline for determining whether constructive changes had occurred because the proposal was not incorporated into the contract. See also *Consolidated Security Servs. Corp.*, GSBCA 7714, 86-1 BCA ¶ 18,597, holding that the details of a pricing proposal were not part of a contract. This result conformed with the Contract Award solicitation provision in FAR 52.215-16, which stated that neither financial data nor representations concerning facilities or financing would "form part of the resulting contract." This helpful language was removed from the FAR by the FAR Part 15 rewrite.

There have also been problems with contractual statements that do not contain clear promissory language. See, for example, *Hamilton Securities Advisory Servs., Inc. v. United States*, 60 Fed. Cl. 144 (2004), denying a government claim that the contractor breached the contract because it could find no clear promise, stating at 158-59:

> The United States Court of Appeals for the Federal Circuit has advised that the "requirement of certainty in contracts serves two purposes. One is the need to determine whether the parties in fact intended to contract at all, and the other relates to the ability of a court to determine when a breach has occurred and to formulate any appropriate remedy." *Aviation Contractor Employees, Inc. v. United States*, 945 F.2d 1568, 1572 (Fed. Cir. 1991) (citing RESTATEMENT § 33) ("The terms of a contract are reasonably certain if they provide a basis for determining the existence of a breach and for giving an appropriate remedy.") and *Neeley* v. *Bankers Trust Co.*, 757 F.2d 621 (5th Cir. 1985), wherein the United States Court of the Fifth Circuit held that:
>
> > the entire contract falls with the failure of indefinite promises. . . . Like most questions of contract law, whether a promise or other term forms an essential part of an agreement depends primarily upon the intent of the parties. Thus, an *"essential" promise denotes one that the parties reasonably regarded, at the time of contracting,* as a vitally important ingredient in their bargain. Failure to fulfill such a promise, in other words, would seriously frustrate the expectations of one or more of the parties as to what would constitute sufficient performance of the contract as a whole. *Courts refuse to enforce agreements that contain indefinite promises or terms they deem essential precisely because judicial clarification of the uncertainty entails great danger of creating intentions and expectations that the parties themselves never entertained.*
>
> *Id.* at 628 (emphasis added); *see also Ace-Federal Reporters, Inc. v. Barram*, 226 F.3d 1329, 1332 (Fed. Cir. 2002); *Modern Sys. Tech. Corp.* v. *United States*, 979 F.2d 200, 202 (Fed. Cir. 1992); *Brookhaven Housing Coalition* v. *Solomon*, 583 F.2d 584, 593 (2nd Cir. 1978) (holding that "a court cannot decree performance of an agreement unless it can discern with reasonable certainty and particularity what the terms of the agreement are. *To consummate an enforceable agreement, the parties must not only believe that they have made a contract, they must also have expressed their intent in a manner that is susceptible of judicial interpretation.*") (emphasis added).

In *United Techs. Corp.*, ASBCA 46880, 97-1 BCA ¶ 28,818, the board interpreted nonpromissory language as promissory because the Secretary of the Navy had made a firm promise to the contractor but the contracting officer had used nonpromissory language in the contract (using the terms "intends to permit the Contractor to compete" for future work when the Secretary had guaranteed the right to compete). The board based its decision to a large degree on the fact that the contractor had sought to obtain promissory language and had been told by a number of officials that "intends" would be interpreted to mean "agrees."

B. Time for Acceptance

Once an offer expires the government loses the power to form a contract by acceptance. The Instructions to Offerors — Competitive Acquisition solicitation provision in FAR 52.215-1 specifies the time that an offeror holds its offer open:

> (d) *Offer expiration date.* Proposals in response to this solicitation will be valid for the number of days specified in the solicitation cover sheet (unless a different period is proposed by the offeror).

Block 4 of OF 308 follows this provision by stating that offers will be valid for 60 days unless a different period is entered in the block. The standard solicitation forms, SF 33 and SF 1442, used to solicit both sealed bids and competitive proposals, contain statements that offerors agree to be bound by their offers if they are accepted within a stated number of days. While these provisions were written to require bidders on sealed bid procurements to submit firm bids, they also appear to limit the time in which a competitive proposal can be accepted. The GAO has ruled, however, that, although these provisions contain dates when the offers expire, the agency can accept an expired offer after all offers have expired if the offeror waives the expiration date. See *Fletcher Constr. Co.*, Comp. Gen. Dec. B-248977, 92-2 CPD ¶ 246, reasoning:

> Even assuming that protester's interpretation of the acceptance period clause on the SF 1442 on which BAFOs were submitted is correct, and that all offers including the protester's had expired by the time of award, it is not improper for an agency to accept an expired offer for a proposed award without reopening negotiations. *Protective Materials Co., Inc.*, B-225495, Mar. 18, 1987, 87-1 CPD ¶ 303. Where the acceptance period has expired on all offers, the contracting officer may allow the successful offeror to waive the expiration of its proposal acceptance period without reopening negotiations to make an award on the basis of the offer as submitted, since waiver under these circumstances is not prejudicial to the competitive system. *Sublette Elec., Inc.*, B-232586, Nov. 30, 1988, 88-2 CPD ¶ 540.

This rule has been followed in *Scot, Inc.*, Comp. Gen. Dec. B-295569, 2005 CPD ¶ 66 (procurement with expiration date in RFP); *Pride Mobility Products Corp.*, Comp. Gen. Dec. B-292822.5, 2005 CPD ¶ 72 (procurement with expiration date in RFP amendment); and *CDA Investment Techs., Inc.*, Comp. Gen. Dec. B-272093.3, 97-1 CPD ¶ 102, *recons. denied*, 97-1 CPD ¶ 103 (procurement using SF 33). In *Krug Life Sciences, Inc.*, Comp. Gen. Dec. B-258669.2, 95-1 CPD ¶ 111, the GAO permitted waiver of the expiration date when the protester had kept its acceptance period open by sending in unsolicited extensions but the winning offeror had permitted its offer to expire. See also *BioGenesis Pacific, Inc.*, Comp. Gen. Dec. B-283738, 99-2 CPD ¶ 109, rejecting a contention that the agency improperly issued an amendment to the RFP extending the expiration date after it expired.

If an offeror submits an offer with an expiration date shorter than that required by the RFP, it will not be permitted to waive the expiration date after its offer has expired because that is prejudicial to the competitive system. See *Camden Shipping Corp. v. United States*, 89 Fed. Cl. 433 (2009), stating at 440:

> Permitting revival of an offer would compromise the integrity of the competitive process if the offeror designated a shorter acceptance period than that requested by the solicitation, and other offerors specified the longer period. *Espirit Int'l Corp.,* [Comp. Gen. Dec. B-276294, 97-1 CPD ¶ 106], at 1; *The Vemo Co.,* [Comp. Gen. Dec. B-243390, 91-2 CPD ¶ 443], at 2; *Fred Rutledge,* [63 Comp. Gen. 253 (B-213474),] 84-1 CPD ¶ 297, at 1; . . . If an offeror shortens the length of time its offer is open, it faces less exposure to the market risk of price fluctuation than other offerors. *Postmaster Gen.,* at 4; *see also Espirit Int'l Corp.,* at 1. Permitting an offeror to revive its offer after the shorter acceptance period has expired would be unfair, because it would allow the offeror to take its risk in increments, assessing after its offer expired whether the market situation had changed, while other offerors have no such opportunity.

The same result was reached in *Data Express*, Comp. Gen. Dec. B-234468, 89-1 CPD ¶ 507, where the protester had allowed its offer to expire by not acknowledging an amendment to the RFP that extended the expiration date of offers. See also *NECCO Inc.*, Comp. Gen. Dec. B-258131, 94-2 CPD ¶ 218, following the same reasoning in a case where the bidder on a sealed bid procurement responded to a request for an extension of the expiration date of a bid with an agreement to extend the date for a shorter length of time and then had its bid expire.

If neither the RFP nor the offer contain an expiration date, to be valid an award must be made within a reasonable time after receipt of a proposal or final proposal revisions. However, once a reasonable time has expired, the offer will no longer be open for award. See *Western Roofing Serv.*, 70 Comp. Gen. 323 (B-232666.4), 91-1 CPD ¶ 242, *recons. denied*, 91-1 CPD ¶ 566, where the agency had delayed action on a procurement for over a year and then reopened the procurement by requesting another round of BAFOs. When one of the original offerors protested because it had never received the request for a BAFO, the GAO denied the protest holding that the agency was correct in assuming that the earlier BAFO had expired and, hence, award could be made only to an offeror that had submitted a new BAFO. The GAO reasoned that the offer had expired in view of the statutory mandate for agencies to award promptly, 41 U.S.C. § 253b(d)(4), and the *Uniform Commercial Code* rule that offers without expiration dates remain open only for a reasonable time, U.C.C. § 2-205. The GAO found that the 13 months that had passed between the submission of the BAFO and the award was too long a period to constitute a reasonable time. See *M.J.S., Inc.*, Comp. Gen. Dec. B-244410, 91-2 CPD ¶ 344, holding that a BAFO with no expiration date could clearly be accepted one month after submission.

Generally, contracting officers obtain proposal extensions from offerors when they find that there will be substantial delays in awarding the contract. The GAO has found this to be proper when the agency has valid reasons for extending the time of award, *Saco Def., Inc.*, Comp. Gen. Dec. B-240603, 90-2 CPD ¶ 462 (11-month delay to permit a small business reasonable time to cure a responsibility problem and to conduct discussions); *Trim-Flite, Inc.*, 67 Comp. Gen. 550 (B-229926.4), 88-2 CPD ¶ 124 (eight-month delay to correct agency errors); *American Identification Prods., Inc.*, Comp. Gen. Dec. B-227599, 87-2 CPD ¶ 42 (six-month delay to evaluate samples). In *Ocean Tech., Inc.*, Comp. Gen. Dec. B-236470, 89-2 CPD ¶ 189, the GAO denied a protest claiming that the proposal extension had been signed by an unauthorized employee of the offeror because the award could have been made even if the offer expired.

If an offeror agrees to hold its offer open and is later awarded the contract, it takes the risk of cost increases that may have occurred in the intervening period. See *Magna Enters., Inc.*, ASBCA 51188, 02-1 BCA ¶ 31660, stating at 156,419-20:

> Magna voluntarily extended its offer repeatedly, and used that time to resolve the Government's serious concerns over Magna's ability to perform. Although the offer remained open for a protracted period, that time was not shown to be unreasonable under the circumstances. Magna assumed the risk in this fixed-price supply contract that potential subcontractors or suppliers might become unavailable, or that prices could increase. *Consolidated Airborne Systems, Inc. v. United States*, 348 F.2d 941 (Ct. Cl. 1965); *D.W. Clark, Inc.*, ASBCA No. 45562, 94-3 BCA ¶ 27,132. A contractor is properly terminated for default when it fails to perform due to price increases during an extended offer period.

See also *Ordnance Parts & Eng'g Co.*, ASBCA 44327, 93-2 BCA ¶ 25,690, where the contractor was properly terminated for default when it failed to perform because of significant price increases that had occurred in the year that it held its offer open.

C. Delay of Award by Protest

When a preaward protest is filed, the award is generally delayed until the protest is resolved. This imposes the burden on the winning offeror if such delayed award increases its costs of performance or otherwise makes it more difficult to perform the work. However, a winning offeror is not required to remain available for award in the face of a protest.

If an agency decides to withhold award pending the outcome of a protest, the selected offeror and other offerors that might be in line for award will normally be requested to keep their offers open. In addition, the protester's offer will be held to have remained open by virtue of the protest, 50 Comp. Gen. 357 (B-170178) (1970). Upon conclusion of the protest, the agency will normally be able to make award in accordance with the original procurement if that is the proper course of action, *Skyline Credit Corp.*, Comp. Gen. Dec. B-209193, 83-1 CPD ¶ 257. The GAO has permitted this outcome by holding that expiration dates may be waived and offers revived by the offeror in negotiated procurements because the only right conferred by expiration dates is the right of the offeror to refuse to waive the expiration date, *Riggins & Williamson Mach. Co.*, 54 Comp. Gen. 783 (B-182801), 75-1 CPD ¶ 168. The GAO has specified that revival of offers or waiver of expiration dates for the purpose of awarding the contract must be done "on the basis of the offer as submitted," *Donald N. Humphries & Assocs.*, 55 Comp. Gen. 432 (B-183292), 75-2 CPD ¶ 275. Under these circumstances, the GAO has repeatedly held that because the offer was not altered, no reopening of negotiations was necessary, as it was not prejudicial to the competitive system. See *Sublette Elec., Inc.*, Comp. Gen. Dec. B-232586, 88-2 CPD ¶ 540; *Protective Materials Co.*, Comp. Gen. Dec. B-225495, 87-1 CPD ¶ 303; and *Medical Coaches, Inc.*, Comp. Gen. Dec. B-196339.2, 79-2 CPD ¶ 308, where the offers were not altered and, therefore, no further discussions were found to have been held by the agency. In *Ocean Tech., Inc.*, Comp. Gen. Dec. B-236470, 89-2 CPD ¶ 189, and *Data Tech. Indus., Inc.*, Comp. Gen. Dec. B-197858, 80-2 CPD ¶ 2, the GAO specifically noted that the actual request that an offeror waive the expiration date of its offer did not constitute discussions requiring the reopening of negotiations with all offerors. See also *Rentfrow, Inc.*, Comp. Gen. Dec. B-243215, 91-2 CPD ¶ 25, holding that it was proper to request a waiver of the expiration date only from the winning offeror.

Offerors that elect to keep their offers open during the protest period and are subsequently awarded the contract have no recourse thereafter. The GAO has refused to grant delay damages in such circumstances. See *Trim-Flite, Inc.*, 67 Comp. Gen. 550 (B-229926.4), 88-2 CPD ¶ 124, stating at 550:

> A delay in meeting procurement milestones generally is a procedural deficiency which does not provide a basis of protest because it has no effect on the validity of the procurement, *American Identification Products, Inc.*, B-227599, July 13, 1987, 87-2 CPD ¶ 42. While an agency is required to award a contract with reasonable promptness, the 8-month period here from closing date to award is not unreasonable per se given the attempts by the agency to correct the matters raised in offerors' complaints and protests through reevaluations. *See Id*. The fact that the delays may have been the result of initial agency errors in the procurement is irrelevant; once the errors occurred . . . the [agency's] proper course of action was to take steps to correct the errors. The award delay was merely an unfortunate, but necessary, by-product of the [agency's] proper action.

Subsequently, the GAO ruled that delay in award of a contract is not a protestable issue, *Federal Sales Serv., Inc.*, Comp. Gen. Dec B-237978, 90-1 CPD ¶ 249. See also

M.A. Mortenson Co. v. United States, 843 F.2d 1360 (Fed. Cir. 1988), where the court denied a price adjustment when the contractor had extended its bid expiration date by 77 days and later claimed additional compensation to reflect the fact that this time extension had forced it to perform in winter weather. Similarly, in *DeMatteo Constr. Co. v. United States*, 220 Ct. Cl. 579, 600 F.2d 1384 (1979), the contractor was denied compensation for a suspension of work when it extended its expiration date pending the outcome of a protest. On the other hand, if performance is stayed after award, the contractor is entitled to compensation under the Protest After Award clause in FAR 52.233-3.

D. Date of Award

There has been controversy on the date that an award through government acceptance of a firm's offer creates a binding contract. This issue can be important when a firm attempts to withdraw its offer before it has received the government's acceptance but finds that the acceptance was place in the mail before the withdrawal. The traditional common-law rule was that the contract was binding when acceptance of the offer is dispatched (the "mailbox" rule). However, this rule was rejected by the Court of Claims in *Emeco Indus., Inc. v. United States*, 202 Ct. Cl. 1006, 485 F.2d 652 (1973), and *Rhode Island Tool Co. v. United States*, 130 Ct. Cl. 698, 128 F. Supp. 417 (1955), where the court, relying on postal regulations allowing the retrieval of mailed documents from the mail by the sender, reasoned that award does not occur until the offeror receives the dispatch. See also *Titan Atlantic Constr. Corp./The Gallegos Corp., a Joint Venture*, ASBCA 26007, 83-2 BCA ¶ 16,791, following this rule in determining that acceptance of a government offer by the contractor was not binding until the government received the acceptance. This decision contains a complete history of the evolution of this rule. Following the *Emeco* decision, some of the government forms stated that acceptance was effective when placed in the mail (adopting the old "mailbox" rule), and several appeals boards held that these forms governed. See *Adaptive Concepts, Inc.*, ASBCA 73123, 96-1 BCA ¶ 28,248; *G.E. Sales & Rentals v. General Servs. Admin.*, GSBCA 13304, 1995 GSBCA LEXIS 409; *Singleton Contracting Corp.*, IBCA-1770-1-84, 86-2 BCA ¶ 18,800; *Computer Wholesale Corp.*, GSBCA 4217, 76-1 BCA ¶ 11,859; and *IMCO Precision Prods., Inc.*, ASBCA 17572, 73-2 BCA ¶ 10,250. The GAO also concluded that the language in these forms was controlling in making the "mailbox" rule applicable, *Wolverine Diesel Power Co.*, 57 Comp. Gen. 468 (B-189789), 78-1 CPD ¶ 375 (telegraphic acceptance effective when dispatched). Although no decisions have been found on this issue, since the Instruction to Offerors – Competitive Acquisition solicitation provision in FAR 52.215-1 contains language essentially the same as that construed by the board and GAO decisions, it would appear that acceptance will be effective when the government mails the signed SF 33, SF 1442 or OF 307. The solicitation provision states in ¶ (f):

> (10) A written award or acceptance of proposal mailed or otherwise furnished to the successful offeror within the time specified in the proposal shall result in a binding contract without further action by either party.

The parties may agree to an effective date of the contract other than the date of execution of the contract document. In *Northrop Worldwide Aircraft Servs., Inc.*, ASBCA 45216, 96-2 BCA ¶ 28,574, the agency amended Standard Form 26 to read "conditional/award," whereby the parties agreed that the contract effective date would be the date on which it received approval from the secretary of the agency. The approval occurred subsequent to the date the form was executed, and it was this later date that the board recognized as the effective date of the contract.

II. NOTICES AND DEBRIEFINGS

Agencies are required to notify offerors when they are eliminated from the competition and to provide debriefings when requested. Section 1014 of The Federal Acquisition Streamlining Act of 1994 (FASA), amending 10 U.S.C. § 2305(b), and § 1064 of the FASA, amending 41 U.S.C. § 253b, added new, detailed guidance on postaward debriefings. Section 4104 of the Clinger-Cohen Act of 1996 further amended 10 U.S.C. § 2305(b) and 41 U.S.C. § 253b to add a new provision on preaward debriefings. These statutes are implemented in FAR 15.605 and FAR 15.606.

A. Preaward Notices and Debriefings

Preaward notices and debriefings serve a number of purposes. Early notice of exclusion from the competition will permit excluded offerors to turn their attention to other contracting opportunities. It will also conserve resources because offerors will be on notice that investing further expense on the procurement would not be productive. These purposes were noted in the promulgation comments of the FAR Part 15 rewrite at 62 Fed. Reg. 51226 (1997):

> This final rule insures that offerors with little probability of success are advised early on that their competitive position does not merit additional expense in a largely futile attempt to secure the contract.

> This knowledge will benefit both large and small entities, but will be especially beneficial to small entities that have constrained budgets. These entities will be able to conserve scarce bid and proposal funds and employ their resources on more productive business opportunities.

Another function of the preaward notice is that it provides an offeror an opportunity to challenge its elimination from the competition by requesting a preaward debriefing and determining whether to file a preaward protest or request alternative dispute resolution of its objection to the exclusion. Although additional effort may be required of procurement personnel and delays in the procurement result if protests are filed, early resolution will be to the public's advantage if the exclusion was not appropriate. Corrective action is less time-consuming and expensive to all parties if undertaken while the procurement is in process rather than after award.

1. *Preaward Notices*

Although the procurement statutes do not specifically state that preaward notice of exclusion from competition is to be given, the requirement for such notice is implicit in the offeror's right to request a preaward debriefing. Thus, FAR 15.503(a) requires preaward notices of exclusion as follows:

> Preaward notices — (1) Preaward notices of exclusion from competitive range. The contracting officer shall notify offerors promptly in writing when their proposals are excluded from the competitive range or otherwise eliminated from the competition. The notice shall state the basis for the determination and that a proposal revision will not be considered.

The phrase "or otherwise eliminated from the competition" is not defined. It apparently is meant to implement the statutory phrase "or otherwise excludes such an offeror from further consideration prior to the final source selection decision" providing for preaward debriefing, 10 U.S.C. § 2305(b)(6)(A) and 41 U.S.C. § 253b(f)(1). Determinations of exclusion that would qualify for such notice would include determinations that an offeror is not responsible or otherwise not eligible for award or that an offer is inexcusably late (FAR 15.208(c)) or is unacceptable. It might also be argued that an offeror is "eliminated from the competition" when another offeror is selected for award. Contradicting such an interpretation is the statutory language providing for preaward debriefing for an excluded offeror "prior to the final source selection decision." Although the FAR would be free to go beyond the statutory mandate, it is doubtful if this is the correct interpretation because FAR 15.503(a)(2) specifically provides for post-selection, preaward notice for small business set-asides, as follows:

> Preaward notices for small business set-asides. In addition to the notice in paragraph (a)(1) of this section, when using a small business set-aside (see Subpart 19.5), upon completion of negotiations and determinations of responsibility, but prior to award, the contracting officer shall notify each offeror in writing of the name and location of the apparent successful offeror. The notice shall also state that
>
> > (i) The Government will not consider subsequent revisions of the offeror's proposal; and
> >
> > (ii) No response is required unless a basis exists to challenge the small business size status of the apparent successful offeror. The notice is not required when the contracting officer determines in writing that the urgency of the requirement necessitates award without delay or when the contract is entered into under the 8(a) program (see 19.805-2).

2. *Preaward Debriefings*

The statutory provisions for preaward debriefings at 10 U.S.C. § 2305(b)(6)(A) and 41 U.S.C. § 253b(f) are implemented in FAR 15.505, as follows:

Offerors excluded from the competitive range or otherwise excluded from the competition before award may request a debriefing before award (10 U.S.C. 2305(b)(6)(A) and 41 U.S.C. 253b(f)–(h)).

(a)(1) The offeror may request a preaward debriefing by submitting a written request for debriefing to the contracting officer within 3 days after receipt of the notice of exclusion from the competition.

(2) At the offeror's request, this debriefing may be delayed until after award. If the debriefing is delayed until after award, it shall include all information normally provided in a postaward debriefing (see 15.506(d)). Debriefings delayed pursuant to this paragraph could affect the timeliness of any protest filed subsequent to the debriefing.

(3) If the offeror does not submit a timely request, the offeror need not be given either a preaward or a postaward debriefing. Offerors are entitled to no more than one debriefing for each proposal.

(b) The contracting officer shall make every effort to debrief the unsuccessful offeror as soon as practicable, but may refuse the request for a debriefing if, for compelling reasons, it is not in the best interests of the Government to conduct a debriefing at that time. The rationale for delaying the debriefing shall be documented in the contract file. If the contracting officer delays the debriefing, it shall be provided no later than the time postaward debriefings are provided under 15.506. In that event, the contracting officer shall include the information at 15.506(d) in the debriefing.

(c) Debriefings may be done orally, in writing, or by any other method acceptable to the contracting officer.

(d) The contracting officer should normally chair any debriefing session held. Individuals who conducted the evaluations shall provide support.

(e) At a minimum, preaward debriefings shall include —

(1) The agency's evaluation of significant elements in the offeror's proposal;

(2) A summary of the rationale for eliminating the offeror from the competition; and

(3) Reasonable responses to relevant questions about whether source selection procedures contained in the solicitation, applicable regulations, and other applicable authorities were followed in the process of eliminating the offeror from the competition.

(f) Preaward debriefings shall not disclose —

(1) The number of offerors;

(2) The identity of other offerors;

(3) The content of other offerors' proposals;

(4) The ranking of other offerors;

(5) The evaluation of other offerors; or

(6) Any of the information prohibited in 15.506(e).

(g) An official summary of the debriefing shall be included in the contract file.

Because ¶ (a)(3) limits offerors to a single debriefing and ¶ (a)(2) permits offerors to elect a postaward debriefing in lieu of a preaward debriefing, they must exercise care in deciding the type of debriefing to request when they have been excluded from the competition prior to the award decision. If they believe that they have been unfairly eliminated from the competition, they will undoubtedly elect a preaward debriefing to determine the basis for the agency's action. However, because the procurement is ongoing, ¶ (f) severely limits the amount of information that can be given to the offeror in this type of debriefing. Thus, in cases where the offeror does not intend to challenge its exclusion from the competition but desires to learn how to improve its competitive position in future procurements, a postaward debriefing is a sensible election because far more information can be obtained in a postaward debriefing. This election also benefits the procuring agency because it permits debriefing at a time when the workload of the source selection team is likely to be smaller than it would be prior to award. Great care should be exercised by offerors in this regard because if they elect a postaward debriefing and learn therein that they were excluded from the competitive range because of deficiencies in their proposal, a protest of faulty evaluation may be held to be untimely. This occurred in *United Int'l Investigative Servs., Inc.*, Comp. Gen. Dec. B-286327, 2000 CPD ¶ 173, where the GAO rejected the protest as being untimely, stating:

> As stated in our timeliness rules, a post-debriefing protest will be considered timely if filed as late as 10 days after the debriefing, even as to issues that should have been known before the debriefing, if that debriefing is "required." [However,] Congress specifically addressed the issue of when agencies are required to give post-award debriefings to offerors excluded from the competitive range, stating that such debriefings are required "only if that [excluded] offeror requested and was refused a preaward debriefing." 41 U.S.C. § 253b(f).

> Here, the record is clear that UIIS did not request a pre-award debriefing. Rather, UIIS expressly requested that its debriefing be delayed until after award. Accordingly, we do not view the debriefing provided by the agency on September 19 as being "required" as contemplated by the controlling statute and our Bid Protest Reg-

ulations. Thus, UIIS may not properly rely on its own decision to request a delayed debriefing as a basis to extend the period for filing its protest by more than 3 months after UIIS received notification of its exclusion from the competitive range.

Since UIIS's debriefing does not fall within the exception to the general requirement, stated above, that protests must be filed no later than 10 days after the basis of the protest is known or should have been known, 4 C.F.R. § 21.2(a)(2), we next consider whether UIIS's decision to delay seeking the information on which its protest is based was consistent with the obligation to diligently pursue that information. A protester may not passively await information providing a basis for protest; rather, a protester has an affirmative obligation to diligently pursue such information, *Automated Med. Prods. Corp.*, B-275835, Feb. 3, 1997, 97-1 CPD ¶ 52 at 2-3, and a protester's failure to utilize the most expeditious information-gathering approach may constitute a failure to meet its obligation in this regard. See, e.g., *Thomas May Constr. Co.*, B-255683, Mar. 23, 1994, 94-1 CPD ¶ 210 (protester did not diligently pursue its basis for protest where it waited until after it received notice of award to file Freedom of Information Act requests to seek information that was publicly available at bid opening). Our timeliness rules reflect the dual requirements of giving parties a fair opportunity to present their cases and resolving protests expeditiously without unduly disrupting or delaying the procurement process. *Air Inc. — Recon.*, B-238220.2, Jan. 29, 1990, 90-1 CPD ¶ 129 at 2.

The GAO will not review an agency's decision that it is in the government's best interest to delay the debriefing in a particular procurement until after award, *Global Eng'g & Constr.*, Comp. Gen. Dec. B-275999.3, 97-1 CPD ¶ 77. In that case, Global requested a preaward debriefing after the agency excluded its proposal from the competitive range. The agency denied Global's request on the ground that preaward debriefings in the procurement would not be in the government's best interest. The agency also stated that a preaward debriefing would require redirecting the agency's resources "which would not best serve our customers' needs or be a wise expenditure of U.S. tax dollars." The GAO stated that the offeror would not be prejudiced by the denial of the preaward debriefing because it would be entitled to receive a postaward debriefing and, if it filed a protest after award, work on the procurement would be stayed. In the GAO's view, an agency postponing the debriefing "may find it difficult to marshall the resources to defend its earlier decision" and that "simply may prejudice the agency in defending the protest." Although the GAO found that Global presented several valid reasons why preaward debriefings should be encouraged, it still denied the protest, stating:

> The arguments Global makes all are valid reasons why preaward debriefings should be encouraged no matter what the procurement circumstances. For example, honest exchange of information in a preaward debriefing may well obviate the need for, or discourage, a bid protest; competitive range evaluation results for excluded offerors always are "fresher" in the preaward than in the postaward timeframe; and since a protest potentially could result in a disruption to correct a procurement deficiency it generally would be better to correct the problem at an earlier time whenever possible.

Nevertheless, we will not review the [agency's] determination that it is not in the government's best interest to provide preaward debriefings in this procurement. In adding the preaward debriefing requirement to 10 U.S.C. § 2305 through section 4104 of the Clinger-Cohen Act the Congress also expressly recognized that it may not be in the government's best interests to conduct a debriefing until after award. In other words, the Congress determined that despite the considerations that make preaward debriefings important elements of government procurements, agencies need to retain the discretion to decide that the government's interests may warrant delaying debriefings in certain circumstances.

The same agency indicated its intention not to grant a preaward debriefing in another decision, *Siebe Envtl. Controls*, Comp. Gen. Dec. B-275999.2, 97-1 CPD ¶ 70. In denying relief the GAO stated that the protest process was not to be used to determine why a contractor had been eliminated from the procurement and suggested that the information could be obtained by seeking information under the Freedom of Information Act. The GAO's refusal to review such actions would appear to permit the agency to arbitrarily deny a preaward debriefing. Whether that is consistent with the intent of the statute is questionable.

The GAO has ruled on the requirement that a preaward debriefing be requested within three days of receipt of the notice of exclusion from the competitive range. See *International Resources Group*, Comp. Gen. Dec. B-286663, 2001 CPD ¶ 35, holding that when the notice of exclusion is sent by the agency electronically after business hours, the first day for the computation should be the first business day after the day that the notice was sent.

B. Postaward Notices and Debriefings

Postaward notices and debriefings serve a number of functions in addition to those served by preaward notices and debriefings. Besides advising offerors that their offers are no longer under consideration and providing them with information to challenge the selection, postaward debriefings can provide offerors with "an indication of how those offerors can improve their chances for success in future procurements," Sen. Rep. 103-258 accompanying the FASA, Pub. L. No. 103-355. By identifying the source selected, postaward notices also provide information that other offerors may use for subcontracting opportunities.

1. Postaward Notices

The procurement statutes require notice of contract award to be given to "all other offerors within 3 days after date of contract award in writing or by electronic means of the rejection of their proposals," 10 U.S.C. § 2305(b)(4)(c) and 41 U.S.C. § 253b(d)(3). This requirement is implemented in FAR 15.503(b), as follows:

Postaward notices. (1) Within 3 days after the date of contract award, the contracting officer shall provide written notification to each offeror whose proposal was in the competitive range but was not selected for award (10 U.S.C. 2305(b)(5) and 41 U.S.C. 253b(c)) or had not been previously notified under paragraph (a) of this section. The notice shall include —

(i) The number of offerors solicited;

(ii) The number of proposals received;

(iii) The name and address of each offeror receiving an award;

(iv) The items, quantities, and any stated unit prices of each award. If the number of items or other factors makes listing any stated unit prices impracticable at that time, only the total contract price need be furnished in the notice. However, the items, quantities, and any stated unit prices of each award shall be made publicly available, upon request; and

(v) In general terms, the reason(s) the offeror's proposal was not accepted, unless the price information in paragraph (b)(1)(iv) of this section readily reveals the reason. In no event shall an offeror's cost breakdown, profit, overhead rates, trade secrets, manufacturing processes and techniques, or other confidential business information be disclosed to any other offeror.

(2) Upon request, the contracting officer shall furnish the information described in paragraph (b)(1) of this section to unsuccessful offerors in solicitations using simplified acquisition procedures in Part 13.

(3) Upon request, the contracting officer shall provide the information in paragraph (b)(1) of this section to unsuccessful offerors that received a preaward notice of exclusion from the competitive range.

2. Postaward Debriefings

The statutory requirements for postaward debriefings, 10 U.S.C. § 2305(b)(5) and 41 U.S.C. § 253b(e), are implemented in FAR 15.506, which provides:

(a)(1) An offeror, upon its written request received by the agency within 3 days after the date on which that offeror has received notification of contract award in accordance with 15.503(b), shall be debriefed and furnished the basis for the selection decision and contract award.

(2) To the maximum extent practicable, the debriefing should occur within 5 days after receipt of the written request. Offerors that requested a postaward debriefing in lieu of a preaward debriefing, or whose debriefing was delayed for compelling reasons beyond contract award, also should be debriefed within this time period.

(3) An offeror that was notified of exclusion from the competition (see 15.505(a)), but failed to submit a timely request, is not entitled to a debriefing.

(4)(i) Untimely debriefing requests may be accommodated.

(ii) Government accommodation of a request for delayed debriefing pursuant to 15.505(a)(2), or any untimely debriefing request, does not automatically extend the deadlines for filing protests. Debriefings delayed pursuant to 15.505(a)(2) could affect the timeliness of any protest filed subsequent to the debriefing.

(iii) Debriefings of successful and unsuccessful offerors may be done orally, in writing, or by any other method acceptable to the contracting officer.

(b) Debriefings of successful and unsuccessful offerors may be done orally, in writing, or by any other method acceptable to the contracting officer.

(c) The contracting officer should normally chair any debriefing session held. Individuals who conducted the evaluations shall provide support.

(d) At a minimum, the debriefing information shall include —

(1) The Government's evaluation of the significant weaknesses or deficiencies in the offeror's proposal, if applicable;

(2) The overall evaluated cost or price (including unit prices) and technical rating, if applicable, of the successful offeror and the debriefed offeror, and past performance information on the debriefed offeror;

(3) The overall ranking of all offerors, when any ranking was developed by the agency during the source selection;

(4) A summary of the rationale for award;

(5) For acquisitions of commercial items, the make and model of the item to be delivered by the successful offeror; and

(6) Reasonable responses to relevant questions about whether source selection procedures contained in the solicitation, applicable regulations, and other applicable authorities were followed.

(e) The debriefing shall not include point-by-point comparisons of the debriefed offeror's proposal with those of other offerors. Moreover, the debriefing shall not reveal any information prohibited from disclosure by 24.202 or exempt from release under the Freedom of Information Act (5 U.S.C. 552) including —

(1) Trade secrets;

(2) Privileged or confidential manufacturing processes and techniques;

(3) Commercial and financial information that is privileged or confidential, including cost breakdowns, profit, indirect cost rates, and similar information; and

(4) The names of individuals providing reference information about an offeror's past performance.

(f) An official summary of the debriefing shall be included in the contract file.

Congress has given protesters more rights by making the stay from proceeding with performance of an awarded contract in the event of a protest dependent on the debriefing. Prior to the FASA, this stay was put in effect (absent urgency) only if the protest was received no more than 10 days from contract award. Under § 1402 of the FASA, the stay will go into effect if a protest is received within five days after the debriefing is conducted. This provision penalizes agencies that do not conduct their postaward debriefings in a timely fashion. Although agencies can wait, by doing so they lengthen the time that a protester has to evaluate the merits of any projected protest.

A debriefing must be timely requested and acted upon in order to preserve the offeror's rights. First, the right to the statutory stay from proceeding with performance after award will be lost if the protest is not filed within five days after a debriefing date *offered* by the agency, FAR 33.103(f)(3), not the actual date of the debriefing. Second, the right to protest to the GAO will be lost if the protest is not filed within 10 days of the date a debriefing is *offered* by the agency. See *Pentec Envtl., Inc.*, Comp. Gen. Dec. B-276874.2, 97-1 CPD ¶ 199, where a protest was found untimely because the protester delayed the debriefing one month after the date offered by the agency in order to obtain information through a Freedom of Information Act request. See also *Professional Rehabilitation Consultants, Inc.*, Comp. Gen. Dec. B-275871, 97-1 CPD ¶ 94, dismissing a postaward debriefing protest because the protester waited two months to request a debriefing after it was informed that it had not received the award, stating:

> [P]rotesters have an affirmative obligation to diligently pursue information that forms the basis for their protests. If they do not do so within a reasonable time, we will dismiss the protest as untimely. *Horizon Trading Co., Inc.; Drexel Heritage Furnishings, Inc.*, B-231177; B-231177.2, July 26, 1988, 88-2 CPD ¶ 86; *see also General Physics Federal Sys. Inc.*, B-274795, Jan. 6, 1997, 97-1 CPD ¶ 8.

> Since this procurement was conducted on the basis of competitive proposals, PRC was entitled to request and receive a post-award debriefing. Federal Acquisition Regulation 15.1004 (FAC 90-27). The requirement to diligently pursue the information on which a protest is based includes diligently pursuing a debriefing, which allows protesters to determine whether they have a basis for protest and, if so, what it is.

Inadequate debriefings have not created a protestable issue in the GAO because such challenges are procedural matters that do not affect the validity of an award decision, *Thermolten Tech., Inc.*, Comp. Gen. Dec. B-278408, 98-1 CPD ¶ 35; *McShade*

Enters., Comp. Gen. Dec. B-278851, 98-1 CPD ¶ 90; *CACI Field Servs., Inc.*, Comp. Gen. Dec. B-234945, 89-2 CPD ¶ 97; *Haworth, Inc.*, Comp. Gen. Dec. B-215638.2, 84-2 CPD ¶ 461. However, an inadequate debriefing can extend the time that an offeror has to protest even if the time to stay the performance of the contract has passed. For example, in *Geo-Centers, Inc.*, Comp. Gen. Dec. B-276033, 97-1 CPD ¶ 182, the GAO sustained a protest that was filed three months after contract award and two months after a debriefing that did not contain sufficient details to disclose the basis for the protest, ruling that the protest was timely because it was filed within 10 days after the protester learned of the grounds for protest in a response to a request for the information pursuant to the Freedom of Information Act. Similarly, in *Biospherics, Inc.*, Comp. Gen. Dec. B-278278, 98-1 CPD ¶ 161, the protester asserted that the agency failed to inform it of adverse past performance information during discussions. The agency countered that this argument was not timely because it had informed the protester during debriefing that the protester had been ranked lower than the awardee under the past performance factor and it did not receive a perfect score on this factor. The GAO held that the protest filed more than 10 days of the debriefing was timely because the protester was not informed during the debriefing of the degree to which its proposal was downgraded under this factor and did not know the specific adverse past performance information being considered by the agency.

A losing firm may obtain more relief in the Court of Federal Claims where the protest timeliness requirements are not as strict. See, for example, *Tin Mills Props., LLC v. United States*, 82 Fed. Cl. 584 (2008), where the court ordered the contracting officer to inform the protester of the precise reasons for its exclusion from the competitive range when the debriefing had been extremely cursory, even after repeated requests by the protester for detailed information.

C. Information Available to Unsuccessful Offerors

FAR 15.506(e) prohibits disclosure in a postaward debriefing of information that would not be made available under the Freedom of Information Act, 5 U.S.C. § 552, giving four examples of the types of information that should not be disclosed. FAR 15.505(f) prohibits disclosure in preaward debriefings of this same information and five other specific types of information. However, this guidance is incomplete because disclosure of information is covered by three statutes that give considerable guidance on the types of information that may be disclosed during the procurement process and agency officials are bound by these statutes without regard to the provisions of the FAR. These statutes are: (1) the procurement integrity provisions of the Office of Procurement Policy Act of 1989, 41 U.S.C. § 423, (2) the Trade Secrets Act, 18 U.S.C. § 1905, and (3) the Freedom of Information Act.

1. *Procurement Integrity Provisions (41 U.S.C. § 423)*

Because this statute applies only before award of a contract, as discussed in Chapter 1, it pertains only to preaward debriefings. With regard to such debriefings, it prohibits any person from disclosing "contractor bid or proposal information" or "source selection information," to any unauthorized person, 41 U.S.C. § 423(a). These terms are defined in the statute (see Chapter 1) and in FAR 3.104-1, with minor modifications, as follows:

> *Contractor bid or proposal information* means any of the following information submitted to a Federal agency as part of or in connection with a bid or proposal to enter into a Federal agency procurement contract, if that information has not been previously made available to the public or disclosed publicly:
>
>> (1) Cost or pricing data (as defined by 10 U.S.C. 2306a(h) with respect to procurements subject to that section, and section 304A(h) of the Federal Property and Administrative Services Act of 1949 (41 U.S.C. 254b(h)), with respect to procurements subject to that section).
>>
>> (2) Indirect costs and direct labor rates.
>>
>> (3) Proprietary information about manufacturing processes, operations, or techniques marked by the contractor in accordance with applicable law or regulation.
>>
>> (4) Information marked by the contractor as "contractor bid or proposal information" in accordance with applicable law or regulation.
>>
>> (5) Information marked in accordance with 52.215-1(e).
>
> *Source selection information* means any of the following information which is prepared for use by a Federal agency for the purpose of evaluating a bid or proposal to enter into a Federal agency procurement contract, if that information has not been previously made available to the public or disclosed publicly:
>
>> (1) Bid prices submitted in response to a Federal agency invitation for bids, or lists of those bid prices before bid opening.
>>
>> (2) Proposed costs or prices submitted in response to a Federal agency solicitation, or lists of those proposed costs or prices.
>>
>> (3) Source selection plans.
>>
>> (4) Technical evaluation plans.
>>
>> (5) Technical evaluations of proposals.
>>
>> (6) Cost or price evaluations of proposals.
>>
>> (7) Competitive range determinations that identify proposals that have a reasonable chance of being selected for award of a contract.

(8) Rankings of bids, proposals, or competitors.

(9) Reports and evaluations of source selection panels, boards, or advisory councils.

(10) Other information marked as "SOURCE SELECTION INFORMA-TION — SEE FAR 3.104" based on a case-by-case determination by the head of the agency or designee, or the contracting officer, that its disclosure would jeopardize the integrity or successful completion of the Federal agency procurement to which the information relates.

See Chapter 1 for a discussion of the statutory savings provisions, which permit some limited disclosure of this type of information. However, for practical purposes these limitations should be read in conjunction with the limitations in FAR 15.505(f) to determine the full scope of information that should not be disclosed in preaward debriefings.

2. Trade Secrets Act (18 U.S.C. § 1905)

This criminal statute applies to all conduct of government officials and thus applies to both preaward and postaward debriefings. It contains a very broad description of information that may not be released by government agencies:

Whoever, being an officer or employee of the United States or of any department or agency thereof, . . . publishes, divulges, discloses, or makes known in any manner or to any extent not authorized by law any information coming to him in the course of his employment or official duties or by reason of any examination or investigation made by, or return, report or record made to or filed with, such department or agency or officer or employee thereof, which information concerns or relates to the trade secrets, processes, operations, style of work, or apparatus, or to the identity, confidential statistical data, amount or source of any income, profits, losses, or expenditures of any person, firm, partnership, corporation, or association; or permits any income return or copy thereof or any book containing any abstract or particulars thereof to be seen or examined by any person except as provided by law; shall be fined not more than $1,000, or imprisoned not more than one year, or both; and shall be removed from office or employment.

It has been held that this Act covers only information submitted to the government in confidence and that it would not apply to unintentional disclosures of information, *United States v. Wallington*, 889 F.2d 573 (5th Cir. 1989).

3. Freedom of Information Act (5 U.S.C. § 552)

The other major guidance on the information that can be given to unsuccessful offerors is contained in the regulations and court decisions under the Freedom of Information Act (FOIA), 5 U.C.S. § 552. The Act is controlling because it has been held that a contractual promise not to release information cannot override the Act, *Petkas v. Staats*, 501 F.2d 887 (D.C. Cir. 1974). Thus, the Act defines the outer limit of information obtainable through the debriefing process and constitutes a mechanism that can be used by an unsuccessful offeror to obtain information denied during the debriefing. This Act contains mandatory disclosure requirements pertaining to all "agency records." The Act provides that "each agency, upon any request for records which (A) reasonably describes such records, and (B) is made in accordance with published rules stating the time, place, fees (if any), and procedures to be followed, shall make the records promptly available to any person." The Act may be used by any person, including persons not party to a controversy, and is mandatory for all executive agencies as well as government corporations and independent regulatory agencies, 5 U.S.C. § 552(a)(3). The Act requires that requested records be furnished unless one of nine statutory exemptions applies, 5 U.S.C. § 552(b). The right to obtain information under the Act depends primarily on two issues: what constitutes an agency record and the scope of the exemptions set forth in 5 U.S.C. § 552(b).

a. Agency Record

The Act does not define "agency record." However, the term is broad and includes existing data in any form pertaining to the operations of an agency. Agency record is defined in the Department of Defense Freedom of Information Act Program Regulation 5400.7-R, 62 Fed. Reg. 35351, July 1, 1997:

> Agency record. (1) The products of data compilation, such as all books, papers, maps, and photographs, machine readable materials, inclusive of those in electronic form or format, or other documentary materials, regardless of physical form or characteristics, made or received by an agency of the United States Government under Federal law in connection with the transaction of public business and in Department of Defense possession and control at the time the FOIA request is made. Care should be taken not to exclude records from being considered agency records, unless they fall within one of the categories of paragraph (2) of this definition.

> (2) The following are not included within the definition of the word "record":

>> (i) Objects or articles, such as structures, furniture, vehicles and equipment, whatever their historical value, or value as evidence.

>> (ii) Anything that is not tangible or documentary record, such as an individual's memory or oral communication.

>> (iii) Personal records of an individual not subject to agency creation or retention requirements, created and maintained primarily for the convenience of an agency employee, and not distributed to other agency employees for their official use. Personal papers fall into three categories: those created before entering Government service; private materials brought

into, created, or received in the office that were not created or received in the course of transacting Government business; and work-related personal papers that are not used in the transaction of Government business.

(3) A record must exist and be in the possession and control of the Department of Defense at the time of the request to be considered subject to this part and the FOIA. There is no obligation to create, compile, or obtain a record to satisfy a FOIA request. See § 286.4(g)(2) creating a record in the electronic environment.

(4) Hard copy of electronic records, that are subject to FOIA requests under 5 U.S.C. 552(a)(3), and that are available to the public through an established distribution system, or through the Federal Register, the National Technical Information Service, or the Internet, normally need not be processed under the provisions of the FOIA. If a request is received for such information, DoD Components shall provide the requester with guidance, inclusive of any written notice to the public, on how to obtain the information. However, if the requester insists that the request be processed under the FOIA, then the request shall be processed under the FOIA. If there is any doubt as to whether the request must be processed, contact the Directorate for Freedom of Information and Security Review.

This definition reflects the fact that records in electronic format are agency records which must be made available in that format if so requested. This requirement was added to the FOIA in 1996 by Pub. L. No. 104-231. It is clear that computer programs that embody databases are agency records, but it is not clear whether computer programs that do not contain data constitute agency records. See *Long v. IRS*, 596 F.2d 362 (9th Cir. 1979), holding that computer tapes were agency records, and *Cleary v. HHS*, 844 F. Supp. 770 (D.D.C. 1993), holding that computer programs that were "uniquely suited to [their] underlying database" were agency records because they "preserve information" and "perpetuate knowledge." The Office of Hearings and Appeals of the Department of Energy has ruled that pure computer programs that neither contain information nor manipulate information are not agency records, *John Gilmore*, D.O.E. No. LFA-0388, June 29, 1994. The 1995 version of DOD Regulation 5400.7-R had stated that "computer software, including source code, object code, and listings of source and object codes" were not agency records, but this was deleted from the current version of the regulation.

For something to be an agency record, it must be in both the possession and control of the agency. The fact that the government has control over information in the possession of a third party, by virtue of a right to require delivery to the agency, does not constitute the possession necessary to establish the existence of an agency record. In *Forsham v. Harris*, 445 U.S. 169 (1980), for example, the government properly denied a FOIA request to obtain raw data underlying a report submitted to the Department of Health, Education and Welfare (HEW) under a federally funded grant. Although HEW had rights under the grant to acquire the data, it had not exercised those rights, and the data remained in the exclusive possession of the grantee. This rule was modified by the Omnibus Consolidated and

Emergency Supplemental Appropriations Act for Fiscal Year 1999, Pub. L. No. 105-277, requiring OMB to modify its Circular A-110, Grants and Agreements with Institutions of Higher Education, Hospitals, and Other Non-Profit Organizations, to provide for the furnishing, pursuant to FOIA requests, research data that has been used to develop agency regulations that impact the public. The OPEN Government Act of 2007, Pub. L. No. 110-175, Dec. 31, 2007, broadens this policy by defining agency records to include records "maintained for an agency by an entity under Government contract, for the purposes of records management." See *Chicago Tribune Co. v. Dep't of Health & Human Servs.*, No. 95 C 3917 (N. D. Ill. 1999) (the underlying data used in a study made by a contractor subject to release under FOIA because the data was part of the agency's record of regulatory action); and *Burka v. Dep't of Health & Human Servs.*, 87 F.3d 508 (D.C. Cir. 1996) (research data held by a contractor an agency record because the agency intended to take possession of the data when all technical articles had been published). Compare *Missouri ex rel. Garstang v. Dep't of the Interior*, 297 F.3d 745 (8th Cir. 2002), holding that records in the possession of a private organization partially funded by the federal government were not agency records because the records played no role in the agency's performance of its official duties.

Control of a record in the possession of an agency is not generally an issue unless the record has been created by a third party. See, for example, *McGehee v. CIA*, 697 F.2d 1095 (D.C. Cir. 1983), where the court rejected an agency's argument that a record in its possession was not an agency record because it had been created by another agency. The court reasoned that denying that the possessing agency had control of the record would frustrate the purpose of the Act by permitting agencies to split possession and control. Lack of control has been found, primarily, with regard to records created by the legislative and judicial branches, which are not subject to FOIA. See *Goland v. CIA*, 607 F.2d 339 (D.C. Cir. 1978), *cert. denied*, 445 U.S. 927 (1980) (transcripts of hearings held in the House of Representatives concerning the CIA were congressional documents, not agency records, even though they were possessed by the CIA, because they remained exclusively under congressional control); *GTE Sylvania, Inc. v. Consumers Union*, 445 U.S. 375 (1980) (documents in control of court because court had enjoined their release). However, if control of the record has passed to the agency, it will be an agency record. See *Dep't of Justice v. Tax Analysts*, 492 U.S. 136 (1989) (court decisions requested by the respondent were under the exclusive control of the Tax Division of the Department of Justice and were therefore found to be agency records); *Paisley v. CIA*, 712 F.2d 686 (D.C. Cir. 1983) (documents created by congressional committee were agency records because they contained no "external indicia of control or confidentiality"); and *Ryan v. Dep't of Justice*, 617 F.2d 781 (D.C. Cir. 1980) (questionnaires filled out by U.S. senators were in control of the Attorney General and Department of Justice and were therefore considered agency records). Compare *Judicial Watch, Inc. v. Dep't of Energy*, 310 F. Supp.2d 271 (D.D.C. 2004), holding that if an agency details personnel to an organization not subject to FOIA, the records gathered by those personnel are in the "constructive control" of the agency for which the employee works.

Agency records that have been properly destroyed in accordance with an agency's records retention policies are not subject to FOIA because the agency no longer has possession of the records, *Jones v. FBI*, 41 F.3d 238 (6th Cir. 1994). See also *Laughlin v. Commissioner*, 103 F. Supp.2d 1219 (S.D. Cal. 1999) (no need to recreate properly discarded records); *Rothschild v. Dep't of Energy*, 6 F. Supp.2d 38 (D.D.C. 1998) (properly discarded drafts of documents). However, an agency cannot merely claim that the records were probably destroyed in accordance with its normal disposal practices without making a diligent search for the records, *Schrecker v. Dep't of Justice*, 254 F.3d 162 (D.C. Cir. 2001); *Valencia-Lucena v. Coast Guard*, 180 F.3d 321 (D.C. Cir. 1999). In the latter case, the court rejected a "generalized claim" of destruction of records.

It has been argued that data will not be an agency record if it is found to be valuable property but there is no clear holding to this effect. In *Consumers Union of the United States, Inc. v. Veterans Admin.*, 301 F. Supp. 796 (S.D.N.Y. 1969), *aff'd*, 436 F.2d 1363 (2d Cir. 1971), the court refused to conclude that results of a Veterans Administration hearing-aid testing program concept "might have merit with respect to formula, designs, and drawings." In *SDC Dev. Corp. v. Mathews*, 542 F.2d 1116 (9th Cir. 1976), the court allowed the Secretary of HEW not to release documentation of its library system, which was in the form of a computer database. The court held that because the database was available in book form and was information of value and usually purchased by customers, it did not constitute an agency record. In contrast, in *Siemens v. Dep't of Defense*, Civ. No. 78-0385 (D.D.C. 1979), the magistrate appointed by the district court to make recommended findings of facts and conclusions of law rejected the government's argument that valuable technical reports concerning electronic beam lithography that had been submitted to the government under contracts were not agency records under FOIA. See also *Soucie v. David*, 448 F.2d 1067 (D.C. Cir. 1971) (report on federal supersonic air transportation not deemed exempt as valuable trade or commercial information).

b. Exemptions

Even if documents are agency records, they may still be withheld from release by the agency when they fall within any of the nine statutory FOIA exemptions set forth in 5 U.S.C. § 552(b):

(1)(A) specifically authorized under criteria established by an Executive order to be kept secret in the interest of national defense or foreign policy and (B) are in fact properly classified pursuant to such Executive order;

(2) related solely to the internal personnel rules and practices of an agency;

(3) specifically exempted from disclosure by statute (other than section 552b of this title) provided that such statute (A) requires that the matters be withheld from the public in such a manner as to leave no discretion on the issue, or (B) estab-

lishes particular criteria for withholding or refers to particular types of matters to be withheld;

(4) trade secrets and commercial or financial information obtained from a person and privileged or confidential;

(5) inter-agency or intra-agency memorandums or letters which would not be available by law to a party other than an agency in litigation with the agency;

(6) personnel and medical files and similar files the disclosure of which would constitute a clearly unwarranted invasion of personal privacy;

(7) records or information compiled for law enforcement purposes, but only to the extent that the production of such law enforcement records or information (A) could reasonably be expected to interfere with enforcement proceedings, (B) would deprive a person of a right to a fair trial or an impartial adjudication, (C) could reasonably be expected to constitute an unwarranted invasion of personal privacy, (D) could reasonably be expected to disclose the identity of a confidential source, including a State, local, or foreign agency or authority or any private institution which furnished information on a confidential basis and, in the case of a record or information compiled by criminal law enforcement authority in the course of a criminal investigation or by an agency conducting a lawful national security intelligence investigation, information furnished by a confidential source, (E) would disclose techniques and procedures for law enforcement investigations or prosecutions, or would disclose guidelines for law enforcement investigations or prosecutions if such disclosure could reasonably be expected to risk circumvention of the law, or (F) could reasonably be expected to endanger the life or physical safety of any individual;

(8) contained in or related to examination, operating, or condition reports prepared by, on behalf of, or for the use of an agency responsible for the regulation or supervision of financial institutions; or

(9) geological or geophysical information and data, including maps, concerning wells.

It has been held that these exemptions are to be narrowly construed in light of the purpose of FOIA to "pierce the veil of administrative secrecy," *Dep't of the Air Force v. Rose*, 425 U.S. 352 (1979) (law students allowed the requested summaries of ethics code and honor violation hearings from the Air Force Academy).

The legislative history to the 1974 amendments to FOIA makes clear that when material falls within an exemption, the agency may withhold but is not precluded from releasing the material, S. Rep. No. 93-854, 93rd Cong., 2d Sess. (1974), at 6. However, in certain circumstances a decision to release exempt material might constitute an abuse of agency discretion. Disclosure of exempt material in violation of 18 U.S.C. § 1905, prohibiting release of trade secrets, would be improper as an abuse of discretion under the Administrative Procedures Act, 5 U.S.C. § 702, *Chrysler Corp. v. Brown*, 441 U.S. 281 (1979); *Acumenics Research & Tech. v. Dep't of Justice*, 843 F.2d 800 (4th Cir. 1988); *National Organization for Women v. DHHS*, 736 F.2d 727 (D.C. Cir. 1984).

In addition, an agency decision to release exempt material without considering all relevant factors, including the needs and motives of the requester, may be an abuse of discretion, *Pennzoil Co. v. Federal Power Comm'n*, 534 F.2d 627 (5th Cir. 1976). See *RSR Corp. v. EPA*, 588 F. Supp. 1251 (N.D. Tex. 1984) (the EPA's release of documents that detailed RSR's smelting techniques to members of the public considered an abuse of discretion where the record showed that the agency did not consider all the relevant factors regarding the information's release); *Charles River Park, Inc. v. Dep't of Housing & Urban Dev.*, 519 F.2d 935 (D.C. Cir. 1975) (release of confidential financial information by the Department of Housing and Urban Development to Boston's Commissioner of Assessing questioned based on evidence that some factors were not taken into account).

Where a document contains both exempt and nonexempt material, the agency is required to disclose any "reasonably segregable" nonexempt material, *Florence v. Dep't of Defense*, 415 F. Supp. 156 (D.D.C. 1976) (DOD network of documents, some of which were labeled as classified and some were not, permitted release of documents not classified). In *Nadler v. Dep't of Justice*, 955 F.2d 1479 (11th Cir. 1992), however, where the releasable and exempt materials were intertwined in short documents and disclosure of the factual information requested would necessarily result in exposure of the exempt material, the court ruled that disclosure was not required.

Much of the information included in offerors' proposals is protected under exemptions three and four, while exemption five covers much of the agency documentation of the source selection process.

(1) EXEMPTION THREE

There are two types of statutes that exempt source selection information from disclosure under the FOIA. The 1997 National Defense Authorization Act, Pub. L. No. 104-201, Sept. 23, 1996, adopted specific provisions that preclude the release of information in proposals in most circumstances. See 10 U.S.C. § 2305(g) and 41 U.S.C. § 253b(m) stating:

Prohibition on release of contractor proposals.

(1) Except as provided in paragraph (2), a proposal in the possession or control of the Department of Defense may not be made available to any person under section 552 of title 5.

(2) Paragraph (1) does not apply to any proposal that is set forth or incorporated by reference in a contract entered into between the Department and the contractor that submitted the proposal.

(3) In this subsection, the term "proposal" means any proposal, including a technical, management, or cost proposal, submitted by a contractor in response to the requirements of a solicitation for a competitive proposal.

This statute was held to be an Exemption 3 statute in *Hombostel v. Dep't of Interior*, No. 02-2523, 2003 WL 23303294 (D.D.C. 2003).

10 U.S.C. § 130 precludes the disclosure of unclassified technical data subject to export controls, as follows:

(a) Notwithstanding any other provision of law, the Secretary of Defense may withhold from public disclosure any technical data with military or space application in the possession of, or under the control of, the Department of Defense, if such data may not be exported lawfully outside the United States without an approval, authorization, or license under the Export Administration Act of 1979 (50 U.S.C. App. 2401–2420) or the Arms Export Control Act (22 U.S.C. 2751 et seq.). However, technical data may not be withheld under this section if regulations promulgated under either such Act authorize the export of such data pursuant to a general, unrestricted license or exemption in such regulations.

*   *   *

(c) In this section, the term "technical data with military or space application" means any blueprints, drawings, plans, instructions, computer software and documentation, or other technical information that can be used, or be adapted for use, to design, engineer, produce, manufacture, operate, repair, overhaul, or reproduce any military or space equipment or technology concerning such equipment.

The procedures implementing this statute are set forth in Executive Order 12470, 49 Fed. Reg. 13099, April 3, 1984, and DOD Directive 5230.25, Withholding of Unclassified Technical Data from Public Disclosure, 32 C.F.R. § 250.4.

(2) EXEMPTION FOUR

Exemption four permits nondisclosure of two classes of information: (1) trade secrets and (2) commercial or financial information obtained from a person and privileged or confidential. These categories would appear to overlap. However, in *Public Citizen Health Research Group v. FDA*, 704 F.2d 1280 (D.D. Cir. 1983), the court indicated that, for FOIA purposes, trade secrets consist of technical information used for "making, preparing, compounding, or processing trade commodities." The court reasoned that to define the term more broadly would encompass the second prong of exemption four. In *Anderson v. Dep't of Health & Human Servs.*, 907

F.2d 936 (10th Cir. 1990), the narrower definition was also employed and the case was remanded because the lower court had applied the broader definition of trade secrets and had left it unclear under which exemption the information fell. Other courts have used a broader, more traditional definition of trade secrets that includes other types of commercial information.

(A) VOLUNTARY VS. REQUIRED INFORMATION

The D.C. Circuit has fashioned two tests for determining whether information falls within exemption four, *Critical Mass Energy Project v. Nuclear Regulatory Comm'n*, 975 F.2d 871 (D.C. Cir. 1992), *cert. denied*, 507 U.S. 984 (1993). If the information was submitted *voluntarily*, the court held that it would fall within the exemption when it was "of a kind that would customarily not be released to the public by the person from whom it was obtained." If the information was *required* to be submitted, the court held that it would fall within the exemption when it met the following test stated in *National Parks & Conservation Ass'n v. Morton*, 498 F.2d 765 (D.C. Cir. 1974), at 770:

> [C]ommercial or financial matter is "confidential" for purposes of the exemption if disclosure of the information is likely to have either of the following effects: (1) to impair the Government's ability to obtain necessary information in the future; or (2) to cause substantial harm to the competitive position of the person from whom the information was obtained.

No other circuit courts have adopted this distinction between voluntarily submitted information and required information, with the result that some district courts follow it and others use the *National Parks* test for all data. See *Frazee v. Forest Serv.*, 97 F.3d 367 (9th Cir. 1996), recognizing the distinction but refusing to rule whether it would be followed because the case involved required information. In the fourth circuit two district judges have reached different conclusions. See *Comdisco, Inc. v. General Servs. Admin.*, 864 F. Supp. 510 (E.D. Va. 1994), rejecting the *Critical Mass* distinction, and *Environmental Tech., Inc. v. Environmental Protection Agency*, 822 F. Supp. 1226 (E.D. Va. 1993), adopting the *Critical Mass* distinction.

Because the choice to submit a bid or proposal is voluntary, there is some disagreement as to whether information that is required to be submitted as a part of the bid or proposal is voluntary or required information. The majority view is that such information is *required* because a proposal will not be considered unless the requested information is submitted, *Canadian Commer. Corp. v. Dep't of the Air Force*, 442 F. Supp.2d 15 (D.D.C. 2006), *aff'd* 514 F.3d 37 (D.C. Cir. 2008); *Frazee v. Forest Serv.*, 97 F.3d 367 (9th Cir. 1996). Two judges in the eastern district of Virginia have reached the opposite conclusion from the rest of the courts. See *Comdisco, Inc. v. General Servs. Admin.*, 864 F. Supp. 510 (E.D. Va. 1994), and *Environmental Tech., Inc. v. Environmental Protection Agency*, 822 F. Supp. 1226 (E.D. Va. 1993). Compare *Cortez III Serv. Corp. v. National Aeronautics & Space Admin.*, 921 F. Supp.

8 (D.D.C. 1996), where the court held that a G&A ceiling, which was submitted by the contractor in response to a written question from the contracting officer asking whether the offeror would be willing to propose a cap on the G&A rates, was voluntarily submitted information. The court reasoned that this was not a requirement of the solicitation but was a request for a voluntary submission of information.

(B) TEST FOR VOLUNTARY INFORMATION

Because almost all the recent cases have found that the contested information was required to be submitted, there has been very little interpretation of the more lenient test in *Critical Mass*. However, the decision provides considerable guidance within its four corners. First, the court makes it clear that the test is whether the information is "of a kind that would customarily not be released to the public by *the person from whom it was obtained*" [emphasis added] not by other parties such as other members of the industry. Thus, the initial inquiry is to the practices of the submitter of the information.

Second, the submitter will be given the protection of the test even if it has released the information to numerous other parties, as long as it has not been released to the public. This was the case in *Critical Mass,* where the lower court found that the contested information had been widely released to parties that signed nondisclosure agreements (644 F. Supp. 344 (D.D.C. 1986)). Yet the D.C. circuit held that the information was protected from release because the organization had a policy of not releasing it to the public at large.

Finally, the court stated in *Critical Mass* that the agency deciding to withhold voluntarily submitted information, following this reasoning, must meet the burden of proving that the provider had a "custom" of nondisclosure of this type of information. This means, of course, that the provider must submit facts to the agency demonstrating its custom at the time it is informed of the FOIA request and claims that the information is confidential. In *Cortez III Serv. Corp. v. National Aeronautics & Space Admin.*, 921 F. Supp. 8 (D.D.C. 1996), the court was satisfied with "unrefuted" affidavits stating that the contractor did not regularly disclose G&A ceilings to the public. See also *Delta, Ltd. v. Customs & Border Protection Bureau*, 393 F. Supp.2d 15 (D.D.C. 2005) (declaration that company information, such as an IRS number, submitted to government agency investigating a smuggling scheme, was not normally given to the public); *Parker v. Bureau of Land Mgmt.*, 141 F. Supp.2d 71 (D.D.C. 2001) (declarations describing internal distribution only on a "need to know" basis and employee confidentiality agreements); *McDonnell Douglas Corp. v. EEOC*, 922 F. Supp. 235 (E.D. Mo. 1996) (evidence showing that documents were marked and carefully guarded within the company and that discovery had been successfully opposed in court cases); *Allnet Comm. Servs., Inc. v. FCC*, 800 F. Supp. 984 (D.D.C. 1992) ("specific, affirmative evidence that no unrestricted disclosure" had occurred). See also *Center for Auto Safety v. Nat'l Highway Traffic Safety Ad-*

min., 244 F.3d 144 (D.C. Cir. 2001), where the court rejected the argument that selling a product in the open market was equivalent to releasing information about the product and directed the lower court to review the declarations of the submitter of the information to determine what its customary practices were.

(C) TEST FOR REQUIRED INFORMATION

Because most of the contested information has been held to fall in the required category, there have been a significant number of cases applying the *National Parks* two-pronged test. The first prong, impairment of the government's ability to obtain the information in the future, has rarely been dispositive when the agency has decided to release proposal-related information. See *McDonnell Douglas Corp. v. National Aeronautics & Space Admin.*, 981 F. Supp. 12 (D.D.C. 1997), where the court stated the normal reasoning on this issue at 15:

> Although MDA contends that release of this information will impair the government's ability to procure future participants in government contracts, this position lacks merit. Government contracting involves millions of dollars and it is unlikely that release of this information will cause NASA difficulty in obtaining future bids. See *Martin Marietta Corp. v. Dalton*, 974 F. Supp. 37, 1997 WL 459831, at 3 (D.D.C. 1997); *McDonnell I*, 895 F. Supp. at 318; *Racal-Milgo Gov't Systems, Inc. v. Small Business Admin.*, 559 F. Supp. 4, 6 (D.D.C 1981). Also, as the government points out, the administrative agency has an incentive not to release information which will impair its future ability to successfully contract for launch missions. See *CC Distribs. v. Kinzinger*, No. 94-1330, 1995 U.S. Dist. LEXIS 21641, 1995 WL 405445, at 4 (D.D.C. June 28, 1995) (concluding that the government is in the best position to determine the effect of disclosure on future bidding situations). As a result, this court should defer to the administrative agency's determination that release will not cause impairment. *Id.* (deferring to the government agency's determination that disclosure would not dissuade firms from contracting with the government in the future).

The second prong, substantial harm to the competitive position of the submitter, has been the focus of almost all of the litigation. It seems clear from the decided cases that to prove substantial harm, the submitter of the information must demonstrate that release of the information will reveal specific business information as to its competitive strategies. General allegations of competitive harm are infrequently accepted. However, "evidence revealing (1) actual competition and (2) a likelihood of substantial competitive injury is sufficient to bring commercial information under Exemption 4," *GC Micro Corp. v. Defense Logistics Agency*, 33 F.3d 1109 (9th Cir. 1994) (quoting *Sharyland Water Supply Corp. v. Block*, 755 F.2d 397 (5th Cir.), *cert. denied*, 471 U.S. 1137 (1985)); *Gulf & Western Indus., Inc. v. United States*, 615 F.2d 527 (D.C. Cir. 1979). In *National Parks & Conservation Ass'n v. Kleppe*, 547 F.2d 673 (D.C. Cir. 1976), the court found substantial injury to be "virtually axiomatic" if detailed financial data was disclosed to actual competitors.

Many of the earlier cases involve proposal information. For example, in *Fidell v. United States Coast Guard*, Civ. No. 80-2291, 28 Cont. Cas. Fed. (CCH) ¶ 81,141 (D.D.C. 1981), the court applied the *National Parks* test in upholding an agency decision to withhold information in the successful offeror's proposal concerning the offeror's methods of performance, costs, and staffing and organizational resources. It reasoned that disclosure of these unique design aspects of the proposal would place the contractor at a competitive disadvantage in future procurements by permitting others to copy its methods and undermine its bid prices. The court also concluded that disclosure would impair the government's ability to obtain valuable information in future procurements by deterring potential offerors from submitting detailed, innovative proposals. Similarly, in *Audio Tech. Servs., Ltd. v. Dep't of the Army*, 487 F. Supp. 779 (D.D.C. 1979), information in a successful proposal concerning design concepts, customer lists, and data on personnel was found to have been properly withheld on the basis of exemption four where disclosure would "threaten the competitive position of the submitter and clearly thwart the Government's interest in obtaining such information in the future." In *Orion Research, Inc. v. Environmental Protection Agency*, 615 F.2d 551 (1st Cir.), *cert. denied*, 449 U.S. 833 (1980), the court denied an unsuccessful offeror access to the winning technical proposal. See also *BDM Corp. v. Small Business Admin.*, Civ. No. 80-1180, 28 Cont. Cas. Fed. (CCH) ¶ 80,950 (D.D.C. 1980), holding that an agency properly withheld information from a requester protesting an awardee's qualification for award on a small business set-aside. The court concluded that the awardee's financial statements, business plans, customer lists, and sales and profit projection fell within the scope of exemption four.

Portions of the successful offeror's technical proposal were found not to constitute privileged commercial or financial information in *Dynalectron Corp. v. Dep't of the Air Force*, Civ. No. 83-3399 (D.D.C. 1984). The Air Force had decided, pursuant to a FOIA request, to release a detailed table of contents, a cross-referencing key, various title pages, and summaries of personnel experience. Although Dynalectron claimed that release would deter contractors from submitting detailed technical proposals in the future, this claim was rejected as the government was willing to release the material without evident concern about jeopardizing the quality of future proposals. As long as the Air Force withheld "meaty details," the court concluded, access to necessary information in proposals should remain unobstructed. Also rejected was Dynalectron's claim that allowing competitors to imitate its "successful style of proposal submission" would constitute substantial competitive harm. Similarly, in *SMS Data Prods. Group, Inc. v. Dep't of the Air Force*, Civ. No. 88-0481-LFO (D.D.C. 1989), while disclosure of pricing strategies and technical information regarding a corporation in the laptop computer business was considered by the court to fall under exemption four, general data regarding its corporate organization, history, and production capabilities were properly released.

Detailed financial information submitted by contractors has generally been determined to be barred from release because it would cause substantial harm. See

Cortez III Servs. Corp. v. NASA, 921 F. Supp. 8 (D.D.C. 1996) (G&A rates); *Braintree Elec. Light Co. v. Dep't of Energy,* 494 F. Supp. 287 (D.D.C. 1980) (selling prices and profit margins); *Gulf & Western Indus., Inc. v. United States,* 615 F.2d 527 (D.C. Cir. 1979) (profit rate, learning curves, and G&A expense rate included in the Armed Services Board of Contract Appeals Rule 4 file); *Burroughs Corp. v. Schlesinger,* 403 F. Supp. 633 (E.D. Va. 1975) (pricing and discount practices); See also *Continental Oil Co. v. FPC,* 519 F.2d 31 (5th Cir. 1975), *cert. denied sub nom., Superior Oil Co. v. FPC,* 425 U.S. 971 (1976), holding that specific contract information was "confidential" but general "composite" information on marketing techniques was subject to disclosure. Compare *Canadian Commer. Corp. v. Dep't of the Air Force,* 442 F. Supp.2d 15 (D.D.C. 2006), *aff'd,* 514 F.3d 37 (D.C. Cir. 2008), holding that fully loaded labor rates should be disclosed because they did not reveal the elements of the rates, and *Common Cause v. Dep't of the Army,* Civ. No. 79-1008 (D.D.C. 1980), holding that information contained in five year old audit reports prepared by the Defense Contract Audit Agency, including the contractor's aggregate costs and number of employees, was not exempt from disclosure.

The most contentious issue has concerned the release of prices being paid by the government. Earlier cases almost uniformly held that prices on the face of the contract should be disclosed because contracts are public documents. For example, in *Acumenics Research & Tech. v. Dep't of Justice,* 843 F. 2d 800 (4th Cir. 1988), the contractor argued that release of unit prices in a service contract subject to the Service Contract Act wage rates would permit the competitors to figure out the markups used by the contractor to win the competition. The court analyzed the situation and rejected the contractor's contention because there were numerous variables in the pricing of the contract. Similarly, in *CC Distributors, Inc. v. Kinzinger,* No. 94-1330(NHJ) (D.D.C. 1995), the Air Force decided to release the unit prices on a requirements contract for resale items that had been awarded pursuant to sealed bidding procedures. The contractor argued that release of the unit prices would disclose its pricing strategy and the concessions it had obtained from its suppliers. The court rejected the argument because the contractor had not been specific enough in proving its allegation. See also *Trifid Corp. v. National Imagery & Mapping Agency,* No. 4:97-CV-2163 CAS (E.D. Mo. 1998) (unit prices for software); *Martin Marietta Corp. v. Dalton,* 974 F. Supp. 37 (D.D.C. 1997) (contract line items containing estimated costs and fees); *Comdisco, Inc. v. GSA,* 864 F. Supp. 510 (E.D. Va. 1994) (some prices disclosed and some withheld); *General Dynamics Corp. v. Dep't of the Air Force,* Civ. No. 88-3272 (D.D.C. 1992) (contract price for launch vehicles); *Brownstein, Zeidman & Schomer v. Dep't of the Air Force,* Civ. No. 90-1582 (D.D.C. 1991) (unit prices for computers); *Pacific Architects & Eng'rs, Inc. v. Dep't of State,* 906 F.2d 1345 (9th Cir. 1990) (fixed hourly rates for categories of service personnel); and *Racal-Milgo Gov't Sys., Inc. v. Small Business Admin.,* 559 F. Supp. 4 (D.D.C. 1981) (unit prices of computer system components).

In contrast, several later decisions have required the disclosure of contract prices. See *McDonnell Douglas Corp. v. NASA,* 180 F.3d 303 (D.C. Cir. 1999), holding that release of the satellite launch prices specified in a NASA contract would cause substantial competitive harm. The court accepted the contractor's argument that the release of line item pricing information would cause it competitive harm for two reasons: it would permit its commercial customers to bargain down ("ratchet down") its prices more effectively, and it would help its domestic and international competitors to underbid it (the company claimed that disclosure of the line item pricing data would allow competitors to calculate its actual costs with a high degree of precision). The Department of Justice FOIA Guide contains the following analysis of this decision:

> In response to the government's petition for rehearing – which was denied – D.C. Circuit Court Judge Silberman, the author of the opinion, ameliorated the government's concerns regarding prior D.C. Circuit precedent by first expressly clarifying that the McDonnell Douglas decision did not hold that "line item pricing would invariably" be protected. Rather, he explained, the court had held "only that the agency's explanation of its position [in that particular case] bordered on the ridiculous." Second, Judge Silberman seemingly sought to reconcile prior D.C. Circuit cases with the McDonnell Douglas decision by commenting that "[o]ther than in a monopoly situation[,] anything that undermines a supplier's relationship with its customers must necessarily aid its competitors." (footnotes omitted)

The same result was reached in *Chemical Waste Mgmt., Inc. v. O'Leary,* 1995 WL 115894 (D.D.C. 1995), where the court found the likelihood of substantial competitive harm in release of unit prices in an indefinite-quantity subcontract. See also *MCI Worldcom, Inc. v. GSA*, 163 F. Supp.2d 28 (D.D.C. 2001), where the court held that long tables of "pricing elements" were not unit prices and were, therefore, protectable under Exemption 4. The court further stated that even if the elements were unit prices, they were not disclosable under FAR 15.506(d) requiring disclosure of unit prices in debriefings, because FAR 15.506(e) limits this provision by precluding disclosure of information that is exempt from release under FOIA. Disclosure was required in *McDonnell Douglas Corp. v. Dep't of the Air Force*, 215 F. Supp.2d 200 (D.D.C. 2002), where the court sustained the agency's decision to release option prices, vendor prices, and "over and above" prices based on the fact that the agency had "presented reasoned accounts of the effect of disclosure based on its experiences with government contracting" to support its conclusion that release of this information would cause no competitive harm. This decision was reversed as to option prices and vendor prices and sustained as to "over and above" prices in *McDonnell Douglas Corp. v. Dep't of the Air Force*, 375 F.3d 1182 (D.C. Cir. 2004). As to the option prices, the court stated at 1189:

> [R]elease of the option year prices in the present contract would likely cause McDonnell Douglas substantial competitive harm because it would significantly increase the probability McDonnell Douglas's competitors would underbid it in the event the Air Force rebids the contract. See *Gulf & W. Indus.*, 615 F.2d at 530 (substantial competitive harm likely where disclosure "would allow competitors to estimate, and undercut, its bids"). Because price is the only objective, or at

least readily quantified, criterion among the six criteria for awarding government contracts, submitting the lowest price is surely the most straightforward way for a competitor to show its bid is superior. Indeed, price is by statute the only factor that "*must* be considered in the evaluation of a proposal." 10 U.S.C. § 2305(a)(3)(A)(ii) (emphasis added). Whether price will be but one of several factors to be weighted equally in any future RFP, therefore, is necessarily somewhat speculative.

As to contract line items that were composed primarily of vendor prices, the court stated at 1190-91:

> McDonnell Douglas argues the release of prices for certain CLINs composed predominantly of the costs of materials and services it procures from other vendors would enable its competitors to derive the percentage (called the "Vendor Pricing Factor") by which McDonnell Douglas marks up the bids it receives from subcontractors. McDonnell Douglas argues release of the disputed CLINs would likely harm its competitive position because Lockheed "most likely obtained quotations from the same vendors," with "the same or nearly the same pric[es]."

> In explaining its decision to release those CLINs the Air Force stated it is "entirely possible," indeed "not uncommon," for a subcontractor to "quote different prices . . . to different prime contractors." Therefore, the Air Force reasoned, McDonnell Douglas's competitors could not "with any degree of certainty" derive its Vendor Pricing Factor from disclosure of the Vendor Pricing CLINs and hence McDonnell Douglas is unlikely to suffer substantial competitive harm.

> The problem with this line of reasoning is its premise, namely, the mere supposition that McDonnell Douglas and Lockheed received — or may well have received — significantly different prices from the same vendors bidding for the same subcontract. The Air Force provided no actual evidence, nor did it claim special knowledge based upon its experience, to support this proposition, apart from the rather casual observations that it was "entirely possible" and "not uncommon." This is tantamount to the Air Force saying it would "not be surprised" if the rival bidders had received different prices from subcontractors, but it is far short of asserting (let alone substantiating) that it was "likely" they did so. Nor does it seem probable as a matter of economic theory. In a competitive market for subcontracted work, a rational subcontractor would quote each prime contractor the lowest price consistent with covering its costs. Any difference in the prices it quotes different prime contractors should, in theory, reflect differences in the costs of supplying them. Therefore, it is reasonable to presume, as McDonnell Douglas did in its submissions to the Air Force, that its "competitors obtained similar pricing from various vendors to support those tasks." (Footnotes omitted)

In a later decision on contract prices, *Canadian Commercial Corp. v. Dep't of the Air Force*, 442 F. Supp.2d 15 (D.D.C. 2006), *aff'd*, 514 F.3d 37 (D.C. Cir. 2008), the court held that contract line item prices should be released but option prices should not be disclosed. Two subsequent district court decisions barred release of contract prices, *Essex Electro Engineers, Inc. v. United States*, 686 F. Supp.2d 91 (D.D.C. 2010) (unit prices on contract); *General Electric Co. v. Dep't of the Air*

Force, 648 F. Supp.2d 95 (D.D.C. 2009) (contract prices of spare parts for jet engines). Compare *Houck Ltd. v. Dep't of Veterans Affairs*, CBCA 1509, 09-1 BCA ¶ 34113, refusing to place the unit prices for the base year of a contract under a protective order.

(3) Exemption Five

Exemption five, permitting nondisclosure of inter-agency or intra-agency memoranda that would not be available to a party in litigation with the agency, protects much of the government's documentation of the source selection process. The Supreme Court has held that this exemption applies to those documents normally privileged in the civil discovery context, *NLRB v. Sears Roebuck & Co.*, 421 U.S. 132 (1975) (traditional attorney work-product privileges applied to memoranda produced in anticipation of litigation). At least three types of privileges available to the government in civil litigation are incorporated into this exemption.

The privilege for confidential intra-agency advisory opinions (called the executive privilege), disclosure of which would be injurious to the deliberative and executive process of government agencies, was discussed by the Court in *NLRB v. Sears Roebuck*, at 151–52:

> Manifestly, the ultimate purpose of this long-recognized privilege is to prevent injury to the quality of agency decisions. The quality of a particular agency decision will clearly be affected by the communications received by the decision maker on the subject of the decision prior to the time the decision is made. However, it is difficult to see how the quality of a decision will be affected by communications with respect to the decision occurring after the decision is finally reached; and therefore equally difficult to see how the quality of the decision will be affected by forced disclosure of such communications, as long as prior communications and the ingredients of the decisionmaking process are not disclosed. Accordingly, the lower courts have uniformly drawn a distinction between predecisional communications, which are privileged . . . and communications made after the decision and designed to explain it, which are not. . . . This distinction is supported not only by the lesser injury to the decisionmaking process flowing from disclosure of postdecisional communications, but also, in the case of those communications which explain the decision, by the increased public interest in knowing the basis of agency policy already adopted.

To fall within this privilege, the material must be both predecisional and deliberative, *Florida House of Representatives v. Dep't of Commerce*, 961 F.2d 941 (11th Cir. 1992). In this case the court held that to meet this dual test, the documents had to consist of advice or opinions given in the formation of policies as opposed to factual determinations. The *Sears Roebuck* case held, however, that predecisional agency documents that are later expressly adopted or incorporated by reference into final agency opinions are no longer exempt as predecisional. In those situations reference to deliberative advice in the context of adopting it as policy is merely a form of "shorthand" for the decision; therefore, the document is treated as a post-decisional statement of final agency opinion. See also *Nat'l Council of La Raza v. Dep't of Justice*, 411 F.3d 350 (2d Cir. 2005).

Most internal documents evaluating proposals would fall within this category. See *Brownstein, Zeidman & Schomer v. Dep't of the Air Force*, Civ. No. 90-1582 (D.D.C. 1991), holding that reports of the source selection evaluation board and the source selection advisory council were predecisional documents falling within the scope of exemption five; and *Audio Tech. Servs., Ltd. v. Dep't of the Army*, 487 F. Supp. 779 (D.D.C. 1979), holding that documents prepared by proposal evaluators were within this exemption. Another example of the application of this privilege to precontract materials is illustrated by the decision of the Department of Energy Office of Hearings and Appeals (OHA) in an appeal to the Department concerning the withholding of certain information from a requester under the FOIA, *Holmes & Narver, Inc.*, Case No. HFA-0037, 9 DOE ¶ 80,140 (1982) (CCH Energy Management Service). The request was made after the selection but before the award of a contract. The requester asked for DOE's evaluation rating of the technical, business, business/ management, and cost proposals of the submitter and the party selected for negotiating; all background data concerning the modification of evaluation criteria; and the total proposed cost of the winner. Although a number of documents were released, withheld under exemption five were the entire report of the source evaluation board (SEB) and portions of the forms used by the SEB in evaluating proposals. OHA reviewed these documents page by page and concluded that certain factual material was neither predecisional nor deliberative and should therefore be disclosed. In a prior decision, *Exxon Nuclear Co.*, 5 DOE ¶ 80,151 (1980), OHA had required disclosure of the table of contents, factual summaries of the SEB method of operation, dates and descriptions of significant events, and material already public (list of parties obtaining the RFP, list of offerors, etc.). Applying this decision and the predecisional/deliberative tests, OHA required release of the names of the board members, a summary of the RFP, a description of the work required, a list of evaluation criteria, and blank forms containing the evaluation weights. OHA also found that the evaluation criteria weights established by the SEB were final opinions of the SEB, which, although predecisional in that they were established by the SEB before a selection was made, were not deliberative nor recommended but were the final actual criteria used by the SEB. Thus, the evaluation weights were released. Withheld from release was the application of the weights to each proposal, evaluation statements by board members, and the total price of the winner (under exemption four). See also *Casad v. Dep't of Health & Human Servs.*, 301 F.3d 1247 (10th Cir. 2002), holding that the privilege covers summaries of the peer group evaluations used to award training grants. This privilege covers predecisional documents even if they are not used to make a decisions, *Moye, O'Brien, O'Rourke, Hogan & Pickart v. Nat'l R.R. Passenger Corp.*, 376 F.3d 1270 (11th Cir. 2004); *Schell v. Dep't of Health & Human Servs.*, 843 F.2d 933 (6th Cir. 1988).

Exemption five also incorporates the attorney work-product privileges generally available to litigants, *NLRB v. Sears Roebuck & Co.*, 421 U.S. 132 (1975). This privilege does not extend to routine reports in the ordinary course of an agency's business, but is limited to documents prepared in anticipation of a particular litigation or related to a specific claim which is likely to lead to litigation, *Rockwell Int'l Corp. v. Dep't of Justice*, 235 F.3d 598 (D.C. Cir. 2001); *Coastal States Gas Corp. v. Dep't of Energy*, 617 F.2d 854 (D.C. Cir. 1980); *Robbins Tire & Rubber Co. v. NLRB*, 563 F.2d 724 (5th Cir. 1977), *rev'd*, 437 U.S. 214 (1978). In *FTC v. Grolier, Inc.*, 462 U.S. 19 (1983), the Supreme Court resolved a split in the circuits by holding that the termination of litigation does not invalidate protection for records properly categorized as attorney work-product. The privilege has been found applicable in several instances. For example, in *Nadler v. Dep't of Justice*, 955 F.2d 1479 (11th Cir. 1992), certain handwritten notes were deemed by the court to be indicative of mental impressions and legal theories of an attorney in anticipation of prosecution of Nadler and were found exempt from a FOIA request under attorney work product privileges. Similarly, in *Chilivis v. SEC*, 673 F.2d 1205 (11th Cir. 1982), the court relied on exemption five and found a detailed index of documents to be exempt from disclosure, as the index was prepared by agency attorneys and legal employees in preparation for litigation and contained sufficient information to constitute work product. In *Shermco Indus., Inc. v. Secretary of the Air Force*, 613 F.2d 1314 (5th Cir. 1980), the court relied on the attorney work-product exemption in denying an unsuccessful bidder access to a legal memorandum prepared by the agency in anticipation of an impending bid protest. See also *Murphy v. Dep't of the Army*, 613 F.2d 1151 (D.C. Cir. 1979), holding that a memorandum prepared by the general counsel of the agency concerning the legal adequacy of a contract was covered by this exemption. This privilege is broader than the executive privilege in that it covers factual as well as deliberative materials, *Judicial Watch, Inc. v. Dep't of Justice*, 432 F.3d 366 (D.C. Cir. 2005). See also *Martin v. Office of Special Counsel*, 819 F.2d 1181 (D.C. Cir. 1987) ("The work-product privilege simply does not distinguish between factual and deliberative material"); *Norwood v. FAA*, 993 F.2d 570 (6th Cir. 1993) (work-product privilege protects documents regardless of status as factual or deliberative); and *Manchester v. DEA*, 823 F. Supp. 1259 (E.D. Pa. 1993) ("segregation is not required where 'factual information is incidental to, and bound with, privileged' information"). Compare *Mone v. Dep't of the Navy*, 353 F. Supp. 2d 193 (D. Mass. 2005), ordering in camera inspection of a litigation report to determine if there were any "reasonably segregable" portions.

The attorney-client privilege is also incorporated under exemption five, *NLRB v. Sears Roebuck & Co.*, 421 U.S. 132 (1975). Written requests for legal advice and other such communications of facts and opinions between attorneys and clients have been ruled to fall within the scope of exemption five, *Murphy v. Tennessee Valley Authority*, 571 F. Supp. 502 (D.D.C. 1983). See also *Murphy v. Dep't of the Army*, 613 F.2d 1151 (D.C. Cir. 1979), in which a document was ruled exempt from disclosure regardless of whether the originating party considered it confidential or not, as it reflected legal advice.

The Supreme Court has held that exemption five also incorporates a qualified privilege permitting withholding of "confidential commercial information . . . generated by the Government itself." In *Federal Open Market Comm'n v. Merrill*, 443 U.S. 340 (1978), the Supreme Court applied this privilege in upholding an agency's refusal to immediately disclose monetary policy directives that served as guidance to federal officials making decisions relative to buying and selling of securities in the open market. The Court distinguished this special privilege from the exemption five "executive privilege," as well as from the type of confidential information covered by exemption four, stating at 359:

> The purpose of the privilege for predecisional deliberations is to insure that a decision-maker will receive the unimpeded advice of the associates. The theory is that if advice is revealed, associates may be reluctant to be candid and frank. It follows that documents shielded by executive privilege remain privileged even after the decision to which they pertain may have been effected, since disclosure at any time could inhibit the free flow of advice, including analysis, reports, and expression of opinion within the agency. The theory behind a privilege for confidential commercial information generated in the process of awarding a contract, however, is not that the flow of advice may be hampered, but that the Government will be placed at a competitive disadvantage or that the consummation of the contract may be endangered. Consequently, the rationale for protecting such information expires as soon as the contract is awarded or the offer withdrawn.

> We are further convinced that recognition of an Exemption 5 privilege for confidential commercial information generated in the process of awarding a contract would not substantially duplicate any other FOIA exemption. The closest possibility is Exemption 4, which applies to "trade secrets and commercial or financial information obtained from a person and privileged or confidential." 5 U.S.C. § 552(b)(4). Exemption 4, however, is limited to information obtained from a person, that is, information obtained outside the Government. 5 U.S.C. § 551(2). The privilege for confidential information about Government contracts recognized by the House Report, in contrast, is necessarily confined to information generated by the Federal Government itself.

This privilege was used to deny a prospective bidder historical cost data that the Army was using to prepare its estimate of the cost of in-house performance of various functions pursuant to OMB Circular A-76, *Morrison-Knudsen Co. v. Dep't of the Army*, 595 F. Supp. 352 (D.D.C. 1984), *aff'd*, 762 F.2d 138 (D.C. Cir. 1985). The district court stated at 355:

> While the papers being withheld will not reveal the precise bid to be made by the Army against M-K's prospective bid, the evidence shows that they will enable an informed bidder such as M-K to make a closer approximation than would be possible on the basis of the information to be released with the bid invitation and other available data. See *Timken Co. v. United States Custom Service*, 491 F. Supp. 557, 559 (D.D.C. 1080). The Court therefore accepts the Army's view that in this instance release may not only chill competition and place the Army at a "competitive disadvantage" in "bidding" to continue doing the work in-house, but might also discourage commercial firms from taking the initiative to come

forward with more innovative techniques for cutting costs in the hope of under-bidding a more uncertain Army "bid."

Further examples of agency documents falling within the privileges encompassed by exemption five are provided in DOD Regulation 5400.7-R:

(i) The nonfactual portions of staff papers, to include after-action reports, lessons learned, and situation reports containing staff evaluations, advice, opinions or suggestions.

(ii) Advice, suggestions, or evaluations prepared on behalf of the Department of Defense by individual consultants or by boards, committees, councils, groups, panels, conferences, commissions, task forces, or other similar groups that are formed for the purpose of obtaining advice and recommendations.

(iii) Those nonfactual portions of evaluations by DOD Component personnel of contractors and their products.

(iv) Information of a speculative, tentative, or evaluative nature or such matters as proposed plans to procure, lease or otherwise acquire and dispose of materials, real estate, facilities or functions, when such information would provide undue or unfair competitive advantage to private personal interests or would impede legitimate government functions.

(v) Trade secret or other confidential research development, or commercial information owned by the Government, where premature release is likely to affect the Government's negotiating position or other commercial interests.

(vi) Records that are exchanged among agency personnel and within and among DOD Components or Agencies as part of the preparation for anticipated administrative proceeding by an Agency or litigation before any Federal, State, or military court, as well as records that qualify for attorney-client privilege.

(vii) Those portions of official reports of inspection, reports of the Inspector Generals, audits, investigations, or surveys pertaining to safety, security, or the internal management, administration, or operation of one or more DOD Components, when these records have traditionally been treated by the courts as privileged against disclosure in litigation.

CHAPTER 11

CONTRACT AWARD CONTROVERSIES

Contract award controversies have become a substantial part of the procurement process. Offerors, prospective offerors, and other parties often seek to challenge procurement actions. For a long time, these challenges were heard without specific statutory authority. However, beginning in 1982, Congress began to take an active role in formalizing the process by adopting a number of statutes dealing with award controversies. Presently, there are three forums where contract award controversies may be heard — the procuring agencies, the Comptroller General (the head of the General Accountability Office (GAO)), and the Court of Federal Claims. **Figure 11-1** summarizes the major features of each of these forums.

The boards of contract appeals have not generally been involved in contract award controversies. See *Coastal Corp. v. United States*, 713 F.2d 728 (Fed. Cir. 1983), holding that the board's jurisdiction under the Contract Disputes Act of 1978, 41 U.S.C. §§ 601-613, does not extend to implied contracts to consider bids and proposals fairly. A notable exception was the General Services Administration Board of Contract Appeals (GSBCA). In 1984 the GSBCA was granted authority to hear protests on Brooks Act automatic data processing equipment (now, information technology) procurements, 40 U.S.C. § 759(h). However, § 5101 of the Clinger-Cohen Act of 1996, Pub. L. No. 104-106, repealed this authority. During this tenure, the board rendered numerous decisions dealing with various phases of the award process. Those decisions and the decisions of the Court of Appeals for the Federal Circuit dealing with them can be helpful in resolving current award controversies.

Except for the time period between 1970 and 2001, the district courts have not been an available forum for protesters. The Supreme Court ruled in 1940 in *Perkins v. Lukens Co. v. United States*, 310 U.S. 113 (1940), that no one had a right to a government contract; as a result, it was held that disappointed bidders were not entitled to have their protests heard in court. Then, in *Scanwell Labs., Inc. v. United States*, 424 F.2d 859 (D.C. Cir. 1970), the court held that the Administrative Procedure Act (APA), 5 U.S.C. § 702, gave offerors a right to bring an action challenging agency action in the process of awarding contracts. The jurisdiction of the district courts over protests was affected by the passage of the Federal Courts Improvement Act of 1982, Pub. L. No. 97-164. This Act established the Claims Court (renamed the Court of Federal Claims by the Federal Courts Administrative Act of 1992, Pub. L. No. 102-572) and provided the court jurisdiction over preaward protests. The Act allowed the Claims Court "to afford complete relief on any contract claim brought before the contract is awarded." This Act created confusion as to whether the Claims Court possessed exclusive jurisdiction to hear preaward protests. Postaward judicial authority remained with the district courts. The Administrative Dispute Resolution

Act (ADRA) of 1992, Pub. L. No. 104-320, § 12(d) resolved the issue by granting the Court of Federal Claims and the district courts concurrent jurisdiction to hear both preaward and postaward protests. The ADRA, however, provided that bid protest jurisdiction in the district courts would expire on January 1, 2001, unless extended by Congress. Congress did not renew the jurisdiction of the district courts over bid protests with the result that the Court of Federal Claims is now the exclusive judicial forum over preaward and postaward bid protests.

This chapter first deals with the distinction between contract award controversies that may be brought by a third party and contract performance disputes. It then considers, in detail, the features of each of the three forums.

Forum	Procuring Agency	Court of Federal Claims (COFC)	GAO
Who May Protest	Interested Parties	Non-procurement contract offerors with implied contract for good faith consideration of offer and procurement contract offerors that are interested parties	Interested Parties
Jurisdiction	FAR 33.103	28 U.S.C. § 1491(a)(1) and (b)(2)	31 U.S.C. § 3551, with deference to actions in other forums
Time for Protest	Pre- and postaward	Pre- and postaward	Pre- and postaward
Time for Decision	No designated time	No designated time	100 calendar days (65 calendar days C express option)
Burden of Proof	Probably same as GAO	Clear and convincing evidence of violation	Presumption of correctness of agency action
Standards of Review	Probably same as GAO	No rational basis or clear violation of statute or regulation	No rational basis or clear violation of statute or regulation
Interim Remedies	Agency must delay award or suspend performance unless CICA override	Discretionary temporary restraining order or preliminary injunction	Agency must delay award or suspend performance unless CICA override

Remedies	Any appropriate actions	Injunction or declaratory judgment if consistent with national defense; bid or proposal costs	Recommend that agency recompete, terminate, or award; contract costs; attorneys' fees; bid or proposal costs
Appeals	If within jurisdictional time period, begin action again in either GAO or COFC	Federal Circuit	Indirectly through suit in the COFC

Figure 11-1

I. AWARD VERSUS PERFORMANCE CONTROVERSIES

Contract award controversies must be distinguished from controversies arising during contract performance. As a general rule, performance controversies occur between the parties to a contract, and third parties cannot challenge actions that occur during the performance of a contract. See, for example, *Gull Airborne Instruments, Inc. v. Weinberger*, 694 F.2d 838 (D.C. Cir. 1982), denying a competitor a right to obtain an injunction ordering the contracting officer to terminate the contract for default based on the contractor's alleged failure to perform as proposed. This rule has been incorporated in the protest regulations of the GAO at 4 C.F.R. § 21.5(a), which states: "The administration of an existing contract is within the discretion of the contracting agency." In *Data Monitor Sys., Inc. (DMS) v. United States*, 74 Fed. Cl.66 (2006), the court held that it lacked jurisdiction to enjoin termination of a contract and refused to enjoin re-solicitation. The matter arose in the aftermath of T Square Logistics Corporation's protest against award of a contract to DMS. T Square protested to GAO, alleging "improper agency evaluation and lack of discussions regarding that rating." The Air Force contended that it did not conduct discussions with T Square because it did not regard the matter in question as "a deficiency, weakness or adverse past performance information which [sic] could be resolved or corrected via discussions." The Air Force informed GAO that it would take corrective action but did not state that it would reopen discussions. The Air Force again indicated DMS as the successful offeror. T Square again protested to GAO, after which the Air Force informed GAO that it would, among other things, terminate DMS's contract and reopen discussions. DMS then sued in the Court of Federal Claims contending that the "proposed termination was wrongful and that the decision to resolicit was arbitrary and unlawful." The court ruled that it lacked jurisdiction to enjoin the termination, stating that it was reviewable only under the CDA. Other court cases denying jurisdiction because the issue was a matter involving contract administration include *Griffy's Landscape Maint. LLC v. United States*, 51 Fed. Cl. 667 (2001) (awardee of a contract may not challenge the decision to terminate that contract by invoking the court's bid protest jurisdiction); *Davis/HRGM Joint Venture v. United States*, 50 Fed. Cl. 539 (2001) (contractor's challenge to a termination for convenience "does not fall within the express language of [28 U.S.C.] § 1491(b) because it does not relate to an interested party's objection to a solicitation, a proposed award, or an award"); *Control Data Sys., Inc. v. United States*, 32 Fed. Cl. 520 (1994) (decision not to exercise an option); *C.M.P., Inc. v. United States*, 8 Cl. Ct. 743 (1985) (exercise of an option in competitor's contract); and *Willow Beach Resort, Inc. v. United States*, 5 Cl. Ct. 241 (1984) (refusal of agency to treat "preferential right" in contract as a promise to buy only from protester).

GAO decisions finding the matter involved contract administration include *Petro Star, Inc.*, Comp. Gen. Dec. B-401108, 2009 CPD ¶ 92 (seeking contract reformation); *Solar Plexus, LLC*, Comp. Gen. Dec. B-402061, 2009 CPD ¶ 256 (whether awardee complies with RFP requirements); *Nilson Van & Storage, Inc.*, Comp. Gen. Dec. B-310485, 2007 CPD ¶ 224 (whether awardee complies with performance work statement standard to conduct background check on prospective employees); *Murray-Benjamin Elec. Co., LP*, Comp. Gen. Dec. B-298481, 2006 CPD ¶ 129 (whether agency violated its obligation to procure items under one of the contractor's existing vehicles); *Catapult Tech., Ltd.*, Comp. Gen. Dec. B-294936, 2005 CPD ¶ 14 (exercise of an option); *Public Facility Consortium I, LLC*, Comp. Gen. Dec. B-295911, 2005 CPD ¶ 170 (whether awardee performs in accordance with solicitation requirements); *Military Agency Servs. Pty., Ltd.*, Comp. Gen. Dec. B-290414, 2002 CPD ¶ 130 (whether services were required to be ordered under contractor's multiple award schedule); *Magney Grande Distribution, Inc.*, Comp. Gen. Dec. B-286981, 2001 CPD ¶ 56 (whether awardee will be held to the RFP's performance testing requirements); *AT&T Corp.*, Comp. Gen. Dec. B-270344, 96-1 CPD ¶ 117 (challenge to the termination of its contract); *Digital Sys. Group, Inc.*, Comp. Gen. Dec. B-252080.2, 93-1 CPD ¶ 228, and *AVW Elec. Sys., Inc.*, Comp. Gen. Dec. B-252399, 93-1 CPD ¶ 386 (exercise of an option); *Anderson Columbia Co.*, Comp. Gen. Dec. B-249475.3, 92-2 CPD ¶ 288 (whether awardee may violate contract requirement for use of U.S. flag vessels); *Sierra Techs., Inc.*, Comp. Gen. Dec. B-251460, 92-2 CPD ¶ 427 (failure to continue making dual awards on acquisition program); *RGI, Inc.*, Comp. Gen. Dec. B-243387.2, 91-2 CPD ¶ 572 (use of less qualified individuals by the awardee than originally proposed to fill positions under the contract); and *American Instrument Corp.*, Comp. Gen. Dec. B-239997, 90-2 CPD ¶ 287 (whether awardee complies with Buy American Act certification).

A. Actions Compromising Competition

Where the contract action is considered to clearly compromise the competition that led to the award, it will be considered a contract award controversy, *Webcraft Packaging, Div. of Beatrice Foods Co.*, Comp. Gen. Dec. B-194087, 79-2 CPD ¶ 120 (agency should have resolicited rather than relax specifications in contract for specialty product produced by only a few sources). Thus, the contract award controversy process will be available where a contract modification alters the contract requirement to the extent that the modified contract is outside the scope of the original competition, *AT&T Communications, Inc. v. Wiltel, Inc.*, 1 F.3d 1201 (Fed. Cir. 1993). This is determined by analyzing the entire contract to determine whether the original competitors would have anticipated that the modification would be issued under the contract. See *Cardinal Maint. Serv., Inc. v. United States*, 63 Fed. Cl. 98 (2004) (changes were not of the type that were specifically authorized or even foreseen in the original contract); *CW Gov't Travel v. United States*, 61 Fed. Cl. 559 (2004), *reh'g denied*, 63 Fed. Cir. 459 (2005), *aff'd*, 163 Fed. Appx. 853 (2005) (new services were so far removed from the original requirements that they should have been independently solicited through full and open competition); and *CCL, Inc. v. United States*, 39 Fed. Cl. 780 (1997) (modification increasing the number of locations where computer maintenance services were to be performed). For GAO decisions, see *Poly-Pacific Techs.*, Comp. Gen. Dec. B-296029, 2005 CPD ¶ 105 (RFP did not anticipate that contractor could be relieved of the recycling requirement or that a disposal effort could be ordered in lieu of recycling); *Sprint Communications Co.*, Comp. Gen. Dec. B-278407.2, 98-1 CPD ¶ 60 (modification adding transmission services were outside the scope because the initial procurement had stated that such services were not required); *MCI Telecommunications Corp.*, Comp. Gen. Dec. B-276659.2, 97-2 CPD ¶ 90 (modification permitting contractor to design, operate, and maintain customized networks beyond the scope of FTS 2000 contract for telecommunications services because this was a different type of service than those called for in original contract); *Marvin J. Perry & Assocs.*, Comp. Gen. Dec. B-277684, 97-2 CPD ¶ 128 (modification of Federal Supply Schedule to substitute stained ash for red oak furniture beyond scope because ash was substantially cheaper); *Neil R. Gross & Co.*, Comp. Gen. Dec. B-237434, 90-1 CPD ¶ 212 (modification adding new court reporting services with substantial increased costs was outside scope of original competition); *Avtron Mfg., Inc.*, 67 Comp. Gen. 404 (B-229972), 88-1 CPD ¶ 458 (modifying the speed drive of the equipment would materially alter the terms of the original contract); and *American Air Filter Co.*, 57 Comp. Gen. 567 (B-188408), 78-1 CPD ¶ 443 (modification requiring units to operate on diesel fuel rather than gasoline was outside scope of original competition).

Cases finding that the modification did not trigger the competition requirements in CICA include *Overseas Lease Group, Inc.*, Comp. Gen. Dec. B-402111, 2010 CPD ¶ 34 (contract modification within scope where solicitation's differentiating between "non-tactical" and "up-armored" vehicles was sufficient to put protester on notice that term "non-tactical" was intended to refer to unarmored vehicles); *Lasmer Indus., Inc.*, Comp. Gen. Dec. B-400866.2, 2009 CPD ¶ 77 (part was specifically included in the contract, and the contract allowed the agency to order the part under a negotiated delivery schedule); *Armed Forces Hospitality*, Comp. Gen. Dec. B-298978.2, 2009 CPD ¶ 192 (lack of definitiveness in the original SOW provided the Army with additional contractual flexibility and latitude to reduce the number of rooms to be renovated and extend performance); *Chapman Law Firm Co. v. United States*, 81 Fed. Cl. 323 (2008) (geographic expansion of service and possibility of new pricing were changes clearly contemplated in the contracts); *Sallie Mae, Inc.*, Comp. Gen. Dec. B-400486, 2008 CPD ¶ 221 (statement of objective clearly placed offerors on notice that the agency intended to award a contract for the management of all types of student loans); *CWT/ Alexander Travel, Ltd. v. United States*, 78 Fed. Cl. 486 (2007) (given the nature of services required under the contract, price changes were viewed as inevitable); *DOR Biodefense, Inc.*, Comp. Gen. Dec. B-296358.3, 2006 CPD ¶ 35 (type of work under the contract as modified remained substantially unchanged because the RFP advised offerors that the government reserves the right to change the list of vaccine sertoypes to add or delete products as need may arise); *HDM Corp. v. United States*, 69 Fed. Cl. 243 (2005) (modification to a contract for management of medical insurance records not outside scope because consolidating responsibility for the crossover function was consistent with the broad objectives of the original contract); *CESC Plaza Ltd. Partnership v. United States*, 52 Fed. Cl. 91 (2002) (modifications did not materially alter the contract's cash flow features or shift the risk of performance); *HG Properties A, LP*, Comp. Gen. Dec. B-290416, 2002 CPD ¶ 128 (lease modification changing location of site for construction of offered building space remains within the scope of the underlying lease where the property location requirements were only general in nature and scope with wide location boundaries); *VMC Behavioral Healthcare Servs., Div. of Vasquez Group, Inc. v. United States*, 50 Fed. Cl. 328 (2001) (solicitation was for level of effort contract for employee assistance services, subject to modification as additional agencies were added to the contract's coverage); *Hughes Space & Communications Co.*, Comp. Gen. Dec. B-276040, 97-1 CPD ¶ 158 (modification to a satellite communications services contract that added "system preemptible" satellite transponder leases to the contract, which previously specified only "non-preemptible" transponder leases, did not exceed scope because fundamental nature and purpose of contract was not changed); and *Arjay Elecs. Corp.*, Comp. Gen. Dec. B-243080, 91-2 CPD ¶ 3 (contract price was not adjusted, period of time for delivery was not extended, and there was no evidence that changes in the item descriptions were significant; thus, no evidence that field of competition changed due to contract modification).

B. Task and Delivery Orders

The Federal Acquisition Streamlining Act of 1994 (FASA), Pub. L. No. 103-355, task and delivery order authority precluded protests concerning the issuance of orders under task and delivery order contracts except for a protest on the ground that the order increases the scope, period, or maximum value of the contract under which the order is issued. Section 843 of the National Defense Authorization Act (NDAA) of Fiscal Year 2008, Pub. L. No. 110-181, modified FASA's prior limitations on task order protests. Specifically, the NDAA provides that, in addition to previously permitted task order protests on the ground that the order increases the scope, period, or maximum value of the contract, a protest at the GAO is also authorized with regard to "an order valued in excess of $10,000,000." This grant of jurisdiction is subject to a three-year sunset provision and is set to expire on May 27, 2011. See 10 U.S.C. § 2304c(e) and 41 U.S.C. § 253j(e) providing:

> (1) A protest is not authorized in connection with the issuance or proposed issuance of a task or delivery order except for

(A) a protest on the ground that the order increases the scope, period, or maximum value of the contract under which the order is issued; or

(B) a protest of an order valued in excess of $10,000,000.

(2) Notwithstanding section 3556 of title 31, the Comptroller General of the United States shall have exclusive jurisdiction of a protest authorized under paragraph (1)(B).

(3) This subsection shall be in effect for three years, beginning on the date that is 120 days after the date of the enactment of the National Defense Authorization Act for Fiscal Year 2008.

The rule is implemented in FAR 16.505.

Other than protests challenging the scope, period, or maximum value of the underlying contract, GAO's jurisdiction is limited to task or delivery protests over $10,000,000, *LaBarge Prods., Inc.*, Comp. Gen. Dec. B-402280, 2010 CPD ¶ 31 (no jurisdiction because the value of the delivery order is below $10 million); and *e-Management Consultants, Inc.*, Comp. Gen. Dec. B-400585.2, 2009 CPD ¶ 39 (the record is undisputed that the value of the task order is less than $10 million). In *ESCO Marine, Inc.*, Comp. Gen. Dec. B-401438, 2009 CPD ¶ 234, for purposes of determining whether the $10 million threshold has been met, the GAO held that it was not limited to consideration of the offerors' proposed prices, but properly included consideration of the estimated ship scrap values. In connection with the task order for dismantling ships, offerors were required to sell the scrap resulting from the ship dismantling, were permitted to retain the scrap sale proceeds, and were required to offset their proposed prices with the scrap sale proceeds. Essentially, the task order provided the contractor with two different forms of payment — the price and payment-in-kind (the right to keep the scrap sale proceeds). In *Armorworks Enters., LLC*, Comp. Gen. Dec. B-401671.3, 2009 CPD ¶ 225, the GAO held that it did not have jurisdiction to consider a protest challenging the agency's decision to issue three separate delivery orders for body armor plates, where each of the delivery orders was valued below the statutory threshold of $10 million, and the record did not support the protester's contention that the agency's decision to procure the plates by separate delivery orders was a deliberate effort to evade GAO's bid protest jurisdiction.

The $10 million dollar threshold is not applicable to a blanket purchase agreement (BPA), since a BPA is not a task or delivery order contract, *C&B Constr., Inc.*, Comp. Gen. Dec. B-401988.2, 2010 CPD ¶ 1. See also *Envirosolve LLC*, Comp. Gen. Dec. B-294974.4, 2005 CPD ¶ 106 (sustaining protest against orders placed under multiple-award BPAs where orders were valued under $100,000).

Protests of task and delivery orders at the GAO are decided following the same rules that apply to other protests, *Triple Canopy, Inc.*, Comp. Gen. Dec. B-310566.4,

2008 CPD ¶ 207; *Bay Area Travel, Inc.*, Comp. Gen. Dec. B-400442, 2009 CPD ¶ 65. Thus, protests objecting to the terms of the task order solicitation are subject to the GAO timeliness rules. In *Innovative Tech. Corp.*, Comp. Gen. Dec. B-401689, 2009 CPD ¶ 235, the GAO dismissed as untimely the protest of alleged improprieties apparent on the face of the task order solicitation, filed after issuance of the task order, because the protester knew or should have known, upon receipt and review of the RFP, that the task order would be issued for an amount in excess of $10 million, given that it was the incumbent contractor and its initial proposal price exceeded $10 million.

A task and delivery order ombudsman will review complaints from contractors holding multiple-award task order or delivery order contracts to ensure that they are afforded a fair opportunity to be considered for task or delivery orders. 10 U.S.C. § 2304c(f) and 41 U.S.C. § 253j(f) provide:

> Each head of an agency who awards multiple task or delivery order contracts pursuant to section 2304a(d)(1)(B) or 2304b(e) of this title shall appoint or designate a task and delivery order ombudsman who shall be responsible for reviewing complaints from the contractors on such contracts and ensuring that all of the contractors are afforded a fair opportunity to be considered for task or delivery orders when required under subsection (b). The task and delivery order ombudsman shall be a senior agency official who is independent of the contracting officer for the contracts and may be the agency's competition advocate.

FAR 16.505(b)(6) incorporates this requirement with slightly different wording. While the statute appears to limit the ombudsman's role to multiple-award situations, the FAR seems to extend it to all aspects of all task and delivery order contracts, whether single or multiple award.

Task and delivery orders, regardless of the dollar value, can be challenged through the contract award controversy process if they increase the scope, period, or maximum value of the contract under which the order is issued. See *Anteon Corp.*, Comp. Gen. Dec. B-293523, 2004 CPD ¶ 51 (physical deliverables under the task order request not reasonably within the scope of GSA's smart card contract); *Floro & Assocs.*, Comp. Gen. Dec. B-285451.3, 2000 CPD ¶ 172 (task order beyond the scope of a contract for noncomplex integration services of commercially available off-the-shelf hardware and software where it required the contractor to provide management services to assist in support of distance learning product lines); *Ervin v. Assocs., Inc.*, Comp. Gen. Dec. B-278850, 98-1 CPD ¶ 89 (task order beyond the scope when the work was not mentioned in the original solicitation); *Dynamac Corp.*, Comp. Gen. Dec. B-252800, 93-2 CPD ¶ 37 (order for support of a computerized information system outside the scope of a contract that was intended to provide engineering support for an agency's information resources management systems because the original solicitation for the contract did not adequately advise offerors of the potential for this type of order); *Data Transformation Corp.*, Comp. Gen. Dec. B-274629, 97-1 CPD ¶ 10 (operation of a nationwide debt collection system outside the scope of a litigation support contract); and *Comdisco, Inc.*, Comp. Gen. Dec. B-277340, 97-2 CPD ¶ 105 (agency exceeded the scope of its task orders for computer equipment and related services by permitting computer hardware/software to constitute more than its allotted share of a contract).

Task orders were found to be within the scope of the underlying contract in *Outdoor Venture Corp.*, Comp. Gen. Dec. B-401628, 2009 CPD ¶ 260 (delivery order requirement for full concealment covers within scope since the SOW listed variations of Ultra Lightweight Camouflage Net Systems to be procured and noted that other versions not specifically identified could also be procured); *Morris Corp.*, Comp. Gen. Dec. B-400336, 2008 CPD ¶ 204 (logical connection between the broad scope of food service operations delineated in the IDIQ contract — the feeding of individuals housed within a specified Iraqi training camp and/or coalition base — and the food service operations required to feed detainees located within the camp); *Colliers Int'l*, Comp. Gen. Dec. B-400173, 2008 CPD ¶ 147 (task order to conduct feasibility study within scope of IDIQ contract which was broad and specifically provided for unidentified "special studies"); *Relm Wireless Corp.*, Comp. Gen. Dec. B-298715, 2006 CPD ¶ 190 (tactical radio within scope of IDIQ contract because RFP's definition of Land Mobile Radio covered similar assets designated for contingency, tactical or war ready material purposes); *Specialty Marine, Inc.*, Comp. Gen. Dec. B-293871, 2004 CPD ¶ 130 (SOW language encompassed a broad category of ships without limitation to size); *Symetrics Indus., Inc.*, Comp. Gen. Dec. B-289606, 2002 CPD ¶ 65 (retrofitting reasonably falls within definition of depot level maintenance); *Ervin & Assocs., Inc.*, Comp. Gen. Dec. B-279083, 98-1 CPD ¶ 126 (relevant language in the solicitation's statement of work sets forth the anticipated services in broad, general, and flexible terms); *Techno-Sciences, Inc.*, Comp. Gen. Dec. B-277260.3, 98-1 CPD ¶ 138 (tasks within scope where the contract specifically contemplated that operations, maintenance, and technical support would include whatever was necessary to support mission); *Exide Corp.*, Comp. Gen. Dec. B-276988, 97-2 CPD ¶ 51 (delivery orders in excess of maximum order limitation and to be delivered after contract expiration within scope when its terms provided for such flexibility); *Master Security, Inc.*, Comp. Gen. Dec. B-274990.2, 97-1 CPD ¶ 21 (addition of number of hours and contract sites not considered material change); *LDDS WorldCom*, Comp. Gen. Dec. B-266257, 96-1 CPD ¶ 50 (the added services could have been anticipated from the face of the contract and were not materially different than the services currently rendered under the contract); *Liebert Corp.*, Comp. Gen. Dec. B-232234.5, 91-1 CPD ¶ 413 (work within scope but quantity beyond maximum stated in contract outside scope); and *Information Ventures, Inc.*, Comp. Gen. Dec. B-240458, 90-2 CPD ¶ 414 (tasks "logically related to the overall purpose" of the agreement).

II. PROCURING AGENCIES AND OMBUDSMEN

Persons seeking to contest a procurement have always had the option of lodging a complaint with the procuring agency, and some agencies have adopted procedures to handle these protests. Until the mid-1990s, however, there were no governmentwide regulations dealing with agency protests. On October 25, 1995, President Clinton issued Exec. Order No. 12979, 60 Fed. Reg. 55171, requiring all agencies to establish administrative procedures for resolving bid protests. These procedures are required to:

(a) emphasize that whenever conduct of a procurement is contested, all parties should use their best efforts to resolve the matter with agency contracting officers;

(b) to the maximum extent practicable, provide for inexpensive, informal, procedurally simple, and expeditious resolution of protests, including where appropriate and as permitted by law, the use of alternative dispute resolution techniques, third party neutrals, and another agency's personnel;

(c) allow actual or prospective bidders or offerors whose direct economic interests would be affected by the award or failure to award the contract to request a review, at a level above the contracting officer, of any decision by a contracting officer that is alleged to have violated a statute or regulation and, thereby, caused prejudice to the protester.

The provisions of the executive order are implemented in FAR 33.103. This section considers the various ways in which the agencies have responded to the executive order and the FAR.

A. Jurisdiction

There are no jurisdictional limitations on agency protests because any agency of the government has inherent authority to consider a protest alleging some defect in one of its procurements. The agency protest procedures mandated by FAR Subpart 33.1 apply to all "executive agencies," FAR 2.101. The meaning of this term is discussed in the next section on protests to the GAO.

B. Who May Protest

The FAR contains no rule limiting the parties that may file a protest with an agency. Agencies may consider protests from any party that raises legitimate concerns about the conduct of a procurement; and it is clear that some agency officials, such as the NASA ombudsman, will consider such protests. To determine the scope of an agency's protest procedures, each agency regulation must be reviewed.

FAR 33.102(e) does "encourage" an "interested party" wishing to protest to seek resolution within the procuring activity. FAR 33.101 defines "interested party" as "an actual or prospective offeror whose direct economic interest would be affected by the award of a contract or by the failure to award a contract." This is the same definition as used by the GAO.

C. Time for Protest

FAR 33.103(e) states very formal rules, patterned on the GAO rules, on the time for submitting protests to an agency. Protests based on alleged apparent improprieties in a solicitation must be filed prior to bid opening or the closing date for receipt of proposals. In all other cases protests must be filed not later than 10 days after the basis of the protest is known or should have been known, whichever is earlier. The agency may, for good cause shown or where the protest raises issues significant to the agency's acquisition system, consider the merits of any protest that is not timely filed. In addition, there is nothing in the FAR that precludes an agency from considering untimely protests on other bases.

The FAR provides some assurance to protesters that an executive agency will not moot a protest by permitting contract performance during the consideration of the protest. FAR 33.103(f)(1) provides that if an agency protest is filed before award, award will not be made unless it is justified in writing for "urgent and compelling reasons or is determined, in writing, to be in the best interests of the Government." This decision to award in the face of a protest must be made "at a level above the contracting officer, or by another official pursuant to agency procedures." With respect to agency protests received within 10 days after award, or within 5 days after a debriefing, whichever is later, the contracting officer must immediately suspend performance unless continued performance is justified for urgent and compelling reasons or is determined to be in the best interest of the government, FAR 33.103(f)(3). Such justification or determination must be approved at a level above the contracting officer, or by another official pursuant to agency procedures, FAR 33.103(f)(3).

Pursuing an agency protest does not extend the time for obtaining a stay at GAO. Agencies may, however, include as part of the agency protest process, a voluntary suspension period when agency protests are denied and the protester subsequently files at GAO. See, for example, DOLAR 2933.103(m):

> If the protest is denied, and contract performance has been suspended under paragraph (i) of this section, the contracting officer will not lift such suspension until five (5) days after the protest decision has been issued, to allow the protester to file a protest with the General Accounting Office, unless the HCA makes a new finding under FAR 33.103(f)(3). The contracting officer shall consider allowing such suspension to remain in effect pending the resolution of any GAO proceeding.

D. Procedures

Protests to the contracting agency should be submitted to the person designated in the solicitation. Under the standard Service of Protest clause in FAR 52.233-2, this is generally expected to be the contracting officer, but each agency may designate the official to which protests may be sent. When the protester sends in its protest, it may "request an independent review at a level above the contracting officer," FAR 33.103(d)(4).

Agency-level protests should include a complete statement of the complaint that the protester has with the procurement. In adopting procedures for agency-level protests, FAR 33.103(d) sets forth the following legalistic guidance modeled on the GAO protest procedures:

> The following procedures are established to resolve agency protests effectively, to build confidence in the Government's acquisition system, and to reduce protests outside of the agency:
>
> (1) Protests shall be concise and logically presented to facilitate review by the agency. Failure to substantially comply with any of the requirements of paragraph (d)(2) of this section may be grounds for dismissal of the protest.
>
> (2) Protests shall include the following information:
>
> > (i) Name, address, and fax and telephone numbers of the protester.
> >
> > (ii) Solicitation or contract number.
> >
> > (iii) Detailed statement of the legal and factual grounds for the protest, to include a description of resulting prejudice to the protester.
> >
> > (iv) Copies of relevant documents.
> >
> > (v) Request for a ruling by the agency.
> >
> > (vi) Statement as to the form of relief requested.
> >
> > (vii) All information establishing that the protester is an interested party for the purpose of filing a protest.
> >
> > (viii) All information establishing the timeliness of the protest.

Agencies are encouraged to resolve agency protests within 35 days after the protest is filed, FAR 33.103(g). Written protest decisions should be sent to the protester and should be well reasoned and explain the agency position, FAR 33.103(h).

The Army Materiel Command (AMC) has successfully used agency-level protests since 1991. Under the AMC's protest procedures, a protest may be filed with either the contracting officer or the AMC Office of Command Counsel. Within 10 working days after the protest is filed, the contracting officer, with the assistance of legal counsel, is required to file an administrative report responsive to the protest to the AMC Office of Command Counsel. The AMC protest decision authority will issue a written decision within 20 working days after the filing of the protest. For good cause, the AMC protest decision authority may grant an extension of time for filing the administrative report and for the issuance of the written decision. The written decision is binding on the AMC and its contracting activities. See Office of Command Counsel at www.amc.army.mil/pa.

DOE also has detailed guidance on agency-level protests. See DOE Acquisition Guide, Chapter 33.1 (October 2008). Generally the protest will be decided by the head of the contracting activity, but it may be decided by the Senior Procurement Executive under certain circumstances. Decisions are issued within 35 calendar days, unless a longer period of time is needed. The guidance provides that the contracting officer should make every attempt to resolve the protest through direct negotiations with the offeror with due regard for the need to take corrective action, if appropriate.

One technique used to resolve an agency protest is to appoint an ombudsman. NASA has created an ombudsman program, NFS Subpart 1815.70. The contracting officer must insert a clause substantially the same as the one at NFS 1852.215-84, Ombudsman, in all solicitations (including draft solicitations) and contracts:

(a) An ombudsman has been appointed to hear and facilitate the resolution of concerns from offerors, potential offerors, and contractors during the preaward and postaward phases of this acquisition. When requested, the ombudsman will maintain strict confidentiality as to the source of the concern. The existence of the ombudsman is not to diminish the authority of the contracting officer, the Source Evaluation Board, or the selection official. Further, the ombudsman does not participate in the evaluation of proposals, the source selection process, or the adjudication of formal contract disputes. Therefore, before consulting with an ombudsman, interested parties must first address their concerns, issues, disagreements, and/or recommendations to the contracting officer for resolution.

(b) If resolution cannot be made by the contracting officer, interested parties may contact the installation ombudsman, _____ [Insert name, address, telephone number, facsimile number, and e-mail address]. Concerns, issues, disagreements, and recommendations which cannot be resolved at the installation may be referred to the NASA ombudsman, the Director of the Contract Management Division, at 202-358-0422, facsimile 202-358-3083, e-mail sthomps1@hq.nasa.gov. Please do not contact the ombudsman to request copies of the solicitation, verify offer due date, or clarify technical requirements. Such inquiries shall be directed to the Contracting Officer or as specified elsewhere in this document.

The scope of this ombudsman's duties extends beyond protests orders — covering all matters concerning contracts with the agency.

E. Alternative Dispute Resolution

Another procedure for resolving a protest in lieu of either protesting with the GAO or litigation is alternative dispute resolution. Alternative dispute resolution includes any procedure or combination of procedures voluntarily used to resolve issues in controversy. These techniques are now recognized and encouraged by the Administrative Dispute Resolution Act, 5 U.S.C. §§ 571-584, as implemented by FAR Subpart 33.2. FAR 33.103(c) provides:

> The agency should provide for inexpensive, informal, procedurally simple, and expeditious resolution of protests. Where appropriate, the use of alternative dispute resolution techniques, third party neutrals, and another agency's personnel are acceptable protest resolution methods.

F. Standards of Review

The FAR is not clear on the standards of review that will be used in dealing with agency-level protests. Its initial guidance is the broad statement that contracting officers "shall consider all protests," FAR 33.102(a). See also FAR 33.103(b), which states:

> Prior to submission of an agency protest, all parties shall use their best efforts to resolve concerns raised by an interested party at the contracting officer level through open and frank discussions.

This guidance indicates that a potential offeror can obtain the contracting officer's review of any concern regarding the procurement. In particular, this type of protest would be appropriate when a potential offeror has questions about the meaning of a solicitation or concerns that a solicitation is not properly drafted.

If the more formal "agency protest" procedure is used, FAR 33.102(b) states that the standard of review will be whether a solicitation, proposed award, or award complies with "the requirements of law and regulation." It appears that this is too narrow a statement of the standard of review that will be applied to formal agency protests, because such protests will also consider whether the actions of the contracting agency are reasonable (as that requirement is construed by the GAO and the courts). In addition, agencies may adopt broader standards of review in accordance with their own internal procedures.

G. Prejudice

As discussed below, the GAO and the courts have refused to grant relief on a protest unless they find that the protester has been prejudiced by the improper agency action. There is no reason why this rule should be followed in an agency protest, because agencies should correct a problem that has occurred in the procurement process as soon as they are aware of the problem.

H. Remedies

The contracting officer or an agency protest authority with broad powers, such as the NASA ombudsman, can take any action necessary to resolve a protest that is brought to it. If a protest is brought to the head of an agency using the FAR agency protest procedures, the FAR provides that the agency can take any action that could have been recommended by the Comptroller General had the protest been filed with the GAO. FAR 33.102(b) states:

> If, in connection with a protest, the head of an agency determines that a solicitation, proposed award, or award does not comply with the requirements of law or regulation, the head of the agency may —
>
> (1) Take any action that could have been recommended by the Comptroller General had the protest been filed with the Government Accountability Office;
>
> (2) Pay appropriate costs as stated in 33.104(h); and
>
> (3) Require the awardee to reimburse the Government's costs, as provided in this paragraph, where a postaward protest is sustained as the result of an awardee's intentional or negligent misstatement, misrepresentation, or miscertification. In addition to any other remedy available, and pursuant to the requirements of Subpart 32.6, the Government may collect this debt by offsetting the amount against any payment due the awardee under any contract between the awardee and the Government.
>
>> (i) When a protest is sustained by GAO under circumstances that may allow the Government to seek reimbursement for protest costs, the contracting officer will determine whether the protest was sustained based on the awardee's negligent or intentional misrepresentation. If the protest was sustained on several issues, protest costs shall be apportioned according to the costs attributable to the awardee's actions.
>>
>> (ii) The contracting officer shall review the amount of the debt, degree of the awardee's fault, and costs of collection, to determine whether a demand for reimbursement ought to be made. If it is in the best interests of the Government to seek reimbursement, the contracting officer shall notify the contractor in writing of the nature and amount of the debt, and the intention to collect by offset if necessary. Prior to issuing a final decision, the contracting officer shall afford the contractor an opportunity to inspect and copy agency records pertaining to the debt to the extent permitted by statute and regulation, and to request review of the matter by the head of the contracting activity.

(iii) When appropriate, the contracting officer shall also refer the matter to the agency debarment official for consideration under Subpart 9.4.

Because this provision is permissive, there appear to be no restrictions preventing the agency from granting other requested relief following review of an agency-level protest. This includes the authority to allow correction or withdrawal in mistake cases, *Unico Constr. Co.*, Comp. Gen. Dec. B-258862, 95-1 CPD ¶ 42; *National Heat & Power Corp.*, Comp. Gen. Dec. B-212923, 84-1 CPD ¶ 125. However, the granting of relief from mistakes in sealed bid procurements is subject to a number of restrictions within the executive agencies. Contracting officers are permitted to correct clerical mistakes apparent on the face of the bid, FAR 14.407-2, but relief for other types of mistakes must be granted by the agency heads who may delegate their authority to a limited number of central authorities, FAR 14.407-3(e). In all mistake cases, the concurrence of legal counsel within the agency is required before a determination is made, FAR 14.407-3(f). Numerous subsidiary regulations implement the FAR and contain delegations of authority to grant relief for mistakes prior to award. See, e.g., DFARS 214.407-3, NFS 1814.407, and GSAR 514.407-3. The current FAR guidance on mistakes in negotiated procurements is unclear. See the discussions in Chapter 5 and Chapter 8.

III. GOVERNMENT ACCOUNTABILITY OFFICE

For many years the only forum to consider contract award controversies was the GAO, headed by the Comptroller General of the United States. It began to hear protests from disappointed bidders early in its existence, e.g., 10 Comp. Gen. 480 (A-36067) (1931); 11 Comp. Gen. 220 (A-39095) (1931). The GAO took these protests and issued decisions under the predecessors of 31 U.S.C. § 3526 and § 3529. These statutes give the GAO the authority to settle and adjust the accounts of accountable officers and the obligation to render advance decisions to certifying and disbursing officers on questions concerning the legality of payments. The procuring agencies generally acquiesced in the decisions, with the result that the GAO protest procedure became firmly embedded in the procurement process.

It was not until 1984 that the GAO was given specific statutory authority to hear protests, 31 U.S.C. § 3551 et seq. As originally enacted, this statute gave the GAO the authority to order a stay of performance longer than the period specified in the statute, 31 U.S.C. § 3554(a)(1). This raised questions as to the constitutionality of the provision given that the GAO is an office in the legislative branch and procurement is an executive function. However, this provision was deleted by § 8139 of the 1989 Department of Defense Appropriations Act, Pub. L. No. 100-463. As a result, *United States Army Corps of Eng'rs v. Ameron, Inc.*, 809 F.2d 979 (3d Cir. 1986), *cert. granted*, 485 U.S. 958 (1988), *mot. denied*, 488 U.S. 809 (1988), *cert. dismissed*, 488 U.S. 918 (1988), which had been scheduled for argument to determine the constitutionality of the statute, was dismissed at the request of the Solicitor General.

A. Jurisdiction

The GAO has slightly different authority to hear protests under 31 U.S.C. § 3551 et seq. than under its prior nonstatutory authority.

1. Statutory Authority

The jurisdiction of the GAO under its statutory authority depends on the status of the agency conducting the procurement and the nature of the transaction. 31 U.S.C. § 3551 defines "protest" as a written objection to a "procurement of property or services" by a "federal agency" as defined in 40 U.S.C. § 472.

a. Status of Agency

The term "federal agency" covers virtually all agencies of the government that operate with appropriated funds. Protests have been taken on procurements of the Tennessee Valley Authority, *Monarch Water Sys., Inc.*, 64 Comp. Gen. 756 (B-218441), 85-2 CPD ¶ 146, *recons. denied*, 85-2 CPD ¶ 335; the Federal Housing Administration Fund, *CoMont, Inc.*, 65 Comp. Gen. 66 (B-219730), 85-2 CPD ¶ 555; the Bonneville Power Administration, *International Line Bldrs.*, 67 Comp. Gen. 8 (B-227811), 87-2 CPD ¶ 345, *recons. denied*, 87-2 CPD ¶ 472; the Federal Reserve Board, *Computer Support Sys., Inc.*, 69 Comp. Gen. 644 (B-239034), 90-2 CPD ¶ 94; Federal Prison Industries, *USA Fabrics*, Comp. Gen. Dec. B-295737, 2005 CPD ¶ 82. See, however, *P.O.M., Inc.*, 64 Comp. Gen. 488 (B-218178), 85-1 CPD ¶ 467, where the GAO held that the District of Columbia government is not a federal agency for purposes of the statute, citing 40 U.S.C. § 472, and *United Way of National Capital Area*, Comp. Gen. Dec. B-311235, 2008 CPD ¶ 96, holding that a Local Fund Campaign Committee is not a federal agency. Mixed-ownership corporations are not considered federal agencies, *Kennan Auction Co.*, Comp. Gen. Dec. B-248965, 92-1 CPD ¶ 503 (Resolution Trust Corporation); *Chas. G. Stott & Co.*, Comp. Gen. Dec. B-220302, 85-2 CPD ¶ 333 (Federal Deposit Insurance Corporation). Nonappropriated fund instrumentalities, as well, are not considered federal agencies, *LDDS Worldcom*, Comp. Gen. Dec. B-270109, 96-1 CPD ¶ 45. The House of Representatives also is not considered to be a federal agency, *Court Reporting Servs., Inc.*, Comp. Gen. Dec. B-259492, 94-2 CPD ¶ 236.

The GAO's protest jurisdiction does not depend on the intended use of the items being acquired or on the source of the funds for the acquisition, *CPT Text-Computer GmbH*, Comp. Gen. Dec. B-222037.2, 86-2 CPD ¶ 29. The key factor in determining applicability is that the procurement is conducted by a federal agency. See *Artisan Builders*, 65 Comp. Gen. 240 (B-220804), 86-1 CPD ¶ 85, holding that the statutory bid protest authority is applicable to a procurement that the Air Force conducted for a base golf course, a nonappropriated fund activity. In *Professional Pension Termination Assocs.*, Comp. Gen. Dec. B-230007.2, 88-1 CPD ¶

498, the GAO found that it had jurisdiction over a protest even though the procurement was partially funded with trust funds, because the Pension Benefit Guaranty Corporation, which conducted the procurement, was a federal agency. Similarly, a procurement by a federal agency for a foreign government is subject to the statute, *Cosmos Eng'rs, Inc.*, Comp. Gen. Dec. B-220000.3, 86-1 CPD ¶ 186 (procurement by Agency for International Development for foreign government); *Yoosung T&S, Ltd.*, Comp. Gen. Dec. B-291407, 2002 CPD ¶ 204 (procurement conducted by the Army, but funded by the Republic of Korea); *Ahntech-Korea Co.*, Comp. Gen. Dec. B-400145.2, 2008 CPD ¶ 169 (although Republic of Korea made the award decision, the Army conducted the procurement — it issued the solicitation, evaluated the proposals, and made the award recommendation). But see *Environmental Tectonics Corp.*, 65 Comp. Gen. 504 (B-222483), 86-1 CPD ¶ 377, where the GAO denied jurisdiction although the contract was financed by a federal agency, because the solicitation was issued and award made by the government of Egypt. See also *Peter Bauwens Bauunternehmung GmbH & Co. KG*, Comp. Gen. Dec. B-277734, 97-2 CPD ¶ 98, where the GAO dismissed a protest for lack of jurisdiction because the procurements were conducted by an agency of the government of Germany.

The GAO will consider a protest when a nonappropriated fund instrumentality is acting only as a mere conduit for an agency, *Premiere Vending*, Comp. Gen. Dec. B-256560, 94-2 CPD ¶ 8 (protester alleged that agency was diverting vending machine requirements to employees' association in order to avoid applicable procurement statutes and regulations). In *Americable Int'l, Inc.*, Comp. Gen. Dec. B-251614, 93-1 CPD ¶ 336, the GAO dismissed a protest, holding that the award of franchise contracts for cable television services and telephone services by a nonappropriated fund instrumentality was beyond the scope of the GAO's jurisdiction. The protester argued that the nonappropriated fund activity was acting as an agent for the Navy. The GAO found that there was no evidence of significant Navy participation in the procurement process, stating:

> [T]here was no participation by Navy contracting officials in the agreements finally ratified, and no suggestion that the Navy was ever intending to sign the agreement. Nor is there any evidence to suggest that agency contracting officials dictated the terms of the franchise contracts.
>
> In our view, this evidence does not constitute the kind of pervasive involvement required for our Office to conclude that an entity that is not a federal agency has become a mere conduit for the agency. See *St. Mary's Hosp. and Med. Center of San Francisco, Cal.*, [70 Comp. Gen. 579 (B-243061, 91-1 CPD ¶ 597]; *Perkin-Elmer Corp., Metco Div.*, [Comp. Gen. Dec. B-237076, 89-2 CPD ¶ 604]. Without evidence of such involvement by a federal agency, and since there is no question that the franchise contracts were awarded by a NAFI, we have no jurisdiction over the procurements here.

Agencies may be exempted from the protest statute by provisions in their own statutes. See *Falcon Sys., Inc.*, 65 Comp. Gen. 584 (B-222549), 86-1 CPD ¶ 462, finding that United States Postal Service contracts were not subject to the protest statute based upon 39 U.S.C. § 410(a), which states that the Postal Service is exempted from any federal law dealing with public or federal contracts except those listed. Because the protest statute is not listed, it does not apply. The Court of Appeals for the Federal Circuit has reached the same conclusion that the United States Postal Service is not subject to GAO jurisdiction in *Emery Worldwide Airlines, Inc. v. United States*, 264 F.3d 1071 (Fed. Cir. 2001). Under Pub. L. No. 104-50, § 348, codified at 49 U.S.C. § 106, Congress directed the Federal Aviation Administration (FAA) to develop and implement a new Acquisition Management System and exempted the FAA from most provisions of federal acquisition law, one being the procurement protest system. Under the FAA management system, protesters should first seek informal resolution of any issues concerning protests with the contracting officer. If resolution at the contracting officer level is not desired or successful, offerors may file a protest with the FAA's Office of Dispute Resolution for Acquisition. Although initially Transportation Security Administration (TSA) procurements were placed under FAA's Acquisition Management System, Congress repealed this provision in order to place all Department of Homeland Security entities under the same system. GAO issued a final rule stating that it would hear protests of TSA procurements covered by TSA solicitations issued on or after June 23, 2008, 73 Fed. Reg. 32,427, 32,429, June 9, 2008. The Presidio Trust is not subject to GAO jurisdiction because the Trust is statutorily exempt from all federal laws and regulations governing procurement by federal agencies, and CICA is not included in the list of statutes made applicable to the Trust, *Performance Excavators, Inc.*, Comp. Gen. Dec. B-291771, 2003 CPD ¶ 63. But see *MFM Lamey Group*, Comp. Gen. Dec. B-402377, 2010 CPD ¶ 81, where the GAO held that the Overseas Private Investment Corporation (OPIC) was subject to GAO bid protest jurisdiction because the Foreign Assistance Act neither expressly exempts OPIC from FPASA, as amended by CICA, nor otherwise authorizes procurement procedures apart from CICA.

The GAO, in considering protests concerning the "procurement of property or services," will not take jurisdiction of protests over the procedures used in other types of transactions. Thus, jurisdiction will be denied over protests concerning grants or cooperative agreements as defined in 31 U.S.C. § 6303, *SBMA, Inc.*, Comp. Gen. Dec. B-255780, 93-2 CPD ¶ 292; cooperative research and development agreements under 15 U.S.C. § 3710a, *Spice Corp.*, Comp. Gen. Dec. B-258267, 94-2 CPD ¶ 257; and "other transactions" under 10 U.S.C. § 2371, *Energy Conversion Devices, Inc.*, Comp. Gen. Dec. B-260514, 95-2 CPD ¶ 121. See also *Exploration Partners*, Comp. Gen. Dec. B-298804, 2006 CPD ¶ 201 (NASA's issuance of Space Act agreements pursuant to its "other transactions authority" is not tantamount to the award of contracts for the procurement of goods and services); *Fred Schreiber*, Comp. Gen. Dec. B-272181, 96-2 CPD ¶ 71 (protests against nonselection of vocational rehabilitation counselors not a procurement of goods or services); and *Michael J. O'Kane*, Comp. Gen. Dec. B-257384, 94-2 CPD ¶ 120 (nonselection of attorneys for inclusion on a list from which attorneys will be selected for appointment to represent financially eligible defendants under the Criminal Justice Act not a procurement of goods or services). The GAO will review a protest that an agency is improperly using one of these instruments instead of a procurement contract, *Rocketplane Kistler*, Comp. Gen. Dec. B-310741, 2008 CPD ¶ 22 (protest alleged that agency improperly used Space Act agreement to avoid the requirements of procurement statutes and regulations). See also *Strong Environmental, Inc.*, Comp. Gen. Dec. B-311005, 2008 CPD ¶ 57 (no basis to conclude that the Library of Congress was required to use a procurement contract, or that it was improper for the library to use a cooperative agreement); *Sprint Communications Co., L.P.*, Comp. Gen. Dec. B-256586, 94-1 CPD ¶ 300 (cooperative agreement was properly used — not to avoid the requirements of procurement statutes and regulations).

The GAO lacks jurisdiction to consider a protest challenging the award of a "pure" concession contract; that is, a no-cost contract that merely authorizes a concessionaire to provide goods or services to the public, as opposed to the government, *Crystal Cruises, Inc.*, Comp. Gen. Dec. B-238347, 90-1 CPD ¶ 141. However, the GAO has recognized that some concession contracts are hybrids that require the delivery of goods and/or services to the government. Where a transaction includes the delivery of goods or services of more than *de minimus* value to the government, it is a contract for the procurement of property or services within the meaning of CICA, *Great South Bay Marina, Inc.*, Comp. Gen. Dec. B-296335, 2005 CPD ¶ 135. See *Shields & Dean Concessions, Inc.*, Comp. Gen. Dec. B-292901.2, 2004 CPD ¶ 42, *recon. denied*, 2004 CPD ¶ 71 (concessionaire required to provide maintenance, repair and other services for government facility as well as facility improvement valued at over $800,000); *Starfleet Marine Transp., Inc.*, Comp. Gen. Dec. B-290181, 2002 CPD ¶ 113 (concessionaire for ferryboat services required to provide janitorial services for agency's docks and piers, equip ferries with public address systems for use by park rangers, and provide transportation for rangers). But see *White Sands Concessions, Inc.*, Comp. Gen. Dec. B-295932, 2005 CPD ¶ 62 (only services that concessionaire is required to furnish are those pertaining to the upkeep of the space in which it operates its business).

The GAO will not exercise jurisdiction over subcontractor procurements unless specifically requested to do so by the agency, 4 C.F.R. § 21.5(h). This rule is derived from *U.S. West Communications Servs., Inc. v. United States*, 940 F.2d 622 (Fed. Cir. 1991). In that case the court of appeals, construing language similar to that applicable to the GAO, held that the GSBCA did not have jurisdiction over subcontract procurements that were conducted "for" a federal agency. In light of this decision, the GAO stated in *Compugen, Ltd.*, Comp. Gen. Dec. B-261769, 95-2 CPD ¶ 103, that it will not exercise jurisdiction over subcontract procurements for the government without a written request from the agency that awarded the contract. Previously, the GAO reviewed subcontractor procurements in cases where the contractor was acting "by or for the government," *St. Mary's Hosp. & Medical Ctr. of San Francisco, Cal.*, 70 Comp. Gen. 579 (B-243061), 91-1 CPD ¶ 597; *Ocean Enters., Ltd.*, 65 Comp. Gen. 585 (B-221851), 86-1 CPD ¶ 479. In *STR, LLC*, Comp. Gen. Dec. B-297421, 2006 CPD ¶ 11, the GAO held that it would not consider a protest of an award of a subcontract as "by" the government where the contractor drafted the portion of the solicitation pertaining to evaluation of vendor responses, participated substantially in the evaluation of responses and selection of a product for award, and would be responsible for administration of the subcontract. In its analysis, the GAO articulated the distinction between "for" and "by" the government, as follows:

> We continue to take jurisdiction where the subcontract is "by" the government. *RGB Display Corp.*, B-284699, May 17, 2000, 2000 CPD ¶ 80 at 3. We have considered a subcontract procurement to be "by" the government where the agency handled substantially all the substantive aspects of the procurement and, in effect, "took over" the procurement, leaving to the prime contractor only the procedural aspects of the procurement, i.e., issuing the subcontract solicitation and receiving proposals. *See St. Mary's Hosp. and Med. Ctr. of San Francisco, Calif., supra*, at 5-6; *University of Mich.; Industrial Training Sys. Corp.*, B-225756, B-225756.2, June 30, 1987, 87-1 CPD ¶ 643 at 5-6. In such cases, the prime contractor's role in the procurement was essentially ministerial, such that it was merely acting as a conduit for the government. On the other hand, we have found subcontractor procurements were not "by" the government where the prime contractor handled other meaningful aspects of the procurement, such as preparing the subcontract solicitation and evaluation criteria, evaluating the offers, negotiating with the offerors, and selecting an awardee. *See Kerr-McGee Chem. Corp — Recon.*, B-252979.2, Aug. 25, 1993, 93-2 CPD ¶ 120 at 4-6; *ToxCo, Inc.*, B-235562, Aug. 23, 1989, 89-2 CPD ¶ 170 at 4-5.

See also *Baron Servs., Inc.*, Comp. Gen. Dec. B-402109, 2009 CPD ¶ 264 (DOE's approval of the issuance of the RFP does not demonstrate that DOE took over the procurement); *Alatech Healthcare, LLC*, Comp. Gen. Dec. B-400925, 2009 CPD ¶ 57 (agency review, comment, and discussion of RFP with contractor did not show that procurement was "by" the government, where the contractor was responsible for significant aspects of the procurement); and *Addison Constr., Inc.*, Comp. Gen. Dec. B-293805, 2004 CPD ¶ 105 (contractor drafted the sections of the solicitation pertaining to the evaluation, evaluated the bids, and selected the awardee).

2. Nonstatutory Authority

The GAO's nonstatutory protests are conducted under its advance decision statute, 31 U.S.C. § 3529. This statute authorizes the GAO to issue a decision on a question involving a payment the disbursing officer or head of an agency will make or a voucher presented to a certifying official for certification. Pursuant to 4 C.F.R. § 21.13, the GAO will hear procurement protests from a government agency not included in the definition of "federal agency" and protests involving sales of property from any government agency only if the agency agrees in writing to have the GAO decide its protests. See, for example, *Delta Timber Co.*, Comp. Gen. Dec. B-290710, 2002 CPD ¶ 161 (protest involving timber sales); *OSRAM SYLVANIA Prods., Inc.*, Comp. Gen. Dec. B-287468, 2001 CPD ¶ 158 (protest involving Defense National Stockpile Center); *Total Spectrum Mfg., Inc.*, Comp. Gen. Dec. B-225400, 86-2

CPD ¶ 673 (procurements by the Architect of the Capitol, which is not a federal agency under the definition); and *Victory Salvage Co.*, Comp. Gen. Dec. B-253006, 93-2 CPD ¶ 92 (protest involving surplus property sales).

B. Who May Protest

The GAO is required to decide protests submitted by interested parties, 31 U.S.C. § 3553(a). 31 U.S.C. § 3551(2) states that an interested party is "an actual or prospective bidder or offeror whose direct economic interest would be affected by the award of the contract or by failure to award the contract." This definition is the same as that under the repealed GSBCA protest authority statute, 40 U.S.C. § 759(h)(9). Because the General Services Board applied the same definition and used the same rationale as that of the GAO, GSBCA cases are included in this section for illustrative purposes. The key phrases in the definition are "actual or prospective bidder or offeror" and "direct economic interest." The protester must meet both tests. The protest must relate to a particular solicitation or to the proposed award or award of a particular contract, *A. Moe & Co.*, 64 Comp. Gen. 755 (B-219762), 85-2 CPD ¶ 144 (protest against the denial of its application for a master agreement for repair and alteration of vessels does not pertain to a particular solicitation or to the proposed award or award of a particular contract and, thus, does not constitute a protest within the statute).

1. *Actual or Prospective Bidder or Offeror*

Because *actual* bidders or offerors are determined by those who submit bids or proposals to the government, the major difficulties in this area have arisen in determining whether a party is a *prospective* bidder or offeror. The term has been taken to mean a potential competitor for the type of work being procured, *Tumpane Servs. Corp.*, Comp. Gen. Dec. B-220465, 86-1 CPD ¶ 95 (protester did not bid but would have if specifications were not defective). Parties are not potential competitors and, thus, are not interested parties, if they do not participate or do not have the capacity to participate in the market involved, *Polycon Corp.*, Comp. Gen. Dec. B-218304.2, 85-1 CPD ¶ 714 (firm's mere characterization of itself as a "prospective prime contractor" ineffective when it was a material supplier and had not bid for construction contract awards); *Julie Research Labs., Inc.*, Comp. Gen. Dec. B-219370, 85-2 CPD ¶ 185, *recons. denied*, 85-2 CPD ¶ 294 (offeror was required to do more than provide manufactured equipment, which was the only function the party contended it could perform); *Signal Corp.*, 69 Comp. Gen. 659 (B-240450), 90-2 CPD ¶ 116, *recons. denied*, 69 Comp. Gen. 725 (B-240450.2), 90-2 CPD ¶ 236 (party voluntarily released its proposed team and unequivocally asserted that it did not want to be further considered in the procurement). In *Federal Data Corp. v. United States*, 911 F.2d 699 (Fed. Cir. 1990), the court held that Federal Data was not an interested party because it knowingly removed itself from the bidding. The court also stated that the protester's desire to compete in a later solicitation if the board found the government's conduct unlawful was not sufficient to make Federal Data an interested party. See also *Robotic Sys. Tech.*, Comp. Gen. Dec. B-271760, 96-1 CPD ¶ 229, where the GAO found that the protester was not an interested party where the protester during negotiations withdrew its proposed pricing with a promise to perform the contract at pricing to be provided in its best and final offer (BAFO) but then did not submit a BAFO or otherwise confirm its earlier offer by the time specified for receipt of BAFOs. But see *McRae, Indus., Inc.*, Comp. Gen. Dec. B-287609.2, 2001 CPD ¶ 127, involving a protest that the agency improperly waived the RFP's end-item test requirements which had deterred it from submitting a proposal. The GAO stated that inasmuch as the appropriate relief, were it to sustain the protest, would be for the protester and other offerors to be given an opportunity to compete based on a revised RFP, it considered the protester to have a sufficiently direct economic interest in the outcome to be deemed an interested party, notwithstanding the fact that it did not submit an offer. Similarly, in *Poly-Pacific Techs., Inc.*, Comp. Gen. Dec. B-296029, 2005 CPD ¶ 105, although Poly-Pacific did not submit a proposal because it was not a qualified provider, the GAO held that it was an interested party to protest a modification of the awarded contract that permitted the contractor to provide a product that Poly-Pacific was qualified to provide. Thus, the GAO held that Poly-Pacific was a prospective offeror whose direct economic interest would be affected by the award of a contract or the failure to award a contract.

Prospective suppliers or subcontractors are not considered interested parties, *PPG Indus., Inc.*, Comp. Gen. Dec. B-272126, 96-1 CPD ¶ 285 (protester did not manufacture or sell equipment); *U.S. Polycon Corp.*, Comp. Gen. Dec. B-254655.3, 94-2 CPD ¶ 53 (protester was only a potential supplier to the ultimate awardee); *Allied Tube & Conduit*, Comp. Gen. Dec. B-252371, 93-1 CPD ¶ 345 (prospective supplier of pipe); *Control Techs., Inc.*, Comp. Gen. Dec. B-251335, 93-1 CPD ¶ 16 (mechanical and electrical subcontractor); *Industrial Combustion*, Comp. Gen. Dec. B-222043, 86-1 CPD ¶ 201 (manufacturer that may supply its product to bidders); *Polycon Corp.*, 64 Comp. Gen. 523 (B-218304), 85-1 CPD ¶ 567, *recons. denied*, 85-1 CPD ¶ 714 (protester that was solely a subcontractor/supplier); *ADB-ALNACO, Inc.*, 64 Comp. Gen. 577 (B-218541), 85-1 CPD ¶ 633 (manufacturer that supplied equipment to potential bidders or offerors).

Associations or organizations that do not perform contracts are not interested parties and cannot bring protests in their own name, *American Fed'n of Gov. Employees*, Comp. Gen. Dec. B-219590.3, 86-1 CPD ¶ 436 (government employees' union, protesting contracting-out cost comparison); *Northwest Forest Workers Assocs.*, Comp. Gen. Dec. B-218891.2, 85-1 CPD ¶ 685 (association representing organizations, some of which submitted bids); *Don Strickland's Consultant & Advisory Serv.*, Comp. Gen. Dec. B-217178, 85-1 CPD ¶ 141 (consultant who refused to identify prospective bidders it was representing). Compare *Windet Hotel Corp.*, Comp. Gen. Dec. B-220987, 86-1 CPD ¶ 138, accepting a protest filed by a representative on behalf of an identified interested party. Although an agent may represent an interested party in a protest where it files the protest on behalf of a specified party and has been authorized to act for that party, *E&R, Inc.*, Comp. Gen. Dec. B-255868, 94-1 CPD ¶ 218, the agent is not itself a prospective bidder or offeror and, thus, is not an interested party to protest on its own behalf, *Bulloch Int'l*, Comp. Gen. Dec. B-265982, 96-1 CPD ¶ 5; *Priscidon Enters., Inc.*, Comp. Gen. Dec. B-220278, 85-2 CPD ¶ 549. See *Total Procurement Servs., Inc.*, Comp. Gen. Dec. B-272343.2, 96-2 CPD ¶ 92, holding that a value-added network used to submit quotes by trading partners via FACNET was not an actual or prospective supplier because it did not submit quotes on its own behalf. Persons acting as private attorneys general are not interested parties, *Julie Research Labs., Inc.*, GSBCA 8070-P-R, 86-2 BCA ¶ 18,881.

Federal employees and/or their representatives qualify as "interested parties" for the purpose of protesting public-private competitions conducted pursuant to OMB Circular A-76, 4 C.F.R. § 21.0(a)(2). In 2004, GAO concluded that an in-house competitor in an A-76 competition did not meet the statutory definition of an "interested party," *Dan Duefrene*, Comp. Gen. Dec. B-293590.2, 2004 CPD ¶ 82. Following this decision, Congress enacted legislation that expanded the definition of an interested party. First, under the Ronald Reagan National Defense Authorization Act for Fiscal Year 2005, Pub. L. No. 108-375, the agency tender official became an interested party for GAO bid protest purposes for A-76 studies involving more than 65 FTE employees initiated on or after January 26, 2005. See *James C. Trump*, Comp. Gen. Dec. B-2999370, 2007 CPD ¶ 40. Subsequently, under the National Defense Authorization Act for Fiscal Year 2008, Pub. L. No. 110-181, the definition of an interested party was again amended, eliminating the prior limitations with regard to the number of affected FTEs, and expanding the definition to include a designated employee agent. The Act provides:

> (b)(1) In the case of an agency tender official who is an interested party under section 3551(2)(B) of this title, the official may file a protest in connection with the public-private competition for which the official is an interested party. At the request of a majority of the employees of the Federal agency who are engaged in the performance of the activity or function subject to such public-private competition, the official shall file a protest in connection with such public-private competition unless the official determines that there is no reasonable basis for the protest.

The Act also provided that, with regard to then-ongoing A-76 competitions, the expanded "interested party" definition was only applicable to a protest that "challenges final selection of the source of performance." See *Gary Johnson — Designated Employee Agent*, Comp. Gen. Dec. B-310910.3, 2009 CPD ¶ 22 (since none of the issues raised by the DEA's protest challenge the agency's source selection decision, the DEA was not an interested party).

2. *Direct Economic Interest*

In order to have a direct economic interest, an actual or prospective offeror must be in line for award or be able to compete for award if its position in the protest is upheld. In reversing a holding of the General Services Board that the fourth lowest bidder in a sealed bid procurement had a sufficient economic interest to protest, the Federal Circuit held in *United States v. International Bus. Machs. Corp.*, 892 F.2d 1006 (Fed. Cir. 1989), that "Congress intended the phrase 'interested party' to be a meaningful limitation on the authority of the board to entertain" a protest. The court stated at 1011:

> The board was troubled by the "logic" that would allow the award of a question-able procurement to go unchallenged if the second-lowest bidder did not file a protest. It believed this result would be "contrary to the notions of full and open and fair and equal competition and would significantly undermine the integrity of the procurement and protest processes." *Id*. But, as the Supreme Court has said in an analogous context,
>
>> the requirement that a party seeking review must allege facts showing that he is himself adversely affected does not insulate executive action from ju-dicial review, nor does it prevent any public interests from being protected through the judicial process. It does serve as at least a rough attempt to put the decision as to whether review will be sought in the hands of those who have a direct stake in the outcome.
>
> *Sierra Club*, 405 U.S. at 740. Congress has decided that the coincidence of a dis-appointed bidder's "direct economic" interest with the public interest adequately accommodates both. By striking a different balance more solicitous of the latter, the board has upset this congressional scheme. Congress simply did not intend for the board to entertain the protests of innumerable disappointed bidders who have little or no chance of receiving the contract.

In negotiated procurement it is much more difficult to determine whether the protester has a direct economic interest in the award. The GAO defined the problem in *Meridian Mgmt. Corp.*, Comp. Gen. Dec. B-271557, 96-2 CPD ¶ 64, as follows:

> Determining whether a party is interested involves consideration of a variety of factors, including the nature of the issue raised, the benefit of relief sought by the protester, and the party's status in relation to the procurement. *Black Hills Refuse Serv.*, 67 Comp. Gen. 261 (1988), 88-1 CPD ¶ 151. A protester is not an interested party where it would not be in line for contract award were its protest to be sus-tained. *ECS Composites, Inc.*, B-235849.2, Jan. 3, 1990, 90-1 CPD ¶ 7.

It is easy to establish that a protester is an interested party if the relief being requested is to permit all the offerors to submit revised proposals. For example, in *Meridian*, the protester was held to be an interested party because it was arguing that the agency had improperly waived a mandatory contract requirement in selecting the winner. The GAO reasoned that because the proper relief was notifying all offer-ors of the waiver and permitting them to submit revised proposals, all offerors were interested parties. Similarly, in *Loral Infrared & Imaging Sys., Inc.*, Comp. Gen. Dec. B-247127.3, 92-2 CPD ¶ 52, the protester was found to be an interested party because it claimed that the agency should have established a competitive range and conducted discussions instead of awarding without discussions, and the GAO found that Loral's proposal would have been in the competitive range.

A protester will also be found to be an interested party if it claims that its proposal was improperly evaluated and that proper evaluation would have put it in line for award, *International Data Prods. Corp.*, Comp. Gen. Dec. B-274654, 97-1 CPD ¶ 34. See *Northwest EnviroService, Inc.*, 71 Comp. Gen. 453 (B-247380.2), 92-2 CPD ¶ 38 (contention that had its past performance been properly assessed, protester would have been the best value for the agency); *Rome Research Corp.*, Comp. Gen. Dec. B-245797.4, 92-2 CPD ¶ 194 (contention that proper evaluation of management experience and technical qualifications would have made protester the best value because it was the lowest-cost offeror); *A.G. Personnel Leasing, Inc.*, Comp. Gen. Dec. B-238289, 90-1 CPD ¶ 416 (contention that proper evaluation of its proposal would have placed protester in competitive range); and *SAMCA*, Comp. Gen. Dec. B-237981.3, 90-1 CPD ¶ 413 (contention that protester should have been placed in competitive range because deficiencies in its proposal were easily correctable).

If an offeror is challenging the evaluation of the winning offeror and not claiming that its proposal was improperly evaluated, it must challenge all higher-ranked offerors to be an interested party. See *Joint Mgmt. & Tech. Servs.*, Comp. Gen. Dec. B-294229.2, 2004 CPD ¶ 208, where the GAO stated that the protester's proposal would have been ranked behind Firm A's, even if it had assumed that the protester's proposal should have received higher ratings than it did. Thus, since Firm A would be in line for award ahead of the protester, and the protester did not challenge the evaluation of Firm A's proposal, the protester was not an interested party. In *Dyn-Corp Int'l LLC*, Comp. Gen. Dec. B-294232, 2004 CPD ¶ 187, the GAO concluded that the agency reasonably decided that DynCorps proposal was ineligible for award as written, and since there was another technically acceptable proposal in line for award, even if it were to sustain DynCorps challenges, Offeror A would be in line for award, not DynCorp. Thus, DynCorp lacked the direct economic interest necessary to pursue challenges. In *Abre Enters., Inc.*, Comp. Gen. Dec. B-251569.2, 93-1 CPD ¶ 239, the contracting officer's price analysis/source selection document showed that the protester was the lowest technically rated, second lowest-priced offeror. The protester did not challenge the evaluation of its own proposal nor the evaluation of the second rated proposal, and had the third highest combined total score for technical and price. The GAO found that even if the protester's allegations against the awardee were sustained, the protester was not next in line for award based on the evaluation results and, therefore, not an interested party. See also *OMV Medical, Inc.*, Comp. Gen. Dec. B-281388, 99-1 CPD ¶ 53 (even if protester was correct that awardee should not have been awarded contract, all offerors were found technically acceptable with a low performance risk rating and that the protester submitted the fourth lowest priced proposal); *Quaker Valley Meats, Inc./Supreme Sales, GmbH (J.V.)*, Comp. Gen. Dec. B-279217, 98-1 CPD ¶ 163 (protester's proposal was ranked third technically and the protester did not challenge the intervening offeror); *Property Analysts, Inc.*, Comp. Gen. Dec. B-277266, 97-2 CPD ¶ 77 (offeror that had submitted the highest priced of three technically equal proposals was not an interested party because price was the determinative factor and the protester would not be in line for award if the protest was sustained); *Government Tech. Servs., Inc.*, Comp. Gen. Dec. B-258082.2, 94-2 CPD ¶ 93 (protesters did not challenge the agency's evaluation of the proposals of the higher-ranked offerors vis-a-vis their own rankings); *Panhandle Venture V; Sterling Inv. Properties, Inc.*, Comp. Gen. Dec. B-252982.3, 93-2 CPD ¶ 142 (protesters were fourth and sixth lowest offerors and neither challenged the eligibility of the intervening offerors for award); *ATD-American Co. — Recons.*, Comp. Gen. Dec. B-275926.2, 97-1 CPD ¶ 188 (even if the protest were sustained, the protester would not be next in line for award); and *Ogden Support Servs., Inc. — Recons.*, Comp. Gen. Dec. B-270354.3, 97-1 CPD ¶ 212 (protester did not challenge the evaluation of a higher-ranked, lower-priced intervening proposal).

If an offeror not only challenges the award but also claims that evaluation of other proposals was inconsistent with stated evaluation factors and that its proposal represented the best value to the government, it will be found to be an interested party, *Wyle Labs., Inc.*, 69 Comp. Gen. 648 (B-239113), 90-2 CPD ¶ 107. See *Native American Indus. Distributors Inc.*, Comp. Gen. Dec. B-310737.3, 2008 CPD ¶ 76 (offeror in a best value procurement whose price was low is an interested party even though another offeror had a higher technical score); *The Arora Group, Inc.*, Comp. Gen. Dec. B-288127, 2001 CPD ¶ 154 (recognizing an offeror whose proposal was ranked fifth as an interested party only because its protest challenged the agency's application of the evaluation criteria in general, and, if successful, could have placed the contractor in line for the award).

Parties that are ineligible for award do not have a direct economic interest in the award. Thus, they will normally not be interested parties unless they are contesting their ineligibility, *Para Scientific Co.*, Comp. Gen. Dec. B-310976, 2008 CPD ¶ 54 (firm did not qualify as a small business concern under the appropriate NAICS code identified for the procurement); *ECI Defense Group*, Comp. Gen. Dec. B-400177, 2008 CPD ¶ 141 (protester had not acknowledged material amendment); *Boehringer Ingelheim Pharmaceuticals, Inc.*, Comp. Gen. Dec. B-294944.3, 2005 CPD ¶ 32 (protester's drug had not been shown to be effective in the treatment of either of the two medical conditions identified in the solicitations); *Sterling Servs., Inc.*, Comp. Gen. Dec. B-291625, 2003 CPD ¶ 26 (protester had not acknowledged material amendment); *Yoosung T&S, Ltd.*, Comp. Gen. Dec. B-291407, 2002 CPD ¶ 204 (even if Army were to determine protester was a responsible prospective contractor, another offer, which submitted the only technically acceptable offer would still be in line for award); and *Qwest Communications Int'l, Inc.*, Comp. Gen. Dec. B-287459, 2001 CPD ¶ 117 (protester was subject to restrictions imposed by Communications Act and therefore was unable to offer service). But see *Designer Assocs., Inc.*, Comp. Gen. Dec. B-293226, 2004 CPD ¶ 114, where the GAO found the protester to be an interested party despite fact that the protester was not an 8(a) contractor, and the procurement was conducted under the 8(a) program, because the protester challenged the procurement on the basis that the decision to place the procurement under the 8(a) program was improper.

Ineligibility for a procurement may result from the offeror's suspension or debarment, *Triton Elec. Enters, Inc.*, Comp. Gen. Dec., B-294221, 2004 CPD ¶ 139 (protester was proposed for debarment); *S.A.F.E. Export Corp.*, Comp. Gen. Dec. B-215022, 84-2 CPD ¶ 58 (protester was debarred). Ineligibility may also result from the restrictive nature of the procurement, *Sales Resources Consultants, Inc.*, Comp. Gen. Dec. B-284943, 2000 CPD ¶ 102 (SRC is not an FSS vendor and thus is ineligible to compete for orders under the FSS program); *Air Transport Ass'n*, Comp. Gen. Dec. B-278621, 98-1 CPD ¶ 56 (protester was not a small business concern and RFP was properly set aside for small business); *Precision Kinetics*, Comp. Gen. Dec. B-249975.2, 93-1 CPD ¶ 226 (protester was not an approved source); *S.A. SABER*, Comp. Gen. Dec. B-249874, 92-2 CPD ¶ 403 (protester not a small disadvantaged business (SDB) in procurement properly set aside for SDBs); and *Cable Antenna Sys.*, 65 Comp. Gen. 313 (B-220752), 86-1 CPD ¶ 168, *recons. denied*, 86-1 CPD ¶ 298 (incumbent was not permitted to participate in a procurement intended to establish a second source for future competition).

Winners of multiple-award contracts are not interested parties because their economic interest is too speculative. In *Recon Optical, Inc.*, Comp. Gen. Dec. B-272239, 96-2 CPD ¶ 21, two awardees protested awards to each other under a solicitation for competitive proposals that proposed award of two contracts to develop an innovative product. The protests were dismissed on the ground that these parties lacked a direct stake in the outcome of the protests because neither protester could credibly allege that its contract would be reduced, increased, or otherwise affected by the other contract that had been awarded. The GAO reasoned:

> While both protesters allege that they do have a direct economic interest in the protest because the contract awarded to the other protester essentially obligates funds which the agency would otherwise be able to apply to their own contract should the proposed costs of their respective proposal not be sufficient to cover the development and testing of the prototype camera, this type of speculative economic interest is not sufficiently direct to render the protesters interested parties. See *Travenol Laboratories, Inc.*, B-215739; B-216961, Jan. 29, 1985, 85-1 CPD ¶ 114.

A potential competitor is an interested party in challenging the propriety of a sole source procurement, *Julie Research Labs., Inc.*, GSBCA 8070-P, 85-3 BCA ¶ 18,375. However, once the sole source procurement has been held to be proper, the potential competitor is no longer an interested party, *Julie Research Labs., Inc.*, GSBCA 8070-P, 85-3 BCA ¶ 18,375. See also *International Training, Inc.*, Comp. Gen. Dec. B-272699, 96-2 CPD ¶ 132, where the GAO ruled that a protester was not an interested party to protest the failure of a contracting agency to follow sole source acquisition procedures because the solicitation contained restrictive requirements that made the protester ineligible for award, and the protester did not challenge these restrictive provisions.

C. Time for Protest

Prior to the enactment of the statutory protest authority, the GAO had adopted very restrictive time limitations on the filing of protests in order to ensure that the impact of protests on the procurement process was minimized. Although these time limitations remain in effect under the statutory protest authority, the statutes also contain additional protections when protests are timely filed — providing for limitations on contract award when a protest is filed before award and a stay of performance if the protest is filed quickly after award.

Neither a protester's unfamiliarity with GAO regulations. *Optical Energy Techs., Inc.*, Comp. Gen. Dec. B-401520, 2009 CPD ¶ 153, nor its decision to wait for a response to a congressional inquiry, provides a basis for suspending GAO timeliness regulations, *Professional Office Ctr.*, Comp. Gen. Dec. B-229704, 87-2 CPD ¶ 607. GAO Bid Protest Regulations are published in the Federal Register and the Code of Federal Regulations; protesters are charged with constructive notice of their contents.

1. Protests of Solicitation Improprieties

Protests of improprieties in solicitations are required to be filed before the closing date for receipt of proposals, 4 C.F.R. § 21.2(a)(1). The basis for this strict rule was explained in *Caddell Constr. Co.*, Comp. Gen. Dec. B-401281, 2009 CPD ¶ 130, as follows:

> Underlying our timeliness rules regarding solicitation improprieties is the principle that challenges which go to the heart of the underlying ground rules by which a competition is conducted, should be resolved as early as practicable during the solicitation process, but certainly in advance of an award decision if possible, not afterwards.

There are numerous protests that are dismissed because they concern solicitation improprieties. See, for example, *Ball Aerospace & Techs. Corp.*, Comp. Gen. Dec. B-402148, 2010 CPD ¶ 37 (allegation that evaluation scheme would not determine likely costs to the government is a challenge to the solicitation's terms); *CES Indus., Inc.*, Comp. Gen. Dec. B-401427, 2010 CPD ¶ 43 (allegation that agency improperly conducted the procurement on an unrestricted basis); *Sea Box, Inc.*, Comp. Gen. Dec. B-401523, 2009 CPD ¶ 190 (conflict between the closing date listed on the GSA e-Buy system and the closing date listed on the RFQ constituted a patent ambiguity that was apparent prior to the time set for receipt of quotations); *General Dynamics-Ordnance & Tactical Sys.*, Comp. Gen.

Dec. B-401658, 2009 CPD ¶ 217 (post-award challenge to evaluation scheme that could produce a misleading result); *Armorworks Enters., LLC*, Comp. Gen. Dec. B-400394, 2008 CPD ¶ 176 (allegation that RFP procedures and testing methods were inherently unreliable and deviated from industry practice); *Hart Security Ltd.*, Comp. Gen. Dec. B-400796.2, 2008 CPD ¶ 229 (post-closing challenge to agency's amendment requiring successful offeror to hold a facility security clearance); *Gentex Corp.*, Comp. Gen. Dec. B-400328, 2008 CPD ¶ 186 (challenge to inclusion of Federal Prison Industries in competition when it was apparent, prior to closing time for receipt of proposals, that it was a potential competitor); *Apptis, Inc.*, Comp. Gen. Dec. B-299457, 2008 CPD ¶ 49 (challenge that third-party contractor that was to assist in the evaluation of proposals had an OCI was known or should have been known before the closing date for receipt of proposals); *CAMSS Shelters*, Comp. Gen. Dec. B-309784, 2007 CPD ¶ 199 (allegation that brand name product itself fails to meet certain salient characteristics); *K9 Operations, Inc.*, Comp. Gen. Dec. B-299923, 2007 CPD ¶ 146 (challenge to evaluation provisions and that offeror's status as a service-disabled veteran would not be a factor in the evaluation process); *TransAtlantic Lines LLC*, Comp. Gen. Dec. B-296245, 2005 CPD ¶ 147 (challenge that RFP failed to include mandatory provision regarding limitations on subcontracting); *Pitney Bowes Inc.*, Comp. Gen. Dec. B-294868, 2005 CPD ¶ 10 (challenge of patent ambiguity); *South-West Critical Care Assocs.*, Comp. Gen. Dec. B-279773, 98-2 CPD ¶ 22 (alleged defect in RFP); *Envirodyne Sys. Inc.*, Comp. Gen. Dec. B-279551.2, 98-1 CPD ¶ 174 (allegation of unduly restrictive specifications); *Thermolten Tech., Inc.*, Comp. Gen. Dec. B-278408.2, 98-1 CPD ¶ 35 (challenge of use of term "mature technology"); *Neal R. Gross & Co.*, Comp. Gen. Dec. B-275066, 97-1 CPD ¶ 30 (postaward protest that solicitation failed to provide for adequate evaluation of price); *Agriculture Tech. Partners*, Comp. Gen. Dec. B-272978, 96-2 CPD ¶ 226 (allegation that RFP failed to define "complexity," which was used to evaluate each offeror's corporate experience); and *Executive Court Reporters, Inc.*, Comp. Gen. Dec. B-272981, 96-2 CPD ¶ 227 (failure of RFP to include estimate quantities of the various types of transcripts).

Alleged solicitation improprieties that did not exist in the initial solicitation but which are subsequently incorporated into the solicitation by amendment, must be filed prior to the next closing time for receipt of proposals, 4 C.F.R. § 21.2(a)(1). GAO has recognized an exception, however, where a protester does not have a reasonable opportunity to file its protest before the due date for proposals. The cases where GAO has concluded that an offeror did not have a reasonable opportunity to protest solicitation terms, and thus applied the exception are those where the protester faced an extremely limited time within which to challenge the solicitation provisions at issue. See, for example, *Dube Travel Agency & Tours, Inc.*, Comp. Gen. Dec. B-270438, 96-1 CPD ¶ 141 (amendment not received until 1 day before proposals due); *Skyline Indus., Inc.*, Comp. Gen. Dec. B-257340, 94-2 CPD ¶ 111 (time for receipt of proposals was "practically simultaneous with solicitation itself"); *Ling Dynamic Sys., Inc.*, Comp. Gen. Dec. B-252091, 93-1 CPD ¶ 407 (protester learned basis for challenging solicitation only 2 hours before bid opening); *G. Davidson Co.*, Comp. Gen. Dec. B-249331, 92-2 CPD ¶ 21 (2 hours and 45 minutes not a reasonable period of time within which to file a protest); *Bardes Servs., Inc.*, Comp. Gen. Dec. B-242581, 91-1 CPD ¶ 419 (protester was informed of basis of protest only one day before proposals due); *ImageMatrix, Inc.*, Comp. Gen. Dec. B-243170, 91-1 CPD ¶ 270 (protester received amendment only one day before proposals were due); *Culligan, Inc.*, 58 Comp. Gen. 307 (B-192581) (1979) (protester received solicitation amendment less than 3 hours before bid opening); and *Ampex Corp.*, Comp. Gen. Dec. B-190529, 78-1 CPD ¶ 212 ("the time for receipt of proposals was practically simultaneous with the solicitation, the entire process apparently taking only 10 minutes"). However, where there is a reasonable opportunity to file a protest, the GAO will not waive the timeliness rule. See *WareOnEarth Communications, Inc.*, Comp. Gen. Dec. B-298408, 2006 CPD ¶ 107 (protester received the amendments 4 days — or, as the protester describes them, 2 working days — before revised proposals were due and was able to prepare and timely submit the revised pricing information required by the agency); *Concepts to Operations, Inc.*, Comp. Gen. Dec. B-248606, 92-2 CPD ¶ 164 (3 calendar days, one business day, was sufficient time to file protest); *Mobile/Modular Express*, Comp. Gen. Dec. B-246183, 91-2 CPD ¶ 459 (2 days reasonable period of time to file protest); *Pacific Instruments, Inc.*, Comp. Gen. Dec. B-228274, 87-2 CPD ¶ 380 ("only 2 working days" as argued by protester was reasonable opportunity to file protest); *R&B Equip. Co.*, Comp. Gen. Dec. B-219560.2, 85-2 CPD ¶ 272 (afforded "only 2 working days"); and *Reliance Steel Prods. Co.*, Comp. Gen. Dec. B-206754, 83-1 CPD ¶ 77 (2 days reasonable).

Protests of the ground rules of how a procurement will be conducted will be treated as challenges to the terms of a solicitation. See, for example, *Domain Name Alliance Registry*, Comp. Gen. Dec. B-310803.2, 2008 CPD ¶ 168 (post-closing argument that agency should have held discussions with protester is untimely where agency unequivocally indicated prior to closing that agency did not contemplate holding discussions as part of corrective action). Similarly, in *Caddell Constr. Co.*, Comp. Gen. Dec. B-401281, 2009 CPD ¶ 130, the agency structured the procurement to allow for the prequalification of firms' eligibility as United States persons and publicly identified prequalified firms. This specifically provided offerors with an opportunity to challenge the eligibility of other potential offerors before the submission of proposals and would have allowed for the early resolution of any eligibility questions. GAO stated:

> Although, as a general rule, a protester is not required to protest that another firm should be excluded from the competition until after the firm has been selected for award, see, e.g., *REEP, Inc.*, B-290688, Sept. 20, 2002, 2002 CPD ¶ 158 at 1-2 (protest that awardee had impermissible organizational conflict of interest), we have applied a different rule where a protester is aware of the facts giving rise to its allegation that another firm should be ineligible to compete and where the protester has been expressly advised that the agency has determined that the firm in question is eligible. See *Abt Assocs., Inc.*, B-294130, Aug. 11, 2004, 2004 CPD ¶ 174 at 2; *International Sci. & Tech. Inst., Inc.*, B-259648, Jan. 12, 1995, 95-1

CPD ¶ 16 at 3-4. In such cases, we have found that the protester cannot wait until an award has been made to file its protest, but instead must protest before the closing time for receipt of proposals.

Generally where a solicitation for an IDIQ contract gives clear notice of an agency's intention to procure particular requirements under an IDIQ contract, any protest to those terms of the solicitation must be filed before the closing date for receipt of task order proposals. However, where the work statement is broad or vague and it is unclear what work will be placed under the task order a different rule has emerged. In *LBM, Inc.*, Comp. Gen. Dec. B-290682, 2002 CPD ¶ 157, the Army argued that LBM's protest of the transfer of the Fort Polk motor pool services to the LOGJAMSS contract should be dismissed as untimely. The Army believed that LBM should have been on notice from the LOGJAMSS solicitation that the Fort Polk motor pool services "could" be ordered under the LOGJAMSS contracts. The GAO disagreed, stating:

> We have recognized that the increasing use of ID/IQ contracts with very broad and often vague statements of work may place an unreasonable burden upon potential offerors, who may be required to guess as to whether particular work, for which they are interested in competing, will be acquired under a particular ID/IQ contract. *See Valenzuela Eng'g, Inc.*, B-277979, Dec. 9, 1997, 98-1 CPD ¶ 51 (Letter to the Acting Sec'y of the Army, Jan. 26, 1998, at 2). This burden may be particularly problematic for small businesses. *Id.* In our view, it is unreasonable to require a small business that believes that one specific acquisition should continue to be set aside for small businesses to identify the possibility, at the time proposals for ID/IQ contracts to perform a broad and undefined scope of work are solicited, that the specific, and relatively small, acquisition it is interested in may ultimately be transferred to the ID/IQ contracts.

> The breadth and vagueness of the LOGJAMSS scope of work illustrate this, since it encompassed a "wide range of logistical functions and supporting tasks" and was undefinitized at the time the LOGJAMSS contracts were solicited. Accordingly, we conclude that LBM could not reasonably be aware, and required to protest, at the time the LOGJAMSS contracts were being competed (and apparently years before the Army considered using those contracts for the Fort Polk motor pool services), that the broad and nonspecific scope of work in the LOGJAMSS solicitation could be improperly used as a vehicle for the agency to perform the motor pool services at Fort Polk without first taking the steps legally required regarding a possible further acquisition of that work under a small business set-aside.

Similarly in *N&N Travel & Tours, Inc.*, Comp. Gen. Dec. B-285164.2, 2000 CPD ¶ 146, the GAO found timely a challenge that travel management services must be set aside for small businesses, although not filed before the time set for receipt of proposals. Here, the agency advised and issued a draft solicitation that made clear that it would not use GSA's IDIQ contract for the Travis AFB travel service needs but rather would use DOD's contract and would set the procurement aside for small businesses. See also *Ocuto Blacktop & Paving Co.*, Comp. Gen. Dec.

B-284165, 2000 CPD ¶ 32 (protest filed at time of task order for landfill capping is timely where solicitations for IDIQ contracts "do not provide clear notice that the [agency] will use these contracts to procure environmental remediation work at [particular] sites"). However, where the solicitation for the IDIQ contract is not broad and vague, but rather gives clear notice of the agency's intention to procure particular requirements under an IDIQ contract, any protest to those terms of the solicitation must be filed before the solicitation closing date, *Datamaxx Group, Inc.*, Comp. Gen. Dec. B-400582, 2008 CPD ¶ 231 (protest untimely where EAGLE solicitation provided clear notice that software development services would be acquired); and *MadahCom, Inc.*, Comp. Gen. Dec. B-297261.2, 2005 CPD ¶ 209 (protest that a solicitation improperly restricts competition to multiple-award task order contract holders, and that the task orders will exceed the scope of the underlying contracts timely when filed before the closing date for receipt of proposals).

2. Protests Not Apparent in Solicitation

Protests on any other ground are required to be filed at the GAO within 10 calendar days after the basis of the protest is known or should have been known, whichever is earlier, 4 C.F.R. § 21.2(a)(2). See, for example, *Rhonda Podojil — Agency Tender Official*, Comp. Gen. Dec. B-311310, 2008 CPD ¶ 94 (protest by agency tender official in competition conducted pursuant to OMB Circular A-76 dismissed as untimely where the ATO filed the protest more than 10 days after it knew or should have known basis of protest); *Armorworks Enters., LLC*, Comp. Gen. Dec. B-400394, 2008 CPD ¶ 176 (challenge to solicitation amendment, issued after initial proposals had been submitted, and which did not provide offerors with an opportunity to submit revised proposals, should have been filed within 10 days of issuance of the amendment); *General Physics Fed. Sys. Inc.*, Comp. Gen. Dec. B-274795, 97-1 CPD ¶ 8 (protester's argument against the acceptance of an offer that included a particular subcontractor could and should have been made shortly after award); *Learjet, Inc.*, Comp. Gen. Dec. B-274385, 96-2 CPD ¶ 215 (protest over the interpretation of solicitation requirements untimely because it was not raised within 10 days after the protester was informed in writing during discussions of the agency's interpretation); and *Harris Corp.*, Comp. Gen. Dec. B-274566, 96-2 CPD ¶ 205 (postaward complaint untimely because protester was challenging a defect in the procurement process that should have been raised well before discussions were concluded and an award was made).

There is an exception for protests challenging a procurement conducted on the basis of competitive proposals where a debriefing is requested and, when requested, is required. In this case, with respect to any protest basis that is known or should have been known either before or as a result of the debriefing, the initial protest cannot be filed before the debriefing date offered to the protester but must be filed not later than 10 calendar days after the date on which the debriefing is held, 4 C.F.R. § 21.2(a)(2). In other words, a post-debriefing protest will be considered timely if filed as late as

10 days after the debriefing, even as to issues that should have been known before the debriefing, if that debriefing is "required." See *Dominion Aviation, Inc. — Recons.*, Comp. Gen. Dec. B-275419.4, 98-1 CPD ¶ 62 (challenge to protester's evaluation of its performance history as marginal untimely where not filed within 10 days of debriefing); *Black & Veatch Special Projects Corp.*, Comp. Gen. Dec. B-279492.2, 98-1 CPD ¶ 173 (protester had 10 days from date of debriefing to file protest concerning issues it first learned at debriefing); *WP Photographic Servs.*, Comp. Gen. Dec. B-278897.4, 98-1 CPD ¶ 151 (protester had 10 days to raise particular objections concerning the evaluation of its proposal after debriefing); *Global Eng'g & Constr. J.V.*, Comp. Gen. Dec. B-275999.4, 97-2 CPD ¶ 125 (protest untimely where issues were raised one month after they were addressed in written debriefing).

"Requested and required" debriefings also preclude protests submitted prior to the debriefing, *Real Estate Ctr.*, Comp. Gen. Dec. B-274081, 96-2 CPD ¶ 74. This rule is designed to encourage early and meaningful debriefings but to preclude strategic or defensive protests. See also *Minotaur Eng'g*, Comp. Gen. Dec. B-276843, 97-1 CPD ¶ 194.

The rule giving protesters 10 days to file a protest after a "requested and required" debriefing is inapplicable where a protester's proposal is eliminated from a competition prior to award, and the protester chooses to delay receipt of a debriefing regarding elimination until after award. See 10 U.S.C. § 2305(b)(6)(A); 41 U.S.C. § 253b(f); FAR 15.505(a)(2); *United Int'l Investigative Servs., Inc.*, Comp. Gen. Dec. B-286327, 2000 CPD ¶ 173. In this situation, a protester may not passively await information providing a basis for protest; rather, a protester has an affirmative obligation to diligently pursue such information, *Automated Med. Prods. Corp.*, Comp. Gen. Dec. B-275835, 97-1 CPD ¶ 52. See *University of Mass. Donahue Inst.*, Comp. Gen. Dec. B-400870.3, 2009 CPD ¶ 173, where the protester delayed debriefing regarding the elimination of its proposal until after award. The GAO held that challenging the agency's elimination of the proposal, filed more than three months after the protester received notice of the proposal's elimination, was untimely where the protester received all of the information on which the protest was based at the time the proposal was eliminated from the competition.

Protests originally filed with an agency must be filed at the GAO within 10 days of actual or constructive knowledge of initial adverse agency action, 4 C.F.R. § 21.2(a)(3); *International Garment Processors*, Comp. Gen. Dec. B-299743, 2007 CPD ¶ 130; *Lifecare Mgmt. Partners*, Comp. Gen. Dec. B-297078, 2006 CPD ¶ 8; *IBP, Inc.*, Comp. Gen. Dec. B-275259, 96-2 CPD ¶ 169; *Orbit Advanced Techs., Inc.*, Comp. Gen. Dec. B-275046, 96-2 CPD ¶ 228. In *Timothy J. Penny*, Comp. Gen. Dec. B-221710, Feb. 20, 1986, *Unpub.*, the GAO held that these time limitations could not be avoided by having the protest filed through a member of Congress. A requested debriefing does not toll the requirement that a protest be filed within 10 days of adverse action on an agency-level protest, *RTI Techs., LLC*, Comp. Gen. Dec. B-401075, 2009 CPD ¶ 86; *M2 Global Tech., Ltd.*, Comp. Gen. Dec. B-400946, 2009 CPD ¶ 13.

For the purposes of timeliness rules, the mechanical receipt of email during a firm's regular business hours constitutes notice of an agency's award. In *Golight, Inc.*, Comp. Gen. Dec. B-401866, 2009 CPD ¶ 184, the protester did not contend that the agency's email was received after the firm's business hours on Friday, but based the timeliness of its protest filing upon the fact that the protester's employee (to whom the email was directed) had left for the day and did not open the email until the following Monday. Because the email was available to be opened during regular business hours on Friday, GAO considered the email to have been received by the protester on that date. Accordingly, the protester knew or should have known the basis of its protest allegations on that Friday when it received the agency's email notification of award, and, to be timely filed, the protest was required to be filed within 10 calendar days of that date. See also *American Office Servs., Inc.*, Comp. Gen. Dec. B-290511, 2002 CPD ¶ 122 (protester on notice of protest basis as of date of receipt of agency email containing proposal deficiency information). Compare *Supreme Edgelight Devices, Inc.*, Comp. Gen. Dec. B-295574, 2005 CPD ¶ 58 (receipt of an agency-level protest decision on a non-business day did not constitute actual or constructive knowledge of initial adverse agency action). Where an e-mail notification of exclusion from the competitive range enters an offeror's computer system after close of business on a weekday or on a weekend or holiday and is not opened before the following business day, receipt of the notice is considered to have occurred on that business day, *International Res. Group*, Comp. Gen. Dec. B-286663, 2001 CPD ¶ 35. The GAO stated that to construe receipt of an e-mail notification as occurring when the notification enters the offeror's computer system outside of normal business hours would lead to a reduction of the 3-day period for requesting a debriefing granted by the FAR to a single day when the notification is transmitted after close of business on Friday or on Saturday of a weekend followed by a Monday holiday.

Constructive notice of award, starting the running of the 10 day period, will be found where posting of the notice is made to FedBizOpps, *CBMC, Inc.*, Comp. Gen. Dec. B-295586, 2005 CPD ¶ 2. But see *Worldwide Language Resources, Inc.*, Comp. Gen. Dec. B-296984, 2005 CPD ¶ 206 (announcement of award on DOD's official website, www.DefenseLink.mil, did not place protesters on constructive notice of award and thus require protesters to file within 10 days of the announcement because DefenseLink has not been designated by statute or regulation as the public medium for announcement of procurement actions).

The GAO regulations permit consideration of late protests for "good cause" or if the protest raises "issues significant to the procurement system," 4 C.F.R. § 21.2(c). The GAO, in order to maintain the value of the time limitations, has construed these exceptions strictly. The good cause exception is available only for a compelling reason beyond the protester's control, *Oracle Corp.*, Comp. Gen. Dec. B-260963, 95-1 CPD ¶ 231 (argument that dismissal of protest would be "particularly unfair" did not meet good cause exception); *John Cuneo, Inc.*, Comp. Gen. Dec. B-227983.2, 87-2 CPD ¶ 147 (protester's lack of awareness of the bid protest timeliness requirements not a good cause); *Arian Fashions, Inc.*, Comp. Gen. Dec. B-247314.3, 92-1 CPD ¶ 223 (fact that basis of protest arose during a holiday was not a good cause).

The "significant interest" exception is also applied strictly. See, for example, *Merck & Co.*, Comp. Gen. Dec. B-248655, 92-1 CPD ¶ 454, where the GAO, refusing to decide on a protest issue raised late, stating that "we strictly construe and seldom use the exception, limiting it to protests that raise issues of widespread interest to the procurement community." See also *Goel Servs., Inc.*, Comp. Gen. Dec. B-310822.2, 2008 CPD ¶ 99 (argument that HUBZone price evaluation preference should have been included in solicitation not significant issue of widespread interest); *Ervin & Assocs., Inc.*, Comp. Gen. Dec. B-279083, 98-1 CPD ¶ 126 (alleged overbreadth of the statement of work for an indefinite-quantity task order contract not of widespread interest to procurement community); *Source Diversified, Inc.*, Comp. Gen. Dec. B-259034, 95-1 CPD ¶ 119 (issue of whether a delegation of procurement authority should have been obtained for a particular procurement not of widespread interest to the procurement community); *International Science & Tech. Inst., Inc.*, Comp. Gen. Dec. B-259648, 95-1 CPD ¶ 16 (organizational conflict of interest of awardee was not a significant issue of widespread interest); *Pardee Constr. Co.*, Comp. Gen. Dec. B-256414, 94-1 CPD ¶ 372 (propriety of solicitation provisions that were incorporated by amendment neither unique nor of widespread interest); *American Material Handling, Inc.*, Comp. Gen. Dec. B-255467.2, 94-1 CPD ¶ 158 (protest involving the solicitation specifications not significant issue of widespread interest); *Julie Research Labs., Inc.*, Comp. Gen. Dec. B-219364, 85-2 CPD ¶ 222 (no significant issue because there were numerous decisions on the issue).

For cases where the GAO has found a significant issue and, thus, considered a late protest, see *Tiger Truck, LLC*, Comp. Gen. Dec. B-400685, 2009 CPD ¶ 19 (the interplay between the obligation to conduct meaningful discussions and the rules governing TAA procurements is not one that GAO has previously decided and is one that can be expected to arise in future TAA procurements); *Celadon Labs., Inc.*, Comp. Gen. Dec. B-298533, 2006 CPD ¶ 158 (the application of conflict of interest regulations to peer review evaluators in Small Business Innovation Research (SBIR) procurements was not one that GAO had previously decided and was one that could be expected to arise again in future SBIR procurements); *Gene Quigley, Jr.*, 70 Comp. Gen. 273 (B-241565), 91-1 CPD ¶ 182 (protests involving newly promulgated regulations on individual sureties); *Discount Mach. & Equip., Inc.*, 70 Comp. Gen. 108 (B-240525), 90-2 CPD ¶ 420 (failure of an agency to refer an adverse agency nonresponsibility determination on a small business to Small Business Administration); *Golden North Van Lines, Inc.*, 69 Comp. Gen. 610 (B-238874), 90-2 CPD ¶ 44 (failure to specify whether option prices would be evaluated); *Baszile Metal Serv.*, Comp. Gen. Dec. B-237925, 90-1 CPD ¶ 378 (DOD's regulatory requirements that SDB regular dealers provide a product manufactured by a small business concern when there is no SDB manufacturer in order to be eligible for an SDB evaluation preference in unrestricted procurements); *Cincinnati Milacron Mktg. Co.*, Comp. Gen. Dec. B-237619, 90-1 CPD ¶ 241 (interpretation of a congressional restriction on the use of appropriated funds); and *F.J. O'Hara & Sons, Inc.*, 69 Comp. Gen. 274 (B-237410), 90-1 CPD ¶ 197 (statutory restriction on the purchase of food). Earlier protest decisions were more liberal in using this exception to the timeliness rules. See *Dep't of the Navy; Fairchild Weston Sys., Inc.*, Comp. Gen. Dec. B-230013.2, 88-2 CPD ¶ 100 (unreasonable exclusion of a protester from the competitive range); *Sinclair Radio Labs, Inc.*, 67 Comp. Gen. 66 (B-227474.2), 87-2 CPD ¶ 470 (exclusion of a small business from competition); *Adrian Supply Co.*, 66 Comp. Gen. 367 (B-225440.2), 87-1 CPD ¶ 357 (actions by the contracting agency that are inconsistent with statute and regulation); and *Topley Realty Co.*, 65 Comp. Gen. 510 (B-221459), 86-1 CPD ¶ 398 (questionable application of definitive responsibility criteria).

3. Statutory Stay

Although the statutes do not limit the filing times for jurisdictional purposes, they do contain provisions that delay award or suspend contract performance pending the decision on a protest. These provisions were enacted to ensure that effective relief could be obtained by successful protesters. If a protest is filed before award, 31 U.S.C. § 3553(c) provides that while a protest is pending, "a contract may not be awarded in any procurement after the federal agency has received notice of the protest" from the GAO. If a protest is filed after award but within specified time limitations, 31 U.S.C. § 3553(d) provides that the federal agency shall, on receipt of notice of the protest from the GAO, "immediately direct the contractor to cease performance under the contract." Both of these stay provisions have exceptions based on urgency or compelling circumstances, 31 U.S.C. § 3553(c)(2) and (d)(3)(C). In addition, performance of a contract awarded prior to receipt of a protest may be continued during a protest based on a finding that it is "in the best interests of the United States," 31 U.S.C. § 3553(d)(3)(C). These findings must be made by "the head of the procuring activity," and the authority to make such findings may not be delegated, 31 U.S.C. § 3553(e).

The period for notice of the protest begins "on the date of contract award and ends on the later of — (A) the date that is 10 [calendar] days after the date of the contract award; or (B) the date that is 5 [calendar] days after the debriefing date offered to an unsuccessful offeror for any debriefing that is requested and, when requested, is required." Thus, an agency must suspend contract performance if it receives notice of a protest by the tenth calendar day following contract award or the fifth calendar day following the offered date of a timely requested debriefing, whichever is later, 31 U.S.C. § 3553.

Under 31 U.S.C. § 3553, an agency is required to suspend performance of a contract only if the agency receives notice *from the Comptroller General* within 10 days of contract award. See *BDM Mgmt. Servs. Co.*, Comp. Gen. Dec. B-228287, 88-1 CPD ¶ 93, holding that there was no duty to suspend contract performance where the protest was filed on the eighth day after award (a Friday) and the agency was notified within one working day, on the eleventh day after award (a Monday). There is no recourse if GAO fails to notify the agency of the protest, *Florida Professional Review Org.*, Comp. Gen. Dec. B-253908.2, 94-1 CPD ¶ 17. Notice by the protester to the agency is insufficient to trigger suspension of contract performance, *Technology for Communications Int'l v. Garrett*, 783 F. Supp. 1446 (D.D.C. 1992) (although protester notified Navy of protest, GAO did not notify the agency until the fourteenth day after contract award).

An agency can override a stay on a finding of urgent and compelling circumstances or, in the case of postaward protests, on a finding of urgent and compelling circumstances *or* if the override is in the government's best interests, 31 U.S.C. § 3553(c)(2) and (d)(3)(C). If an agency decides to award a contract or to proceed with performance in spite of the statutory stay, the GAO has no authority to challenge this action. However, a protester can challenge the agency's decision to override the stay requirement by filing a suit in the Court of Federal Claims under the Administrative Procedure Act (APA), 5 U.S.C. § 706(2)(a). See *RAMCOR Servs. Group, Inc. v. United States*, 185 F.3d 1286 (Fed. Cir. 1999), holdng that the Court of Federal Claims had jurisdiction to rule on the validity of an agency's decision to override the automatic stay when a timely protest was filed in the GAO. This extends both to 31 U.S.C. § 3553(d)(3)(C) determinations premised upon asserted "best interests of the United States" as well as those based upon asserted "urgent and compelling circumstances that significantly affect interests of the United States, *PGBA, LLC v. United States*, 57 Fed. Cl. 655 (2003). Review of override decisions is guided by the standards set forth in the APA — that the decision was arbitrary, capricious, an abuse of discretion, or otherwise not in accordance with law.

Although early Court of Federal Claims decisions suggested a more deferential standard of review should apply to judicial review of overrides, see, e.g., *Spherix, Inc. v. United States*, 62 Fed. Cl. 497 (2004), the Court of Federal Claims has taken a far less deferential stance to agency override determinations since its decision in *Reilly's Wholesale Produce, Inc. v. United States*, 73 Fed. Cl. 705 (2006). In *Reilly's*, the court narrowed the scope of agency decision, and identified the relevant factors an agency must consider and address when considering both "best interest" and "urgent and compelling circumstances" overrides. The factors include:

> (i) whether significant adverse consequences will necessarily occur if the stay is not overridden; (ii) conversely, whether reasonable alternatives to the override exist that would adequately address the circumstances presented; (iii) how the potential cost of proceeding with the override, including the costs associated with the potential that the GAO might sustain the protest, compare to the benefits associated with the approach being considered for addressing the agency's needs; and (iv) the impact of the override on competition and the integrity of the procurement system, as reflected in the Competition in Contracting Act.

In addition to these factors, the Court of Federal Claims has identified issues that the agency should not consider in exercising its override rights. For instance, the government's decision to override a stay may not be based simply on its view that the new contract is better than the old one or that the agency simply prefers to override the stay rather than await GAO's decision, *Advanced Sys. Dev., Inc. v. United States*, 72 Fed. Cl. 25 (2006) ("The allegation that the new contract is better than the old one in terms of cost or performance is not enough to justify a best interests determination."); *Superior Helicopter LLC v. United States*, 78 Fed. Cl. 181 (2007) (Forest Service's conclusion that exclusive-use contracts were more "advantageous" than the CWN contracts is an invalid justification for overriding an automatic stay).

Justifications based on agency claims of cost savings have proven not likely to withstand judicial review, *Nortel Gov't Solutions, Inc. v. United States*, 84 Fed. Cl. 243 (2008) (rejecting government cost saving arguments on grounds that "similar amounts have been found insufficient to support a best interests override"); *E-Management Consultants, Inc. v. United States*, 84 Fed. Cl. 1 (2008) (avoiding termination costs of any replacement contract and maintaining uninterrupted performance beyond the calendar year "not the sorts of benefits envisioned in the cost-benefit calculation"); *Automation Techs., Inc. v. United States*, 72 Fed. Cl. 723 (2006) (estimated $103,196.27 per month cost saving during an expected delay of almost three months in the context of an anticipated five-year $49,500,000 contract with options insufficient to support override). If the agency will lose money without a stay, it may be able to justify the override, *Chapman Law Firm Co. v. United States*, 67 Fed. Cl. 188 (2005) (without the override the agency estimated it would lose $3 million per month and that government properties would be unmanaged and subject to vandalism).

When several offerors are available to perform the work or mechanisms like bridge contracts are available, the court is likely to sustain a challenge to the override, *Nortel Gov't Solutions, Inc. v. United States*, 84 Fed. Cl. 243 (2008) (agency override was arbitrary and capricious, in part, because the bridge contract provided a reasonable alternative); *Keeton Corrections, Inc. v. United States*, 59 Fed. Cl. 753 (2004) (agency override lacked a rational basis where the agency could have continued awarding short term sole source contracts to incumbent). But see *Alion Science & Tech. Corp. v. United States*, 69 Fed. Cl. (2005) (upholding override noting the time-critical nature of the contract and the lack of multiple vendors).

In considering the effect of the override on the integrity of the procurement system, the court will not permit an agency to point to a protesting party's likelihood of ultimately winning the contract. In *E-Management Consultants, Inc. v. United States*, 84 Fed. Cl. 1 (2008), the court held that the agency failed to consider the impact of its override on the procurement system and that the override memorandum failed to meet even the deferential standards of APA review, stating at 10:

> [T]he OM [override memorandum] failed to offer any reasoning that shows that
> it actually considered the integrity of the procurement system Congress created

in CICA. *See id.* at 2-3. The text of the paragraphs in which the consideration is mentioned reads in full as follows:

> I considered the impact on competition and on the integrity of the procurement process, should the agency decline to suspend performance.
>
> In my view, the competition process is best served by allowing the awardee to proceed. As noted above, I conclude from discussions with the relevant agency officials that the agency has a reasonable chance of prevailing. Moreover, the protester is not next in line for award. Taken together, these two points lead me to conclude that allowing the awardee to proceed is the fairest approach. As an extra safeguard, however, the awardee's performance will be limited to essential efforts during the pendency of the protest.

Id.

The claimed consideration of the impact on the procurement system do not recognize or vindicate the purpose of the automatic stay. NHTSA first states that it "has a reasonable chance of prevailing." *Id.* at 3. This observation does not relate to the integrity of the procurement system. It relates to the merits of the protest, not to the automatic stay in CICA. NHTSA also states that the protestor is not "next in line." *Id.* Again, this is not an appropriate evaluation of the impact of the override on the procurement system. The purpose of the procurement system as envisioned in CICA is a fair process in which disappointed bidders can seek review at GAO. GAO was given the automatic stay in CICA to promote these policies. *See* H.R. Rep. No 98-861 at 1435-36 (Conf. Rep.). NHTSA then states that it has "limited [Centech's performance] to essential efforts during the pendency of the protest." AR 3. Again, this statement has nothing to do with the integrity of the procurement process. The CICA stay was meant to prevent the "fait accompli" of a contractor establishing a relationship in a new contract with an agency long before GAO issued its decision. *See* H.R. Rep. No. 99-138, at 4-5. Limiting the contractor to "essential efforts," AR 3, does not address Congress' concerns.

The agency must be able to demonstrate that its override determination was not arbitrary, capricious, or an abuse of discretion based upon the evidence in the record at the time the determination was made, *Advanced Sys. Dev., Inc. v. United States,* 72 Fed. Cl. 25 (2006) (rejecting notion that override "can be an evolving document"). See also *Cigna Gov't Servs., LLC v. United States,* 70 Fed. Cl. 100 (2006) (rationale for overriding the statutory stay in complex, costly procurement for Medicare claims processing was contained in a three and one-half page memorandum with little explanation and generalized conclusions); *PGBA, LLC v. United States,* 57 Fed. Cl. 65 (2003) (finding "nakedness of . . . assumption undercut other critical findings").

Some Court of Federal Claims judges have declined to apply the *Reilly* factors. In *PlanetSpace Inc. v. United States,* 86 Fed. Cl. 566 (2009), the court held that when considering injunctive relief in override cases, the court should only apply the APA four-factor test for injunctive relief and not the additional four *Reilly* factors. The court held that "Congress limited the court's review on an agency's decision in a CICA override action to the Administrative Procedure Acts standards." Similarly in *Analysis Group, LLC v. United States*, 2009 U.S. Claims Lexis 349, the court stated that while these four additional factors may be helpful in analyzing the agency's override decision, they are not dispositive. The court went on to reason that even applying the *Reilly* factors, it is clear that GSA FEDSIM justified its override of the stay. Imposing a stay of performance would jeopardize the Air Force's ability to meet its ongoing national security obligation such as its on going international treaties, health and welfare of military personnel, H1N1 virus planning, troop deployments, air flight planning for military operations in Afghanistan and similar locations, Air Force Counter-Radiological Warfare capabilities, and the implementation of toxins handling procedures and recommendations. Thus, the national security factor was the significant factor in the court's decision. Overrides related to procurements involving national defense and security are more likely to withstand challenge, *Maden Tech Consulting Inc. v. United States*, 74 Fed. Cl. 786 (2006) (procurement of electromagnetic spectrum engineering services to support war fighters in Iraq and Afghanistan); *Kropp Holdings, Inc. v. United States*, 63 Fed. CL. 537 (2005) ("where legitimate 'interests of national defense and national security' are raised and established to the court's satisfaction, the circumstances under which the court should find it 'necessary' to reach the merits of an override decision should be the exception, rather than the rule"); and *SDS Int'l, Inc. v. United States*, 55 Fed. Cl. 363 (2003) (absolutely essential to the success of the Weapons School and to the quality of our warriors that courseware development, production and presentation, as well as the contractor aircrew training not receive further interruption).

D. Intervenors

4 C.F.R. § 21.0 defines an "intervenor" as

an awardee if the award has been made or, if no award has been made, all bidders or offerors who appear to have a substantial prospect of receiving an award if the protest is denied.

Potential intervenors become aware of a protest by the fact that the contracting agency must immediately give notice of a protest to the awardee, if award has been made or, if award has not been made, to all bidders or offerors who appear to have a reasonable prospect of receiving an award, 4 C.F.R. § 21.3(a). Most often it is the awardee that files as an intervenor, e.g., *The Boeing Co.*, Comp. Gen. Dec. B-311344, 2008 CPD ¶ 114 (awardee filed as intervenor when protester challenged technical and cost evaluations of proposals); *B.L. Harbert-Brasfield & Gorrie, JV*, Comp. Gen. Dec. B-402229, 2010 CPD ¶ 69 (awardee filed as intervenor when protester challenged award on basis of organizational conflict of interest); *Source One Mgmt., Inc.*, Comp. Gen. Dec. B-278044.4, 98-2 CPD ¶ 11 (awardee filed as intervenor when protester challenged technical evaluation of proposals); *EBA Eng'g,*

Inc., Comp. Gen. Dec. B-275818, 97-1 CPD ¶ 127 (awardee filed as intervenor when protester alleged that awardee used bait-and-switch tactics with proposed key personnel). However, offerors that are likely to win an award may also file as intervenors, e.g., *Hoechst Marion Roussel, Inc.*, Comp. Gen. Dec. B-279073, 98-1 CPD ¶ 127 (Forest Pharmaceuticals filed as intervenor in protest concerning solicitation terms); *Government Tech. Servs., Inc.*, Comp. Gen. Dec. B-258082.2, 94-2 CPD ¶ 93 (intervenor next offeror in line). Upon receiving notification of a protest, any intervenor may file a request for dismissal, it if believes that a protest or specific protest allegations should be dismissed before submission of an agency report, 4 C.F.R. § 21.3(b). If the protest is not dismissed, the agency must prepare the agency report and, subject to any protective order, simultaneously furnish a copy to the protester and any intervenors, 4 C.F.R. § 21.3(e). As with protesters, intervenors have 10 days after receipt of the agency report to provide comments, 4 C.F.R. § 21.3(i). These comments must be given to the contracting agency and all other participating parties, 4 C.F.R. § 21.3(i).

Sometimes a party will find itself in the position of filing as an intervenor after having been a protester on the procurement. In *Executive Conference Ctr., Inc.*, Comp. Gen. Dec. B-275882.2, 97-1 CPD ¶ 138, the intervenor, Howard Johnson, had previously protested the procurement because its bid was deemed nonresponsive for failing to acknowledge an amendment. In considering Howard Johnson's protest, the contracting officer concluded that the amendment was not material and waived Howard Johnson's failure to properly acknowledge the amendment. The award to Executive Conference Center was terminated, and the contract awarded to Howard Johnson. Following the award to Howard Johnson, the GAO sustained Executive Conference's protest, holding that the amendment was material. In *Alice Roofing & Sheet Metal Works, Inc.*, Comp. Gen. Dec. B-275477, 97-1 CPD ¶ 86, the intervenor, Port Enterprises, had previously filed a protest, asserting that the bid of the awardee, Alice Roofing, had been unbalanced. In preparing a response to the protest, the contracting officer reviewed the pricing and determined that the bid was, in fact, unbalanced. The agency terminated Alice Roofing's contract and awarded the contract to Port Enterprises. Alice Roofing filed a protest with the GAO challenging the decision that its bid was unbalanced. The GAO denied the protest.

E. Procedures

Protests in the GAO are governed by its protest procedures, 4 C.F.R. Part 21. The procedures can be found at *www.gao.gov*.

1. Filing a Protest

Protests are filed directly with the GAO, not with the contracting agency. A copy of the protest, however, must be sent promptly to the contracting agency.

a. *Manner of Protest*

Protests must be filed in writing, 4 C.F.R. § 21.1(b). They may be hand delivered or sent by mail, commercial carrier, facsimile, or other electronic means. The filing party bears the risk that the delivery method chosen will not result in timely receipt at GAO. Protests are properly filed on a day if they are received by 5:30 p.m., eastern time, 4 C.F.R. § 21.0(g). The entire text of the protest must be received prior to this deadline in order for the protest to be timely, *Peacock, Myers & Adams*, Comp. Gen. Dec. B-279327, 98-1 CPD ¶ 94 (last page of protest received at 5:31 p.m.). Where a protest is transmitted to GAO (either by email or fax) outside of business hours, GAO will consider the protest to have been filed at the time GAO next opens for business following receipt of the submissions, *FitNet Purchasing Alliance*, Comp. Gen. Dec. B-400553, 2008 CPD ¶ 177; *Guam Shipyard*, Comp. Gen. Dec. B-294287, 2004 CPD ¶ 181.

Protests should be addressed to:

General Counsel

General Accountability Office

441 G Street, N.W.

Washington, D.C. 20548

Attention: Procurement Law Control Group

4 C.F.R. § 21.1(c) provides that the protest must:

(1) Include the name, street address, electronic mail address, and telephone and facsimile numbers of the protester,

(2) Be signed by the protester or its representative,

(3) Identify the contracting agency and the solicitation and/or contract number,

(4) Set forth a detailed statement of the legal and factual grounds of protest including copies of relevant documents,

(5) Set forth all information establishing that the protester is an interested party for the purpose of filing a protest,

(6) Set forth all information establishing the timeliness of the protest,

(7) Specifically request a ruling by the Comptroller General of the United States, and

(8) State the form of relief requested.

In addition, ¶ (d) provides that a protest may:

(1) Request a protective order,

(2) Request specific documents, explaining the relevancy of the documents to the protest grounds, and

(3) Request a hearing, explaining the reasons that a hearing is needed to resolve the protest.

Failure to specifically request a ruling by the GAO or to state the form of relief requested has not been considered a fatal defect to the consideration of the protest on the merits, *Air Shunt Instruments*, Comp. Gen. Dec. B-293766, 2004 CPD ¶ 125; *Carolina Auto Processing*, Comp. Gen. Dec. B-226841, 87-2 CPD ¶ 8; *Container Prods. Corp.*, 64 Comp. Gen. 641 (B-218556), 85-1 CPD ¶ 727.

b. Copy to Contracting Agency

The protester must furnish a copy of the protest to the agency official designated in the solicitation — or if there is no such designation, to the contracting officer — within one day of filing at the GAO, 4 C.F.R. § 21.1(e). A delay in providing a copy to the agency will not be considered prejudicial to the merits of the protest if the delay is not unreasonable and does not delay the preparation of the procuring agency's report to the GAO, 4 C.F.R. § 21.1(i). For cases where notification to the agency was delayed but was not deemed prejudicial, see *Container Prods. Corp.*, 64 Comp. Gen. 641 (B-218556), 85-1 CPD ¶ 727 (delay of one day), and *Land Mark Realty, Inc.*, Comp. Gen. Dec. B-224323, 86-2 CPD ¶ 620 (delay of two working days). But see *Alan Scott Indus.*, Comp. Gen. Dec. B-226012, 87-1 CPD ¶ 338, where a protest was dismissed because the copy to the procuring agency was received four working days after it was filed at the GAO.

c. Detailed Statement

The protest must include a detailed statement of its legal and factual grounds, 4 C.F.R. § 21.1(c). In *Mercer Prods. & Mfg. Co.*, Comp. Gen. Dec. B 251126, 92-2 CPD ¶ 385, the GAO dismissed a request for reconsideration because the protester did not provide a detailed statement as to why it believed the awards to be improper. In *Image Contracting, Inc.*, Comp. Gen. Dec. B-245599, 91-2 CPD ¶ 588, the GAO found that a detailed statement of the protest was insufficient because it merely stated that the technical specifications for the project were inadequate. In discussing the importance of the detailed statement, the GAO stated:

> This requirement is intended to provide us and the agency with a sufficient understanding of the grounds for the protest and with an opportunity to consider and resolve the matter without disrupting the orderly process of government procurement.

In *Coffman Specialists, Inc.*, Comp. Gen. Dec. B-400706.2, 2008 CPD ¶ 211, the GAO held that the protester failed to state sufficient legal and factual grounds for it to consider the protest. The GAO stated that, "by [the protester's] own admission, in filing its protest 'prematurely,' it made 'certain assumptions . . . on the basis of belief,' acknowledging that it 'still does not have knowledge that the bases it makes [in its] protest are true and accurate,' and that it 'makes the allegations based on its good faith belief.'" See also *FPM Remediations, Inc.*, Comp. Gen. Dec. B-401017.2, 2009 CPD ¶ 88 (protester's failure to receive a small business award resulted from its inaccurate representation that it was eligible for a HUBZone award, not from any violation of procurement law or regulation by the agency); *Med-South, Inc.*, Comp. Gen. Dec. B-401214, 2009 CPD ¶ 112 (no evidence to support contentions that the three offerors that responded to the solicitation cannot meet a solicitation requirement to be "established" in the state of Alabama and cannot comply with the "non-manufacturing rule" requirement); *View One., Inc.*, Comp. Gen. Dec. B-400346, 2008 CPD ¶ 142 (bare allegations that the agency "failed to perform a proper price/technical tradeoff" with neither evidence nor explanation to support it's theory); *Pacific Photocopy & Research Servs.*, Comp. Gen. Dec. B-278698, 98-1 CPD ¶ 69 (protest allegation that estimates were not accurate not supported by sufficient factual information); *Siebe Envtl. Controls*, Comp. Gen. Dec. B-275999.2, 97-1 CPD ¶ 70 (protester's belief that it has been and would be a good contractor and that it submitted a proposal that met all necessary criteria so that it should not have been excluded from competitive range); *Tidewater Marine, Inc.*, Comp. Gen. Dec. B-270602.5, 96-2 CPD ¶ 2 (protest failed to articulate how or why the proposed work commencement date was unduly restrictive); *Automated Power Sys., Inc.*, Comp. Gen. Dec. B-257178, 95-1 CPD ¶ 76 (protest that merely listed allegedly ambiguous specifications without details or explanation); *Federal Computer Int'l Corp.*, Comp. Gen. Dec. B-257618, 94-2 CPD ¶ 24 (protest that evaluation of proposals was improper without an explanation); *TAAS Israel Indus., Inc.*, Comp. Gen. Dec. B-251789, 94-1 CPD ¶ 197 (mere allegation that the agency's determination was wrong); *Imaging Equip. Servs., Inc.*, Comp. Gen. Dec. B-247201, 92-1 CPD ¶ 50 (unsupported assertion that agency's stated requirements were overly restrictive); *Blackhorse Servs. Co.*, Comp. Gen. Dec. B-244545, 91-2 CPD ¶ 30 (protest by a low bidder against a higher bidder without setting out and responding to the agency's basis for rejection); and *Herley Indus., Inc.*, Comp. Gen. Dec. B-242903, 91-1 CPD ¶ 449 (allegation that item did not meet salient characteristics of brand-name-or-equal specification without identifying the particular characteristics not met).

2. Actions Following Receipt of Protest

Upon receipt of a protest, an agency has two courses of action. It can either take corrective action or fight the protest.

a. Solving the Problem

Prior to the GAO resolving a protest, an agency may, on its own initiative, take corrective action. In such cases the GAO will dismiss the protest, *Canon USA, Inc.*, Comp. Gen. Dec. B-272414.7, 96-2 CPD ¶ 235.

(1) DISCRETION TO TAKE CORRECTIVE ACTION

Contracting officials in negotiated procurements have broad discretion to take corrective action in response to a protest when the agency determines that such action is necessary to ensure fair and impartial competition, *MayaTech Corp.*, Comp. Gen. Dec. B-400491.4, 2009 CPD ¶ 55; *Patriot Contract Servs., LLC*, Comp. Gen. Dec. B-278276.11, 98-2 CPD ¶ 77; *Oshkosh Truck Corp.*, Comp. Gen. Dec. B-237058.2, 90-1 CPD ¶ 274. When an agency informs GAO that it is taking corrective action, the protest will generally be dismissed as being moot.

The only constraint on this authority is that the corrective action must be appropriate to remedy the impropriety, *Computing Devices Int'l*, Comp. Gen. Dec. B-258554.3, 94-2 CPD ¶ 162. As long as the agency acts in good faith, the GAO will find that the agency's corrective action is appropriate. In *ZAFER Constr. Co.*, Comp. Gen. Dec. B-401871.4, 2010 CPD ¶ 66, the protester argued that the Army's corrective action to permit new and complete proposals, including price revisions, was overbroad and contradicted the explicit representations from the agency counsel that the corrective action would be limited to the project management plan page-limitation issue. The Army stated that due to the time lapse between proposal submission and the corrective action, the agency was concerned that the original price proposals submitted by the offerors would not longer accurately reflect the offerors' costs for the project. The Army also stated that the need to take corrective action also provided an opportunity to allow offerors to improve the quality of their technical submissions by revising their proposals to account for any changed circumstances between the original proposal submission and the time of corrective action. The GAO denied the protest holding that the agency has considerable discretion in these matters and GAO will not substitute its views for the Army's on how best to proceed, absent a showing that this discretion is being abused. In *Honeywell Tech. Solutions, Inc.*, Comp. Gen. Dec. B-400771.6, 2009 CPD ¶ 49, the protester argued that the agency's corrective action did not go far enough, insofar as offerors should be permitted to submit unlimited proposal revisions. The GAO denied the protest finding that NASA's decision to update the past performance information from each offeror was a reasonable way to remedy the identified procurement impropriety while not affecting other portions of offerors' proposals and the evaluation thereof. See also *ICON Consulting Group, Inc.*, Comp. Gen. Dec. B-310431.2, 2008 CPD ¶ 38 (corrective action reasonable which allowed protester opportunity to compete for an award with remaining unsuccessful offerors, but did not permit protester to compete for one of the two 8(a) contracts already awarded); *CMC & Maint., Inc.*, Comp. Gen. Dec. B-293803.2, 2004 CPD ¶ 243 (within the agency's discretion to reevaluate the quotations and make a new award determination based on a fully documented evaluation record); *Hyperbaric Techs., Inc.*, Comp. Gen. Dec. B-293047.2, 2004 CPD ¶ 87 (corrective action to solicit and evaluate revised proposals and make a new best value determination reasonable); *PCA Aerospace, Inc.*, Comp. Gen Dec. B-293042.3, 2004 CPD ¶ 65 (corrective action of rescinding contract reasonable where dramatic price differentials may reasonably be interpreted to suggest that offerors had dissimilar understandings of the requirements); *Strand Hunt Constr., Inc.*, Comp. Gen. Dec. B-292415, 2003 CPD ¶ 167 (corrective action of terminating contract reasonable); *Computer Assocs. Int'l, Inc.*, Comp. Gen. Dec. B-292077.2, 2003 CPD ¶ 157 (limited request for price information from each vendor reasonable way to remedy the suspected procurement impropriety while not affecting other portions of vendor's quotes and the evaluation thereof); *Fisher-Cal Indus., Inc.*, Comp. Gen. Dec. B-285150.2, 2000 CPD ¶ 115 (agency's corrective action of terminating the contract was appropriate); *Landmark Constr. Corp.*, Comp. Gen. Dec. B-281957.3, 99-2 CPD ¶ 75 (proposed corrective action reasonable where agency will allow the improperly awarded IDIQ contract to expire, and will place no new delivery orders under the contract but will allow delivery orders already issued to be performed pending recompetition and new award); *Patriot Contract Servs.*, Comp. Gen. Dec. B-278276.11, 98-2 CPD ¶ 77 (rescinding contracts, amending the solicitation, reopening negotiations, and requesting a second round of BAFOs reasonable); *NavCom Defense Elecs., Inc.*, Comp. Gen. Dec. B-276163.3, 97-2 CPD ¶ 126 (reopening discussions with all offerors in the competitive range and by requesting a second BAFO reasonable). It is not necessary for an agency to conclude that the protest is certain to be sustained before it may take corrective action. Even if the protest could be denied, the agency still has the prerogative to take corrective action, *Main Bldg. Maint., Inc.*, Comp. Gen. Dec. B-279191.3, 98-2 CPD ¶ 47.

Cases where the GAO reinstated a protest because the corrective action taken by the agency is found to be unreasonable include *Saltwater, Inc. — Recon.*, Comp. Gen. Dec. B-294121.3, 2005 CPD ¶ 33 (where an agency's implementation of promised corrective action, which caused GAO to dismiss a protest as academic, is such that the issue in controversy in fact has not been resolved, GAO will consider the protest's merits in response to a reconsideration request); *SYMVIONICS, Inc.*, Comp. Gen. Dec. B-293824.2, 2004 CPD ¶ 204 (agency provided material information concerning solicitation requirements to a single competitor in a post-award debriefing and the agency subsequently reopened the competition without providing the other competitors with the same information); *Gulf Copper Ship Repair, Inc.*, Comp. Gen. Dec. B-293706.5, 2004 CPD ¶ 108 (agency in taking corrective action conducted discussions only with the awardee, rather than with all offerors whose proposals were in the competitive range); *Ridoc Enters., Inc./Myers Investigative & Sec. Servs., Inc.*, Comp. Gen. Dec. B-293045.2, 2004 CPD ¶ 153 (after restoring offerors to the competitive range in order to resolve an earlier protest, and having already conducted discussions with offeror that had continued to be in the competitive range, the agency failed to conduct any discussions with the reinstated offerors); and *Security Consultants Group, Inc.*, Comp. Gen. Dec. B-293344.2, 2004 CPD ¶ 53 (agency's decision to reopen competition, after making award to protester, in order to correct solicitation defect was unreasonable where record does not establish a reasonable possibility that any offeror was prejudiced by the defect; reopening of competition thus did not provide any benefit to the procurement system that would justify competitive harm to protester from resoliciting after exposure of protester's price).

The Court of Federal Claims similarly recognizes contracting officals' broad discretion to take corrective action where the agency determines that such action is necessary to ensure fair and impartial competition, *DGS Contract Serv., Inc. v. United States*, 43 Fed. Cl. 227 (1999). See also *Consolidated Eng'g Servs., Inc. v. United States*, 64 Fed. Cl. 617 (2005) (agency's decision to expand the scope of the corrective action to permit revisions to key personnel and subcontactors was reasonable, as was its decision to limit revisions to those aforementioned areas). In *Carahsoft Tech. Corp. v. United States*, 86 Fed. Cl. 325 (2009), following GAO outcome prediction indicating that it intended to sustain plaintiff's protest with regard to its competitor's proposed noncompliant indemnification clause, the agency called for another round of final proposal revisions, allowing revised price proposals, but not allowing technical proposals and allowing the competitor to propose a compliant indemnification clause. Plaintiff argued that when a negotiated procurement is reopened for revised offers, it must allow any revision to those offers the offeror may care to make. The court disagreed, finding that the ability to limit proposals derives from contracting officials' broad discretion to take corrective action.

(2) Types of Corrective Action

The cases discussed above demonstrate that agencies can take a wide variety of actions to correct a defect in the original procurement. At a minimum, it is clear that agencies may take any corrective action that the GAO would be recommend by GAO if the protest went to decision, such as amending the solicitation and requesting proposal revisions, *Computing Devices Int'l*, Comp. Gen. Dec. B-258554.3, 94-2 CPD ¶ 162; *Federal Security Sys., Inc.*, Comp. Gen. Dec. B-281745.2, 99-1 CPD ¶ 86; *International Res. Group*, Comp. Gen. Dec. B-286683, 2001 CPD ¶ 35; canceling the solicitation and resoliciting, *Noelke GmbH*, Comp. Gen. Dec. B-278324.2, 98-1 CPD ¶ 46; reopening negotiations, *Rockville Mailing Serv., Inc.*, Comp. Gen. Dec. B-270161.2, 96-1 CPD ¶ 184; terminating the contract and reevaluating proposals, *Strand Hunt Constr., Inc.*, Comp. Gen. Dec. B-292415, 2003 CPD ¶ 167; *Aquidneck Sys. Int'l, Inc.*, Comp. Gen. Dec. B-257170.2, 94-2 CPD ¶ 122; or payment of the protester's proposal preparation costs, *Southern Techs., Inc.*, Comp. Gen. Dec. D-278030, 97-2 CPD ¶ 167. In addition, subsequent to an ADR "outcome prediction," an agency may re-open a solicitation and allow offerors to make only limited revisions to their proposals, *Consolidated Eng'g Servs., Inc. v. United States*, 64 Fed. Cl. 617 (2005).

b. *Conducting the Protest*

The Clinger-Cohen Act of 1996 shortened the time for the GAO to decide a protest to 100 calendar days. To comply with this requirement, the GAO protest procedures specify the precise times when the parties must take actions or deliver documents. These times are set to permit the parties adequate time to prepare documents while giving the GAO time to decide the protest.

(1) Notification

The GAO has one day to notify the contracting agency of the GAO's receipt of the protest, 31 U.S.C. § 3553(b)(1); 4 C.F.R. § 21.3(a). As discussed above, the time for invoking a suspension of contract performance under 31 U.S.C § 3553(d) continues to run until the agency receives notice of the protest from the GAO, and there is no recourse if the GAO fails to comply with this one-day notification requirement.

(2) Requests for Dismissal

The GAO may summarily dismiss a protest because the protest is untimely, the protester does not qualify as an interested party, or the protest fails to meet the requirement of specificity, 4 C.F.R. § 21.5. In addition, the GAO rules specifically state that the GAO will not consider the following issues:

1. A matter of contract administration
2. A matter that is in the purview of the SBA
3. Affirmative determinations of responsibility not involving definitive responsibility criteria
4. Violations of subsections (a), (b), c), or (d) of Section 27 of the Procurement Integrity Act where the protester failed to report the information it believed constituted evidence of the offense to the federal agency responsible for the procurement within 14 days after the protester first discovered the possible violation; see *DME Corp.*, Comp. Gen. Dec. B-401924, 2010 CPD ¶ 44; *Honeywell Tech. Solutions, Inc.*, Comp. Gen. Dec. B-400771, 2009 CPD ¶ 49; *Frank A. Bloomer — Agency Tender Official*, Comp. Gen. Dec. B-401482, 2009 CPD ¶ 174.
5. Protests not filed in GAO or the contracting agency within the time limits
6. Protests which lack a detailed statement of the legal and factual grounds or which fail to clearly state legally sufficient grounds
7. Procurements by other than federal agencies as defined in Section 3 of the Federal Property and Administrative Services Act of 1949; i.e., U.S. Postal Service, the Federal Deposit Insurance Corporation, and nonappropriated fund activities
8. Subcontract protests
9. Suspensions and debarments
10. Assertions that the protester's proposal should not have been included or kept in the competitive range
11. Decision of an agency tender official to file a protest or not file a protest in connection with a public-private competition

(3) Early Request for Documents

A protest may include a request for the early release of documents relevant to the protest, 4 C.F.R. § 21.1(d)(2). In such cases the agency should send the documents to the protester as quickly as possible or arrange for an on-site review of documents. When such a request is made, the contracting agency must provide to all parties and the GAO a list of the documents released and the documents that the agency intends to withhold from the protester, as well as the reasons for such withholding, 4 C.F.R. § 21.3(c). Objections to any proposed withholdings must be submitted to the GAO within two days of the receipt of the list.

This procedure is intended to facilitate the resolution of disputes about the release of documents and to enable the protester to more easily meet the time limitations imposed after receipt of the agency report, 61 Fed. Reg. 39041, July 26, 1996. However, the procedure is required only when the protester submits a specific request for release of documents at the time the protest is filed.

(4) Agency Report

31 U.S.C. § 3553(f) requires that a protest file be made available to the parties to the protest. The contracting agency must file its report within 30 calendar days from the date it receives telephone notification from the GAO of receipt of protest, 4 C.F.R. § 21.3(c). The agency must simultaneously send a copy of the report to the protester and any intervenors, 4 C.F.R. § 21.3(e). If a protective order has been issued, parties under the protective order will receive the entire file. Those not under the protective order will receive only a redacted version. If no protective order has been issued, only the GAO will receive protected documents.

4 C.F.R. § 21.3(d) provides that the agency report should include

the contracting officer's statement of the relevant facts, including a best estimate of the contract value, a memorandum of law, and a list and a copy of all relevant documents, or portions of documents, not previously produced, including, as appropriate: the protest; the bid or proposal submitted by the protester; the bid or proposal of the firm which is being considered for award, or whose bid or proposal is being protested; all evaluation documents; the solicitation, including the specifications; the abstract of bids or offers; and any other relevant documents. In appropriate cases, the contracting agency may request that the protester produce relevant documents, or portions of documents, that are not in the agency's possession.

The procuring agency may request an extension of time for submission of the agency report, 4 C.F.R. § 21.3(f). The GAO will grant an extension of time on a case-by-case basis, *Blue Rock Structures, Inc.*, Comp. Gen. Dec. B-400811, 2009 CPD ¶ 26; *Military Agency Servs. Pty., Ltd.*, Comp. Gen. Dec. B-290414, 2002 CPD

¶ 130; *Land Mark Realty, Inc.*, Comp. Gen. Dec. B-224323, 86-2 CPD ¶ 620; *Adrian Supply Co.*, Comp. Gen. Dec. B-227022.6, 88-1 CPD ¶ 417.

(5) Reverse Discovery

In appropriate cases, the contracting agency may request that the protester produce relevant documents, or portions of documents, that are not in the agency's possession, 4 C.F.R. § 21.3(d). This is known as the reverse discovery rule. This rule is narrowly construed. In *Boeing Co.*, Comp. Gen. Dec. B-311344, 2008 CPD ¶ 114, the Air Force requested that Boeing produce certain broad categories of documents bearing upon, among other things, Boeing's interpretation of the solicitation and several of its protest allegations. Boeing objected to that request, asserting that the documents sought were not relevant. The agency responded that its request was reasonable and limited, and sought relevant documents, which would be "necessary to allow GAO to perform a complete and accurate review of the issues in Boeing's protests. The GAO denied the Air Force request stating that the bid protest regulations do not provide for wide-open discovery requests by the agency on broad categories.

(6) Additional Documents

If a protester becomes aware of the existence of relevant documents after submission of the initial protest, it has two days from the time it first knew or should have known of the existence of additional documents to submit a written request for them to the GAO and the agency, 4 C.F.R. § 21.3(g). The agency must then respond within two days either with the documents, or a portion of the documents, and a list or with an explanation for why it is not required to produce the documents.

The GAO will decide any dispute that arises concerning the release of withheld documents and whether this should be done under a protective order, 4 C.F.R. § 21.3(h). When withheld documents are provided, the protester's comments on the agency report must be filed within the original comment filing period unless GAO determines that an extension is appropriate, 4 C.F.R. § 21.3(h).

(7) Comments on Agency Report

Comments on the agency report must be filed by the protester with the GAO within 10 calendar days after receipt of the report, with a copy provided to the contracting agency and other participating parties, 4 C.F.R. § 21.3(i). Under this provision, if the protester fails to file comments or a written statement expressing continuing interest within the deadline, the GAO will dismiss the protest, *Keymiaee Aero-Tech, Inc. — Recons.*, Comp. Gen. Dec. B-274803.3, 97-1 CPD ¶ 163; *Carmon Constr., Inc.*, Comp. Gen. Dec. B-271316.2, 96-2 CPD ¶ 3. In addition, if the protester fails to respond to the rebuttal of any protest issue, the GAO will consider that the protester has abandoned that issue, *Dynamic Instruments, Inc.*, Comp. Gen. Dec. B-291071, 2002 CPD ¶ 183; *Strategic Resources, Inc.*, Comp. Gen. Dec. B-287398, 2001 CPD ¶ 131; *O. Ames Co.*, Comp. Gen. Dec. B-283943, 2000 CPD ¶ 20; *Analex Space Sys., Inc.*, Comp. Gen. Dec. B-259024, 95-1 CPD ¶ 106; *Carter Chevrolet Agency, Inc.*, Comp. Gen. Dec. B-254813, 94-1 CPD ¶ 5; *J.M. Yurick Assocs.*, Comp. Gen. Dec. B-243806.2, 91-2 CPD ¶ 245; *The Big Picture Co.*, Comp. Gen. Dec. B-220859.2, 86-1 CPD ¶ 218. Protests are rarely sustained where the protester does not file substantive comments on the report. See, for example *DUCOM, Inc.*, Comp. Gen. Dec. B-285485, 2000 CPD ¶ 144, where the GAO noted that the Army provided a detailed response to each evaluation challenge raised in DUCOM's protest. DUCOM's comments on the agency report specifically addressed just 2 issues, which involved only 6 of 20 disadvantages noted by the SSEB. In the absence of any argument from DUCOM to the contrary, the GAO held it had no basis to find the Army's evaluation unreasonable.

(8) Supplemental Issues

A protester may raise new grounds for protest if the new grounds were first discovered upon receipt of the agency report and the protester raises these supplemental issues within 10 days of its receipt of the agency report, *Anteon Corp.*, Comp. Gen. Dec. B-293523, 2004 CPD ¶ 51 (allowing supplemental protest issues that were first discovered from agency report, and raised within 10 days of receipt of agency report); *Planning & Dev. Collaborative Int'l*, Comp. Gen. Dec. B-299041, 2007 CPD ¶ 28 (supplemental protest issues first discovered from agency report were untimely because they were raised in protester's comments filed more than 10 days after receipt of agency report; extension for filing comments does not authorize extension for raising supplemental protest issues).

(9) Further Submissions

Although no further submissions are specifically provided for in the rules, the GAO may permit or request further submissions by the parties, 4 C.F.R. § 21.3(j).

3. *Protective Orders*

The GAO is authorized by statute to issue protective orders, 31 U.S.C. § 3553(f)(2). 4 C.F.R. § 21.4(a) provides:

> At the request of a party or on its own initiative, GAO may issue a protective order controlling the treatment of protected information. Such information may include proprietary, confidential, or source-selection-sensitive material, as well as other information the release of which could result in a competitive advantage to one or more firms. The protective order shall establish procedures for applica-

tion for access to protected information, identification and safeguarding of that information, and submission of redacted copies of documents omitting protective information. Because a protective order serves to facilitate the pursuit of a protest by a protester through counsel, it is the responsibility of protester's counsel to request that a protective order be issued and to submit timely applications for admission under that order.

If there is no protective order, proprietary and procurement-sensitive documents must be furnished to the GAO but not to nongovernmental parties, 4 C.F.R. § 21.4(b).

a. Admissible Parties

Three kinds of parties may be admitted under the protective order: (1) outside counsel, (2) in-house counsel, and (3) experts or consultants.

In determining whether counsel should be admitted under a protective order, the GAO will look to whether the attorney is involved in the competitive decision-making process, *Allied-Signal Aerospace Co.*, Comp. Gen. Dec. B-250822, 93-1 CPD ¶ 201. Where an attorney is involved in competitive decision-making, the attorney will not be granted access to proprietary data of another company because there is an unacceptable risk of inadvertent disclosure of protected material, *U.S. Steel Corp. v. United States*, 730 F.2d 1465 (Fed. Cir. 1984).

Although it is often easier to establish that outside counsel is not involved in the decision-making process, *International Tech. Corp.*, GSBCA 9967-P, 89-2 BCA ¶ 21,746, the GAO will determine the admission of counsel on a case-by-case basis. See *Allied-Signal Aerospace Co.*, Comp. Gen. Dec. B-250822, 93-1 CPD ¶ 201, where the GAO excluded outside counsel because they were also officials involved in competitive decision making for the firms they represented. In *Colonial Storage Co.*, Comp. Gen. Dec. B-253501.5, 93-2 CPD ¶ 234, the GAO did not admit an interested party's counsel under a protective order because the counsel had represented the interested party at a presolicitation conference and had also participated in price discussions between the interested party and the agency. Compare *AirTrak Travel*, Comp. Gen. Dec. B-292101, 2003 CPD ¶ 117, where the agency objected to the admission of outside counsel on the grounds they were involved in advising the companies during competitions but were unable to submit proof of this assertion. Although an individual outside counsel may be excluded from admission under the protective order, other attorneys from the same law firm may be admitted if adequate procedures are in place to guarantee access by only those attorneys admitted, *Mine Safety Appliances Co.*, Comp. Gen. Dec. B-242379.2, 91-2 CPD ¶ 506.

In-house counsel who are not involved in competitive decision-making may be admitted under a protective order when the risk of inadvertent disclosure of proprietary or procurement-sensitive information is small, *Robbins-Gioia, Inc.*, Comp.

Gen. Dec. B-274318, 96-2 CPD ¶ 222. In *Earle Palmer Brown Cos.*, Comp. Gen. Dec. B-243544, 91-2 CPD ¶ 134, the GAO stated:

> In determining whether to grant access to protected material, we consider such factors as whether counsel primarily advises on litigation matters or also advises on pricing and production decisions, including the review of bids and proposals, the degree of physical separation and security with respect to those who participate in competitive decision-making and level of supervision to which in-house counsel is subject.

Here, the GAO denied admittance under the protective order, stating that the direct relationship between the chief executive officer of the company and in-house counsel made the risk of inadvertent disclosure too high. Similarly in *McDonnell Douglas Corp.*, Comp. Gen. Dec. B-259694.2, 95-2 CPD ¶ 51, the GAO denied admittance under the protective order because the in-house counsel were in the position of advising the firm's competitive strategists. See also *TRW, Inc.*, Comp. Gen. Dec. B-243450.2, 91-2 CPD ¶ 160, where, in denying admittance under the protective order, the GAO stated that there were only two attorneys in the office and, thus, the general legal counsel would likely be relied on to render legal advice on many subjects, including business-related decisions.

Similarly, with regard to experts or consultants, if the risk of inadvertent disclosure is too high, the GAO will not admit such individuals under a protective order. In *Systems Research & Applications Corp.*, Comp. Gen. Dec. B-299818, 2008 CPD ¶ 28, the GAO held that admission of a consultant to a GAO protective order was appropriate, over the objection that the consultant once held a position with the protester and that the consultant's daughter was currently employed by the protester. The GAO stated that the record showed that the consultant had no continuing interest in the protester and the consultant's daughter held a relatively low-level position with the protester in a division that was unrelated to the work to be performed under the protested contract. In *Restoration & Closure Servs., LLC*, Comp. Gen. Dec. B-295663.12, 2005 CPD ¶ 92, the GAO denied the consultants' applications for admission to the protective order because the applications agreed to restrict the consultants' activities only with regard to the particular site for the procurement being protested and thus permitted the consultants to engage or assist in the preparation of proposals for the same type of work at other sites where a party to the protest might be a competitor. *Bendix Field Eng'g Corp.*, Comp. Gen. Dec. B-246236, 92-1 CPD ¶ 227, is an interesting case where the agency requested that admission of experts to a protective order be made contingent upon a promise to avoid participation in future procurements for the same type of work for a period of five years. The GAO found this to be reasonable given the large dollar value of the contract and the competition-sensitive nature of the information to be made available to the experts.

Even if there is little risk of inadvertent disclosure, if the information is highly sensitive, the GAO may decline to admit experts or consultants, *EER Sys. Corp.*,

Comp. Gen. Dec. B-256383, 94-1 CPD ¶ 354 (information contained highly sensitive and proprietary engineering approaches and solutions that would be invaluable to any practicing engineer).

Where a protester does not retain counsel, the protester may be at a disadvantage in that it will not have access to information that is available under a protective order. In *Dominion Aviation, Inc., — Recons.*, Comp. Gen. Dec. B-275419.4, 98-1 CPD ¶ 62, the GAO issued a protective order in the original matter in order to protect proposal and detailed evaluation information. The protester did not retain counsel and, therefore, did not have access to all relevant information concerning the awardee's proposal and its evaluation. After the protest was denied, the protester sought reconsideration based on information first learned from the publicly available copy of the GAO decision. The GAO denied reconsideration stating that the protester had made a business decision not to retain counsel and obtain access to information under the protective order and could not later raise protest grounds based on information it essentially opted not to receive earlier. In *JoaQuin Mfg. Corp.*, Comp. Gen. Dec. B-275185, 97-1 CPD ¶ 48, the GAO held that because no protective order was issued during a protest since protester was not represented by counsel, the protester was not entitled to receive and review protected information. See also *TEAM Support Servs., Inc.*, Comp. Gen. Dec. B-279379.2, 98-1 CPD ¶ 167, where, in a footnote, the GAO noted that the protester was not represented by counsel and, therefore, was provided only redacted versions of the agency report and supporting documentation. The GAO reviewed in camera unredacted copies of all evaluation and source selection documents in light of the protest arguments raised by the protester. The GAO stated that because much of the information reviewed was source selection sensitive and proprietary in nature, its decision of the evaluation would be limited.

If the terms of the protective order are violated, both counsel and client are subject to a variety of sanctions, including dismissal of the protect. See *PWC Logistics Servs. Co. KSC(c)*, Comp. Gen. Dec. B-310559, 2008 CPD ¶ 25 (GAO dismissed protest after protester's attorney, who had been admitted under protective order, revealed protected information to protester); *Network Securities Tech., Inc.*, Comp. Gen. Dec. B-290741.2, 2002 CPD ¶ 193 (GAO provides notice that, in a future case, it may impose the sanction of dismissal where protester's attorney discloses protected information to client).

b. Procedure

An individual seeking admission under a protective order must submit an application to the GAO with copies furnished to all other parties, 4 C.F.R. § 21.4(c). See Guide to GAO Protective Orders, GAO-09-770SP, June 2009, for sample forms. Although there is no time limit for filing an application, it should be done as soon as possible. Parties have two days to object to the applicant's admission, 4 C.F.R. § 21.4(c). The GAO may, however, consider objections raised after that time.

4. *Alternative Dispute Resolution*

GAO has also adopted alternative dispute resolution procedures to more efficiently resolve protests. 4 C.F.R. 21.0(h) provides:

> Alternative dispute resolution encompasses various means of resolving cases expeditiously, without a written decision, including techniques such as outcome prediction and negotiation assistance.

GAO may use alternative dispute resolution procedures at the request of one or more of the parties, or where GAO deems appropriate. This may take the form of negotiation assistance either before or after a protest is filed, or outcome prediction, where GAO will advise the parties of the likely outcome of the protest in order to allow the party likely to be unsuccessful to take appropriate action to resolve the protest without a written decision.

With negotiation assistance ADR, a GAO attorney acts as a facilitator. If settlement is reached, the protest is withdrawn or rendered academic. If no settlement is reached, GAO will issue a written decision.

The more common form of ADR is outcome prediction where the GAO attorney concludes, based on precedent and/or facts and with the concurrence of supervising attorneys that one party is very likely to prevail. It is initiated either by a party's request or by the GAO attorney. The purpose is to share the view of GAO regarding the likely outcome, therein saving the parties' time and resources.

5. *Hearings*

In 1991 the GAO revised its bid protest regulations to permit a hearing on the protest at the request of one of the parties or on its own initiative, 4 C.F.R. § 21.7(a). The hearing replaced the former administrative conference proceedings. A hearing is not automatic but, rather, is held at the discretion of the GAO, *Jack Faucett Assocs.*, Comp. Gen. Dec. B-254421, 94-2 CPD ¶ 72. Requests for hearings must set forth the reasons why a hearing is necessary, 4 C.F.R. § 21.7(a). Although hearing have been conducted more frequently in recent years, they will be denied if they are not justified. See *Spectrum Sys., Inc.*, Comp. Gen. Dec. B-401130, 2009 CPD ¶ 110 (request for hearing denied because the protester provided no reasonable basis for the necessity of a hearing and no legitimate reason for a hearing was apparent).

A prehearing conference (usually by telephone) is generally conducted prior to the hearing to decide on the timing, the procedures to be followed, the issues to be considered, and the witnesses who will be called to testify, 4 C.F.R. § 21.7(b).

Generally, hearings are conducted as soon as practicable after receipt by the parties of the agency report and relevant documents, 4 C.F.R. § 21.7(c). Hearings are usually limited to one day and are conducted at the GAO in Washington, D.C., or, at the discretion of the GAO, at other locations, 4 C.F.R. § 21.7(c).

Witnesses are not sworn but are reminded that false testimony may subject them to criminal penalties. If a witness fails to appear or to answer a question, the GAO may draw inferences unfavorable to the party for whom the witness would have testified, 4 C.F.R. § 21.7(f). In *HEROS, Inc.*, Comp. Gen. Dec. B-292043, 2003 CPD ¶ 111, the agency refused to provide any witnesses, including the two specifically requested. As discussed at the hearing, one of the matters about which GAO would have sought information from the agency witnesses was whether or not its "secret" data had been reduced to any tangible form. GAO held that its review of the record, along with the agency's refusal to permit any cross-examination of its declarents led GAO to conclude it had not. See also *Network Security Techs., Inc.*, Comp. Gen. Dec. B-290741.2, 2002 CPD ¶ 193 (GAO drew unfavorable inference regarding a violation of a protective order because of former counsel's failure to appear at GAO hearing).

Post-hearing comments are permitted but must be submitted within five days of the hearing unless the GAO sets a different time, 4 C.F.R. ¶ 21.7(g).

6. Time for Decision

Under the original statute establishing GAO protest authority, the GAO was given 90 working days to resolve a protest. The FASA restated this time as 125 calendar days. The Clinger-Cohen Act of 1996 shortened this time to 100 calendar days.

a. Statutory Deadline

The 100-day deadline for a GAO decision on a protest starts on the day after the date the protest is submitted to the GAO, 31 U.S.C. § 3554(a)(1). Although there is no specific exception authorizing an extension of time, where supplemental protests have been filed, the GAO may "roll over" a protest — that is, dismiss the earlier protest and incorporate it into the last supplemental protest, 31 U.S.C. § 3554(a)(2). This, in effect, can extend the time taken to have the protest decided well beyond the 100-calendar-day period.

b. Express Option

In cases that can be decided on an expeditious basis, the GAO may decide to use the "express option procedures." The FASA amended the express option process to require completion within 65 working days, Pub. L. No. 103-355, § 1403(a). The Clinger-Cohen Act of 1996 shortened this to 65 calendar days. A request for use of the express option may be submitted by any party in writing and must be received by the GAO within five days after the protest or supplemental protest is filed, 4 C.F.R.

§ 21.10(c). When the express option is used, the following schedule applies, as set forth in 4 C.F.R. § 21.10(d):

(1) The contracting agency shall file a complete report with GAO and the parties within 20 days after it receives notice from GAO that the express option will be used.

(2) Comments on the agency report shall be filed with GAO and the other parties within 5 days after receipt of the report.

(3) If a hearing is held, no separate comments on the agency report under paragraph (d)(2) of this section should be submitted unless specifically requested by GAO. Consolidated comments on the agency report and hearing shall be filed within 5 days after the hearing was held or as specified by GAO.

(4) Where circumstances demonstrate that a case is no longer suitable for resolution using the express option, GAO shall establish a new schedule for submissions by the parties.

For cases using the express option procedures, see *B&S Transp., Inc.*, Comp. Gen. Dec. B-299144, 2007 CPD ¶ 16 (granted agency's request to use the express option where agency contended that fast-tracking would allow it to meet its deadlines in the Army's Base Realignment and Closure plan); *AshBritt Inc.*, Comp. Gen. Dec. B-297889, 2006 CPD ¶ 48 (express option used pursuant to agency request); *Aalco Forwarding, Inc.*, Comp. Gen. Dec. B-277241.20, 98-2 CPD ¶ 1 (express option utilized in procurement with 99 protesters); and *Possehn Consulting*, Comp. Gen. Dec. B-278579, 98-1 CPD ¶ 10 (express option used to decide whether protester was properly excluded from competition based on low price).

c. *Summary Decision and Accelerated Schedule*

At the request of a party or on its own initiative, the GAO may set up an accelerated schedule for deciding a protest and may issue a summary decision on a protest, 4 C.F.R. § 21.10(e).

d. *Decision Distribution*

A hard copy of the decision is to be made available to each of the parties, as well as to the public, unless the decision is protected. If the decision is protected, only the parties under the protective order and the contracting agency will receive copies. Protected decisions are redacted and then made available to the public. Protest decisions are available electronically, 4 C.F.R. § 21.12, at http://www.gao.gov/

7. Reconsideration

The GAO will reconsider a protest decision at the request of a protester, an intervenor, or a federal agency involved in the protest, 4 C.F.R. § 21.14. Copies of the request must be sent to all parties that participated in the protest.

The request for reconsideration must be filed within 10 calendar days of the date the basis for the request for reconsideration was or should have been known, 4 C.F.R. § 21.14(b). Normally, that is 10 days after receipt of the decision, but if the protester learns of the decision in some other way, the 10-day rule will be enforced strictly. See *Speedy Food Serv., Inc.*, Comp. Gen. Dec. B-274406.2, 97-1 CPD ¶ 5, where the request for reconsideration was dismissed as untimely because it was not filed within 10 days of the time the protester saw the decision on the Internet. In *Sodexho Mgmt., Inc. — Costs*, Comp. Gen. Dec. B-289605.3, 2003 CPD ¶ 136, the Navy learned the basis for its request for reconsideration when Sodexho submitted its initial cost claim and supporting documentation but did not request reconsideration until it filed its response to that claim. The GAO held that the delay was unreasonable and the Navy's request untimely.

The request for reconsideration must do more than restate the arguments in the initial protest. 4 C.F.R. § 21.14(a) provides:

> GAO will not consider a request for reconsideration that does not contain a detailed statement of the factual and legal grounds upon which reversal or modification is deemed warranted, specifying any errors of law made or information not previously considered.

In *Tri-Star Indus.*, Comp. Gen. Dec. B-254767.3, 94-1 CPD ¶ 388, the GAO stated that the request for reconsideration must be based on (1) the failure to consider evidence that should have been considered, (2) newly discovered evidence that the party could not reasonably have furnished for the initial consideration, or (3) errors of law. See *MadahCom, Inc. — Recons.*, Comp. Gen. Dec. B-297261.2, 2005 CPD ¶ 209 (wrong timeliness standard applied); *Dep't of the Navy*, Comp. Gen. Dec. B-237342.2, 90-2 CPD ¶ 39 (GAO misread agency record); and *Gracon Corp.*, Comp. Gen. Dec. B-236603.2, 90-1 CPD ¶ 496 (labor hours for electrical work considered in prior protest were in error). More often, the protester fails to provide a basis for reconsideration. See *Small Business Administration — Recons.*, Comp. Gen. Dec. B-401057.2, 2009 CPD ¶ 148 (SBA's request for reconsideration primarily states its disagreement with GAO legal analysis regarding the statutory requirements for HUBZone set-asides); *Metro Machine Corp. — Recons. & Modification of Recommendation*, Comp. Gen. Dec. B-311245.5, 2008 CPD ¶ 167 (awardee/requester showed no error in, but simply disagreed with, GAO recommendation that the agency conduct meaningful discussions); *Shields & Dean Concessions, Inc. — Recons.*, Comp. Gen. Dec. B-292901.4, 2004 CPD ¶ 71 (decision contained no errors of fact or law, or present information not previously considered); *Social Se-*

curity Admin. — Recons., Comp. Gen. Dec. B-286201.4, 2001 CPD ¶ 157 (GAO decision did not err in identifying $[DELETED] as the approximate potential value of Rockwell's price reduction under a fair and proper competition); and *RGII Techs., Inc. — Recons. & Protest*, Comp. Gen. Dec. B-278352.2, 98-1 CPD ¶ 130 (repetition of arguments made during consideration of the original protest and mere disagreement with GAO decision do not meet standard for reconsideration).

The GAO rarely finds that the protester is offering newly discovered evidence that could not possibly have been furnished during the initial consideration, *Dep't of the Navy — Request for Modification of Remedy*, Comp. Gen. Dec. B-401102.3, 2009 CPD ¶ 162 (information not new where Navy failed to mention the DOD memoranda during the protest; it cannot now proffer this information and the associated arguments for the first time on reconsideration); *Allstate Van & Storage, Inc.*, Comp. Gen. Dec. B-270744.2, 96-2 CPD ¶ 72 (information proffered seven months after the protester had learned of the evidence not new).

There is no statutory deadline for issuing a decision on reconsideration. Also, there is no requirement to withhold award or suspend performance during the pendency of the reconsideration, 4 C.F.R. § 21.14(c).

F. Standards of Review

31 U.S.C. § 3554(b)(1) provides that the GAO will review an agency action to determine if it "complies with statute or regulation." Under this standard, a protester must establish that the contracting agency has prejudicially violated a statute or regulation or has taken a discretionary action without a rational basis. The GAO has given agencies considerable latitude in applying this rational basis standard to discretionary actions. The Federal Circuit has made clear that administrative protest authorities are not permitted to substitute their judgment for that of the agency, *Unisys Corp. v. Dep't of the Air Force*, GSBCA 13129-P, 95-2 BCA ¶ 27,622, *rev'd*, 98 F.3d 1325 (Fed. Cir. 1996).

The GAO traditionally acted in accordance with this guidance of the court, as shown by standard language in GAO decisions in protests challenging the rationality of discretionary decisions of contracting agencies. See, for example, *Red River Serv. Corp.*, Comp. Gen. Dec. B-253671.2, 94-1 CPD ¶ 385, which states:

> Where, as here, the RFP provides that technical considerations will be more important than cost, source selection officials have broad discretion in determining the manner in which they will make use of the technical and cost evaluation results in arriving at a source selection decision. *University of Dayton Research Inst.*, B-245431, Jan. 2, 1992, 92-1 CPD ¶ 6. Such cost/technical tradeoffs are governed only by the test of rationality and consistency with the RFP's stated evaluation criteria. *Miller Bldg. Corp.*, B-245488, Jan. 3, 1992, 92-1 CPD ¶ 21.

See also *JB Indus.*, Comp. Gen. Dec. B-251118.2, 93-1 CPD ¶ 297 (award to offeror with 13% higher price to obtain lower risk of unsuccessful performance); *University of Dayton Research Inst.*, Comp. Gen. Dec. B-245431, 92-1 CPD ¶ 6 (award to offeror with 27% higher cost and fee to obtain lower risk of technical failure). In none of these three cases was there any quantification of the technical and management evaluations. The GAO stated a slightly different formulation of the standard in *Technology Vectors, Inc.*, Comp. Gen. Dec. B-252518.2, 94-1 CPD ¶ 345:

> Since the RFP here stated that award would be made to the offeror whose proposal was determined to be most advantageous to the government, considering price and other factors, the agency had the discretion to determine whether the technical advantages associated with [the winning offeror's] proposal was worth its higher price. Our Office will not object to that determination if the agency reasonably determined that the price premium involved is justified by the technical superiority of the proposal.

See *Ameriko Maint. Co.*, Comp. Gen. Dec., B-253274.2, 93-2 CPD ¶ 121 (award to higher-priced offeror to obtain more extensive experience); *D'Wiley's Servs., Inc.*, Comp. Gen. Dec., B-251912, 93-1 CPD ¶ 377, *DynCorp*, Comp. Gen. Dec. B-257037.2, 95-1 CPD ¶ 34, and *Scheduled Airlines Traffic Offices, Inc.*, Comp. Gen. Dec. B-257292.9, 95-2 CPD ¶ 113 (award to higher-priced offeror to obtain better staffing); *Centro Mgmt., Inc.*, Comp. Gen. Dec., B-249411.2, 92-2 CPD ¶ 387, and *Hornet Joint Venture*, Comp. Gen. Dec. B-258430.2, 95-1 CPD ¶ 55 (award to higher-priced offeror to obtain better staffing and lower risk of poor performance); *EG&G Team*, Comp. Gen. Dec. B-259917.2, 95-2 CPD ¶ 138 (award to higher-price offeror to obtain benefits of higher-rated proposal); *TRW, Inc.*, Comp. Gen. Dec. B-260623, 95-2 CPD ¶ 92 (award to higher-priced offeror to obtain lower risk); and *Tidewater Homes Realty, Inc.*, Comp. Gen. Dec. B-274689.5, 98-2 CPD ¶ 40 (award to lower-priced, lower-rated offer proper where agency determined that higher-rated offer was not so significantly superior as to be worth the associated cost premium). However, in *Strum, Ruger & Co.*, Comp. Gen. Dec. B-250193, 93-1 CPD ¶ 42, the GAO overturned an award that required the agency to pay a large premium to an offeror that was rated only marginally superior to the protester. The source selection authority had selected the offeror with the highest technical score without making any tradeoff analysis. The GAO stated that the source selection authority had "misapprehended applicable law" and sent the matter back to the agency to "document a reasoned source selection decision."

The GAO continues to follow this broad standard of review. See *John Blood*, Comp. Gen. Dec. B-402133, 2010 CPD ¶ 30, stating:

> In reviewing a protest against the propriety of an evaluation, it is not our function to independently evaluate proposals and substitute our judgment for that of the contracting activity. *Barents Group, L.L.C.*, B-276082, B-276082.2, May 9, 1997, 97-1 CPD ¶ 164 at 6. Rather, we will review an evaluation to ensure that it was reasonable and consistent with the evaluation criteria in the solicitation and applicable procurement statutes and regulations; a protester's mere disagreement with the evaluation does not show it lacked a reasonable basis. *Id*. On the record

here, we see no basis to question the evaluation of the protester's quotation or the source selection decision.

A protester's mere disagreement with the agency's judgment in its determination of the relative merit of competing proposals or quotes does not establish that the evaluation was unreasonable, *C. Lawrence Constr. Co.*, Comp. Gen. Dec. B-287066, 2001 CPD ¶ 70 (agency's judgment of past performance was reasonable and consistent with the stated evaluation criteria and applicable statutes and regulations). See also *La Dolce Vida Catering*, Comp. Gen. Dec. B-402421, 2010 CPD ¶ 96 (contracting officer concluded that proposal was most advantageous to the agency and selected it for award, noting various strengths in the proposal); *Domain Name Alliance Registry*, Comp. Gen. Dec. B-310803.2, 2008 CPD ¶ 168 (evaluation of an offeror's proposal or quote, including experience, is a matter within the agency's discretion). However, agencies must show that they actually considered the relative merits of the proposals in making the selection decision. See *Preferred Sys. Solutions, Inc.*, Comp. Gen. Dec. B-292322, 2003 CPD ¶ 166, where, the GAO found the decision not reasonably based, stating:

> [T]he propriety of a cost/technical tradeoff turns not on the difference in technical score, per se, but on whether the contracting agency's judgment concerning the significance of that difference was reasonable in light of the solicitation's evaluation scheme. Where cost is secondary to technical considerations under a solicitation's evaluation scheme, as here, the selection of a lower-priced proposal over a proposal with a higher technical rating requires an adequate justification, i.e., one showing the agency reasonably concluded that notwithstanding the point or adjectival differential between the two proposals, they were essentially equal in technical merit, or that the differential in the evaluation ratings between the proposals was not worth the cost premium associated with selection of the higher technically rated proposal.

See also *Shumaker Trucking & Excavating Contractors, Inc.*, Comp. Gen. Dec. B-290732, 2002 CPD ¶ 169 (decision to select a higher technically rated, higher priced proposal unreasonable where agency mechanically applied the solicitation's evaluation methodology; neither the source selection documentation nor the evaluation record establish a valid rationale for why the agency found the higher priced, higher technically rated proposal to be most advantageous to the government)

G. Prejudice

Competitive prejudice is an essential element of every viable protest, 51 Comp. Gen. 678 (B-174367) (1972); *Lithos Restoration Ltd.*, 71 Comp. Gen. 367 (B-247003.2), 92-1 CPD ¶ 379. The protester must establish that but for the agency's actions, it would have had a substantial chance of receiving the award, *Armorworks Enter's., LLC*, Comp. Gen. Dec. B-400394.3, 2009 CPD ¶ 79. This is the same test as used in the courts, *Statistica, Inc. v. United States*, 102 F.3d 1577 (Fed. Cir. 1996); *Bannum, Inc. v. United States*, 404 F.3d 1346 (Fed. Cir. 2005);

Galen Med. Assocs., Inc. v. United States, 369 F.3d 1324 (Fed. Cir. 2004); *Info. Tech. & Applications Corp. v. United States*, 316 F.3d 1312 (Fed. Cir. 2003). In some instances the GAO states the test as a "reasonable possibility that the protester would have otherwise been the successful offeror as a sufficient basis for sustaining a protest," *CDA Investment Techs., Inc.*, Comp. Gen. Dec. B-272093.3, 97-1 CPD ¶ 103; *Truetech, Inc.*, Comp. Gen. Dec. B-402536.2, 2010 CPD ¶ 129. The court in *Statistica* stated that "reasonable likelihood" should be interpreted to be the same as "substantial chance."

General allegations of prejudice will not suffice. See *MCI Constructors, Inc.*, Comp. Gen. Dec. B-274347, 96-2 CPD ¶ 210, where the GAO found a failure to show prejudice when the protester failed to present information showing how it could reduce its price by the nearly $7 million margin with the low offeror. See also *Labrador Airways Ltd.*, Comp. Gen. Dec. B-241608, 91-1 CPD ¶ 167, where the protester did not demonstrate that it was prejudiced because the agency relaxed specifications for commercial flight services for one offeror. The protester alleged in general terms that on past contracts this requirement resulted in a net cost to the protester, but failed to provide any information showing how it calculated this cost or how much of this cost was included in its offer. Protesters have most readily demonstrated prejudice when they have been denied the opportunity to revise their proposals in the same manner as a competitor. For example, in *Global Assocs., Ltd.*, Comp. Gen. Dec. B-271693, 96-2 CPD ¶ 100, the GAO found that the protester was prejudiced when the agency conducted discussions with only the awardee after the submission of best and final offers.

The failure to conduct meaningful discussions may be prejudicial. In *Cogent Sys., Inc.*, Comp. Gen. Dec. B-295990.4, 2005 CPD ¶ 179, the GAO sustained a protest challenging the award of a contract for an automated fingerprint identification system because the agency's technical evaluators assigned the protester a significant weakness that was based upon the erroneous belief that the flatbed scanner offered in the protester's final proposal, which met technical requirements, was the same as the noncompliant flatbed scanner offered in the protester's initial proposal. The Army failed to raise this perceived significant weakness with the protester during discussions. Failure to conduct meaningful discussions with the protester with respect to this aspect of the agency's evaluation was prejudicial. See also *Ogden Support Servs., Inc.*, Comp. Gen. Dec. B-270354, 96-1 CPD ¶ 175, where the GAO sustained a protest because the agency did not inform the protester of the evaluated weaknesses and deficiencies in its proposal. The GAO concluded that the protester was prejudiced because it would have had an opportunity to improve its score to a level approaching the awardee's score and its proposal may well have remained low in cost. See also *Alliant Techsystems, Inc.*, Comp. Gen. Dec. B-260215.4, 95-2 CPD ¶ 79, where the GAO stated that in these circumstances, it would "resolve any doubts concerning the prejudicial effect of the agency's action in favor of the protester." But see *McDonald-Bradley*, Comp. Gen. Dec. B-270126, 96-1 CPD ¶ 54, where an allegation that the protester was misled during discussions was denied because the protester did not demonstrate a reasonable possibility that it was prejudiced. The protester argued that the agency misled the firm during discussions into believing that its proposed wages had to be consistent with the Service Contract Act requirements, but the GAO found no proof that the protester would have lowered its wages further in its BAFO or that an adjustment to the protester's price would have made its price competitive. Similarly, in *Alliance Tech. Servs., Inc.*, Comp. Gen. Dec. B-311329, 2008 CPD ¶ 108, the GAO held that the protester was not prejudiced by any failure by the agency to provide meaningful discussions. Even had the protester received a perfect score under the particular subfactor where the discussions were allegedly not meaningful, the total evaluated score would have remained lower technically than the other two awardees' proposals, and its price would remain higher than both awardees' prices. Thus, the protester would not have been in line for award even if it prevailed on this aspect of its protest. See also *D.N. American, Inc.*, Comp. Gen. Dec. B-292557, 2003 CPD ¶ 188 (protester had not shown that it would have or could have identified contracts of a larger size or that its subcontractor's references would have included other than contracts for hardware support had these issues been raised during discussions).

Prejudice has also been demonstrated when the agency makes errors in initiating the procurement. In *Comint Sys. Corp.*, Comp. Gen. Dec. B-274853, 97-1 CPD ¶ 14, the agency's letter offering a requirement to the SBA for acceptance into the 8(a) program failed to give complete and accurate information regarding the proposed offering. The GAO found prejudice because the failure to provide the information deprived the SBA of the opportunity to make a fully informed decision with respect to the acquisition and deprived the protester of a potential opportunity to participate in the procurement.

Prejudice has been found where an agency relaxes its requirements. See *George Hyman Constr. Co.*, Comp. Gen. Dec. B-265798, 95-2 CPD ¶ 173, where the agency relaxed a go/no-go key personnel experience evaluation criterion. The GAO noted that the key personnel experience requirements were very restrictive and that a prospective offeror had requested that the requirements be amended to be less restrictive, which the agency declined to do. Additionally, one offeror was rejected as technically unacceptable for failing to meet these requirements. Thus, the GAO held that there was a reasonable possibility of prejudice by relaxing these requirements for the awardee. In *Lockheed Martin Corp.*, Comp. Gen. Dec. B-295402, 2005 CPD ¶ 24, the record showed that performance requirements, and associated evaluation criteria, were altered to delete a significant requirement and an evaluation factor under which the protester was viewed as having an advantage. A senior procurement official, who was involved in discussions that culminated in the deletion of the requirement, acknowledged bias in favor of the ultimate awardee. The GAO sustained the protest on the basis that the agency failed to demonstrate that the senior official's acknowledged bias did not prejudice the protester and that the integrity of the procurement process was not compromised. However, where a proposal deviates from a specification by a negligible amount, prejudice is unlikely to be found.

See *First Federal Corp. — Costs*, Comp. Gen. Dec. B-293373.2, 2004 CPD ¶ 94 (one-half mile deviation from the 25-mile requirement appears minor on its face and protester did not show how it would have altered its proposal to improve its competitive standing had it been given an opportunity to respond to the relaxed requirement); *Gulf Copper Ship Repair, Inc.*, Comp. Gen. Dec. B-292431, 2003 CPD ¶ 155 (deviation of 1 inch water depth specification); *L.A. Sys., Inc.*, Comp. Gen. Dec. B-276349, 97-1 CPD ¶ 206 (although agency relaxed the stated requirements, there was no reasonable possibility that the protester was prejudiced by the relaxation); and *Magnaflux Corp.*, Comp. Gen. Dec. B-211914, 84-1 CPD ¶ 4 (agency permitted to waive deviation from specification which was minor and did not result in prejudice).

Prejudice has also been found where an agency changes its requirements but does not issue an amendment to the solicitation. See *Symetrics Indus., Inc.*, Comp. Gen. Dec. B-274246.3, 97-2 CPD ¶ 59, where the GAO sustained the protest, finding that the agency was required to amend the solicitation upon receiving information that funds were unavailable for the purchase of a significant portion of an estimated quantity included in the RFP for an indefinite-quantity, indefinite-delivery contract. The GAO stated that the change in quantity was material and there was a reasonable possibility that the protester was prejudiced by the failure to amend the solicitation. But see *M.K. Taylor Contractors, Inc.*, Comp. Gen. Dec. B-291730.2, 2003 CPD ¶ 97 (although agency improperly failed to issue amendment of the changed requirements, no prejudice found since, by protester's own calculations, increased quantities would not have led protester to reduce its price sufficiently to give it a substantial chance of receiving the award).

When the procurement defect is a failure to evaluate proposals properly, the protester must show that proper evaluation would have given it a chance to win the competition. This test was met in *Labat-Anderson, Inc.*, 71 Comp. Gen. 252 (B-246071), 92-1 CPD ¶ 193, where the agency had so significantly deviated from its evaluation scheme that it was not clear how a reevaluation would have scored the competitors. Prejudice will not be found where the outcome of the evaluation is unchanged. In *Calnet, Inc.*, Comp. Gen. Dec. B-402558.2, 2010 CPD ¶ 130, the GAO held that even if the protester were correct that the agency improperly failed to consider the protester's third past performance questionnaire, there was no prejudice. Including the scores of the third questionnaire in the calculation would have given the protester and awardee the same overall score. The awardee offered a lower price and therefore remained in line for award ahead of the protester. See also *Alsalam Aircraft Co.*, Comp. Gen. Dec. B-401298.4, 2010 CPD ¶ 23 (even if DynCorp failed to include the fringe benefit costs, a cost realism adjustment would not overcome the awardee's $11.4 million advantage over the protester's overall price); *PM Servs. Co.*, Comp. Gen. Dec. B-310762, 2008 CPD ¶ 42 (even agreeing with protester regarding the agency's evaluation of its proposal, awardee's proposal remained technically superior and was offered at a 4.4.% lower cost); *American Cybernetic Corp.*, Comp. Gen. Dec. B-310551.2, 2008 CPD ¶ 40 (even assuming that protester's technical proposal should have been assigned the highest possible rating, no reasonable possibly that the contracting officer would have concluded that protester's proposal was worth paying more than twice the price); *Med Optical*, Comp. Gen. Dec. B-296231.2, 2005 CPD ¶ 169 (even if protester received perfect scores in both areas where it challenged the agency's evaluation, its proposal would still be lower rated technically and substantially higher priced that the awardee's); *Restoration & Closure Servs., LLC*, Comp. Gen. Dec. B-295663.6, 2005 CPD ¶ 92 (protester's evaluated cost was $47 million higher than awardee's, and the protester made no claim that it would have been able to reduce its proposed costs); and *AV-CARD*, Comp. Gen. Dec. B-293775.2, 2004 CPD ¶ 9 (given that protester's proposal was significantly higher priced than the awardee's, in order to prevail in its protest, protester would have had to demonstrate that agency should have rated proposal higher than awardee's proposal in at least one of the non-price evaluation areas to demonstrate prejudice).

When the evaluation errors are minor, prejudice is difficult to prove. See *SWR, Inc.*, Comp. Gen. Dec. B-294835, 2005 CPD ¶ 7 (although agency improperly failed to take into account the relative weights of the evaluation factors in scoring proposals, there was no basis for finding that correctly weighted scoring would have had any significant impact on the award decision); *Wadsworth Bldrs., Inc.*, Comp. Gen. Dec. B-291633, 2003 CPD ¶ 43 (even assuming the agency should have regarded a cited project as relevant and considered it in evaluating the protester's past performance, there was no basis to conclude that this would have resulted in an increase in protester's past performance rating); *Innovative Mgmt., Inc.*, Comp. Gen. Dec. B-291375, 2003 CPD ¶ 11 (no prejudice by the agency's alleged error in not having protester's original transparencies available for use during its oral presentation); *SBC Federal Sys.*, Comp. Gen. Dec. B-283693, 2000 CPD ¶ 5 (although agency may have improperly performed a price/technical tradeoff in violation of the solicitation's evaluation scheme, awardee was not prejudiced because protester's proposal was technically unacceptable); *Conwal, Inc.*, Comp. Gen. Dec. B-279260, 98-1 CPD ¶ 153 (even if protester's allegations concerning the reasonableness of the agency's evaluation of the awardee's cost proposal had merit, the minor amount of an adjustment would not show prejudice); *Advanced Data Concepts, Inc.*, Comp. Gen. Dec. B-277801.4, 98-1 CPD ¶ 145 (although evaluated weaknesses were double-counted under one of two personnel subcriteria, slightly higher score would not have changed overall evaluation); *Northport Handling, Inc.*, Comp. Gen. Dec. B-274615, 97-1 CPD ¶ 3 (no prejudice by any errors that may have occurred during evaluation because even if agency assigned the highest rating to protester's performance as the incumbent, it would have no impact on past performance rating); *CDA Investment Techs., Inc.*, Comp. Gen. Dec. B-272093, 97-1 CPD ¶ 102 (no prejudice by any errors that may have occurred in the evaluation of awardee's proposed use of a subcontractor because the subcontractor's task comprises only a relatively minor portion of the overall effort); *Agriculture Tech. Partners*, Comp. Gen. Dec. B-272978, 96-2 CPD ¶ 226 (even if agency improperly evaluated staff evaluation factor, there were several superior proposals and protester had no reasonable chance for award); and *Executive Court Reporters, Inc.*, Comp. Gen. Dec. B-272981, 96-2 CPD ¶ 227 (the slightly unequal weighting of the three factors in the evaluation did not have a material effect on protester's proposal score and resulting competitive position).

Prejudice will not be found in circumstances where the protester does not demonstrate that it could have won the competition. See *SERAPH, Inc.*, Comp. Gen. Dec. B-297452, 2006 CPD ¶ 18 (no prejudice for alleged improper evaluation of key personnel because proposal was not selected for award due to the agency's evaluation conclusion that the proposal represented a moderate risk under the understanding of work evaluation factor, and not because of lack of experience); *Information Ventures, Inc.*, Comp. Gen. Dec. B-297225, 2005 CPD ¶ 216 (protester made no attempt to show that it could have met the agency's requirement, regardless of the time provided); *United Valve Co.*, Comp. Gen. Dec. B-295879, 2005 CPD ¶ 85 (agency had waived schedule specified in the solicitation for both competitors, and protester did not show competitive prejudice, since its own requested schedule was already longer than schedule granted to awardee, and protester's proposal offered a higher price); *United Enter. & Assocs.*, Comp. Gen. Dec. B-295742, 2005 CPD ¶ 67 (although SBA did not follow applicable certificate of competency procedures, the protester was not prejudiced because SBA agreed with the procuring agency that the 8(a) vendor was not responsible for this requirement, and thus SBA would not have exercised its right to appeal the agency's determination not to contract with that vendor, which was the only action under applicable regulations that SBA could take to contest the procuring agency's determination); *CourtSmart Digital Sys., Inc.*, Comp. Gen. Dec. B-292995.8, 2005 CPD ¶ 28 (protester did not show that it could or would have modified its quotation had it known of the agency's interpretation of the "field-tested" requirement); *Kloppenburg Enters.*, Inc., Comp. Gen. Dec. B-294709, 2004 CPD ¶ 246 (although GAO recognizes that an agency is obligated to ensure that prospective contractors are registered in the CCR database before award, no prejudice where agency made award only after confirming that awardee would promptly register in the CCR database); *DuRette Constr. Co.*, Comp. Gen. Dec. B-294379, September 15, 2004, *Unpub.* (even assuming that the disclosure of protester's suggestion was improper, no prejudice because both the protester's initial and final proposals were based on using the concrete block sizes described in the RFP, not the smaller block sizes that the protester mentioned during discussions); *Cross Match Techs., Inc.*, Comp. Gen. Dec. B-293024.3, 2004 CPD ¶ 193 (solicitation provision that provides for incorporating into a BPA additional, unevaluated items, in quantities for which no estimates are provided in the solicitation, and at prices that are subsequently to be negotiated was improper, but record showed that the amount involved could have accounted for no more than small portion of awardee's overall price advantage); *Frasca Int'l, Inc.*, Comp. Gen. Dec. B-293299, 2004 CPD ¶ 38 (to the extent that protester was unable to compete, it was due to breakdown of teaming discussions caused by protester's untimely proposals submission, not by bundling); *Bath Iron Works Corp.*, Comp. Gen. Dec. B-290470, 2002 CPD ¶ 133 (agency's denial of protester's use of a decommissioned destroyer for testing while allowing the awardee to use such constituted unequal treatment but was not prejudicial because record showed protester would have obtained no material technical benefit or evaluation advantage had it been allowed to use of the destroyer); *Si-Nor, Inc.*, Comp. Gen. Dec. B-286910, 2001 CPD ¶ 1 (small disadvantaged business not prejudiced by agency's failure to apply 10% SDB evaluation preference provided for in the solicitation where the awardee was an SDB so the preference would not apply in any case and there was no basis to conclude that protester inflated its bid price in reliance on application of the preference); *Charleston Marine Containers, Inc.*, Comp. Gen. Dec. B-283393, 99-2 CPD ¶ 84 (although agency failed to hold discussions, it was apparent from the record that the protester could not have improved its proposal enough through discussions to be in competition for award); *Motorola, Inc.*, Comp. Gen. Dec. B-277862, 97-2 CPD ¶ 155 (protester not prejudiced by an agency decision to ignore a requirement in the statement of work); *Brown & Root, Inc.*, Comp. Gen. Dec. B-270505.2, 96-2 CPD ¶ 143 (no evidence that had the protester been aware of the waiver of the security clearance requirement, it would have submitted a different proposal); and *Safety-Kleen Corp.*, Comp. Gen. Dec. B-274176, 96-2 CPD ¶ 200 (improper waiver of provision requiring a certificate of environmental impairment liability insurance did not prejudice protester because it did not assert that it would have refrained from providing the insurance coverage had it known it was unnecessary).

Prejudice cannot be proved if the protester is ineligible for award. See *Wyeth-Lederle Vaccines & Pediatrics*, Comp. Gen. Dec. B-274490, 96-2 CPD ¶ 229, where the protester was found to have suffered no prejudice as a result of the agency's inclusion of the single-award clause in the solicitation because even if the single-award clause were removed, the protester would still be ineligible for award because it did not possess the required license.

Prejudice will not be found where the agency accepts an expired offer if no changes are permitted to be made to the proposal, *Scot, Inc.*, Comp. Gen. Dec. B-295569, 2005 CPD ¶ 66.

H. Remedies

The GAO can make recommendations to the agency but does not have the authority to direct the agency to take action or to refrain from doing so. Only in rare cases, however, do agencies fail to follow these recommendations. The GAO is required to report annually to Congress all cases in which procuring agencies do not fully implement the GAO's recommendations, 31 U.S.C. § 3554(e)(2). There are only a few instances where the GAO's recommendations were not fully implemented by the respective agencies. See *Mission Critical Solutions*, Comp. Gen. Dec. B-401057, 2009 CPD ¶ 93; *Symplicity Corp.*, Comp. Gen. Dec. B-291902, 2003 CPD ¶ 89; *Consolidated Eng'g Servs., Inc.*, Comp. Gen. Dec. B-291345, 2002 CPD ¶ 220; *Rockwell Elec. Commerce Corp.*, Comp. Gen. Dec. B-286201.6, 2001 CPD ¶ 162, *modified*, 2002 CPD ¶ 47; *Aberdeen Tech. Servs., Inc.*, Comp. Gen. Dec.

B-283727.2, 2000 CPD ¶ 46. See GAO Bid Protest Annual Reports to the Congress (Fiscal Years 2000-2008) available at *www.gao.gov/*.

1. *Nonmonetary Remedies*

The GAO can recommend a variety of nonmonetary remedies. 31 U.S.C. § 3554(b)(1) states:

> If the Comptroller General determines that the solicitation, proposed award, or award does not comply with a statute or regulation, the Comptroller General shall recommend that the Federal agency —
>
> (A) refrain from exercising any of his options under the contract;
>
> (B) recompete the contract immediately;
>
> (C) issue a new solicitation;
>
> (D) terminate the contract;
>
> (E) award a contract consistent with the requirements of such statute and regulation;
>
> (F) implement any combination of recommendations under clauses (A), (B), (C), (D), and (E); or
>
> (G) implement such other recommendations as the Comptroller General determines to be necessary in order to promote compliance with procurement statutes and regulations.

If award has already been made, the GAO, in making recommendations, is prohibited from considering any cost or disruption resulting from the termination, recompetition, or reaward of the contract, 31 U.S.C. § 3554(b)(2). In *Price Waterhouse*, Comp. Gen. Dec. B-220049, 86-1 CPD ¶ 333, an agency requested reconsideration of a decision that sustained a protest and recommended possible contract termination. The GAO held that its decision would not be reconsidered based upon the estimated costs of termination where the agency proceeded with performance of the contract upon a finding that to do so would be in the best interests of the government. See also *Spherix, Inc.*, Comp. Gen. Dec. B-294572, 2005 CPD ¶ 3; *Dep't of the Navy*, Comp. Gen. Dec. B-274944.4, 97-2 CPD ¶ 16; and *World-Wide Sec. Serv., Inc.*, 66 Comp. Gen. 195 (B-224277) 87-1 CPD ¶35.

The GAO may recommend that the agency amend the solicitation, *FC Business Sys., Inc.*, Comp. Gen. Dec. B-278730, 98-2 CPD ¶ 9 (where RFP did not provide a common definition of a staff year, agency should amend solicitation to explain how it will take into consideration the differences in the number of hours per staff year proposed by the offerors or otherwise establish a uniform basis for preparing and evaluating offers); *Hoescht Marion Roussel, Inc.*, Comp. Gen. Dec. B-279073, 98-1 CPD ¶ 127 (where solicitation fails to realistically state agency's estimated requirements for various drug dosages, agency should amend RFP); *Comark Fed. Sys.*, Comp. Gen. Dec. B-278343.2, 98-1 CPD ¶ 34 (where agency failed to advise vendors of the basis for the source selection, agency should amend RFQ to advise firms holding basic purchasing agreements of agency's needs, including whether agency is willing to conduct a cost/technical tradeoff).

The GAO may recommend that the agency make a new competitive range determination, *Trifax Corp.*, Comp. Gen. Dec. B-279561, 98-2 CPD ¶ 24. The GAO may also recommend the reinstatement of a wrongfully disqualified offeror to the competitive range, *KPMG Peat Marwick*, Comp. Gen. Dec. B-251902.3, 93-2 CPD ¶ 272.

The agency may recommend that the agency conduct new oral presentations, *e-LYNXX Corp.*, Comp. Gen. Dec. B-292761, 2003 CPD ¶ 219. See also *Kathpal Techs., Inc.*, Comp. Gen. Dec. B-283137.3, 2000 CPD ¶ 6 (GAO recommended agency either afford all technically acceptable offerors an opportunity to make oral presentations or amend the solicitation to properly inform offerors that oral presentations would not be considered as part of offerors' proposals and obtain revised proposals).

A common remedy in negotiated procurement is to reopen discussions, request new revised proposals and reevaluate proposals, *Haworth, Inc.*, Comp. Gen. Dec. B-297077, 2005 CPD ¶ 215 (agency erroneously concluded that awardee's quotation met the stated requirements and erroneously downgraded protester's under the "environmental factors" evaluation factor); *Technical Support Servs., Inc.*, Comp. Gen. Dec. B-279665.2, 98-2 CPD ¶ 26 (agency disregarded the solicitation's stated best value evaluation scheme); *Century Envtl. Hygiene, Inc.*, Comp. Gen. Dec. B-279378, 98-1 CPD ¶ 164 (evaluation of protester's proposal was inconsistent with the solicitation evaluation criteria); *Biosperics, Inc.*, Comp. Gen. Dec. B-278278, 98-1 CPD ¶ 161 (agency failed to inform firm that its cost/pricing was considered unrealistically low but instead twice encouraged the firm to reduce its proposed price); *Hughes STX Corp.*, Comp. Gen. Dec. B-278466, 98-1 CPD ¶ 52 (cost evaluation was unreasonable and discussions with the protester concerning its proposed direct labor rates were not meaningful); *CitiWest Properties, Inc.*, Comp. Gen. Dec. B-274689.4, 98-1 CPD ¶ 3 (agency failed to conduct meaningful discussions); *Gardiner, Kamya & Assocs.*, Comp. Gen. Dec. B-258915.2, 95-1 CPD ¶ 193 (agency unreasonably downgraded protester's proposal); *National Med. Staffing, Inc.*, Comp. Gen. Dec. B-259402, 95-1 CPD ¶ 163 (agency did not conduct meaningful and equal discussions).

In some cases the GAO recommends that discussions be reopened but that they be of limited nature, *Boeing Sikorsky Aircraft Support*, Comp. Gen. Dec. B-277263.2, 97-2 CPD ¶ 91. There, the GAO recommended that the agency reopen negotiations regarding costs and fees with offerors in the competitive range and allow them to submit revised cost proposals.

In some instances the GAO may recommend termination of the task order or contract. See *Tarheel Specialties, Inc.*, Comp. Gen. Dec. B-298197, 2006 CPD ¶ 140 (recommended that the agency terminate the task order, assess its requirements, and determine whether it was appropriate to obtain these services under the FSS program, and then either resolicit under the FSS program or conduct full and open competition).

In rare cases the GAO recommends that award be made to the protester. See *Spectrum Security Servs., Inc.*, Comp. Gen. Dec. B-297320.2, 2005 CPD ¶ 227 (recommended that contract be terminated and that the agency consider award to protester or the other small business offeror); *Dismas Charities, Inc.*, Comp. Gen. Dec. B-292091, 2003 CPD ¶ 125 (in the event proposal is selected for award, the agency should terminate awardee's contract, and award a contract to the protester); *R. & W. Flammann GmbH*, Comp. Gen. Dec. B-278486, 98-1 CPD ¶ 40 (where agency improperly canceled procurement, GAO recommended that award be made to protester on the basis of its low offer); *For Your Information, Inc.*, Comp. Gen. Dec. B-278352, 97-2 CPD ¶ 164 (where agency had improperly awarded contract to technically unacceptable offeror, GAO recommended that the agency terminate the contract and make award to the protester, which was the only offeror that submitted a technically acceptable proposal); *Tri-State Gov't Servs., Inc.*, Comp. Gen. Dec. B-277315.2, 97-2 CPD ¶ 143 (where agency improperly accepted nonconforming offer, GAO recommended that contract be terminated and award be made to protester); *Aetna Gov't Health Plans, Inc.*, Comp. Gen. Dec. B-254397, 95-2 CPD ¶ 129 (where agency failed to recognize the significance of the organizational conflict of interest, GAO recommended that the agency terminate the existing contract and make award to protester); and *L&E Assocs.*, Comp. Gen. Dec. B-258808.4, 95-1 CPD ¶ 288 (where the record showed that the agency considered two technical proposals to be essentially equal, the GAO recommended that award be made to the protester who offered a lower price and whose proposal had been improperly rejected for allegedly not providing firm labor rates).

2. Monetary Remedies

The monetary remedies that protesters have been able to recover are the costs of pursuing the protest, including attorneys' fees and the costs of preparing the bid or proposal. Recovery of anticipated profits has been uniformly denied, *Baker Support Servs., Inc.*, Comp. Gen. Dec. B-256192.3, 95-1 CPD ¶ 75.

When the GAO recommends payment of protest costs and/or bid or proposal preparation costs, it leaves it to the parties to agree on the amount. The protester is required to submit to the procuring agency a detailed and certified claim within 60 calendar days after receipt of the GAO recommendation that the costs be paid, 4 C.F.R. § 21.8(f)(1). The protester seeking to recover the costs of pursuing its protest must submit sufficient evidence to support its monetary claim, *Consolidated Bell, Inc.*, 70 Comp. Gen. 358 (B-220425.4), 91-1 CPD ¶ 325. In *Wind Gap Knitwear, Inc.*, Comp. Gen. Dec. B-251411.2, 95-2 CPD ¶ 94, the GAO denied a claim for costs where the protester failed to file an adequately detailed claim with the agency within 60 days after the protester received a copy of the decision awarding protest costs. See also *Custom Production Mfg., Inc.*, Comp. Gen. Dec. B-235431.8, 95-2 CPD ¶ 40 (protester submitted its claim four and a half years after it was entitled to such costs).

The procuring agency must decide the claim "as soon as practicable after the claim is filed" and notify the GAO within 60 calendar days after the GAO decision recommending the payment of costs, 4 C.F.R. § 21.8(f)(3). If the parties cannot reach agreement on the amount within a reasonable time, the protester may refer the matter to the GAO for decision, 4 C.F.R. § 21.8(f)(2). A protester must diligently pursue a claim for protest costs, *Aalco Forwarding, Inc. — Costs*, Comp. Gen. Dec. B-277241.30, 99-2 CPD ¶ 36. Failure to timely pursue a claim may result in forfeiture of the right to recover protest costs, *Holloway & Co., PLLC — Costs*, Comp. Gen. Dec. B-311342.5, 2009 CPD ¶ 146 (request for recommendation for reimbursement of protest costs not diligently pursued where protester delayed filing at GAO until more than 8 months had passed without receiving a response from the contracting agency); *L-3 Communications Corp., Ocean Systems Div. — Costs*, Comp. Gen. Dec. B-281784.5, 2004 CPD ¶ 40 (although protester filed its claim with the agency in a timely fashion, the protester failed to continue pursuit of the claim for an extended period of time, nearly 3 years). The GAO will not ordinarily recommend the amount of costs to be paid for pursuing the claim, *Princeton Gamma-Tech, Inc.*, 68 Comp. Gen. 401 (B-228052.5), 89-1 CPD ¶ 401, except where the parties cannot agree on the amount, 4 C.F.R. § 21.8(f)(2). See *ViON Corp.*, Comp. Gen. Dec. B-256363.3, 95-1 CPD ¶ 219, where the GAO determined the amount of protest costs because the protester and the agency were unable to reach agreement. The GAO, if determining the amount of costs to be paid, may also recommend that the agency pay the costs of pursuing this claim for costs before the GAO, 4 C.F.R. § 21.8(f)(2).

a. Bid or Proposal Preparation Costs

31 U.S.C. § 3554(c)(1)(B) permits the GAO to award the costs of preparing a bid or proposal to a successful protester. However, bid or proposal costs are not awarded merely if a protest is sustained; rather, recovery is appropriate only when a protester is unreasonably excluded from the competition and no other remedy is appropriate. This is often the case when performance of the contract is complete or when it is impractical to terminate the contract because performance has reached its latter stages. In *Data Integrators, Inc.*, Comp. Gen. Dec. B-310928, 2008 CPD ¶ 27, GAO recommended that the protester be reimbursed its costs of quotation preparation and of filing and pursuing the protest, including reasonable attorneys' fees, because delivery has been completed. See also *Mechanical Contractors, S.A.*, Comp. Gen. Dec. B-277916.2, 98-1 CPD ¶ 68 (protester entitled to proposal preparation costs because 25% of the work had already been completed and the agency had determined that urgent and compelling circumstances existed and it would take several additional weeks to conduct discussions and reevaluate proposals); *Aerospace Design & Fabrication, Inc.*, Comp. Gen. Dec. B-278896.2, 98-1 CPD ¶ 139

(protester entitled to its proposal preparation costs because unique circumstances created a situation where reevaluation and reconsideration of the selection decision could not return the parties to their respective positions prior to the agency error); *Jack Faucett Assocs., Inc.*, Comp. Gen. Dec. B-279347, 98-1 CPD ¶ 155 (protester entitled to quotation preparation costs because the services at issue had been substantially performed); *International Data Sys.*, Comp. Gen. Dec. B-277385, 97-2 CPD ¶ 96 (protester entitled to proposal preparation costs as well as the reasonable costs of filing and pursing protest where contract for personal computers fully performed); *Adelaide Blomfield Mgmt. Co.*, Comp. Gen. Dec. B-253128.4, 95-1 CPD ¶ 7 (protester entitled to its bid preparation and protest costs because the GAO was unable to recommend termination of the awarded lease contract when the lease did not contain a termination for convenience clause); and *Bush Painting, Inc.*, Comp. Gen. Dec. B-239904.3, 91-2 CPD ¶ 159 (protester entitled to its bid preparation costs because it was impracticable to terminate performance of a contract that was 90% complete).

The GAO will not award proposal costs if the protester would not have been in line for the award, *Temps & Co.*, 65 Comp. Gen. 819 (B-221846.2), 86-2 CPD ¶ 236. But see *EHE Nat'l Health Servs.*, Inc., 65 Comp. Gen. 1 (B-219361.2), 85-2 CPD ¶ 362, where the GAO found that a protester had a substantial chance of receiving the award when the protester was one of three firms in line for award.

If a solicitation is canceled for valid reasons not related to the protest, no bid or proposal preparation costs will be awarded. In *Orange Personnel Servs., Inc.*, Comp. Gen. Dec. B-256164.2, 95-1 CPD ¶ 26, cancellation precluded the award of bid preparation costs although the protester was in line for award. See also *Quan-Tech, Inc.*, Comp. Gen. Dec. B-278380.3, 98-1 CPD ¶ 165 (no proposal preparation costs awarded where agency reasonably canceled procurement in order to take corrective action); and *Fischer & Porter Co.*, Comp. Gen. Dec. B-227941.3, 88-1 CPD ¶ 327 (no bid preparation costs awarded where legislation passed subsequent to a GAO decision sustaining a protest had the effect of rendering moot the decision).

No bid or proposals costs will be awarded if the agency takes corrective action in response to the protest. GAO has reached this conclusion because its regulation on remedies, 4 C.F.R. § 21.8(e), only provides for the award of protests costs in discussing corrective action. See *Mapp Bldg. Servs. — Costs*, Comp. Gen. Dec. B-289160.2, 2002 CPD ¶ 60 ("[O]ur regulations do not provide for recovery of such costs where an agency has taken corrective action"); *Moon Eng'g Co. — Request for Declaration of Entitlement to Costs*, Comp. Gen. Dec. B-247053.6, 92-2 CPD ¶ 129. See also *Yardney Tech. Prods., Inc. — Costs*, Comp. Gen. Dec. B-297648.3, 2006 CPD ¶ 60 (fact that corrective action will mean effort on original proposal was "wasted" not relevant when regulations don't provide for such costs).

A protester is generally not entitled to the award of bid or proposal preparation costs if it will have an opportunity to compete for award of the contract under a resolicitation conducted as a result of its protest, *Lockheed Martin Corp. — Costs*, Comp. Gen. Dec. B-295402.2, 2005 CPD ¶ 192; *KIME Enters.*, Comp. Gen. Dec. B-241996.5, 91-2 CPD ¶ 523; *Koehring Co.*, 65 Comp. Gen. 268 (B-219667.2), 86-1 CPD ¶ 135. However, the GAO may recommend reimbursement where changed circumstances render no longer relevant a proposal that was previously submitted. In *COBRO Corp.*, Comp. Gen. Dec. B-287578.2, 2001 CPD ¶ 181, the GAO recommended the award of bid and proposal costs where the protester had expended substantial cost and effort on a proposal which was likely to have virtually no value under a recompetition. The GAO stated that the reissued solicitation was likely to represent a requirement that was fundamentally different from that which was presented under the defective solicitation. See also *Rockwell Elec. Commerce Corp. — Modification of Recommendation,* Comp. Gen. Dec. B-286201.8, 2002 CPD ¶ 47, where the GAO recommended the reimbursement of Rockwell's proposal preparation costs since the agency stated it would not follow GAO's recommendation to cure the improprieties in the competition. GAO held that since the agency would not take appropriate corrective action, Rockwell would not have a meaningful opportunity to compete based on the proposal submitted. See *Aberdeen Tech. Servs. — Modification of Recommendation*, Comp. Gen. Dec. B-283727.3, 2001 CPD ¶ 146, where the GAO modified its recommendation to include reimbursement of protester's costs of preparing its proposal where the agency canceled the solicitation and acknowledged it would be unable to issue a new solicitation for "some 2 years" after the GAO's original decision and recommendation.

The GAO has awarded bid preparation costs where a protester bid was improperly rejected even though the agency's subsequent review of the bid determined that it was not eligible for award, *Industrial Storage Equipment-Pacific*, Comp. Gen. Dec. B-228123.2, 88-1 CPD ¶ 328.

b. Protest Costs

The GAO has the authority to grant protest costs, including reasonable attorneys' fees, 31 U.S.C. § 3554(c). Protest costs can be granted even when other corrective action is taken in a sustained protest, *Norse Inc.*, Comp. Gen. Dec. B-233534, 89-1 CPD ¶ 293 (protester was both reinstated into the contract competition and granted protest costs).

The GAO has consistently rejected assertions that its cost reimbursement authority under CICA is properly applied to litigation costs incurred in connection with matters brought in another forum, since the GAO does not view those costs as having been incurred in filing and pursuing a protest with GAO, *Sodexho Mgmt., Inc. — Costs*, Comp. Gen. Dec. B-289605.3, 2003 CPD ¶ 136 (GAO statutory authority to recommend reimbursement of costs does not extend to the costs associated with Sodexho's administrative appeal of the initial A-76 cost comparison). See also *Rice Servs., Ltd. — Costs*, Comp. Gen. Dec. B-284997.2, 2001 CPD ¶ 88; *Diverco, Inc., — Claim for Costs*, Comp. Gen. Dec. B-240639.5, 92-1 CPD ¶ 460.

(1) GROUNDS FOR PROTEST COSTS

Generally, no protest costs will be granted if the GAO has not made a decision on the merits, *Signal Corp.*, 69 Comp. Gen. 659 (B-240450), 90-2 CPD ¶ 116; *Moody Bros.*, Comp. Gen. Dec. B-237278.3, 89-2 CPD ¶ 590. For instance, if an agency decides to cancel a solicitation, the protester will not be entitled to recover the costs of filing and pursuing its protest, *H. Watt & Scott Gen. Contractors, Inc.*, Comp. Gen. Dec. B-257776.3, 95-1 CPD ¶ 183 (cancellation based on inability to proceed with work due to weather conditions); *Digital Sys. Group, Inc.*, Comp. Gen. Dec. B-257835.2, 95-1 CPD ¶ 173 (agency did not receive any proposals that satisfied requirement); *Red River Serv. Corp.*, Comp. Gen. Dec. B-259462.2, 95-2 CPD ¶ 106 (bid acceptance period had expired).

As a general rule, GAO recommends that a successful protester be reimbursed costs incurred with respect to all issues pursued, not merely those upon which it prevails, *AAR Aircraft Servs. — Costs*, Comp. Gen. Dec. B-291670.6, 2003 CPD ¶ 100; *Main Bldg. Maint., Inc.*, Comp. Gen. Dec. B-260945.6, 97-2 CPD ¶ 163. However, in appropriate cases the GAO will limit its recommendation for the award of protest costs where a part of their costs is allocable to a protest issue that is so clearly severable as to essentially constitute a separate protest, *Interface Floorings Sys., Inc. — Claim for Attorney Fees*, Comp. Gen. Dec. B-225439.5, 87-2 CPD ¶ 106. See *KAES Enters., LLC—Protest & Costs*, Comp. Gen. Dec. B-402050.4, 2010 CPD ¶ 49 (costs limited to specific ground on which protester was likely to prevail — agency's failure to consider price when excluding the firm's proposal from the competitive range); *Panacea Consulting, Inc. — Costs*, Comp. Gen. Dec. B-299307.3, 2007 CPD ¶ 133 (recovery of protest costs is limited to those issues upon which protester prevailed). In determining whether protest issues are so clearly severable as to essentially constitute separate protests, GAO considers, among other things, the extent to which the claims are interrelated or intertwined — i.e., the successful and unsuccessful claims share a common core set of facts, are based on related legal theories, or are otherwise not readily severable, *Sodexho Mgmt., Inc. — Costs*, Comp. Gen. Dec. B-289605.3, 2003 CPD ¶ 136. In *BAE Tech. Servs., Inc. — Costs*, Comp. Gen. Dec. B-296699.3, 2006 CPD ¶ 122, the GAO held that the protester was entitled to recover costs attributed to almost all of the issues raised as they are "largely intertwined parts of [its] basic objection that the [agency] misevaluated proposals and treated offerors unequally." See also *Burns & Roe Servs. Corp. — Costs*, Comp. Gen. Dec. B-310828.2, 2008 CPD ¶ 81, holding that the misevaluation of proposals, failure to hold meaningful discussions and treating offerors unequally involve the same core facts. In *T Square Logistics Servs. Corp., Inc. — Costs*, Comp. Gen. Dec. B-297790.6, 2007 CPD ¶ 108, the Air Force argued that T Square should recover only those reasonable costs relating to the protest issue that the GAO attorney identified as a "probable sustain" during the outcome prediction ADR, which was the failure to conduct meaningful discussions. The Air Force argued that because T Square did not attempt to separate the costs relating to this issue from the other issues it raised, all of its claimed costs should be disallowed. GAO disagreed, finding that all of T Square's arguments pertained to the reasonableness of the agency's evaluation of proposals under the past performance factor and the Air Force's failure to conduct meaningful discussions based on its evaluation, such that the arguments were interconnected and based on common factual underpinnings. See also *Blue Rock Structures, Inc. — Costs*, Comp. Gen. Dec. B-293134.2, 2005 CPD ¶ 190 (all of protester's arguments pertained to the reasonableness of the agency's evaluation of proposals and source selection determination). But see *Al Qabandi United Co. — Costs*, Comp. Gen. Dec. B-310600.3, 2008 CPD ¶ 112, recommending that the protester be reimbursed the reasonable costs of filing and pursuing its protest only as related to its challenge to the price evaluation. The protester's challenge to the affirmative determination of the awardee's responsibility and its assertion that the Army improperly relaxed performance requirements after award did not involve the same set of core facts as did its clearly meritorious challenge to the price evaluation. See also *Honeywell Tech. Solutions, Inc. — Costs*, Comp. Gen. Dec. B-296860.3, 2005 CPD ¶ 226, where the GAO did not recommend reimbursement of costs associated with the unresolved issues, which were severable from the organizational conflict of interest issue addressed during ADR.

(2) CORRECTIVE ACTION

Where the contracting agency decides to take corrective action in response to a protest, the GAO may recommend that the protester be reimbursed the reasonable costs of filing and pursuing the protest, including attorneys' fees and consultant and expert witness fees, 4 C.F.R. § 21.8(e). To be eligible for protest costs when the agency takes corrective action, the protester is required to file with the GAO within 15 calendar days after being advised of the procuring agency's decision to take corrective action, 4 C.F.R. § 21.8(e). The protester must also file a copy with the procuring agency, which then has 15 calendar days to respond. A protester will not be reimbursed its costs in every case in which an agency decides to take corrective action; rather, a protester should be reimbursed its costs where an agency *unduly delayed* its decision to take corrective action in the face of a *clearly meritorious* protest, *Griner's-A-One Pipeline Servs., Inc. — Entitlement to Costs*, Comp. Gen. Dec. B-255078.3, 94-2 CPD ¶ 41.

If the procuring agency unduly delays taking corrective action in a clearly meritorious protest, 4 C.F.R. § 21.8(e) provides that the GAO may recommend payment of protest costs. See *Core Tech Int'l Corp. — Costs*, Comp. Gen. Dec. B-400047.2, 2009 CPD ¶ 59 (corrective action occurring only after the agency report and the ADR is unduly delayed); *World Communications Center, Inc. — Costs*, Comp. Gen. Dec. B-310398.4, 2008 CPD ¶ 19 (agency did not terminate the award and cancel the solicitation until after the agency had produced its report, the protester had filed its comments on the report, and the GAO attorney assigned to the protest had requested additional information); *Salvation Army Community Corrections Program*, Comp. Gen. Dec. B-298866.3, 2007 CPD ¶ 165 (agency did not elect to take corrective action until after the protester filed its comments on the agency report and the GAO informed the parties that a hearing would be conducted); *EBSCO Publishing, Inc. —*

Costs, Comp. Gen. Dec. B-298918.4, 2007 CPD ¶ 90 (agency did not take corrective action until after the filing of the agency report); *Johnson Controls World Servs., Inc. — Costs*, Comp. Gen. Dec. B-295529.4, 2005 CPD ¶ 162 (issues raised in the initial protest filing clearly identified deficiencies in the agency's determination that in-house performance would be more economical than contracting out, the agency admitted that it did not investigate the protest allegations, and the agency withheld relevant protest documents until more than 70 days after the initial protest filing); *Miller Elevator Serv. Co. — Costs*, Comp. Gen. Dec. B-284870.3, 2000 CPD ¶ 126 (GSA did not propose corrective action until well after the agency had submitted its report and the protester had incurred the time and expense necessary to respond to it); *The Real Estate Center — Costs*, Comp. Gen. Dec. B-274081.7, 98-1 CPD ¶ 105 (Veterans Administration took three months and two weeks to acknowledge evaluation decision was insupportable and convene new evaluation panel); *Pemco Aeroplex, Inc.*, Comp. Gen. Dec. B-275587.5, 97-2 CPD ¶ 102 (agency allow four months to pass without revising the solicitation); *Chant Eng'g Co.*, Comp. Gen. Dec. B-274871.2, 97-2 CPD ¶ 58; *Custom Printing Co.*, Comp. Gen. Dec. B-275798.3, 97-2 CPD ¶ 9 (agency did not promptly or adequately investigate protest grounds and took corrective action only 21 days before GAO decision was due); *Multi-Bloc, Inc.*, Comp. Gen. Dec. B-259182.2, 95-1 CPD ¶ 217; *Tucson Mobilephone, Inc.*, Comp. Gen. Dec. B-252659.3, 94-1 CPD ¶ 12 (agency failed to promptly or adequately investigate clearly meritorious protest but only took corrective action when the hearing testimony showed the bases for the sole source awards were unfounded); and *Commercial Energies, Inc.*, 71 Comp. Gen. 97 (B-243718.2), 91-2 CPD ¶ 499 (agency took five months to perform the promised corrective action).

For cases finding that the protester was not entitled to award of costs of filing and pursuing its protest because the agency took prompt corrective action, see *Intercontinental Constr. Contracting, Inc. — Costs*, Comp. Gen. Dec. B-400729.3, 2009 CPD ¶ 44 (once the protester articulated its challenge, the agency promptly determined its evaluation was flawed and took corrective action within 18 days after the protester submitted its comments on the agency report); *Security Consultants Group, Inc. — Costs*, Comp. Gen. Dec. B-293344.6, 2004 CPD ¶ 228 (agency took prompt corrective action in cancelling the solicitation and notifying GAO of intent to reinstate protester's contract prior to the due date for the agency's report); *PTI Supply Co.*, Comp. Gen. Dec. B-276559.3, 97-2 CPD ¶ 11 (agency took responsive corrective action the same day); *Carlson Wagonlit Travel*, Comp. Gen. Dec. B-266337.3, 96-2 CPD ¶ 99 (38 working days before corrective agency action not unreasonable where four separate protests were filed against the agency); *Bionetics Corp.*, Comp. Gen. Dec. B-270323.3, 96-2 CPD ¶ 70 (where agency took prompt corrective action and remaining changes were due to base closure); *Veda Inc.*, Comp. Gen. Dec. B-265809.2, 96-2 CPD ¶ 27 (delay of almost five months not unreasonable); *Atlas Powder Int'l, Ltd.*, 73 Comp. Gen. 122 (B-254408.5), 94-1 CPD ¶ 278 (even though corrective action not taken for nearly two months, delay not unreasonable where corrective action taken within eight working days of telephone conference between the parties); *Locus Sys., Inc.*, 71 Comp. Gen. 243 (B-241441.5), 92-1 CPD

¶ 177 (agency promptly investigated the protester's allegations and subsequently resolicited the requirement after determining that the protester was correct); *Metters Indus., Inc.*, Comp. Gen. Dec. B-240391.5, 91-2 CPD ¶ 535 (agency promptly initiated an investigation and, in conjunction with the preparation of a lawsuit filed by another offeror during the investigation, discovered potential regulatory and statutory violations, which led to the cancellation of the solicitation two days after the agency report was due to be filed); and *Oklahoma Indian Corp.*, 70 Comp. Gen. 558 (B-243785.2), 91-1 CPD ¶ 558 (agency took corrective action within two weeks of protest being filed).

Generally the GAO will consider corrective action to be prompt if it is taken before the due date for the agency report responding to the protest. See *Apptis Inc. — Costs*, Comp. Gen. Dec. B- 402146.3, 2010 CPD ¶ 123 (agency's corrective action took place prior to the submission of its supplemental agency report); *AGFA HealthCare Corp. — Costs*, Comp. Gen. Dec. B-400733.6, 2009 CPD ¶ 90 (agency took corrective action on the date comments were due on the second supplemental); *Coronet Mach. Corp — Costs*, Comp. Gen. Dec. B-400197.2, 2008 CPD ¶ 213 (Army initiated corrective action 10 days prior to the report due date); *Alaska Structures, Inc. — Costs*, Comp. Gen. Dec. B-298156.2, 2006 CPD ¶ 109 (decision to cancel the solicitation occurred prior to the date set for the filing of the agency's report); *DuraMed Enters., Inc.*, Comp. Gen. Dec. B-271793.2, 96-2 CPD ¶ 135 (corrective action taken on day agency report was due); and *Boaz Towing, Inc.*, Comp. Gen. Dec. B-257883.2, 95-1 CPD ¶ 109 (initiation of corrective action took place approximately when agency report was due).

Even if corrective action is unduly delayed, GAO will not recommend the payment of protest costs unless the protest was clearly meritorious, i.e., not a close question, *J.F. Taylor, Inc. — Entitlement to Costs*, Comp. Gen. Dec. B-266039.3, 96-2 CPD ¶ 5; *Baxter Healthcare Corp. — Entitlement to Costs*, Comp. Gen. Dec. B-259811.3, 95-2 CPD ¶ 174; *GVC Cos. — Entitlement to Costs*, Comp. Gen. Dec. B-254670.4, 94-1 CPD ¶ 292. A protest is "clearly meritorious" when a reasonable agency inquiry into the protester's allegations would show facts disclosing the absence of a defensible legal position, *Yardney Tech. Prods., Inc.*, Comp. Gen. Dec. B-297648.3, 2006 CPD ¶ 65; *Dep't of the Army — Recons.*, Comp. Gen. Dec. B-270860.5, 96-2 CPD ¶ 23. The mere fact that an agency decides to take corrective action does not establish that a statute or regulation clearly has been violated, *Sun Chemical Corp. — Cost*, Comp. Gen. Dec. B-288466.4, 2001 CPD ¶ 199; *Spar Applied Sys. — Declaration of Entitlement*, Comp. Gen. Dec. B-276030.2, 97-2 CPD ¶ 70. See *Triple Canopy, Inc. — Costs*, Comp. Gen. Dec. B-310566.9, 2009 CPD ¶ 62 (while acknowledging that the issues presented were "close questions, protests not clearly meritorious). In *Yardney* the GAO found that which party's position was correct was not apparent from the original record. Rather, in order to reach a decision on the matter, GAO would have required, at a minimum, a supplemental report from the agency and comments on that report by Yardney. Following this further development of the record, GAO stated that it would have had to conduct substantial further analysis of the parties' positions. In such cases, GAO does not consider the protest grounds to be clearly meritorious.

Cases where the GAO found the protest to be not clearly meritorious include *AGFA HealthCare Corp. — Costs*, Comp. Gen. Dec. B-400733.6, 2009 CPD ¶ 90 (although agency's failure to evaluate alleged noncompliance with mandatory standards in RFP was a serious issue, GAO did not agree that the issue was so clearly meritorious as to reveal the absence of any defensible legal position); *New England Radiation Therapy Mgmt, Servs., Inc. — Costs*, Comp. Gen. Dec. B-297397.3, 2006 CPD ¶ 30 (whether or not solicitation was ambiguous and whether awardee's price was or was not in accordance with the RFP schedule was not apparent from the record); *LENS, JV — Costs*, Comp,. Gen. Dec. B-295952.4, 2006 CPD ¶ 9 (resolution of the protest required further record development such as a hearing to complete and clarify the record); *Sandi-Sterling Consortium — Costs*, Comp. Gen. Dec. B-296246.2, 2005 CPD ¶ 173 (merits of protest would have required development of the protest record — including a complete agency report and the protester' comments on the report — and GAO would have had to conduct substantial further legal analysis); *East Penn Mfg. Co. — Costs*, Comp. Gen. Dec. B-291503.4, 2003 CPD ¶ 83 (decision would have required further steps to complete and clarify the record); and *J.F. Taylor, Inc.*, Comp. Gen. Dec. B-266039.3, 96-2 CPD ¶ 5 (decision would have required interpretation of the solicitation's requirements and the awardee's compliance with the requirements).

Clearly meritorious protests include *Commercial Design Group, Inc. — Costs*, Comp. Gen. Dec. B-400923.3, 2009 CPD ¶ 126 (had the agency conducted a reasonable review of the allegations in initial protest, it would have discovered that awardee's proposed computer-aided design manager's resume did not provide a sufficient basis to conclude that he met RFP requirements); *ManTech Sys. Eng'g Corp.*, Comp. Gen. Dec. B-401542.6, 2010 CPD ¶ 14 (notwithstanding clear misevaluation of cost proposal, agency elected to defend protest); *Pond Sec. Group Italia JV — Costs*, Comp. Gen. Dec. B-400149.2, 2009 CPD ¶ 61 (alleged defect affected protester's ability to compete at the time the protest was pending); *Salvation Army Community Corrections Program — Costs*, Comp. Gen. Dec. B-298866.3, 2007 CPD ¶ 165 (no reasonable explanation in the record for the agency's evaluation in a number of areas); *Shindong-A Express Tour Co., Ltd. — Costs*, Comp. Gen. Dec. B-292459.3, 2004 CPD ¶ 75 (initial protest provided ample information to permit the Army to conclude that the awardee's proposal was unacceptable under the solicitation's stated evaluation scheme); *Martin Elecs., Inc. — Costs*, Comp. Gen. Dec. B-291732.2, 2003 CPD ¶ 84 (agency's selection of one awardee unreasonable and unsupported and agency's evaluation of another awardee's proposal inconsistent with the solicitation's stated evaluation criteria); *Georgia Power Co.*, Comp. Gen. Dec. B-289211.5, 2002 CPD ¶ 81 (agency did not reasonably evaluate whether awardee's past performance was for services similar in size, magnitude, and complexity to the solicitation requirement); *PADCO, Inc. — Costs*, Comp. Gen. Dec. B-289096.3, 2002 CPD ¶ 135 (in making cost realism analysis of the awardee's proposed indirect costs agency accepted, without any analysis, the awardee's unexplained final proposed rates, which were substantially less than those initially proposed, its historical rates, and its proposed ceiling rates); *Miller Elevator Serv. Co. — Costs*, Comp. Gen. Dec. B-284870.3, 2000 CPD ¶ 126 (evaluation deficiencies would reduce 6-point technical advantage and increase protester's price advantage, necessitating a new price/technical tradeoff); and *Browning-Ferris Indus. of Hawaii, Inc.*, Comp. Gen. Dec. B-278051.2, 98-1 CPD ¶¶ 122 (an inquiry into the protester's allegations would have revealed that estimates in the solicitation had no reasonable basis).

GAO's willingness to inform the parties through outcome prediction ADR that a protest is likely to be sustained is generally an indication that the protest is viewed as clearly meritorious, *National Opinion Research Ctr. — Costs*, Comp. Gen. Dec. B-289044.3, 2002 CPD ¶ 55. See *KAES Enters., LLC — Protest & Costs*, Comp. Gen. Dec. B-402050.4, 2010 CPD ¶ 49 (protest costs awarded with regard to issue identified during the ADR conference — exclusion of KAES's proposal from the competitive range without consideration of its price); *Panacea Consulting, Inc. — Costs*, Comp. Gen. Dec. B-299307.3, 2007 CPD ¶ 133 (ADR found that the record showed that the agency had weighted the evaluation criteria differently during the evaluations than the manner stated in the solicitation); and *TyeCom, Inc.*, Comp. Gen. Dec. B-287321.3, 2002 CPD ¶ 101 (during ADR conference the GAO attorney explained that protest was likely to be sustained because the agency had made an award to an offer which had submitted a substantially lower-rated technical proposal, on the basis of low proposed cost under a cost-reimbursement contract, without performing any meaningful cost realism analysis).

(3) No Corrective Action Possible

When the contract has been substantially performed at the time the protest is granted, the GAO will recommend the award of protest costs. See *International Program Group, Inc.*, Comp. Gen. Dec. B-400278, 2008 CPD ¶ 172 (GAO recommended that the agency reimburse the protester its costs of filing and pursuing the protest where the order for the requirement was completely performed); *Information Ventures, Inc.*, Comp. Gen. Dec. B-293518, 2004 CPD ¶ 76 (since GAO could not recommend disturbing the award where contract for educational services was largely completed, protester was entitled to costs associated with filing and pursuing this protest, including reasonable attorneys' fees).

(4) Amount Recoverable

The GAO will award only those protest costs that are related to the protest. Related costs have included the salaries of the protester's president and other employees for the time they worked on the protest, *Ultraviolet Purification Sys., Inc.*, Comp. Gen. Dec. B-226941.3, 89-1 CPD ¶ 376. See, however, *Berkshire Computer Prods.*, Comp. Gen. Dec. B-240327.3, 95-1 CPD ¶ 6, denying the award of protest costs because the protester did not establish that the costs claimed to have been paid to an unsalaried consultant and an attorney were related to the protest. A protester's time spent soliciting help from members of Congress is not related to the protest; thus, the cost is not recoverable, *Omni Analysis*, 69 Comp. Gen. 433 (B-233372.4), 90-1 CPD ¶ 436.

The GAO will not allow the recovery of costs that may be related to the protest but are not properly documented, *W. S. Spotswood & Sons*, 69 Comp. Gen. 622 (B-236713.3), 90-2 CPD ¶ 50. The burden is on the protester to adequately document the costs incurred, and the protester cannot rely on standard rates to substantiate its claim. See *John Peeples*, 70 Comp. Gen. 661 (B-233167.2), 91-2 CPD ¶ 125. The GAO will also disallow legal expenses or fees that are not adequately documented by the law firm, *Diverco, Inc.*, Comp. Gen. Dec. B-240639.5, 92-2 CPD ¶ 460. In *W. S. Spotswood & Sons*, the GAO disallowed costs due to data insufficiency. The protester submitted evidence showing the type and amount of work performed by the employees but did not demonstrate how the hourly rates were calculated or whether the rates claimed reflected actual compensation plus reasonable overhead and fringe benefits. In *Solutions Lucid Group, LLC — Costs*, Comp Gen. Dec. B-400967.2, 2009 CPD ¶ 198, the GAO denied the protester's request for recommendation that it be reimbursed $52,800 in protest costs where the protester failed to furnish sufficient evidence to establish the number of hours worked and rates of compensation for the individuals who worked on the protest. See also *DTV Transition Group., Inc. — Costs*, Comp. Gen. Dec. B-401466.2, 2010 CPD ¶ 84 (claim not adequately documented where protester did not submit requested additional documentation — i.e., copies of the analysis performed by experts, documentation of attorneys' fees, and supporting records such as timesheets, calendars, expense reports, billing statements, and receipts); *Al Long Ford — Costs*, Comp. Gen. Dec. B-297807.2, 2007 CPD ¶ 189 (claim did not identify the dates on which the hours were worked or the nature of the tasks performed, nor did it include documentation supporting the claimed rates of compensation or establishing protester's obligation to compensate the consultant); *TRS Research — Costs*, Comp. Gen. Dec. B-290644.2, 2003 CPD ¶ 112 (protester did not demonstrate the reasonableness of outside counsel's hourly rates); *CAN Indus. Eng'g, Inc.*, Comp. Gen. Dec. B-271034.2, 97-2 CPD ¶ 149 (hours charged were unreasonable where sole supporting documentation consisted of a matrix showing only the employees' names, terse and very general descriptions of the type of work that each employee was doing over time periods of a week or two, and the total number of hours that the employees allegedly worked during those time periods); *Innovative Refrigeration Concepts*, Comp. Gen. Dec. B-258655.2, 97-2 CPD ¶ 19 (documentation failed to demonstrate how hourly rates were calculated or that the claimed rates reflected actual rates of compensation); *Custom Prod. Mfg., Inc.*, Comp. Gen. Dec. B-235431.7, 95-1 CPD ¶ 236 (claim consisted of lump-sum figures that prevented both the agency and the GAO from reviewing the reasonableness of the amount claimed); and *McNeil Techs., Inc.*, Comp. Gen. Dec. B-254909.3, 95-1 CPD ¶ 207 (protester failed to identify which employees were involved in specific aspects of pursuing the protest, the purposes of the employees' claimed efforts, or what cost elements were reflected in the different hourly rates calculated for each individual).

In the case where issues are severable and information submitted to support a claim is not detailed enough to establish how much of the claimed amount was incurred in pursuit of the successful protest issues, the GAO has recognized a "page count" method — that is, an estimate based on the number of pages in the protester's submissions to GAO that were devoted to a particular issue — is a reasonable means of determining this amount, *ViON Corp. — Costs*, Comp. Gen. Dec. B-256363.3, 95-1 CPD ¶ 219. In *Intercon Assocs., Inc. — Costs*, Comp. Gen. Dec. B-296697.2, 2006 CPD ¶ 95, GAO held that given the absence of more probative evidence from Intercon, it was reasonable for the agency to use a page count to determine the amount of the claimed costs attributable to Intercon's restrictive specification argument. The estimate was based on the number of pages devoted to that issue in Intercon's comments, as compared to the number of pages devoted to Intercon's bias allegation in that same pleading. See also *BAE Tech. Servs., Inc. — Costs*, Comp. Gen. Dec. B-296699.3, 2006 CPD ¶ 122, finding that the contemporaneous records documenting the time spent on the protest by BAE's attorneys and other legal staff were not sufficiently detailed to permit an allocation of hours to the two severable issues. GAO found it appropriate to use a page count to determine the amount of the claimed costs attributable to the issues. BAE estimated through use of a page count (which the agency has not shown to be inaccurate) that approximately 5.5% of the total number of pages in its submissions to GAO were devoted to the two severable issues. Accordingly, GAO recommended that BAE's claim of $ 421,323.91 for legal services (including both attorney and other legal staff time) be reduced by 5.5%, or $23,172.82, leaving the remaining amount of the claim at $398,151.09.

(5) ATTORNEYS' FEES AND CONSULTANT AND EXPERT FEES

The most common costs sought are attorneys' fees, consultant or expert fees, internal labor, and other direct costs.

(A) ATTORNEYS' FEES

Attorneys' fees usually are the primary component of a claim for protest costs. GAO generally accepts the number of attorney hours claimed, unless the agency identifies specific hours as excessive and articulates a reasonable analysis as to why payment for those hours should be disallowed, *Data Based Decisions, Inc. — Costs*, Comp. Gen. Dec. B-232663.3, 89-2 CPD ¶ 538. Simply concluding that the hours claimed are excessive or suggest duplication of effort is inadequate to justify denying a claim for protest costs, *Princeton Gamma-Tech, Inc. — Claim for Costs*, Comp. Gen. Dec. B-228052.5, 89-1 CPD ¶ 401; *Omni Analysis*, 69 Comp. Gen. 433 (B-233372.4), 90-1 CPD ¶ 436. In *BAE Tech. Servs., Inc. — Costs*, Comp. Gen. Dec. B-296699.3, 2006 CPD ¶ 122, the GAO stated that when the Air Force annotated each time charge by each BAE attorney for each day to indicate that the agency considered the hours claimed to be excessive, the agency did not explain the basis for its assertions. The GAO held that such unsupported claims that the hours were excessive was insufficient to justify denying or reducing a claim as it related to attorney time.

The GAO will examine the reasonableness of the attorney hours claimed to determine whether they exceed, in nature and amount, what a prudent person would incur in pursuit of his or her protest, *SKJ & Assocs., Inc.*, Comp. Gen. Dec. B-291533.3, 2003 CPD ¶ 130; *Price Waterhouse — Claim for Costs*, Comp. Gen. Dec. B-254492.3, 95-2 CPD ¶ 38. In *Pulau Elecs. Corp. — Costs*, Comp. Gen. Dec. B-280048.11, 2000 CPD ¶ 122, the GAO held that Pulau's use of a five-person team was not unreasonable in the context of these substantively and procedurally demanding protests. In *Galen Med. Assocs., Inc. — Costs*, Comp. Gen. Dec. B-288661.6, 2002 CPD ¶ 114, Galen's claim included a request that it be reimbursed for a total of 938.5 hours for various individuals at various hourly rates: 346.25 hours for an outside attorney, 220 hours for a consultant and 363 hours for Galen's president. The GAO held that these claimed hours were far beyond what should have been necessary to reasonably pursue the protest. GAO stated its file in this case was only open for approximately 9 weeks, and yet these hours amount to 8.6 full-time (40-hour) work weeks for the attorney, 9 full-time work weeks for Galen's president and 5.5 full-time work weeks for Galen's consultant. The issues were relatively limited and straightforward in nature. The primary bases for protest were that the agency misevaluated proposals and engaged in activities that amounted to procurement integrity violations. There was no hearing in the matter and the documents involved were not voluminous. The core exhibit for purposes of the allegations — the evaluation materials, including all of the individual evaluator worksheets for the protester, the awardee, and a third offeror whose evaluation the protester did not challenge — amounted to only 39 pre-printed evaluation form pages with little or no additional narrative material included; 13 of those pages related to the third offeror. The protester's submissions to GAO amounted to only 22 pages. The claim equated to approximately 42 hours and approximately $7,154 per page. GAO found this amount excessive and well beyond what a prudent person would have expended in pursuit of the protest. See also *Armour of Am., Inc.*, Comp. Gen. Dec. B-237690.2, 92-1 CPD ¶ 257, where the GAO determined that legal fees were excessive even though well documented. There, the GAO disallowed all 36 hours of the attorneys' billed time for pursuit of issues that were clearly untimely, disallowed one fourth of Armour's attorneys' hours attributable to legal research and writing, and disallowed one third of the total time claimed by Armour's attorneys for travel to and from the informal bid protest conference held at the GAO offices. In *Price Waterhouse*, Comp. Gen. Dec. B-254492.3, 95-2 CPD ¶ 38, the GAO reviewed each hour billed to determine the reasonableness of the attorney hours claimed. The GAO found that although 13.5 hours seemed to be high in preparing a protective order, it was not excessive. However, 4.5 hours to review the agency's notice to authorize contract performance pursuant to the statutory best interest clause was considered excessive by the GAO.

See also *Fritz Cos., Inc. — Costs*, Comp. Gen. Dec. B-246736.7, 94-2 CPD ¶ 58 (request for reimbursement denied where billing records showed that multiple attorneys performed duplicative work, and did not demonstrate a need for such efforts).

31 U.S.C. § 3554(c)(2)(B) places a cap on attorneys' fees and expert and consultant fees, except where the protester is a small business concern. The top rate reimbursable to large businesses for attorneys' fees is $150 per hour unless the procuring agency determines, on the recommendation of the GAO, that a higher fee is justified. The attorney fee cap may be increased where "the agency determines, based on the recommendation of the GAO on a case by case basis, that an increase in the cost of living or a special factor, such as the limited availability of qualified attorneys for the proceedings involved, justifies a higher fee."

The justification for an upward departure from the $150 cap is self-evident if the claimant asserts that the cost of living has increased, as measured by the Department of Labor's (DOL) Consumer Price Index (CPI), *Sodexho Mgmt., Inc — Costs*, Comp. Gen. Dec. B-289605.3, 2003 CPD ¶ 136. Since *Sodexho*, the GAO has recommended higher fee rates based on this calculation. See, for example, *Transportation Security Admin. — Costs*, Comp. Gen. Dec. B-400340.8, 2010 CPD ¶ 119 (fee rates of $ 210.77 to $ 211.12 per hour (depending on the month of billing) properly calculated using DOL's CPI — All Urban Consumers); *Core Tech Int'l Corp. — Costs*, Comp. Gen. Dec. B-400047.3, 2009 CPD ¶ 121 (protester provided a detailed explanation of its calculation of the $ 239.74 to $ 248.35 rate per hour using DOL's CPI — All Urban Consumers); *EBSCO Publishing, Inc. — Costs*, Comp. Gen. Dec. B-298918.4, 2007 CPD ¶ 90 (upward adjustment of attorney fees to $ 197.00 per hour per the applicable CPI); *Dep't of the Army — Costs*, B-296783.4, 2006 CPD ¶ 72 (upward adjustment of attorney fees at a rate of $238 per hour using DOL's CPI for All Urban Consumers, U.S. City Average for Legal Services); and *Dep't of State — Costs*, Comp. Gen. Dec. B-295352.5, 2005 CPD ¶ 145 (fees at rates of $ 196.89 to $ 197.77 per hour properly computed using DOL's CPI for All Urban Consumers).

Because of the lack of a fee cap for small business concern's attorneys' fees, GAO will consider whether the rates charged by an attorney are consistent with customary rates for similar work in the community, as well as the experience, reputation and ability of the practitioner, *Public Communications Servs., Inc. — Costs*, Comp. Gen. Dec. B-400058.4, 2009 CPD ¶ 131 (finding reasonable an hourly rate of $705 per hour). The GAO will also look to surveys of area law firms' hourly rates to determine the reasonableness of rates, *CourtSmart Digital Sys., Inc. — Costs*, Comp. Gen. Dec. B-292995.7, 2005 CPD ¶ 47 (hourly rate of $475 reasonable for an attorney experienced in government procurement law who was a partner in a Washington, D.C. firm; noting that according to an article published in the January 2003 edition of Legal Times, the hourly rates for partners from 19 Washington, D.C. area law firms surveyed ranged from $185 to $750). But see *TRS Research — Costs*, Comp. Gen. Dec. B-290644.2, 2003 CPD ¶ 112 (despite numerous requests by the agency, protester did not submit any documentation to show that the $425 hourly rate claimed by TRS counsel was representative of that charged for similar services in the Philadelphia area where he practices). The GAO will also consider, where relevant and appropriate, the fee rates found allowable by it in other similarly complex proceedings, *Blue Rock Structures, Inc. — Costs*, Comp. Gen. Dec. B-293134.2, 2005 CPD ¶ 190 ("Given our approval of $475 as a reasonable hourly rate for a partner in a Washington firm in *CourtSmart*, we see no basis to object to the lower rate billed by Blue Rock's attorney, who is also a partner in a Washington firm.").

The GAO will permit a protester to recover the work of support staff such as paralegals, but not library services, which the GAO deems more appropriately included in overhead, *Public Communications Servs., Inc. — Costs*, Comp. Gen. Dec. B-400058.4, 2009 CPD ¶ 131; *Pulau Elecs. Corp. — Costs*, Comp. Gen. Dec. B-280048.11, 2000 CPD ¶ 122.

(B) LABOR COSTS

A protester's internal labor costs for preparing a bid or proposal may be recovered where the rates reflect "actual rates of compensation plus reasonable overhead and fringe benefits," *Sodexho Mgmt., Inc — Costs*, Comp. Gen. Dec. B-289605.3, 2003 CPD ¶ 136. However, a protester must not recover a profit, *Celadon Labs, Inc.*, Comp. Gen. Dec. B-298533.2, 2008 CPD ¶ 208; *SKJ & Assocs., Inc.*, Comp. Gen. Dec. B-291533.3, 2003 CPD ¶ 130. A protester may reasonably show the hours spent by employees through a general explanation of the tasks conducted and estimate of the time spent by those employees. See *Data Based Decisions, Inc. — Costs*, 69 Comp. Gen. 122 (B-232663.3), 89-2 CPD ¶ 538, recommending reimbursement of the time spent by the company's president discussing the protest with the attorneys that was corroborated by the attorneys' records. Compare *CNA Indus. Eng;g, Inc. — Costs*, Comp. Gen. Dec. B-271034.2, 97-2 CPD ¶ 149, denying compensation for employees that had spent more time than the attorneys but had no access to key documents because they were not admitted to the protective order.

(C) OUTSIDE CONSULTANTS & EXPERT WITNESSES

Under 31 U.S.C. § 3554(c)(2)(B), the top rate for consultants and expert witnesses for large businesses is the "highest rate of compensation for expert witnesses paid by the Federal Government." Reimbursement of protest costs associated with use of consultants is limited to highest rate of pay for a federal employee (GS-15, step 10), even where the consultant billed at a higher rate, *Dep't of the Army*, Comp. Gen. Dec. B-296783.4, 2006 CPD ¶ 72.

3. Revision of Remedies

Section 2741(a) of the Competition in Contracting Act, Pub. L. No. 98-369, Div. B., Title VII, codified at 31 U.S.C. § 3554(e), required that "the head of procuring activity responsible for the solicitation, proposed award or award of the contract shall report to the GAO, if the federal agency has not implemented those recommendations within 60 days of receipt of the Comptroller General's recommendations." Section 1403(b)(3) of the Federal Acquisition Streamlining Act of 1994, Pub. L. No. 103-355, removed the statutory requirement that an agency report its noncompliance with the GAO recommendation and replaced it with a mandate to GAO to report promptly to the Senate's Committee on Governmental Affairs and Committee on Appropriations and the House's Committee on Government Reform and Oversight and the Committee on Appropriations any case in which a federal agency fails to implement fully a recommendation of the Comptroller General. See 31 U.S.C. § 3554(e)(1). The report is required to include "a comprehensive review of the pertinent procurement including the circumstances of the failure of the Federal agency to implement a recommendation of the Comptroller General," 31 U.S.C. § 3554(e)(1)(A). The report must also include a recommendation regarding whether "in order to correct an inequity or to preserve the integrity of the procurement process," Congress should consider (1) private relief legislation, (2) legislative recission or cancellation of funds, (3) further investigation by Congress, or (4) other action, 31 U.S.C. § 3554(e)(1)(B).

The details of implementing GAO recommendations for corrective action are within the sound discretion and judgment of the contracting agency, *Rel-Tek Sys. & Design, Inc. — Modification of Remedy*, Comp. Gen. Dec. B-280463.7, 99-2 CPD ¶ 1. Such discretion must be exercised reasonably and in a fashion that remedies the procurement impropriety that was the basis for the GAO protest recommendation. In *Futures Group Int'l*, Comp. Gen. Dec. B-281274.5, 2000 CPD ¶ 148, the GAO had sustained the protest because the contemporaneous record did not evidence that USAID reasonably found the awardee's proposed rates realistic. In response to this decision the agency took corrective action by determining that the awardee's probable costs were the lowest and confirming award to that firm. The GAO held this to be unreasonable because the agency was advised by the DCAA that the awardee's proposed uncapped indirect rates were understated by an amount that would have affected the outcome of the competition. In *Rockwell Elec. Commerce Corp.*, Comp. Gen. Dec. B-286201.6, 2001 CPD ¶ 162, the GAO found that the agency did not act reasonably in its response to an earlier sustained decision by reopening discussions and requesting proposal revisions from only one offeror in the competitive range. See also *Cooperativa Muratori Riuniti*, Comp. Gen. Dec. B-294980.5, 2005 CPD ¶ 144, stating that where an agency amends the RFP after closing and permits offerors to submit revised proposals, it should permit offerors to revise aspects of their proposals that were not the subject of the amendment absent evidence that the amendment could not reasonably have any effect on other aspects of proposals, or that allowing such revisions would have a detrimental impact on the competitive process. Compare *Pemco Aeroplex, Inc.*, Comp. Gen. Dec. B-310372.3, 2008 CPD ¶ 126 (since prior GAO decision was based on an informational deficiency in the agency's evaluation record, it was not unreasonable for the agency to correct that deficiency by performing and documenting the required analyses based on the information that was already available; protester's assertion that the agency was obligated to reopen discussions with all offerors is without merit); *Johnson Controls World Servs., Inc.*, Comp. Gen. Dec. B-286714.3, 2001 CPD ¶ 145 (corrective action on organizational conflict of interest protest reasonable which included requiring party to terminate its teaming relationship with conflicted organization and making the contents of a database available to mitigate prior awardee's potential competitive advantage and potential impaired objectivity); *Southern Techs., Inc.*, Comp. Gen. Dec. B-278030, 97-2 CPD ¶ 167 (paying costs rather than recompeting procurement reasonable).

In some circumstances it may not be feasible or practicable for an agency to follow the GAO's recommendation. In such cases the agency may request that the GAO modify its recommendation for corrective action. See *Dep't of Commerce — Recons.*, Comp. Gen. Dec. B-277260.4, 98-2 CPD ¶ 35 (recommendation modified because agency established, through a site visit by the GAO, that a significant portion of the contract work had been completed and that it would be impracticable to disturb award); *Dep't of Transportation — Recons. & Modification of Remedy*, Comp. Gen. Dec. B-278466.2, 98-1 CPD ¶ 140 (recommendation modified where original remedy would endanger agency's ability to address Year 2000 problem); *Aeronautics & Space Admin. — Recons. & Modification*, Comp. Gen. Dec. B-274748.3, 97-1 CPD ¶ 159 (recommendation modified where it was not practicable to return the items because they had already been delivered and paid for); *ABA Indus., Inc. — Recons.*, Comp. Gen. Dec. B-250186.2, 93-1 CPD ¶ 415 (recommendation modified where only awardee could meet delivery schedule). Compare *Dep't of the Army — Request for Modification of Recommendation*, Comp. Gen. Dec. B-290682.2, 2003 CPD ¶ 23 (modification of recommendation to open competition to all eligible small business concerns denied because CICA provides for full and open competition among eligible small business concerns for acquisitions required to be set aside for small businesses; *Dep't of Commerce — Request for Modification of Recommendation*, Comp. Gen. Dec. B-283137.7, 2000 CPD ¶ 27 (modification of recommendation to permit offerors the opportunity to make oral presentations or amend the solicitation denied because the evaluation scheme would not be materially changed after receipt of proposals without providing offerors an opportunity to submit revised proposals based on the revised scheme); *Kumasi Ltd./Kukawa Ltd. — Recons.*, 72 Comp. Gen. 331 (B-247975.12), 93-2 CPD ¶ 195 (modification of recommendation to reopen negotiations denied, rejecting agency claim that continued performance of the contracts after best interest determination made implementation of recommendation impracticable); and *Gunn Van Lines-Recons.*, Comp. Gen. Dec. B-248131.2, 92-2 CPD ¶ 246 (modification of recommendation to terminate contract denied even though only one month remained on contract) Although an agency is not required to "formally" request modification before taking different corrective action, generally it will do so because of the requirement that the GAO report noncompliance to Congress.

The GAO may modify its recommendation if it finds the agency's request to be reasonable. See *Dep't of the Treasury, Bureau of Engraving & Printing — Request for Modification Remedy*, Comp. Gen. Dec. B-296490.6, 2007 CPD ¶101 (modification request on recommendation to reevaluate proposals and make new source selection decision granted where agency determined that its needs would be best met by splitting original requirements and competing under two new solicitations); *Dep't of State — Reconsideration and Modification of Recommendation*, Comp. Gen. Dec. B-295352.3, 2005 CPD ¶ 81 (modification request on recommendation to terminate reasonable in view of security concerns at the embassy as well as significant change in the agency's needs for guard service); *SMF Sys. Tech. Corp.*, Comp. Gen. Dec. B-292419.3, 2003 CPD ¶ 203 (disruption to agency's mission to provide medical services was considered in fashioning modification of recommendation); and *J & J/BMAR Joint Venture, LLP — Costs*, Comp. Gen. Dec. B-290316.7, 2003 CPD ¶ 129 (wartime exigencies provide reasonable basis for delay in implementing corrective action).

The agency may decide to perform the work in-house, rather than take corrective action. In *Pemco Aeroplex, Inc.*, Comp. Gen. Dec. B-275587.9, 98-2 CPD ¶ 17, the agency, in response to a protest, decided to revise the solicitation, conduct discussions, solicit BAFOs, and reevaluate proposals. Shortly thereafter, it decided not to complete the proposed corrective action but rather to perform the work in-house. In addition to arguing that the agency improperly failed to take the corrective action that it had promised and that its actions were calculated to punish the company for protesting, the protesters argued that there was no reasonable basis for canceling the RFP. The GAO denied the protest, stating:

> [S]o long as there is a reasonable basis for doing so, an agency may cancel a solicitation after the announcement of a different course of action in response to a GAO protest. *See Atlantic Scientific & Technology Corp.*, [Comp. Gen. Dec. B-276334.2, 97-2 CPD ¶ 116] at 1-2. In addition, if there is a reasonable basis for canceling a solicitation, notwithstanding some element of personal animus, we will not object to the cancellation. *Dr. Robert J. Telepak*, [Comp. Gen. Dec. B-247681, 92-2 CPD ¶ 4] at 4. Here, the protesters have offered no credible evidence showing that the cancellation was based upon animus toward either firm. In any event, since the Air Force has provided a reasonable basis for canceling the solicitation, neither the timing of the announcement of that basis nor the possibility of personal animus provides grounds for sustaining this protest.

See also *Southwest Anesthesia Servs.*, Comp. Gen. Dec. B-279176.2, 98-2 CPD ¶ 28, finding it proper to cancel a procurement and perform the services in-house, rather than take action, as promised.

In an unusual case, the Air Force defied a GAO recommendation. In *Pemco Aeroplex, Inc.*, Comp. Gen. Dec. B-280397, 98-2 CPD ¶ 79, the GAO sustained a protest challenging the Air Force's decision to consolidate its depot work-load requirements into a single solicitation. The GAO recommended that the Air Force cancel the current solicitation and resolicit its requirements without bundling the workloads. The Air Force subsequently announced that it had gone ahead with the consolidated procurement, stating that awarding the depot work to one contractor will save up to $ 638 million during the nine-year life of the contract. In another interesting case, Symplicity contested the Office of Personnel Management's (OPM) award of a task order to TMP Worldwide, Inc. (Monster) for online employment information services. The GAO sustained the protest, recommending that OPM reopen discussions and request revised quotations from vendors, *Symplicity Corp.*, Comp. Gen. Dec. B-291902, 2003 CPD ¶ 89. In July 2003 OPM formally declined to follow the GAO's recommendation, on the basis that the recommendation was "incompatible with the best interest of Federal Government" and national security." See GAO Bid Protest Annual Report to the Congress for Fiscal Year 2003, B-158766 (2004). In August 2003, GAO reported the matter to Congress pursuant to 31 U.S.C. § 3554 and recommended that Congress consider an inquiry into OPM's failure to fully implement GAO's recommendation. Congressional hearings were held and the appropriations act for OPM was amended to cut funding for the procurement until OPM complied with GAO recommendations from the *Symplicity* decision. Funding was later restored in conference committee presumably after OPM agreed to cancel its contract with Monster and reopen the solicitation. Upon resolicitation of the procurement, OPM again awarded the contract to Monster. Another interesting case is *Mission Critical Solutions*, Comp. Gen. Dec. B-401057, 2009 CPD ¶ 93, *recons. denied*, 2009 CPD ¶ 148, where the GAO held that HUBZone set-asides take precedence over the 8(a) program. Following the GAO decision, on July 10, 2009 the Office of Management and Budget issued a memorandum directing executive branch agencies to disregard GAO's ruling pending legal review by the executive branch. On August 21, 2009, the Office of Legal Counsel (OLC) of the U.S. Department of Justice issued an opinion addressing the issues raised in MCS's protest. The OLC disagreed with the GAO's analysis, arguing that the SBA was correct in ruling that the HUB-Zone statute establishes "parity" with the 8(a) program. OLC stated further that the OLC opinion is binding on the executive branch while the GAO's decision is not, and directed agencies to disregard GAO decisions that are inconsistent with its opinion. Subsequently, the Court of Federal Claims reached the same conclusion as the GAO, *Mission Critical Solutions v. United States*, 91 Fed. Cl. 386 (2010), and the GAO continued to grant protests when the HUBZone priority was not honored, *DGR Assocs, Inc.*, Comp. Gen. Dec. B-402494, 2010 CPD ¶ 15; Rice Servs., Inc., Comp. Gen. Dec. B-402966.2, 2010 CPD ¶ 217. The matter was resolved by a statutory amendment providing for parity among the programs.

IV. COURT OF FEDERAL CLAIMS

The Court of Federal Claims and its predecessors initially relied upon the Tucker Act, 28 U.S.C. § 1491(a)(1), to take jurisdiction over contract award controversies. This statute gives the court jurisdiction over claims "founded either upon the Constitution, or any Act of Congress, or any regulation of an executive department, or upon any express or implied contract with the United States." As early as 1956, the Court of Claims used the government's "implied contract to consider bids fairly" in holding that a disappointed bidder would be entitled to bid preparation costs if it could show that its bid had not been evaluated in good faith, *Heyer Prods. Co. v. United States*, 135 Ct. Cl. 63, 140 F. Supp. 409 (1956). The court again held that its jurisdiction extended to implied contracts to consider bids and proposals fairly and honestly in *Keco Indus., Inc. v. United States*, 203 Ct. Cl. 566, 492 F.2d 1200 (1974). However, lacking general equitable powers, the court could not grant injunctive relief but could only award damages.

Injunctive relief became available in 1982 when the following provision granting equitable powers to the Claims Court (renamed the Court of Federal Claims) was added to 28 U.S.C. § 1491(b)(3):

> To afford complete relief on any contract claim brought before the contract is awarded, the court shall have exclusive jurisdiction to grant declaratory judgments and such equitable and extraordinary relief as it deems proper, including but not limited to injunctive relief. In exercising this jurisdiction, the court shall give regard to the interests of national defense and national security.

The court held that this grant of jurisdiction also was limited to the implied contract to consider bids and proposals fairly and honestly in *United States v. John C. Grimberg Co.*, 702 F.2d 1362 (Fed. Cir. 1983).

The Administrative Dispute Resolution Act of 1996 (ADRA), Pub. L. No. 104-320, repealed this provision but gave new "bid protest" jurisdiction to the court by enacting 28 U.S.C. § 1491(b), which states:

> (1) [T]he United States Court of Federal Claims . . . shall have jurisdiction to render judgment on any action by an interested party objecting to a solicitation by a Federal agency for bids or proposals for a proposed contract or to a proposed award or the award of a contract or any alleged violation of statute or regulation in connection with a procurement or a proposed procurement. . . . [T]he United States Court of Federal Claims . . . shall have jurisdiction to entertain such an action without regard to whether suit is instituted before or after award.

> (2) To afford relief in such an action, the courts may award any relief that the court considers proper, including declaratory and injunctive relief except that any monetary relief shall be limited to bid preparation and proposal costs.

Subsequently, some judges in the Court of Federal Claims decided that it had protest jurisdiction under both 28 U.S.C. § 1491(a)(1) (damages) and 28 U.S.C. § 1491(b)(1) (injunction and/or damages). The Federal Circuit in *Resource Conservation Group, LLC v. Dep't of Navy*, 597 F.3d 1238 (Fed. Cir. 2010), raised questions about this dual jurisdiction, holding that relief in the "procurement" context is exclusive under 28 U.S.C. § 1491(b)(1), while relief under 28 U.S.C. § 1491(a)(1) is still available when a claim arises from a federal solicitation which is not a procurement. In *Resource Conservation*, the protest arose from a solicitation to lease federal land and the protester contended that the Court of Federal Claims had jurisdiction under 28 U.S.C. § 1491(a)(1) to consider a claimed breach of an implied contract of fair and honest consideration. The Court of Federal Claims dismissed the protest, holding it no longer had jurisdiction after the enactment of the ADRA to adjudicate the claim under § 1491(a)(1). The Court of Federal Claims also held it did not have jurisdiction under 28 U.S.C. § 1491(b)(1) over a bid protest involving a lease of government land, because relief under § 1491(b)(1) is limited to the procurement context, and the lease of land by the government is not a procurement. In addressing the question of implied-in-fact contract jurisdiction under § 1491(a)(1), the court noted the legislative history clearly showed the ADRA was intended to unify bid protest law in one court under one standard, and § 1491(b)(1) jurisdiction was to be exclusive where § 1491(b)(1) provided a remedy. However, the Federal Circuit found it unlikely Congress intended § 1491(b)(1) to deny a pre-existing remedy without providing a new remedy. Here, because the protest involved a nonprocurement solicitation, the Court of Federal Claims had implied-in-fact contract jurisdiction under § 1491(a)(1). Two judges of the Court of Federal Claims have ruled that this dicta does not deprive the court of dual jurisdiction under § 1491(a)(1) and § 1491(b)(1), *FAS Support Servs., LLC v. United States*, 93 Fed. Cl. 687 (2010); *L-3 Communications Integrated Sys., L.P. v. United States*, 94 Fed. Cl. 394 (2010). Two judges have followed *Resource Conservation, Metropolitan Van & Storage, Inc. v. United States*, 92 Fed. Cl. 232 (2010); *Linc Gov't Servs., LLC v. United States*, No. 10-375-C, November 5, 2010. A fifth judge has held that a protester can assert breach of the implied contract to consider proposals fairly as part of its claim under §1491(b)(1), *Bilfinger Berger AG Sede Secondaria Italiana v. United States*, 94 Fed. Cl. 389 (2010).

A. Jurisdiction

Aside from the issue of whether the Court of Federal Claims has dual jurisdiction or only jurisdiction over "procurement" protests under 28 U.S.C. § 1491(b), there are other issued that must be addressed in deciding whether the court has jurisdiction.

1. Procurement Protests

28 U.S.C. § 1491(b)(1) gives the court jurisdiction to hear protests in connection with a procurement of a "federal agency."

a. Federal Agency

While the bid protest statute does not define the term "federal agency," it is defined in 40 U.S.C. § 472 as

> any executive agency or any establishment in the legislative or judicial branch of the Government, including any wholly owned Government corporation.

The term "federal agency" is defined in other statutes, as well. Some definitions seem to be very broad. For example, 22 U.S.C. § 4802 states that "federal agency" "includes any department or agency of the United States Government." Some definitions do not include the legislative or judicial branches of the government within the definition. For example, 40 U.S.C. § 304e defines "federal agency" as "any executive department, independent establishment, commission, board, bureau, or office in the executive branch, or other agency of the United States." See also 5 U.S.C. § 804, which states that "federal agency" means any agency as is defined in § 551(1). This section defines "agency" as "each authority of the Government of the United States, whether or not it is within or subject to review by another agency, but does not include such entities as Congress, the courts, territories or possessions of the United States, the government of the District of Columbia, and courts martial and military commissions." Other statutory definitions include the legislative and judicial branches of the government. For example, 5 U.S.C. § 7901 defines "federal agency" as "an Executive agency as defined under Section 105 of title 5, United States Code, and shall include any agency of the legislative or judicial branch of Government." 40 U.S.C. § 612 is similar but excludes the Senate, the House of Representatives, and the Architect of the Capitol and any activities under his direction. 40 U.S.C. § 762 and 41 U.S.C. § 423 state that "federal agency" "has the meaning given such term by Section 3(b) of the Federal Property and Administrative Services Act of 1949" (40 U.S.C. § 472). The 28 U.S.C. § 451 definition of the term "agency" may also be used in bid protest cases. See *Emery Worldwide Airlines, Inc. v. United States*, 264 F.3d 1071 (Fed. Cir. 2001) (USPS is a "federal agency" within the meaning of the Tucker Act and the definition of "agency" in 28 U.S.C. § 451 governs that determination); *Hewlett-Packard Co. v. United States*, 41 Fed. Cl. 99 (1998) (Tucker Act as amended by the Administrative Disputes Resolution Act confers jurisdiction on court to hear protests challenging procurement decisions of the Postal Service).

b. In Connection with a Procurement

The phrase "in connection with a procurement" is very sweeping in scope. As long as a statute has a connection to a procurement proposal, an alleged violation suffices to supply bid protest jurisdiction, *RAMCOR Servs. Group, Inc. v. United States*, 185 F.3d 1286 (Fed. Cir. 1999). See also *LABAT-Anderson, Inc. v. United States*, 65 Fed. Cl. 570 (2005) (even though the protest did not involve review of a solicitation or award, it involved a government decision not to conduct a solicitation and thus was a challenge to an "alleged violation of statute or regulation in connection with a procurement"); and *Knowledge Connections, Inc. v. United States*, 79 Fed. Cl. 750 (2007) (court does not lose jurisdiction over a bid protest "because [an agency] allegedly only violated the APA, not a procurement statute"). In *Distributed Solutions, Inc. v. United States*, 539 F.3d 1340 (Fed. Cir. 2008), the Federal Circuit reversed the Court of Federal Claims decision, determining that the court possessed jurisdiction to entertain the complaint because 28 U.S.C. § 491(b) expressly permits the filing of protests of pre-procurement decisions, such as an agency's determination of a need for property or services. The court adopted the definition of "procurement" from 41 U.S.C. § 403(2). This statute defines "procurement" as including "all stages of the process of acquiring property or services, beginning with the process for determining a need for property or services and ending with contract completion and closeout." The court concluded that "[t]o establish jurisdiction pursuant to this definition the contractors must demonstrate that the Government at least initiated a procurement, or initiated 'the process for determining a need' for acquisition and assistance solutions for JAMMS." Thus, it held that when the government issued an RFI to solicit information to determine the scope of services it required, there was jurisdiction to review such pre-procurement decisions. See also *Savantage Fin. Servs. v. United States*, 81 Fed. Cl. 300 (2008) (DHS's decision to migrate to the Oracle and SAP constituted a procurement because it reflected DHS's determination of a need to consolidate its financial management software systems, and its selection of the Oracle and SAP systems to meet that need); *K-LAK Corp. v. United States*, 54 CCF ¶ 79,390 (2010) (claims challenging the decision to exit the 8(a) program and use the FSS the concerned an alleged violation of statutes and regulations in connection with a procurement). But see *R&D Dynamics Corp. v. United States*, 80 Fed. Cl. 715 (2007) (declining to assume jurisdiction over a postaward protest related to the Army's Small Business Innovation Research Program because the claim did not arise "in connection with a procurement or proposed procurement" despite plaintiff's argument that the GAO has routinely held that it has jurisdiction over protest actions related to the SBIR program). See also *Resource Conservation Group, LLC v. United States*, 597 F.3d 1238 (Fed. Cir. 2010), agreeing with the Court of Federal Claims (86 Fed. Cl. 475 (2009)) that the court lacked jurisdiction under § 1491(b)(1) to adjudicate bid protests involving leases of land where the government is the lessor, because such as action is not "in connection with a procurement or proposed procurement."

2. Implied-in-Fact Jurisdiction

28 U.S.C. § 1491(a)(1) confers jurisdiction over "any express or implied contract with the United States."

a. Contract of the United States

The language of 28 U.S.C. § 1491(a)(1) permitting monetary relief is extremely broad, extending to "any contract of the United States." The following nonappropriated fund activities are included within the definition of the United States:

Army and Air Force Exchange Service

Navy Exchanges

Marine Corps Exchanges

Coast Guard Exchanges

Exchange Councils of the National Aeronautics and Space Administration

The only government agency excluded from coverage is the Tennessee Valley Authority, 28 U.S.C. § 1491(c). Cases considering whether an entity is covered under the statute include *McDonald's Corp. v. United States*, 926 F.2d 1126 (Fed. Cir. 1991) (Navy resale and services support office was covered even though it was not specifically listed in the statute because the legislative history showed that Congress intended to waive sovereign immunity for military organizations funded by resale activities); *Wolverine Supply, Inc. v. United States*, 17 Cl. Ct. 190 (1989) (Eielson AFB central base fund not covered because it was not included in the NAFI military exchanges set forth in the statute); *Eubanks v. United States*, 25 Cl. Ct. 131 (1992) (United States was not a party to the contract between housing authority and property owner, and its funding and regulating program did not establish any contractual obligation).

b. Type of Actions

Relief under 28 U.S.C. § 1491(a)(1) is available where an issue arises from a federal solicitation which is not a "procurement," i.e. where the federal solicitation concerns a sale, not an acquisition, or where a federal solicitation concerns the lease of federal real property, and not a federal "procurement" of property or services, *Resource Conservation Group, LLC v. Dep't of Navy*, 597 F.3d 1238 (Fed. Cir. 2010). It is not clear whether procurement actions remain viable under § 1491(a)(1). Some courts have read *Resource Conservation* to suggest that § 1491(a) no longer serves as a predicate for jurisdiction in a bid protest. However, in *L-3 Communications Integrated Sys., L.P. v. United States*, 94 Fed. Cl. 394 (2010), the court stated that it did not read the dicta in *Resource Conservation* as an effort by the Federal Circuit to repeal the § 1491(a) jurisdiction with regard to procurement contracts, stating at 396-97:

> Without addressing the entire universe of what type of § 1491(a) actions survived the enactment of § 1491(b)(1), the Federal Circuit held that one type of breach of the implied contract of fair dealing — a breach in connection with a lease — did survive and remains actionable under § 1491(a). While the Federal Circuit characterized a viable action predicated on § 1491(a) jurisdiction as including "claims where the new statute does not provide a remedy," that characterization should not be read to eliminate other facets of the Court's § 1491(a) jurisdiction. There may well be procurement bid protests that do not fall within the ambit of § 1491(b), and such protests should not be left without a judicial forum when that was not the intent of Congress. As the Federal Circuit in *Resource Conservation* acknowledged: "it

seems quite unlikely that Congress would intend that statute to deny a pre-existing remedy without providing a remedy under the new statute." 597 F.3d at 1246.

See also *FAS Support Servs., LLC v. United States*, 93 Fed. Cl. 687 (2010) (conferring jurisdiction in a bid protest challenging a suspension or debarment process).

B. Standing — Who May Protest

"Standing is a threshold jurisdictional issue, which . . . may be decided without addressing the merits of a determination," *Castle v. United States*, 301 F.3d 1328 (Fed. Cir. 2002). Before addressing the merits of a plaintiff's protest, a court must therefore determine whether a plaintiff has standing to invoke the court's jurisdiction.

1. Interested Party

The threshold issue in determining whether a party has standing is whether a protester qualifies as an "interested party" under § 1491(b)(1), *Am. Fed'n of Gov't Employees v. United States*, 258 F.3d 1294 (Fed. Cir. 2001). The Federal Circuit has used the definition of "interested party" in 31 U.S.C. § 3551(2)(A) governing protests to GAO. See *Rex Serv. Corp. v. United States*, 448 F.3d 1305 (Fed. Cir. 2006). A two-part test is applied to determine whether a protester is an "interested party:" (1) the protestor must show that it was an actual or prospective bidder; and (2) the protester must have a direct economic interest in the procurement, *Distributed Solutions, Inc. v. United States*, 539 F.3d 1340 (Fed. Cir. 2008).

a. Actual or Prospective Bidder

Where the claim is that the government failed to engage in a competitive procurement, the plaintiff need not show that it would have received the award in a competition with other hypothetical bidders, but rather must show that it would have been a qualified bidder, *Myers Investigative & Sec. Servs., Inc. v. United States*, 275 F.3d 1366 (Fed. Cir. 2002). See *Savantage Fin. Servs. v. United States*, 81 Fed. Cl. 300 (2008) (plaintiff currently supplied a competitive financial management system to DHS and clearly could have competed for the contract if DHS had bid it out). In *RhinoCorps Ltd. Co. v. United States*, 87 Fed. Cl. 261 (Fed. Cl. 2009), the court found that the plaintiff had standing to continue its protest despite the fact that the company did not bid on the protested solicitation because the protest had been pending since well before the solicitation was issued and the protester claimed the solicitation was issued as a pretext to keep it from being awarded a follow-on contract. However, eventually Rhinocorps lost on the merits. See also *Magnum Opus Techs., Inc. v. United States*, 94 Fed. Cl. 512 (2010) (protester suing on its own rights as a prospective bidder in a new competition, not on the joint venture's rights); and *Totolo/King v. United States*, 87 Fed. Cl. 680 (2009) (prospective bidder if the solicitation were issued as a SDVOSB or small business set-aside). But see *Space Exploration Techs. Corp. v. United States*, 68 Fed. Cl. 1 (2005) (plaintiff is not an actual or prospective bidder and cannot qualify as an interested party with standing under the ADRA because it did not anticipate having full launch capability until the following fiscal year).

b. Direct Economic Interest

A showing of direct economic interest requires the plaintiff to demonstrate that any alleged errors caused prejudice, *Myers Investigative & Sec. Servs., Inc. v. United States*, 275 F.3d 1366 (Fed. Cir. 2002) (prejudice is a necessary element of standing). To prove a direct economic interest, the offeror is required to establish that it had a substantial chance of receiving the contract, *Info. Tech. & Applications v. United States*, 316 F.3d 1312 (Fed. Cir. 2003). Prejudice for standing is something less than prejudice on the merits, see Section G, *supra*. Cases finding prejudice for standing include *Coastal Int'l Sec., Inc. v. United States*, 93 Fed. Cl. 502 (2010) (plaintiff was in competitive range and record indicated that the competition between the two proposals was very close); *Hunt Bldg. Co. v. United States*, 61 Fed. Cl. 243 (2004) (protester was one of two offerors in the competitive range, with both deemed by the agency to be outstanding); *PGBA, LLC, v. United States*, 60 Fed. Cl. 196 (2004) (proposal was fully within the zone of consideration for a contractual award, and agency's handling of the data-access element showed unequal and unfair treatment). In *Systems Plus, Inc. v. United States*, 69 Fed. Cl. 757 (2006), the court held that the protester would have had a substantial chance of wining the contract. The protester was a qualified small business and its proposal was found to be technically acceptable. Also, as the incumbent supplier on many deliverables under the agreement, the protester demonstrated it was capable of performing the contract. But see *Homesource Real Estate Asset Servs., Inc. v. United States*, 94 Fed. Cl. 466 (2010), where the court held that even if plaintiff's protest grounds were sustained, there were eight vendors that did not receive any award and had higher technical ratings than plaintiff. Any of these eight vendors would have provided a better choice to the government. Therefore, even if plaintiff were to succeed in its protest on the merits, there was not a substantial chance it would be awarded the contract.

In a pre-award context, a protester can establish the prejudice necessary for standing by showing a non-trivial injury which can be addressed by judicial relief, *Weeks, Marine, Inc. v. United States*, 575 F.3d 1352 (Fed. Cir. 2009). In *Weeks Marine*, the court observed that in a pre-award protest it is difficult for a prospective offeror to make the showing of prejudice because "there is no factual foundation for a 'but for' prejudice analysis." The court stated it would apply the standard used by the Court of Federal Claims that had previously been articulated in *WinStar Communications, Inc. v. United States*, 41 Fed. Cl. 748 (1998), in which standing is established by alleging "a non-trivial competitive injury which can be redressed by judicial relief." The Federal Circuit determined that this standard "strikes the appropriate balance" between § 1491(b)(1)'s "interested party" requirements and Article III standing requirements, and agreed that it is the appropriate standard to apply in a pre-award challenge to an agency's solicitation. The court subsequently determined that Weeks had standing because it had alleged a facial defect in the solicitation that would materially affect how Weeks would be required to do business with the Corps for the duration of the IDIQ contract. See *Magnum Opus Techs., Inc. v. United States*, 94 Fed. Cl. 512 (2010) (if Magnum Opus succeeds in the protest, then it will be able to compete in any re-solicitation for the services it alleges should have been subject to competition); *Knowledge Connections, Inc. v. United States*, 76 Fed. Cl. 6 (2007) (offeror had standing because it had effectively renewed its offer). But see *Camden Shipping Constr. Co. v. United States*, 89 Fed. Cl. 433 (2009) (protester's offer did not remain open for the required period).

2. Disappointed Bidders

The most common form of implied contract in contract award cases under § 1491(a)(1) arose when the government issued a solicitation, thereby making an offer to honestly and fairly consider responses, and the prospective contractor accepted this offer by submitting a bid or proposal, *Keco Indus., Inc. v. United States*, 192 Ct. Cl. 773, 428 F.2d 1233 (1970); *United States v. John C. Grimberg Co.*, 702 F.2d 1362 (Fed. Cir. 1983); *National Forge Co. v. United States*, 779 F.2d 665 (Fed. Cir. 1985). Such cases are usually characterized as "disappointed bidder" cases. In order to obtain jurisdiction on the basis of such implied contracts, the "disappointed bidder" must plead that it has accepted the government's offer contained in the solicitation. Thus, a party that did not submit a bid or proposal has no contract claim because it did not furnish the government the consideration requested for its promise, *Hero, Inc. v. United States*, 3 Cl. Ct. 413 (1983). In that case the plaintiff expended effort in preparing a bid but did not submit the bid, contending that the specifications were defective. The court refused to grant an injunction preventing award under the solicitation, reasoning that the mere expenditure of effort and money in preparing a bid without actually submitting it is not sufficient consideration for the government's implied promise. In *Harris Sys. Int'l, Inc. v. United States*, 5 Cl. Ct. 253 (1984), the court found no jurisdiction in an action by a small-business minority firm that had not submitted a proposal because the procuring agency had demanded that the SBA nominate another firm under the 8(a) set-aside. The court also held that the fact that the SBA had originally nominated the plaintiff to the Air Force did not establish an implied contract. In *Eagle Constr. Corp. v. United States*, 4 Cl. Ct. 470 (1984), the court found that the government's cancellation of a solicitation after technical proposals were received was not improper under the circumstances. Thus, the plaintiff who submitted a proposal under that solicitation but failed to submit one under the new solicitation for the same work had no disappointed bidder status under the new solicitation. See also *Control Data Sys., Inc. v. United States*, 32 Fed. Cl. 520 (1994) (incumbent contractor did not submit a proposal for follow-on contract, and the plaintiff's claim was therefore not a preaward protest within the jurisdiction of the court); *Howard v. United States*, 21 Cl. Ct. 475 (1990) (proposal submitted after closing date for receipt of proposals; thus, no valid offer that the government could accept); *Durable Metals Prods., Inc. v. United States*, 27 Fed. Cl. 472 (1993) (no jurisdiction because offeror withdrew from procurement); and *Data Transformation Corp. v. United States*, 13 Cl. Ct. 165 (1987) (informal presentation made to an agency of the plaintiff's technical ability to perform the work called for under the planned program was not the same as a response to a solicitation and did not create an implied-in-fact contract). While the court's rationale in nonbidder cases is clearly supportable where the plaintiff has not expended effort in reliance on the solicitation or decides to forgo the procurement, it is questionable where expenditures have been made in reliance on a solicitation that contains defective specifications or is otherwise improper.

The mere submission of a bid or proposal will not establish the necessary contractual relationship; the submission must be responsive to the invitation for bids. In *Yachts Am., Inc. v. United States*, 3 Cl. Ct. 447 (1983), *aff'd*, 779 F.2d 656 (Fed. Cir. 1985), the documents and letter submitted to the agency were found to be wholly nonresponsive and, thus, failed to give the plaintiff the status of a disappointed bidder. However, the court will review the bid and the solicitation to determine whether it is responsive and, if it so finds, will exercise its jurisdiction, *Olympia USA, Inc. v. United States*, 6 Cl. Ct. 550 (1984). See also *Blount, Inc. v. United States*, 22 Cl. Ct. 221 (1990) (court exercised jurisdiction to determine whether a clause in the IFB not addressed by the bid related to bidder responsiveness or responsibility). The disappointed bidder must also be able to show actual or threatened injury. In *Caddell Constr. Co. v. United States*, 9 Cl. Ct. 610 (1986), the court held that an offeror ranked sixth had no substantial chance for award and, thus, had no standing to sue. In addition, the firm submitting the offer must be eligible to receive the award, *ATL, Inc. v. United States*, 735 F.2d 1343 (Fed. Cir. 1984) (bids following a firm's suspension or debarment could not create implied contract because such firms are ineligible for award); *Gibraltar Indus., Inc. v. United States*, 2 Cl. Ct. 589 (1983), *vacated as moot*, 726 F.2d 747 (Fed. Cir. 1984) (bidder determined not to be a small business could not create implied contract by bidding on small business set-aside). However, a suspension or debarment issued after a bid or proposal has been submitted does not deprive the disappointed offeror of jurisdiction over such a previous bid or proposal, *Sterlingwear of Boston, Inc. v. United States*, 11 Cl. Ct. 517 (1987); *Electro-Methods, Inc. v. United States*, 728 F.2d 1471 (Fed. Cir. 1984). The court will take jurisdiction over claims alleging that the agency has improperly applied responsibility standards to an offeror, *Hayes Int'l Corp. v. United States*, 7 Cl. Ct. 681 (1985). See also *Skytech Aero, Inc. v. United States*, 26 Cl. Ct. 251 (1992), where an unsuccessful bidder alleged that the Army acted arbitrarily and capriciously by awarding a contract to a bidder that was not responsible and whose bid was nonresponsive. The court exercised jurisdiction and held that a preaward survey conducted by the Army allowed a reasonable conclusion that the bidder was responsible. The Court of Federal Claims has jurisdiction to review certificate of competency determinations by the SBA, *Cavalier Clothes, Inc. v. United States*, 810 F.2d 1108 (Fed. Cir. 1987); *Stapp Towing, Inc. v. United States*, 34 Fed. Cl. 300 (1995); *Related Indus., Inc. v. United States*, 2 Cl. Ct. 517 (1983).

In several rare cases the court has found preaward implied contracts to exist in situations other than disappointed bidder cases. See *Western Pioneer, Inc. v. United States*, 8 Cl. Ct. 291 (1985), where the court held that a letter requesting that the plaintiff submit its proposed operating plan constituted "a sufficient request . . . such as to form an implied contract to fairly and honestly consider [the] responding proposal." See also *Standard Mfg. Co. v. United States*, 7 Cl. Ct. 54 (1984), where the plaintiff alleged that it responded to a *Commerce Business Daily* (CBD) notice in which the Air Force stated its intention to award a sole source contract and invited interested parties to identify interests in the procurement or to submit proposals for the work. The court held that such facts are sufficient to create an implied promise for the Air Force to give fair and impartial consideration to the response. Similarly, in *Magnavox Elec. Sys. Co. v. United States*, 26 Cl. Ct. 1373 (1992), the court held that a CBD notice of intent to conduct a sole source procurement and plaintiff's response that it could perform the work resulted in an implied contract to give plaintiff's response fair and impartial consideration. However, in *Motorola, Inc. v. United States*, 988 F.2d 113 (Fed. Cir. 1993), the court affirmed a decision of the Court of Federal Claims denying jurisdiction over a suit filed by a company that assisted the government in drafting the procurement specification but did not submit an offer because a bid sample was required. The Federal Circuit adopted the Court of Federal Claims decision, which disagreed with the rationale in *Standard Manufacturing*, stating that government requests for information and responses from prospective bidders are not the equivalents of offer and acceptance. The Federal Circuit quoted the Court of Federal Claims at 116:

> Such exchanges are not carried on with an expectation to presently affect legal relations. Rather, the parties are dealing — as they were here — exclusively with an eye to the future, each being free, in the meantime, to withdraw from the dialogue.

> The situation, therefore, is quite unlike that encountered where a bid has been submitted. In that circumstance there is a promise — the contractor's bid — which empowers the Government, upon acceptance, to bind the contractor to the terms of the solicitation. The essence of the contractor's engagement — the manifestation of an intention to be bound — warrants reading into the situation a reciprocal commitment from the Government, *i.e.*, a promise to fairly and honestly consider the contractor's bid. *Heyer Products Co. v. United States*, 135 Ct. Cl. 63, 69, 140 F. Supp. 409, 412 (1956).

See also *Garchik v. United States*, 37 Fed. Cl. 52 (1996), where the court denied jurisdiction over a proposal submitted in response to a CBD announcement that the agency proposed to enter into a sole source lease. In *American Hoist & Derrick, Inc. v. United States*, 3 Cl. Ct. 198 (1983), the plaintiff was a large business that was precluded from bidding on a solicitation because the procurement was set-aside for small businesses. However, the court took jurisdiction on the basis of an implied contract alleged to have been formed when the plaintiff released its proprietary data to the government in exchange for an agreement that it would be permitted to bid on the procurement. See also *Yachts Am., Inc. v. United States*, 3 Cl. Ct. 447 (1983), *aff'd*, 779 F.2d 656 (Fed. Cir. 1985). In *Airborne Data, Inc. v. United States*, 702 F.2d 1350 (Fed. Cir. 1983), the court held that an implied contract was formed when an unsolicited proposal was received in response to regulations inviting the submittal of such proposals. In *Pressman v. United States*, 33 Fed. Cl. 438 (1995), the court held that the agency's regulations prohibiting the release of confidential information did not give rise to an implied contract not to disclose confidential information contained in unsolicited proposals. The court distinguished *Airborne Data*, stating that in that case the text of the regulations contained an explicit promise of confidentiality, whereas in *Pressman* the regulations, although binding on the agency, could not be construed as suggesting that the agency was directing an offer to the general public to confidentially consider unsolicited proposals.

C. Time for Protest

Unlike agency-level or GAO protests, there are no regulatory time limits for filing at the court, However, the Federal Circuit has established a waiver rule by stating that "a party who has the opportunity to object to the terms of a government solicitation containing a patent error and fails to do so prior to the close of the bidding process waives its ability to raise the same objection afterwards in a § 1491(b) action in the Court of Federal Claims," *Blue & Gold Fleet, L.P. v. United States*, 492 F.3d 1308 (Fed. Cir. 2007). *Blue & Gold* has been consistently interpreted as standing for the proposition that "[t]he proper time to challenge the provisions of a prospectus is before bids are required to be submitted," *Frazier v. United States*, 79 Fed. Cl. 148 (2007). Among the many reasons for this rule cited by the Federal Circuit is the need for "'expeditious resolution'" of bid protests before this court. The waiver rule thus "avoids costly after the fact litigation," *Infrastructure Def. Techs., LLC v. United States*, 81 Fed. Cl. 375 (2008). See *Shamrock Foods Co. v. United States*, 92 Fed. Cl. 339 (2010) (protest of terms of the solicitation); *Unisys Corp. v. United States*, 89 Fed. Cl. 126 (2009) (propriety of a price evaluation methodology that was explicitly described in the RFQ); *Blackwater Lodge & Training Center, Inc. v. United States*, 86 Fed. Cl. 488 (2009) (failure to challenge the terms of solicitation); *Moore's Cafeteria Servs. v. United States*, 77 Fed. Cl. 180 (2007) (protest of solicitation amendment); *Scott v. United States*, 78 Fed. Cl. 151 (2007) (protest of terms of solicitation after contract award); and *Erinys Iraq Ltd. v. United States*, 78 Fed. Cl. 518 (2007) (protest of solicitation terms). But see *Allied Materials & Equip. Co. v. United States*, 81 Fed. Cl. 448 (2008), in which Allied did not waive protest right because it had no knowledge of defect in solicitation until after the date for submission of proposals. In *DGR Assoc's, Inc. v. United States*, 94 Fed. Cl. 189 (2010), the court distinguished *Blue & Gold Fleet* and found a protest to a challenge to the solicitation impropriety timely even though it was not filed before the close of the bidding process. DGR had challenged the Air Force's solicitation before the closing date for receipt of proposals with an agency-level protest. When those actions proved unsuccessful DGR timely protested to the GAO. At each step DGR followed applicable FAR and GAO protest procedures. The court held that the correct interpretation of *Blue & Gold Fleet* is that, if a party has challenged a solicitation impropriety before the close of the bidding process, the party is not precluded from later filing its protest at the Court of Federal Claims. A party must do something before the closing date to preserve its rights, and must thereafter pursue its position in a timely manner.

D. Intervenors

Intervenors are permitted under the Rules of the United States Court of Federal Claims (RCFC) 24, which states:

(a) Intervention of Right. On timely motion, the court must permit anyone to intervene who:

(1) is given an unconditional right to intervene by a federal statute; or

(2) claims an interest relating to the property or transaction that is the subject of the action, and is so situated that disposing of the action may as a practical matter impair or impede the movant's ability to protect its interest, unless the existing parties adequately represent that interest.

(b) Permissive Intervention.

(1) *In General.* On timely motion, the court may permit anyone to intervene who:

(A) is given a conditional right to intervene by a federal statute; or

(B) has a claim or defense that shares with the main action a question of law or fact.

(2) *By a Government Officer or Agency.*

[Not used.]

(3) *Delay or Prejudice.* In exercising its discretion, the court must consider whether the intervention will unduly delay or prejudice the adjudication of the original parties' rights.

This rule thus provides for both intervention of right and permissive intervention.

The court has held that the requirements for intervention are to be construed in favor of intervention, *Cherokee Nation of Okla. v. United States*, 69 Fed. Cl. 148 (2005). Intervention is authorized where the applicant has an interest relating to the subject of the action and is so situated that disposition of the action may impair or impede its ability to protect that interest. Such intervention of right is mandated when the applicant's interests are not adequately represented by the existing parties to the litigation, *Che Consulting, Inc. v. United States*, 452 F.3. 1371 (2006). Here, the applicant to the motion to intervene asserted that its interests and the government's interests did not completely coincide. As a result, it argued that there was a likelihood that its interests would not be adequately protected by the government. The court agreed, stating that the issue before the court has a direct affect on the applicant, which may not be adequately articulated by the government, making intervention appropriate. See also *Northrop Grumman Information Tech., Inc. v. United States*, 74 Fed. Cl. 407 (2006), where the court granted the motion to intervene finding the intervenor's trade secrets and proprietary information constituted sufficient property interests to justify intervention. The record indicated a denial of the right to intervene might directly impair the intervenor's ability to protect its intellectual property. However, the court will not allow intervention to protect indirect or contingent interests, *American Maritime Transp. v. United States*, 870 F.2d 1559 (Fed. Cir. 1989); *Hage v. United States*, 35 Fed. Cl. 737 (1996).

A motion to intervene must be timely filed. Three factors are used to determine whether an intervention is timely: (1) the length of time during which the would-be intervenors actually knew or reasonably should have known of their rights; (2) whether the prejudice to the rights of existing parties by allowing intervention outweighs the prejudice to the would-be intervenors by denying intervention; and (3) the existence of unusual circumstances militating either for or against a determination that the application is timely, *Belton Indus., Inc. v. United States*, 6 F.3d 756 (Fed. Cir. 1993). See *Wackenhut Servs., Inc. v. United States*, 85 Fed. Cl. 273 (2008) (motion submitted two days after complaint, no party opposed motion and the court was unaware of any prejudice to the existing parties or any unusual circumstances); and *Information Sciences Corp. v. United States*, 73 Fed. Cl. 70 (2006) (submitted seven days after complaint, neither party opposed intervention, and court was unaware of any prejudice to existing parties or any unusual circumstances militating against intervention). However, in *TRW Envtl. Safety Sys., Inc. v. United States*, 16 Cl. Ct. 516 (1989), the Claims Court held that an unsuccessful bidder's motion to intervene in another unsuccessful bidder's suit for injunctive relief was untimely: the bidder waited 84 days from knowing of the suit before moving to intervene.

E. Procedures

The Court of Federal Claims follows the rules set forth in the Rules of the United States Court of Federal Claims (RCFC) (as amended through January 11, 2010). These rules are based upon the Federal Rules of Civil Procedure. Appendix C to the RCFC, which is entitled "Procedures in Procurement Protest Cases Pursuant to 28 U.S.C. § 1491(b)" describes standard practices in Court of Federal Claims bid protest cases.

1. Commencement of Action

a. Complaint and Service of Summons

A civil action in the Court of Federal Claims is commenced by filing a complaint with the clerk of court, RCFC 3. Service is made by the party, attorney of record, or any other person acting under the attorney of record's direction by executing a certificate of service, which contains the date and manner of service, the person or entity served, and the method of service employed, e.g., in person, by mail, or by electronic or other means, RCFC 5.3(a). The plaintiff must file an original and seven copies of the complaint with the court, RCFC 5.5. To serve a complaint on the United States, the clerk must deliver five copies of the complaint to the Attorney General or to an agent designated by authority of the Attorney General, RCFC 4(a). When serving a complaint, the clerk must enter the fact of service on the docket, and this entry will be prima facie proof of service, RCFC 4(b).

In order to expedite the proceeding, Appendix C to the RCFC requires that protester's "counsel must (except in exceptional circumstances to be described in moving papers) provide at least 24-hour advance notice of filing a protest" to the DOJ's Commercial Litigation Branch, the COFC Clerk, the procuring agency, and the apparently successful offeror(s) (if any)," Appendix C(2).

b. Filing Fee

A $350 filing fee must be paid to the clerk of the court when the action is commenced.

2. Pleadings and Motions

a. Claim for Relief

Rule 8(a) states that the complaint must contain the following:

(1) a short and plain statement of the grounds for the court's jurisdiction, unless the court already has jurisdiction and the claim needs no new grounds to support;

(2) a short and plain statement of the claim showing that the pleader is entitled to relief; and

(3) a demand for the relief sought, which may include relief in the alternative or different types of relief.

In all averments of fraud or mistake, the circumstances constituting fraud or mistake must be stated with particularity, RCFC 9(b). See *Keco Indus., Inc. v. United States*, 203 Ct. Cl. 566, 492 F.2d 1200 (1974), where the court held that a disappointed bidder's pleadings lacked particularity. In reaching this finding, the court stated that alleging general violations of the Armed Services Procurement Regulations fell far short of the specificity called for in the rule. See also *Baskett v. United States*, 2 Cl. Ct. 356 (1983) (although the Claims Court has adopted the notice pleading system found in the federal courts, this system does not do away with the requirement of particularity; unclear allegations of fraud and misrepresentation in pleadings of plaintiff are dismissed).

b. Preliminary Hearings

Evidentiary hearings may be conducted by the Court of Federal Claims, RCFC 12(d). This rule provides that the following defenses must be heard and determined at a preliminary hearing unless the court orders deferral until trial:

(1) lack of subject-matter jurisdiction;

(2) lack of personal jurisdiction;

(3) improper venue [not used];

(4) insufficient process;

(5) insufficient service of process;

(6) failure to state a claim upon which relief can be granted; and

(7) failure to join a party under RCFC 19.

c. Administrative Record Supplementation

The "administrative record" refers to materials that the United States is required to file with the Court of Federal Claims in response to a protest, RCFC App. C, provision 21. RCFC App. C provision 22 provides a detailed list as guidance regarding the type of documents that may be appropriate for the United States to include as "core documents" in the administrative record, to include:

(a) the agency's procurement request, purchase request, or statement of requirements;

(b) the agency's source selection plan;

(c) the bid abstract or prospectus of bid;

(d) the Commerce Business Daily or other public announcement of the procurement;

(e) the solicitation, including any instructions to offerors, evaluation factors, solicitation amendments, and requests for best and final offers;

(f) documents and information provided to bidders during any pre-bid or pre-proposal conference;

(g) the agency's responses to any questions about or requests for clarification of the solicitation;

(h) the agency's estimates of the cost of performance;

(i) correspondence between the agency and the protester, awardee, or other interested parties relating to the procurement;

(j) records of any discussions, meetings, or telephone conferences between the agency and the protester, awardee, or other interested parties relating to the procurement;

(k) records of the results of any bid opening or oral motion auction in which the protester, awardee, or other interested parties participated;

(*l*) the protester's, awardee's, or other interested parties' offers, proposals, or other responses to the solicitation;

(m) the agency's competitive range determination, including supporting documentation;

(n) the agency's evaluations of the protester's, awardee's, or other interested parties' offers, proposals, or other responses to the solicitation, including supporting documentation;

(o) the agency's source selection decision including supporting documentation;

(p) pre-award audits, if any, or surveys of the offerors;

(q) notification of contract award and the executed contract;

(r) documents relating to any pre- or post-award debriefing;

(s) documents relating to any stay, suspension, or termination of award or performance pending resolution of the bid protest;

(t) justifications, approvals, determinations, and findings, if any, prepared for the procurement by the agency pursuant to statute or regulation; and

(u) the record of any previous administrative or judicial proceedings relating to the procurement, including the record of any other protest of the procurement.

Motions to supplement the administrative record are governed by the Federal Circuit's decision in *Axiom Resource Mgmt., Inc. v. United States*, 564 F.3d 1374 (Fed. Cir. 2009). In *Axiom*, the court emphasized that "the parties' ability to supplement the administrative record is limited," and that the "focus of judicial review of agency action" remains on the administrative record, which should be supplemented only if the existing record is insufficient to permit meaningful review consistent with the Administrative Procedure Act. The court stated that determination of whether to order supplementation of the administrative record depends on whether supplementation is "necessary in order not 'to frustrate effective judicial review'" (quoting *Camp v. Pitts*, 411 U.S. 138, 142-43 (1973)). See also *Impresa Construzioni Geom.*

Domenico Garufi v. United States, 238 F.3d 1324 (Fed. Cir. 2001). In a motion seeking testimony, the court in *Global Computer Enters., Inc. v. United States*, 88 Fed. Cl. 52 (2009), permitted supplementation of the administrative record because of the complexity of the case, the multitude of issues presented with respect to both jurisdiction and merits, the voluminous amount of information presented by the parties, and the necessity for supplementation in order to avoid frustrating judicial review. See also *Blue & Gold Fleet, LP v. United States*, 70 Fed. Cl. 487 (2006), *aff'd*, 492 F.3d 1308 (Fed. Cir. 2007) (supplementation is justified "when it is necessary for a full and complete understanding of the issues"); and *Mike Hooks, Inc. v. United States*, 39 Fed. Cl. 147 (1997) (considering evidence supplementing the record because it "help[s] explain the highly technical nature of the issues").

Supplementation of the administrative record is limited to cases in which "the omission of extra-record evidence precludes effective judicial review," *Murakami v. United States*, 46 Fed. Cl. 731, 735 (2000), *aff'd*, 389 F.3d 1342 (Fed. Cir. 2005). The *Murakami* court stated that the purpose of limiting review to the record actually before the agency is to guard against courts using new evidence to "convert the 'arbitrary and capricious' standard into effectively 'de novo review.'" However, to perform an effective review pursuant to the APA, the court must have a record containing the information upon which the agency relied when it made its decision as well as any documentation revealing the agency's decision-making process. See *Citizens to Preserve Overton Park, nc. v. Volpe*, 401 U.S. 402, 420 (1971) ("[S]ince the bare record may not disclose the factors that were considered or the Secretary's construction of the evidence[,] it may be necessary for the [d]istrict [c]ourt to require some explanation in order to determine if the Secretary acted within the scope of his authority and if the Secretary's action was justifiable under the applicable standard."), abrogated in an unrelated respect by *Califano v. Sanders*, 430 U.S. 99, 105 (1977) (APA does not constitute an implied grant of subject matter jurisdiction to review agency actions). See also *Montana Fish, Wildlife, & Parks Found., Inc. v. United States*, 91 Fed. Cl. 434 (2010).

Cases permitting supplementation of the administrative record with declarations include *Totolo/King, a Joint Venture v. United States*, 87 Fed. Cl. 680 (2009) (affidavit attempted to explain why the government's failure to specify a bond estimate was unreasonable); and *Academy Facilities Mgmt. v. United States*, 87 Fed. Cl. 680 (2009) (affidavit of a source selection authority was an appropriate supplement to the record because it explicitly answered a question on a critical issue that was not clear in the administrative record). Cases rejecting supplementation include *DataMill, Inc. v. United States*, 91 Fed. Cl. 722 (2010) (rejecting supplementation of the record, stating that supplementation is justified (1) when required for meaningful judicial review, and (2) when necessary for a full and complete understanding of the issues); *Allied Tech. Group, Inc. v. United States & Monster Gov't Solutions, LLC*, 92 Fed. Cl. 226 (2010) (declarations offered by both parties were not included in the protest record because they were not before the contracting officer at the time the protested decision was made; they also constituted opinion testimony that would not assist the court in determining whether the agency's award decision was rational); and *L-3 Communications Eotech, Inc. v United States*, 87 Fed. Cl. 565 (2009) (proffered documents were irrelevant to the court's APA review of the protester's elimination from competition and where other documents constituted "post-hoc contentions of fact and argument" that were not before the agency as it made its decision).

The court may permit supplementation of the record with information that the protester argues the agency either did consider or should have considered in making the protested decision. See *Allied Tech. Group, Inc. v. United States*, 92 Fed. Cl. 226 (2010) (supplementation of record with Internet materials such as memoranda from the Office of Personnel Management and the Office of Management and Budget, Internet articles, and a screen shot of an agency website); *PlanetSpace, Inc. v. United States*, 90 Fed. Cl. 1 (2009) (introduced 146 pages of documents received in response to a Freedom of Information Act request); and *Kerr Contractors, Inc. v. United States*, 89 Fed. Cl. 312 (2009) (agency's responses to questions regarding clarification of the solicitation).

Where bias is alleged, the administrative record frequently will not be complete or suffice to prove or disprove the allegation, *Pitney Bowes Gov't Solutions, Inc. v. United States*, 93 Fed. Cl. 327 (2010). Consequently, to address bias, the court will entertain extra-record evidence and permit discovery when there has been a "strong showing of bad faith or improper behavior" such that without discovery the administrative record cannot be trusted, *Alabama Aircraft Indus., Inc. v. United States*, 82 Fed. Cl. 757 (2008). The strong showing must have an evidentiary foundation and not rest merely on counsel's argument, suspicion, or conjecture, *Madison Servs., Inc. v. United States*, 92 Fed. Cl. 120 (2010). In *Pitney Bowes* the court determined that there were indicia of bias, including affidavits regarding pre-procurement discussions. The court ordered limited deposition testimony of the individual technical evaluation panel members in order to determine their views prior to finalization of the consensus reports. See also *L-3 Communications Integrated Sys., L.P. v United States*, 91 Fed. Cl. 347 (2010) ("[A]llegations of bad faith and bias [must be] sufficiently well grounded to warrant supplementation of the [a]dministrative [r]ecord, [and] based upon hard facts."). A threshold showing of either a motivation for the governmental employee to have acted in bad faith or of conduct that is hard to explain absent bad faith is required, *Beta Analytics Int'l, Inc. v. United States*, 61 Fed. Cl. 223 (2004). Although the agency decision is entitled to a presumption of regularity, *Impresa Construzioni Geom. Domenico Garufi v. United States*, 238 F.3d 1324 (Fed. Cir. 2001), this presumption may be rebutted by an appropriate factual predicate, *OTI Am., Inc. v. United States*, 68 Fed. Cl. 108 (2005). Further, allowing for deposition testimony of the contracting officer or other governmental official in a bid protest, where appropriate, "may enable the court to satisfy its statutory duty to give due regard to the need for expeditious resolution of the action," *Asia Pac. Airlines v. United States*, 68 Fed. Cl. 8 (2005) (allowing supplementation where rationale of decision makers was not apparent from the administrative record). See also

Impressa Construzioni Geom. Domenico Garufi, 238 F.3d 1324 (Fed. Cir. 2001) (allowing deposition of contracting officer to elucidate grounds for his decisions and determine whether a rational basis was lacking).

In some instances, a plaintiff will move to introduce portions of a prior GAO protest record into the court protest record. In *Bannum v. United States*, 89 Fed. Cl. 184 (2009), the court determined that documents related to contract performance should be supplements to the administrative record because without the documents, the court would not be able to assess whether the contracting agency provided a coherent and reasonable explanation of its exercise of discretion. In its reasoning the court cited RCFC App. C, Provision 22(u), which explicitly anticipated the inclusion of the agency report submitted to GAO in the record in a subsequent protest filed at the Court of Federal Claims that involves the same procurement. See also *Holloway & Co., PLLC v. United States*, 87 Fed. Cl. 381 (2009), noting that the purpose of RCFC App. C, provision 22(u) is to ensure that the full record of all proceedings related to the procurement is before the court for review. The court allowed supplementation of the record with six documents generated before GAO because provision 22(u) indicates that core documents include the record of the previous protest. But see *Allied Tech. Group, Inc. v. United States*, 92 Fed. Cl. 226 (2010), stating that inclusion of documents in the record of a GAO protest is not automatic. The court held that the declarations were opinion testimony proclaiming the alleged superiority of the competing products, and were not before the contracting officer at the time of the award decision, and were not necessary to organize or understand the administrative record.

The court may allow the introduction of information relevant to a remedy, rather that the merits of the protest. See *AshBritt, Inc. v. United States*, 87 Fed. Cl. 344 (2009), where the court stated at 366-67:

> In general, it is appropriate to add evidence pertaining to prejudice and the factors governing injunctive relief to the record in a bid protest — not as a supplement to the AR, but as part of this Court's record. Evidence directed at prejudice and remedy necessarily would not be before an agency decision maker effecting a procurement decision such as a source selection award. Rather, evidence of the prejudicial effect vel non of a procurement decision or the ramifications of injunctive relief would necessarily post date and flow from such agency decision.

4. *Depositions and Discovery*

Parties may conduct discovery by one oral examination (RCFC 30) or by written questions (RCFC 31). The scope of discovery is set forth in RCFC 26(b)(1):

> Parties may obtain discovery regarding any nonprivileged matter that is relevant to any party's claim or defense — including the existence, description, nature, custody, condition, and location of any documents or other tangible things and the identity and location of persons who know of any discoverable matter. For

good cause, the court may order discovery of any matter relevant to the subject matter involved in the action. Relevant information need not be admissible at the trial if the discovery appears reasonably calculated to lead to the discovery of admissible evidence. All discovery is subject to the limitations imposed by RCFC 26(b)(2)(C).

Discovery sought in an effort to establish alleged bias of the agency in the procurement process is difficult to obtain. In *Information Tech. & Applications Corp. v. United States*, 316 F.3d 1312 (Fed. Cir. 2003), the appellant argued that the Court of Federal Claims improperly refused to allow discovery regarding alleged bias of the Air Force in the procurement process. In denying discovery, the Federal Circuit addressed the standard for allowing discovery on a bias allegation in a bid protest. It explained at 1323, fn2:

> An agency decision is entitled to a presumption of regularity. [D]iscovery of the contracting officer's reasoning is not lightly to be ordered and should not be ordered unless record evidence raises serious questions as to the rationality of the contracting officer's [decision]. In this case, ITAC has pointed to no record evidence of bias. Instead it has merely reiterated its contentions that the Air Force erred in evaluating the proposals. This is not evidence of bias, and it is insufficient to overcome the presumption that the contracting officer acted in good faith.

Discovery must be conducted in a timely fashion early in the proceedings. If a party finds that unforeseen discovery is necessary during the argument of a case, it must request discovery at that time. In *Vanguard Sec., Inc. v. United States*, 20 Cl. Ct. 90 (1990), the plaintiff found, while arguing summary judgment motions, that the government was asserting new grounds to support the cancellation of a solicitation. The plaintiff did not indicate at the time that it needed discovery but made the request in its post-argument brief. The court denied this request, holding that it was untimely.

It is very difficult to obtain sanctions for failing to comply with discovery requests. In *ViON Corp. v. United States*, 906 F.2d 1564 (Fed. Cir. 1990), the court reversed the board's dismissal of a protest on the grounds that it was frivolous because the protester had not provided good faith answers to the government's interrogatories. The court quoted the board's reasoning, 90-1 BCA ¶ 22,287 at 111,941:

> Since this protest was filed, however, we have had the opportunity to observe the actions of protester first hand. We have reviewed in detail the answers ViON has provided to critical discovery requests. We have concluded that they were inadequate. We have likewise seen protester disregard important provisions in the Board's order authorizing discovery, with the result that the Board's control over the discovery process was diminished and the discovery accomplished was less efficient and less productive. In the absence of some redress from the Board, all of these actions on the part of ViON make it increasingly difficult for the agency to prepare a timely defense and, to that extent, provide ViON with an unfair advantage in pursuing the protest.

The court found that the interrogatories for which the board considered ViON non-responsive did not relate to a matter that ViON had the burden to prove and held that a protest cannot be dismissed as frivolous unless the protest lacks an arguable basis in fact or law. The court held that noncompliance with a discovery order on issues that the protester did not have to prove and a finding by the board that the motive of the protester was not genuine did not make the protest frivolous. However, the court added in a footnote at 1566:

> This is not to say that the refusal to respond promptly and adequately to proper discovery request might not, in this or some other case, give rise to an inference that the protester's case lacks merits because the protester does not have the facts required for an arguable case.

5. Protective Orders

When a party responding to a discovery request believes that it will have to provide confidential material, it can seek a protective order limiting the people that can review the material. RCFC 26(c) governs protective orders, providing that:

> A party or any person from whom discovery is sought may move for a protective order. The motion must include a certification that the movant has in good faith conferred or attempted to confer with other affected parties in an effort to resolve the dispute without any court action. The court may, for good cause, issue an order to protect a party or person from annoyance, embarrassment, oppression, or undue burden or expense, including one or more of the following: . . . (G) requiring that a trade secret or other confidential research, development, or commercial information not be revealed or revealed only in a specific way. . . .

See *Forest Prods. Northwest, Inc. v. United States*, 453 F.3d 1355 (Fed. Cir. 2006), affirming the denial of a protective order because the party had not met the "good cause" standard by submitting evidence that the material sought to be protected affected "its business operations, its public persona, or the privacy of its principals." In *Lakeland Partners, LLC v. United States*, 88 Fed. Cl. 124 (2009), the court described the "good cause" standard as "strict," stating at 133:

> "The party . . . must make a particularized factual showing of the harm that would be sustained if the court did not grant a protective order." Arthur R. Miller, *Confidentiality, Protective Orders, and Public Access to Courts*, 105 Harv. L. Rev. 427, 433 (1991). "[T]he party seeking the protective order must show good cause by demonstrating a particular need for protection." *Cipollone v. Liggett Group, Inc.*, 785 F.2d 1108, 1121 (3d Cir. 1986). Thus, broad allegations of harm, unsubstantiated by specific examples, are insufficient to justify issuance of a protective order.

In contrast, when competitors are involved in litigation, such as a protest including an intervenor, courts frequently issue blanket protective orders as a means of allowing discovery to proceed efficiently, *Armour of America v. United States*, 73 Fed. Cl. 597 (2006) (emphasizing that such an order is not a determination that the protected material is proprietary). RCFC Form 8 is a standard form protective order to be used in protest cases. This form specifies that the only persons allowed access to protected information are "counsel for a party and independent consultants and experts assisting such counsel in connection with this litigation" as well as paralegal, clerical and administrative support personnel assisting counsel. Persons other than counsel must sign a RCFC Form 9 indicating that they have read and will abide by the order. Government attorneys and agency personnel are permitted access to protected material without any formalities.

A protective order can also deny discovery of confidential material when the court determines that the party does not need the information to pursue the litigation. Where a party seeking a protective order has shown that the information sought is confidential and that its disclosure might be harmful, the burden shifts to the party seeking discovery to establish that the disclosure of trade secrets and confidential information is relevant and necessary to its case, *American Standard, Inc. v. Pfizer, Inc.*, 828 F.2d 734 (Fed. Cir. 1987); *Heat & Control, Inc. v. Hester Indus., Inc.*, 785 F.2d 1017 (Fed. Cir. 1986). See *Pikes Peak Family Housing, LLC v. United States*, 40 Fed. Cl. 673 (1998), where the court held that the successful offeror was not entitled to a protective order forbidding disclosure of certain information by counsel for the disappointed offeror to its client. The court stated that the information, whether already in the administrative record or obtained through discovery, was pertinent to the disappointed offeror's own proposal. Thus, it was clear that discovery was not being used as a vehicle for the acquisition of proprietary information and trade secrets of other offerors.

The Court of Federal Claims can impose sanctions on attorneys that violate a protective order, *Pacific Gas & Elec. Co. v. United States*, 82 Fed. Cl. 474 (2008) (ordering attorney to pay costs incurred by government).

F. Standard of Review

The proper standard to be applied in bid protest cases is provided by 5 U.S.C. § 706(2)(A), which provides a reviewing court shall set aside the agency action if it is arbitrary, capricious, an abuse of discretion, or otherwise not in accordance with law, *Banknote Corp. of Am. v. United States*, 365 F.3d 1345 (2004). The arbitrary and capricious standard is highly deferential, *Advanced Data Concepts, Inc. v. United States*, 216 F.3d 1054 (Fed. Cir. 2000).

This appears to be essentially the same standards that the court uses in its contract jurisdiction. In cases alleging that the government has violated its implied promise to honestly and fairly consider bids or proposals, the standard of review used by the Court of Federal Claims is to determine if the government's conduct toward the protester was arbitrary or capricious. But see *Information Sciences Corp. v. United States*, 85 Fed. Cl. 195 (standards of review is different under § 1491(b); only "fairly and honestly considered" standard under § 1491(a)(1)). In *Keco Indus.,*

Inc. v. United States, 203 Ct. Cl. 566, 492 F.2d 1200 (1974), the court indicated that arbitrary or capricious action would not result from mere negligence by the government, but may be proved in a number of ways, stating at 574:

> One is that subjective bad faith on the part of the procuring officials, depriving a bidder of the fair and honest consideration of his proposal, normally warrants recovery of bid preparation costs. *Heyer Products Co. v. United States*, 135 Ct. Cl. 63, 140 F. Supp. 409 (1956). A second is that proof that there was "no reasonable basis" for the administrative decision will also suffice, at least in many situations. *Continental Business Enterprises v. United States*, 196 Ct. Cl. 627, 637-38, 452 F.2d 1016, 1021 (1971). The third is that the degree of proof of error necessary for recovery is ordinarily related to the amount of discretion entrusted to the procurement officials by applicable statutes and regulations. *Continental Business Enterprises v. United States, supra*, 196 Ct. Cl. at 637, 452 F.2d at 1021 (1971); *Keco Industries, Inc. v. United States, supra*, 192 Ct. Cl. at 784, 428 F.2d at 1240. The fourth is that proven violation of pertinent statutes or regulations can, but need not necessarily, be a ground for recovery.

In *Impresa Construzioni Geom. Domenico Garufy v. United States*, 238 F.3d 1324 (Fed. Cir. 2001), the Federal Circuit held that 28 U.S.C. § 1491(b), by its plain terms and according to its legislative history, "applies the Administrative Dispute Resolution Act standard of review previously applied by the district courts." Thus, the standards outlined in *Scanwell Labs., Inc. v. Shaffer*, 424 F.2d 859 (D.C. Cir. 1970) and the line of cases following that decision apply. Under the APA standard as applied in the *Scanwell* line of cases, and now in ADRA cases, a bid award may be set aside if either (1) the procurement official's decision lacked a rational basis or (2) the procurement procedure involved a violation of statute or regulation.

In considering whether the government acted in bad faith, the court requires the protester to prove that the government acted with specific intent to injure it. See *Galen Medical Assocs. v. United States*, 369 F.3d 1324 (Fed. Cir. 2004), stating at 1330:

> [W]hen a bidder alleges bad faith, "in order to overcome the presumption of good faith [on behalf of the government], the proof must be irrefragable." *Info. Tech. Applications Corp. v. United States*, 316 F.3d 1312, 1323 n.2 (Fed. Cir. 2003). "Almost irrefragable proof" amounts to "clear and convincing evidence," *Am-Pro Protective Agency, Inc. v. United States*, 281 F.3d 1234, 1239-40 (Fed. Cir. 2002). "In the cases where the court has considered allegations of bad faith, the necessary 'irrefragable proof' has been equated with evidence of some specific intent to injure the plaintiff." *Torncello v. United States*, 231 Ct. Cl. 20, 681 F.2d 756, 770 (1982).

See also *Aviation Enters., Inc. v. United States*, 8 Cl. Ct. 1 (1985) (refusing to find bad faith on the basis of "speculation and innuendo"); and *Shields Enters., Inc. v. United States*, 28 Fed. Cl. 615 (1993) (no evidence that the government specifically intended to injure the plaintiff or that the government operated with any prejudice toward the plaintiff). However, in *Parcel 49C Limited Partnership v. United States*, 39 Cont. Cas. Fed. (CCH) ¶ 76,689, *aff'd*, 31 F.3d 1147 (Fed. Cir. 1994), the court held that the General Services Administration abused its discretion when it canceled a solicitation for the lease of office space allegedly based on changes in the needs of the using agency. The court found that the using agency's needs did not change until five years into the future and concluded that the GSA had relied upon this interpretation merely as a pretext for ridding itself of the procurement. In a fact pattern similar to *Parcel 49C*, the court in *126 Northpoint Plaza L.P. v. United States*, 34 Fed. Cl. 105 (1995), found bad faith when GSA officials canceled a solicitation in an effort to accommodate the Immigration and Naturalization Service, which was trying to avoid contracting with a particular offeror.

Absent bad faith, the protester must establish with clear and convincing evidence that the agency's determination lacked any rational basis or violated applicable statutes or regulations, *Vanguard Sec., Inc. v. United States*, 20 Cl. Ct. 90 (1990); *Northern Telecom, Inc. v. United States*, 8 Cl. Ct. 376 (1985). In finding that there was no rational basis for the action, the court in *Rockwell Int'l Corp. v. United States*, 4 Cl. Ct. 1 (1983), stated that: "To have a reasoned or rational basis, there must be a rational connection between the facts established and the choice made." See also *Prineville Sawmill Co. v. United States*, 859 F.2d 905 (Fed. Cir. 1988) (decision by Forest Service to reject all bids in timber sale had no reasonable basis). In *R.R. Donnelly & Sons, Co. v. United States*, 38 Fed. Cl. 518 (1997), the court rejected the argument that a postaward protester must prove a case by "clear and convincing" evidence and held that the burden was only "high." The court applied the standards traditionally applied in bid protests under *Keco Industries* but denied summary judgment because of unresolved factual issues between the parties.

If an award decision is challenged on the basis that it was made without a rational basis, the court will determine whether the contracting agency provided a coherent and reasonable explanation of its exercise of discretion, and the disappointed bidder bears a heavy burden of showing that the award decision had no rational basis, *Centech Group, Inc. v. United States*, 554 F.3d 1029 (Fed. Cir. 2009). The court will sustain an agency action unless the action does not evince rational reasoning and consideration of relevant factors, *Weeks Marine, Inc. v. United States*, 575 F.3d 1352 (Fed. Cir. 2009). In *Weeks Marine*, a dredging contractor, filed a pre-award bid protest challenging the Army Corps of Engineers' decision to solicit proposals for regional maintenance dredging and shore protection projects using multiple award, indefinite delivery/indefinite quantity (IDIQ) task order contracts, rather than sealed bidding procedures. The Court of Federal Claims granted Weeks's motion for judgment on the administrative record, ruling that the Corps' solicitation violated 10 U.S.C. § 2304(a)(2), which provides that sealed bidding must be used when an agency plans to award a contract based solely on price and price-related factors, and finding that the Corps lacked a rational basis for departing from its traditional district-by-district procurement strategy, in which individual dredging efforts were sourced locally through sealed bidding. On appeal, the Federal Circuit reversed, holding that the solicitation for the regional multiple award contracts did call for evaluation of non-price factors, and that the solicitation was rationally designed to address several of the Corps' goals. But see *Savantage Fin. Servs. v. United States*,

595 F.3d 1282 (Fed. Cir. 2010), where the court found no reasonable basis for the sole source decision because all the reasons cited by DHS in the justification as supporting its decision to use Oracle and SAP as the financial software system baseline were equally applicable to the Savantage system.

In negotiated procurement the court takes a more deferential view of whether an agency's actions were rational or reasonable than it does in sealed bidding, *Logicon, Inc. v. United States*, 22 Cl. Ct. 776 (1991). There, the court found that the government had a rational basis for reopening negotiations on a contract after having initially decided to award the contract to the plaintiff. In *Overstreet Elec. Co. v. United States*, 59 Fed. Cl. 99 (2003), the court characterized the standard of review as "near draconian." Further, in *Galen Med. Assocs., Inc. v. United States*, 369 F.3d 1324 (Fed. Cir. 2004), the court stated at 1330:

> Because the bid protest at issue here involved a "negotiated procurement," the protestor's burden of proving that the award was arbitrary, capricious, an abuse of discretion, or otherwise not in accordance with law is greater than in other types of bid protests. *LeBarge Prods., Inc. v. West*, 46 F.3d 1547, 1555 (Fed. Cir. 1995) (citing *Burroughs Corp. v. United States*, 617 F.2d 590, 597-98 (Ct. Cl. 1980)). "The higher burden exists because the contracting officer engages in what is 'inherently a judgmental process.'" *Omega World Travel v. United States*, 54 Fed. Cl. 570, 578 (2002) (citing *Burroughs*, 617 F.2d at 598). "[T]he greater the discretion granted to a contracting officer, the more difficult it will be to prove the decision was arbitrary and capricious." *Burroughs*, 617 F.2d at 597. "In formally advertised bidding the pertinent statutes and regulations are far more strict about the conduct of the procurement than in a negotiated one, consequently in negotiated procurement the contracting officer is entrusted with a relatively high degree of discretion." *Id.*

See *Blackwater Lodge & Training Ctr. v. United States*, 86 Fed. Cl. 488 (2009) (government reasonably determined awardee had instituted policies and procedures to resolve safety problems and there was no reason to disturb this judgment); *Medical Dev. Int'l, Inc. v. United States*, 89 Fed. Cl. 691 (2009) (government did not act arbitrarily or capriciously in conducting competitive range determination three months after the firm prices had expired because the contracting officer reasonably viewed the offers as definite enough to become binding upon the government's acceptance); *Dyonyx, L.P. v. United States*, 83 Fed. Cl. 460 (2008) (rational basis to exclude plaintiff from competitive range); *PHT Supply Corp. v. United States*, 71 Fed. Cl. 1 (2006) (risk rating based on past performance upheld because the solicitation did not limit the government's review to technically relevant contracts and assessment of the awardee's risk had a rational basis); *Avtel Servs., Inc. v. United States*, 70 Fed. Cl. 173 (2005) (contracting officer's decision not to disqualify the eventual awardee from competition was not arbitrary and capricious); *Gulf Group, Inc. v. United States*, 61 Fed. Cl. 338 (2004) (risk rating based on past performance not arbitrary or capricious); *Mantech Telecomm. & Info. Sys. Corp. v. United States*, 49 Fed. Cl. 57 (2001) (proposed corrective action neither arbitrary, capricious nor otherwise contrary to law); *Cincom Sys., Inc., v. United States*, 37 Fed. Cl. 993 (1997) (government's award of software contract was supported by rational basis);

Delbert Wheeler Constr., Inc. v. United States, 39 Fed. Cl. 239 (1997) (contracting officer's award to offeror who, in his opinion, provided best value, was reasonable); *W&D Ships Deck Works, Inc. v. United States*, 39 Fed. Cl. 638 (1997) (proposal was properly excluded from competitive range); *Compubahn, Inc. v. United States*, 33 Fed. Cl. 677 (1995) (offeror not entitled to relief because there was no evidence that the evaluators acted in bad faith or without a reasonable basis, notwithstanding the fact that four of the five evaluators were incapable of assessing the proposed technology); *IMS Servs., Inc. v. United States*, 33 Fed. Cl. 167 (1995) (Navy did not act arbitrarily, capriciously, or contrary to law when it reopened procurement competition and conducted new round of BAFOs). Compare *Turner Constr. Co. v. United States*, 94 Fed. Cl. 561 (2010) (agency acted arbitrarily in following GAO recommendation to cancel award and reopen competition because of an organizational conflict of interest of awardee); *Magnum Opus Techs., Inc. v. United States*, 94 Fed. Cl. 512 (2010) (agency arbitrarily exercised options that had no firm prices); *Systems Plus, Inc. v. United States*, 69 Fed. Cl. 757 (2006) (agency's price evaluation arbitrary because the contracting officer's methodology calculated a simple, non-weighted arithmetic formula to derive an average hourly rate for each bidder); *United Int'l Investigative Servs. v. United States*, 41 Fed. Cl. 312 (1998) (agency acted unreasonably in allowing an individual member of the technical evaluation board to rescore the offeror's technical proposal).

G. Prejudice

In order for a protester to prevail in a bid protest, it must show not only that there was a significant error in the procurement process, but also that the error was prejudicial, *Data General Corp. v. United States*, 78 F.3d 1556 (Fed. Cir. 1996). In that case the court stated that the test was whether there was a "reasonable likelihood" that the protester would obtain award. In *Statistica, Inc. v. United States*, 102 F.3d 1577 (Fed. Cir. 1996), the court stated that to establish competitive prejudice, a protester must demonstrate that but for the alleged error, there was a "substantial chance" that it would receive an award. It concluded, however, that there was no difference between the "reasonable likelihood" test in *Data General* and the "substantial chance" test that had been used in older cases such as *CACI, Inc. — Fed. v. United States*, 719 F.2d 1567 (Fed. Cir. 1983), and *Morgan Bus. Assocs. v. United States*, 223 Ct. Cl. 325, 619 F.2d 892 (1980). The more recent Federal Circuit cases all state a party has been prejudiced when it can show that but for the error, it would have had a substantial chance of securing the contract, *Labatt Food Serv., Inc. v. United States*, 577 F.3d 1375 (Fed. Cir. 2009); *Bannum, Inc. v. United States*, 404 F.3d 1346 (Fed. Cir. 2005); *Galen Med. Assocs., Inc. v. United States*, 369 F.3d 1324 (Fed. Cir. 2004). In *Afghan American Army Servs. Corp. v. United States*, 90 Fed. Cl. 341 (2009), the highest-priced offeror in a multiple-award competition for indefinite-deliver/indefinite-quantity trucking services contracts was prejudiced by the government's evaluation and selection errors because its proposal was within the competitive range, and it established there was a reasonable likelihood it would have received an award but for the errors. The protester was the most expensive offeror in a best-value procurement where price was weighed as approximately equal to past performance, past experience, and security approach and it received lower technical ratings than four other offerors also not awarded contracts. However, the result could have been different if the government had performed a proper price realism analysis, best-value tradeoff, and past experience evaluation. See also *Red River Holdings, LLC v. United States*, 87 Fed. Cl. 768 (2009) (improper evaluation of the awardee's proposal prejudicial).

De minimis errors by the agency are not sufficient grounds for overturning a contract award, *Andersen Consulting Co. v. United States*, 959 F.2d 929 (Fed. Cir. 1992) ("Any good lawyer can pick lint off any Government procurement, pundits say. We will not set aside an award, even if violations of law are found, unless those violations have some significance," quoting the GSBCA decision at 91-1 BCA ¶ 23,474). See also *Labatt Food Serv., Inc. v. United States*, 577 F.3d 1375 (Fed. Cir. 2009) (plaintiff did not show that government's improper acceptance of emails throughout the bid process interfered with its ability to receive the contract award); *Grumman Data Sys. Corp. v. Widnall*, 15 F.3d 1044 (Fed. Cir. 1994) (Air Force departure from standard accounting principles in conducting its best value analysis may have violated some technical accounting principles but was de minimis); and *Cubic Applications, Inc. v. United States*, 37 Fed. Cl. 345 (1997) (failure to follow statutory procedures in awarding the contract not prejudicial and thus nullification of the award was not warranted).

If there is a significant difference in price, the court is unlikely to make a finding of prejudice. In *Electronic Data Sys., LLC v. United States*, 93 Fed. Cl. 416 (2010), the court found the large price differential to preclude a finding of prejudice, stating at 436:

> The difficulty for plaintiff in this regard is the sheer size of the differential between its price and that of BAE — in raw terms, slightly more than $50 million, representing nearly a 29 percent spread. This differential is the proverbial elephant in the parlor — and, strive as it might, plaintiff cannot squeeze that pachyderm out the door. That price variance weighed heavily on Treasury's best value determination because the two offerors had nearly identical merit ratings — ratings, to be sure, that plaintiff has challenged before this court, albeit unsuccessfully. While plaintiff correctly notes that prejudice may be found despite the existence of a price differential, it cannot be gainsaid that a significant difference in price, when accompanied by nearly identical technical ratings, can and often does preclude such a finding. And the cases so indicate. See, e.g., *Axiom Res. Mgmt., Inc. v. United States*, 78 Fed. Cl. 576, 590 (2007) (no prejudice where significant differences in price); *see also Data Gen.*, 78 F.3d at 1563 (indicating that price differential is a factor that may be considered in assessing prejudice).

See also *Allied Tech. Group, Inc. v. United States*, 92 Fed. Cl. 226 (2010) (assigning higher technical rating would not have affected award as evaluated price was at least 218% higher than Monster's); *Axiom Res. Mgmt., Inc. v. United States*, 78 Fed. Cl. 576 (2007) (despite apparent errors in the plaintiff's technical approach and past performance ratings, the awardee's lower price still trumped plaintiff's price); *Galen Med. Assocs., Inc. v. United States*, 369 F.3d 1324 (Fed. Cir. 2004) (denying existence of prejudice when proposal did not have requisite facilities required by the solicitation); *Candle Corp. v. United States*, 40 Fed. Cl. 658 (1998) (even if the government had complied with its legal obligations, the plaintiff's price still would have been considerably more expensive than the awardee's); *Analytical & Research Tech., Inc. v. United States*, 39 Fed. Cl. 34 (1997) (no prejudice where protester's price was 35% higher than the awardee's despite a violation of procurement laws); and *Data Gen. Corp. v. United States*, 78 F.3d 1556 (Fed. Cir. 1996) (prejudice not found when, despite pricing error, protester's prices remained substantially higher). See, however, *Alfa Laval Separation, Inc. v. United States*, 40 Fed. Cl. 215 (1998), *rev'd*, 175 F.3d 1365 (Fed. Cir. 1999), where the Federal Circuit reversed a Court of Federal Claims' decision that a specification was not prejudicial because there was a $5 million price difference between proposals. There, Alfa Laval protested a procurement in which a minimum mandatory requirement of the RFP had been waived for its competitor. The Court of Federal Claims found that the contractor could not establish prejudice because its conforming bid was significantly higher priced than its competitor. In reversing the court concluded that the plaintiff had established prejudice because "[t]he only bid competing with Alfa Laval was unacceptable under the standards set out in the RFP," adding that because the plaintiff "submitted the only bid meeting all of the government's requirements, ... it must have had a substantial chance to receive the contract award." As to the large differential in pricing, the court stated that "while price differential may be taken into account, it is not solely dispositive; we must consider all the surrounding circumstances in determining whether there was a substantial chance that a protester would have received an award but for a significant error in the procurement process."

In a best value procurement, an offeror has a relatively heavy burden to show that its position in the procurement was prejudiced, *Systems Plus, Inc. v. United States*, 69 Fed. Cl. 757 (2006). There, the court found that although the government's methodology for evaluating proposals excluded pertinent pricing considerations and was irrational and arbitrary, the protester failed to demonstrate it was prejudiced by those errors. The contracting officer had broad discretion to determine how important each of the criteria would be in the evaluation. It thus appeared that the contracting officer determined the awardee's proposal to be sufficiently superior to the other offerors' proposals that it should be selected for award regardless of which measure of price was evaluated. The court in *Textron, Inc. v. United States*, 74 Fed. Cl. 11 (2006), would likely have ruled differently. The *Textron* court stated that if the court finds that the government has acted arbitrarily and capriciously, the analysis stops at that finding. There should be no need to continue to prejudice because a finding that the government has acted arbitrarily and capriciously invalidates the procurement.

H. Remedies

The ultimate remedy sought by a protester is to receive award of the contract. However, such relief is granted in only the rarest of cases. More often, the agency will be directed to cure a defect in the procurement, and pending the action, the award of a contract will be delayed or the work under a contract will be suspended. In some cases the remedy may involve declarations of the rights of the parties or directions to recompete the contract. Monetary relief may also be granted. See 28 U.S.C. § 1491(b)(2) "[T]he courts may award any relief that the court considers proper, including declaratory and injunctive relief except that any monetary relief shall be limited to bid and proposal costs."

The court has discretion to award *both* injunctive relief and bid preparation costs, *CNA Corp. v. United States*, 83 Fed. Cl. 1 (2008), *aff'd*, 332 Fed. Appx. 638 (Fed. Cir. 2009). In *Alabama Aircraft Indus., Inc. — Birmingham v. United States*, 85 Fed. Cl. 558, *rev'd on other grounds*, 586 F.3d 1372 (Fed. Cir. 2009), in addition to the prior decision enjoining the Air Force from proceeding with a contract and requiring a resolicitation, the court determined the award of bid preparation and proposal costs to be necessary to place Alabama Aircraft in its rightful position. Here, without defendant's errors, Alabama Aircraft would have had to submit only one proposal. Due to those errors, Alabama Aircraft was now required to pay for and submit another proposal in a continuing effort to obtain an award of the contract. In *Geo-Seis Helicopters, Inc. v. United States*, 77 Fed. Cl. 633 (2007), when an injunction issued by the court was partial and only set aside part of the contract in question, the court found it appropriate to include bid preparation and proposal costs as part of the award. Other cases also have awarded complete, permanent injunctive relief along with bid preparation and proposal costs. See *United Payors & United Providers Health Servs., Inc. v. United States*, 55 Fed. Cl. 323 (2002) (required the defendant to terminate the contract, allowed resolicitation of bids, and awarded bid preparation and proposal costs to the plaintiff); *MVM, Inc. v. United States*, 47 Fed. Cl. 361 (2000) (awarded proposal and preparation costs in addition to the injunction previously awarded); *Seattle Sec. Servs. v. United States*, 45 Fed. Cl. 560 (2000) (awarded injunctive relief and bid preparation costs). But see *Ashbritt, Inc. v. United States*, 87 Fed. Cl. 344 (2009), where the court declined to award both injunctive and monetary relief because Ashbritt had achieved the goal of its protest — to secure, through injunctive relief, the chance to compete for further awards under the procurement on an even playing field.

1. *Nonmonetary Remedies*

The types of nonmonetary remedies that a protester may obtain in the Court of Federal Claims are either provisional (temporary restraining order (TRO) or preliminary injunction) or final relief (declaratory relief or permanent injunction).

The rules for granting a TRO or preliminary injunction are identical to those followed by the district courts. See RCFC 65. The four factors the court examines when determining whether a preliminary injunction should be granted are the same as in the district courts: (1) reasonable likelihood of success on the merits, (2) irreparable harm if the injunction is not granted, (3) substantial harm to the other parties if the stay is granted, and (4) consideration of the public interest, *Hydro Eng'g, Inc. v. United States*, 37 Fed. Cl. 448 (1997). The court seldom grants either a TRO or a preliminary injunction. As a general rule, courts should interfere with the government procurement process "only in extremely limited circumstances," *Banknote Corp. of Am., Inc. v. United States*, 56 Fed. Cl. 377 (2003) (quoting *United States v. John C. Grimberg Co.*, 702 F.2d 1362 (Fed. Cir. 1983)), *aff'd*, 365 F.3d 1345 (Fed. Cir. 2004). In *Magellan Corp. v. United States*, 27 Fed. Cl. 446 (1993), the court denied a request for preliminary injunction, stating that the disruption to the ongoing procurement process would not be justified in view of the unlikelihood of success on the merits. In discussing its review of requests for preliminary injunctions, the court stated at 447:

> The court has the authority to enter an injunction blocking the award to any bidder other than Magellan. 28 U.S.C. § 1491(a)(3). The limited question is whether the status quo ante should be maintained while the plaintiff undertakes discovery and proofs on its request for permanent relief. Prior decisions of this court and of the United States Court of Appeals for the Federal Circuit, however, make it clear that such authority should not be routinely exercised. As the Federal Circuit wrote in *United States v. John C. Grimberg Co.*, 702 F.2d 1362 (Fed. Cir. 1983), equitable powers "should be exercised in a way which best limits judicial interference in contract procurement." *Id.* at 1372.

The decision on whether or not to grant an injunction is within the sound discretion of the trial court, *FMC Corp. v. United States*, 3 F.3d 424 (Fed. Cir. 1993); *Asociacion Colombiana de Exportadores de Flores v. United States*, 916 F.2d 1571 (Fed. Cir. 1990). Confirming the difficult nature of obtaining injunctive relief in a bid protest case, the Federal Circuit has stated that even if a trial court finds that the government's actions in soliciting and awarding a contract were arbitrary, capricious, or not in accordance with law, the trial court retains discretion on whether to issue an injunction, *PGBA, LLC v. United States*, 389 F.3d 1219 (Fed. Cir. 2004). In *PGBA*, the court reasoned that the statutory scheme for reviewing procurement decision "does not deprive a court of its equitable discretion in deciding whether injunctive relief is appropriate," and that 28 U.S.C. § 1491(b)(4) "does not automatically require a court to set aside an arbitrary, capricious, or otherwise unlawful contract award." Once injunctive relief is denied, "the movant faces a heavy burden of showing that the trial court abused its discretion, committed an error of law, or seriously misjudged the evidence," *FMC Corp. v. United States*, 3 F.3d 424 (Fed. Cir. 1993).

The court will examine whether a plaintiff can establish success on the merits before looking at the other factors for injunctive relief. In *Logicon, Inc. v. United* States, 22 Cl. Ct. 776 (1991), the court denied injunctive relief, finding that the agency's decision to reopen negotiations and conduct another round of BAFOs was not irrational or unreasonable; thus, the offeror did not establish by clear and convincing evidence a strong likelihood of success on the merits. In *Career Training Concepts, Inc. v. United States*, 83 Fed. Cl. 215 (2008), the court denied plaintiff's motion for injunctive relief, finding that an awardee's proposal was deemed timely because the contracting officer properly extended the deadline for receipt of proposals through a formal notice posted on the website used to conduct the solicitation, and the awardee submitted its offer within the extension period. The protester's attempt to characterize the extension as invalid based on the fact the contracting officer notified offerors of the extension via e-mail, rather than a formal solicitation amendment, was rejected. Similarly in *The Centech Group, Inc. v. United States*, 78 Fed. Cl. 496 (2007), *aff'd*, 554 F.3d 1029 (2009), the court held that Centech did not meet the first requisite for injunctive relief — demonstrated success on the merits. Here, Centech's proposal was unacceptable because it failed to comply with the Limitation on Subcontracting clause — a mandatory, material solicitation requirement. However, in *Isratex, Inc. v. United States*, 25 Cl. Ct. 223 (1992), the court granted a TRO upon finding a strong likelihood of success on the merits. The offeror was excluded from further participation in a negotiated procurement on the ground that its demonstration model did not satisfy one of the factors listed in the RFP, but the court found no indication in the RFP that automatic exclusion would follow from test failure.

When assessing irreparable injury, "[t]he relevant inquiry in weighing this factor is whether the plaintiff has an adequate remedy in the absence of an injunction," *Magellan Corp. v. United States*, 27 Fed. Cl. 446 (1993). In *Serco, Inc. v. United States*, 81 Fed. Cl. 463 (2008), the government was enjoined from proceeding with awards made under a government-wide acquisition contract because it conducted an improper and flawed evaluation. The protesters demonstrated they would suffer irreparable injury if an injunction were not granted because the only other available relief — the potential for recovery of bid preparation costs — would not compensate them for the loss of valuable business over the course of the contract term.

The public interest must weigh in favor of injunctive relief, *Klinge Corp. v. United States*, 82 Fed. Cl. 127 (2008) (public interest weighs in favor of preventing the government from awarding a contract in contravention of the Trade Agreements Act and in preventing the government from failing to make proper inquiry into compliance when it had a duty to do so). The public interest is served by ensuring that the government conduct fair and legal procurement procedures, giving honest and fair consideration to all bids, *Aeroplate Corp. v. United States*, 67 Fed. Cl. 4 (2005). Preserving the integrity of the public procurement system is in the public interest, *MVM, Inc. v. United States*, 46 Fed. Cl. 137 (2000); *Day & Zimmerman Servs. v. United States*, 38 Fed. Cl. 591 (1997). The integrity of the procurement process includes the requirement that government officials follow applicable procurement law and regulation, *Rotech Healthcare, Inc. v. United States*, 71 Fed. Cl. 393 (2006) (procurement approach adopted by the VA violated the letter and the spirit of the non-manufacturer rule and the Small Business Act as a whole). In *Serco, Inc. v. United States*, 81 Fed. Cl. 463 (2008), the court found the public interest would be served by granting the injunction, particularly in the context of a massive procurement that will impact the public potentially for a decade.

When an appeal is taken to the Federal Circuit, an appellant may request a stay of contract award pending appeal under RCFC 62(c). However, the court follows a stringent test in determining whether to issue a stay pending appeal. This test mirrors the TRO test: "(1) a strong likelihood that the movant will prevail on the merits of the appeal; (2) irreparable injury to the movant unless the stay is granted; (3) no substantial harm to the other parties if the stay is granted; and (4) consideration of the public interest," *Aerolease Long Beach & Satsuma Inv., Inc. v. United States*, 31 Fed. Cl. 342 (1994).

The final relief by the Court of Federal Claims may take the form of a declaratory judgment or a permanent injunction. The test for a permanent injunction is almost identical to that for a temporary restraining order or preliminary injunction, but rather that the likelihood of success on the merits, a permanent injunction requires actual success on the merits, *Amoco Prod. Co. v. Vill. of Gambill, Alaska*, 480 U.S.

531 (1987). In *PGBA, LLC v. United States*, 389 F.3d 1219 (Fed. Cir. 2004), the Federal Circuit set out the test for a permanent injunction, stating at 1228-29, that a court must consider:

> (1) whether, as it must, the plaintiff has succeeded on the merits of the case; (2) whether the plaintiff will suffer irreparable harm if the court withholds injunctive relief; (3) whether the balance of hardships to the respective parties favors the grant of injunctive relief; and (4) whether it is in the public interest to grant injunctive relief.

The injunction may prohibit the agency from undertaking some activity or it may be mandatory, directing that certain actions be taken. See *Klinge Corp. v. United States*, 82 Fed. Cl. 127 (2008) (directed to terminate the contract); *Informatics Corp. v. United States*, 40 Fed. Cl. 508 (1998) (award of contract enjoined and re-evaluation of plaintiff's proposal ordered); *ATA Defense Indus., Inc. v. United States*, 38 Fed. Cl. 489 (1997) (permanent injunction prohibiting continued performance of legally defective procurement); *Day & Zimmermann, Inc. v. United States*, 38 Fed. Cl. 591 (1997) (contract award enjoined unless and until discussions were held and resulting BAFOs were considered); and *126 Northpoint Plaza L.P. v. United States*, 34 Fed. Cl. 105 (1995) (original solicitation reinstated).

The court has limited injunctive relief in an otherwise meritorious protest for national defense/national security considerations, *Gentex Corp. v. United States*, 58 Fed. Cl. 634 (2003) (plaintiff found not to have met burden of demonstrating that injunctive relief is warranted, given urgency of procurement for the nation's military); *Geo-Seis Helicopters v. United States*, 77 Fed. Cl. 633 (2007) (national security considerations caused injunction to be limited in scope); *Filtration Dev. Co. v. United States*, 60 Fed. Cl. 371 (2004); (limited injunctive relief in light of national defense considerations); and *Cincom Sys. v. United States*, 37 Fed. Cl. 226 (1997) (application for TRO and motion for preliminary injunction denied for national security reasons).

2. *Monetary Remedies*

The monetary remedies that protesters have been able to recover are generally limited to the costs of preparing the bid or proposal. In some instances the protester may receive attorneys' fees and expenses under the Equal Access to Justice Act (EAJA). Recovery of anticipated profits (or lost profits) has been uniformly denied. See *Keco Indus., Inc. v. United States*, 203 Ct. Cl. 566, 492 F.2d 1200 (1974) (improper to award lost profits in the absence of a contract and no certainty that protester would have received award); *Rockwell Int'l Corp. v. United States*, 8 Cl. Ct. 662 (1985) (prior precedent flatly precludes such an award); *La Strada Inn, Inc. v. United States*, 12 Cl. Ct. 110 (1987) (disappointed bidder may not recover anticipated profits on a contract improperly awarded to another); *Finley v. United States*, 31 Fed. Cl. 704 (1994) (lost profits are speculative in nature and have consistently been denied); and *Gentex Corp. v. United States*, 61 Fed. Cl. 49 (2004) (protester's attempt to recover a 15% "markup" on its bid and preparation costs was unsuccessful because profit is not an allowable cost).

a. Bid or Proposal Preparation Costs

The Court of Federal Claims may award bid proposal and preparation costs in a bid protest action, 28 U.S.C. § 1491(a)(1); 28 U.S.C § 1491(b)(2). The successful protester that has not received award may recover the costs of preparing its bid or proposal if it had a substantial chance for award, *Morgan Bus. Assocs. v. United States*, 223 Ct. Cl. 325, 619 F.2d 892 (1980). See also *AT&T Techs., Inc. v. United States*, 18 Cl. Ct. 315 (1989).

A losing competitor may recover the costs of preparing its unsuccessful proposal if it can establish that the government's consideration of the proposal submitted was arbitrary or capricious or in violation of applicable statute or regulation, *Gentex Corp. v. United States*, 58 Fed. Cl. 634 (2003). *Keco Indus., Inc. v. United States*, 203 Ct. Cl. 566 (1974) set forth this standard. In *Keco*, the court described four factors to consider in assessing a claim for bid or proposal preparation costs: (1) whether the agency acted in bad faith, (2) whether there was a reasonable basis for the agency's decision or action, (3) the amount of discretion the agency is afforded in the area being questioned, and (4) whether a procurement statute or regulation was violated. See also *Crux Computer Corp. v. United States*, 24 Cl. Ct. 223 (1991). If the court finds that an agency breached its obligation to fairly and honestly consider a bid or proposal, or that it violated a procurement statute or regulation, the court may award bid or proposal preparation costs. Such actions on the part of the government are considered to be arbitrary and capricious. However, the protester must demonstrate by clear and convincing proof that the agency's evaluation of offers and/or award of the contract was arbitrary and capricious, *Paxson Elec. Co. v. United States*, 14 Cl. Ct. 634 (1988). See *Concept Automation, Inc. v. United States*, 41 Fed. Cl. 361 (1998), where the court held that the protesters were entitled to proposal preparation costs because the government breached its implied-in-fact contract to treat proposals fairly and honestly, acted in an arbitrary and capricious fashion, and unreasonably awarded the contract to unqualified offerors. However, in *Finley v. United States*, 31 Fed. Cl. 704 (1994), the court held that because there was no evidence of bad faith in the evaluation process, the protester had no basis for the award of proposal preparation costs. In *Stapp Towing, Inc. v. United States*, 34 Fed. Cl. 300 (1995), the court held that the bidder was not entitled to bid preparation costs because there was no showing that the SBA's decision denying a certificate of competency was arbitrary and capricious. Even if an agency violates a procurement statute or regulation, an offeror will not necessarily receive proposal preparation costs unless it can show that it was prejudiced, *E.W. Bliss Co. v. United States*, 33 Fed. Cl. 123 (1995), *aff'd*, 77 F.3d 445 (Fed. Cir. 1996). In *Alfa Laval Separation, Inc. v. United States*, 47 Fed. Cl. 305 (2000), the protester failed to include a claim for bid and proposal costs in its original complaint, but sought them after the Federal Circuit had reversed and remanded the Court of Federal Claims' initial decision denying the protest. The Court of Federal Claims held that it was too late to seek bid and proposal costs, because the protester had only proven that the agency's action was in violation of procurement regulations, but had not shown it to be arbitrary, capricious, or unreasonable.

Bid preparation and proposal costs are treated as allocable when they are "incurred specifically for the contract," *Coflexip & Servs., Inc. v. United States*, 961 F.2d 951 (Fed. Cir. 1992). In *Coflexip*, the court distinguished between recoverable postsubmission costs that are incurred as a result of ongoing negotiations and nonrecoverable costs incurred in anticipation of contract award, stating at 953:

> [I]n a negotiated procurement, the costs a contractor incurs *pursuant to ongoing negotiations* with the government and in support of a revised proposal, i.e., postsubmission costs, can be proposal preparation costs. However, costs which do not support an initial or revised proposal are costs which a contractor incurs in an effort to better position itself to perform any contract it should be awarded. These latter costs, incurred in *anticipation of* contract award, are not proposal preparation costs. The contractor assumes the risk that it will not be awarded the contract, and, accordingly, these contract preparation costs will not be recoverable. [emphasis added]

The court stated that none of the plaintiff's costs in that case had been incurred for the purpose of preparing its proposal but, rather, to place it in a position to perform the contract had it received the award. Because the court could not determine whether the prototype was built pursuant to ongoing negotiations or in anticipation of contract award, the court remanded the case to the Claims Court. In *Beta Analytics Int'l, Inc. v. United States*, 75 Fed. Cl. 155 (2007), bid and proposal costs incurred before a solicitation issued were disallowed because the protester did not establish the activities were related to proposal preparation. Although it was appropriate to allow pre-solicitation costs "incurred in anticipation of competing for the specific contract at issue," the protester's employee time records and invoices for publishing services failed to show employee time claimed before the date of the solicitation was spent on proposal preparation or segregated from unrelated activities. In addition, pre-solicitation invoices for publishing services did not refer to the proposal and predated the protester's proposal preparation work. Similarly, in *Alabama Aircraft Indus., Inc. v. United States*, 85 Fed. Cl. 558 (2009), the court stated that bid preparation and proposal costs have been awarded to a successfully protesting offeror for costs sustained prior to the solicitation only when it was working on its own proposal. The fact that Alabama Aircraft was in part able to incorporate its work in assisting Boeing into its own proposal was not sufficient to support recovery of the costs it experienced while working with Boeing. The efforts it undertook while working with Boeing might have better positioned Alabama Aircraft to perform any contract that might be awarded, but the expenses of those efforts did not constitute costs of preparing Alabama Aircraft's own proposal. In *Naplesyacht.com, Inc. v. United States*, 49 CCF ¶ 78,366 (2005), the government had contested the costs as appearing to be related to procurements conducted under the GSA supply schedule and otherwise unrelated to the disputed solicitation. The court found, however, that the record sufficiently detailed that the protester began to prepare its proposal when it responded to requests for sources from the government. In addition, other correspondence established that the government conducted pre-solicitation activities, including site visits to the protester's facilities. Email correspondence described the government's need for a specified foot length and other requirements that it later included in the boat manufacturing solicitation. The court found the costs allocable as related to research and preparation of the protester's initial and final proposals. In *Lion Raisins, Inc. v. United States*, 52 Fed. Cl. 115 (2002), the costs of litigating a Small Business Administration size protest and obtaining a Certificate of Competency were not reimbursable bid and proposal preparation costs, because they were not incurred specifically for the bid. Here, the solicitation did not reference a set-aside for small business, eligibility to bid was not predicated on size, and the resolution of the protest was irrelevant to contract award.

b. Protest Costs

The costs of pursuing a protest in the Court of Federal Claims are not recoverable except under the Equal Access to Justice Act (EAJA), 28 U.S.C. § 2412, *Grumman Data Sys. Corp. v. United States*, 28 Fed. Cl. 803 (1993). See also *Coflexip & Servs., Inc. v. United States*, 20 Cl. Ct. 412 (1990) (court is without jurisdiction to award protest costs in the absence of a waiver of sovereign immunity); and *AT&T Techs., Inc. v. United States*, 18 Cl. Ct. 315 (1989) (damages for breach of the implied contract to fairly and honestly consider offers are limited exclusively to bid and proposal preparation costs).

Under the EAJA, an award of reasonable attorneys' fees may be made to a qualifying "party" who prevails in an action by or against the United States, provided that certain criteria are met, 28 U.S.C. § 2412(d)(1)(A).

A qualifying "party" is a corporation or other organization with a net worth of less than $7 million and 500 or fewer employees, 28 U.S.C. § 2412(d)(2)(B). In *Lion Raisins, Inc. v. United States*, 57 Fed. Cl. 505 (Fed. Cl. 2003), the court held that the net worth of two other business related to an entity that requested attorneys' fees and costs under the EAJA was irrelevant for purposes of determining whether the EAJA claimant was eligible to collect attorneys' fees and costs under EAJA. The government had asserted that Lion Raisins was an affiliate of two other business entities and that the net worth of these entities should be aggregated in determining Lion Raisin's net worth. The court explained that the plain language of EAJA counseled against aggregation, stating at 510:

> The jurisprudence makes clear that aggregation, if required at all, is necessary only when the underlying litigation pursued by the . . . claimant substantially benefitted another party, or if the claimant was not the real party in interest to the underlying litigation. This is not the situation in the case at bar. . . . Most important to the issue of aggregation, only plaintiff had a direct interest in the underlying lawsuit. While . . . [the other entities] may profit from plaintiff's ability to perform government contracts, even the more restrictive formulations of EAJA eligibility would not require aggregation for this type of attenuated benefit from the underlying litigation.

See also *Information Sciences Corp. v. United States*, 78 Fed. Cl. 673 (2007), where the government contended that the intervenor's net worth should include the assets and liabilities of its "working partners" and perhaps its principles. The court found that the intervenor did not have a formal legal or contractual relationship with any entity, and even if it had an implicit contractual relationship with its working partners, mere affiliation did not justify aggregating the net worth of affiliated companies under the EAJA. An applicant must present evidence showing its net worth was less than $7 million at the time the action is filed, *Ghanim Combined Group Co. v. United States*, 67 Fed. Cl. 494 (2005) (applicant's self-serving, non-probative affidavit claiming a net worth below the threshold was inadequate to establish that its net worth did not exceed $7 million for purposes of EAJA).

Eligibility for such an award requires that: (1) the claimant be a "prevailing party;" (2) the government's position was not "substantially justified;" (3) no "special circumstances make an award unjust;" and (4) any fee application be submitted to the court within 30 days of final judgment in the action and be supported by an itemized statement, *Commissioner, INS v. Jean*, 496 U.S. 154 (1990); *Loomis v. United States*, 74 Fed. Cl. 350 (2006); *Lion Raisins, Inc. v. United States*, 57 Fed. Cl. 505 (2003).

The burden of establishing substantial justification rests upon the government, *White v. Nicholson*, 412 F.3d 1314 (Fed. Cir. 2005). In determining substantial justification, the court must "look at the entirety of the government's conduct [both prior to and during litigation] and make a judgment call whether the government's overall position had a reasonable basis in both law and fact," *Chiu v. United States*, 948 F.2d 711 (Fed. Cir. 1991). See also *Doty v. United States*, 71 F.3d 384 (Fed. Cir. 1995) ("[T]he term 'position of the United States' [in the EAJA] refers to the government's position throughout the dispute, including not only its litigating position but also the agency's administrative position."). See *Universal Fidelity LP v. United States*, 70 Fed. Cl. 310 (2006) (restrictions were unreasonable and the government took corrective action late in the proceedings); and *Dubinsky v. United States*, 44 Fed. Cl. 360 (1999) (government assertion that procurement was conducted in accordance with simplified acquisition procedures was not reasonable because the protester successfully showed that the solicitation was conducted as a standard procurement, consequently making the government's discussions with the awardee improper). But see *Klinge Corp. v. United States*, 53 CCF ¶ 79,183 (2009), where an application for attorneys' fees and expenses under the EAJA was dismissed because the government's overall litigation position in the protest was substantially justified. In its EAJA application, the protester argued the government's decision to cancel the solicitation was based on its unreasonable conclusion that the protester did not comply with the Trade Agreements Act. Even though the government was mistaken in fact and law, the court found no government bad faith or animus toward the protester and no government desire to help the awardee.

The government's position will not be found to be reasonable or substantially justified when explicit, unambiguous regulations directly contradict that position, *Information Sciences Corp. v. United States*, 78 Fed. Cl. 673 (2007) (even though court resolved most of the protest challenges in the government's favor and did not rule the contracting officer's and SSA's decisions were unreasonable, violations of the FAR were ipso facto unreasonable in law); *Hillensbeck v. United States*, 74 Fed. Cl. 477 (2006) (government's position conflicted with unambiguous statutory definition and regulations); *Loomis v. United States*, 74 Fed. Cl. 350 (2006) (military failed to comply with its own regulations); *Filtration Dev., Co. v. United States*, 63 Fed. Cl. 612 (2005) (government position contradicted unambiguous regulatory requirements relating to organizational conflicts of interest). In *Geo-Seis Helicopters, Inc. v. United States*, 79 Fed. Cl. 74 (2007), the government argued that its position in the underlying litigation was justified because there was significant GAO precedent supporting the contracting officer's position. The court determined that the plain language of the FAR precluded the government's position. The court held that the FAR and not GAO or the court, establish the parameters for the contracting officer's position.

The government's position may be found to be substantially justified even though the court previously overturned the government's actions. See *RAMCOR Servs. Group, Inc. v. United States*, 185 F.3d 1286 (Fed. Cir. 1999) ("Although INS had lost the underlying action, that outcome does not alone show that its position had no substantial justification.").

The court follows the Supreme Court's decision in *Buckhannon Board & Care Home, Inc. v. West Virginia Dep't of Health and Human Resources*, 532 U.S. 598 (2001) in deciding prevailing party status under EAJA, *Brickwood Contractors, Inc. v. United States*, 288 F.3d 1371 (Fed. Cir. 2002). In *Buckhannon*, the Supreme Court rejected the catalyst theory and set forth standards for a party to prevail under attorney fees statutes. Under the catalyst theory, a party "prevails" because the lawsuit brought about a voluntary change in the defendant's conduct. The Court found the catalyst theory insufficient because "[i]t allows an award where there is no judicially sanctioned change in the legal relationship of the parties." The Court then proceeded to construe the phrase "prevailing party" as requiring some judicial action that changes the legal relationship between the parties on the merits of the claim. In other words, to prevail, a party must have received a judicial imprimatur tantamount to a judgment in favor of that party on the merits of the original claim. That judicial action could take the form of a consent decree settling the claim in favor of the plaintiff, a judgment on the merits, or an award of damages. In *Rice Servs., LTD v. United States*, 405 F.3d 1017 (2005), an award of legal fees under the EAJA was reversed on appeal because the protester did not achieve prevailing party status as a result of the government's voluntary decision to withdraw a solicitation. The protester sought a reevaluation of the bids pursuant to the terms of the solicitation for dining services. The Court of Federal Claims granted the government's motion to dismiss the case, but included in its order a provision directing the government to follow through with its promise to reevaluate the solicitation. Subsequently, the protester was awarded its litigation costs as a prevailing party on the basis the dismissal order altered the parties' legal relationship. The Federal Circuit reversed finding that the dismissal order was not an enforceable judgment because the court did not reach the merits, and there was no evidence the order embodied an agreement between the parties and was incorporated into a consent decree. See also *Universal Fidelity LP v. United States*, 70 Fed. Cl. 310 (2006) (contractor was a "prevailing party" because the court's order advised the parties the solicitation would be enjoined, the matter had been fully briefed, and the court and the parties agreed no hearing was necessary; the court's conclusions were legal in nature, exhibited an essence of finality and were made late in the proceedings, and an opinion granting injunctive relief would have been issued had the government declined curative action); and *Filtration Dev. Co., LLC v. United States*, 63 Fed. Cl. 612 (2005) (protester was a prevailing party because a permanent injunction granted in its favor altered the legal relationship between the parties). However, in *Knowledge Connections, Inc. v. United*, 76 Fed. Cl. 612 (2007), a court order remanding a bid protester's claim to the government procuring agency for further consideration was not sufficient to establish "prevailing party" status because the order did not grant any relief and the Court of Federal Claims retained jurisdiction over the appeal. Here, the remand order did not provide any resolution to the key question on the merits, which concerned whether the solicitation at issue was defective in a manner that prejudiced the protester. Accordingly the court held that a final judgment and a determination of whether the protester is a prevailing party will be achieved only after the court has had an opportunity to assess the government agency's determination on remand. The court ruled protester's EAJA application premature and denied without prejudice. Similarly in *Advanced Sys. Tech., Inc. v. United States*, 74 Fed. Cl. 171 (2006), the protester filed an EAJA application, arguing it obtained "prevailing party" status when the court issued the preliminary injunction suspending the award pending the outcome of an SBA appeal. The court held that when a preliminary injunction only grants temporary relief preserving the status quo, "prevailing party" status is not conferred, because such a preliminary injunction is not a judicially sanctioned material alteration of the parties' legal relationship." Moreover, the remand to the SBA resulted from an agreement between the parties, not an adjudication of the court.

Attorney fees are compensable under the EAJA if adequately documented, specific to the protest, necessary, and reasonable, *Information Sciences Corp. v. United States*, 78 Fed. Cl. 673 (2007). There, attorneys' expenses were compensable. The intervenor submitted law firm records itemizing miscellaneous expenses and confirmed the expenses were limited to the protest before the Court of Federal Claims, not the preceding GAO protest. The consultant worked for two days assisting the intervenor's counsel to review the administrative record, which the intervenor characterized as too large for an attorney to review unassisted. Given the consultant's expertise in reviewing administrative records in bid protests and assistance in preparing for the hearing within a small time-frame, the court held that his work was necessary and the associated fees were reasonable.

Attorneys' fees are capped at $125 per hour unless the court makes special findings justifying a higher fee. See *Geo-Seis Helicopters, Inc. v. United States*, 79 Fed. Cl. 74 (2007) (entitled to cost of living adjusted allowing rate of $167.27). The fee application with supporting documentation must be submitted to the court within 30 days of final judgment.

V. Federal Tort Claims Act

Unsuccessful offerors and bidders have attempted to obtain relief in district court under the Federal Tort Claims Act (FTCA), 28 U.S.C. § 1346(b), but such actions have generally not been successful. In *Scanwell Labs., Inc. v. Thomas*, 521 F.2d 941 (D.C. Cir. 1975), *cert. denied*, 425 U.S. 910 (1976), an unsuccessful bidder bought an FTCA action in district court while its claim for recovery of bid preparation costs was pending in the Court of Claims, alleging in both actions that the government had violated its procurement regulations by awarding the contract to a nonresponsive bidder. The court first concluded that it need not decide the question of whether the plaintiff would be limited to proceeding under "one theory or the other," but stated that its "solution" would be "merely to prevent a double recovery." Turning then to the merits of the tort action, the court held that the plaintiff's claim was based upon alleged negligent misrepresentation and was therefore barred by the FTCA exceptions under 28 U.S.C. § 2680(h). The court in *Scanwell* also held that the government's action in evaluating the bids fell within the discretionary function exception to the Act, 28 U.S.C. § 2680(a), even though it had held in prior litigation that there was "no discretion to ignore the regulations regarding responsiveness of bids."

In *Edelman v. Federal Housing Admin.*, 382 F.2d 594 (2d Cir. 1967), the Second Circuit found that a claim by a disappointed bidder alleging that the government had failed to fairly consider its bid was barred by the misrepresentation exception. In *Covington v. United States*, 303 F. Supp. 1145 (N.D. Miss. 1969), a claim alleging that the government had fraudulently misrepresented the amount of funds available for the solicited work, causing the bid to be rejected as nonresponsive for exceeding the funding limitation, was held to fall within this same exception. See also *Armstrong & Armstrong, Inc. v. United States*, 356 F. Supp. 514 (E.D. Wash. 1973), *aff'd*, 514 F.2d 402 (9th Cir. 1975), where the court held that a claim by an unsuccessful bidder that the Bureau of Reclamation had acted "negligently, arbitrarily, and capriciously" in denying it award of a contract was a claim based upon interference with contract rights and was thus barred under 28 U.S.C. § 2680(h), which expressly excepts claims based upon interference with contract rights from the waiver of sovereign immunity under 28 U.S.C. § 1336(b). It is evident from these decisions that even where disappointed bidders have succeeded in convincing a court that claims arising out of contract award decisions sound in tort, the breadth of the exceptions to the waiver of immunity set forth in 28 U.S.C. § 2680(a)-(m) has effectively precluded that class of plaintiffs from obtaining relief under the FTCA. See, however, *Myers & Myers, Inc. v. United States Postal Serv.*, 527 F.2d 1252 (2d Cir. 1975), where the Second Circuit held that refusal to renew a contract based upon a nonresponsibility determination might be a de facto debarment requiring a hearing and remanded the case to the district court for decision under the FTCA, with instructions that the discretionary function exception to the Act would not apply if it was found that the procurement official had "behave[d] unconstitutionally or outside the scope of . . . authority." In *Cecile Indus., Inc. v. United States*, 793 F.2d 97 (3d Cir. 1986), the court held that the government's failure to follow debarment regulations did not constitute actionable fraud.

VI. INTERRELATIONSHIP OF FORUMS AND APPEALS

The current system gives protesters more than one available forum to hear protests; thus, protesters are able to select the forum best suited to their needs. This freedom of choice is recognized in the GAO bid protest statute, 31 U.S.C. § 3556, which states that it "does not give the Comptroller General exclusive jurisdiction over protests" and that nothing "shall affect the right of any interested party" to bring suit in the Court of Federal Claims. However, care must be taken in selecting the forum because the filing of a protest may be held to be a binding election of that forum by the protester. There are a number of statutory provisions dealing with this issue.

A. Government Accountability Office

The GAO protest regulations provide that the GAO will dismiss any protest where "the matter involved" is before a court of competent jurisdiction or where the matter has been decided on the merits by a court, unless the court requests a decision by the GAO, 4 C.F.R. § 21.11(b). This rule applies to both initial protests and requests for reconsideration. 4 C.F.R. § 21.11(a) requires a protester to notify the GAO immediately of any court proceedings that involve the subject matter of a protest and to file all relevant documents with the GAO.

When the subject matter is before a court of competent jurisdiction, GAO will dismiss the protest. In *Oahu Tree Experts*, Comp. Gen. Dec. B-282247, 99-1 CPD ¶ 69, the matter involved whether the contracting agency knew the "marginal" CPAR ratings to be motivated by bias, instead of an impartial assessment of the protester's performance. To answer this question, the GAO stated that it must first determine whether bias did, in fact, taint the ratings — the same question posed in Oahu's federal complaint. The GAO held that while Oahu correctly observed that its federal complaint does not mention the instant procurement and seeks different relief (i.e., the correction of the CPAR rather than the termination of the awardee's contract), these differences do not overcome the fact that Oahu has placed the same facts in issue before both the GAO and the federal court.

A later-filed court action will also divest the GAO of jurisdiction. In *Prince George's Contractors, Inc.*, 64 Comp. Gen. 786 (B-218640.2), 85-2 CPD ¶ 195, the protest was dismissed because the protester filed suit in the district court after filing a protest with the GAO. In addition, the GAO will not consider a request for costs and attorneys' fees for an action that was adjudicated in a court decision, *Pitney Bowes, Inc.*, 64 Comp. Gen. 623 (B-218241), 85-1 CPD ¶ 696. In that case the protest was first filed at the GAO; but when the agency refused to suspend contract performance, the protester went to court and obtained an injunction. The GAO ruled that its authority to award such remedies was ancillary to its jurisdiction to rule on the protest and that the district court injunction ousted it from jurisdiction in the case.

In determining whether the matter involved is before a court, the GAO has ruled that it will not consider a protest where the court proceeding pertains to a matter that "might have been decided" by the court, even though it was not decided, *Santa Fe Corp.*, 64 Comp. Gen. 429 (B-218234.2), 85-1 CPD ¶ 361, *recons. denied*, 85-1 CPD ¶ 499; *Affiliated Textiles, Inc.*, Comp. Gen. Dec. B-242970.2, 91-2 CPD ¶ 127; *Techniarts Eng'g — Recons.*, Comp. Gen. Dec. B-238520.7, 92-1 CPD ¶ 504. In *Meisel Rohrbau GmbH & Co.*, 67 Comp. Gen. 380 (B-228152.3), 88-1 CPD ¶ 371, the GAO concluded that a pending court case requesting reinstatement of a prior solicitation was relevant to the current protest contesting the cancellation of the replacement solicitation. See also *North Shore Strapping Co.*, Comp. Gen. Dec. B-248003, 92-1 CPD ¶ 532, where the GAO dismissed a protest alleging the use of restrictive specifications because it was within the scope of a pending court suit alleging unfair treatment of the protester by the procuring agency. But if the matter before the court is not relevant to the protest, the GAO will not dismiss the protest. See *Rix Indus., Inc.*, Comp. Gen. Dec. B-241498, 91-1 CPD ¶ 165, where the GAO found that a pending litigation involving an offeror's alleged theft of trade secrets concerning the product to be manufactured under the contract was not relevant to the issue of whether that offeror could perform the pending contract. *Sprint Communications Co. LP; Global Crossing Telecommunications, Inc.*, Comp. Gen. Dec. B-288413.11, 2002 CPD ¶ 171, is an interesting case in that the facts surrounding the inaccurate financial information were in flux due to the actions pending in other forums. The GAO stated that it hesitated to judge the degree of relevance or importance of such facts — such as the nature of culpability for acts causing the inaccuracies — before the other forums determine them. Thus, although the precise matter being protested (the award of the DREN contract) was not the subject of litigation before a court of competent jurisdiction the GAO held that it did not believe it appropriate to "get ahead" of this process in the context of this protest and thus dismissed the protest and request for reconsideration.

The GAO dismisses protests when there is a case pending in court even if a party other than the protester files the court suit. See, for example, *Dawson Constr. Co.*, Comp. Gen. Dec. B-208547.2, 83-1 CPD ¶ 327, where the GAO dismissed a protest of the cancellation of a procurement because a competitor had filed a suit in the Claims Court concerning the same procurement. This can result in a protest being dismissed because another party filed a subsequent suit in a court. *Test Sys. Assocs.*, Comp. Gen. Dec. B-256813.6, 96-2 CPD ¶ 161, is a good example of the peculiar nature of these cases. In that case the agency awarded a contract to TSAI. The unsuccessful offeror filed a protest at the GAO and shortly thereafter in district court. On its own initiative, the agency took corrective action and terminated TSAI's contract. The agency notified TSAI of its intention to award to Dixon. TSAI filed its first protest with GAO (B-256813.3) on the basis of an ambiguous clause and for terminating its contract and rejecting its offer. In the meantime, Dixon choose not to withdraw its civil action in district court. The GAO advised TSAI to intervene in Dixon's court action, but it did not. The GAO then dismissed TSAI's protest, stating that the dispositive issue was before the district court. In *Geronimo Serv. Co.*, Comp. Gen. Dec. B-242331.3, 91-1 CPD ¶ 321, the agency made award to Global, and an unsuccessful offeror, Emerald, protested at the GAO and in district court. The court requested an advisory opinion from the GAO. Subsequently, the other unsuccessful offeror, Geronimo, filed a protest at the GAO. The GAO stated that Geronimo chose not to intervene in the district court action and that GAO was therefore precluded from issuing an advisory opinion. Geronimo requested the GAO to reconsider its position, stating that the court could not review the merits of Geronimo's case and that dismissal of the protest would effectively preclude Geronimo from obtaining any relief on its protest. The GAO disagreed and dismissed the protest, stating: "If the court agrees with Emerald's position that the Air Force improperly awarded the contract to Global, the court could direct that award be made to another firm." An action filed in court will also deprive the government of the ability to obtain reconsideration by the GAO if the protester files a suit in court after winning the protest, *Dep't of the Navy — Recons.*, Comp. Gen. Dec. B-253129.4, 96-1 CPD ¶ 175.

A court may specifically request that the GAO provide an advisory opinion on the merits of a protest, *Academy Facilities Mgmt.Advisory Opinion*, Comp. Gen. Dec. B-401094.3, 2009 CPD ¶ 139; *Career Training Concepts, Inc. — Advisory Opinion*, Comp. Gen. Dec. B-311429, 2009 CPD ¶ 97; *Patriot Contract Servs. — Advisory Opinion*, Comp. Gen. Dec. B-294777.3, 2005 CPD ¶ 10; *TEAC Am. Corp., Inc.*, Comp. Gen. Dec. B-259831, 95-1 CPD ¶ 273; *Test Sys. Assocs.*, Comp. Gen. Dec. B-256813.5, 94-2 CPD ¶ 153; *Florida Professional Review Org., Inc.*, Comp. Gen. Dec. B-253908.2, 94-1 CPD ¶ 17. In such cases the GAO will rule on the protest even if it would have been untimely if filed with the GAO, *Adelaide Blomfield Mgmt.Co.*, 72 Comp. Gen. 335 (B-253128.2), 93-2 CPD ¶ 197. Once the GAO gives a decision to the court, it will not reconsider that decision unless the court requests such action, *Ace Fed. Reporters, Inc.*, Comp. Gen. Dec. B-241309.3, 91-1 CPD ¶ 54.

B. Appeals

There is no specified appeals procedure from GAO decisions because they are not in the nature of judicial decisions. If a protester is dissatisfied with a GAO decision, an action may be brought in the Court of Federal Claims, assuming that all requirements for jurisdiction are met, 31 U.S.C. § 3556. It is the agency's procurement award decision, not the GAO's recommendation, that is subject to review by the court, *Advanced Constr. Servs., Inc. v. United States*, 51 Fed. Cl. 362 (2002) ("Construing § 1491(b)(1) in the expansive manner advocated by [the protester] would violate the well-established principle that it is the agency's decision, not the decision of the GAO that is the subject of judicial review when a bid protester protests an award previously reviewed by the GAO."); *Cubic Applications, Inc. v. United States*, 37 Fed. Cl. 339 (1997). Although the court is conducting its review of the agency's award decision under the APA, the GAO recommendation is considered to be part of the agency record, 31 U.S.C. § 3556.

In these cases, the agency has almost always followed the recommendation of the GAO at the time the case is heard in the Court of Federal Claims. As a result, review of the agency's procurement decision necessarily requires the court to determine whether the GAO's recommendation was rational, *Honeywell, Inc. v.*

United States, 870 F.2d 644 (Fed. Cir. 1989). There, the contracting officer held that a competitor's bid was not responsive, but the GAO ruled to the contrary and recommended that the Army award the contract to the competitor. When the Army stated that it would follow that recommendation, Honeywell, Inc., the second low bidder on the contract, filed suit in the Claims Court to enjoin the award. The Claims Court held that the GAO did not have a rational basis for its recommendation and enjoined the award. The Court of Appeals for the Federal Circuit reversed. In its analysis, the Federal Circuit stated at 647:

> The question before the Claims Court was whether the Army justifiably followed the GAO's recommendation that the bid identified Haz-Tad as the bidder and therefore was responsive to the solicitation. The Claims Court recognized that the controlling inquiry in deciding that question was whether the GAO's decision was a rational one. After paying lip service to that standard, however, the Claims Court impermissibly undertook what can fairly be characterized only as its own independent de novo determination of whether the bid documents identified Haz-Tad as the bidder. Based upon its own weighing and evaluation of those materials, the Claims Court concluded that the GAO had "ignored the blatantly ambiguous wording of the bid, as well as its underlying meaning."

Carothers Constr., Inc. v. United States, 18 Cl. Ct. 745 (1989), further articulated the scope of review at 751:

> Although Carothers Construction Inc. (Carothers) was not required to file a protest with the GAO, it elected to do so. This election precludes the Claims Court from conducting its own independent de novo determination. *Honeywell*, 870 F.2d at 647.

> Even if the court would come to a different conclusion, the procurement agency's decision to follow the Comptroller General's recommendation is proper, unless the Comptroller General's decision itself was irrational. *Honeywell*, 870 F.2d at 648. "If the court finds a reasonable basis for the agency's action, the court should stay its hand even though it might, as an original proposition, have reached a different conclusion as to the proper administration and application of the procurement regulations." *Id.* at 648 (citing *M. Steinthal & Co. v. Seamans*, 147 U.S. App. D.C. 221, 455 F.2d 1289, 1301 (D.C. Cir. 1971).

In *The Centech Group, Inc. v. United States*, 79 Fed. Cl. 562 (2007), *aff'd*, 554 F.3d 1029 (2009), Centech argued that the Air Force irrationally ignored the responsibility determination by SBA and followed GAO's independent finding of unacceptability. The court stated that since Centech's proposal did not offer to provide what the RFP requested, it was not responsive to the RFP. The proposal therefore was unacceptable and could not serve as the basis for contract award. Under these circumstances, GAO's recommendation to solicit revised proposals for the contract was rational. It thus was proper for the Air Force to follow GAO's recommendation.

The court found an agency decision to follow an irrational GAO decision itself irrational in *Turner Constr. Co. v. United States*, 94 Fed. Cl. 586 (2010). There, the court concluded that the GAO conducted an improper de novo review of the contracting officer's OCI determination without giving the agency the deference it was due. The GAO had overturned the contracting officer's determination without highlighting any hard facts to base its OCI determination. The court held that the Army was arbitrary and capricious in implementing the GAO's decision, stripping Turner of the contract.

There may be instances where the court will overturn agency actions that were validated by the GAO, *Latecoere Int'l Inc. v. Dep't of the Navy*, 19 F.3d 1342 (11th Cir. 1994). There, the court disagreed with the GAO's finding that the arbitrary rating of a proposal did not prejudice Latecoere. The court stated that the GAO based its conclusion that "Latecoere was not prejudiced by the arbitrary elevation of [the other offeror's] ratings on two assumptions, one of which has no support in the record, and the other of which is flatly contradicted by the record." In *E.W. Bliss Co. v. United States*, 33 Fed. Cl. 123 (1995), *aff'd*, 77 F.3d 445 (Fed. Cir. 1996), the court, although acknowledging that GAO decisions should be given a high degree of deference, stated: "The Court of Claims is not bound by the views of the Comptroller General nor do they operate as a legal or judicial determination of the rights of the parties," quoting *Burroughs Corp. v. United States*, 223 Ct. Cl. 53, 63, 617 F.2d 590, 597 (1980) (citing *Font v. United States*, 219 Ct. Cl. 335, 593 F.2d 388 (1979)). In distinguishing *Honeywell*, the *Bliss* court stated that the Federal Circuit decision focused on the fact that the Claims Court did not give deference to either the GAO or the contracting officer's decision but, rather, engaged in an independent de novo analysis. Thus, *Honeywell* should not be read as conferring on the GAO a degree of deference beyond that set forth in *Burroughs*. The court stated at 135:

> The weight of precedent instructs that, although the review is not de novo and the GAO's decision is accorded deference, the court is to answer the question whether the agency's procurement decision or the GAO's decision on the protest was reasonable based on the record before the contracting officer or the GAO.

Although the court went to great lengths in analyzing the scope of its review, it in fact agreed with the GAO's decision. Similarly, in *SP Sys., Inc. v. United States*, 86 Fed. Cl. 1 (2009), SP Systems originally won a NASA award, but, after the GAO sustained a protest against the evaluations of cost realism, management approach, and past performance that led to that award, the agency followed the GAO's specific recommendations for corrective action and (after re-evaluation) awarded the contract to a competitor. SP Systems then filed suit in the Court of Federal Claims, which found both the GAO's decision and the agency's decision to follow it, reasonable, even though there were other ways the agency might have re-evaluated proposals.

If the GAO recommendation is plainly contrary to a statutory or regulatory requirement, that decision is irrational and an agency is not justified in following it. In *Firth Constr. Co. v. United States*, 36 Fed. Cl. 268 (1996), an offeror was the apparent low bidder but had failed to submit a completed Standard Form (SF) 1442. After bid opening, the offeror faxed a completed SF 1442 to the agency and was awarded the contract. Following a protest, the Office of Counsel of the agency advised the contracting division that the award was improper because the bid was nonresponsive due to the lack of an original signature on the SF 1442. Given this advice, the contracting officer canceled the award. The offeror protested to the GAO, and the GAO sustained the protest. The agency announced its intention to follow the GAO's recommendation and award the contract to the offeror, and Firth Construction filed suit in the Court of Federal Claims. The court determined that the bid was nonresponsive because it lacked an original signature. Thus, the court held that the GAO's decision was irrational and that the agency would be arbitrary and capricious to follow it. Similarly in *Grunley Walsh Int'l, LLC v. United States*, 78 Fed. Cl. 35 (2007), the Department of State disqualified plaintiff's prequalification based upon the GAO's recommended interpretation of a statutory business-volume requirement. In holding that the GAO's recommended interpretation is afforded no deference because it plainly lacked a reasonable basis and thus was arbitrary and capricious, the court stated at 43-44:

> Although the court does not specifically reach the question of whether the GAO afforded proper deference to the DOS's original interpretation under *Chevron, U.S.A., Inc. v. Natural Res. Def. Council, Inc.*, 467 U.S. 837 (1984), the court must address defendant's argument for affording deference to the DOS's new interpretation. Adoption of defendant's position would effectively strip this court of any real review in any case where the agency followed a recommendation of the GAO on an interpretation of a statute or regulation. The court declines to play that shell game. In entrusting this court with bid protest jurisdiction under APA standards, Congress necessarily meant for the court to undertake a meaningful review of agency action.

> Defendant cites *Honeywell, Inc. v. United States*, 870 F.2d 644 (Fed. Cir. 1989), in support of its argument. *Honeywell* stands for the rule that "a procurement agency's decision to follow the [GAO]'s recommendation . . . was proper unless the [GAO]'s decision itself was irrational." 870 F.2d at 648. In order to review an agency's action when it is based upon the recommendation of the GAO, it is necessary to examine the underlying decision of the GAO. *See Firth Const. Co. v. United States*, 36 Fed. Cl. 268, 271-72 (1996) (citing and applying *Honeywell* to overturn agency action that was based on a decision of the GAO). The GAO decision constitutes the very reason(s) for the agency action. Put another way, an agency action is not insulated from meaningful review simply because the GAO recommended it.

See also *Geo-Seis Helicopters, Inc. v. United States*, 77 Fed. Cl. 636 (Fed. Cl. 2007), where the Military Sealift Command accepted amendments to the winning bid after the bid closing date in reliance on GAO precedent allowing agencies to issue amendments that extend the closing date after the closing date has passed. Geo-Seis argued that the Sealift Command violated the late is late rule. GAO denied the protest and then Geo-Seis filed suit in the Court of Federal Claims. The court held that the Military Sealift Command violated the APA by relying on GAO precedent. The court stated that the refusal of the contracting officer to "adhere to the categorical reality of the 'late is late' rule renders arbitrary her decision to accept [the winning bidder's] first and second revised proposals."

C. Appellate Review of Court of Federal Claims Protest Decisions

The Federal Circuit has jurisdiction over appeals from the Court of Federal Claims, 28. U.S.C. § 1295(a)(3). An appeal must be filed within 60 days from the date of entry of the judgment or order, Fed. R. App. P. 4(a)(1); R.C.F.C. 72. The Federal Circuit reviews legal decisions of the Court of Federal Claims *de novo* and applies the same standard of review as the Court of Federal Claims, *Dysart v. United States*, 369 F.3d 1303 (Fed. Cir. 2004).

D. Precedential Authority

The Court of Federal Claims is bound by the decisions of the United States Supreme Court, the precedential decisions of the Federal Circuit, and the published decisions of the Federal Circuit's predecessor courts, the Court of Claims and the Court of Customs and Patent Appeals, *South Corp. v. United States*, 690 F.2d 1368 (Fed. Cir. 1982) (adopting as precedent the decisions of the predecessor Court of Claims and Court of Customs and Patent Appeals). Court of Federal Claims judges are not bound by the decisions of other Court of Federal Claims judges, *Casa De Cambio Comdiv S.A., de C.V. v. United States*, 291 F.3d 1356 (Fed. Cir. 2002).

APPENDIX 1

FAR PART 15

15.000 Scope of part.

This part prescribes policies and procedures governing competitive and noncompetitive negotiated acquisitions. A contract awarded using other than sealed bidding procedures is a negotiated contract (see 14.101).

15.001 Definitions.

As used in this part—

Deficiency is a material failure of a proposal to meet a Government requirement or a combination of significant weaknesses in a proposal that increases the risk of unsuccessful contract performance to an unacceptable level.

Proposal modification is a change made to a proposal before the solicitation closing date and time, or made in response to an amendment, or made to correct a mistake at any time before award.

Proposal revision is a change to a proposal made after the solicitation closing date, at the request of or as allowed by a contracting officer, as the result of negotiations.

Weakness means a flaw in the proposal that increases the risk of unsuccessful contract performance. A "significant weakness" in the proposal is a flaw that appreciably increases the risk of unsuccessful contract performance.

15.002 Types of negotiated acquisition.

(a) *Sole source acquisitions.* When contracting in a sole source environment, the request for proposals (RFP) should be tailored to remove unnecessary information and requirements; *e.g.,* evaluation criteria and voluminous proposal preparation instructions.

(b) *Competitive acquisitions.* When contracting in a competitive environment, the procedures of this part are intended to minimize the complexity of the solicitation, the evaluation, and the source selection decision, while maintaining a process designed to foster an impartial and comprehensive evaluation of offerors' proposals, leading to selection of the proposal representing the best value to the Government (see 2.101).

Subpart 15.1—Source Selection Processes and Techniques

15.100 Scope of subpart.

This subpart describes some of the acquisition processes and techniques that may be used to design competitive acquisition strategies suitable for the specific circumstances of the acquisition.

15.101 Best value continuum.

An agency can obtain best value in negotiated acquisitions by using any one or a combination of source selection approaches. In different types of acquisitions, the relative importance of cost or price may vary. For example, in acquisitions where the requirement is clearly definable and the risk of unsuccessful contract performance is minimal, cost or price may play a dominant role in source selection. The less definitive the requirement, the more development work required, or the greater the performance risk, the more technical or past performance considerations may play a dominant role in source selection.

15.101-1 Tradeoff process.

(a) A tradeoff process is appropriate when it may be in the best interest of the Government to consider award to other than the lowest priced offeror or other than the highest technically rated offeror.

(b) When using a tradeoff process, the following apply:

(1) All evaluation factors and significant subfactors that will affect contract award and their relative importance shall be clearly stated in the solicitation; and

(2) The solicitation shall state whether all evaluation factors other than cost or price, when combined, are significantly more important than, approximately equal to, or significantly less important than cost or price.

(c) This process permits tradeoffs among cost or price and non-cost factors and allows the Government to accept other than the lowest priced proposal. The perceived benefits of the higher priced proposal shall merit the additional cost, and the rationale for tradeoffs must be documented in the file in accordance with 15.406.

15.101-2 Lowest price technically acceptable source selection process.

(a) The lowest price technically acceptable source selection process is appropriate when best value is expected to result from selection of the technically acceptable proposal with the lowest evaluated price.

(b) When using the lowest price technically acceptable process, the following apply:

(1) The evaluation factors and significant subfactors that establish the requirements of acceptability shall be set forth in the solicitation. Solicitations shall specify that award will be made on the basis of the lowest evaluated price of proposals meeting or exceeding the acceptability standards for non-cost factors. If the contracting officer documents the file pursuant to 15.304(c)(3)(iii), past performance need not be an evaluation factor in lowest price technically acceptable source selections. If the contracting officer elects to consider past performance as an evaluation factor, it shall be evaluated in accordance with 15.305. However, the comparative assessment in 15.305(a)(2)(i) does not apply. If the contracting officer determines that a small business' past performance is not acceptable, the matter shall be referred to the Small Business Administration for a Certificate of Competency determination, in accordance with the procedures contained in Subpart 19.6 and 15 U.S.C. 637(b)(7)).

(2) Tradeoffs are not permitted.

(3) Proposals are evaluated for acceptability but not ranked using the non-cost/price factors.

(4) Exchanges may occur (see 15.306).

15.102 Oral presentations.

(a) Oral presentations by offerors as requested by the Government may substitute for, or augment, written information. Use of oral presentations as a substitute for portions of a proposal can be effective in streamlining the source selection process. Oral presentations may occur at any time in the acquisition process, and are subject to the same restrictions as written information, regarding timing (see 15.208) and content (see 15.306). Oral presentations provide an opportunity for dialogue among the parties. Pre-recorded videotaped presentations that lack real-time interactive dialogue are not considered oral presentations for the purposes of this section, although they may be included in offeror submissions, when appropriate.

(b) The solicitation may require each offeror to submit part of its proposal through oral presentations. However, representations and certifications shall be submitted as required in the FAR provisions at 52.204-8(d) or 52.212-3(b), and a signed offer sheet (including any exceptions to the Government's terms and conditions) shall be submitted in writing.

(c) Information pertaining to areas such as an offeror's capability, past performance, work plans or approaches, staffing resources, transition plans, or sample tasks (or other types of tests) may be suitable for oral presentations. In deciding what information to obtain through an oral presentation, consider the following:

(1) The Government's ability to adequately evaluate the information;

(2) The need to incorporate any information into the resultant contract;

(3) The impact on the efficiency of the acquisition; and

(4) The impact (including cost) on small businesses. In considering the costs of oral presentations, contracting officers should also consider alternatives to on-site oral presentations (*e.g.,* teleconferencing, video teleconferencing).

(d) When oral presentations are required, the solicitation shall provide offerors with sufficient information to prepare them. Accordingly, the solicitation may describe—

(1) The types of information to be presented orally and the associated evaluation factors that will be used;

(2) The qualifications for personnel that will be required to provide the oral presentation(s);

(3) The requirements for, and any limitations and/or prohibitions on, the use of written material or other media to supplement the oral presentations;

(4) The location, date, and time for the oral presentations;

(5) The restrictions governing the time permitted for each oral presentation; and

(6) The scope and content of exchanges that may occur between the Government's participants and the offeror's representatives as part of the oral presentations, including whether or not discussions (see 15.306(d)) will be permitted during oral presentations.

(e) The contracting officer shall maintain a record of oral presentations to document what the Government relied upon in making the source selection decision. The method and level of detail of the record (*e.g.,* videotaping, audio tape recording, written record, Government notes, copies of offeror briefing slides or presentation notes) shall be at the discretion of the source selection authority. A copy of the record placed in the file may be provided to the offeror.

(f) When an oral presentation includes information that the parties intend to include in the contract as material terms or conditions, the information shall be put in writing. Incorporation by reference of oral statements is not permitted.

(g) If, during an oral presentation, the Government conducts discussions (see 15.306(d)), the Government must comply with 15.306 and 15.307.

Subpart 15.2—Solicitation and Receipt of Proposals and Information

15.200 Scope of subpart.
This subpart prescribes policies and procedures for—
(a) Exchanging information with industry prior to receipt of proposals;
(b) Preparing and issuing requests for proposals (RFPs) and requests for information (RFIs); and
(c) Receiving proposals and information.

15.201 Exchanges with industry before receipt of proposals.
(a) Exchanges of information among all interested parties, from the earliest identification of a requirement through receipt of proposals, are encouraged. Any exchange of information must be consistent with procurement integrity requirements (see 3.104). Interested parties include potential offerors, end users, Government acquisition and supporting personnel, and others involved in the conduct or outcome of the acquisition.

(b) The purpose of exchanging information is to improve the understanding of Government requirements and industry capabilities, thereby allowing potential offerors to judge whether or how they can satisfy the Government's requirements, and enhancing the Government's ability to obtain quality supplies and services, including construction, at reasonable prices, and increase efficiency in proposal preparation, proposal evaluation, negotiation, and contract award.

(c) Agencies are encouraged to promote early exchanges of information about future acquisitions. An early exchange of information among industry and the program manager, contracting officer, and other participants in the acquisition process can identify and resolve concerns regarding the acquisition strategy, including proposed contract type, terms and conditions, and acquisition planning schedules; the feasibility of the requirement, including performance requirements, statements of work, and data requirements; the suitability of the proposal instructions and evaluation criteria, including the approach for assessing past performance information; the availability of reference documents; and any other industry concerns or questions. Some techniques to promote early exchanges of information are—

(1) Industry or small business conferences;

(2) Public hearings;

(3) Market research, as described in Part 10;

(4) One-on-one meetings with potential offerors (any that are substantially involved with potential contract terms and conditions should include the contracting officer; also see paragraph (f) of this section regarding restrictions on disclosure of information);

(5) Presolicitation notices;

(6) Draft RFPs;

(7) RFIs;

(8) Presolicitation or preproposal conferences; and

(9) Site visits.

(d) The special notices of procurement matters at 5.205(c), or electronic notices, may be used to publicize the Government's requirement or solicit information from industry.

(e) RFIs may be used when the Government does not presently intend to award a contract, but wants to obtain price, delivery, other market information, or capabilities for planning purposes. Responses to these notices are not offers and cannot be accepted by the Government to form a binding contract. There is no required format for RFIs.

(f) General information about agency mission needs and future requirements may be disclosed at any time. After release of the solicitation, the contracting officer must be the focal point of any exchange with potential offerors. When specific information about a proposed acquisition that would be necessary for the preparation of proposals is disclosed to one or more potential offerors, that information must be made available to the public as soon as practicable, but no later than the next general release of information, in order to avoid creating an unfair competitive advantage. Information provided to a potential offeror in response to its request must not be disclosed if doing so would reveal the potential offeror's confidential business strategy, and is protected under 3.104 or Subpart 24.2. When conducting a presolicitation or preproposal conference, materials distributed at the conference should be made available to all potential offerors, upon request.

15.202 Advisory multi-step process.

(a) The agency may publish a presolicitation notice (see 5.204) that provides a general description of the scope or purpose of the acquisition and invites potential offerors to submit information that allows the Government to advise the offerors about their potential to be viable competitors. The presolicitation notice should identify the information that must be submitted and the criteria that will be used in making the initial evaluation. Information sought may be limited to a statement of qualifications and other appropriate information (*e.g.,* proposed technical concept, past performance, and limited pricing information). At a minimum, the notice shall contain sufficient information to permit a potential offeror to make an informed decision about whether to participate in the acquisition. This process should not be used for multi-step acquisitions where it would result in offerors being required to submit identical information in response to the notice and in response to the initial step of the acquisition.

(b) The agency shall evaluate all responses in accordance with the criteria stated in the notice, and shall advise each respondent in writing either that it will be invited to participate in the resultant acquisition or, based on the information submitted, that it is unlikely to be a viable competitor. The agency shall advise respondents considered not to be viable competitors of the general basis for that opinion. The agency shall inform all respondents that, notwithstanding the advice provided by the Government in response to their submissions, they may participate in the resultant acquisition.

15.203 Requests for proposals.

(a) Requests for proposals (RFPs) are used in negotiated acquisitions to communicate Government requirements to prospective contractors and to solicit proposals. RFPs for competitive acquisitions shall, at a minimum, describe the—

(1) Government's requirement;

(2) Anticipated terms and conditions that will apply to the contract:

(i) The solicitation may authorize offerors to propose alternative terms and conditions, including the contract line item number (CLIN) structure; and

(ii) When alternative CLIN structures are permitted, the evaluation approach should consider the potential impact on other terms and conditions or the requirement (*e.g.,* place of performance or payment and funding requirements) (see 15.206);

(3) Information required to be in the offeror's proposal; and

(4) Factors and significant subfactors that will be used to evaluate the proposal and their relative importance.

(b) An RFP may be issued for OMB Circular A-76 studies. See Subpart 7.3 for additional information regarding cost comparisons between Government and contractor performance.

(c) Electronic commerce may be used to issue RFPs and to receive proposals, modifications, and revisions. In this case, the RFP shall specify the electronic commerce method(s) that offerors may use (see Subpart 4.5).

(d) Contracting officers may issue RFPs and/or authorize receipt of proposals, modifications, or revisions by facsimile.

(1) In deciding whether or not to use facsimiles, the contracting officer should consider factors such as—

(i) Anticipated proposal size and volume;

(ii) Urgency of the requirement;

(iii) Availability and suitability of electronic commerce methods; and

(iv) Adequacy of administrative procedures and controls for receiving, identifying, recording, and safeguarding facsimile proposals, and ensuring their timely delivery to the designated proposal delivery location.

(2) If facsimile proposals are authorized, contracting officers may request offeror(s) to provide the complete, original signed proposal at a later date.

(e) Letter RFPs may be used in sole source acquisitions and other appropriate circumstances. Use of a letter RFP does not relieve the contracting officer from complying with other FAR requirements. Letter RFPs should be as complete as possible and, at a minimum, should contain the following:

(1) RFP number and date;

(2) Name, address (including electronic address and facsimile address, if appropriate), and telephone number of the contracting officer;

(3) Type of contract contemplated;

(4) Quantity, description, and required delivery dates for the item;

(5) Applicable certifications and representations;

(6) Anticipated contract terms and conditions;

(7) Instructions to offerors and evaluation criteria for other than sole source actions;

(8) Proposal due date and time; and

(9) Other relevant information; *e.g.,* incentives, variations in delivery schedule, cost proposal support, and data requirements.

(f) Oral RFPs are authorized when processing a written solicitation would delay the acquisition of supplies or services to the detriment of the Government and a notice is not required under 5.202 (*e.g.,* perishable items and support of contingency operations or other emergency situations). Use of an oral RFP does not relieve the contracting officer from complying with other FAR requirements.

(1) The contract files supporting oral solicitations should include—

(i) A description of the requirement;

(ii) Rationale for use of an oral solicitation;

(iii) Sources solicited, including the date, time, name of individuals contacted, and prices offered; and

(iv) The solicitation number provided to the prospective offerors.

(2) The information furnished to potential offerors under oral solicitations should include appropriate items from paragraph (e) of this section.

15.204 Contract format.

The use of a uniform contract format facilitates preparation of the solicitation and contract as well as reference to, and use of, those documents by offerors, contractors, and contract administrators. The uniform contract format need not be used for the following:

(a) Construction and architect-engineer contracts (see Part 36).

(b) Subsistence contracts.

(c) Supplies or services contracts requiring special contract formats prescribed elsewhere in this regulation that are inconsistent with the uniform format.

(d) Letter requests for proposals (see 15.203(e)).

(e) Contracts exempted by the agency head or designee.

15.204-1 Uniform contract format.

(a) Contracting officers shall prepare solicitations and resulting contracts using the uniform contract format outlined in Table 15-1 of this subsection.

(b) Solicitations using the uniform contract format shall include Parts I, II, III, and IV (see 15.204-2 through 15.204-5). Upon award, contracting officers shall not physically include Part IV in the resulting contract, but shall retain it in the contract file. (See 4.1201(c).) Section K shall be incorporated by reference in the contract.

TABLE 15-1—UNIFORM CONTRACT FORMAT

Section	Title
	Part I—The Schedule
A	Solicitation/contract form
B	Supplies or services and prices/costs
C	Description/specifications/statement of work
D	Packaging and marking
E	Inspection and acceptance
F	Deliveries or performance
G	Contract administration data
H	Special contract requirements
	Part II—Contract Clauses
I	Contract clauses
	Part III—List of Documents, Exhibits, and Other Attachments
J	List of attachments
	Part IV—Representations and Instructions
K	Representations, certifications, and other statements of offerors or respondents
L	Instructions, conditions, and notices to offerors or respondents
M	Evaluation factors for award

15.204-2 Part I—The Schedule.

The contracting officer shall prepare the contract Schedule as follows:

(a) Section A, Solicitation/contract form.

(1) Optional Form (OF) 308, Solicitation and Offer—Negotiated Acquisition, or Standard Form (SF) 33, Solicitation, Offer and Award, may be used to prepare RFPs.

(2) When other than OF 308 or SF 33 is used, include the following information on the first page of the solicitation:

(i) Name, address, and location of issuing activity, including room and building where proposals or information must be submitted.

(ii) Solicitation number.

(iii) Date of issuance.

(iv) Closing date and time.

(v) Number of pages.

(vi) Requisition or other purchase authority.

(vii) Brief description of item or service.

(viii) Requirement for the offeror to provide its name and complete address, including street, city, county, state, and ZIP code, and electronic address (including facsimile address), if appropriate.

(ix) Offer expiration date.

(b) *Section B, Supplies or services and prices/costs.* Include a brief description of the supplies or services; *e.g.,* item number, national stock number/part number if applicable, nouns, nomenclature, and quantities. (This includes incidental deliverables such as manuals and reports.)

(c) *Section C, Description/specifications/statement of work.* Include any description or specifications needed in addition to Section B (see Part 11, Describing Agency Needs).

(d) *Section D, Packaging and marking.* Provide packaging, packing, preservation, and marking requirements, if any.

(e) *Section E, Inspection and acceptance.* Include inspection, acceptance, quality assurance, and reliability requirements (see Part 46, Quality Assurance).

(f) *Section F, Deliveries or performance.* Specify the requirements for time, place, and method of delivery or performance (see Subpart 11.4, Delivery or Performance Schedules, and 47.301-1).

(g) *Section G, Contract administration data.* Include any required accounting and appropriation data and any required contract administration information or instructions other than those on the solicitation form. Include a statement that the offeror should include the payment address in the proposal, if it is different from that shown for the offeror.

(h) *Section H, Special contract requirements.* Include a clear statement of any special contract requirements that are not included in Section I, Contract clauses, or in other sections of the uniform contract format.

15.204-3 Part II—Contract Clauses.

Section I, Contract clauses. The contracting officer shall include in this section the clauses required by law or by this regulation and any additional clauses expected to be included in any resulting contract, if these clauses are not required in any other section of the uniform contract format. An index may be inserted if this section's format is particularly complex.

15.204-4 Part III—List of Documents, Exhibits, and Other Attachments.

Section J, List of attachments. The contracting officer shall list the title, date, and number of pages for each attached document, exhibit, and other attachment. Cross-references to material in other sections may be inserted, as appropriate.

15.204-5 Part IV—Representations and Instructions.

The contracting officer shall prepare the representations and instructions as follows:

(a) *Section K, Representations, certifications, and other statements of offerors.* Include in this section those solicitation provisions that require representations, certifications, or the submission of other information by offerors.

(b) *Section L, Instructions, conditions, and notices to offerors or respondents.* Insert in this section solicitation provisions and other information and instructions not required elsewhere to guide offerors or respondents in preparing proposals or responses to requests for information. Prospective offerors or respondents may be instructed to submit proposals or information in a specific format or severable parts to facilitate evaluation. The instructions may specify further organization of proposal or response parts, such as—

(1) Administrative;

(2) Management;

(3) Technical;

(4) Past performance; and

(5) Certified cost or pricing data (see Table 15-2 of 15.408) or data other than certified cost or pricing data.

(c) *Section M, Evaluation factors for award.* Identify all significant factors and any significant subfactors that will be considered in awarding the contract and their relative importance (see 15.304(d)). The contracting officer shall insert one of the phrases in 15.304(e).

15.205 Issuing solicitations.

(a) The contracting officer shall issue solicitations to potential sources in accordance with the policies and procedures in 5.102, 19.202-4, and Part 6.

(b) A master solicitation, as described in 14.203-3, may also be used for negotiated acquisitions.

15.206 Amending the solicitation.

(a) When, either before or after receipt of proposals, the Government changes its requirements or terms and conditions, the contracting officer shall amend the solicitation.

(b) Amendments issued before the established time and date for receipt of proposals shall be issued to all parties receiving the solicitation.

(c) Amendments issued after the established time and date for receipt of proposals shall be issued to all offerors that have not been eliminated from the competition.

(d) If a proposal of interest to the Government involves a departure from the stated requirements, the contracting officer shall amend the solicitation, provided this can be done without revealing to the other offerors the alternate solution proposed or any other information that is entitled to protection (see 15.207(b) and 15.306(e)).

(e) If, in the judgment of the contracting officer, based on market research or otherwise, an amendment proposed for issuance after offers have been received is so substantial as to exceed what prospective offerors reasonably could have anticipated, so that additional sources likely would have submitted offers had the substance of the amendment been known to them, the contracting officer shall cancel the original solicitation and issue a new one, regardless of the stage of the acquisition.

(f) Oral notices may be used when time is of the essence. The contracting officer shall document the contract file and formalize the notice with an amendment (see Subpart 4.5, Electronic Commerce in Contracting).

(g) At a minimum, the following information should be included in each amendment:

(1) Name and address of issuing activity.

(2) Solicitation number and date.

(3) Amendment number and date.

(4) Number of pages.

(5) Description of the change being made.

(6) Government point of contact and phone number (and electronic or facsimile address, if appropriate).

(7) Revision to solicitation closing date, if applicable.

15.207 Handling proposals and information.

(a) Upon receipt at the location specified in the solicitation, proposals and information received in response to a request for information (RFI) shall be marked with the date and time of receipt and shall be transmitted to the designated officials.

(b) Proposals shall be safeguarded from unauthorized disclosure throughout the source selection process. (See 3.104 regarding the disclosure of source selection information (41 U.S.C. 423)). Information received in response to an RFI shall be safeguarded adequately from unauthorized disclosure.

(c) If any portion of a proposal received by the contracting officer electronically or by facsimile is unreadable, the contracting officer immediately shall notify the offeror and permit the offeror to resubmit the unreadable portion of the proposal. The method and time for resubmission shall be prescribed by the contracting officer after consultation with the offeror, and documented in the file. The resubmission shall be considered as if it were received at the date and time of the original unreadable submission for the purpose of determining timeliness under 15.208(a), provided the offeror complies with the time and format requirements for resubmission prescribed by the contracting officer.

15.208 Submission, modification, revision, and withdrawal of proposals.

(a) Offerors are responsible for submitting proposals, and any revisions, and modifications, so as to reach the Government office designated in the solicitation by the time specified in the solicitation. Offerors may use any transmission method authorized by the solicitation (*i.e.,* regular mail, electronic commerce, or facsimile). If no time is specified in the solicitation, the time for receipt is 4:30 p.m., local time, for the designated Government office on the date that proposals are due.

(b)(1) Any proposal, modification, or revision, that is received at the designated Government office after the exact time specified for receipt of proposals is "late" and will not be considered unless it is received before award is made, the contracting officer determines that accepting the late proposal would not unduly delay the acquisition; and—

(i) If it was transmitted through an electronic commerce method authorized by the solicitation, it was received at the initial point of entry to the Government infrastructure not later than 5:00 p.m. one working day prior to the date specified for receipt of proposals; or

(ii) There is acceptable evidence to establish that it was received at the Government installation designated for receipt of proposals and was under the Government's control prior to the time set for receipt of proposals; or

(iii) It was the only proposal received.

(2) However, a late modification of an otherwise successful proposal, that makes its terms more favorable to the Government, will be considered at any time it is received and may be accepted.

(c) Acceptable evidence to establish the time of receipt at the Government installation includes the time/date stamp of that installation on the proposal wrapper, other documentary evidence of receipt maintained by the installation, or oral testimony or statements of Government personnel.

(d) If an emergency or unanticipated event interrupts normal Government processes so that proposals cannot be received at the Government office designated for receipt of proposals by the exact time specified in the solicitation, and urgent Government requirements preclude amendment of the solicitation closing date, the time specified for receipt of proposals will be deemed to be extended to the same time of day specified in the solicitation on the first work day on which normal Government processes resume.

(e) Proposals may be withdrawn by written notice at any time before award. Oral proposals in response to oral solicitations may be withdrawn orally. The contracting officer must document the contract file when oral withdrawals are made. One copy of withdrawn proposals should be retained in the contract file (see 4.803(a)(10)). Extra copies of the withdrawn proposals may be destroyed or returned to the offeror at the offeror's request. Where practicable, electronically transmitted proposals that are withdrawn must be purged from primary and backup data storage systems after a copy is made for the file. Extremely bulky proposals must only be returned at the offeror's request and expense.

(f) The contracting officer must promptly notify any offeror if its proposal, modification, or revision was received late, and must inform the offeror whether its proposal will be considered, unless contract award is imminent and the notice prescribed in 15.503(b) would suffice.

(g) Late proposals and modifications that are not considered must be held unopened, unless opened for identification, until after award and then retained with other unsuccessful proposals.

(h) If available, the following must be included in the contracting office files for each late proposal, modification, revision, or withdrawal:

(1) The date and hour of receipt.

(2) A statement regarding whether the proposal was considered for award, with supporting rationale.

(3) The envelope, wrapper, or other evidence of date of receipt.

15.209 Solicitation provisions and contract clauses.

When contracting by negotiation—

(a) The contracting officer shall insert the provision at 52.215-1, Instructions to Offerors—Competitive Acquisition, in all competitive solicitations where the Government intends to award a contract without discussions.

(1) If the Government intends to make award after discussions with offerors within the competitive range, the contracting officer shall use the basic provision with its Alternate I.

(2) If the Government would be willing to accept alternate proposals, the contracting officer shall alter the basic clause to add a new paragraph (c)(9) substantially the same as Alternate II.

(b)(1) Except as provided in paragraph (b)(2) of this section, the contracting officer shall insert the clause at 52.215-2, Audit and Records—Negotiation (10 U.S.C. 2313, 41 U.S.C. 254d, and OMB Circular No. A-133), in solicitations and contracts except those for—

(i) Acquisitions not exceeding the simplified acquisition threshold;

(ii) The acquisition of utility services at rates not exceeding those established to apply uniformly to the general public, plus any applicable reasonable connection charge; or

(iii) The acquisition of commercial items exempted under 15.403-1.

(2)(i) When using funds appropriated or otherwise made available by the American Recovery and Reinvestment Act of 2009 (Pub. L. 111-5)—

(A) The exceptions in paragraphs (b)(1)(i) through (b)(1)(iii) are not applicable; and

(B) Use the clause with its Alternate I.

(ii)(A) In the case of a bilateral contract modification that will use funds appropriated or otherwise made available by the American Recovery and Reinvestment Act of 2009, the contracting officer shall specify applicability of Alternate I to that modification.

(B) In the case of a task- or delivery-order contract in which not all orders will use funds appropriated or otherwise made available by the American Recovery and Reinvestment Act of 2009, the contracting officer shall specify the task or delivery orders to which Alternate I applies.

(3) For cost-reimbursement contracts with State and local Governments, educational institutions, and other nonprofit organizations, the contracting officer shall use the clause with its Alternate II.

(4) When the head of the agency has waived the examination of records by the Comptroller General in accordance with 25.1001, use the clause with its Alternate III.

(c) When issuing a solicitation for information or planning purposes, the contracting officer shall insert the provision at 52.215-3, Request for Information or Solicitation for Planning Purposes, and clearly mark on the face of the solicitation that it is for information or planning purposes.

(d) [Reserved]

(e) The contracting officer shall insert the provision at 52.215-5, Facsimile Proposals, in solicitations if facsimile proposals are authorized (see 15.203(d)).

(f) The contracting officer shall insert the provision at 52.215-6, Place of Performance, in solicitations unless the place of performance is specified by the Government.

(g) [Reserved]

(h) The contracting officer shall insert the clause at 52.215-8, Order of Precedence—Uniform Contract Format, in solicitations and contracts using the format at 15.204.

15.210 Forms.

Prescribed forms are not required to prepare solicitations described in this part. The following forms may be used at the discretion of the contracting officer:

(a) Standard Form 33, Solicitation, Offer and Award, and Optional Form 308, Solicitation and Offer—Negotiated Acquisition, may be used to issue RFPs and RFIs.

(b) Standard Form 30, Amendment of Solicitation/ Modification of Contract, and Optional Form 309, Amendment of Solicitation, may be used to amend solicitations of negotiated contracts.

(c) Optional Form 17, Offer Label, may be furnished with each request for proposal.

Subpart 15.3—Source Selection

15.300 Scope of subpart.

This subpart prescribes policies and procedures for selection of a source or sources in competitive negotiated acquisitions.

15.301 [Reserved]

15.302 Source selection objective.

The objective of source selection is to select the proposal that represents the best value.

15.303 Responsibilities.

(a) Agency heads are responsible for source selection. The contracting officer is designated as the source selection authority, unless the agency head appoints another individual for a particular acquisition or group of acquisitions.

(b) The source selection authority shall—

(1) Establish an evaluation team, tailored for the particular acquisition, that includes appropriate contracting, legal, logistics, technical, and other expertise to ensure a comprehensive evaluation of offers;

(2) Approve the source selection strategy or acquisition plan, if applicable, before solicitation release;

(3) Ensure consistency among the solicitation requirements, notices to offerors, proposal preparation instructions, evaluation factors and subfactors, solicitation provisions or contract clauses, and data requirements;

(4) Ensure that proposals are evaluated based solely on the factors and subfactors contained in the solicitation (10 U.S.C. 2305(b)(1) and 41 U.S.C. 253b(d)(3));

(5) Consider the recommendations of advisory boards or panels (if any); and

(6) Select the source or sources whose proposal is the best value to the Government (10 U.S.C. 2305(b)(4)(B) and 41 U.S.C. 253b(d)(3)).

(c) The contracting officer shall—

(1) After release of a solicitation, serve as the focal point for inquiries from actual or prospective offerors;

(2) After receipt of proposals, control exchanges with offerors in accordance with 15.306; and

(3) Award the contract(s).

15.304 Evaluation factors and significant subfactors.

(a) The award decision is based on evaluation factors and significant subfactors that are tailored to the acquisition.

(b) Evaluation factors and significant subfactors must—

(1) Represent the key areas of importance and emphasis to be considered in the source selection decision; and

(2) Support meaningful comparison and discrimination between and among competing proposals.

(c) The evaluation factors and significant subfactors that apply to an acquisition and their relative importance, are within the broad discretion of agency acquisition officials, subject to the following requirements:

(1) Price or cost to the Government shall be evaluated in every source selection (10 U.S.C. 2305(a)(3)(A)(ii) and 41 U.S.C. 253a(c)(1)(B)) (also see Part 36 for architect-engineer contracts);

(2) The quality of the product or service shall be addressed in every source selection through consideration of one or more non-cost evaluation factors such as past performance, compliance with solicitation requirements, technical excellence, management capability, personnel qualifications, and prior experience (10 U.S.C. 2305(a)(3)(A)(i) and 41 U.S.C. 253a(c)(1)(A)); and

(3)(i) Except as set forth in paragraph (c)(3)(iii) of this section, past performance shall be evaluated in all source selections for negotiated competitive acquisitions expected to exceed the simplified acquisition threshold.

(ii) For solicitations involving bundling that offer a significant opportunity for subcontracting, the contracting officer must include a factor to evaluate past performance indicating the extent to which the offeror attained applicable goals for small business participation under contracts that required subcontracting plans (15 U.S.C. 637(d)(4)(G)(ii)).

(iii) Past performance need not be evaluated if the contracting officer documents the reason past performance is not an appropriate evaluation factor for the acquisition.

(4) The extent of participation of small disadvantaged business concerns in performance of the contract shall be evaluated in unrestricted acquisitions expected to exceed $650,000 ($1.5 million for construction) subject to certain limitations (see 19.201 and 19.1202).

(5) For solicitations involving bundling that offer a significant opportunity for subcontracting, the contracting officer must include proposed small business subcontracting participation in the subcontracting plan as an evaluation factor (15 U.S.C. 637(d)(4)(G)(i)).

(6) If telecommuting is not prohibited, agencies shall not unfavorably evaluate an offer that includes telecommuting unless the contracting officer executes a written determination in accordance with FAR 7.108(b).

(d) All factors and significant subfactors that will affect contract award and their relative importance shall be stated clearly in the solicitation (10 U.S.C. 2305(a)(2)(A)(i) and 41 U.S.C. 253a(b)(1)(A)) (see 15.204-5(c)). The rating method need not be disclosed in the solicitation. The general approach for evaluating past performance information shall be described.

(e) The solicitation shall also state, at a minimum, whether all evaluation factors other than cost or price, when combined, are—

(1) Significantly more important than cost or price;

(2) Approximately equal to cost or price; or

(3) Significantly less important than cost or price (10 U.S.C. 2305(a)(3)(A)(iii) and 41 U.S.C. 253a(c)(1)(C)).

15.305 Proposal evaluation.

(a) Proposal evaluation is an assessment of the proposal and the offeror's ability to perform the prospective contract successfully. An agency shall evaluate competitive proposals and then assess their relative qualities solely on the factors and subfactors specified in the solicitation. Evaluations may be conducted using any rating method or combination of methods, including color or adjectival ratings, numerical weights, and ordinal rankings. The relative strengths, deficiencies, significant weaknesses, and risks supporting proposal evaluation shall be documented in the contract file.

(1) *Cost or price evaluation.* Normally, competition establishes price reasonableness. Therefore, when contracting on a firm-fixed-price or fixed-price with economic price adjustment basis, comparison of the proposed prices will usually satisfy the requirement to perform a price analysis, and a cost analysis need not be performed. In limited situations, a cost analysis (see 15.403-1(c)(1)(i)(B))

may be appropriate to establish reasonableness of the otherwise successful offeror's price. When contracting on a cost-reimbursement basis, evaluations shall include a cost realism analysis to determine what the Government should realistically expect to pay for the proposed effort, the offeror's understanding of the work, and the offeror's ability to perform the contract. (See 37.115 for uncompensated overtime evaluation.) The contracting officer shall document the cost or price evaluation.

(2) *Past performance evaluation.*

(i) Past performance information is one indicator of an offeror's ability to perform the contract successfully. The currency and relevance of the information, source of the information, context of the data, and general trends in contractor's performance shall be considered. This comparative assessment of past performance information is separate from the responsibility determination required under Subpart 9.1.

(ii) The solicitation shall describe the approach for evaluating past performance, including evaluating offerors with no relevant performance history, and shall provide offerors an opportunity to identify past or current contracts (including Federal, State, and local government and private) for efforts similar to the Government requirement. The solicitation shall also authorize offerors to provide information on problems encountered on the identified contracts and the offeror's corrective actions. The Government shall consider this information, as well as information obtained from any other sources, when evaluating the offeror's past performance. The source selection authority shall determine the relevance of similar past performance information.

(iii) The evaluation should take into account past performance information regarding predecessor companies, key personnel who have relevant experience, or subcontractors that will perform major or critical aspects of the requirement when such information is relevant to the instant acquisition.

(iv) In the case of an offeror without a record of relevant past performance or for whom information on past performance is not available, the offeror may not be evaluated favorably or unfavorably on past performance.

(v) The evaluation should include the past performance of offerors in complying with subcontracting plan goals for small disadvantaged business (SDB) concerns (see Subpart 19.7), monetary targets for SDB participation (see 19.1202), and notifications submitted under 19.1202-4(b).

(3) *Technical evaluation.* When tradeoffs are performed (see 15.101-1), the source selection records shall include—

(i) An assessment of each offeror's ability to accomplish the technical requirements; and

(ii) A summary, matrix, or quantitative ranking, along with appropriate supporting narrative, of each technical proposal using the evaluation factors.

(4) *Cost information* Cost information may be provided to members of the technical evaluation team in accordance with agency procedures.

(5) S*mall business subcontracting evaluation.* Solicitations must be structured to give offers from small business concerns the highest rating for the evaluation factors in 15.304(c)(3)(ii) and (c)(5).

(b) The source selection authority may reject all proposals received in response to a solicitation, if doing so is in the best interest of the Government.

(c) For restrictions on the use of support contractor personnel in proposal evaluation, see 37.203(d).

15.306 Exchanges with offerors after receipt of proposals.

(a) *Clarifications and award without discussions.*

(1) Clarifications are limited exchanges, between the Government and offerors, that may occur when award without discussions is contemplated.

(2) If award will be made without conducting discussions, offerors may be given the opportunity to clarify certain aspects of proposals (*e.g.,* the relevance of an offeror's past performance information and adverse past performance information to which the offeror has not previously had an opportunity to respond) or to resolve minor or clerical errors.

(3) Award may be made without discussions if the solicitation states that the Government intends to evaluate propos-
als and make award without discussions. If the solicitation contains such a notice and the Government determines it is necessary to conduct discussions, the rationale for doing so shall be documented in the contract file (see the provision at 52.215-1) (10 U.S.C. 2305(b)(4)(A)(ii) and 41 U.S.C. 253b(d)(1)(B)).

(b) *Communications with offerors before establishment of the competitive range.* Communications are exchanges, between the Government and offerors, after receipt of proposals, leading to establishment of the competitive range. If a competitive range is to be established, these communications—

(1) Shall be limited to the offerors described in paragraphs (b)(1)(i) and (b)(1)(ii) of this section and—

(i) Shall be held with offerors whose past performance information is the determining factor preventing them from being placed within the competitive range. Such communications shall address adverse past performance information to which an offeror has not had a prior opportunity to respond; and

(ii) May only be held with those offerors (other than offerors under paragraph (b)(1)(i) of this section) whose exclusion from, or inclusion in, the competitive range is uncertain;

(2) May be conducted to enhance Government understanding of proposals; allow reasonable interpretation of the proposal; or facilitate the Government's evaluation process. Such communications shall not be used to cure proposal deficiencies or material omissions, materially alter the technical or cost elements of the proposal, and/or otherwise revise the proposal. Such communications may be considered in rating proposals for the purpose of establishing the competitive range;

(3) Are for the purpose of addressing issues that must be explored to determine whether a proposal should be placed in the competitive range. Such communications shall not provide an opportunity for the offeror to revise its proposal, but may address—

(i) Ambiguities in the proposal or other concerns (*e.g.,* perceived deficiencies, weaknesses, errors, omissions, or mistakes (see 14.407)); and

(ii) Information relating to relevant past performance; and

(4) Shall address adverse past performance information to which the offeror has not previously had an opportunity to comment.

(c) *Competitive range.*

(1) Agencies shall evaluate all proposals in accordance with 15.305(a), and, if discussions are to be conducted, establish the competitive range. Based on the ratings of each proposal against all evaluation criteria, the contracting officer shall establish a competitive range comprised of all of the most highly rated proposals, unless the range is further reduced for purposes of efficiency pursuant to paragraph (c)(2) of this section.

(2) After evaluating all proposals in accordance with 15.305(a) and paragraph (c)(1) of this section, the contracting officer may determine that the number of most highly rated proposals that might otherwise be included in the competitive range exceeds the number at which an efficient competition can be conducted. Provided the solicitation notifies offerors that the competitive range can be limited for purposes of efficiency (see 52.215-1(f)(4)), the contracting officer may limit the number of proposals in the competitive range to the greatest number that will permit an efficient competition among the most highly rated proposals (10 U.S.C. 2305(b)(4) and 41 U.S.C. 253b(d)).

(3) If the contracting officer, after complying with paragraph (d)(3) of this section, decides that an offeror's proposal should no longer be included in the competitive range, the proposal shall be eliminated from consideration for award. Written notice of this decision shall be provided to unsuccessful offerors in accordance with 15.503.

(4) Offerors excluded or otherwise eliminated from the competitive range may request a debriefing (see 15.505 and 15.506).

(d) *Exchanges with offerors after establishment of the competitive range.* Negotiations are exchanges, in either a competitive or sole source environment, between the Government and offerors, that are undertaken with the intent of allowing the offeror to revise its proposal. These negotiations may include bargaining. Bargaining includes persuasion, alteration of assumptions and positions, give-and-take, and may apply to price, schedule, technical requirements, type of contract, or other terms of a proposed contract. When negotiations are conducted in a competitive acquisition, they take place after establishment of the competitive range and are called discussions.

(1) Discussions are tailored to each offeror's proposal, and must be conducted by the contracting officer with each offeror within the competitive range.

(2) The primary objective of discussions is to maximize the Government's ability to obtain best value, based on the requirement and the evaluation factors set forth in the solicitation.

(3) At a minimum, the contracting officer must, subject to paragraphs (d) (5) and (e) of this section and 15.307(a), indicate to, or discuss with, each offeror

still being considered for award, deficiencies, significant weaknesses, and adverse past performance information to which the offeror has not yet had an opportunity to respond. The contracting officer also is encouraged to discuss other aspects of the offeror's proposal that could, in the opinion of the contracting officer, be altered or explained to enhance materially the proposal's potential for award. However, the contracting officer is not required to discuss every area where the proposal could be improved. The scope and extent of discussions are a matter of contracting officer judgment.

(4) In discussing other aspects of the proposal, the Government may, in situations where the solicitation stated that evaluation credit would be given for technical solutions exceeding any mandatory minimums, negotiate with offerors for increased performance beyond any mandatory minimums, and the Government may suggest to offerors that have exceeded any mandatory minimums (in ways that are not integral to the design), that their proposals would be more competitive if the excesses were removed and the offered price decreased.

(5) If, after discussions have begun, an offeror originally in the competitive range is no longer considered to be among the most highly rated offerors being considered for award, that offeror may be eliminated from the competitive range whether or not all material aspects of the proposal have been discussed, or whether or not the offeror has been afforded an opportunity to submit a proposal revision (see 15.307(a) and 15.503(a)(1)).

(e) *Limits on exchanges.* Government personnel involved in the acquisition shall not engage in conduct that—

(1) Favors one offeror over another;

(2) Reveals an offeror's technical solution, including unique technology, innovative and unique uses of commercial items, or any information that would compromise an offeror's intellectual property to another offeror;

(3) Reveals an offeror's price without that offeror's permission. However, the contracting officer may inform an offeror that its price is considered by the Government to be too high, or too low, and reveal the results of the analysis supporting that conclusion. It is also permissible, at the Government's discretion, to indicate to all offerors the cost or price that the Government's price analysis, market research, and other reviews have identified as reasonable (41 U.S.C. 423(h) (1)(2));

(4) Reveals the names of individuals providing reference information about an offeror's past performance; or

(5) Knowingly furnishes source selection information in violation of 3.104 and 41 U.S.C. 423(h)(1)(2).

15.307 Proposal revisions.

(a) If an offeror's proposal is eliminated or otherwise removed from the competitive range, no further revisions to that offeror's proposal shall be accepted or considered.

(b) The contracting officer may request or allow proposal revisions to clarify and document understandings reached during negotiations. At the conclusion of discussions, each offeror still in the competitive range shall be given an opportunity to submit a final proposal revision. The contracting officer is required to establish a common cut-off date only for receipt of final proposal revisions. Requests for final proposal revisions shall advise offerors that the final proposal revisions shall be in writing and that the Government intends to make award without obtaining further revisions.

15.308 Source selection decision.

The source selection authority's (SSA) decision shall be based on a comparative assessment of proposals against all source selection criteria in the solicitation. While the SSA may use reports and analyses prepared by others, the source selection decision shall represent the SSA's independent judgment. The source selection decision shall be documented, and the documentation shall include the rationale for any business judgments and tradeoffs made or relied on by the SSA, including benefits associated with additional costs. Although the rationale for the selection decision must be documented, that documentation need not quantify the tradeoffs that led to the decision.

Subpart 15.4—Contract Pricing

15.400 Scope of subpart.

This subpart prescribes the cost and price negotiation policies and procedures for pricing negotiated prime contracts (including subcontracts) and contract modifications, including modifications to contracts awarded by sealed bidding.

15.401 Definitions.

As used in this subpart—

Price means cost plus any fee or profit applicable to the contract type.

Subcontract (except as used in 15.407-2) also includes a transfer of commercial items between divisions, subsidiaries, or affiliates of a contractor or a subcontractor (10 U.S.C. 2306a(h)(2) and 41 U.S.C. 254b(h)(2)).

15.402 Pricing policy.

Contracting officers shall—

(a) Purchase supplies and services from responsible sources at fair and reasonable prices. In establishing the reasonableness of the offered prices, the contracting officer—

(1) Shall obtain certified cost or pricing data when required by 15.403-4, along with data other than certified cost or pricing data as necessary to establish a fair and reasonable price; or

(2) When certified cost or pricing data are not required by 15.403-4, obtain data other than certified cost or pricing data as necessary to establish a fair and reasonable price, generally using the following order of preference in determining the type of data required:

(i) No additional data from the offeror, if the price is based on adequate price competition, except as provided by 15.403-3(b).

(ii) Data other than certified cost or pricing data such as—

(A) Data related to prices (*e.g.*, established catalog or market prices, sales to non-governmental and governmental entities), relying first on data available within the Government; second, on data obtained from sources other than the offeror; and, if necessary, on data obtained from the offeror. When obtaining data from the offeror is necessary, unless an exception under 15.403-1(b) (1) or (2) applies, such data submitted by the offeror shall include, at a minimum, appropriate data on the prices at which the same or similar items have been sold previously, adequate for evaluating the reasonableness of the price.

(B) Cost data to the extent necessary for the contracting officer to determine a fair and reasonable price.

(3) Obtain the type and quantity of data necessary to establish a fair and reasonable price, but not more data than is necessary. Requesting unnecessary data can lead to increased proposal preparation costs, generally extend acquisition lead time, and consume additional contractor and Government resources. Use techniques such as, but not limited to, price analysis, cost analysis, and/or cost realism analysis to establish a fair and reasonable price. If a fair and reasonable price cannot be established by the contracting officer from the analyses of the data obtained or submitted to date, the contracting officer shall require the submission of additional data sufficient for the contracting officer to support the determination of the fair and reasonable price.

(b) Price each contract separately and independently and not—

(1) Use proposed price reductions under other contracts as an evaluation factor; or

(2) Consider losses or profits realized or anticipated under other contracts.

(c) Not include in a contract price any amount for a specified contingency to the extent that the contract provides for a price adjustment based upon the occurrence of that contingency.

15.403 Obtaining certified cost or pricing data.

15.403-1 Prohibition on obtaining certified cost or pricing data (10 U.S.C. 2306a and 41 U.S.C. 254b).

(a) Certified cost or pricing data shall not be obtained for acquisitions at or below the simplified acquisition threshold.

(b) *Exceptions to certified cost or pricing data requirements.* The contracting officer shall not require certified cost or pricing data to support any action (contracts, subcontracts, or modifications) (but may require data other than certified cost or pricing data as defined in FAR 2.101 to support a determination of a fair and reasonable price or cost realism)—

(1) When the contracting officer determines that prices agreed upon are based on adequate price competition (see standards in paragraph (c)(1) of this subsection);

(2) When the contracting officer determines that prices agreed upon are based on prices set by law or regulation (see standards in paragraph (c)(2) of this subsection);

(3) When a commercial item is being acquired (see standards in paragraph (c)(3) of this subsection);

(4) When a waiver has been granted (see standards in paragraph (c)(4) of this subsection); or

(5) When modifying a contract or subcontract for commercial items (see standards in paragraph (c)(3) of this subsection).

(c) *Standards for exceptions from certified cost or pricing data requirements*—

(1) *Adequate price competition.* A price is based on adequate price competition if—

(i) Two or more responsible offerors, competing independently, submit priced offers that satisfy the Government's expressed requirement and if—

(A) Award will be made to the offeror whose proposal represents the best value (see 2.101) where price is a substantial factor in source selection; and

(B) There is no finding that the price of the otherwise successful offeror is unreasonable. Any finding that the price is unreasonable must be supported by a statement of the facts and approved at a level above the contracting officer;

(ii) There was a reasonable expectation, based on market research or other assessment, that two or more responsible offerors, competing independently, would submit priced offers in response to the solicitation's expressed requirement, even though only one offer is received from a responsible offeror and if—

(A) Based on the offer received, the contracting officer can reasonably conclude that the offer was submitted with the expectation of competition, *e.g.,* circumstances indicate that—

(1) The offeror believed that at least one other offeror was capable of submitting a meaningful offer; and

(2) The offeror had no reason to believe that other potential offerors did not intend to submit an offer; and

(B) The determination that the proposed price is based on adequate price competition, is reasonable, and is approved at a level above the contracting officer; or

(iii) Price analysis clearly demonstrates that the proposed price is reasonable in comparison with current or recent prices for the same or similar items, adjusted to reflect changes in market conditions, economic conditions, quantities, or terms and conditions under contracts that resulted from adequate price competition.

(2) *Prices set by law or regulation.* Pronouncements in the form of periodic rulings, reviews, or similar actions of a governmental body, or embodied in the laws, are sufficient to set a price.

(3) *Commercial items.*

(i) Any acquisition of an item that the contracting officer determines meets the commercial item definition in 2.101, or any modification, as defined in paragraph (3)(i) of that definition, that does not change the item from a commercial item to a noncommercial item, is exempt from the requirement for certified cost or pricing data. If the contracting officer determines that an item claimed to be commercial is, in fact, not commercial and that no other exception or waiver applies, (*e.g.* the acquisition is not based on adequate price competition; the acquisition is not based on prices set by law or regulation; and the acquisition exceeds the threshold for the submission of certified cost or pricing data at 15.403-4(a)(1)) the contracting officer shall require submission of certified cost or pricing data.

(ii) In accordance with section 868 of Pub. L. 110-417:

(A) When purchasing services that are not offered and sold competitively in substantial quantities in the commercial marketplace, but are of a type offered and sold competitively in substantial quantities in the commercial marketplace, they may be considered commercial items (thus meeting the purpose of 41 U.S.C. 254b and 10 U.S.C. 2306a for truth in negotiations) only if the contracting officer determines in writing that the offeror has submitted sufficient information to evaluate, through price analysis, the reasonableness of the price of such services.

(B) In order to make this determination, the contracting officer may request the offeror to submit prices paid for the same or similar commercial items under comparable terms and conditions by both Government and commercial customers; and

(C) If the contracting officer determines that the information described in paragraph (c)(3)(ii)(B) of this section is not sufficient to determine the reasonableness of price, other relevant information regarding the basis for price or cost, including information on labor costs, material costs and overhead rates may be requested.

(iii) The following requirements apply to minor modifications defined in paragraph (3)(ii) of the definition of a commercial item at 2.101 that do not change the item from a commercial item to a noncommercial item:

(A) For acquisitions funded by any agency other than DoD, NASA, or Coast Guard, such modifications of a commercial item are exempt from the requirement for submission of certified cost or pricing data.

(B) For acquisitions funded by DoD, NASA, or Coast Guard, such modifications of a commercial item are exempt from the requirement for submission of certified cost or pricing data provided the total price of all such modifications under a particular contract action does not exceed the greater of the threshold for obtaining certified cost or pricing data in 15.403-4 or 5 percent of the total price of the contract at the time of contract award.

(C) For acquisitions funded by DoD, NASA, or Coast Guard such modifications of a commercial item are not exempt from the requirement for submission of certified cost or pricing data on the basis of the exemption provided for at 15.403-1(c)(3) if the total price of all such modifications under a particular contract action exceeds the greater of the threshold for obtaining certified cost or pricing data in 15.403-4 or 5 percent of the total price of the contract at the time of contract award.

(iv) Any acquisition for noncommercial supplies or services treated as commercial items at 12.102(f)(1), except sole source contracts greater than $17.5 million, is exempt from the requirements for certified cost or pricing data (41 U.S.C. 428a).

(4) *Waivers.* The head of the contracting activity (HCA) may, without power of delegation, waive the requirement for submission of certified cost or pricing data in exceptional cases. The authorization for the waiver and the supporting rationale shall be in writing. The HCA may consider waiving the requirement if the price can be determined to be fair and reasonable without submission of certified cost or pricing data. For example, if certified cost or pricing data were furnished on previous production buys and the contracting officer determines such data are sufficient, when combined with updated data, a waiver may be granted. If the HCA has waived the requirement for submission of certified cost or pricing data, the contractor or higher-tier subcontractor to whom the waiver relates shall be considered as having been required to provide certified cost or pricing data. Consequently, award of any lower-tier subcontract expected to exceed the certified cost or pricing data threshold requires the submission of certified cost or pricing data unless—

(i) An exception otherwise applies to the subcontract; or

(ii) The waiver specifically includes the subcontract and the rationale supporting the waiver for that subcontract.

15.403-2 Other circumstances where certified cost or pricing data are not required.

(a) The exercise of an option at the price established at contract award or initial negotiation does not require submission of certified cost or pricing data.

(b) Certified cost or pricing data are not required for proposals used solely for overrun funding or interim billing price adjustments.

15.403-3 Requiring data other than certified cost or pricing data.

(a) *General.*

(1) In those acquisitions that do not require certified cost or pricing data, the contracting officer shall—

(i) Obtain whatever data are available from Government or other secondary sources and use that data in determining a fair and reasonable price;

(ii) Require submission of data other than certified cost or pricing data, as defined in 2.101, from the offeror to the extent necessary to determine a fair and reasonable price (10 U.S.C. 2306a(d)(1) and 41 U.S.C. 254b(d)(1)) if the contracting officer determines that adequate data from sources other than the offeror are not available. This includes requiring data from an offeror to support a cost realism analysis;

(iii) Consider whether cost data are necessary to determine a fair and reasonable price when there is not adequate price competition;

(iv) Require that the data submitted by the offeror include, at a minimum, appropriate data on the prices at which the same item or similar items have previously been sold, adequate for determining the reasonableness of the price unless an exception under 15.403-1(b)(1) or (2) applies; and

(v) Consider the guidance in section 3.3, chapter 3, volume I, of the Contract Pricing Reference Guide cited at 15.404-1(a)(7) to determine the data an offeror shall be required to submit.

(2) The contractor's format for submitting the data should be used (see 15.403-5(b)(2)).

(3) The contracting officer shall ensure that data used to support price negotiations are sufficiently current to permit negotiation of a fair and reasonable price. Requests for updated offeror data should be limited to data that affect the adequacy of the proposal for negotiations, such as changes in price lists.

(4) As specified in section 808 of the Strom Thurmond National Defense Authorization Act for Fiscal Year 1999 (Pub. L. 105-261), an offeror who does not comply with a requirement to submit data for a contract or subcontract in accordance with paragraph (a)(1) of this subsection is ineligible for award unless the HCA determines that it is in the best interest of the Government to make the award to that offeror, based on consideration of the following:

(i) The effort made to obtain the data.

(ii) The need for the item or service.

(iii) Increased cost or significant harm to the Government if award is not made.

(b) *Adequate price competition.* When adequate price competition exists (see 15.403-1(c)(1)), generally no additional data are necessary to determine the reasonableness of price. However, if there are unusual circumstances where it is concluded that additional data are necessary to determine the reasonableness of price, the contracting officer shall, to the maximum extent practicable, obtain the additional data from sources other than the offeror. In addition, the contracting officer should request data to determine the cost realism of competing offers or to evaluate competing approaches.

(c) *Commercial items.*

(1) At a minimum, the contracting officer must use price analysis to determine whether the price is fair and reasonable whenever the contracting officer acquires a commercial item (see 15.404-1(b)). The fact that a price is included in a catalog does not, in and of itself, make it fair and reasonable. If the contracting officer cannot determine whether an offered price is fair and reasonable, even after obtaining additional data from sources other than the offeror, then the contracting officer shall require the offeror to submit data other than certified cost or pricing data to support further analysis (see 15.404-1). This data may include history of sales to non-governmental and governmental entities, cost data, or any other information the contracting officer requires to determine the price is fair and reasonable. Unless an exception under 15.403-1(b)(1) or

(2) applies, the contracting officer shall require that the data submitted by the offeror include, at a minimum, appropriate data on the prices at which the same item or similar items have previously been sold, adequate for determining the reasonableness of the price.

(2) *Limitations relating to commercial items (10 U.S.C. 2306a(d)(2)* and 41 U.S.C. 254b(d)(2)).

(i) The contracting officer shall limit requests for sales data relating to commercial items to data for the same or similar items during a relevant time period.

(ii) The contracting officer shall, to the maximum extent practicable, limit the scope of the request for data relating to commercial items to include only data that are in the form regularly maintained by the offeror as part of its commercial operations.

(iii) The Government shall not disclose outside the Government data obtained relating to commercial items that is exempt from disclosure under 24.202(a) or the Freedom of Information Act (5 U.S.C. 552(b)).

(3) For services that are not offered and sold competitively in substantial quantities in the commercial marketplace, but are of a type offered and sold competitively in substantial quantities in the commercial marketplace, see 15.403-1(c)(3)(ii).

15.403-4 Requiring certified cost or pricing data (10 U.S.C. 2306a and 41 U.S.C. 254b).

(a)(1) The contracting officer shall obtain certified cost or pricing data only if the contracting officer concludes that none of the exceptions in 15.403-1(b) applies. However, if the contracting officer has reason to believe exceptional circumstances exist and has sufficient data available to determine a fair and reasonable price, then the contracting officer should consider requesting a waiver under the exception at 15.403-1(b)(4). The threshold for obtaining certified cost or pricing data is $700,000. Unless an exception applies, certified cost or pricing data are required before accomplishing any of the following actions expected to exceed the current threshold or, in the case of existing contracts, the threshold specified in the contract:

(i) The award of any negotiated contract (except for undefinitized actions such as letter contracts).

(ii) The award of a subcontract at any tier, if the contractor and each higher-tier subcontractor were required to furnish certified cost or pricing data (but see waivers at 15.403-1(c)(4)).

(iii) The modification of any sealed bid or negotiated contract (whether or not certified cost or pricing data were initially required) or any subcontract covered by paragraph (a)(1)(ii) of this subsection. Price adjustment amounts must consider both increases and decreases (*e.g.*, a $200,000 modification resulting from a reduction of $500,000 and an increase of $300,000 is a pricing adjustment exceeding $700,000). This requirement does not apply when unrelated and separately priced changes for which certified cost or pricing data would not otherwise be required are included for administrative convenience in the same modification. Negotiated final pricing actions (such as termination settlements and total final price agreements for fixed-price incentive and redeterminable contracts) are contract modifications requiring certified cost or pricing data if—

(A) The total final price agreement for such settlements or agreements exceeds the pertinent threshold set forth at paragraph (a)(1) of this subsection; or

(B) The partial termination settlement plus the estimate to complete the continued portion of the contract exceeds the pertinent threshold set forth at paragraph (a)(1) of this subsection (see 49.105(c)(15)).

(2) Unless prohibited because an exception at 15.403-1(b) applies, the head of the contracting activity, without power of delegation, may authorize the contracting officer to obtain certified cost or pricing data for pricing actions below the pertinent threshold in paragraph (a)(1) of this subsection, provided the action exceeds the simplified acquisition threshold. The head of the contracting activity shall justify the requirement for certified cost or pricing data. The documentation shall include a written finding that certified cost or pricing data are necessary to determine whether the price is fair and reasonable and the facts supporting that finding.

(b) When certified cost or pricing data are required, the contracting officer shall require the contractor or prospective contractor to submit to the contracting officer (and to have any subcontractor or prospective subcontractor submit to the prime contractor or appropriate subcontractor tier) the following in support of any proposal:

(1) The certified cost or pricing data and data other than certified cost or pricing data required by the contracting officer to determine that the price is fair and reasonable.

(2) A Certificate of Current Cost or Pricing Data, in the format specified in 15.406-2, certifying that to the best of its knowledge and belief, the cost or pricing data were accurate, complete, and current as of the date of agreement on price or, if applicable, an earlier date agreed upon between the parties that is as close as practicable to the date of agreement on price.

(c) If certified cost or pricing data are requested and submitted by an offeror, but an exception is later found to apply, the data must not be considered certified cost or pricing data as defined in 2.101 and must not be certified in accordance with 15.406-2

(d) The requirements of this subsection also apply to contracts entered into by an agency on behalf of a foreign government.

15.403-5 Instructions for submission of certified cost or pricing data and data other than certified cost or pricing data.

(a) Taking into consideration the policy at 15.402, the contracting officer shall specify in the solicitation (see 15.408 (l) and (m))—

(1) Whether certified cost or pricing data are required;

(2) That, in lieu of submitting certified cost or pricing data, the offeror may submit a request for exception from the requirement to submit certified cost or pricing data;

(3) Any requirement for data other than certified cost or pricing data; and

(4) The requirement for necessary preaward or postaward access to offeror's records.

(b)(1) *Format for submission of certified cost or pricing data.* When certification is required, the contracting officer may require submission of certified cost or pricing data in the format indicated in Table 15-2 of 15.408, specify an alternative format, or permit submission in the contractor's format (See 15.408(l)(1)), unless the data are required to be submitted on one of the termination forms specified in Subpart 49.6.

(2) *Format for submission of data other than certified cost or pricing data.* When required by the contracting officer, data other than certified cost or pricing data may be submitted in the offeror's own format unless the contracting officer decides that use of a specific format is essential for evaluating and determining that the price is fair and reasonable and the format has been described in the solicitation.

(3) *Format for submission of data supporting forward pricing rate agreements.* Data supporting forward pricing rate agreements or final indirect cost proposals shall be submitted in a form acceptable to the contracting officer.

15.404   Proposal analysis.

15.404-1   Proposal analysis techniques.

(a) *General.* The objective of proposal analysis is to ensure that the final agreed-to price is fair and reasonable.

(1) The contracting officer is responsible for evaluating the reasonableness of the offered prices. The analytical techniques and procedures described in this subsection may be used, singly or in combination with others, to ensure that the final price is fair and reasonable. The complexity and circumstances of each acquisition should determine the level of detail of the analysis required.

(2) Price analysis shall be used when certified cost or pricing data are not required (see paragraph (b) of this subsection and 15.404-3).

(3) Cost analysis shall be used to evaluate the reasonableness of individual cost elements when certified cost or pricing data are required. Price analysis should be used to verify that the overall price offered is fair and reasonable.

(4) Cost analysis may also be used to evaluate data other than certified cost or pricing data to determine cost reasonableness or cost realism when a fair and reasonable price cannot be determined through price analysis alone for commercial or non-commercial items.

(5) The contracting officer may request the advice and assistance of other experts to ensure that an appropriate analysis is performed.

(6) Recommendations or conclusions regarding the Government's review or analysis of an offeror's or contractor's proposal shall not be disclosed to the offeror or contractor without the concurrence of the contracting officer. Any discrepancy or mistake of fact (such as duplications, omissions, and errors

in computation) contained in the certified cost or pricing data or data other than certified cost or pricing data submitted in support of a proposal shall be brought to the contracting officer's attention for appropriate action.

(7) The Air Force Institute of Technology (AFIT) and the Federal Acquisition Institute (FAI) jointly prepared a five-volume set of Contract Pricing Reference Guides to guide pricing and negotiation personnel. The five guides are: I Price Analysis, II Quantitative Techniques for Contract Pricing, III Cost Analysis, IV Advanced Issues in Contract Pricing, and V Federal Contract Negotiation Techniques. These references provide detailed discussion and examples applying pricing policies to pricing problems. They are to be used for instruction and professional guidance. However, they are not directive and should be considered informational only. They are available via the internet at *http://www.acq.osd.mil/ dpap/cpf/contract_pricing_reference_guides.html*.

(b) *Price analysis for commercial and non-commercial items.*

(1) Price analysis is the process of examining and evaluating a proposed price without evaluating its separate cost elements and proposed profit. Unless an exception from the requirement to obtain certified cost or pricing data applies under 15.403-1(b)(1) or (b)(2), at a minimum, the contracting officer shall obtain appropriate data, without certification, on the prices at which the same or similar items have previously been sold and determine if the data is adequate for evaluating the reasonableness of the price. Price analysis may include evaluating data other than certified cost or pricing data obtained from the offeror or contractor when there is no other means for determining a fair and reasonable price. Contracting officers shall obtain data other than certified cost or pricing data from the offeror or contractor for all acquisitions (including commercial item acquisitions), if that is the contracting officer's only means to determine the price to be fair and reasonable.

(2) The Government may use various price analysis techniques and procedures to ensure a fair and reasonable price. Examples of such techniques include, but are not limited to, the following:

(i) Comparison of proposed prices received in response to the solicitation. Normally, adequate price competition establishes a fair and reasonable price (see 15.403-1(c)(1)).

(ii) Comparison of the proposed prices to historical prices paid, whether by the Government or other than the Government, for the same or similar items. This method may be used for commercial items including those "of a type" or requiring minor modifications.

(A) The prior price must be a valid basis for comparison. If there has been a significant time lapse between the last acquisition and the present one, if the terms and conditions of the acquisition are significantly different, or if the reasonableness of the prior price is uncertain, then the prior price may not be a valid basis for comparison.

(B) The prior price must be adjusted to account for materially differing terms and conditions, quantities and market and economic factors. For similar items, the contracting officer must also adjust the prior price to account for material differences between the similar item and the item being procured.

(C) Expert technical advice should be obtained when analyzing similar items, or commercial items that are "of a type" or requiring minor modifications, to ascertain the magnitude of changes required and to assist in pricing the required changes

(iii) Use of parametric estimating methods/application of rough yardsticks (such as dollars per pound or per horsepower, or other units) to highlight significant inconsistencies that warrant additional pricing inquiry.

(iv) Comparison with competitive published price lists, published market prices of commodities, similar indexes, and discount or rebate arrangements.

(v) Comparison of proposed prices with independent Government cost estimates.

(vi) Comparison of proposed prices with prices obtained through market research for the same or similar items.

(vii) Analysis of data other than certified cost or pricing data (as defined at 2.101) provided by the offeror.

(3) The first two techniques at 15.404-1(b)(2) are the preferred techniques. However, if the contracting officer determines that information on competitive proposed prices or previous contract prices is not available or is insufficient to determine that the price is fair and reasonable, the contracting officer may use any of the remaining techniques as appropriate to the circumstances applicable to the acquisition.

(4) Value analysis can give insight into the relative worth of a product and the Government may use it in conjunction with the price analysis techniques listed in paragraph (b)(2) of this section.

(c) *Cost analysis.*

(1) Cost analysis is the review and evaluation of any separate cost elements and profit or fee in an offeror's or contractor's proposal, as needed to determine a fair and reasonable price or to determine cost realism, and the application of judgment to determine how well the proposed costs represent what the cost of the contract should be, assuming reasonable economy and efficiency.

(2) The Government may use various cost analysis techniques and procedures to ensure a fair and reasonable price, given the circumstances of the acquisition. Such techniques and procedures include the following:

(i) Verification of cost data or pricing data and evaluation of cost elements, including—

(A) The necessity for, and reasonableness of, proposed costs, including allowances for contingencies;

(B) Projection of the offeror's cost trends, on the basis of current and historical cost or pricing data;

(C) Reasonableness of estimates generated by appropriately calibrated and validated parametric models or cost-estimating relationships; and

(D) The application of audited or negotiated indirect cost rates, labor rates, and cost of money or other factors.

(ii) Evaluating the effect of the offeror's current practices on future costs. In conducting this evaluation, the contracting officer shall ensure that the effects of inefficient or uneconomical past practices are not projected into the future. In pricing production of recently developed complex equipment, the contracting officer should perform a trend analysis of basic labor and materials, even in periods of relative price stability.

(iii) Comparison of costs proposed by the offeror for individual cost elements with—

(A) Actual costs previously incurred by the same offeror;

(B) Previous cost estimates from the offeror or from other offerors for the same or similar items;

(C) Other cost estimates received in response to the Government's request;

(D) Independent Government cost estimates by technical personnel; and

(E) Forecasts of planned expenditures.

(iv) Verification that the offeror's cost submissions are in accordance with the contract cost principles and procedures in Part 31 and, when applicable, the requirements and procedures in 48 CFR Chapter 99 (Appendix to the FAR looseleaf edition), Cost Accounting Standards.

(v) Review to determine whether any cost data or pricing data, necessary to make the offeror's proposal suitable for negotiation, have not been either submitted or identified in writing by the offeror. If there are such data, the contracting officer shall attempt to obtain and use them in the negotiations or make satisfactory allowance for the incomplete data.

(vi) Analysis of the results of any make-or-buy program reviews, in evaluating subcontract costs (see 15.407-2).

(d) *Cost realism analysis.*

(1) Cost realism analysis is the process of independently reviewing and evaluating specific elements of each offeror's proposed cost estimate to determine whether the estimated proposed cost elements are realistic for the work to be performed; reflect a clear understanding of the requirements; and are consistent with the unique methods of performance and materials described in the offeror's technical proposal.

(2) Cost realism analyses shall be performed on cost-reimbursement contracts to determine the probable cost of performance for each offeror.

(i) The probable cost may differ from the proposed cost and should reflect the Government's best estimate of the cost of any contract that is most likely to result from the offeror's proposal. The probable cost shall be used for purposes of evaluation to determine the best value.

(ii) The probable cost is determined by adjusting each offeror's proposed cost, and fee when appropriate, to reflect any additions or reductions in cost elements to realistic levels based on the results of the cost realism analysis.

(3) Cost realism analyses may also be used on competitive fixed-price incentive contracts or, in exceptional cases, on other competitive fixed-price-type contracts when new requirements may not be fully understood by competing

offerors, there are quality concerns, or past experience indicates that contractors' proposed costs have resulted in quality or service shortfalls. Results of the analysis may be used in performance risk assessments and responsibility determinations. However, proposals shall be evaluated using the criteria in the solicitation, and the offered prices shall not be adjusted as a result of the analysis.

(e) *Technical analysis.*

(1) The contracting officer should request that personnel having specialized knowledge, skills, experience, or capability in engineering, science, or management perform a technical analysis of the proposed types and quantities of materials, labor, processes, special tooling, equipment or real property, the reasonableness of scrap and spoilage, and other associated factors set forth in the proposal(s) in order to determine the need for and reasonableness of the proposed resources, assuming reasonable economy and efficiency.

(2) At a minimum, the technical analysis should examine the types and quantities of material proposed and the need for the types and quantities of labor hours and the labor mix. Any other data that may be pertinent to an assessment of the offeror's ability to accomplish the technical requirements or to the cost or price analysis of the service or product being proposed should also be included in the analysis.

(3) The contracting officer should request technical assistance in evaluating pricing related to items that are "similar to" items being purchased, or commercial items that are "of a type" or requiring minor modifications, to ascertain the magnitude of changes required and to assist in pricing the required changes.

(f) *Unit prices.*

(1) Except when pricing an item on the basis of adequate price competition or catalog or market price, unit prices shall reflect the intrinsic value of an item or service and shall be in proportion to an item's base cost (*e.g.,* manufacturing or acquisition costs). Any method of distributing costs to line items that distorts the unit prices shall not be used. For example, distributing costs equally among line items is not acceptable except when there is little or no variation in base cost.

(2) Except for the acquisition of commercial items, contracting officers shall require that offerors identify in their proposals those items of supply that they will not manufacture or to which they will not contribute significant value, unless adequate price competition is expected (10 U.S.C. 2304 and 41 U.S.C. 254(d)(5) (A)(i)). Such information shall be used to determine whether the intrinsic value of an item has been distorted through application of overhead and whether such items should be considered for breakout. The contracting officer should require such information in all other negotiated contracts when appropriate.

(g) *Unbalanced pricing.*

(1) Unbalanced pricing may increase performance risk and could result in payment of unreasonably high prices. Unbalanced pricing exists when, despite an acceptable total evaluated price, the price of one or more contract line items is significantly over or understated as indicated by the application of cost or price analysis techniques. The greatest risks associated with unbalanced pricing occur when—

(i) Startup work, mobilization, first articles, or first article testing are separate line items;

(ii) Base quantities and option quantities are separate line items; or

(iii) The evaluated price is the aggregate of estimated quantities to be ordered under separate line items of an indefinite-delivery contract.

(2) All offers with separately priced line items or subline items shall be analyzed to determine if the prices are unbalanced. If cost or price analysis techniques indicate that an offer is unbalanced, the contracting officer shall—

(i) Consider the risks to the Government associated with the unbalanced pricing in determining the competitive range and in making the source selection decision; and

(ii) Consider whether award of the contract will result in paying unreasonably high prices for contract performance.

(3) An offer may be rejected if the contracting officer determines that the lack of balance poses an unacceptable risk to the Government.

15.404-2 Data to support proposal analysis.

(a) *Field pricing assistance.*

(1) The contracting officer should request field pricing assistance when the information available at the buying activity is inadequate to determine a fair and reasonable price. The contracting officer shall tailor requests to reflect the minimum essential supplementary information needed to conduct a technical or cost or pricing analysis.

(2) The contracting officer shall tailor the type of information and level of detail requested in accordance with the specialized resources available at the buying activity and the magnitude and complexity of the required analysis. Field pricing assistance is generally available to provide—

(i) Technical, audit, and special reports associated with the cost elements of a proposal, including subcontracts;

(ii) Information on related pricing practices and history;

(iii) Information to help contracting officers determine commerciality and a fair and reasonable price, including—

(A) Verifying sales history to source documents;

(B) Identifying special terms and conditions;

(c) Identifying customarily granted or offered discounts for the item;

(D) Verifying the item to an existing catalog or price list;

(E) Verifying historical data for an item previously not determined commercial that the offeror is now trying to qualify as a commercial item; and

(F) Identifying general market conditions affecting determinations of commerciality and a fair and reasonable price.

(iv) Information relative to the business, technical, production, or other capabilities and practices of an offeror.

(3) When field pricing assistance is requested, contracting officers

are encouraged to team with appropriate field experts throughout the acquisition process, including negotiations. Early communication with these experts will assist in determining the extent of assistance required, the specific areas for which assistance is needed, a realistic review schedule, and the information necessary to perform the review.

(4) When requesting field pricing assistance on a contractor's request for equitable adjustment, the contracting officer shall provide the information listed in 43.204(b)(5).

(5) Field pricing information and other reports may include proprietary or source selection information (see 2.101). This information must be appropriately identified and protected accordingly.

(b) *Reporting field pricing information.*

(1) Depending upon the extent and complexity of the field pricing review, results, including supporting rationale, may be reported directly to the contracting officer orally, in writing, or by any other method acceptable to the contracting officer.

(i) Whenever circumstances permit, the contracting officer and field pricing experts are encouraged to use telephonic and/or electronic means to request and transmit pricing information.

(ii) When it is necessary to have written technical and audit reports, the contracting officer shall request that the audit agency concurrently forward the audit report to the requesting contracting officer and the administrative contracting officer (ACO). The completed field pricing assistance results may reference audit information, but need not reconcile the audit recommendations and technical recommendations. A copy of the information submitted to the contracting officer by field pricing personnel shall be provided to the audit agency.

(2) Audit and field pricing information, whether written or reported telephonically or electronically, shall be made a part of the official contract file (see 4.807(f)).

(c) *Audit assistance for prime contracts or subcontracts.*

(1) The contracting officer should contact the cognizant audit office directly, particularly when an audit is the only field pricing support required. The audit office shall send the audit report, or otherwise transmit the audit recommendations, directly to the contracting officer.

(i) The auditor shall not reveal the audit conclusions or recommendations to the offeror/contractor without obtaining the concurrence of the contracting officer. However, the auditor may discuss statements of facts with the contractor.

(ii) The contracting officer should be notified immediately of any information disclosed to the auditor after submission of a report that may significantly affect the audit findings and, if necessary, a supplemental audit report shall be issued.

(2) The contracting officer shall not request a separate preaward audit of indirect costs unless the information already available from an existing audit, completed within the preceding 12 months, is considered inadequate for

determining the reasonableness of the proposed indirect costs (41 U.S.C. 254d and 10 U.S.C. 2313).

(3) The auditor is responsible for the scope and depth of the audit. Copies of updated information that will significantly affect the audit should be provided to the auditor by the contracting officer.

(4) General access to the offeror's books and financial records is limited to the auditor. This limitation does not preclude the contracting officer or the ACO, or their representatives, from requesting that the offeror provide or make available any data or records necessary to analyze the offeror's proposal.

(d) *Deficient proposals.* The ACO or the auditor, as appropriate, shall notify the contracting officer immediately if the data provided for review is so deficient as to preclude review or audit, or if the contractor or offeror has denied access to any records considered essential to conduct a satisfactory review or audit. Oral notifications shall be confirmed promptly in writing, including a description of deficient or denied data or records. The contracting officer immediately shall take appropriate action to obtain the required data. Should the offeror/contractor again refuse to provide adequate data, or provide access to necessary data, the contracting officer shall withhold the award or price adjustment and refer the contract action to a higher authority, providing details of the attempts made to resolve the matter and a statement of the practicability of obtaining the supplies or services from another source.

15.404-3 Subcontract pricing considerations.

(a) The contracting officer is responsible for the determination of a fair and reasonable price for the prime contract, including subcontracting costs. The contracting officer should consider whether a contractor or subcontractor has an approved purchasing system, has performed cost or price analysis of proposed subcontractor prices, or has negotiated the subcontract prices before negotiation of the prime contract, in determining the reasonableness of the prime contract price. This does not relieve the contracting officer from the responsibility to analyze the contractor's submission, including subcontractor's certified cost or pricing data.

(b) The prime contractor or subcontractor shall—

(1) Conduct appropriate cost or price analyses to establish the reasonableness of proposed subcontract prices;

(2) Include the results of these analyses in the price proposal; and

(3) When required by paragraph (c) of this subsection, submit subcontractor certified cost or pricing data to the Government as part of its own certified cost or pricing data.

(c) Any contractor or subcontractor that is required to submit certified cost or pricing data also shall obtain and analyze certified cost or pricing data before awarding any subcontract, purchase order, or modification expected to exceed the certified cost or pricing data threshold, unless an exception in 15.403-1(b) applies to that action.

(1) The contractor shall submit, or cause to be submitted by the subcontractor(s), certified cost or pricing data to the Government for subcontracts that are the lower of either—

(i) $12.5 million or more; or

(ii) Both more than the pertinent certified cost or pricing data threshold and more than 10 percent of the prime contractor's proposed price, unless the contracting officer believes such submission is unnecessary.

(2) The contracting officer should require the contractor or subcontractor to submit to the Government (or cause submission of) subcontractor certified cost or pricing data below the thresholds in paragraph (c)(1) of this subsection and data other than certified cost or pricing data that the contracting officer considers necessary for adequately pricing the prime contract.

(3) Subcontractor certified cost or pricing data shall be submitted in the format provided in Table 15-2 of 15.408 or the alternate format specified in the solicitation.

(4) Subcontractor certified cost or pricing data shall be current, accurate, and complete as of the date of price agreement, or, if applicable, an earlier date agreed upon by the parties and specified on the contractor's Certificate of Current Cost or Pricing Data. The contractor shall update subcontractor's data, as appropriate, during source selection and negotiations.

(5) If there is more than one prospective subcontractor for any given work, the contractor need only submit to the Government certified cost or pricing data for the prospective subcontractor most likely to receive the award.

15.404-4 Profit.

(a) *General*. This subsection prescribes policies for establishing the profit or fee portion of the Government prenegotiation objective in price negotiations based on cost analysis.

(1) Profit or fee prenegotiation objectives do not necessarily represent net income to contractors. Rather, they represent that element of the potential total remuneration that contractors may receive for contract performance over and above allowable costs. This potential remuneration element and the Government's estimate of allowable costs to be incurred in contract performance together equal the Government's total prenegotiation objective. Just as actual costs may vary from estimated costs, the contractor's actual realized profit or fee may vary from negotiated profit or fee, because of such factors as efficiency of performance, incurrence of costs the Government does not recognize as allowable, and the contract type.

(2) It is in the Government's interest to offer contractors opportunities for financial rewards sufficient to stimulate efficient contract performance, attract the best capabilities of qualified large and small business concerns to Government contracts, and maintain a viable industrial base.

(3) Both the Government and contractors should be concerned with profit as a motivator of efficient and effective contract performance. Negotiations aimed merely at reducing prices by reducing profit, without proper recognition of the function of profit, are not in the Government's interest. Negotiation of extremely low profits, use of historical averages, or automatic application of predetermined percentages to total estimated costs do not provide proper motivation for optimum contract performance.

(b) *Policy.*

(1) Structured approaches (see paragraph (d) of this subsection) for determining profit or fee prenegotiation objectives provide a discipline for ensuring that all relevant factors are considered. Subject to the authorities in 1.301(c), agencies making noncompetitive contract awards over $100,000 totaling $50 million or more a year—

(i) Shall use a structured approach for determining the profit or fee objective in those acquisitions that require cost analysis; and

(ii) May prescribe specific exemptions for situations in which mandatory use of a structured approach would be clearly inappropriate.

(2) Agencies may use another agency's structured approach.

(c) *Contracting officer responsibilities.*

(1) When the price negotiation is not based on cost analysis, contracting officers are not required to analyze profit.

(2) When the price negotiation is based on cost analysis, contracting officers in agencies that have a structured approach shall use it to analyze profit. When not using a structured approach, contracting officers shall comply with paragraph (d)(1) of this subsection in developing profit or fee prenegotiation objectives.

(3) Contracting officers shall use the Government prenegotiation cost objective amounts as the basis for calculating the profit or fee prenegotiation objective. Before applying profit or fee factors, the contracting officer shall exclude from the pre-negotiation cost objective amounts the purchase cost of contractor-acquired property that is categorized as equipment, as defined in FAR 45.101, and where such equipment is to be charged directly to the contract. Before applying profit or fee factors, the contracting officer shall exclude any facilities capital cost of money included in the cost objective amounts. If the prospective contractor fails to identify or propose facilities capital cost of money in a proposal for a contract that will be subject to the cost principles for contracts with commercial organizations (see Subpart 31.2), facilities capital cost of money will not be an allowable cost in any resulting contract (see 15.408(i)).

(4)(i) The contracting officer shall not negotiate a price or fee that exceeds the following statutory limitations, imposed by 10 U.S.C. 2306(d) and 41 U.S.C. 254(b):

(A) For experimental, developmental, or research work performed under a cost-plus-fixed-fee contract, the fee shall not exceed 15 percent of the contract's estimated cost, excluding fee.

(B) For architect-engineer services for public works or utilities, the contract price or the estimated cost and fee for production and delivery of designs, plans, drawings, and specifications shall not exceed 6 percent of the estimated cost of construction of the public work or utility, excluding fees.

(C) For other cost-plus-fixed-fee contracts, the fee shall not exceed 10 percent of the contract's estimated cost, excluding fee.

(ii) The contracting officer's signature on the price negotiation memorandum or other documentation supporting determination of fair and reasonable price documents the contracting officer's determination that the statutory price or fee limitations have not been exceeded.

(5) The contracting officer shall not require any prospective contractor to submit breakouts or supporting rationale for its profit or fee objective but may consider it, if it is submitted voluntarily.

(6) If a change or modification calls for essentially the same type and mix of work as the basic contract and is of relatively small dollar value compared to the total contract value, the contracting officer may use the basic contract's profit or fee rate as the prenegotiation objective for that change or modification.

(d) *Profit-analysis factors—*

(1) *Common factors.* Unless it is clearly inappropriate or not applicable, each factor outlined in paragraphs (d)(1)(i) through (vi) of this subsection shall be considered by agencies in developing their structured approaches and by contracting officers in analyzing profit, whether or not using a structured approach.

(i) *Contractor effort.* This factor measures the complexity of the work and the resources required of the prospective contractor for contract performance. Greater profit opportunity should be provided under contracts requiring a high degree of professional and managerial skill and to prospective contractors whose skills, facilities, and technical assets can be expected to lead to efficient and economical contract performance. The subfactors in paragraphs (d)(1)(i)(A) through (D) of this subsection shall be considered in determining contractor effort, but they may be modified in specific situations to accommodate differences in the categories used by prospective contractors for listing costs—

(A) *Material acquisition.* This subfactor measures the managerial and technical effort needed to obtain the required purchased parts and material, subcontracted items, and special tooling. Considerations include the complexity of the items required, the number of purchase orders and subcontracts to be awarded and administered, whether established sources are available or new or second sources must be developed, and whether material will be obtained through routine purchase orders or through complex subcontracts requiring detailed specifications. Profit consideration should correspond to the managerial and technical effort involved.

(B) *Conversion direct labor.* This subfactor measures the contribution of direct engineering, manufacturing, and other labor to converting the raw materials, data, and subcontracted items into the contract items. Considerations include the diversity of engineering, scientific, and manufacturing labor skills required and the amount and quality of supervision and coordination needed to perform the contract task.

(C) *Conversion-related indirect costs.* This subfactor measures how much the indirect costs contribute to contract performance. The labor elements in the allocable indirect costs should be given the profit consideration they would receive if treated as direct labor. The other elements of indirect costs should be evaluated to determine whether they merit only limited profit consideration because of their routine nature, or are elements that contribute significantly to the proposed contract.

(D) *General management*. This subfactor measures the prospective contractor's other indirect costs and general and administrative (G&A) expense, their composition, and how much they contribute to contract performance. Considerations include how labor in the overhead pools would be treated if it were direct labor, whether elements within the pools are routine expenses or instead are elements that contribute significantly to the proposed contract, and whether the elements require routine as opposed to unusual managerial effort and attention.

(ii) *Contract cost risk*.

(A) This factor measures the degree of cost responsibility and associated risk that the prospective contractor will assume as a result of the contract type contemplated and considering the reliability of the cost estimate in relation to the complexity and duration of the contract task. Determination of contract type should be closely related to the risks involved in timely, cost-effective, and efficient performance. This factor should compensate contractors proportionately for assuming greater cost risks.

(B) The contractor assumes the greatest cost risk in a closely priced firm-fixed-price contract under which it agrees to perform a complex undertaking on time and at a predetermined price. Some firm-fixed-price contracts may entail substantially less cost risk than others because, for example, the contract task is less complex or many of the contractor's costs are known at the time of price agreement, in which case the risk factor should be reduced accordingly. The contractor assumes the least cost risk in a cost-plus-fixed-fee level-of-effort contract, under which it is reimbursed those costs determined to be allocable and allowable, plus the fixed fee.

(C) In evaluating assumption of cost risk, contracting officers shall, except in unusual circumstances, treat time-and-materials, labor-hour, and firm-fixed-price, level-of-effort term contracts as cost-plus-fixed-fee contracts.

(iii) *Federal socioeconomic programs*. This factor measures the degree of support given by the prospective contractor to Federal socioeconomic programs, such as those involving small business concerns, small business concerns owned and controlled by socially and economically disadvantaged individuals, women-owned small business concerns, veteran-owned, HUBZone, service-disabled veteran-owned small business concerns, handicapped sheltered workshops, and energy conservation. Greater profit opportunity should be provided contractors that have displayed unusual initiative in these programs.

(iv) *Capital investments*. This factor takes into account the contribution of contractor investments to efficient and economical contract performance.

(v) *Cost-control and other past accomplishments*. This factor allows additional profit opportunities to a prospective contractor that has previously demonstrated its ability to perform similar tasks effectively and economically. In addition, consideration should be given to measures taken by the prospective contractor that result in productivity improvements, and other cost-reduction accomplishments that will benefit the Government in follow-on contracts.

(vi) *Independent development*. Under this factor, the contractor may be provided additional profit opportunities in recognition of independent development efforts relevant to the contract end item without Government assistance. The contracting officer should consider whether the development cost was recovered directly or indirectly from Government sources.

(2) *Additional factors*. In order to foster achievement of program objectives, each agency may include additional factors in its structured approach or take them into account in the profit analysis of individual contract actions.

15.405 Price negotiation.

(a) The purpose of performing cost or price analysis is to develop a negotiation position that permits the contracting officer and the offeror an opportunity to reach agreement on a fair and reasonable price. A fair and reasonable price does not require that agreement be reached on every element of cost, nor is it mandatory that the agreed price be within the contracting officer's initial negotiation position. Taking into consideration the advisory recommendations, reports of contributing specialists, and the current status of the contractor's purchasing system, the contracting officer is responsible for exercising the requisite judgment needed to reach a negotiated settlement with the offeror and is solely responsible for the final price agreement. However, when significant audit or other specialist recommendations are not adopted, the contracting officer should provide rationale that supports the negotiation result in the price negotiation documentation.

(b) The contracting officer's primary concern is the overall price the Government will actually pay. The contracting officer's objective is to negotiate a contract of a type and with a price providing the contractor the greatest incentive for efficient and economical performance. The negotiation of a contract type and a price are related and should be considered together with the issues of risk and uncertainty to the contractor and the Government. Therefore, the contracting officer should not become preoccupied with any single element and should balance the contract type, cost, and profit or fee negotiated to achieve a total result—a price that is fair and reasonable to both the Government and the contractor.

(c) The Government's cost objective and proposed pricing arrangement directly affect the profit or fee objective. Because profit or fee is only one of several interrelated variables, the contracting officer shall not agree on profit or fee without concurrent agreement on cost and type of contract.

(d) If, however, the contractor insists on a price or demands a profit or fee that the contracting officer considers unreasonable, and the contracting officer has taken all authorized actions (including determining the feasibility of developing an alternative source) without success, the contracting officer shall refer the contract action to a level above the contracting officer. Disposition of the action should be documented.

15.406 Documentation.

15.406-1 Prenegotiation objectives.

(a) The prenegotiation objectives establish the Government's initial negotiation position. They assist in the contracting officer's determination of fair and reasonable price. They should be based on the results of the contracting officer's analysis of the offeror's proposal, taking into consideration all pertinent information including field pricing assistance, audit reports and technical analysis, fact-finding results, independent Government cost estimates and price histories.

(b) The contracting officer shall establish prenegotiation objectives before the negotiation of any pricing action. The scope and depth of the analysis supporting the objectives should be directly related to the dollar value, importance, and complexity of the pricing action. When cost analysis is required, the contracting officer shall document the pertinent issues to be negotiated, the cost objectives, and a profit or fee objective.

15.406-2 Certificate of Current Cost or Pricing Data.

(a) When certified cost or pricing data are required, the contracting officer shall require the contractor to execute a Certificate of Current Cost or Pricing Data, using the format in this paragraph, and must include the executed certificate in the contract file.

CERTIFICATE OF CURRENT COST OR PRICING DATA

This is to certify that, to the best of my knowledge and belief, the cost or pricing data (as defined in section 2.101 of the Federal Acquisition Regulation (FAR) and required under FAR subsection 15.403-4) submitted, either actually or by specific identification in writing, to the Contracting Officer or to the Contracting Officer's representative in support of _____* are accurate, complete, and current as of _____**. This certification includes the cost or pricing data supporting any advance agreements and forward pricing rate agreements between the offeror and the Government that are part of the proposal.

Firm _____

Signature _____

Name _____

Title _____

Date of execution*** _____

* Identify the proposal, request for price adjustment, or other submission involved, giving the appropriate identifying number (*e.g.,* RFP No.).

** Insert the day, month, and year when price negotiations were concluded and price agreement was reached or, if applicable, an earlier date agreed upon between the parties that is as close as practicable to the date of agreement on price.

*** Insert the day, month, and year of signing, which should be as close as practicable to the date when the price negotiations were concluded and the contract price was agreed to.

(END OF CERTIFICATE)

(b) The certificate does not constitute a representation as to the accuracy of the contractor's judgment on the estimate of future costs or projections. It applies to the data upon which the judgment or estimate was based. This distinction between fact and judgment should be clearly understood. If the contractor had information reasonably available at the time of agreement showing that the negotiated price was not based on accurate, complete, and current data, the contractor's responsibility is not limited by any lack of personal knowledge of the information on the part of its negotiators.

(c) The contracting officer and contractor are encouraged to reach a prior agreement on criteria for establishing closing or cutoff dates when appropriate in order to minimize delays associated with proposal updates. Closing or cutoff dates should be included as part of the data submitted with the proposal and, before agreement on price, data should be updated by the contractor to the latest closing or cutoff dates for which the data are available. Use of cutoff dates coinciding with reports is acceptable, as certain data may not be reasonably available before normal periodic closing dates (*e.g.,* actual indirect costs). Data within the contractor's or a subcontractor's organization on matters significant to contractor management and to the Government will be treated as reasonably available. What is significant depends upon the circumstances of each acquisition.

(d) Possession of a Certificate of Current Cost or Pricing Data is not a substitute for examining and analyzing the contractor's proposal.

(e) If certified cost or pricing data are requested by the Government and submitted by an offeror, but an exception is later found to apply, the data shall not be considered certified cost or pricing data and shall not be certified in accordance with this subsection.

15.406-3 Documenting the negotiation.

(a) The contracting officer shall document in the contract file the principal elements of the negotiated agreement. The documentation (*e.g.,* price negotiation memorandum (PNM)) shall include the following:

(1) The purpose of the negotiation.

(2) A description of the acquisition, including appropriate identifying numbers (*e.g.,* RFP No.).

(3) The name, position, and organization of each person representing the contractor and the Government in the negotiation.

(4) The current status of any contractor systems (*e.g.,* purchasing, estimating, accounting, and compensation) to the extent they affected and were considered in the negotiation.

(5) If certified cost or pricing data were not required in the case of any price negotiation exceeding the certified cost or pricing data threshold, the exception used and the basis for it.

(6) If certified cost or pricing data were required, the extent to which the contracting officer—

(i) Relied on the certified cost or pricing data submitted and used them in negotiating the price;

(ii) Recognized as inaccurate, incomplete, or noncurrent any certified cost or pricing data submitted; the action taken by the contracting officer and the contractor as a result; and the effect of the defective data on the price negotiated; or

(iii) Determined that an exception applied after the data were submitted and, therefore, considered not to be certified cost or pricing data.

(7) A summary of the contractor's proposal, any field pricing assistance recommendations, including the reasons for any pertinent variances from them, the Government's negotiation objective, and the negotiated position. Where the determination of a fair and reasonable price is based on cost analysis, the summary shall address each major cost element. When determination of a fair and reasonable price is based on price analysis, the summary shall include the source and type of data used to support the determination.

(8) The most significant facts or considerations controlling the establishment of the prenegotiation objectives and the negotiated agreement including an explanation of any significant differences between the two positions.

(9) To the extent such direction has a significant effect on the action, a discussion and quantification of the impact of direction given by Congress, other agencies, and higher-level officials (*i.e.,* officials who would not normally exercise authority during the award and review process for the instant contract action).

(10) The basis for the profit or fee prenegotiation objective and the profit or fee negotiated.

(11) Documentation of fair and reasonable pricing.

(b) Whenever field pricing assistance has been obtained, the contracting officer shall forward a copy of the negotiation documentation to the office(s) providing assistance. When appropriate, information on how advisory field support can be made more effective should be provided separately.

15.407 Special cost or pricing areas.

15.407-1 Defective certified cost or pricing data.

(a) If, before agreement on price, the contracting officer learns that any certified cost or pricing data submitted are inaccurate, incomplete, or noncurrent, the contracting officer shall immediately bring the matter to the attention of the prospective contractor, whether the defective data increase or decrease the contract price. The contracting officer shall consider any new data submitted to correct the deficiency, or consider the inaccuracy, incompleteness, or noncurrency of the data when negotiating the contract price. The price negotiation memorandum shall reflect the adjustments made to the data or the corrected data used to negotiate the contract price.

(b)(1) If, after award, certified cost or pricing data are found to be inaccurate, incomplete, or noncurrent as of the date of final agreement on price or an earlier date agreed upon by the parties given on the contractor's or subcontractor's Certificate of Current Cost or Pricing Data, the Government is entitled to a price adjustment, including profit or fee, of any significant amount by which the price was increased because of the defective data. This entitlement is ensured by including in the contract one of the clauses prescribed in 15.408(b) and (c) and is set forth in the clauses at 52.215-10, Price Reduction for Defective Certified Cost or Pricing Data, and 52.215-11, Price Reduction for Defective Certified Cost or Pricing Data-Modifications. The clauses give the Government the right to a price adjustment for defects in certified cost or pricing data submitted by the contractor, a prospective subcontractor, or an actual subcontractor.

(2) In arriving at a price adjustment, the contracting officer shall consider the time by which the certified cost or pricing data became reasonably available to the contractor, and the extent to which the Government relied upon the defective data.

(3) The clauses referred to in paragraph (b)(1) of this subsection recognize that the Government's right to a price adjustment is not affected by any of the following circumstances:

(i) The contractor or subcontractor was a sole source supplier or otherwise was in a superior bargaining position;

(ii) The contracting officer should have known that the certified cost or pricing data in issue were defective even though the contractor or subcontractor took no affirmative action to bring the character of the data to the attention of the contracting officer;

(iii) The contract was based on an agreement about the total cost of the contract and there was no agreement about the cost of each item procured under such contract; or

(iv) Certified cost or pricing data were required; however, the contractor or subcontractor did not submit a Certificate of Current Cost or Pricing Data relating to the contract.

(4) Subject to paragraphs (b)(5) and (6) of this subsection, the contracting officer shall allow an offset for any understated certified cost or

pricing data submitted in support of price negotiations, up to the amount of the Government's claim for overstated pricing data arising out of the same pricing action (*e.g.,* the initial pricing of the same contract or the pricing of the same change order).

(5) An offset shall be allowed only in an amount supported by the facts and if the contractor—

(i) Certifies to the contracting officer that, to the best of the contractor's knowledge and belief, the contractor is entitled to the offset in the amount requested; and

(ii) Proves that the certified cost or pricing data were available before the "as of" date specified on the Certificate of Current Cost or Pricing Data but were not submitted. Such offsets need not be in the same cost groupings (*e.g.,* material, direct labor, or indirect costs).

(6) An offset shall not be allowed if—

(i) The understated data were known by the contractor to be understated before the "as of" date specified on the Certificate of Current Cost or Pricing Data; or

(ii) The Government proves that the facts demonstrate that the price would not have increased in the amount to be offset even if the available data had been submitted before the "as of" date specified on the Certificate of Current Cost or Pricing Data.

(7)(i) In addition to the price adjustment, the Government is entitled to recovery of any overpayment plus interest on the overpayments. The Government is also entitled to penalty amounts on certain of these overpayments. Overpayment occurs only when payment is made for supplies or services accepted by the Government. Overpayments do not result from amounts paid for contract financing, as defined in 32.001.

(ii) In calculating the interest amount due, the contracting officer shall—

(A) Determine the defective pricing amounts that have been overpaid to the contractor;

(B) Consider the date of each overpayment (the date of overpayment for this interest calculation shall be the date payment was made for the related completed and accepted contract items; or for subcontract defective pricing, the date payment was made to the prime contractor, based on prime contract progress billings or deliveries, which included payments for a completed and accepted subcontract item); and

(C) Apply the underpayment interest rate(s) in effect for each quarter from the time of overpayment to the time of repayment, utilizing rate(s) prescribed by the Secretary of the Treasury under 26 U.S.C. 6621(a)(2).

(iii) In arriving at the amount due for penalties on contracts where the submission of defective certified cost or pricing data was a knowing submission, the contracting officer shall obtain an amount equal to the amount of overpayment made. Before taking any contractual actions concerning penalties, the contracting officer shall obtain the advice of counsel.

(iv) In the demand letter, the contracting officer shall separately include—

    (A) The repayment amount;

    (B) The penalty amount (if any);

    (C) The interest amount through a specified date; and

    (D) A statement that interest will continue to accrue until repayment is made.

(c) If, after award, the contracting officer learns or suspects that the data furnished were not accurate, complete, and current, or were not adequately verified by the contractor as of the time of negotiation, the contracting officer shall request an audit to evaluate the accuracy, completeness, and currency of the data. The Government may evaluate the profit-cost relationships only if the audit reveals that the data certified by the contractor were defective. The contracting officer shall not reprice the contract solely because the profit was greater than forecast or because a contingency specified in the submission failed to materialize.

(d) For each advisory audit received based on a postaward review that indicates defective pricing, the contracting officer shall make a determination as to whether or not the data submitted were defective and relied upon. Before making such a determination, the contracting officer should give the contractor an opportunity to support the accuracy, completeness, and currency of the data in question. The contracting officer shall prepare a memorandum documenting both the determination and any corrective action taken as a result. The contracting officer shall send one copy of this memorandum to the auditor and, if the contract has been assigned for administration, one copy to the administrative contracting officer (ACO). A copy of the memorandum or other notice of the contracting officer's determination shall be provided to the contractor. When the contracting officer determines that the contractor submitted defective cost or pricing data, the contracting officer, in accordance with agency procedures, shall ensure that information relating to the contracting officer's final determination is reported in accordance with 42.1503(f). Agencies shall ensure updated information that changes a contracting officer's prior final determination is reported into the FAPIIS module of PPIRS in the event of a—

    (1) Contracting officer's decision in accordance with the Contract Disputes Act;

    (2) Board of Contract Appeals decision; or

    (3) Court decision.

(e) If both the contractor and subcontractor submitted, and the contractor certified, or should have certified, cost or pricing data, the Government has the right, under the clauses at 52.215-10, Price Reduction for Defective Certified Cost or Pricing Data, and 52.215-11, Price Reduction for Defective Certified Cost or Pricing Data—Modifications, to reduce the prime contract price if it was significantly increased because a subcontractor submitted defective data. This right applies whether these data supported subcontract cost estimates or supported firm agreements between subcontractor and contractor.

(f) If Government audit discloses defective subcontractor certified cost or pricing data, the information necessary to support a reduction in prime contract and subcontract prices may be available only from the Government. To the extent necessary to secure a prime contract price reduction, the contracting officer should make this information available to the prime contractor or appropriate subcontractors, upon request. If release of the information would compromise Government security or disclose trade secrets or confidential business information, the contracting officer shall release it only under conditions that will protect it from improper disclosure. Information made available under this paragraph shall be limited to that used as the basis for the prime contract price reduction. In order to afford an opportunity for corrective action, the contracting officer should give the prime contractor reasonable advance notice before determining to reduce the prime contract price.

(1) When a prime contractor includes defective subcontract data in arriving at the price but later awards the subcontract to a lower priced subcontractor (or does not subcontract for the work), any adjustment in the prime contract price due to defective subcontract data is limited to the difference (plus applicable indirect cost and profit markups) between the subcontract price used for pricing the prime contract, and either the actual subcontract price or the actual cost to the contractor, if not subcontracted, provided the data on which the actual subcontract price is based are not themselves defective.

(2) Under cost-reimbursement contracts and under all fixed-price contracts except firm-fixed-price contracts and fixed-price contracts with economic price adjustment, payments to subcontractors that are higher than they would be had there been no defective subcontractor certified cost or pricing data shall be the basis for disallowance or nonrecognition of costs under the clauses prescribed in 15.408(b) and (c). The Government has a continuing and direct financial interest in such payments that is unaffected by the initial agreement on prime contract price.

15.407-2   Make-or-buy programs.

(a) *General.* The prime contractor is responsible for managing contract performance, including planning, placing, and administering subcontracts as necessary to ensure the lowest overall cost and technical risk to the Government. When make-or-buy programs are required, the Government may reserve the right to review and agree on the contractor's make or-buy program when necessary to ensure negotiation of reasonable contract prices, satisfactory performance, or implementation of socioeconomic policies. Consent to subcontracts and review of contractors' purchasing systems are separate actions covered in Part 44.

(b) *Definition.* "Make item," as used in this subsection, means an item or work effort to be produced or performed by the prime contractor or its affiliates, subsidiaries, or divisions.

(c) *Acquisitions requiring make-or-buy programs.*

(1) Contracting officers may require prospective contractors to submit make-or-buy program plans for negotiated acquisitions requiring certified cost or pricing data whose estimated value is $12.5 million or more, except when the

proposed contract is for research or development and, if prototypes or hardware are involved, no significant follow-on production is anticipated.

(2) Contracting officers may require prospective contractors to submit make-or-buy programs for negotiated acquisitions whose estimated value is under $12.5 million only if the contracting officer—

(i) Determines that the information is necessary; and

(ii) Documents the reasons in the contract file.

(d) *Solicitation requirements.* When prospective contractors are required to submit proposed make-or-buy programs, the solicitation shall include—

(1) A statement that the program and required supporting information must accompany the offer; and

(2) A description of factors to be used in evaluating the proposed program, such as capability, capacity, availability of small, small disadvantaged, women-owned, veteran-owned, HUBZone, and service-disabled veteran-owned small business concerns for subcontracting, establishment of new facilities in or near labor surplus areas, delivery or performance schedules, control of technical and schedule interfaces, proprietary processes, technical superiority or exclusiveness, and technical risks involved.

(e) *Program requirements.* To support a make-or-buy program, the following information shall be supplied by the contractor in its proposal:

(1) *Items and work included.* The information required from a contractor in a make-or-buy program shall be confined to those major items or work efforts that normally would require company management review of the make-or-buy decision because they are complex, costly, needed in large quantities, or require additional equipment or real property to produce. Raw materials, commercial items (see 2.101), and off-the-shelf items (see 46.101) shall not be included, unless their potential impact on contract cost or schedule is critical. Normally, make-or-buy programs should not include items or work efforts estimated to cost less than 1 percent of the total estimated contract price or any minimum dollar amount set by the agency.

(2) The offeror's program should include or be supported by the following information:

(i) A description of each major item or work effort.

(ii) Categorization of each major item or work effort as "must make," "must buy," or "can either make or buy."

(iii) For each item or work effort categorized as "can either make or buy," a proposal either to "make" or to "buy."

(iv) Reasons for categorizing items and work efforts as "must make" or "must buy," and proposing to "make" or to "buy" those categorized as "can either make or buy." The reasons must include the consideration given to the evaluation factors described in the solicitation and must be in sufficient detail to permit the contracting officer to evaluate the categorization or proposal.

(v) Designation of the plant or division proposed to make each item or perform each work effort, and a statement as to whether the existing or proposed new facility is in or near a labor surplus area.

(vi) Identification of proposed subcontractors, if known, and their location and size status (also see Subpart 19.7 for subcontracting plan requirements).

(vii) Any recommendations to defer make-or-buy decisions when categorization of some items or work efforts is impracticable at the time of submission.

(viii) Any other information the contracting officer requires in order to evaluate the program.

(f) *Evaluation, negotiation, and agreement.* Contracting officers shall evaluate and negotiate proposed make-or-buy programs as soon as practicable after their receipt and before contract award.

(1) When the program is to be incorporated in the contract and the design status of the product being acquired does not permit accurate precontract identification of major items or work efforts, the contracting officer shall notify the prospective contractor in writing that these items or efforts, when identifiable, shall be added under the clause at 52.215-9, Changes or Additions to Make-or-Buy Program.

(2) Contracting officers normally shall not agree to proposed "make items" when the products or services are not regularly manufactured or provided by the contractor and are available—quality, quantity, delivery, and other essential factors considered—from another firm at equal or lower prices, or when they are regularly manufactured or provided by the contractor, but are available—quality, quantity, delivery, and other essential factors considered—from another firm at lower prices. However, the contracting officer may agree to these as "make items" if an overall lower Governmentwide cost would result or it is otherwise in the best interest of the Government. If this situation occurs in any fixed-price incentive or cost-plus-incentive-fee contract, the contracting officer shall specify these items in the contract and state that they are subject to paragraph (d) of the clause at 52.215-9, Changes or Additions to Make-or-Buy Program (see 15.408(a)). If the contractor proposes to reverse the categorization of such items during contract performance, the contract price shall be subject to equitable reduction.

(g) *Incorporating make-or-buy programs in contracts.* The contracting officer may incorporate the make-or-buy program in negotiated contracts for—

(1) Major systems (see Part 34) or their subsystems or components, regardless of contract type; or

(2) Other supplies and services if—

(i) The contract is a cost-reimbursable contract, or a cost-sharing contract in which the contractor's share of the cost is less than 25 percent; and

(ii) The contracting officer determines that technical or cost risks justify Government review and approval of changes or additions to the make-or-buy program.

15.407-3 Forward pricing rate agreements.

(a) When certified cost or pricing data are required, offerors are required to describe any forward pricing rate agreements (FPRAs) in each specific pricing proposal to which the rates apply and to identify the latest cost or pricing data already submitted in accordance with the FPRA. All data submitted in connection with the FPRA, updated as necessary, form a part of the total data that the offeror certifies to be accurate, complete, and current at the time of agreement on price for an initial contract or for a contract modification. (See the Certificate of Current Cost or Pricing Data at 15.406-2.)

(b) Contracting officers will use FPRA rates as bases for pricing all contracts, modifications, and other contractual actions to be performed during the period covered by the agreement. Conditions that may affect the agreement's validity shall be reported promptly to the ACO. If the ACO determines that a changed condition invalidates the agreement, the ACO shall notify all interested parties of the extent of its effect and status of efforts to establish a revised FPRA.

(c) Contracting officers shall not require certification at the time of agreement for data supplied in support of FPRA's or other advance agreements. When a forward pricing rate agreement or other advance agreement is used to price a contract action that requires a certificate, the certificate supporting that contract action shall cover the data supplied to support the FPRA or other advance agreement, and all other data supporting the action.

15.407-4 Should-cost review.

(a) *General.*

(1) Should-cost reviews are a specialized form of cost analysis. Should-cost reviews differ from traditional evaluation methods because they do not assume that a contractor's historical costs reflect efficient and economical operation. Instead, these reviews evaluate the economy and efficiency of the contractor's existing work force, methods, materials, equipment, real property, operating systems, and management. These reviews are accomplished by a multi-functional team of Government contracting, contract administration, pricing, audit, and engineering representatives. The objective of should-cost reviews is to promote both short and long-range improvements in the contractor's economy and efficiency in order to reduce the cost of performance of Government contracts. In addition, by providing rationale for any recommendations and quantifying their impact on cost, the Government will be better able to develop realistic objectives for negotiation.

(2) There are two types of should-cost reviews—program should-cost review (see paragraph (b) of this subsection) and overhead should-cost review (see paragraph (c) of this subsection). These should-cost reviews may be performed together or independently. The scope of a should-cost review can range from a large-scale review examining the contractor's entire operation (including plant-wide overhead and selected major subcontractors) to a small-scale tailored review examining specific portions of a contractor's operation.

(b) *Program should-cost review.*

(1) A program should-cost review is used to evaluate significant elements of direct costs, such as material and labor, and associated indirect costs, usually associated with the production of major systems. When a program should-

cost review is conducted relative to a contractor proposal, a separate audit report on the proposal is required.

(2) A program should-cost review should be considered, particularly in the case of a major system acquisition (see Part 34), when—

(i) Some initial production has already taken place;

(ii) The contract will be awarded on a sole source basis;

(iii) There are future year production requirements for substantial quantities of like items;

(iv) The items being acquired have a history of increasing costs;

(v) The work is sufficiently defined to permit an effective analysis and major changes are unlikely;

(vi) Sufficient time is available to plan and adequately conduct the should-cost review; and

(vii) Personnel with the required skills are available or can be assigned for the duration of the should-cost review.

(3) The contracting officer should decide which elements of the contractor's operation have the greatest potential for cost savings and assign the available personnel resources accordingly. The expertise of on-site Government personnel should be used, when appropriate. While the particular elements to be analyzed are a function of the contract work task, elements such as manufacturing, pricing and accounting, management and organization, and subcontract and vendor management are normally reviewed in a should-cost review.

(4) In acquisitions for which a program should-cost review is conducted, a separate program should-cost review team report, prepared in accordance with agency procedures, is required. The contracting officer shall consider the findings and recommendations contained in the program should-cost review team report when negotiating the contract price. After completing the negotiation, the contracting officer shall provide the ACO a report of any identified uneconomical or inefficient practices, together with a report of correction or disposition agreements reached with the contractor. The contracting officer shall establish a follow-up plan to monitor the correction of the uneconomical or inefficient practices.

(5) When a program should-cost review is planned, the contracting officer should state this fact in the acquisition plan or acquisition plan updates (see Subpart 7.1) and in the solicitation.

(c) *Overhead should-cost review.*

(1) An overhead should- cost review is used to evaluate indirect costs, such as fringe benefits, shipping and receiving, real property, and equipment, depreciation, plant maintenance and security, taxes, and general and administrative activities. It is normally used to evaluate and negotiate an FPRA with the contractor. When an overhead should-cost review is conducted, a separate audit report is required.

(2) The following factors should be considered when selecting contractor sites for overhead should-cost reviews:

(i) Dollar amount of Government business.

(ii) Level of Government participation.

(iii) Level of noncompetitive Government contracts.

(iv) Volume of proposal activity.

(v) Major system or program.

(vi) Corporate reorganizations, mergers, acquisitions, or takeovers.

(vii) Other conditions (*e.g.,* changes in accounting systems, management, or business activity).

(3) The objective of the overhead should-cost review is to evaluate significant indirect cost elements in-depth, and identify and recommend corrective actions regarding inefficient and uneconomical practices. If it is conducted in conjunction with a program should-cost review, a separate overhead should-cost review report is not required. However, the findings and recommendations of the overhead should-cost team, or any separate overhead should-cost review report, shall be provided to the ACO. The ACO should use this information to form the basis for the Government position in negotiating an FPRA with the contractor. The ACO shall establish a follow-up plan to monitor the correction of the uneconomical or inefficient practices.

15.407-5 Estimating systems.

(a) Using an acceptable estimating system for proposal preparation benefits both the Government and the contractor by increasing the accuracy and reliability of individual proposals. Cognizant audit activities, when it is appropriate to do so, shall establish and manage regular programs for reviewing selected contractors' estimating systems or methods, in order to reduce the scope of reviews to be performed on individual proposals, expedite the negotiation process, and increase the reliability of proposals. The results of estimating system reviews shall be documented in survey reports.

(b) The auditor shall send a copy of the estimating system survey report and a copy of the official notice of corrective action required to each contracting office and contract administration office having substantial business with that contractor. Significant deficiencies not corrected by the contractor shall be a consideration in subsequent proposal analyses and negotiations.

15.408 Solicitation provisions and contract clauses.

(a) *Changes or Additions to Make-or-Buy Program.* The contracting officer shall insert the clause at 52.215-9, Changes or Additions to Make-or-Buy Program, in solicitations and contracts when it is contemplated that a make-or-buy program will be incorporated in the contract. If a less economical "make" or "buy" categorization is selected for one or more items of significant value, the contracting officer shall use the clause with—

(1) Its Alternate I, if a fixed-price incentive contract is contemplated; or

(2) Its Alternate II, if a cost-plus-incentive-fee contract is contemplated.

(b) *Price Reduction for Defective Certified Cost or Pricing Data.* The contracting officer shall, when contracting by negotiation, insert the clause at 52.215-10, Price Reduction for Defective Certified Cost or Pricing Data, in solicitations and contracts when it is contemplated that certified cost or pricing data will be required from the contractor or any subcontractor (see 15.403-4).

(c) *Price Reduction for Defective Certified Cost or Pricing Data—Modifications.* The contracting officer shall, when contracting by negotiation, insert the clause at 52.215-11, Price Reduction for Defective Certified Cost or Pricing Data—Modifications, in solicitations and contracts when it is contemplated that certified cost or pricing data will be required from the contractor or any subcontractor (see 15.403-4) for the pricing of contract modifications, and the clause prescribed in paragraph (b) of this section has not been included.

(d) *Subcontractor Certified Cost or Pricing Data.* The contracting officer shall insert the clause at 52.215-12, Subcontractor Certified Cost or Pricing Data, in solicitations and contracts when the clause prescribed in paragraph (b) of this section is included.

(e) *Subcontractor Certified Cost or Pricing Data—Modifications.* The contracting officer shall insert the clause at 52.215-13, Subcontractor Certified Cost or Pricing Data—Modifications, in solicitations and contracts when the clause prescribed in paragraph (c) of this section is included.

(f) *Integrity of Unit Prices.*

(1) The contracting officer shall insert the clause at 52.215-14, Integrity of Unit Prices, in solicitations and contracts except for-

(i) Acquisitions at or below the simplified acquisition threshold;

(ii) Construction or architect-engineer services under Part 36;

(iii) Utility services under Part 41;

(iv) Service contracts where supplies are not required;

(v) Acquisitions of commercial items; and

(vi) Contracts for petroleum products.

(2) The contracting officer shall insert the clause with its Alternate I when contracting without adequate price competition or when prescribed by agency regulations.

(g) *Pension Adjustments and Asset Reversions.* The contracting officer shall insert the clause at 52.215-15, Pension Adjustments and Asset Reversions, in solicitations and contracts for which it is anticipated that certified cost or pricing data will be required or for which any preaward or postaward cost determinations will be subject to part 31.

(h) *Facilities Capital Cost of Money.* The contracting officer shall insert the provision at 52.215-16, Facilities Capital Cost of Money, in solicitations expected to result in contracts that are subject to the cost principles for contracts with commercial organizations (see Subpart 31.2).

(i) *Waiver of Facilities Capital Cost of Money.* If the prospective contractor does not propose facilities capital cost of money in its offer, the contracting officer shall insert the clause at 52.215-17, Waiver of Facilities Capital Cost of Money, in the resulting contract.

(j) *Reversion or Adjustment of Plans for Postretirement Benefits (PRB) Other Than Pensions.* The contracting officer shall insert the clause at 52.215-18, Reversion or Adjustment of Plans for Postretirement Benefits (PRB) Other Than

Pensions, in solicitations and contracts for which it is anticipated that certified cost or pricing data will be required or for which any preaward or postaward cost determinations will be subject to Part 31.

(k) *Notification of Ownership Changes.* The contracting officer shall insert the clause at 52.215-19, Notification of Ownership Changes, in solicitations and contracts for which it is contemplated that certified cost or pricing data will be required or for which any preaward or postaward cost determination will be subject to Subpart 31.2.

(l) *Requirements for Certified Cost or Pricing Data and Data Other Than Certified Cost or Pricing Data.* Considering the hierarchy at 15.402, the contracting officer shall insert the provision at 52.215-20, Requirements for Certified Cost or Pricing Data and Data Other Than Certified Cost or Pricing Data, in solicitations if it is reasonably certain that certified cost or pricing data or data other than certified cost or pricing data will be required. This provision also provides instructions to offerors on how to request an exception from the requirement to submit certified cost or pricing data. The contracting officer shall—

(1) Use the provision with its Alternate I to specify a format for certified cost or pricing data other than the format required by Table 15-2 of this section;

(2) Use the provision with its Alternate II if copies of the proposal are to be sent to the ACO and contract auditor;

(3) Use the provision with its Alternate III if submission via electronic media is required; and

(4) Replace the basic provision with its Alternate IV if certified cost or pricing data are not expected to be required because an exception may apply, but data other than certified cost or pricing data will be required as described in 15.403-3.

(m) *Requirements for Certified Cost or Pricing Data and Data Other Than Certified Cost or Pricing Data—Modifications.* Considering the hierarchy at 15.402, the contracting officer shall insert the clause at 52.215-21, Requirements for Certified Cost or Pricing Data and Data Other Than Certified Cost or Pricing Data—Modifications, in solicitations and contracts if it is reasonably certain that certified cost or pricing data or data other than certified cost or pricing data will be required for modifications. This clause also provides instructions to contractors on how to request an exception from the requirement to submit certified cost or pricing data. The contracting officer shall—

(1) Use the clause with its Alternate I to specify a format for certified cost or pricing data other than the format required by Table 15-2 of this section;

(2) Use the clause with its Alternate II if copies of the proposal are to be sent to the ACO and contract auditor;

(3) Use the clause with its Alternate III if submission via electronic media is required; and

(4) Replace the basic clause with its Alternate IV if certified cost or pricing data are not expected to be required because an exception may apply, but data other than certified cost or pricing data will be required as described in 15.403-3.

(n) Limitations on Pass-Through Charges.

(1) The contracting officer shall insert the provision at 52.215-22, Limitations on Pass-Through Charges-Identification of Subcontract Effort, in solicitations containing the clause at 52.215-23.

(2)(i) Except as provided in paragraph (n)(2)(ii), the contracting officer shall insert the clause 52.215-23, Limitations on Pass-Through Charges, in solicitations and contracts including task or delivery orders as follows:

(A) For civilian agencies, insert the clause when—

(1) The total estimated contract or order value exceeds the simplified acquisition threshold as defined in section 2.101 and

(2) The contemplated contract type is expected to be a cost-reimbursement type contract as defined in Subpart 16.3; or

(B) For DoD, insert the clause when—

(1) The total estimated contract or order value exceeds the threshold for obtaining cost or pricing data in 15.403-4; and

(2) The contemplated contract type is expected to be any contract type except—

(i) A firm-fixed-price contract awarded on the basis of adequate price competition;

(ii) A fixed-price contract with economic price adjustment awarded on the basis of adequate price competition;

(iii) A firm-fixed-price contract for the acquisition of a commercial item; or

(iv) A fixed-price contract with economic price adjustment, for the acquisition of a commercial item.

(ii) The clause may be used when the total estimated contract or order value is below the thresholds identified in 15.408(n)(2)(i) and for any contract type, when the contracting officer determines that inclusion of the clause is appropriate.

(iii) Use the clause 52.215-23 with its Alternate I when the contracting officer determines that the prospective contractor has demonstrated that its functions provide added value to the contracting effort and there are no excessive pass-through charges.

TABLE 15-2—INSTRUCTIONS FOR SUBMITTING COST/PRICE PROPOSALS WHEN CERTIFIED
COST OR PRICING DATA ARE REQUIRED

This document provides instructions for preparing a contract pricing proposal when certified cost or pricing data are required.
Note 1. There is a clear distinction between submitting certified cost or pricing data and merely making available books, records, and other documents without identification. The requirement for submission of certified cost or pricing data is met when all accurate certified cost or pricing data reasonably available to the offeror have been submitted, either actually or by specific identification, to the Contracting Officer or an authorized representative. As later data come into your possession, it should be submitted promptly to the Contracting Officer in a manner that clearly shows how the data relate to the offeror's price proposal. The requirement for submission of certified cost or pricing data continues up to the time of agreement on price, or an earlier date agreed upon between the parties if applicable.
Note 2. By submitting your proposal, you grant the Contracting Officer or an authorized representative the right to examine records that formed the basis for the pricing proposal. That examination can take place at any time before award. It may include those books, records, documents, and other types of factual data (regardless of form or whether the data are specifically referenced or included in the proposal as the basis for pricing) that will permit an adequate evaluation of the proposed price.
I. General Instructions
A. You must provide the following information on the first page of your pricing proposal:
(1) Solicitation, contract, and/or modification number;
(2) Name and address of offeror;
(3) Name and telephone number of point of contact;
(4) Name of contract administration office (if available);
(5) Type of contract action (that is, new contract, change order, price revision/redetermination, letter contract, unpressed order, or other);
(6) Proposed cost; profit or fee; and total;
(7) Whether you will require the use of Government property in the performance of the contract, and, if so, what property;
(8) Whether your organization is subject to cost accounting standards; whether your organization has submitted a CASB Disclosure Statement, and if it has been determined adequate; whether you have been notified that you are or may be in noncompliance with your Disclosure Statement or CAS (other than a noncompliance that the cognizant Federal agency official has determined to have an immaterial cost impact), and, if yes, an explanation; whether any aspect of this proposal is inconsistent with your disclosed practices or applicable CAS, and, if so, an explanation; and whether the proposal is consistent with your established estimating and accounting principles and procedures and FAR Part 31, Cost Principles, and, if not, an explanation;
(9) The following statement: This proposal reflects our estimates and/or actual costs as of this date and conforms with the instructions in FAR 15.403-5(b)(1) and Table 15-2. By submitting this proposal, we grant the Contracting Officer and authorized representative(s) the right to examine, at any time before award, those records, which include books, documents, accounting procedures and practices, and other data, regardless of type and form or whether such supporting information is specifically referenced or included in the proposal as the basis for pricing, that will permit an adequate evaluation of the proposed price.
(10) Date of submission; and
(11) Name, title, and signature of authorized representative.

B. In submitting your proposal, you must include an index, appropriately referenced, of all the certified cost or pricing data and information accompanying or identified in the proposal. In addition, you must annotate any future additions and/or revisions, up to the date of agreement on price, or an earlier date agreed upon by the parties, on a supplemental index.

C. As part of the specific information required, you must submit, with your proposal—

(1) Certified cost or pricing data (as defined at FAR 2.101). You must clearly identify on your cover sheet that certified cost or pricing data are included as part of the proposal.

(2) Information reasonably required to explain your estimating process, including—

(i) The judgmental factors applied and the mathematical or other methods used in the estimate, including those used in projecting from known data; and

(ii) The nature and amount of any contingencies included in the proposed price.

D. You must show the relationship between contract line item prices and the total contract price. You must attach cost-element breakdowns for each proposed line item, using the appropriate format prescribed in the "Formats for Submission of Line Item Summaries" section of this table. You must furnish supporting breakdowns for each cost element, consistent with your cost accounting system.

E. When more than one contract line item is proposed, you must also provide summary total amounts covering all line items for each element of cost.

F. Whenever you have incurred costs for work performed before submission of a proposal, you must identify those costs in your cost/price proposal.

G. If you have reached an agreement with Government representatives on use of forward pricing rates/factors, identify the agreement, include a copy, and describe its nature.

H. As soon as practicable after final agreement on price or an earlier date agreed to by the parties, but before the award resulting from the proposal, you must, under the conditions stated in FAR 15.406-2, submit a Certificate of Current Cost or Pricing Data.

II. Cost Elements

Depending on your system, you must provide breakdowns for the following basic cost elements, as applicable:

A. *Materials and services.* Provide a consolidated priced summary of individual material quantities included in the various tasks, orders, or contract line items being proposed and the basis for pricing (vendor quotes, invoice prices, etc.). Include raw materials, parts, components, assemblies, and services to be produced or performed by others. For all items proposed, identify the item and show the source, quantity, and price. Conduct price analyses of all subcontractor proposals. Conduct cost analyses for all subcontracts when certified cost or pricing data are submitted by the subcontractor. Include these analyses as part of your own certified cost or pricing data submissions for subcontracts expected to exceed the appropriate threshold in FAR 15.403-4. Submit the subcontractor certified cost or pricing data and data other than certified cost or pricing data as part of your own certified cost or pricing data as required in paragraph IIA(2) of this table. These requirements also apply to all subcontractors if required to submit certified cost or pricing data.

(1) *Adequate Price Competition.* Provide data showing the degree of competition and the basis for establishing the source and reasonableness of price for those acquisitions (such as subcontracts, purchase orders, material order, etc.) exceeding, or expected to exceed, the appropriate threshold set forth at FAR 15.403-4 priced on the basis of adequate price competition. For interorganizational transfers priced at other than the cost of comparable competitive commercial work of the division, subsidiary, or affiliate of the contractor, explain the pricing method (see FAR 31.205-26(e)).

(2) *All Other*. Obtain certified cost or pricing data from prospective sources for those acquisitions (such as subcontracts, purchase orders, material order, etc.) exceeding the threshold set forth in FAR 15.403-4 and not otherwise exempt, in accordance with FAR 15.403-1(b) (*i.e.*, adequate price competition, commercial items, prices set by law or regulation or waiver). Also provide data showing the basis for establishing source and reasonableness of price. In addition, provide a summary of your cost analysis and a copy of certified cost or pricing data submitted by the prospective source in support of each subcontract, or purchase order that is the lower of either $12.5 million or more, or both more than the pertinent certified cost or pricing data threshold and more than 10 percent of the prime contractor's proposed price. Also submit any information reasonably required to explain your estimating process (including the judgmental factors applied and the mathematical or other methods used in the estimate, including those used in projecting from known data, and the nature and amount of any contingencies included in the price). The Contracting Officer may require you to submit cost or pricing data in support of proposals in lower amounts. Subcontractor certified cost or pricing data must be accurate, complete and current as of the date of final price agreement, or an earlier date agreed upon by the parties, given on the prime contractor's Certificate of Current Cost or Pricing Data. The prime contractor is responsible for updating a prospective subcontractor's data. For standard commercial items fabricated by the offeror that are generally stocked in inventory, provide a separate cost breakdown, if priced based on cost. For interorganizational transfers priced at cost, provide a separate breakdown of cost elements. Analyze the certified cost or pricing data and submit the results of your analysis of the prospective source's proposal. When submission of a prospective source's certified cost or pricing data is required as described in this paragraph, it must be included as part of your own certified cost or pricing data. You must also submit any data other than certified cost or pricing data obtained from a subcontractor, either actually or by specific identification, along with the results of any analysis performed on that data.

B. *Direct Labor*. Provide a time-phased (*e.g.,* monthly, quarterly, etc.) breakdown of labor hours, rates, and cost by appropriate category, and furnish bases for estimates.

C. *Indirect Costs*. Indicate how you have computed and applied your indirect costs, including cost breakdowns. Show trends and budgetary data to provide a basis for evaluating the reasonableness of proposed rates. Indicate the rates used and provide an appropriate explanation.

D. *Other Costs*. List all other costs not otherwise included in the categories described above (*e.g.*, special tooling, travel, computer and consultant services, preservation, packaging and packing, spoilage and rework, and Federal excise tax on finished articles) and provide bases for pricing.

E. *Royalties*. If royalties exceed $1,500, you must provide the following information on a separate page for each separate royalty or license fee:

(1) Name and address of licensor.

(2) Date of license agreement.

(3) Patent numbers.

(4) Patent application serial numbers, or other basis on which the royalty is payable.

(5) Brief description (including any part or model numbers of each contract item or component on which the royalty is payable)

(6) Percentage or dollar rate of royalty per unit.

(7) Unit price of contract item.

(8) Number of units.

(9) Total dollar amount of royalties.

(10) If specifically requested by the Contracting Officer, a copy of the current license agreement and identification of applicable claims of specific patents (see FAR 27.202 and 31.205-37).

F. *Facilities Capital Cost of Money.* When you elect to claim facilities capital cost of money as an allowable cost, you must submit Form CASB-CMF and show the calculation of the proposed amount (see FAR 31.205-10).

III. Formats for Submission of Line Item Summaries

A. *New Contracts (including letter contracts).*

Cost Elements	Proposed Contract Estimate—Total Cost	Proposed Contract Estimate—Unit Cost	Reference
(1)	(2)	(3)	(4)

Column		Instruction
(1)		Enter appropriate cost elements.
(2)		Enter those necessary and reasonable costs that, in your judgment, will properly be incurred in efficient contract performance. When any of the costs in this column have already been incurred (*e.g.,* under a letter contract), describe them on an attached supporting page. When preproduction or startup costs are significant, or when specifically requested to do so by the Contracting Officer, provide a full identification and explanation of them.
(3)		Optional, unless required by the Contracting Officer.
(4)		Identify the attachment in which the information supporting the specific cost element may be found.
		(Attach separate pages as necessary.)

B. *Change Orders, Modifications, and Claims.*

Cost Elements	Estimated Cost of All Work Deleted	Cost of Deleted Work Already Performed	Net Cost To Be Deleted	Cost of Work Added	Net Cost of Change	Reference
(1)	(2)	(3)	(4)	(5)	(6)	(7)

Column		Instruction
(1)		Enter appropriate cost elements.
(2)		Include the current estimates of what the cost would have been to complete the deleted work not yet performed (not the original proposal estimates), and the cost of deleted work already performed.
(3)		Include the incurred cost of deleted work already performed, using actuals incurred if possible, or, if actuals are not available, estimates from your accounting records. Attach a detailed inventory of work, materials, parts, components, and hardware already purchased, manufactured, or performed and deleted by the change, indicating the cost and proposed disposition of each line item. Also, if you desire to retain these items or any portion of them, indicate the amount offered for them.
(4)		Enter the net cost to be deleted, which is the estimated cost of all deleted work less the cost of deleted work already performed. Column (2) minus Column (3) equals Column (4).

(5)		Enter your estimate for cost of work added by the change. When nonrecurring costs are significant, or when specifically requested to do so by the Contracting Officer, provide a full identification and explanation of them. When any of the costs in this column have already been incurred, describe them on an attached supporting schedule.
(6)		Enter the net cost of change, which is the cost of work added, less the net cost to be deleted. Column (5) minus Column (4) equals Column (6). When this result is negative, place the amount in parentheses.
(7)		Identify the attachment in which the information supporting the specific cost element may be found.
		(Attach separate pages as necessary.)

C. Price Revision/Redetermination.

CUTOFF DATE		NUMBER OF UNITS COMPLETED	NUMBER OF UNITS TO BE COMPLETED	CONTRACT AMOUNT	REDETERMINATION PROPOSAL AMOUNT		DIFFERENCE
(1)		(2)	(3)	(4)	(5)		(6)

COST ELEMENTS	INCURRED COST— PREPRODUCTION	INCURRED COST— COMPLETED UNITS	INCURRED COST—WORK IN PROGRESS	TOTAL INCURRED COST	ESTIMATED COST TO COMPLETE	ESTIMATED TOTAL COST	REFERENCE
(7)	(8)	(9)	(10)	(11)	(12)	(13)	(14)

(Use as applicable)

Column		Instruction
(1)		Enter the cutoff date required by the contract, if applicable.
(2)		Enter the number of units completed during the period for which experienced costs of production are being submitted.
(3)		Enter the number of units remaining to be completed under the contract.
(4)		Enter the cumulative contract amount.
(5)		Enter your redetermination proposal amount.
(6)		Enter the difference between the contract amount and the redetermination proposal amount. When this result is negative, place the amount in parentheses. Column (4) minus Column (5) equals Column (6).
(7)		Enter appropriate cost elements. When residual inventory exists, the final costs established under fixed-price-incentive and fixed-price-redeterminable arrangements should be net of the fair market value of such inventory. In support of subcontract costs, submit a listing of all subcontracts subject to repricing action, annotated as to their status.

(8)		Enter all costs incurred under the contract before starting production and other nonrecurring costs (usually referred to as startup costs) from your books and records as of the cutoff date. These include such costs as preproduction engineering, special plant rearrangement, training program, and any identifiable nonrecurring costs such as initial rework, spoilage, pilot runs, etc. In the event the amounts are not segregated in or otherwise available from your records, enter in this column your best estimates. Explain the basis for each estimate and how the costs are charged on your accounting records (*e.g.,* included in production costs as direct engineering labor, charged to manufacturing overhead). Also show how the costs would be allocated to the units at their various stages of contract completion.
(9)		Enter in Column (9) the production costs from your books and records (exclusive of preproduction costs reported in Column (8)) of the units completed as of the cutoff date.
(10)		Enter in Column (10) the costs of work in process as determined from your records or inventories at the cutoff date. When the amounts for work in process are not available in your records but reliable estimates for them can be made, enter the estimated amounts in Column (10) and enter in column (9) the differences between the total incurred costs (exclusive of preproduction costs) as of the cutoff date and these estimates. Explain the basis for the estimates, including identification of any provision for experienced or anticipated allowances, such as shrinkage, rework, design changes, etc. Furnish experienced unit or lot costs (or labor hours) from inception of contract to the cutoff date, improvement curves, and any other available production cost history pertaining to the item(s) to which your proposal relates.
(11)		Enter total incurred costs (Total of Columns (8), (9), and (10)).
(12)		Enter those necessary and reasonable costs that in your judgment will properly be incurred in completing the remaining work to be performed under the contract with respect to the item(s) to which your proposal relates.
(13)		Enter total estimated cost (Total of Columns (11) and (12)).
(14)		Identify the attachment in which the information supporting the specific cost element may be found.
		(Attach separate pages as necessary.)

Subpart 15.5—Preaward, Award, and Postaward Notifications, Protests, and Mistakes

15.501 Definition.

Day, as used in this subpart, has the meaning set forth at 33.101.

15.502 Applicability.

This subpart applies to competitive proposals, as described in 6.102(b), and a combination of competitive procedures, as described in 6.102(c). The procedures in 15.504, 15.506, 15.507, 15.508, and 15.509, with reasonable modification, should be followed for sole source acquisitions and acquisitions described in 6.102(d)(1) and (2).

15.503 Notifications to unsuccessful offerors.

(a) *Preaward notices—*

(1) *Preaward notices of exclusion from competitive range.* The contracting officer shall notify offerors promptly in writing when their proposals are excluded from the competitive range or otherwise eliminated from the competition. The notice shall state the basis for the determination and that a proposal revision will not be considered.

(2) *Preaward notices for small business programs.*

(i) In addition to the notice in paragraph (a)(1) of this section, the contracting officer shall notify each offeror in writing prior to award, upon completion of negotiations, determinations of responsibility, and, if necessary, the process in 19.304(d)—

(A) When using a small business set-aside (see Subpart 19.5);

(B) When a small disadvantaged business concern receives a benefit based on its disadvantaged status (see Subpart 19.11 and 19.1202) and is the apparently successful offeror;

(C) When using the HUBZone procedures in 19.1305 or 19.1307; or

(D) When using the service-disabled veteran-owned small business procedures in 19.1405.

(ii) The notice shall state—

(A) The name and address of the apparently successful offeror;

(B) That the Government will not consider subsequent revisions of the offeror's proposal; and

(C) That no response is required unless a basis exists to challenge the small business size status, disadvantaged status, HUBZone status, or service-disabled veteran-owned status of the apparently successful offeror.

(iii) The notice is not required when the contracting officer determines in writing that the urgency of the requirement necessitates award without delay or when the contract is entered into under the 8(a) program (see 19.805-2).

(b) *Postaward notices.*

(1) Within 3 days after the date of contract award, the contracting officer shall provide written notification to each offeror whose proposal was in the competitive range but was not selected for award (10 U.S.C. 2305(b)(5) and 41 U.S.C. 253b(c)) or had not been previously notified under paragraph (a) of this section. The notice shall include—

(i) The number of offerors solicited;

(ii) The number of proposals received;

(iii) The name and address of each offeror receiving an award;

(iv) The items, quantities, and any stated unit prices of each award. If the number of items or other factors makes listing any stated unit prices impracticable at that time, only the total contract price need be furnished in the notice. However, the items, quantities, and any stated unit prices of each award shall be made publicly available, upon request; and

(v) In general terms, the reason(s) the offeror's proposal was not accepted, unless the price information in paragraph (b)(1)(iv) of this section readily reveals the reason. In no event shall an offeror's cost breakdown, profit, overhead rates, trade secrets, manufacturing processes and techniques, or other confidential business information be disclosed to any other offeror.

(2) Upon request, the contracting officer shall furnish the information described in paragraph (b)(1) of this section to unsuccessful offerors in solicitations using simplified acquisition procedures in Part 13.

(3) Upon request, the contracting officer shall provide the information in paragraph (b)(1) of this section to unsuccessful offerors that received a preaward notice of exclusion from the competitive range.

15.504 Award to successful offeror.

The contracting officer shall award a contract to the successful offeror by furnishing the executed contract or other notice of the award to that offeror.

(a) If the award document includes information that is different than the latest signed proposal, as amended by the offeror's written correspondence, both the offeror and the contracting officer shall sign the contract award.

(b) When an award is made to an offeror for less than all of the items that may be awarded and additional items are being withheld for subsequent award, each notice shall state that the Government may make subsequent awards on those additional items within the proposal acceptance period.

(c) If the Optional Form (OF) 307, Contract Award, Standard Form (SF) 26, Award/Contract, or SF 33, Solicitation, Offer and Award, is not used to award the contract, the first page of the award document shall contain the Government's acceptance statement from Block 15 of that form, exclusive of the Item 3 reference language, and shall contain the contracting officer's name, signature, and date. In addition, if the award document includes information that is different than the signed proposal, as amended by the offeror's written correspondence, the first page shall include the contractor's agreement statement from Block 14 of the OF 307 and the signature of the contractor's authorized representative.

15.505 Preaward debriefing of offerors.

Offerors excluded from the competitive range or otherwise excluded from the competition before award may request a debriefing before award (10 U.S.C. 2305(b)(6)(A) and 41 U.S.C. 253b(f) - (h)).

(a)(1) The offeror may request a preaward debriefing by submitting a written request for debriefing to the contracting officer within 3 days after receipt of the notice of exclusion from the competition.

(2) At the offeror's request, this debriefing may be delayed until after award. If the debriefing is delayed until after award, it shall include all information normally provided in a postaward debriefing (see 15.506(d)). Debriefings delayed pursuant to this paragraph could affect the timeliness of any protest filed subsequent to the debriefing.

(3) If the offeror does not submit a timely request, the offeror need not be given either a preaward or a postaward debriefing. Offerors are entitled to no more than one debriefing for each proposal.

(b) The contracting officer shall make every effort to debrief the unsuccessful offeror as soon as practicable, but may refuse the request for a debriefing if, for compelling reasons, it is not in the best interests of the Government to conduct a debriefing at that time. The rationale for delaying the debriefing shall be documented in the contract file. If the contracting officer delays the debriefing, it shall be provided no later than the time postaward debriefings are provided under 15.506. In that event, the contracting officer shall include the information at 15.506(d) in the debriefing.

(c) Debriefings may be done orally, in writing, or by any other method acceptable to the contracting officer.

(d) The contracting officer should normally chair any debriefing session held. Individuals who conducted the evaluations shall provide support.

(e) At a minimum, preaward debriefings shall include—

(1) The agency's evaluation of significant elements in the offeror's proposal;

(2) A summary of the rationale for eliminating the offeror from the competition; and

(3) Reasonable responses to relevant questions about whether source selection procedures contained in the solicitation, applicable regulations, and other applicable authorities were followed in the process of eliminating the offeror from the competition.

(f) Preaward debriefings shall not disclose—

(1) The number of offerors;

(2) The identity of other offerors;

(3) The content of other offerors' proposals;

(4) The ranking of other offerors;

(5) The evaluation of other offerors; or

(6) Any of the information prohibited in 15.506(e).

(g) An official summary of the debriefing shall be included in the contract file.

15.506 Postaward debriefing of offerors.

(a)(1) An offeror, upon its written request received by the agency within 3 days after the date on which that offeror has received notification of contract award in accordance with 15.503(b), shall be debriefed and furnished the basis for the selection decision and contract award.

(2) To the maximum extent practicable, the debriefing should occur within 5 days after receipt of the written request. Offerors that requested a postaward debriefing in lieu of a preaward debriefing, or whose debriefing was delayed for compelling reasons beyond contract award, also should be debriefed within this time period.

(3) An offeror that was notified of exclusion from the competition (see 15.505(a)), but failed to submit a timely request, is not entitled to a debriefing.

(4)(i) Untimely debriefing requests may be accommodated.

(ii) Government accommodation of a request for delayed debriefing pursuant to 15.505(a)(2), or any untimely debriefing request, does not automatically extend the deadlines for filing protests. Debriefings delayed pursuant to 15.505(a)(2) could affect the timeliness of any protest filed subsequent to the debriefing.

(b) Debriefings of successful and unsuccessful offerors may be done orally, in writing, or by any other method acceptable to the contracting officer.

(c) The contracting officer should normally chair any debriefing session held. Individuals who conducted the evaluations shall provide support.

(d) At a minimum, the debriefing information shall include—

(1) The Government's evaluation of the significant weaknesses or deficiencies in the offeror's proposal, if applicable;

(2) The overall evaluated cost or price (including unit prices) and technical rating, if applicable, of the successful offeror and the debriefed offeror, and past performance information on the debriefed offeror;

(3) The overall ranking of all offerors, when any ranking was developed by the agency during the source selection;

(4) A summary of the rationale for award;

(5) For acquisitions of commercial items, the make and model of the item to be delivered by the successful offeror; and

(6) Reasonable responses to relevant questions about whether source selection procedures contained in the solicitation, applicable regulations, and other applicable authorities were followed.

(e) The debriefing shall not include point-by-point comparisons of the debriefed offeror's proposal with those of other offerors. Moreover, the debriefing shall not reveal any information prohibited from disclosure by 24.202 or exempt from release under the Freedom of Information Act (5 U.S.C. 552) including—

(1) Trade secrets;

(2) Privileged or confidential manufacturing processes and techniques;

(3) Commercial and financial information that is privileged or confidential, including cost breakdowns, profit, indirect cost rates, and similar information; and

(4) The names of individuals providing reference information about an offeror's past performance.

(f) An official summary of the debriefing shall be included in the contract file.

15.507 Protests against award.

(a) Protests against award in negotiated acquisitions shall be handled in accordance with Part 33. Use of agency protest procedures that incorporate the alternative dispute resolution provisions of Executive Order 12979 is encouraged for both preaward and postaward protests.

(b) If a protest causes the agency, within 1 year of contract award, to—

(1) Issue a new solicitation on the protested contract award, the contracting officer shall provide the information in paragraph (c) of this section to all prospective offerors for the new solicitation; or

(2) Issue a new request for revised proposals on the protested contract award, the contracting officer shall provide the information in paragraph (c) of this section to offerors that were in the competitive range and are requested to submit revised proposals.

(c) The following information will be provided to appropriate parties:

(1) Information provided to unsuccessful offerors in any debriefings conducted on the original award regarding the successful offeror's proposal; and

(2) Other nonproprietary information that would have been provided to the original offerors.

15.508 Discovery of mistakes.

Mistakes in a contractor's proposal that are disclosed after award shall be processed substantially in accordance with the procedures for mistakes in bids at 14.407-4.

15.509 Forms.

Optional Form 307, Contract Award, Standard Form (SF) 26, Award/Contract, or SF 33, Solicitation, Offer and Award, may be used to award negotiated contracts in which the signature of both parties on a single document is appropriate. Note however, if using the SF 26 for a negotiated procurement, block 18 is not to be used. If these forms are not used, the award document shall incorporate the agreement and award language from the OF 307.

Subpart 15.6—Unsolicited Proposals

15.600 Scope of subpart.

This subpart sets forth policies and procedures concerning the submission, receipt, evaluation, and acceptance or rejection of unsolicited proposals.

15.601 Definitions.

As used in this subpart—

Advertising material means material designed to acquaint the Government with a prospective contractor's present products, services, or potential capabilities, or designed to stimulate the Government's interest in buying such products or services.

Commercial item offer means an offer of a commercial item that the vendor wishes to see introduced in the Government's supply system as an alternate or a replacement for an existing supply item. This term does not include innovative or unique configurations or uses of commercial items that are being offered for further development and that may be submitted as an unsolicited proposal.

Contribution means a concept, suggestion, or idea presented to the Government for its use with no indication that the source intends to devote any further effort to it on the Government's behalf.

15.602   Policy.

It is the policy of the Government to encourage the submission of new and innovative ideas in response to Broad Agency Announcements, Small Business Innovation Research topics, Small Business Technology Transfer Research topics, Program Research and Development Announcements, or any other Government-initiated solicitation or program. When the new and innovative ideas do not fall under topic areas publicized under those programs or techniques, the ideas may be submitted as unsolicited proposals.

15.603   General.

(a) Unsolicited proposals allow unique and innovative ideas or approaches that have been developed outside the Government to be made available to Government agencies for use in accomplishment of their missions. Unsolicited proposals are offered with the intent that the Government will enter into a contract with the offeror for research and development or other efforts supporting the Government mission, and often represent a substantial investment of time and effort by the offeror.

(b) Advertising material, commercial item offers, or contributions, as defined in 15.601, or routine correspondence on technical issues, are not unsolicited proposals.

(c) A valid unsolicited proposal must—

(1) Be innovative and unique;

(2) Be independently originated and developed by the offeror;

(3) Be prepared without Government supervision, endorsement, direction, or direct Government involvement;

(4) Include sufficient detail to permit a determination that Government support could be worthwhile and the proposed work could benefit the agency's research and development or other mission responsibilities;

(5) Not be an advance proposal for a known agency requirement that can be acquired by competitive methods; and

(6) Not address a previously published agency requirement.

(d) Unsolicited proposals in response to a publicized general statement of agency needs are considered to be independently originated.

(e) Agencies must evaluate unsolicited proposals for energy-savings performance contracts in accordance with the procedures in 10 CFR 436.33(b).

15.604   Agency points of contact.

(a) Preliminary contact with agency technical or other appropriate personnel before preparing a detailed unsolicited proposal or submitting proprietary information to the Government may save considerable time and effort for both parties (see 15.201). Agencies must make available to potential offerors of unsolicited proposals at least the following information:

(1) Definition (see 2.101) and content (see 15.605) of an unsolicited proposal acceptable for formal evaluation.

(2) Requirements concerning responsible prospective contractors (see subpart 9.1), and organizational conflicts of interest (see subpart 9.5).

(3) Guidance on preferred methods for submitting ideas/concepts to the Government, such as any agency: upcoming solicitations; Broad Agency Announcements; Small Business Innovation Research programs; Small Business Technology Transfer Research programs; Program Research and Development Announcements; or grant programs.

(4) Agency points of contact for information regarding advertising, contributions, and other types of transactions similar to unsolicited proposals.

(5) Information sources on agency objectives and areas of potential interest.

(6) Procedures for submission and evaluation of unsolicited proposals.

(7) Instructions for identifying and marking proprietary information so that it is protected and restrictive legends conform to 15.609.

(b) Only the cognizant contracting officer has the authority to bind the Government regarding unsolicited proposals.

15.605 Content of unsolicited proposals.

Unsolicited proposals should contain the following information to permit consideration in an objective and timely manner:

(a) Basic information including—

(1) Offeror's name and address and type of organization; e.g., profit, nonprofit, educational, small business;

(2) Names and telephone numbers of technical and business personnel to be contacted for evaluation or negotiation purposes;

(3) Identification of proprietary data to be used only for evaluation purposes;

(4) Names of other Federal, State, or local agencies or parties receiving the proposal or funding the proposed effort;

(5) Date of submission; and

(6) Signature of a person authorized to represent and contractually obligate the offeror.

(b) Technical information including—

(1) Concise title and abstract (approximately 200 words) of the proposed effort;

(2) A reasonably complete discussion stating the objectives of the effort or activity, the method of approach and extent of effort to be employed, the nature and extent of the anticipated results, and the manner in which the work will help to support accomplishment of the agency's mission;

(3) Names and biographical information on the offeror's key personnel who would be involved, including alternates; and

(4) Type of support needed from the agency; e.g., Government property or personnel resources.

(c) Supporting information including—

(1) Proposed price or total estimated cost for the effort in sufficient detail for meaningful evaluation;

(2) Period of time for which the proposal is valid (a 6-month minimum is suggested);

(3) Type of contract preferred;

(4) Proposed duration of effort;

(5) Brief description of the organization, previous experience, relevant past performance, and facilities to be used;

(6) Other statements, if applicable, about organizational conflicts of interest, security clearances, and environmental impacts; and

(7) The names and telephone numbers of agency technical or other agency points of contact already contacted regarding the proposal.

15.606   Agency procedures.

(a) Agencies shall establish procedures for controlling the receipt, evaluation, and timely disposition of unsolicited proposals consistent with the requirements of this subpart. The procedures shall include controls on the reproduction and disposition of proposal material, particularly data identified by the offeror as subject to duplication, use, or disclosure restrictions.

(b) Agencies shall establish agency points of contact (see 15.604) to coordinate the receipt and handling of unsolicited proposals.

15.606-1   Receipt and initial review.

(a) Before initiating a comprehensive evaluation, the agency contact point shall determine if the proposal—

(1) Is a valid unsolicited proposal, meeting the requirements of 15.603(c);

(2) Is suitable for submission in response to an existing agency requirement (see 15.602);

(3) Is related to the agency mission;

(4) Contains sufficient technical information and cost-related or price-related information for evaluation;

(5) Has overall scientific, technical, or socioeconomic merit;

(6) Has been approved by a responsible official or other representative authorized to obligate the offeror contractually; and

(7) Complies with the marking requirements of 15.609.

(b) If the proposal meets these requirements, the contact point shall promptly acknowledge receipt and process the proposal.

(c) If a proposal is rejected because the proposal does not meet the requirements of paragraph (a) of this subsection, the agency contact point shall promptly inform the offeror of the reasons for rejection in writing and of the proposed disposition of the unsolicited proposal.

15.606-2   Evaluation.

(a) Comprehensive evaluations shall be coordinated by the agency contact point, who shall attach or imprint on each unsolicited proposal, circulated for evaluation, the legend required by 15.609(d). When performing a comprehensive evaluation of an unsolicited proposal, evaluators shall consider the following factors, in addition to any others appropriate for the particular proposal:

(1) Unique, innovative and meritorious methods, approaches, or concepts demonstrated by the proposal;

(2) Overall scientific, technical, or socioeconomic merits of the proposal;

(3) Potential contribution of the effort to the agency's specific mission;

(4) The offeror's capabilities, related experience, facilities, techniques, or unique combinations of these that are integral factors for achieving the proposal objectives;

(5) The qualifications, capabilities, and experience of the proposed principal investigator, team leader, or key personnel critical to achieving the proposal objectives; and

(6) The realism of the proposed cost.

(b) The evaluators shall notify the agency point of contact of their recommendations when the evaluation is completed.

15.607   Criteria for acceptance and negotiation of an unsolicited proposal.

(a) A favorable comprehensive evaluation of an unsolicited proposal does not, in itself, justify awarding a contract without providing for full and open competition. The agency point of contact shall return an unsolicited proposal to the offeror, citing reasons, when its substance—

(1) Is available to the Government without restriction from another source;

(2) Closely resembles a pending competitive acquisition requirement;

(3) Does not relate to the activity's mission; or

(4) Does not demonstrate an innovative and unique method, approach, or concept, or is otherwise not deemed a meritorious proposal.

(b) The contracting officer may commence negotiations on a sole source basis only when—

(1) An unsolicited proposal has received a favorable comprehensive evaluation;

(2) A justification and approval has been obtained (see 6.302–1(a)(2)(i) for research proposals or other appropriate provisions of subpart 6.3, and 6.303–2(b));

(3) The agency technical office sponsoring the contract furnishes the necessary funds; and

(4) The contracting officer has complied with the synopsis requirements of subpart 5.2.

15.608   Prohibitions.

(a) Government personnel shall not use any data, concept, idea, or other part of an unsolicited proposal as the basis, or part of the basis, for a solicitation or in negotiations with any other firm unless the offeror is notified of and agrees to the intended use. However, this prohibition does not preclude using any data, concept, or idea in the proposal that also is available from another source without restriction.

(b) Government personnel shall not disclose restrictively marked information (see 3.104 and 15.609) included in an unsolicited proposal. The disclosure of such information concerning trade secrets, processes, operations, style of work, apparatus, and other matters, except as authorized by law, may result in criminal penalties under 18 U.S.C. 1905.

15.609   Limited use of data.

(a) An unsolicited proposal may include data that the offeror does not want disclosed to the public for any purpose or used by the Government except for evaluation purposes. If the offeror wishes to restrict the data, the title page must be marked with the following legend:

Use and Disclosure of Data

This proposal includes data that shall not be disclosed outside the Government and shall not be duplicated, used, or disclosed—in whole or in part—for any purpose other than to evaluate this proposal. However, if a contract is awarded to this offeror as a result of—or in connection with—the submission of these data, the Government shall have the right to duplicate, use, or disclose the data to the extent provided in the resulting contract. This restriction does not limit the Government's right to use information contained in these data if they are obtained from another source without restriction. The data subject to this restriction are contained in Sheets [*insert numbers or other identification of sheets*].

(b) The offeror shall also mark each sheet of data it wishes to restrict with the following legend: Use or disclosure of data contained on this sheet is subject to the restriction on the title page of this proposal.

(c) The agency point of contact shall return to the offeror any unsolicited proposal marked with a legend different from that provided in paragraph (a) of this section. The return letter will state that the proposal cannot be considered because it is impracticable for the Government to comply with the legend and that the agency will consider the proposal if it is resubmitted with the proper legend.

(d) The agency point of contact shall place a cover sheet on the proposal or clearly mark it as follows, unless the offeror clearly states in writing that no restrictions are imposed on the disclosure or use of the data contained in the proposal:

Unsolicited Proposal—Use of Data Limited

All Government personnel must exercise extreme care to ensure that the information in this proposal is not disclosed to an individual who has not been authorized access to such data in accordance with FAR 3.104, and is not duplicated, used, or disclosed in whole or in part for any purpose other than evaluation of the proposal, without the written permission of the offeror. If a contract is awarded on the basis of this proposal, the terms of the contract shall control disclosure and use. This notice does not limit the Government's right to use information contained in the proposal if it is obtainable from another source without restriction. This is a Government notice, and shall not by itself be construed to impose any liability upon the Government or Government personnel for disclosure or use of data contained in this proposal.

(e) Use the notice in paragraph (d) of this section solely as a manner of handling unsolicited proposals that will be compatible with this subpart. However, do not use this notice to justify withholding of a record, or to improperly deny the public access to a record, where an obligation is imposed by the Freedom of Information Act (5 U.S.C. 552). An offeror should identify trade secrets, commercial or financial information, and privileged or confidential information to the Government (see paragraph (a) of this section).

(f) When an agency receives an unsolicited proposal without any restrictive legend from an educational or nonprofit organization or institution, and an evaluation outside the Government is necessary, the agency point of contact shall—

(1) Attach a cover sheet clearly marked with the legend in paragraph (d) of this section;

(2) Change the beginning of this legend to read "All Government and non-Government personnel * * * "; and

(3) Require any non-Government evaluator to agree in writing that data in the proposal will not be disclosed to others outside the Government.

(g) If the proposal is received with the restrictive legend (see paragraph (a) of this section), the modified cover sheet shall also be used and permission shall be obtained from the offeror before release of the proposal for evaluation by non-Government personnel.

(h) When an agency receives an unsolicited proposal with or without a restrictive legend from other than an educational or nonprofit organization or institution, and evaluation by Government personnel outside the agency or by experts outside of the Government is necessary, written permission must be obtained from the offeror before release of the proposal for evaluation. The agency point of contact shall—

(1) Clearly mark the cover sheet with the legend in paragraph (d) or as modified in paragraph (f) of this section; and

(2) Obtain a written agreement from any non-Government evaluator stating that data in the proposal will not be disclosed to persons outside the Government.

APPENDIX 2

DFARS PART 215

Subpart 215.2—Solicitation and Receipt of Proposals and Information

215.203-70   Requests for proposals—tiered evaluation of offers.

(a) The tiered or cascading order of precedence used for tiered evaluation of offers shall be consistent with FAR part 19.

(b) Consideration shall be given to the tiers of small businesses (*e.g.* , 8(a), HUBZone small business, service-disabled veteran-owned small business, small business) before evaluating offers from other than small business concerns.

(c) The contracting officer is prohibited from issuing a solicitation with a tiered evaluation of offers unless—

(1) The contracting officer conducts market research, in accordance with FAR Part 10 and Part 210, to determine—

(i) Whether the criteria in FAR part 19 are met for setting aside the acquisition for small business; or

(ii) For a task or delivery order, whether there are a sufficient number of qualified small business concerns available to justify limiting competition under the terms of the contract; and

(2) If the contracting officer cannot determine whether the criteria in paragraph (c)(1) of this section are met, the contracting officer includes a written explanation in the contract file as to why such a determination could not be made (Section 816 of Public Law 109–163).

215.270   Peer Reviews.

Agency officials shall conduct Peer Reviews in accordance with 201.170.

Subpart 215.3—Source Selection

215.303   Responsibilities.

(b)(2) For high-dollar value and other acquisitions, as prescribed by agency procedures, the source selection authority shall approve a source selection plan before the solicitation is issued. Follow the procedures at PGI 215.303(b)(2) for preparation of the source selection plan.

215.304   Evaluation factors and significant subfactors.

(c)(i) In acquisitions that require use of the clause at FAR 52.219–9, Small Business Subcontracting Plan, other than those based on the lowest price technically acceptable source selection process (see FAR 15.101–2), the extent of participation of small businesses and historically black colleges or universities and minority institutions in performance of the contract shall be addressed in source selection. The contracting officer shall evaluate the extent to which offerors identify and commit to small business and historically black college or university and minority institution performance of the contract, whether as a joint venture, teaming arrangement, or subcontractor.

(A) See PGI 215.304(c)(i)(A) for examples of evaluation factors.

(B) Proposals addressing the extent of small business and historically black college or university and minority institution performance may be separate from subcontracting plans submitted pursuant to the clause at FAR 52.219–9 and should be structured to allow for consideration of offers from small businesses.

(C) When an evaluation assesses the extent that small businesses and historically black colleges or universities and minority institutions are specifically identified in proposals, the small businesses and historically black colleges or universities and minority institutions considered in the evaluation shall be listed in any subcontracting plan submitted pursuant to FAR 52.219–9 to facilitate compliance with 252.219–7003(g).

(ii) In accordance with 10 U.S.C. 2436, consider the purchase of capital assets (including machine tools) manufactured in the United States, in source selections for all major defense acquisition programs as defined in 10 U.S.C. 2430.

(iii) See 247.573–2(c) for additional evaluation factors required in solicitations for the direct purchase of ocean transportation services.

215.305   Proposal evaluation.

(a)(2) *Past performance evaluation.* When a past performance evaluation is required by FAR 15.304, and the solicitation includes the clause at FAR 52.219–8, Utilization of Small Business Concerns, the evaluation factors shall include the past performance of offerors in complying with requirements of that clause. When a past performance evaluation is required by FAR 15.304, and the solicitation includes the clause at FAR 52.219–9, Small Business Subcontracting Plan, the evaluation factors shall include the past performance of offerors in complying with requirements of that clause.

215.370   Evaluation factor for employing or subcontracting with members of the Selected Reserve.

215.370-1   Definition.

Selected Reserve, as used in this section, is defined in the provision at 252.215–7005, Evaluation Factor for Employing or Subcontracting with Members of the Selected Reserve.

215.370-2   Evaluation factor.

In accordance with Section 819 of the National Defense Authorization Act for Fiscal Year 2006 (Pub. L. 109–163), the contracting officer may use an evaluation factor that considers whether an offeror intends to perform the contract using employees or individual subcontractors who are members of the Selected Reserve. See PGI 215.370–2 for guidance on use of this evaluation factor.

215.370-3   Solicitation provision and contract clause.

(a) Use the provision at 252.215–7005, Evaluation Factor for Employing or Subcontracting with Members of the Selected Reserve, in solicitations that include an evaluation factor considering whether an offeror intends to perform the contract using employees or individual subcontractors who are members of the Selected Reserve.

(b) Use the clause at 252.215–7006, Use of Employees or Individual Subcontractors Who are Members of the Selected Reserve, in solicitations that include the provision at 252.215–7005. Include the clause in the resultant contract only if the contractor stated in its proposal that it intends to perform the contract using employees or individual subcontractors who are members of the Selected Reserve, and that statement was used as an evaluation factor in the award decision.

Subpart 215.4—Contract Pricing

215.402   Pricing policy.

Follow the procedures at PGI 215.402 when conducting cost or price analysis, particularly with regard to acquisitions for sole source commercial items.

215.403   Obtaining cost or price data.

215.403-1   Prohibition on obtaining cost or pricing data (10 U.S.C. 2306a and 41 U.S.C. 254b).

(b) *Exceptions to cost or pricing data requirements.* Follow the procedures at PGI 215.403–1(b).

(c) *Standards for exceptions from cost or pricing data requirements* —(1) *Adequate price competition.* For acquisitions under dual or multiple source programs:

(A) The determination of adequate price competition must be made on a case-by-case basis. Even when adequate price competition exists, in certain cases it may be appropriate to obtain additional information to assist in price analysis.

(B) Adequate price competition normally exists when—

(*i*) Prices are solicited across a full range of step quantities, normally including a 0–100 percent split, from at least two offerors that are individually capable of producing the full quantity; and

(*ii*) The reasonableness of all prices awarded is clearly established on the basis of price analysis (see FAR 15.404–1(b)).

(3) *Commercial items.*

(A) Follow the procedures at PGI 215.403–1(c)(3)(A) for pricing commercial items.

(B) By November 30th of each year, departments and agencies shall provide a report to the Director, Defense Procurement and Acquisition Policy (DPAP), ATTN: DPAP/CPF, of all contracting officer determinations that commercial item exceptions apply under FAR 15.403–1(b)(3), during the previous fiscal year, for any contract, subcontract, or modification expected to have a value of $15,000,000 or more. See PGI 215.403–1(c)(3)(B) for the format and guidance for the report. The Director, DPAP, will submit a consolidated report to the congressional defense committees.

(4) *Waivers.* (A) The head of the contracting activity may, without power of delegation, apply the exceptional circumstances authority when a determination is made that—

(*1*) The property or services cannot reasonably be obtained under the contract, subcontract, or modification, without the granting of the waiver;

(*2*) The price can be determined to be fair and reasonable without the submission of certified cost or pricing data; and

(*3*) There are demonstrated benefits to granting the waiver. Follow the procedures at PGI 215.403–1(c)(4)(A) for determining when an exceptional case waiver is appropriate, for approval of such waivers, for partial waivers, and for waivers applicable to unpriced supplies or services.

(B) By November 30th of each year, departments and agencies shall provide a report to the Director, DPAP, ATTN: DPAP/CPF, of all waivers granted under FAR 15.403–1(b)(4), during the previous fiscal year, for any contract, subcontract, or modification expected to have a value of $15,000,000 or more. See PGI 215.403–1(c)(4)(B) for the format and guidance for the report. The Director, DPAP, will submit a consolidated report to the congressional defense committees.

(C) DoD has waived the requirement for submission of cost or pricing data for the Canadian Commercial Corporation and its subcontractors.

(D) DoD has waived cost or pricing data requirements for nonprofit organizations (including education institutions) on cost-reimbursement-no-fee contracts. The contracting officer shall require—

(*1*) Submission of information other than cost or pricing data to the extent necessary to determine reasonableness and cost realism; and

(*2*) Cost or pricing data from subcontractors that are not nonprofit organizations when the subcontractor's proposal exceeds the cost or pricing data threshold at FAR 15.403–4(a)(1).

215.403-3   Requiring information other than cost or pricing data.
Follow the procedures at PGI 215.403–3.

215.404   Proposal analysis.

215.404-1   Proposal analysis techniques.
(1) Follow the procedures at PGI 215.404–1 for proposal analysis.
(2) For spare parts or support equipment, perform an analysis of—

(i) Those line items where the proposed price exceeds by 25 percent or more the lowest price the Government has paid within the most recent 12-month period based on reasonably available information;

(ii) Those line items where a comparison of the item description and the proposal price indicates a potential for overpricing;

(iii) Significant high-dollar-value items. If there are no obvious high-dollar-value items, include an analysis of a random sample of items; and

(iv) A random sample of the remaining low-dollar value items. Sample size may be determined by subjective judgment, e.g., experience with the offeror and the reliability of its estimating and accounting systems.

215.404-2   Information to support proposal analysis.

See PGI 215.404–2 for guidance on obtaining field pricing or audit assistance.

215.404-3   Subcontract pricing considerations.

Follow the procedures at PGI 215.404–3 when reviewing a subcontractor's proposal.

215.404-4   Profit.

(b) *Policy.* (1) Contracting officers shall use a structured approach for developing a prenegotiation profit or fee objective on any negotiated contract action when cost or pricing data is obtained, except for cost-plus-award-fee contracts (see 215.404–74, 216.405–2, and FAR 16.405–2) or contracts with Federally Funded Research and Development Centers (FFRDCs) (see 215.404–75). There are three structured approaches—

(A) The weighted guidelines method;

(B) The modified weighted guidelines method; and

(C) An alternate structured approach.

(c) *Contracting officer responsibilities.* (1) Also, do not perform a profit analysis when assessing cost realism in competitive acquisitions.

(2) When using a structured approach, the contracting officer—

(A) Shall use the weighted guidelines method (see 215.404–71), except as provided in paragraphs (c)(2)(B) and (c)(2)(C) of this subsection.

(B) Shall use the modified weighted guidelines method (see 215.404–72) on contract actions with nonprofit organizations other than FFRDCs.

(C) May use an alternate structured approach (see 215.404–73) when—

(*1*) The contract action is—

(*i*) At or below the cost or pricing data threshold (see FAR 15.403–4(a)(1));

(*ii*) For architect-engineer or construction work;

(*iii*) Primarily for delivery of material from subcontractors; or

(*iv*) A termination settlement; or

(2) The weighted guidelines method does not produce a reasonable overall profit objective and the head of the contracting activity approves use of the alternate approach in writing.

(D) Shall use the weighted guidelines method to establish a basic profit rate under a formula-type pricing agreement, and may then use the basic rate on all actions under the agreement, provided that conditions affecting profit do not change.

(E) Shall document the profit analysis in the contract file.

(5) Although specific agreement on the applied weights or values for individual profit factors shall not be attempted, the contracting officer may encourage the contractor to—

(A) Present the details of its proposed profit amounts in the weighted guidelines format or similar structured approached; and

(B) Use the weighted guidelines method in developing profit objectives for negotiated subcontracts.

(6) The contracting officer must also verify that relevant variables have not materially changed (e.g., performance risk, interest rates, progress payment rates, distribution of facilities capital).

(d) *Profit-analysis factors* —(1) *Common factors.* The common factors are embodied in the DoD structured approaches and need not be further considered by the contracting officer.

215.404-70   DD Form 1547, Record of Weighted Guidelines Method Application.

Follow the procedures at PGI 215.404–70 for use of DD Form 1547 whenever a structured approach to profit analysis is required.

215.404-71   Weighted guidelines method.

215.404-71-1   General.

(a) The weighted guidelines method focuses on four profit factors—

(1) Performance risk;

(2) Contract type risk;

(3) Facilities capital employed; and

(4) Cost efficiency.

(b) The contracting officer assigns values to each profit factor; the value multiplied by the base results in the profit objective for that factor. Except for the cost efficiency special factor, each profit factor has a normal value and a designated range of values. The normal value is representative of average conditions on the prospective contract when compared to all goods and services acquired by DoD. The designated range provides values based on above normal or below normal conditions. In the price negotiation documentation, the contracting officer need not explain assignment of the normal value, but should address conditions that justify assignment of other than the normal value. The cost efficiency special factor has no normal value. The contracting officer shall exercise sound business judgment in selecting a value when this special factor is used (see 215.404–71–5).

215.404-71-2 Performance risk.

(a) *Description.* This profit factor addresses the contractor's degree of risk in fulfilling the contract requirements. The factor consists of two parts:

(1) Technical—the technical uncertainties of performance.

(2) Management/cost control—the degree of management effort necessary—

(i) To ensure that contract requirements are met; and

(ii) To reduce and control costs.

(b) *Determination.* The following extract from the DD Form 1547 is annotated to describe the process.

	Contractor risk factors	Assigned weighting	Assigned value	Base (item 20)	Profit objective
21	Technical	(1)	(2)	N/A	N/A
22	Management/Cost Control	(1)	(2)	N/A	N/A
23	Performance Risk (Composite)	N/A	(3)	(4)	(5)

(1) Assign a weight (percentage) to each element according to its input to the total performance risk. The total of the two weights equals 100 percent.

(2) Select a value for each element from the list in paragraph (c) of this subsection using the evaluation criteria in paragraphs (d) and (e) of this subsection.

(3) Compute the composite as shown in the following example:

	Assigned weighting (percent)	Assigned value (percent)	Weighted value (percent)
Technical	60	5.0	3.0
Management/Cost Control	40	4.0	1.6
Composite Value	100		4.6

(4) Insert the amount from Block 20 of the DD Form 1547. Block 20 is total contract costs, excluding facilities capital cost of money.

(5) Multiply (3) by (4).

(c) Values: Normal and designated ranges.

	Normal value (percent)	Designated range
Standard	5	3% to 7%
Technology Incentive	9	7% to 11%

(1) *Standard.* The standard designated range should apply to most contracts.

(2) *Technology incentive.* For the technical factor only, contracting officers may use the technology incentive range for acquisitions that include development, production, or application of innovative new technologies. The technology incentive range does not apply to efforts restricted to studies, analyses, or demonstrations that have a technical report as their primary deliverable.

(d) *Evaluation criteria for technical.* (1) Review the contract requirements and focus on the critical performance elements in the statement of work or specifications. Factors to consider include—

(i) Technology being applied or developed by the contractor;

(ii) Technical complexity;

(iii) Program maturity;

(iv) Performance specifications and tolerances;

(v) Delivery schedule; and

(vi) Extent of a warranty or guarantee.

(2) *Above normal conditions.* (i) The contracting officer may assign a higher than normal value in those cases where there is a substantial technical risk. Indicators are—

(A) Items are being manufactured using specifications with stringent tolerance limits;

(B) The efforts require highly skilled personnel or require the use of state-of-the-art machinery;

(C) The services and analytical efforts are extremely important to the Government and must be performed to exacting standards;

(D) The contractor's independent development and investment has reduced the Government's risk or cost;

(E) The contractor has accepted an accelerated delivery schedule to meet DoD requirements; or

(F) The contractor has assumed additional risk through warranty provisions.

(ii) Extremely complex, vital efforts to overcome difficult technical obstacles that require personnel with exceptional abilities, experience, and professional credentials may justify a value significantly above normal.

(iii) The following may justify a maximum value—

(A) Development or initial production of a new item, particularly if performance or quality specifications are tight; or

(B) A high degree of development or production concurrency.

(3) *Below normal conditions.* (i) The contracting officer may assign a lower than normal value in those cases where the technical risk is low. Indicators are—

(A) Requirements are relatively simple;

(B) Technology is not complex;

(C) Efforts do not require highly skilled personnel;

(D) Efforts are routine;

(E) Programs are mature; or

(F) Acquisition is a follow-on effort or a repetitive type acquisition.

(ii) The contracting officer may assign a value significantly below normal for—

(A) Routine services;

(B) Production of simple items;

(C) Rote entry or routine integration of Government-furnished information; or

(D) Simple operations with Government-furnished property.

(4) *Technology incentive range.* (i) The contracting officer may assign values within the technology incentive range when contract performance includes the introduction of new, significant technological innovation. Use the technology incentive range only for the most innovative contract efforts. Innovation may be in the form of—

(A) Development or application of new technology that fundamentally changes the characteristics of an existing product or system and that results in increased technical performance, improved reliability, or reduced costs; or

(B) New products or systems that contain significant technological advances over the products or systems they are replacing.

(ii) When selecting a value within the technology incentive range, the contracting officer should consider the relative value of the proposed innovation to the acquisition as a whole. When the innovation represents a minor benefit, the contracting officer should consider using values less than the norm. For innovative efforts that will have a major positive impact on the product or program, the contracting officer may use values above the norm.

(e) *Evaluation criteria for management/cost control.* (1) The contracting officer should evaluate—

(i) The contractor's management and internal control systems using contracting office information and reviews made by field contract administration offices or other DoD field offices;

(ii) The management involvement expected on the prospective contract action;

(iii) The degree of cost mix as an indication of the types of resources applied and value added by the contractor;

(iv) The contractor's support of Federal socioeconomic programs;

(v) The expected reliability of the contractor's cost estimates (including the contractor's cost estimating system);

(vi) The adequacy of the contractor's management approach to controlling cost and schedule; and

(vii) Any other factors that affect the contractor's ability to meet the cost targets (e.g., foreign currency exchange rates and inflation rates).

(2) *Above normal conditions.* (i) The contracting officer may assign a higher than normal value when there is a high degree of management effort. Indicators of this are—

(A) The contractor's value added is both considerable and reasonably difficult;

(B) The effort involves a high degree of integration or coordination;

(C) The contractor has a good record of past performance;

(D) The contractor has a substantial record of active participation in Federal socioeconomic programs;

(E) The contractor provides fully documented and reliable cost estimates;

(F) The contractor makes appropriate make-or-buy decisions; or

(G) The contractor has a proven record of cost tracking and control.

(ii) The contracting officer may justify a maximum value when the effort—

(A) Requires large scale integration of the most complex nature;

(B) Involves major international activities with significant management coordination (e.g., offsets with foreign vendors); or

(C) Has critically important milestones.

(3) *Below normal conditions.* (i) The contracting officer may assign a lower than normal value when the management effort is minimal. Indicators of this are—

(A) The program is mature and many end item deliveries have been made;

(B) The contractor adds minimal value to an item;

(C) The efforts are routine and require minimal supervision;

(D) The contractor provides poor quality, untimely proposals;

(E) The contractor fails to provide an adequate analysis of subcontractor costs;

(F) The contractor does not cooperate in the evaluation and negotiation of the proposal;

(G) The contractor's cost estimating system is marginal;

(H) The contractor has made minimal effort to initiate cost reduction programs;

(I) The contractor's cost proposal is inadequate;

(J) The contractor has a record of cost overruns or another indication of unreliable cost estimates and lack of cost control; or

(K) The contractor has a poor record of past performance.

(ii) The following may justify a value significantly below normal—

(A) Reviews performed by the field contract administration offices disclose unsatisfactory management and internal control systems (e.g., quality assurance, property control, safety, security); or

(B) The effort requires an unusually low degree of management involvement.

215.404-71-3 Contract type risk and working capital adjustment.

(a) *Description.* The contract type risk factor focuses on the degree of cost risk accepted by the contractor under varying contract types. The working capital adjustment is an adjustment added to the profit objective for contract type risk. It only applies to fixed-price contracts that provide for progress payments. Though it uses a formula approach, it is not intended to be an exact calculation of the cost of working capital. Its purpose is to give general recognition to the contractor's cost of working capital under varying contract circumstances, financing policies, and the economic environment.

(b) *Determination.* The following extract from the DD 1547 is annotated to explain the process.

Item	Contractor risk factors		Assigned value	Base (item 20)	Profit objective
24.	CONTRACT type risk		(1)	(2)	(3)
		Cost financed	Length factor	Interest rate	
25.	WORKING capital (4)	(5)	(6)	(7)	(8)

(1) Select a value from the list of contract types in paragraph (c) of this subsection using the evaluation criteria in paragraph (d) of this subsection.

(2) Insert the amount from Block 20, i.e., the total allowable costs excluding facilities capital cost of money.

(3) Multiply (1) by (2).

(4) Only complete this block when the prospective contract is a fixed-price contract containing provisions for progress payments.

(5) Insert the amount computed per paragraph (e) of this subsection.

(6) Insert the appropriate figure from paragraph (f) of this subsection.

(7) Use the interest rate established by the Secretary of the Treasury (see *http://www.treasurydirect.gov/govt/rates/tcir/tcir_opdirsemi.htm*). Do not use any other interest rate.

(8) Multiply (5) by (6) by (7). This is the working capital adjustment. It shall not exceed 4 percent of the contract costs in Block 20.

(c) *Values: Normal and designated ranges.*

Contract type		Normal value (percent)	Designated range (percent)
Firm-fixed-price, no financing	(1)	5.0	4 to 6.
Firm-fixed-price, with performance-based payments	(6)	4.0	2.5 to 5.5
Firm-fixed-price, with progress payments	(2)	3.0	2 to 4.
Fixed-price incentive, no financing	(1)	3.0	2 to 4.
Fixed-price incentive, with performance-based payments	(6)	2.0	0.5 to 3.5.
Fixed-price with redetermination provision	(3)		
Fixed-price incentive, with progress payments	(2)	1.0	0 to 2.
Cost-plus-incentive-free	(4)	1.0	0 to 2.
Cost-plus-fixed-fee	(4)	0.5	0 to 1.
Time-and-materials (including overhaul contracts priced on time-and-materials basis)	(5)	0.5	0 to 1.
Labor-hour	(5)	0.5	0 to 1.
Firm-fixed-price, level-of-effort	(5)	0.5	0 to 1.

(1) "No financing" means either that the contract does not provide progress payments or performance-based payments, or that the contract provides them only on a limited basis, such as financing of first articles. Do not compute a working capital adjustment.

(2) When the contract contains provisions for progress payments, compute a working capital adjustment (Block 25).

(3) For the purposes of assigning profit values, treat a fixed-price contract with redetermination provisions as if it were a fixed-price incentive contract with below normal conditions.

(4) Cost-plus contracts shall not receive the working capital adjustment.

(5) These types of contracts are considered cost-plus-fixed-fee contracts for the purposes of assigning profit values. They shall not receive the working capital adjustment in Block 25. However, they may receive higher than normal values within the designated range to the extent that portions of cost are fixed.

(6) When the contract contains provisions for performance-based payments, do not compute a working capital adjustment.

(d) *Evaluation criteria* —(1) *General.* The contracting officer should consider elements that affect contract type risk such as—

(i) Length of contract;

(ii) Adequacy of cost data for projections;

(iii) Economic environment;

(iv) Nature and extent of subcontracted activity;

(v) Protection provided to the contractor under contract provisions (e.g., economic price adjustment clauses);

(vi) The ceilings and share lines contained in incentive provisions;

(vii) Risks associated with contracts for foreign military sales (FMS) that are not funded by U.S. appropriations; and

(viii) When the contract contains provisions for performance-based payments—

(A) The frequency of payments;

(B) The total amount of payments compared to the maximum allowable amount specified at FAR 32.1004(b)(2); and

(C) The risk of the payment schedule to the contractor.

(2) *Mandatory.* The contracting officer shall assess the extent to which costs have been incurred prior to the definitization of the contract action (*also see* 217.7404–6(a) and 243.204–70–6). The assessment shall include any reduced contractor risk on both the contract before definitization and the remaining portion of the contract. When costs have been incurred prior to definitization, generally regard the contract type risk to be in the low end of the designated range. If a substantial portion of the costs have been incurred prior to definitization, the contracting officer may assign a value as low as 0 percent, regardless of contract type.

(3) *Above normal conditions.* The contracting officer may assign a higher than normal value when there is substantial contract type risk. Indicators of this are—

(i) Efforts where there is minimal cost history;

(ii) Long-term contracts without provisions protecting the contractor, particularly when there is considerable economic uncertainty;

(iii) Incentive provisions (e.g., cost and performance incentives) that place a high degree of risk on the contractor;

(iv) FMS sales (other than those under DoD cooperative logistics support arrangements or those made from U.S. Government inventories or stocks) where the contractor can demonstrate that there are substantial risks above those normally present in DoD contracts for similar items; or

(v) An aggressive performance-based payment schedule that increases risk.

(4) *Below normal conditions.* The contracting officer may assign a lower than normal value when the contract type risk is low. Indicators of this are—

(i) Very mature product line with extensive cost history;

(ii) Relative short-term contracts;

(iii) Contractual provisions that substantially reduce the contractor's risk;

(iv) Incentive provisions that place a low degree of risk on the contractor;

(v) Performance-based payments totaling the maximum allowable amount(s) specified at FAR 32.1004(b)(2); or

(vi) A performance-based payment schedule that is routine with minimal risk.

(e) *Costs financed.* (1) Costs financed equal total costs multiplied by the portion (percent) of costs financed by the contractor.

(2) Total costs equal Block 20 (i.e., all allowable costs excluding facilities capital cost of money), reduced as appropriate when—

(i) The contractor has little cash investment (e.g., subcontractor progress payments liquidated late in period of performance);

(ii) Some costs are covered by special financing provisions, such as advance payments; or

(iii) The contract is multiyear and there are special funding arrangements.

(3) The portion that the contractor finances is generally the portion not covered by progress payments, i.e., 100 percent minus the customary progress payment rate (see FAR 32.501). For example, if a contractor receives progress payments at 80 percent, the portion that the contractor finances is 20 percent. On contracts that provide progress payments to small businesses, use the customary progress payment rate for large businesses.

(f) *Contract length factor.* (1) This is the period of time that the contractor has a working capital investment in the contract. It—

(i) Is based on the time necessary for the contractor to complete the substantive portion of the work;

(ii) Is not necessarily the period of time between contract award and final delivery (or final payment), as periods of minimal effort should be excluded;

(iii) Should not include periods of performance contained in option provisions; and

(iv) Should not, for multiyear contracts, include periods of performance beyond that required to complete the initial program year's requirements.

(2) The contracting officer—

(i) Should use the following table to select the contract length factor;

(ii) Should develop a weighted average contract length when the contract has multiple deliveries; and

(iii) May use sampling techniques provided they produce a representative result.

Table

Period to perform substantive portion (in months)	Contract length factor
21 or less	.40
22 to 27	.65
28 to 33	.90
34 to 39	1.15
40 to 45	1.40
46 to 51	1.65
52 to 57	1.90
58 to 63	2.15
64 to 69	2.40
70 to 75	2.65
76 or more	2.90

(3) Example: A prospective contract has a performance period of 40 months with end items being delivered in the 34th, 36th, 38th, and 40th months of the contract. The average period is 37 months and the contract length factor is 1.15.

215.404-71-4   Facilities capital employed.

(a) *Description.* This factor focuses on encouraging and rewarding capital investment in facilities that benefit DoD. It recognizes both the facilities capital that the contractor will employ in contract performance and the contractor's commitment to improving productivity.

(b) *Contract facilities capital estimates.* The contracting officer shall estimate the facilities capital cost of money and capital employed using—

(1) An analysis of the appropriate Forms CASB–CMF and cost of money factors (48 CFR 9904.414 and FAR 31.205–10); and

(2) DD Form 1861, Contract Facilities Capital Cost of Money.

(c) *Use of DD Form 1861.* See PGI 215.404–71–4(c) for obtaining field pricing support for preparing DD Form 1861.

(1) *Purpose.* The DD Form 1861 provides a means of linking the Form CASB–CMF and DD Form 1547, Record of Weighted Guidelines Application. It—

(i) Enables the contracting officer to differentiate profit objectives for various types of assets (land, buildings, equipment). The procedure is similar to applying overhead rates to appropriate overhead allocation bases to determine contract overhead costs.

(ii) Is designed to record and compute the contract facilities capital cost of money and capital employed which is carried forward to DD Form 1547.

(2) *Completion instructions.* Complete a DD Form 1861 only after evaluating the contractor's cost proposal, establishing cost of money factors, and establishing a prenegotiation objective on cost. Complete the form as follows:

(i) List overhead pools and direct-charging service centers (if used) in the same structure as they appear on the contractor's cost proposal and Form CASB–CMF. The structure and allocation base units-of-measure must be compatible on all three displays.

(ii) Extract appropriate contract overhead allocation base data, by year, from the evaluated cost breakdown or prenegotiation cost objective and list against each overhead pool and direct-charging service center.

(iii) Multiply each allocation base by its corresponding cost of money factor to get the facilities capital cost of money estimated to be incurred each year. The sum of these products represents the estimated contract facilities capital cost of money for the year's effort.

(iv) Total contract facilities cost of money is the sum of the yearly amounts.

(v) Since the facilities capital cost of money factors reflect the applicable cost of money rate in Column 1 of Form CASB–CMF, divide the contract cost of money by that same rate to determine the contract facilities capital employed.

(d) *Preaward facilities capital applications.* To establish cost and price objectives, apply the facilities capital cost of money and capital employed as follows:

(1) *Cost of Money.* (i) *Cost Objective.* Use the imputed facilities capital cost of money, with normal, booked costs, to establish a cost objective or the target cost when structuring an incentive type contract. Do not adjust target costs established at the outset even though actual cost of money rates become available during the period of contract performance.

(ii) *Profit Objective.* When measuring the contractor's effort for the purpose of establishing a prenegotiation profit objective, restrict the cost base to normal, booked costs. Do not include cost of money as part of the cost base.

(2) *Facilities Capital Employed.* Assess and weight the profit objective for risk associated with facilities capital employed in accordance with the profit guidelines at 215.404–71–4.

(e) *Determination.* The following extract from the DD Form 1547 has been annotated to explain the process.

Item	Contractor facilities capital employed	Assigned value	Amount employed	Profit objective
26	Land	N/A	(2)	N/A
27	Buildings	N/A	(2)	N/A
28	Equipment	(1)	(2)	(3)

(1) Select a value from the list in paragraph (f) of this subsection using the evaluation criteria in paragraph (g) of this subsection.

(2) Use the allocated facilities capital attributable to land, buildings, and equipment, as derived in DD Form 1861, Contract Facilities Capital Cost of Money.

(i) In addition to the net book value of facilities capital employed, consider facilities capital that is part of a formal investment plan if the contractor submits reasonable evidence that—

(A) Achievable benefits to DoD will result from the investment; and

(B) The benefits of the investment are included in the forward pricing structure.

(ii) If the value of intracompany transfers has been included in Block 20 at cost (i.e., excluding general and administrative (G&A) expenses and profit), add to the contractor's allocated facilities capital, the allocated facilities capital attributable to the buildings and equipment of those corporate divisions supplying the intracompany transfers. Do not make this addition if the value of intracompany transfers has been included in Block 20 at price (i.e., including G&A expenses and profit).

(3) Multiply (1) by (2).

(f) *Values: Normal and designated ranges.* These are the normal values and ranges. They apply to all situations.

Asset type	Normal value (percent)	Designated range
Land	0	N/A
Buildings	0	N/A
Equipment	17.5	10 to 25

(g) *Evaluation criteria.* (1) In evaluating facilities capital employed, the contracting officer—

(i) Should relate the usefulness of the facilities capital to the goods or services being acquired under the prospective contract;

(ii) Should analyze the productivity improvements and other anticipated industrial base enhancing benefits resulting from the facilities capital investment, including—

(A) The economic value of the facilities capital, such as physical age, undepreciated value, idleness, and expected contribution to future defense needs; and

(B) The contractor's level of investment in defense related facilities as compared with the portion of the contractor's total business that is derived from DoD; and

(iii) Should consider any contractual provisions that reduce the contractor's risk of investment recovery, such as termination protection clauses and capital investment indemnification.

(2) *Above normal conditions.* (i) The contracting officer may assign a higher than normal value if the facilities capital investment has direct, identifiable, and exceptional benefits. Indicators are—

(A) New investments in state-of-the-art technology that reduce acquisition cost or yield other tangible benefits such as improved product quality or accelerated deliveries; or

(B) Investments in new equipment for research and development applications.

(ii) The contracting officer may assign a value significantly above normal when there are direct and measurable benefits in efficiency and significantly reduced acquisition costs on the effort being priced. Maximum values apply only to those cases where the benefits of the facilities capital investment are substantially above normal.

(3) *Below normal conditions.* (i) The contracting officer may assign a lower than normal value if the facilities capital investment has little benefit to DoD. Indicators are—

(A) Allocations of capital apply predominantly to commercial item lines;

(B) Investments are for such things as furniture and fixtures, home or group level administrative offices, corporate aircraft and hangars, gymnasiums; or

(C) Facilities are old or extensively idle.

(ii) The contracting officer may assign a value significantly below normal when a significant portion of defense manufacturing is done in an environment characterized by outdated, inefficient, and labor-intensive capital equipment.

215.404-71-5   Cost efficiency factor.

(a) This special factor provides an incentive for contractors to reduce costs. To the extent that the contractor can demonstrate cost reduction efforts that benefit the pending contract, the contracting officer may increase the prenegotiation profit objective by an amount not to exceed 4 percent of total objective cost (Block 20 of the DD Form 1547) to recognize these efforts (Block 29).

(b) To determine if using this factor is appropriate, the contracting officer shall consider criteria, such as the following, to evaluate the benefit the contractor's cost reduction efforts will have on the pending contract:

(1) The contractor's participation in Single Process Initiative improvements;

(2) Actual cost reductions achieved on prior contracts;

(3) Reduction or elimination of excess or idle facilities;

(4) The contractor's cost reduction initiatives (e.g., competition advocacy programs, technical insertion programs, obsolete parts control programs,

spare parts pricing reform, value engineering, outsourcing of functions such as information technology). Metrics developed by the contractor such as fully loaded labor hours (i.e., cost per labor hour, including all direct and indirect costs) or other productivity measures may provide the basis for assessing the effectiveness of the contractor's cost reduction initiatives over time;

(5) The contractor's adoption of process improvements to reduce costs;

(6) Subcontractor cost reduction efforts;

(7) The contractor's effective incorporation of commercial items and processes; or

(8) The contractor's investment in new facilities when such investments contribute to better asset utilization or improved productivity.

(c) When selecting the percentage to use for this special factor, the contracting officer has maximum flexibility in determining the best way to evaluate the benefit the contractor's cost reduction efforts will have on the pending contract. However, the contracting officer shall consider the impact that quantity differences, learning, changes in scope, and economic factors such as inflation and deflation will have on cost reduction.

215.404-72   Modified weighted guidelines method for nonprofit organizations other than FFRDCs.

(a) *Definition.* As used in this subpart, a nonprofit organization is a business entity—

(1) That operates exclusively for charitable, scientific, or educational purposes;

(2) Whose earnings do not benefit any private shareholder or individual;

(3) Whose activities do not involve influencing legislation or political campaigning for any candidate for public office; and

(4) That is exempted from Federal income taxation under section 501 of the Internal Revenue Code.

(b) For nonprofit organizations that are entities that have been identified by the Secretary of Defense or a Secretary of a Department as receiving sustaining support on a cost-plus-fixed-fee basis from a particular DoD department or agency, compute a fee objective for covered actions using the weighted guidelines method in 215.404–71, with the following modifications:

(1) *Modifications to performance risk (Blocks 21–23 of the DD Form 1547).* (i) If the contracting officer assigns a value from the standard designated range (see 215.404–71–2(c)), reduce the fee objective by an amount equal to 1 percent of the costs in Block 20 of the DD Form 1547. Show the net (reduced) amount on the DD Form 1547.

(ii) Do not assign a value from the technology incentive designated range.

(2) *Modifications to contract type risk (Block 24 of the DD Form 1547).* Use a designated range of −1 percent to 0 percent instead of the values in 215.404–71–3. There is no normal value.

(c) For all other nonprofit organizations except FFRDCs, compute a fee objective for covered actions using the weighted guidelines method in 215.404–71, modified as described in paragraph (b)(1) of this subsection.

215.404-73   Alternate structured approaches.

(a) The contracting officer may use an alternate structured approach under 215.404–4(c).

(b) The contracting officer may design the structure of the alternate, but it shall include—

(1) Consideration of the three basic components of profit—performance risk, contract type risk (including working capital), and facilities capital employed. However, the contracting officer is not required to complete Blocks 21 through 30 of the DD Form 1547.

(2) Offset for facilities capital cost of money.

(i) The contracting officer shall reduce the overall prenegotiation profit objective by the amount of facilities capital cost of money under Cost Accounting Standard (CAS) 414, Cost of Money as an Element of the Cost of Facilities Capital (48 CFR 9904.414). Cost of money under CAS 417, Cost of Money as an Element of the Cost of Capital Assets Under Construction (48 CFR 9904.417), should not be used to reduce the overall prenegotiation profit objective. The profit amount in the negotiation summary of the DD Form 1547 must be net of the offset.

(ii) This adjustment is needed for the following reason: The values of the profit factors used in the weighted guidelines method were adjusted to recognize the shift in facilities capital cost of money from an element of profit to an element of contract cost (see FAR 31.205–10) and reductions were made directly to the profit factors for performance risk. In order to ensure that this policy is applied to all DoD contracts that allow facilities capital cost of money, similar adjustments shall be made to contracts that use alternate structured approaches.

215.404-74   Fee requirements for cost-plus-award-fee contracts.

In developing a fee objective for cost-plus-award-fee contracts, the contracting officer shall—

(a) Follow the guidance in FAR 16.405–2 and 216.405–2;

(b) Not use the weighted guidelines method or alternate structured approach;

(c) Apply the offset policy in 215.404–73(b)(2) for facilities capital cost of money, i.e., reduce the base fee by the amount of facilities capital cost of money; and

(d) Not complete a DD Form 1547.

215.404-75   Fee requirements for FFRDCs.

For nonprofit organizations that are FFRDCs, the contracting officer—

(a) Should consider whether any fee is appropriate. Considerations shall include the FFRDC's—

(1) Proportion of retained earnings (as established under generally accepted accounting methods) that relates to DoD contracted effort;

(2) Facilities capital acquisition plans;

(3) Working capital funding as assessed on operating cycle cash needs; and

(4) Provision for funding unreimbursed costs deemed ordinary and necessary to the FFRDC.

(b) Shall, when a fee is considered appropriate, establish the fee objective in accordance with FFRDC fee policies in the DoD FFRDC Management Plan.

(c) Shall not use the weighted guidelines method or an alternate structured approach.

215.404-76 Reporting profit and fee statistics.

Follow the procedures at PGI 215.404–76 for reporting profit and fee statistics.

215.406-1 Prenegotiation objectives.

Follow the procedures at PGI 215.406–1 for establishing prenegotiation objectives.

215.406-3 Documenting the negotiation.

Follow the procedures at PGI 215.406–3 for documenting the negotiation.

215.407-2 Make-or-buy programs.

(e) *Program requirements* —(1) *Items and work included.* The minimum dollar amount is $1.5 million.

215.407-3 Forward pricing rate agreements.

(b)(i) Use forward pricing rate agreement (FPRA) rates when such rates are available, unless waived on a case-by-case basis by the head of the contracting activity.

(ii) Advise the ACO of each case waived.

(iii) Contact the ACO for questions on FPRAs or recommended rates.

215.407-4 Should-cost review.

See PGI 215.407–4 for guidance on determining whether to perform a program or overhead should-cost review.

215.407-5 Estimating systems.

215.407-5-70 Disclosure, maintenance, and review requirements.

(a) *Definitions.* (1) *Acceptable estimating system* is defined in the clause at 252.215–7002, Cost Estimating System Requirements.

(2) *Contractor* means a business unit as defined in FAR 2.101.

(3) *Estimating system* is as defined in the clause at 252.215–7002, Cost Estimating System Requirements.

(4) *Significant estimating system deficiency* means a shortcoming in the estimating system that is likely to consistently result in proposal estimates for total cost or a major cost element(s) that do not provide an acceptable basis for negotiation of fair and reasonable prices.

(b) *Applicability.* (1) DoD policy is that all contractors have acceptable estimating systems that consistently produce well-supported proposals that are acceptable as a basis for negotiation of fair and reasonable prices.

(2) A large business contractor is subject to estimating system disclosure, maintenance, and review requirements if—

(i) In its preceding fiscal year, the contractor received DoD prime contracts or subcontracts totaling $50 million or more for which cost or pricing data were required; or

(ii) In its preceding fiscal year, the contractor received DoD prime contracts or subcontracts totaling $10 million or more (but less than $50 million) for which cost or pricing data were required and the contracting officer, with concurrence or at the request of the ACO, determines it to be in the best interest of the Government (e.g., significant estimating problems are believed to exist or the contractor's sales are predominantly Government).

(c) *Responsibilities.* (1) The contracting officer shall—

(i) Through use of the clause at 252.215–7002, Cost Estimating System Requirements, apply the disclosure, maintenance, and review requirements to large business contractors meeting the criteria in paragraph (b)(2)(i) of this subsection;

(ii) Consider whether to apply the disclosure, maintenance, and review requirements to large business contractors under paragraph (b)(2)(ii) of this subsection; and

(iii) Not apply the disclosure, maintenance, and review requirements to other than large business contractors.

(2) The cognizant ACO, for contractors subject to paragraph (b)(2) of this subsection, shall—

(i) Determine the acceptability of the disclosure and system; and

(ii) Pursue correction of any deficiencies.

(3) The cognizant auditor, on behalf of the ACO, serves as team leader in conducting estimating system reviews.

(4) A contractor subject to estimating system disclosure, maintenance, and review requirements shall—

(i) Maintain an acceptable system;

(ii) Describe its system to the ACO:

(iii) Provide timely notice of changes in the system; and

(iv) Correct system deficiencies identified by the ACO.

(d) *Characteristics of an acceptable estimating system* —(1) *General.* An acceptable system should provide for the use of appropriate source data, utilize sound estimating techniques and good judgment, maintain a consistent approach, and adhere to established policies and procedures.

(2) *Evaluation.* In evaluating the acceptability of a contractor's estimating system, the ACO should consider whether the contractor's estimating system, for example—

(i) Establishes clear responsibility for preparation, review, and approval of cost estimates;

(ii) Provides a written description of the organization and duties of the personnel responsible for preparing, reviewing, and approving cost estimates;

(iii) Assures that relevant personnel have sufficient training, experience, and guidance to perform estimating tasks in accordance with the contractor's established procedures;

(iv) Identifies the sources of data and the estimating methods and rationale used in developing cost estimates;

(v) Provides for appropriate supervision throughout the estimating process;

(vi) Provides for consistent application of estimating techniques;

(vii) Provides for detection and timely correction of errors;

(viii) Protects against cost duplication and omissions;

(ix) Provides for the use of historical experience, including historical vendor pricing information, where appropriate;

(x) Requires use of appropriate analytical methods;

(xi) Integrates information available from other management systems, where appropriate;

(xii) Requires management review including verification that the company's estimating policies, procedures, and practices comply with this regulation;

(xiii) Provides for internal review of and accountability for the acceptability of the estimating system, including the comparison of projected results to actual results and an analysis of any differences;

(xiv) Provides procedures to update cost estimates in a timely manner throughout the negotiation process; and

(xv) Addresses responsibility for review and analysis of the reasonableness of subcontract prices.

(3) *Indicators of potentially significant estimating deficiencies.* The following examples indicate conditions that may produce or lead to significant estimating deficiencies—

(i) Failure to ensure that historical experience is available to and utilized by cost estimators, where appropriate;

(ii) Continuing failure to analyze material costs or failure to perform subcontractor cost reviews as required;

(iii) Consistent absence of analytical support for significant proposed cost amounts;

(iv) Excessive reliance on individual personal judgments where historical experience or commonly utilized standards are available;

(v) Recurring significant defective pricing findings within the same cost element(s);

(vi) Failure to integrate relevant parts of other management systems (e.g., production control or cost accounting) with the estimating system so that the ability to generate reliable cost estimates is impaired; and

(vii) Failure to provide established policies, procedures, and practices to persons responsible for preparing and supporting estimates.

(e) *Review procedures.* Follow the procedures at PGI 215.407–5–70(e) for establishing and conducting estimating system reviews.

(f) *Disposition of survey team findings.* Follow the procedures at PGI 215.407–5–70(f) for disposition of the survey team findings.

(g) *Impact of estimating system deficiencies on specific proposals.* (1) Field pricing teams will discuss identified estimating system deficiencies and their impact in all reports on contractor proposals until the deficiencies are resolved.

(2) The contracting officer responsible for negotiation of a proposal generated by an estimating system with an identified deficiency shall evaluate whether the deficiency impacts the negotiations. If it does not, the contracting officer should proceed with negotiations. If it does, the contracting officer should consider other alternatives, e.g.—

(i) Allowing the contractor additional time to correct the estimating system deficiency and submit a corrected proposal;

(ii) Considering another type of contract, e.g., FPIF instead of FFP;

(iii) Using additional cost analysis techniques to determine the reasonableness of the cost elements affected by the system's deficiency;

(iv) Segregating the questionable areas as a cost reimbursable line item;

(v) Reducing the negotiation objective for profit or fee; or

(vi) Including a contract (reopener) clause that provides for adjustment of the contract amount after award.

(3) The contracting officer who incorporates a reopener clause into the contract is responsible for negotiating price adjustments required by the clause. Any reopener clause necessitated by an estimating deficiency should—

(i) Clearly identify the amounts and items that are in question at the time of negotiation;

(ii) Indicate a specific time or subsequent event by which the contractor will submit a supplemental proposal, including cost or pricing data, identifying the cost impact adjustment necessitated by the deficient estimating system;

(iii) Provide for the contracting officer to unilaterally adjust the contract price if the contractor fails to submit the supplemental proposal; and

(iv) Provide that failure of the Government and the contractor to agree to the price adjustment shall be a dispute under the Disputes clause.

215.408   Solicitation provisions and contract clauses.

(1) Use the clause at 252.215–7000, Pricing Adjustments, in solicitations and contracts that contain the clause at—

(i) FAR 52.215–11, Price Reduction for Defective Cost or Pricing Data—Modifications;

(ii) FAR 52.215–12, Subcontractor Cost or Pricing Data; or

(iii) FAR 52.215–13, Subcontractor Cost or Pricing Data—Modifications.

(2) Use the clause at 252.215–7002, Cost Estimating System

requirements, in all solicitations and contracts to be award on the basis of cost or pricing data.

215.470   Estimated data prices.

(a) DoD requires estimates of the prices of data in order to evaluate the cost to the Government of data items in terms of their management, product, or engineering value.

(b) When data are required to be delivered under a contract, include DD Form 1423, Contract Data Requirements List, in the solicitation. See PGI 215.470(b) for guidance on the use of DD Form 1423.

(c) The contracting officer shall ensure that the contract does not include a requirement for data that the contractor has delivered or is obligated to deliver to the government under another contract or subcontract, and that the successful offeror identifies any such data required by the solicitation. However, where duplicate data are desired, the contract price shall include the costs of duplication, but not of preparation, of such data.

APPENDIX 3

PGI PART 215

Subpart 215.3—Source Selection

215.303 Responsibilities.

(b)(2) The source selection plan—

(A) Shall be prepared and maintained by a person designated by the source selection authority or as prescribed by agency procedures;

(B) Shall be coordinated with the contracting officer and senior advisory group, if any, within the source selection organization; and

(C) Shall include, as a minimum—

(1) The organization, membership, and responsibilities of the source selection team;

(2) A statement of the proposed evaluation factors and any significant subfactors and their relative importance;

(3) A description of the evaluation process, including specific procedures and techniques to be used in evaluating proposals; and

(4) A schedule of significant events in the source selection process, including documentation of the source selection decision and announcement of the source selection decision.

215.304 Evaluation factors and significant subfactors.

(c)(i)(A) Evaluation factors may include—

(1) The extent to which such firms are specifically identified in proposals;

(2) The extent of commitment to use such firms (for example, enforceable commitments are to be weighted more heavily than non-enforceable ones);

(3) The complexity and variety of the work small firms are to perform;

(4) The realism of the proposal;

(5) Past performance of the offerors in complying with requirements of the clauses at FAR 52.219-8, Utilization of Small Business Concerns, and 52.219-9, Small Business Subcontracting Plan; and

(6) The extent of participation of such firms in terms of the value of the total acquisition.

215.370 Evaluation factor for employing or subcontracting with members of the Selected Reserve.

215.370-2 Evaluation factor.

(1) This evaluation factor may be used as an incentive to encourage contractors to use employees or individual subcontractors who are members of the Selected Reserve.

(2) As with all evaluation factors and subfactors, the contracting officer should consider the impact the inclusion of this factor will have on the resulting contract and weight it accordingly.

(3) The solicitation provision at 252.215-7005 requires an offeror to provide supporting documentation when stating an intent to use members of the Selected Reserve in the performance of the contract.

Subpart 215.4—Contract Pricing

215.402 Pricing policy.

(1) Contracting officers must purchase supplies and services from responsible sources at fair and reasonable prices. The Truth in Negotiations Act (TINA) (10 U.S.C. 2306a and 41 U.S.C. 254b) requires offerors to submit cost or pricing data if a procurement exceeds the TINA threshold and none of the exceptions to cost or pricing data requirements applies. Under TINA, the contracting officer obtains accurate, complete, and current data from offerors to establish a fair and reasonable price (see FAR 15.403). TINA also allows for a price adjustment remedy if it is later found that a contractor did not provide accurate, complete, and current data.

(2) When cost or pricing data are not required, and the contracting officer does not have sufficient data or information to determine price reasonableness, FAR 15.402(a)(2) requires the offeror to provide whatever information or data the contracting officer needs in order to determine fair and reasonable prices.

(3) Obtaining sufficient data or information from the offeror is particularly critical in situations where an item is determined to be a commercial item in accordance with FAR 2.101 and the contract is being awarded on a sole source basis. This includes commercial sales information of items sold in similar quantities and, if such information is insufficient, cost data to support the proposed price.

(4) See PGI 215.404-1 for more detailed procedures for obtaining data or information needed to determine fair and reasonable prices.

215.403 Obtaining cost or pricing data. (No Text)

215.403-1 Prohibition on obtaining cost or pricing data (10 U.S.C. 2306a and 41 U.S.C. 254b).

(b) *Exceptions to cost or pricing data requirements.* Even if an exception to cost or pricing data applies, the contracting officer is still required to determine price reasonableness. In order to make this determination, the contracting officer may require information other than cost or pricing data, including information related to prices and cost information that would otherwise be defined as cost or pricing data if certified.

(c)(3) *Commercial items.*

(A)*(1)* Contracting officers must exercise care when pricing a commercial item, especially in sole source situations. The definition of a commercial item at FAR 2.101 requires the product or service be one—

(i) That is of a type customarily used by the general public or by non-governmental entities for other than governmental purposes; and

(ii) That—

(A) Has been sold, leased, or licensed to the general public;

(B) Has been offered for sale, lease, or license to the general public; or

(C) Has evolved or been modified from such products or services.

(2) Therefore, some form of prior non-government sales data, or the fact that the item was sold, leased, licensed, or offered for sale (either the specific product or service or the product or service from which the item evolved) must be obtained.

(3) The fact that an item has been determined to be a commercial item does not, in and of itself, prohibit the contracting officer from requiring information other than cost or pricing data. This includes information related to prices and cost information that would otherwise be defined as cost or pricing data if certified. Obtaining sufficient data or information from the offeror is particularly critical in situations where an item is determined to be a commercial item in accordance with FAR 2.101 and the contract is being awarded on a sole source basis. See PGI 215.404-1 for more detailed procedures for use when obtaining information and data from the offeror to determine price reasonableness.

(B)*(1) Report Content.* The annual report of commercial item exceptions to Truth in Negotiations Act (TINA) requirements shall include the following:

Title: Commercial Item Exceptions to TINA Requirements
(1) Contract number, including modification number, if applicable, and program name.
(2) Contractor name.
(3) Contracting activity.
(4) Total dollar amount of exception.
(5) Brief explanation of the basis for determining that the item(s) are commercial.
(6) Brief description of the specific steps taken to ensure price reasonableness.

(2) Pricing Actions Reported. The intent of this requirement is to report when a commercial item exception was determined. Therefore, the reporting of the commercial item exceptions are for pricing actions at the point the contracting officer makes a determination that the commercial item exception applies. For example—

> *Example 1*: The contracting officer determined that a commercial item exception applies for an entire indefinite-delivery indefinite-quantity (IDIQ) contract and expected the subsequent orders to exceed $15 million (based on the estimated maximum amount for the IDIQ or other supportable estimate of future orders). The organization would report this in accordance with DFARS 215.403-1(c)(3) for the period in which the IDIQ contract was awarded, and would include the total dollar amount of subsequent orders under the exception expected at the time of award.

> *Example 2*: The contracting officer awards an IDIQ contract with no commercial item exceptions anticipated. The contracting officer later modifies the contract for an order that will meet commercial item exceptions, and the subsequent order(s) are expected to exceed $15 million. Reporting (in the year the modification was issued) will include this IDIQ contract, the amount of this order, and any other expected future orders that will use the exception.

(i) For the above examples, after the contract is reported as receiving the exception with expected awards over $15 million, there would be no further report, e.g., when a subsequent order under that contract exceeds $15 million, because reporting for that contract was already accomplished.

(ii) When explaining price reasonableness in accordance with paragraph (c)(3)(B)*(1)*(6) of this subsection, if pricing was accomplished when the IDIQ contract was awarded, also explain how price reasonableness was determined. In circumstances where pricing will take place on the order at a future date, explain how pricing techniques at FAR 15.404-1 will be used, including obtaining cost information, if that is the only way to determine price reasonableness.

(4) *Waivers.*

(A) *Exceptional case TINA waiver.*

(1) In determining that an exceptional case TINA waiver is appropriate, the head of the contracting activity must exercise care to ensure that the supplies or services could not be obtained without the waiver and that the determination is clearly documented. *See DPAP March 23, 2007, policy memorandum.* The intent is not to relieve entities that normally perform Government contracts subject to TINA from an obligation to certify that cost or pricing data are accurate, complete, and current. Instead, waivers must be used judiciously, in situations where the Government could not otherwise obtain a needed item without a waiver. A prime example would be when a particular company offers an item that is essential to DoD's mission but is not available from other sources, and the company refuses to submit cost or pricing data. In such cases,

a waiver may be appropriate. However, the procuring agency should, in conjunction with the waiver, develop a strategy for procuring the item in the future that will not require such a waiver (e.g., develop a second source, develop an alternative product that satisfies the department's needs, or have DoD produce the item).

(2) Senior procurement executive coordination. An exceptional case TINA waiver that exceeds $100 million shall be coordinated with the senior procurement executive prior to granting the waiver.

(3) Waiver for part of a proposal. The requirement for submission of cost or pricing data may be waived for part of an offeror's proposed price when it is possible to clearly identify that part of the offeror's cost proposal to which the waiver applies as separate and distinct from the balance of the proposal. In granting a partial waiver, in addition to complying with the requirements in DFARS 215.403-1(c)(4), the head of the contracting activity must address why it is in the Government's best interests to grant a partial waiver, given that the offeror has no objection to certifying to the balance of its cost proposal.

(4) Waivers for unpriced supplies or services. Because there is no price, unpriced supplies or services cannot be subject to cost or pricing data certification requirements. The Government cannot agree in advance to waive certification requirements for unpriced supplies or services, and may only consider a waiver at such time as an offeror proposes a price that would otherwise be subject to certification requirements.

(B) The annual report of waiver of TINA requirements shall include the following:

Title: Waiver of TINA Requirements

(1) Contract number, including modification number, if applicable, and program name.

(2) Contractor name.

(3) Contracting activity.

(4) Total dollar amount waived.

(5) Brief description of why the item(s) could not be obtained without a waiver. *See DPAP March 23, 2007, policy memorandum.*

(6) Brief description of the specific steps taken to ensure price reasonableness.

(7) Brief description of the demonstrated benefits of granting the waiver.

215.403-3 Requiring information other than cost or pricing date.

To the extent that cost or pricing data are not required by FAR 15.403-4 and there is no other means for the contracting officer to determine that prices are fair and reasonable, the offeror is required to submit "information other than cost or pricing data" (see definition at FAR 2.101). In accordance with FAR 15.403-3(a), the offeror must provide appropriate information on the prices at which the same or similar items have previously been sold, adequate for determining the reasonableness of the price. The following clarifies these requirements:

(1) *Information other than cost or pricing data.* When cost or pricing data are not required, the contracting officer must obtain whatever information is necessary in order to determine the reasonableness of the price. The FAR defines this as "information other than cost or pricing data." When TINA does not apply and there is no other means of determining that prices are fair and reasonable, the contracting officer must obtain appropriate information on the prices at which the same or similar items have been sold previously, adequate for evaluating the reasonableness of the price. Sales data must be comparable to the quantities, capabilities, specifications, etc., of the product or service proposed. Sufficient steps must be taken to verify the integrity of the sales data, to include assistance from the Defense Contract Management Agency, the Defense Contract Audit Agency, and/or other agencies if required. See PGI 215.404-1 for more detailed procedures for obtaining information and data from offerors to determine price reasonableness.

(2) *Previously been sold.* Contracting officers shall request offerors to provide information related to prior sales (or "offered for sale") in support of price reasonableness determinations.

(3) *Adequacy of sales data for pricing.* The contracting officer must determine if the prior sales information is sufficient for determining that prices are fair and reasonable. If the sales information is not sufficient, additional information shall be obtained, including cost information if necessary. See PGI 215.404-1 for more detailed procedures for obtaining whatever data or information is needed to determine fair and reasonable prices.

(4) *Reliance on prior prices paid by the Government.* Before relying on a prior price paid by the Government, the contracting officer must verify and document that sufficient analysis was performed to determine that the prior price was fair and reasonable. Sometimes, due to exigent situations, supplies or services are purchased even though an adequate price or cost analysis could not be performed. The problem is exacerbated when other contracting officers assume these prices were adequately analyzed and determined to be fair and reasonable. The contracting officer also must verify that the prices previously paid were for quantities consistent with the current solicitation. Not verifying that a previous analysis was performed, or the consistencies in quantities, has been a recurring issue on sole source commercial items reported by oversight organizations. Sole source commercial items require extra attention to verify that previous prices paid on Government contracts were sufficiently analyzed and determined to be fair and reasonable. At a minimum, a contracting officer reviewing price history shall discuss the basis of previous prices paid with the contracting organization that previously bought the item. These discussions shall be documented in the contract file.

215.403-5 [Removed]

215.404 Proposal analysis.

215.404-1 Proposal analysis techniques.
    (a) *General.*
        (i) The objective of proposal analysis is to ensure that the final agreed-to price is fair and reasonable. When the contracting officer needs information to determine price reasonableness and the offeror will not furnish that information, use the following sequence of steps to resolve the issue:
        (A) The contracting officer should make it clear what information is required and why it is needed to determine fair and reasonable prices, and should be flexible in requesting data and information in existing formats with appropriate explanations from the offeror.
        (B) If the offeror refuses to provide the data, the contracting officer should elevate the issue within the contracting activity.
        (C) Contracting activity management shall, with support from the contracting officer, discuss the issue with appropriate levels of the offeror's management.
        (D) If the offeror continues to refuse to provide the data, contracting activity management shall elevate the issue to the head of the contracting activity for a decision in accordance with FAR 15.403-3(a)(4).
        (E) The contracting officer shall document the contract file to describe—
        (1) The data requested and the contracting officer's need for that data;
        (2) Why there is currently no other alternative but to procure the item from this particular source; and
        (3) A written plan for avoiding this situation in the future (e.g., develop a second source by...; bring the procurement in house to the Government by...).
        (F) Consistent with the requirements at FAR 15.304 and 42.1502 and the DoD Guide to Collection and Use of Past Performance Information, Version 3, dated May 2003, the contracting officer shall provide input into the past performance system, noting the offeror's refusal to provide the requested information.
        (ii) In some cases, supplies or services that are not subject to TINA may require a cost analysis (see paragraph (b)(iv) of this section). This will occur when a price analysis is not sufficient for determining prices to be fair and reasonable. In such cases, the contracting officer should consider the need for a Defense Contract Audit Agency audit of the cost data.
        (iii) Particular attention should be paid to sole source commercial supplies or services. While the order of preference at FAR 15.402 must be followed, if the contracting officer cannot determine price reasonableness without obtaining information or cost data from the offeror, at a minimum, the contracting officer must obtain appropriate information on the prices at which the same or similar items have been sold previously (often previous sales information was the basis of the commercial item determination and must be requested during price analysis of the information or data provided by the offeror). If previous sales

information is not sufficient to determine price reasonableness, the contracting officer must obtain "information other than cost or pricing data" and, if necessary, perform a cost analysis.

(b) *Price analysis.*

(i) Price analysis should generally be performed on supplies or services that are not subject to TINA. Available commercial sales, published catalogs or prices, etc., can sometimes be obtained through market research and can provide a basis for determining if the proposed prices are fair and reasonable.

(ii) In some cases, commercial sales are not available and there is no other market information for determining fair and reasonable prices. This is especially true when buying supplies or services that have been determined to be commercial, but have only been "offered for sale" or purchased on a sole source basis with no prior commercial sales upon which to rely. In such cases, the contracting officer must require the offeror to submit whatever cost information is needed to determine price reasonableness.

(iii) The following procedures shall be adhered to when executing the price analysis steps at FAR 15.404-1(b)(2):

(A) When the contracting officer is relying on information obtained from sources other than the offeror, the contracting officer must obtain and document sufficient information to confirm that previous prices paid by the Government were based on a thorough price and/or cost analysis. For example, it would not be sufficient to use price(s) from a database paid by another contracting officer without understanding the type of analysis that was performed to determine the price(s), and without verifying that the quantities were similar for pricing purposes. This does not necessarily need to be another analysis, but there should be coordination with the other office that acknowledges an analysis was performed previously.

(B) When purchasing sole source commercial items, the contracting officer must request non-Government sales data for quantities comparable to those in the solicitation. In addition, if there have not been any non-Government sales, "information other than cost or pricing data" shall be obtained and a price or cost analysis performed as required.

(iv) When considering advice and assistance from others, the contracting officer must pay particular attention to supplies or services that are not subject to TINA because they are "of a type" customarily used by the general public or "similar to" the item being purchased. There must be a thorough analysis of—

(A) The available price information for the similar-type item;

(B) The changes required by the solicitation; and

(C) The cost of modifying the base item.

(v) In some cases, the contracting officer will have to obtain "information other than cost or pricing data" from the offeror because there is not sufficient information from other sources to determine if prices are fair and reasonable. The contracting officer must use business judgment to determine the level of information needed from the offeror, but must ensure that the information is sufficient for making a reasonableness determination. For example, the offeror may have significant sales of the item in comparable quantities to non-Government entities, and that may be all the information needed, once the sales information is appropriately verified. On the other hand, there may be no non-Government sales and the contracting officer may be required to obtain cost information, and should do so. The request for additional information shall be limited to only that needed to determine prices to be fair and reasonable. For example, assume the proposal is 40 percent purchase parts, 30 percent labor, and the balance indirect rates. Also assume that the Defense Contract Management Agency (DCMA) has a forward pricing rate agreement with the offeror. It may be sufficient to limit requests to historical purchase records and/or vendor quotes and the proposed labor hours. Based on this information and the forward pricing rates from DCMA, the contracting officer may be able to determine price reasonableness.

(c) *Cost analysis.*

(i) When the contracting officer cannot obtain sufficient information to perform a price analysis in accordance with the pricing steps in FAR 15.404-1(b), a cost analysis is required.

(ii) When a solicitation is not subject to TINA and a cost analysis is required, the contracting officer must clearly communicate to the offeror the cost information that will be needed to determine if the proposed price is fair and reasonable.

(iii) To the extent possible, when cost or pricing data are not required to be submitted in accordance with Table 15-2 of FAR 15.408, the contracting officer should accept the cost data in a format consistent with the offeror's records.

(iv) The contracting officer must always consider the need for field pricing support from the Defense Contract Management Agency, the Defense Contract Audit Agency, and/or other agencies.

(e) *Technical analysis.* Requesting technical assistance is particularly important when evaluating pricing related to items that are "similar to" items being purchased or commercial items that are "of a type" or require "minor modifications." Technical analysis can assist in pricing these types of items by identifying any differences between the item being acquired and the "similar to" item. In particular, the technical review can assist in evaluating the changes that are required to get from the "similar to" item, to the item being solicited, so the contracting officer can determine sufficient price/cost analysis techniques when evaluating that the price for the item being solicited is fair and reasonable.

215.404-2 Information to support proposal analysis.

(a) *Field pricing assistance.*

(i) The contracting officer should consider requesting field pricing assistance (See PGI 215.404-2(c) for when audit assistance should be requested) for—

(A) Fixed-price proposals exceeding the cost or pricing data threshold;

(B) Cost-type proposals exceeding the cost or pricing data threshold from offerors with significant estimating system deficiencies (see DFARS 215.407-5-70(a)(4) and (c)(2)(i)); or

(C) Cost-type proposals exceeding $10 million from offerors without significant estimating system deficiencies.

(ii) The contracting officer should not request field pricing support for proposed contracts or modifications in an amount less than that specified in paragraph (a)(i) of this subsection. An exception may be made when a reasonable pricing result cannot be established because of—

(A) A lack of knowledge of the particular offeror; or

(B) Sensitive conditions (e.g., a change in, or unusual problems with, an offeror's internal systems).

(c) *Audit assistance for prime contracts or subcontracts.*

(i) The contracting officer should consider requesting audit assistance from DCAA for—

(A) Fixed-price proposals exceeding $10 million;

(B) Cost-type proposals exceeding $100 million.

(ii) The contracting officer should not request DCAA audit assistance for proposed contracts or modifications in an amount less than that specified in paragraph (c)(i) of this subsection unless there are exceptional circumstances explained in the request for audit. (See PGI 215.404-2(a)(i) for requesting field pricing assistance without a DCAA audit.)

(iii) If, in the opinion of the contracting officer or auditor, the review of a prime contractor's proposal requires further review of subcontractors' cost estimates at the subcontractors' plants (after due consideration of reviews performed by the prime contractor), the contracting officer should inform the administrative contracting officer (ACO) having cognizance of the prime contractor before the review is initiated.

(iv) Notify the appropriate contract administration activities when extensive, special, or expedited field pricing assistance will be needed to review and evaluate subcontractors' proposals under a major weapon system acquisition. If audit reports are received on contracting actions that are subsequently cancelled, notify the cognizant auditor in writing.

(v) Requests for audit assistance for subcontracts should use the same criteria as established in paragraphs (c)(i) and (c)(ii) of this subsection.

215.404-3 Subcontract Pricing Considerations

(a) The contracting officer should consider the need for field pricing analysis and evaluation of lower-tier subcontractor proposals, and assistance to prime contractors when they are being denied access to lower-tier subcontractor records.

(i) When obtaining field pricing assistance on a prime contractor' proposal, the contracting officer should request audit or field pricing assistance to analyze and evaluate the proposal of a subcontractor at any tier (notwithstanding availability of data or analyses performed by the prime contractor) if the contracting officer believes that such assistance is necessary to ensure the reasonableness of the total proposed price. Such assistance may be appropriate when, for example-

(A) There is a business relationship between the contractor and the subcontractor not conducive to independence and objectivity;

(B) The contractor is a sole source supplier and the subcontract costs represent a substantial part of the contract cost;

(C) The contractor has been denied access to the subcontractor' records;

(D) The contracting officer determines that, because of factors such as the size of the proposed subcontract price, audit or field pricing assistance for a subcontract at any tier is critical to a fully detailed analysis of the prime contractor's proposal;

(E) The contractor or higher-tier subcontractor has been cited for having significant estimating system deficiencies in the area of subcontract pricing, especially the failure to perform adequate cost analyses of proposed subcontract costs or to perform subcontract analyses prior to negotiation of the prime contract with the Government; or

(F) A lower-tier subcontractor has been cited as having significant estimating system deficiencies.

(ii) It may be appropriate for the contracting officer or the ACO to provide assistance to a contractor or subcontractor at any tier, when the contractor or higher-tier subcontractor has been denied access to a subcontractor' records in carrying out the responsibilities at FAR 15.404-3 to conduct price or cost analysis to determine the reasonableness of proposed subcontract prices. Under these circumstances, the contracting officer or the ACO should consider whether providing audit or field pricing assistance will serve a valid Government interest.

(iii) When DoD performs the subcontract analysis, DoD shall furnish to the prime contractor or higher-tier subcontractor, with the consent of the subcontractor reviewed, a summary of the analysis performed in determining any unacceptable costs included in the subcontract proposal. If the subcontractor withholds consent, DoD shall furnish a range of unacceptable costs for each element in such a way as to prevent disclosure of subcontractor proprietary data.

(iv) Price redeterminable or fixed-price incentive contracts may include subcontracts placed on the same basis. When the contracting officer wants to reprice the prime contract even though the contractor has not yet established final prices for the subcontracts, the contracting officer may negotiate a firm contract price-

(A) If cost or pricing data on the subcontracts show the amounts to be reasonable and realistic; or

(B) If cost or pricing data on the subcontracts are too indefinite to determine whether the amounts are reasonable and realistic, but-

(1) Circumstances require prompt negotiation; and

(2) A statement substantially as follows is included in the repricing modification of the prime contract:

As soon as the Contractor establishes firm prices for each subcontract listed below, the Contractor shall submit (in the format and with the level of detail specified by the Contracting Officer) to the Contracting Officer the subcontractor's cost incurred in performing the subcontract and the final subcontract price. The Contractor and the Contracting Officer shall negotiate an equitable adjustment in the total amount paid or to be paid under this contract to reflect the final subcontract price.

(v) If the selection of the subcontractor is based on a trade-off among cost or price and other non-cost factors rather than lowest price, the analysis supporting subcontractor selection should include a discussion of the factors considered in the selection (also see FAR 15.101 and 15.304 and DFARS 215.304). If the contractor's analysis is not adequate, return it for correction of deficiencies.

(vi) The contracting officer shall make every effort to ensure that fees negotiated by contractors for cost-plus-fixed-fee subcontracts do not exceed the fee limitations in FAR 15.404-4(c)(4).

215.404-70 DD Form 1547, Record of Weighted Guidelines Method Application.

(1) The DD Form 1547—

(i) Provides a vehicle for performing the analysis necessary to develop a profit objective;

(ii) Provides a format for summarizing profit amounts subsequently negotiated as part of the contract price; and

(iii) Serves as the principal source document for reporting profit statistics to DoD's management information system.

(2) The military departments are responsible for establishing policies and procedures for feeding the DoD-wide management information system on profit and fee statistics (see PGI 215.404-76).

(3) The contracting officer shall-

(i) Use and prepare a DD Form 1547 whenever a structured approach to profit analysis is required by DFARS 215.404-4(b) (see DFARS 215.404-71, 215.404-72, and 215.404-73 for guidance on using the structured approaches). Administrative instructions for completing the form are in PGI 253.215-70.

(ii) Ensure that the DD Form 1547 is accurately completed. The contracting officer is responsible for the correction of any errors detected by the management system auditing process.

215.404-71 Weighted guidelines method. (No Text)

215.404-71-4 Facilities capital employed.

(c) *Use of DD Form 1861- Field pricing support.*

(i) The contracting officer may ask the ACO to complete the forms as part of field pricing support.

(ii) When the Weighted Guidelines Method is used, completion of the DD Form 1861 requires information not included on the Form CASB-CMF, i.e., distribution percentages of land, building, and equipment for the business unit performing the contract. Choose the most practical method for obtaining this information, for example-

(A) Contract administration offices could obtain the information through the process used to establish factors for facilities capital cost of money or could establish advance agreements on distribution percentages for inclusion in field pricing reports;

      (B) The corporate ACO could obtain distribution percentages; or

      (C) The contracting officer could request the information through a solicitation provision.

215.404-76 Reporting profit and fee statistics.

    (1) Contracting officers in contracting offices that participate in the management information system for profit and fee statistics must send completed DD Forms 1547 on actions that exceed the cost or pricing data threshold, where the contracting officer used the weighted guidelines method, an alternate structured approach, or the modified weighted guidelines method, to their designated office within 30 days after contract award.

    (2) Participating contracting offices and their designated offices are-

Contracting Office	*Designated Office*
ARMY	
All	*
NAVY	
All	Commander Fleet and Industrial Supply Center, Norfolk Washington Detachment, Code 402 Washington Navy Yard Washington, DC 20374-5000
AIR FORCE	
Air Force Materiel Command (all field offices)	*

*Use the automated system, Profit Weighted Guidelines and Application at *https://www.wgl.wpafb.af.mil/wgl*, as required by your department.

(3) When the contracting officer delegates negotiation of a contract action that exceeds the cost or pricing data threshold to another agency (e.g., to an ACO), that agency must ensure that a copy of the DD Form 1547 is provided to the delegating office for reporting purposes within 30 days after negotiation of the contract action.

(4) Contracting offices outside the United States and its outlying areas are exempt from reporting.

(5) Designated offices send a quarterly (non-cumulative) report of DD Form 1547 data to-

Washington Headquarters Services Directorate for Information Operations and Reports (WHS/DIOR) 1215 Jefferson Davis Highway Suite 1204 Arlington, VA 22202-4302

(6) In preparing and sending the quarterly report, designated offices—

(i) Perform the necessary audits to ensure information accuracy;

(ii) Do not enter classified information;

(iii) Transmit the report using approved electronic means; and

(iv) Send the reports not later than the 30th day after the close of the quarterly reporting periods.

(7) These reporting requirements have been assigned Report Control Symbol DD-AT&L(Q)1751.

215.406-1 Prenegotiation objectives.

(a) Also consider—

(i) Data resulting from application of work measurement systems in developing prenegotiation objectives; and

(ii) Field pricing assistance personnel participation in planned prenegotiation and negotiation activities.

(b) Prenegotiation objectives, including objectives related to disposition of findings and recommendations contained in preaward and postaward contract audit and other advisory reports, shall be documented and reviewed in accordance with departmental procedures.

215.406-3 Documenting the negotiation.

(a)(7) Include the principal factors related to the disposition of findings and recommendations contained in preaward and postaward contract audit and other advisory reports.

(10) The documentation—

(A) Must address significant deviations from the prenegotiation profit objective;

(B) Should include the DD Form 1547, Record of Weighted Guidelines Application (see DFARS 215.404-70), if used, with supporting rationale; and

(C) Must address the rationale for not using the weighted guidelines method when its use would otherwise be required by DFARS 215.404-70.

215.407-4 Should-cost review.

(b) *Program should-cost review.*

(2) DoD contracting activities should consider performing a program should-cost review before award of a definitive contract for a major system as defined by DoDI 5000.2. See DoDI 5000.2 regarding industry participation.

(c) *Overhead should-cost review.*

(1) Contact the Defense Contract Management Agency (DCMA) (*http://www.dcma.mil/*) for questions on overhead should-cost analysis.

(2)(A) DCMA or the military department responsible for performing contract administration functions (e.g., Navy SUPSHIP) should consider, based on risk assessment, performing an overhead should-cost review of a contractor business unit (as defined in FAR 2.101) when all of the following conditions exist:

(1) Projected annual sales to DoD exceed $1 billion;

(2) Projected DoD versus total business exceeds 30 percent;

(3) Level of sole-source DoD contracts is high;

(4) Significant volume of proposal activity is anticipated;

(5) Production or development of a major weapon system or program is anticipated; and

(6) Contractor cost control/reduction initiatives appear inadequate.

(B) The head of the contracting activity may request an overhead should-cost review for a business unit that does not meet the criteria in paragraph (c)(2)(A) of this subsection.

(C) Overhead should-cost reviews are labor intensive. These reviews generally involve participation by the contracting, contract administration, and contract audit elements. The extent of availability of military department, contract administration, and contract audit resources to support DCMA-led teams should be considered when determining whether a review will be conducted. Overhead should-cost reviews generally should not be conducted at a contractor business segment more frequently than every 3 years.

215.407-5 Estimating systems. (No Text)

215.407-5-70 Disclosure, maintenance, and review requirements.

(e) *Review procedures.* Cognizant audit and contract administration activities shall—

(1) Establish and manage regular programs for reviewing selected contractors' estimating systems.

(2) Conduct reviews as a team effort.

(i) The contract auditor will be the team leader.

(ii) The team leader will—

(A) Coordinate with the ACO to ensure that team membership includes qualified contract administration technical specialists.

(B) Advise the ACO and the contractor of significant findings during the conduct of the review and during the exit conference.

(C) Prepare a team report.

(1) The ACO or a representative should—

(i) Coordinate the contract administration activity's review;

(ii) Consolidate findings and recommendations; and

(iii) When appropriate, prepare a comprehensive written report for submission to the auditor.

(2) The contract auditor will attach the ACO's report to the team report.

(3) Tailor reviews to take full advantage of the day-to-day work done by both organizations.

(4) Conduct a review, every 3 years, of contractors subject to the disclosure requirements. The ACO and the auditor may lengthen or shorten the 3-year period based on their joint risk assessment of the contractor's past experience and current vulnerability.

(f) *Disposition of survey team findings.*

(1) *Reporting of survey team findings.* The auditor will document the findings and recommendations of the survey team in a report to the ACO. If there are significant estimating deficiencies, the auditor will recommend disapproval of all or portions of the estimating system.

(2) *Initial notification to the contractor.* The ACO will provide a copy of the team report to the contractor and, unless there are no deficiencies mentioned in the report, will ask the contractor to submit a written response in 30 days, or a reasonable extension.

(i) If the contractor agrees with the report, the contractor has 60 days from the date of initial notification to correct any identified deficiencies or submit a corrective action plan showing milestones and actions to eliminate the deficiencies.

(ii) If the contractor disagrees, the contractor should provide rationale in its written response.

(3) *Evaluation of contractor's response.* The ACO, in consultation with the auditor, will evaluate the contractor's response to determine whether—

(i) The estimating system contains deficiencies that need correction;

(ii) The deficiencies are significant estimating deficiencies that would result in disapproval of all or a portion of the contractor's estimating system; or

(iii) The contractor's proposed corrective actions are adequate to eliminate the deficiency.

(4) *Notification of ACO determination.* The ACO will notify the contractor and the auditor of the determination and, if appropriate, of the Government's intent to disapprove all or selected portions of the system. The notice shall—

(i) List the cost elements covered;

(ii) Identify any deficiencies requiring correction; and

(iii) Require the contractor to correct the deficiencies within 45 days or submit an action plan showing milestones and actions to eliminate the deficiencies.

(5) *Notice of disapproval.* If the contractor has neither submitted an acceptable corrective action plan nor corrected significant deficiencies within 45 days, the ACO shall disapprove all or selected portions of the contractor's estimating system. The notice of disapproval must-

(i) Identify the cost elements covered;

(ii) List the deficiencies that prompted the disapproval; and

(iii) Be sent to the cognizant auditor, and each contracting and contract administration office having substantial business with the contractor.

(6) *Monitoring contractor's corrective action.* The auditor and the ACO will monitor the contractor's progress in correcting deficiencies. If the contractor fails to make adequate progress, the ACO shall take whatever action is necessary to ensure that the contractor corrects the deficiencies. Examples of actions the ACO can take are: bringing the issue to the attention of higher level management, reducing or suspending progress payments (see FAR 32.503-6), and recommending nonaward of potential contracts.

(7) *Withdrawal of estimating system disapproval.* The ACO will withdraw the disapproval when the ACO determines that the contractor has corrected the significant system deficiencies. The ACO will notify the contractor, the auditor, and affected contracting and contract administration activities of the withdrawal.

215.470 Estimated data prices.

(b)(i) The form and the provision included in the solicitation request the offeror to state what portion of the total price is estimated to be attributable to the production or development of the listed data for the Government (not to the sale of rights in the data). However, offerors' estimated prices may not reflect all such costs; and different offerors may reflect these costs in a different manner, for the following reasons-

(A) Differences in business practices in competitive situations;

(B) Differences in accounting systems among offerors;

(C) Use of factors or rates on some portions of the data;

(D) Application of common effort to two or more data items; and

(E) Differences in data preparation methods among offerors.

(ii) Data price estimates should not be used for contract pricing purposes without further analysis.

APPENDIX 4

GSAR PART 515

Subpart 515.2—Solicitation and Receipt of Proposals and Information

515.204 Contract format.

515.204-1 Uniform contract format.

(a) The uniform contract format is not required for leases of real property.

(b) Each solicitation and contract must include the two notices in paragraphs (b)(1) and (b)(2) of this section, except that acquisitions of interests in real property, must include only the notice in (b)(1):

(1) "The information collection requirements contained in this solicitation/contract are either required by regulation or approved by the Office of Management and Budget pursuant to the Paperwork Reduction Act and assigned OMB Control No. 3090–0163."

(2) "GSA's hours of operation are 8:00 a.m. to 4:30 p.m. Requests for preaward debriefings postmarked or otherwise submitted after 4:30 p.m. will be considered submitted the following business day. Requests for postaward debriefings delivered after 4:30 p.m. will be considered received and filed the following business day."

515.205 Issuing solicitations.

Potential sources, as used in FAR 15.205, include both of the following:

(a) The incumbent contractor, except when its written response to the notice of contract action under FAR subpart 5.2 states a negative interest.

(b) Offerors that responded to recent solicitations for the same or similar items.

515.209 Solicitation provisions and contract clauses.

515.209-70 Examination of records by GSA clause.

Clause for Other Than Multiple Award Schedules

(a) For other than multiple award schedule (MAS) contracts, insert the clause at 552.215–70, Examination of Records by GSA, in solicitations and contracts over $100,000, including acquisitions of leasehold interests in real property, that meet any of the following conditions:

(1) Involve the use or disposition of Government-furnished property.

(2) Provide for advance payments, progress payments based on cost, or guaranteed loan.

(3) Contain a price warranty or price reduction clause.

(4) Involve income to the Government where income is based on operations under the control of the contractor.

(5) Include an economic price adjustment clause where the adjustment is not based solely on an established, third party index.

(6) Are requirements, indefinite-quantity, or letter type contracts as defined in FAR part 6.

(7) Are subject to adjustment based on a negotiated cost escalation base.

(8) Contain the provision of FAR 52.223–4, Recovered Material Certification.

(b) You may modify the clause at 552.215–70 to define the specific area of audit (e.g., the use or disposition of Government-furnished property, compliance with the price reduction clause). Counsel and the Assistant Inspector General—Auditing or Regional Inspector General—Auditing, as appropriate, must concur in any modifications to the clause.

Clause for Multiple Award Schedules

(c) Insert the clause at 552.215–71, Examination of Records by GSA (Multiple Award Schedule), in solicitations and contracts for MAS contracts.

(d) With the Senior Procurement's Executive approval, you may modify the clause at 552.215–71 to provide for post-award access to and the right to examine records to verify that the pre-award/modification pricing, sales or other data related to the supplies or services offered under the contract which formed the basis for the award/modification was accurate, current, and complete. The following procedures apply:

(1) Such a modification of the clause must provide for the right of access to expire 2 years after award or modification.

(2) Before modifying the clause, you must make a determination that absent such access there is a likelihood of significant harm to the Government and submit it to the Senior Procurement Executive for approval.

(3) The determinations under paragraph (d)(2) of this section must be made on a schedule-by-schedule basis.

Subpart 515.3—Source Selection

515.305   Proposal evaluation.

(a) *Restrictions placed on a proposal by the submitter.* If you receive a proposal with more restrictive conditions than those in the provision at FAR 52.215–1(e), ask whether the submitter is willing to accept the conditions of the paragraph at FAR 52.215–1(e). If the submitter refuses, consult with legal counsel on whether to accept the proposal as marked or return it.

(b) *Actions before releasing proposal.* Before releasing any proposal to an evaluator you must take all the following actions:

(1) Obtain the signed original "Conflict of Interest Acknowledgment and Nondisclosure Agreement" from each Government and nongovernment individual serving as an evaluator. Use the Acknowledgment/Agreement in Figure 515.3–1.

(i) For employees of other Executive agencies, replace the reference in paragraph (c) of the Acknowledgement/Agreement to GSA's supplemental standards with a reference to the applicable agency.

(ii) for nongovernment evaluators, substitute paragraph (c) of the Acknowledgement/Agreement with the following language and delete paragraph (h):

(c) I have read and understand the requirements of subsection 27(a) and 27(b) of the Office of Federal Procurement Policy Act (41 U.S.C. 423).

(2) Attach to each proposal a cover page bearing the following notice:

Government Notice for Handling Proposals

To anyone receiving this proposal or proposal abstract:

(1) This proposal must be used and disclosed for evaluation purposes only.

(2) You must apply a copy of this Government notice to any reproduction or abstract of this proposal.

(3) You must comply strictly with any authorized restrictive notices which the submitter places on this proposal.

(4) You must *not* disclose this proposal outside the Government for evaluation purposes except to the extent authorized by, and in accordance with, the procedures in 48 CFR 515.305–71.

515.305-70   Use of outside evaluators.

(a) *Conditions.* To use outside evaluators, you must meet the restrictions in FAR 37.203 and 537.2.

(b) *Limitations on disclosing proposal information.* You may disclose proposal information outside the Government before the Government's decision as to contract award only to the extent authorized in this section. Disclosure and handling must comply with FAR 3.1 and 503.1.

(c) *Solicitation notice.* Include in the solicitation a notice substantially as follows:

Notice About Releasing Proposals

(1) The Government intends to disclose proposals received in response to this solicitation to nongovernment evaluators.

(2) Each evaluator will sign and provide to GSA a "Conflict of Interest Acknowledgment and Nondisclosure Agreement."

Figure 515.3–1—Conflict of Interest Acknowledgment and Nondisclosure Agreement

Conflict of Interest Acknowledgment and Nondisclosure Agreement

For proposals submitted in response to GAS solicitation no. _____, I agree to the following:

(a) To the best of my knowledge and belief, no conflict of interest exists that may either:

(1) Diminish my capacity to impartially review the proposals submitted.

(2) Or result in a biased opinion or unfair advantage.

(b) In making the above statement, I have considered all the following factors that might place me in a position of conflict, real or apparent, with the evaluation proceedings:

(1) All my stocks, bonds, other outstanding financial interests or commitments.

(2) All my employment arrangements (past, present, and under consideration).

(3) As far as I know, all financial interests and employment arrangements of my spouse, minor children, and other members of my immediate household.

(c) I have read and understand the requirements of the Standards of Ethical Conduct for Employees of the Executive Branch (5 CFR Part 2635) and Supplemental Standards of Ethical Conduct for Employees of the General Service Administration (5 CFR Part 6701).

(d) I have a continuing obligation to disclose any circumstances that may create an actual or apparent conflict of interest. If I learn of any such conflict, I will report it immediately to the Contracting Officer. I will perform no more duties related to evaluating proposals until I receive instructions on the matter.

(e) I will use proposal information for evaluation purposes only. I understand that any authorized restriction on disclosure placed on the proposal by the prospective contractor, prospective subcontractor, or the Government applies to any reproduction or abstracted information of the proposal.

(f) I will use my best efforts to safeguard proposal information physically. I will not disclose the contents of, nor release any information about, the proposals to anyone other than:

(1) The Source Selection Evaluation Board or other panel assembled to evaluate proposals submitted in response to the solicitation identified above.

(2) Other individuals designed by the contracting Officer.

(g) After completing evaluation, I will return to the Government all copies of the proposals and any abstracts.

(h) GSA Appropriations Act restriction: These restrictions are consistent with and do not supersede, conflict with or otherwise alter the employee obligations, rights, or liabilities created by Executive Order No. 12958; section 7211 of title 5, United States Code (governing disclosure of Congress); section 1034 of title 10, United States Code, as amended by the Military Whistleblower Protection Act (governing disclosure to Congress by members of the military); section 2302(b)(8) of title 5, United States Codes, as amended by the Whistleblower Protection Act (governing disclosures of illegality, waste, fraud, abuse or public health or safety threats); the Intelligence Identities Protection Act of 1982 (50 U.S.C. 421 *et seq.*) (governing disclosures that could expose confidential Government agents); and the statutes which protect against disclosure that may compromise the national security, including sections 641, 793, 794, 798, and 952 of title 18, United States Code, and section 4(b) of the Subversive Activities Act of 1950 (50 U.S.C. 783(b). The definitions, requirements, obligations, rights, sanctions, and liabilities created by said Executive order and listed statutes are incorporated into this agreement and are controlling.

——————————
(Enter name of evaluator and organization)

——————————
Date

Subpart 515.4—Contract Pricing

515.408   Solicitation provisions and contract clauses.
MAS Requests for Information Other Than Cost or Pricing Data
(a) You should use Alternative IV of the FAR provision at 52.215–20, Requirements for Cost or Pricing Data or Information Other than Cost or Pricing Data, for MAS contracts to provide the format for submission of information other than cost or pricing data for MAS contracts. To provide uniformity in request under the MAS program, you should insert the following in paragraph (b) of the provision:

(1) An offer prepared and submitted in accordance with the clause at 552.212–70, Preparation of Offer (Multuiple Award Schedule).

(2) Commercial sales practices. The Offeror shall submit information in the format provided in this solicitation in accordance with the instructions at Figure 515.4 of the GSA Acquisition Regulation (48 CFR 515–2), or submit information in the Offeror's own format.

(3) Any additional supporting information requested by the Contracting Officer. The Contracting Officer may require additional supporting information, but only to the extent necessary to determine whether the price(s) offered is fair and reasonable.

(4) By submission of an offer in response to this solicitation, the Offeror grants the Contracting Officer or an authorized representative the right to examine, at any time before initial award, books, records, documents, papers, and other directly pertinent records to verify the pricing, sales and other data related to the supplies or services proposed in order to determine the reasonableness of price(s). Access does not extend to Offeror's cost or profit information of other data relevant solely to the Offeror's determination of the prices to be offered in the catalog or marketplace.

(b) Insert the following format for commercial sales practices in the exhibits or attachments section of the solicitation and resulting contract (see FAR 12.303).

Commercial Sales Practices Format

Name of Offeror _____ SIN(s) ____
Note: Please refer to Clause 552.212–70, Preparation of Offer (Multiple Award Schedule), for additional information concerning your offer. Provide the following information for each SIN (or group of SINs or SubSIN for which information is the same).

(1) Provide the dollar value of sales to the general public at or based on an established catalog or market price during the previous 12-month period or the offerors last fiscal year: $_____. State beginning and ending of the 12 month period. Beginning _____ ending _____. In the event that a dollar value is not an appropriate measure of the sales, provide and describe your own measure of the sales of the item(s).

(2) Show your total projected annual sales to the Government under this contract for the contract term, excluding options, for each SIN offered. If you currently hold a Federal Supply Schedule contract for the SIN the total projected annual sales should be based on your mostrecent 12 months of sales under that contract.

SIN _____ $_____

SIN _____ $_____

SIN _____ $_____

(3) Based on your written discounting policies (standard commercial sales practices in the event you do not have written discounting policies), are the discounts and any concessions which you offer the Government equal to or better than your best price (discount and concessions in any combination) offered to any customer acquiring the same items regardless of quantity or terms and conditions? YES__ NO__ (See definition of "concession" and "discount" in 552.212–70.)

(4)(a) Based on your written discounting policies (standard commercial sales practices in the event you do not have written discounting policies), provide information as requested for each SIN (or group of SINs for which the information is the same) in accordance with the instructions at Figure 515.4, which is provided in this solicitation for your convenience. The information should be provided in the chart below or in an equivalent format developed by the offeror. Rows should be added to accommodate as many customers as required.

Column 1 Customer	Column 2 Discount	Column 3 Quantity/Volume	Column 4 FOB Term	Column 5 Concessions

(b) Do any deviations from your written policies or standard commercial sales practices disclosed in the above chart ever result in better discounts (lower prices) or concessions than indicated? YES_ NO_. If YES, explain deviations in accordance with the instructions at Figure 515.4, which is provided in this solicitation for your convenience.

(5) If you are a dealer/reseller without significant sales to the general public, you should provide manufacturers' information required by paragraphs (1) through (4) above for each item/SINoffered, if the manufacturer's sales under any resulting contract are expected to exceed $500,000. You must also obtain written authorization from the manufacturer(s) for Government access, at any time before award or before agreeing to a modification, to the manufacturer's sales records for the purpose of verifying the information submitted by the manufacturer. The information is required in order to enable the Government to make a determination that the offered price is fair and reasonable. To expedite the review and processing of offers, you should advise the manufacturer(s) of this requirement. The contracting officer may require the information be submitted on electronic media with commercially available spreadsheet(s). The information may be provided by the manufacturer directly to the Government. If the manufacturer's item(s) is being offered by multiple dealers/resellers, only one copy of the requested information should be submitted to the Government. In addition, you must submit the following information along with a listing of contact information regarding each of the manufacturers whose products and/or services are included in the offer (include the manufacturer's name, address, the manufacturer's contact point, telephone number, and FAX number) for each model offered by SIN:

(a) Manufacturer's Name.

(b) Manufacturer's Part Number.

(c) Dealer's/Reseller's Part Number.

(d) Product Description.

(e) Manufacturer's List Price.

(f) Dealer's/Reseller's percentage discount from list price or net prices.

(End of format)

(c) Include the instructions for completing the commercial sales practices format in Figure 515.4 in solicitations issued under the MAS program.

Figure 515.4—Instructions for Commercial Sales Practices Format

If you responded "yes" to question (3), on the Commercial Sales Practices Format in paragraph (b) of this section, complete the chart in question (4)(a) for the customer(s) who receive your best discount. If you responded "no", complete the chart in question (4)(a) showing your written policies or standard sales practices for all customers or customer categories to whom you sell at a price (discounts and concessions in combination) that is equal to or better than the price(s) offered to the Government under this solicitation or with which the Offeror has a current agreement to sell at a discount which equals or exceeds the discount(s) offered under this solicitation. Such agreement shall be in effect on the date the offer is submitted or contain an effective date during the proposed multiple award schedule contract period. If your offer is lower than your price to other customers or customers categories, you will be aligned with the customer or category of customer that receives your best price for purposes of the Price Reductions clause at 552.238–75. The Government expects you to provide information required by the format in accordance with these instructions that is, to the best of your knowledge and belief, current, accurate, and complete as of 14 calender days prior to its submission. You must also disclose any changes in your price list(s), discounts and/or discounting policies which occur after the offer is submitted, but before the close of negotiations. If your discount practices vary by model or product line, the discount information should be by model or product line as appropriate. You may limit the number of models or product lines reported to those which exceed 75% of actual historical Government sales (commercial sales may be substituted if Government sales are unavailable) value of the special item number (SIN).

Column 1—Identify the Applicable Customer or Category of Customer

A "customer" is any entity, except the Federal Government, which acquires supplies or services from the Offeror. The term customer includes, but is not limited to original equipment manufacturers, value added resellers, state and local Governments, distributors, educational institutions (an elementary, junior high, or degree granting school which maintains a regular faculty and established curriculum and an organized body of students), dealers, national accounts, and end users. In any instance where the Offeror is asked to disclose information for a customer, the Offeror may disclose information by category of customer if the Offeror's discount policies or practices are the same for all customers in the category. (Use a separate line for each customer or category of customer.)

Column 2—Identify the Discount

The term "discount" is as defined in solicitation clause 552.212–70, Preparation of Offer (Multiple Award Schedule). Indicate the best discount (based on your written discounting policies or standard commercial discounting practices if you do not have written discounting policies) at which you sell to the customer or category of customer identified in column 1, without regard to quantity; terms and conditions of the agreements under which the discounts are given; and whether the agreements are written or oral. Net prices or discounts off of other price lists should be expressed as percentage discounts from the price list which is the basis of your offer. If the discount disclosed is a combination of various discounts (prompt payment, quantity, etc.), the percentage should be broken out for each type of discount. If the price lists which are the basis of the discounts given to the customers identified in the chart are different than the price list submitted upon which your offer is based, identify the type or title and date of each price list. The contracting officer may require submission of these price lists. To expedite evaluation, offerors may provide these price lists at the time of submission.

Column 3—Identify the Quantity or Volume of Sales

Insert the minimum quantity or sales volume which the identified customer or category of customer must either purchase/order, per order or within a specified period, to earn a discount indicate the time period.

Column 4—Indicate the FOB Delivery Term for Each Identified Customer

See FAR 47.3 for an explanation of FOB delivery terms.

Column 5—Indicate Concessions Regardless of Quantity Granted to the Identified Customer or Category of Customer

Concessions are defined in solicitation clause 552.12–70, Preparation of Offers (Multiple Award Schedule). If the space provided is inadequate, the disclosure should be made on a separate sheet by reference.

If you respond "yes" to question 4(b) in the Commercial Sales Practices Format, provide an explanation of the circumstances under which you deviate from your written policies or standard commercial sales practices disclosed in the chart on the Commercial Sales Practices Format and explain how often they occur. Your explanation should include a discussion of situations that lead to deviations from standard practice, an explanation of how often they occur, and the controls you employ to assure the integrity of your pricing. Examples of typical deviations may include, but are not limited to, one time goodwill discounts to charity organizations or to compensate an otherwise disgruntled customer; a limited sale of obsolete or damaged goods; the sale of sample goods to a new customer, or the sales of prototype goods for testing purposes.

If deviations from your written policies or standard commercial sales practices disclosed in the chart on the Commercial Sales Practices Format are so significant and/or frequent that the Contracting Officer cannot establish whether the price(s) offered is fair and reasonable, then you may be asked to provide additional information. The Contracting Officer may ask for information to demonstrate that you have made substantial sales of the item(s) in the commercial market consistent with the information reflected on the chart on the Commercial Sales Practices Format, a description of the conditions surrounding those sales deviations, or other information that may be necessary in order for the Contracting Officer to determine whether your offered price(s) is fair and reasonable. In cases where additional information is requested the Contracting Officer will target the request in order to limit the submission of data to that needed to establish the reasonableness of the offered price.

(End of figure)

(d) Insert the clause at 552.215–72, Price Adjustment—Failure to Provide Accurate Information, in solicitations and contracts under the MAS program.

(e) You should use Alternate IV of FAR 52.215–21, Requirements for Cost or Pricing Data or Information Other Than Cost or Pricing Data—Modifications, to provide for submission of information other than cost or pricing data for MAS contracts. To provide for uniformity in requests under the MAS program, you should insert the following in paragraph (b) of the clause:

(1) Information required by the clause at 552.243–72, Modifications (Multiple Award Schedule).

(2) Any additional supporting information requested by the Contracting Officer. The Contracting Officer may require additional supporting information, but only to the extent necessary to determine whether the price(s) offered is fair and reasonable.

(3) By submitting a request for modification, the Contractor grants the Contracting Officer or an authorized representative the right to examine, at any time before agreeing to a modification, books, record, documents, papers, and other directly pertinent records to verify the pricing, sales and other data related

to the supplies or services proposed in order to determine the reasonableness of price(s). Access does not extent to Contractor's cost or profit information or other data related solely to the Contractor's determination of the prices to be offered in the catalog or marketplace.

Subpart 515.5—Preaward, Award, and Postaward Notifications, Protests, and Mistakes

515.506   Postaward debriefing of offerors.

For purposes of determining the date of receipt of a request for a post award debriefing, GSA's hours of operation are 8:00 a.m. to 4:30 p.m. Request received after 4:30 p.m. will be considered received the following business day.

Subpart 515.70—Use of Samples

515.7002   Procedures.

(a) *Unsolicited samples.* The reference to FAR 14.404–2(d) in FAR 14.202–4(g) does not apply. However, qualifications in the proposal that are at variance with the Government's requirements, constitute deficiencies. Resolve these as provided in FAR 15.306.

(b) *Solicitation requirements.* (1) Use the clause at FR 52.214–20. The second sentence in paragraph (c) of the clause does not apply. Substitute a sentence substantially as follows: Failure of the bid samples to conform to all the required characteristics listed in the solicitation constitutes a deficiency in the proposal (see FAR 15.306).

(2) In addition to listing subjective characteristics that you cannot adequately describe in the specification, you may list and evaluate objective characteristics. To include objective characteristics, you must determine that examination of such characteristics is essential to the acquisition of any acceptable product. Base your determination on past experience or other valid considerations.

(c) FAR 52.215–1(c)(3) applies to samples received after the time set for receipt of offers.

DEAR PART 915

Subpart 915.2—Solicitation and Receipt of Proposals and Information

915.200   Scope of subpart.

The 48 CFR subpart 15.2 is not applicable to Program Opportunity Notices for Commercial Demonstrations (See subpart 917.72) or Program Research and Development Announcements (See subpart 917.73).

915.201   Exchanges with industry before receipt of proposals. (DOE coverage—paragraph (e)).

(e) Approval for the use of solicitations for information or planning purposes shall be obtained from the Head of the Contracting Activity.

915.207   Handling proposals and information.

915.207-70   Handling proposals and information during evaluation.

(a) Proposals furnished to the Government are to be used for evaluation purposes only. Disclosure outside the Government for evaluation is permitted only to the extent authorized by, and in accordance with, the procedures in this subsection.

(b) While the Government's limited use of proposals does not require that the proposal bear a restrictive notice, proposers should, if they desire to maximize protection of their trade secrets or confidential or privileged commercial and financial information contained in them, apply the restrictive notice prescribed in paragraph (e) of the provision at 48 CFR 52.215–1 to such information. In any event, information contained in proposals will be protected to the extent permitted by law, but the Government assumes no liability for the use or disclosure of information (data) not made subject to such notice in accordance with paragraph (e) of the provision at 48 CFR 52.215–1.

(c) If proposals are received with more restrictive conditions than those in paragraph (e) of the provision at 48 CFR 52.215–1, the contracting officer or coordinating officer shall inquire whether the submitter is willing to accept the conditions of paragraph (e). If the submitter does not, the contracting officer or coordinating officer shall, after consultation with counsel, either return the proposal or accept it as marked. Contracting officers shall not exclude from consideration any proposals merely because they contain an authorized or agreed to notice, nor shall they be prejudiced by such notice.

(d) Release of proposal information (data) before decision as to the award of a contract, or the transfer of valuable and sensitive information between competing offerors during the competitive phase of the acquisition process, would seriously disrupt the Government's decision-making process and undermine the integrity of the competitive acquisition process, thus adversely affecting the Government's ability to solicit competitive proposals and award a contract which would best meet the Government's needs and serve the public interest. Therefore, to the extent permitted by law, none of the information (data) contained in proposals, except as authorized in this subsection, is to be disclosed outside the Government before the Government's decision as to the award of a contract. In the event an outside evaluation is to be obtained, it shall be only to the extent authorized by, and in accordance with the procedures of, this subsection.

(e)(1) In order to maintain the integrity of the procurement process and to assure that the propriety of proposals will be respected, contracting officers shall assure that the following notice is affixed to each solicited proposal prior to distribution for evaluation:

Government Notice for Handling Proposals

This proposal shall be used and disclosed for evaluation purposes only, and a copy of this Government notice shall be applied to any reproduction or abstract thereof. Any authorized restrictive notices which the submitter places on this proposal shall also be strictly complied with. Disclosure of this proposal outside the Government for evaluation purposes shall be made only to the extent authorized by, and in accordance with, the procedures in DEAR subsection 915.207–70.

(End of notice)

(2) The notice at FAR 15.609(d) for unsolicited proposals shall be affixed to a cover sheet attached to each such proposal upon receipt by DOE. Use of the notice neither alters any obligation of the Government, nor diminishes any rights in the Government to use or disclose data or information.

(f)(1) Normally, evaluations of proposals shall be performed only by employees of the Department of Energy. As used in this section, "proposals" includes the offers in response to requests for proposals, sealed bids, program opportunity announcements, program research and development announcements, or any other method of solicitation where the review of proposals or bids is to be performed by other than peer review. In certain cases, in order to gain necessary expertise, employees of other agencies may be used in instances in which they will be available and committed during the period of evaluation. Evaluators or advisors who are not Federal employees, including employees of DOE management and operating contractors, may be used where necessary. Where such non-Federal employees are used as evaluators, they may only participate as members of technical evaluation committees. They may not serve as members of the Source Evaluation Board or equivalent board or committee.

(2)(i) Pursuant to section 6002 of Pub. L. 103–355, a determination is required for every competitive procurement as to whether sufficient DOE personnel with the necessary training and capabilities are available to evaluate the proposals that will be received. This determination, discussed at FAR 37.204, shall be made in the memorandum appointing the technical evaluation committee by the Source Selection Official, in the case of Source Evaluation Board procurements, or by the Contracting Officer in all other procurements.

(ii) Where it is determined such qualified personnel are not available within DOE but are available from other Federal agencies, a determination to that effect shall be made by the same officials in the same memorandum. Should such qualified personnel not be available, a determination to use non-Federal evaluators or advisors must be made in accordance with paragraph (f)(3) of this subsection.

(3) The decision to employ non-Federal evaluators or advisors, including employees of DOE management and operating contractors, in Source Evaluation Board procurements must be made by the Source Selection Official with the concurrence of the Head of the Contracting Activity. In all other procurements, the decision shall be made by the senior program official or designee with the concurrence of the Head of the Contracting Activity. In a case where multiple solicitations are part of a single program and would call for the same resources for evaluation, a class determination to use non-Federal evaluators may be made by the Senior Procurement Executive.

(4) Where such non-Federal evaluators or advisors are to be used, the solicitation shall contain a provision informing prospective offerors that non-Federal personnel may be used in the evaluation of proposals.

(5) The nondisclosure agreement as it appears in paragraph (f)(6) of this subsection shall be signed before DOE furnishes a copy of the proposal to non-Federal evaluators or advisors, and care should be taken that the required handling notice described in paragraph (e) of this subsection is affixed to a cover sheet attached to the proposal before it is disclosed to the evaluator or advisor. In all instances, such persons will be required to comply with nondisclosure of information requirements and requirements involving Procurement Integrity, see FAR 3.104; with requirements to prevent the potential for personal conflicts of interest; or, where a non-Federal evaluator or advisor is acquired under a contract with an entity other than the individual, with requirements to prevent the potential for organizational conflicts of interest.

(6) Non-Federal evaluators or advisors shall be required to sign the following agreement prior to having access to any proposal:

Nondisclosure Agreement

Whenever DOE furnishes a proposal for evaluation, I, the recipient, agree to use the information contained in the proposal only for DOE evaluation purposes and to treat the information obtained in confidence. This requirement for confidential treatment does not apply to information obtained from any source, including the proposer, without restriction. Any notice or restriction placed on the proposal by either DOE or the originator of the proposal shall be conspicuously affixed to any reproduction or abstract thereof and its provisions strictly complied with. Upon completion of the evaluation, it is agreed all copies of the proposal and abstracts, if any, shall be returned to the DOE office which initially furnished the proposal for evaluation. Unless authorized by the Contracting Officer, I agree that I shall not contact the originator of the proposal concerning any aspect of its elements.

Recipient:_____
Date:_____

(End of agreement)

(g) The submitter of any proposal shall be provided notice adequate to afford an opportunity to take appropriate action before release of any information (data) contained therein pursuant to a request under the Freedom of Information Act (5 U.S.C. 552); and, time permitting, the submitter should be consulted to obtain assistance in determining the eligibility of the information (data) in question as an exemption under the Act. (See also 48 CFR 24.2, Freedom of Information Act.)

Subpart 915.3—Source Selection

915.305   Proposal evaluation.

(d) Personnel from DOE, other Government agencies, consultants, and contractors, including those who manage or operate Government-owned facilities, may be used in the evaluation process as evaluators or advisors when their services are necessary and available. When personnel outside the Government, including those of contractors who operate or manage Government-owned facilities, are to be used as evaluators or advisors, approval and nondisclosure procedures as required by 48 CFR (DEAR) 915.207–70 shall be followed and a notice of the use of non-Federal evaluators shall be included in the solicitation. In all instances, such personnel will be required to comply with DOE conflict of interest and nondisclosure requirements.

Subpart 915.4—Contract Pricing

915.404   Proposal analysis.

915.404-2   Information to support proposal analysis.

(a)(1) Field pricing assistance as discussed in FAR 15.404–2(a) is not required for the negotiation of DOE contract prices or modifications thereof. The term "field pricing assistance" refers to the Department of Defense (DOD) system for obtaining a price and/or cost analysis report from a cognizant DOD field level contract management office wherein requests for the review of a proposal submitted by an offeror are initiated and the recommendations made by the various specialists of the management office are consolidated into a single report that is forwarded to the office making the contract award for use in conducting negotiations. In the DOE, such review activities, except for reviews performed by professional auditors, are expected to be accomplished by pricing support personnel located in DOE Contracting Activities. The DOE contracting officer shall formally request the assistance of appropriate pricing support personnel, other than auditors, for the review of any proposal that exceeds $500,000, unless the contracting officer has sufficient data to determine the reasonableness of the proposed cost or price. Such pricing support may be requested for proposals below $500,000, if considered necessary for the establishment of a reasonable pricing arrangement. Contracting officers, however, are not precluded by this section from requesting pricing assistance from a cognizant DOD contract management office, provided an appropriate cross-servicing arrangement for pricing support services exists between the DOE and the servicing agency.

(c)(1) When an audit is required pursuant to 915.404–2–70, "Audit as an aid in proposal analysis," the request for audit shall be sent directly to the Federal audit office assigned cognizance of the offeror or prospective contractor. When the cognizant agency is other than the Defense Contract Audit Agency or the Department of Health and Human Services, and an appropriate interagency agreement has not been established, the need for audit assistance shall be coordinated with the Office of Policy, within the Headquarters procurement organization.

(2)(i) The request for audit shall establish the due date for receipt of the auditor's report and in so doing shall allow as much time as possible for the auditor's review.

(ii) Copies of technical analysis reports prepared by DOE technical or other pricing support personnel shall not normally be provided to the auditor. The contracting officer or the supporting price, cost, or financial analyst at the contracting activity shall determine the monetary impact of the technical findings.

915.404-2-70   Audit as an aid in proposal analysis.

(a) When a contract price will be based on cost or pricing data submitted by the offerors, the DOE contracting officer or authorized representative shall request a review by the cognizant Federal audit activity prior to the negotiation of any contract or modification including modifications under advertised contracts in excess of—

(1) $500,000 for a firm fixed-price contract or a fixed-price contract with economic price adjustment provisions; or adjustment provisions; or

(2) $1,000,000 for all other contract types, including initial prices, estimated costs of cost-reimbursement contracts, interim and final price redeterminations, and target and settlement of incentive contracts.

(b) The requirement for auditor reviews of proposals which exceed the thresholds specified in paragraph (a) of this section may be waived at a level above the contracting officer when the reasonableness of the negotiated contract price can be determined from information already available. The contract file shall be documented to reflect the reason for any such waiver, provided, however, that independent Government estimates of cost or price shall not be used as the sole justification for any such waiver.

915.404-4   Profit.

(c)(4)(i) *Contracting officer responsibilities.* The statutory limitations on profit and fees as set forth in FAR 15.404–4(c)(4)(i) shall be followed, except as exempted for DOE architect-engineer contracts covering Atomic Energy Commission (AEC) and Bonneville Power Administration (BPA) functions. Pursuant to section 602(d) (13) and (20) of the Federal Property and Administration Services Act of 1949, as amended, those former AEC functions, as well as those of the BPA, now being performed by DOE are exempt from the 6 percent of cost restriction on contracts for architect-engineer services. The estimated costs on which the maximum fee is computed shall include facilities capital cost of money when this cost is included in cost estimates.

(6) In cases where a change or modification calls for substantially different work than the basic contract, the contractor's effort may be radically changed and a detailed analysis of the profit factors would be a necessity. Also, if the dollar amount of the change or contract modification is very significant in comparison to the contract dollar amount, a detailed analysis should be made.

(d) *Profit-analysis factors.* A profit/fee analysis technique designed for a systematic application of the profit factors in FAR 15.404–4(d) provides contracting officers with an approach that will ensure consistent consideration of the relative value of the various factors in the establishment of a profit objective and the conduct of negotiations for a contract award. It also provides a basis for documentation of this objective, including an explanation of any significant departure from it in reaching a final agreement. The contracting officer's analysis of these prescribed factors is based on information available prior to negotiations. Such information is furnished in proposals, audit data, performance reports, preaward surveys and the like.

915.404-4-70   DOE structured profit and fee system.

This section implements FAR 15.404–4(b) and (d).

915.404-4-70-1   General.

(a) *Objective.* It is the intent of DOE to remunerate contractors for financial and other risks which they may assume, resources they use, and organization, performance and management capabilities they employ. Profit or fee shall be negotiated for this purpose; however, when profit or fee is determined as a separate element of the contract price, the aim of negotiation should be to fit it to the acquisition, giving due weight to effort, risk, facilities investment, and special factors as set forth in this subpart.

(b) *Commercial (profit) organization.* Profit or fee prenegotiation objectives for contracts with commercial (profit) organizations shall be determined as provided in this subpart.

(c) *Nonprofit organizations.* It is DOE's general policy to pay fees in contracts with nonprofit organizations other than educational institutions and governmental bodies; however, it is a matter of negotiation whether a fee will be paid in a given case. In making this decision, the DOE negotiating official should consider whether the contractor is ordinarily paid fees for the type of work involved. The profit objective should be reasonable in relation to the task to be performed and the requirements placed on the contractor.

(d) *Educational institutions.* It is DOE policy not to pay fees under contracts with educational institutions.

(e) *State, local and Indian tribal governments.* Profit or fee shall not be paid under contracts with State, local, and Indian tribal Governments.

915.404-4-70-2   Weighted guidelines system.

(a) To properly reflect differences among contracts and the circumstances relating thereto and to select an appropriate relative profit/fee in consideration of these differences and circumstances, weightings have been developed for application by the contracting officer to standard measurement bases representative of the prescribed profit factors cited in FAR 15.404–4(d) and paragraph (d) of this section. This is a structured system, referred to as weighted guidelines. Each profit factor or subfactor, or component thereof, has been assigned weights relative to their value to the contract's overall effort. The range of weights to be applied to each profit factor is also set forth in paragraph (d) of this section. Guidance on how to apply the weighted guidelines is set forth in 915.404–4–70–8.

(b) Except as set forth in 915.404–4–70–4, the weighted guidelines shall be used in establishing the profit objective for negotiation of contracts where cost analysis is performed.

(c) The negotiation process does not contemplate or require agreement on either estimated cost elements or profit elements. Accordingly, although the details of analysis and evaluation may be discussed in the fact-finding phase of the negotiation process in order to develop a mutual understanding of the logic of the respective positions, specific agreement on the exact weights of values of the individual profit factors is not required and need not be attempted.

(d) The factors set forth in the following table are to be used in determining DOE profit objectives. The factors and weight ranges for each factor shall be used in all instances where the weighted guidelines are applied.

Profit factors	Weight ranges (percent)
I. Contractor Effort (Weights applied to cost):	
A. Material acquisitions:	
1. Purchased parts	1 to 3.
2. Subcontracted items	1 to 4.
3. Other materials	1 to 3.
B. Labor skills:	
1. Technical and managerial:	
a. Scientific	10 to 20.
b. Project management/administration	8 to 20.
c. Engineering	8 to 14.
2. Manufacturing	4 to 8.
3. Support services	4 to 14.
C. Overhead:	
1. Technical and managerial	5 to 8.
2. Manufacturing	3 to 6.
3. Support services	3 to 7.
D. Other direct costs	3 to 8.
E. G&A (General Management) expenses	5 to 7.
II. Contract Risk (type of contract-weights applied to total cost of items IA thru E)	0 to 8.
III. Capital Investment (Weights applied to the net book value of allocable facilities)	5 to 20.
IV. Independent Research and Development:	
A. Investment in IR&D program (Weights applied to allocable IR&D costs)	5 to 7.
B. Developed items employed (Weights applied to total of profit $ for items IA thru E)	0 to 20.
V. Special Program Participation (Weights applied to total of Profit $ for items IA thru E)	−5 to +5.
VI. Other Considerations (Weights applied to total of Profits $ for items 1A thru E)	−5 to +5.
VII. Productivity/Performance (special computation)	(N/A).

915.404-4-70-3 Documentation.

Determination of the profit or fee objective, in accordance with this subpart shall be fully documented. Since the profit objective is the contracting officer's pre-negotiation evaluation of a total profit allowance for the proposed contract, the amounts developed for each category of cost will probably change in the course of negotiation. Furthermore, the negotiated amounts will probably vary from the objective and from the pre-negotiation detailed application of the weighted guidelines technique to each element of the contractor's input to total performance. Since the profit objective is viewed as a whole rather than as its component parts, insignificant variations from the pre-negotiation profit objective, as a result of changes to the contractor's input to total performance, need not be documented in detail. Conversely, significant deviations from the profit objective necessary to reach a final agreement on profit or fee shall be explained in the price negotiation memorandum prepared in accordance with FAR 15.406–3.

915.404-4-70-4 Exceptions.

(a) For contracts not expected to exceed $500,000, the weighted guidelines need not be used; however, the contracting officer may use the weighted guidelines for contracts below this amount if he or she elects to do so.

(b) For the following classes of contracts, the weighted guidelines shall not be used—

(1) Commercialization and demonstration type contracts;

(2) Management and operating contracts;

(3) Construction contracts;

(4) Construction management contracts;

(5) Contracts primarily requiring delivery of material supplied by subcontractors;

(6) Termination settlements; and

(7) Contracts with educational institutions.

(c) In addition to paragraphs (a) and (b) of this section, the contracting officer need not use the weighted guidelines in unusual pricing situations where the weighted guidelines method has been determined by the DOE negotiating official to be unsuitable. Such exceptions shall be justified in writing and shall be authorized by the Head of the Contracting Activity. The contract file shall include this documentation and any other information that may support the exception.

(d) If the contracting officer makes a written determination that the pricing situation meets any of the circumstances set forth in this section, other methods for establishing the profit objective may be used. For contracts other than those subject to subpart 917.6, the selected method shall be supported in a manner similar to that used in the weighted guidelines (profit factor breakdown and documentation of profit objectives); however, investment or other factors that would not be applicable to the contract shall be excluded from the profit objective determination. It is intended that the methods will result in profit objectives for noncapital intensive contracts that are below those generally developed for capital intensive contracts.

915.404-4-70-5   Special considerations—contracts with nonprofit organizations (other than educational institutions).

(a) For purposes of identification, nonprofit organizations are defined as those business entities organized and operated exclusively for charitable, scientific, or educational purposes, of which no part of the net earnings inure to the benefit of any private shareholder or individual, of which no substantial part of the activities is attempting to influence legislation or participating in any political campaign on behalf of any candidate for public office, and which are exempt from Federal income taxation under section 501 of the Internal Revenue Code.

(b) In computing the amount of profit or fee to be paid, the DOE negotiating official shall take into account the tax benefits received by a nonprofit organization. While it is difficult to establish the degree to which a remuneration under any given contract contributes to an organization's overall net profit, the DOE negotiating official should assume that there is an element of profit in any amount to be paid.

(c) In order to assure consideration of the tax posture of nonprofit organizations during a profit or fee negotiation, the DOE negotiating official shall calculate the fee as for a contract with a commercial concern and then reduce it at least 25 percent. However, depending on the circumstances, the contracting officer may pay profit or fees somewhere between this amount and the appropriate profit or fee as if it were a commercial concern. When this is the case, the contract file shall be documented to specifically state the reason or reasons.

(d) Where a contract with a nonprofit organization is for the operation of Government-owned facilities, the fee should be calculated using the procedures and schedules applicable to operating contracts as set forth in part 970.

915.404-4-70-6   Contracts with educational institutions.

In certain situations the DOE may contract with a university to manage or operate Government-owned laboratories. These efforts are generally apart from, and not in conjunction with, their other activities, and the complexity and magnitude of the work are not normally found in standard university research or study contracts. Such operating contracts are subject to the applicable provisions set forth in part 970.

915.404-4-70-7   Alternative techniques.

(a) Profit or fees to be paid on construction contracts and construction management contracts shall be determined in accordance with the applicable profit/fee technique for such contracts set forth in 915.404–4–71.

(b) Profit and fee to be paid on contracts under $500,000, not using the weighted guidelines, shall be judgmentally developed by the contracting officer by assigning individual dollar amounts to the factors appropriate to DOE profit considerations discussed in 915.404–4–70–2(d).

(c) Contracts which require only delivery or furnishing of goods or services supplied by subcontractors shall include a fee or profit which, in the best judgment of the contracting officer, is appropriate. It would be expected that there would be a declining relationship of profit/fee dollars in relation to total costs. The higher the cost of subcontracts, for example, the lower the profit/fee ratio to these costs.

(d) Profit/Fee considerations in termination settlements are often a question of equity. They are a matter of negotiation. They should not, however, exceed what would have otherwise been payable under weighted guidelines had the termination not occurred.

915.404-4-70-8 Weighted guidelines application considerations.

The Department has developed internal procedures to aid the contracting officer in the application of weighted guidelines and to assure a reasonable degree of uniformity across the Department.

915.404-4-71 Profit and fee-system for construction and construction management contracts.

915.404-4-71-1 General.

(a) Business concerns awarded a DOE construction or construction management contract shall be paid a profit or fee if requested or solicited. The profit or fee objective for a construction or construction management contract shall be an amount appropriate for the type of effort contained therein. It is the intent of DOE to

(1) Reward contractors based on the complexity of work;

(2) Reward contractors who demonstrate and establish excellent records of performance; and

(3) Reward contractors who contribute their own resources, including facilities and investment of capital.

(b) Standard fees or across-the-board agreements will not be used or made. Profit or fee objectives are to be determined for each contract according to the effort or task contracted thereunder.

(c) Profit or fee payable on fixed-price and cost-reimbursable construction or construction management contracts shall be established in accordance with the appropriate procedures and schedules set forth in this subpart.

915.404-4-71-2 Limitations.

Amounts payable under construction and construction management contracts shall not exceed amounts derived from the schedules established for this purpose. Requests to pay fees in excess of these levels shall be forwarded to the Senior Procurement Executive for review and approval.

915.404-4-71-3 Factors for determining fees.

(a) The profit policy stated in 915.404–4–71–1(a) reflects, in a broad sense, recognition that profit is compensation to contractors for the entrepreneurial function of organizing and managing resources (including capital resources), and the assumption of risk that all costs of performance (operating and capital) may not be reimbursable.

(b) The best approach calls for a structure that allows judgmental evaluation and determination of fee dollars for prescribed factors which impact the need for, and the rewards associated with, fee or profit, as follows—

(1) Management risk relating to performance, including the—

(i) Quality and diversity of principal work tasks required to do the job;

(ii) Labor intensity of the job;

(iii) Special control problems; and

(iv) Advance planning, forecasting and other such requirements;

(2) The presence or absence of financial risk, including the type and terms of the contract;

(3) The relative difficulty of work, including consideration of technical and administrative knowledge, skill, experience and clarity of technical specifications;

(4) Degree and amount of contract work required to be performed by and with the contractor's own resources, including the extent to which the contractor contributes plant, equipment, computers, or working capital (labor, etc.);

(5) Duration of project;

(6) Size of operation;

(7) Benefits which may accrue to the contractor from gaining experience and know-how, from establishing or enhancing a reputation, or from being enabled to hold or expand a staff whose loyalties are primarily to the contractor; and

(8) Other special considerations, including support of Government programs such as those relating to small, small disadvantaged, and women-owned small business in subcontracting, energy conservation, etc.

(c) The total fee objective and amount for a particular negotiation is established by judgmental considerations of the factors in paragraph (b) of this section, assigning fee values as deemed appropriate for each factor and totaling the resulting amounts.

(d) In recognition of the complexities of this process, and to assist in promoting a reasonable degree of consistency and uniformity in its application, fee schedules have been developed which set forth maximum fee amounts that contracting activities are allowed to negotiate for a particular transaction without obtaining prior approval of the Senior Procurement Executive. In addition, the fee negotiation objective established in accordance with 915.404–4–71–3(a), (b), and (c) shall not exceed the applicable fee schedule amounts without prior approval of the Senior Procurement Executive. To facilitate application to a contract, the fee amounts are related to the total cost base which is defined as total operating and capital costs.

915.404-4-71-4   Considerations affecting fee amounts.

(a) In selecting final fee amounts for the various factors in 915.404–4–71–3 of this section, the DOE negotiating official will have to make several judgments as discussed in this subsection.

(b) Complexity of a construction project shall be considered by analysis of its major parts. For a project which includes items of work of different degrees of complexity, a single average classification should be considered, or the work should be divided into separate classifications. The following class identifications are appropriate for proper fee determinations.

(1) *Class A* —Manufacturing plants involving operations requiring a high degree of design layout or process control; nuclear reactors; atomic particle accelerators; complex laboratories or industrial units especially designed for handling radioactive materials.

(2) *Class B* —Normal manufacturing processes and assembly operations such as ore dressing, metal working plant and simple processing plants; power plants and accessory switching and transformer stations; water treatment plants; sewage disposal plants; hospitals; and ordinary laboratories.

(3) *Class C* —Permanent administrative and general service buildings, permanent housing, roads, railroads, grading, sewers, storm drains, and water and power distribution systems.

(4) *Class D* —Construction camps and facilities and other construction of a temporary nature.

(c) Normal management elements of principal tasks relating to a construction contract cover several categories of tasks with differing rates of application throughout the construction period. The principal elements of management effort are outlined in this paragraph. Although each project has a total management value equal to 100% for all elements, the distribution of effort among the various elements will be different for each project due to differences in project character or size. The basic management elements and the normal range of efforts expected to apply for a normal sized project are as follows. When the normally expected effort will not be performed by a contractor, this fact should be considered in arriving at appropriate fee amounts.

Management elements	Effort range	
	Minimum	Maximum
I. *Broad project planning.* Overall project planning and scheduling, establishment of key project organization and consultation with the A-E and DOE. Performed by highest level of contractor's officers, technical personnel and project manager	15	25
II. *Field planning.* Mobilization and demobilization of top field organization from the contractor's existing organization and from other sources as necessary. Detailed project planning and scheduling for construction of facilities. Performed by the project manager and top field professional staff	18	28
III. *Labor supervision.* Direct supervision of manual employees. Performed by contractor's subprofessional staff, such as superintendents and foremen (some salaried and some hourly rate). This includes the contractor's personnel to coordinate and expedite the work of Subcontractors	12	16
IV. *Acquisition and subcontracting.* Acquisition of other than special equipment. Selection of subcontractors and execution and administration of subcontracts. Performed by contractor's staff under supervision and direction of elements I and II	12	16
V. *Labor relations and recruitment (manual).* Performed by the contractor's staff under supervision and direction of elements I, II and III. This includes demobilization of work forces	7	11
VI. *Recruitment of supervisory staff.* Staffing required to supplement the organization under elements I and II, and demobilization during completion of the project. Performed by contractor's permanent staff and recruitment personnel under supervision and direction of management elements I and II	4	6
VII. *Expediting.* Expediting contracting performed by contractor's staff and by subcontractors. Performed by contractor's staff under supervision and direction of elements I and II	4	6
VIII. *Construction equipment operations.* This includes mobilization and demobilization. Performed by contractor's staff under supervision, direction and coordination of elements I, II, and IV	4	6
IX. *Other services.* Timekeeping, cost accounting, estimating, reporting, security, etc., by the contractor's staff under supervision and direction of elements I and II	4	6

(d) Fee considerations dealing with the duration of a project are usually provided by the consideration given to the degree of complexity and magnitude of the work. In only very unusual circumstances should it be necessary to separately weight, positively or negatively, for the period of services or length of time involved in the project when determining fee levels.

(e) The size of the operation is to a considerable degree a continuation of the complexity factor, and the degree and amount of work required to be performed by and with the contractor's own resources. Generally, no separate weighting, positively or negatively, is required for consideration of those factors.

(f) The degree and amount of work required to be performed by and with the contractor's own resources affect the level of fees. Reasonable fees should be based on expectations of complete construction services normally associated with a construction or construction management contract. In the case of a construction contract, reduced services can be in the form of excessive subcontracting or supporting acquisition actions and labor relations interfaces being made by the government. If an unusual amount of such work is performed by other than the contractor, it will be necessary to make downward adjustments in the fee levels to provide for the reduction in services required.

(g) The type of contract to be negotiated and the anticipated contractor cost risk shall be considered in establishing the appropriate fee objective for the contract.

(h) When a contract calls for the contractor to use its own resources, including facilities and equipment, and to make its own cost investment (i.e., when there is no letter-of-credit financing), a positive impact on the fee amount shall be reflected.

915.404-4-71-5   Fee schedules.

(a) The schedules included in this paragraph, adjusted in accordance with provisions of this section and 915.404–4–71–6, provide maximum fee levels for construction and construction management contracts. The fees are related to the estimated cost (fee base) for the construction work and services to be performed. The schedule in paragraph (d) of this section sets forth the basic fee schedule for construction contracts. The schedule in paragraph (f) of this section sets forth the basic fee schedule for construction management contracts. A separate schedule in paragraph (h) of this section has been developed for determining the fee applicable to special equipment purchases and to reflect a differing level of fee consideration associated with the subcontractor effort under construction management contracts. (See 915.404–4–71–6(c) and 915.404–4–71–6(d)).

(b) The schedules cited in paragraph (a) of this section provide the maximum fee amount for a CPFF contract arrangement. If a fixed-price type contract is to be awarded, the fee amount set forth in the fee schedules shall be increased by an amount not to exceed 4 percent of the fee base.

(c) The fee schedule shown in paragraphs (d) and (f) of this section assumes a letter of credit financing arrangement. If a contract provides for or requires the contractor to make their own cost investment for contract performance (i.e., when there is no letter-of-credit financing), the fee amounts set forth in the fee schedules shall be increased by an amount equal to 5 percent of the fee amount as determined from the schedules.

(d) The following schedule sets forth the base for construction contracts:

Construction Contracts Schedule

Fee base (dollars)	Fee (dollars)	Fee (per cent)	Incr. (per cent)
Up to $1 Million			5.47
1,000,000	54,700	5.47	3.88
3,000,000	132,374	4.41	3.28
5,000,000	198,014	3.96	2.87
10,000,000	341,328	3.41	2.60
15,000,000	471,514	3.14	2.20
25,000,000	691,408	2.77	1.95
40,000,000	984,600	2.46	1.73
60,000,000	1,330,304	2.22	1.56
80,000,000	1,643,188	2.05	1.41
100,000,000	1,924,346	1.92	1.26
150,000,000	2,552,302	1.70	1.09
200,000,000	3,094,926	1.55	0.80
300,000,000	3,897,922	1.30	0.68
400,000,000	4,581,672	1.15	0.57
500,000,000	5,148,364	1.03	
Over $500 Million	5,148,364		0.57

(e) When using the Construction Contracts Schedule for establishing maximum payable basic fees, the following adjustments shall be made to the Schedule fee amounts for complexity levels, excessive subcontracting, normal contractor services performed by the government or another contractor:

(1) The target fee amounts, set forth in the fee schedule, shall not be adjusted for a Class A project, which is maximum complexity. A Class B project requires a 10 percent reduction in amounts. Class C and D projects require a 20 percent and 30 percent reduction, respectively. The various classes are defined in 915.404–4–71–4(b).

(2) The target fee schedule provides for 45 percent of the contract work to be subcontracted for such things as electrical and other specialties. Excessive subcontracting results when such efforts exceed 45 percent of the total contract work. To establish appropriate fee reductions for excessive subcontracting, the negotiating official should first determine the amount of subcontracting as

a percentage of the total contract work. Next, the negotiating official should determine a percentage by which the prime contractor's normal requirement (based on a requirement for doing work with its own forces) is reduced due to the excessive subcontracting and, finally, multiply the two percentages to determine a fee reduction factor.

(3) If acquisition or other services normally expected of the contractor (see 915.404–4–71–4(c)) are performed by the government, or another DOE prime or operating contractor, a fee reduction may also be required. The negotiating official should first determine what percentage of the total procurement or other required services is performed by others. Then the negotiating official should apply this percentage reduction to the normally assigned weightings for the management services or effort as discussed in 915.404–4–71–4(c) to arrive at the appropriate reduction factor.

(f) The following schedule sets forth the base for construction management contracts:

Construction Management Contracts Schedule

Fee base (dollars)	Fee (dollars)	Fee (per cent)	Incr. (per cent)
Up to $1 Million			5.47
1,000,000	54,700	5.47	3.88
3,000,000	132,374	4.41	3.28
5,000,000	198,014	3.96	2.87
10,000,000	341,328	3.41	2.60
15,000,000	471,514	3.14	2.20
25,000,000	691,408	2.77	1.95
40,000,000	984,600	2.46	1.73
60,000,000	1,330,304	2.22	1.56
80,000,000	1,643,188	2.05	1.41
100,000,000	1,924,346	1.92	1.26
150,000,000	2,552,302	1.70	1.09
200,000,000	3,094,926	1.55	0.80
300,000,000	3,897,922	1.30	0.68
400,000,000	4,581,672	1.15	0.57
500,000,000	5,148,364	1.03	
Over $500 Million	5,148,364		0.57

(g) When applying the basic Construction Management Contracts Schedule for determining maximum payable fees, no adjustments are necessary to such payable fees for contractor Force account labor used for work which should otherwise be subcontracted until such Force account work exceeds, in the aggregate, 20 percent of the base. Excessive use of Force account work results when such effort exceeds 20 percent of the fee base; and, when this occurs, appropriate fee reductions for such excessive Force account labor shall be computed as follows:

(1) Determine the percentage amount of Force account work to total contractor effort.

(2) Determine the percentage amount of subcontract work reduced due to the use of Force account work.

(3) Multiply the two percentages to determine the fee reduction factor. It is not expected that reductions in the Construction Management Contracts Schedule fee amounts will be made for complexity, reduced requirements and similar adjustments as made for construction contracts.

(h) The schedule of fees for consideration of special equipment purchases and for consideration of the subcontract program under a construction management contract is as follows:

Special Equipment Purchases/Subcontract Work Schedule

Fee base (dollars)	Fee (dollars)	Fee (per cent)	Incr. (per cent)
Up to $1 Million			1.64
1,000,000	16,410	1.64	1.09
2,000,000	27,350	1.37	0.93
4,000,000	45,948	1.15	0.77
6,000,000	61,264	1.02	0.71
8,000,000	75,486	0.94	0.66
10,000,000	88,614	0.89	0.61
15,000,000	119,246	0.79	0.53
25,000,000	171,758	0.69	0.47
40,000,000	242,868	0.61	0.43
60,000,000	329,294	0.55	0.39
80,000,000	406,968	0.51	0.37
100,000,000	480,266	0.48	0.28
150,000,000	619,204	0.41	0.23
200,000,000	732,980	0.37	0.13
300,000,000	867,542	0.29	
Over $300 Million	867,542		013

915.404-4-71-6   Fee base.

(a) The fee base shown in the Construction Contracts Schedule and Construction Management Contracts Schedule represents that estimate of cost to which a percentage factor is applied to determine maximum fee allowances. The fee base is the estimated necessary allowable cost of the construction work or other services which are to be performed. It shall include the estimated cost for, but is not limited to, the following as they may apply in the case of a construction or construction management contract:

(1) Site preparation and utilities.

(2) Construction (labor-materials-supplies) of buildings and auxiliary facilities.

(3) Construction (labor-materials-supplies) to complete/construct temporary buildings.

(4) Design services to support the foregoing.

(5) General management and job planning cost.

(6) Labor supervision.

(7) Procurement and acquisition administration.

(8) Construction performed by subcontractors.

(9) Installation of government furnished or contractor acquired special equipment and other equipment.

(10) Equipment (other than special equipment) which is to become Government property (including a component of Government property).

(b) The fee base for the basic fee determination for a construction contract and construction management contract shall include all necessary and allowable costs cited in paragraph (a) of this section as appropriate to the type of contract; except, any home office G&A expense paid as a contract cost per cost principle guidance and procedures shall be excluded from the fee base. The fee base shall exclude:

(1) Cost of land.

(2) Cost of engineering (A&E work).

(3) Contingency estimate.

(4) Equipment rentals or use charges.

(5) Cost of government furnished equipment or materials.

(6) Special equipment.

(c) A separate fee base shall be established for special equipment for use in applying the Special Equipment Purchases or Subcontract Work Schedule (see 915.404–4–71–5(h)). The fee base for determination of applicable fees on special equipment shall be based on the estimated purchase price of the equipment.

(d) The fee base under the Construction Management Contracts Schedule for a maximum basic fee determination for a construction management contract shall be comprised of only the costs of the construction manager's own efforts. However, it is recognized that in the case of construction management contracts, the actual construction work will be performed by subcontractors. In most cases the subcontract awards for the construction work will be made by the construction management contractor. Occasionally the contract may involve management of construction performed under a contract awarded by the Department or by one of the Department's operating contractors. In these cases, the actual cost of the subcontracted construction work shall be excluded from the fee base used to determine the maximum basic fee (under the Construction Management Contracts Schedule) applicable to a construction management contract. A separate fee base for additional allowances (using the Special Equipment Purchases or Subcontract Work Schedule) shall be established, which shall be comprised of those subcontract construction costs, special equipment purchases, and other items' costs that are contracted for or purchased by the construction manager.

915.404-4-72   Special considerations for cost-plus-award-fee contracts.

(a) When a contract is to be awarded on a cost-plus-award-fee basis several special considerations are appropriate. Fee objectives for management and operating contracts or other contracts as determined by the Senior Procurement Executive, including those using the Construction, Construction Management, or Special Equipment Purchases/Subcontract Work schedules from 915.404–4–71–5, shall be developed pursuant to the procedures set forth in 970.15404–4–8. Fee objectives for other cost-plus-award-fee contracts shall be in accordance with 916.404–2 and be developed as follows:

(1) The base fee portion of the fee objective of an award fee contract may range from 0% up to the 50% level of the fee amount for a Cost-Plus-Fixed-Fee (CPFF) contract, arrived at by using the weighted guidelines or other techniques (such as those provided in 915.404–4–71 for construction and construction management contracts). However, the base amount should not normally exceed 50% of the otherwise applicable fixed fee. In the event this 50% limit is exceeded, appropriate documentation shall be entered into the contract file. In no event shall the base fee exceed 60% of the fixed fee amount.

(2) The base fee plus the amount included in the award fee pool should normally not exceed the fixed fee (as subjectively determined or as developed from the fee schedule) by more than 50%. However, in the event the base fee is to be less than 50% of the fixed fee, the maximum potential award fee may be increased proportionately with the decreases in base fee amounts.

(3) The following maximum potential award fees shall apply in award fee contracts: (percent is stated as percent of fee schedule amounts).

Base fee percent	Award fee percent	Maximum total percentage
50	100	150
40	120	160
30	140	170
20	160	180
10	180	190
0	200	200

(b) Prior approval of the Senior Procurement Executive, is required for total fee (base plus award fee pool) exceeding the guidelines in 915.404–4–72(a)(3).

915.408 Solicitation provisions and contract clauses.

915.408-70 Key personnel clause.

The contracting officer (after deleting "under the clause at 970.5203–3, Contractor's Organization" from paragraph (a) if not a management and operating contract) shall insert the clause at 952.215–70, Key Personnel, in contracts under which performance is largely dependent on the expertise of specific key personnel.

Subpart 915.6—Unsolicited Proposals

915.602 Policy.

(a) Present and future needs demand the involvement of all resources in exploring alternative energy sources and technologies. To achieve this objective, it is DOE policy to encourage external sources of unique and innovative methods, approaches, and ideas by stressing submission of unsolicited proposals for government support. In furtherance of this policy and to ensure the integrity of the acquisition process through application of reasonable controls, the DOE:

(1) Disseminates information on areas of broad technical concern whose solutions are considered relevant to the accomplishment of DOE's assigned mission areas;

(2) Encourages potential proposers to consult with program personnel before expending resources in the development of written unsolicited proposals;

(3) Endeavors to distribute unsolicited proposals to all interested organizations within DOE;

(4) Processes unsolicited proposals in an expeditious manner and, where practicable, keeps proposers advised as discrete decisions are made;

(5) Assures that each proposal is evaluated in a fair and objective manner; and, (6) Assures that each proposal will be used only for its intended purpose and the information, subject to applicable laws and regulations, contained therein will not be divulged without prior permission of the proposer.

915.603 General.

(f) Unsolicited proposals for the performance of support services are, except as discussed in this paragraph, unacceptable as the performance of such services is unlikely to necessitate innovative and unique concepts. There may be rare instances in which an unsolicited proposal offers an innovative and unique approach to the accomplishment of a support service. If such a proposal offers a previously unknown or an alternative approach to generally recognized techniques for the accomplishment of a specific service(s) and such approach will provide significantly greater economy or enhanced quality, it may be considered for acceptance. Such acceptance shall, however, require approval of the acquisition of support services in accordance with applicable DOE Directives and be processed as a deviation to the prohibition in this paragraph.

915.605 Content of unsolicited proposals.

(b)(5) Unsolicited proposals for nonnuclear energy demonstration activities not covered by existing formal competitive solicitations or program opportunity notices may include a request for federal assistance or participation, and shall be subject to the cost sharing provisions of subpart 917.70.

915.606 Agency procedures.

(b) Unless otherwise specified in a notice of program interest, all unsolicited proposals should be submitted to the Unsolicited Proposal Manager, U.S. Department of Energy, National Energy Technology Laboratory P.O. Box 10940, MS 921–107, Pittsburgh, PA 15236–0940. If the proposer has ascertained the cognizant program office through preliminary contacts with program staff, the proposal may be submitted directly to that office. In such instances, the proposer should separately send a copy of the proposal cover letter to the unsolicited proposal coordinator to assure that the proposal is logged in the Department's automated tracking system for unsolicited proposals.

915.607 Criteria for acceptance and negotiation of an unsolicited proposal.

(c) DOE's cost participation policy, at subpart 917.70, shall be followed in determining the extent to which the DOE will participate in the cost for the proposed effort.

APPENDIX 6

NFS PART 1815

Subpart 1815.2—Solicitation and Receipt of Proposals and Information

1815.203-72   Risk management.

In all RFPs and RFOs for supplies or services for which a technical proposal is required, proposal instructions shall require offerors to identify and discuss risk factors and issues throughout the proposal where they are relevant, and describe their approach to managing these risks.

1815.207   Handling proposals and information.

1815.207-70   Release of proposal information.

(a) NASA personnel participating in any way in the evaluation may not reveal any information concerning the evaluation to anyone not also participating, and then only to the extent that the information is required in connection with the evaluation. When non-NASA personnel participate, they shall be instructed to observe these restrictions.

(b)(1) Except as provided in paragraph (b)(2) of this section, the procurement officer is the approval authority to disclose proposal information outside the Government. If outside evaluators are involved, this authorization may be granted only after compliance with FAR 37.2 and 1837.204, except that the determination of unavailability of Government personnel required by FAR 37.2 is not required for disclosure of proposal information to JPL employees.

(2) Proposal information in the following classes of proposals may be disclosed with the prior written approval of a NASA official one level above the NASA program official responsible for the overall conduct of the evaluation. If outside evaluators are involved, the determination of unavailability of Government personnel required by FAR 37.2 is not required for disclosure in these instances.

(i) Proposals submitted in response to broad agency announcements such as Announcements of Opportunity and NASA Research Announcements;

(ii) Unsolicited proposals; and

(iii) SBIR and STTR proposals.

(3) If JPL personnel, in evaluating proposal information released to them by NASA, require assistance from non-JPL, non-Government evaluators, JPL must obtain written approval to release the information in accordance with paragraphs (b)(1) and (b)(2) of this section.

1815.207-71 Appointing non-Government evaluators as special Government employees.

(a) Except as provided in paragraph (c) of this section, non-Government evaluators, except employees of JPL, shall be appointed as special Government employees.

(b) Appointment as a special Government employee is a separate action from the approval required by paragraph 1815.207–70(b) and may be processed concurrently. Appointment as a special Government employee shall be made by:

(1) The NASA Headquarters personnel office when the release of proposal information is to be made by a NASA Headquarters office; or

(2) The installation personnel office when the release of proposal information is to be made by the installation.

(c) Non-Government evaluators need not be appointed as special Government employees when they evaluate:

(1) Proposals submitted in response to broad agency announcements such as Announcements of Opportunity and NASA Research Announcements;

(2) Unsolicited proposals; and

(3) SBIR and STTR proposals.

1815.208 Submission, modification, revision, and withdrawal of proposals. (NASA supplements paragraph (b))

(b) The FAR late proposal criteria do not apply to Announcements of Opportunity, NASA Research Announcements, and Small Business Innovative Research (SBIR) Phase I and Phase II solicitations, and Small Business Technology Transfer (STTR) solicitations. For these solicitations, proposals or proposal modifications received from qualified firms after the latest date specified for receipt may be considered if a significant reduction in cost to the Government is probable or if there are significant technical advantages, as compared with proposals previously received. In such cases, the project office shall investigate the circumstances surrounding the late submission, evaluate its content, and submit written recommendations and findings to the selection official or a designee as to whether there is an advantage to the Government in considering it. The selection official or a designee shall determine whether to consider the late submission.

1815.209 Solicitation provisions and contract clauses. (NASA supplements paragraph (a))

(a) The contracting officer shall insert FAR 52.215–1 in all competitive negotiated solicitations.

1815.209-70 NASA solicitation provisions.

(a) The contracting officer shall insert the provision at 1852.215–77, Preproposal/Pre-bid Conference, in competitive requests for proposals and invitations for bids where the Government intends to conduct a prepoposal or pre-bid conference. Insert the appropriate specific information relating to the conference.

(b) When it is not in the Government's best interest to make award for less than the specified quantities solicited for certain items or groupings of items, the contracting officer shall insert the provision at 1852.214–71, Grouping for Aggregate Award. *See* 1814.201–670(b).

(c) When award will be made only on the full quantities solicited, the contracting officer shall insert the provision at 1852.214–72, Full Quantities. *See* 1814.201–670(c).

(d) The contracting officer shall insert the provision at 1852.215–81, Proposal Page Limitations, in all competitive requests for proposals.

Subpart 1815.3—Source Selection

1815.305-70 Identification of unacceptable proposals.

(a) The contracting officer shall not complete the initial evaluation of any proposal when it is determined that the proposal is unacceptable because:

(1) It does not represent a reasonable initial effort to address the essential requirements of the RFP or clearly demonstrates that the offeror does not understand the requirements;

(2) In research and development acquisitions, a substantial design drawback is evident in the proposal, and sufficient correction or improvement to consider the proposal acceptable would require virtually an entirely new technical proposal; or

(3) It contains major efficiencies or omissions or out-of-line costs which discussions with the offeror could not reasonably be expected to cure.

(b) The contracting officer shall document the rationale for discontinuing the initial evaluation of a proposal in accordance with this section.

1815.306 Exchanges with offerors after receipt of proposals. (NASA supplements paragraphs (c), (d), and (e))

(c)(2) A total of no more than three proposals shall be a working goal in establishing the competitive range. Field installations may establish procedures for approval of competitive range determinations commensurate with the complexity or dollar value of an acquisition.

(e)(1) In no case shall the contacting officer relax or amend RFP requirements for any offeror without amending the RFP and permitting the other offerors an opportunity to propose against the relaxed requirements.

Subpart 1815.4—Contract Pricing

1815.403 Obtaining cost or pricing data.

1815.403-170 Waivers of cost or pricing data.

(a) NASA has waived the requirement for the submission of cost or pricing data when contracting with the Canadian Commercial Corporation (CCC). This waiver applies to the CCC and its subcontractors. The CCC will provide assurance of the fairness and reasonableness of the proposed price. This assurance should be relied on; however, contracting officers shall ensure that the appropriate level of information other than cost or pricing data is submitted by subcontractors to support any required proposal analysis, including a technical analysis and a cost realism analysis. The CCC also will provide for follow-up audit activity to ensure that any excess profits are found and refunded to NASA.

(b) NASA has waived the requirement for the submission of cost or pricing data when contracting for Small Business Innovation Research (SBIR) program Phase II contracts. However, contracting officers shall ensure that the appropriate level of information other than cost or pricing data is submitted to determine price reasonableness and cost realism.

1815.404-471   NASA structured approach for profit or fee objective.

1815.404-472   Payment of profit or fee under letter contracts.
NASA's policy is to pay profit or fee only on definitized contracts.

1815.407   Special cost or pricing areas.

1815.407-2   Make-or-buy programs. (NASA supplements paragraph (e))
(e)(1) Make-or-buy programs should not include items or work efforts estimated to cost less than $500,000.

1815.408   Solicitation provisions and contract clauses.

1815.408-70   NASA solicitation provisions and contract clauses.
(a) The contracting officer shall insert the provision at 1852.215–78, Make-or-Buy Program Requirements, in solicitations requiring make-or-buy programs as provided in FAR 15.407–2(c). This provision shall be used in conjunction with the clause at FAR 52.215–9, Changes or Additions to Make-or-Buy Program. The contracting officer may add additional paragraphs identifying any other information required in order to evaluate the program.

(b) The contracting officer shall insert the clause at 1852.215–79, Price Adjustment for "Make-or-Buy" Changes, in contracts that include FAR 52.215–9 with its Alternate I or II. Insert in the appropriate columns the items that will be subject to a reduction in the contract value.

Subpart 1815.5—Preaward, Award, and Postaward Notifications, Protests, and Mistakes

1815.504   Award to successful offeror.
The reference to notice of award in FAR 15.504 on negotiated acquisitions is a generic one. It relates only to the formal establishment of a contractual document

obligating both the Government and the offeror. The notice is effected by the transmittal of a fully approved and executed definitive contract document, such as the award portion of SF 33, SF 26, SF 1449, or SF 1447, or a letter contract when a definitized contract instrument is not available but the urgency of the requirement necessitates immediate performance. In this latter instance, the procedures for approval and issuance of letter contracts shall be followed.

Subpart 1815.6—Unsolicited Proposals

1815.602 Policy. (NASA paragraphs (1) and (2))

(1) An unsolicited proposal may result in the award of a contract, grant, cooperative agreement, or other agreement. If a grant or cooperative agreement is used, the NASA Grant and Cooperative Agreement Handbook (NPR 5800.1) applies.

(2) Renewal proposals (i.e., those for the extension or augmentation of current contracts) are subject to the same FAR and NFS regulations, including the requirements of the Competition in Contracting Act, as are proposals for new contracts.

1815.604 Agency points of contact. (NASA supplements paragraph (a))

(a)(6) Information titled "Guidance for the Preparation and Submission of Unsolicited Proposals" is available on the Internet at *http://ec.msfc.nasa.gov/ hq/library/unSol-Prop.html.* A deviation is required for use of any modified or summarized version of the Internet information or for alternate means of general dissemination of unsolicited proposal information.

1815.606 Agency procedures. (NASA supplements paragraphs (a) and (b))

(a) NASA will not accept for formal evaluation unsolicited proposals initially submitted to another agency or to the Jet Propulsion Laboratory (JPL) without the offeror's express consent.

1815.606-70 Relationship of unsolicited proposals to NRAs.

An unsolicited proposal for a new effort or a renewal, identified by an evaluating office as being within the scope of an open NRA, shall be evaluated as a response to that NRA (see 1835.016–71), provided that the evaluating office can either:

(a) State that the proposal is not at a competitive disadvantage, or

(b) Give the offeror an opportunity to amend the unsolicited proposal to ensure compliance with the applicable NRA proposal preparation instructions. If these conditions cannot be met, the proposal must be evaluated separately.

1815.609 Limited use of data.

1815.609-70 Limited use of proposals.

Unsolicited proposals shall be evaluated outside the Government only to the extent authorized by, and in accordance with, the procedures prescribed in, 1815.207–70.

1815.670 Foreign proposals.

Unsolicited proposals from foreign sources are subject to NPD 1360.2, Initiation and Development of International Cooperation in Space and Aeronautics Programs.

Subpart 1815.70—Ombudsman

1815.7001 NASA Ombudsman Program.

NASA's implementation of an ombudsman program is in NPR 5101.33, Procurement Advocacy Programs.

1815.7003 Contract clause.

The contracting officer shall insert a clause substantially the same as the one at 1852.215–84, Ombudsman, in all solicitations (including draft solicitations) and contracts. Use the clause with its Alternate I when a task or delivery order contract is contemplated.

APPENDIX 7

HSAR PART 3015

Subpart 3015.2—Solicitation and Receipt of Proposals and Information

3015.204-3 Contract clauses.

The contracting officer shall insert clause (HSAR) 48 CFR 3052.215–70, Key Personnel or Facilities, in solicitations and contracts when the selection for award is substantially based on the offeror's possession of special capabilities regarding personnel or facilities.

3015.207-70 Handling proposals and information.

(b) Proposals and information may be released outside the Government for evaluation and similar purposes if qualified personnel are not available to thoroughly evaluate or analyze proposals or information. The contracting officer shall document the file in such cases.

Subpart 3015.6—Unsolicited Proposals

3015.602 Policy.

The Department of Homeland Security (DHS) encourages new and innovative proposals and ideas that will sustain or enhance the DHS mission.

3015.603 [Reserved]

3015.604 Agency points of contact.

(a) The DHS does not have a central clearinghouse for distributing information or assistance regarding unsolicited proposals. Each HCA is responsible for disseminating the information required at (FAR) 48 CFR 15.604(a). General information concerning DHS's scope of responsibilities and functions is available at *http://www.dhs.gov/dhspublic/*.

3015.606 Agency procedures.

(a) The agency authority to establish procedures for receiving, reviewing and evaluating, and timely disposing of unsolicited proposals, consistent with the requirements of (FAR) 48 CFR 15.6 and this subpart, is delegated to each HCA.

(b) The agency authority to establish points of contact (see (FAR) 48 CFR 15.604) to coordinate the receipt and handling of unsolicited proposals is delegated to each HCA. Contracting offices are designated as the receiving point for unsolicited proposals. Persons within DHS (e.g., technical personnel) who receive proposals shall forward them to their cognizant contracting office.

3015.606-1   Receipt and initial review.

(a) The agency contact point shall make an initial review determination within seven calendar days after receiving a proposal.

(b) If the proposal meets the requirements at (FAR) 48 CFR 15.606–1(a), the agency contact point shall acknowledge receipt within three calendar days after making the initial review determination and advise the offeror of the general timeframe for completing the evaluation.

(c) If the proposal does not meet the requirements of (FAR) 48 CFR 15.606–1(a), the agency contact point shall return the proposal within three calendar days after making the determination. The offeror shall be informed, in writing, of the reasons for returning the proposal.

3015.606-2   Evaluation.

(a) Comprehensive evaluations should be completed within sixty calendar days after making the initial review determination. If additional time is needed, then the agency contact point shall advise the offeror accordingly and provide a new evaluation completion date. The evaluating office shall neither reproduce nor disseminate the proposal to other offices without the consent of the contracting office from which the proposal was received for evaluation. If the evaluating office requires additional information from the offeror, the evaluator shall convey this request to the responsible contracting office. The evaluator shall not directly contact the proposal originator.

(b) If the evaluators recommend accepting the proposal, the responsible contracting officer shall ensure compliance with all of the requirements of (FAR) 48 CFR 15.607.

APPENDIX 8

COMMON AGENCY SOURCE SELECTION GUIDANCE

Agency	Agency Guidance
DOD	DOD Directive 5000.01, The Defense Acquisition System (May 12, 2003)
	DOD Instruction 5000.02, Operation of the Defense Acquisition System (Dec. 8, 2008)
	DFARS Procedures, Guidance and Instruction (PGI) 215-Contracting by Negotiation
	Office of Defense Acquisition, Technology, and Logistics, Commercial Item Handbook (Draft Version 2.0, 2009)
Navy	Department of the Navy Acquisition Planning Guide (Mar. 2007)
	Navy Acquisition Procedures Supplement (NAPS)
Army	AFARS—Appendix AA Army Source (Feb. 26, 2009)
Air Force	AFFARS *Informational Guidance* 5315.303 (Dec. 2008)
	AFFARS Mandatory Procedure 5315.3
Naval Sea Systems Command	NAVSEA Source Selection Guide (Jan. 24, 2001).
Army Materiel Command	*Contracting for Best Value: A Best Practice Guide to Source Selection*, AMC-P 715-3 (Jan. 1, 1998)
National Aeronautics and Space Administration	NASA Source Selection Guide
Department of Energy	DOE's Acquisition Guide (Jan. 2009)
	Department of Energy Order 413.3A Program and Project Management for the Acquisition of Capital Assets (Nov. 17, 2008)
	DOE G 413.3-18 Integrated Project Teams Guide for Use with DOE O 413.3A (Sept. 24, 2008)
	DOE G 413.3-13 U.S. Department of Energy Acquisition Strategy Guide for Capital Asset Projects (July 22, 2008)
	DOE Manual 413.3-1, Project Management and the Project Management Manual (2003)
Department of Homeland Security	DHS HSAM Chapter 3007, Acquisition Planning DHS Acquisition Planning Guide, Version 6.0 (Aug. 1, 2010) (Appendix H)
Housing and Urban Development	HUD Handbook 2210.3, Procurement Policies and Procedures (http://www.hud.gov)
General Services Administration	GSA Order, Acquisition Planning (OGP 2800.1) (Appendix 507A)
	GSA's Acquisition Planning Wizard (https://apw.gsa.gov)

SUBJECT INDEX